Networks

# Networks

## An Economics Approach

Sanjeev Goyal

The MIT Press
Cambridge, Massachusetts
London, England

The MIT Press would like to thank the anonymous peer reviewers who provided comments on drafts of this book. The generous work of academic experts is essential for establishing the authority and quality of our publications. We acknowledge with gratitude the contributions of these otherwise uncredited readers.

This book was set in TimesNewRoman by Westchester Publishing Services. Printed and bound in the United States of America.

Library of Congress Cataloging-in-Publication Data
Names: Goyal, Sanjeev, author.
Title: Networks : an economics approach / Sanjeev Goyal.
Description: Cambridge, Massachusett : The MIT Press, [2023] | Includes bibliographical references and index.
Identifiers: LCCN 2022021505 (print) | LCCN 2022021506 (ebook) | ISBN 9780262048033 (hardcover) | ISBN 9780262374071 (epub) | ISBN 9780262374088 (pdf)
Subjects: LCSH: Social networks—Economic aspects. | Economics, Mathematical. | Social networks—Mathematics.
Classification: LCC HM741 .G693 2023 (print) | LCC HM741 (ebook) | DDC 330.0151—dc23/eng/20220519
LC record available at https://lccn.loc.gov/2022021505
LC ebook record available at https://lccn.loc.gov/2022021506

10 9 8 7 6 5 4 3 2 1

In loving memory of my parents

# Contents

# Preface

Our lives are immersed in networks that range across physical infrastructure to tangible economic ties and encompass the subtle and delicate ties that connect us to friends and family. The aim of this book is to provide an introduction to the structure of these networks and the principles that govern their formation and functioning.

Networks are extraordinarily diverse, so the principles we will develop must be general. In this book, I view networks through the lens of economics. This means that we will view activity in networks and the formation of networks as arising out of trade-offs that we make between the costs and benefits of different courses of action. One virtue of this approach is that it suggests a natural point of reference for assessing performance: how well does a network deliver on the goals of the actors who created it? An assessment of performance will guide us to ways in which different types of interventions can improve matters.

I would like this book to be readable for people with different backgrounds. With this in mind, every chapter will begin with an introduction to a high-level phenomenon that will be illustrated with the help of case studies used to motivate lines of formal inquiry. The core of each chapter will be a theoretical model. The insights from the analysis of this model will be developed through simple examples that will be followed by a statement of general results. Formal proofs will be provided to help readers develop a deeper appreciation of the structure of the argument. Where possible, we will return to the original motivating phenomenon and show how the theory in question helps us understand it better.

## Organization of the Book

The book starts with a short introduction and then has four parts:

I Foundations

II Economic Networks

III Social Networks

IV Broader Themes

Part I contains four chapters. Chapter 1 introduces the main themes of the book through a discussion of a number of real-world networks and the definition of basic network concepts. Chapter 2 begins our study of how networks are formed through an introduction to the theory of random graphs. Chapter 3 describes the basic elements of an economic approach to the formation of networks. Chapter 4 provides an introduction to how networks shape human activity through the study of games played on networks. Taken together, chapters 1–4 provide the theoretical concepts that are used in the rest of the book.

Part II contains six chapters, each of which takes up a specific economic sector or theme. Chapter 5 studies the determinants of the input-output network and how its structure shapes economic activity. Chapter 6 looks at infrastructure networks. Chapter 7 discusses the security of networks that face natural and human threats. Chapter 8 studies how network effects give rise to market power. Chapter 9 studies the role of interconnections in propagating shocks in financial networks. Chapter 10 takes up the study of inter-linked wars.

Part III contains five chapters on social networks. Chapter 11 discusses the origins of specialization and unequal information in networks. Chapter 12 considers how interaction patterns shape the coordination of human activity. Chapter 13 studies problems of communication and learning in social networks. Chapter 14 studies the diffusion of ideas and epidemics in networks. Chapter 15 examines questions at the intersection of social and economic networks and impersonal markets.

Part IV contains four chapters that locate social and economic networks in a broader context, in conjunction with cultural beliefs, impersonal exchange, and the nature of the state. Chapter 16 takes up the study of networked markets, where trading restrictions and structures are modeled as networks. Chapter 17 looks at the role of communities in economic development. Chapter 18 takes up the question of trust. Chapter 19 studies the relation between groups, impersonal exchange, and the state.

## Possible Course Outlines

Parts of this material have been used to teach networks courses. Here are two ways of organizing the material for a 10-week course:

1. Applied course: Chapter 1, chapters 3–4; chapters 5–6, chapters 8–9; chapters 16–19
2. Theoretically oriented course: Chapters 1–4; chapters 5–6; chapters 11–15

Here are two ways of organizing the material for a 15-week course:

1. Applied course: Chapters 1–4; chapters 5–6, chapters 8–10; chapters 11, 15, 17–19
2. Theoretically oriented course: Chapters 1–4; chapters 5–7; chapters 11–19

# Acknowledgments

I started writing this book in January 2020, when I arrived in New York to visit Columbia University, and I am completing it in February 2022, at the New York University Abu Dhabi. In between these visits, my office at the Faculty of Economics in Cambridge offered me the perfect place to work during the long months of COVID. It is difficult to convey in words the gratitude I feel for the support of these institutions, offered graciously and unconditionally, in what have been very difficult times.

This is a long book, and it reports on a research program that has been in the making for many years. In this time, I have been singularly lucky to have worked with some wonderful people who have shared their ideas and their thoughts with me generously. I would especially like to thank Venkatesh Bala, Francis Bloch, Yann Bramoullé, Syngjoo Choi, Partha Dasgupta, Lorenzo Ductor, Bhaskar Dutta, Marcin Dziubinski, Matthew Elliott, Marcel Fafchamps, Julien Gagnon, Andrea Galeotti, Christian Ghiglino, Ben Golub, Matthew Jackson, Maarten Janssen, Sumit Joshi, Michael Kearns, Marco van der Leij, Dunia Lopez-Pintado, Frederic Moisan, Jose Luis Moraga-González, Stephanie Rosenkranz, Omer Tamuz, Fernando Vega-Redondo, Adrien Vigier, and Leeat Yariv for their collaboration and for their friendship.

I have had the good fortune to interact closely and learn from some outstanding doctoral students and post doctoral fellows at Erasmus, Essex, and Cambridge: Ana Babus, Oliver Baetz, Leonie Baumann, Diego Cerdiero, George Charlson, Shoumitro Chatterjee, Vessela Daskalova, Sihua Ding, Julien Gagnon, Andrea Galeotti, Fulin Guo, Sam Jindani, Joerg Kalbfuss, Willemein Kets, Alexander Konovalov, Rohit Lamba, Marco van der Leij, David Minarsch, Manu Munoz, Gustavo Nicolas Paez, Roberto Parra-Seguro, Anja Prummer, Ruohan Qin, Bryony Reich, James Rutt, Klaas Staal, Eduard Talamas, Tony To, Adrien Vigier, and Alan Walsh.

More broadly, I have learned a great deal from a number of friends and colleagues who are far too numerous for me to mention exhaustively. It would be remiss of me, however, not to thank Daron Acemoglu, Arun Agrawal, Sinan Aral, Larry Blume, Timothy Besley, Vasco Carvalho, Antonio Cabrales, Antonio Calvo-Armengol, Gabriele Demange,

Steven Durlauf, David Easley, Drew Fudenberg, Aditya Goenka, Mark Granovetter, William Janeway, Navin Kartik, Jon Kleinberg, Rachel Kranton, Eric Masken, Jim Mirrlees, Markus Mobius, Dilip Mookherjee, Stephen Morris, Lin Peng, Andrea Prat, Raghavendra Rau, Debraj Ray, Santanu Roy, Hamid Sabourian, Larry Samuelson, Arun Sundararajan, Eva Tardos, Coen Teulings, Jean Tirole, Duncan Watts, Asher Wolinsky, Myrna Wooders, Muhamet Yildiz, Peyton Young, and Yves Zenou.

Francis Bloch, Sihua Ding, Matthew Elliott, Mark Granovetter, Fulin Guo, Sam Jindani, Ruohan Qin, Bryony Reich, Evan Sadler, Misha Safronov, Ricky Vohra, and Michael Xu read an earlier draft of this book and made comments and suggestions and pointed out several errors: to all of them, I am deeply grateful. I thank Mohammad Akbarpour, Yann Bramoullé, Michele Barnes, Antonio Cabrales, Ozan Candogan, Vasco Carvalho, George Charlson, Krishna Dasaratha, Dave Donaldson, Marcin Dziubinski, Marcel Fafchamps, Maryam Farboodi, Ben Golub, Michel König, Dunia Lopez-Pintado, Miguel-Angel Melendez, Markus Mobius, James Moody, Stephen Nei, Lin Peng, Agathe Pernoud, Ruohan Qin, Edouard Schaal, and Yves Zenou for sharing insights and materials and for comments on specific chapters of the book.

I would like to thank Ying Gao, from the MIT Economics Department, who worked as research assistant on the book, for detailed and very helpful comments on every chapter of the book. Most of all, I thank Tony To, my PhD student at Cambridge, who has been a research assistant throughout the writing of the book. Tony's contributions show up on almost every page—he has produced most of the pictures and tables in the book, he has offered suggestions and comments on the exposition, and he has proposed questions for a number of the chapters.

The remaining errors in the book are solely my responsibility; corrections from readers would be much appreciated.

Emily Taber at MIT Press helped steer me toward the textbook style that the book now has; I started with rather different ideas. It is a pleasure to thank her for all her help in bringing this project to fruition. I am also grateful to three anonymous referees, who offered encouraging and very helpful comments on an earlier draft of the manuscript.

My wife, Pauline Rutsaert, has supported me with great patience as the weeks rolled into months and the months became years, and the book still continued to take up most of my time. She also made a number of suggestions that have helped me improve the presentation of the material at several points in the book. Our older son, Dilip, read large parts of the book and set me right on many points of presentation, and also offered me the benefit of a student's perspective. Our younger son, Sachin, entertained the right level of detachment and kept up an unfailing sense of humour during our long months of joint seclusion. My sister, Shama Goyal, and brother-in-law, Devadathan Sen, and their daughters, Sneha and Soumya, inquired about the progress of the book regularly, and by doing so, they kept me going. My parents-in-law, Monique and Paul Rutsaert, have supported me and my family with great generosity as we have moved across the Netherlands, England, and France. I thank them all for their support.

This book is dedicated to the memory of my parents Prem Chand Jain and Lakshmi Jain. My father, many years ago, first got me started on the road to asking questions about how the world works and why things often don't work well. He always encouraged me to work out my own answers. My father was a civil engineer with a taste for solving concrete problems, and I think he would have liked the style of the book. My mother offered me her love and her unflinching support without which I would not have started out at all.

# Introduction

## Why Networks?

Economics is concerned with the allocation of scarce resources to meet desired ends. For the decisions to be made correctly, it is important that the appropriate information is available to the decision-makers in a timely manner. Networks are key to understanding the fundamental processes concerning production, consumption, and information. Firms located in production and supply networks combine labor, knowledge, and material inputs to supply goods and services. Production and consumption rest on the movement of goods and services and of people on infrastructure networks like roads, trains, airlines, and the Internet. The flow of information takes place in networks of social interaction. Individuals build friendships and social ties that give them access to information, shape their values, and ultimately determine who they become. Economic exchange rests on trust, but trust, combining elements of beliefs and behaviors, is a feature of personal ties and group relations.

Twentieth-century economics has made major advances in the study of these fundamental processes. Economists have developed sophisticated theoretical methods for studying decision-making in both small and large groups. For small groups, the models are based on strategic reasoning and for large groups the models are based on ideas of perfect competition.

A background assumption in the strategic models is that everyone interacts uniformly with everyone else. This is true, for instance, in models of buyer-seller trading, oligopoly, matching, and auctions. However, due to social, geographic, and economic constraints, there are often restrictions on who can interact with whom. For instance, traders within a city trade freely with all other traders in the same city, but there may be ties between a select few traders that are located in different cities (this may be costs of transport or costs of cultural distance, reflected in lower trust). Networks provide us a framework to accommodate these restrictions

In the study of large-scale interactions, economists use models of competitive interaction and the background assumption is that agents are anonymous. In a production network or on Twitter, the system as a whole is very large, with hundreds of thousands of entities, but individual entities interact with only a small subset of the population. The average firm will have a few input suppliers and a few output purchasers; similarly, the average individual will form a few subsequent links to some Twitter account holders. These interactions can hardly be said to be anonymous. Networks provide us a framework that accommodates local and personalized interactions and also allows a large number of entities. This versatility offers the possibility to develop methods for the study of a central problem in economics (and in the other social sciences)—the so-called *problem of aggregation*, which is concerned with developing an understanding of large-scale phenomenon through microfounded reasoning that applies to small-scale settings.

Graphically, we may think of a network as a collection of points joined by lines. The points are called "nodes" or "vertices," and the lines are called "links" or "edges." This graphical and abstract nature of a network is helpful, as we can easily adapt language to describe very different systems. The nodes/vertices may be individuals, firms, and countries, and the links/edges may refer to friendships, supply relations, physical contiguity, or alliances. The nodes/vertices may be physical objects or locations, and the links/edges may refer to tangible connections like cables, trains, roads, and airline routes.

Starting in the early 1990s, economists started to develop models that incorporate networks alongside the familiar concepts of purposeful individual actions, strategic reasoning, competition, externalities, and asymmetric information. The initial models grew out of an interest in how social connections shape information diffusion and social learning. This early work pointed to the powerful effects of networks and led to the study of the origins of different types of networks (i.e., to the theory of network formation). These two ideas—that networks affect behavior and individuals strive to create networks that are beneficial for themselves—have given rise to a new research program in economics that over time has taken on progressively broader and more ambitious themes. As a result, networks are now central to our understanding of macroeconomic volatility and cycles, patterns of trade and intermediation, contagion in financial networks, diffusion and epidemics in social systems, resilience of infrastructure and supply chains, wars, economic development, unemployment and inequality, the nature of trust, and a host of other important phenomena.

The aim of this book is to offer an introduction to this body of research.

## Examples of Networks

The production of goods or services involves a set of firms that are linked through buyer/seller relations. Similarly, the financial system consists of banks, insurance companies, and other institutions connected through borrowing, lending, and other relations. In many cases, the linkages crisscross national boundaries, so events such as floods and earthquakes can have an impact on us as they travel through these connections. To get a first, high-level impression, we present a snapshot of the network of production in the US in figure 0.1. In this network, a node corresponds to a sector of the US economy. Every edge

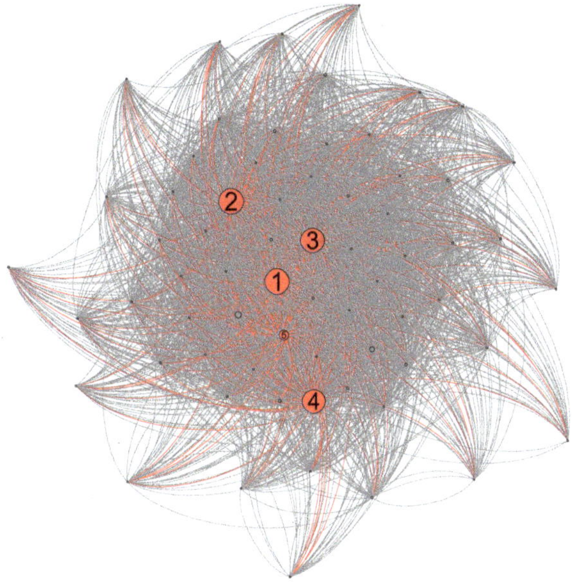


**Figure 0.1**
US production economy 2020. *Source*: Bureau of Economic Analysis.

corresponds to an input-supply relation between two sectors. Larger (red) nodes, closer to the center of the network, represent sectors that supply inputs to many other sectors. There are sixty-six sectors in all. The largest five highlighted sectors correspond to (1) Professional, scientific, and technical services, (2) Real estate, (3) Administrative and support services, (4) Insurance carriers and related activities, and (5) Management of companies and services. The presence of these hub sectors means that most other sectors are close to each other, as they are often connected to the hub sectors.

The presence of prominent and large sectors that are hubs and the small average distances between the sectors raise a number of questions about the functioning of the economy. Why are some sectors so large relative to the rest of the economy, how do hubs matter for the transmission of shocks, and how should governments target public policy in order to have maximum impact? Indeed, very similar questions arise when we consider the impact of shocks on banks and financial institutions. For instance, what was it about the production and financial network that allowed a financial shock in the real-estate sector of the US in 2007–2008 to spread to the rest of the world and create a global recession?

We next turn to infrastructure networks such as trains, roads, airlines, pipelines, shipping, canals, and the Internet. Figure 0.2 presents the routing network of British Airways, which resembles a hub and spoke, with one highly connected central city that links to all other cities (who are not otherwise linked). The train network in many countries has a similar hub-spoke structure, with major cities serving as hubs. As opposed to the airline and rail

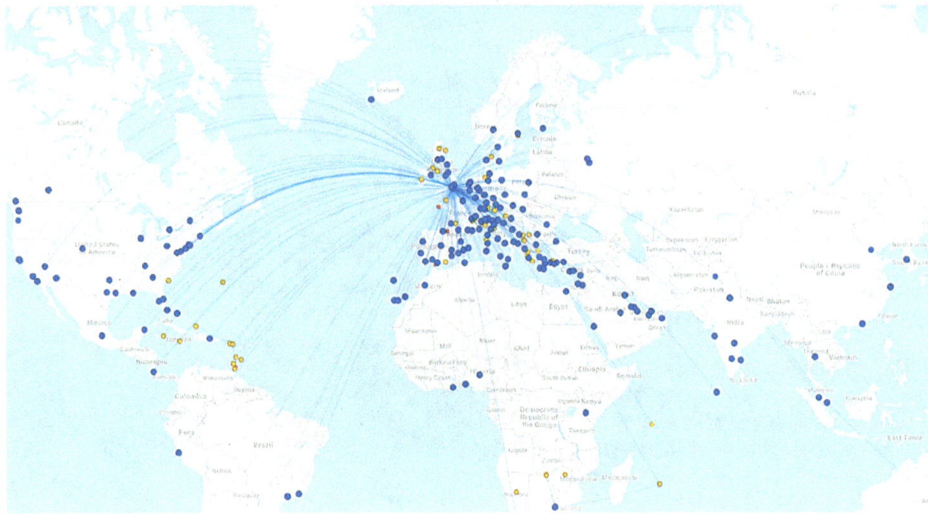

**Figure 0.2**
British Airways network. *Source*: www.ch-aviation.com/portal/.

networks, the road network in many cities around the world has a grid structure. Figure 0.3 depicts the original urban plan for Philadelphia, which stretched two miles from east to west between two rivers, the Delaware and Schuylkill. It comes from Thomas Holme's 1683 "A Portraiture of the City of Philadelphia in the Province of Pennsylvania." At the center is a civic square, and this structure is echoed in each quadrant by a spacious park that is planted with trees. The grid plan became central to the division of land during the westward expansion across America. This proposal was used as a basis for the city plan of Philadelphia and was an inspiration for the design of many cities in America. Indeed, it continues to shape city planning across the world to this day.

Finally, we take up social networks. Prominent examples of social networks include kinship-based groups like the family, friends and colleagues, and professional relationships such as co-authorships and online social networks. Figure 0.4 presents the friendship network in an American high school in 1994. We can see that pupils have similar numbers of ties. The colour of each node represents the race of the pupil: we see that most pupils form friendships with others of the same race. Moreover, we see that within the same colour, there a further partition of nodes, which reflects the year of the class. We see that links form between pupils of the same year and the same race—a tendency we will term *homophily*. Pupils share information and ideas, take part in joint activities, and develop shared values through friendships. This leads us to explore questions such as how the number of friends and location in a school network shape a pupil's performance, and what the effects of relatively segregated groups on pupil and school performance are? To answer such

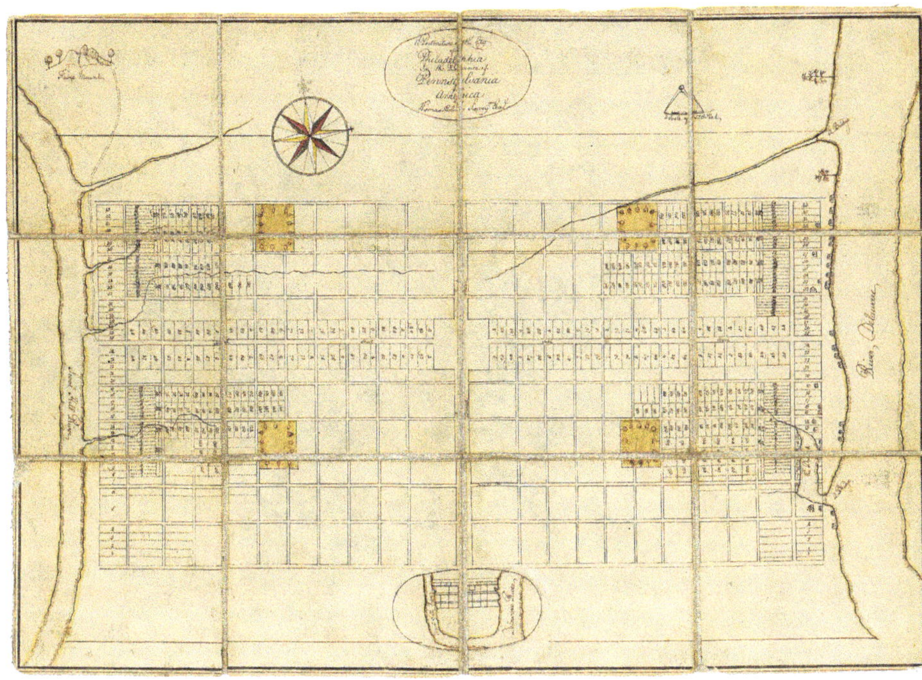

**Figure 0.3**
Plan for Philadelphia, 1683. *Source*: https://explorepahistory.com.

questions, we need a theory of how social structure affects individual values and behavior. A challenge in thinking about these questions is that individuals themselves create these friendship networks, so we need to take great care to separate cause from effect.

Large-scale online social networks like Twitter, WhatsApp, Instagram, TikTok, and Facebook are a defining aspect of social life in the early twenty-first century. On Twitter, a user can send messages known as "tweets." The tweets are seen by other users who "follow" this user. An important feature of Twitter is that "followers" can forward the tweets that they receive; this "retweet" is seen by their followers in turn, and the messages can be retweeted further. Thus Twitter creates the possibility for messages to be passed from one user to another, through this network of links. In figure 0.5, we present the network of Twitter users who have over a million followers. The size of the nodes scales with the number of links and tweets.

As Twitter is used by individuals, firms, and governments to share ideas and information, we would like to understand how far information travels on Twitter and how it depends on the point at which it is first tweeted, what the influence of different individuals is, and how this influence is related to the network of connections. Does the truth prevail, or do mutually

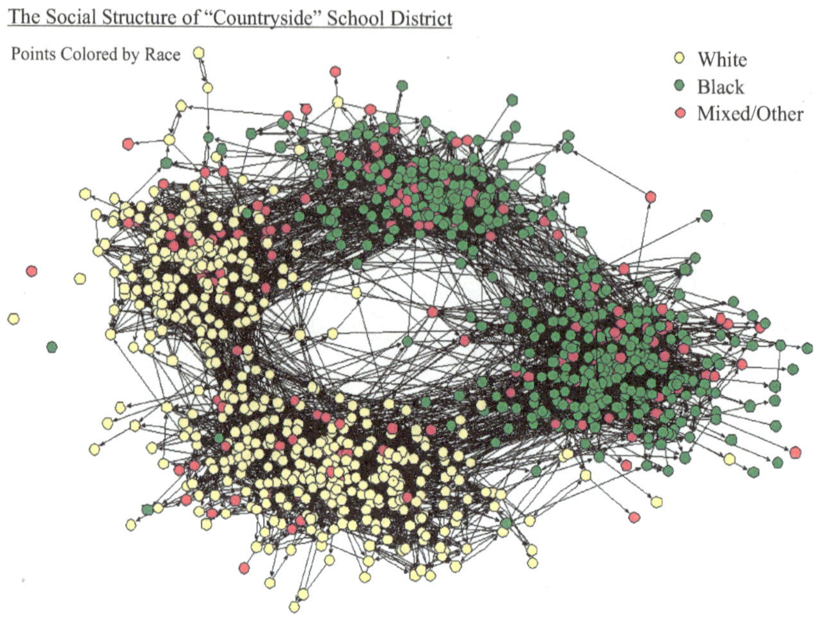


**Figure 0.4**
Countryside High School friendship network. Courtesy: James Moody.

contradictory views persist over long periods of time in the network? What are optimal nodes to target to maximize influence or to minimize the spread of false information?

We conclude this section by discussing a network that combines elements of a social interaction, professional relations, and information sharing. Scientists collaborate to conduct research, and co-authorship is perhaps the most concrete form that this takes. The patterns of co-authorship can have a profound effect on what questions economists study, how well informed they are, and thus what methods they use to conduct their research. Figure 0.6 presents the local network of a prominent economist, Daron Acemoglu, for the period 2000–2009. In this network, we start with Acemoglu (in blue) and trace his coauthors (represented in yellow) and their coauthors (in green). The thickness of an edge reflects the number of papers that the two authors have written together. This diagram leads us to explore the process that gives rise to such a collaboration network. What are its implications for the productivity of individual scholars, and how does it shape the performance of the profession of economics research as a whole?

These examples give a first impression of the extraordinary variety of tasks that networks perform and their diverse structure. They pose three high-level questions: What are the processes of network formation, and how do they explain the networks that we observe in the world? What are the effects of the networks? How can individuals (and firms and governments) use networks to achieve their objectives?

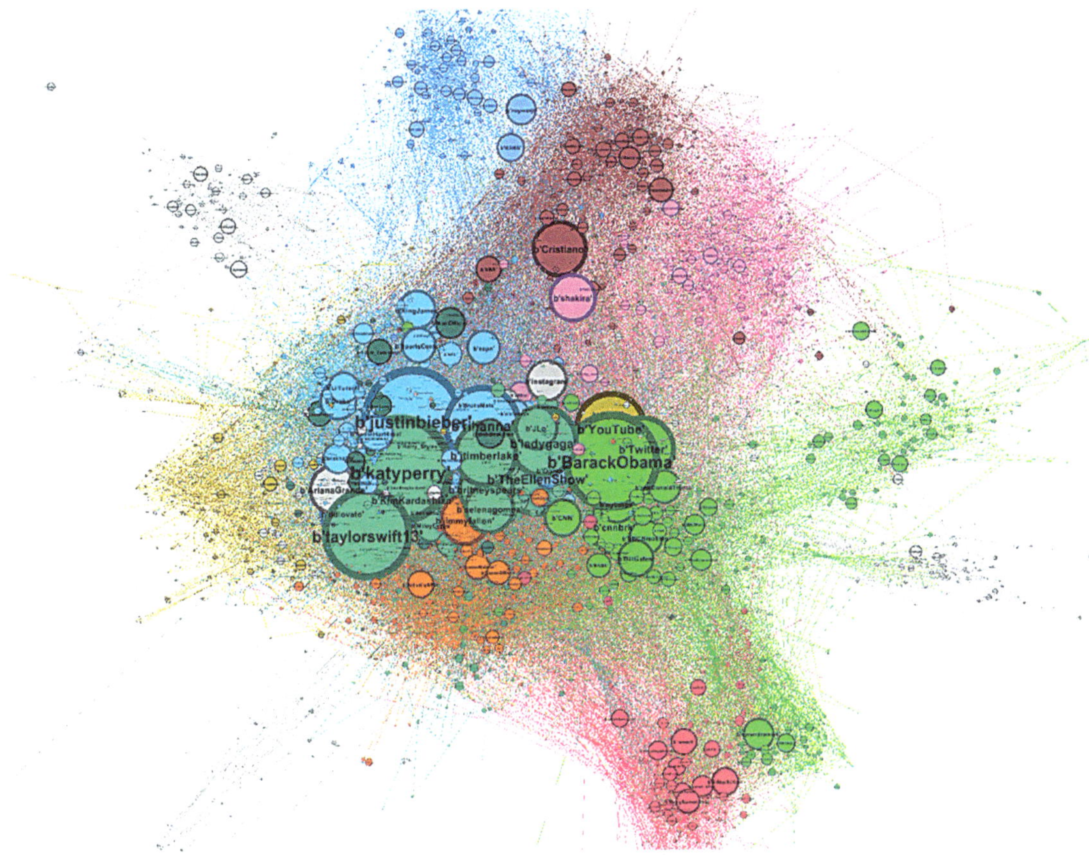


**Figure 0.5**
Twitter Millionaire Club, plotted in Gephi by Brian Srebrenik. Based on data from "Twitter Network Edges" by Luca Hammer.

## Properties of Networks

A network consists of points and the lines that connect these points: this parsimony and abstraction allow us to represent a wide variety of important social, physical, and economic systems as networks. The advances in data collection methods and our computational capacity over the past three decades allow us to collect progressively richer data on networks and the different processes that take place on networks. In this section, we draw attention to aspects of networks that play an important role in economics. Formal definitions of network concepts and measurements are presented in chapter 1.

A fundamental building block for much of network theory is the simple idea of connections: how many connections does a node possess? The nodes with which a node has a

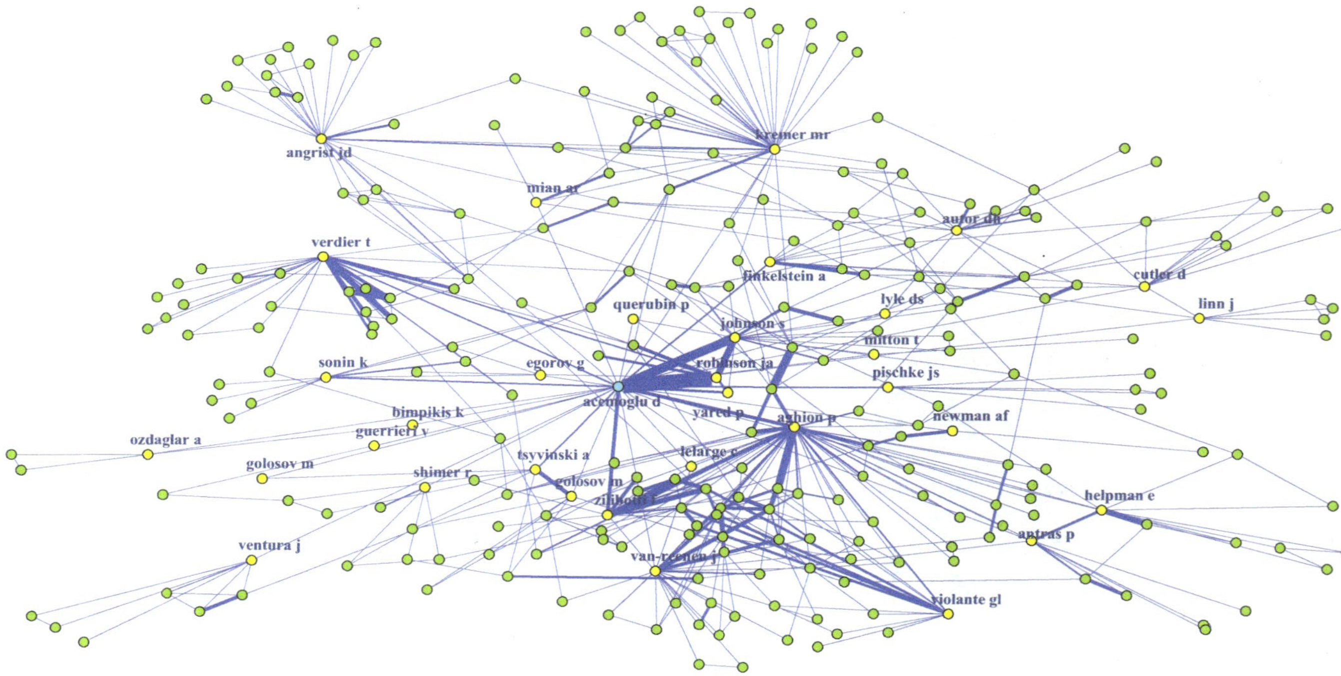


**Figure 0.6**
Coauthors of Daron Acemoglu, 2000–2009. *Note*: Some economists might appear twice or are missing due to the use of different initials or misspellings in EconLit. The width denotes the strength of a tie. The figure was created by the software program Pajek.

connection are called its "neighbors," and the number of neighbors is called the "degree" of the node. In a production network, the links refer to input and output relations and have a directionality. Similarly, on Twitter, individuals follow others—that is, a directed relation. In these cases, it will be useful to use the term "in-degree" for incoming links and "out-degree" for out going links. A recurring theme in this book is that networks contain hubs (i.e., they have very high degrees), and on the other hand, very many nodes have very low degrees. The *degree distribution* of a network will be an important object of study. We will be led to study the processes and circumstances that give rise to unequal degree distributions, and we will examine the performance of networks with unequal degree distributions on a number of dimensions.

Another important topic of study is how far apart are nodes in a network. It is customary to define the distance between two nodes in a network, the "geodesic-distance," as the minimum number of edges one would have to cross to get from one node to the other. The distance between two linked nodes is 1, the distance between two nodes that are not linked but have a common neighbor is 2, and so forth. A distinctive feature of many networks of interest is that nodes will on average be very close to one another. We commented on this in our discussion on production networks in the previous section. This has given rise to the well-known expression—the *small world*, in which one can get from any node to any other node with just six hops in the network, the so-called *six-degrees of separation*.

The role of a node in a network may depend on how *central* it is. Degree is a natural measure of centrality, but there are also other notions of centrality that play an important role. For instance, centrality may rest on proximity, and then a node with a few connections with nodes that have many connections may be very central. This suggests a *recursive* definition of centrality: a node is central if it is connected to nodes that are central. Google's PageRank is an example of a measure of centrality that rests on such a recursive definition. We will present a number of notions of centrality.

Another feature of network is the idea of community. The interest in community draws attention to the local structure of a network. We will introduce a number of ideas relating to the local structure of a network, such as *cliques* and *clustering*. In the example of friendships, we saw that pupils have friends from the same year and ethnicity. This draws attention to the notion of *homophily*, an idea that lies somewhere between the local and the global. We will present definitions of homophily and use them to study important phenomena such as diversity in social norms and the persistence of different opinions in a society.

## Outline of the Book

The book consists of four parts.

Part I of the book consists of chapters 1–4, and it provides the theoretical foundation for the rest of the book. Chapter 1 introduces the main network concepts and measures that we use throughout the book. It also illustrates these concepts by presenting computations on simple examples and applying them to measure a range of real-world networks. Chapter 2 introduces the theory of random graphs to help the reader to appreciate the mechanics of how linking processes shapes the essential properties of networks, such as degree distribution, average distances, and clustering. Chapter 3 introduces the basic elements of the economic theory of network formation. In this theory, individuals use links to create networks in order to achieve their objectives. This discussion draws attention to the central role of *directedness* or *undirectedness* of a link in shaping networks. We present the role of *externalities* and *strategic considerations* in the process of linking. This leads us to draw attention to a fundamental *tension* between strategically stable networks and collectively desirable or efficient networks. Chapter 4 presents a theoretical framework in which individuals interact locally with neighbors who are embedded in broader chains of interaction. This model offers us a simple model where behavior in small groups can be scaled up to very large populations through a sequence of overlapping neighborhoods. It illustrates an important high-level function of networks: they offer a language that can allow us to talk at one and the same time about the fine-grained interactions within an extended family and the pathways that lead from individual lives to engagements that they have with the world at large. The chapter also draws attention to the role of the *content of interaction*—whether individuals' actions generate positive or negative spillovers on their neighbors and nonneighbors and whether the actions of different individuals are *strategic complements* or *strategic substitutes*.

Part II of the book consists of chapters 5–10, and it covers economic and infrastructure networks. Chapter 5 introduces the production economy as a network and studies how properties of networks such as degree distributions and centrality shape the size and behavior of individual sectors, and how that determines the resilience of an economy. We also discuss the role of profit-making incentives of firms in shaping the structure of networks and their robustness to shocks. Chapter 6 takes up the study of infrastructure networks such as airlines, trains, and roads. We present case studies of prominent infrastructure networks and then develop theoretical models that help explain the economic factors that give rise to grid and hub-and-spoke networks. In addition, we study the implications of these networks for the distribution of goods, the mobility of labor, and the performance of the system. Chapter 7 studies the robustness of different infrastructure networks to natural and artificial shocks. It draws attention to the circumstances that support the robustness of dense (gridlike) networks and sparse (hub-and-spoke) networks, respectively. Chapter 8 studies the effects of network size and the role of intermediaries (such as platforms). It also presents a theoretical model that examines the role of pricing protocols in shaping intermediation networks. Chapter 9 takes up the role of networks in financial contagion. We develop the basic economics that give rise to links across financial institutions. We then study the role of networks in propagating shocks to individual institutions. Finally, we examine the role of complexity of connections in giving rise to the possibility of bank runs in financial networks. Chapter 10 takes up the study of wars among interconnected parties. It draws attention to the versatility of networks: we may think of links as reflecting defense alliances or physical contiguity. The chapter uses theoretical models of conflict on networks to provide a better understanding of the Great War of Congo, the reduction in the number of wars after World War II, and the growth of empires in history.

Part III of the book consists of chapters 11–15, and it covers social networks. Chapter 11 revisits the subject of personal influence and presents a theoretical model to understand an important feature of the social network of communication: the law of the few, which says that such networks are characterized by specialization in linking and in information gathering. It also presents an experiment that brings out in sharp relief the dynamics of linking and information purchase and how they feed into extreme levels of specialization in linking and information purchase. Chapter 12 studies social coordination. Almost all human activity involves coordination, ranging from our use of time, when and how we eat, what to wear, and our use of particular languages and technologies (such as fax machines or telephones). As coordination is so central to our lives, it is important for societies to have norms or standards. In this chapter, we explore how the patterns of interaction—who interacts with whom—matter as societies work their way toward developing norms, how they respond to new circumstances and arrive at new norms, and how they navigate the tension between differing personal tastes and the benefits of coordination on common norms. Chapter 13 takes up the study of how information flows in a network and how that shapes beliefs and opinions and the optimality of long-run decisions. The chapter presents theoretical models of Bayesian learning and bounded rational learning and shows how these models lead to similar predictions on the role of networks. The chapter presents experimental evidence in support of the main theoretical predictions. The final part of the chapter proposes a model of verification of news in social networks and the incentives of an external information provider and uses it to study the amount and quality of information that circulates in social networks. Chapter 14 studies the dynamics of diffusion. The first part takes up the study of diseases and examines how disease characteristics and network structure determine the size of an epidemic. The second part examines the diffusion of ideas and modern technology and identifies circumstances under which the seeding of nodes can make a big difference to the extent of diffusion. In chapter 15, we study the role of social networks in the functioning of product, labor, and financial networks.

Part IV of the book consists of chapters 16–19 and it studies networks in a broader context. Chapter 16 studies markets as networks. We take the view that bonds of trust and cooperation lead to personalized relations, and geographical distance and national boundaries place restrictions on who can undertake exchanges with whom. These restrictions may be formulated in terms of (either present or absent) ties within a network. The chapter presents models of networked markets that help us understand the ways in which prices and quantities are determined in such settings. In chapter 17, we take up the role of communities in the process of economic development—here, the interest is in the relation between group-based ties of family, lineage, tribe and caste, and how they interact with the arrival of modern technologies and with impersonal exchange. In chapter 18, we take up the fundamental notion of trust. Trust is central to most economic exchange, but the level of trust varies greatly across countries and across communities within the same country. We discuss trust in small groups and in society at large, and we explore the fundamental question of how trust scales up from the small scale to the large scale, as well as how the structure of the social network matters in this process. Chapter 19 goes one step further and introduces the role of the state. We lay out a theoretical framework to study the scale and efficiency of economic exchange in a context that combines elements of civic capital, impersonal exchange, and state capacity.

## Reading Notes

For an introduction to the use of networks in economics, see Goyal (2016, 2017). The opening lines of this introduction, on the nature of economics, paraphrase the definition of the subject offered in 1932 by Lionel Robbins (for a recent imprint of this essay, see Robbins [2007]). Hayek (1945) offers an influential statement on the central role of information and knowledge in economic systems. Bramoullé, Galeotti, and Rogers (2016) present a panoramic overview of the literature on the economics of networks.

# I FOUNDATIONS

# 1 Concepts and Measures

## 1.1 Introduction

The introduction drew attention to the extraordinary diversity of networks and described in very general terms a broad set of properties of networks. This chapter begins our formal study of networks. We introduce definitions of network concepts and use them to compute different properties of prominent real-world networks.

## 1.2 Concepts and Terminology

We introduce concepts from graph theory in this section. The discussion will concentrate on the main concepts that we use in the book and it is therefore selective and brief; for a more systematic and comprehensive coverage of the theory of graphs and networks, the interested reader is referred to Newman (2018) and Bollobas (1998).

We shall think of a network as a collection of nodes and edges. An edge between two nodes signifies a direct relation between them. Recalling the examples from the Introduction, in a production network, an edge represents an input-output relation; in an airline network, it is a route between two cities; in a social network, it may be a friendship; on Twitter, it is a "following" relation; and in a scientific collaboration network, it reflects coauthorship. In this book, we will use the terms "edge" and "link" interchangeably.

Let the set of nodes be given by $N = \{1, 2, 3, \ldots, n\}$, where $n \geq 2$ is the number of nodes. In the simplest case, a relationship or link between two nodes $i$ and $j$ is represented by the number 0 or 1, so a link is either absent or present. This is for instance the case of a following link on Twitter and a friendship link on Facebook. In other cases, such as a production network, a link may have different weights depending on the input levels.

A directed link $g_{ij}$ indicates a directionality from $i$ to $j$, so, in Twitter, it may mean that "$i$ follows $j$" while in a production network, it may refer to the flow of inputs from sector $i$ to sector $j$ (as is clear from these examples in the Introduction, there may be no flows going the other way). An undirected link has no directionality (or equivalently, the values in both directions are equal), so $g_{ij} = g_{ji}$. An example could be friendship, a research collaboration,

**Table 1.1**
Adjacency matrix

| | 1 | 2 | 3 |
|---|---|---|---|
| 1 | 0 | 1 | 0 |
| 2 | 1 | 0 | 1 |
| 3 | 0 | 1 | 0 |

or a transport link between two cities. The nodes $N$ and the links between them $\{g_{ij}\}$ define a network $g$. The set of all networks on $n$ nodes is denoted by $\mathcal{G}_n$.

A network may be described through an enumeration of all the links in it. For instance, in a network with three nodes $N = \{1, 2, 3\}$, where nodes 1 and 2 are linked and 2 and 3 are linked, we may write the network as $g = \{g_{12}, g_{23}\}$. Here, $g_{ij}$ refers to the presence of a link. Sometimes we will find it more convenient to describe the network in matrix form: the three-node two-link network is represented as an adjacency matrix in table 1.1.

A matrix representation allows us to represent directed and undirected links. Moreover—and this will be useful in some applications—it also allows us to consider networks in which the links have weights, that is, they may take on positive or negative real numbers, not just the values 0 and 1.

It is important to note that even a small number of nodes gives rise to a very large set of networks. To see this, suppose $n = 100$, and let us consider undirected links. There are approximately 5,000, that is $\binom{100}{2}$, distinct pairs of nodes. Note that this is also the number of potential undirected links possible in a network with 100 nodes. As every link is either present or absent, there are $2^{5000}$ possible networks. This is greater than the number of atoms in the observable universe! Given a network $g$, let $N_i(g) = \{j \neq i | g_{ij} = 1\}$ be the set of nodes with whom $i$ has a link. The set $N_i(g)$ will be referred to as the set of neighbors of node $i$ in network $g$. We will define the *degree* of node $i$ in network $g$, $d_i(g)$, to be the number of neighbors of $i$, that is, $d_i(g) = |N_i(g)|$.

### 1.2.1 Regular and Irregular Networks

A network is said to be *regular* if every node has the same number of links. Figure 1.1 presents some examples of regular networks. In the empty network, the degree is 0; in the circle, the degree is 2; and in a complete network, it is $n - 1$. As we add links in a regular network, all the while maintaining the equal degree property, we trace out a progressively denser network. We see this as we move from panel (a) to (b) to (c) to (d) in figure 1.1.

We next take up *irregular* networks: these are networks in which the degree of at least one pair of nodes is different. A prominent member of this class of networks is the *core-periphery* network. This network contains two types of nodes—the core and the periphery. Figure 1.2 presents two types of core-periphery networks. In both cases, the nodes in the core are fully connected among themselves. The difference lies in the degree of the periphery nodes. In one case, the periphery node has a single link as in figure 1.2(b), while in the other, it may be linked to a subset of the members of the core as in figures 1.2(c) and 1.2(d). The

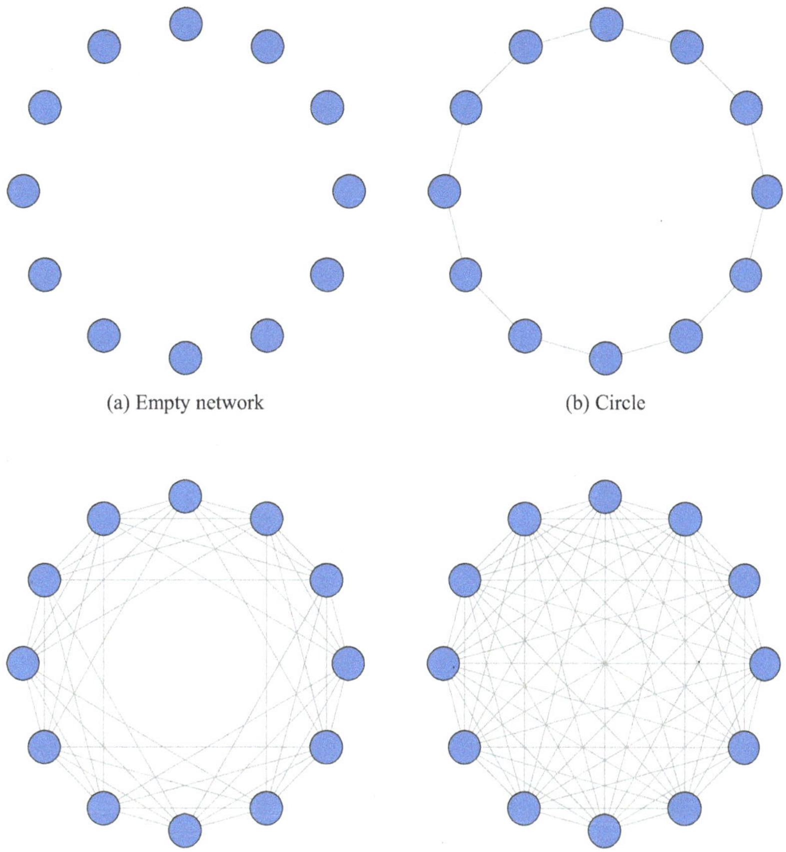

(a) Empty network

(b) Circle

(c) Degree 8 network

(d) Complete network

**Figure 1.1**
Regular networks.

*star* network in figure 1.2(a) is perhaps the best-known special case of the core-periphery network, with a singleton core member. We will sometimes refer to the star as a *hub-spoke network*.

A *line* network has the form of a line, where two nodes with one link each are at the two ends of the line while the nodes with two links are in between. Figure 1.3 presents a line network.

Sometimes, as when we study Twitter or the production network of firms, we are interested in large networks with hundreds of thousands of nodes. In the study of large networks, a complete description of all nodes and each and every link is not practical, and we will find it useful to work with summary statistics of the network.

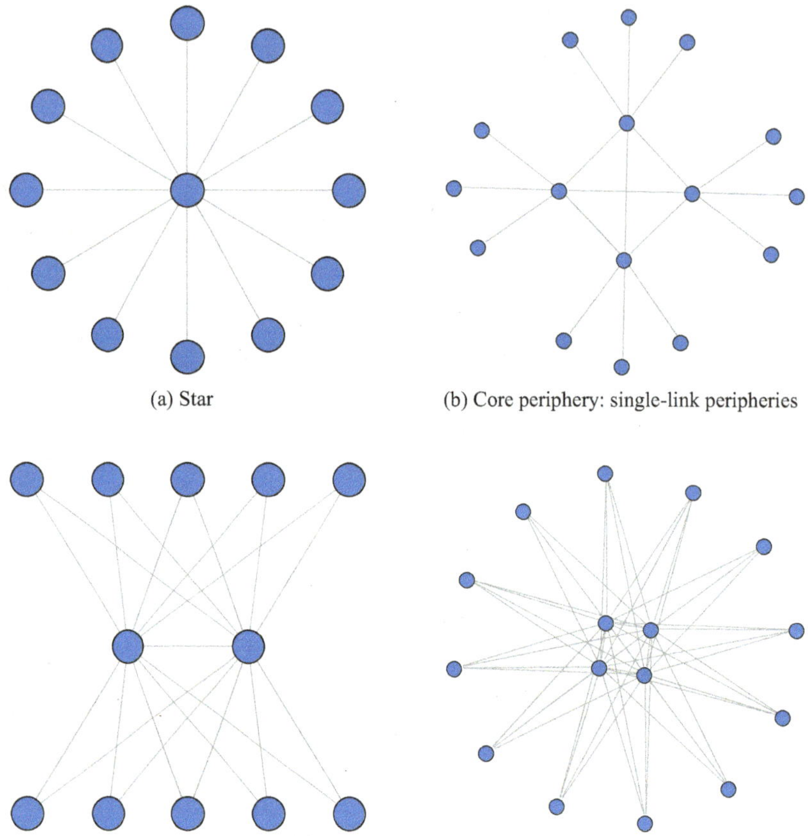

(a) Star

(b) Core periphery: single-link peripheries

(c) Core periphery: two-link peripheries

(d) Core periphery: four-link peripheries

**Figure 1.2**
Core-periphery networks.

**Figure 1.3**
Line network.

### 1.2.2 Degree Distributions

A natural way to describe the links in large networks is to consider their *degree distribution*. Let $P(d)$ be the frequency or fraction of nodes with degree $d$. To develop a feel for degree distributions, we discuss some examples of simple and well known networks. The degree distribution of a regular network will take on a simple form—$P(d) = 1$ for a single degree and zero for all other degrees. Next, consider an irregular network. For the star network, the degrees take on the values 1 and $n-1$, with $n-1$ nodes having degree

1 and 1 node having degree $n-1$. The degree distribution is as follows: $P(n-1)=1/n$, $P(1)=(n-1)/n$, and $P(d)=0$ for all other degrees $d \in \{0,\ldots,n-1\}$. Finally, in the core-periphery network given in figure 1.2(b), the degree distribution is given by $P(6)=4/n$, $P(1)=(n-4)/n$, and $P(d)=0$ for all other degrees $d \in \{0,\ldots,n-1\}$.

The *mean* (or average) degree in network $g$ is the sum of degrees across nodes divided by the number of nodes:

$$d(g)=\sum_{i\in N}\frac{d_i(g)}{n}=\sum_{d}P(d)d. \tag{1.1}$$

Sometimes, in subsequent chapters, we will find it convenient, for ease of exposition, to denote the mean degree of a network by $\hat{d}$ (and drop the $g$).

The mean degree in a regular network is the same as the degree of every node, while the mean degree of a star network is $2-2/n$ (which is approximately equal to 2 when the number of nodes is large). The mean degree of a line network is the same as that of a star because they have the same number of links (which is $n-1$ in a network with $n$ nodes).

The *variance* of the degree distribution is given by

$$\text{var}(g)=\sum_{d=0}^{n-1}P(d)[d(g)-d]^2. \tag{1.2}$$

To develop a feel for degree distributions of large networks, we next consider two widely used examples—the Poisson and the Pareto distributions. Under a Poisson distribution, the probability that a randomly selected node has degree $d$ is given by

$$\frac{e^{-\lambda}\lambda^d}{d!}, \tag{1.3}$$

where $\lambda$ is the mean number of links. Figure 1.4 presents a network containing 25 nodes with a Poisson degree distribution ($\lambda=4, 5,$ and 6) and the corresponding degree distributions. An important feature of the Poisson distribution is that most of the nodes will have degrees close to the mean degree $\lambda$. We also note that the variance of this degree distribution is equal to its mean, $\lambda$.

Under a Pareto distribution, the probability that a node has degree $d$ is

$$P(d)=cd^{-\gamma}, \tag{1.4}$$

where $c$ is a positive constant that normalizes the sum of probabilities to 1 and $\gamma \in (1,3)$. Figure 1.5 presents networks with coefficient values of $\gamma=1.5, 2, 2.5$ (the mean degree is $3.76 \approx 4$). As we raise the value of $\gamma$, we see that this leads to a network with a few very highly linked nodes and a large number of poorly linked nodes. The variance of the Pareto distribution is undefined if $\gamma \in (1,2)$, and it grows without bound (in the number of nodes) if $\gamma \in (2,3)$ (for a derivation of this property, see chapter 2, on random graphs).

As the probability in the Pareto distribution scales with a power coefficient, this degree distribution is also commonly referred to as a *power-law degree distribution*. Figure 1.6

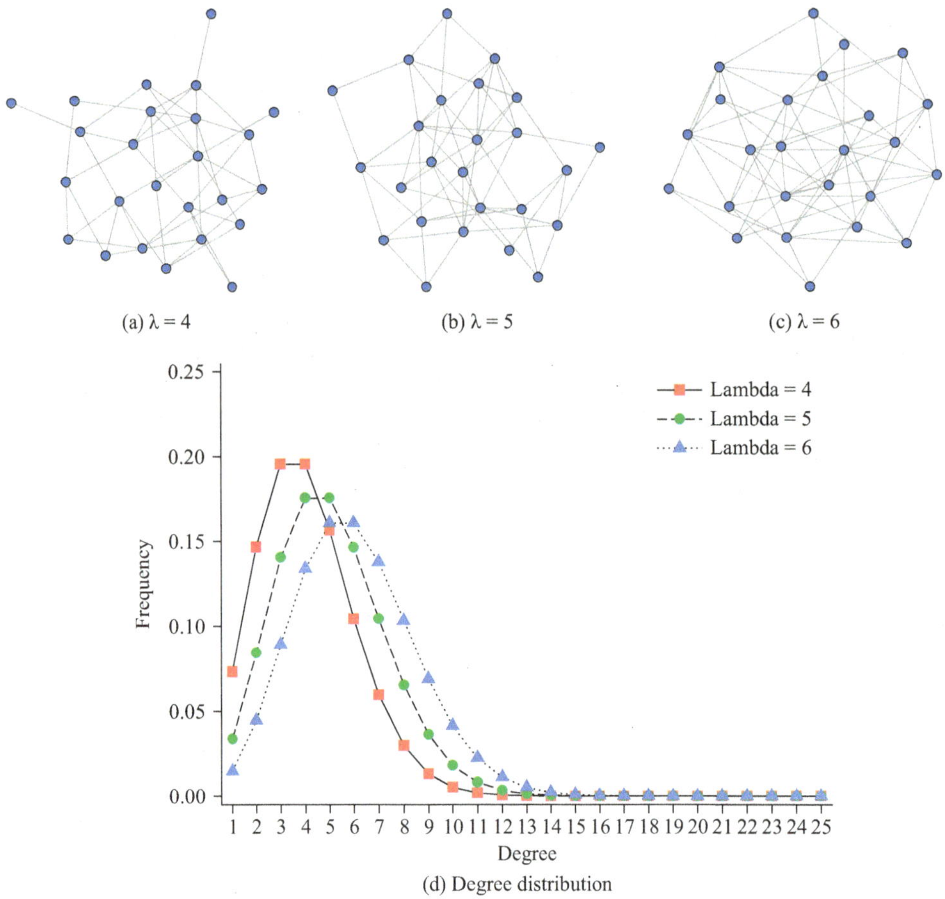


**Figure 1.4**
Networks with Poisson degree distribution.

draws attention to a distinctive and interesting feature of Pareto degree distributions. It shows that the probability falls at a rate that is independent of the degree, and this suggests a widely used name for such distributions—the *scale-free* distribution.

To appreciate the differences between Poisson and Pareto degree distributions, it is helpful to plot them on the same scale. Figure 1.7 presents the degree distributions for Poisson and Pareto distributions (where both the $x$-axis and $y$-axis are on a log scale). We note that there is a larger fraction of less connected and also a significantly larger fraction of more highly connected nodes under the Pareto distribution compared with the Poisson degree distribution.

In a small network, it is easy to describe what happens when we add a link to the network. We write the operation of adding or deleting a link as $g+g_{ij}$ and $g-g_{ij}$. In large

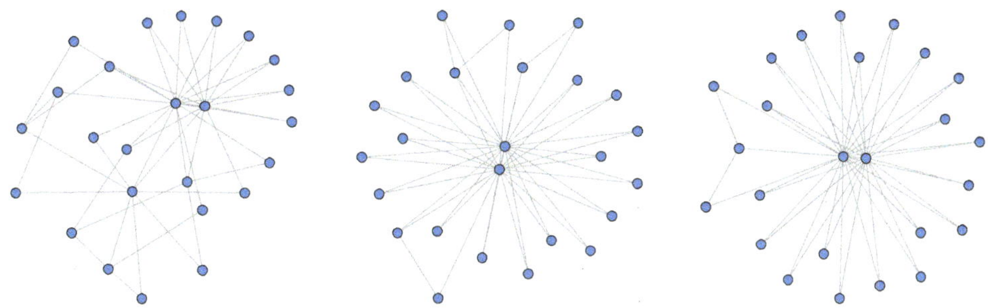

(a) $\gamma = 1.5$ (b) $\gamma = 2$ (c) $\gamma = 2.5$

**Figure 1.5**
Networks with Pareto degree distribution. *Note*: Average degree = 4.

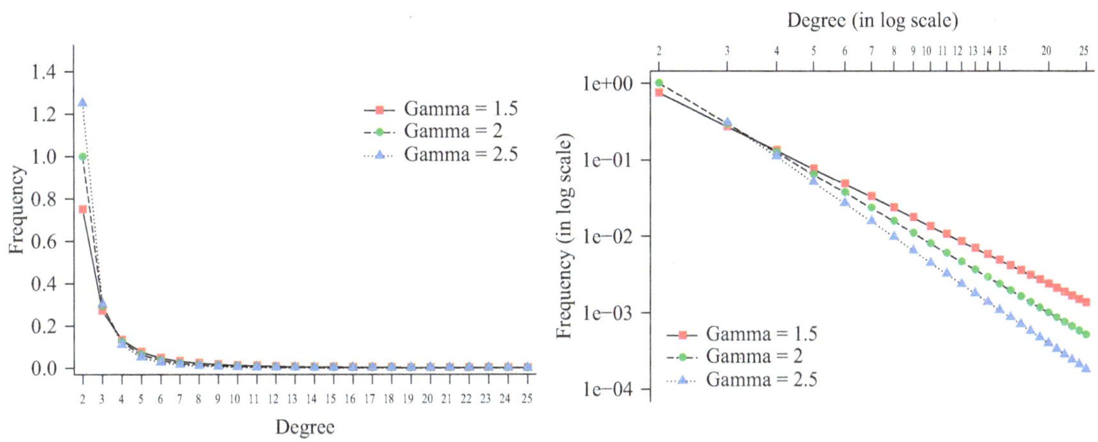


(a) Standard scale (b) On log-log scale

**Figure 1.6**
Pareto degree distributions.

networks, degree distributions allow us to conduct the same thought experiment as follows. Given a degree distribution $P$, let the cumulative distribution function be denoted by $\mathcal{P}$: $\{1, 2, \ldots, n-1\} \rightarrow [0, 1]$, where

$$\mathcal{P}(d) = \sum_{x=0}^{d} P(x). \tag{1.5}$$

Let $P$ and $P'$ be two degree distributions and $\mathcal{P}$ and $\mathcal{P}'$ be their corresponding cumulative distribution functions.

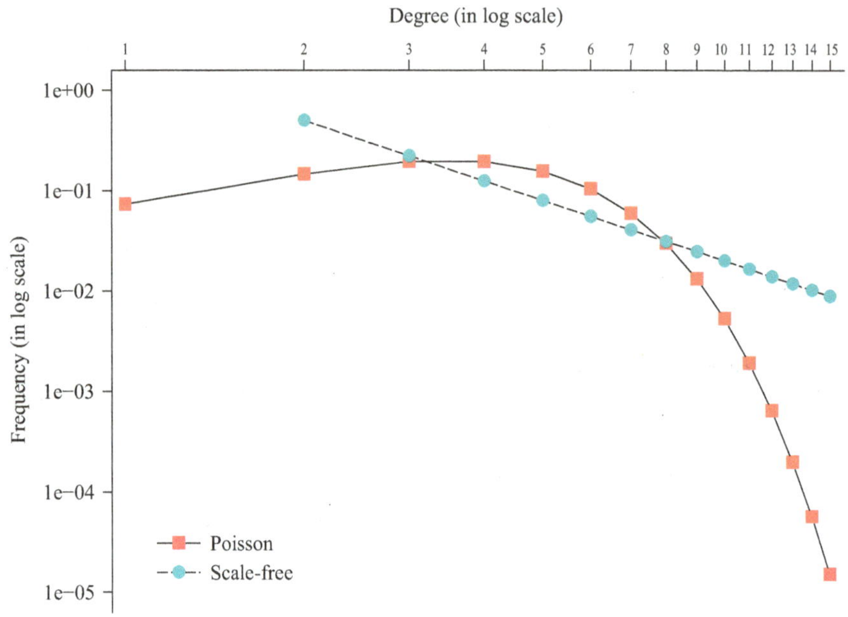


**Figure 1.7**
Poisson versus Pareto. *Note*: $\lambda = 4$, $\gamma = 1.5$.

In a large network, the notion of adding links is reflected in the concept of first-order stochastic dominance shifts in degree distributions.

**Definition 1.1** *P first-order stochastically dominates (FOSD) $P'$ if and only if $\mathcal{P}(k) \leq \mathcal{P}'(k)$ for every $k \in \{1, 2, \ldots, n-1\}$.*

So the plot of the cumulative degree distribution, $\mathcal{P}(d)$, will lie weakly below the cumulative degree distribution $\mathcal{P}'(d)$ for every $d$.

Motivated by these observations on Poisson and Pareto distributions, we now study the dispersion of degrees. Our interest is in understanding if the degrees of one network are more dispersed than those of another network. The idea of dispersion is captured by second-order stochastic dominance and a mean-preserving spread, which we now define formally as follows.

**Definition 1.2** *P second-order stochastically dominates $P'$ if and only if $\sum_{k=1}^{x} \mathcal{P}(k) \leq \sum_{k=1}^{x} \mathcal{P}'(k)$ for every $x \in \{1, 2, \ldots, n-1\}$.*

**Definition 1.3** *$P'$ is a mean-preserving spread of $P$ if and only if $P$ and $P'$ have the same mean and $P$ second-order stochastically dominates $P'$.*

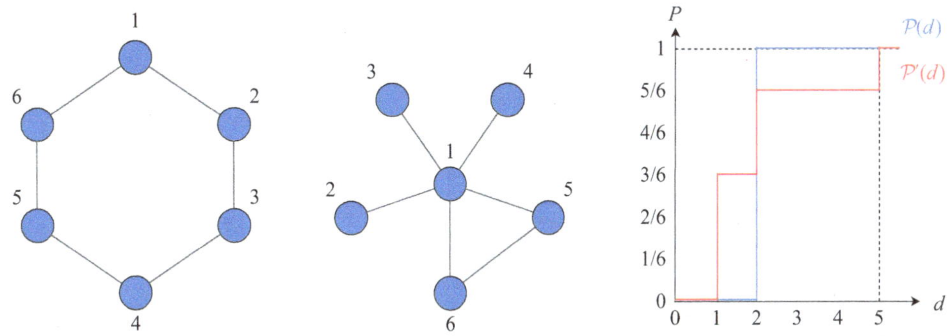


**Figure 1.8**
Mean preserving spread of degrees.

A simple example of first-order stochastic shift in degree distribution arises when we move from a regular network with degree $k$ to a regular network with degree $k+1$. An example of a second-order shift arises when we move from a cycle to a hub-spoke network with one pair of spokes connected. Figure 1.8 illustrates this in the case of a network with six nodes.

### 1.2.3 Distances

A *path* exists between two nodes $i$ and $j$ if $g_{ij}=1$ or if there is a sequence of distinct intermediate nodes $j_1, j_2, \ldots, j_n$ such that $g_{ij_1}=g_{j_1j_2}=\cdots=g_{j_nj}=1$. A *component* is a maximal group of nodes such that there is a path between every pair of them. A network is *connected* if there is a path between every pair of nodes.

The *geodesic* distance between two nodes $i$ and $j$, $d(i,j;g)$ is the length of the shortest path between them. The *diameter* of a connected network is equal to the geodesic distance between the pair of nodes that are farthest apart in that network. The *mean distance* between nodes in a connected network $g$, then, is the arithmetic mean of distances across all pairs of nodes:

$$AD(g)=\frac{\sum_{i\in N}\sum_{j\in N\setminus\{i\}} d(i,j;g)}{n(n-1)}. \tag{1.6}$$

By way of illustration, let us examine the distances in two simple networks: the star and the line. The mean distance in a star is $2-2/n$, and the mean distance in a line network is (approximately) $n/3$. The difference in average distances between the star and the line grows without bound with the number of nodes. This contrast is worth noting, given that both networks have $n-1$ links.

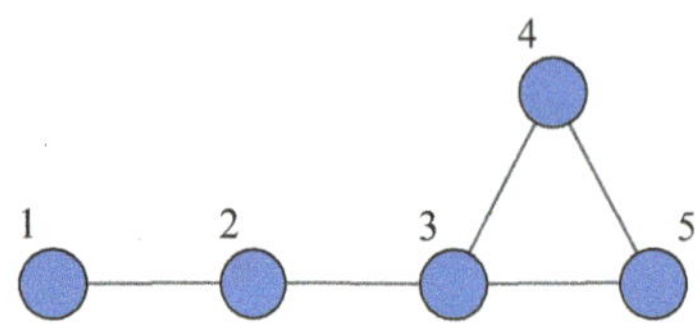


**Figure 1.9**
Network concepts: walk (2,3,4,3,2), cycle (3,4,5,3), path (2,3,4,5).

**Table 1.2**
$\mathbf{G}^2$: Walks of length 2

| | 1 | 2 | 3 |
|---|---|---|---|
| 1 | 1 | 0 | 1 |
| 2 | 0 | 2 | 0 |
| 3 | 1 | 0 | 1 |

In some contexts, it is helpful to consider more general ways of traversing the network. An elementary notion is a *walk*, which is a sequence of nodes in which two nodes have a link between them in the network (i.e., they are neighbors). A node or a link may appear more than once in a walk: a walk is the most general sequence of nodes and links possible in a network, subject to the restriction that any two consecutive nodes must have a link in the network. The length of a walk is simply the number of links it crosses. A walk with three or more nodes, with no duplication of links, and where the initial and the end nodes are the same is called a *cycle*.

It is helpful to illustrate these ideas with the help of figure 1.9. A possible walk in this network is 2, 3, 4, 3, 2. This walk contains the links $g_{23}$ and $g_{34}$ twice, and the nodes 2 and 3 also appear twice in this walk. The walk 3, 4, 5, 3 constitutes a cycle, and the walk 2, 3, 4, 5 is a path.

The matrix representation of a network is helpful with figuring out walks of varying lengths between nodes of a network. To see this, let us recall the simple three-node line network represented in table 1.1. In this network, there is one walk of length 1 between 1 and 2 and no such walks between 1 and 3. We can infer the number of walks of length 2 by writing the matrix $\mathbf{G}^2$ as given in table 1.2. Table 1.2 reveals that there is one walk of length 2 between 1 and 1 and between 3 and 3, and two walks of length 2 between 2 and 2. There are no other walks of length 2 in this network.

### 1.2.4 Local Structure

A simple example of a local measure is the number of triangles in the neighborhood of a node. In the context of social networks, this is motivated by the following intuitive idea: if A has two close friends, B and C, then sooner or later, A will introduce them to each other, thereby making it likely that B and C will also become friends. The *clustering-coefficient* of a node $i$ (that has two or more links) is defined as

$$Cl_i(g) = \frac{\sum_{l,k \in N_i, l \neq k} g_{lk}}{d_i(g)(d_i(g)-1)}. \tag{1.7}$$

The numerator is the number of pairs of neighbors of $i$ who have a link while the denominator is the number of all possible pairs among the neighbors.

By way of illustration, let us compute the *clustering-coefficient* of nodes in some of the networks in figures 1.1 and 1.2. The clustering for every node in a circle is zero as none of the neighbors has a link. Moving on to the core-periphery networks, in figure 1.2(b), clustering for the hub is 1/5 and clustering for the spoke is not defined; in figure 1.2(c) clustering for the hub is 2/11 and for the spoke is 1; in figure 1.2(d), clustering for the hub is 13/35 and for the spoke is 1.

The clustering of a network $g$ can be expressed in two ways. One is to take the average across the clustering of individual nodes. This is simply the mean of clustering across all nodes that have degree two or more and is given by

$$Cl(g) = \sum_{i \in N} \frac{Cl_i(g)}{n}. \tag{1.8}$$

The clustering in the star is therefore zero, as none of the triangles involving the links of the center is present, and clustering in the complete network is equal to 1, as it contains all possible links and hence all possible triangles. An alternative way to proceed is to weigh the nodes by their degree. Define *weighted* or *overall clustering* in a network $g$ as

$$Cl_w(g) = \frac{\sum_{i;j\neq i;k\neq j;k\neq i} g_{ij}g_{ik}g_{jk}}{\sum_i g_{ij}(g)_{ik}}. \tag{1.9}$$

The two measures can differ quite significantly if there is a strong correlation between the degrees and the clustering coefficient. A question at the end of the chapter examines the relation between these two measures of clustering.

The study of local structure can be generalized beyond three nodes to a larger group of nodes. A *clique* in a network $g$ is a complete subgraph of $g$—that is, a set of nodes $I = \{i_1, i_2, \ldots, i_k\} \subset N$ such that for every pair $i, j \in I$, $g_{ij} = 1$. In a complete network, the clique consists of all the nodes. In a core-periphery network, the clique consists of the nodes in the core (see figure 1.2).

### 1.2.5 Centrality

The centrality of a node in a network captures a number of ideas relating to its prominence. Perhaps the simplest notion pertains to the idea of how many links a node has: in this spirit, *degree centrality* measures the relative prominence of a node vis-à-vis other nodes in terms of its degree. The standard degree centrality of a node $i$ is its degree divided by the maximum

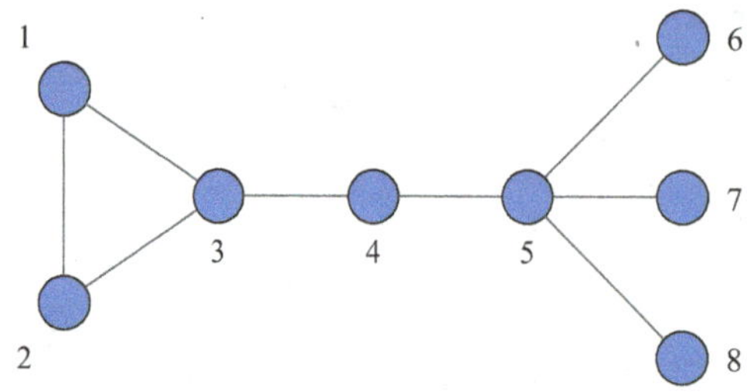


**Figure 1.10**
Network for centrality computations.

**Table 1.3**
Centrality measures

| Nodes | 1, 2 | 3 | 4 | 5 | 6, 7, 8 |
|---|---|---|---|---|---|
| Degree | 0.29 | 0.43 | 0.29 | 0.57 | 0.14 |
| Closeness | 0.37 | 0.50 | 0.58 | 0.58 | 0.39 |
| Betweenness | 0.00 | 0.48 | 0.57 | 0.71 | 0.00 |
| Eigenvector | 0.40 | 0.52 | 0.40 | 0.40 | 0.17 |
| Katz prestige | 0.32 | 0.47 | 0.32 | 0.63 | 0.16 |
| Katz prestige-2, $a = 1/3$ | 3.12 | 4.25 | 3.50 | 4.25 | 1.75 |
| Bonacich $b = 1/3, a = 1$ | 9.38 | 12.75 | 10.50 | 12.75 | 5.25 |
| Bonacich $b = 1/4, a = 1$ | 4.96 | 6.88 | 5.61 | 7.57 | 2.89 |
| Bonacich $b = 1/5, a = 1$ | 3.85 | 5.41 | 4.32 | 6.21 | 2.24 |

possible degree:

$$C_d(i;g) = \frac{d_i(g)}{n-1}. \tag{1.10}$$

By way of illustration, consider the network presented in figure 1.10. We see that nodes 6, 7, and 8 have the lowest degree centrality, node 5 has the highest degree centrality, and nodes 1, 2, 3 and 4 lie in between. This measure lies between 0 and 1.

Another notion of centrality derives from the idea of proximity: a node is said to be central in a network if the distance from other nodes is small. The total distance from node $i$ to all other nodes in the network $g$ is given by $\sum_{j \neq i} d(i,j;g)$. To account for the number of nodes, we normalize the measure by multiplying it by the minimum possible total distance in any network, $n-1$. The *closeness centrality* of node $i$ in network $g$ is defined as

$$C_c(i;g) = \frac{n-1}{\sum_{j \neq i} d(i,j;g)}. \tag{1.11}$$

This measure of centrality lies between 0 and 1. Table 1.3 presents the closeness centrality measures of nodes in the network in figure 1.10. In line with intuition, we see that nodes 1, 2, 6, 7, and 8 have the lowest levels, nodes 4 and 5 have the highest levels, and node 3 has an intermediate level of closeness centrality.

In some contexts, a node's status may arise from its location between other nodes, for example, due to possibilities of intermediation and brokerage. With this idea in mind, let us define *betweenness* for a node $i$ with respect to a pair of other nodes, $j$ and $k$:

$$b_i^{jk}(g) = \frac{\#\,\text{shortest paths between } j \text{ and } k \text{ on which } i \text{ lies}}{\#\,\text{shortest paths between } j \text{ and } k}. \tag{1.12}$$

Aggregating across all possible other pairs yields us the *betweenness centrality* of a node

$$C_b(i,g) = \frac{2}{(n-1)(n-2)} \sum_{j,k \neq i} b_i^{jk}(g), \tag{1.13}$$

where the denominator is the set of all possible pairs of remaining nodes in the network, $\binom{n-1}{2}$. Betweenness centrality of a node lies between 0 and 1.

The betweenness centrality for the nodes in the network in figure 1.10 is presented in table 1.3. We see that nodes 1, 2, 6, 7, and 8 do not lie on the shortest paths for any other pair of nodes, so they have 0 betweenness centrality. On the other hand, nodes 3, 4, and 5 lie on some shortest paths; and node 5 has the highest betweenness centrality, as it lies on the shortest paths of nodes 6, 7, 8 in addition to connecting 6, 7, 8 with the rest of the population.

A natural idea is that a person's standing in a society depends on the standing of their associates. This leads us to consider prestige or influence recursively. In this spirit, Katz (1953) proposed that a node's *prestige* is given by

$$P_i^K(g) = \sum_{j \neq i} g_{ij} \frac{P_j^K(g)}{d_j(g)}. \tag{1.14}$$

Let us set $\hat{g}_{ij} = g_{ij}/d_j$—that is, we normalize the weight of a link with the degree of the corresponding neighbor. We can then write the *Katz first prestige measure* in matrix form as

$$[I - \hat{G}]P^K(g) = 0, \tag{1.15}$$

where $P^K$ is a $n \times 1$ vector, $I$ is the identity matrix, and $\hat{G}$ is the degree-adjusted adjacency matrix of the network.

In other words, calculating prestige requires us to find the unit eigenvector of the adjacency matrix $\hat{G}$. Katz prestige values are presented in table 1.3. We note that the weighting of a neighbor's prestige by their degree is important: we see that nodes 6, 7, and 8 have the lowest measure in spite of their being connected to the most prestigious node, 5: this is because node 5 has degree 4. Moreover, node 5 has a higher prestige than node 4 because node 5 is linked to 6, 7, and 8, which are only linked to 5 (thus having a low degree).

We may also define a recursive notion of prestige that does not normalize for degrees of neighbors: this yields us the *eigenvector centrality* of a node. The eigenvector centrality of a node is proportional to the sum of the eigenvector centrality of its neighbors—that is,

$$\lambda C_i^e(g) = \sum_{j \neq i} g_{ij} C_j^e(g), \tag{1.16}$$

where $\lambda$ is a proportionality factor. In matrix notation, we write this as

$$\lambda C^e(g) = GC^e(g). \tag{1.17}$$

$C^e(g)$ is an eigenvector of $G$, and $\lambda$ is an eigenvalue of the matrix. In general, there are many eigenvalues for which a nonzero eigenvector solution exists. However, since the entries in the adjacency matrix are nonnegative, there is a unique largest eigenvalue that is real and positive (this is a consequence of the Perron-Frobenius theorem; see Seneta 2006). The eigenvector is defined only up to a common factor. To define an absolute score, one can normalize the eigenvector (e.g., by requiring that it be unit valued). Table 1.3 presents computations for eigenvector centrality for the nodes in figure 1.10. The contrast with Katz prestige measures, especially with regard to node 5, brings out the role of normalization by degree.

Katz (1953) also introduced a second measure of centrality in which the prestige of a node is a weighted sum of the walks that emanate from it, and a walk of length $k$ is worth $a^k$ for some parameter $0 < a < 1$. Katz's *second prestige measure* is given by

$$P^{K2}(g; a) = [I - aG]^{-1} aG\mathbf{1}, \tag{1.18}$$

where $I$ is the identity matrix, $\mathbf{1}$ is the $n$ (column) vector of 1s, and $a$ is sufficiently small. Table 1.3 presents the computations for Katz's second prestige measure. We see that nodes 3 and 5 have the highest prestige while nodes 6, 7, and 8 have the lowest prestige. Node 4 has intermediate prestige.

We can generalize Katz's second prestige measure to obtain the *Bonacich measure of centrality*:

$$CB(g; a, b) = [I - bG]^{-1} aG\mathbf{1}, \tag{1.19}$$

where $a > 0$ and $b > 0$ are scalars and $b$ is sufficiently small. Bonacich centrality values are presented in table 1.3. Observe that parameter $b$ now provides us the weights for walk length, and in line with intuition, we see that as $b$ declines from 1/3 to 1/5, the longer walks become less weighted and the centrality measure gets closer to the corresponding degree of centrality measure. We have covered local measures such as clustering and cliques, and global measures such as centrality. We next take up a measure that lies somewhere in between: homophily.

### 1.2.6 Homophily

*Homophily* is the tendency of nodes to be linked to others like themselves (Lazarsfeld and Merton [1954]). For example, individuals with an interest in the same sport would like to link with each other. In high school, pupils who are the same gender or who are in the same year group may be more likely to form links with one another.

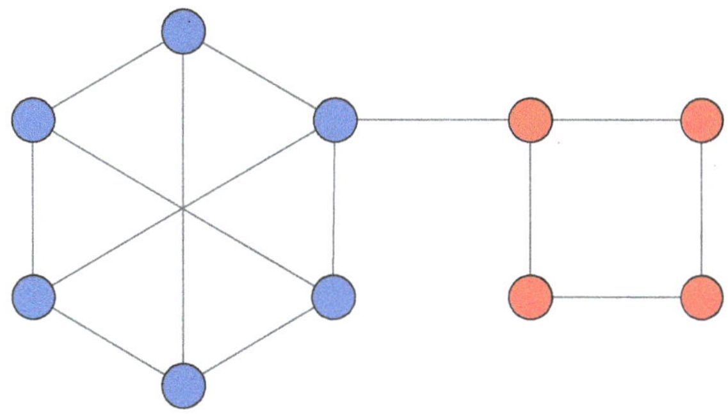

**Figure 1.11**
Homophily in a network.

**Table 1.4**
Gender homophily

| $H_{blue}$ | $H_{red}$ | $w_{blue}$ | $w_{red}$ | $RH_{blue}$ | $RH_{red}$ | $IH_{blue}$ | $IH_{red}$ |
|---|---|---|---|---|---|---|---|
| 0.9 | 0.8 | 0.6 | 0.4 | 0.3 | 0.4 | 0.75 | 0.67 |

For simplicity, let us define the notion of homophily with reference to gender. Denote the fraction of men in the population by $w_m$ and the share of women by $w_f$, where $w_f = 1 - w_m$. Let $H_m$ denote the mean share of male links among links of men.

*Relative homophily* captures a straightforward idea: we say that a group of men displays relative homophily if the fraction of links that men have with other men is larger than the fraction of males in the population; a similar notion of relative homophily applies to women. Let us define the relative homophily of group $i$ as $RH_i = H_i - w_i$ for $i = m, f$.

*Inbreeding homophily* goes a step further and measures the proportion of links within the same group (such as gender) in relation to the fraction of the population that belongs to this group and then normalizes the difference by the maximum bias that a group could possess (this measure was introduced by Coleman 1958). Inbreeding homophily for group $s$ is defined as follows:

$$IH_s = \frac{H_s - w_s}{1 - w_s}, \quad \text{for } s \in \{f, m\}. \tag{1.20}$$

A positive $IH_s$ indicates homophily, while a negative $IH_s$ indicates heterophily. The definitions of relative and inbreeding homophily can be extended in a natural way to cover multiple groups in a population.

To illustrate the definitions of relative and inbreeding homophily, we present an example of a network with ten nodes in figure 1.11. In this network, there are six men (indicated in blue) and four women (indicated in red). The homophily statistics for this network are given in table 1.4.

We next apply the network concepts introduced in this section to measure a number of prominent real-world networks.

## 1.3 Measuring Networks

### 1.3.1 US Production Network

In the US production network, a node is a sector, and the $(i,j)$ link represents the flow of inputs from $j$ to $i$. In plotting the production network, a link is said to exist from $j$ to $i$ if it constitutes over 1 percent of $i$'s purchases in the year 2002. The data is taken from the US Bureau of Economic Analysis (BEA) Commodity-by-Commodity Direct Requirements Detailed tables (https://www.bea.gov/). The data classifies the US economy into 417 sectors. The resulting network presented in figure 1.12(a) accounts for about 80 percent of the value of intermediate input trade in the US economy in the year 2002. Our discussion draws on Carvalho and Tahbaz-Salehi (2014).

In this figure, we note that the highlighted five sectors refer to (313) Wholesale Trade, (270) Real Estate, (297) Electric Power Generation and Distribution, (145) Management of Companies and Enterprises, and (21) Iron and Steel Mills. Turning to the properties of the network, the first thing to note is that the network is very sparse: there are only 5,217 links; thus the network density is 0.03. The mean degree, 11, is very small relative to the total number of sectors in the network. There is significant heterogeneity across sectors pertaining to their role as input suppliers. To develop a feel for this, let us define $w_{ij} \in [0, 1]$ as the weighted input from sector $j$ to sector $i$—that is, this is the input coming from sector $j$ as a share of total input coming into sector $i$. With this in hand, let us define the weighted out-degree of a sector $j$ as

$$d^j_{out} = \sum_{i=1}^{n} w_{ij}. \tag{1.21}$$

This measure ranges from zero (if a sector does not supply inputs to any other sector) to $n$ (if a single sector is the sole input supplier of every sector). The mean weighted out-degree of the US production network is 0.5. An average input-supplying technology is cutting tools manufacturing—with a weighted out-degree of 0.45—that supplies seven other sectors. By contrast, consider iron and steel mills: they have a weighted out-degree of 5.5 and supply 100 other sectors!

Figure 1.12(b) illustrates the empirical degree distribution associated with the 2002 input-output data. The $x$-axis is the weighted out-degree for each sector and is presented on a log scale. The $y$-axis (also in log scale) gives the probability that a sector selected at random has an out-degree larger than or equal to $x$. The weighted out-degree measure is skewed: in particular, the right tail of this distribution is well approximated by a Pareto degree distribution with coefficient $\gamma = 1.44$ as shown in the two panels of figure 1.12(b).

The presence of hubs means that many sectors are close to each other, as they are all connected to the hub sectors. Indeed, the diameter of the network is approximately 10, and

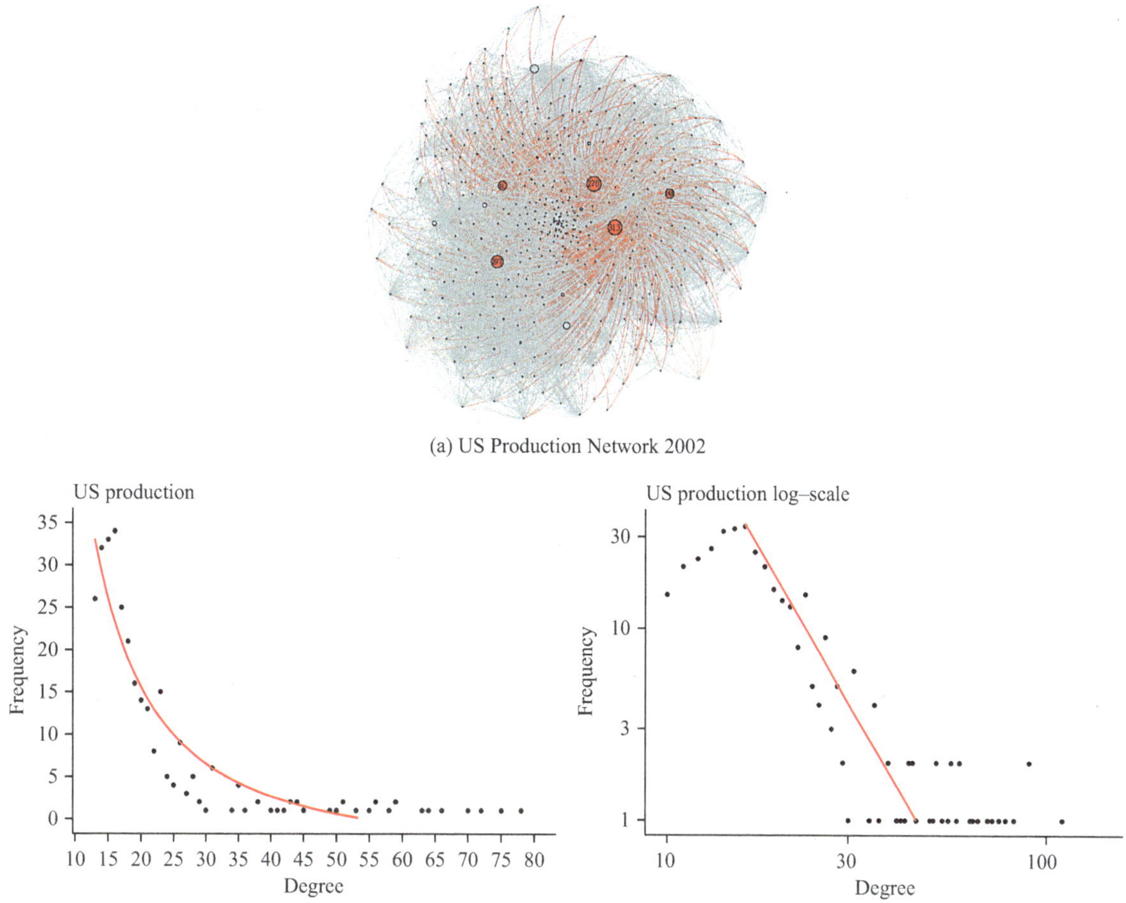


(a) US Production Network 2002

(bi) Out-degrees of US economy 2002

(bii) Degrees on log scale

**Figure 1.12**
US Production Economy 2002. A power law degree distribution. *Source*: US Bureau of Economic Analysis.

the mean distance is only 4. This mean distance is very small, bearing in mind that there are 417 sectors in the economy and the mean degree is only 11.

The scale-free degree distribution, the presence of hubs, and the small average distances between sectors raise a number of questions about the functioning of the economy. Why are some sectors so central to the rest of the economy? How do hubs matter for the transmission of shocks? How should governments target public policy to have the maximum impact on the economy?

Later in this book, we will examine the determinants of networks with scale-free degree distributions (chapter 2), the impact of shocks on production networks (chapter 5), and financial contagion (chapter 9). We will also examine the choices of traders and firms located in such networks (chapter 16) and their incentives to create networks (chapters 3, 5, 7 and 8). This study will also help us understand the forces that make systems robust on some dimensions but fragile on others.

### 1.3.2 Airline Networks

Next, we discuss the routing network of two airlines—British Airways and Southwest Airlines. The data in this section is taken from the website FlightsFrom.com (https://www.flightsfrom.com/top-100-airlines).

British Airways is the flagship airline of the United Kingdom. It began operating in 1974. As of February 2020, the airline serves 183 cities (which correspond to the nodes in the network). There are roughly 400 routes operated, but practically all the flights are routed through one of three airports in London—Heathrow, London City, and Gatwick. Figure 1.13 illustrates this network. For all practical purposes, it is a hub-spoke network, with a significant fraction of passengers using indirect flights that are routed via London. The mean distance in the network is close to 2. Singapore Airlines, Emirates, Lufthansa, and several other major airlines operate a similar hub-spoke network.

Southwest Airlines began operating in 1971 and serves 103 cities. As of February 2020, the airline operated flights on 2,980 city pairs. Figure 1.14 illustrates the Southwest Airline network. While it is by no means a complete network, its density—the ratio of operated routes to all possible routes—is 0.56. So, more than half of all possible city pairs are served with a point-to-point flight. To appreciate the extraordinarily high density of the Southwest network, note that in a hub-spoke network with 103 nodes, the density would be 0.02. The distances in this network are correspondingly low, while there is significant clustering. Well-known low-cost airlines like Ryanair and easyJet similarly operate a very dense network (in fact, Ryanair allows passengers to purchase only point-to-point tickets).

In later chapters, we will examine how transport networks shape economic activity, what economic forces drive these structures toward a grid or hub-spoke structure, and how that in turn shapes the location of economic activity (see especially chapter 6, on infrastructure). Given the central role of infrastructure networks in modern economies, we will also study the robustness of different networks to human attacks, as well as to natural disasters (see chapter 7).

### 1.3.3 Friendship Networks

We study the friendship network at a high school in the United States in 1994. Our data is taken from Moody (2001) and forms part of the first-wave component of the US National Longitudinal Study of Adolescent Health (often referred to as "Add Health"). The nodes in this network are the 673 students from a school that we will refer to as the "Countryside High School." A directed link from node A to node B is a nomination by A that B is their friend.

**Figure 1.13**
British Airways network. *Source*: www.flightsfrom.com/top-100-airlines.

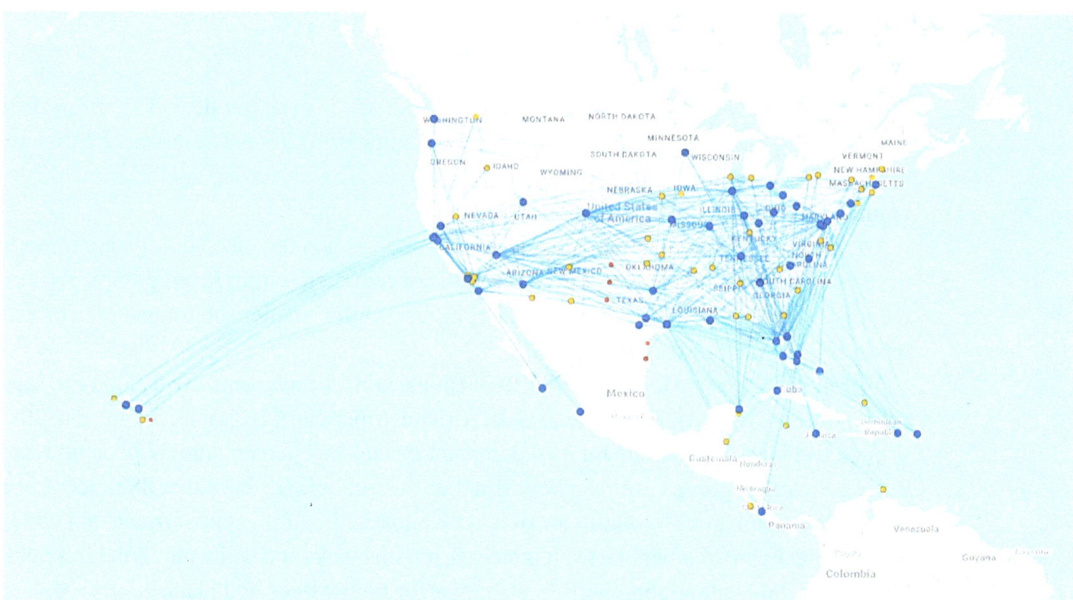


**Figure 1.14**
Southwest Airlines routing network. *Source*: https://www.flightsfrom.com/top-100-airlines.

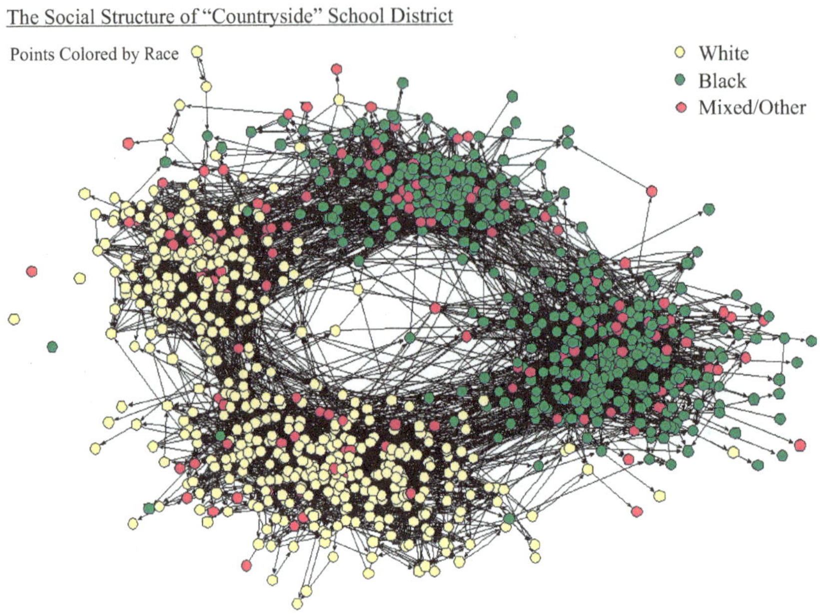


**Figure 1.15**
Countryside High School friendship network. *Source*: Courtesy of James Moody.

Students were asked to nominate up to 10 friends (5 of each gender). The mean degree was 5, so the network is relatively sparse. The diameter of the network was 9 (if we were to interpret every nomination as an undirected link). The clustering coefficient was 0.165. Figure 1.15 presents this friendship network.

The network shows that pupil characteristics such as gender, race, and age are important in shaping the network. We note that links are concentrated within racial groups. And even within a racial group, there appear to be strong ties within smaller subgroups, each of which represents the year of the students.

Turning to a closer examination of friendships, table 1.5 presents the data on the role of race. There are five groups: White, Black (African-American), Hispanic, Asian, and Others. Whites and blacks constitute the two dominant groups (49 percent and 39 percent, respectively); the other groups are relatively small at this school. Observe that 88 percent of the friendship nominations by whites are of other whites, while 81 percent of friendship nominations by blacks are of other blacks. It is clear that both blacks and white pupils exhibit relative homophily. Inbreeding homophily is also high for both whites and black pupils—0.76 and 0.68, respectively.

Table 1.6 presents evidence on the role of year: as one would expect, most of the friends of a student would be his/her classmates. Finally, table 1.7 provides evidence of the role of

**Table 1.5**
Racial homophily in friendships

| Race | Number | Fraction | Nominated | Nominated/Fraction |
|---|---|---|---|---|
| White | 333 | 0.49 | 0.88 | 1.79 |
| Black | 263 | 0.39 | 0.81 | 2.09 |
| Hispanic | 33 | 0.05 | 0.02 | .48 |
| Asian | 3 | 0.00 | 0.00 | 0.00 |
| Other | 47 | 0.07 | 0.09 | 1.28 |

**Table 1.6**
Year homophily in friendships

| Grade | Number | Fraction | Nominated | Nominated/Fraction |
|---|---|---|---|---|
| 9 | 239 | 0.35 | 0.66 | 1.87 |
| 10 | 167 | 0.25 | 0.52 | 2.12 |
| 11 | 140 | 0.21 | 0.65 | 3.17 |
| 12 | 135 | 0.20 | 0.69 | 3.51 |

**Table 1.7**
Gender homophily in friendships

| Gender | Number | Fraction | Nominated | Nominated/Fraction |
|---|---|---|---|---|
| Male | 336 | 0.49 | 0.54 | 1.11 |
| Female | 346 | 0.51 | 0.58 | 1.14 |

gender: in this school, gender appears to play a relatively minor role in shaping friendships. A student's friends of the same gender are roughly in line with the fraction of own-gender pupils in the school (the gender balance in friendships may be an artifact of the requirement in the survey that students nominate up to five friends of each gender).

Pupils share information and ideas, take part in joint activities, and develop shared values through friendships. This leads us to ask: How does the number of friends and the location in a school network shape a pupil's performance? What are the effects of relatively segregated groups on pupil and school performance? To answer such questions, we need a theory of how social structure affects individual values and behavior. A challenge to thinking about these questions is that individuals themselves create these friendship networks; thus we need to take great care to separate cause from effect. In later chapters, we will examine how the network of relations among individuals arises (see chapters 2 and 3) and how it shapes the spread of norms and of information and the formation of opinions (see chapters 4, 11, 12, 13, 18, and 19). In these chapters, we will pay special attention to the role of homophily.

### 1.3.4 Chains of Affection: Romantic and Sexual Relations

We describe the network of romantic and sexual relationships in an American high school, named Jefferson High School, over the period 1993–1995. Our data is taken from Bearman, Moody, and Stovel (2004) and forms part of the first-wave component of the Add Health study. This high school has roughly 1,000 students, and it is located in a mid-sized midwestern town. The town is over an hour's drive from the nearest large city. In all, 90 percent of the students on the school roster participated in the in-school survey, and over the course of the study period, 83 percent of them completed in-home interviews.

Jefferson is a close-knit, insular, predominantly working-class community that offers few activities for young people. The relative isolation of the community helps us build a relatively complete picture of all relationships in the high school.

Jefferson High is similar to other American schools with regard to many dimensions, such as grades, prevalence of smoking, religious affiliation, and alcohol consumption. More than half of all the students report having had sexual intercourse, a rate comparable to the national average and only slightly higher than observed for similar schools with respect to race and size.

Adolescents were asked if they were currently in or had been involved in a special romantic relationship at some point during the past 18 months (1993–1994). Adolescents involved in such relationships were asked to describe their three most recent ones (including any current relationships). In addition, adolescents were asked to identify up to three individuals with whom they had a nonromantic sexual relationship in the past 18 months. A nonromantic sexual relationship was defined as a relationship involving sexual intercourse that the respondent did not identify as special and in which the partners did not kiss, hold hands, or say that they liked each other. A little less than one-quarter of all Jefferson students reported no romantic or nonromantic sexual relationship.

Figure 1.16 presents the network of romantic and sexual relations among adolescents attending high school in Jefferson. It maps the actual network structure that connects the 573 students involved in a romantic or sexual relationship with another student at Jefferson High. In this network, a node is a student, and an edge is a romantic or sexual relation between the two nodes.

The diagram reveals a number of interesting facts. Recall from section 1.2.3, that a component is a subgraph of a network in which all nodes are reachable through paths from other nodes in the subgraph. A component is the natural object of study for the diffusion of diseases if infection can spread only via close contact. We first note that dyads (two individuals whose only partnership is with each other) are relatively common (appearing 63 times). Thus 126 students are involved in isolated dyadic relations. In addition, a large number of other individuals have a single relationship, but their partners have multiple partners. Triads composed of one male and two females occur 12 times, and triads composed of one female and two males occur 9 times. In all, 189 students at Jefferson (roughly 35 percent of the romantically active students) are involved in components containing three or fewer students.

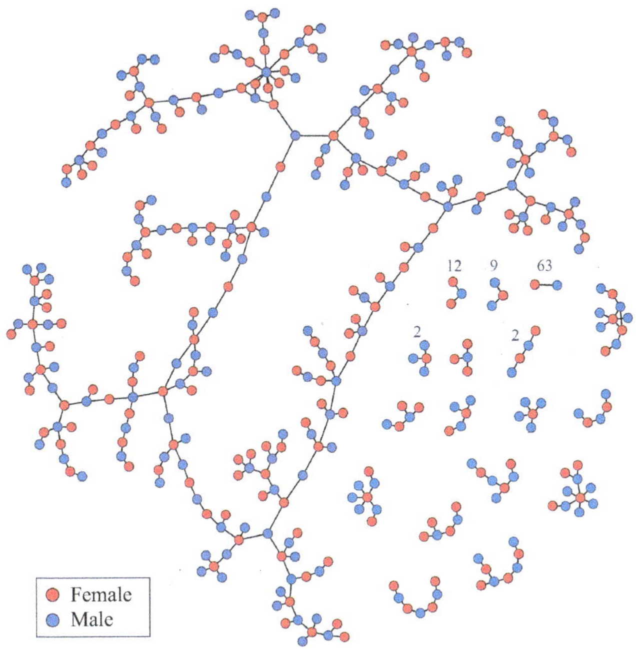


**Figure 1.16**
Romantic and sexual relations network at "Jefferson School," 1993–1994. *Source*: Bearman, Moody, and Stovel (2004).

Another interesting feature of the network is the existence of a giant component involving 288 students (52 percent of the romantically involved students at Jefferson). This giant component contains many individuals with multiple partners, and it has short branches and a large diameter: the two most distant individuals are 37 steps apart. Interestingly, though perhaps not surprisingly, it contains no short cycles.

The romantic relations network has some striking properties—a large component size, long paths, gender heterophily in links, and the absence of small cycles. In later chapters, we will draw attention to the wide range of individual motives that shape linking behavior and determine the architecture of social networks (chapters 2 and 3) and how the structure of the network shapes behavior (chapters 4–13), and the spread of opinions, norms, and diseases (chapters 12, 13, and 14).

### 1.3.5 Caste Networks in Rural India

We describe the social network in a village in the Indian state of Karnataka in the year 2006. This data is taken from a large-scale study conducted by Abhijit Banerjee, Arun Chandrashekhar, Esther Duflo, and Matthew Jackson (2013). The nodes in this network are 413 households. A link reflects a variety of social interactions, ranging across labor exchange, advice, and monetary transfers, to the exchange of daily necessities (such as cooking fuel). There were 1,756 ties between these households. The mean degree was 8.50; hence the network is very sparse.

Let us examine the local features of the network next. There was significant overlap in neighbors: the clustering-coefficient of the network was 0.40! This is very high, considering that only 2.5 percent of the potential links were realized. This suggests that if links were formed at random, then clustering would be roughly 0.025.

To understand the drivers of link formation, we now turn to the role of individual characteristics. In Indian society, caste is an important category. It is therefore useful as a first step to categorize this village in terms of general groups based on the following legally defined categories of castes and tribes: Other Backward Caste (OBC), Scheduled Caste (SC), Scheduled Tribe (ST), and General (G). Figure 1.17 presents the network of social relations in the village, and we see that there is a significant concentration of social relations within castes and tribes.

Table 1.8 presents the evidence on subcaste-based relations. Four subcaste categories are covered: OBC, SC, ST, and G. OBC and SC constitute 69 percent and 26 percent of the population, respectively.

Here, we examine the distribution within and across links through the lens of caste-based homophily. As an example, consider SC: its members constitute 26 percent of the population but 80 percent of their links are within their own group, yielding am inbreeding homophily of 0.73 (for a definition of inbreeding homophily, see section 1.2). Similarly, consider the case of ST; its members constitute only 2 percent of the population of the village, but 31 percent of their social relations are with other ST members, yielding an inbreeding homophily ratio of 0.30.

Favor exchange is an important element in these social networks. As these networks sustain trust and cooperation, the sparsity of links across caste groups raises the possibility that many potentially beneficial exchanges do not occur. In later chapters, we will examine the role of network structure in shaping the magnitude and patterns of cooperation. In those discussions, we will also take up the questions of how trust and cooperation at the level of a community scale up, how they are related to generalized trust (the possibility of cooperation at a society level), and how such communities interact with other institutions like the market and the state to sustain high economic performance. These issues are examined in chapters 12, 17, 18, and 19.

### 1.3.6 Twitter

Twitter is an online information network that was established in May 2006. It allows users to keep up to date with messages from other users, a relation that is referred to as "following." If A is following B, then tweets received by A from B can be passed on to their followers. In other words, a tweet may be "retweeted." This creates the possibility of users spreading

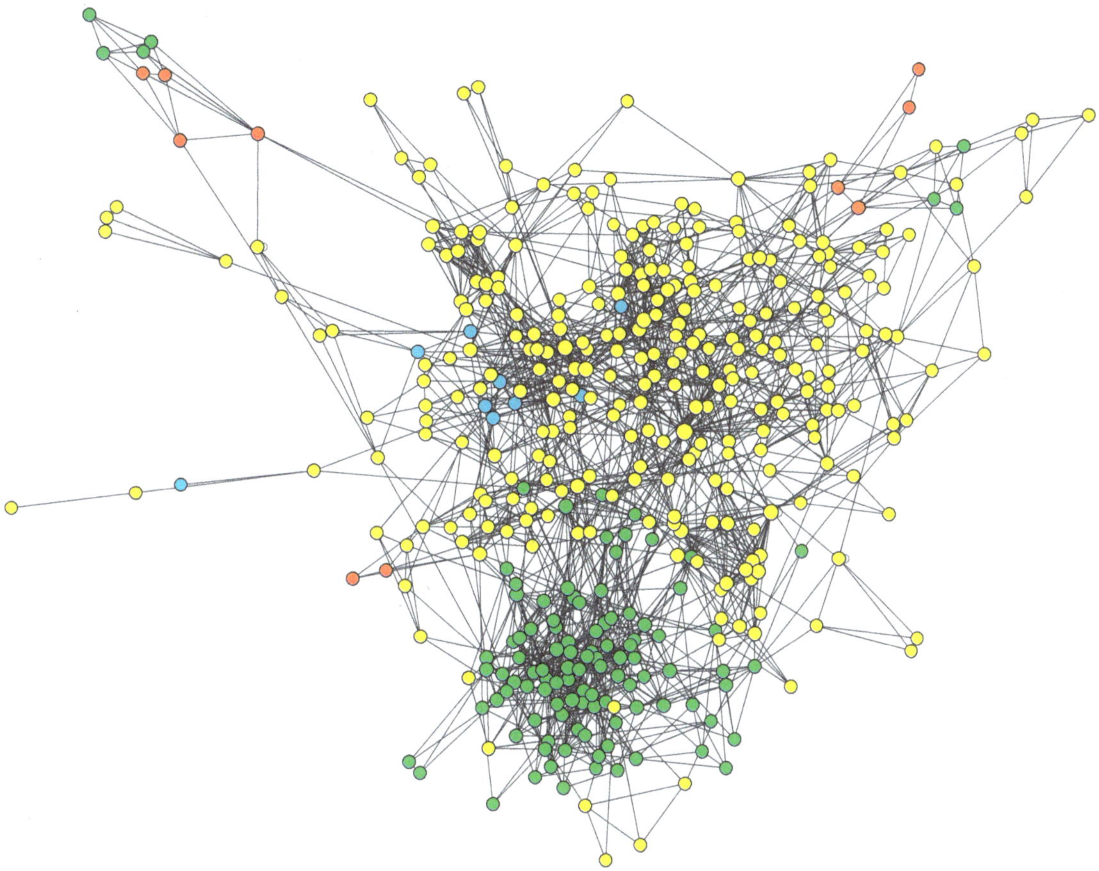

**Figure 1.17**
Networks in an Indian village. *Note*: OBC is presented in yellow; SC is in green; ST is in red; and G is in blue. *Source*: Banerjee et al. (2013).

**Table 1.8**
Caste homophily and social relations

| | Fraction | Nomination | Nom/Fraction |
|---|---|---|---|
| OBC | 69 | 89 | 1.2 |
| SC | 26 | 80 | 3 |
| ST | 2 | 31 | 13 |
| G | 2 | 15 | 7 |

information of their choice beyond the neighborhood of the original tweeter, along the paths of the Twitter social network.

In a 2018 study conducted by the Pew Research Center, Twitter had 321 million users (Wojcik and Hughes, 2019). The median in-degree was 25, while the median out-degree was 89: the median out-degree is therefore much greater than the median in-degree (recall that the in-degree of a node refers to the number of followers, while the out-degree refers to the number of people a person is following). This gives a first sense of the imbalance in Twitter, which suggests that in-degree distribution is very unequal compared to out-degree distribution.

There are also very large differences in the level of activity, which correlate strongly with the network structure. The top 10 percent of tweeters made 138 tweets on average, and these users were responsible for 80 percent of all tweets. In this set of highly active tweeters, the median in-degree was 387, while the median out-degree was 456. Users like Donald Trump, Barack Obama, and Katy Perry had over 25 million followers apiece. These statistics are in sharp contrast to the behavior of the bottom 90 percent of tweeters. This last category made 2 tweets per month, their median in-degree was 19, and their median out-degree was 74.

As Twitter is used by individuals, firms, and governments to share ideas and information, we would like to understand how far information travels on Twitter and how it depends on the point at which it is first tweeted, as well as the influence of different individuals and how this influence is related to the network of connections. Does the truth prevail, or do mutually contradictory views persist over long periods of time in the network? What are the optimal nodes to target to maximize influence or to minimize the spread of false information? These questions are the subject of much contemporary research; we will study them in chapters 11, 13, and 14.

Later in this book, we will also examine how such sparse and unequal networks emerge (chapters 2, 3, and 11), their implications for the amount of information acquired (chapter 11), how they shape the spread of information (chapter 13), and how the structure of such a network can be exploited for the more effective diffusion of ideas (chapter 15).

### 1.3.7 World Wide Web

The World Wide Web is a network in which links connect pieces of information. Our discussion draws on Broder, Kumar, Maghoul, et al. (2000), Kleinberg (1998), and Easley and Kleinberg (2010).

The Web was designed by Tim Berners-Lee between 1989 and 1991. At a basic level, it is an application designed for people to share information with each other over the Internet. The Web has two central elements: One, it provides a way to make documents (in the form of web pages) easily available to anyone on the Internet. Two, it provides a way for others to easily access the web pages using a browser that can connect to public spaces on computers across the Internet.

Web pages make use of hypertext that allows the designer to annotate any portion of the document with a virtual link to another Web page. This allows a reader to move directly from one page to another. The set of Web pages thereby becomes a graph, which is in fact a directed graph.

We draw attention to two features of the Web. The first feature pertains to the connectivity of the network. We shall say that a directed graph is *strongly connected* if there is a path from every node to every other node. When a directed graph is not strongly connected, it's important to be able to identify the nodes that are "reachable" from other nodes using directed paths. The key is to find the right notion of a "component" for directed graphs, and in fact, one can do this with a definition that strictly mirrors the formal definition of a component in an undirected graph. A strongly connected component (SCC) in a directed graph is a subset of the nodes such that every node in the subset has a path to every other one, and the subset is *not* part of a larger set with the property that every node can reach every other one.

With these definitions in hand, we turn to the description of the network structure of the Web. Our description is based on a study of the Web by Broder, Kumar, Maghoul, et al. (2000), done when the Web had been in place for about a decade. For their raw data, the researchers used the index of pages and links from one of the largest commercial search engines at the time, AltaVista.

First, we note that it is not possible for us to present a "map" of the Web, given the scale and complexity of the network being analyzed. So we will take a more abstract, high-level perspective: we will divide the Web into a few large pieces and then show how the pieces fit together. Figure 1.18 presents a plot of the network at this high level of abstraction.

The first observation is that the Web contains a giant SCC. Let us now discuss the constituents of this SCC. It consists of a number of major search engines and other "starting page" sites with links leading to directory-type pages from which one can in turn reach the home pages of major educational institutions, large companies, and governmental agencies. From here, one can reach most of these pages within each of these large sites. Further, many of the pages within these sites link back to the search engines and starting pages themselves. Thus, all these pages can mutually reach one another and all belong to the same SCC.

The second step is to position all the remaining SCCs in relation to the giant one. We consider groups of nodes in terms of reachability from the SCC. There is a set of IN nodes that can reach the giant SCC but cannot be reached from it, and there is a set of OUT nodes that can be reached from the giant SCC but cannot reach it.

When we put the SCC and the IN and OUT nodes together, there is the visual effect of IN and OUT as large lobes hanging off the central SCC. These are the considerations that lie behind the 'bow-tie picture" of the Web in figure 1.18.

There are nodes that do not lie in SCC or in IN or OUT, and they can be further classified as follows. There are the "tendrils" of the bow-tie, which consist of (1) the nodes reachable from IN that cannot reach the giant SCC, and (2) the nodes that can reach OUT but cannot

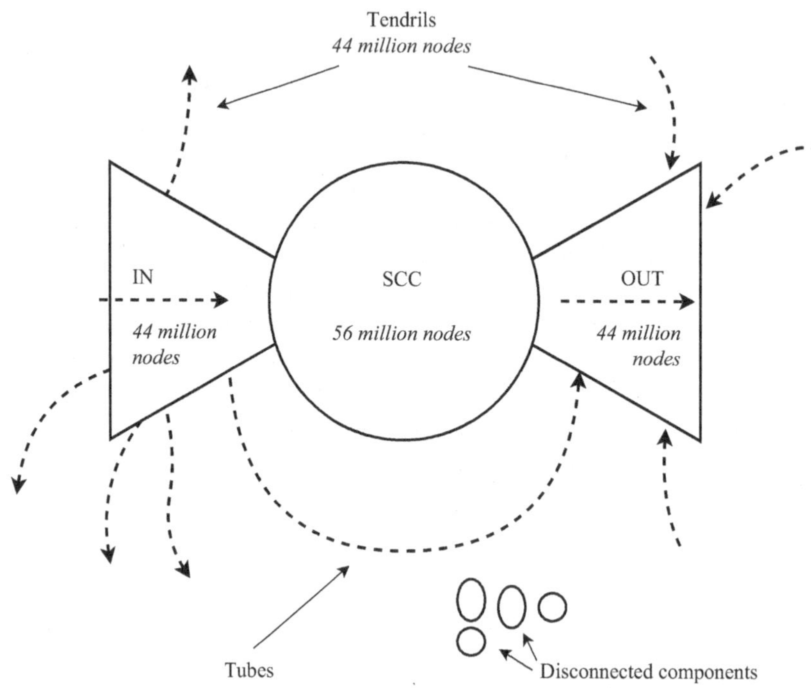


**Figure 1.18**
Architecture of the World Wide Web. *Source*: Based on Broder, Kumar, Maghoul, et al. (2000).

be reached from the giant SCC. It is possible for a tendril node to satisfy both (1) and (2), in which case it forms part of a "tube" that travels from IN to OUT without touching the giant SCC. Finally, there are nodes that are disconnected: nodes that do not have a path to the giant SCC even if we ignore the directionality of the edges.

Thus we see that the Web contains a central "core" containing many of its most prominent pages, with many other nodes that lie "upstream," "downstream," or "off to one side" relative to this core. It is important to keep in mind that the high-level snapshot reveals an order that persists in spite of the extraordinarily dynamic nature of the Web. Every day, people create pages and links and so, at the micro level, the constituent pieces of the bow-tie are constantly shifting their boundaries, with nodes entering (and leaving) the giant SCC over time. But the aggregate or high-level picture has remained essentially unchanged.

The fundamental function of the Web is that it allows information to be shared. A first thought would be that a Web page's information is shared in proportion to how many links point to it (i.e., its in-degree). Early studies suggest that the in-degrees are extremely unequal and they follow a scale-free distribution. In particular, a number of early researchers found that the fraction of Web pages that have k links is approximately proportional to $k^{-2}$ (see for e.g., Broder et al. 2000). Over the years, a number of studies have been done with regard to the degree distribution: they suggest that both the high-level bow-tie structure and the great inequality in connections are robust features of the Web.

This description raises the question of how powerful or influential a Web page is compared to other Web pages. To understand questions like this, we need to dig deeper into the details of the Web's network structure and to develop a theory of how information travels through a network. The discussion on centrality measures in section 1.2.5 reveals that the power or influence of a node can be understood recursively in terms of the influence of the Web pages that point to it. In particular, traditional concepts from matrix algebra (such as eigenvector centrality) are closely related to the notion of Page Rank (PR), an algorithm used by Google Search to rank Web pages in their search engine results. Roughly, Page Rank works by counting the number and quality of links to a page to determine an estimate of how important the website is.

These striking features of the Web motivate a closer examination of the processes that lead to the bow-tie structure and the great inequality in links, and invite further study of the implications of such structures for information sharing and opinion formation. These questions are explored in chapters 2 and 3 (which discuss the formation of networks) and chapters 11 and 13 (which take up the generation and flow of information in networks).

### 1.3.8 Scientific Collaboration: The Case of Coauthorship

Scientists collaborate to conduct research. Coauthorship is perhaps the most concrete form of such collaboration. The patterns of collaboration can potentially have a profound effect on the questions that scientists study, how well informed they are, what methods they use to conduct their research, and most of all, how fast they make progress. These considerations motivate the study of coauthor networks. Our discussion draws on Goyal, van der Leij, and Moraga-González (2006), Ductor, Fafchamps, Goyal, and Van der Leij (2014), and Ductor, Goyal, and Prummer (2022).

We discuss the network of coauthorships among economists over the 10-year period of 2000–2009. The data is taken from Econlit, a publicly available data set (https://www.aeaweb.org/econlit/). In this period, over 151,000 authors published papers. The mean or average number of coauthors (1.95), was very small, given the period of time and the number of potential coauthors. Our first observation is that this network is very sparse. On the other hand, the most connected 100 authors had an average degree of 25: this suggests that the coauthor network is very unequal.

Next, we turn to the local structure: the clustering-coefficient was large (0.17). To get a sense of why this is a very large figure, note that if coauthors were found at random, then the clustering ratio would correspond to the average number of coauthors divided by the total number of authors—a number that is close to zero!

Next, consider the macro-level properties of the network. An interesting feature is that it is relatively well integrated. The largest component contained over 67,000 nodes (this is over 44 percent of all the authors), with a mean distance of only 9.80. At first, this average distance should come as a surprise: if individual authors have two coauthors on average, then an author will have two authors who are neighbors of neighbors, and so forth. Thus the number of nodes reached only grows by a factor of 2 at every step. How can we reconcile the size of the largest component with its small average distance?

The key to understanding the puzzle is to recall the great difference in average or mean distance in a line network and a star network. They have roughly the same average degree, but very different mean distances. Indeed, in the economic coauthor network, there are some very highly connected authors (as noted previously). To see this in the simplest way, suppose that we were to delete 5 percent of authors at random: this has practically no impact on mean distance in the largest component. But the deletion of the 5 percent most connected authors completely fragments it. Thus the most connected authors span the research profession and hold it together. The figure of the local network of Daron Acemoglu presented in the introduction and the local network of Jean Tirole from the 1990–1999 period presented in figure 1.19 illustrate this point.

We may wonder if authors of different ethnicities or genders have very different modes of collaboration. Ductor, Goyal, and Prummer (2022) study the role of gender and find

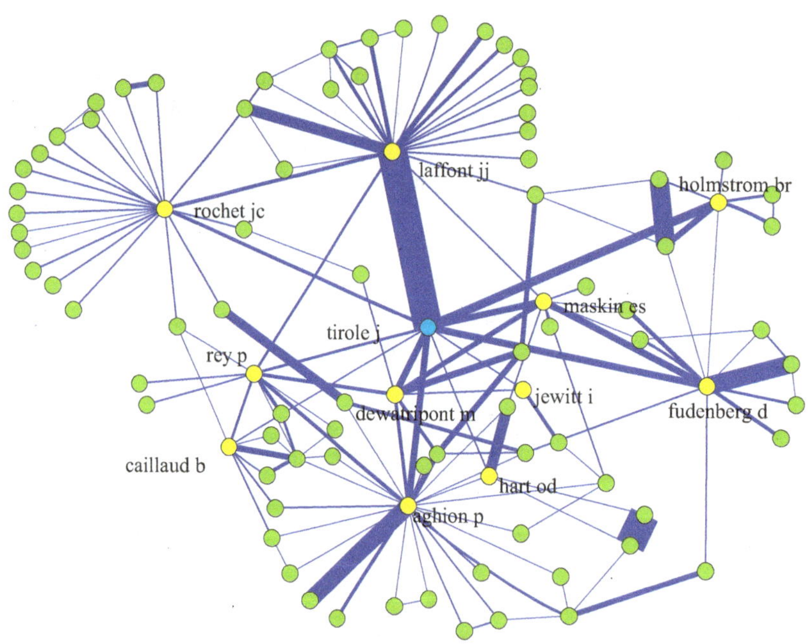


**Figure 1.19**
Local coauthor network of Jean Tirole, 1990–1999. *Data source*: www.aeaweb.org/econlit/ *Note*: The figure shows all authors within distance 2 of J. Tirole, as well as the links among them all. The width denotes the strength of a tie. Some economists might appear twice or are missing due to the use of different initials or misspellings in EconLit. The figure was created by the software program Pajek.

that the economics coauthor network exhibits homophily along the lines of gender, a male economist (a female economist) coauthors more often with men (women) than their fraction in the population of economists. On average, 81 percent of men's collaborations are with other men; the fraction of men in the economist population was 72 percent. Similarly, for women, 33 percent of their collaborations are with other women on average, while the ratio of women in the population is 27 percent. Perhaps more surprisingly, men and women differ in their degree and clustering: women have roughly 23 percent lower-degree and 6 percent higher-degree clustering compared to men. By way of illustration, figure 1.20 presents the coauthor networks of the three 2019 economics Nobel laureates—Abhijit Banerjee, Esther Duflo and Michael Kremer (over the period 2000–2009). Banerjee had a degree of 22 and a clustering-coefficient of 0.09, Duflo had a degree of 19 and a clustering-coefficient of 0.14, and Kremer has a degree of 34 and a clustering coefficient of 0.04.

Later in this book, we will explore how such unequal networks of collaboration and exchange emerge (chapters 2, 3, and 16), and their implications for individual productivity (chapters 4, 11, and 16) and for the creation of norms and standards (chapters 12, 17, and 18). In these discussions, we will pay special attention to the relation between networks and inequality.

## 1.4 Reading Notes

There are many excellent textbooks on networks. As networks are studied across many disciplines, the books are written with different questions in mind. For books written from an economics perspective, see Goyal (2007), Jackson (2008), and Vega-Redondo (2008). Bramoullé, Galeotti, and Rogers (2016) provide a panoramic overview of the economics research on networks. The role of networks in economics analysis may be traced to papers written in the mid-1990s. For a discussion of the methodological issues raised by such interactions and the introduction of graph theory in the toolkit of economists, see Goyal (2016) and Goyal (2017).

For a comprehensive introduction to the study of the theory of networks, see Newman (2018). Networks have been studied in sociology for a very long time; see Burt (1994), Granovetter (1994), Smelser and Swedberg (2005), and Wasserman and Faust (1994). For a mathematical treatment of graph theory, see Bollobas (1998) and Harary (1969). For a physics perspective, see Barabási (2016) and Watts (1999), and for a computer science perspective, see Parkes and Seuken (2016) and Pass (2019). For a book that combines the economics and computer science perspective, see Easley and Kleinberg (2010).

The material on network concepts in the chapter draws on Goyal (2007), Jackson (2008), and research papers by Katz (1953), Coleman (1958), Bonacich (1987), and Freeman (1979).

The study of personal influence starts with the classical work of Katz and Lazarsfeld (1966) and Lazarsfeld, Berelson, and Gaudet (1948). For an engaging popular introduction

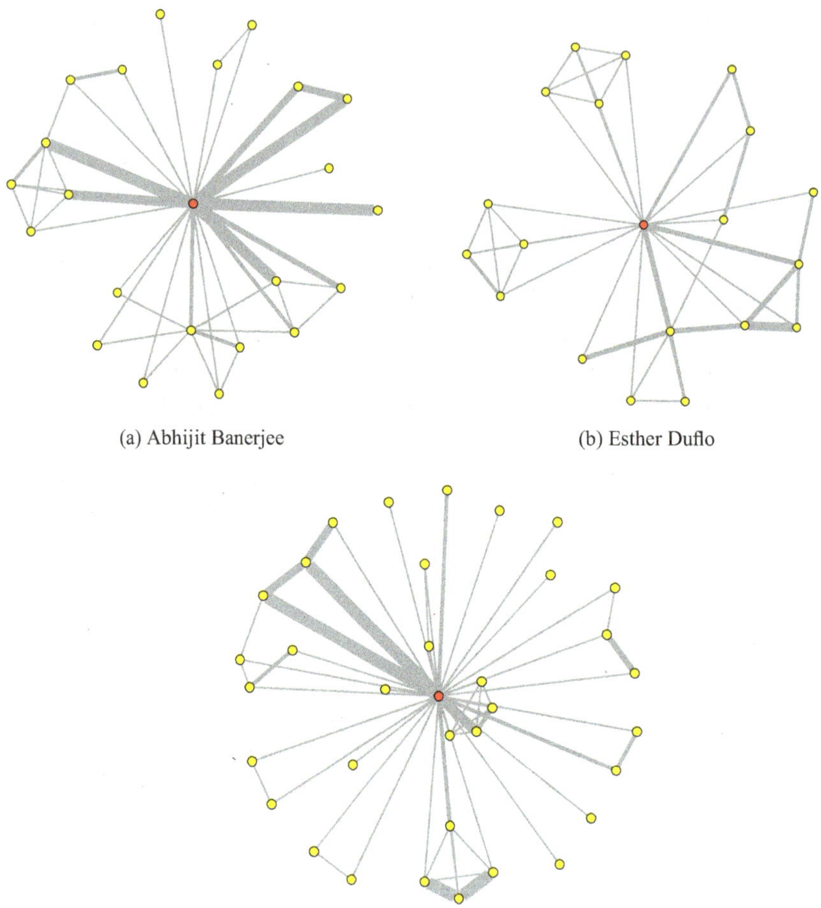

(a) Abhijit Banerjee

(b) Esther Duflo

(c) Michael Kremer

**Figure 1.20**
Gender and networks, 2000–2009. *Data source*: www.aeaweb.org/econlit/.

to the subject of personal influence in social networks, see Gladwell (2006). The data on Twitter is drawn from Wojcik and Hughes (2019).

There is a sizable body of literature on the structure and the functioning of the World Wide Web and large social media sites like Twitter. Our description of the Web drew heavily on the seminal empirical study of Broder, Kumar, Maghoul, et al. (2000). Their study has since been replicated on other, larger snapshots of the Web, including an early index of Google's search engine (Bharat, Chang, Henzinger, and Ruhl [2001]) and large research collections of Web pages (Donato, Laura, Leonardi, and Millozzi [2007]).

The study of input-output methods in economics can be traced to the work of Wassily Leontief in the 1940s; for an overview of his work, see Leontief (1941). The recent revival of input-output networks is due to the influence of Long and Plosser (1983) and Acemoglu, Carvalho, Ozdaglar, and Tahbaz-Salehi (2012). The material on the US production network is taken from Carvalho (2014). For an overview of the research on production networks, see Carvalho and Tahbaz-Salehi (2019).

The study of the sociological aspects of the process of science and its production was pioneered by Robert Merton; for a collection of his essays on this subject, see Merton (1973). Scientific collaboration is a central element in the process of the production and dissemination of knowledge. The material on coauthorship in economics is taken from Goyal, van der Leij, and Moraga-González (2006) and follow-up research by the authors. The findings on gender and collaboration are taken from Ductor, Goyal, and Prummer (2022).

The study of friendships as a social process may be traced to Lazarsfeld and Merton (1954) and Coleman (1958). Our discussion on American high school friendships draws on Moody (2001); the data reported here was kindly provided by James Moody.

Robert Fogel pioneered the quantitative study of the role of transport networks in economic growth (see Fogel, 1964). Transport networks and infrastructure are now widely studied in economics; for recent surveys, see Donaldson (2015) and Redding and Rossi-Hansberg (2017). For an early study of economic reasons for hub-spokes in airline networks, see Hendricks, Piccione, and Tan (1995). The data on airline networks is taken from https://www.flightsfrom.com/top-100-airlines. A well-known early example of the urban grid has come down to us from the ancient city of Mohenjodaro in the Indus Valley civilization.

The study of caste has a long history. Notable modern sociological works on caste include Beteille (1965, 1969), Srinivas (1987), and Mayer (1960). The data on the caste networks in the Indian villages of Karnataka is available at https://economics.mit.edu/faculty/eduflo/social.

## 1.5 Questions

1. Prove the following facts about graphs:
   (a) A connected tree with $n$ nodes has exactly $n-1$ links.
   (b) A leaf in a network is a node that has exactly one link. Show that there are at least two leaves in every tree network.
   (c) In a connected tree network, there is a unique path between every pair of nodes.
2. Compute the mean degree and the variance in degrees of the networks presented in figure 1.2.
3. Compute the average distance in the networks presented in figures 1.1 and 1.2.

4. Let $i^*$ be the node with the highest degree—or, equivalently, degree centrality—in $g$, and let us denote this centrality by $C_d(i^*;g)$. The *degree centralization* of network $g$ is defined relative to the maximum attainable centralization:

$$C_d(g) = \frac{\Sigma_{i=1}^{n}[C_d(i^*;g) - C_d(i;g)]}{\max_{g\in\mathcal{G}}\left[\Sigma_{i=1}^{n}[C_d(i^*;g) - C_d(i;g)]\right]}. \tag{1.22}$$

   (a) The denominator is the maximum possible centrality of a network: show that this is given by $(n-2)(n-1)/(n-1)$. Using this value in the denominator, show that the degree centralization of a network $g$ is given by

$$C_d(g) = \frac{\Sigma_{i=1}^{n}[C_d(i^*;g) - C_d(i;g)]}{(n-2)}. \tag{1.23}$$

   (b) What is the degree centralization of a star and a regular network?

5. We define closeness centrality of a network as follows: Let $i^*$ be the node that attains the highest closeness centrality across all nodes, and let $C_c(i^*;g)$ be this centrality. The centralization of a network is defined in terms of the difference between this maximum and the centralities of all nodes, and we normalize the measure to make sure it lies between 0 and 1.

   (a) Show that this leads us to define the *closeness centrality* of a network $g$ as

$$C_c(g) = \frac{\Sigma_{i=1}^{n}[C_c(i^*;g) - C_c(i;g)]}{[(n-2)(n-1)]/(2n-3)}. \tag{1.24}$$

   (b) Show that the maximum closeness centrality value of 1 is attained by a star, while a cycle attains the minimum value of 0.

6. Consider a three-node network in which there exist two links $g_{12} = g_{23} = 1$.

   (a) Leo Katz (1953) defined prestige of node $i$ in network $g$ as

$$P_i^K(g) = \sum_{j\neq i} g_{ij}\frac{P_j^k(g)}{d_j(g)}. \tag{1.25}$$

   Let us set $\hat{g}_{ij} = g_{ij}/d_j$ for every link. We can then write Katz's first prestige measure in matrix form as

$$[I - \hat{G}]P^K(g) = 0, \tag{1.26}$$

   where $P^K$ is the $n \times 1$ vector and $I$ is the identity matrix. Calculate this prestige measure for the three nodes in our network and compare it to degree centrality.

   (b) Compute the closeness centrality of nodes 1, 2, and 3 in this tree node network.

7. Define an independent set of nodes as a collection of nodes that have no links among them. Define a maximal independent set as an independent set that is not a strict subset of any independent set.

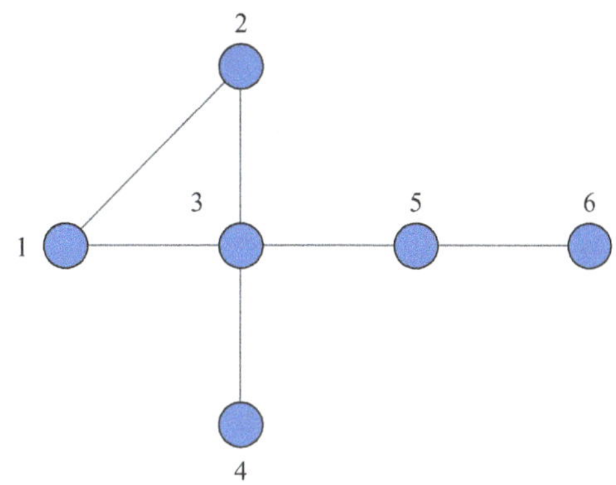


**Figure 1.21**
Network for centrality computations.

(a) Identify the maximal independent sets in a star network.

(b) Identify the maximal independent sets in a cycle network.

8. A node $i$ is a said to be critical for two nodes $j$ and $k$ in a network $g$ if it lies on all paths between $j$ and $k$ in that network.

   (a) What are the critical nodes in a star network and a cycle network?

   (b) Compute the betweenness centrality of nodes in the star and a cycle network.

9. Compute the degree centrality, closeness centrality, betweenness centrality, the Katz first prestige, eigenvector centrality, and Bonacich centrality for the nodes in the network shown in figure 1.21.

10. Explore the structure of the Facebook network of friendships. Discuss similarities and differences between the Facebook and the Twitter networks.

11. The clustering coefficient for a node is given by $Cl_i(g)$. One way to define the clustering coefficient of a network $g$ is as the "average" across nodes:

$$Cl_u(g) = \frac{1}{n}\sum_{i=1}^{n} Cl_i(g). \tag{1.27}$$

Alternatively, we can look at the fraction of potential triads that are actually present in the network. Define weighted or overall clustering in a network $g$ as

$$Cl_w(g) = \frac{\sum_{i;j\neq i;k\neq j;k\neq i} g_{ij}g_{ik}g_{jk}}{\sum_i g_{ij}g_{ik}}. \tag{1.28}$$

Compare the average and weighted clustering coefficients in a network when clustering is increasing and decreasing in degree, respectively.

# 2 Random Origins

## 2.1 Introduction

In this chapter, we will begin the journey of understanding how networks form. We will start with the building blocks of networks, the nodes and the linking protocols that connect them, and then we will see how varying these protocols gives rise to various degree distributions, connectivity levels, distances and clustering.

We will start with a presentation of the following basic model: there are $n$ nodes and an identical and independent probability $p$ that a link forms between any pair of nodes. In the literature, this is known as the *Erdős-Rényi model* of random graphs. Observe that for fixed $n$ and $p$, as links are random, a wide range of networks, ranging from the empty all the way to the complete, can arise with positive probability. An important insight of the research with this model is that as we raise $n$ and adjust $p$ in such a manner that $np$ remains unchanged, the structure of the resulting networks acquires a very definite pattern: the degrees in the resulting network exhibit the Poisson distribution. There is a threshold value of $np$, above which the resulting network is connected and below which it is not connected. This threshold draws attention to a general theme in network formation: small changes in underlying conditions can lead to dramatic changes in the structure of networks. Next, we discuss various properties of this network, such as average distances and clustering. We introduce homophily into this model by defining groups and specifying different probabilities of linking within and across groups. This richer model is known as the *stochastic block model.*

This model of random graphs is simple and the properties are intuitive. However, as we saw in chapter 1, the degree distribution of empirical networks is often highly skewed and is better approximated by a power law (and therefore is quite unlike the Poisson distribution). This leads us to consider models of growing networks in which nodes arrive over time and a new node links to an existing node in proportion to the number of its links, giving rise to a rich-get-richer property. In the literature, this is known as the *preferential attachment model.* We will derive the degree distributions generated by preferential attachment and develop conditions under which they exhibit a power law.

The Erdős-Rényi random graph model and the preferential attachment model give rise to specific degree distributions. From a theoretical point of view, as well as for empirical purposes, it would be helpful to have a random graph model that accommodates general degree distributions. This is the motivation behind the construction of the *configuration model*. We next present this network model and discuss its properties.

As we noted in chapter 1, a distinctive feature of social networks is that they exhibit short path lengths *and* significant clustering. The economics coauthor network discussed in the previous chapter provides one illustration. The Poisson graphs and the networks based on the preferential attachment process generate small distances, but they exhibit negligible clustering. We next turn to a network formation process that is able to accommodate both these properties. The approach is to start with an initial network of $n$ nodes arranged around a cycle, and each node is connected to its nearest two neighbors on either side. So there are $2n$ links in all. The diameter is $n/4$, while the clustering coefficient is $1/2$. Observe that in this initial network, the mean distance and the clustering are both large. The key idea is a "rewiring" of links: with a very small probability $p$, a link is reoriented away from a neighbor to someone picked at random from the rest of the network. As we move across links, due to the small value of $p$, only a very small fraction of the links are actually rewired. Thus the clustering remains virtually unchanged. However, the few links that are reordered reduce mean distance greatly, as a link to someone across the cycle significantly shortens the length of a very large number of paths. Thus the rewiring generates a sparse network with a small diameter and also high clustering. In the literature, this is known as the *small-world model*.

The preferential attachment model delivers skewed degree distributions but fails to account for clustering, while the small-world model provides an account for clustering but exhibits relatively uniform degrees. The chapter concludes with a model of a growing network in which a new node creates new links through two routes—random linking with older existing nodes and linking with contacts of these nodes. The possibility of linking based on the connections of others generates networks that exhibit both a power law degree distribution and also a high clustering. In the literature, this is known as the *network-based linking model*.

## 2.2 Erdős-Rényi Graphs

This section introduces the Erdős-Rényi model of random graphs and studies some of its main properties. There are $n$ nodes and an equal probability, $p \in [0, 1]$, for a link to form between any two of the nodes. What is the structure of the network generated through this process? For instance, what is the distribution of connections? Are most nodes in the network connected? What is the distance between the nodes? It will turn out that the answers to these questions can be formulated in terms of the relation between the two parameters $p$ and $n$. The model and the principal results in this section originate from the work of Solomonoff

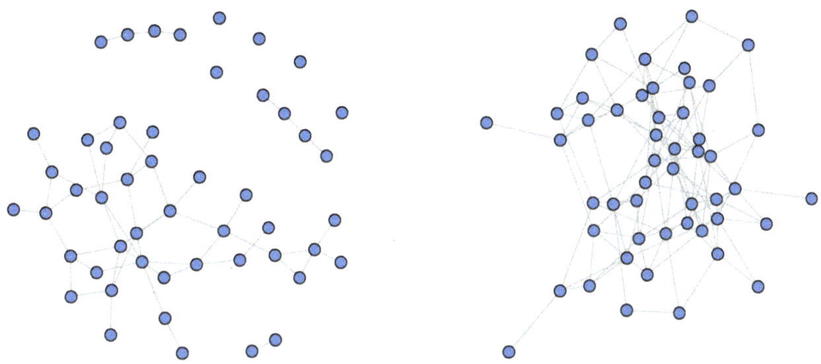

(a) Probability of linking, $p = 0.05$ (b) Probability of linking, $p = 0.10$

**Figure 2.1**
Random graphs with 50 nodes.

and Rapoport (1951) and Erdős-Rényi (1959, 1960, 1961). The presentation in this section draws on Bollobás (1998, 2004), Jackson (2008), and Newman (2018).

To get a first impression of this model, let us consider a few examples of Erdős-Rényi graphs. Figure 2.1(a) and (b) plot two graphs with 50 nodes, with the probability of linking given by $p = 0.05$ and $p = 0.10$, respectively. In panel (a), there are multiple components, and the largest group of connected nodes—the so-called giant component—is relatively small. By contrast, the graph in panel (b) is connected (i.e., it contains only one component). This brings out the point that raising the probability of linking from 0.05 to 0.10 can have powerful effects on the connectivity of the graph.

Let us next consider a thought experiment in which the probability of linking is kept constant but the number of nodes is raised. Fix $p = 0.05$. As the number of nodes increases from 25 to 50 to 100, the expected degree ($np$) grows roughly from 1.25 to 2.5 to 5. This leads to a progressively more integrated network and suggests that as we increase the number of nodes $n$, a smaller value of $p$ would suffice to ensure the connectivity of the network. Figure 2.2 plots the three random graphs corresponding to this exercise. It shows how, for a fixed probability of links $p$, raising the number of nodes raises the average number of connections for every node, and therefore enhances the connectivity of the network as a whole.

Turning to the higher-level (macroscopic) properties of the network, consider the probability that a network has $k$ links: recall that the probability of a single link is $p$ and all links are independent: so the probability of a specific set of $k$ links is $p^k(1-p)^{\frac{n(n-1)}{2}-k}$. A total of $n(n-1)/2$ links are possible, so the probability of $k$ links in a network with $n$ nodes may be written as

$$\frac{(n(n-1)/2)!}{(n(n-1)/2-k)!k!}p^k(1-p)^{\frac{n(n-1)}{2}-k}. \quad (2.1)$$

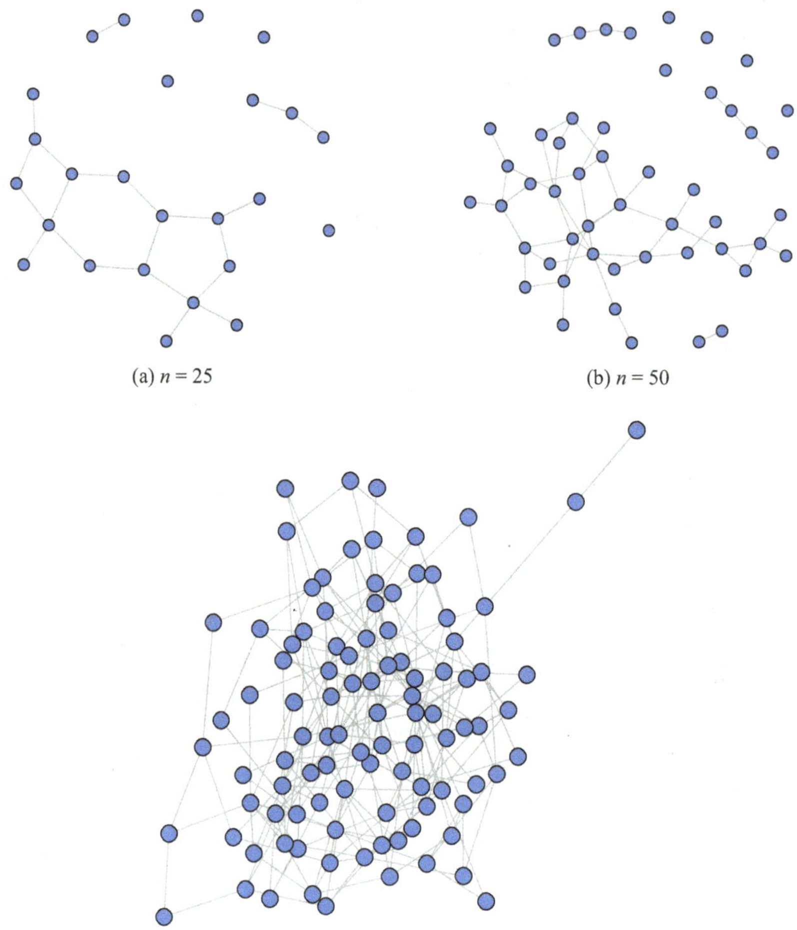

(a) $n = 25$ (b) $n = 50$ (c) $n = 100$

**Figure 2.2**
Random graphs with $p = 0.05$.

For any given node $i$, there are $n-1$ other nodes; so the probability that a node $i$ has degree $k$ is

$$P(k) = \frac{(n-1)!}{(n-1-k)!k!} p^k (1-p)^{n-1-k}. \tag{2.2}$$

For fixed $n$ and $p$, any network—ranging from empty to complete—has a positive probability of being realized. An important insight of the Erdős-Rényi approach is that the structure of the network can be sharply delineated as we take limits and consider a very

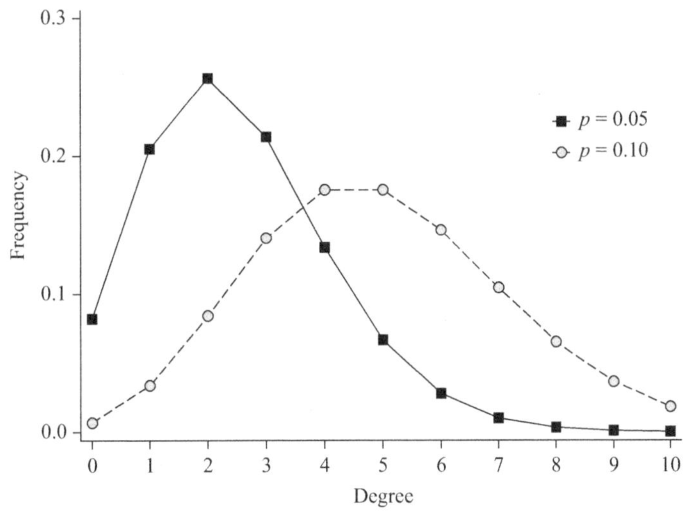


**Figure 2.3**
Degree distribution with 50 nodes.

large number of nodes. We next turn to developing this point with respect to the distribution of connections.

**Degree distribution** Suppose that the number of nodes gets very large and the average degree remains finite. The simplest way to do this is to suppose that $np$ is a fixed number. Suppose that $pn = \lambda$. Then it is possible to write the probability that a node has $k$ links as follows:

$$\begin{aligned}\lim_{n\to\infty} P(k) &= \lim_{n\to\infty} \tfrac{n!}{(n-k)!k!}\left(\tfrac{\lambda}{n}\right)^k \left(1-\tfrac{\lambda}{n}\right)^{n-k-1}\\ &= \lim_{n\to\infty} \tfrac{n!}{(n-k)!k!}\left(\tfrac{\lambda}{n}\right)^k \left(1-\tfrac{\lambda}{n}\right)^{n} \left(1-\tfrac{\lambda}{n}\right)^{-k-1}\\ &= \lim_{n\to\infty} \tfrac{n}{n}\tfrac{n-1}{n}\cdots\tfrac{n-k+1}{n}\left(\tfrac{\lambda^k}{k!}\right) \left(1-\tfrac{\lambda}{n}\right)^{n} \left(1-\tfrac{\lambda}{n}\right)^{-k-1}\\ &= \tfrac{e^{-\lambda}\lambda^k}{k!}.\end{aligned} \tag{2.3}$$

Here, we are using $n$ and $k$ instead of $n-1$ and $k-1$; for large $n$, the difference is immaterial. This formula corresponds to the well-known Poisson distribution. A property of the Poisson degree distribution is that the probability of degrees drops sharply as we move away from the mean. Figure 2.3 illustrates the Poisson degree distribution for $n = 50$, with the probability of linking given by $p = 0.05$ and $p = 0.10$, respectively.

**Connectivity** We next discuss the relationship between the number of nodes $n$, the probability of linking $p$, and the connectedness of the network. A key building block in the analysis is the concept of *threshold function*. As we vary $p$ and $n$, we would like to ask if connectedness holds. The examples illustrated in figure 2.2 suggest that as we increase $n$, connectedness would be possible for lower $p$. With this idea in mind, let us define the probability of linking as a function of the number of nodes, $p(n)$. Our aim is to understand whether there is some property of $p(n)$ that generates connected and disconnected networks. Let $A(N)$ be the set of networks that exhibit a property (e.g., particular nodes have some number of links or connectedness of the graph as a whole). A threshold function for this property, $A(N)$, is a function $t(n)$ such that

$$\begin{aligned} Pr[A(N)|p(n)] &\to 1 \text{ if } \frac{p(n)}{t(n)} \to \infty \\ Pr[A(N)|p(n)] &\to 0 \text{ if } \frac{p(n)}{t(n)} \to 0. \end{aligned} \tag{2.4}$$

If such a function exists, then we shall say that there is a phase transition at the threshold: the qualitative properties of the networks generated undergo a marked transformation when we move from slightly below to slightly above the threshold. In principle, the threshold will differ as we examine different properties of graphs.

To develop a feel for threshold functions, let us take up the property that node 1 has at least one link. In this case, $A(N) = \{g | d_1(g) \geq 1\}$. In the Poisson graph with $n$ nodes, the probability that node 1 has zero links is $(1-p)^{n-1}$. Thus the probability that $A(N)$ holds is $1-(1-p)^{n-1}$. How does this probability vary as we move across $p(n)$: for what functions is this probability equal to 1 and 0? Let us consider the function

$$t(n) = \frac{r}{n-1}. \tag{2.5}$$

Recalling a standard definition of the exponential function (i.e., for some number $x$, $\lim_{n\to\infty}(1+x/n)^n = e^x$), it follows that

$$\lim_n (1-t(n))^{n-1} = \lim_n \left(1 - \frac{r}{n-1}\right)^{n-1} = e^{-r}. \tag{2.6}$$

Thus if $p(n)$ is proportional to $1/(n-1)$, then the probability that node 1 has one or more links lies between 0 and 1. We will build on this observation to show that $t(n) = 1/n$ is a threshold function. Consider $p(n)/t(n) \to \infty$, which means that $p(n) \geq r/(n-1)$ for any $r$ and a large enough $n$. From equation (2.6), it follows that $\lim_n (1-p(n))^{n-1} \leq e^{-r}$ for every $r$, implying that $\lim_n (1-p(n))^{n-1} = 0$. Similarly, we can verify that for $p(n) < 1/(n-1)$, $\lim_n (1-p(n))^{n-1} = 1$. In other words, $t(n) = 1/(n-1)$ is a threshold function for the property that node 1 has one or more links.

We now develop the threshold function for connectedness. For a network to be connected, it must contain no isolated nodes. In a Poisson degree distribution, the probability that a node has degree 0 is approximately $e^{-(n-1)p}$. If one node is isolated, the fraction of isolated nodes is $1/n$. Equating the two yields $e^{-(n-1)p} = 1/n$. Taking logs on both sides, we obtain

$$-(n-1)p = log\left(\frac{1}{n}\right). \tag{2.7}$$

When $(n-1)p > \log n$, the fraction of degree zero nodes becomes small, while for $(n-1)p < \log n$, the fraction of degree zero nodes becomes large. The function $(\log n)/n$ is thus a threshold. The probability of linking $p$ must decline roughly in line with this threshold as $n$ grows. For any function $p$ of $n$ that remains above the threshold, the network will contain no isolated nodes, and for any function $p$ of $n$ that lies below this threshold, the network will contain many isolated nodes.

For connectedness to be obtained, not only must isolated notes not exist, but there must also be no distinct components. As we scale up the number of nodes, a component with any fixed number of nodes becomes like a single node. Thus this argument on isolated nodes can be extended to cover finite-sized components. Finally, consider the possibility of multiple components that grow with the network. As the network scales up, two components, each with an unbounded number of nodes, cannot be sustained, as the sheer number of outgoing links in each component makes the probability of the two components being unconnected negligible. So the probability of no links across the component will go to 0. This discussion is summarized in a celebrated result that we can state as follows.

**Proposition 2.1** *Consider the Poisson random graph model. The function* $(\log(n))/n$ *represents a threshold for the connectedness of the network: for* $p(n)$ *that lies above this threshold, the network is connected, and for* $p(n)$ *below this threshold, the network is disconnected, with probability 1.*

As the reasoning underlying this result is the basis of a number of key results in the theory of random graphs, we now provide a proof.

*Proof.* There are two steps in the proof. In the first step, we will consider the existence of isolated nodes: clearly, for a network to be connected, it must contain no isolated nodes. We will show that the postulated threshold suffices to rule out isolated nodes. The second step will take up components of size 2 until n/2, and we will show that for probability $p(n)$ respecting the threshold, the expected number of such components goes to zero for large $n$.

*Step 1*: In a network with $n$ nodes and with a probability $p(n)$ of a link, the probability that a node forms no links is given by $(1-p(n))^{n-1}$. As $p(n)$ becomes progressively small and goes to 0 in large $n$, this probability of zero links is approximately equal to $(1-p(n))^n$. Moreover, as $p(n)/n \to 0$, we can approximate the probability by $e^{-np(n)}$. In developing the threshold result, we will work with the function $p(n) = \frac{log(n)-f(n)}{n}$, where $f(n) \to \infty$ and $f(n) < logn$. With this functional specification, the probability of zero links is given by $e^{f(n)}/n$. The expected number of isolated nodes is simply $e^{f(n)}$. This grows without bound in $n$. We build on this observation to establish that the required property of the postulated function is $log(n)/n$.

Let $X^n$ denote the random number of isolated nodes. Let $\mu^n = E[X^n]$. We show that the variance of $X^n$, $E[(X^n)^2] - E[X^n]^2$ is at most twice as large as $\mu^n$. Observe that the expected number of isolated ordered pairs, $E[X^n(X^n-1)]$, is given by $n(n-1)(1-p)^{2n-3}$: this corresponds to the absence of links from each member of the pair to all the others and the link between the pair themselves. We may write $E[X^n(X^n-1)] = E[(X^n)^2] - E[X^n]$. With this in hand,

$$\begin{aligned} E[(X^n)^2] - E[X^n]^2 &= n(n-1)(1-p)^{2n-3} + E[X^n] - E[X^n]^2 \\ &= n(n-1)(1-p)^{2n-3} + E[X^n] - n^2(1-p)^{2n-2} \\ &\leq E[X^n] + pn^2(1-p)^{2n-3} \\ &= E[X^n](1+pn(1-p)^{n-2}) \\ &\leq E[X^n]\left(1+(log(n)-f(n))e^{-log(n)+f(n)}(1-p)^{-2}\right) \\ &\leq E[X^n]. \end{aligned} \tag{2.8}$$

We use this upper bound along with Chebyshev's inequality (Billingsley [2008]). Recall that Chebyshev's inequality says that for a random variable $X$, with mean $\mu$ and standard deviation $\sigma$, $Pr[|X-\mu| > r\sigma] < \frac{1}{r^2}$ for every $r$. In particular, from this derivation of the upper bound on the variance of $X^n$, relative to $\mu$, it follows that

$$Pr[X^n < \mu - r\sqrt{2\mu}] < \frac{1}{r^2} \tag{2.9}$$

for all $r > 0$. As $\mu \to \infty$, this implies that probability $X^n$ will be arbitrarily large converges to 1 as $n$ grows. In other words, most networks will lie close to networks with an unbounded number of isolated nodes. To complete the proof of step 1, with regard to the threshold for isolated nodes, we need to show that if $p(n)/t(n) \to \infty$, then the probability of isolated nodes goes to 0 as $n$ grows. Take a function $p(n) = (log(n) + f(n))/n$, where $f(n) \to \infty$, but $f(n)/n \to 0$. We now construct a variant of this argument to show that the expected number of isolated nodes grows as $e^{-f(n)}$ with $n$. This expectation tends to 0 with $n$. This can happen only if the probability of at least one isolated node tends to 0 in n. This completes step 1 of the proof.

*Step 2*: This step of the proof shows that the expected number of components of size 2 to $n/2$ converges to zero when $f(n)$ gets close to the postulated threshold function. Let us say that $X_k$ is the number of components of size $k$. Let $p(n) = (log(n) + f(n))/n$, where, as before, $f(n) \to \infty$ and $f(n)/n \to 0$:

$$\begin{aligned} E\left[\sum_{k=2}^{n/2} X_k\right] &\leq \sum_{k=2}^{n/2} \binom{n}{k}(1-p)^{k(n-k)} \\ &= \sum_{k=2}^{n^{3/4}} \binom{n}{k}(1-p)^{k(n-k)} + \sum_{k=n^{3/4}}^{n/2} \binom{n}{k}(1-p)^{k(n-k)} \end{aligned}$$

$$\leq \sum_{k=2}^{n^{3/4}} \left(\frac{en}{k}\right)^k e^{-knp} e^{k^2 p} + \sum_{k=n^{3/4}}^{n/2} \left(\frac{en}{k}\right)^k e^{-knp} e^{k^2 p} \tag{2.10}$$

$$\leq \sum_{k=2}^{n^{3/4}} e^{k(1-f(n))} k^{-k} e^{2k^2 \log(n)/n} + \sum_{k=n^{3/4}}^{n/2} \left(\frac{en}{k}\right)^k e^{-knp/2}$$

$$\leq 3e^{-f(n)} + n^{\frac{-n^{3/4}}{5}}.$$

We explain the reasoning underlying the last three inequalities. The first inequality holds because we abstract from the probability of links within the components. The second inequality holds because of Sterling's formula ($\binom{n}{k} \leq (en/k)^k$). The third inequality holds because, for $k \in [n^{3/4}, n/2]$, $k^2 p \leq knp/2$ (and therefore $e^{-knp} e^{k^2 p} \leq e^{-knp/2}$), and because $e^{k^2 p} = e^{k^2 \frac{\log(n)+f(n)}{n}} \leq e^{k^2 \frac{\log(n)+\log(n)}{n}}$. ■

**Distances and diameter** In many contexts of interest—spread of information or disease is one example—we are interested in how far nodes are from each other. One way to get a sense of distances in a network is to measure the diameter of the graph. Recall from chapter 1 that the diameter of a connected graph is the largest geodesic distance across all pairs of nodes.

Our interest is in large networks, and we consider the case where $pn$ is a constant so that $p$ declines with $n$. To develop a sense of diameters in such a graph, it is helpful to imagine a sparse network in which most nodes have similar degrees. With these remarks in place, we study diameter in a tree network in which every node has exactly $d$ degrees or degree 1. Furthermore, to make the computation simpler, suppose that there is a root node that is exactly distance $\ell$ from all the leaves. Start from this root node $i$. Each of its neighbors has $d$ links. This means that there are $d + d(d-1)$ nodes within distance 2 of node $i$. Extrapolating, we see that the number of nodes within distance $k$ of root node $i$ is

$$d + d(d-1) + d(d-1)^2 + \cdots + d(d-1)^{k-1}. \tag{2.11}$$

Simplifying, the sum of nodes within distance $k$ may be written as

$$d\left[\frac{(d-1)^k - 1}{d-1-1}\right] = \frac{d}{d-2}((d-1)^k - 1). \tag{2.12}$$

So it follows that if we want to cover $n-1$ nodes, it would suffice to have an $\ell$ neighborhood, where $\ell$ solves the following equation:

$$\frac{d}{d-2}((d-1)^\ell - 1) \geq n - 1. \tag{2.13}$$

To get an approximate diameter in a tree network, we can solve for $(d-1)^\ell = n-1$. Taking logs on both sides, it follows that $\ell$ is of order $\log(n-1)/\log(d-1)$. The diameter is at most $2\ell$. The key point to note is that the diameter grows very slowly as $n$ grows. To see this, consider a few examples. Suppose that the degree of every node is 11. The diameter for a network with 1,000 nodes is 6, and for a network with 100,000 nodes, it is 10.

**Homophily** In chapter 1, we discussed the network of friendships in an American high school and a social network of favor exchange among households in Indian villages. We noted there that a distinctive feature of these networks was *homophily*: the tendency of individuals to form links with others of their own type. Depending on the context, the type would correspond to gender, year, race, or caste. In the Erdős-Rényi model, the probability of linking is the same between every pair of individuals. We now extend the basic model to illustrate how it can accommodate homophily. A simple way to think of homophily in the Erdős-Rényi model is to suppose that there are many groups, and that the probability of a link between two individuals within a group is different from the probability of a link between two individuals in different groups. Let there be $M$ groups, and suppose that the probability of linking within group $i$ is given by $p_{ii} \in [0, 1]$, while the probability of a link between two individuals belonging to groups $i$ and $j$ is given by $p_{ij} \in [0, 1]$. These different probabilities define a random graph that is referred to as the stochastic block model (Holland, Laskey, and Leinhardt [1983]).

A special case is where $p_{ii} = p_s$ while $p_{ij} = p_d$, where $p_s > p_d$. Figure 2.4 illustrates networks in a society with 50 individuals that consists of two equal-sized groups, Blue and Red. In panel (a), we have a uniform Erdős-Rényi graph, with average degree 4. In panel (b), we have a graph in which the probability within the group is 0.15, while the probability of linking across groups is 0.03. The two graphs have a similar average degree, but the differential probabilities of linking create strong homophily effects. In panel (c), we have a uniform Erdős-Rényi graph with average degree 8, and in panel (d), we have a graph in which the probability within the group is 0.30, while the probability of linking across groups is 0.01. The average degree in the two networks is the same, and again we see that the density of links is significantly higher within each group compared to pairs of individuals across groups.

The Erdős-Rényi random graph model is probably the most widely studied model of networks. The reason for its popularity is that it is easy to present and provides insights into the most fundamental questions concerning networks: the determinants of the degree distribution, the connectivity, and the diameter of the graph. A major attraction of this model is that the methods of analysis are transparent and prove useful when we go beyond the basic model and study variations. The stochastic block model provides one illustration of this flexibility. At many points in this book, when we study diffusion and epidemics, games on networks, and network interventions, we will return to this model.

While the model is theoretically very attractive, from an empirical point of view it has some serious weaknesses. One problem is that for large graphs, the network will display *negligible* clustering—observe that since link probability is independent across pairs of nodes,

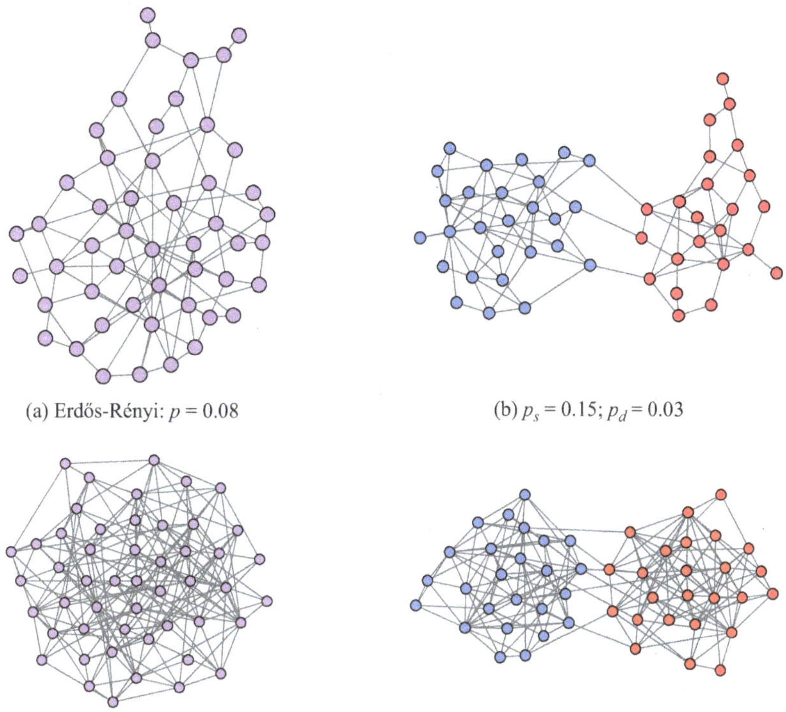

(a) Erdős-Rényi: $p = 0.08$

(b) $p_s = 0.15$; $p_d = 0.03$

(c) Erdős-Rényi: $p = 0.16$

(d) $p_s = 0.30$; $p_d = 0.01$

**Figure 2.4**
Stochastic block random graphs.

the clustering will be of the order of probability of linking and this probability gets close to zero in large graphs (it is of order $\lambda/n$).

To get a sense of the numbers, let us revisit economics coauthor networks. Table 2.1 (based on Goyal, Leij, and Moraga-González [2006]) presents some aspects of the economics coauthor network through the period 1970–2010. We see that, in the 2000–2010 period, the average degree is around 2: if links were formed at random, the clustering would be equal to the probability of a link and would be tiny (smaller than 0.001). However, the clustering coefficient in the empirical network is 0.17. This is a general feature of social networks: they exhibit very large clustering relative to what would arise in the Erdős-Rényi network with a similar mean degree.

The random graph differs from real-world networks in one other critical dimension—degree distribution. Table 2.1 gives us a first sense of this discrepancy: the average degree at 2 is very small, but the variance around 6.75 is much larger. In a Poisson random graph, the variance would be around 2. Thus the variance is greatly in excess of what a Poisson graph

**Table 2.1**
Coauthorship network in economics: 1970–2010

| Decade | 1970s | 1980s | 1990s | 2000s |
|---|---|---|---|---|
| Total authors | 32,936 | 46,181 | 82,135 | 151,953 |
| Average degree | 0.894 | 1.268 | 1.617 | 1.951 |
| Standard deviation of degree | 1.358 | 1.793 | 2.204 | 2.539 |
| Size of giant component | 4,962 | 13,134 | 30,689 | 67,158 |
| —as percentage | 0.15 | 0.28 | 0.37 | 0.44 |
| Clustering coefficient | 0.19 | 0.18 | 0.17 | 0.17 |
| Average distance | 12.39 | 10.83 | 10.00 | 9.81 |

*Source*: www.aea.org/econlit/; Goyal, van der Leij, and Moraga-González (2006).

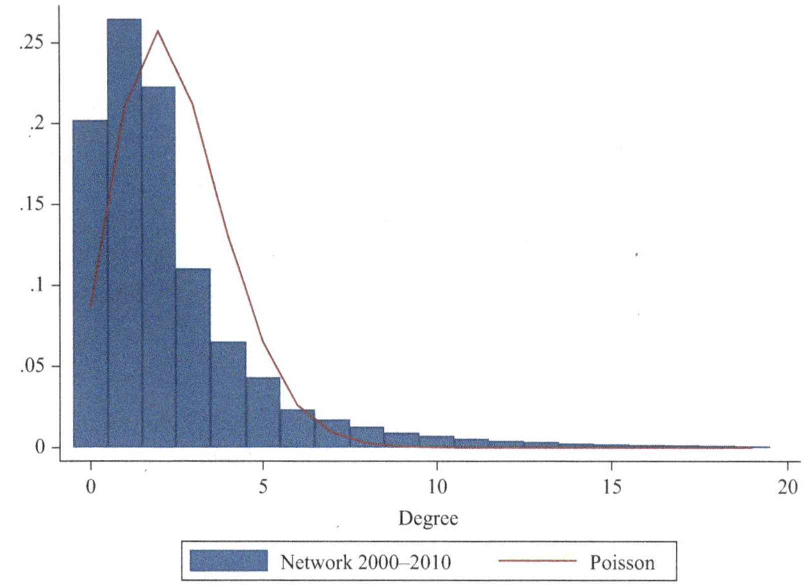


**Figure 2.5**
Coauthor network: Empirical versus Poisson distribution. *Source*: www.aea.org/econlit/; Goyal, van der Leij, and Moraga-González (2006).

would generate. Let us examine the degree distribution in a little more detail. Figure 2.5 plots the empirical degree distribution alongside the Poisson plot (for a comparable average degree). We see that the empirical degree distribution has many more low- and high-degree nodes compared to the corresponding Poisson network. These differences between the Poisson graph and empirical networks motivate the study of alternative models of networks. At this point, we turn to models that can address the issue of skewed distributions.

## 2.3 Preferential Attachment

The empirical study of skewed distributions originates with the Italian sociologist and economist Vilfredo Pareto. Pareto found that across a range of countries, the distribution of income and wealth is very unequal. Skewed distributions have also been documented in a number of other contexts, such as upstream and downstream linkages in input-output networks, the number of coauthors, and the citations of scientific papers. These skewed distributions are sometimes described as exhibiting a power law or being scale-free. The wide occurrence of these distributions encourages us to think of a general mechanism that may be at work.

The theoretical study of the mechanisms underlying skewed distributions may be traced to an early paper by Simon (1955). This rich-get-richer story is central to the study of processes leading to power laws. The existence of power law degrees in networks was first noted in the context of citation networks by de Solla Price (1965). Motivated by this empirical finding, de Solla Price proposed a theoretical model built on the rich-get-richer mechanism identified by Simon (1955). In subsequent work, this mechanism has been termed *preferential attachment* by Barabási and Albert (1999). We will first present the directed link model from de Solla Price (1976), and then we will present the undirected link model from Barabási and Albert (1999). The exposition in this section draws on Easley and Kleinberg (2010), Newman (2018), and Jackson (2008).

Recall from chapter 1, a fact concerning the World Wide Web: the fraction of web pages that have $k$ links is approximately proportional to $k^{-2}$ (see e.g., Broder, Kumar, Maghoul, et al. [2000]). As the fraction varies in proportion to $k^{-2}$, the degree distribution was said to contain a *power law*. More generally, the fraction of nodes with degree $k$ is given by $P(k) = a/k^c$ for some positive constants $a$ and $c$. If we take logs on both sides, we get the following equation:

$$logP(k) = log(a) - c\ log(k). \tag{2.14}$$

Expressed in this way, we see that the log of probability is a linear function of the log of degree. Thus the rate of fall in probability is independent of the degree, giving rise to the term "scale-free distribution." Given any empirical degree distribution, it is then possible to ask what values of $a$ and $c$ offer the best fit. The interest is mainly in the value of $c$—sometime referred to as the "Pareto coefficient" or the "power-law coefficient"—as $a$ is mostly used for the purposes of normalization.

Figure 2.6 presents the degree-distribution plots in the production network of four economies, the US, China, India, and Germany (the Pareto coefficients of the fitted curves are 1.65, 2.28, 2.25, and 1.84, respectively). These plots draw attention to the magnitude of the power-law coefficients: they often lie in the range $2 \leq c \leq 3$, with occasional values slightly outside this interval. A second general point to bear in mind is that the empirical distribution does not generally follow the power law over its entire range. For example, in

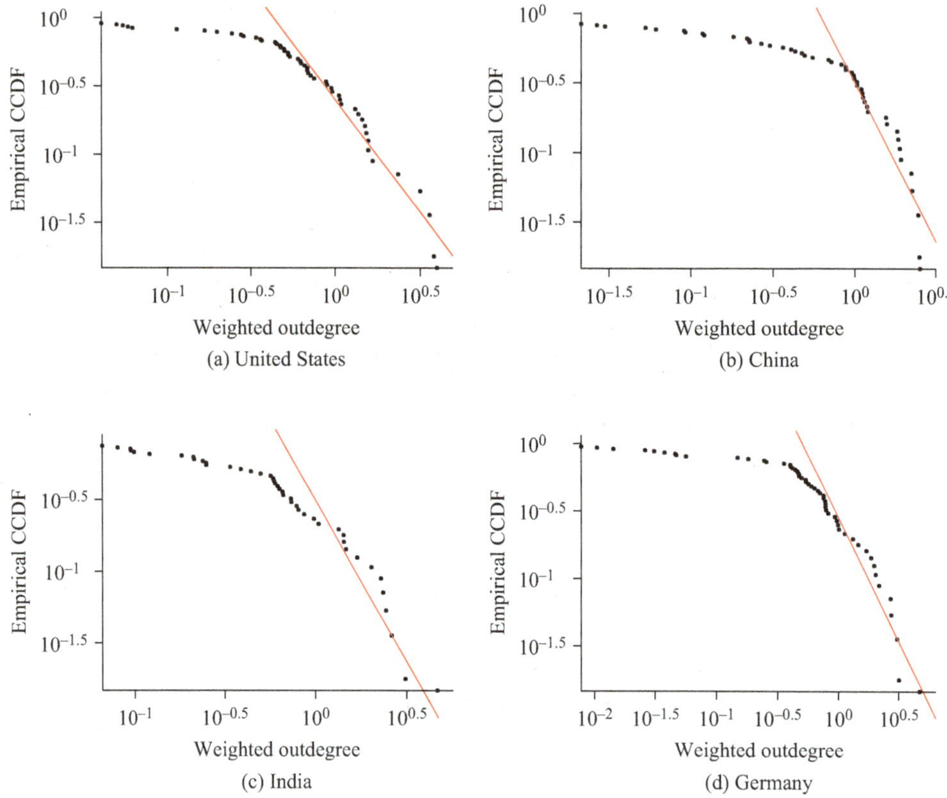


**Figure 2.6**
Production network degree distribution (2014). Data from World Input-Output Database. *Source*: www.wiod.org.

figure 2.6, the power law distribution provides a good fit for the higher degrees, but not for the lower degrees. In line with common practice, we say that a degree distribution follows a power law if the empirical degrees match the function for high degrees above some cutoff point. We now present a simple model of a growing network that generates skewed degree distributions.

**de Solla Price model of directed linking** Suppose that links are directed. By way of motivation, think of the process of linking on the World Wide Web: pages are created at regular intervals and numbered 1, 2, 3. . . . When page $j$ is created, it creates a link to an existing web page. With probability $p$, the link is created at random with one of the existing nodes, and with probability $1-p$, page $j$ picks a node $i$ at random, but then forms a link with the page to which $i$ is linked. The linking based on copying gives rise to a rich-get-richer dynamic: in this case, the probability of linking with page $\ell$ is directly proportional to the number of incoming links of $\ell$. So we can rephrase the copying part of the linking process as follows: with probability $1-p$, page $j$ chooses page $\ell$ with probability that is proportional to $\ell$'s current incoming links. This is the essence of the preferential attachment: currently highly connected nodes are likely to receive more new links.

If we run this process for many pages, the fraction of pages with $k$ incoming links will be distributed approximately according to a power law $1/k^c$, where the value of the exponent $c$ depends, in an intuitively plausible way, on the choice of $p$. As $p$ becomes smaller, most of the linking is driven by the copying element, which means that the rich-get richer element gets correspondingly stronger. We now present the details of this process and explicitly compute the value of coefficient $c$ as a function of $p$.

Let $d_i(t)$ be the links of node $i$ at time $t$. The new link to page $i$, therefore, can arise in two ways: (1) the new page picks page $i$ at random, and (2) the new page picks page $j$ and then links to $i$ because $j$ is linked to $i$. Observe that it is the second route that creates the rich-gets-richer pressure, as the probability of $j$ being linked to $i$ is greater the more links $i$ has. These two routes to an additional link for $i$ are captured in the following formula:

$$\frac{p}{t}+(1-p)\frac{d_i(t)}{t}. \tag{2.15}$$

In principle, there is uncertainty in the growth of links of nodes, as the links are probabilistic, but we can get a good understanding of the process by considering a simpler deterministic analog. To write out and solve the deterministic process, we need to specify the starting point and the rate of change over time. Let us say that at the start, every node has an in-degree of 0. We write the rate of change as being equal to the expected change in incoming links:

$$\frac{d}{dt}d_i(t)=\frac{p}{t}+(1-p)\frac{d_i(t)}{t}. \tag{2.16}$$

Dividing both sides by $p+(1-p)d_i$, we get

$$\frac{1}{p+(1-p)d_i}\frac{d}{dt}d_i=\frac{1}{t}. \tag{2.17}$$

Integrating both sides and rearranging terms, we arrive at

$$log(p+(1-p)d_i)=(1-p)logt+c, \tag{2.18}$$

where $c$ is a constant. Taking exponents on both sides and setting $A=e^c$, we get

$$p+(1-p)d_i=At^{(1-p)}. \tag{2.19}$$

The degree of node $i$ at time $t$ is then given by

$$d_i(t)=\frac{1}{1-p}(At^{1-p}-p). \tag{2.20}$$

Noting that $d_i(i)=0$, we can obtain $A=p/i^{1-p}$. This allows us to rewrite $d_i(t)$ as

$$d_i(t)=\frac{1}{1-p}\left[p(\left(\frac{t}{i}\right)^{1-p}-1)\right]. \tag{2.21}$$

Equipped with this formula, we proceed and compute the fraction of nodes/pages that have a degree more than $k$ at time $t$. Given $k$, using equation (2.21), it is possible to compute the point of entry of a node that has degree $k$ at time $t$. Define this $i$ as $i_t(k)$:

$$\frac{i_t(k)}{t}=\left[\frac{1-p}{p}k+1\right]^{-1/1-p}. \tag{2.22}$$

Given the deterministic process of linking, the nodes with a degree greater than $k$ at time $t$ are the nodes that were born before $i_t(k)$. This means the fraction of nodes with a degree greater than $k$ is

$$\left[\frac{1-p}{p}k+1\right]^{-1/(1-p)}. \tag{2.23}$$

The negative of the derivative of this expression with respect to $k$ gives the frequency of degrees with in-degree $k$:

$$P(k)=\frac{1}{p}\left[\frac{1-p}{p}k+1\right]^{-(1+1/(1-p))}. \tag{2.24}$$

Our discussion may be summarized in the following result.

**Proposition 2.2** *In the preferential attachment model of linking, with a large number of nodes, the fraction of pages with in-degree k is proportional to* $k^{-(1+1/(1-p))}$. *This yields a power-law distribution with exponent* $1+1/(1-p)$.

If $p$ is close to 1, the linking is mostly random, the reinforcement is minimal, and the coefficient takes on very large values. This means that large in-degrees are very unlikely. On the other hand, if $p$ is very small, the reinforcement aspect of linking is strong: the coefficient is close to (but larger than) 2. Figures 2.7(a) to 2.7(c) illustrate networks with 50 nodes corresponding to three values of the exponent—2.25, 2.5, and 3, respectively. Figure 2.7(d) plots the degree distributions of these networks. Observe also that as the coefficient increases from 2.25, to 2.5, to 3, the probability of higher degrees falls, which is reflected in the red curve being located above the blue curve, which in turn is located above the green curve.

**Barabási and Albert (1999)'s model of undirected linking** Let us now take up the undirected linking version of the preferential attachment model. Suppose that nodes are born at times $i\in\{0,1,\ldots t,\ldots\}$ and form $m$ links with distinct existing nodes when they

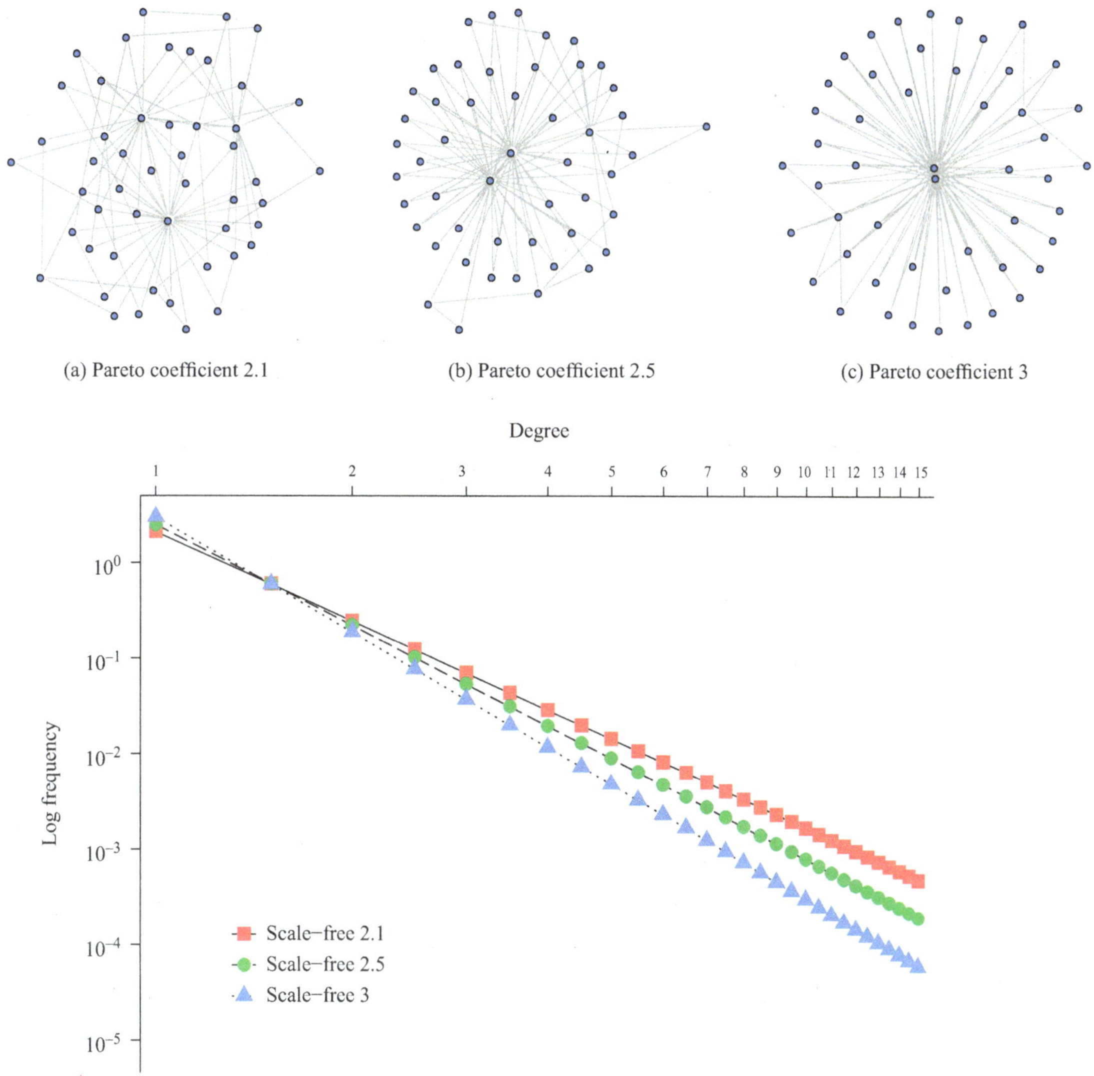


(a) Pareto coefficient 2.1

(b) Pareto coefficient 2.5

(c) Pareto coefficient 3

(d) Pareto degree distributions

**Figure 2.7**
Networks with preferential attachment.

enter. To keep matters simple, assume that there are enough nodes at the start and they have the same number of links. A new node forms links with an existing node with a probability that is proportional to its links (relative to the total links). Let $d_i(t)$ be the links of node $i$ at time $t$. Then the probability of a new link for node $i$ at time $t$ is given by

$$m\frac{d_i(t)}{\sum_j d_j(t)}. \tag{2.25}$$

Since $m$ links are created by every $i$, it follows that at time $t$, there are $mt$ links and $2mt$ degrees. So the probability may be written as

$$\frac{d_i(t)}{2t}. \tag{2.26}$$

In principle, this is a stochastic process, but following the approach outlined in the de Solla model presented earlier, we will examine the deterministic approximation in which the rate of change of degree is equated to this probability of change in degree. With this in mind, we write the rate of change of degree as

$$\frac{d}{dt}d_i(t) = \frac{d_i(t)}{2t}. \tag{2.27}$$

The differential equation with initial condition $d_i(i) = m$ has the solution

$$d_i(t) = m\left(\frac{t}{i}\right)^{\frac{1}{2}}. \tag{2.28}$$

We can use the solution to explicitly derive the long-run degree distribution. Given $d$, we can compute the point of entry of a node that has degree $d$ at time $t$, using equation (2.28). Define this $i$ as $i_t(d)$:

$$\frac{i_t(d)}{t} = \left(\frac{m}{d}\right)^2 \tag{2.29}$$

The nodes with a degree greater than $d$ at time $t$ are simply the nodes that were born before $i_t(d)$. This means the fraction of nodes with a degree greater than $d$ is $(m/d)^2$, which in turn means that the distribution function is

$$F(d) = 1 - m^2 d^{-2}. \tag{2.30}$$

The frequency of degrees is then simply the derivative, given by

$$f(d) = 2m^2 d^{-3}. \tag{2.31}$$

The Barabási-Albert model has a striking simplicity. However, from an empirical point of view, this model is somewhat restrictive, as it yields an exact Pareto coefficient of 3. There are a number of directions in which the model has been extended. For instance, we can allow multiple links to be formed by new entering nodes, the removal of edges, non-linear preferential attachment, and nodes of varying quality.

The central motivation for the preferential attachment model was the degree distribution. Let us examine the Pareto coefficient more closely, as it offers a way to tune the degree distribution. A key feature of the degree distribution is inequality in degrees. We now examine this issue of degree inequality through a study of dispersion in power-law networks. Recall that the mean of a degree distribution $P(d)$ is

$$\langle d \rangle = \sum_{d=1}^{\infty} d p_d. \tag{2.32}$$

The second moment is the mean square:

$$\langle d^2 \rangle = \sum_{d=1}^{\infty} d^2 p_d. \tag{2.33}$$

More generally, we may write the $m$th moment as

$$\langle d^m \rangle = \sum_{d=1}^{\infty} d^m p_d. \tag{2.34}$$

Suppose that the degree distribution obeys a power law with coefficient $a$ for degrees above $d_{min}$. Then we may write the expression for the $m$th moment as

$$\langle d^m \rangle = \sum_{d=1}^{d_{min}-1} d^m p_d + a \sum_{d=d_{min}}^{\infty} d^{m-c}. \tag{2.35}$$

As the probability is slowly moving for large $d$, we can approximate the second term by an integral so that

$$\langle d^m \rangle = \sum_{d-1}^{d_{min}-1} d^m p_d + a \int_{d=d_{min}}^{\infty} d^{m-c} dd \tag{2.36}$$

$$= \sum_{d=1}^{d_{min}-1} d^m p_d + \frac{a}{m-c+1} \left[ d^{m-c+1} \right]_{d_{min}}^{\infty}. \tag{2.37}$$

The first term is a finite number whose value depends on the (possibly non-power law) probability distribution for low degrees. The second term depends on the values of $m$ and $c$. If $m-c+1 < 0$, then the bracketed term has a finite value; if $m-c+1 > 0$, then the bracketed sum diverges. Thus $\langle d^m \rangle$ is finite if and only if $m+1 < c$. So, for instance, $\langle d^2 \rangle$, which is the variance in degrees, will be bounded if and only if $c > 3$.

The raison d'être for the preferential attachment model is on providing a mechanism that can account for an empirically observed power law degree distribution. The great power of the model in explaining power laws has led researchers to investigate other properties of the networks, such as connectivity, network diameter, and clustering. In networks that exhibit a power law degree distribution, the presence of highly connected hubs brings nodes closer to each other, suggesting that the network is connected and the diameter is smaller than the diameter in a Poisson random graph with a similar average degree (especially for large networks). The clustering coefficient becomes negligible in large networks (although it declines at a slower rate with respect to the number of nodes compared to the Poisson graph). See Barabási (2016) and Newman (2018) for a comprehensive study of the properties of networks generated by the preferential attachment model.

## 2.4 The Configuration Model

The degree distribution provides a bridge between the micro and the macro aspects of networks and it has received a great deal of attention. Interest in more general degree distributions that go beyond the Poisson and the power law distributions has grown with our expanding empirical knowledge of networks. In this section, we present a widely studied model called the "configuration model." Early contributions to the study of the configuration model include Molloy and Reed (1995), Newman, Strogatz, and Watts (2001) and Chung and Lu (2002a). Our exposition draws on Newman (2018) and Jackson (2008).

The configuration model may be seen as a model of a random graph with a given degree sequence. The exact degree of each individual node in the network is fixed. This in turn means that the number of edges is fixed. Given the sequence of degrees $d_1, d_2, ..d_n$, the number of edges is $m = \sum_{i=1}^{n} d_i/2$. Let us now describe the mechanics of how the degree sequence is constructed.

Let us start with an arbitrary degree sequence $d_1, .., d_n$ for $n$ nodes. We can create a random graph with this degree sequence as follows: Assign node $i$, $d_i$ stubs. There are thus $\sum_i d_i = 2m$ stubs. We choose two stubs uniformly at random and connect them. We then take two more stubs from the remaining $2m - 2$ stubs, and so forth. This yields a network in which every node has the degree that we started with. Moreover, as we move across possible matchings of stubs, we will traverse the various possible networks that are all consistent with the original degree sequence. The configuration model is then an ensemble of networks in which each matching of stubs obtains with equal probability. The uniform distribution over matchings has an important implication: each stub is equally likely to be matched with every other stub. This allows us to interpret the resulting network as being random and permits use to analyze a number of interesting questions, such as the size of the giant component and its diameter.

Before we turn to these questions, we need to clarify a couple of technical issues in the construction of the configuration model outlined above. First, the network may contain self-edges (if two stubs from the same node are matched) and/or multiple edges (if multiple pairs of stubs from two nodes are matched). However, because the numbers of such self-edges and multiple edges are constant, as we raise the number of nodes, they become progressively negligible and therefore can be ignored when we consider large populations. A second remark pertains to the specification of the model in terms of degree sequence: often our interest is in the degree distribution rather than the degree sequence. If we start with degree distribution $p_{(d)}$, then we can compute the probability of a specific degree sequence $\{d_i\}$ as $\Pi_i p_{d_i}$. We can use this definition to study the average value of objects of interest in the network ensemble with degree distribution $p_d$.

The configuration model has attracted a great deal of attention over the past two decades. Due to space constraints, we will restrict ourselves to a discussion of the diameter of general random graphs. For a comprehensive exposition of the configuration model, the interested reader is urged to consult Newman (2018).

We build here on the ideas proposed in Newman, Strogatz, and Watts (2001) and Chung and Lu (2002a), to provide approximate estimates for the diameter in general random graphs. For expositional simplicity, we will consider a tree network with degree distribution $P(d)$ and mean $\langle d \rangle$. Suppose that the degrees of nodes are at least approximately independent (this is true in a Poisson random graph when $n$ is large). How many degrees does a neighbor node picked at random have?

To answer this question, it is useful to consider the following related question: Suppose that we randomly pick a link in the network. What is the degree of one of the ends of the link? Consider a simple example, in which nodes have either degree 1 or degree 2 and the two degrees are equally likely (i.e., $P(1) = P(2) = 1/2$). In the case of four nodes, let network $g = \{g_{12}, g_{23}, g_{34}\}$. If we fix a node and pick one of its links at random, we will connect with a node of degree 2 with probability 2/3 and a node of degree 1 with probability 1/3. This is intuitive, as nodes with degree 2 are more present in links than are nodes with degree 1. Building on this argument, we say that for a network with degree distribution $P(d)$, if we were to pick a link at random and then look at the degree of an end of the link (picked with equal probability), the degree distribution of that node would be given by

$$\tilde{P}(d) = \frac{P(d)d}{\langle d \rangle}. \tag{2.38}$$

This degree distribution is sometimes referred to as the "excess degree distribution." Note that this distribution is a property of random graphs when the degrees of neighbors are independent: this means that the degree of the node at the other end does not depend on the degree of the initial starting node.

Applying this excess degree distribution, we may infer that the expected number of new neighbors of a neighbor is

$$\sum_d (d-1)\tilde{P}(d) = \frac{\langle d^2 \rangle - \langle d \rangle}{\langle d \rangle}. \tag{2.39}$$

Before proceeding further, it is worth noting the slightly unexpected nature of this excess degree distribution and its implications. In particular, note that the expected degree of a neighbor is

$$\frac{\langle d^2\rangle}{\langle d\rangle}. \tag{2.40}$$

And the difference between the average neighbor degree and the average degree in the network is

$$\frac{\langle d^2\rangle}{\langle d\rangle} - \langle d\rangle = \frac{1}{\langle d\rangle}(\langle d^2\rangle - \langle d\rangle^2). \tag{2.41}$$

Thus the average degree of a neighbor is larger than the average degree in the network, so long as there is a positive variance in degrees. This is known as the "friendship paradox" (Feld, S. L. 1991).

Building on equation (2.39), we can write the expected number of $i$'s second neighbors (i.e., the neighbors of neighbors of $i$) as

$$\langle d\rangle \frac{\langle d^2\rangle - \langle d\rangle}{\langle d\rangle}^2. \tag{2.42}$$

Reasoning as in the simple tree example here, as we reach outward from node $i$ to distance $\ell$, we cover

$$\sum_{k=1}^{\ell} \langle d\rangle \left[\frac{\langle d^2\rangle - \langle d\rangle}{\langle d\rangle}\right]^{k-1} = \langle d\rangle \left[\frac{\left(\frac{\langle d^2\rangle - \langle d\rangle}{\langle d\rangle}\right)^{\ell} - 1}{\left(\frac{\langle d^2\rangle - \langle d\rangle}{\langle d\rangle}\right) - 1}\right]. \tag{2.43}$$

To estimate the diameter of the graph, we require a number $\ell$ that covers $n-1$ nodes; that is,

$$\langle d\rangle \left[\frac{\left(\frac{\langle d^2\rangle - \langle d\rangle}{\langle d\rangle}\right)^{\ell} - 1}{\left(\frac{\langle d^2\rangle - \langle d\rangle}{\langle d\rangle}\right) - 1}\right] = n - 1. \tag{2.44}$$

Taking logs and simplifying, we get

$$\ell = \frac{log[(n-1)(\langle d^2\rangle - 2\langle d\rangle) + \langle d\rangle^2] - log[\langle d\rangle^2]}{log[\langle d^2\rangle - \langle d\rangle] - log[\langle d\rangle]}. \tag{2.45}$$

Recall that in the Poisson degree distribution, $\langle d^2\rangle = \langle d\rangle + \langle d\rangle^2$. In the Poisson case, we can then rewrite equation (2.45) as follows:

$$\ell = \frac{log\left((n-1)\frac{\langle d\rangle - 1}{\langle d\rangle} + 1\right)}{log[\langle d\rangle]}. \tag{2.46}$$

We see that if the expected degree is large, then the expression may be approximated by $\ell = log(n-1)/log(\langle d \rangle)$, which looks similar to the original derivation for the simplest case of a tree with a unique root. Thus if we abstract from cycles, the ratio of logs of the number of nodes and the average degree offers a rough estimate of $\ell$ (and also therefore the diameter). While these numbers are approximate, our discussion suggests that in large random graphs, the diameter is likely to be small.

We conclude with the remark that, as in the Poisson random graph, clustering becomes very small for large values of $n$ in networks generated through a configuration model.

## 2.5 Small-World Networks

In chapter 1 (and earlier in this chapter), we discussed the network of economics coauthors. In addition to having a small average distance, the network exhibits a high clustering coefficient. The Poisson random graph model and the preferential attachment model both generate small distances, but they exhibit negligible clustering. How can we reconcile high clustering and small distance?

To develop a sense of the difficulty of reconciling small path lengths and clustering, consider the following simple example. Suppose that everyone has 100 friends. As I have 100 friends, and each of my friends has 100 friends, if none of the friends overlap, I will have 10,000 distance 2 friends. Extrapolating on this, I would have 1 million distance 3 friends, and 100 million distance 4 friends. So short distances are natural in this world, and indeed would be in any network with reasonable degree that is a tree. However, in this example, observe that we are assuming that there is no overlap among friends—in other words, no triangles. To see the impact of this assumption in its extreme form, suppose that all my friends are friends of each other. In that case, distance 2 friends will be the same as my immediate friends, as all the friends of my friends are also my friends. Indeed, the circle of friends of 100 will constitute a distinct (and disconnected) clique and therefore will have no paths to other cliques. In other words, the average distance between nodes in the network will be unbounded. While this is a very extreme example, it helps bring out the point that reconciling small average distance and high clustering may be challenging.

In a celebrated paper, Watts and Strogatz (1998) proposed a resolution to this tension with the help of the following simple model. Their approach has an initial network of $n$ nodes arranged around a cycle, which are connected to their nearest 2 neighbors on either side. So there are $2n$ links in all. The degree distribution is perfectly equal: everyone has degree 4. The diameter in this network is roughly $n/4$ (the average distance is roughly $n/8$), and the clustering is $1/2$. Observe that as $n$ grows, the diameter will grow too. Figure 2.8(a) illustrates this starting point. How can we contain the growth of the mean distance as $n$ grows?

The key idea is the "rewiring" of links: pick a link $(A, B)$, with a very small probability $p$, fix one side to node $A$ (for example), and then pick a new partner selected at random

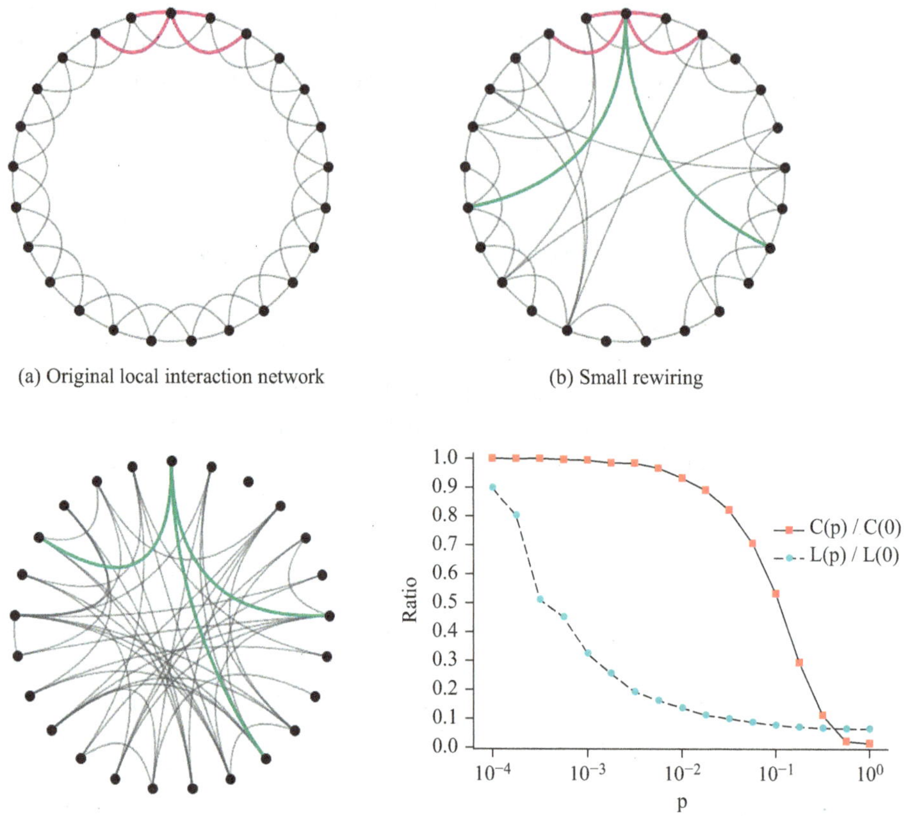


(a) Original local interaction network

(b) Small rewiring

(c) Complete rewiring

(d) Clustering versus distance

**Figure 2.8**
Link rewiring and small-world networks, based on Watts and Strogatz (1998).

from all the other nodes. The surprising finding of Watts and Strogatz (1998) is that for low and modest values of $p$, the average distance falls very sharply, while the clustering remains high and stable.

To get a sense of the numbers here, suppose that $n = 25$, so there is a total of 50 links; the network is presented in figure 2.8(a). Let us rewire 6 links; this leads us to figure 2.8(b). An inspection of the network suggests that the average distances have come down rather sharply. When we rewire all links (i.e., $p = 1$), we arrive at figure 2.8(c), a random network with very small average distances. Let us examine the changes more systematically.

The two objects of interest are the mean distance or the average path length $L(p)$ and the clustering coefficient $C(p)$. Recall that $L(p)$ is defined as the number of edges in the shortest path between two vertices, averaged over all the pairs of vertices. Recall also that the clustering coefficient $C(p)$ is defined as follows: If node $v$ has $k_v$ neighbors, then there can be at most $k_v(k_v - 1)/2$ edges between them. $C_v$ is the fraction of these edges that actually exist in the network. Define $C(p)$ as the average of $C_v$ over all $v$. Figure 2.8(d) presents a simulation of this thought experiment in which we vary the values of $p$ and examine the effects on $L(p)$ and $C(p)$. It presents a summary of simulation runs: on the $x$-axis we vary the fraction of rewired links all the way from 0 to 1. The $y$-axis shows that there is a wide range of rewiring probability—ranging from .001 to .01—for which clustering remains close to the original local interaction network, while the average distance falls precipitously relative to distance in the original network.

How can we account for this pattern? The intuition for this is that a large number of long paths are shortened through the relocation of a few links from short to far range. Meanwhile, as only 6 out of 50 links are affected, most of the links remain as before, so the clustering is only marginally lowered.

We may summarize our short discussion as follows: *In the structure of small worlds, starting with a sparse graph on a cycle, the clustering remains stable for a broad range of rewiring probabilities, while the diameter comes down sharply with a small probability of rewiring.*

We conclude this section on a more general note by narrating the history of the idea of small worlds.

### 2.5.1 A Brief History of the Small-World Idea

The origins of the small-world idea may be traced to the Hungarian writer Frigyes Karinthy, who wrote a short story called "Lancszemek," in which two characters believed that any two individuals on Earth could be connected to each other through a chain of no more than five acquaintances (Karinthy [1929]). These literary origins were followed by academic research in the 1950s by Ithiel de Sola Pool and Manfred Kochen, who wrote a paper titled "Contacts and Influence," which proposed a number of ideas relating to social networks and discussed ways of quantifying the distance between people through chains of connections. The article eventually appeared as de Sola Pool and Kochen (1978–79).

The next major development were the experiments undertaken by the social psychologist Stanley Milgram. In his first experiment, there were 296 randomly chosen starting individuals (located in Nebraska, a state in the US). Each starter was asked to forward a letter to a target individual. The personal details of the target—the name and the address (a suburb of Boston, Massachusetts) and the profession (stockbroker)—were provided. The starter was asked to forward the letter to someone known on a first-name basis so it would reach the target as quickly as possible. The letter therefore passed through a chain of acquaintances until it arrived at the target. In all, 64 letters (out of the 296) arrived at the target; the rest did not. The path lengths ranged from 1 to 11, with a median value of 6. In the Milgram study, the sample size was small, and even within this small sample, the vast majority of the chains did not actually reach the target. These concerns have motivated a number of follow-up empirical studies on small-world properties of social networks (see e.g., Dodds, Muhamad, and Watts, 2003).

It is worth commenting on the relation between these small-world experiments and the network models of small worlds. In the model of small worlds, there are short paths between individuals that create the possibility of communication across the network using short paths. However, the problem posed in the original Milgram experiments (as well as the follow-up experiments) asks an individual to find someone through chains in the network: this requires knowledge of where people are located in a network. In other words, the Milgram problem is one of navigating a network to find someone whose whereabouts may or may not be known. Networks that have very short average distances may nevertheless be difficult to navigate. For instance, consider a core-periphery network in which the large core is a clique and every member of the core is linked to a large number of individuals. The diameter in this network is 3, so the average distances are small. However, navigation may be difficult. Suppose that every node knows the identity of its neighbors. Now suppose that the origin and the target are both peripheral nodes and an individual can search through one link at a time. It could in principle take a very long time for a peripheral node to locate such an anonymous target. The navigation problem would be a lot simpler if the potential target had clear markers of identity and these markers were in turn highly correlated with the corresponding core node to which they were linked. These remarks draw our attention to the importance of correlations between the links individuals have and their types or their characteristics.

## 2.6 Network-Based Linking

The preferential attachment model delivers skewed degree distributions but fails to account for clustering, while the small-world model provides an account for clustering but exhibits relatively similar degrees. We now present a model of a growing network that combines features of preferential attachment with an additional feature—links are formed with neighbors of nodes found at random. This model generates networks with skewed degree distribution, as well as significant clustering levels. Our presentation is based on Vazquez (2003) and Jackson and Rogers (2007).

Let us suppose that time proceeds in discrete steps ($t = 1, 2, 3, \ldots$), and at each point $t > 1$, a new node enters. So $N_t$ is the set of nodes at time $t$. There is a contacting process followed by a linking process. Let us describe the contact process first. At birth, a node picks randomly, and without replacement, $m_r$ nodes from set $N_{t-1}$ and forms links to them. She then picks $m_n$ nodes randomly, without replacement, from the neighbors of the $m_r$ nodes picked at random. Thus we can say that $m = m_r + m_n$ is the number of outward links formed by every entering new node. It is important to bear in mind that the neighbor of $i$ is a node $j$ such that $g_{ij} = 1$. In other words, we are using only incoming links for the indirect linking part of the process.

To make sure that the process is well defined, let us suppose that there are enough nodes and links at the start. Suppose that at the start of time $t$, node $i$ has $d_i(t)$ incoming links. What is the probability that it gets another link in period $t$? We note that links are formed via random draws uniformly from the population and indirectly by following outlinks from other nodes that have been picked uniformly at random. Putting together these two ways of forming links, we may write the expected number of new links for node $i$ as

$$\frac{m_r}{t} + \frac{m_r d_i(t)}{t}\left(\frac{m_n}{m_r(m_r+m_n)}\right). \tag{2.47}$$

Substituting $m = m_r + m_n$ in equation (2.47) yields us:

$$\frac{m_r}{t} + \frac{m_n d_i(t)}{mt}, \tag{2.48}$$

which is increasing linearly in $d_i(t)$. Thus the probability of getting a new link is increasing in the number of existing links. This is the preferential attachment aspect of this model.

Observe that this is a complicated model because the evolution of the network depends on network-based links and the network is itself stochastic. As in the study of the preferential attachment models described previously, we can employ a deterministic approximation to solve the model.

Using the deterministic approximation, we may write the rate of change in links as

$$\frac{d}{dt}d_i(t) = \frac{m_r}{t} + \frac{m_n d_i(t)}{mt} \tag{2.49}$$

Let us set the initial condition for this differential equation, $d_i(i) = d_0 \geq 0$. Define $r = (m_r)/(m_n)$ as the ratio of random to network-based links.

The solution to the differential equation is given by

$$d_i(t) = (d_o + rm)\left(\frac{t}{i}\right)^{1/(1+r)} - rm, \tag{2.50}$$

where $d_i(t)$ is the in-degree of node $i$ at time $t \geq i$. We use this formula to develop the degree distribution of the network. Using methods similar to those in the preferential attachment model, we can conclude that the in-degree distribution of this mean-field process has a cumulative distribution function of

$$F_t(d) = 1 - \left(\frac{d_0 + rm}{d + rm}\right)^{1+r}. \tag{2.51}$$

for $d \geq d_0$ and each time $t$.

Starting with the in-degree equation (2.50) and with the help of equation (2.51), we get the formula for the tail distribution:

$$log(1 - F(d)) = \frac{m}{m_n}\left[log(d_0 + rm) - log(d + rm)\right]. \tag{2.52}$$

Equation (2.52) permits us to make a number of observations. First, note that if $d$ is large relative to $rm$, the tail probability is roughly linear in $log(d)$. Second, for small $r$, the distribution is roughly linear in $d$ and exhibits a power law. On the other hand, if $r$ is large, most links are random and the distribution is close to a random linking model with a growing number of nodes.

We next turn to clustering levels in this network. Recall that the clustering coefficient in the directed network may be described as the fraction of transitive triples:

$$C^T(g) = \frac{\sum_{i:j\neq i\neq k} g_{ij}g_{jk}g_{ik}}{\sum_{i:j\neq i,k\neq i} g_{ij}g_{jk}}. \tag{2.53}$$

A newborn connects to $m_r$ parent nodes, and each one has $m$ outgoing links. Thus an upper bound of potential triples (for a single node $i$) is given by $m^2$. But each newborn forms $m_n$ connections with the neighbors of parents, so we get the following expression as a lower bound for clustering:

$$\frac{m_n}{m^2} = \frac{1}{(1+r)m}. \tag{2.54}$$

So, for instance, if $m=4$ and $r=1$, then the lower bound for clustering-coefficient is given by 0.125. Moreover, in line with our intuition, it is falling in the fraction of randomly drawn links.

## 2.7 A Concluding Remark

This chapter has provided a brief introduction to models of random graphs—the Erdős-Rényi model (and its variant, the stochastic block model), the configuration model, the preferential attachment model, the small-world model, and a model of random and neighbor linking. This introduction helps us appreciate how different mechanics of linking give rise to network properties such as connectivity, degree distributions, small distances, and clustering.

In the rest of this book, we will locate the network concepts introduced in chapter 1 and our understanding of the mechanics of linking introduced in this chapter within a perspective that sees networks as arising out of the goal-driven activity of individuals and collective entities (like firms and the state).

## 2.8 Reading Notes

The chapter proposes a number of models of random graphs. At a basic level, one may imagine a random graph as specifying a number of nodes, $n$, and a number of links/edges, $m$. The links may be ordered in different ways, and this gives rise to different networks. Say that every possible arrangement of the $m$ links is equally likely. This model gives rise to an ensemble of networks, denoted by $G(n, m)$. We may ask what the properties of these networks are, say, in terms of their connectivity or of distances. As the model describes an ensemble of networks, it is reasonable to ask questions about the average properties of the networks. Some properties of these networks, such as the average degree, are easy to derive; however, it turns out that others, like connectivity or diameter, are less easy to calculate. Interest has focused on a slightly different model, which allows much more complete answers with regard to the properties of networks.

This model is known as the "$G(n,p)$ model." In this model, the number of nodes is $n$ and there is an identical and independent probability $p$ for the formation of a link between any pair of nodes. Thus the number of links is no longer fixed but varies depending on the realization of random draws. As in the original $G(n,m)$ model, the model describes an ensemble of networks. We can pose questions about degree distribution and connectivity with regard to the average network generated by this process. The $G(n,p)$ model was first studied in Solomonoff and Rapoport (1951). However, the model is often referred to as the "Erdős-Rényi random graph model" due to three papers published by Paul Erdős and Alfred Rényi in the late 1950s and early 1960s. The Erdős-Rényi model is sometimes also called the "Poisson random graph model" or the "Bernoulli random graph model." There is a vast body of literature on this model and its variants. For excellent overviews of this work, see Bollobás (1998, 2004).

In chapter 1, we drew attention to the presence of very highly connected nodes—also called "hubs"—in a variety of real-world networks. This preponderance of hubs is accompanied at the other end of the distribution by the existence of a very large number of nodes with very small degrees. The degree distribution thus appears to be quite different from a Poisson degree distribution, where the vast majority of nodes have degrees close to the mean degree. The study of unequal networks may be traced to an early paper by Derek de Solla Price (1965), in which he showed that the distribution of citations was similarly very skewed both toward the bottom and the top.

Building on Simon (1955) (and earlier literature in statistics), de Solla Price (1976) proposed a network model of linking that generated a power law degree distribution. The work of de Solla Price went relatively unnoticed until a revival of interest in networks in the 1990s, when Barabási and Albert (1999) present a simpler and undirected link version of the original Price model. It also brings it closer to a broad range of empirical applications. For a systematic and wide-ranging overview of various aspects of the model, see Barabási (2016) and Newman (2018). For a fascinating experimental study of how information releases can give rise to power laws, see Salganik, Dodds, and Watts (2006).

Having studied the Poisson and power law degree distributions, it is only natural that we should consider a framework that allows general degree distributions. The configuration model is an example of such a framework. A model of specific degree sequence was proposed and studied in the context of the existence of giant components by Molloy and Reed (1995). Watts, Dodds, and Newman (2002) study a number of properties of this model, such as the phase transition at which a giant component first forms, the mean component size, the size of the giant component (if one exists), and properties of excess degree distributions and average distances. Chung and Lu (2002b) propose a smoother version of the model with expected degrees and obtain results on the relation between the power law coefficients and average distances in the network. There is a large body of literature that examines various aspects of the model. For a deeper and more comprehensive overview of these developments, see Newman (2018).

The presence of power laws has been noted in a number of contexts, such as city population size, number of copies of a gene in a genome, and firm size (we have already mentioned the distribution of citations). At first sight, it is puzzling that there is a similar macroscopic property in very different contexts. The fact that the rich-get-richer process can provide a common account is interesting, but we should note that there are alternative explanations for such networks. A parallel thread of research argues that power laws may arise due to optimization in the presence of constraints. An early paper by Mandelbrot (1953) introduces this perspective, and it has been elaborated upon by a number of authors since then. In chapter 3 (on an economic theory of network formation), chapter 7 (on network security), and chapter 11 (on the law of the few), we will present economic models where both the decentralized formation of networks and the optimization of networks leads to hubs and highly unequal networks.

The model with rewiring of links giving rise to networks with small average distance and high clustering comes from Watts and Strogatz (1998). This model has given rise to a vast body of research; see Watts (2004) and Newman (2018) for an overview of this work. The discussion on small-world experiments draws on the fascinating early papers by Milgram (1967) and the follow-up by Travers and Milgram (1969). With the advances in computing and information technology, the small-world problem has been explored by a number of more recent papers; prominent contributions include Dodds, Muhamad, and Watts (2003). The small-world experiments have given rise to the study of the problem of navigation in networks. An important element of whether a network is navigable lies in the connection between network structure and individual identity. For theoretical investigations on this subject, see Kleinberg (2000) and Watts, Dodds, and Newman (2002).

Finally, in an attempt to reconcile unequal degrees with clustering, we have presented a model that combines growing network with network-based linking. The model is taken from Vazquez (2003) and Jackson and Rogers (2007). For a more comprehensive exposition of this model, see Jackson (2008).

## 2.9 Questions

1. Consider the Erdős-Rényi model of random graphs. Let $P$ be the degree distribution corresponding to a probability of linking $p$ and $P'$ be the degree distribution corresponding to a probability of linking $p'$. Show that if $p' > p$, then the degree distribution $P'$ first-order

stochastically dominates degree distribution $P$ (for definitions of stochastic dominance, see chapter 1).

2. Show that $p(n-1) = 1$ is a threshold for the emergence of a giant component in the Erdős-Rényi model of random graphs.
3. Consider the Erdős-Rényi model of random graphs. Show that $t(n) = 1/n^2$ is a threshold function for having at least one link.
4. The preferential attachment process gives early moving nodes large advantages. Discuss. Hint: Suppose that in a every period, a new node is born. Use the formulas in this chapter to ask how long it would take a node born in period 10 to have the same number of connections as the firstborn node in period 10.
5. This question is inspired by an experiment on popularity ratings reported in Salganik, Dodds, and Watts (2006). Prominent news sites like that of the BBC and the *Guardian* present links to their stories; readers can click on these links to access various pieces of news. We may define the popularity of a news item by the number of readers who click on the corresponding link. Suppose that a news company is considering adding a counter next to a news link that would show the number of readers who have already clicked on that link. Discuss the effects of such readership information on the popularity distribution of news items.
6. Consider the model of growing network presented in section 2.3. But now suppose that a newborn node forms $k$ links with uniform probability with each of the existing nodes. Derive the master equations corresponding to this process for the growth in in-degree (for large $n$) and show that (in the limit of large $n$) the in-degree distribution have an exponential distribution: $p(d) = Ce^{-\lambda d}$, where $C$ is a normalization constant and $\lambda = log(1 + 1/k)$.
7. Consider the Jackson-Rogers model of growing networks discussed in section 2.6. Show that as we raise the fraction of random linking from $r$ to $r'$, the corresponding degree distribution is less skewed; that is, $P'$ second-order stochastically dominates $P$ (for definitions of stochastic dominance, see chapter 1).

# 3 The Costs and Benefits of Links

## 3.1 Introduction

In a number of the networks presented in the Introduction and chapter 1, links are chosen by purposeful agents. For example, firms decide on whom to source their inputs from, and this gives rise to production networks. Airline companies decide on the routing network they operate. Similarly, individual economists decide on whom to coauthor with and school pupils choose whom to be friends with. It is therefore reasonable to approach the formation of networks through an examination of the motivations that individuals or firms have in forming links. This chapter provides an introduction to a theory of network formation in which purposeful entities create links based on their costs and benefits.

A fundamental dimension of linking is who can decide on a link. For instance, on Twitter, an individual user can decide on whom to follow, while on Facebook, a friendship link requires that both parties agree. We may think of a link on Twitter as being unilateral or one-sided, while a link on Facebook is bilateral or two-sided.

We start with a consideration of the following simple scenario: There is a group of individuals who each have some information that is valuable to everyone. Each player can form links with a subset of others. The model is taken from Goyal (1993) and Bala and Goyal (2000a). In this model, the linking decisions of individuals give rise to a directed network. The benefits to an individual in this network depend on the number of other people that they have a directed path to, and the costs depend on the number of links they have formed. Thus an individual's links create paths for others. This potential for a link between two individuals, A and B, to be used by another individual, C, is a central feature of the process. One-sided link formation can be formulated as a noncooperative game. We study the networks that arise in the Nash equilibrium of the game.

We find that economic models of linking lead to sharp transitions in network structure especially with regard to connectedness—at certain thresholds that relate to the costs and benefits of links. A second finding is that there is a tension between strategically stable and efficient networks. The sharp transitions in network architecture and the tension between individual incentives and collective interests and ideas will be a recurring theme in our study of linking and network formation throughout the book.

We then turn to a study of bilateral or two-sided links—a link between A and B requires the assent of both of them. Following Jackson and Wolinsky (1996), we are led to study the incentives of not just one person, but of joint interests. This leads to the notion of pairwise stability. A comparison of pairwise stable networks and Nash networks (from the one-sided model) helps us understand the role of the link formation protocol in shaping network architecture.

The economics literature on network formation has been a very active and fruitful field of research over the past quarter-century. As linking activity occurs across a very wide range of contexts, the literature has expanded to accommodate a number of issues that include the dynamics of linking, the study of linking in combination with assorted activities, weighted graphs, and nonspecific networking. We provide an overview of these strands of work and point to subsequent chapters of this book where these subjects are explored at greater length.

In chapter 2, our study of random graphs drew attention to thresholds and sharp transitions in networks. These transitions also arise in an economic approach. But perhaps the central distinguishing feature of an economic approach is its attention to goal-driven linking by individuals. The central role of individual choice calls for an explicit consideration of the preferences, knowledge, and rationality of individuals. In particular, our discussion will draw attention to how linking by one individual creates benefits (and costs) for other individuals. We will refer to the effect of one person on the payoffs of others as an "externality." In many applications of interest, the links of one person also affect the marginal returns from links for others; this gives rise to strategic interaction and games of linking.

These spillovers give rise to two fundamental issues that will recur throughout the book. One, externalities in linking create a tension between what individuals choose and what is in their collective interest. Two, strategic interactions create the possibility of multiple equilibria. This draws attention to coordination failures in the linking process. These two phenomena—tension between individual and collective interest and coordination failure—motivate a study of appropriate policy interventions in networks.

The ideas we explore in the current chapter are central to an economic approach to the study of networks. The formal arguments we develop will be useful throughout the book, especially in chapters 5–12 and in chapters 16, 17, and 19.

## 3.2 One-Sided Links

This section presents an approach to network formation in which individuals can unilaterally decide to form links with others. This approach gives rise to a noncooperative game that can be solved using the concept of the Nash equilibrium. The model is taken from Goyal (1993) and Bala and Goyal (2000a).

We consider a set of players given by $N = \{1, \ldots, n\}$, with $n \geq 2$; let $i$ and $j$ be typical members of this set. A strategy of player $i \in N$ is a row vector $s_i = (s_{i,1}, \ldots, s_{i,i-1}, s_{i,i+1}, \ldots, s_{i,n})$, where $s_{i,j} \in \{0, 1\}$ for each $j \in N \backslash \{i\}$. Player $i$ has a *link* to $j$ if $s_{i,j} = 1$. The set of pure strategies of player $i$ is denoted by $\mathcal{S}_i$. A strategy profile is denoted by $s = (s_1, \ldots, s_n)$, with the set of all strategies given by $\mathcal{S} = \prod_{i=1}^{n} \mathcal{S}_i$. There is an equivalence between a strategy profile and a directed network. Let $\mathcal{G}$ be the set of directed networks on $n$ nodes. We shall say that $N_i^d(g) = \{j \in N | g_{ij} = 1\}$ is the set of players with whom player $i$ forms a link and define $\eta_i^d(g) = |N_i^d(g)|$ as the number of connections of player $i$ in network $g$. Note that in the definition here, the superscript $d$ refers to the directed nature of the link. Similarly, define $N_{-i}^d(g) = \{j \in N | g_{ji} = 1\}$ as the set of players who form a link with player $i$ and define $\eta_{-i}^d(g) = |N_{-i}^d(g)|$ as the number of players who form links with player $i$. Recall that $\eta_i^d(g)$ is the out-degree and $\eta_{-i}^d(g)$ the in-degree of player $i$ in network $g$. In the directed network $g$, let $\mathcal{N}_i(g) = \{k \mid i \xrightarrow{g} k\}$ be the set of individuals accessed through a directed path by $i$. We follow the convention that a player accesses themselves, so the total number of players accessed by player $i$ in network $g$ is given by $n_i(g) \equiv |\mathcal{N}_i(g)| + 1$.

Given a strategy profile $s$, let $\Pi_i(s)$ be the payoff of player $i$. A Nash equilibrium is a profile of strategies $s^* = (s_1^*, \ldots, s_n^*)$, such that for every player $i \in N$, $\Pi_i(s_i^*, s_{-i}^*) \geq \Pi_i(s_i, s_{-i}^*)$, for every $s_i \in \mathcal{S}_i$, i.e., every player is choosing the highest payoff strategy, given the strategies of the other players. A Nash equilibrium $s^*$ is said to be strict if all players choose a strict best response, i.e., the inequalities defining the equilibrium are strict for every player.

In the study of network formation, an important concern will be the relation between equilibrium/stable networks and socially desirable networks. Two aspects of social desirability will be touched upon: efficiency and equity.

Two notions of efficiency are used: Pareto efficiency and aggregate efficiency. A network $g$ yields a profile of individual payoffs $\Pi(g) = (\Pi_1(g), \Pi_2(g), \ldots, \Pi_n(g))$. A network $g$ is said to Pareto-dominate another network $g'$ if $\Pi_i(g) \geq \Pi_i(g')$, for all players $i \in N$, and there is a player $j$ such that $\Pi_j(g) > \Pi_j(g')$. A network $g$ is Pareto efficient if there is no other network $g' \in \mathcal{G}$ which Pareto-dominates it.

In the networks literature, a simpler aggregate notion of efficiency has been more widely used. Define aggregate welfare from a network $g$ as

$$W(g) = \sum_{i \in N} \Pi_i(g). \tag{3.1}$$

Network $g$ is said to be efficient if $W(g) \geq W(g')$ for all $g' \in \mathcal{G}$.

Consider next the issue of equity. In sociology and political science, social and economic networks have traditionally been associated with the origins and perpetuation of inequality. At several points in this book, we will discuss the inequality of network outcomes. Inequality can be measured in various ways; we will draw upon the voluminous literature on economic inequality (for an introduction to the subject, see Sen [1997]). Standard measures of inequality include the range, variance, and Gini coefficient. We will sometimes also consider the ratio of maximum versus minimum (or the ratio of maximum/median payoffs).

The range of the payoffs in a network is given by

$$R(g) = \max_{i \in N} \Pi_i(g) - \min_{j \in N} \Pi_j(g), \tag{3.2}$$

where max refers to the maximum individual payoff and min refers to the minimum payoff level in network $g$. The variance of payoffs in network $g$ is given by

$$Var(g) = \frac{\sum_i^n \left[\Pi_i(g) - \overline{\Pi}(g)\right]^2}{n}, \tag{3.3}$$

where $\overline{\Pi}(g)$ is the average payoff.

### 3.2.1 The One-Way Flow Model

To illustrate the trade-offs that arise in the one-sided linking approach, we present the one-way flow model taken from Bala and Goyal (2000a). Denote the set of nonnegative integers as $\mathcal{Z}_+$. Let $\phi : \mathcal{Z}_+^2 \to \mathbb{R}_+$ be such that $\phi(x, y)$ is strictly increasing in $x$ and strictly decreasing in $y$. Define each player's payoff function $\Pi_i : \mathcal{G} \to \mathbb{R}_+$ as

$$\Pi_i(g) = \phi\left(n_i(g), \eta_i^d(g)\right). \tag{3.4}$$

We may interpret $n_i(g)$ as the benefit that player $i$ receives from the network, while $\eta_i^d(g)$ measures the cost associated with maintaining their links. Note that the assumptions on the payoff function $\phi(.,.)$ allow both increasing and decreasing marginal returns from connections. The linear payoff function is a simple example that satisfies these properties:

$$\Pi_i(g) = n_i(g) - \eta_i^d(g)k, \text{ where } k > 0 \text{ is the cost of a link.} \tag{3.5}$$

In other words, player $i$'s payoffs are the number of players they observe less the total cost of link formation.

What is the architecture of networks that arise? To answer this question, we will examine the Nash equilibria of the game. We start by developing an important property of Nash equilibrium networks: either no one forms any links and the network is empty or every individual accesses everyone else, and the network is connected. (We are using the term connected slightly loosely here: as the network is directed, the property we are after requires a directed path from every player to every other player. In graph theory, this property is referred to as "strongly" connected. For ease of exposition, however, we will retain the simpler term "connected" here). The argument underlying this property is sketched below.

Suppose that $i$ has paths to the most players and $i$ does not observe everyone. Then there must be a player $j$ who is not observed by $i$ and who does not observe $i$ (otherwise, $j$ would access more players than $i$). We argue that $j$ can earn a strictly higher payoff by forming a single link with $i$. To see this in the simplest way, suppose that $j$ has formed links that include a link with $k$. By deleting all their current links and forming a single link with $i$, they will access strictly more players than $i$, since they have the additional benefit of observing $i$.

Since $j$ was observing weakly fewer individuals than $i$ in their original strategy, and they are forming weakly fewer links in this deviation, $j$ strictly increases their payoff through this deviation. This contradiction means that $i$ must observe everyone in the society.

Building on this property, we can show that every other agent will have an incentive to either link with $i$ or to observe them through a sequence of links (i.e., the network is connected). Moreover, the network must be minimally connected: if it is not, then there are two paths between a pair of individuals and a player can delete a link and still observe all the players, which would contradict the optimality of actions in a Nash equilibrium.

Figure 3.1 presents examples of Nash networks in the linear payoffs shown in equation (3.5). We see that networks can have a variety of architectures, ranging from a hub-spoke network to a cycle containing all players and a number of intermediate structures with smaller cycles (we refer to them as "petals"). We note that a given architecture can be supported in various ways: for instance, any of the $n$ players can occupy the hub place in the hub-spoke network—therefore, there are $n$ equilibria that support that architecture. Similarly, the cycle network can be supported by any permutation of players on the nodes of the cycle (i.e., there are $n!$ Nash equilibria supporting that architecture). Indeed, the number of Nash networks increases quite rapidly with the number of players; it is possible to show that there are 5, 58, 1,069, and in excess of 20,000 Nash networks as $n$ takes on the values of 3, 4, 5, and 6, respectively. Thus the Nash equilibrium is a fairly permissive requirement. Is there some way to restrict the set of networks further based on individual incentives alone?

We observe that in the star network, the spoke player is indifferent between a link with the central player and any other spoke. In other words, the spoke player has multiple best responses, which creates the possibility that the individual may drift away from the star over time, as no payoff losses are associated with a switch in links. This motivates the study of a strict Nash equilibrium. Recall that a Nash equilibrium is strict if every player chooses a strict best response. It turns out that the requirement of strictness is powerful and eliminates all but two network architectures as candidate networks in our game.

The key step is a simple switching argument: in a Nash equilibrium, if two players $i$ and $j$ have a link with the same player $\ell$, then player $i$ will be indifferent between forming a link with $\ell$ and forming a link with $j$. This means that every player has one and only one player who initiates a link with them; thus a nonempty strict Nash network has exactly $n$ links. From the arguments above, we know that a (nonempty) equilibrium network is connected. It can be shown that the cycle is the unique connected (directed) network with exactly $n$ links. Putting together these arguments, we arrive at the following result on Nash and strict Nash equilibrium networks.

**Proposition 3.1** *In the one-sided model with one-way flow, a Nash equilibrium network is either connected or empty. A strict Nash network is either a cycle containing all players or the empty network. In particular, (a) If $\phi(x+1,x) > \phi(1,0)$ for some $x \in \{1,2,\ldots,n\}$, then the cycle is the unique strict Nash equilibrium. (b) If $\phi(x+1,x) < \phi(1,0)$ for all $x \in \{1,2,\ldots,n-1\}$ and $\phi(n,1) > \phi(1,0)$, then* *the empty network and the cycle are both strict Nash equilibrium. (c) If* $\phi(x+1, x) < \phi(1, 0)$ *holds for all* $x \in \{1, 2, \ldots, n-1\}$ *and* $\phi(n, 1) < \phi(1, 0)$*, then the empty network is the unique strict Nash equilibrium.*

For concreteness, let us apply this result to the linear payoffs in equation (3.5). Proposition 3.1 says that the cycle containing all players is a unique strict Nash equilibrium if $k < 1$, the cycle and the empty network are strict Nash equilibria when $k \in (1, n-1)$, and

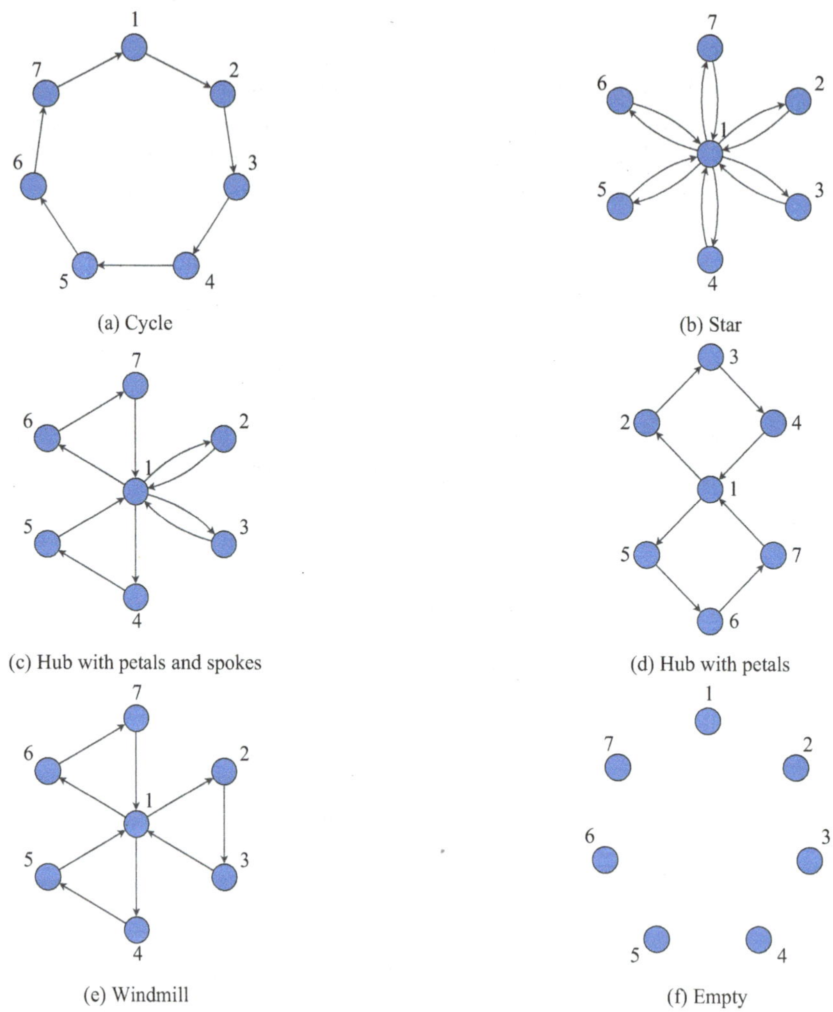


**Figure 3.1**
Nash networks: one-sided links model.

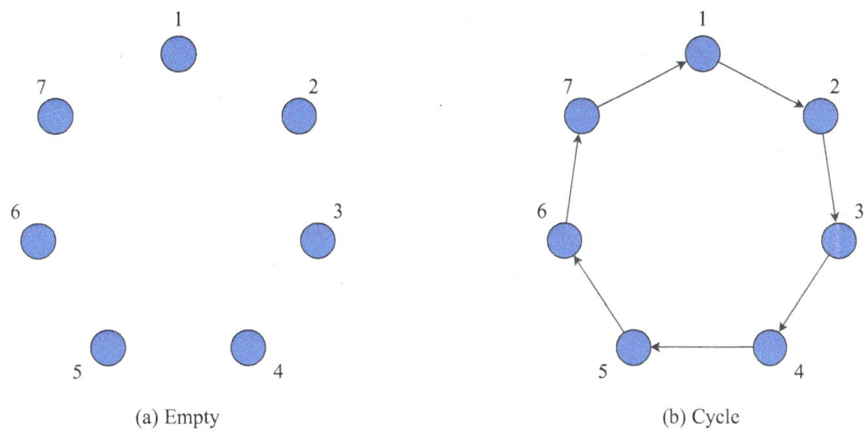


**Figure 3.2**
Strict Nash networks: one-sided link model.

the empty network is a unique strict Nash equilibrium when $k > n - 1$. Figure 3.2 depicts these equilibrium networks for $n = 7$. Note that in this diagram, a link formed by player $i$ with player $j$ is represented by a line joining $i$ and $j$, and the arrow points toward $j$.

Three aspects of this result are worth highlighting. The first is that there is an intimate relation between the costs and benefits of of links and the architecture of the network: when the costs are smaller than stand-alone benefits, the network is connected, while when the costs of accessing everyone are larger than the benefits, the network must be empty. In addition, for an intermediate range of values, both empty and connected networks are possible.

The second is that there is a sharp threshold separating the connected from the empty network at $k = n - 1$: just below that level of cost, we get a connected network, and just above that level, we get an empty network.

The third point is that in the range $k \in (1, n - 1)$, there are multiple equilibria that have extreme properties—one is empty with no links while the other is connected. This multiplicity is a recurring theme in strategic models of networks because it reflects a fundamental dimension of linking activity: the marginal returns to an individual from forming a link depend on how many links others have created. In this example, the marginal returns are 1 in the absence of any links but may be $n - 1$ if a player forms a link with someone who accesses everyone else. Thus for a cost $k \in (1, n - 1)$, the profitability of a link depends on whether others have formed links.

As economic incentives to form links will be invoked in different contexts throughout the subsequent chapters in this book, it is valuable to develop a deeper formal understanding of how to combine graph theoretic concepts with strategic reasoning and we therefore present a proof of the result here.

*Proof of Proposition 3.1.* The first step in the proof is to show that a Nash network is either empty or minimally connected. The focus is on the case $\phi(n, 1) > \phi(1, 0)$; the proof for the case $\phi(n, 1) \leq \phi(1, 0)$ is straightforward and is therefore omitted.

Suppose that $g$ is a nonempty Nash network. Choose a player $i \in \text{argmax}_{k\in N} n_k(g)$. Since $g$ is nonempty, the set of individuals accessed by $i$, $x_i = n_i(g) \geq 2$, and the number of their links $y_i = \eta_i^d(g) \geq 1$. Furthermore, since $g$ is Nash, $\Pi_i(g) = \phi(x_i, y_i) \geq \phi(1, 0)$. It is shown that $x_i = n$. Suppose instead that $x_i < n$. Then there exists $j \notin \mathcal{N}_i(g)$. Clearly, $i \notin \mathcal{N}_j(g)$, for otherwise player $j$ would access strictly more players than player $i$. Suppose that $y_j = 0$: in this case, player $j$ can strictly increase their payoffs by forming a link with $i$ because $\phi(x_i + 1, 1) > \phi(x_i, 1) \geq \phi(x_i, y_i) \geq \phi(1, 0)$. Hence $y_j \geq 1$. Now a variant of the same argument can be used to show that player $j$ can strictly increase their payoffs by deleting all their current links and instead form a direct link with player $i$. This contradicts the hypothesis of the Nash equilibrium. It also implies that $j \in \mathcal{N}_i(g)$, and since $j$ was arbitrary, this in turn means that $x_i = n$ in a Nash network.

Let $i$ be a player with $x_i = n$ as before. A player $j$ is critical to player $i$ if $n_i(g_{-j}) < n_i(g)$. Let $E$ be the set of noncritical players for player $i$ in network $g$. If $j \in \text{argmax}_{j'\in N} d(i, j'; g)$, then $j$ is noncritical, so $E$ is clearly nonempty. Next, it is shown that if $j \in E$, then $n_j(g) = n$. Suppose that this is not true. If $\eta_j^d(g) = 0$, then from the earlier argument, there is a deviation for player $j$ that increases her payoff strictly. Thus $\eta_j^d(g) \geq 1$. If $x_j = n_j(g) < n$, then player $j$ can delete all their links and instead form a single link with player $i$. The earlier argument step concerning access of all players in a Nash equilibrium can be used to show that they benefit strictly from such a deviation. Thus $g$ is not a Nash network. This contradiction implies that $n_j(g) = n$ for all $j \in E$.

The next step in the proof of connectedness establishes that for every $j_1 \notin E \cup \{i\}$, there exists $j \in E$ such that $j \in N_{j_1}(g)$. Since $j_1$ is critical, there exists $j_2 \in N_{j_1}(g)$ such that every path from $j_2$ to $i$ involves $j_1$. Hence $d(i, j_2; g) > d(i, j_1; g)$. If $j_2 \in E$, then the claim is proved; otherwise, by a similar argument, there exists a player $j_3 \in N_{j_2}(g)$ such that $d(i, j_3; g) > d(i, j_2; g)$. Since $i$ accesses every player and $n$ is finite, repeating this argument no more than $n - 2$ times will yield a player $j \in E$ such that $j \in N_{j_1}(g)$. Since $n_j(g) = n$, it follows that $n_{j_1}(g) = n$ as well. Hence $g$ is connected. If $g$ is Nash but not minimal, then a player can delete a link and the network still remains connected. This means that the player can strictly increase their payoffs by deleting a link, contradicting the definition of a Nash equilibrium. We have therefore shown that a nonempty network is minimally connected.

The *second* part of this proof shows that the cycle with all players is the unique, nonempty, strict equilibrium network. Let $g \in \mathcal{G}$ be a nonempty, strict Nash network. It is shown that for every player $k$, there is one and only one player $i$ such that $g_{ik} = 1$. First, note that since $g$ is nonempty and an equilibrium, it must be minimally connected. So for every player $k$, there is a player $i$ such that $g_{i,k} = 1$. Suppose that there is another player $j \neq i$ such that $g_{jk} = 1$. Since $g$ is minimal, it follows that $g_{ij} = 0$. Now consider a strategy $g_i'$ for player $i$ in which they delete the link with $k$ and instead form a link with $j$ and define $g_i' = g_i - g_{ik} + g_{ij}$.

Then $\eta_i^d(g) = \eta_i^d(g')$. Furthermore, since $k \in N_j^d(g) = N_j^d(g')$, clearly $n_i(g') \geq n_i(g)$. Hence $i$ earns weakly higher payoffs from this new strategy, $g_i'$, which contradicts the hypothesis that $g$ is a strict Nash network. As each player has exactly one player forming a link with them and the network is connected, it follows that the network must be a cycle that contains all players. Parts (a)–(c) now follow by direct verification. ■

A central theme in the economic study of networks is the question of performance. We start with a consideration of efficiency. We will say that a network is efficient if it maximizes the sum total of payoffs across the set of all possible networks. Let us make some preliminary observations to delimit the range of possible efficient networks. First, consider the class of connected networks. Every such network contains at least $n$ links because every player accesses everyone else in such a network and therefore must form at least one link. The cycle network containing all players has $n$ links, so it must maximize aggregate payoffs in the class of connected networks. As the cycle is the only connected network with $n$ links, we know that if a connected network is efficient, it must be a cycle.

The second observation concerns network externalities: if an efficient network contains some links, it must be connected (i.e., a partially connected network with multiple components is never efficient). Thus an efficient network is either empty or the cycle. The following result builds on these observations to provide a complete description of efficient networks.

**Proposition 3.2** *Suppose that the payoffs are given by (3.4). If $\phi(n,1) > \phi(1,0)$, then the unique efficient architecture is the cycle containing all players, while if $\phi(n,1) < \phi(1,0)$, the unique efficient architecture is the empty network.*

*Proof.* Let $F$ be the set of values $(n_i(g), \eta_i^d(g))$ as $g$ ranges over $\mathcal{G}$. If $\eta_i(g) = 0$, then $n_i(g) = 1$. If $\eta_i^d(g) \in \{1, \ldots, n-1\}$, then $n_i(g) \in \{\eta_i^d(g) + 1, n\}$. Thus $F \subset \{1, \ldots, n\} \times \{1, \ldots, n-1\} \cup \{0, 1\}$. Given $(x, y) \in F \setminus \{(1, 0)\}$, we have $\phi(n, 1) \geq \phi(n, y) \geq \phi(x, y)$ since $\phi$ is decreasing in its second argument and increasing in its first. For the cycle network $g^\ell$, note that $n_i(g^\ell) = n$ and $\eta_i = 1$ for all $i \in N$. Next, consider any other network $g \neq g^\ell$: for each $i \subset N$, if $\eta_i^d(g) \geq 1$, then $n_i(g) \leq n$, while if $\eta_i^d(g) = 0$, then $n_i(g) = 1$. In either case,

$$\Pi_i(g) = \phi(n, 1) \geq \phi(n_i(g), \eta_i^d(g)) = \pi_i(g), \tag{3.6}$$

where we have assumed that $\phi(n, 1) > \phi(1, 0)$. It follows that aggregate payoffs are given by

$$W(g^\ell) = \sum_{i \in N} \phi(n, 1) \geq \sum_{i \in N} \phi(n_i(g), \eta_i^d(g)) = W(g). \tag{3.7}$$

Thus $g^\ell$ is an efficient architecture.

To show uniqueness, note that our assumptions on $\phi$ imply that equation (3.6) holds with strict inequality if $\eta_i^d(g) \neq 1$ or $n_i(g) < n$. Let $g \neq g^\ell$ be given; if $\eta_i(g) \neq 1$ for even one player $i$, then the inequality in equation (3.6) is strict, which means that $W(g^\ell) > W(g)$. On the other hand, suppose that $\eta_i^d(g) = 1$ for all $i \in N$. As the cycle is the only connected network with $n$ agents and $n$ links and $g \neq g^{\ell}$, there must be an agent $j$ such that $n_i(g) < n$. Thus equation (3.6) again implies that there is a strict inequality for player $j$ and $W(g^{\ell}) > W(g)$, proving uniqueness.

For the case where $\phi(n, 1) < \phi(1, 0)$, let $g$ be different from the empty network $g^e$. Then there is an agent $j$ such that $\eta_i^d(g) \geq 1$. For this player,

$$\Pi_j(g^e) = \phi(1, 0) > \phi(n, 1) \geq \phi(n_j(g), \eta_i(g)) = \Pi_j(g), \tag{3.8}$$

while for every other player $i$,

$$\Pi_i(g^e) = \phi(1, 0) \geq \phi(n_i(g), \eta_i^d(g)) = \Pi_i(g). \tag{3.9}$$

The result follows by summing across $\Pi_j(g^e)$ and all other players $i$, $\Pi_i(g^e)$. ■

This result tells us in particular that for the linear payoffs case given by equation (3.5), the unique efficient network for $0 < k < n-1$ is the cycle containing all players and for $k > n-1$, it is the empty network. Thus efficient and equilibrium networks both exhibit sharp transitions at key threshold points.

A second point is worth noting: when we compare proposition 3.1 to proposition 3.2, we see that for the cost values in the range $0 < k < n-1$ and $k > n-1$, an efficient network is sustainable as a Nash equilibrium, but in the range $1 < k < n-1$, an efficient network is a cycle, while the empty network is also a (strict) Nash equilibrium. Thus there is the possibility of coordination failure: individuals may create an empty network even though they could create a connected network in equilibrium. A final remark is that the cycle is perfectly symmetric in terms of the number of links and the number of payoffs.

In the basic model discussed here, the value of accessing someone remains constant across path length. We now consider a more natural setting, in which value declines with distance. To appreciate the implications of this change, we restrict our attention to the linear payoffs model in equation (3.5) and introduce a decay parameter that is given by $\delta \in [0, 1]$. Given network $g$, if agent $i$ has a link with another agent $j$ (i.e., $g_{ij} = 1$), then $i$ receives information of value $\delta$ from $j$. More generally, if the shortest (directed) path in the network from $j$ to $i$ has $q > 1$ links, then the value of player $j$ to player $i$ is $\delta^q$. The cost of link formation is still taken to be $c$ per link. The payoff to a player $i$ in the network $g$ is

$$\Pi_i(g) = 1 + \sum_{j \in N \setminus \{i\}} \delta^{d(i,j;g)} - \eta_i^d(g)c, \tag{3.10}$$

where $d(i,j;g)$ is the geodesic distance from $j$ to $i$. The original linear model of equation (3.5) corresponds to $\delta = 1$. We will follow the convention that if there is no path between two individuals in a network, then the distance between them is set equal to infinity.

The trade-off between the costs of link formation and the benefits of short paths to overcome transmission losses is key to understanding the architecture of networks in this setting.

Building on the arguments in proposition 3.1, it can be shown that a strict Nash equilibrium network is connected or empty. A question at the end of the chapter develops the argument for this property. We next turn to other properties of Nash equilibrium networks.

If $k < \delta - \delta^2$, the marginal return from replacing an indirect link by a direct one exceeds the cost of link formation. It is a dominant strategy for a player to form links with everyone: the complete network is the unique Nash equilibrium. On the other hand, if $\delta - \delta^2 < k < \delta$, a player would want to directly or indirectly access everyone, meaning that the network must be connected. And, since $k > \delta - \delta^2$, if there is someone who has links with every other player, then everyone in the society will be content to form a single link with him (i.e., a star is a Nash equilibrium network). Next, observe that if $k > \delta$, then the empty network is a Nash network, as everyone wishes to form no links if no one has formed any links. However, other nonempty networks like the cycle reach equilibrium for $k > \delta$ and $\delta$ close to 1. Thus sharp transition thresholds and multiple equilibria remain salient, as in the baseline model with no decay.

We conclude this section with a brief comment on the role of decay in shaping network architecture. The high-level idea here is that smaller decay—higher values of $\delta$—pushes toward greater distances. We illustrate this in figure 3.3 by focusing on networks that range from a single cycle to a hub to which all are connected. For a fixed cost of linking, the size of the cycle sustainable in a Nash equilibrium expands as we increase the value of $\delta$ (keeping $k < \delta$).

## 3.3 Two-Sided Links

This section presents a model of network formation in which a link between two players requires the approval of both of them. In such games, for any pair of individuals, it is always a best response for each of them to offer to form no link if the other does so. This difficulty leads us to consider solution concepts that allow coordination and cooperation between pairs of individuals. We propose the concept of pairwise stability and its elaborations in order to study games with two-sided links. The discussion will describe pairwise stable networks and efficient networks and the relation between the two. We will also draw out the role of the linking protocol by comparing the architecture of the Nash equilibrium in the one-sided model with pairwise stable networks in the two-sided links model.

Following Myerson (1991), we consider a link announcement game. Every player announces a set of *intended* links. An intended link is a binary variable, $s_{i,j} \in \{0, 1\}$, where $s_{i,j} = 1$ ($s_{i,j} = 0$) means that player $i$ intends to (does not intend to) form a link with player $j$. A pure strategy for player $i$ is $s_i = \{s_{i,j}\}_{j \in N \setminus \{i\}}$, with $S_i$ denoting the strategy set of player $i$. A strategy profile for all players is denoted by $s = (s_1, \ldots, s_n)$, with the set of all strategies given by $\mathcal{S} = \prod_{i=1}^{n} \mathcal{S}_i$. Define $g_{ij} = \min\{s_{i,j}, s_{j,i}\}$. A strategy profile $s$ therefore induces a corresponding *undirected* network $g(s)$. Define $\Pi_i : \mathcal{S} \to \mathcal{R}$ as the payoff function of player $i$ in network $g$.

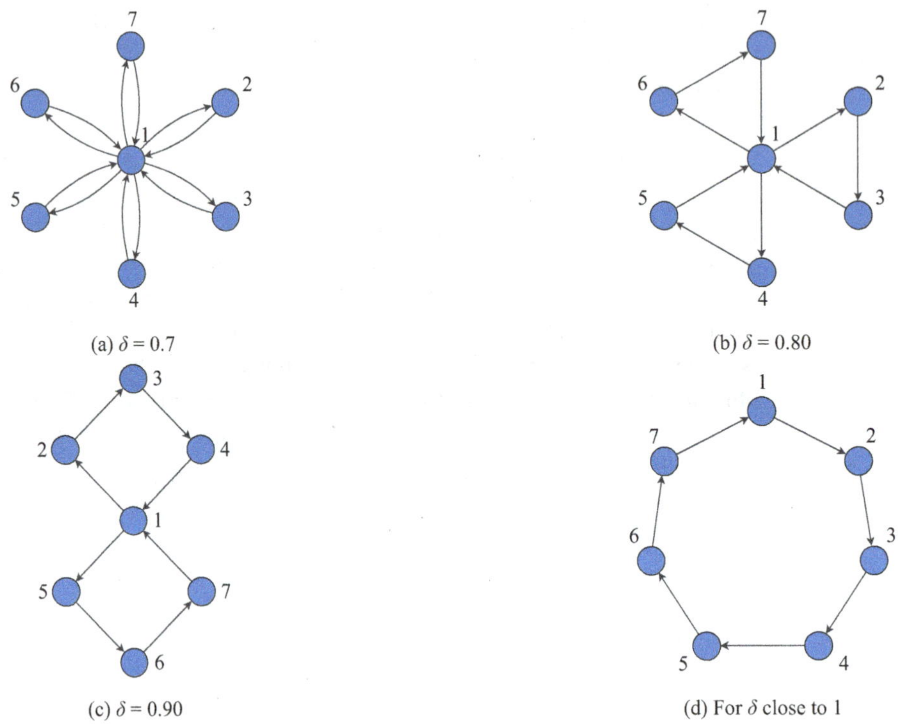


**Figure 3.3**
Nash networks with decay: $n = 7, k = 0.5$.

To develop an appreciation of the linking protocol, we will consider linear payoffs as in equation (3.5) (but now in an undirected network setting). Let $n_i(g)$ be the benefit that player $i$ receives from each player that they access through an undirected path in the network, and let $\eta_i(g)$ be the number of links they form. Given an undirected network $g$, the payoff to individual $i$ is given by

$$\Pi_i(g) = n_i(g) - \eta_i(g)k. \tag{3.11}$$

In other words, player $i$'s payoffs are the number of players they access less the cost of the links they form.

We start the analysis of this game with a consideration of the familiar notion of the Nash equilibrium, as this will illustrate some of the conceptual issues that arise with the study of network formation with two-sided links. Recall that a strategy profile $s^* = (s_1^*, \ldots, s_n^*)$ is a Nash equilibrium if $\Pi_i(g(s_i^*, s_{-i}^*)) \geq \Pi_i(g(s_i, s_{-i}^*))$, for all $s_i \in \mathcal{S}_i$ and all $i \in N$. This means that if every player announces that they want to form no links, then a best response of player $i$ is to announce that they want to form no links as well. In other words, the empty network is a Nash equilibrium for any network formation game.

The concept of pairwise stability from Jackson and Wolinsky (1996) is designed to overcome this coordination issue.

**Definition 3.1** *A network g is pairwise stable if*

1. *For every* $g_{ij}=1$, $\Pi_i(g) \geq \Pi_i(g-g_{ij})$ *and* $\Pi_j(g) \geq \Pi_j(g-g_{ij})$.
2. *For* $g_{ij}=0$, $\Pi_i(g+g_{ij}) > \Pi_i(g) \implies \Pi_j(g+g_{ij}) < \Pi_j(g)$.

Pairwise stability looks at the attractiveness of links in a network $g$ *one at a time*. The first condition requires that every link in a stable network must be weakly profitable for the players involved in the link. The second condition requires that for every link that is not present in the network, it must be the case that if one player strictly gains from the link, then the other player must be strictly worse off.

Let us work through the trade-offs introduced by the two-sided nature of linking. First, observe that there cannot be two paths between any two players in a pairwise stable network. This is because if there were such a link, since there is no decay and distances don't matter, a player could strictly increase their payoff by deleting a link that retained the connectivity of a component. Thus a pairwise stable network must be acyclic.

Next, we argue that a pairwise stable network is either empty or connected. To see why this is true, consider a nonempty network that is pairwise stable but has multiple components. Let $C_1$ be the largest component. As this is not a singleton and it is acyclic, there is a player $i$ who has a single link with a player $j$: the payoff to this player is $|C_1|-k$, and this payoff must exceed 1 (which the player could earn on their own in a singleton component): thus $|C_1|-k-1 \geq 0$. Now consider a player, $\ell$, who lies outside component $C_1$: such a player can propose a link with $j$ that would yield a net marginal benefit of $|C_1|-k > |C_1|-1-k \geq 0$. In other words, player $\ell$ can strictly increase their payoff by forming a link with player $j$. Moreover, player $j$ would not be worse off with the link, as they were happy with the link with player $i$. We have therefore shown that $\ell$ has a strict incentive and $j$ has at least a weak incentive to form a link. But then the original network $g$ would not be pairwise stable.

Next, observe that if $k<1$, then every pair of players has an incentive to access each other: a pairwise stable network must be connected. Moreover, if $k>1$, then no player would be willing to form a link with an isolated player.

Let us next describe the efficient networks in this model. A preliminary remark is that there cannot be two paths between any pair of individuals in an efficient network: if there were two paths, then a link can be deleted without affecting the connectivity of the component and this new network would yield strictly higher welfare, as it would contain one link less with no effect on benefits. So an efficient network must be acyclic. Note that a minimally connected network with $n$ nodes has exactly $n-1$ links.We next establish that an efficient network must be empty or connected.

To see this, consider a nonempty network with two components (each of which is minimal) with $\ell \geq 2$ and $m \geq 2$ nodes, respectively. The aggregate payoffs in the two components

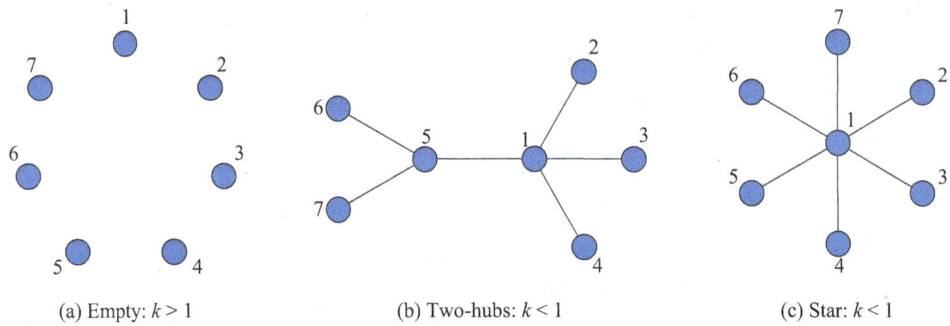


**Figure 3.4**
Pairwise stable networks: two-sided link model.

are $\ell^2 - 2(\ell-1)k$ and $m^2 - 2(m-1)k$, respectively. As the network is efficient, the components must generate payoffs greater than the corresponding empty networks (i.e., $\ell^2 - 2(\ell-1)k \geq \ell$ and $m^2 - 2(m-1)k \geq m$). If we aggregate the two components to create one minimal component, the total payoffs are $(\ell+m)^2 - 2(\ell+m-1)k$. It is clear that

$$(\ell+m)^2 - 2(\ell+m-1)k > \ell^2 - 2(\ell-1)k + m^2 - 2(m-1)k, \tag{3.12}$$

given that $\ell^2 - 2(\ell-1)k \geq \ell$ and $m^2 - 2(m-1)k \geq m$. Thus an efficient network is either minimally connected or it is empty. A minimally connected network yields a total payoff of $n^2 - 2(n-1)k$, while the empty network yields total payoffs equal to $n$. Thus the connected network dominates the empty network if and only if $k < n/2$.

Our discussion is summarized in the following result.

**Proposition 3.3** *Suppose that the payoffs are given by equation (3.11). If $k < 1$, then a pairwise stable network is minimally connected and if $k > 1$ then the unique pairwise stable network is empty. If $k < n/2$, then an efficient network is minimally connected, while if $k > n/2$, then the efficient network is empty.*

Figures 3.4 and 3.5 present pairwise stable and efficient networks in the two-sided links model. The study of two-sided links networks draws attention to the two themes that were also mentioned in the discussion of the one-sided links model above: (1) there are sharp transitions at thresholds from a connected to an empty network and (2) there is a tension between stability and efficiency. However, there are also important differences between the Nash equilibrium of the one-sided model and the pairwise stable networks of the two-sided model. In particular, in the one-sided links model, directed cycles are a recurring feature of Nash networks, while they do not arise in pairwise stable networks of the two-sided model (cf. figures 3.1 and 3.4).

Turning to the question of payoffs, observe that in an efficient network like the star, the central player earns $n-(n-1)k$, while the periphery player earns $n-k$. This is a more

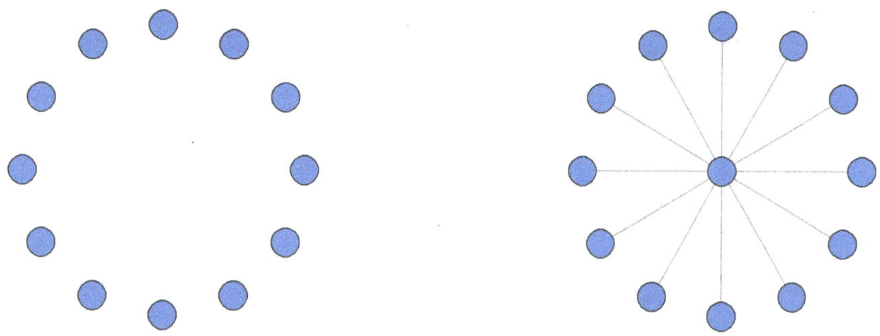

(a) Empty: $k > n/2$ (b) Star: $k < n/2$

**Figure 3.5**
Efficient networks: two-sided links model.

general feature of efficient networks: even in a line network, the leaves earn $n - k$, while all other players earn $n - 2k$. Thus the marginal return to the leaf from a link is significantly larger than the marginal return to the nonleaf from linking with the leaf. In all minimally connected networks, there is this great asymmetry in marginal returns, which goes some way toward understanding why the efficient network is not pairwise stable.

For completeness, we now discuss the two-sided link model with decay; following Jackson and Wolinsky (1996), this is known as the "connections model." Let $\delta \in [0, 1]$ be the rate of decay in value as it moves across links. Given a strategy profile $s$, the payoffs to player $i$ in a network $g(s)$ are

$$\Pi_i(s) = 1 + \sum_{j \neq i} \delta^{d(i,j;g(s))} - \eta_i(g(s))k, \tag{3.13}$$

where $k > 0$ is the cost of forming a link (for each player) and $\delta \in [0, 1]$ is the decay in value as it passes through paths of the network. The value of $\delta = 0$ reflects full decay and no flow of value, while $\delta = 1$ indicates the absence of any decay. The existence of decay creates an incentive for players to locate themselves close to others.

**Proposition 3.4** *Suppose that payoffs are given by equation (3.13). A pairwise stable network is either connected or empty. For $k < \delta - \delta^2$, the unique pairwise stable network is the complete network. For $\delta - \delta^2 < k < \delta$, a star is a pairwise stable network. For $\delta < k$, the empty network is pairwise stable and any pairwise stable network that is nonempty is such that each player has at least two links.*

The first part of this proof follows from agglomeration arguments as in the baseline model without decay. The rest of the result follows from straightforward computations. Figure 3.6 illustrates some pairwise stable networks. We note that dense networks like the complete network, as well as sparse and small average distance networks like the star, can be pairwise stable networks.

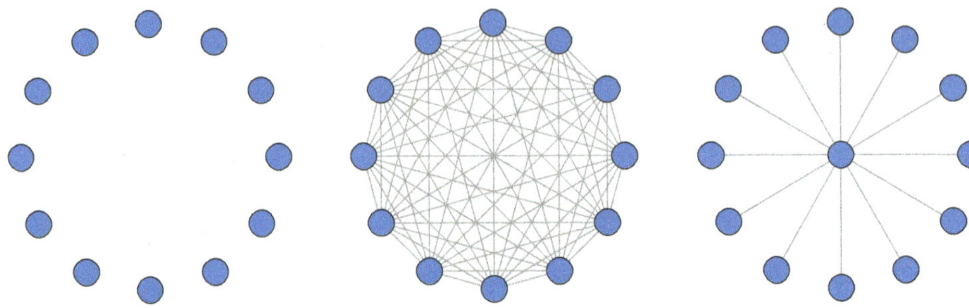


**Figure 3.6**
Pairwise stable networks: two-sided model with decay.

We next turn to an assessment of the performance of networks. Recall that a network is efficient if it maximizes the sum of individual payoffs in the set of all networks. In addition to the trade-offs introduced in proposition 3.3, the presence of decay creates a further trade-off now. If the costs of linking are very small, expressed as $k < (\delta - \delta^2)$, it is socially desirable to form a direct link between every pair of individuals. If, on the other hand, the costs of links are very large, then it is clear that no links would be justifiable. We also note that the star network is attractive because it economizes on the number of links and simultaneously keeps the average distance between individuals very low (there are $n - 1$ links in a star, the minimum number of links it takes to connect $n$ nodes) and the average distance is less than 2. These preliminary remarks help pin down efficient networks very sharply, as the following result confirms.

**Proposition 3.5** *Suppose that payoffs are given by equation (3.13). The unique efficient network in the connections model is (1) the complete network if $k < \delta - \delta^2$, (2) the star if $\delta - \delta^2 < k < \delta + (n-2)\delta^2/2$, and (3) the empty network if $k > \delta + (n-2)\delta^2/2$.*

The arguments underlying this result resurface at different points in subsequent chapters. It is therefore important to develop a thorough understanding of these arguments, and so we present a proof of the result.

*Proof.* The joint marginal gains to players $i$ and $j$ from forming a link are bounded from below by $2[\delta - \delta^2]$. If $2k < 2[\delta - \delta^2]$, then forming a link increases social welfare. Thus any incomplete network is welfare-dominated by the complete network, so long as $k < [\delta - \delta^2]$: that is, the complete network is uniquely efficient.

Next, fix component $C_1$ in $g$, with $|C_1| = m$. Suppose that $m \geq 3$, and let $l \geq m - 1$ be the number of links in the component. Then the welfare in $C_1$ is bounded above by

$$m + l(2\delta - 2k) + [m(m-1) - 2l]\delta^2. \tag{3.14}$$

This is because a link ensures direct benefits of $2\delta$ to each of the connected pairs, the cost of a link is $k$, and the closest all other pairs of individuals could be is distance 2. If the component is a star, then social welfare is

$$m + (m-1)[2\delta - 2k] + (m-1)(m-2)\delta^2, \tag{3.15}$$

where $m$ reflects stand-alone benefits, the second term collects the direct benefits less the costs of links, and the third term reflects the benefits of all pairs who are distance 2 apart.

Under the hypothesis that $(\delta - \delta^2) < k$, equation (3.14) can never exceed equation (3.15), and the two are exactly equal for $l = m - 1$. It can be checked that the star is the only network with $m$ players and $m - 1$ links in which every pair of players is at a distance of 2 or less. Hence any other network with $m - 1$ links must have at least one pair of players who are at a distance of 3 or more. This implies that social welfare in any other network with $l = m - 1$ links is strictly less than social welfare in the star. Thus in an efficient network, a component must be a star.

Consider next an efficient network with two stars and $m$ and $m'$ individuals, respectively. As the network is efficient, each of the component must have nonnegative welfare. It can be shown by direct computation that a single component with $m + m'$ players has higher social welfare than two components with the star structure. Thus a single star maximizes social welfare in the class of all nonempty networks. Social welfare in a star is given by equation (3.15), but we substitute $m$ with $n$. It can be checked that welfare in the star exceeds welfare in the empty network if $\delta + (n-2)\delta^2/2 > k$. This completes the proof. ∎

The analysis of the connections model reveals a number of features that are of general interest. We start by noting that a wide range of network architectures are pairwise stable—they range from the complete network to the empty network and include the star network. We next comment on the role of decay. In the model with no decay, the complete network is never an equilibrium because the equilibrium network cannot be cyclic: thus introducing decay makes denser networks strategically stable. On the other hand, decay also presses toward bringing individuals closer to each other: this makes the star especially attractive from a payoff point of view, as it economizes on links and also has small average distances.

The second point pertains to the sharp transition in network structure—both for stability and efficiency—that occurs at critical cost values. This is again reminiscent of the thresholds in the one-way flow model (and in the random graph models).

The third point to note is that there is a tension between individual incentives and collective welfare. The star is efficient for a wide range of parameters—if $\delta - \delta^2 < k < \delta + (n-2)\delta^2$—but it cannot be sustained as a pairwise stable network for $k > \delta$. This is reminiscent of the tension previously noted in the one-way flow model. It points to the positive externalities created by individual linking: when the hub forms links with the spokes, it creates value for all spokes that it does not take into account.

We conclude our discussion of the two-sided model by drawing attention to the role of the linking protocol: in the one-sided model, Nash equilibrium (and efficient) networks will generally contain (directed) cycles, while in the two-sided linking model, both pairwise stability (and efficiency) push toward acyclic networks.

## 3.4 General Considerations

Up to now, we have presented the elements of an economic approach to network formation. For expositional reasons, we have concentrated on distinguishing between one- and two-sided links, and we have focused on a very simple model of benefits and costs. The economics literature on network formation has made major advances over the past two decades in terms of the generality of the theory, as well as in terms of the reach of the applications. The aim of this section is to introduce some of the general features of the theoretical models in this literature. In subsequent chapters, these general features will be further elaborated upon in a number of applications, such as production networks, infrastructure, brokerage and intermediaries, security, online social media, social coordination, and networked markets.

### 3.4.1 Dynamics

Networks change as individuals add and delete links over time. This raises the natural question of whether the process of link formation settles down and what networks arise. What is the relation between the networks that arise in the long run and the networks that are Nash equilibria or pairwise stable networks of the static network formation game? To develop a first impression of how dynamics can be used to understand networks, we present the dynamics of the one-sided model of linking.

Perhaps the simplest way to approach the dynamics of networks is to think of a world in which individuals get an opportunity to revise their links, form links with some new players, maintain some of the existing links, and delete some of the other links. The structure of the existing network will determine the rewards from linking with different individuals. The possibility that current linking activity will alter incentives for others (and hence shape future linking activity) may be an important factor as well. The importance of longer-term effects will depend on how quickly the network changes, as well as on how patient the players are.

For expositional simplicity, and in line with most of the research in the field, let us suppose that individuals are perfectly impatient: they care only about the immediate returns and ignore the longer-term effects entirely. This leads to the myopic best-response model of dynamics that we now outline.

Time is a discrete variable and indexed by $t = 1, 2, 3, \ldots$. Let $g^t$ be the network/strategy profile at the start of time $t$. In each period, with probability $p \in (0, 1)$, a player gets an opportunity to revise their strategy. They know the network that exists at that point in time, and they choose links that maximize the payoff. In making these choices, they assume that the links of all other players do not change. If more than one profile of links is optimal, then a player randomly picks one of them. Denote the strategy of a player $i$ in period $t$ by $g_i^t$. If player $i$ is not active in period $t$, then it follows that $g_i^t = g_i^{t-1}$. This simple best-response strategy revision rule generates a transition probability function of $P_{gg'} : \mathcal{G} \times \mathcal{G} \rightarrow [0, 1]$, with $\sum_{g'} P_{gg'} = 1$ for every $g \in \mathcal{G}$. The dynamics of networks $g^t$ obey this transition probability function. This defines a Markov chain: a strategy profile (or state) $g$ is said to be an absorbing state of the Markov chain if the dynamic process cannot escape from that state (i.e., $P_{gg} = 1$).

In some cases, the process may not converge; in such instances, we will talk of absorbing sets of networks. An absorbing set is a collection of networks such that once the process reaches one of the networks in this set, then it remains within this set forever after. Note that the set of all networks is clearly an absorbing set of the process.

A preliminary observation is that if the dynamics settle on a network, the absorbing state is a strict Nash equilibrium: clearly the absorbing network must be a Nash network, as otherwise at least one of the players has an alternative, more profitable profile of links and will deviate in due course. In addition, we note that the randomization among best responses means that a nonstrict Nash equilibrium cannot be an absorbing network for the dynamic.

By way of illustration, figure 3.7 presents the dynamics of linking in the one-sided link formation model. We suppose that payoffs have a linear specification as in equation (3.5) and $k \in (0, 1)$. The initial network (labeled $t = 1$) has been drawn at random from the set of all directed networks with five agents. In the periods $t \geq 2$, the choices of agents who exhibit inertia have been drawn in solid lines, while the links of those who are active are drawn in dashed lines. Figure 3.7 suggests that the choices of individuals evolve rapidly and settle down by period 11: the limit network is a cycle.

This simulation motivates a more general question: under what conditions—the structure of payoffs, the size of the society, and the initial network—does the dynamic process converge? Convergence of the dynamic process would suggest that individuals who are myopically pursuing self-interested goals, with no assistance from a central coordinator, are able to arrive at a stable network over time. It is possible to show that such a decentralized process does converge in the one-way flow model under fairly general circumstances; for the details of the arguments involved, see Bala and Goyal (2000a).

In this example of the linear model with $k \in (0, 1)$, the cycle is the unique strict Nash network, but if $k \in (1, n-1)$, then there are two strict Nash networks: the cycle and the empty network. A possible question is whether one of the two networks is more stable or more likely to be picked by the dynamics. The problem of selection among strict Nash equilibria—through the introduction of trembles—has been widely studied in the literature of evolutionary game theory. We will have to leave the subject here; for an elegant introduction to evolutionary approaches to equilibrium selection, see Young (1998).

So far we have assumed that individual players know the network that they are located in, and therefore they can calculate the costs and benefits from various links. However,

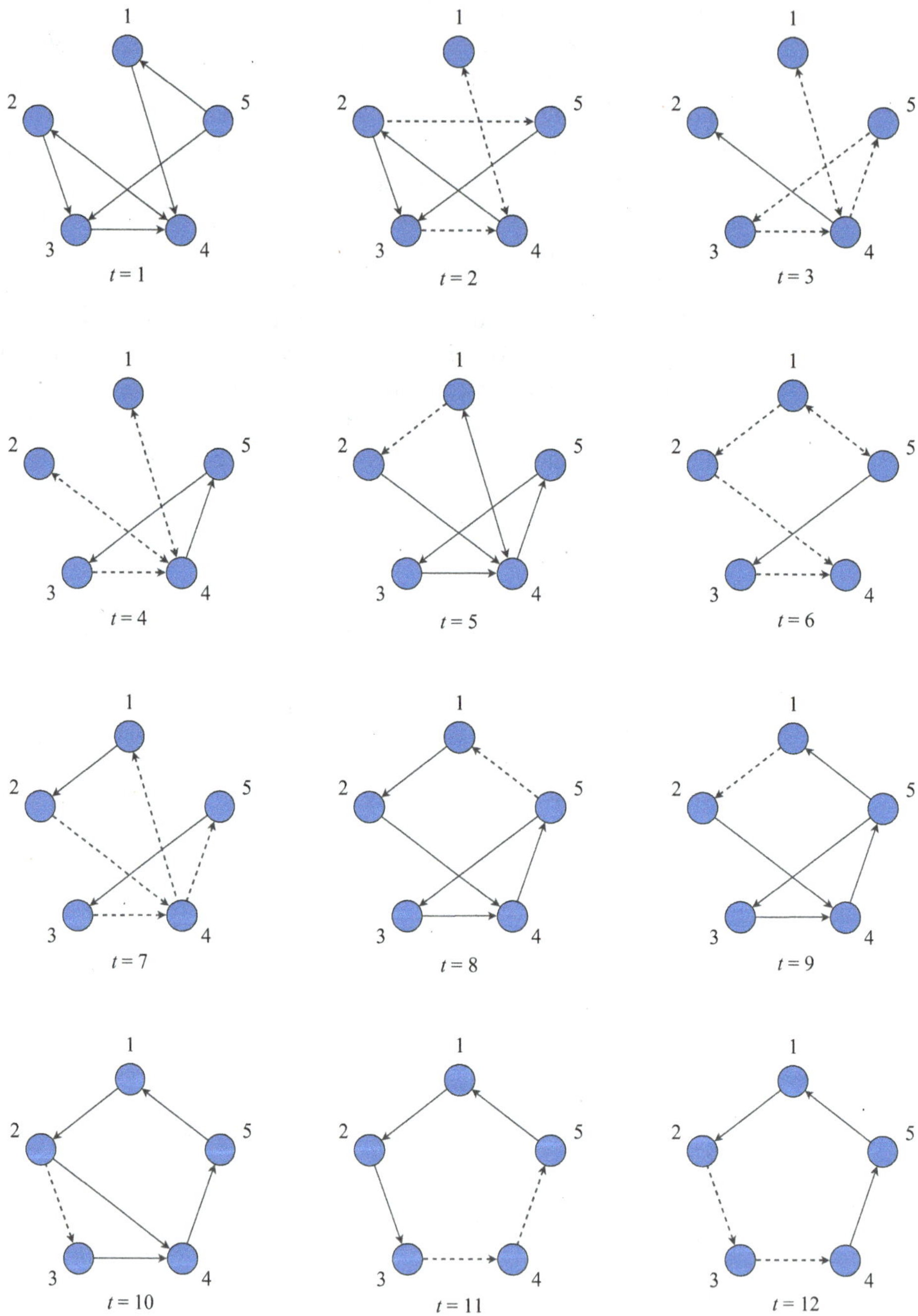


**Figure 3.7**
Best response network dynamics: taken from Bala and Goyal (2000a).

networks are complicated objects, and even with a few players, a great many structures can arise. Moreover, the fact that networks are subject to subtle transformations typically carried out at a local level suggests that it may be difficult for players to keep informed about the details of the evolving network. In chapter 11, we will present experiments on the dynamics of linking, and we will then see that the question of knowledge and the complexity of networks is important for understanding network formation.

### 3.4.2 Richer Models of Links

We have studied models in which links are binary—a link is either present or absent. This is in keeping with most of the literature to date. However, it is clear that in many contexts, it is not just the existence of a link but the quality that is important. For instance, take the case of information on jobs. In his classical study, "The Strength of Weak Ties," Granovetter (1973) drew attention to the distinct roles of strong and weak ties in shaping the flow of information about jobs in a society. Following on this, Scott Boorman (1975) proposed a model of costly investments in strong and weak ties that help communicate information on jobs. However, the modeling of weighted links presents a number of conceptual and mathematical challenges, and progress has been slow. The discussion in this section draws attention to some of the these challenges.

We start with an approach that builds directly on the basic models of binary links presented in sections 3.2 and 3.3. The model is taken from Bloch and Dutta (2009). The authors focus on an interpretation of communication networks—networks where agents derive benefits from the agents with whom they are connected, with the benefits decreasing as the distance increases between two agents. Their point of departure is that links may have different qualities, depending on the investments that individuals make. Assume that every individual has resources $T$ that they can allocate across the links with the other $n-1$ individuals. Formally, for investments $g_{ij}, g_{ji} \in \mathbb{R}_+$ by individuals $i$ and $j$, let the quality of the link between them be $q_{ij} : \mathbb{R}_+ \times \mathbb{R}_+ \rightarrow [0, 1]$. Observe that by suitably varying the nature of function $q_{ij}$, we can obtain the one- and two-sided linking models discussed earlier as special cases.

To develop intuitions on the forces driving the formation of weighted networks let us focus on a simple special case: suppose that the quality of the link is defined as an additive and separable function of individual investments. Moreover, suppose that the returns to individual investments have increasing returns:

$$q_{ij} = \phi(g_{ij}) + \phi(g_{ji}), \tag{3.16}$$

where $\phi$ is an increasing and convex function with $\phi(0) = 0$ and $\phi(T) < 1/2$.

We next define the quality of a path as a product of the quality of the links on the path. As an example, the quality of a path consisting of three individuals A, B, and C is simply

$q_{AB}q_{BC}$. In this formulation, observe that it is not just the length of a path, but also the quality of the links in it that matters. We discuss efficient and equilibrium networks in this setting.

Our first observation is that the efficient network is a star. The argument for this result builds on the following intuitions. A star is connected (thus everyone accesses all other individuals), every peripheral agent concentrates their investment on a single link (which enhances quality of the link), and the distance between two nodes that are not directly connected is minimized. All these features contribute to making the star the natural candidate for the efficient network. Turning to the Nash equilibrium, if link strength is a strictly convex function of individual investments, then the unique Nash equilibrium network is a star whose center invests fully on just one link. The intuition for this result builds on the strict convexity of $\phi$: it implies that an individual will invest in at most one link. This more or less rules out all networks other than the star.

This discussion shows how the arguments presented in the context of the baseline binary model need to be modified to understand weighted networks. They also suggest that some of the results on the efficiency and stability of network architecture can be generalized to settings with richer linking possibilities. In this model, the investments of the individuals can be substituted in building up the quality of links (as the investments enter in a separable form). We next turn to a setting in which the individual investments are complements in shaping the quality of the link.

We discuss a model taken from Baumann (2021). Individuals allocate their resource $T$ between a private activity $t_{ii}$, and link-specific activities $t_{ij}$, for $j \in N \backslash \{i\}$. An individual's strategy is given by a vector $t_i = (t_{i1}, \ldots, t_{ii}, \ldots, t_{in})$. A link between two individuals $i$ and $j$ exists if both of them make positive investments, $t_{ij} > 0$ and $t_{ji} > 0$. Given a strategy profile $s = (t_1, \ldots, t_n)$, the utility of individual $i$ is

$$u_i(t) = \sum_{j \neq i} t_{ij}^{\beta} t_{ji}^{1-\beta} + f(t_{ii}), \tag{3.17}$$

where $\beta \in (0, 1)$ and $t_{ij}^{\beta} t_{ji}^{1-\beta}$ refers to returns from relations in which individuals $i$ and $j$ contribute $t_{ij}$ and $t_{ji}$, respectively. The term $f(t_{ii})$ refers to the return from contribution $t_{ii}$ in own activities. It is assumed that the return is increasing and concave, specifically that $f' > 0, f'' < 0, f' \to \infty$ if $t_{ii} \to 0$ and $f'(T)$ is "low enough." Note that in this model, the payoffs depend only on the quality of links with immediate neighbors. This simplification helps us to obtain sharp results on patterns of investment in equilibrium.

Given the assumptions on reward function, it follows that in a Nash equilibrium, every individual must fully use all their resources allocation:

$$\sum_{j \in N} t_{ij} = T. \tag{3.18}$$

Moreover, due to the form of the link function, in a Nash equilibrium, if $t_{ji}=0$ then $t_{ij}=0$. Finally, if $t_{ji}>0$, then $t_{ij}>0$ and

$$\beta\left(\frac{t_{ji}}{t_{ij}}\right)^{1-\beta}=f'(t_{ii}). \tag{3.19}$$

In addition, it follows from the assumption $f'(t)\to\infty$ for $t\to 0$ that $t_{ii}>0$ for all individuals in a Nash equilibrium.

Observe that due to the complementarity in link quality, there is always an equilibrium in which no one invests in any links with others. Our interest is in equilibria that contain "active" links. In such an equilibrium, the marginal returns to investment in own activity must equal the marginal return to investment in any link; that is,

$$\beta\left(\frac{t_{ji}}{t_{ij}}\right)^{1-\beta}=\beta\left(\frac{t_{ki}}{t_{ik}}\right)^{1-\beta}=f'(t_{ii}). \tag{3.20}$$

This means that the ratio of investments for individual $i$ must be the same for every link in which they are active: let us define

$$q_i=\frac{t_{ji}}{t_{ij}}=\frac{t_{ki}}{t_{ik}}. \tag{3.21}$$

In equilibrium, a neighbor of $i$ faces a ratio $q_j$ that is the inverse of $q_i$:

$$q_j=\frac{t_{ij}}{t_{ji}}=\frac{1}{q_i}. \tag{3.22}$$

Consider a connected network of active ties. In such an equilibrium network, if the ratio of effort for an individual is not 1, then the ratios will alternate across neighbors. Therefore, in a connected network of active links, the individual ratios must take on two values, $q'$ and $1/q'$. This yields a simple characterization of Nash networks:

1. Reciprocal: $q_i=1$ for all $i$. Every player chooses the same self-investment $t_b$, where $\beta=f'(t_b)$.
2. Nonreciprocal: Concentrated $q_i>1$ for $i$ with self-investment $t_c$, where $\beta(1/q_i)^{1-\beta}=f'(t_c)$ and diversified $q_j<1$ for a $j$ with self-investment $t_d$, where $\beta(q_i)^{1-\beta}=f'(t_d)$.

Given a nonreciprocal network $t$ and a reciprocal network $t'$,

$$\beta\left(\frac{1}{q'}\right)^{1-\beta}=f'(t_c)<\beta=f'(t'_b)<\beta(q')^{1-\beta}=f'(t_d). \tag{3.23}$$

As $f$ is concave, this yields the following ranking of investment in links: $t_d<t'_b<t_c$. This in turn induces an ordering of utility levels:

$$u_i(t_d)>u_i(t_b)>u_i(t_c). \tag{3.24}$$

(a) Reciprocal ties (b) Nonreciprocal ties

**Figure 3.8**
Weighted Nash networks.

Figure 3.8 presents examples of reciprocal and nonreciprocal Nash networks.

Let us draw out implications of reciprocal and nonreciprocal investments for network topologies. First, observe that regular networks are sustainable via reciprocal investments. On the other hand, a network with a leaf cannot be sustained in a reciprocal equilibrium in a connected network with three or more individuals: this is because reciprocity would mean that $q = 1$ for a leaf and its neighbor. This would in turn rule out investments in other links by the nonleaf individual. Observe that leaves are easily sustained in nonreciprocal networks.

This brief discussion does not do justice to the large body of literature on the subject of weighted networks. The aim here has been much more modest: to draw attention to some of the challenges of moving from binary to weighted links. We see that the results on network topologies obtained in the binary link model can sometimes be extended to weighted counterparts (though the arguments are significantly more complicated), but there arise interesting asymmetries in patterns of investment between neighbors that are intimately connected to the network topology. The area of weighted networks remains a very active field of research; section 3.6 provides a number of references for further reading.

### 3.4.3 Generic Investments and Random Linking

In the models presented here, we have taken the view that individuals make decisions on individual links and in computing their costs and benefits they are informed about all the links in the entire network. In some contexts, including parent-teacher associations, neighborhood groups, and professional conferences, it is perhaps more plausible to think of the network in a more generic sense and imagine that individuals contemplate the issue in terms of how much time or resources they will allocate to interacting with different groups of individuals (such as friends, neighbors, professional colleagues, and sports contacts). In these contexts, we are interested in the amount of time and other resources that different groups of individuals spend in these forums and how that would affect the returns to taking part in them. In this approach, the exact details of who links with whom no longer occupy central stage. Rather, we are interested in the "thickness" of interactions or the macroscopic level of the network. These considerations suggest a simpler and more direct approach to the problem of network formation. This section discusses a strand of the literature that takes this "social investments" perspective.

We start with a model taken from Cabrales, Calvo-Armengol, and Zenou (2011), in which individuals make two decisions that pertain to "production" and "socialization." Individual payoffs depend on own and others' production efforts and these spillovers are mediated through the social links between individuals.

There are $n$ players with types/values $0 < b_1 < \cdots < b_n$. Player $i$ chooses a strategy, $s_i = (e_i, g_i)$, comprising productive effort $e_i$ and a synergy effort $g_i$. Both socialization and effort are costly, and the returns depend on the strength of synergy between individuals. Given a profile of strategies $s = (s_1, \ldots, s_n)$, the payoffs to player $i$ are

$$u_i(s) = b_i e_i + \sum_j g_{ij} e_i e_j - \frac{c}{2} e_i^2 - \frac{1}{2} g_i^2, \tag{3.25}$$

where $c > 0$ refers to the relative cost of productive effort. The link quality or intensity is constructed as follows: given a profile of investments $g = (g_1, \ldots, g_n)$, for any pair $i, j$ the link intensity is

$$g_{ij}(g) = \frac{g_i g_j}{\sum_k g_k}. \tag{3.26}$$

This formula captures two intuitive ideas: (1) the weight of a link between two individuals is increasing in each of their investments and (2) it is decreasing in the sum total of all investments of everyone.

As in the earlier models with two-sided links, there is a coordination aspect to investing in social interaction: specifically, if everyone else chooses zero social interaction, then there is no return to investing in social interaction; therefore, zero investment is always an equilibrium. The more interesting case concerns positive social investments. An important feature of the model is the complementarity between social interaction and efforts—reflected in the term $\sum_j g_{ij} e_i e_j$—and this can give rise to multiple interior equilibria. In other words, there are a low interaction plus modest effort equilibrium and a high interaction plus high effort equilibrium. As the game exhibits complementarities, the effects of changes in parameters can be studied using classical methods from the theory of supermodular games. (e.g., Topkis [1998]).

A second strand of the literature examines models of linking in which individuals propose a single scalar number, as in the model described just previously, but the payoffs depend on the macroscopic properties (such as connectedness and giant component) of the random graph that they create. We will present a model taken from Dasaratha (2021) that takes this approach.

Suppose there are $N = \{1, \ldots, n\}$, $n \geq 3$ firms. Every firm has a distinct idea, $a_i \in \mathbb{N}$. A firm can earn payoffs only if they have access to a technology that consists of $L > 1$ ideas. Moreover, due to competition, a firm earns this payoff only if they uniquely have these $L$ ideas. We may think of the size of $L$ as a measure of the complexity of the technology.

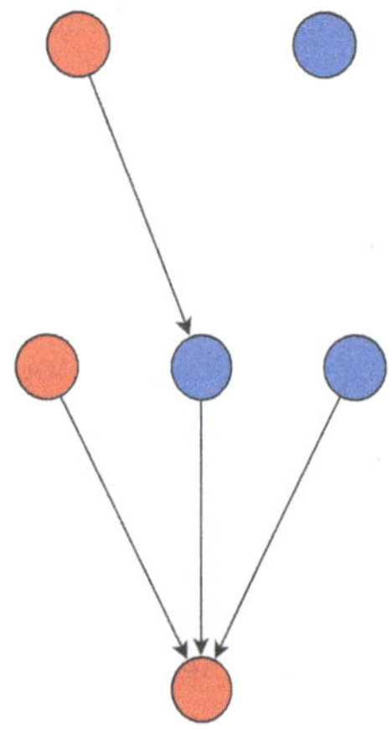


**Figure 3.9**
Exclusive technology for firm $i$: $L = 3$.

The goal of a firm is to form connections to access $L$ distinct ideas. The firm accesses ideas from others by choosing a level of openness, $q_i \in [0, 1]$. This level of openness refers to how secretive or collaborative it will be (e.g., should it be located near or far from other firms, or should it be liberal in sharing its intellectual advances with employees and encouraging informal interactions of its employees).

Greater openness is, however, a double-edged sword: it facilitates access to other firms' ideas, but it also makes its own idea more easily accessible to other firms. Given openness $q_i$ and $q_j$, we say that a firm $i$ learns the idea of firm $j$ with probability

$$p_i(q_i, q_j) = q_i q_j. \tag{3.27}$$

A key element of the process is that the learning is directed: so firm $i$ may learn from firm $j$ without the converse being true (i.e., the random variable $p_{ij}$ is realized independent of $p_{ji}$). Importantly, however, notice that increasing $q_i$ leads to a higher learning probability for both firms $i$ and $j$.

The next important element is indirect learning: when $i$ learns from $j$, it also gains access to the ideas that $j$ has learned from other firms. Conditional on connecting with $j$, there is a probability given by $\delta \in [0, 1]$ that it learns the ideas that firm $j$ has learned directly or indirectly through its connections. To complete the description of the learning process, we note that the realizations with respect to learning are independent and occur simultaneously.

Let us say a few words on the notion of a technology here. A technology, $t$, is defined as a set of $L$ distinct ideas. We will say that firm $i$ has exclusive access to technology $t$ if it contains $i$'s idea, $a_i \in t$, firm knows all the ideas contained in $t$, and no other individual knows all these ideas. Figure 3.9 illustrates the exclusive access of individual $i$ to a technology consisting of ideas from three individuals. An individual earns 1 from every technology to which it has exclusive access. We can consider these technologies as proprietary technologies for $i$. On the other hand, $i$ receives zero payoff from those technologies that they know along with other individuals. Given a profile of openness choices $q$, the expected earnings of firm $i$ are simply the expected number of exclusive technologies; that is,

$$U_i(q) = E[PT_{ij}], \tag{3.28}$$

where $PT_i$ is the number of exclusive technologies of individual $i$. We next study Nash equilibria in openness levels and comment on their social efficiency.

Let us start by drawing out some of the economic forces at work. First, note that profile $q$ gives rise to a directed graph that tells us who will have access to which ideas. The value of openness to a firm will depend on how open other firms are. Greater openness of other individuals creates two conflicting pressures. On the one hand, it makes them more likely to have more ideas to share, which increases the value of accessing them; but on the other hand, as each of them has access to many ideas, it is not necessary to access many of them, which lowers the value of openness. This conflicting impact of openness of others is central to an understanding of equilibrium.

The analysis will build on our previous discussion of random graphs, and in particular on the thresholds of sharp transitions (which were identified in the chapter 2 on random graphs). As in the case of random graphs, the arguments will apply as the number of individuals, $n$, gets large. We will say that the symmetric level of openness $q$ is subcritical if the expected number of links where an individual learns indirectly is less than 1 (i.e., $p_i(q, q)\delta n < 1$), it is critical if the other ideas learned is 1, and it is supercritical if the expected number of new ideas learned is greater than 1.

These thresholds are helpful as we can apply methods from random graph theory to infer that the number of ideas learned by an individual in each region can be pinned down as follows. In the subcritical region, all firms learn at most $o(n)$ ideas (i.e., the number of ideas is negligible relative to the value of $n$ when $n$ is large); in the critical region, firms learn an intermediate number of ideas, while in the supercritical region, a positive fraction of firms learn $\gamma n$ ideas for $\gamma \in (0, 1)$, while all other firms learn $o(n)$ ideas. Figure 3.10 illustrates the role of openness—and the number of links—in shaping access to others' ideas.

In this setting, it can be shown that for *large enough n, a symmetric equilibrium has a critical level of openness*.

Let us discuss the intuition underlying this result as it gives us a first glimpse of the forces driving knife-edge properties of equilibrium networks that are also obtained in other applications such as financial networks and supply chains. By definition, at the optimal level of openness, $q$, the marginal cost of raising openness must be equal to the marginal return from openness. The marginal cost comes in the form of giving up possible exclusivity to technologies, while the marginal return arises from potentially exclusive access to new technologies. Marginal costs to links increase with the number of links, as a firm has more to

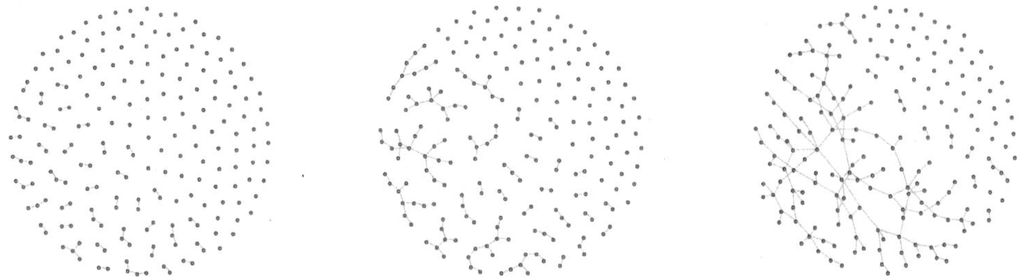

(a) Subcritical: edges = 50 (b) Critical: edges = 100 (c) Supercritical: edges = 150

**Figure 3.10**
Regions and component sizes: $n = 200$.

lose from their idea leaking through the increased openness of everyone. So to sustain a high interaction rate equilibrium, marginal returns to links must also increase in overall openness. In other words, we need the openness of different individuals to be complements. However, in the supercritical region, the network will contain a giant component, and adding openness serves to lower exclusivity (i.e., the levels of openness of individuals are substitutes). On the other hand, in the subcritical region, the marginal cost of losing access to exclusive technologies is small, as there are no large components. This pushes up the openness level. In this way, economic pressures push individuals to create networks at the critical threshold.

In these models, individuals choose a single level of interaction that helps define a probability of being connected to any other individual. It is possible to take this one step further and say that individuals choose a number of links. This is the approach proposed by Goyal and Sadler (2021). In their model, choices of the number of links are mapped onto a degree distribution using the configuration model (for a discussion of the configuration model, see chapter 2). The motivation is similar to the model of linking and assorted activity discussed previously. Players can invest effort in obtaining a discrete piece of information, and they can also invest in costly links that can transmit information. Individuals choose the probability of obtaining the information, $x \in X = [0, 1]$, and the number of links $d \in \mathbb{N}_+$. The types of individuals lie in the set $T = \mathbb{R}_+$; they assume that the distribution of $F$ types is continuous with full support. They interpret $x \in X$ as the probability with which a player independently obtains the information and $t \in T$ as the cost of a link. A player learns the information either if they discover it themselves or if they are path-connected to a player who learns it. Learning the information yields a payoff of 1, but choosing strategy $(x, d)$ incurs the cost $x^2 + td$. Hence, player $i$ earns the expected payoff

$$u_i = \mathbb{P}\,(i \text{ learns the information}) - x_i^2 - t_i d_i. \tag{3.29}$$

The game proceeds as follows: Players realize their private costs and make investments $x$ and link requests $d$, the network forms, and payoffs are realized. A symmetric strategy profile $\sigma(t) = (d(t), x(t))$ specifies how many links to request and how much to invest in information as a function of the link cost parameter $t$. It is possible to show that given a type distribution, there is a symmetric equilibrium (in which a player's strategy is only a function of their type). This equilibrium generates a degree distribution and a probability of learning the information and the corresponding payoffs. Lower cost types form more links and exert less personal effort, have a higher probability of learning the true state, and they earn higher payoffs. We leave the discussion of this model here; the interested reader is referred to Goyal and Sadler (2021) for further details.

### 3.4.4 Combining Linking with Assorted Activity

In the baseline models, individuals choose links with each other. In many of the examples studied in chapter 1, individual entities choose links and make choices on related activities. For instance, on Twitter, they choose links and the level of tweeting and retweeting; on Facebook, they choose friendship links and various types of participation. Similarly, a researcher or a firm chooses whom to collaborate with and how much effort and investment to put in these collaborations. If we reflect on these examples, we see that the level of activity will affect the rewards of linking and vice versa. This consideration motivates a large and very active body of economics literature that explores models of network formation alongside related activities. In this section, we illustrate the interaction between linking and related activity by adding an activity alongside linking in the one-sided link model from section 3.2. We will then comment briefly on a range of assorted activities and discuss the potential role of linking.

Let us begin by adding an effort dimension to the one-sided linking model in section 3.2. An individual chooses links with a subset of others, $g_i$, and an effort level of $x_i \in \mathbb{R}_+$. A strategy of individual $i$ is given by $s_i = (g_i, x_i)$, and the profile of strategies is denoted by $s = (s_1, \ldots, s_n)$. We set $N_i^l(g)$ as the set of individuals who lie at distance $l$ of $i$ in the directed network $g$. Following Galeotti and Goyal (2010), we shall say that given a strategy profile $s$, the payoffs of an individual $i$ are

$$\Pi_i(s) = f(x_i + \sum_{l=1}^{l=n-1} a_l \sum_{j \in N_i^l(g)} x_j) - cx_i - d_i(g)k, \tag{3.30}$$

where $a_l \geq 0$, and $a_{l+1} \leq a_l$ for all $l \geq 1$, $f(.)$ is a strictly increasing and concave function, with $f(0) = 0$, $c > 0$ and $k > 0$, and $d_i(g)$ is the number of links created and paid for by individual $i$. To see how activity and linking can powerfully shape networks, we use a specific functional form for the reward function (Goyal, Rosenkranz, Weitzel, and Buskens (2017):

$$f(y) = \begin{cases} y(29 - y) & \text{if } y \leq 14 \\ 196 + y & \text{else.} \end{cases} \tag{3.31}$$

Suppose that the per-unit cost of information $c = 11$ and $a_l = 1$ for all $l \geq 1$ (i.e., there is no decay). Recall that in the one-sided model with no decay, the cycle containing all nodes is the unique nonempty equilibrium network (see proposition 3.1). Let us see how adding an effort level alters this prediction.

Consider an individual in isolation who chooses effort 9. Observe that this is the optimal effort level for someone in isolation under reward function $f$. What would be the response of the other individuals? To fix ideas, consider an individual and label them as B: how much effort should they exert, and should they link with A? B accesses 9 units if they link with A. The cost of this effort is $11 \times 9 = 99$, and it costs $k$ to access A. So it is in their interest to link with A if $k < 99$. Observe that once an individual links with A, they have access to 9 units of effort, so the incremental value of additional information is smaller than the cost of information: they will choose the personal effort level 0. The same reasoning applies to all individuals other than A. Therefore, the star network with A choosing effort 9, all other individuals choosing effort 0, and a link forming with A constitutes an equilibrium.

This argument helps bring out the dramatic impact of adding an effort dimension to the basic linking problem: we move from a cycle containing all individuals to a star network in which the spokes form a link with the hub and make zero effort, while the hub forms no links and chooses effort 9. Chapter 11, on the law of the few, will develop the theoretical arguments more fully and also describe an experiment.

The economics literature has developed a range of models to explore the interplay between linking and assorted activity. We next discuss some of the important lines of inquiry that deal with coordination, cooperation, exchange and intermediation, and collaboration and competition, and we point to chapters where these topics are discussed at length.

**The problem of coordination** The problem of coordination arises in its simplest form when the optimal course of action for an individual is to conform to what others are doing. If there is more than one possible course of action, then individuals have to coordinate on one of these actions. One simple example is the choice of software to draft documents or communicate. As we work with colleagues, we have a preference to choose the software that they are using. This suggests that the network of interaction could shape the ways in which individuals solve their coordination problems; in a highly integrated group, individuals may opt for a common course of action, while in fragmented groups, segments might follow different courses of action. The reasoning can well flow the other way: individuals may organize into different segments and choose different actions if they have different preferences over these actions. What are the circumstances under which we expect to see social conformism and diversity? Can societies get locked into inefficient courses of action? How does the network shape the openness of a society to change and movement from an inefficient to an efficient norm? Chapter 12, on social coordination, studies the role of linking in shaping social coordination.

**The problem of cooperation** This arises in its simplest form when we consider situations that arise over time: an individual needs support at a point in time that can be provided by another individual. The key point to note is that the benefit to the recipient is greater than the cost of support to the provider. To the extent that individuals need support over time, it is in their collective interest to provide mutual support. However, at any instant in time, an individual who is asked to provide support is better off by *not* offering it. As is clear from this description, the potential provider may be persuaded to provide support through an appeal to enlightened self-interest: by refusing to provide support today, they forgo the chance of receiving help in the future from the person currently in need. This bilateral cost-benefit, however, may not be sufficient, as such opportunities may arise insufficiently often. This brings into play the possibility that connections with other individuals may be brought into play as well. This points to the role of networks of mutual support. A large body of work has studied the role of social structure in sustaining cooperation. More recent work has incorporated the idea that the network itself is evolving and endogenous. Economists have traditionally studied questions of cooperation, norms, and trust using models of repeated games. The chapters 18 and 19 present models of networks, repeated games, trust, and cooperation.

**Exchange, intermediation, and brokerage** The terms on which individuals carry out exchanges with each other will depend on the outside options they have. Here, an exchange may be direct when a buyer purchases an object from a seller, or it may be indirect when a buyer purchases something from a seller, but through intermediaries. In the first case, for example, a buyer who has links with many potential sellers is likely to have greater bargaining power. In the second case of indirect exchange, a pair consisting of a buyer and a seller are likely to pay less to intermediaries if there are multiple paths of intermediaries available to them. These observations have led to a study of the ways in which networks shape the terms of exchange among individuals. As networks can potentially have large effects on terms of trade and earnings, it is natural for individuals to try to shape the networks within which they conduct exchanges. The formation of exchange networks has been the subject of an extensive body of research in economics (as well as computer science and sociology). The problem of exchange in networks is studied in chapter 16, on networked markets, while brokerage rents are studied in the chapter 8 on market power and intermediation.

**Collaboration and competition** Firms collaborate to share knowledge and innovate and to become more competitive in the market; similarly, individual researchers collaborate to explore ideas and conduct research. An important feature of such collaborations is that they are extensive and nonexclusive (A may collaborate with B, who may collaborate with C, but A and C do not collaborate with each other). These collaborations shape the speed and level of innovation and can have a decisive impact on the relative performance of firms/individuals. Discussions on empirical aspects of scientific collaboration networks are spread across different chapters of the book; chapter 16 takes up models of oligopolists forming research collaboration networks to compete in a market.

## 3.5 Appendix: Advanced Material on Solution Concepts

An important part of the appeal of pairwise stability is its great simplicity. In this section, we elaborate on some aspects of this concept and develop conditions for its existence. We also discuss elaborations on the concept. The results are taken from Jackson and Watts (2001), and the exposition is based on Goyal (2007).

We will exploit the ideas of improving paths and cycles, from Jackson and Watts (2001). An improving path is a sequence of networks that can emerge when individuals form or sever links based on individual payoff considerations.

**Definition 3.2** *An improving path from a network g to network $g'$ is a finite sequence of networks $g^1, g^2, \ldots, g^k$, with $g^1 = g$ and $g^k = g'$, such that for every $l \in \{1, 2, \ldots, k-1\}$, either*

1. $g^{l+1} = g^l - g_{ij}$ *for some* $g^l_{i,j} = 1$ *and* $\Pi_k(g^l - g_{ij}) > \Pi_k(g^l)$ *for* $k \in \{i, j\}$, *or*
2. $g^{l+1} = g^l + g_{ij}$ *for some* $g^l_{i,j} = 0$ *and* $\Pi_i(g^l + g_{ij}) > \Pi_i(g^l)$ *and* $\Pi_j(g^l + g_{ij}) \geq \Pi_j(g^l)$.

A set of networks $\hat{\mathcal{G}}$ forms a *cycle* if for any $g, g' \in \hat{\mathcal{G}}$ (which includes $g = g'$), there exists an improving path from $g$ to $g'$. A cycle $\hat{\mathcal{G}}$ is *maximal* if it is not a proper subset of any other cycle, while a cycle $\hat{\mathcal{G}}$ is *closed* if no network in $\hat{\mathcal{G}}$ lies on an improving path leading to a network that does not lie in $\hat{\mathcal{G}}$.

A sufficient condition for the existence of a pairwise stable network is that there is not an improving path starting from every network; in a game with a finite number of players (and therefore also a finite number of networks), a sufficient condition for this is that there are no cycles of improving paths in the network. We develop conditions on payoff functions in network formation games that rule out cycles. These conditions suggest that payoffs should exhibit a form of monotonicity.

It is convenient to write a network formation game slightly more generally as follows. There is a set of players $N = \{1, 2, \ldots, n\}$; a value function $V : \mathcal{G} \to R$, which defines the aggregate value generated by any network $g$; and an allocation function $\Pi : \mathcal{G} \to R^n$, which specifies, for each network $g$, the payoff accruing to every player in the network.

The following from Jackson and Watts (2001), provides a result about existence.

**Proposition 3.6** *For any value function V and any allocation function $\Pi$, there is at least one pairwise stable network or a closed cycle of networks.*

*Proof.* Start with network $g$. If it is pairwise stable, then the proof is done. So suppose that it is not pairwise stable. This means that there is an improving path leading away from it. If this improving path ends at some network, that network is pairwise stable, and the proof is done. So suppose that there is no end network: given the finiteness of the game, there must be a cycle. So suppose there is no pairwise stable network. First, note that since $G$ is finite, there must be a maximal cycle. Second, consider the set of maximal cycles, and note that at least one of them must have no path leaving it. If all maximal cycles had paths leaving them, then there would be a larger cycle containing two or more of such cycles, which would be a contradiction to the hypothesis that these cycles are maximal. Thus at least one maximal cycle must be closed. ■

Ruling out closed cycles is one simple way to guarantee the existence of pairwise stable networks. The following terminology is used in the next result. For a given game of network formation, denote the existence of an improving path from $g$ to $g'$ as $g \to g'$. Clearly, $\to$ is a transitive relation, and so it follows that there are no cycles if and only if $\to$ is asymmetric. Two networks $g$ and $g'$ are *adjacent* if they differ by only one link. $V$ and $\Pi$ exhibit no indifference if, for any two adjacent networks $g$ and $g'$, either $g$ defeats $g'$ or vice versa. Note that a network $g$ defeats another network $g'$ if there is an improving path from $g'$ to $g$. Our next result provides a useful characterization of the existence of cycles.

**Proposition 3.7** *Fix a value function $V$ and an allocation function $\Pi$. If there is a function $\mathcal{W}$: $\mathcal{G} \to \mathcal{R}$ such that* [$g'$ defeats $g$] $\Leftrightarrow$ [$\mathcal{W}(g') > \mathcal{W}(g)$ and $g$ and $g'$ are adjacent], *then there are no cycles. Conversely, if $V$ and $\Pi$ exhibit no indifference, then there are no cycles only if there is a function, $\mathcal{W}: \mathcal{G} \to R$, such that* [$g'$ defeats $g$] $\Leftrightarrow$ [$\mathcal{W}(g') > \mathcal{W}(g)$ and $g'$ and $g$ are adjacent].

*Proof.* Consider the first statement of the proposition. This is equivalent to saying that if there is a cycle, then there cannot be such a $\mathcal{W}$. Suppose that is not so, and there is such a $\mathcal{W}$ function. Then by transitivity of $>$, it follows that $\mathcal{W}(g) > \mathcal{W}(g)$, which is impossible. So the existence of cycles precludes any $\mathcal{W}$ function that satisfies the mentioned properties.

Now consider the second statement. Assume that there are no cycles, and also that for any adjacent pair of networks $g$ and $g'$, either $g$ defeats $g'$ or vice versa. The proof shows that there is such a $\mathcal{W}$ that satisfies the desired properties. This step exploits proposition 3.2 in Kreps (2018), which is stated in lemma 3.1 for easy reference. A binary relation $b$ is negatively transitive if the converse relation *not-b* is transitive.

**Lemma 3.1** *If $X$ is a finite set and $b$ is a binary relation, then there is $\mathcal{W}: X \to R$ such that $\mathcal{W}(x) > \mathcal{W}(y) \Leftrightarrow xby$, if and only if $b$ is asymmetric and negatively transitive.*

Since there are no cycles, the binary relation $\to$ is acyclic and therefore asymmetric. The relation $\to$ is transitive by the definition of an improving path. However, the relation *not* $\to$ is not necessarily transitive.

Here is an example: Let $n = 5$ and start with a cycle network, $g^{cycle}$. Suppose that in the network $g^{cycle} + g_{12}$, the payoffs of players 1 and 2 fall by 1 each, while all other payoffs remain the same, relative to $g^{cycle}$. Proceed next to a network $g^{cycle} + g_{12} + g_{34}$, in which the payoffs of players 3 and 4 fall by 1 each, relative to network $g^{cycle} + g_{12}$. Finally, consider the network $g^{cycle} + g_{34}$, in which the payoffs of players 1 and 2 fall by 1 each, while the payoffs of players 3 and 4 increase by 2 each, relative to $g^{cycle} + g_{12} + g_{34}$. The payoff of player 5 remains unchanged throughout. So we have a situation in which $g^{cycle} + g_{12}$ *not* $\to$ $g^{cycle} + g_{12} + g_{34}$ *not* $\to$ $g^{cycle} + g_{34}$, but $g^{cycle} + g_{12}$ *not* $\to$ $g^{cycle} + g_{34}$ does not hold, since there is an improving path $g^{cycle} + g_{12} \to g^{cycle} \to g^{cycle} + g_{34}$.

Therefore, a relation $b$ has to be constructed such that (1) $g \to g'$ implies that $g'\, b\, g$; (2) if $g$ and $g'$ are adjacent, then $g \to g'$ if and only if $g'\, b\, g$; and (3) $b$ is asymmetric and negatively transitive. Then lemma 3.1 can be applied to obtain $\mathcal{W}$, and proposition 3.7 follows from property (2). The construction of $b$ is now presented for two cases.

*Case 1:* For every distinct pair of networks, $g$ and $g'$, at least one of the following holds: $g \to g'$ and $g' \to g$. Set $g'\, b\, g$ if and only if $g \to g'$. We show that this relation is negatively transitive. Define $g\, nb\, g'$ if $g\, b\, g'$ fails to obtain. Suppose that $g\, nb\, g'$ and $g'\, nb\, g''$. Given the definition of $b$, this means that $g'\, b\, g$ and $g''\, b\, g'$. It then follows from the transitivity of $b$ that $g''\, b\, g$, which in turn implies, by asymmetry of $b$ and definition of $nb$, that $g\, nb\, g''$.

*Case 2:* There are distinct $g$ and $g'$ (which are not adjacent) such that $g$ not $\to g'$ and $g'$ not $\to g$. Define the binary relation $b_1$ as follows. Let $g''\, b_1\, g'''$ if and only if $g''' \to g''$, except on $g$ and $g'$ where set $g'\, b_1\, g$. Note that by construction, (1) and (2) are satisfied, and also note that $b_1$ is acyclic (and hence asymmetric). To see the acyclicity of $b_1$, note that if there is a cycle, then it would have to include $g$ and $g'$, as this is the only point at which $b_1$ and $\to$ disagree. However, the existence of such a cycle would imply that $g' \to g$, which is a contradiction. Next, define $b_2$ by taking all the transitive implications of $b_1$. Again, (1) and (2) are true of $b_2$. By construction, $b_2$ is transitive. Then it is shown (by construction) that $b_2$ is acyclic. Add one implication from $b_1$ and transitivity at a time, and verify acyclicity at each step. Consider the first new implication that is added, and suppose that there is a cycle. Let $g'''$ and $g''$ be the networks in question. So $g''\, b_1\, g'''$ and $g'''\, nb_1\, g''$, but $g'''\, b_2\, g''$, and there is a sequence of networks $\{g_o, g_1, \ldots, g_r\}$ such that $g'''\, b_1\, g_0\, b_1\, g_1 \ldots .b_1\, g_r\, b_1\, g''$. This implies that there is a cycle under $b_1$, which is a contradiction. Iterating this argument implies that $b_2$ is acyclic.

Now consider cases 1 and 2 when $b_2$ is substituted for $\to$. Iterations on this process lead to a case where $b_k$ has been constructed and relative to $b_k$–namely, case 1. Iterating on the argument under case 2, it follows that (1) and (2) will be true of $b_k$ and $b_k$ will be transitive and asymmetric. Then by the argument under Case 1, $b_k$ will be negatively transitive. Set $b = b_k$, and the proof is complete. ■

While pairwise stability is a useful first check for strategic stability, only a relatively small set of possible deviations are ruled out—for instance, the deletion of only one link is contemplated, and the simultaneous addition and deletion of links is not allowed. We briefly discuss ways in which these considerations can be taken into account.

Let us consider example 3.1, in which the deletion or addition of a link by itself is not profitable, but the deviation in which several links are deleted together is profitable.

**Example 3.1** *Deleting a subset of links*

Suppose that $n = 4$. Assume that the payoffs satisfy $\Pi_i(g^c) = 10$ for all players, while $\Pi_i(g) = 15$ in every network $g$ in which player $i$ has no links. In network $g$ where two players have 3 links each and two players have 2 links each, the payoffs to players with 3 links are 9, while the payoffs with 2 links are 8. The complete network is clearly pairwise stable since no player has an incentive to delete a single link. However, a player would strictly profit from deleting all the links. ■

The notion of a pairwise equilibrium addresses this concern directly by supplementing the idea of a Nash equilibrium with the requirement that no pair of players wishes to form an additional link.

**Definition 3.3** *A network $g^*$ can be sustained in a pairwise equilibrium if*

1. *There is a Nash equilibrium $s^*$ that yields $g^*$.*
2. *For any $g_{ij}(s^*) = 0$, $\Pi_i(g(s^*) + g_{ij}) > \Pi_i(g(s^*)) \implies \Pi_j(g(s^*) + g_{ij}) < \Pi_j(g(s^*))$.*

A feature of pairwise stability is that deviations in which each member of a pair of players deletes one or more links *and/or* adds a link in a coordinated manner are not allowed. In some games, it is possible that deleting a subset of links is not profitable for any single player *and* adding a link is not profitable for any pair of players, but it is profitable for a pair of players to simultaneously delete a subset of their current links and add a link. Example 3.2 illustrates this possibility.

**Example 3.2** *Simultaneous deletion and addition of a link*

Consider a game with $n = 4$. Assume the following payoffs: Any isolated player earns 0; in a line network the two central players earn 25 each, while the end players earn 10 each; in a cycle network, every player earns 20 each; in a network with a cycle and an additional link, the payoffs of the players with two links each is 20; and the payoffs of the three link players is 15 each. Then it follows that the cycle is a pairwise equilibrium. However, if players can delete links and add a link at the same time, then two players in the cycle can make a coordinated move—which yields a line network with themselves as the central players—and thereby increase their payoffs. Thus the cycle is not stable with respect to coordinated deviations. ■

The notion of bilateral equilibrium addresses these concerns by introducing the possibility of players deviating in a coordinated manner. Define $s_{-i-j}$ as the strategy profile $s$ less the strategies of players $i$ and $j$; that is, $s_{-i-j} = \{s_1, \ldots, s_{i-1}, s_{i+1}, \ldots, s_{j-1}, s_{j+1}, \ldots, s_n\}$.

**Definition 3.4** *A network $g^*$ is a bilateral equilibrium if*

1. *There is a Nash equilibrium strategy profile $s^*$ that yields $g^*$.*
2. *For any pair of players $i, j \in N$, and every strategy pair $(s_i, s_j)$,*

$$\Pi_i(g(s_i, s_j, s^*_{-i-j})) > \Pi_i(g(s^*_i, s^*_j, s^*_{-i-j})) \Rightarrow \Pi_j(g(s_i, s_j, s^*_{-i-j})) < \Pi_j(g(s^*_j, s^*_j, s^*_{-i-j}). \quad (3.32)$$

Thus a given network can be supported in a bilateral equilibrium if no player or pair of players can deviate (unilaterally or bilaterally, respectively) and benefit from the deviation (at least one of them strictly). We note that the bilateral equilibrium is a special case of the well-known concept of the strong equilibrium—it is special in the sense that only two player subsets are allowed (the strong equilibrium was introduced by Aumann [1959]). The characterization of conditions on payoffs for the existence of bilateral equilibrium appears to be an open problem.

## 3.6 Reading Notes

The beginnings of an economic approach to network formation can be traced to an early paper by Boorman (1975), that studied workers who form links to learn about jobs. The model he proposed captures two key ideas in the theory of network formation: link formation has costs and benefits for the individual and also generates externalities on others (for a brief overview of the Boorman model see chapter 15).

In an early paper, Myerson (1977b) studied a variation of the Shapley value for games when players in a component can form coalitions. This is now referred to as the "Myerson value." In a subsequent paper, Aumann and Myerson (1988) introduced an explicit extensive-form game of link formation with the following rules: Pairs of players are ordered, and in each period, one pair is given the opportunity to form a link. Linking is irreversible. Once every pair of players has had a chance and decided whether to form a link, the game ends. The paper examined some examples to illustrate that subgame perfect equilibrium networks of this process may be socially inefficient. In his game theory textbook, Myerson (1991) proposed a simultaneous link-formation model: every player announces a subset of links which they intend to form, and a link between two players is formed if and only if both players express a wish to do so.

Following these early attempts at network formation, the systematic study of linking processes and network formation games may be traced to traced to Goyal (1993), Bala and Goyal (2000), and Jackson and Wolinsky (1996). For extended surveys of this research, the interested reader is referred to Demange and Wooders (2005), Dutta and Jackson (2003), Goyal (2007), Jackson (2008), Mauleon and Vannetelbosch (2016), and Bramoullé, Galeotti, and Rogers (2016).

The chapter starts with a discussion of a model of network formation in which individuals can unilaterally decide to form links. Unilateral link formation has the advantage of allowing the use of the tools of noncooperative game theory to analyze the games of linking. This facilitates a study of a number of questions using familiar methods. This approach was introduced in Goyal (1993) and was systematically developed in Bala and Goyal (2000a). In many contexts, such as friendships and coauthorships, it is more natural to consider link formation as a two-sided process: both individuals must agree to the link. In our discussion, we follow Jackson and Wolinsky (1996), which proposes the solution concept of pairwise stability and offers a general introduction to this approach. The study of pairwise stability has been developed in a large body of literature. Richer solution concepts have been explored by these works, and we briefly discussed some of the more widely used notions. The pairwise equilibrium is formally defined in Goyal and Joshi (2006b) and Belleflamme and Bloch (2004). The existence of pairwise stable networks is established by Jackson and Watts (2001). The basic ideas underlying the proof of the efficiency result in the two-sided model with decay were provided in a paper on airlines by Hendricks, Piccione, and Tan (1995). Overviews of solution concepts for network formation games are presented in Gilles and Sarangi (2004), Gilles, Chakrabarti, and Sarangi (2012), Bloch and Jackson (2006), and Bloch and Dutta (2011). For discussions of ways to reconcile one-sided and two-sided linking protocols, see Ding (2021) and Olaizola and Valenciano (2015).

With the basic models studied in sections 3.2 and 3.3, we assumed that individuals were symmetric: everyone had the same payoff function. Differences across individuals may be important with regard to both costs and benefits. These heterogeneities can shape networks in important ways. For an early examination of network formation with heterogeneous individuals, see Galeotti, Goyal, and Kamphorst (2006), Galeotti (2006), and Gilles and Johnson (2000). A prominent development in this line of work is the incorporation of homophily in linking; for an early model of network formation with homophily, see Currarini, Jackson, and Pin (2009).

A recurring theme is the tension between pairwise stability and equilibrium networks and efficiency. The literature has explored the scope of this tension and proposed ways of mitigating it. We refer to Jackson and Wolinsky (1996) and Dutta and Mutuswami (1997), on centralized mechanisms, and Bloch and Jackson (2007), on decentralized transfers between the players. For overviews of this work, see Jackson (2008) and Goyal (2007).

The literature on network formation has grown greatly over the past twenty-five years, so a number of variations on the basic models presented in sections 3.2 and 3.3 have been developed. The chapter discusses four themes in the literature: dynamics, weighted links, generic social investments, and linking and assorted activities. The dynamics of linking were studied early by Bala and Goyal (2000a), Watts (2001), and Jackson and Watts (2002a). For an early overview of the research in this field, see Goyal (2007) and Jackson (2008); for more recent surveys, see Bramoullé, Galeotti, and Rogers (2016) and Benhabib, Bisin, and Jackson (2011).

Turning to weighted links, an early discussion of related issues is presented in Goyal (2005). A number of papers have examined the formation of weighted networks and some of these papers have also studied specific empirical contexts; for example, see Bloch and Dutta (2009), Deroian (2009), Rogers (2006), Brueckner (2006), Goyal, Moraga-González, and Konovalov (2008), Van der Leij and Goyal (2011), and Skyrms and Pemantle (2009). Recent contributions include Baumann (2021), Ding (2021), Salonen (2015), and Griffith (2020).

Fairly early, a number of researchers realized that nonspecific linking may offer a more tractable framework to study network formation in large populations, and it would also help with obtaining more realistic network architectures. Early contributions using this approach include Durieu, Haller, and Sola (2011) and Cabrales, Calvo-Armengol, and Zenou (2011). This line of work has been recently elaborated upon by Albornoz, Cabrales, and Hauk (2019) and Canen, Jackson, and Trebbi (2020).

A strand of this literature examines models of linking in which individuals propose a single scalar number, as in section 3.4.3, but the payoffs depend on the macroscopic properties (such as connectedness and giant component) of the random graph that they create. A number of other papers have explored a similar approach and have drawn attention to the economic incentives for creating networks that exist at the knife edge of macroscopic properties like connectedness (or the existence of a giant component); for example, see Dasaratha (2021), Blume, Easley, Kleinberg, et al. (2013), Elliott, Golub, and Leduc (2020), Golub and Livne (2010), and Goyal and Sadler (2021).

There is a very large body of literature on linking and assorted activities. For a survey of the theoretical aspects of the interplay between linking and related activities, see Vega-Redondo (2016). A recent paper by Sadler and Golub (2021) further explores some of the issues in this field. The chapter discusses contexts relating to coordination, cooperation and trust, cooperation and competition among firms, and brokerage and intermediation, where this perspective has been further developed.

The solution concepts discussed in the chapter focus on one- and two-player deviations. The ideas can be extended further to include groups of players to shape pairwise links and allow many-player links. Consider first the issue of larger group deviations within a pairwise link context. Suppose that a group of players of any size can determine the nature of networks among them, as well as determine the links between members of the group and the players who are not in the group. Group-level incentives are traditionally studied using notions of strong equilibrium and coalition equilibrium. Jackson and Van den Nouweland (2005) study strongly stable networks and derive conditions for the existence of such networks. Building on the work of Chwe (1994), there is also a strand of research that examines far-sighted network formation. The interested reader is referred to Dutta and Mutuswami (1997), Bloch and Jackson (2006), and Herings, Mauleon, and Vannetelbosch (2009) for alternative solution concepts in the context of network formation.

At a more fundamental level, however, there is the issue of why links should be bilateral. Indeed, in well-known applications, such as co-authoring, collaboration between firms, and free-trade agreements between countries, links often involve more than two players. This suggests that the level of linking should itself be viewed as endogenous. Allowing larger groups in network formation brings the framework closer to the coalitions framework, with one major difference: a distinctive feature of the coalitions model is that membership is exclusive. A player can be a member of one or the other group, but not of several groups. By contrast, the network literature restricts group formation to the level of pairs of players, but allows a player to be a member of any number of two-player groups at the same time. Extending the network framework to allow links between general many-player groups and nonexclusive membership of groups would therefore yield a general framework for studying coalitions as well as networks.

We may generalize coalitions and networks using the concept of *hypergraphs*: a hypergraph allows for a link to be formed between any subset of two or more nodes. A network is thus a special type of hypergraph in which only subsets of two nodes are permitted. This general framework would also permit a study of endogenous group size and exclusivity. Hypergraphs are used in Dziubiński and Goyal (2017) in the context of network defense (see chapter 7, on network security). For studies of the formation of hypergraphs, see Page and Wooders (2010), Chen, Elliott, and Koh (2020), Martinez, Rostek, and Yoon (2019), Ding, Dziubinski, and Goyal (2021) and Fershtman and Persitz (2021).

The formation of networks is subject to a variety of technological, economic, and social forces. It is therefore only natural that network formation is studied across a number of disciplines. Early work on network formation in mathematics and bibliometrics used the metaphor of random graphs; chapter 2 presented an introduction to this topic. There is a rich body of work in mathematical sociology that studies network formation and dynamics (for an introduction to this literature, see Wasserman and Faust [1994]). More recently, network formation has been the subject of research in computer science (Fabrikant, Luthra, Maneva, et al. [2003], Roughgarden [2005] and Easley and Kleinberg [2010]), physics (Barabási and Albert [1999], Watts and Strogatz [1998]) and business strategy (Gulati [2007]).

## 3.7 Questions

1. (From Bala and Goyal [2000a]). Consider the one-way flow model with decay from section 3.2.
   (a) Suppose $n=4$. Show that a strict Nash equilibrium network is either connected or empty.
   (b) Suppose $n=6$. Construct an example of a Nash network that is nonempty and not connected.
   (c) Suppose $n=4$. A network is efficient if it maximizes the sum of individual utilities. Derive the efficient networks as a function of decay $\delta$ and the costs of linking $c$.
2. Consider the one-way flow model with linear payoffs discussed in section 3.2. Fix $n=10$.
   (a) Derive the conditions on decay, $\delta$, and cost of link, $c$, under which a single hub with 9 spokes and a hub with windmill network with three equal size petals is a Nash equilibrium.
   (b) Derive the conditions on decay, $\delta$, and cost of link, $c$, under which a cycle containing all the nodes is a Nash equilibrium.

3. Recall that the social welfare of a network is the sum of utilities of players. In a game, define the price of anarchy as the ratio of first-best social welfare to the social welfare attained in the worst Nash equilibrium. Define the price of stability as the ratio of first-best social welfare to the social welfare attained in the best Nash equilibrium
   (a) Show that in the two-sided linking model, the price of anarchy is unbounded for a wide range of cost parameters.
   (b) Show that in the one-sided linking model with one-way benefits, the price of anarchy is unbounded for a wide range of cost parameters.
   (c) Comment on the price of stability in the one-way and the two-way flow models.
4. Consider an $n$ player network formation game. Suppose that two players $i$ and $j$ can form a link if they both agree, and pay a cost $c > 0$. The network created by this bilateral linking is denoted by $g$. The payoffs to player $i$ under network $g$ are

$$\Pi_i(g) = 1 + \sum_{j \neq i} \delta^{d(i,j;g)} - \eta_i^d(g)c, \tag{3.33}$$

   where $d(i,j;g)$ is the (geodesic) distance between $i$ and $j$ in network g and $\delta \in (0,1)$ is the decay factor.
   (a) Define a pairwise stable network.
   (b) Fix $n = 6$. Provide the range of parameter values, $c$ and $\delta$, for which the empty, the complete, and star networks are pairwise stable.
   (c) Fix $n = 6$. A network is efficient if it maximizes players' payoffs across all networks. Provide a characterization of efficient networks for different values of $c$ and $\delta$.
5. (From Jackson and Wolinsky [1996]). Consider a group of researchers, each of whom has a fixed amount of time available, which they can allocate across projects. The payoffs to a player $i$ in network $g$ are given by

$$\Pi_i(g) = \sum_{j \in N_i(g)} \left[ \frac{1}{d_i(g)} + \frac{1}{d_j(g)} + \frac{1}{d_i(g)d_j(g)} \right] = 1 + \left(1 + \frac{1}{d_i(g)}\right) \sum_{j \in N_i(g)} \frac{1}{d_j(g)}. \tag{3.34}$$

   if $d_i(g) > 0$, and $\Pi_i(g) = 0$, if $d_i(g) = 0$. A researcher allocates equal time across projects and productivity depends on the time spent on the project $1/d_i(g) + 1/d_j(g)$ and a synergy in the production process, captured by the interactive term $1/(d_i(g).d_j(g))$.
   (a) Show that in a network constituted of distinct pairs, every player earns a payoff of 3.
   (b) Next, consider the effects of an author starting a new project. Show that a coauthor with two links earns $[1/2 + 1 + 1/2]$ from an old project and $[1/2 + 1/2 + 1/4]$ from the new one. Show that if everyone has two projects, then the payoff for each player would be $5/2$.

(c) Let $n$ be an even number. Show that a network with $n/2$ separate pairs maximizes social welfare.

(d) Any pairwise stable network can be partitioned into complete components of unequal size. In particular, if $m$ is the size of a component and $m'$ is the size of the next larger component, then $m' > m^2$.

6. (From Bala and Goyal [2000b]). Suppose that every individual has information of value 1. Individuals can access each other's information via direct or indirect links. A link is costly. However, in contrast to the models described in this chapter, suppose that the reliability of a link is uncertain and given by $p \in [0, 1]$.

   (a) Discuss the trade-offs that arise as we vary $p$, $c$ and $n$. A network is super connected if deleting a link leaves the network connected. Show that for fixed $c$ and $p \in (0, 1)$, as we increase $n$, an efficient network must be super connected.

   (b) Next, suppose that reliability can be increased through investments. Discuss how the convexity/concavity of costs of increasing reliability will shape the architecture of efficient networks.

7. (From Galeotti et al. [2006] and Jackson and Rogers [2005]). Consider a model of network formation in which agents belong to groups: individuals are alike except that the costs of forming links within groups are less than the costs of linking across groups, and there is a decay in value as it flows through paths of the network. Building on the arguments in the chapter, show how these group-based cost differences and decay can give rise to a core-periphery network in which a few agents from different groups constitute hubs. Comment on the relation between this network architecture and small worlds networks (discussed in chapter 2).

8. (From Goyal and Joshi [2006]). Consider a game of link announcement. A strategy profile $s$ induces an undirected network $g(s)$. Let $L(g)$ be the total number of links in network $g$. Define $g_{-i}$ as the network obtained by deleting player $i$ and all their links from the network $g$ and $L(g_{-i}) = \sum_{j \neq i} \eta_j(g_{-i})$ as the total number of links in $g_{-i}$. The payoffs to a player $i$ are given by:

$$\Pi_i(g(s_i, s_{-i})) = \Phi(\eta_i(g), L(g_{-i})) - c.\eta_i(g). \tag{3.35}$$

where $c > 0$ is the cost of forming a link. We will say that the payoffs of player $i$ are convex (concave) in own links if for every $y \geq 0$, the marginal returns $\Phi(x+1, y) - \Phi(x, y)$ are strictly increasing (decreasing) in $x$ for $x \geq 0$. Next we say that the payoffs of player $i$ satisfy the strategic substitutes property if for $y' > y \geq 0$, $\Phi(x+1, y') - \Phi(x, y') < \Phi(x+1, y) - \Phi(x, y)$, for every $x \geq 0$, while they satisfy the strategic complements property if for $y' > y \geq 0$, $\Phi(x+1, y') - \Phi(x, y') > \Phi(x+1, y) - \Phi(x, y)$, for every $x \geq 0$.

(a) Suppose payoffs (3.35) are convex in own links. Then a pairwise equilibrium network is either empty, complete or a dominant group network (a dominant group network consists of a clique of nodes and a set of isolated nodes). Comment on how complements versus substitutes affects network architecture.

(b) Suppose that payoffs (3.35) are concave in own links and exhibit strategic complements across others links. Then a regular pairwise equilibrium network always exists. In any irregular pairwise equilibrium network, all nonmaximally linked nodes are mutually linked.

9. Ductor, Goyal, and Prummer (2022) show that male and female economists have different coauthor networks: women have fewer coauthors, form stronger ties, and have higher clustering (for a discussion, see chapter 1). Using the ideas of purposeful linking introduced in this chapter, discuss the role of preferences and the environment in explaining these network differences.

10. Bearman, Moody, and Stovel (2004) show that romantic and sexual networks are heterophilous and contain a large component with long cycles (for a discussion, see chapter 1). Propose a model of relationship formation and use it to reason about the role of preferences and constraints in shaping such a network.

11. Currarini, Jackson, and Pin (2009) present empirical evidence on school friendships: pupils from larger communities have more friends and there is inbreeding homophily (see chapter 1 for a definition of this concept). Propose a model of friendships with the following features—individuals belong to groups, individuals are matched at random with each other, the benefits of within group links are on average larger than benefits from cross group links, and there are costs to forming links. Use this model to reason about these empirical patterns.

# 4 Network Structure and Human Behavior

## 4.1 Introduction

In a democracy, a citizen votes in city, regional, and national elections. To inform themself on the issues and the competing candidates, they read newspapers and magazines, and they also exchange views with their family, friends, and colleagues. As there is a wide range of problems and the issues are often complex, who they talk to will play a role in determining how well informed they are and how they vote. Families decide on whether to vaccinate their children against infectious diseases such as measles and mumps. The risk of contracting a disease depends on its prevalence in the neighborhood, something that is determined by the vaccination decisions of friends and neighbors. A person decides on whether to take up a life of crime; they will be more likely to succeed if they learn tricks from others who are engaged in crime. The skills of these others in turn depend on their connections. The quality of research a scientist undertakes depends on their efforts and the efforts of collaborators. The availability of collaborators in turn depends on the other collaborations they are engaged in.

In each of these instances, an inquiry into individual behavior pushes us toward a study of a broader set of relationships within which individuals and their contacts are embedded. We are led to such questions as: What are the effects of connections on individual behavior? How does behavior respond to changes in a network? Are some networks better for the attainment of socially desirable outcomes? How can policy interventions alter behavior in a network? The aim of this chapter is to develop a theoretical framework that helps to precisely formulate these questions and to introduce concepts that will help us to understand how embeddedness shapes human behavior.

The framework we propose will have two ingredients: (1) a formal description of the pattern of relationships among individual entities, and (2) a description of the cross effects that an individual's actions create for other individuals and how these are mediated by the pattern of ties among them. We introduced networks in chapters 1–3. In this chapter, we will introduce a number of concepts that help us to organize the different ways in which networks mediate the effects of others' actions on individual payoffs.

Our starting point is the observation is that the same action carried out by two individuals, A and B, will have a different effect on C depending on their locations vis-à-vis C. A simple way of formalizing this point is to think of effects as being either *local* or *global*: an individual $j$ is said to be a *neighbor* of $i$ if $i$ and $j$ have a tie. In this case, the actions of $j$ have a local effect on $i$. All players who are not neighbors are referred to as *nonneighbors* and are treated alike, and their effects on $i$ are said to be global.

We will be especially interested in two dimensions of such effects. The first is the effect of $j$'s action on $i$'s total payoffs—the actions of others are said to create a *positive externality* if an increase in the action raises an individual's payoffs; they are said to create a *negative externality* if an increase in an action lowers an individual's payoff. The second dimension of effect is intimately connected to individual incentives: if an increase in an other's actions raises the marginal returns from one's own actions, the actions are said to be *strategic complements*; if an increase in an other's actions lowers the marginal returns from one's own actions, then the actions are said to be *strategic substitutes*.

The effects of others' actions can be mixed, depending on their location in the network: the actions of neighbors may generate positive effects while actions of nonneighbors may generate negative effects, and vice versa. This points to the potentially complex interplay between action externalities and network location. We will refer to these payoff effects as the *content* of interaction. In section 4.2, we present a number of examples that help us appreciate the rich possibilities with regard to the content of interaction.

Our analysis of games on networks begins with two classical binary action games: the *best-shot* game and the *weakest-link* game. The analysis of these games draws attention to an important general point about embedded human activity: individual behavior is shaped by both the structure of the network and the content of interaction. In the best-shot game, individual activity can be understood in terms of *maximal independent sets* of the network; in the weakest-link game, activity can be understood in terms of the *q-core* of the network. The difference between these two network properties shows how the content of interaction—strategic substitutes versus complements—is decisive for identifying a network dimension that defines individual behavior.

In our study of the best-shot and weakest-link games, we assume that individuals know all details of the network. In a large network, it is unlikely that individuals will have complete knowledge of all details of the network. Rather, we expect individuals to know some aspects of their local environment (such as the number of their neighbors) and some global aspects of the network (such as its overall connectivity), but not other features—such as, for example, the links among other nodes in the network. In this setting, it is natural to define the strategy of an individual as a function of their degree and we are led to a study of the Bayes-Nash equilibrium of a game of incomplete information. The analysis yields sharp predictions: equilibrium strategy is monotonically decreasing (increasing) in degree in best-shot (weakest-link) games. Earnings are increasing in degree in both types of games. We are also able to study the effects of changes in the network on individual behavior.

We then turn to games with a continuum of actions. In this context, networks have smoother effects on behavior. Take a game of complements: if an individual raises their action, then their neighbors will best respond by raising their own actions. This will in turn affect their neighbors, and so forth. These raised efforts will feed back to the original individual, with the magnitude of the positive pressure depending on the number and length of "walks" of the initial player in the network. Recall from chapter 1 that the *Katz-Bonacich centrality* of a node is a summary statistic of the number and length of all walks from a node to all other nodes. Our analysis in this chapter will yield the following insight: the equilibrium action of an individual is proportional to their Katz-Bonacich centrality. However, the centrality of different nodes in a network turns on the nature of the strategic effects: for instance, in games of strategic complements, the hub of the star network has highest centrality and chooses the largest action; by contrast, in games of strategic substitutes, the hub has the lowest centrality and hence chooses the smallest action.

A central feature of games on networks that we have discussed so far is the presence of externalities: in an equilibrium of the game, individual actions will therefore generally not be socially optimal. The tension between what individuals do and what is in their collective interest is an important motivation for intervening in a network. Our study of the network intervention problem draws attention to the value of targeting nodes in proportion to their presence in different principal components/eigenvectors of the matrix of interactions.

## 4.2 Choice in Networks

This section presents a framework for the study of individual choice in networked environments. There are two essential ingredients. The first is the content of interaction: What is the form of activity being contemplated? More precisely, we are interested in incentives of individuals to undertake different actions, and so by the content of interaction, we mean how actions of others affect an individual's total and marginal returns to activity. The second is the structure of interaction: Who is connected to whom? We start by laying out some basic notations on individuals, their actions, and the network they are embedded in. Our exposition draws on Goyal (2007).

Consider a set of individuals $N = \{1, 2, \ldots, n\}$, where $n \geq 2$. Individuals are located in a network $g$. The set of networks is denoted by $\mathcal{G}$. Individuals make their choices simultaneously: let the strategy of individual $i$ be given by $s_i \in \mathcal{S}$. It will be assumed that $0, 1 \in S$ and both discrete and "continuous" action sets are allowed. The vector of strategies is denoted by $s = (s_1, \ldots, s_n)$, where $s \in \mathcal{S}^n$. In what follows, $s_{-i} = (s_1, s_2, \ldots, s_{i-1}, s_{i+1}, \ldots, s_n)$ refers to the profile of strategies of all players other than player $i$. The payoff (utility or reward) to player $i$ under the profile of actions $s = (s_1, \ldots, s_n)$ is given by $\Pi_i : S^n \times \mathcal{G} \to \mathbb{R}$.

In games where the action set is continuous, we assume that $S$ is also convex (recall that a set $S$ is said to be convex if, for every pair of elements $x, y \in S$ and for any $\lambda \in [0, 1]$, $\lambda x + (1 - \lambda) y \in S$). Individuals are located in a network $g$. Recall that the neighbors of $i$ in a network, denoted by $N_i(g)$, are individuals with whom the individual $i$ has a link, that is, $N_i(g) = \{j \in N | g_{ij} = 1\}$. Also recall that the degree of $i$, $d_i(g)$ is the number of neighbors of $i$ in network $g$. An individual's payoffs depend on their actions and the actions of others. Given a profile of strategies $s$ and a network $g$, let $s_{N_i(g)}$ refer to the strategies of $i$'s neighbors in network $g$. It will be useful to define higher and lower actions of neighbors: we say that a vector $s'_{N_i(g)}$ is greater than the vector $s_{N_i(g)}$, $s'_{N_i(g)} > s_{N_i(g)}$, if for every neighbor $j \in N_i(g)$, $s'_j \geq s_j$, and for some neighbor $k$, $s'_k > s_k$.

In the examples mentioned in the introduction, it is reasonable to suppose that the action of a neighbor has a greater impact on an individual compared with the action of nonneighbors. This leads us to classify "others" into two groups, *neighbors* and *nonneighbors*, and to treat members in each group alike. This distinction between neighbors and nonneighbors naturally suggests a corresponding distinction between *local* and *global* spillovers. In a game of local spillovers, the payoffs of an individual depend only on their own actions and the actions of their neighbors. Given a strategy profile $s$, an individual $i$'s payoff is

$$\Pi_i(s|g) = \Phi(s_i, s_{N_i(g)}), \tag{4.1}$$

where $\Phi(.,.) : S^{d_i(g)+1} \rightarrow \mathbb{R}$ and $d_i(g) = |N_i(g)|$ is the degree of individual $i$ in network $g$.

We assume that the payoff functions of two players with the same degree are identical, and so payoffs do not depend on the identity of the player. This simplifying assumption is reasonable as our primary interest is in network effects. At a later point, we may wish to add specific forms of individual heterogeneity—such as gender or race or age—depending on the particular application under study. We will also assume that payoffs are anonymous with regard to choices of neighbors' actions. This means that if $s'_{N_i(g)}$ is a permutation of actions in $s_{N_i(g)}$, then $\Phi(s_i, s'_{N_i(g)}) = \Phi(s_i, s_{N_i(g)})$.

Going beyond the pure local case, we will also be interested in situations where neighbors and nonneighbors matter. An important special case arises when an individual's payoff depends only on one's own action, the sum of neighbors' actions, and the sum of nonneighbors' actions. Given a profile $s = (s_1, \ldots, s_n)$ and a network $g$, an individual $i$'s payoff is

$$\Pi_i(s|g) = \Phi\left(s_i, \sum_{j \in N_i(g)} s_j, \sum_{k \notin N_i(g) \cup \{i\}} s_k\right). \tag{4.2}$$

In this chapter, we will restrict attention to the cases where we treat all neighbors and all nonneighbors alike. It is possible to generalize this formulation so that effects depend on the distances in a network. In chapter 11, on the Law of the Few, we will present an example that illustrates this possibility.

We now turn to how others' actions matter for payoffs. A game of local effects exhibits *positive externality* if payoffs are increasing in the actions of neighbors, and it exhibits *negative externality* if they are decreasing in the actions of neighbors. As players are homogeneous (other than network differences) and as we are assuming that actions are anonymous, we can simplify strategy of neighbors $s_{N_i(g)}$ and write it as $s_d$ for a player with degree $d$. With this simplification in place, let us define positive and negative externality.

**Definition 4.1** *A game with pure local effects exhibits positive externality if, for every* $d \in \{1, 2, \ldots, n-1\}$, *for every* $s_i \in S$, *and for every pair of neighbors' strategies* $s_d, s'_d \in S^d$, $s_d \geq s'_d$ *implies* $\Phi(s_i, s_d) \geq \Phi(s_i, s'_d)$.

*A game with pure local effects exhibits negative externality if, for every* $d \in \{1, 2, \ldots, n-1\}$, *for every* $s_i \in S$, *and for every pair of neighbors' strategies* $s_d, s'_d \in S^d$, $s_d \geq s'_d$ *implies* $\Phi(s_i, s_d) \leq \Phi(s_i, s'_d)$.

The game exhibits strict (positive or negative) externality if the corresponding payoff inequalities are strict whenever $s_d \gneq s'_d$.

We now turn to the effects of neighbors' actions on incentives of an individual. The incentives will depend on how an individual's marginal returns are affected by neighbors' actions. Building on Bulow, Geanakoplos, and Klemperer (1985), we shall say that a game with pure local effects exhibits *strategic complements* or *strategic substitutes* depending on whether the marginal returns to one's own action for player $i$ are increasing or decreasing in the efforts of their neighbors.

**Definition 4.2** *A game with pure local effects exhibits strategic complements if, for every* $d \in \{1, 2 \ldots, n-1\}$, *for every pair of one's own strategies* $s_i > s'_i$, *and every pair of neighbors' strategies* $s_d, s'_d \in S^d$, $s_d \geq s'_d$ *implies that* $\Phi(s_i, s_d) - \Phi(s'_i, s_d) \geq \Phi(s_i, s'_d) - \Phi(s'_i, s'_d)$.

*A game with pure local effects exhibits strategic substitutes if, for every* $d \in \{1, 2 \ldots, n-1\}$, *for every pair of one's own strategies* $s_i > s'_i$ *and every pair of neighbors' strategies* $s_d, s'_d \in S^d$, $s_d \geq s'_d$ *implies that* $\Phi(s_i, s_d) - \Phi(s'_i, s_d) \leq \Phi(s_i, s'_d) - \Phi(s'_i, s'_d)$.

The payoffs exhibit strict complements and substitutes if these payoff inequalities are strict whenever $s_d \gneq s'_d$.

Games on networks are solved using the concept of Nash equilibrium. A strategy profile $s^* = (s^*_1, \ldots, s^*_n)$ is a Nash equilibrium of a network game if, for each player $i$, given the strategies of other players $s^*_{-i}$, $s^*_i$ maximizes their payoffs. Formally, a strategy profile $s^* = (s^*_i, s^*_{-i})$ is a Nash equilibrium in network g if, for all $i \in N$,

$$\Pi_i(s^*_i, s^*_{-i}|g) \geq \Pi_i(s_i, s^*_{-i}|g), \forall s_i \in S. \tag{4.3}$$

The conditions for the existence of a Nash equilibrium have been studied extensively; we refer the interested reader to Osborne and Rubinstein (1994).

We now present examples to illustrate the scope of this framework.

### 4.2.1 Examples

The aim of this section is to formally represent social and economic situations where connections matter, and to draw out the relationship with strategic complements and substitutes.

We start with binary games and then turn to continuous action games. The two binary action games—the best-shot game and the weakest-link game—are taken from Hirshleifer (1983).

**Example 4.1** *Best-shot game*

There are two actions, 0 and 1. Action 0 denotes inactivity and is costless. Action 1 denotes a costly activity. Examples of action 1 include collecting information on the best route to a destination, the availability and location of a product, and facts about a political candidate. The individual utility is 1 if and only if the sum of their action and their neighbors' actions adds up to 1 or more. For simplicity, suppose that action 1 costs $c \in (0, 1)$. Observe that if an individual is choosing 0, an increase in action of the other player raises the individual's payoff from 0 to 1. If they are choosing 1, such an increase in action by another player leaves the individual's payoff unaffected. Thus an increase in action by another player raises their payoffs or leaves them unchanged. Next, observe that in this game, there is a return to choosing a costly action 1 if and only if the neighbors do not choose 1. Thus the marginal returns to choosing 1 are falling in the other player's choice—that is, the individual action and the actions of neighbors are strategic substitutes. Following Galeotti, Goyal, Jackson et al. (2010), we locate this game in a network. Given a network $g$ and a strategy profile $s$, the payoffs of individual $i$ are

$$\Pi_i(s|g) = \begin{cases} 1-c & \text{if } s_i = 1 \\ 1 & \text{if } s_i = 0 \text{ and } \sum_{j \in N_i(g)} s_j \geq 1 \\ 0 & \text{if } s_i = 0 \text{ and } \sum_{j \in N_i(g)} s_j = 0. \end{cases} \tag{4.4}$$

Observe that it does not matter who among the neighbors chooses which action, only the sum of actions matters. This is an instance of a general feature of such contexts: these payoffs are anonymous, that is, all individuals with the same degree have the same payoff function, and this payoff function is symmetric with regard to the actions of different neighbors. We also see that individual payoffs are increasing in the actions of others, so this is a game with positive externalities. ■

**Example 4.2** *Weakest-link game*

In a classroom, the returns from learning a new computer language depend on how many others are learning the same language. Learning a language takes time and effort and is a costly endeavor. Observe that if an individual chooses not to learn (i.e., action 0), then an increase in action of another player has no effect on an individual's payoff. If an individual chooses to learn a new language, action 1, then such an increase in action by the other player raises the individual's payoff from $-c$ to $1-c$. Thus the marginal returns to choosing action 1 are increasing in the choice of the other player, and so the actions of an individual and her classmates are complements. Following Galeotti, Goyal, Jackson et al. (2010) we locate this interaction within a network. Given a network $g$ and a strategy profile $s$, the payoffs of an individual $i$ are

$$\Pi_i(s|g) = s_i \sum_{j \in N_i(g)} s_j - cs_i. \tag{4.5}$$

This is therefore a game with positive externalities. ■

We now present a number of examples of games where the action set is continuous.

**Example 4.3** *Local public goods*

In a wide class of situations, an individual makes a costly contribution that not only brings them closer to their ideal level of a "good," but also raises the "good" enjoyed by their neighbors. Prominent examples include (1) the case of an individual who reads extensively on public affairs and shares this information with their friends and colleagues; (2) contributions to improve physical neighborhoods, such as residents clearing snow or improving their garden; and (3) protective measures against infectious disease, such as getting vaccinated or wearing masks. These examples have motivated a widely studied model of local public goods proposed by Bramoullé and Kranton (2007a); for elaborations on this model, see Galeotti and Goyal (2010), Allouch (2015), and Galeotti, Golub, and Goyal (2020).

Suppose that each individual $i$ contributes effort $s_i$ to the public good. Then the amount of public good that $i$ experiences is

$$x_i = \tilde{b}_i + s_i + \tilde{\beta} \sum_{j \in N_i(g)} g_{ij} s_j, \tag{4.6}$$

where $0 < \tilde{\beta} < 1$. The utility of $i$ is

$$U_i(s, g) = -\frac{1}{2}(\tau - x_i)^2 - \frac{1}{2} s_i^2, \tag{4.7}$$

where $\tilde{b}_i < \tau$.

The optimal level of public good in the absence of any costs is $\tau$; this can be thought of as the maximum that can be provided (thus, $x_i \leq \tau$). Individual $i$ has access to a base level $\tilde{b}_i$ of the public good. Each agent can expend a costly effort $s_i$ to augment this base level to $\tilde{b}_i + s_i$. If $i$'s neighbor $j$ expends effort $s_j$, then $i$ has access to an additional $\tilde{\beta} g_{ij} s_j$ units of the public good, where $\tilde{\beta} < 1$.

As higher efforts of others raise an individual's utility, this is a game of positive externality. Simple computations also reveal that a greater effort by neighbors lowers an individual's marginal returns from higher efforts, so this is a game of strategic substitutes. ■

**Example 4.4** *Crime*

There exist very large differences in rates of crime across space (this holds true across countries, across cities within the same country, and also across precincts within the same city).

Glaeser, Sacerdote, and Scheinkman (1996) show that these differences cannot be accounted for by differences in local social and economic conditions. This leads them to argue that positive covariance across agents' decisions about crime must be an important part of the explanation for such dispersion in crime.

Building on the rational-actor approach to crime introduced in Becker (1968), we propose the following model of criminal activity. As criminal activity is illegal, individuals acquire proficiency in it through personal interaction with other trusted people. This suggests that the level of criminal activity exhibits a form of "complementarity:" individual incentives to engage in crime increase with the criminal activity of nearby people. Developing this reasoning, we are led to the view that the level of criminal activity will depend on the direct and indirect connections of individuals. We present a model of crime taken from Ballester, Calvó-Armengol, and Zenou (2006) that captures these ideas.

There are $n$ individuals, each of whom chooses, a level of criminal activity $s_i$. The payoffs to player $i$ under strategy profile $s$ are given by

$$\Pi_i(s) = \alpha s_i - \frac{1}{2}s_i^2 + \rho \sum_{j \neq i} g_{ij} s_i s_j. \tag{4.8}$$

Assume that $\alpha > 0$ and $\rho > 0$. We can see that an increase in actions of neighbors raises an individual's payoffs, implying that this a game of positive spillovers. Taking cross-partial derivatives with respect to a neighbor's action, reveals that this is a game of strategic complements. ■

**Example 4.5** *Research collaboration among firms*

Firms collaborate with each other to create new products and to reduce their costs of production. The study of business management provides extensive evidence on the role of such collaborations (see Hagedoorn 2002; Gulati 2007). Two features of this collaborative activity are worth noting. The first feature is that firms enter into a number of relationships that are nonexclusive. The second feature is that firms often collaborate with other firms within the same market, giving rise to a complex relation which combines cooperation and competition, thus giving rise to a form of *coopetition* (Nalebuff and Brandenburger 1997). We present a model of research collaboration among firms taken from Goyal and Moraga-González (2001), which embodies this perspective.

Suppose that demand is linear and given by $Q = 1 - p$ and that the initial marginal cost of production in a firm is $\bar{c}$, and assume that $n\bar{c} < 1$. Each firm $i$ chooses a level of research effort given by $s_i \in S = [0, \bar{c}]$. The marginal costs of production of a firm $i$ in a network $g$, facing a profile of efforts $s$, are given by

$$c_i(s|g) = \bar{c} - \left( s_i + \sum_{j \in N_i(g)} s_j \right). \tag{4.9}$$

Efforts involve allocation of scarce resources; let us suppose that this cost is given by $Z(s_i) = \alpha s_i^2/2$, where $\alpha > 0$. Given costs $c = \{c_1, c_2, \ldots, c_n\}$, firms choose quantities to maximize profits. The costs of firms are positive so long as $\alpha$ is sufficiently large.

Firms choose quantities $\{q_i\}_{i \in N}$, with $Q = \sum_{i \in N} q_i$. Thus, the profits of firm $i$ in a collaboration network $g$ are given by

$$\Pi_i(s|g) = \left[ 1 - q_i(g) - \sum_{j \neq i} q_j(g) - c_i(s|g) \right] q_i(g) - \alpha \frac{s_i^2(g)}{2}. \tag{4.10}$$

From the theory of oligopoly, we know that, given a cost vector $c = (c_1, \ldots, c_n)$, firm $i$ will choose "quantity" given by

$$q_i = \left( 1 - nc_i + \sum_{j \neq i} c_j \right) / (n+1). \tag{4.11}$$

Bearing this in mind, the payoffs of a firm $i$ located in network $g$, faced with a research profile $s$, are given by

$$\Pi_i(s|g) = \left[ \frac{1 - \bar{c} + s_i[n - \eta_i(g)] + \sum_{j \in N_i(g)} s_j[n - \eta_j(g)] - \sum_{l \in N \setminus \{i\} \cup N_i} s_l[1 + \eta_l(g)]}{n+1} \right]^2 - \alpha \frac{s_i^2(g)}{2}. \tag{4.12}$$

It can be checked that this payoff function exhibits positive externality across neighbors' actions and negative externality across nonneighbors' actions. Moreover, the actions of neighbors are strategic complements, while the actions of nonneighbors are strategic substitutes. We see here how a rather simple game of collaboration can generate a very rich set of externalities and strategic effects. ■

**Example 4.6** *Competition among firms*

Consider the classical problem of a set of firms, each producing a distinct good and choosing a price for that good. Following Singh and Vives (1984), let us say that demand for good $i$ is

$$Q_i(p) = a - \beta p_i + \sum_{j \neq i} \gamma_{ij} p_j, \tag{4.13}$$

where $p = (p_1, \ldots, p_n)$ is the price vector, $\beta$ is the firm's price effect, and $\gamma_{ij}$ is the effect of price $j$ on the demand for good $i$. Given a price vector $p$, the profit for firm $i$ is

$$\Pi_i(p) = p_i Q_i(p) = p_i \left( a - \beta p_i + \sum_{j \neq i} \gamma_{ij} p_j \right). \tag{4.14}$$

We may summarize the parameters of the demand system $\beta$ and $\gamma_{ij}$ in an adjacency matrix $D$, where $\beta$ occupies the diagonal cells and $\gamma_{ij}$ is the element in cell $ij$ of the matrix. The adjacency matrix $D$ may be seen reflecting a network of demand cross-dependencies across different goods. Let us assume that $\gamma_{ij} = \gamma_{ji}$. We notice that the nature of effects between firms $i$ and $j$ will depend on the sign and magnitude of the parameter $\gamma_{ij}$; $\gamma_{ij} > 0$ will imply that raising the price of $j$ confers a positive externality on $i$, and $\gamma_{ij} < 0$ implies that raising the price of $j$ confers a negative externality on $i$. Similarly, $\gamma_{ij} > 0$ signifies a relation of strategic complements between the prices of $i$ and $j$, and $\gamma_{ij} < 0$ signifies a relation of strategic substitutes. ■

**Example 4.7** *Keeping up with the Joneses*

Individuals and families often define the quality of their lives in relation to the standard of living of their relatives and neighbors. A distinguished strand of literature starting with the celebrated work of Torsten Veblen (1973) studies the consequences of the "keeping up with the Joneses effect." (See Duesenberry (1949) for an early discussion of the implications of such effects.) For empirical evidence on the presence of relative consumption effects, see Luttmer (2005) and Kuhn et al. (2011). We present a model, taken from Ghiglino and Goyal (2010), that studies consumer choice in a setting where individuals care about relative consumption.

We consider a group of households who have the same income $\omega$ and spend it on two goods $x$ and $y$. The households have Cobb-Douglas preferences; the novel feature of the preferences is that the good $y$ is a relative consumption good. The utility of individual $i$ facing a consumption profile $(x_i, y_i)_{i \in N}$ is

$$u_i(x_i, y_i, y_{-i}) = x_i^{\sigma} \left[ y_i + \alpha \eta_i \left( y_i - \frac{1}{d_i} \sum_{j \in N_i(g)} y_j \right) \right]^{1-\sigma}, \qquad (4.15)$$

where $y_{-i}$ is the consumption of all households other than household $i$, $\sigma \in (0, 1)$ and $\alpha > 0$ represent the strength of social comparisons, $\eta_i$ is the number of neighbors of $i$ in network, and $d_i$ is the number of neighbors. We can check that the consumption of good $y$ is a strategic complement across neighbors. ■

With this general discussion in place, we now analyze different classes of games on networks. As a first step we solve binary action games.

## 4.3 Binary Games

We commence our analysis of behavior in networks with a study of two simple games: the best-shot game and the weakest-link game. This binary choice environment offers us a basic framework within which we can develop a general message—behavior is jointly shaped by the content of interaction (as reflected in the payoff externalities in an activity) and the structure of the network.

### 4.3.1 Best-Shot Games

Let us consider the best-shot game; the discussion here is based on Bramoullé and Kranton (2007a). A preliminary observation is that, since $c \in (0, 1)$, in a Nash equilibrium it must be the case that an individual either chooses 1 for themself or one of the individual's neighbors chooses 1. Moreover, the strong substitutability of actions among neighbors implies that an individual will choose 1 if and only if all the neighbors will choose 0. So in any network, a Nash equilibrium can be constructed using the following algorithm: number the players from 1 to $n$. Say that player 1 chooses 1; assign 1 to the set of active players $A$. Next, consider players starting from 2 onward: check if 2 is a neighbor of 1; if not, then add this person to the set of players A who choose 1. If 2 is a neighbor, put him in the set B that chooses 0. Proceed next to 3: check if this individual is a neighbor of anyone in set A. If 3 is not, then place them in set A; if is a neighbor of someone in set A, then place them in set B. Proceed next to player 4 and so forth. Once we complete this procedure with player $n$, we will have partitioned the players into two sets, A and B (every player lies either in A or in B but never in both). Indeed, the set of active individuals correspond to a *maximally independent set* of the network. Formally, an independent set is a collection of nodes $N'$ so that no pair of nodes $i, j \in N'$ has a link. An independent set is maximal if it is not a strict subset of any other independent set in the network. A question at the end of this chapter works through properties of maximal independent sets.

Every player in set A chooses 1 while every player in the set B chooses 0. By construction of the sets A and B, observe that these actions are optimal for every individual. Consider a player $i \in A$: every neighbor lies in set B and chooses 0, so it is optimal for player $i$ to choose 1. Similarly, for any player $j \in B$, there must be a neighbor in set A; otherwise, player $j$ would themself be in set A. But everyone in set A chooses 1, so it is optimal for everyone in set B to choose 0. This simple process thus yields a Nash equilibrium for the best-shot game. By suitably reordering the players, we can in fact trace any Nash equilibrium on a given network. Finally, as we have not invoked any special feature of a network, note that the same procedure would apply to any network.

Figures 4.1 and 4.2 provide examples of maximally independent sets. In figure 4.1, we consider Erdős-Rényi graphs and see that the number of nodes in the maximal independent set can vary widely (in this case, from 6 to 10). This is a more general feature of maximal independent sets. Figure 4.2 presents two simple networks—the star and the circle—and their corresponding maximal independent sets. In the star, the maximal independent sets vary from size 1 to $n - 1$, while in the circle, the number varies from $n/3$ to $n/2$.

Some features of maximal independent sets are worth noting. There is no simple relation between an individual's connections and that individual's presence in a maximal independent set: behavior in the best-shot game thus depends on the social structure broadly construed. The multiplicity of maximal independent sets gives rise to the problem of multiple Nash equilibria.

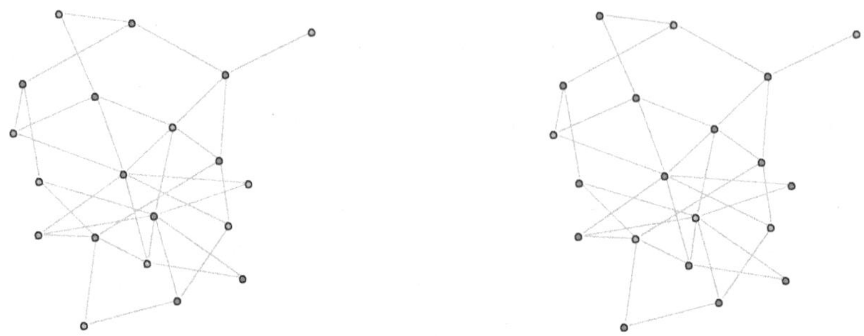

(a) Largest (b) Smallest

**Figure 4.1**
Maximal independent sets (indicated in orange) in E-R graph ($n = 20, p = 20$).

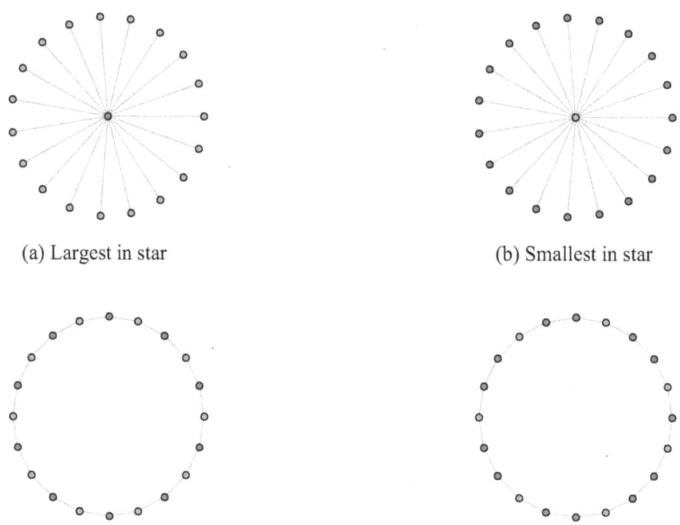

(a) Largest in star (b) Smallest in star

(c) Largest in circle (d) Smallest in circle

**Figure 4.2**
Maximal independent sets in simple networks (indicated in orange).

The multiplicity of equilibria poses a challenge when we wish to understand the effects of changes in a network. To see this, let us start from a network that contains two distinct stars and add a link that connects the two hubs. The effect of this change can be radically different depending on which maximally independent set is active. Figure 4.3 illustrates this point: in the top-left panel (figure 4.3(a)), there is a network with two stars, and in each star the hub (represented in red) is active and the spokes (represented in blue) are passive. A link is added between the two hubs to create a connected network. Figure 4.3(b), presents

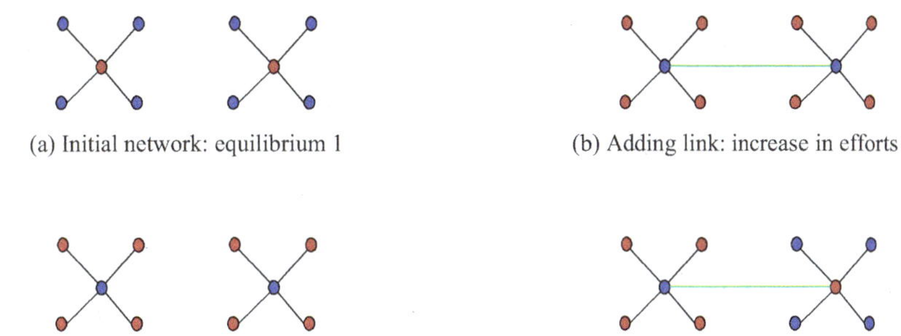

(a) Initial network: equilibrium 1

(b) Adding link: increase in efforts

(c) Initial network: equilibrium 2

(d) Adding link: fall in efforts

**Figure 4.3**
Adding links: multiplicity in outcomes (active players in red).

an equilibrium in the connected network in which spokes are active (represented in red) and both the hubs are passive (represented in blue). This shows that a link can lead to significant increase in activity. By contrast, consider the bottom panel on the left (figure 4.3[c]), there is an equilibrium in which the hubs are passive (represented in blue) while the spokes are active (represented in red). In the bottom right panel (figure 4.3[d]), after the addition of the links, the equilibrium changes—one hub is active and the corresponding spokes are passive, while the other hub is passive but the corresponding spokes are active (active in red and passive in blue). Thus the effects of adding a link—whether it increases or decreases aggregate activity—depend very much on the initial starting situation. It is easy to see that this ambiguity is also true if we look at the effects of additional links on payoffs.

The following result summarizes our discussion of best-shot games.

**Proposition 4.1** *Consider the best-shot game played on a network. In an equilibrium, the set of active players is given by a maximal independent set of the network. Starting from any network g, adding links may increase or decrease the level of activity. Similarly, adding links may increase or lower the payoffs of individuals.*

We conclude our discussion of best-shot games with some remarks on social welfare. As in chapter 3, let us define social welfare as the sum of individual utilities. Observe that since $c \in (0, 1)$, in an equilibrium every individual must have access to at least one unit of activity. Thus any variations that arise in social welfare must be due to the number of active players. Indeed, it follows that social welfare is falling in the size of the maximal independent set. In the star network, therefore, differences in social welfare across equilibria are very large: 1 versus $n - 1$.

### 4.3.2 Weakest-Link Games

We next take up weakest-link games: our discussion is based on Gagnon and Goyal (2017). Note that the state where everyone is choosing action 0 is always an equilibrium. However, there will typically exist other equilibria. To develop a better sense of how networks matter, let us fix the cost of action 1 to be $c = 4.1$. So an individual will only choose action 1 if the returns of choosing 1 cover the cost 4.1. From the payoff given in equation (12.5), this means that at least five of the individual's neighbors must also choose action 1. However, these neighbors will choose action 1 only if each of them has at least four other neighbors choosing 1 (in addition to the first player mentioned). Thus for an individual to choose 1, they must be part of a set of nodes in a network, each of whom has at least five links with others who have five links, and so on. This discussion motivates the study of the q-core of a network.

**Definition 4.3** *The q-core of a network g, denoted by $g^q$, is the largest subgraph of g such that all individuals in $g^q$ have strictly more than q links to other individuals in $g^q$.*

Here is a simple procedure for obtaining the q-core of a network. Start with a network g. In step 1, delete all the nodes (and their links) in g for which degree $k \leq q$. Label the residual graph $g_1$. In step 2, delete all the nodes (and their links) in $g_1$ for which $k \leq q$. Iterate until no node with $k \leq q$ remains (i.e., when $g_t = g_{t+1}$). The residual graph in this last step is the q-core.

By way of illustration, consider the network in figure 4.4. Suppose that we want to find the 4-core. First, find all the nodes with $k \leq 4$, and delete them and their links. In step 2, delete the nodes with four or fewer links in the residual network from step 1. Proceed likewise until no node with $k \leq 4$ remains. The remaining nodes form the 4-core. A question at the end of the chapter works through some properties of the q-core.

To return to our example with $c = 4.1$, observe that everyone in the 4-core choosing action 1 and everyone outside choosing action 0 constitutes a Nash equilibrium of the weakest-link game. By definition, everyone in the 4-core has at least five neighbors, and so their return from choosing action 1 is at least $5 - 4.1 = 0.9$. Moreover, no one outside the set has five or more neighbors who belong to the 4-core. Finally, we note that, by definition of the 4-core, this is also the largest set of individuals who can choose action 1 in an equilibrium in this network.

Observe that the zero activity outcome remains an equilibrium for every network. Taken together, the zero equilibrium and the equilibrium corresponding to the q-core define the minimal and the maximal level of activity in a network. Figure 4.5 illustrates the 1-core and 2-core in an Erdős-Rényi network and in a stochastic block random graph with two communities (and an equal average degree). We observe that in Erdős-Rényi graphs, the q-core is either extensive and covers much of the graph or is very small. This is because Erdős-Rényi graphs have a fairly homogeneous structure, with most nodes having a degree close to the average degree. As we move from the Erdős-Rényi to the stochastic random graph model, this changes slightly, and we see that a part of one community constitutes a q-core while the other one lies outside the q-core. To see how this homogeneity matters, let us consider another classical network: the core-periphery network. Figure 4.6 shows that the q-core in this network has a very different reach compared with the Erdős-Rényi graph.

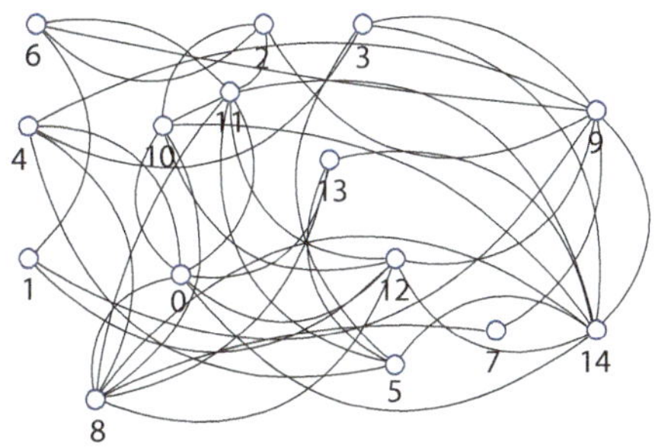


(a) Initial graph

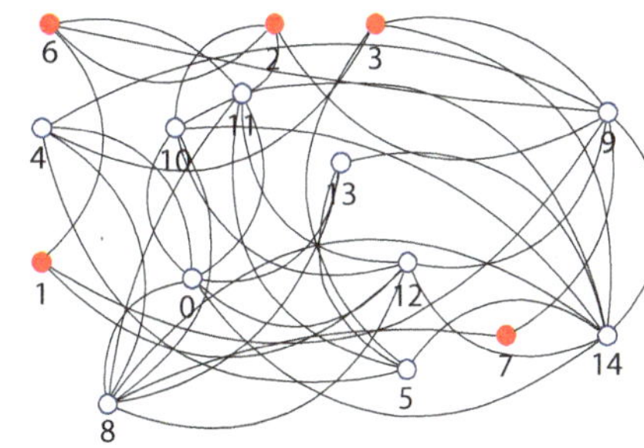


(b) Delete nodes with less than 5 links

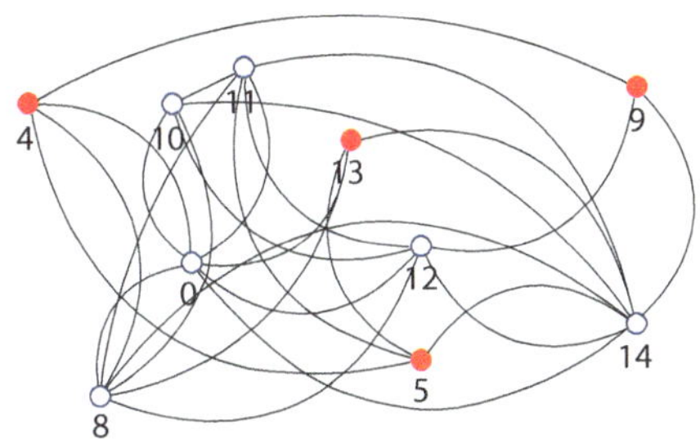


(c) Among the nodes remaining, delete nodes with less than 5 links

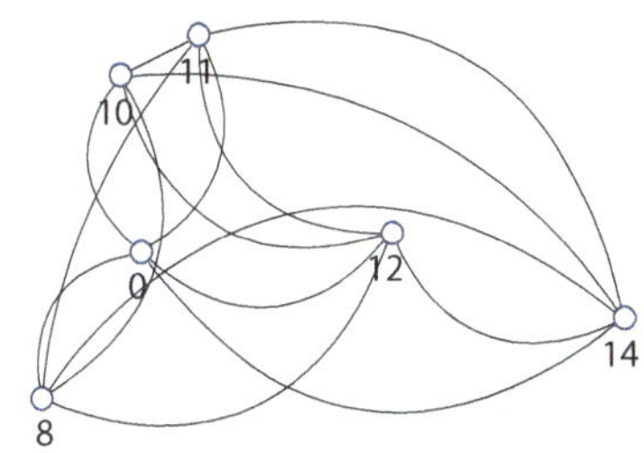


(d) The 4-core is obtained when no further iteration is possible

**Figure 4.4**
The 4-core. *Source*: Gagnon and Goyal (2017).

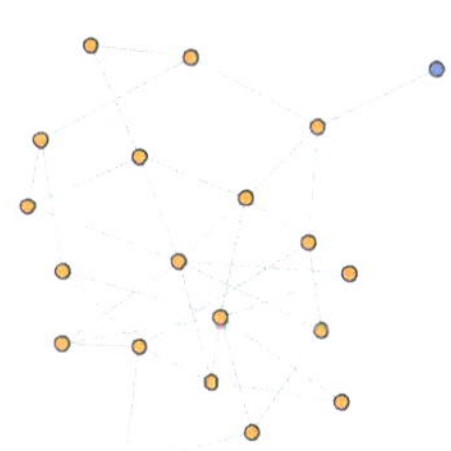

(a) 1-core (E-R network, $p = 0.2$)

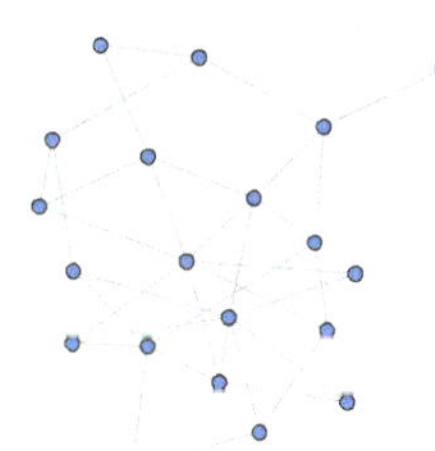

(b) 2-core (E-R network: $p = 0.2$)

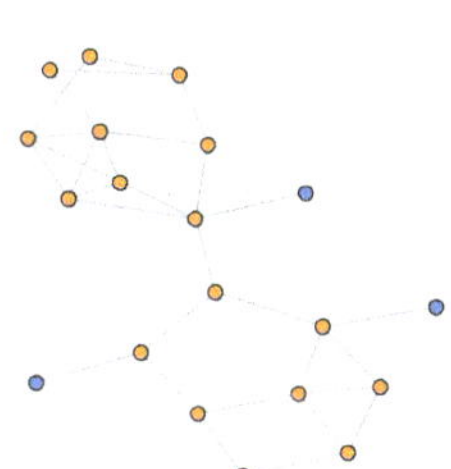

(c) 1-core (St. block, $p^I = 0.45$, $p^O = 0.023$)

(d) 2-core: (St. block, $p^I = 0.45$, $p^O = 0.023$)

**Figure 4.5**
Q-cores (in orange): $n = 20$.

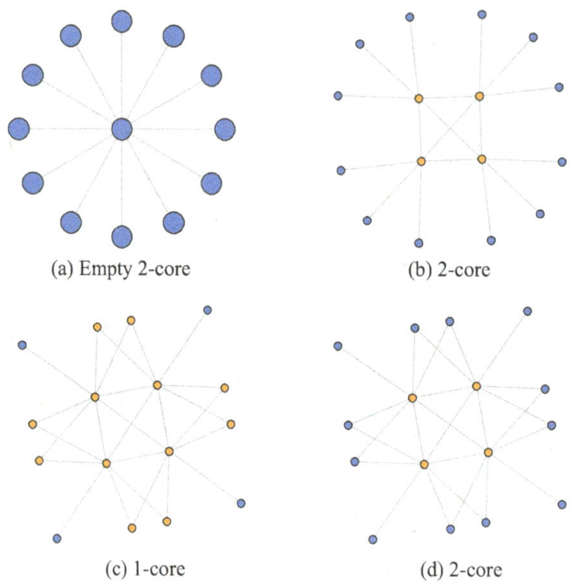


**Figure 4.6**
Q-cores (in orange).

On the effects of changes in a network, note that adding a link to a network will either leave the q-core unaffected or will expand it, so adding a link to a network can only weakly raise the maximal equilibrium.

A final remark concerns utility: the payoffs to an individual who chooses 0 are zero while the potential payoffs of an active agent are increasing in the number of neighbors who choose action 1. So given a positive cost $c$, it follows that payoffs are larger for nodes in the q-core as compared with those outside it. It then follows as a simple corollary that, for any network, aggregate social welfare is maximized in the equilibrium corresponding to the q-core. Hence, adding links to a network has the potential to raise social welfare that is therefore maximized in the complete network.

Define $\lceil x \rceil$ as the smallest integer at least as large as $x$. The following result summarizes our analysis of the weakest-link game.

**Proposition 4.2** *Consider the weakest-link game played on a network. In every network, there exists a zero activity equilibrium. The maximal activity equilibrium is defined by the q-core of the network, where $q = \lceil c - 1 \rceil$. Starting from any network g, adding links expands the q-core and has the potential to increase the level of activity. The payoffs of players are larger in more active equilibria; thus, adding links can potentially increase payoffs.*

A comparison of propositions 4.1 and 4.2 brings out the general point that individual behavior and utility are jointly shaped by the content of interaction and the structure of the network. In particular, in the best-shot game, the strategic-substitutes property leads us to a focus on maximal independent sets; in the weakest-link game, the strategic-complements property leads us to a focus on the q-core of the network.

A feature of both types of games is that, even in simple networks, there exist multiple equilibria. This means that it is often difficult to clearly relate an individual's location with their behavior and utility. So, for instance, we cannot say whether highly connected individuals choose higher or lower actions and earn more or less than less connected individuals. This multiplicity also places limits on what we can say on the effects of network change.

A key assumption underlying the analysis in this section has been that individuals know the entire network. This is a reasonable assumption for small networks but is unlikely to hold for large networks. The next section takes up the study of human behavior in large networks.

## 4.4 Binary Games on Random Networks

Many networks of interest—such as coauthor networks, Twitter, and Facebook—are very large, containing hundreds of thousands to millions of users. In such large networks, complete knowledge of every node and every link is not a plausible assumption. It is more reasonable to assume that individuals will have limited information on the details of who is connected to whom. An individual may know who their friends are, and they may have a rough idea about the overall distribution of connections. This section explores human behavior when individuals have limited knowledge of the network. Our discussion is based on Galeotti, Goyal, Jackson et al. (2010).

Let us revisit the best-shot game. Now suppose that an individual has degree $d$ and knows that this is their degree. Should they choose action 0 or action 1? The returns to choosing 1 remain the same as before $(1-c)$, but the returns from choosing 0 are less clear. If any of her neighbors chooses 1, then their best choice is 0; if all the neighbors choose 0, then their best action is 1. To make the decision, they therefore need to have a view on what actions their neighbors are choosing. Their choices will depend on the number of connections they have. To make progress in this problem, one way to proceed is as follows: we define individual strategy as a function of the individual's degree, $s_i : \mathbb{N} \rightarrow \{0, 1\}$. Next, we need to consider an individual's perspective on the behavior of their neighbors: as their behavior depends on their degree, they need to have a view on the degrees of each of their neighbors. For concreteness, let us suppose that they believe that the network arises out of an Erdős-Rényi random linking process with probability $p \in (0, 1)$. With this belief, she believes that the probability that any randomly selected neighbor is of degree $k$ is the probability that the neighbor is connected to $k-1$ additional agents of the remaining $n-2$ agents. This probability may be written as

$$Q(k;p) = \binom{n-2}{k-1} p^{k-1} (1-p)^{N-k-1}. \tag{4.16}$$

In principle, since the network is undirected, an individual's own degree is related to the degree of others, and in particular to the degrees of her neighbors. However, as $n$ gets large, this correlation becomes progressively smaller. Let us make one final assumption: suppose that everyone with the same degree chooses the same action. We now have all the ingredients to fully solve for the optimal individual strategy.

We show that the optimal strategy has a threshold property: there is a cutoff value $d^*$, such that everyone below $d^*$ chooses 1 and everyone above $d^*$ chooses 0. To see why this must be true, suppose that it is optimal for someone with degree $k$ to choose action 1. As degrees of neighbors are uncorrelated, it follows that each of the neighbors of someone with degree $k-1$ has the same degree distribution as a neighbor of someone with degree $k$. As a neighbor's degree is independent of an individual's own degree, this means that someone with degree $k-1$ must expect less activity in the aggregate from their neighborhood compared to someone with $k$ neighbors. As this is a game of strategic substitutes, it follows that the marginal returns to choosing action 1 are higher for the individual with degree $k-1$ than for the individual with degree $k$. If action 1 is optimal for degree $k$, it must also be optimal for the individual with degree $k-1$. Thus there is a threshold property to optimal choice.

Suppose that every individual is following the threshold strategy with a threshold $t$. Let us compute this threshold. First, note that the individual payoff from action 1 is $1-c$. The payoff from action 0 depends on whether one of the neighbors chooses action 1. What is the probability that at least one of the neighbors chooses 1? This is 1 minus the probability that none of the neighbors chooses 1:

$$1-\left[1-\sum_{k=1}^{t} Q(k;p))\right]^{t}. \tag{4.17}$$

To compute $t$, we equate the expected payoff from action 0, given in equation (4.17), with the payoff from action 1, $1-c$. In other words, we are looking for $t$ such that $1-c$ lies between the values of equation (4.17) evaluated at $t$ as opposed to $t+1$. It is possible to show that this equilibrium is the only equilibrium in strategies that condition only on degree. Moreover, the strategy is (monotonically) decreasing in degree: degrees below the threshold choose action 1, and degrees above the threshold choose action 0.

We now turn to the issue of how changes in the network affect behavior. An individual conditions their behavior on their own degree, so it is natural to study changes in the network in terms of changes in the degree distribution. Let us again consider the Erdős-Rényi random graph: here, changes in the degree distribution can be studied in terms of an increase in the probability of linking, $p$. Let us consider an increase from $p$ to a higher $p'$. Note that a higher $p$ means that for every $t$,

$$\sum_{k=1}^{t} Q(k;p') \leq \sum_{k=1}^{t} Q(k;p). \tag{4.18}$$

**Table 4.1**
Equilibrium in best-shot game on Erdős-Rényi network

| | |
|---|---|
| Number of nodes | 20 |
| Probability of link | 0.1 |
| Cost of action | 0.5 |
| Threshold | 2 |
| Prob. at least 1 neighbor chooses 1: | 0.70 |
| Expected utility of threshold degree (s=0) | 0.70 |
| Expected utility (s=1) | 0.50 |

**Table 4.2**
Best-shot thresholds in Erdős-Rényi networks: varying $p$

| Prob. of link, $p$ | 0.1 | 0.2 | 0.3 | 0.4 | 0.5 |
|---|---|---|---|---|---|
| Best-shot threshold | 2 | 3 | 4 | 6 | 7 |

Recall from chapter 1 that a change from $p$ to $p'$ induces a first-order stochastic shift in the degree distribution.

Consider the threshold that we computed under $p$. Under a first-order stochastic dominant shift, the term $\sum_{k=1}^{t} Q(k;p'))$ is smaller and the expected payoff from action 0 at threshold t is strictly smaller than the payoff from action 1. This means that the new threshold $t'$ under $p'$ will be higher, $t' \geq t$.

To develop a feel for these features of behavior, it is helpful to compute some thresholds. Table 4.1 presents thresholds in an Erdős-Rényi network with $n = 20$ and the probability of linking $p = 0.1$. The threshold is 2, so degrees 1 and 2 choose action 1, and all degrees above 2 choose 0. Table 4.2 presents thresholds for different levels of $p$ in the best-shot game: we see that the threshold is increasing in connectivity level $p$.

The increase in threshold means that effort remains unchanged for individuals with degrees lower than $t$ or greater than $t'$, and *increases* for all individuals with degrees between $t$ and $t'$. The change in threshold also has another implication: the probability that any randomly selected neighbor chooses effort falls; in other words, $\sum_{k=1}^{t'} Q(k;p') \leq \sum_{k=1}^{t} Q(k;p)$. Thus the threshold only increases if, for a given degree, the total of neighbors' equilibrium efforts is greater under the original $p$ than under $p'$, which implies that the probability of any selected neighbor choosing effort must be lower under $p'$.

The computations here were made in the context of Erdős-Rényi networks. However, nothing essential in these computations rests on the details of the Erdős-Rényi construction. Recall from chapter 2 that starting from some degree distribution $P$, using the configuration model, the approximate degree distribution for neighbors is

$$\tilde{P}(d) = \frac{P(d)d}{E[d]}, \tag{4.19}$$

where $E(d)$ is the expected degree under distribution $P$. The probability that a neighbor who uses strategy $s(.)$ chooses 1 is given by

$$p_s = \sum_d s(d)\tilde{P}(d). \tag{4.20}$$

The probability that $m$ out of $d_i$ neighbors choose action 1 is given by

$$\binom{d_i}{m} p_s^m (1-p_s)^{d_i-m}. \tag{4.21}$$

The expected utility of a player choosing action $x_i$ is then given by

$$U_{d_i}(x_i, s(.)) = \sum_{m=0}^{d_i} u_{d_i}(x_i, m)\binom{d_i}{m} p_s^m (1-p_s)^{d_i-m}. \tag{4.22}$$

The arguments used to derive the thresholds in the Erdős-Rényi network can easily be used to derive thresholds for an arbitrary degree distribution $P$ (simply by substituting the formula from equation (4.23) in the place of the expressions corresponding to the Erdős-Rényi degree distribution in equations (4.16), (4.17), and (4.19). With these remarks in mind, we may summarize our discussion as follows.

**Proposition 4.3** *Consider the best-shot game played on a random network in which degrees of neighbors are independent. There exists a unique equilibrium in threshold strategies. Degrees below the threshold degree choose action 1, while degrees above the threshold choose 0. Thus activity level is (weakly) falling and therefore utility is (weakly) increasing in degree.*

*A first-order stochastic shift in neighbors' degree distribution from P to P' leads to a (weak) increase in degree threshold in the equilibrium strategy. Thus more connected networks exhibit a (weakly) higher level of activity, for every degree. This implies that for every degree, the expected level of activity of a neighbor must go down.*

We provide a sketch of the argument for uniqueness here; the interested reader is referred to Galeotti, Goyal, Jackson et al. (2010) for the details of the proof. Suppose there exist two equilibria with distinct thresholds $t > t'$. So there is a degree $t' + 1$ that is weakly lower than $t$: this degree chooses action 0 under $t'$ and action 1 under threshold $t$. However, that degree $t' + 1$ expects a higher sum of activity in the $t$ equilibria, and so her marginal returns from action 1 will be lower than the marginal returns from action 1 for the same degree under the threshold $t'$. Given that $t' + 1$ finds it optimal to choose action 0, this contradicts the optimality of choosing action 1 under threshold $t$.

We conclude our discussion of the best-shot game on random graphs with some remarks on social welfare. Let us say that social welfare is given by the expected payoff of a randomly chosen player (according to the prevailing degree distribution). This result tells us that every degree does weakly less well under the more connected network. However, utility is increasing in degree, and there is a higher fraction of individuals in the more connected network. It is therefore possible that even though every degree does less well, the average individual does better in the more connected network.

We next turn to the weakest-link game played by individuals located in a large random graph. Recall that payoffs in the weakest-link game are given by

$$s_i \sum_{j \in N_i(g)} s_j - c s_i. \tag{4.23}$$

We will show that equilibrium is characterized by a unique threshold. As before, suppose that individuals inhabit an Erdős-Rényi model with link probability given by $p$. If the number of nodes is large enough, the degrees of neighbors are (close to) independent. This means that the probability of a neighbor choosing action 1 is independent of their own degree: in turn, this implies that expected activity is increasing in the number of neighbors; that is, $\sum_{j \in N_i}(g)x_j$ is increasing in degree of $i$. If someone with degree $t$ chooses action 1, then the property of strategic complements tells us that the marginal returns to action 1 are strictly larger for individuals with a degree greater than $t$. In other words, optimal action obeys a threshold: there is some $t$, individuals with a degree lower than $t$ choose 0, while those with a degree greater than $t$ choose 1.

Building on this argument, we can say that, for sufficiently large $p$, there exists $t < N - 1$, for which

$$(t-1) \sum_{k=t}^{N-1} Q(k;p) < c \text{ and } t \sum_{k=t}^{N-1} Q(k;p) \geq c. \tag{4.24}$$

Marginal returns are increasing in expected activity in neighborhood. As their own degree is independent of the neighbor's degree, higher degree means higher expected activity level in the neighborhood. From strategic complementarity, this implies that the optimal strategy is monotonically increasing in the degree of an individual. As individuals can always earn 0 by choosing action 0, it follows that expected payoffs are increasing in degree as well.

Let us now take up the effects of changes in the network: consider an increase in probability of linking from $p$ to $p'$, where $p' > p$. This means that the degree distribution under $p'$ first-order dominates the degree distribution under $p$; that is, for any $t$, $\sum_{k=t}^{N-1} Q(k;p') > \sum_{k=t}^{N-1} Q(k;p)$. Intuitively, the shift from $p$ to $p'$ increases connectivity of neighbors, and this raises the probability that a neighbor would choose 1. From the property of strategic complements, this raises the returns from action 1 and lowers the threshold. Iterating on this process, we generate a new threshold, $t' < t$. A lower threshold means that the probability that a neighbor chooses 1 increases: this is because for any $t$, the probability of degree greater than $t$ is higher under $p'$.

To develop a feel for these features of behavior, we compute some thresholds in Erdős-Rényi networks. Table 4.3 presents the computation of active equilibrium threshold for a network with twenty nodes ($n = 20$) and with the probability of linking $p = 0.2$. The threshold is 3: this means that all those with degrees 1 and 2 choose action 0, while players

**Table 4.3**
Equilibrium in weakest-link game on Erdős-Rényi network

| | |
|---|---|
| Number of nodes | 20 |
| Probability of link | 0.2 |
| Cost of action | 2 |
| Threshold | 3 |
| Prob. a neighbor's degree $\geq 3$: | 0.72 |
| Expected utility ($s = 0$) | 0 |
| Expected utility of threshold degree ($s = 1$) | 0.19 |

**Table 4.4**
Weakest-link thresholds in Erdős-Rényi networks: varying $p$

| Prob. of link, $p$ | 0.1 | 0.2 | 0.3 | 0.4 | 0.5 |
|---|---|---|---|---|---|
| Weakest-link threshold | 3 | 2 | 2 | 2 | 2 |

with degree 3 and higher choose action 1. Table 4.4 presents thresholds for different levels of $p$ in the weakest-link game: we see that the threshold is declining in connectivity level $p$.

The following result summarizes our discussion on weakest-link games on random graphs.

**Proposition 4.4** *Consider the weakest-link game played on a random graph where degrees of neighbors are independent. There exists a zero activity equilibrium in every network. In addition, there may be an equilibrium with positive activity. A positive-activity equilibrium strategy exhibits a threshold property: degrees below the threshold degree choose action 0, while degrees above the threshold choose 1. Thus activity level is (weakly) rising in the degree of an individual.*

*A first-order shift in degree distribution of neighbors leads to a (weak) decrease in the degree threshold. Thus more connected networks exhibit a (weakly) higher level of activity, for every degree.*

We conclude our discussion of the weakest-link game with some remarks on social welfare. As before, we measure social welfare by the expected payoff of a randomly chosen player. This result tells us that every degree does weakly better under the more connected network. Moreover, utility is increasing in degree, and there is a higher fraction of higher-degree individuals in the more connected network. It therefore follows that in the active equilibrium of the weakest-link game, the average individual does better in the more connected network.

Our study of best-shot and weakest-link games in random graphs provides a nice illustration of how the content of interaction interacts with networks to shape behavior. The structure of interaction is captured by the degree distribution, while the content of interaction is reflected in whether the game is one of substitutes or complements. Equilibrium strategy is monotonically decreasing in degree under strategic substitutes, while it is monotonically increasing under strategic complements. Higher-degree individuals earn higher payoffs in both cases. Increases in connectivity of neighbors have contrasting implications for behavior: under strategic substitutes, there is a fall in expected efforts of each neighbor, while under strategic complements, there is an increase in expected efforts from each neighbor.

### 4.4.1 Experimental Evidence

The previous discussion derives a simple rule for behavior in large networks when individuals have limited information on the network. We found that equilibria involve simple thresholds that determine whether to be active or passive. The level of the threshold depends on the degree distribution of the network, the costs of activity, and whether the game is one of substitutes or complements. In this section, we present a laboratory experiment that tests these predictions: do experimental subjects use threshold rules, and do the thresholds adapt as the underlying network is changed? Our discussion is based on Charness, Feri, Meléndez-Jiménez, and Sutter (2014).

At the outset, it is worth drawing attention to a few potential difficulties faced by subjects. Subjects need to work their way toward understanding how degrees and strategic considerations interact. In addition, there is the potential challenge of choosing the right threshold. In the best-shot game, there is a unique threshold; in the weakest-link game, there typically are multiple equilibria, ranging from the zero activity outcome to the positive activity outcome. As actions are costly, there is a difference in the level of security/risk associated with each equilibrium: choosing action 0 guarantees a payoff, while choosing action 1 exposes the individual to an uncertain payoff that depends on how many neighbors choose action 1. Thus attitudes toward uncertainty may come into play, in addition to the thresholds.

We consider three networks that are displayed in figure 4.7. Let $p$ be the probability that the Orange network is picked, with the other two networks being picked with equal probability given by $(1-p)/2$. Observe that the Orange network has higher connectivity than the other two networks (the Orange network is obtained by adding link 24 to the Green network, and it is obtained from the Purple network by adding link 34). An increase in $p$ can therefore be interpreted as an increase in connectivity of the networks. Two values of $p$ are considered: $p=0.2$ and $p=0.8$. So there were four treatments in all—two for substitutes and two for complements. There were two sessions per treatment and 20 subjects per session, so there were 160 subjects in all. The experiment was conducted at the University of Innsbruck.

The theoretical analysis tells us that the equilibria are defined by a threshold. In the best-shot game, the parameters are as follows: a player earns 100 if either they or one of their neighbors is active, and earns zero otherwise. Action 1 costs 50. In the weakest-link game, if a player is inactive, they earn 50, and if they are active, they earn 33.33 times the number

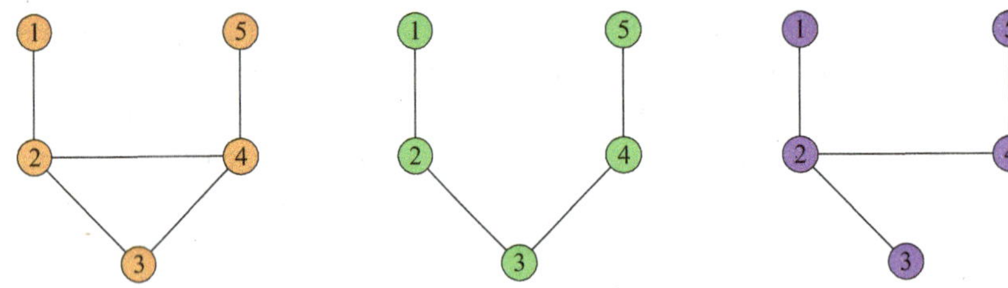


(a) Orange network (b) Green network (c) Purple network

**Figure 4.7**
Networks for experiment 1. *Source*: Charness, Feri, Meléndez-Jiménez, and Sutter (2014).

**Table 4.5**
Equilibrium in games

| | | Active degrees | Inactive degrees |
|---|---|---|---|
| Substitutes | p=0.20 | 1 | 2,3 |
| | p=0.80 | 1, 2 | 3 |
| Complements | p=0.20 | — | 1,2,3 |
| | p=0.80 | — | 1,2,3 |
| | | 2,3 | 1 |

of neighbors who are active. Thus they require at least two neighbors to be active to justify choosing action 1 themselves.

Table 4.5 summarizes the theoretical analysis for these parameters. In the case of strategic substitutes, the theoretical prediction is that players with degree 1 (degree 3) are active (inactive) in both treatments with $p = 0.2$ and $p = 0.8$. Players with degree 2 are active when $p = 0.8$ and inactive when $p = 0.2$. With strategic complements, the unique theoretical prediction is zero activity with $p = 0.2$. With $p = 0.8$, in addition to the zero activity, there is a positive action equilibrium in which degrees 2 and 3 are active, while degree 1 is inactive (it is worth bearing in mind that the degrees of neighbors may be correlated due to the size of networks; a question at the end of the chapter explores this issue further).

Figure 4.8 (top panel) shows the evolution of behavior across networks and across the 40 periods in the game of strategic substitutes (the best-shot game). For strategic substitutes, we observe that subjects behave very much in line with the (unique) threshold equilibrium: this is especially true for degrees 1 and 3, but slightly less so for degree 2.

Next, let us consider the effect of degree on behavior. Subjects with degree 2 are much less likely to choose an activity than those with degree 1; this decrease is large when $p = 0.2$ and somewhat smaller when $p = 0.8$. Comparing degree 3 to degree 2, the probability of choosing 1 is significantly lower for subjects with degree 3; this difference is large when

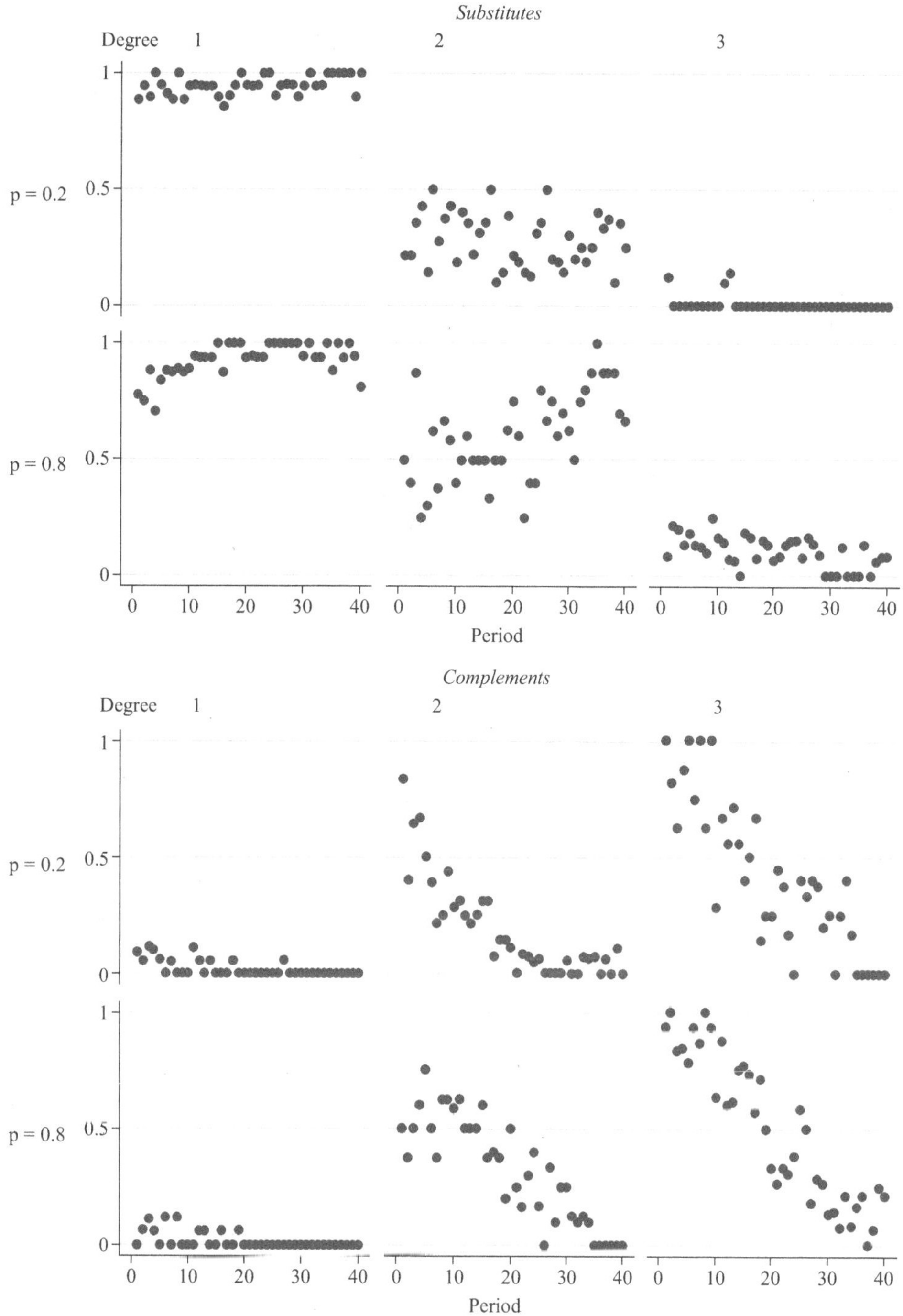


**Figure 4.8**
Experiment 1—relative frequencies of choices by degree. *Source*: Charness, Feri, Meléndez-Jiménez, and Sutter (2014).

$p = 0.8$, and it is smaller when $p = 0.2$. Overall, the behavior in the laboratory is in line with the theoretical prediction.

Turning to the effects of greater connectivity (recall that higher values of $p$ imply higher connectivity), there is no significant change for degree 1. The degree 2 individuals do increase activity with a move from $p = 0.2$ to $p = 0.8$. For subjects with degree 3, there is a slight increase in the probability of action 1.

To summarize, *in the best-shot game, subjects consistently choose the unique equilibrium and the probability of activity is decreasing with the degree and increasing with network connectivity.*

We next report on the game of strategic complements (the weakest-link game). When $p = 0.2$, the zero-action outcome is the unique equilibrium. Play by subjects with degrees 1 and 2 is strongly consistent with the equilibrium prediction. Subjects with degree 3 are inactive with significant probability. When $p = 0.8$, in addition to the zero action outcome, there is the activity equilibrium, in which subjects with degrees 2 and 3 are active. The behavior of subjects with degree 1 is strongly consistent, but the evidence on the behavior of degree 2 and 3 subjects is mixed.

Turning to the effects of changing $p$, the behavior of subjects with degree 1 does not change significantly, but subjects with degrees 2 and 3 are significantly more likely to choose 1 for higher values of $p$. However, these attempts are largely unsuccessful over time and subjects eventually converge to the secure and inefficient equilibrium.

Concerning the effect of the degree, a person with degree 2 is significantly more likely to be active than a person of degree 1; this difference is considerably larger with $p = 0.8$ than with $p = 0.2$. This qualitatively supports the theoretical prediction of a lowering of threshold with an increase in connectivity.

To summarize: *in the weakest-link game, subjects choose the secure zero activity equilibrium with low connectivity. The probability of activity increases with the degree and with connectivity. Under the high-connectivity network, there is eventually convergence to the inefficient (but secure) zero activity equilibrium.*

Let us summarize what we have learned in our study of binary games on large networks. We took the view that individuals will know some aspects of the local network (such as their own degree) and general aspects of the network as a whole (such as its degree distribution). In such a setting, individual strategy will be a mapping from degree to action. The theoretical analysis of binary games with limited network knowledge yields a number of sharp and intuitive predictions. Equilibrium strategies exhibit a simple threshold structure: in games of substitutes, individuals below a threshold choose action 1, while those above the threshold choose action 0. In games of complements, individuals above a threshold choose action 1, while those below the threshold choose action 0. An increase in the connectivity of the network has clear-cut effects on these cutoff thresholds. We have presented the findings of a laboratory experiment that offers support for these theoretical predictions.

## 4.5 Continuous Action Games

In the previous two sections, we studied binary action games. We now enrich the action possibilities open to individuals: we allow them to chose from a continuum of options. We will focus on games that admit a linear best response for individuals. As in the case of binary games, we will start by considering a setting in which individuals know the entire network. Our analysis will yield a powerful insight: the behavior of individuals is proportional to their Katz-Bonacich centrality in the network. We will comment on the social welfare of the equilibrium outcomes. The section concludes with remarks on continuous action games with incomplete network information. The discussion draws on the papers by Ballester, Calvó-Armengol, and Zenou (2006), Bramoullé and Kranton (2007a), and Galeotti, Goyal, Jackson et al. (2010).

Recall that there is a set of players $N=\{1,\ldots,n\}$, with $n\geq 2$. Individuals simultaneously choose an action: individual $i$ chooses an action, $s_i\in\mathbb{R}_+$. Individuals are located in a network $g$. The network has a corresponding adjacency matrix, given by $G$. In the matrix $G$, entry $g_{ij}$ reflects the strength of the relationship that $i$ has with $j$. For expositional simplicity, we will assume that $g_{ij}=g_{ji}$: in other words, the links (and the networks) are symmetric. It will be assumed that there are no own links ($g_{ii}=0$). The vector of actions is denoted by $\boldsymbol{s}\in\mathbb{R}^n_+$. The payoff to individual $i$ depends on this vector, $\boldsymbol{s}$, the undirected network (with adjacency matrix) $\boldsymbol{G}$, and other parameters, described as follows:

$$U_i(\boldsymbol{s},\boldsymbol{G})=\underbrace{s_i\left(b_i+\beta\sum_{j\in N}g_{ij}s_j\right)}_{\text{returns from own action}}-\underbrace{\frac{1}{2}s_i^2}_{\substack{\text{private costs}\\ \text{of own action}}}+\underbrace{P_i(\boldsymbol{s}_{-i},\boldsymbol{G},\boldsymbol{b})}_{\text{pure externalities}}. \tag{4.25}$$

The marginal returns from action $s_i$ depend on $i$'s action, $s_i$, and on others' actions. The coefficient $b_i\in\mathbb{R}$ corresponds to the part of $i$'s marginal return that is independent of others' actions, and it is called $i$'s stand-alone marginal return. The contribution of others' actions to $i$'s marginal return is given by the term $\beta\sum_{j\in N}g_{ij}s_j$. The parameter $\beta$ captures strategic interdependencies. If $\beta>0$, then actions are strategic complements; and if $\beta<0$, then actions are strategic substitutes. The function $P_i(\boldsymbol{s}_{-i},\boldsymbol{G},\boldsymbol{b})$ captures pure externalities—that is, spillovers that do not affect the best response.

For ease of reference, let us recall a baseline example of a game on networks that satisfies these properties.

**Example 4.8** *The investment game*

Individual $i$ makes an investment $s_i$ at a cost $\frac{1}{2}s_i^2$. The private marginal return on that investment is $b_i+\beta\sum_{j\in N}g_{ij}s_j$, where $b_i$ is individual $i$'s stand-alone marginal return and $\sum_{j\in N}g_{ij}s_j$ is the aggregate local effort. The utility of $i$ is

$$U_i(\boldsymbol{s}, \boldsymbol{G}) = s_i \left( b_i + \beta \sum_{j \in N} g_{ij} s_j \right) - \frac{1}{2} s_i^2. \tag{4.26}$$

The case with $\beta > 0$ reflects investment complementarities. Here, an individual's marginal returns are enhanced when his neighbors work harder; this creates both strategic complementarities and positive externalities. The case of $\beta < 0$ corresponds to strategic substitutes and negative externalities; this can be microfounded via a model of competition in a market after investment decisions $s_i$ have been made. ■

In making their choices, an individual will seek to equate the marginal returns with the marginal costs of action. Differentiating the payoff with respect to their own action, setting it equal to zero, and rearranging the terms yields individual $i$'s best response:

$$s_i = b_i + \beta \sum_{j \in N} g_{ij} s_j. \tag{4.27}$$

Thus a player's best response is their stand-alone marginal benefit $b_i$ plus the sum of the actions of their neighbors: the direction of movement relative to the autarkic optimum $b_i$ is determined by whether $\beta$ is positive or negative (i.e., whether actions are complements or substitutes), and on the level of connectivity (reflected in the values of $g_{ij}$).

### 4.5.1 Equilibrium and Centrality

There are three challenges in the study of such games—the equilibrium may not be interior (so that the first-order conditions are not appropriate), there may be multiple equilibria, or the spillovers are so large that there is no well-defined optimum. A simple way to ensure that the equilibrium is interior and defined by the first-order conditions is to require that spillovers $\beta$ are suitably small in relation to the network. As we start with an interior autarkic optimum, the best response in the game then also remains interior. The early literature in this field essentially used this approach, and we will present the restrictions needed to ensure this now. Let us work through the mechanics of the derivations to develop a feel for how these restrictions operate and how such games are solved. The study of general network effects (i.e., when $\beta$ is large), requires more advanced methods that are not covered here. See Bramoullé, Kranton, and D'Amours (2014) for an introduction to those methods.

The best responses of the individuals as in equation (4.27), constitute a system of $n$ linear equations. Recalling that the matrix $G$ summarizes the cross-dependencies, we may write this system in matrix form. In particular, any (interior) Nash equilibrium action profile $\boldsymbol{s}^*$ of the game satisfies

$$[\boldsymbol{I} - \beta \boldsymbol{G}]\boldsymbol{s}^* = \boldsymbol{b}. \tag{4.28}$$

The *spectral radius* of a matrix is the maximum of its eigenvalues' absolute values. Let us denote the eigenvalues of matrix $G$ by $\lambda_1(G), \ldots, \lambda_n(G)$ and suppose that they are ordered from highest to lowest. The key assumption we will make is as follows.

**Assumption 4.1** *The spectral radius of $\beta \boldsymbol{G}$ is less than 1 (i.e., $\lambda_1(G) < 1/\beta$).*

Under this condition, equation (4.28) is a necessary and sufficient condition for a solution to the game. This condition also ensures the uniqueness (and stability) of the Nash equilibrium. The interested reader is referred to Bramoullé and Kranton (2016) for a discussion on this condition..

The eigenvalues provide us a measure of the amplification of spillovers via connections in the network. The assumption places a bound on the magnitude of the spillovers in relation to the parameter $\beta$: note in particular that the restriction on the matrix is stricter in inverse proportion to the value of $\beta$.

Under assumption 4.1, the unique Nash equilibrium of the game is given by

$$s^* = [\boldsymbol{I} - \beta \boldsymbol{G}]^{-1} \boldsymbol{b}. \tag{4.29}$$

We now use this characterization to develop a relation between network structure and behavior.

If we suppose that $\beta$ is a small enough number, then the inverse

$$[I - \beta \mathbf{G}]^{-1} \mathbf{1}, \tag{4.30}$$

is well defined. Recalling our discussion on Katz-Bonacich centrality vector from chapter 1, we may write

$$C_b(g, \beta) = [I - \beta G]^{-1} \mathbf{1}. \tag{4.31}$$

Recall in particular that Katz-Bonacich centrality summarizes the sum of weighted walks of varying lengths in the network:

$$C_b(i; g, \beta) = \sum_{j=1}^{n} \sum_{k} \beta^{k-1} m_{ij}^{k}(g, \beta), \tag{4.32}$$

where $m_{ij}^{k}(g, \beta)$ is the number of weighted walks of length $k$ between players $i$ and $j$ in network $g$.

These observations are summarized as follows.

**Proposition 4.5** *Suppose assumption 4.1 is satisfied and payoffs are given by equation (4.28). There exists a unique equilibrium*

$$s^* = [\boldsymbol{I} - \beta \boldsymbol{G}]^{-1} \boldsymbol{b}. \tag{4.33}$$

*Equilibrium actions are proportional to Katz-Bonacich centralities of individual players.*

It is helpful to work through some examples to appreciate how the content of interaction (complements versus substitutes) and the structure of the network shapes individual behavior.

Consider example 4.8. The stand-alone benefit $b_i$ is set equal to 1 for every $i \in N$. In the game of substitutes, the spillover parameter is set to $\beta = -0.05$; in the games

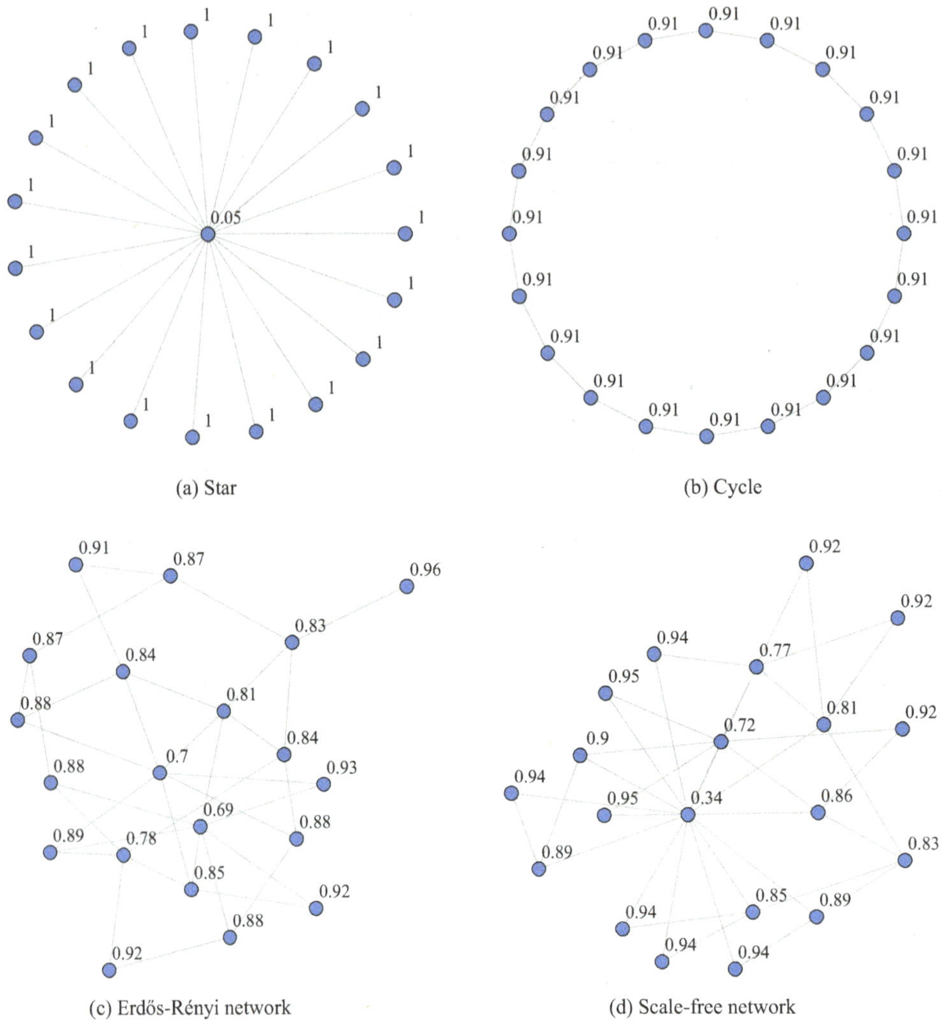


**Figure 4.9**
Centrality and effort: substitutes.

of complements, $\beta = 0.05$. The equilibrium is as in equation (4.29). Figure 4.9 presents equilibrium actions under strategic substitutes in four networks—the star, the cycle, an Erdős-Rényi network (with $n = 20, p = 0.20$) and a scale-free network (with $n = 20$, Pareto coefficient $= 1.33$). Figure 4.10 presents behavior under strategic complements in the same networks.

These figures draw our attention to a number of points. First, we see that in games of complements, as $\beta > 0$, efforts are positively reinforced as we move along a walk. Thus

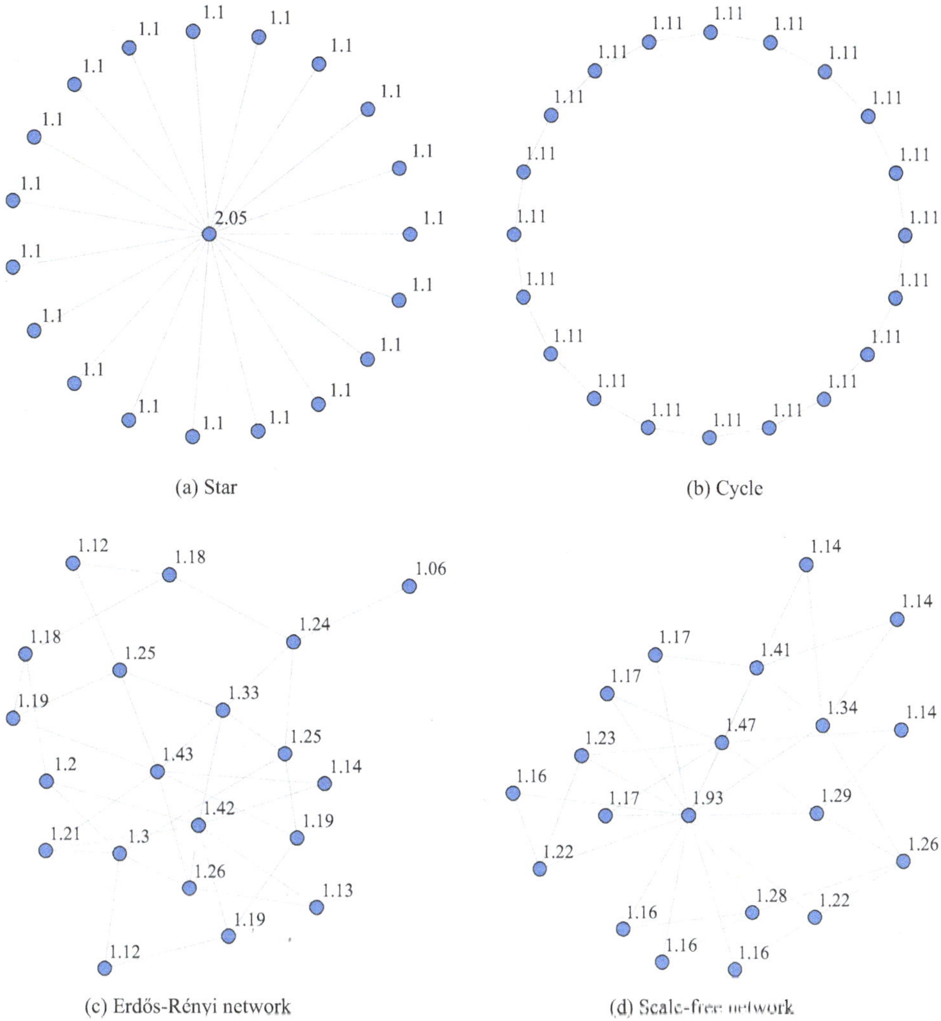


**Figure 4.10**
Centrality and effort: complements.

individuals who are connected to other well-connected individuals have the highest centrality and make the highest efforts. On the other hand, in games of substitutes, as $\beta < 0$, the effects alternate: a higher effort by $i$ lowers the incentives of her neighbors, and this in turn pushes up the incentives of $i$'s neighbors' neighbors, and so forth. This yields the interesting observation that in such games, the hub of the star network chooses the smallest effort. Similar results occur in the scale-free network; the nodes connected to other highly connected nodes choose the highest effort under complements and the smallest effort under substitutes.

The second point to note is that connections raise the effort level in games of complements compared to games of substitutes: in the cycle, players choose a higher activity level under complements. Finally, observe that for games of complements, the range of effort is greater under the scale-free network than under the Erdős-Rényi network with the same average degree (3.5). This is a consequence of the greater dispersion in the centralities in the scale-free network.

The study of continuous action games provides us with a clear prediction of the relation between network location and individual behavior. We now use this characterization to make some remarks on individual utility and social welfare.

We will stay with example 4.8 in this exercise. Consider the star network presented in the figures 4.9 and 4.10. Observe that the hub chooses relatively higher effort in the complements game compared to the strategic substitutes case. The hub also earns a higher payoff in the strategic complements game than in the strategic substitutes game. Thus, in the strategic complements case, centrality yields payoff advantages, and these advantages can be quite large as we move toward scale-free networks. On the other hand, higher connectivity translates into lower payoffs in the strategic substitutes case. Figure 4.11 presents a snapshot of payoffs in selected networks with games of both complements and substitutes to bring out this point.

Turning to social welfare, a first remark is that in games with positive externalities, individual efforts are generally too low relative to what is collectively desirable: this holds true for games of complements. In the game of strategic substitutes the externalities are negative, and, as a result, the efforts are too large relative to the social optimum. This wedge between individual optimum/equilibrium and what is collectively desirable suggests that there is space for interventions that can enhance social welfare. We will study optimal interventions in networks in section 4.6.

Before we conclude, let us note that we have studied games with linear best responses and assumed that players have complete knowledge of the network. It is possible to study such games in a setting with local network knowledge. Indeed, the arguments developed in section 4.4 can be carried over to a fairly general class of payoffs that include games with compact and convex strategy sets (with a restriction that individual payoffs remain anonymous and depend only on the sum of neighbors' actions). See Galeotti, Goyal, Jackson et al. (2010).

With these assumptions in place, it is possible to show that there always exists an equilibrium involving monotone (symmetric) strategies in degrees. In games with strategic substitutes, equilibrium actions are nonincreasing in players' degrees, and in games of strategic complements, equilibrium actions are nondecreasing in the degree of players. In turn, the monotonicity property of equilibrium actions implies that with positive externalities, social connections create personal advantages regardless of whether the game exhibits strategic complements or substitutes: higher degree players earn more than lower degree players. This implies in particular that in games of strategic substitutes, higher degree

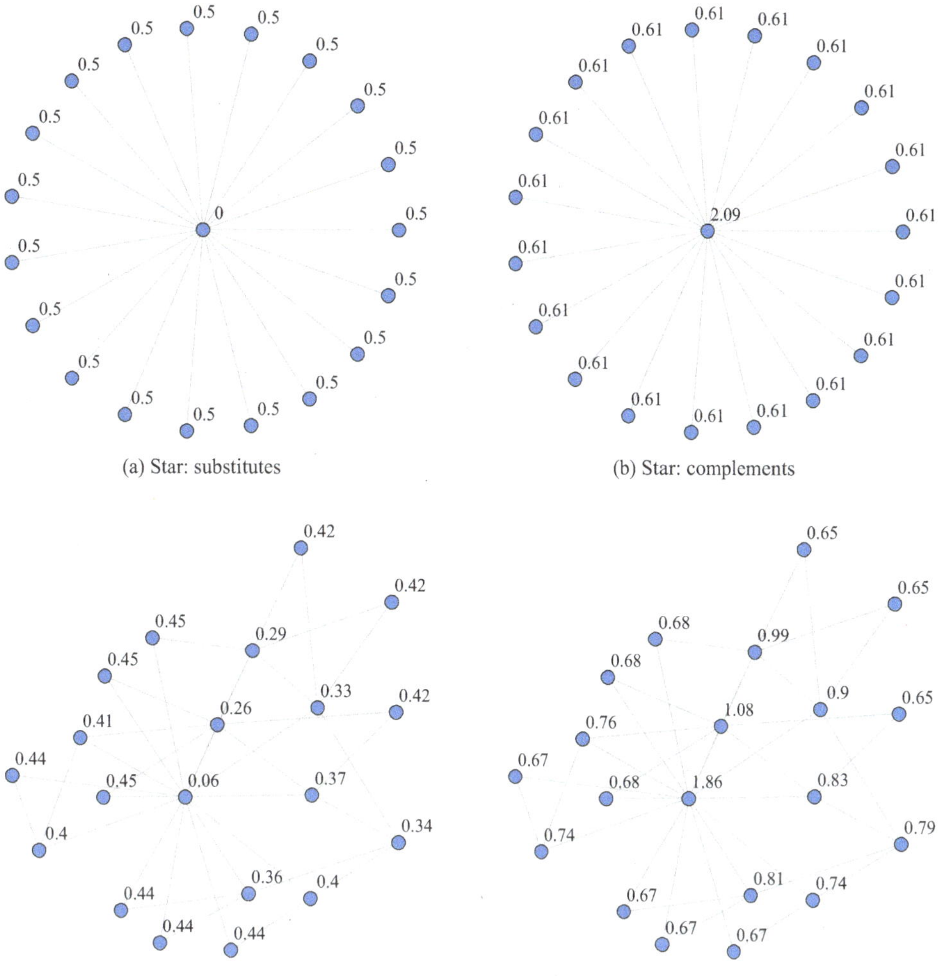


(a) Star: substitutes
(b) Star: complements
(c) Scale free: substitutes
(d) Scale-free: complements

**Figure 4.11**
Centrality and payoffs.

individuals undertake *lower* efforts and earn *higher* payoffs. The results on changes in networks can similarly be extended: an increase in connectivity is modeled in terms of the notion of first-order stochastic dominance of degree distributions. In games of strategic complements, this has unambiguous effects, raising the action for every degree and for the average neighbor. For full statements and proofs of these claims, the interested reader is urged to consult Galeotti, Goyal, Jackson et al. (2010).

## 4.6 Intervening in a Network to Influence Behavior

Our study of strategic interaction on networks reveals that equilibrium outcomes are generally socially suboptimal. This is because individual actions give rise to externalities and individuals do not take these externalities into account in their decision-making. One way to address this problem is to adjust the individual marginal returns in such a way that they are brought more in line with the social returns. However, an intervention on one individual has direct and indirect effects on the incentives of others. For example, suppose that the planner increases a given individual's stand-alone marginal returns to effort, thereby increasing their effort. If actions are strategic complements, this will push up the incentives of the targeted individual's neighbors. That will increase the efforts of the neighbors of these neighbors, and so forth, creating aligned feedback effects throughout the network. If actions are strategic substitutes, the same intervention will discourage the individual's neighbors from exerting effort. However, the effect on those neighbors' neighbors will be positive (i.e., in the same direction as the effect on the targeted agent). This interplay between spillovers and network structure makes targeting interventions a complex problem. The aim of this section is to develop general principles for how to take into account these direct and indirect effects. Our discussion is based on Galeotti, Golub, and Goyal (2020).

We will consider a simultaneous-move game among individuals as analyzed in section 4.5, and assume that links are symmetric and that assumption 4.1 holds. Equipped with these assumptions, we know from section 4.5 that there is a unique Nash equilibrium of the game. For easy reference we recall the equation that characterizes this equilibrium:

$$\boldsymbol{s}^* = [\boldsymbol{I} - \beta \boldsymbol{G}]^{-1}\boldsymbol{b}. \tag{4.34}$$

Let us now turn to the intervention problem: The external agent, the planner, whom we shall think of as a utilitarian, seeks to maximize the sum of utilities. Let us define aggregate utility as follows:

$$W(\boldsymbol{b}, \boldsymbol{G}) = \sum_{i \in N} U_i(\boldsymbol{s}^*, \boldsymbol{G}). \tag{4.35}$$

The planner aims to maximize this aggregate utility by changing a vector of status quo, stand-alone marginal returns $\hat{\boldsymbol{b}}$ to a vector $\boldsymbol{b}$ subject to a budget constraint.

The timing of this intervention is as follows. The planner moves first and chooses their intervention, and then individuals simultaneously choose actions. The planner's maximization problem is given by

$$\max_{\boldsymbol{b}} W(\boldsymbol{b}, \boldsymbol{G}) \tag{4.36}$$

$$\text{s.t.: } \boldsymbol{s}^* = [\boldsymbol{I} - \beta \boldsymbol{G}]^{-1}\boldsymbol{b},$$

$$K(\boldsymbol{b}, \hat{\boldsymbol{b}}) = \sum_{i \in N} \left(b_i - \hat{b}_i\right)^2 \leq C,$$

where $C$ is a given budget. Function $K$ represents an adjustment cost for implementing interventions.

We note that the cost function is separable across individuals and increasing in the magnitude of the change to each individual's incentives. This is a very simple formulation and it helps us to get at the basic insights in a straightforward way.

Our final assumption is as follows.

**Assumption 4.2** *The aggregate equilibrium utility is proportional to the sum of the squares of the equilibrium actions; that is, $W(\boldsymbol{b}, \boldsymbol{G}) = w \cdot (\boldsymbol{s}^*)^\tau \boldsymbol{s}^*$ for some $w \in \mathbb{R}$, where $\boldsymbol{s}^*$ is the Nash equilibrium action profile.*

Assumption 4.2 is satisfied by example 4.8; it is also satisfied by the crime example in section 4.2.

We now introduce a basis for the space of stand-alone marginal returns and actions in which, under our assumptions on $\boldsymbol{G}$, strategic effects and the planner's objective both take a simple form. For expositional simplicity, we restrict attention to networks that are symmetric, i.e., for every pair $i$ and $j$, $g_{ij} = g_{ji}$.

**Fact** *If $\boldsymbol{G}$ is symmetric, then $\boldsymbol{G} = \boldsymbol{U}\boldsymbol{\Lambda}\boldsymbol{U}^\tau$, where*

1. *$\boldsymbol{\Lambda}$ is an $n \times n$ diagonal matrix whose diagonal entries $\Lambda_{\ell\ell} = \lambda_\ell$ are the eigenvalues of $\boldsymbol{G}$ (which are real numbers), ordered from greatest to smallest: $\lambda_1 \geq \lambda_2 \geq \ldots \geq \lambda_n$.*
2. *$\boldsymbol{U}$ is an orthogonal matrix. The $\ell$th column of $\boldsymbol{U}$, which we call $\boldsymbol{u}^\ell$, is a real eigenvector—namely, the eigenvector associated with the eigenvalue $\lambda_\ell$, which is normalized so that $\|\boldsymbol{u}^\ell\| = 1$ (in the Euclidean norm).*

For generic $\boldsymbol{G}$, the decomposition described in Fact above is uniquely determined, except that any column of $\boldsymbol{U}$ is determined only up to multiplication by $-1$. The *$\ell$th* eigenvector of $\boldsymbol{G}$, which we denote by $\boldsymbol{u}^\ell(\boldsymbol{G})$, corresponds to the $\ell$th principal component of $\boldsymbol{G}$.

An important interpretation of this diagonalization is as a decomposition into *principal components*. First, consider the vector that best approximates $\boldsymbol{G}$ in the squared-error sense—equivalently, the vector $\boldsymbol{u}$ such that

$$\sum_{i,j \in N} (g_{ij} - u_i u_j)^2 \tag{4.37}$$

is minimized. The minimizer turns out to be a scaling of the eigenvector $\boldsymbol{u}^1$. Now, if we consider the "residual" matrix $\boldsymbol{G}^{(2)} = \boldsymbol{G} - \boldsymbol{u}^1(\boldsymbol{u}^1)^\tau$, we can perform the same type of decomposition on $\boldsymbol{G}^{(2)}$ and obtain the second eigenvector $\boldsymbol{u}^2$ as the best rank-one approximation. Proceeding further in this way gives a sequence of vectors that constitute an orthonormal basis. At each step, the next vector generates the rank-one matrix that "best summarizes" the remaining structure in matrix $\boldsymbol{G}$.

We can think of the columns of $\boldsymbol{G}$ as $n$ data points. The first principal component of $\boldsymbol{G}$ is defined as the $n$-dimensional vector that minimizes the sum of squares of the distances to

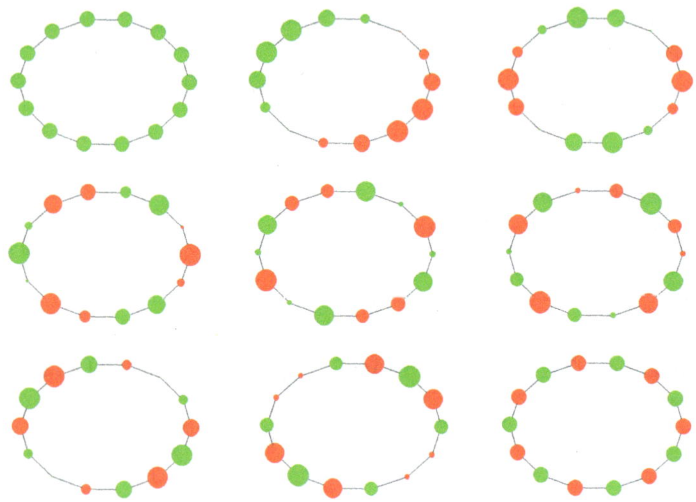

**Figure 4.12**
(top) Eigenvectors 1, 3, 5; (middle) eigenvectors 7, 9, 11; (bottom) eigenvectors 12, 13, 14.

the columns of $\boldsymbol{G}$. The first principal component can therefore be thought of as a fictitious column that "best summarizes" the data set of all columns of $\boldsymbol{G}$. To characterize the next principal component, we orthogonally project all columns of $\boldsymbol{G}$ off this vector and repeat this procedure for the new columns. We continue in this way, projecting orthogonally off the subspace generated by vectors obtained to date, to find the next principal component. A well-known result is that the eigenvectors of $\boldsymbol{G}$ that diagonalize the matrix (i.e., the columns of $\boldsymbol{U}$) are indeed the principal components of $\boldsymbol{G}$ in this sense. Moreover, the eigenvalue corresponding to a given principal component quantifies the residual variation explained by that vector.

Figure 4.12 illustrates some eigenvectors/principal components of a circle network with 14 nodes, where the links all have equal weight, given by 1. For each eigenvector, the color of a node indicates the sign of the entry of that node in that eigenvector (red means negative), while the size of a node indicates the absolute value of that entry. Note that the circle network is invariant to rotations (cyclic permutations) of the nodes, so the eigenvectors are determined only up to a rotation. A general feature worth noting is that the entries of the top eigenvectors (with smaller values of $\ell$) are similar among neighboring nodes, while the bottom eigenvectors (with larger values of $\ell$) tend to be negatively correlated among neighboring nodes.

### 4.6.1 Analysis of the Game Using Principal Components

For any vector $z \in \mathbb{R}^n$, let $\underline{z} = \boldsymbol{U}^\tau z$. We will refer to $\underline{z}_\ell$ as the projection of $z$ onto the $\ell$th principal component or the magnitude of $z$ in that component. Setting the expression $\boldsymbol{G} =$

$\boldsymbol{U}\boldsymbol{\Lambda}\boldsymbol{U}^{\tau}$ into equation (4.28), we obtain

$$[\boldsymbol{I} - \beta \boldsymbol{U}\boldsymbol{\Lambda}\boldsymbol{U}^{\tau}]s^* = \boldsymbol{b}. \tag{4.38}$$

Multiplying both sides of this equation by $\boldsymbol{U}^{\tau}$ gives us an analog of equation (4.34):

$$[\boldsymbol{I} - \beta\boldsymbol{\Lambda}]\underline{s}^* = \underline{\boldsymbol{b}} \qquad \Longleftrightarrow \qquad \underline{s}^* = [\boldsymbol{I} - \beta\boldsymbol{\Lambda}]^{-1}\underline{\boldsymbol{b}}.$$

This system is diagonal, and the $\ell$th diagonal entry of $[\boldsymbol{I} - \beta\boldsymbol{\Lambda}]^{-1}$ is $\frac{1}{1-\beta\lambda_\ell}$. Hence, for every $\ell \in \{1, 2, \ldots, n\}$,

$$\underline{s}^*_\ell = \frac{1}{1-\beta\lambda_\ell}\underline{b}_\ell. \tag{4.39}$$

The principal components of $\boldsymbol{G}$ constitute a basis in which strategic effects are easily described. The equilibrium action $\underline{s}^*_\ell$ in the $\ell$th principal component of $\boldsymbol{G}$ is the product of an amplification factor (determined by the strategic parameter $\beta$ and the eigenvalue $\lambda_\ell$) and $\underline{b}_\ell$, which is simply the projection of $\boldsymbol{b}$ onto that principal component. Under assumption 4.1, for all $\ell$, we have $1 - \beta\lambda_\ell > 0$. This assumption on the spectral radius also implies that $\beta\boldsymbol{\Lambda}$ has no entries larger than 1. Finally, observe that if $\beta > 0$ ($\beta < 0$), the amplification factor is decreasing (increasing) in $\ell$.

We can also use this to give a formula for equilibrium actions in the original coordinates as follows:

$$s_i^* = \sum_{\ell=1}^{n} \frac{1}{1-\beta\lambda_\ell} u_i^\ell \underline{b}_\ell. \tag{4.40}$$

Figure 4.13 depicts the optimal intervention in an example where the budget is large. We consider an 11-node undirected network with binary links containing two hubs, $L_0$ and $R_0$, that are connected by an intermediate node $M$. The network is shown in figure 4.13(a). The

(a) The network and status-quo standalone marginal returns

(b) Eigenvectors and interventions

**Figure 4.13**
An example of optimal interventions with large budgets. Taken from Galeotti, Golub, and Goyal (2020).

numbers next to the nodes are the ex-ante, stand-alone marginal returns; the budget is set to $C=500$ (about 125 times larger than $\|\hat{\boldsymbol{b}}\|^2$). Payoffs are as in example 4.8. For the case of strategic complements, we set $\beta=0.1$, and for strategic substitutes, we set $\beta=-0.1$. The top left of figure 4.13(b) illustrates the first eigenvector, and the top right depicts the optimal intervention in a game with strategic complements. The bottom left of figure 4.13(b) illustrates the last eigenvector, and the bottom right depicts the optimal intervention when the game has strategic substitutes. The node size represents the size of the intervention, $|b_i^* - \hat{b}_i|$; node shading represents the sign of the intervention, with green signifying a positive intervention and red indicating a negative intervention.

For large budgets, $C$, the optimal intervention is guided by the "main" component of the network. Under strategic complements, this is the first (largest-eigenvalue) eigenvector of the network, whose entries are individuals' eigenvector centralities. By increasing the stand-alone marginal return of each individual in proportion to their eigenvector centrality, the planner targets the individuals in proportion to their global contributions to strategic feedback. On the other hand, under strategic substitutes, optimal targeting is determined by the last eigenvector of the network (corresponding to its smallest eigenvalue). The last eigenvector contains information about the local structure of the network: it determines a way to partition the set of nodes into two sets so that most of the links are across individuals in different sets. The optimal intervention increases the stand-alone marginal returns of all individuals in one set and decreases those of individuals in the other set. This asymmetric targeting reduces crowding-out effects that occur due to the strategic substitutes property.

Let us summarize what we have learned in this section: games on networks exhibit positive and negative externalities. The equilibrium of these games will therefore generally be socially suboptimal. We studied the question of how scarce resources can be used to target specific nodes in a network so as to maximize social welfare. The key to the approach we studied is a particular way to organize the direct and indirect spillover effects of interventions in terms of the principal components/eigenvectors of the matrix of interactions. In particular, any change in individual marginal returns can be expressed in terms of these principal components. This formulation allows us to describe the magnitude of the effect of the change in marginal rewards as a product of the intervention and a multiplier that is determined by an eigenvalue of the network corresponding to that principal component. As the principal components are orthogonal, the effects along various principal components can be treated separately. This formulation yields a clear-cut optimal intervention when the budget is large: target the first eigenvector in games of complements and the last eigenvector in games of strategic substitutes.

## 4.7 Reading Notes

This chapter studies how human behavior is shaped by network structure. It is impossible to do justice to the extraordinarily wide-ranging literature on this subject in one chapter. Goyal (2007) and Jackson (2008) provide good reviews of the early literature, while Jackson and Zenou (2015) and Bramoullé and Kranton (2016) provide more recent reviews of the theoretical literature. Jackson, Rogers, and Zenou et al. (2017) give a more general overview of how networks affect behavior.

Games on networks has been an active field of research for close to three decades. In the early 1990s, Blume (1993) and Ellison (1993) introduced the study of binary action coordination problems among players located on simple networks like the cycle and a lattice. The study of coordination problems is taken up in chapter 12, on social coordination. In this chapter, in order to develop a basic understanding of how network structure and the content of interactions matter, we start with two binary games—the best-shot and weakest-link games, inspired from Hirshleifer (1983). Shachter (1986) and Koller and Milch (2003) introduced the notion of multiagent influence diagrams to study social strategic interaction. Kearns, Littman, and Singh (2001) introduced *graphical games* and provided algorithms to solve for Nash equilibria in binary action local interaction games.

We present a number of examples on how networks affect behavior. Let us place these examples in the broader context of the literature. The best-shot and weakest-link games should be seen as a metaphor for a wide range of situations in which actions exhibit substitutes and complements properties. The concepts of strategic complements and substitutes will be useful throughout the book, especially in chapters 5, 7, 8, 10–12, 16–17, and 19.

Research collaboration among firms from Goyal and Moraga-González (2001) is an early example of a continuous action game on a network. There is a large body of literature on research alliances and competition among firms. For an overview of the empirical trends, see Hagedoorn (2002) and König, Rohner, Thoenig, and Zilibotti (2019). We will discuss this application in detail in chapter 16 on networked markets.

Bramoullé and Kranton (2007a) introduce the study of local public goods in networks: they also introduces the concept of *maximally independent sets* as a solution to a game of local public goods in networks. There is a large body of literature that elaborates on various aspects of this game and applies it to various contexts. We will take up models of strategic substitutes in combination with a game of network formation in chapter 11, on the Law of the Few.

The weakest-link game we study in this chapter is a variation on the classical weakest-link game proposed by Hirshleifer (1983). In the original game, payoffs depend on the minimum action, and thus they are positive only if a player and their contacts all choose action 1. We take the smoother variant studied in this chapter from Galeotti, Goyal, Jackson et al. (2010). Gagnon and Goyal (2017) introduce the concept of q-core to solve this game when players have complete information on the network. We will further use the q-core in chapter 17 to study the relation between social networks and markets.

The economic study of criminal activity starts with Becker (1968). Empirical evidence on the role of social interactions in shaping criminal activity is presented in Glaeser, Sacerdote, and Scheinkman (1996). For an overview of the recent literature on criminal networks, see Lindquist and Zenou (2019). The model of criminal activity in networks was taken from Ballester, Calvo-Armengol, and Zenou (2006).

The study of relative consumption effects may be traced to the early work of Veblen (1973) and Duesenbury (1949). In recent decades, interest in relative consumption effects has been revived by the collection of empirical evidence on these effects (e.g., Luttmer (2005); Kuhn, Kooreman, Soetevent, and Kapteyn [2011]). This strand of work is also closely related to the ideas of subjective and relative nature of happiness that has been developed by Richard Layard and others (see e.g., Layard 2011). The model we presented was taken from Ghiglino and Goyal (2010). For further theoretical explorations of the role of relative status in networks, see Immorlica, Kranton, Manea et al. (2017).

Ballester, Calvó-Armengol, and Zenou (2006) study continuous action games with strategic complements. They introduce the concept of *Katz-Bonacich centrality* as a method to solve such games. A large strand of subsequent research applies the idea of Katz-Bonacich centrality to understand behavior in networks; for an overview of some of this work and for references to the literature, see Jackson and Zenou (2015). We will discuss Katz-Bonacich to study behavior in network games again in chapter 5 (on production networks) and in chapter 10 (on the Great War of Congo).

The literature on games with linear-best responses proceeds under the assumption that the spillovers are sufficiently small. In an important advance, Bramoullé, Kranton, and D'Amours (2014) propose an approach, based on potential functions, that generalizes the study of Nash equilibria to allow constrained action sets. The concept of a potential function is proposed by Monderer and Shapley (1996). For an introduction to potential functions and an application to study of coordination problems, see chapter 12.

The models described in sections 4.3 and 4.5 assume that individuals know the entire network. A parallel strand of the literature explores behavior in networks when individuals have only local knowledge of the network. Examples of such games are studied by Sundararajan (2005) and Galeotti and Vega-Redondo (2011). Galeotti, Goyal, Jackson et al. (2010) present a general framework for the study of games when individuals have limited information on the network. Their framework allows binary action games as well as continuous action games (and it also allows for nonlinear best responses). The predictions of these models were experimentally studied in Charness, Feri, Meléndez-Jiménez, and Sutter (2014).

The problem of intervening by targeting "key players" is well known in the networks literature. For an early discussion of "key player" see Borgatti (2003). In the economics literature, the problem of the key player is introduced by Ballester, Calvó-Armengol, and Zenou (2006): they study the issue of which nodes to eliminate in order to minimize the sum of criminal activity in the network. In this chapter, we present the intervention problem of a utilitarian planner with a budget constraint who targets individuals that are playing a game on a network. The problem of network interventions will be taken up again in chapter 10 (on attack and defense in networks), in chapter 15 (on optimal seeds for the diffusion of innovations) and in chapter 16 (on optimal advertising and pricing in networked markets). The "key player" problem may be seen as a specific type of intervention in networks. For an overview of the literature on "key player" problem, see Zenou (2016). The exposition in section 4.6 was based on Galeotti, Golub, and Goyal (2020). For an application of this intervention approach to coordination problems in networks, see Galeotti, Golub, Goyal, and Rao (2021) and for an application to optimal tax-subsidy schemes in oligopoly, see Galeotti, Golub, Goyal et al. (2022).

## 4.8 Questions

1. Show that every network contains a maximal independent set.
2. Show that in any network there is a unique q-core and that the algorithm outlined in the chapter identifies this q-core.
3. Fix $n=6$. Consider the best-shot game. Fix $c=1/2$. Compute the equilibrium in the circle, complete, and star networks. Define social welfare as the sum of individual utilities. Compute social welfare in the different equilibria.
4. Fix $n=6$. Consider the weakest-link game. Set $c=1/2$. Compute the equilibrium in the circle, complete, and star networks. Also, compute social welfare in the active equilibria.
5. Fix $n=6$. Consider the following variant of the weakest-link game. Given a network $g$, and a strategy profile $s$, the payoffs of an individual $i$ are

$$\Pi_i(s|g) = s_i \Pi_{j\in N_i(g)} s_j - cs_i \tag{4.41}$$

   (a) Set $c=1/2$. Compute equilibria in the circle, complete, and star networks. Also, compute social welfare in the active equilibria.
   (b) Set $c=1.2$. Compute equilibria in the circle, complete, and star networks. Also, compute social welfare in the active equilibria.
6. Consider the best-shot game. Set $c=25/64$. Suppose that degrees take on values 1, 2, and 3, and the degrees of neighbors are independent. Therefore, there is a unique symmetric equilibrium that is nonincreasing and it is fully characterized by a threshold. This question works through the computation of thresholds.
   (a) Let us start with initial beliefs $P$ that assign probability one-half to neighboring players having degrees 1 and 2. Show that in the unique symmetric equilibrium, degree 1 players choose 1 with probability 1, whereas degree 2 players choose 1 with probability 0.
   (b) Recall from chapter 1 that a degree distribution $P$ first-order stochastically dominates another degree distribution $P'$ if for every degree $k$, the cumulative distribution $\sum_0^k P(d) \leq \sum_0^k P'(d)$. Consider a first-order stochastic dominance shift of degree distributions such that neighboring players are believed to have degrees 2

and 3 with probability one-half each. Show that the unique equilibrium involves degree 2 players choosing action 1 with probability 3/4, whereas degree 3 players choose 1 with probability 0.

(c) Show that the threshold degree 2 player has lower expectation of action 1 under $P'$ compared to $P$.

7. (Bramoullé and Kranton [2007a]). Consider a game in which $n$ players are located on nodes of an undirected network $g$. Players simultaneously choose actions $x_i \in \mathcal{R}_+$. Let $N_i(g)$ be the set of players with whom player $i$ has a link in network $g$. The payoffs of player $i$ faced with a strategy profile $x$ are given by

$$\Pi_i(x) = f(x_i + \sum_{j \in N_i(g)} x_j) - cx_i, \tag{4.42}$$

where $f(0) = 0, f'(.) > 0$ and $f''(.) < 0$ and $c > 0$. Suppose that there is a number $\hat{x} > 0$, such that $f'(\hat{x}) = c$.

(a) Show that in every nonempty network, there is an equilibrium with specialization: some players choose $\hat{x}$ and others choose 0.

(b) Show that there are only two equilibria in the star network, one in which only the center contributes and the other in which only the spokes contribute.

(c) Define social welfare as the sum of individual utilities. Discuss the merits of different networks from a social welfare point of view.

(d) Define the costs of decentralization as the ratio of social welfare from the social optimum choice of effort versus the social welfare from the lowest welfare Nash equilibrium. Compute this ratio for the star network with $n$ players.

8. (Bramoullé and Kranton [2016]). Consider a simultaneous move game on networks. Suppose that the best response of agent $i \in N$ is given by:

$$s_i(g) = 1 - \delta \sum_{j \neq i} g_{ij} s_j.$$

Suppose that $n = 5$ and let players be located on a line network starting with player 1 at one end and going to player 5 at the other end.

(a) Suppose $\beta = 0.3$. Compute the Nash equilibrium.

(b) Suppose $\beta = -0.3$. Compute the Nash equilibrium.

9. Consider a simultaneous action game played on an undirected network as in the criminal activity example in section 4.2.1. Suppose the payoffs to player $i$ faced under strategy profile $s$ are given by

$$\Pi_i(s) = 0.5 s_i - \frac{1}{2} s_i^2 + 0.01 \sum_{j \neq i} g_{ij} s_i s_j. \tag{4.43}$$

(a) Fix $n = 6$. Compute the equilibrium efforts in a complete, circle, star, and line network.

(b) Fix $n = 6$ Compute the equilibria for complete, circle, star, and line networks when the payoff is

$$\Pi_i(s) = 0.5s_i - \frac{1}{2}s_i^2 + 0.02 \sum_{j \neq i} g_{ij}s_is_j. \tag{4.44}$$

10. (Goyal and Moraga-González [2001]). Consider the model of research collaboration among firms presented in section 4.2.1.

    (a) Consider regular networks of degree $d$. Compute equilibrium in research efforts as a function of the degree $d$. Show that individual effort is falling, firm costs are initially falling but eventually increasing, while firm profits are initially rising but eventually falling as a function of degree $d$.

    (b) Compute the equilibrium efforts and profits of the hub and spoke firms in the star network.

11. (Goyal and Ghiglino [2010]). Consider the relative consumption model that was presented in section 4.2.1. Let the price for good $x$ be a numeraire and set it equal to 1, and let the price of good $y$ be denoted by $p_y$. Suppose that all households have the same initial income given by $\omega$. Fix some network $g$.

    (a) Define the general equilibrium in this economy.

    (b) Compute the general equilibrium prices as a function of network $g$.

    (c) Compute the equilibrium consumption of households as a function of their network position.

12. Consider the networks presented in figure 4.8. Show that the strategies specified as equilibria in the main text are equilibria when we take into the account the correlations in the degree of neighbors.

13. Show that equilibrium in games of example 4.8 satisfies assumption 4.2 in section 4.6.

14. Consider a star network with undirected binary links. Derive the eigenvalues and eigenvectors of the adjacency matrix corresponding to this network.

15. Suppose the game being played is as described in example 4.8. Fix a star network (with symmetric links) and say $n = 5$. Compute optimal interventions for $b_i = 0.10$ for all $i$, and for $\beta = 0.05$ and $\beta = -0.05$ and large budget (say) $C = 300$.

16. (Bourlès, Bramoullé, and Perez-Richet [2017]). There are $n$ agents. Agent $i$ has income $y_i^0 \geq 0$ and makes transfer $t_{ij} \geq 0$ to agent $j$. Income after transfers is equal to

$$y_i = y_i^0 - \sum_j t_{ij} + \sum_k t_{ki} \tag{4.45}$$

where $\sum_j t_{ij}$ represents overall transfers made by $i$, while $\sum_k t_{ki}$ represents overall transfers made to $i$. Agents care about each other. Agent $i$ has a private utility over her own consumption, and she is also potentially altruistic toward others:

$$v_i(\mathbf{y}) = u_i(y_i) + \sum_j \alpha_{ij} u_j(y_j), \tag{4.46}$$

where $u_i$ reflects utility from private consumption (it is twice differentiable and satisfies $u_i' > 0$ and $u_i'' < 00$). The coefficient $\alpha_{ij}$, with $0 \le \alpha_{ij} < 1$, measures the strength of the altruistic link that $i$ has toward $j$. Suppose that all individuals have CARA (Constant absolute risk aversion) utility functions: $\forall i,\ u_i(y) = -e^{-Ay}$.

(a) Consider the two-agent economy and fix initial incomes $y_1^0$ and $y_2^0$, and suppose that $-\ln(\alpha_{ij})/A = -\ln(\alpha_{ji})/A = 1$. Show that a Nash equilibrium in transfers is such that (i) $y_1 - y_2 \le 1$, $y_2 - y_1 \le 1$, $t_{12} > 0 \Rightarrow y_1 - y_2 = 1$ and $t_{21} > 0 \Rightarrow y_2 - y_1 = 1$. (ii) if $|y_1^0 - y_2^0| \le 1 \Leftrightarrow y_1^0 - y_2^0 \le 1$ and $y_2^0 - y_1^0 \le 1$, then no transfers is the unique Nash equilibrium. (iii) If 1 is richer. If 1 is richer than 2 and $y_1^0 - y_2^0 > 1$, then $y_1 - y_2 = 1$ and 1 gives to 2 the amount needed to reach this situation.

(b) Consider a line network with three agents, and with agent 2 at the center; suppose that $y_1^0 = 5$, $y_2^0 = 5$, and $y_3^0 = 1$. Compute the equilibrium.

# II ECONOMIC NETWORKS

# 5 Production and Supply Chains

## 5.1 Introduction

> Layman and professional economist alike, practical planner and the subjects of his regulative activities, all are equally aware of the existence of some kind of interconnection between even the remotest parts of a national economy [...] The presence of these invisible but nevertheless very real ties can be observed whenever expanded automobile sales in New York City increase the demand for groceries in Detroit, [...] when the sudden shutdown of the Pennsylvania coal mines paralyzes the textile mills in New England, and it reasserts itself with relentless regularity in alternative ups and downs of business cycles.
> —Leontief (1941), p. 3.

Following the March 11, 2011, earthquake in Japan, physical infrastructure was destroyed and over 19,000 people lost their lives. But the effects of this earthquake were not limited to the local economy; they were felt widely across the entire Japanese economy. As Kim and Reynolds (2011) reported:

> Supply chain disruptions in Japan have forced at least one global auto maker to delay the launch of two new models and are forcing other industries to shutter plants (...) The auto maker is just one of dozens, if not hundreds, of Japanese manufacturers facing disruptions to their supply chains as a result of the quake, the subsequent tsunami and a still-unresolved nuclear threat.

This episode raises a number of questions. How do shocks spread through a production system, and how can firms mitigate the impact of these shocks?

To study these questions, we develop a model of a production economy. There are a number of sectors, each producing a distinct good. These goods are used in households and can also be used as inputs into production of other goods. An example of such a good is a computer. The quantity of inputs from a sector used by another sector defines a link between the two. Households supply labor to production firms, and they use the income they earn from their work to buy goods and services. In every sector, there is a technology of production;

firms choose a mix of inputs in order to produce an output. Market prices help coordinate input demands and supplies across firms and consumers.

We first take up the issue of what determines the size of a sector. This size will depend on how important it is for other sectors (in other words, how much of its output is used as an input in other sectors). In addition, there is the indirect demand: a sector's output may be used as an input by a few sectors, but these sectors may in turn be used as inputs in a great many other sectors. Thus the size of a sector is determined by the sum of direct and indirect demands of its output. These demands are reflected in the "walks" of various lengths in the production network of the economy. In chapter 1, we showed that the Katz-Bonacich centrality summarizes all the walks in a network. This observation yields us the following insight: the size of a sector will be proportional to its Katz-Bonacich centrality in the production network. Equipped with this result, we examine input-output data from a number of countries. We find that the distribution of the centrality is very unequal: a few sectors dominate their respective economies.

We then study the role of central sectors—the hubs—in amplifying sectoral shocks and in generating large-scale fluctuations in economic activity. Individual sectors face a variety of shocks—some positive and others negative. One might expect that as the sectors face shocks emanating from distinct sources, and as the sectors are individually small, the shocks will cancel out, and in the aggregate, the economy will be relatively unperturbed. The model of a production network allows us to explore the scope of this intuition. We find that sectoral shocks indeed wash out if the sectors are of a similar size, but these shocks are amplified and generate large aggregate fluctuations if the distribution of sectoral centralities is very unequal (more precisely, if it exhibits a power law).

This result motivates an examination of the economics of network formation: what forces give rise to a production network with unequal sectors? The study of the formation of production networks is still at a very early stage. We provide a brief overview of the research on network formation and then turn to firm-level motivations in creating and supporting supply chains.

Firms are aware of the risks of natural and man-made disruptions in the production process and they seek to secure supply by diversifying across input producers. To examine the incentives of a firm, we study a simple supply chain with multiple layers, where layer A supplies input to layer B, layer B supplies to layer C, and so forth. There is a single firm in every layer. Every firm has a baseline reliability level of $1/2$. The supply chain is successful (or delivers) if every firm in the chain is operational. A firm can invest in plant and machinery and in personnel to raise its reliability.

In this setting, we find that returns to a firm are increasing in the investments by firm in other layers: more formally, investments in reliability are strategic complements. This suggests that there may be multiple equilibria with regard to the reliability of the supply chain: a low equilibrium, in which no firm invests in reliability; and a high reliability equilibrium, in which all firms invest. A second insight from this model is that when a firm invests in reliability, it raises the likelihood that the supply chain as whole will deliver, and this therefore raises the earnings of the other firms in the chain. To the extent that a firm cannot completely appropriate these gains, there exists a gap between private and the collective returns to a firm's investments. As a firm is primarily interested in its own profits, firms will underinvest in reliability relative to what is collectively desirable. These results are derived in a setting with one firm per layer of the supply chain. We then take up the question of how many firms will join different layers of the supply chain.

As in the original model, the supply chain is a line starting with a source and ending in a sink. The new element is that multiple firms in a layer are linked to all firms in the adjacent upstream and downstream layers. The study of the entry problem yields a number of insights. The first is that we show that firm entry decisions are strategic complements across layers and are strategic substitutes within a layer. There are thus multiple equilibria in levels of entry. This points to the role of coordination among firms. Further, as in the basic, single-firm supply chain model, firms' incentives to enter will typically be lower than what is collectively desirable. Taking the decisions on reliability and entry into account, we conclude that firms will create supply chains that are less reliable than is socially desirable. This wedge between firms' incentives and the collective good provides the raison d'être for an active public policy. These considerations motivate the following policy statement.

> As the global supply chain becomes more complex and global in scope, it is increasingly at risk from disruptions including natural hazards, accidents, and malicious incidents. Events like Hurricane Katrina in 2005, the eruption of the *Eyjafjallajökull* volcano in Iceland in 2010, and the Japan earthquake and tsunami of 2011; failing infrastructures such as the I-35 bridge collapse in 2007; terrorist attacks such as 9/11, and more recent plots involving air cargo shipments filled with explosives shipped via Europe and the Middle East to the US remind us that even localized disruptions can escalate rapidly and impact US interests and the broader global community. We must collectively address the challenges posed by these threats and strengthen our national and international policies accordingly. *US Supply Chain Policy Fact Sheet 2012.*

## 5.2 Case Study: The 2011 Japanese Earthquake

We commence our exploration of production networks with a brief case study taken from Carvalho, Nirei, Saito, and Tahbaz-Salehi (2021). On March 11, 2011, a magnitude 9.0 earthquake occurred off the northeast coast of Japan. This was the most powerful earthquake in the history of Japan (a country that is prone to earthquakes) and the fifth most powerful across the world since 1900. The earthquake led to significant material damage in one part of the country, it gave rise to a tsunami that flooded 561 square kilometers of the northeast coastline, and it led to the failure of the Fukushima Dai-ichi Nuclear Power Plant. We describe the direct impact of the earthquake and then present evidence on the transmission of the shock and its amplification through the upstream and downstream production linkages emanating from the firms in the physically affected areas and spreading across the Japanese economy.

The direct physical damage was concentrated in the four Pacific coast prefectures of Aomori, Fukushima, Iwate, and Miyagi in the Tohoku region. According to government estimates, the earthquake caused losses of the order of 16.9 trillion yen, including capital losses due to destruction of buildings, plants and buildings, and equipment. There were close to 20,000 deaths (and several thousand people were missing). These massive losses had an impact on economic standards in that year, but also affected the economic growth of the region and the Japanese economy more generally. We now turn to these direct and indirect economic consequences.

First, we note that the gross domestic product (GDP) growth rate of the four disaster-stricken prefectures in the 2011 fiscal year was -1.5 percent; the growth rate in the previous year had been 0.7 percent. This was a large fall in growth rate. The four prefectures account for only 4.6 percent of the total Japanese GDP; therefore, the direct impact of this loss in growth on the national economy should be of the order of $0.046 \times (0.7 - (-1.5)) = 0.1$ percent. However, the actual decline in Japan's growth rate was four times as large, dropping from 2.6 percent in year 2010 to 2.2 percent in 2011. This large aggregate national-level impact motivates an examination of the channels of transmission of the local shock.

The key step in understanding this transmission is the measurement of shocks on firms that are upstream and downstream from the firms in the prefectures hit by the earthquake. To do this requires us to plot the input-output network of connections between firms. Firms that sell to firms in the affected prefectures are immediately upstream, while those that sell these upstream firms are upstream distance 2 from the affected firms, and so forth. A similar notion of distance applies when we consider downstream firms. The network helps us identify how far upstream and downstream firms are from the directly affected firms. With this network in place, it is possible to study the relation between the distance in the network and the magnitude of the shock on sales.

There is evidence of large transmission shocks that are related to the distance in the supply chain network. Specifically, the earthquake led to a 3.8 percent decline in the growth rate of firms with disaster-hit suppliers (upstream) and a 3.1 percent decline in the growth rate of immediate upstream firms and a 3.1 percent decline in the growth rate of immediate downstream firms. The disruption caused by the earthquake also had indirect negative shocks. Turning to indirect downstream effects, we note that disaster-stricken firms' customers' customers experienced a 2.8 percent point reduction in sales growth. On the upstream side, suppliers' suppliers experienced a 2.1 percent decline in sales growth. These observations motivate a number of questions: How do the technological possibilities shape the decisions of firms on inputs? Are some production structures more resilient against shocks than others? What are the incentives that firms have to create buyer and seller relations, and do private decisions give rise to resilient networks? We develop a theoretical framework that helps us to address these questions.

## 5.3 The Input-Output Model of Production

In this section, we will study an economy with a number of sectors. A sector produces a good, and this good can be used as an input in the production of other goods. Further, every good can also be consumed by a household. A sector consists of firms. Firms are given a set of technologies that specify how different combinations of inputs lead to different outputs. Faced with these technologies and a set of prices in the market, a firm makes decisions on how much to produce and what inputs to use in their production. The households supply labor to the firms in the various sectors. Faced with the prices of goods, they use their income to purchase goods. We will be studying the competitive market equilibrium of this economy. Of particular interest is the ways in which production technologies shape the market prices and the size of different sectors. We will use a model from Acemoglu, Carvalho, Ozdaglar, and Tahbaz-Salehi (2012); the exposition draws on Carvalho and Tahbaz-Salehi (2019).

The set of goods is $N=\{1,\ldots,n\}$, where $n\geq 2$. A sector corresponds to a good, so there are $n$ sectors. Each of the goods can be used as an input in the production of the other $n-1$ goods, and every good can also be used by a household.

The output of industry $i$ is given by

$$y_i = z_i \xi_i \ell_i^{\alpha_i} \prod_{j=1}^{n} x_{ij}^{a_{ij}}, \tag{5.1}$$

where $z_i$ is sector $i$–specific productivity, $\ell_i$ is labor employed, $x_{ij}$ is input from industry $j$ used in industry $i$, and $\alpha_i$ is the share of labor. The parameter

$$\xi_i = \alpha_i^{-\alpha_i} \prod_{j=1}^{n} a_{ij}^{-a_{ij}} \tag{5.2}$$

is a normalization constant.

The exponents $a_{ij}$ reflect the role of sector input $j$ in sector $i$: a larger $a_{ij}$ means that good $j$ is a more important input for the production of good $i$, whereas $a_{ij}=0$ means that good $j$ is not needed to produce good $i$. Generally, the relationships between the sectors will not be symmetric, that is $a_{ij}\neq a_{ji}$, as industry $i$'s reliance on industry $j$ as an input supplier may be different from $j$'s dependence on $i$. Furthermore, it may also be the case that $a_{ii}>0$, as good $i$ may itself be used as an intermediate input for production by firms in industry $i$. Finally, note that the assumption that all technologies exhibit constant returns to scale implies that $\alpha_i+\sum_j a_{ij}=1$ for all $i\in N$. In other words, constant returns to scale say that if all factors of production scale by factor $f$, then output scales by the same factor. Moreover, as $\alpha_i>0$ for all $i$, $\sum_j a_{ij}<1$ for all $i\in N$. All variables except for $x_{ij}$ are exogenous; $x_{ij}$ is the choice made by a firm in sector $i$ on how much it will buy from a firm in sector $j$.

There is a representative consumer in the economy. The consumer's utility is given by

$$u(c_1, c_2, .., c_n) = \sum_{i=1}^{n} \beta_i log\left(\frac{c_i}{\beta_i}\right), \tag{5.3}$$

where $\beta_i$ is the weight placed on good $i$ by the consumer. In what follows, for expositional simplicity, we will assume that $\sum_{i=1}^{n} \beta_i = 1$. The consumer owns 1 unit of labor that is supplied inelastically.

There are competitive markets for every product. The price of product $i$ is $p_i$ and the wage for labor is $w$: in other words, firms and the consumer take prices as given.

A representative firm in sector $i$ maximizes profits that are given as follows:

$$\Pi_i = p_i y_i - w\ell_i - \sum_j p_j x_{ij}, \tag{5.4}$$

where the first term is the gross revenue, the second term is the wage bill, and the third term is the total cost of all other inputs.

The consumer maximizes utility subject to their budget constraint as follows:

$$\max\ u(c);\ \text{s.t.}\ \sum_{i=1}^{n} p_i c_i \leq w. \tag{5.5}$$

This completes the description of the economy.

The competitive equilibrium of this economy is defined in the usual way: it consists of a collection of prices and quantities such that (1) the representative household maximizes their utility; (2) the representative firm in each sector maximizes its profits while taking the prices and wages as given; and (3) in all markets demand is equal to the supply, in other words, all markets clear. We shall study the sizes of different sectors of the economy in a competitive equilibrium and relate them to the structures of input and output relations across the sectors.

**Adjacency matrices and Katz-Bonacich centrality** The input-output linkages between various industries are summarized by matrix $A = [a_{ij}]$, which we will call the economy's "input-output matrix." This matrix, along with the vector of productivity shocks $z = (z_1; ..; z_n)$, describes the production side of the economy. Observe that $\alpha_i > 0$ for all $i \in N$ means that $A$ is a nonnegative matrix, with row sums that are strictly less than 1. This in turn means that the spectral radius of $A$—defined as the largest absolute value of its eigenvalues — is strictly less than 1 (for a derivation of these properties, refer to Berman and Plemmons [1979]). Alternatively, we may interpret $A$ as a graph with $n$ nodes, with the weights of the directed edges given by $a_{ij}$. While the production network representation of the economy is equivalent to the representation using the input-output matrix, it can provide a conceptually simpler framework for summarizing (and visualizing) input-output linkages.

The matrix $L = [1 - A]^{-1}$ is known as the *Leontief inverse*. As $A$ is nonnegative with a spectral radius that is strictly less than 1, we can deduce that $[1 - A]$ is a nonsingular M-matrix. This in turn implies that the Leontief inverse $L$ always exists and is element-wise nonnegative. Moreover, since the spectral radius of $A$ is strictly less than 1, the Leontief inverse can be expressed as the infinite sum of the powers of the input-output matrix $A$ (Stewart [1998]):

$$L = [I - A]^{-1} = \sum_{k=0}^{\infty} A^k. \tag{5.6}$$

This decomposition tells us that the $l_{ij}$ value in cell $(i;j)$ of the Leontief inverse measures the importance of industry $j$ as a direct and indirect input supplier to industry $i$ in the economy. Interpreted in terms of the production network representation of the economy, $l_{ij}$ is a measure of all possible directed walks (of different lengths) that connect industry $j$ to industry $i$ over the network. We define $v_i = \sum_i l_{ji}$: this is a variant on the *Katz-Bonacich centrality* of sector $i$, as it provides a measure of walks of different lengths emanating from a sector (for an introduction to Katz-Bonacich centrality, refer to chapter 1).

An important focus of this analysis will be the relative size of different sectors. This is measured by the *Domar weight* of an industry, which is the market value of its output as a ratio of the total output of the economy:

$$\lambda_i = \frac{p_i y_i}{GDP}. \tag{5.7}$$

With these concepts in place, we are now ready to relate the production and consumption and the size of the sectors in this economy to its technology as manifest in the matrix of input-output connections.

### 5.3.1 The Size of Sectors and the Aggregate Economy

The first step is to derive a firm's demands for different inputs. As all firms are identical, we may write demand at the industry level. This demand is derived by differentiating the profit of a firm with respect to labor and inputs. Industry $i$'s demand for labor is

$$\ell_i = \frac{p_i y_i \alpha_i}{w}. \tag{5.8}$$

Similarly, industry $i$'s demand for input from industry $j$ is

$$x_{ij} = \frac{p_i y_i a_{ij}}{p_j}. \tag{5.9}$$

Substituting these demands in the production function yields

$$y_i = z_i \xi_i \left(\frac{p_i y_i \alpha_i}{w}\right)^{\alpha_i} \prod_{j=1}^{n} \left(\frac{p_i y_i a_{ij}}{p_j}\right)^{a_{ij}}. \tag{5.10}$$

Dividing by $y_i$ and taking logs on both sides yields

$$0 = logp_i + logz_i + log\xi_i + \alpha_i log\alpha_i - \alpha_i logw + \sum_{j=1}^{n} a_{ij}(loga_{ij} - logp_j). \tag{5.11}$$

Rearranging terms, we may rewrite equation (5.11) as follows:

$$logp_i - \alpha_i logw = -logz_i - log\xi_i - \alpha_i log\alpha_i - \sum_{j=1}^{n} a_{ij}(loga_{ij} - logp_j). \tag{5.12}$$

Defining $\epsilon_i = logz_i$, recalling the normalization constant, and rearranging we get

$$log\left(\frac{p_i}{w}\right) + (1 - \alpha_i)logw = -\epsilon_i + \sum_{j=1}^{n} a_{ij} logp_j. \tag{5.13}$$

Recalling $\sum_j a_{ij} = 1 - \alpha_i$, we may rewrite equation (5.13) as

$$log\left(\frac{p_i}{w}\right) = \sum_{j=1}^{n} a_{ij} log\left(\frac{p_j}{w}\right) - \epsilon_i. \tag{5.14}$$

It is convenient to define $\hat{p}_i = log(p_i/w)$.

The relationship in equation (5.14) must hold for all industries, so it yields a system of $n$ equations. Rewriting this system of equations in matrix form, we get

$$\hat{p} = A\hat{p} - \epsilon. \tag{5.15}$$

We can rewrite equation (5.15) in inverse form, as follows

$$\hat{p} = -[I - A]^{-1}\epsilon. \tag{5.16}$$

We now turn to consumer demands. Recall that the consumer seeks to maximize utility subject to budget constraints, as in equation (5.5). Differentiating with respect to $c_i$ and simplifying, we get

$$c_j = \frac{\beta_j w}{p_j}. \tag{5.17}$$

The market clearing condition for product $j$ can be written as follows:

$$y_j = c_j + \sum_{i=1}^{n} x_{ij}. \tag{5.18}$$

Substituting firm demand from equation (5.9) and consumer demand from equation (5.17), equation (5.18) can be rewritten as follows:

$$y_j = \frac{\beta_j w}{p_j} + \sum_{i=1}^{n} \frac{a_{ij} p_i y_i}{p_j}. \tag{5.19}$$

Multiplying by $p_j$ and dividing by $w$ on both sides, we get

$$\frac{p_j y_j}{w} = \beta_j + \sum_{i=1}^{n} \frac{a_{ij} p_i y_i}{w}. \tag{5.20}$$

Rewriting this equation in terms of Domar weight, we get

$$\lambda_j = \beta_j + \sum_{i=1}^{n} a_{ij} \lambda_i. \tag{5.21}$$

We note that Domar weight is a function of consumer preference $\beta_j$ and production network $a_{ij}$ and may be written more compactly as

$$\lambda_i = \sum_{j=1}^{n} \beta_j l_{ji}. \tag{5.22}$$

Observe that the industry impact occurs downstream only. This is an artifact of the Cobb-Douglas production function. With this production function, the price and output effects cancel out for upstream firms: if the quantity of good $i$ falls (because of the negative shock), the price of good $i$ increases proportionately, leaving $p_i x_i$ unchanged. Thus there is no upstream impact as a response to productivity shocks. A question at the end of the chapter examines the upstream propagation of shocks.

Rewriting equation (5.22) in matrix form and solving for the vector of Domar weights yields

$$\lambda = [1 - A']^{-1} \beta. \tag{5.23}$$

Finally, recall from equation (5.13) that $log(p_i/w) = -\sum_{j=1}^{n} l_{ij} \epsilon_j$.

Putting these points together, we arrive at the following result on the size of sectors.

**Proposition 5.1** *The log of industry output i is given by*

$$log(y_i) = \sum_{j=1}^{n} l_{ij} \epsilon_j + \delta_i, \tag{5.24}$$

*where* $\delta_i = log(\sum_j \beta_j l_{ji})$ *is a constant that is independent of the shocks* $z_i$.

This result reveals that the output of industry $i$ (i.e., its size) depends on the productivity of every sector, weighted by the entries of the Leontief inverse. In other words, a sector's size is proportional to its Katz-Bonacich centrality in the production network.

The intuition underlying the result is as follows. Suppose that industry $j$ is hit by a negative shock that reduces its production. This will push up its prices. Such an increase in price will negatively affect the industries that use $j$ as an input. This negative impact will then flow downstream through the firms/sectors that use this sector as an input, and so forth. The overall effect of downstream propagation of the initial shock is reflected in the economy's Leontief inverse (and summarized in the Katz-Bonacich centrality).

Let us now consider the relation between the production network and the aggregate output. Recall that

$$log(\frac{p_i}{w}) = -\sum_{j=1}^{n} l_{ij}\epsilon_j. \tag{5.25}$$

If we multiply on both sides by $\beta_i$ and sum across all $i$, we get

$$\sum_{i=1}^{n} \beta_i logp_i - \sum_{i=1}^{n} \beta_i logw = -\sum_{i=1}^{n} \beta_i \sum_{j=1}^{n} l_{ij}\epsilon_j. \tag{5.26}$$

Recalling that GDP is simply the wage earnings of consumers and labor supply is inelastic at 1 unit, the GDP is given by $w$. Substituting for this in equation (5.26) and rearranging, we get

$$log(GDP) = \sum_{i=1}^{n} \beta_i logp_i + \sum_{i=1}^{n} \beta_i \sum_{j=1}^{n} l_{ij}\epsilon_j. \tag{5.27}$$

Define the consumption good bundle $P_c = \prod_{i=1}^{n} p_i^{\beta_i}$ as numeraire and set its price equal to 1. This implies that $\sum_i \beta_i logp_i = 0$.

We are now ready to state the following result on the size of the aggregate economy as it relates to productivity shocks and the input-output matrix.

**Proposition 5.2** *An economy's real value added is given by*

$$log(GDP) = \sum_{i=1}^{n} \lambda_i \epsilon_i \tag{5.28}$$

$$\lambda_i = \frac{p_i y_i}{GDP} = \sum_{j=1}^{n} \beta_j l_{ji}, \tag{5.29}$$

*and $l_{ji}$ is the $(j, i)$ element of the Leontief inverse, $L = [I - A]^{-1}$.*

Thus the log aggregate output is a linear combination of industry-level productivity shocks, with coefficients given by the industries' Domar weights. Importantly, the Domar weight of industry $i$ depends on the downstream linkages from $i$ to all other sectors. This relation is known as "Hulten's theorem" (Hulten, 1978; Gabaix, 2011). The result also shows that with Cobb-Douglas technology and preferences, the Domar weight depends only on the preference shares and the corresponding column of the economy's Leontief inverse.

To appreciate propositions 5.1 and 5.2, it is helpful to work through a few simple production networks.

### 5.3.2 Computations for Simple Economies

Consider the production networks represented in figure 5.1. In these networks, there are six sectors: $n = 6$. Suppose that the share of labor is the same across sectors: $\alpha_i = 0.2$ for all $i \in N$. For simplicity, assume that productivity shocks are given by $z_i = 1$ for every $i$ and consumer

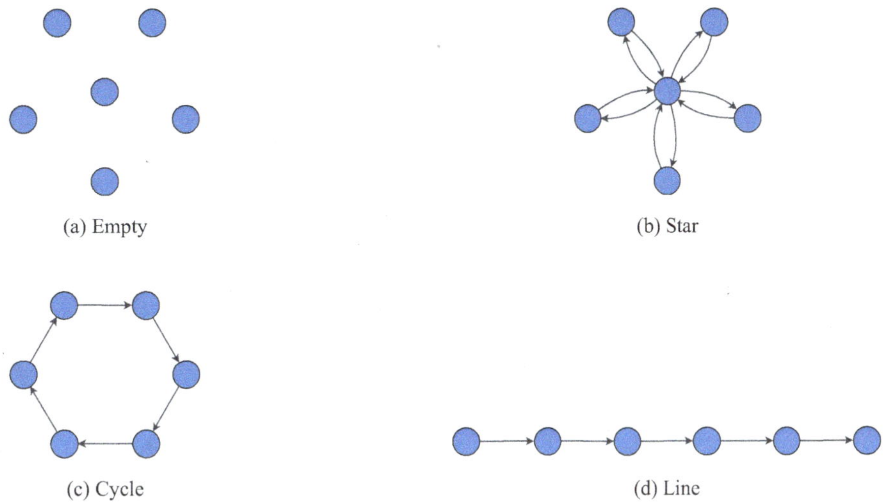


**Figure 5.1**
Simple production networks.

**Table 5.1**
Cycle: production matrix A (left) and Leontief matrix L (right)

| | | | | | | | | | | | |
|---|---|---|---|---|---|---|---|---|---|---|---|
| 0 | 0 | 0 | 0 | 0 | .8 | 1.36 | 0.44 | 0.56 | 0.69 | 0.87 | 1.08 |
| .8 | 0 | 0 | 0 | 0 | 0 | 1.08 | 1.36 | 0.44 | 0.56 | 0.69 | 0.87 |
| 0 | .8 | 0 | 0 | 0 | 0 | 0.87 | 1.08 | 1.36 | 0.44 | 0.56 | 0.69 |
| 0 | 0 | .8 | 0 | 0 | 0 | 0.69 | 0.87 | 1.08 | 1.36 | 0.44 | 0.56 |
| 0 | 0 | 0 | .8 | 0 | 0 | 0.56 | 0.69 | 0.87 | 1.08 | 1.36 | 0.44 |
| 0 | 0 | 0 | 0 | .8 | 0 | 0.44 | 0.56 | 0.69 | 0.87 | 1.08 | 1.36 |

places equal weight on all sectors, $\beta_i = 1/6$ for all $i \in N$. Let us now compute the Leontief inverse and the centralities and Domar weights of sectors in these different economies. Note that in our setting, the Katz-Bonacich centrality is simply the column sum whereas the Domar weight is the column sum weighted by the respective $\beta$'s (this is equivalent to "dividing" by the "number of sectors" here).

For the empty network, the Leontief inverse is simply the identity matrix; the Katz-Bonacich centrality of every node is therefore given by 1. The Domar weight of each sector is given by 0.17.

Table 5.1 presents the adjacency matrix for a cycle network and the corresponding Leontief matrix. We see that as all nodes are symmetric, the Katz-Bonacich centrality for every sector is the same and given by 5. The Domar weight of each sector is given by 0.83.

Table 5.2 presents the adjacency matrix for a star network and the corresponding Leontief matrix. We see that the Katz-Bonacich centrality is 13.89 for the center and 3.22 for each

**Table 5.2**
Star: production matrix A (left) and Leontief matrix L (right)

| | | | | | |
|---|---|---|---|---|---|
| 0 | 0.16 | 0.16 | 0.16 | 0.16 | 0.16 |
| 0.8 | 0 | 0 | 0 | 0 | 0 |
| 0.8 | 0 | 0 | 0 | 0 | 0 |
| 0.8 | 0 | 0 | 0 | 0 | 0 |
| 0.8 | 0 | 0 | 0 | 0 | 0 |
| 0.8 | 0 | 0 | 0 | 0 | 0 |

| | | | | | |
|---|---|---|---|---|---|
| 2.78 | 0.44 | 0.44 | 0.44 | 0.44 | 0.44 |
| 2.22 | 1.36 | 0.36 | 0.36 | 0.36 | 0.36 |
| 2.22 | 0.36 | 1.36 | 0.36 | 0.36 | 0.36 |
| 2.22 | 0.36 | 0.36 | 1.36 | 0.36 | 0.36 |
| 2.22 | 0.36 | 0.36 | 0.36 | 1.36 | 0.36 |
| 2.22 | 0.36 | 0.36 | 0.36 | 0.36 | 1.36 |

**Table 5.3**
Line: production matrix A (left) and Leontief matrix L (right)

| | | | | | |
|---|---|---|---|---|---|
| 0 | 0 | 0 | 0 | 0 | 0 |
| 0.8 | 0 | 0 | 0 | 0 | 0 |
| 0 | 0.8 | 0 | 0 | 0 | 0 |
| 0 | 0 | 0.8 | 0 | 0 | 0 |
| 0 | 0 | 0 | 0.8 | 0 | 0 |
| 0 | 0 | 0 | 0 | 0.8 | 0 |

| | | | | | |
|---|---|---|---|---|---|
| 1.00 | 0.00 | 0.00 | 0.00 | 0.00 | 0.00 |
| 0.80 | 1.00 | 0.00 | 0.00 | 0.00 | 0.00 |
| 0.64 | 0.80 | 1.00 | 0.00 | 0.00 | 0.00 |
| 0.51 | 0.64 | 0.80 | 1.00 | 0.00 | 0.00 |
| 0.41 | 0.51 | 0.64 | 0.80 | 1.00 | 0.00 |
| 0.33 | 0.41 | 0.51 | 0.64 | 0.80 | 1.00 |

spoke. The Domar weight of each of the peripheral sectors is given by 0.54, while the Domar weight of the central sector is given by 2.31.

Table 5.3 presents the adjacency matrix for the line network and the corresponding Leontief matrix. We see that the Katz-Bonacich centrality is 3.69, 3.36, 2.95, 2.44, 1.80, and 1.00 for nodes 1, 2, 3, 4, 5, and 6, respectively. The Domar weight of the sectors is 0.61,0.56, 0.49, 0.41, 0.30, and 0.17, respectively.

### 5.3.3 Remarks on Empirical Production Networks

The theoretical model offers us a useful lens through which to view production economies in the world. Perhaps the most widely used industry-level data is the input-output accounts data compiled by the US Bureau of Economic Analysis (BEA). This database provides a detailed breakdown of the US economy into hundreds of industries. We discussed this data in chapter 1. For easy reference, we briefly recall some important properties of the US network. The industry-level network is highly sparsely connected, in the sense that narrowly defined specialized industries supply inputs on average to only about 11 other industries. Further, the network is dominated by a small number of hubs that are general-purpose industries. The weighted out-degree distribution is highly skewed and close to a Pareto distribution. Next, the network exhibits a "small-world" property: most industry pairs are indirectly linked by hub-like sectors, and thereby the network has short average distances and small diameters. Finally, the network exhibits a highly skewed distribution of sectoral Bonacich centralities (which is also well approximated by a Pareto distribution with diverging second moments).

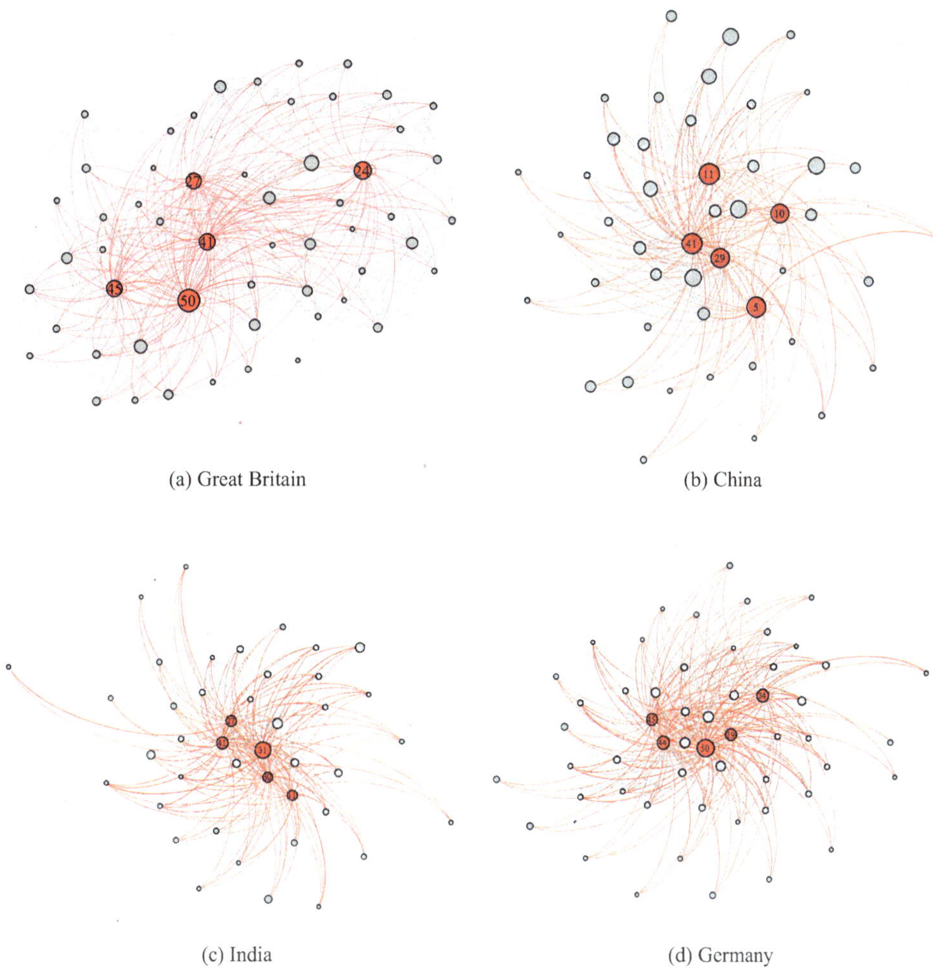

**Figure 5.2**
Production networks, 2014. Node size is proportional to the weighted out-degree. *Source*: World Input-Output Database. www.wiod.org.

These properties of production networks are not limited to the US. To get a sense of the structure of production networks more generally, we present statistics from four other large economies—Great Britain, China, India, and Germany (the data is taken from the World Input-Output Database and is presented at a higher level of aggregation than the BEA data). Define the weighted out-degree of a sector $j$ as

$$d_{out}^{j} = \sum_{i=1}^{n} w_{ij}, \tag{5.30}$$

**Table 5.4**
Comparing top sectors across four leading economies

| Great Britain | China | India | Germany |
|---|---|---|---|
| Administrative/support services | Manufacturing: chemicals/chemical products | Land transport and pipelines | Administrative/support services |
| Electricity/gas/steam/air conditioning | Financial services | Financial services | Real estate activities |
| Financial services | Manufacturing: food, beverages, and tobacco | Construction | Warehousing/support transportation |
| Legal and accounting; management consultancy | Wholesale trade | Retail trade | Legal and accounting; management consulting |
| Manufacturing: coke/refined petroleum | Manufacturing: coke/refined petroleum | Manufacturing: chemicals/chemical products | Wholesale trade |

where $w_{ij}$ is the input weight from $j$ to $i$. This measure ranges from 0 (if a sector does not supply inputs to any other sector) to $n$ (if a single sector is the sole input supplier of every sector). Figure 5.2 presents the production networks of these four countries.

Next, recall from chapter 2, that under the Pareto distribution, the probability of degree $k$ is $P(k) = a/k^c$, for positive constants $a$ and $c$. If we take logs on both sides, we get

$$logP(k) = loga - clogk. \tag{5.31}$$

Expressed in this way, we see that the log of probability is a linear function of the log of degree. Given any empirical distribution, it is then possible to ask what value of $a$ and $c$ offers the best fit. Fitting the Pareto distribution to the weighted out-degree distribution of the four countries, we get the following coefficients: 2.28 for China, 2.25 for India, 1.74 for Great Britain, and 1.84 for Germany.

The top five sectors in terms of size are presented in table 5.4. An interesting aspect of the networks across countries is that, depending on the level of economic development, the networks cluster around various central industries. Table 5.4 illustrates this by comparing the top five sectors in Great Britain, China, India, and Germany. We see that Great Britain and Germany share two sectors out of their top five—administrative/support services and legal and accounting services (it is worth comparing these sectors with the largest sectors in the US, mentioned in chapter 1). Similarly, China and India also have two sectors in common—manufacturing: chemicals and chemical products and financial services. We also note the prominent role of general-purpose sectors like financial services, legal and accounting services, and administrative services, Wholesale Trade, Real Estate, Electric Power Generation and Distribution, Management of Companies and Enterprises, and Iron and Steel Mills.

**Table 5.5**
Comparing top sectors across four leading economies

| Great Britain | China | India | Germany |
|---|---|---|---|
| 8.68% | 5.85% | 11.26% | 9.60% |
| 6.27% | 5.79% | 7.51% | 6.47% |
| 5.90% | 5.68% | 6.33% | 6.27% |
| 5.70% | 5.23% | 5.91% | 5.58% |
| 5.38% | 5.16% | 5.71% | 5.53% |

To appreciate the inequality in sector size, it is instructive to look at the shares of the top five sectors. Table 5.5 presents the shares of the top five sectors from the four economies. We see that the top five sectors make up over 35 percent of the national economy in India, over 30 percent in Great Britain and Germany, and over 25 percent in China.

## 5.4 Network Structure and Aggregate Volatility

We turn next to the relation between network structure and shock propagation in the economy. The traditional view is that independent sector-level shocks will not have a large impact on the aggregate economy (e.g., Lucas, 1977). The intuition is that shocks on the various sectors have distinct origins, and therefore some will be positive and others negative. They will cancel each other out and not have an large aggregate impact. In what follows, we will examine the scope of this argument and show that it hinges crucially on the network structure of the production economy.

To bring out the role of the network structure in the simplest way, we will simplify some aspects of the production process. First, suppose that the productivity shocks are identical and independent across sectors: so $\epsilon_i = \epsilon$ for every sector $i$. Next, suppose that the mean or average shock is of size 0 and its standard deviation is $\sigma$. Finally, assume for simplicity that all sectors use labor in the same way (i.e., $\alpha_i = \alpha > 0$, for all $i \in N$).

Recall from proposition 5.2 that

$$log(GDP) = \sum_{i=1}^{n} \lambda_i \epsilon_i. \tag{5.32}$$

The volatility of the economy may be measured by the standard deviation of the aggregate output, $\sigma_{agg}$. Let us express this standard deviation in terms of the network structure and the production shocks of the economy:

$$\sigma_{agg} = \sqrt{E(logw)^2} = \sqrt{E(\sum_{i=1}^{n} \lambda_i \epsilon_i)^2} = \sqrt{\sum_{i=1}^{n} \lambda_i^2 E(\epsilon_i^2)} = \sqrt{\sum_{i=1}^{n} \lambda_i^2 ((E\epsilon)^2 + \sigma^2)}, \tag{5.33}$$

where $w$ is GDP and we have used the formula for the variance of a random variable $x$, $\sigma_x^2 = Ex^2 - (Ex)^2$. Noting that $E\epsilon = 0$ and $\|\lambda\| = \sqrt{\sum_{i=1}^n \lambda_i^2}$, we obtain the following compact expression:

$$\sigma_{agg} = \sigma \|\lambda\|. \tag{5.34}$$

To appreciate the magnitude of aggregate volatility in an economy, we next turn to the mean and variance of the distribution of its Domar weight. Recall from the discussion in section 5.3.1 that the Domar weight is

$$\lambda_i = \sum_{j=1}^n \beta_j l_{ji}. \tag{5.35}$$

Therefore, the sum of Domar weights is

$$\sum_{i=1}^n \lambda_i = \sum_{i=1}^n \sum_{j=1}^n \beta_j l_{ji} = \frac{1}{\alpha}. \tag{5.36}$$

We can therefore write the mean value of $\lambda_i$, $E(\lambda) = 1/(n\alpha)$. Turning to the variance, note that

$$\begin{aligned}\sum_{i=1}^n \lambda_i^2 &= n\frac{\sum_{i=1}^n \lambda_i^2}{n} = nE(\lambda^2) \\ &= n(E(\lambda)^2 + \sigma^2(\lambda)) = nE(\lambda)^2\left[1 + \frac{\sigma^2(\lambda)}{E(\lambda)^2}\right],\end{aligned} \tag{5.37}$$

where we have again used the formula for a random variable $x$, $\sigma_x^2 = Ex^2 - (Ex)^2$. Substituting for $\sum_{i=1}^n \lambda_i^2$ in equation (5.34), we arrive at

$$\sigma_{agg} = \frac{\sigma/\alpha}{\sqrt{n}}\sqrt{1 + n^2\alpha^2 var(\lambda_1, \lambda_2, \ldots, \lambda_n)}. \tag{5.38}$$

Sector size is central to an understanding of aggregate volatility. To see this, note that if the Domar weights are equal, then $var(\lambda_1, .., \lambda_n) = 0$. Substituting in equation (5.38) yields the expression

$$\sigma_{agg} = \frac{\sigma/\alpha}{\sqrt{n}}. \tag{5.39}$$

As $\sigma$ and $\alpha$ are constants, this means that the fluctuation in aggregate output is proportional to $1/\sqrt{n}$. We have, therefore, arrived at the conventional wisdom: aggregate volatility becomes negligible as the number of sectors $n$ grows.

From proposition 5.1, we know that the Domar weight of a sector is an equilibrium outcome and reflects the production network and consumer demands. To focus on the network, let us further assume that the consumer assigns equal weight to all goods: $\beta_i = 1/n, \forall i \in N$.

Recall that the Domar weight $\lambda_i = v_i/n$, where

$$v_i = \sum_{j=1}^{n} l_{ji} \tag{5.40}$$

is the column sum of the Leontief inverse matrix and indicates the importance of industry $i$ as a supplier to the economy. Substitute for $\lambda_i$ in equation (5.38) and, noting that $\sigma^2(\lambda) = \sigma^2(v)/n^2$, we get

$$\sigma_{agg} = \frac{\sigma}{\sqrt{n}}\sqrt{\alpha^{-2} + var(v_1, \ldots, v_n)}, \tag{5.41}$$

Equation (5.41) suggests that heterogeneity across sectoral centrality/size can give rise to significant aggregate volatility. For example, if $v_i'$ has a Pareto distribution with exponent $\gamma \in (1, 2)$, then it can be shown that $\sigma_{agg}$ will be proportional to $n^{1/\gamma-1}$, and therefore it will be unbounded (the relation between the Pareto coefficient and the variance is discussed in chapter 2). The interested reader should refer to Gabaix (2011) and Acemoglu, Carvalho, Ozdaglar, and Tahbaz-Salehi (2012) for further discussion on this issue.

The intuition underlying this result comes from the propagation mechanism developed in propositions 5.1 and 5.2. Sector-level shocks cancel out at the aggregate level if the sectors are roughly the same size. But when the sectors are very unequal in their roles as input suppliers, shocks to sectors that are more important suppliers propagate more widely and dominate the shocks to less prominent sectors. These observations lie at the heart of the granularity hypothesis: in the presence of significant heterogeneity at the micro level, sector-level shocks can be amplified by the network structure of production.

### 5.4.1 Shock Propagation: Examples

Figure 5.1 takes up four networks to illustrate our analysis of aggregate volatility. Consider first an empty network in which every sector only uses labor as an input. In this economy, shocks to any given sector will not affect production in any other sector: there is no amplification of micro-level volatility.

Next, consider the cycle network, in which every sector acts as an input into one other sector. In this setting, shocks do percolate, but the effects have similar magnitude, as every sector is symmetrically located in the network. More generally, if shocks respect the assumptions of zero mean and equal variance, then they indeed tend to cancel out: the standard deviation declines as the number of nodes grows (in line with the expression $1/\sqrt{n}$).

A supply chain suggests a situation in which inputs flow unidirectionally from a well-defined upstream sector (e.g., rare earth minerals). Its output is successively transformed into magnets that are used in speakers, which are ultimately incorporated in the final downstream sector, the smart phone. This is a simple line network with a source node (the first node, with no incoming links), and a single sink node (the last node, with no outgoing links). The effects of a shock will depend on the location in the chain: for example, a shock at the most upstream source (sector 1) now has a first-round effect on its immediate downstream customer sector 2, a smaller, second-round effect on sector 3, and an even smaller, third-round effect on sector 4. The remaining three sectors contribute in a similar manner except that they are closer to the sink node and hence do not contribute to aggregate volatility, with as many higher-order indirect effects. This source-sink arrangement of the production network draws attention to the disproportionate role of central technologies. The next example, of a star economy, brings out this point clearly.

Finally, consider a setting in which a single, general-purpose technology serves as nearly the only input (in addition to labor) in all other sectors. Moreover, each of the other sectors is an input for the general-purpose technology. Figure 5.1 illustrates this configuration as the star economy. This is a very stylized way to represent the role of sectors such as real estate, construction, and information technology. This network yields the highest volatility across the four networks considered. The reason for this is the large effect of the central hub sector: a shock to this sector has large, first-order effects on all sectors, while a shock to any other sector has a direct effect on one other sector and an indirect effect on every other sector.

These theoretical considerations are of substantive interest as production networks in important economies exhibit great inequality. Recall that the size of a sector is related to its centrality in the production network. With this in mind, figure 5.3 plots the centrality distribution in Great Britain, China, India, and Germany. The Pareto coefficients of the fitted curves are 1.96, 1.67, 1.65, and 1.82, respectively (we fit the coefficient $b$ in the function $y = e^a x^b$).

Decisions on investments and on securing supply chains are ultimately made by firms. To understand whether they will act appropriately—whether they will invest adequately to make their production reliable, what they will use as input suppliers, and which sectors they will enter—it is important to understand the connections at the firm level. The approach of mapping relations at the sector level can be adapted to study interfirm relations: the nodes are now firms, and the links reflect the input relations between firms. The interfirm supply chain networks for a few countries such as Belgium and Japan have been studied. As in the case of sector-level networks, interfirm networks exhibit an extensive heterogeneity that is consistent with power law distributions. In contrast to the sectoral network, the in-degree distribution is also highly skewed. Finally, the size of a firm is positively correlated with both its number of upstream supplier firms and its downstream customer firms.

The discussion has brought out the role of production connections between firms and sectors in transmitting shocks, and it has illustrated the role of hub nodes in amplifying shocks. This motivates a closer study of the economic processes that give rise to hubs.

### 5.4.2 Endogenous Networks

We expect that firms will respond to changes in economic conditions, and this response may entail a change in their technology, suppliers, and trading partners. For instance, they may source new inputs to take advantage of technological innovations or enter relationships with

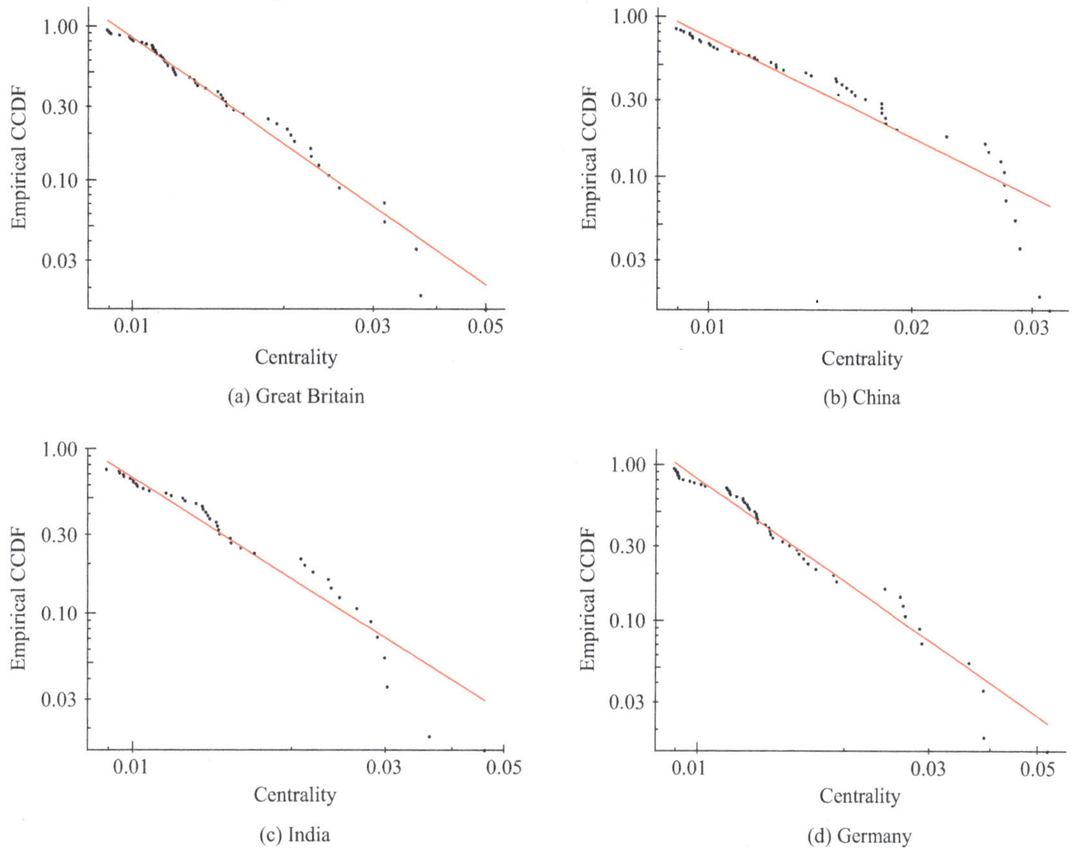


**Figure 5.3**
Tail distribution of centralities, 2014. *Source*: World Input-Output Database. www.wiod.org.

new customers in response to a customer's exit. These changes will give rise to changes in the production network, and this may significantly alter the economy's response to exogenous shocks.

To accommodate these considerations, a small but growing body of literature develops a theory of production and endogenous network formation. The economic forces involved are complex and include the direct and indirect network effects, as well as the combinatorial nature of graphs. A formal presentation of this work is outside the scope of this chapter, so we limit ourselves to mentioning some papers only.

In an early strand of work, this challenge was addressed through statistical models of network formation. Atalay, Hortacsu, Roberts, and Syverson (2011) develop a model in which links between firms are created through a variant of the preferential attachment model (proposed in chapter 2). Carvalho and Voigtlander (2015) propose an industry-level network formation model that builds on the network formation model of Jackson and Rogers (2007) (also presented in chapter 2). In that model, existing input-output linkages are used to search for new inputs for production. Recall that the model generates a scale-free degree distribution and high clustering. Using industry-level data, and consistent with the model's central mechanism, Carvalho and Voigtlander (2015) find that producers are more likely to adopt inputs that are already in use by their current (direct or indirect) upstream suppliers. These statistical models are able to match some of the key attributes of real-world production networks, but they abstract from incentives that depend on the specific inputs and production technologies. Their use for normative and policy purposes is therefore limited.

Oberfield (2018) proposes a model in which firm-level incentives are incorporated. In his model, firms optimally choose one input from a randomly evolving set of suppliers. He finds that such endogenous choice results in the emergence of star suppliers that sell their goods to many other firms for intermediate use. Acemoglu and Azar (2020) consider a model in which firms decide which subset of the other industries to use as input suppliers, with each input combination leading to a different constant returns to scale production technology. The key assumption in the model is that markets are "contestable," that is, a number of firms have access to the same menu of technologies. This assumption ensures that, while making its input combination decisions, each firm can take the production network and all prices as given.

## 5.5 Supply Chains: Fragility and Resilience

In a modern economy, almost any product—be it a cup of coffee or a smart phone—arises out of a supply chain with multiple layers, with the output of one layer forming an essential input in the production of the next layer. Firms are aware of the shocks and uncertainties associated with these multilayer chains and they take steps to mitigate them—they invest in their own reliability, choose which layer of the supply chains to enter opportunistically, and seek to secure their input supply and downstream demand by creating links with multiple suppliers and buyers. As supply chains are complex, these decisions involve complicated interactions with other firms. We present a simple model of a supply chain to explore incentives of firms and the performance of supply chains they create.

The simplest example of a supply chain is a line with a unique source and unique sink: layer A supplies inputs to layer B, layer B supplies inputs to layer C, and so forth. Let us assume that there is a single firm in each layer. For ease of computation, assume that there is a baseline reliability level of $1/2$ for every firm (i.e., this is the probability that a level produces a viable product using inputs from a previous level). There is, then, a probability of $1/2$ that the supply chain with a single layer delivers, a probability of $1/4$ that a chain with two layers delivers, and so forth. A supply chain with $n$ layers, therefore, successfully delivers with a probability of $1/2^n$.

Firms embedded in this supply chain can take steps to improve their performance. Suppose that a firm earns 1 if the supply chain is successful and earns 0 if the chain fails to deliver. Let us say that with an investment $C$, the firm can raise the reliability to 1. In a supply chain with a single firm, a firm compares an expected return of $1/2$ with the expected return of 1. The marginal returns to investment are $1/2$. So the firm will undertake the investment if $C < 1/2$.

Next, consider a supply chain with two layers: an upstream layer and a downstream layer. As before, suppose that a firm earns 1 in case the supply chain delivers successfully. It is instructive to start with a situation with zero investment in reliability. The supply chain delivers with a probability of $1/4$, and both firms expect to earn $1/4$. If the upstream firm alone makes an investment, then it earns 1 if it succeeds (this happens now with a probability of $1/2$) and 0 if it fails (this happens with a probability of $1/2$). The firm thus expects to earn $1/2$ if it invests, hence a marginal return of 1/4. So a firm will make the investment if $C < 1/4$.

To appreciate the strategic relation between investments by firms, suppose next that downstream firm makes investment $C$. This means that the expected returns to an upstream firm without any investment is $1/2$. In this situation, if the upstream firm makes the investment, then the supply chain delivers with certainty and the upstream firm expects to earn 1. So the return to investment is $1/2$. We have thus established that the returns to the upstream firm are larger when the downstream firm invests in reliability. This reveals that the investments in reliability by various firms are strategic complements (see chapter 4 for a definition of strategic complements and substitutes).

We may summarize our computations as follows: a firm will invest in reliability regardless of what the other firm does if $C < 1/4$, it invests only if the other firm invests if $1/4 < C < 1/2$, and it never invests in reliability if $C > 1/2$.

More generally, in a supply chain with $k$ layers (and $k$ firms), a firm always invests if $C < 1/2^k$, it invests so long as all other firms invest if $1/2^k < C < 1/2$, and it never invests if $C > 1/2$. As the chain grows in length, $1/2^k$ becomes progressively smaller. The need for firms to coordinate their investments, therefore, becomes more pressing, but at the same time, the growing supply chain makes coordination more difficult.

Observe next that even if firms can coordinate on their investment decisions, they will never invest if $C > 1/2$. So we know that if $C > 1/2$, then the supply chain will deliver with a probability of $1/2^k$. Thus the likelihood of delivery is small and falling as $k$ grows. Is this a desirable state of affairs? Is this the best that the firms can hope to do?

Consider the collective problem of the firms. If the supply chain is successful, their joint earnings are $k$. The complementarity in investments tells us that we only need to compare the two polar cases: all firms invest versus no firm invests. If all firms invest, the supply chain delivers with certainty. The aggregate net earnings are

$$k - kC = k(1 - C). \tag{5.42}$$

By contrast, if no firm invests, then the joint earnings are $k/2^k$. A comparison of the two expressions tells us that firms should invest if

$$1 - C > 1/2^k. \tag{5.43}$$

As the number of layers grows, the term $1/2^k$ becomes progressively smaller and converges to 0. In other words, all firms should invest so long as $C < 1$. These simple computations reveal a key tension in the supply chain: at an individual level, firms have an incentive to invest only if $C < 1/2$, but it is in their collective interest to invest, so long as $C < 1$. Thus, in the range $1/2 < C < 1$, no firm will invest even though it is in the interest of all firms to do so. These observations are summarized as follows.

**Proposition 5.3** *Consider a line supply chain with k layers and one firm in each layer. The investments of firms across different layers are strategic complements. This gives rise to the possibility of multiple equilibria and firms need to coordinate their investments to achieve a high reliability outcome. There is a wedge between the private benefits to investing in reliability and the collective gains from doing so: as a result, firms will underinvest in reliability. This underinvestment grows with the length of the supply chain.*

### 5.5.1 The Case of Multiple Firms in a Layer

There is one important aspect of actual supply chains that is missing in the model described here—the presence of multiple firms producing the same output. To accommodate this possibility, we extend the model as follows: we suppose, as before, that there is a single line starting with A that supplies to B, which supplies to C, and so forth; but now we allow firms to decide whether they wish to enter a layer of the supply chain. For simplicity, suppose that there are many firms that are interchangeable and can enter one (and only one) layer.

To develop our arguments, it is instructive to start with the simple case of a two-layer network presented in figure 5.4(a). There are two layers: an upstream layer, U, and a downstream layer, D. The supply chain can potentially contain several firms in every layer, and there are links between every firm and firms in the adjacent layers. In this network, every firm in layer D can source inputs from every firm in layer U. In figure 5.4(b), this structure is presented with multiple layers. In other words, the network is a complete multipartite network. As in our original line supply chain, each firm has a baseline probability of $1/2$ of being functional. To keep the computations simple, suppose that the firms face equal and independent shocks (and thus the likelihood of a firm being operational is unrelated to the status of any other firm).

Let us consider the decision of a firm to enter the two-layer supply chain. Entering a production layer entails investments in plant, equipment, and personnel, which are summarized by a fixed cost $F > 0$. The supply chain delivers an output if there is at least one operational firm in each layer. In the simple case, with only one firm per layer, the payoffs

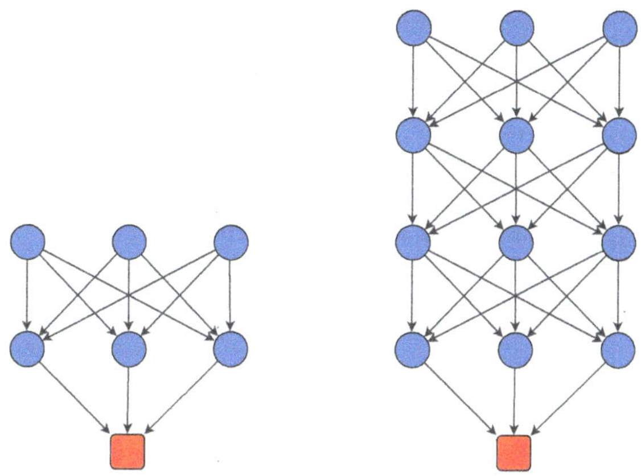

(a) Two-layer (b) Four-layer

**Figure 5.4**
Supply chains.

are simple: if the supply chain delivers, then every operational firm earns 1. A nonoperational firm earns 0 (less the costs of entry $F$), regardless of whether the supply chain delivers or not.

The returns to entering a layer depend on the number of firms in different layers of the supply chain. Consider the two-layer network, and suppose that there is no firm active in any layer of the supply chain. Say that a firm is considering entering the upstream layer. The expected returns are 0 because there are no firms in the downstream layer. So the supply chain cannot deliver the output, regardless of what this firm decides. On the other hand, if there is already a firm in the downstream layer, then there is a positive value to entering upstream. The supply chain delivers only if firms in either layer are operational, so the probability of successful delivery is $1/2 \times 1/2 = 1/4$. Therefore, upon entry, the firm expects to earn $1/4$. The firm will enter, so long as $F < 1/4$.

Let us now consider the entry decision with multiple firms in different layers of the supply chain. Suppose that there is one firm in each of the two layers: what are the returns to a firm from entering the downstream layer? Observe that the supply chain can deliver only if the firm in layer U is operational: this happens with a probability of $1/2$. Given that layer U is functional, the firm in question will earn profits if it is itself operational: this again happens with a probability of $1/2$. There is, however, a further complication—the returns to this firm depend on whether the other firm in layer D is functional and the form of competition with that firm. To keep matters simple, suppose that all firms in a layer produce a perfectly substitutable output. This suggests that a firm A in layer X earns a positive payoff if and only if it is itself operational, all other firms in its layer are *not* operational, and all other layers are operational. Returning to our example with two layers, with one firm in each layer, we can write the expected profits of the firm that enters the downstream layer as

$$\frac{1}{2} \times \frac{1}{2} \times \frac{1}{2} - F. \tag{5.44}$$

Thus the firm will enter if $F < 1/8$.

Suppose that the firm enters the downstream layer, so there are now two firms in layer D and one firm in layer U. What are the returns to a firm from entering layer U? As before, we need to keep track of the likelihood of layer D being operational and the likelihood of the other firm in layer U failing. Keeping these factors in mind, the profits of the firm that enters layer U are

$$\frac{3}{4} \times \frac{1}{2} \times \frac{1}{2} - F. \tag{5.45}$$

Thus the firm will enter the upstream layer if $F < 3/16$.

These computations tell us that firms' incentive to enter a layer

- increase with the number of firms in other layers.
- decrease with the number of firms in that layer.

The first effect says that entry in different layers is complementary: as firms enter in the other layers, a firm has enhanced incentives to enter its chosen layer. The second effect goes in the opposite direction: entering decisions in the same layer are strategic substitutes due to the competition between firms in the same layer.

Let us now define more general supply chains. A supply chain $\ell = \{\ell_1, .., \ell_k\}$, consists of $\ell_i$ firms in layer $i$, where $i = 1, \ldots, k$ denotes the layers. We shall say that a supply chain $\ell$ is *stable* if no firm that is outside wishes to enter and no firm in the supply chain wishes to exit or switch to another layer.

Suppose that a firm is considering whether to enter a supply chain with $m$ firms in every layer. The entry of the firm gives rise to a supply chain in which one layer contains $m+1$ firms and all other layers contain exactly $m$ firms. The complementarity property tells us that new firms will have an even greater incentive to enter one of the remaining layers with $m$ firms. Reasoning through this complementarity, one layer at a time, we can conclude that in a stable supply chain, every layer must contain an equal number of firms.

Consider the stability of a two-layer supply chain with one firm in each layer. A firm prefers to stay if expected returns, $1/4$, are larger than the cost, $F$. On the other hand, no new firm wishes to enter if $F > 1/8$. So a single-firm, two-layer supply chain is stable if

$$\frac{1}{8} < F < \frac{1}{4}, \tag{5.46}$$

Similarly, we can verify that a chain with two firms in each layer is stable if

$$\frac{3}{32} < F < \frac{3}{16}, \tag{5.47}$$

These computations reveal an interesting fact about the strategic structure of the entry problem: there is a range of costs, $2/16 < F < 3/16$, in which a 1-firm-per-layer supply chain and a 2-firm-per-layer supply chain are both stable.

This multiplicity of stable supply chains motivates this question: which of the two supply chains is better, and more generally, what is an optimal supply chain?

In a 1-firm 2-layer supply chain, the collective or joint earnings of the two firms are

$$\frac{1}{2} - 2F, \tag{5.48}$$

From the computations given here, in a 2-firm, 2-layer supply chain, the payoff of a firm is equal to $3/16 - F$. This tells us that the profits of an individual firm are larger in the 1-firm, 2-layer supply chain than in the 2-firm, 2-layer supply chain. Let us next consider the joint profits of the active firms. As all firms are symmetric, the joint earnings of the four firms in the 2-firm, 2-layer supply chain are

$$\frac{12}{16} - 4F. \tag{5.49}$$

It follows that the aggregate profits in the 2-firm, 2-layer supply chain are higher than the aggregate profits in the 1-firm, 2-layer supply chain if

$$F < \frac{1}{8}. \tag{5.50}$$

This means that in the range of costs of $2/16 < F < 3/16$, the 1-firm, 2-layer chain is better for the firms in the chain than the 2-firm, 2-layer supply chain. Thus in the range of costs when both 1-firm and 2-firm-per-layer supply chains are stable, the 1-firm, 2-layer supply chain is better for the firms.

At a higher level, we may say that the purpose of a supply chain is to deliver a good. With this in mind, let us consider the total surplus net of costs of entry. Implicit in the definition of earnings is the idea that in a successful 2-layer supply chain, the value of the good delivered is 2. The likelihood that such a chain will deliver is simply the probability that both layers are operational, which is $9/16$. So the social value of such a chain is

$$2 \times \frac{9}{16} - 4F. \tag{5.51}$$

A comparison of equation (5.51) with the expression for joint profits of firms in equation (5.49) reveals that there is a wedge between the joint profits of the firms and the social value of a 2-firm, 2-layer supply chain. This reflects the competition effect of multiple operational firms in the same layer.

To summarize, the analysis on firms' choices in supply chains brings out a rich set of interactions—a firm's returns on investment depend on the investments in reliability by other firms. In particular, we showed that the investments are strategic complements. This gives rise to the possibility of multiple equilibria. There also exists a wedge between private and collective returns on investment, suggesting that firms will generally underinvest relative to what is in their collective interest. The discussion on entering supply chains reveals rich strategic relations: entry decisions are strategic complements across layers, but strategic substitutes within the same layer. A general message is that there is a need for a policy intervention as firms acting in their private interest will create supply chains that are insufficiently reliable.

## 5.6 Reading Notes

The study of an economy in terms of its input-output relations between its sectors has a long tradition. For an early introduction to the literature, see Leontief (1941, 1951). Following the early work of Wassily Leontief and his collaborators, a large strand of research explored aspects of economic planning and development using input-output models. This work was accompanied with the collection of very detailed data on input-output relations of economies across the world. The more recent interest in input-output relations may be traced to Black (2009), and Long and Plosser (1983). Acemoglu, Carvalho, Ozdaglar, and Tahbaz-Salehi (2012) build on this tradition and combine it with ideas from the economics of networks and the work of Gabaix (2011) on the "granularity hypothesis." For an early empirical study of production networks, see Blöchl, Theis, Vega-Redondo, and Fisher (2011). An important strand of research has emerged following the work of Acemoglu, Carvalho, Ozdaglar, and Tahbaz-Salehi (2012), including Acemoglu, Akcigit, and Kerr (2016) and Baqaee and Farhi (2019), among others. Carvalho (2014) and Carvalho and Tahbaz-Salehi (2019) provide excellent surveys of this work. Our exposition draws heavily on Carvalho and Tahbaz-Salehi (2019).

The data on input-output tables is taken from the University of Groningen website (www.wiod.org).

Supply chains are a major object of study in many disciplines, including economics, operations research, management science, organization theory, and economic sociology. The emergence of a liberal trading regime has been complemented with advances in information technology to give rise to global supply chains. This in turn has been studied extensively by different strands of research. It is not possible to do justice to this large and fascinating body of work here. For important contributions from an economics perspective, see Antras and Chor (2013), Antras and Helpman (2004), and Costinot, Vogel, and Wang (2013). For an influential contribution on the role of complementarities in the reliability of production, see Kremer (1993). Our aim was to develop some basic economics of firm-level decisions in relation to reliability and participation in supply chains. We developed a model that builds on ideas taken from Elliott, Golub, and Leduc (2020) and Bimpikis, Candogan, and Ehsani (2019).

## 5.7 Questions

1. Consider a production economy. Set $n=4$. Firms use a Cobb-Douglas constant returns to scale technology; every industry uses labor in the same proportion, $\alpha_i = 1/5 \in (0, 1)$. Industry $i$ faces productivity shock $z_i$. The consumer has a log utility that assigns equal weight to all four products, so $\beta_i = \beta = 1/4$. The consumer has endowment of 1 unit of labor that they supply inelastically.
   (a) Define a competitive equilibrium for this economy.
   (b) Fix the production network to be an undirected complete network in which every industry uses itself and the other three industries in equal measure (so for all $i, j$, $a_{ij} = 1/5$). Derive the Leontief matrix and the Domar weights for this economy. Compute the equilibrium output and prices. (Feel free to use computer software as needed.)
   (c) Fix the production network as a star network. The hub industry uses itself and the other three industries in equal measure ($1/5$), while the other three industries each uses itself and the hub, with a coefficient of $2/5$ each. Derive the Leontief matrix and the Domar weights for this economy. Compute the equilibrium output and prices.
   (d) Comment on the potential for propagation of industry-level shocks in these two economies.
2. Consider a production economy with four sectors, $n=4$. Firms use a Cobb-Douglas constant returns to scale technology. Every industry uses labor in the same proportion, $\alpha_i = 1/5$. Industry $i$ faces a productivity shock $z_i$. The consumer has a log utility that assigns equal weight to all four products, so $\beta_i = \beta = 1/4$. The consumer has endowment of 1 unit of labor that they supply inelastically.
   (a) Consider the network as in figure 5.5(a). Write the adjacency matrix and derive the Leontief matrix and the Domar weights for this economy. Compute the equilibrium output of different sectors (use computer software as appropriate).
   (b) Consider the network as in figure 5.5(b). Write the adjacency matrix and derive the Leontief matrix and the Domar weights for this economy. Compute the equilibrium output of different sectors (use computer software as appropriate).
3. Consider the model of production from section 5.3, but now suppose the government purchases an exogenously given quantity $q_i$ of good $i$. These demands are financed by lump-sum taxes imposed on consumers. Reason carefully on how such government demands will propagate upstream from the affected markets with high demands to their suppliers and further upstream along the production network.
4. Discuss possible reasons for the unequal size and centrality of sectors in modern economies.

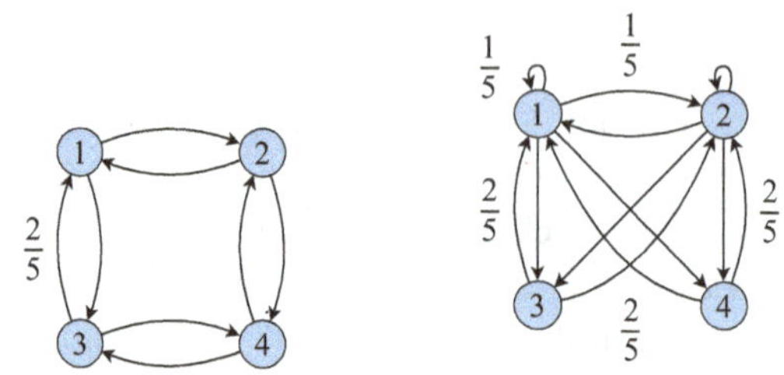


(a) Symmetric network (b) Core-periphery network

**Figure 5.5**
Supply chains.

5. Consider the two-layer supply chain problem discussed in section 5.5. There is one firm in each layer. Suppose that the probability of successful operation for a firm is $p \in (0, 1)$ and it is identical and independent across firms. A firm can raise its reliability level from $p$ to 1 by investing $C > 0$. Derive the equilibrium reliability investments as a function of $C$ and $p$.
6. Consider the two-layer supply chain problem with firm entry discussed in section 5.5. Firms can enter one layer. Suppose that the probability of successful operation for a firm is $p \in (0, 1)$ and its entry into a layer costs $F$. Derive the entry equilibrium as a function of $F$ and $p$.

# 6 Infrastructure

## 6.1 Introduction

Surviving works of infrastructure from antiquity, such as the urban grids of Mohenjo-daro in the Indus Valley, the Roman roads and aqueducts, and the Great Wall of China, continue to impress us, but there is no historical parallel to the extraordinary range of transport and infrastructure networks in the modern world. Examples include airlines, roads and trains, shipping, electricity, pipelines, and the Internet. It is difficult to do justice to this range of networks in the space of a single chapter. To convey a sense of the great diversity of such networks, the chapter will present case studies on three transport networks—airlines, roads, and trains. We will then present theoretical models with a view to developing economic principles that shape the structure of these networks and determine their performance.

We start with airlines. Air travel has grown enormously over the past few decades. Our point of departure is an empirical observation from our discussions in the introduction and chapter 1: most airlines operate a hub-spoke structure, and some recent low-cost airlines operate point-to-point networks. What are the determinants of network structure? We develop a theoretical model with two ingredients—fixed costs in creating links and benefits of flying that are declining in the number of flight transfers. The model predicts that airlines will either choose a *point-to-point* network or a *hub-spoke* network depending on the cost of creating flight links relative to the benefits of direct versus indirect flights. We use this theory to understand the routing networks of different airlines.

We then turn to road and train networks. The discussion begins with case studies on the Roman road network, the Indian railways, and the American railroads. These case studies help to bring out the scale of these networks and to indicate the enormous resources devoted to their creation. They also draw attention to the topological features of these networks. A distinctive feature of these transport networks, as compared to airline networks, is that physical geography has an important influence on the costs of linking. We draw upon the classical work of Robert Fogel and the significant advances made by recent research to develop a theoretical framework to study the relation between transport networks and economic activity. In this approach, the key idea is that transport networks help reduce the costs of shipping goods between locations; thus transport networks determine market access. The integration of markets in turn facilitates better allocation of resources and thereby raises incomes. Thus, on the one hand, transport networks seek to connect locations that are more productive and, on the other hand, the connections themselves shape the flow of goods and labor, and that shapes the scale of activity and the performance of various locations. Thus network design may play a decisive role in determining the fate of these locations.

We conclude with a discussion of the Belt and Road Initiative (BRI) launched by China in 2013. The BRI covers a wide range of infrastructure and involves a large number of countries. The discussion draws attention to the main elements of the initiative and connects them to the theoretical considerations developed in the chapter.

## 6.2 Airlines

The idea of flying goes as far back as the myth of Daedalus and Icarus. Leonardo da Vinci's designs of the fifteenth century brought it closer to reality, but air travel, as we know it really began in the early twentieth century as entrepreneurs, engineers, and governments built on what Orville Wright and Wilbur Wright had started not so long before. In this section, our attention will focus on passenger air travel and the airlines that operate planes. We begin with a brief discussion of the empirical background.

### 6.2.1 Empirical Background

Historically, airlines have been either state owned or heavily regulated. This meant that both the routing and the pricing of services were controlled by public authorities. In the US, private firms were allowed to function but were strictly regulated. In most other parts of the world, air services were provided by a natural monopoly (and this remains the case in many countries). Over the past three decades, there have been a number of major developments. One, passenger traffic has grown greatly: over the past two decades, international passenger numbers have grown by over 5 percent annually in most years. Two, in some large countries like India and China, the rates of growth have been in excess of 10 percent over the past decade (2010–2020) and countries in Africa and Latin America are expected to have high growth rates in the coming decade. Three, many countries have liberalized the airline sector—public-sector airlines have been privatized and a number of new companies have entered. Economy airlines like easyJet, Southwest, and Ryanair have become dominant in Europe and the US.

Airlines use a variety of strategies to compete in the market, which include the flights they operate and the prices they charge for these flights. In addition, airlines form alliances with other airlines to share capacity and facilities and to provide a broader market coverage. In this chapter, we will focus on airlines' decisions regarding their routing network.

In chapter 1, we noted that large international airlines such as British Airways and Singapore Airlines operate a hub-spoke network, while low-cost airlines such as Southwest

**Table 6.1**
A number of leading airlines throughout the world

| Airlines | Destinations | Flights |
|---|---|---|
| British Airways | 226 | 348 |
| Singapore Airlines | 68 | 103 |
| Ryanair | 221 | 1,741 |
| easyJet | 127 | 420 |
| Indigo | 75 | 508 |
| SpiceJet | 68 | 267 |
| Southwest | 109 | 2,641 |
| China Southern | 235 | 960 |
| China Eastern | 210 | 947 |
| American Airlines | 352 | 1,256 |
| United Airlines | 384 | 1,112 |
| EgyptAir | 87 | 118 |

*Source*: https://www.ch-aviation.com/portal/.

Airlines and Ryanair have a dense network that is closer to a point-to-point network. We present data on a few airlines to develop a sense of their sizes and the architecture of their routing networks in table 6.1. These numbers draw attention to the networks of some of the world's biggest airlines. They also highlight marked differences in the density of direct flights across airlines: British Airways, Egypt Air, and Singapore Airlines operate something close to a hub-spoke structure, while other airlines operate dense flight networks (with close to 50 percent of their flights being direct). The data also highlights the growth of new airlines such as Ryanair and easyJet (in Europe), Indigo and SpiceJet (in India), and China Eastern and China Southern. United Airlines and American Airlines lie somewhere in between these two extremes. To help appreciate the differences across airlines, we next plot a few routing networks: Singapore Airlines and Ryanair in figure 6.1 and China Southern and Indigo Airlines in figure 6.2. We now examine the economic factors that shape the architecture of routing networks.

In these networks, there are two types of trips: direct (without stops) and indirect. Passengers prefer a direct flight to a flight with stop-overs and flight changes. On the other hand, operating a flight is costly for an airline: these costs include depreciation of aircraft, personnel salaries, landing slot charges at airports, and costs of selling tickets and checking in passengers.

To develop a feel for the issues let us consider some numbers. Suppose that there is a passenger demand of 20 from every city to every other city. Consider the network in figure 6.3(a). If a plane has a capacity of 60, then a direct flight between a pair of cities entails an excess capacity of 40. Figure 6.3(b) presents a hub-spoke network. In this network, every flight carries 60 passengers: thus every flight operates at full capacity. This is referred to as *economies of density*.

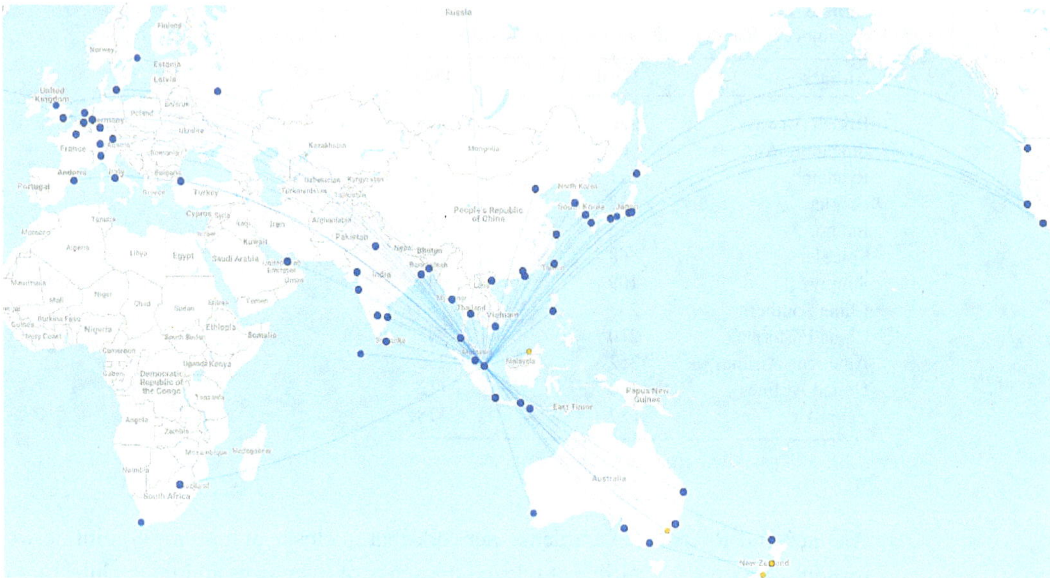


(a) Singapore Airlines

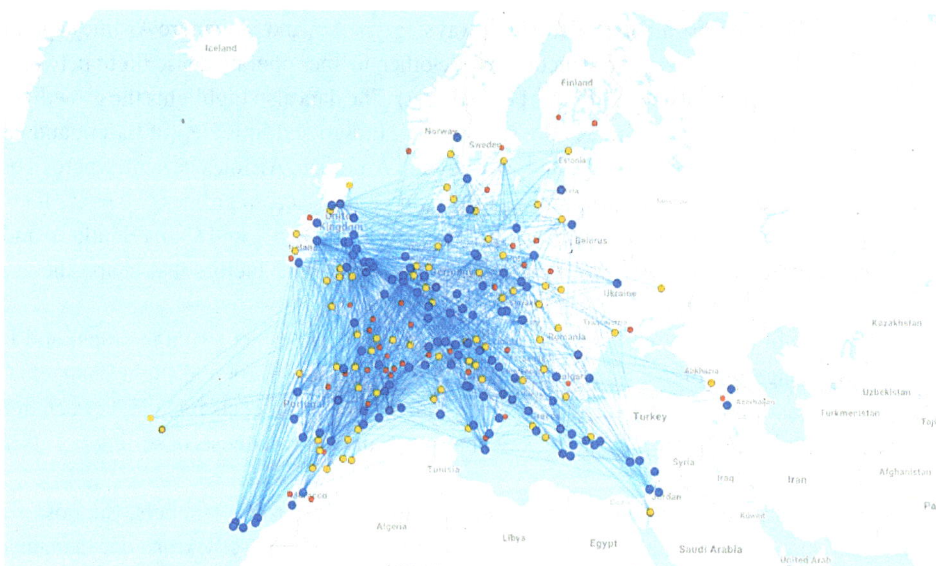


(b) Ryanair

**Figure 6.1**
Airline network examples. *Source*: www.ch-aviation.com/portal/

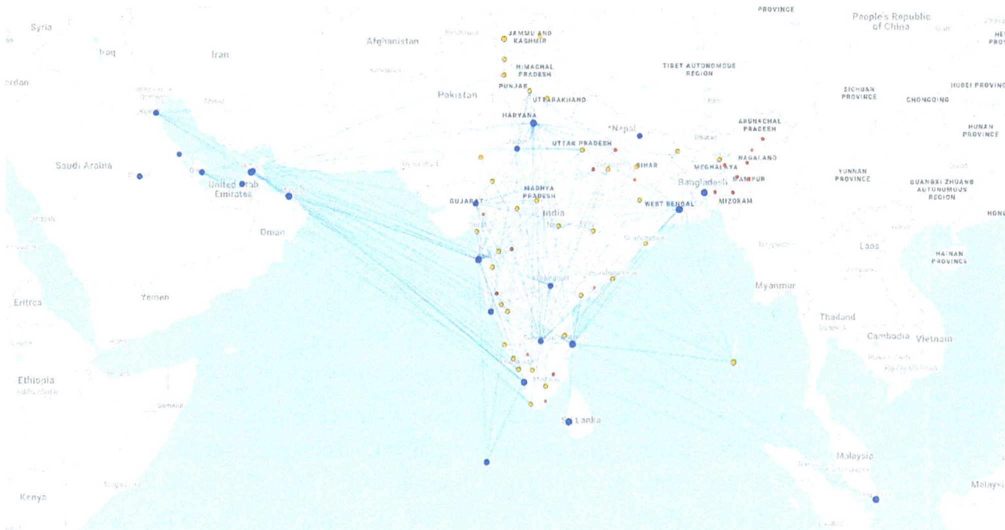


(a) Indigo Airlines

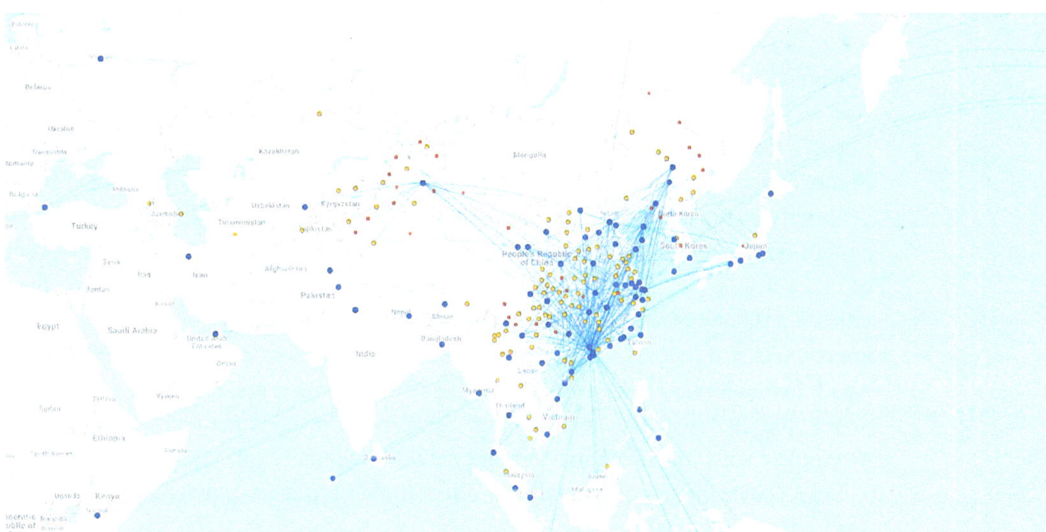


(b) China Southern

**Figure 6.2**
Airline network examples. *Source*: www.ch-aviation.com/portal/

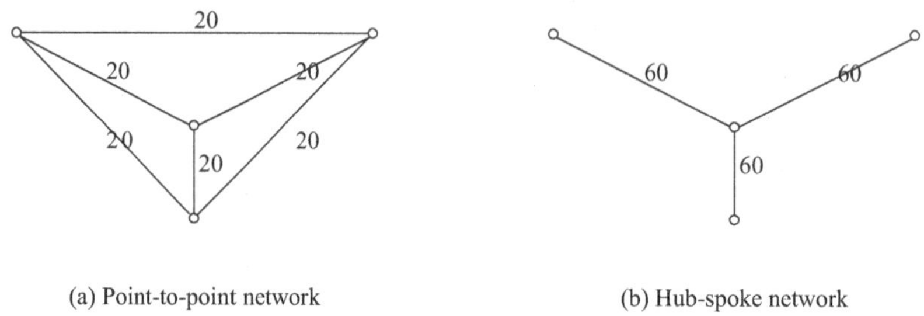


**Figure 6.3**
Capacity use in networks.

In a hub-spoke network, there are more indirect flights, and because passengers dislike making flight changes, this will push the airline to charge lower prices. A question at the end of the chapter examines pricing in airline network. These observations suggest the following trade-off: direct flights entail larger costs of operation, but indirect flights lead to lower prices for the airlines. With these remarks in place, let us now turn to a model of optimal network design.

### 6.2.2 A Simple Model of Airline Routing

We present a model based on Hendricks, Piccione, and Tan (1995). There is a set of $N=\{1,\ldots,n\}$ cities, with $n\geq 2$; people living in each city wish to travel to other cities. Let $A, B$ denote a pair of cities. A *direct connection* is a nonstop flight from $A$ to $B$. A flight-routing network is graph $g$, and a typical link in this network is denoted by $g_{AB}$. For simplicity, suppose that all flights have return flights: so $g_{A,B}=g_{B,A}$, and we can talk of links as signifying a return flight. The number of links in network $g$ is given by $m(g)$. A sequence of cities $A_1, A_2, \ldots, A_{z+1}$ is called a *path* if there is a direct link between two consecutive cities. The length of such a path is $z$: this is the number of direct flights in the path. Two cities are *connected* if there is a path between them. A *network* is said to be *connected* if there is a path between every pair of cities. A hub-spoke network $g$ is said to have size $m$ if there are $m+1$ cities in it, with one hub and $m$ spokes. A point-to-point network $g$ is another name for a complete network; so a point-to-point network with $m$ cities contains $m(m-1)/2$ links.

Let $f>0$ be the cost of operating a direct flight between any two cities. Then the cost of a network with $k$ links is $fk$.

An airline carrier's *operating profits* are calculated as the revenue minus the variable costs. They can therefore be written as the sum of profits across city-market pairs. In each city pair, they depend on the length of the path that a traveler has to traverse: let $\pi(z)$ denote the (gross) returns for a city pair that is distance $z$ apart in the network. As passengers prefer fewer stops we assume that gross profits are falling in distance $z$:

$$\pi(z)\geq\pi(z+1)\geq 0, \forall\, z. \tag{6.1}$$

The profits of an airline therefore depend on the number of flights it operates and the length of the flights that passengers have to traverse. Let $d(A,B;g)$ be the length of the shortest path in network $g$ between two cities, $A$ and $B$. The profits of the airline can be written as:

$$\Pi(g) = \sum_{i,j:i<j} \pi(d(i,j;g)) - fm(g). \tag{6.2}$$

Clearly, no flights would be created if the costs were too large. To rule out empty networks, we assume that

$$(n-1)\pi(1) + \frac{(n-1)(n-2)}{2}\pi(2) > (n-1)f. \tag{6.3}$$

The first term on the left side of equation (6.3) reflects the returns from $n-1$ direct flights between the spokes and the hub, and the second term reflects the returns from all the one-stop indirect flights between the spokes that go through the hub. This assumption therefore says that the benefits of a hub-spoke network outweigh the costs of operating the $n-1$ routes.

The following result provides us a complete description of optimal routing networks in relation to the costs of flights.

**Proposition 6.1** *Suppose equations (6.1) and (6.3) hold. Then there is some* $f^*$ *such that*

(a) *For* $f < f^*$*, the optimal network is the point-to-point network.*
(b) *For* $f > f^*$*, the optimal network is the hub-spoke network.*

Let us develop the arguments underlying this result. First we will show that creating a network with $m < n-1$ links is never optimal. As $m$ is less than $n-1$, we know that the airline cannot connect all the cities. What is the best it can hope to do? Well, it can provide direct flights between $m$ city pairs and provides a one-stop flight between the $m$ pairs of cities. This is possible with a hub-spoke network with $m$ spokes. The airline earns a profit given by

$$m\pi(1) + \frac{m(m-1)}{2}\pi(2) - fm \tag{6.4}$$

using this network. Could such a network ever be optimal for the airline? No. To see why, observe that the last link—the $m$th link—helps connect a city to the hub-spoke network with $m-1$ spoke cities. So the marginal cost of the last flight is $f$, while the marginal return is the difference in the operating profits of the $m-1$ hub-spoke network compared to the $m$ hub-spoke network. This is given by $\pi(1) + (m-1)\pi(2)$. Reasoning similarly, the marginal value of increasing the number of direct flights from $m$ to $m+1$ is $\pi(1) + m\pi(2)$. Thus if link $m$ is profitable, so is link $m+1$. This means that if the airline found it profitable to add flight $m$, it would be even more profitable to add flight $m+1$. This tells us that a network with $0 < m < n-1$ is never optimal. This is an example of agglomeration: once a hub-spoke network begins to form, the marginal returns to connecting grow with the size of the network.

Next, consider a network with exactly $n-1$ direct flights: such a network provides a direct flight between $(n-1)$ city pairs. The shortest path length for all the other $(n(n-1)/2-(n-1))$ city pairs is 2. The hub-spoke network with $n-1$ links attains this best-case scenario. The profits of the airline in this hub-spoke network are

$$(n-1)\pi(1)+\frac{(n-1)(n-2)}{2}\pi(2)-(n-1)f. \tag{6.5}$$

What are the marginal returns to adding a link to this hub-spoke network? The new flight would connect two spoke cities: thus the marginal returns are given by the difference in profit between a direct flight and a one-stop flight: $(\pi(1)-\pi(2))$. It therefore follows that if $f<(\pi(1)-\pi(2))$, then it is profitable for the airline to add a link. Observe that the marginal returns to adding links between any pair of spokes remains unchanged as we connect the spokes. Thus if it is profitable to connect one pair, then it is profitable to connect all pairs (i.e., to create a point-to-point network). We have thus shown that an optimal network is either the hub-spoke network or the point-to-point network.

These arguments provide a very general basis for understanding the optimal networks not only for airlines but also in other settings so it is instructive to present the details.

*Proof.* We show that a network with $n-1<m<n(n-1)/2$ links cannot be optimal. Note that with $m$ links, there are $2m$ direct connections and at most $(n(n-1)-2m)$ connections with 1 stop. Thus gross profits are bounded by the expression

$$m\pi(1)+\left(\frac{n(n-1)}{2}-m\right)\pi(2). \tag{6.6}$$

This payoff is attained by a hub-spoke network of the following type: a hub-spoke network with $(n-1)$ links plus $(m-(n-1))$ direct links between the remaining spoke cities.

Note that the gain from adding direct connection $(m+1)$ is given by $(\pi(1)-\pi(2))$. Thus if $f<(\pi(1)-\pi(2))$, then it is profitable to create an additional link. Otherwise, the $(n-1)$ hub-spoke network generates a higher gross profit than any larger network.

The second step shows that a network with $m<n-1$ links is never optimal. Suppose that $X$ is an optimal network with $m<n-1$ links. Then the maximum payoff from such a network is given by

$$m\pi(1)+\left(\frac{m(m+1)}{2}-m\right)\pi(2)-mf. \tag{6.7}$$

Since $m$ links is preferred to $(m-1)$ links, it must be that the payoff with $m-1$ links is lower:

$$(m-1)\pi(1)+\left(\frac{(m-1)m}{2}-(m-1)\right)\pi(2)-(m-1)f. \tag{6.8}$$

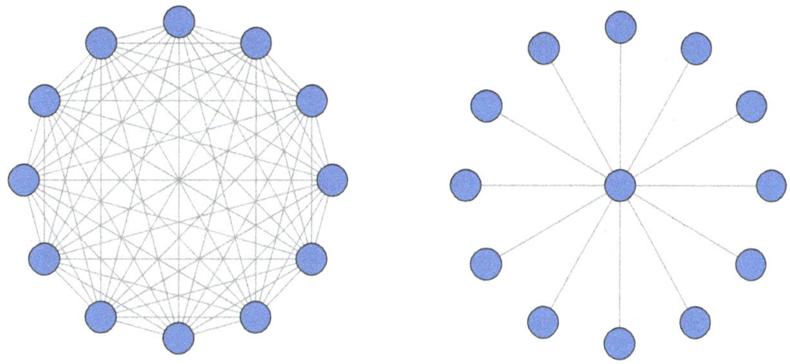

(a) Point-to-point (b) Hub-spoke network

**Figure 6.4**
Optimal airline networks.

As equation (6.7) is greater than equation (6.8), we get

$$\begin{aligned} &\pi(1)(m-(m-1))+\pi(2)\left(\tfrac{m(m-1)}{2}-\tfrac{(m-1)(m-2)}{2}\right)-f>0 \\ \Rightarrow\ &\pi(1)+\pi(2)(m-1)-f>0. \end{aligned} \tag{6.9}$$

The payoff from adding link $m+1$ is given by

$$(m+1)\pi(1)+\left(\frac{(m+1)(m+2)}{2}-(m+1)\right)\pi(2)-(m+1)f. \tag{6.10}$$

Subtracting equation (6.7) from equation (6.10), we get that the benefit of adding another link is

$$\pi(1)((m+1)-m)+\pi(2)\left(\frac{m(m+1)}{2}-\frac{m(m-1)}{2}\right)-f.$$

Simplifying,

$$\pi(1)+\pi(2)m-f. \tag{6.11}$$

Clearly, equation (6.11) is positive, given that equation (6.9) holds. Hence $0<m<n-1$ cannot be profitable. Equation (6.3) rules out the empty network (with $m=0$). The proof is complete. ■

Figure 6.4 presents the optimal networks. We next use the theory as a lens through which to view the structure of airline networks in different parts of the world.

### 6.2.3 Mapping Theory to Empirical Routing Networks

There are a number of forces at work, but as a first step, it is instructive to consider the size of planes as they offer an indication of the costs of a link. Ryanair operates the same aircraft model on all its flights—the Boeing 737-800—with a capacity of 189 passengers.

British Airways uses a range of planes, but for its long-haul flights, it uses the Boeing 777-200 plane, with a capacity ranging from 314 to 451. These differences in capacity can be related to our discussion on the capacity of planes and the shape of the network in figure 6.3: larger-capacity planes are consistent with hub-spoke networks, while smaller-capacity planes are consistent with point-to-point networks.

A second point concerns the airports that the two airlines use. British Airways uses principal airports at major cities, which have high landing fees; by contrast, Ryanair is well known for operating its flights from smaller airports that charge lower landing fees. Both these features lower the fixed cost of operating direct flights for Ryanair. The theory therefore helps us understand why Ryanair operates a dense network (with point-to-point tickets only), whereas British Airways operates a hub-spoke network. Similar considerations arise when we consider the networks of the other airlines listed in table 6.1.

We have assumed that the demand for travel is equal across city pairs. Clearly, larger city pairs will have different demands compared to pairs of small cities. This will shape the routing network in an intuitive way: the airline will operate a hub-spoke network in which the larger cities will also have a direct link. A question at the end of this chapter explores this issue more systematically. We have considered the problem of optimal network design by a monopoly airline. In principle, it is possible that airlines may choose richer and more complicated routing networks when facing competition from other airlines. A question at the end of the chapter examines competition among airlines and develops conditions under which competing airlines will create hub-spoke networks.

Let us summarize what we have learned in this section. Air travel has grown enormously since the 1950s, and this growth has been especially large in the last two decades. This growth has been accompanied with a progressive deregulation of the market for flying. The result has been an expansion of older airlines and the emergence of a number of new airline companies. These airlines compete to serve consumers. Their strategies include the pricing and routing of flights. We have focused on the design of routing networks. Airlines operate a variety of routing networks ranging from the hub-spoke networks to dense point-to-point networks. We explored a simple model of airline network design: in this model, there are two key ingredients—the costs of setting up direct routes and the higher benefits of direct routes. This model yields the following insight—when all city pairs have similar demand for air travel, the optimal network is either a hub-spoke or a point-to-point network (i.e., all other networks are suboptimal).

## 6.3 Roads and Trains

To set the stage, we start with a brief discussion of an ancient transport network—the Roman roads. This is followed by a discussion of two large modern transport networks—US railroads and railways in colonial India. The aim of these short case studies is to bring out the extraordinary scale of these networks, to discuss the goals of the network builders, and to draw attention to the spatial dimension of these networks (that sets them apart from airline networks).

### 6.3.1 Empirical Background

#### Roman roads

At its peak, in the first half of the second century AD, the Roman Empire ranged from Hadrian's Wall (in Scotland) and the banks of the Rhine River in the north to Morocco and Egypt in the south and from Spain in the west all the way to the Euphrates River (in Mesopotamia) in the east. By 125 AD, the Romans had built over 80,000 kilometers of hard-surfaced roads connecting their capital with the frontiers of their far-flung empire. Figure 6.5 presents a map of the principal Roman highway network at the time of Emperor Hadrian. Our discussion here draws on Britannica (2000).

Wars were frequent, and roads were the principal mode of transport for the army and for the incorporation of captured territory into the empire. At the start, highways connected the capital, Rome, with nearby provinces and towns that had recently been taken over by the Romans. The first of the great Roman roads, the Via Appia, started in 312 BC, originally ran southeast from Rome to Tarentum (modern-day Taranto), and was later extended to Brundisium (modern-day Brindisi) on the Adriatic coast. By the beginning of the second century BC, four other great roads radiated from Rome: the Via Aurelia, extending northwest to Genua (modern-day Genoa); the Via Flaminia, running north to the Adriatic, where it joined the Via Aemilia, crossed the Rubicon, and led northwest; the Via Valeria, east across the peninsula by way of Lake Fucinus (Conca del Fucino); and the Via Latina, running southeast and joining the Via Appia near Capua. These major roads were supplemented by numerous feeder roads extending far into the Roman provinces, thereby creating a network with a hub at Rome, giving rise to the expression, "all roads lead to Rome."

In 145 BC, the Romans started constructing the Via Egnatia, an extension of the Via Appia beyond the Adriatic into Greece and Asia Minor, where it joined the ancient Persian Royal Road. In northern Africa, the Romans followed up their conquest of Carthage by building a road system that spanned the south shore of the Mediterranean. In Gaul, they developed a system centred near Lyon, from where the main roads extended to the Rhine, Bordeaux, and the English Channel. In Britain, a network was created with roads stretching out from London. In Gaul and Roman Britain, the principal roads were laid out in a hub-spoke structure, while in Spain, the geography dictated a system of main roads around the periphery of the peninsula (with secondary roads leading into the central plateau). In summary, the network combined key elements of the hub-spoke structure, reached out toward the boundaries of the empire, and respected the physical constraints of geography.

Once in place, the roads came to be used to transport different kinds of agricultural products (oil, olives, wheat, and wine) and for post, by the imperial courier system. The Roman road system continued to serve Europe throughout the Middle Ages; many major modern

Figure 6.5
Roman road network, 125 AD: By Andrein–Own work, CC BY-SA 3.0, https://commons.wikimedia.org/w/index.php?curid=6654575.

roads have been built on old Roman routes, but fragments of the old system survive and remain in use in many parts of Europe to the present day. For a detailed and fascinating study of Roman infrastructure, visit the Stanford University Department of Classics website (https://classics.stanford.edu/). ■

### Trains in colonial India

We next turn to another of history's great transportation projects—the vast network of rail tracks built in colonial India (an area covering modern-day India, Pakistan, and Bangladesh). The first railway line in India, Red Hill Railroad, was built to bring granite for road building in Madras in 1836. However, the start of the construction of a national railway network is generally traced to a railway line that ran from Bombay to Thane and started operations in April 1853. The train network was built during the period 1852–1930, and in the end stretched over 67,000 kilometers. The material in this case study draws on Donaldson (2018).

Prior to the creation of this train network, goods transport within India took place on roads, rivers, and coastal shipping routes. The bulk of inland travel was carried by bullocks along the road network. On the best road surfaces and during optimal weather conditions, bullock carts could cover 20–30 kilometers per day. Trade was also carried by pack bullocks (which carried goods strapped to their backs and generally traveled directly over pastureland), which were considerably slower and riskier than cart bullocks. Water transport was superior to road transport, but it functioned only on the Brahmaputra, Ganges, and Indus river systems. Coastal shipping was available along India's long coastline; steamships were fast and could cover over 100 kilometers per day but only served major seaports. Against this backdrop of costly and slow internal transportation, the potential for economic effects appears to be very large when we note that compared to traditional modes of transport, railroads could ship commodities over 600 kilometers in a day, and at much lower per-unit distance freight rates. It is not surprising that the construction of a train network was discussed as early as 1832.

The decisions on where to lay the train tracks were made by the government of India. The government had three motives for building railroads—military, commercial, and humanitarian. Since its inception, military motives were prominent and appeared at every stage of the development of the network. The military consideration was reinforced after the Indian Mutiny of 1857.

The original plan was to build five trunk lines to connect India's major provincial capitals—Delhi, Bombay, Madras, Calcutta, and Lahore—so as to maximize the political advantages of a train network. These lines were built by 1869. The expansion of the train network is presented in figure 6.6. We see that the network eventually fanned out to all corners of the country, reflecting the strategic considerations underlying its construction. Another aspect of the network was that it is dense in the northern plains and relatively

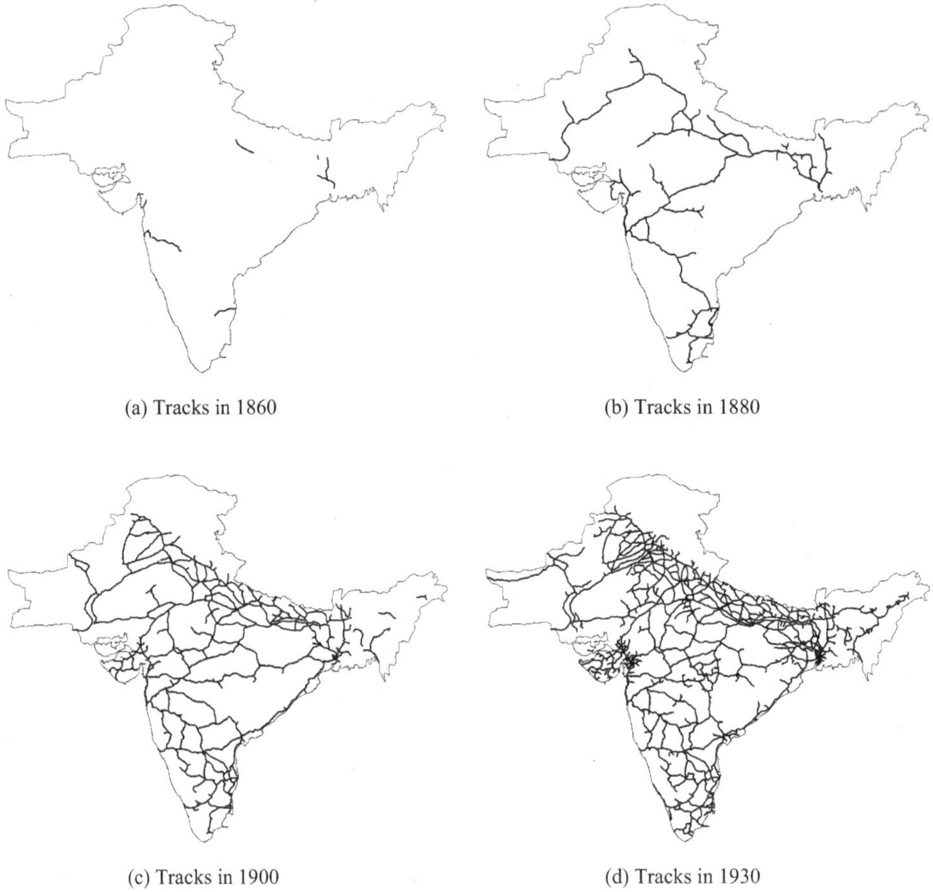

**Figure 6.6**
Expansion of Indian Railways, 1860–1930. Courtesy: Dave Donaldson.

sparse in central India and the north (in Kashmir). Over this period, 1850–1930, the train network was the dominant form of public investment in colonial India. The total mileage of the Indian railways remained relatively unchanged throughout the twentieth century. The Indian Railways is one of the largest employers in the world and the major carrier for freight and passenger traffic in twenty-first-century India. ■

### Railroads in the United States

We next take up the development of the American railroads. The construction of train networks in the US started in the 1820s and by 1900, 215,000 miles of tracks had been laid. The presentation here draws on Britannica (2000) and Donaldson and Hornbeck (2016).

In the 1820s a number of cities on the East Coast, including New York, Boston, Baltimore, and Charleston, began exploring railroad routes to access raw materials and agricultural produce from the inland and to lower transport costs to ship their manufactured goods to the inland markets. The first phase of American railroad development, from 1828 until about 1850, involved connecting pairs of large cities that were close neighbors: New York City and New Haven, Connecticut; Richmond, Virginia, and Washington, D.C.; and Syracuse, New York, and Rochester, New York.

The growth of the railroads stepped up significantly with an extension into the interior of the continent and from the Atlantic to the Pacific. In 1862, the Pacific Railroad Act chartered the Central Pacific and the Union Pacific railroad companies, tasking them with building a transcontinental railroad that would link the US from east to west. The first transcontinental railroad was completed on May 10, 1869. The effects of this railroad on travel times were dramatic: in the 1850s, it took four to six months to travel from the Missouri River to California by wagon, but in 1870, it took approximately seven days to travel on the transcontinental line from New York to San Francisco. Figures 6.7 and 6.8 present an overview of the expansion of the railroads through the period 1830–1900.

By 1871, approximately 45,000 miles of track had been laid. Beginning in the early 1870s, railroad construction increased dramatically, and between 1871 and 1900, another 170,000 miles were added to the railroad system. Much of this growth can be attributed to the transcontinental railroads. By 1900, four additional transcontinental railroads connected the eastern states to the Pacific Coast.

The state and federal governments supported private companies in the construction of this railroad network. The governments offered millions of acres of public land to railroad companies to lay track and earn revenue by selling the land. At the start of the twentieth century, railroads were the primary carrier for both passengers and freight. During the twentieth century, passenger traffic declined as people shifted to automobiles and air travel, but the share of American railroads in freight has remained high today. At the start of the twenty-first century, the railroads carried over 40 percent of all freight in the US. ■

These networks date from different periods in history and are located in different parts of the world. One feature they share, though, is that they were truly monumental in their scale and in the resources devoted to their construction. A second point pertains to the objectives of the network builders: in the case of the Roman Roads and the Indian railways, strategic considerations relating to conquest and consolidation of empire were critical. By contrast, the building of the American railroads was driven primarily by economic considerations. However, regardless of their objectives, builders faced great resource constraints: the network that emerged, therefore, may be seen as a preferred choice in the face of resource (and geographical) constraints. Finally, the case studies draw attention to the topology of the network. Each of these networks spans many more nodes and has a clear physical aspect to it that is closely related to the topography of the countries in which it lies.

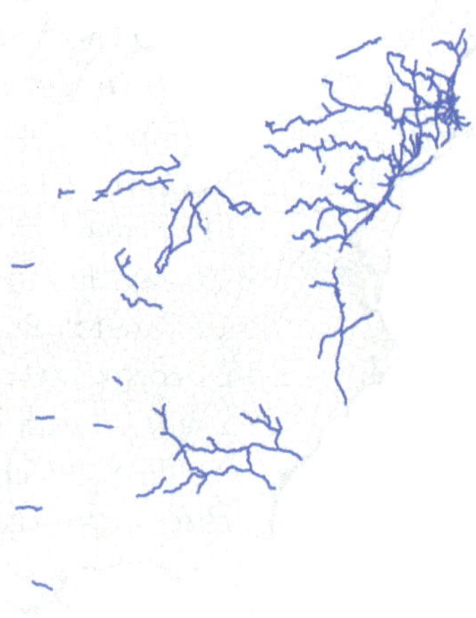

(a) Network in 1850

(b) Network in 1870

**Figure 6.7**
Expansion of US railroads, 1830–1870. *Source*: Donaldson and Hornbeck (2016).

(a) Network in 1880

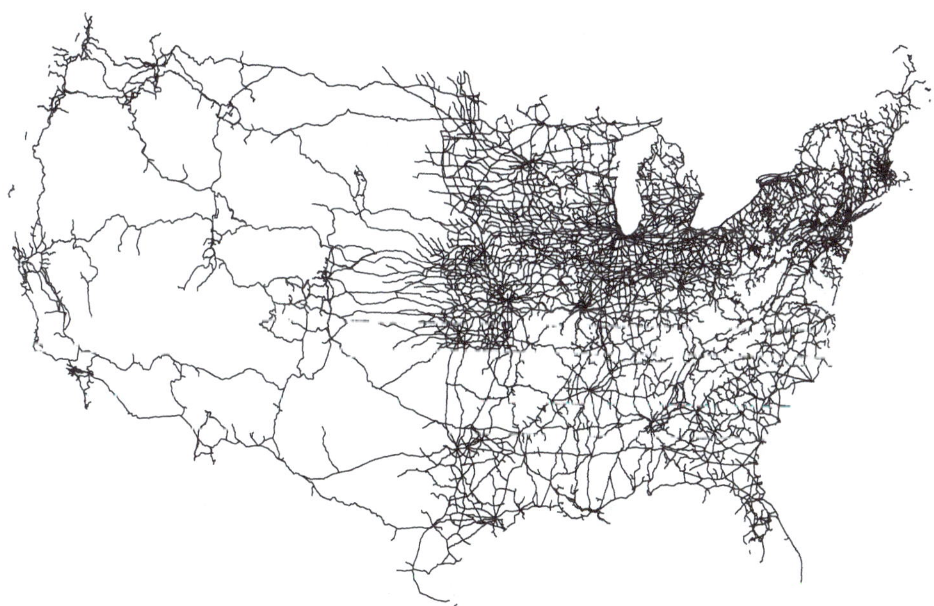

(b) Network in 1900

**Figure 6.8**
Network expansion, 1870–1900. *Source*: Donaldson and Hornbeck (2016).

We now turn to the relation between transport networks and economic activity. Historians and economists have studied the role of train networks extensively. The following passage gives us an impression of the powerful claims that have been made on the economic impact of trains:

> Research ... has further buttressed the idea that the railroad was an imperative of economic growth. Christopher Savage, in his recent *Economic History of Transport*, states that the influence of the railroad in American development "can hardly be over-emphasized" since "agricultural and industrial development and the settlement of the West would scarcely have been possible" without it. W. W. Rostow has administered an even stronger fillip to this view-point. In the projection of his concept of a "take-off into self-sustained growth," Rostow assigns railroads a crucial role. The railroad, he argues, was "historically the most powerful single initiator of take-offs." It "performed the Smithian function of widening the market," it was a "prerequisite in many cases to the development of a major new and rapidly expanding export sector," and most important, it "led on to the development of modern coal, iron and engineering industries." Rostow lists the United States first among the countries in which the influence of the railroad was "decisive." (Fogel 1962, pp. 163–164).

There are a number of ways in which railroads may be important for economic activity. For example, they enable cheaper and speedier transportation of perishable products, they may benefit manufacturing through increased scale and coordination, and by facilitating movement of people, they may also facilitate a better flow of ideas and encourage technological growth. For concreteness, we will focus on one of these, examining the impact of lower costs of moving goods from one location to another. We present a theoretical framework that allows us to study the implication of this cost reduction. We will use the model to comment on the quantitative impact of the American railroads and Indian railways, and then we will use the model to discuss the optimal design of transport networks.

## 6.4 Theoretical Framework for Trains and Roads

We will consider a theoretical model in which the primary benefit of a transport link between two locations is that it allows producers in one location to access and sell goods to consumers in the other location. The costs of a link depend on its quality (a four-lane highway costs more than a one-lane road) and on geography (a river or a mountain lying between the locations may necessitate a bridge or a detour that is costly). The costs of transporting a good in turn depend on the quality of the link—a regular train service or a multilane highway may help move goods faster, and possibly also at a lower cost. The aim is to understand how location and geography shape the network and how network formation in turn shapes the scale and spatial distribution of economic activity.

The model is based on Fajgelbaum and Schaal (2020). The economy consists of a set of locations $\mathcal{J} = \{1, \ldots, J\}$. There are $L_j$ workers at location $j \in \mathcal{J}$; $L = \sum_j L_j$ is the total number of workers. Workers consume a bundle of traded goods and a nontraded good (land or housing, which is in fixed supply). The utility of an individual worker who consumes $c$

units of the traded goods bundle and $h$ units of the nontraded good is $U(c, h)$. The utility function $U$ is homothetic and concave in both its arguments. $C_j$ is the aggregate demand of the traded goods bundle at location $j$, and the per capita consumption of traded goods is $c_j = C_j / L_j$.

There are $n = 1, \ldots N$ traded goods/sectors. These goods are combined to obtain $C_j$:

$$C_j = D_j(D_j^1, \ldots, D_j^N), \tag{6.12}$$

where $D_j^n$ is consumption of good $n$ in location $j$. The aggregator function $D_j(.)$ is assumed to be concave and homogenous of degree 1. In addition, in the examples presented in sections 6.5.1–6.5.2 below, we will assume a constant elasticity to substitution function.

Suppose for simplicity that production uses only labor, and that output is linear in labor input. In the basic model, we will assume that labor is immobile across locations, but mobile across the production sectors of a location. Thus production of good $n$ at location $j$ is given by

$$Y_j^n = L_j^n, \tag{6.13}$$

where $L_j^n$ is the number of workers assigned to sector $n$ at location $j$. In some of the examples here, we will allow for differences in productivity across locations.

The locations $J$ are arranged on an undirected graph $g = (\mathcal{J}, \mathcal{E})$, where $\mathcal{E}$ denotes the set of edges (i.e., unordered pairs of $\mathcal{J}$). For each location $j$, there is a set $N_j(g)$ of connected locations or neighbors. Goods can be shipped only between connected locations; that is, goods shipped from $j$ can be sent to any $k \in N_j(g)$, but to reach any $k \notin N_j(g)$, they must transit through a sequence of linked locations. The transport network is given by $\{I_{jk}\}_{j \in \mathcal{J}}$, $k \in N_j(g)$.

A natural interpretation is that $j$ is a geographic unit such as a county, $N_j(g)$ are its bordering counties, and shipments are done over land. More generally, the neighbors in the model do not need to be geographically contiguous since it could be possible to ship directly between geographically distant locations by land, air, or sea. The fully connected scenario in which every location may ship directly to every other location, $N_j(g) = \mathcal{J}$ for all $j$, is a special case.

Goods may transit through several locations before reaching a point where they are consumed. Let $Q_{jk}^n$ be the quantity of goods in sector $n$ shipped from $j$ to $k \in N_j(g)$ (regardless of where the good was originally produced). There are a number of ways in which transport costs can be modeled. For simplicity, we will assume "iceberg" costs—we will therefore suppose that part of the "good" sent is used up during the transportation. Moreover, it will be assumed that there is no congestion in transportation across goods but there is congestion for individual goods.

Transporting a unit of good $n$ from location $j$ to location $k$ requires $\tau_{jk}^n$ units of the good itself. So $1 + \tau_{jk}^n$ corresponds to the iceberg cost. This per-unit cost is specified as a function of the total quantity $Q_{jk}^n$ of good $n$ shipped on the link $jk$, and of the quality of infrastructure

$I_{jk}$ on that link:

$$\tau_{jk}^{n} = \tau_{jk}(Q_{jk}^{n}, I_{jk}). \tag{6.14}$$

Congestion is an important feature of this model: per-unit cost of transporting is increasing in the quantity shipped:

$$\frac{\partial \tau_{jk}(Q, I)}{\partial Q} \geq 0. \tag{6.15}$$

In short, the more that is shipped, the higher the per-unit shipping cost. This captures higher travel times or road damage, decreasing returns to scale in transportation due to land-intensive fixed factors such as warehousing or specialized inputs.

A second assumption of the model is that better infrastructure lowers the transport costs:

$$\frac{\partial \tau_{jk}(Q, I)}{\partial I} \leq 0. \tag{6.16}$$

The transport technology $\tau_{jk}(Q, I)$ may also depend on $jk$, capturing variations in shipping costs across links for the same quantity shipped and for the same infrastructure. This variation may reflect geographical considerations such as distance or physical landscape. In principle, the per-unit cost function $\tau_{jk}(Q, I)$ may depend on the direction of the flow; for example, if elevation is higher in $j$ than $k$ and it is cheaper to drive downhill, then $\tau_{jk}(Q, I) < \tau_{kj}(Q, I)$.

It follows that at every location, the balance of these flows must hold: for every good $n = 1, \ldots, N$, and for all locations $j = 1, \ldots, J$,

$$D_j^n + \sum_{k \in N_j(g)} (1 + \tau_{jk}^n) Q_{jk}^n \leq Y_j^n + \sum_{i \in N_j(g)} Q_{ij}^n. \tag{6.17}$$

The left side describes location j's consumption $D_j^n$ of good $n$, exports to neighbors $Q_{jk}^n$, and inputs to the transport sector $\tau_{jk}^n Q_{jk}^n$. These flows must be less than or equal to the local production $Y_j^n$ and imports from the neighbors $Q_{ij}^n$ of good $n$.

We let $P_j^n$ be the price of good $n$ at location $j$, which reflects society's valuation of a marginal unit of good $n$ in location $j$.

### 6.4.1 The Economic Returns to Train Networks

We use the theoretical framework proposed here to make some observations about the economic returns to transport networks. We first take up the American railroads. In a famous early contribution, Fogel (1964) proposed measuring the benefits in terms of cost savings generated by the railroads. Viewed in terms of our theoretical framework, this may be seen as calculating the impact of railroads on the total transport costs, $Q_{jk}^n \tau_{jk}^n$, across all goods and all locations.

As transport of agricultural produce from the American Midwest was a central motivation for the building of the railroads, Fogel (1964) focused on cost savings in that sector in 1890. This cost savings may be computed as the sum of savings on interregional trade and the savings on intraregional trade. Interregional trade covered trade from 9 primary markets in the American Midwest to 90 secondary markets in the east and south of the country: here, shipping costs were only moderately cheaper with railroads compared to using natural waterways and canals. The total cost savings amounted to the difference in shipping costs (with and without railroads) times the quantity of transported agricultural goods. Fogel (1964) showed that this number was no more than $73 million, or 0.6 percent of gross national product (GNP).

Intraregional trade covers the shipments from farms to primary markets. In the absence of railroads, farms would incur substantially higher costs in transporting goods by wagon to the nearest waterway before they could be shipped to the closest primary market. In farms more than 40 miles from a waterway, wagon transportation may have become prohibitively expensive. Fogel (1964) deemed all land farther than 40 miles from a navigable waterway as lying in the infeasible region: he bounded the loss in these areas by the value of agricultural land in these areas and arrived at a figure of $154 million lost in annual rent. He then estimated the savings in transportation costs for the feasible region (lying within 40 miles of a waterway): he bounded these by $94 million using a similar approach to the interregional analysis. Thus the total annual intraregional cost saving was bounded above by $248 million (or 2.1 percent of GNP). The total social savings estimate of $321 million—2.7 percent of GNP—is generally regarded as indicating a limited impact of the railroads on the American economy.

Fogel (1964)'s approach was followed by a large body of research studying the value of large infrastructure projects. A natural next step to the cost savings idea is to examine the effects of a railroad network on production, income, and consumption at different locations. This helps us develop a more aggregate economic picture of railroads.

Donaldson and Hornbeck (2016) present a measurement of this aggregate impact. Consider the county as the geographical unit. The railroads lowered the costs of transport between counties and thereby facilitated the integration of county markets. A county's market access increases when it becomes cheaper to trade with another county, particularly when the other county has a larger population and higher trade costs with other counties. So we can see that changes in market access can act as a summary statistic for all direct and indirect impacts on each county from changes in the national railroad network. In an agricultural economy, greater prices and higher output responses will result in higher farm incomes, which will be reflected in higher land values. Donaldson and Hornbeck (2016) estimate that removing all railroads in 1890 would have lowered the total value of agricultural land in the US by 60.2 percent. This reduction in agricultural land value would generate annual economic losses equal to 3.22 percent of GNP. The estimates of Donaldson and Hornbeck (2016) are thus slightly larger than the social savings estimates derived by Fogel (1964).

It is instructive to similarly examine the effects of the Indian railways from a market integration perspective. To begin to appreciate the scale of change brought about by trains, note that prior to the trains, bullocks were the principal model of transport for commodities.

They traveled no more than 30 kilometers per day along India's sparse network of dirt roads. By contrast, railroads could transport commodities over 600 kilometers in a day, and at much lower per-unit distance freight rates.

As in the American case, let us examine the economic implications of the train network in terms of lower costs of transport. Lower transport costs in principle allow a producer in one location to earn a higher price from selling their produce at other locations, and also possibly to sell to new, more distant and erstwhile inaccessible markets. Both these effects should raise their incomes. As India was a predominantly agricultural country at that time, let us consider changes in agricultural income. Using a theoretical framework as in the previous section, Donaldson (2018) shows that the train network did indeed have large effects. First, he shows that in line with the theoretical prediction, as transport costs declined, price differences across locations fell significantly. Moreover, when a district was connected to the rail network, farm incomes rose by 16 percent. To place this in perspective, we note that, over the period 1870–1930, Indian agricultural income grew by a mere 35 percent. Being connected to the railroad, therefore, made a very big difference to a farmer's income.

As transport links lower costs, the structure of the network and the strength of the links across locations matter for economic activity. We now examine how these considerations shape the optimal design of transport networks and how that design affects economic activity.

## 6.5 Optimal Spatial Transport Networks

To formulate the optimal design problem, we introduce the final ingredient of the model: the costs of networks. Building transport infrastructure requires a resource (such as stones, concrete, or asphalt) that is available in a fixed supply, $K$. Thus the opportunity cost of building infrastructure between two locations is simply the value of forgoing infrastructure elsewhere. Building infrastructure $I_{jk}$ on link $jk$ requires an investment of $\delta^I_{jk} I_{jk}$ units of $K$. The network-building constraint is

$$\sum_j \sum_{k \in N_j(g)} \delta^I_{jk} I_{jk} \leq K. \tag{6.18}$$

We note that the infrastructure matrix $\{I_{jk}\}$ defines a weighted directed graph. Thus $I_{jk}$ and $I_{kj}$ may be different.

We are now ready to state the optimal network design problem. The planner's optimization problem consists of three subproblems: (i) allocating consumption and labor across locations, $(c_j, h_j, D^n_j, L^n_j)$, (ii) optimal flows across locations $(Q^n_{jk})$, and (iii) the allocation of resources to construct transport links across locations $(I_{jk})$. Let us define $w_j$ as the weight that the planner assigns to the utilities of workers in location $j$.

The optimization problem can be written as consisting of three nested problems:

$$W = \max_{I_{jk}} \max_{Q^n_{jk}} \max_{c_j, h_j, D^n_j, L^n_j} \sum_j w_j L_j U(c_j, h_j), \tag{6.19}$$

subject to

1. availability of traded commodities:

$$c_j L_j \leq D_j(D^1_j, \ldots, D^N_j), \forall j; \tag{6.20}$$

   and availability of nontraded commodities:

$$h_j L_j \leq H_j, \forall j. \tag{6.21}$$

2. the balanced flow constraint:

$$D^n_j + \sum_{k \in N_j(g)} (1 + \tau_{jk}(Q^n_{jk}, I_{jk}))Q^n_{jk} \leq Y^n_j + \sum_{i \in N_j(g)} Q^n_{ij}, \forall j, n, \tag{6.22}$$

   where $Y^n_j$ is the production of good $n$ in location $j$.

3. the network building constraint:

$$\sum_j \sum_{k \in N_j(g)} \delta^I_{jk} I_{jk} \leq K. \tag{6.23}$$

4. local labor-market clearing:

$$\sum_n L^n_j \leq L_j, \forall j; \tag{6.24}$$

5. nonnegativity constraints on consumption, flows, and factor use:

$$C^n_j, c_j, h_j \geq 0, \forall j \in N_j(g), \tag{6.25}$$

$$Q^n_{jk} \geq 0, \forall j, k \in N_j(g), n, \tag{6.26}$$

$$L^n_j \geq 0, \forall j, n. \tag{6.27}$$

The key to understanding the economics of the problem is to recall that given a transport network $\{I_{jk}\}_{j \in \mathcal{J}}, k \in N_j(g)$, we are in a production and consumption economy that meets all the usual technical assumptions (for an exposition of the standard general equilibrium model with production, see Mas-Colell, Whinston, and Green [1995]). So there are equilibrium prices such that all consumers are maximizing utility and input and local product markets clear. These prices reflect the marginal utility of consumption in different locations. A variation in prices of a good across two locations defines the potential benefits of flows across them. These benefits in turn give us a measure of the advantages of investing in transport links and will be central to working out the optimal transport networks.

With these observations in mind, let us turn to some properties of the optimal flow and allocation. At an optimum, it must be the case that the price differential for a good between two locations must be smaller than the costs of transporting the good between the two locations (and this must also account for the increase in marginal cost of transporting):

$$\frac{P_k^n}{P_j^n} \leq 1 + \tau_{jk}^n + \frac{\partial \tau_{jk}^n}{\partial Q_{jk}^n} Q_{jk}^n. \tag{6.28}$$

Also, note that this expression must hold with equality if $Q_{jk}^n > 0$.

Observe that in the absence of congestion, $\partial \tau_{jk}^n / \partial Q_{jk}^n = 0$, this price differential would be bounded by the trade cost. This no-arbitrage condition helps us understand the nature of flow between locations. Suppose that the transport cost $Q_{jk}^n \tau_{jk}^n$ is convex in the quantity shipped. Then the expression can be inverted, and we can conclude that gross trade flow, $Q_{jk}^n$, is increasing in the price differential.

Turning to the optimal transport network, let $P_K$ be the multiplier of the network-building constraint. This reflects the shadow price of the infrastructure network. For any positive quality link, $I_{jk}$, at the optimum network, the marginal cost of link must be greater than or equal to the marginal returns from the link:

$$P_K \delta_{jk}^I \geq \sum_n P_j^n Q_{jk}^n \left( -\frac{\partial \tau_{jk}^n}{\partial I_{jk}} \right). \tag{6.29}$$

The left side of equation (6.29) is the opportunity cost of building an extra unit of infrastructure along $jk$—the multiplier $P_K$ of the network-building constraint times the rate $\delta_{jk}^I$ at which that resource translates to infrastructure. The right side is the reduction in per-unit shipping costs, $-\partial \tau_{jk}^n / \partial I_{jk}$, applied to the value of the goods used as inputs in the transport technology.

With these general considerations in mind, we now study examples in order to understand the role of transport networks in shaping economic activity. The first set of examples will have only one traded good and one nontraded good, and locations are organized in a $w \times h$ symmetric grid. Preferences are constant relative risk aversion (CRRA) form over a Cobb-Douglas bundle of traded and nontraded goods:

$$U = \frac{(c^\alpha h^{1-\alpha})^{1-\rho}}{1-\rho}, \tag{6.30}$$

with $\alpha = 0.5$ and $\rho = 2$. The total transport costs for the single good being transported are given by

$$T(Q, I) = \frac{1}{1+\gamma} \frac{Q^\beta}{I^\gamma}, \tag{6.31}$$

where $\beta \geq 0$ and $\gamma \geq 0$.

Observe that parameters $\beta$ and $\gamma$ measure the sensitivity of costs of transport to changes in quantity and to transport investment. If $\gamma \leq \beta$, a proportional increase in quantity and

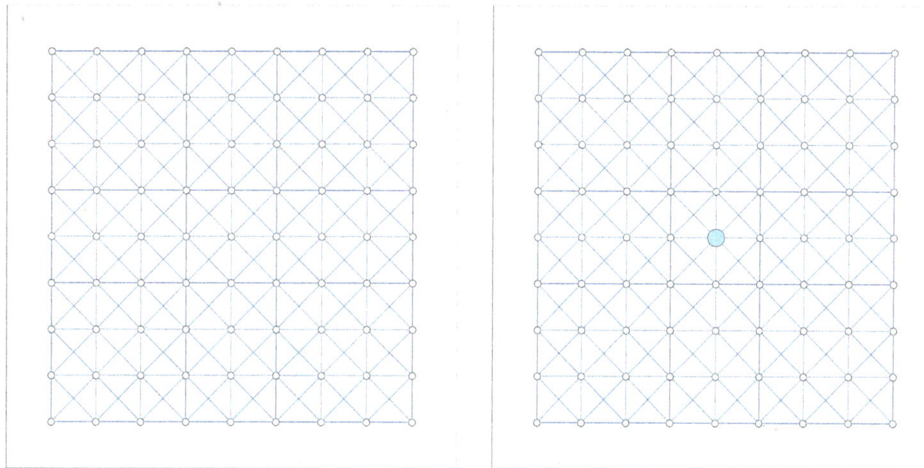

(a) A grid with 8 neighbors (b) Productivity levels

**Figure 6.9**
Physical layout and productivity.

transport investment leads to higher per-unit costs of transport, and the converse is true when $\gamma > \beta$. We shall refer to the former as the *decreasing returns case* and the latter as the *increasing returns case*. Fajgelbaum and Schaal (2020) develop a number of general results on the solution of the optimal network design problem and how it varies with the main economic parameters. We next present some numerical examples to illustrate these results.

### 6.5.1 Size of the Infrastructure Budget

This section shows that as the infrastructure budget grows, the network can reach more deeply from a source into the hinterland, thereby lowering price differentials across space, making consumption more uniform, and enhancing social welfare.

Suppose that $\beta = \gamma = 1$. Thus quantity and transport quality have proportional effects on costs of transport. There is a single traded good and no geographic frictions (i.e., for any pair of locations $jk$, $\delta^{\tau}_{jk} = \delta^{\tau}_{kj} = \delta_{distance}$).

Figure 6.9 presents the geographic configuration and the productivity parameters of this scenario. The geography is represented as a $9 \times 9$ grid, in which every location is connected to 8 neighbors. The existence of the links indicates that a transport link is potentially feasible. Suppose that labor productivity is 1 at the central location (1 unit of labor yields 1 unit of output) and 0.10 at all the other locations. All other features of locations are perfectly symmetric, $(L_j, H_j) = (1, 1)$, for all locations $j \in \mathcal{J}$.

Figure 6.10 presents the optimal network and its economic implications as we raise the infrastructure budget from $K = 1$ to $K = 100$. The panel on top corresponds to $K = 1$, and the

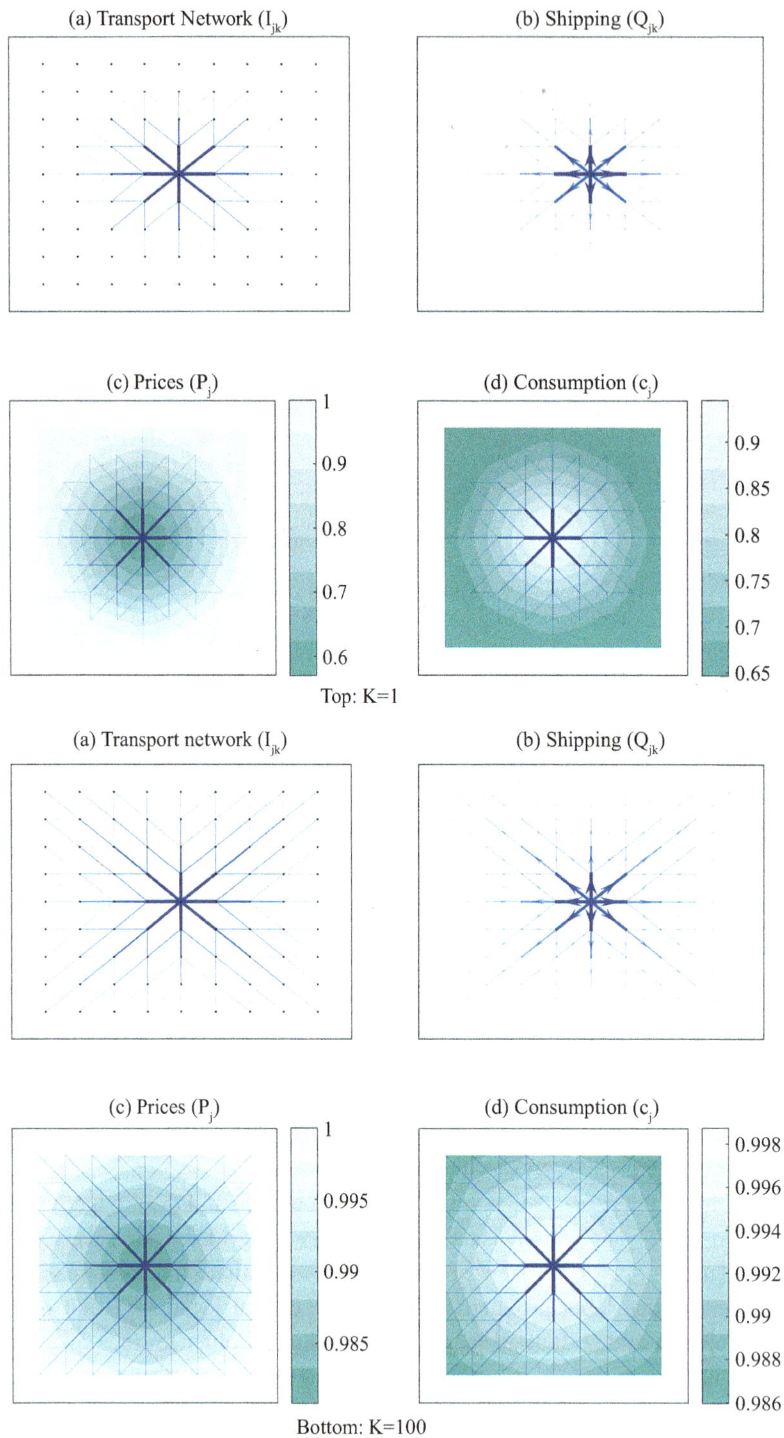


**Figure 6.10**
Optimal networks: effects of the infrastructure budget.

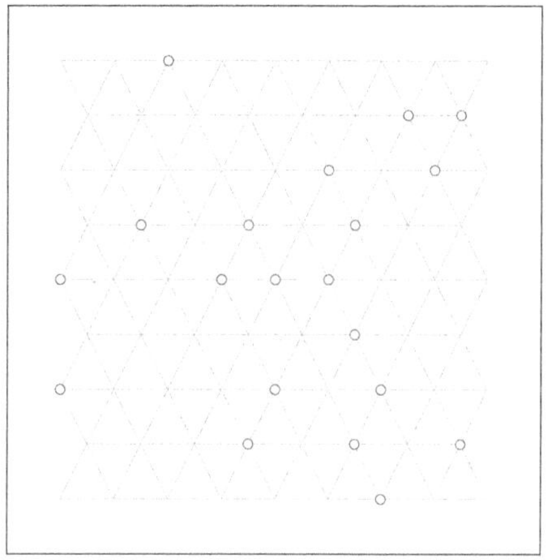

**Figure 6.11**
Spatial configuration of cities.

panel on bottom presents the case for $K = 100$. The optimal link investments radiate from the center, and this has a bearing on the level of shipments. The quality of the network has great economic effects on prices and utility. This is reflected in the heat diagrams plotted in the lower half of each of the panels. With a small budget, the tradable goods are scarcer in the outskirts of the network, and as a result, the price and the marginal utility are higher. A larger infrastructure budget leads to a strengthening of the transport network: it now grows further afield; as a result, the price differentials and the difference in marginal utility shrink across space.

### 6.5.2 The Role of Transport Technology

We now turn to a study of the returns to transport technology—specifically, whether $\beta/\gamma \geq 1$ or $\beta/\gamma \leq 1$—for the design of the optimal transport network. The discussion will develop the following basic intuition: with decreasing returns, it is more economical to have multiple routes between a source and a destination, whereas with increasing returns, it is more economical to have broader single highways connecting a source and a destination. Thus in the former case, optimal networks are dense and consist of weak transport links, while in the latter case, they will be trees.

To bring out this point clearly, we consider 20 locations randomly situated in a space where each location has eight neighbors. Figure 6.11 presents the layout of the cities. Labor $L_j = 1$ in each of the 20 cities and 0 elsewhere. Assume that productivity is 1 at the central city and 0.10 at the other 19 locations.

Figure 6.12 presents the optimal networks and optimal flows. The top panel covers the convex case, when $\beta = \gamma = 1$. The top left figure shows that the optimal network radiates outward from the centre to reach all destinations. Due to congestion on routes, some destinations are reached through multiple routes. But to reach some faraway locations such

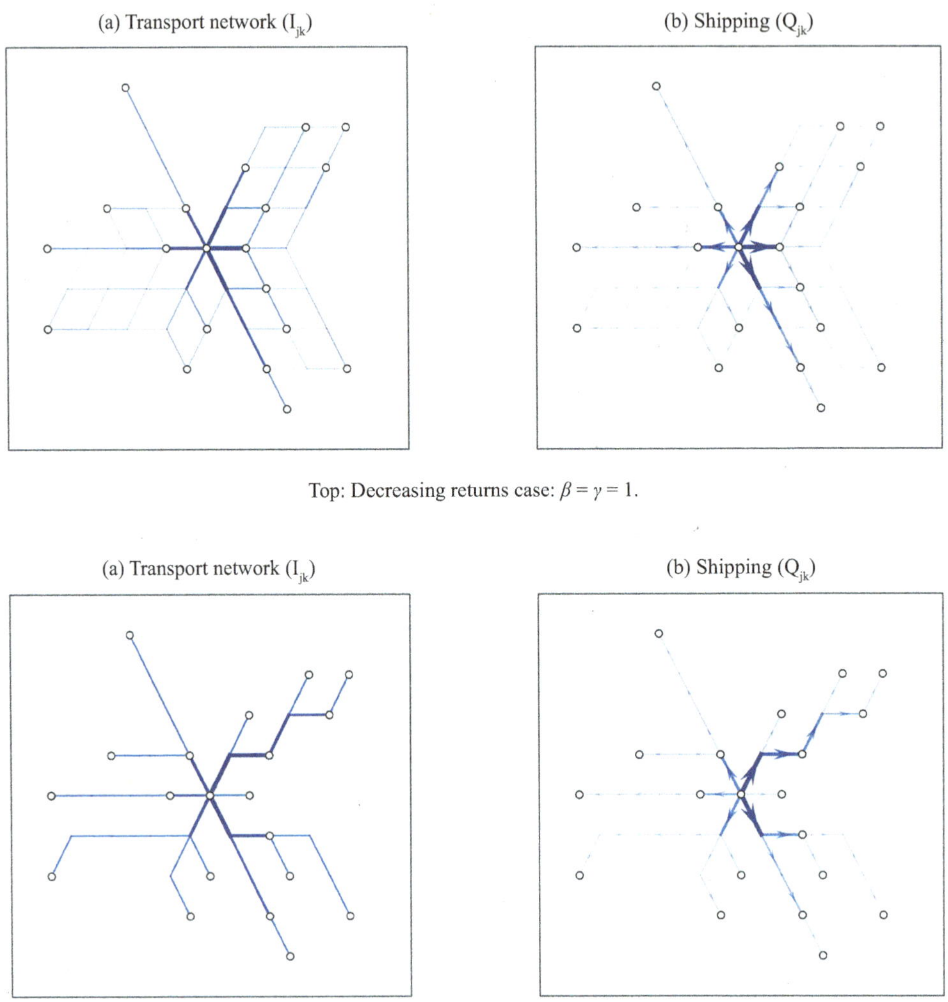


Bottom: Increasing returns: $\beta = 1,\ \gamma = 2$.

**Figure 6.12**
Optimal networks: effects of transport technology.

as the one in the northwest, there is only one route. The figure on the top right shows optimal flows of the good away from the principal producing unit.

The panel at the bottom presents optimal networks and flows with increasing returns to network building, $\gamma = 2 > \beta = 1$. We observe a qualitative change in the network: fewer but larger roads are built. As a result, there is only one route linking any two destinations—the network is a tree in which nodes have a similar number of offshoots.

To elaborate on the effects of transport technology, we next consider multiple locations for production, and to bring out the full impact of transport networks, we extend the baseline spatial economic model to allow labor to move to more attractive locations. This means that, given a network, a profile of prices defines an equilibrium to be in place if in addition to conditions (1)–(3) and (5), no person wishes to change location and aggregate labor demand equals labor supply. In the setting with free labor mobility, utilitarian welfare maximization tells us that individual utility must be equalized across locations: let us denote this utility by $u$. Let us write these conditions formally for completeness.

6. no one wishes to move to another location:

$$U(c_j, h_j) \geq u \ \forall j. \tag{6.32}$$

7. aggregate labor market clearing conditions:

$$\sum_j \sum_n L_j^n = L, \tag{6.33}$$

where $\sum_j L_j = L$.

We compute the optimal transport network in a simple example with five industrial products and one agricultural good. The industrial goods are each produced at only one city, and the agricultural good is produced at all locations outside the cities. The agricultural good is labeled 1, so we have $z_j^1 = 1$ in all countryside locations and $z_j^1 = 0$, in all cities. The five industrial goods are labeled $n = 2, 3, 4, 5, 6$ are each produced in one city, so $z_j^n = 1$ in only one city $j$ each and $z_j^n = 0$ otherwise. These goods are combined via a constant elasticity of substitution aggregator with the elasticity of substitution $\sigma = 2$. Labor continues to be the sole factor of production. As before, labor and nontraded goods are equal at all locations, $L_j = H_j = 1$, for all $j \in \mathcal{J}$.

Figures 6.13(a) and 6.13(b) presents optimal networks in the decreasing and increasing returns cases, respectively. A comparison reveals that, as in the one good case, in the presence of economies of scale in transportation, the optimal network becomes significantly sparser with fewer but wider highways. With $\beta = 1$ and $\gamma = 0.5$, the optimal network connects every industrial city through multiple routes to other locations. By contrast, under $\beta = 1$ and $\gamma = 4$, the optimal network links each industrial city through a unique, wide highway to all other locations; the case is similar for the supply of agricultural locations.

Let us now summarize what we have learned in this section. We have presented a theoretical model with spatial features in which the costs of transport are the central force shaping economic activity. This model allowed us to draw out principles for the design of optimal spatial transport networks, and in particular on the role of returns to transport technology. When these returns are diminishing, the optimal network has many links, but each link is weak (one example is a complete network). By contrast, under increasing returns to scale, the network is sparse and each of the transport links is strong (examples include tree graphs

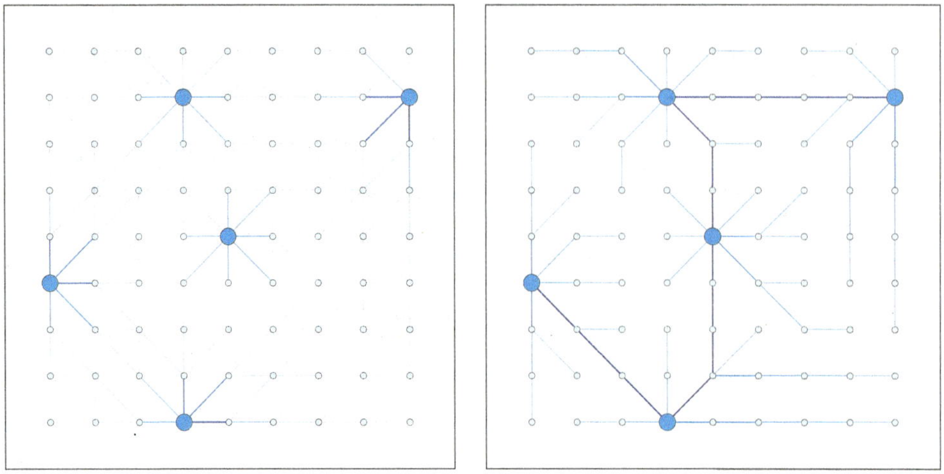

(a) Convex case: $\beta = 1$, $\gamma = 0.5$

(b) Increasing returns: $\beta = 1$, $\gamma = 4$

**Figure 6.13**
Optimal networks: effects of transport technology.

and variants of hub-spokes networks). As increasing returns to transport push toward hub-spoke networks, they could amplify agglomeration forces and lead to a greater concentration of economic activity.

## 6.6 The Belt and Road Initiative

China's Belt and Road Initiative (BRI), sometimes referred to as the New Silk Road, was launched in 2013 by President Xi Jinping. It is a vast collection of development and investment initiatives that would stretch from East Asia to Europe and Africa (a more elaborate version also includes projects in Australia and Latin America). The BRI calls for close cooperation among countries and is expected to improve the region's infrastructure; put in place a secure and efficient network of land, sea and air passages; enhance trade and investment; establish a network of free trade areas; increase financial integration; and enhance cultural exchanges. The BRI has subsequently become an important part of Chinese planning and general policy—it was incorporated into the 13th Five-Year Plan (2016–2020) and was included in the Chinese Communist Party constitution in October 2017. The discussion here draws on a number of sources—OECD (2018), official Chinese government documents, and Maceaes (2018).

The BRI aims to connect East Asian economies at one end with European economies at the other end, and covers a number of countries with a huge potential for economic development in both Eurasia and Africa. There are two components to the infrastructure element—the Silk Road Economic Belt, which is on land, and the twenty-first-century

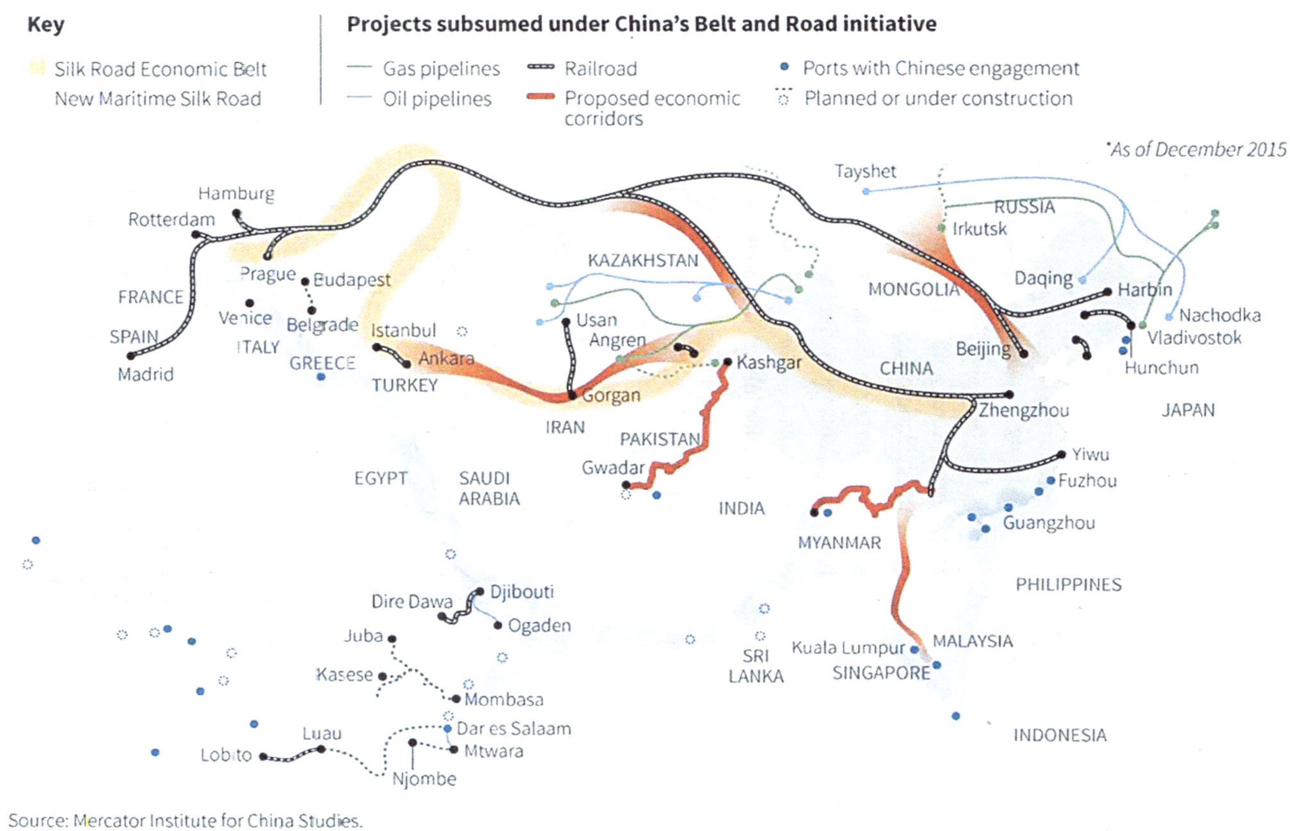


**Figure 6.14**
The BRI. *Source*: Mercator Institute for Chinese Studies.

Maritime Silk Road, which covers seaports and sea routes. Figure 6.14 provides an impression of the vast scope of the BRI. Let us look more closely at some of the principal components of the initiative.

On land, the Silk Road Economic Belt consists of three broad routes—(1) from Northwest China and Northeast China to Europe and Baltic Sea via Central Asia and Russia; (2) from Northwest China to the Persian Gulf and the Mediterranean Sea, passing through Central Asia and West Asia; and (3) from Southwest China through Indochina Peninsula to the Indian Ocean. These three routes are divided into six economic corridors:

1. New Eurasia Land Bridge, involving train connections from China to Europe via Kazakhstan, Russia, Belarus, and Poland.
2. China-Mongolia-Russia Economic Corridor, which would involve rail links and highways and also link to the land bridge.
3. China–Central Asia–West Asia Economic Corridor, which will involve Kazakhstan, Kyrgyztan, Tajikistan, Uzbekistan, Turkmenistan, Iran, and Turkey.
4. China–Indochina Peninsula Economic Corridor, which will involve Vietnam, Thailand, Lao People's Democratic Republic, Cambodia, Myanmar, and Malaysia.
5. China-Pakistan Economic Corridor, connecting Kashgar (in Xinjiang) through a highway to the Pakistan port of Gwadar. The road passes through the Karakoram Mountains in the Himalayas. Gwadar is a deepwater port that can be used for both commercial and military purposes.
6. China-Bangladesh-India-Myanmar Economic Corridor, with investment in infrastructure development and joint exploration and development of mineral, water, and other natural resources.

These economic corridors will involve broad economic integration along various dimensions, but physical integration will be an important feature. This will be facilitated by a transport network consisting of railways, highways, and sea and air routes, together with electric power transmission and telecommunication networks and oil and gas pipelines.

The Maritime Silk Road runs from the Chinese coast to the south via a number of Southeast Asian cities (i.e., Hanoi, Jakarta, Singapore, and Kuala Lumpur) through the Strait of Malacca to Sri Lanka. It then carries on through the southern tip of India via Male to East Africa (i.e., Mombasa and Djibouti). The route continues through the Red Sea via the Suez Canal to the Mediterranean Sea (via Haifa, Istanbul, and Athens) to Italy (Trieste). The route then continues via sea and over land connections to Central Europe and the North Sea. Figure 6.14 illustrates the broad outlines of the Maritime Silk Road.

BRI's geographical scope is constantly evolving as new countries sign up for joint projects and other countries withdraw from them. By 2018, the BRI covered over 70 countries, accounting for about two-thirds of the world's population and around one-third of the world's total income.

Let us next place the BRI in a broader context. Resilient infrastructure is a part of the UN's 17 Goals of Sustainable Development, but it is generally agreed that at the global level there is a large gap in infrastructure. For instance, in 2020, over 840 million people lived more than 2 kilometers from all-weather roads, 1 billion people lacked electricity, and 4 billion people lacked Internet access. For a number of years now, multilateral development institutions such as the World Bank have prioritized infrastructure funding in developing countries. From a Chinese perspective, the BRI is expected to help by providing better access to markets for its manufactured goods. Closer integration across markets in Eurasia will increase demand for its manufactured products and integration with Central Asia and West Asia will raise the reliability of its oil and gas and other natural resource supplies. Closer economic integration between Northwest China and Central and West Asia will help less-developed provinces like Xinjiang. At a more general level, closer integration with the resource-rich but less-developed economies of Central Asia will help China transition out of a middle-income level by gradually relocating certain industries out of China. The BRI may therefore be seen as an attempt by China to fit its policy goals into a leading global challenge—the shortage of infrastructure.

Let us consider the financing of the BRI. It calls for very large investments—in excess of $1 trillion for the decade starting in 2017—and so financing these projects is a major challenge. Large Chinese state financial institutions—the Industrial and Commercial Bank of China, the Agricultural Bank of China, the Bank of China, and the China Construction Bank—are expected to play an important role. But entirely new institutions, such as the Asian Infrastructure Investment Bank (AIIB), have the BRI as a priority too: by mid-2016, the AIIB approved funding in excess of $500 million for projects in Bangladesh, Indonesia, Pakistan, and Tajikistan (these countries lie in the core economic corridor of the BRI). Similarly, the Silk Road Fund was set up to facilitate funding of a variety of projects ranging across hydropower plants in Pakistan, fund acquisition of Italian tyremaker Pirelli, and to make investments in the Russia-based Yamal Liquified Natural Gas project.

Finally, let us comment on some aspects of the network elements underlying of the BRI: the transport network envisaged by the BRI involves a vast number of nodes (located in over 70 countries) and a rich combination of types of edges including roads, train tracks, sea routes, oil pipelines, Internet cables, and financial links. Figure 6.14 draws attention to the importance of oil and gas pipelines. Turning to the topology of the network, the BRI hopes to make Xinjiang the hub for the Silk Road Economic Belt and Fujian the hub for the Maritime Silk Road. There is thus an important sense in which this extraordinarily large and complex network seeks to exploit the network advantages of the hub-spoke structure.

The BRI envisages a close integration of transport infrastructure across Eurasia and Africa with hubs based in China, proposes the financing of this infrastructure through a number of financial institutions based in China, and advances the idea of greater domestic and trade policy coordination across countries. These features have led researchers and commentators to speculate on the longer-term implications of BRI.

To place the BRI in a broader perspective, recall that this chapter has covered a range of transport networks. The discussion drew attention to the scale of train and road networks, the goals of the network builder, and how they interact with resource constraints and physical geography to shape the network. We also presented a theoretical framework that allows us to explore the economic effects of transport networks and the determinants of optimal network design. Keeping these ideas in mind, we conclude this chapter with a general comment on the BRI:

> The Belt and Road Initiative is the name for a global order infused with Chinese political principles and placing China at it heart. In economic terms this means that China will be organizing and leading an increasing share of global supply chains, reserving for itself the most valuable segments of production and creating strong links of collaboration and infrastructure with other countries, whose main role in the system will be to occupy lower value segments. Politically, Beijing hopes to put in place the same kind of feedback mechanism that the West has benefitted from: deeper links of investment, infrastructure, and trade can be used as leverage to shape relations with other countries even more in its favor. The process feeds on itself. (Maceaes, 2018, p. 30)

## 6.7 Reading Notes

Transport networks come in various forms. The aim of this chapter is to bring out the close relation between these networks and economic activity. It discusses roads, trains, and airlines and briefly comments on a shipping network.

As air travel has grown, economic issues in the airline industry have attracted increasing attention. For an overview of developments in airlines, see Petzinger (1996) and Borenstein (1992). A striking and widely commented-on feature of airlines is the hub-spoke network structure. Hendricks, Piccione, and Tan (1995) developed a model in which the basic trade-offs between dense and sparse networks could be studied. This chapter draws on their work to develop an analysis of the optimality of different networks. The discussion focuses on the case of a single airline. Similar arguments can be used to show that competing airlines will create hub-spoke networks; for a formal model of competing airline networks, see Hendricks, Piccione, and Tan (1999). For an exploration of the role of hub-spoke networks as an entry deterrence device, see Hendricks, Piccione, and Tan (1997).

The study of spatial transport networks has a long and distinguished history. Perhaps the best-known work is the study of the effects of American railroads on economic growth by Robert Fogel. Fogel (1964) studied the impact of railroads through a method of counterfactuals—how would the American economy have fared in the absence of any railroads? He examined the cost savings brought about by railroads relative to alternative existing modes of transport, such as rivers and canals. Fogel argued that small differences in freight rates caused some areas to thrive relative to others, but railroads had only a small aggregate impact on the U.S. agricultural sector. This social saving methodology has been widely applied to transportation improvements; for an alternative approach that suggests larger effects, see Fishlow (1965). For a re-evaluation of this hypothesis and a summary of the state of the literature, see Donaldson and Hornbeck (2016). For a general overview of economic issues relating to economic effects of market integration, see Donaldson (2015).

To highlight the general ideas underlying the benefits of transport networks and the possible trade-offs in building different types of networks, the chapter then presents a theoretical model of optimal spatial transport networks. This model builds on the large body of literature in international trade and economic geography and bridges it with the research on optimal flows in networks. For an overview of the trade and geography literature, see Eaton and Kortum (2002) and Redding and Rossi-Hansberg (2017). For an introduction to optimization methods in transport networks, see Galichon (2016). The model presented in section 6.5 is taken from Fajgelbaum and Schaal (2020). The exposition here also draws heavily on that paper.

The BRI is one of the most ambitious infrastructure projects ever undertaken. There is a very large body of popular literature on different aspects of the BRI. However, the initiative is also very controversial due to its vast economic scope and the large political and strategic elements in it. The discussion here draws on a number of official documents and a general introduction to the initiative by Maceaes (2018). Other documents include an Organisation for Economic Co-operation and Development (OECD) study of the BRI (OECD, 2018) and official Chinese government reports taken from http://english.www.gov.cn/beltAndRoad/.

## 6.8 Questions

1. There are $n$ cities, $n \geq 3$. Suppose that demand for travel between any city pair is a function of the price of the ticket and is given by

$$D(p) = kp^{-\alpha}, \quad \alpha \geq 1, \quad k \geq 0. \tag{6.34}$$

   Marginal costs of flying are constant and given by $c$. Compute the optimal prices for direct and indirect (two-step) flights. Then compute the profits for the monopoly airline in the complete and the hub-spoke networks. Finally, compute the threshold value of the costs of links $f^*$ such that the optimal network is complete below $f^*$ and hub-spoke above $f^*$.

2. Consider a scenario with one airline operating a network to serve $n$ cities. Suppose that there are two types of cities, large and small. The demand for air travel is high ($H$) between every pair of large cities and low ($L$) between every other pair of cities. There is a cost $F$ per link between any pair of cities. Direct flights between cities yields profits equal to the size of the demand between the pair of cities, while an indirect (two-step) flight yields profits equal to one-half of the demand. Thus a direct flight between two large cities yields profit $H$, while an indirect flight yields profit $H/2$. Similarly, a direct flight between a pair of cities (in which at least one is not large) yields profit $L$, while an

indirect flight yields a gross profit of $L/2$. Reason carefully and describe the nature of the optimal routing network as a function of the parameters $F$, $L$ and $H$.

3. (Hendricks, Piccione, and Tan [1999]). There are two airlines $i = A, B$ and $N = \{1, 2, \ldots, n\}$, with $n \geq 3$ cities. Let $i, j$ index cities. Airlines choose routing networks, $X^A$ and $X^B$. The size of an airline's routing network is $m^i = \sum_{g,h} X^i(g,h)/2$. Let there be a fixed cost per city-pair link $f > 0$ (as in the model described in section 6.2.2). Let $\pi(z^i z^j)$ denote the revenue in a city pair for airline $i$ with path length $z^i$, faced with a path length $z^j$. Denote by $\pi_M(z) = \pi(z^i, \infty)$ the monopoly revenue from path length $z^i$. Passengers prefer shorter routes: so for any $z$ and $y$, $\pi(z, y) \geq \pi(z+1, y)$. Given $X^i$, define the path length $r: N \times N \to \{1, 2, .., n\}$. Define the set of city pairs of length $r$: $\Gamma(z) = \{(g, h) | r(g, h) = z\}$. We write the payoff to an airline as

$$\Pi(X^i, X^j) = \sum_{z=1}^{\infty} \sum_{\gamma^i(z)} \pi(z, r^j(g, h)) - fm^i. \tag{6.35}$$

Assume (1) $f(\frac{n(n-1)}{2}) > n(n-1)\pi_M(1)$ (2) $(n-1)2\pi_M(1) + (n-1)(n-2)\pi_M(2) > f(n-1)$: part (1) says that a point-to-point network is not profitable even for a monopolist, part (2) says that a hub-spoke network is profitable for a monopolist. Assume (3) $\pi(z, y) + \pi(y, z) \leq \pi_M(\min(y, z))$ (4) $\pi(z, y) \leq \pi_M(z)$; part (3) says the profits of a duopoly cannot exceed the profits of monopoly on the shorter route. Part (4) says that duopoly profit is smaller than monopoly profit. Finally, assume that (5) $\pi_M(z) > 0$ is strictly declining in $z$ (i.e., a longer path lowers profits).

(a) Aggressive competition: $\pi(z, y) = 0$, if $z \geq y$. Show that under (1)–(5) and aggressive competition, the following is true: (A) two hub-spoke networks cannot arise in a Nash equilibrium; and (B) one airline operating a hub-spoke network and the other firm staying out of the market is a Nash equilibrium.

(b) Moderate competition: airlines offering flights of same length can make profits. In particular, replace requirement (2) above with $(n-2)(n-3)\pi(2,2) > f(n-2)$. This means in particular that profits are positive in city-pair markets where both carriers offer a one-stop connection. We will say that $\pi$ is quasi-submodular if, for any pair of positive integers $(z, y)$,

$$\pi(z, y) + \pi(y, z) \geq \pi(z, z) + \pi(y, y). \tag{6.36}$$

The payoff is quasi-supermodular if the converse inequality holds:

(i) Suppose that assumptions (1)–(5) hold. Suppose that $i$ creates a full hub-spoke network. Show that the best response of $j$ is either a hub-spoke network of size $n-1$ or a hub-spoke network of size $n-2$ (which omits the hub node of $i$).

(ii) Define $F_1 = 2\pi(1,1) + 2(n-2)\pi(2,1)$. Suppose that $f < F_1$. Show that if $\pi$ is quasi-supermodular, then two full competing hub-spokes centered on the same hub constitute an equilibrium. If $\pi$ is quasi-submodular, then $X^A, X^B$ with two distinct hub nodes constitutes an equilibrium.

4. (Goyal and Joshi [2006a]). Suppose there are $n$ cities, each with its own market and with a single monopoly firm that can sell in the local city market, as well as in other cities. Suppose that, at the start, transport costs across cities are prohibitive. However, any two cities can build a road that lowers these costs and makes trade feasible. The cost of building a road between any two cities is given by $F > 0$ for each of the cities.

   Let $N_i(g)$ be the set of cities with whom city $i$ is connected by road. Let the output of firm $j$ in city $i$ be denoted by $Q_i^j$. The total output in city $i$ is then given by $Q_i = \sum_{j \in N_i(g)} Q_i^j + Q_i^i$. In each city $i \in N$, there is an identical inverse linear demand given by $P_i = \alpha - Q_i$, $\alpha > 0$. Assume that all firms have zero fixed costs and a constant and identical marginal cost of production, $\gamma > 0$. Assume that $\alpha > \gamma$. Let the initial preroad costs of transport between any two cities be $T > \alpha$. A road between two cities $i$ and $j$ lowers costs of transport between them to zero.

   (a) Given a network of roads $g$, the number of active firms in city/market $i$ is $d_i(g) + 1$, where $d_i(g)$ is the degree of city $i$ in network $g$. Show that if a firm $i$ is active in market $j$, then its output is given by $Q_j^i = (\alpha - \gamma)/(n_j(g) + 2)$.

   (b) Define welfare in a city $i$ as the sum of firm profits and consumers surplus in that city and denote it by $W_i(g)$. Show that the welfare of a city $i$ in a network $g$ is given by

   $$W_i(g) = \frac{1}{2}\left[\frac{(\alpha - \gamma)(d_i(g) + 1)}{d_i(g) + 2}\right]^2 + \sum_{j \in N_i(g)} \left[\frac{\alpha - \gamma}{d_j(g) + 2}\right]^2. \tag{6.37}$$

   (c) Consider the social planner who seeks to maximize the sum of the welfare of cities. Suppose the number of cities is $n = 4$. Describe the utilitarian optimum road network as a function of $\alpha$, $\gamma$ and $F$.

   (d) Next, consider the incentives to build roads. Recall that a network is pairwise stable if every link that exists benefits the two cities involved (at least weakly) and the addition of every link that is missing makes at least one of the two cities strictly worse off. Suppose $n = 4$. Describe pairwise stable networks as a function of parameters $\alpha$ and $\gamma$ and $F$.

   (e) Suppose a city can trade with every city with which it has a path in the road network. Fix $n = 4$. Describe the efficient and pairwise stable networks as a function of $\alpha$, $\gamma$ and $F$.

5. Discuss how the budget for infrastructure and the nature of the transport technology (whether it is increasing or decreasing returns) shape the scale and location of economic activity.

6. Present economic arguments to explain the similarities and differences between airline and train networks.

# 7 Security

## 7.1 Introduction

> Our nation's critical infrastructure is crucial to the functioning of the American economy... (It) is increasingly connected and interdependent and protecting it and enhancing its resilience is an economic and national security imperative. US Office of Infrastructure Protection.
> —Department of Homeland Security (2012).

Infrastructure networks include highways, aviation, shipping, pipelines, train systems, and telecommunications. These networks face a variety of threats, ranging from natural disasters (such as floods, storms, and earthquakes) to human attacks (such as guerrilla attacks, attacks by an enemy country, or nonviolent protests). In this chapter, we study questions relating to the protection and design of infrastructure networks.

To set the stage for a study of the threats, we need a measure of the value of a network and how it is affected by shocks. We present a concept of network value that rests on two ideas: (1) the value of a network is equal to the sum of value of its components, and (2) the value of a component is increasing and convex in its size. Attacks on the network are therefore harmful because they reduce its connectivity. This formulation of network value is the basis of the various models we study.

We take the view that the goal of the defender/designer is to maximize the value of the network in the worst case. This is a realistic assumption in some settings (such as human attacks) because the adversary is intelligent and wishes to maximize damage. In other settings (such as natural disasters), even when the attacks are random, it may be wise to take the worst contingency as a benchmark to guard against especially bad outcomes. This leads us to a model in which the designer/defender moves first, and then the adversary moves. The designer/defender anticipates the optimal attack of the adversary and chooses a strategy (of defense or design) that maximizes the network value, given this optimal attack.

Section 7.3 takes up the study of the design and defense of infrastructure networks that face threats that damage or destroy particular nodes (and links). A network can be made robust to such threats through additional investments in equipment and personnel. As networks are pervasive, the investments needed can be very large; so it is important to target resources at specific parts of the network. What are the key parts of the network that should be protected to ensure maximal functionality? Taking a longer-term view, we then study how networks should be designed so that they are robust to attacks.

The first question we take up pertains to the defense of a given network. As the network value function is increasing and convex in the size of the components, the adversary will find it attractive to target nodes that fragment the network; these are referred to as *separators*. Anticipating this, the designer/defender will choose to block these separators, i.e., choose the most effective *transversals* of the sets of separators.

We then take a longer-term view and ask how a network should be designed so that it remains robust in the face of attacks. This leads us to enrich the model and to allow for both linking and protection decisions. The network's connectivity can be maintained through adding links and via protecting nodes. When the adversary's resources are limited, we show that this gives rise to a trade-off between creating a dense network (that uses extra links to sustain connectivity) and large protection investments in key (hub) nodes that sustain the connectivity of the network. Our analysis shows that there is a simple resolution of this trade-off: either the optimal network is *k-connected* (the network remains connected after the removal of any $k$ nodes) or it is a *hub-spoke network with a protected hub*.

Section 7.4 takes up the question of threats that spread via connections. As energy, communication, travel, and consumer interaction increasingly adopt digital networks, cybersecurity has emerged as a major concern. Relative to other infrastructure, a distinctive feature of many cybersecurity threats is that attacks can travel across the links to capture and control progressively larger sections of a network. This creates a tension between the benefits of connectivity and its costs (in terms of the enhanced dangers of contagion) and motivates the study of the design and defense of networks that face contagious threats. We develop a model of a defender who can design and defend a network and an adversary that chooses which nodes to attack and how to route their attack on the network. The model helps us in identifying circumstances under which a highly centralized network with the protected center is optimal and when a network with multiple hub-nodes or multiple components is desirable.

## 7.2 The Value of a Network

The value of an infrastructure network comes from goods, services, and people being able to move smoothly from one point to another. Similarly, the value of a communication network like the Internet comes from the possibility of information moving from one person to another (or one node to another). In both instances, connectivity of the network is central to its value.

The network consists of nodes and edges. The set of nodes is denoted by $N = \{1, \ldots, n\}$, where $n \geq 2$. A link between two nodes $i$ and $j$ is represented by $g_{ij} \in \{0, 1\}$: we set $g_{ij} = 1$

if there is a link between $i$ and $j$, and $g_{ij}=0$ otherwise. Links are undirected (i.e., $g_{ij}=g_{ji}$). The nodes and the links together define network $g$.

In this chapter, we will use the notions of paths, components, and connectedness of networks; the reader should consult chapter 1 for definitions of these concepts. Let $\mathcal{C}(g)$ be the set of components of $g$ and $C_i(g)$ be the component containing node $i$. We let $|C|$ indicate the cardinality (or size) of the component $C$. A maximum component of $g$ is a component with maximal cardinality in $\mathcal{C}(g)$. Network $g'$ on $N'$ is a subnetwork of $g$ if and only if $N' \subseteq N$, and $g'_{ij}=1 \Rightarrow g_{ij}=1$ and $i,j \in N'$. We let $\mathcal{G}(g)$ denote the set of all subnetworks of $g$.

Following Myerson (1977b), we assume that the value of a network is the sum of the value of its components and the value of any component is a function of its size only. Let the function $f:\mathbb{N}\to\mathbb{R}_+$ specify a value to the component size. We shall assume that this value is increasing and convex in the size of a component.

**Assumption 7.1** *The value of network g is given by*

$$\Phi(g)=\sum_{C\in\mathcal{C}(g)} f(|C|), \tag{7.1}$$

*where $f$ is strictly increasing, strictly convex, and $f(0)=0$.*

Increasing and convex network value functions arise in a number of different contexts. Let us consider some examples.

In the models presented in chapter 3, on the costs and benefits of links, the simplest setting is one where the value of a network to an individual is equal to the number of individuals they can access (in other words, the size of the component). With this payoff function, it follows that the aggregate value to all individuals in a network component of size $x$ would be $x^2$. Moreover, the value of the network will be the sum of the value of the components. This is consistent with Metcalfe's Law on telecommunication networks.

A second example concerns collaborative work. Suppose that every subset of individuals can perform a task and the value of a task is 1. Individuals need to coordinate their activities. A task is carried out by a group of individuals only if they are connected. The value of the network is the total value of all tasks that can be carried out. A component with $m$ nodes thus generates value $2^m$ 1 (as there are exactly $2^m-1$ tasks that $m$ nodes can perform). This yields a network value that is the sum of the network components and exponential in the size of components. This is consistent with Reed's Law on networked systems.

## 7.3 Infrastructure Networks

To develop a feel for the issues involved in the defense of networks, for concreteness, we present the network structure of metro-train services in two major cities, London and Beijing.

Figure 7.1 presents the network of the London Underground. It consists of 309 nodes, representing stations, and 370 links, representing direct journey connections between stations. This network is therefore relatively sparse. The average distance between stations is 13.1, the diameter is 36, and the average degree is 2.38. This sparseness is reflected in a number of long branches reaching to distinct parts of the sprawling city.

Next, we discuss the Beijing Metro Network, presented in figure 7.2. The network consists of 287 stations, the number of direct links is 326, the diameter of the network is 45, and the average degree is 2.27. This is therefore a relatively sparse and again spread-out network. As in the London Underground, there is a core set of stations and a number of long branches reaching to distant parts of the city.

The governments in London and Beijing wish to minimize any possible disruption in their transport networks. We develop a theoretical model that explores the economic trade-offs that arise when nodes are subject to shocks.

In the case of infrastructure such as trains, pipelines, and canals, alterations in the structure of the network takes time, so it is reasonable to take the network as a given in the short to medium term. We therefore first study the problem of how to protect a given network. Taking a longer-term perspective, we then take up the question of the optimal design of networks that face threats.

A threat to the network may come from natural sources (such as storms, earthquakes, or floods) or from human activity (such as violent or peaceful political protestors). In both types of attack, as we explained in the introduction, it is useful to take the perspective that the attack will seek to minimize the value of the network, so the task is to design and defend the network effectively. Building on this idea, we will proceed to construct a game of conflict with two players—a Designer and an Adversary.

### 7.3.1 Defense of a Network

We study a game of conflict that takes the following form: in the first stage, the Defender chooses an allocation of defense resources in the network. In the second stage, after observing the defended network, the Adversary chooses the nodes to attack. Successfully attacked nodes (and their links) are removed from the network, yielding a residual network. The goal of the Defender is to maximize the value of the residual network, while the goal of the Adversary is to minimize this value. The model is taken from Dziubiński and Goyal (2017).

#### 7.3.1.1 A model

Consider a given network $g = (N, E)$ that consists of vertices $N = \{1, \ldots, n\}$ and edges between these vertices. There are two players, the Defender and the Adversary. The Defender chooses a set of nodes to protect, given by $\mathcal{D} \subseteq N$. Observing this defense, the Adversary then chooses a set of nodes $X \subseteq N$ to attack (the attack strategy is thus formally a function of the defense). For simplicity, we shall assume that defense is perfect (i.e., a protected node cannot be removed by an attack). On the other hand, attack on an unprotected node leads to

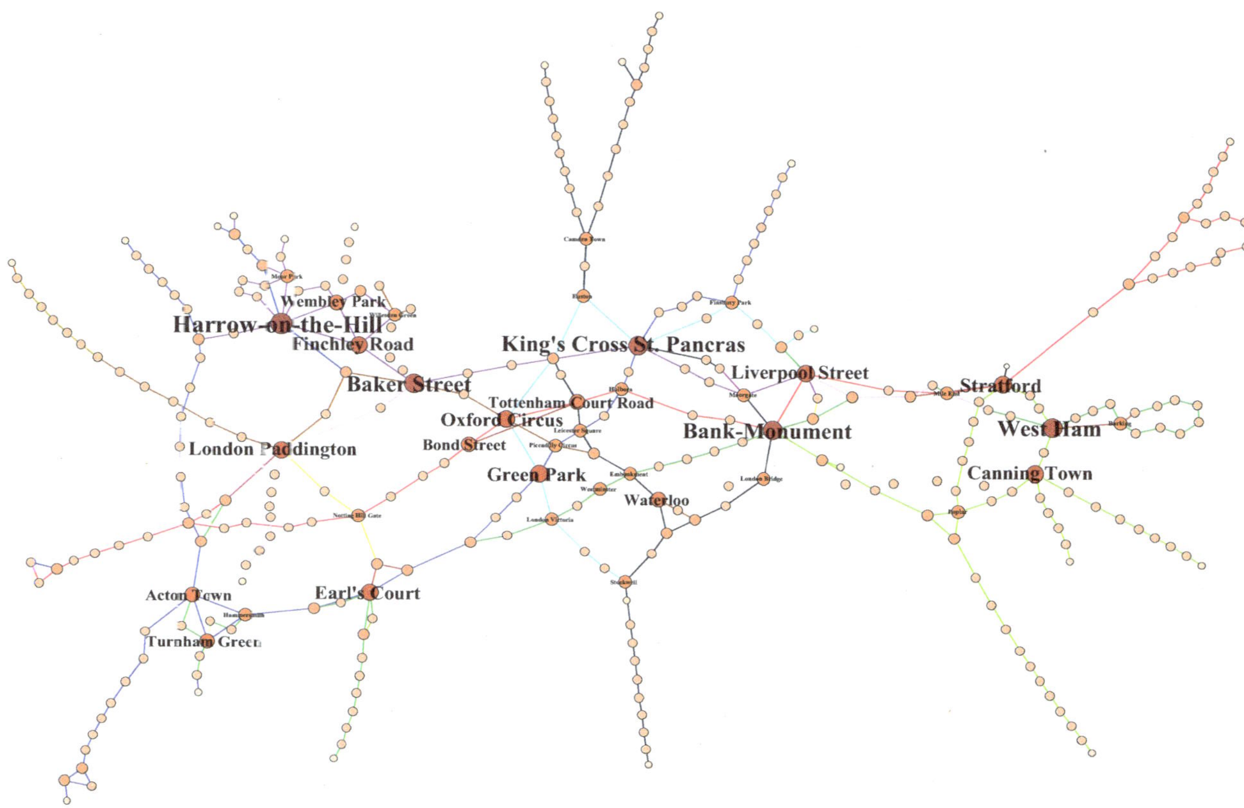


**Figure 7.1**
The London Underground Network. *Source*: https://github.com/jaron/railgraph/blob/master/graphs/tubeDLR.gephi.

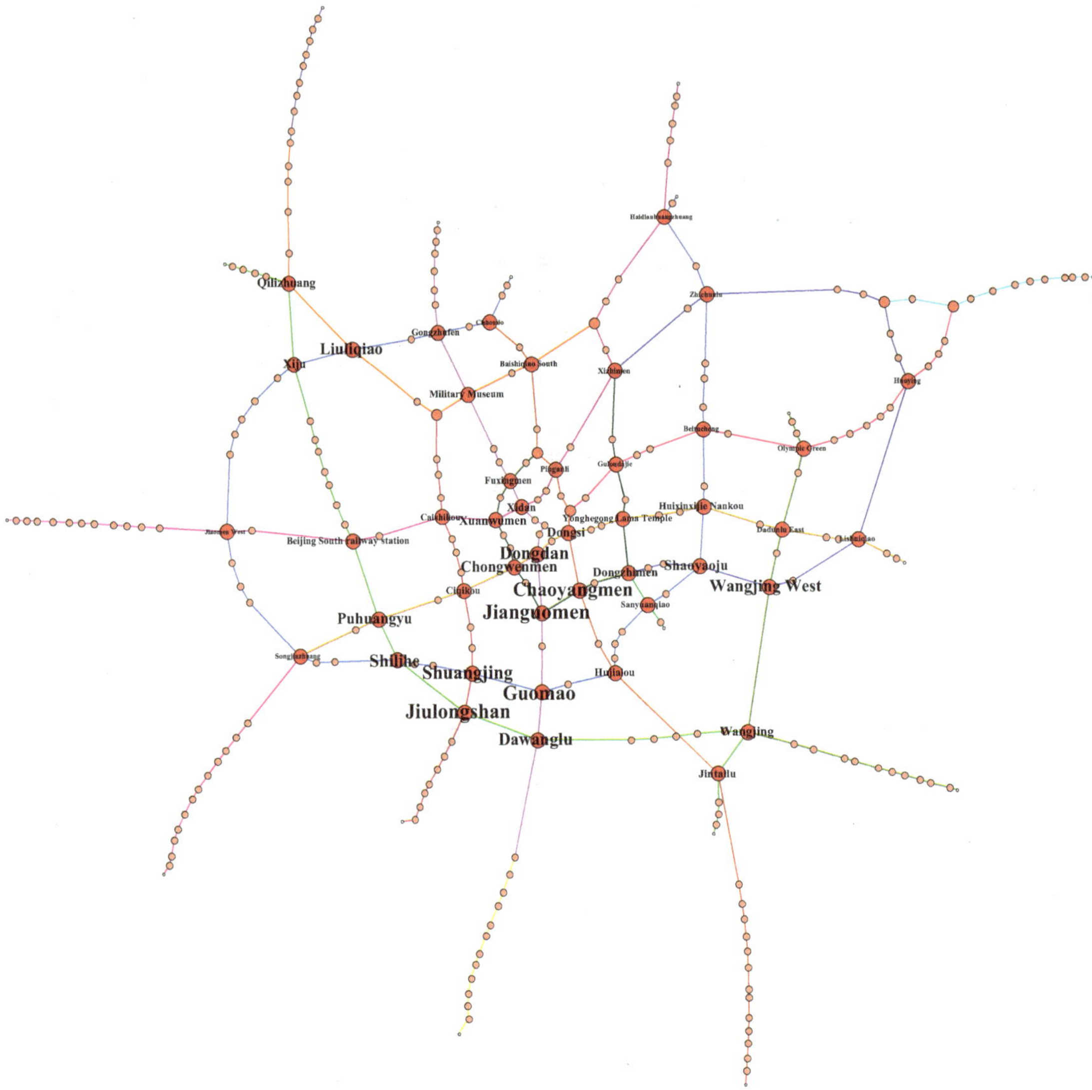


**Figure 7.2**
The Beijing Metro Network. *Source*: http://dvop.github.io/%E5%9C%B0%E9%93%81/2016/01/11/DiTie.html.

the elimination of that node and its links. Given defense $\mathcal{D}$ and attack $X$, define $Y = X \setminus \mathcal{D}$ as the nodes that are removed from the network. This yields a *residual network* $g'$ on $N \setminus Y$ nodes with edges, $\{g_{ij} \in g : i, j \in N\ Y\}$.

Defense is costly: the cost of defending a node is $c_D > 0$. Similarly, attack is costly: the cost of attacking a node is $c_A > 0$. Given a network $g$, the Defender's payoff from strategy $\mathcal{D} \subseteq N$, when faced with the Adversary's strategy $X \subseteq N$, is

$$\Pi^D(\mathcal{D}, X; g, c_D) = \Phi(g - (X \setminus \mathcal{D})) - c_D|\mathcal{D}|. \tag{7.2}$$

Given a defended network $(g, \mathcal{D})$, the payoff to the Adversary from strategy $X \subseteq N$ is

$$\Pi^A(\mathcal{D}, X; g, c_A) = -\Phi(g - (X \setminus \mathcal{D})) - c_A|X|. \tag{7.3}$$

We shall refer to this as the *Network Defense game*.

A subgame perfect equilibrium of this game is a profile of strategies $(\mathcal{D}^*, X^*(\mathcal{D}))$, such that $X^*(.)$ maximizes the payoff of the Adversary given defense $\mathcal{D}$ and $\mathcal{D}^*$ maximizes the payoff of the Defender given attack strategy $X^*(.)$.

A preliminary observation is that because this is a two-stage sequential game with full information and a finite number of actions for both players, we can compute the subgame perfect equilibrium through backward induction. It follows from standard considerations that (for most—that is, generic—parameters of the model) the equilibrium is unique in terms of a player's payoffs, the sizes of defense and attack, and the value of the residual network. In what follows, we will study the nature of this unique equilibrium.

#### 7.3.1.2 Equilibrium attack and defense

To develop a feel for the economics of the defense and attack, it is helpful to start with the star network.

**Example 7.1** *Defense and attack on the star*

Figure 7.3 presents a star network with four nodes. The network value function is $f(x) = x^2$.

Given a defended network, $(g, \mathcal{D})$, we compute the optimal response of the Adversary, $X^*(g, \mathcal{D})$. The Defender compares his payoffs under different $(g, \mathcal{D})$ and picks the one that gives the highest payoffs. Suppose that the Defender protects the hub. In that case, the Adversary can only hope to eliminate single nodes (without affecting the connectivity of the residual network). The payoff to a Defender from eliminating a single node is $f(3)$. By contrast, if the hub is not protected and the Adversary eliminates the hub, they reduce the size of the network and fragment it completely, yielding the Defender a payoff of $3f(1)$. As network value $f(.)$ is increasing and convex, $f(3) > 3f(1)$. This comparison brings out the interaction between the network architecture and the value function in shaping the conflict between the Defender and the Adversary. The Adversary would prefer to attack in a manner

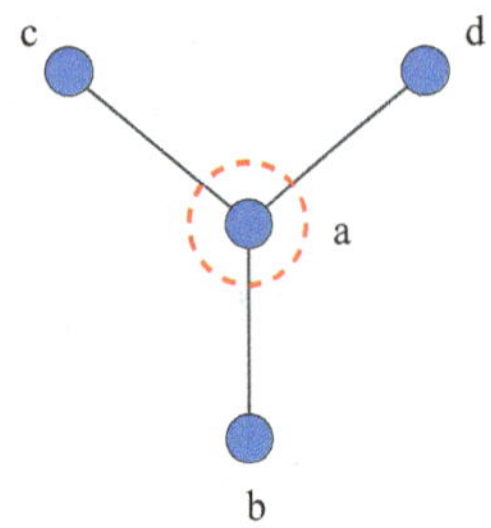


**Figure 7.3**
Star network ($n = 4$).

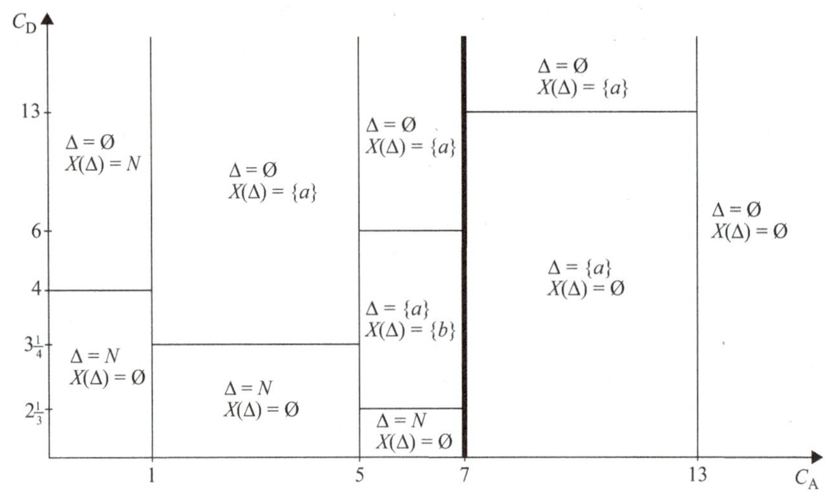


**Figure 7.4**
Equilibrium outcomes: star network ($n = 4$) and $f(x) = x^2$.

that would disconnect the network, and anticipating this, the Defender would like to block such attacks. The details of the equilibrium outcomes are summarized in figure 7.4.

In this equilibrium, two points are worth noting. First, for much of the parameter range, attack and defense are targeted at the on the hub node $a$. There is a threshold cost of the attack level, 7, the Adversary either attacks $a$ or does not attack at all when $c_A > 7$. Second, consider the intensity of conflict, defined as the resources allocated to defense and attack. When the cost of attack is large (e.g., 13) there is no threat to the network, and hence no need for defense. The intensity of conflict is 0. If the cost of attack is small ($c_A < 1$), the intensity of conflict hinges on the costs of defense. When the defense cost is small, all nodes are protected and there is no attack, implying that the intensity of conflict is given by $nc_D$. If defense costs are high, there is no defense and all nodes are eliminated, so the intensity

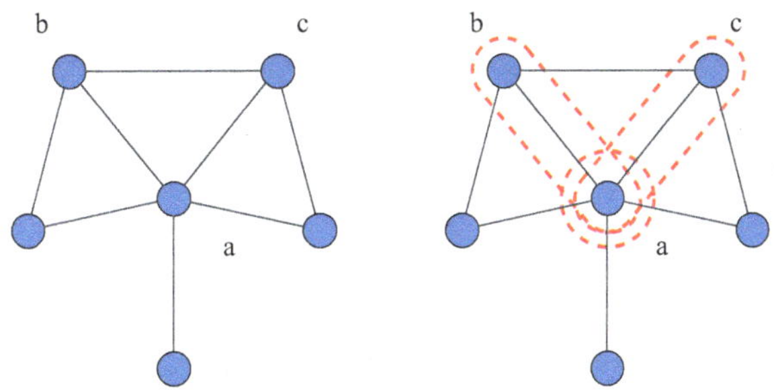


**Figure 7.5**
Essential separators.

of conflict is $nc_A$. For intermediate cost of attack and defense, both the Defender and the Adversary are active. ■

Let us next consider defense and attack in general networks. A set $X \subseteq N$ is a *separator* of the network $g$ if $|\mathcal{C}(g)| < |\mathcal{C}(g - X)|$; in other words, a separator is a set of nodes whose removal strictly increases the number of components in the network. A network will typically contain multiple separators: as the Adversary seeks to maximize their payoffs, they target the most economical separators. A separator $S \subseteq N$ is *essential* for network $g \in \mathcal{G}(N)$ if for every separator $S' \subsetneq S$, $|\mathcal{C}(g - S)| > |\mathcal{C}(g - S')|$ (i.e., a strict subset of eliminated nodes results in a strictly smaller number of components). The set of all essential separators of a network $g$ is denoted by $\mathcal{E}(g)$. Figure 7.5 illustrates the essential separators in a simple network: $\{a\}$, $\{a, b\}$, and $\{a, c\}$.

Example 7.1 suggests that the network defense problem can be divided into two parts depending on the cost of attack. In the low-cost case, the elimination of single nodes is attractive for the Adversary, while in the high-cost case, elimination of a node is justified only if it results in disconnecting the residual network. Let $\Delta f(x) = f(x+1) - f(x)$ be the marginal increase in the value of a component of size $x$ when a single node is added to it. Under assumption 7.1, $\Delta f(x)$ is strictly increasing. High costs occur when $c_A > \Delta f(n-1)$, implying that the Adversary does not want to eliminate single nodes; low costs occur when they may wish to eliminate single nodes, $c_A < \Delta f(n-1)$.

With a high attack cost, an active Adversary must disconnect the network (i.e., choose a separator or not attack the network at all). Given a cost of attack $c_A$ and network $g$, we define the set of individually rational separators as

$$\mathcal{E}(g, c_A) = \{X \in \mathcal{E}(g) : \Phi(g) - \Phi(g - X) \geq c_A |X|\}. \tag{7.4}$$

When the cost of attack is low, it may be profitable for the Adversary to use attacks that merely remove nodes from the network without disconnecting it. A set $R \subseteq N$ is a *reducing*

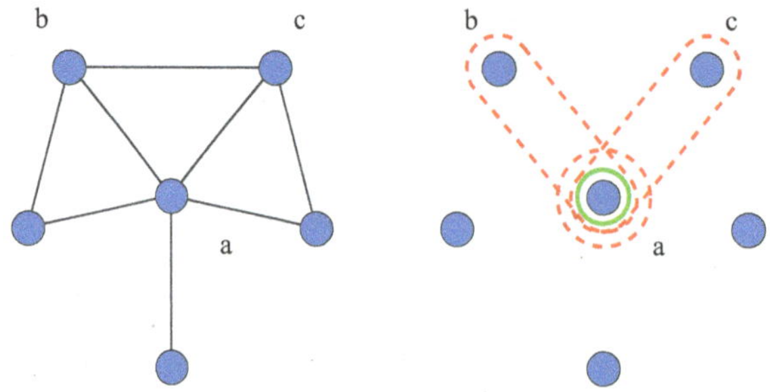


**Figure 7.6**
Minimum transversal, $\{a\}$, of essential separators $\{\{a\}, \{a, b\}, \{a, c\}\}$.

*attack* for a network $g$ if there is no $X \subseteq R$ for which $X$ is a separator for $g$. For a given network, the set of all reducing attacks is denoted by $\mathcal{R}(g)$.

The attack of the Adversary can be decomposed into two parts. First, the Adversary fragments the network by removing a minimal set of nodes needed to obtain the desired components—this is the essential separator. Second, the Adversary reduces the size of the components (but without disconnecting any of them).

Anticipating this attack, the Defender chooses a defense. It is instructive to start with the setting where the cost of attack is high, as we can limit our attention to attacks that disconnect the network. In this case, given the costs of attack, the Adversary will only use separator $\mathcal{E}$ and not use $R$. The optimal strategy of the Defender is to block a subset of the separators in the most economical way. The study of such blocking strategies requires the use of the notion of a *transversal*.

Given a family of sets of nodes $\mathcal{H}$, and a set of nodes $M$, define

$$\mathcal{B}(M, \mathcal{H}) = \{Z \in \mathcal{H} : Z \cap M \neq \varnothing\} \tag{7.5}$$

as the sets in $\mathcal{H}$ that are blocked (or *covered*) by $M$. Set $M$ is called a *transversal of* $\mathcal{H}$ if $\mathcal{B}(M, \mathcal{H}) = \mathcal{H}$. The set of all transversals of $\mathcal{H}$ is denoted by $\mathcal{T}(\mathcal{H})$. Members of $\mathcal{T}(\mathcal{H})$ that are minimal with respect to inclusion are called *minimal* transversals of $\mathcal{H}$. Elements of $\mathcal{T}(\mathcal{H})$ with the smallest size are called *minimum* transversals of $\mathcal{H}$. Let $\tau(\mathcal{H})$ denote the *transversal number* of $\mathcal{H}$ (i.e., the size of a minimum transversal of $\mathcal{H}$). Figure 7.6 illustrates the minimum transversal in a simple network.

We illustrate the concepts of separator and transversal using the example of *trees* and *core-periphery networks*.

**Trees** In any tree network, every nonempty set of internal nodes (nodes that are not leaves) constitutes a separator. Essential separators are nonempty sets of nodes such that any node in a set has at least two neighbors outside that set. Transversals of essential separators are subsets of internal nodes. In particular, there is a unique minimal transversal of the set

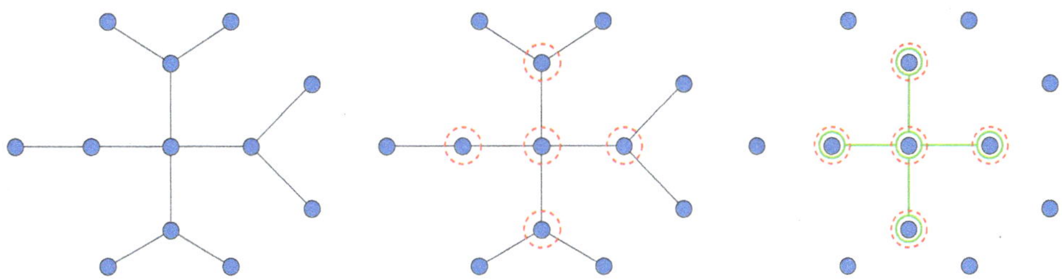

**Figure 7.7**
Tree: separators (in red) and transversals (in green) ($n = 12$).

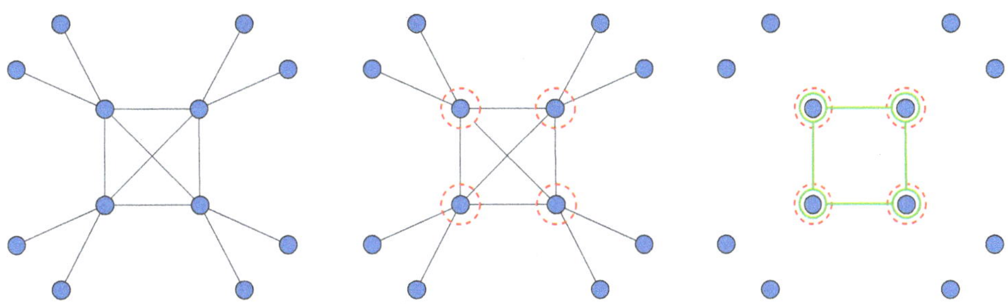

**Figure 7.8**
Core-periphery: separators (in red) and transversals (in green) ($n = 12$).

of all essential separators: the set of all internal nodes. Minimal essential separators and transversal for tree networks are illustrated in figure 7.7.

**Core-periphery networks** Every peripheral node is connected to exactly one node of the core (and the core constitutes a clique). Every subset of the core nodes is an essential separator. There is a unique minimal transversal: the set of all core nodes. Minimal essential separators and transversals for core-periphery networks are illustrated in figure 7.8.

We build on example 7.1 and the discussion of separators and transversal to develop the following result on defense and attack in networks.

**Proposition 7.1** *Consider the Network Defense game. Suppose the network value function is given by equation (7.1) and fix a network g that is connected. Let* $(\mathcal{D}^*, X^*)$ *be an equilibrium.*

1. *If* $c_A < \Delta f(n-1)$, *then*
   - $\mathcal{D}^* = N$ *or* $\mathcal{D}^*$ *is a minimal transversal of* $\mathcal{B}(\mathcal{D}^*, \mathcal{E}(g, c_A))$.
   - $X^*(\mathcal{D}) = E \cup R$, *where* $E \in \mathcal{E}(g, c_A)$ *and* $R \in \mathcal{R}(g - E)$, *with* $X^*(\mathcal{D}) \cap \mathcal{D} = \varnothing$.
2. *If* $c_A > \Delta f(n-1)$, *then*
   - $|\mathcal{D}^*| \leq \tau(\mathcal{E}(g, c_A))$ *and* $\mathcal{D}^*$ *is a minimum transversal of* $\mathcal{B}(\mathcal{D}^*, \mathcal{E}(g, c_A))$.
   - $X^*(\mathcal{D}) = \varnothing$ *if* $\mathcal{D} \in \mathcal{T}(\mathcal{E}(g, c_A))$; $X^*(\mathcal{D}) \in \mathcal{E}(g, c_A)$ *with* $X^*(\mathcal{D}) \cap \mathcal{D} = \varnothing$.

A first message is that no attack will target a protected node. The more general point of this analysis is that essential separators (ones that are effective at fragmenting the network) are key to optimal attack, and economical transversals (that block these separators) are key to optimal defense. A third point is that if the Defender goes beyond blocking the separator and protecting nodes that expand the size of a component, then, due to the convexity of the network value function, it is optimal for them to protect all nodes in the network.

We now outline the arguments underlying the proof of this proposition. Let us start with part 1: when the costs of attack are small, if defense exceeds a minimal transversal (of covered essential separators), then it must include a node that is being protected purely to prevent it from removal. This protection is being done to protect the size of the component. This must mean that, in the absence of defense, the node will be eliminated in the subsequent optimal attack. As $f$ is convex, the marginal return of the expanding size of a component is increasing in its size. Since the cost of node defense is linear, once the Defender decides to protect nodes beyond the minimal transversal, it must be optimal for them to defend all nodes.

Turning to part 2: if the costs are large, the Adversary will not use reducing attacks. So an optimal attack must be either empty or an essential separator. Clearly, optimal defense $\mathcal{D}^*$ cannot be larger than the size of the minimum transversal of $\mathcal{E}(g, c_A)$, as that would be wasteful for the Defender. If $|\mathcal{D}^*| = \tau(\mathcal{E}(g, c_A))$, then $\mathcal{D}^*$ must be a minimum transversal of $\mathcal{E}(g, c_A)$. If $|\mathcal{D}^*| < \tau(\mathcal{E}(g, c_A))$, then $\mathcal{D}^*$ is a minimum transversal of $\mathcal{B}(\mathcal{D}^*, \mathcal{E}(g, c_A))$ in $\mathcal{E}(g, c_A)$. ■

We next apply the insights of proposition 7.1 to the problem of defending the London Underground.

#### 7.3.1.3 Application: London Underground

Let us compute some separators and corresponding tranversals for the London Underground. There are 135 separators of size 1: the large number of separators is due to the many long paths emanating from the core of the network with the key junctions. It then follows that the transversal number $\tau(\mathcal{M}(g, c_A)) = 135$ (where $\mathcal{M}(g, c_A)$ is the set of all minimal separators, given a network $g$ and the cost of attack $c_A$). Consider other separators, which are of size 2: there are 209 additional such separators. This in turn raises the transversal number to 195. Finally, consider separators of size 3: there are 130 such separators, and faced with this attack, the transversal number is 205. One point to note is that as we allow larger separators, there is only a very modest increase in the transversal number.

Let us summarize what we have learned about the optimal defense of infrastructure networks in this section. We have shown that an intelligent Adversary will use an attack strategy that combines separators and reducing cuts. Anticipating this strategy, the Designer will focus on protecting the nodes that block the separators, which gives rise to a transversal-based defense. In the model considered, and indeed throughout this chapter, we will focus on the case with a single Designer and a single Adversary. This is a natural baseline, and it offers some intuitions. However, in many contexts, defense may be left to the nodes (as in

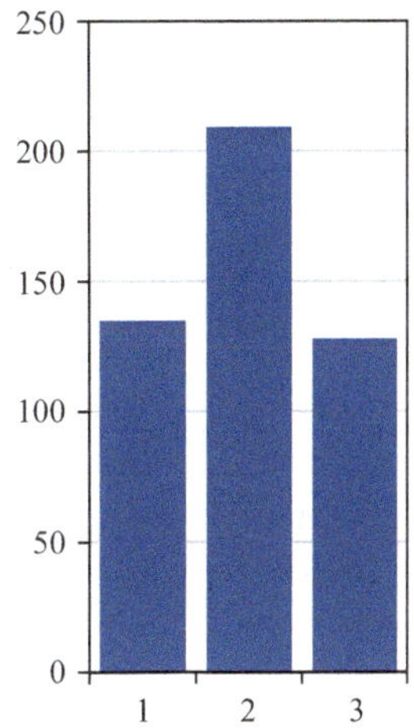


**Figure 7.9**
Minimal separators of London Underground.

cities or states making choices on the protection of their infrastructure). We conclude this section with a discussion of some issues that arise when we allow individual nodes to make decisions on their own protection.

#### 7.3.1.4 Decentralized defense

Here, we consider a two-stage game. In the first stage, each of the nodes in the network decides whether to protect itself or stay unprotected. These choices are observed by the Adversary, which then chooses the nodes to attack.

Let $N = \{1, 2, \ldots, n\}$, with $n \geq 3$ as the set of players, and let $S_i = \{0, 1\}$ denote the strategy set of node $i \in N$. Here, $s_i = 1$ means that the node chooses to defend itself, and $s_i = 0$ refers to the case of no-defense. These choices are made simultaneously. There is a one-to-one correspondence between a strategy profile of the nodes, $\mathbf{s} \in \{0, 1\}^N$, and the resulting set of defended nodes $\Delta \subseteq N$. So we will use $\Delta$ to refer to the strategy profile of the nodes in the first stage.

In the second stage, the Adversary observes the defended network $(g, \Delta)$ and chooses an attack $X \subseteq N$, which leads to a residual network $g - (X \setminus \Delta)$. The payoff to the Adversary remains as in the case of the centralized defense and as defined in equation (7.3). The payoff to a node depends on whether the node is removed by the attack. A removed node receives a payoff of 0. Each of the surviving nodes receives an equal share of the value of its component in the residual network:

$$\Pi^i(\Delta, X; g, c_{\mathrm{D}}) = \begin{cases} 0 & \text{if } i \in X \setminus \Delta, \\ \frac{f(|C(i)|)}{|C(i)|} - s_i c_{\mathrm{D}} & \text{otherwise,} \end{cases} \tag{7.6}$$

where $C(i)$ is the component in the residual network $g - (X \setminus \Delta)$ containing $i$.

This completes the description of the *Decentralized Defense Game*. As in the two-player game, we study the subgame perfect equilibria of this game. We focus on equilibria with no active conflict (these are equilibria in which either the nodes do not defend or the Adversary does not attack), because we are able to provide a characterization, and also because these equilibria suffice for us to discuss the inefficiencies that arise when defense decisions are decentralized. All other equilibria in the Decentralized Defense Game could be characterized in the same spirit as the characterization provided in proposition 7.1 for the Defender-Adversary game discussed above.

As usual, we solve the game backward, starting from the second stage. As in the two-player game, the Adversary chooses either the empty attack or an attack as a combination of an essential separator and a reducing attack. If the cost of attack is low and there is no active conflict, then either the Adversary removes all the nodes or all nodes are protected. In any other outcome, the Adversary must remove at least one node. If the cost of attack is high and there is no active conflict, then either none of the nodes protects or, anticipating the strategy of the Adversary, the nodes choose a defense configuration that blocks all the individually rational essential separators. Therefore, in equilibrium, they must choose a minimal transversal of $\mathcal{E}(g, c_{\mathrm{A}})$. We build on these observations to provide the characterization of equilibria with no active conflict in the Decentralized Defense Game.

**Proposition 7.2** *Consider the Decentralized Defense Game on a connected network g. Let $\Delta^*$ be the equilibrium defense.*

1. *If $c_{\mathrm{D}} > f(n)/n$, then $\Delta^* = \varnothing$ is the unique equilibrium defense.*
2. *If $c_{\mathrm{D}} \leq f(n)/n$, and*
   (a) *$c_{\mathrm{A}} < f(n) - f(n-1)$, then $\Delta^* = N$ is an equilibrium defense.*
   (b) *$c_{\mathrm{A}} > f(n) - f(n-1)$, then any minimal transversal of $\mathcal{E}(g, c_{\mathrm{A}})$ is an equilibrium defense.*

*The equilibrium strategy of the Adversary is as in proposition 7.1.*

We now discuss inefficiencies that may arise due to decentralized protection. This is done via a comparison of the aggregate welfare of the nodes in the equilibrium of the two-player game with the aggregate welfare in the Decentralized Defense Game. Let $\Pi^{\mathrm{D}^*}(g, c_{\mathrm{A}}, c_{\mathrm{D}})$ denote the equilibrium payoff in the two-player game on network $g$ with cost of defense $c_{\mathrm{D}}$ and cost of attack $c_{\mathrm{A}}$. Aggregate welfare in the two-player game, starting from network $g$ and with costs $c_{\mathrm{A}}$ and $c_{\mathrm{D}}$, are

$$W^F(g, c_{\mathrm{A}}, c_{\mathrm{D}}) = \Pi^{\mathrm{D}^*}(g, c_{\mathrm{A}}, c_{\mathrm{D}}). \tag{7.7}$$

Aggregate welfare under defense profile $\Delta$ and attack $X$ of the $n+1$ player game starting from network $g$, and given cost of defense $c_{\mathrm{D}}$, are

$$W^D(\Delta, X; g, c_{\mathrm{D}}) = \sum_{i \in N} \Pi^i(\Delta, X; g, c_{\mathrm{D}}). \tag{7.8}$$

We study the cost of decentralization in terms of the *price of anarchy*: the ratio of welfare in the two-player game to the welfare in the worst equilibrium of the Decentralized Defense Game. Let $E(g, c_A, c_D)$ denote the set of equilibria of the $n+1$ player game on network $g$ with cost of attack $c_A$ and cost of defense $c_D$. The price of anarchy is

$$\text{PoA} = \max_{g, c_A, c_D} \left( \frac{W^F(g, c_A, c_D)}{\min_{(\Delta, X) \in E(g, c_A, c_D)} W^D(\Delta, X(\Delta); g, c_D)} \right). \tag{7.9}$$

We first take up the issue of positive externalities: an individual's protection decision creates benefits for other nodes (that they do not take into account). This can lead to very large welfare losses. To see this, consider a star network and suppose that the cost of attack is high, $c_A > f(n) - f(n-1)$, and $c_D \in (f(n)/n, f(n))$. In the equilibrium of the two-player game, the aggregate welfare $f(n) - c_D$. By contrast, in the equilibrium of the Decentralized Defense Game, the central player does not find it profitable to defend itself, as $c_D > f(n)/n$. So aggregate welfare in the equilibrium of the $n+1$ player game is 0. Thus the ratio of the two is unbounded for the range of costs $c_D \in (f(n)/n, f(n))$.

Protection choices exhibit a threshold property: for a node to find it profitable to protect itself, it is necessary that other nodes belonging to the same minimal transversal also choose to protect themselves. In other words, protection decisions are strategic complements—a property that can give rise to coordination failures. To see this, consider a tree with two hubs, each of whom is linked to $(n-2)/2$ distinct nodes. Suppose that

$$f(n) - f(n-1) < c_A < f(n/2) - (n-2)f(1)/2, \tag{7.10}$$

so the Adversary will only attack hub nodes. If $2f(n/2)/n < c_D < f(n)/n$, then the first best outcome is to defend the two hubs. One hub protecting itself gives incentives to the other hub to protect itself as well: two protected hubs is an equilibrium outcome. However, on its own, a hub node does not have sufficient incentives to protect itself: zero protection is an equilibrium outcome. In this zero-protection equilibrium, the aggregate payoffs equal $(n-2)f(1)$ compared to the first best outcome of $f(n) - 2c_D$. Given that $f()$ is convex, the cost of decentralization can be unbounded.

Third, at the local level, the game is clearly one of strategic substitutes. A node in a separator has incentives to protect itself only if no other node in the separator protects itself. As we saw in the study of local public goods in networks (see chapter 4), the network protection game therefore displays multiple equilibria. This can generate very large efficiency losses. As an example, consider network $g$, depicted in figure 7.10.

Suppose that $f(x) = x^2$, $c_A \in (21, 28)$ and $c_D < 11$. Given this cost of attack, the Adversary will not remove a node without disconnecting the network. The set of individually rational essential separators is the combination of sets depicted in figure 7.10. Notice that the minimum transversal of $\mathcal{E}(g, c_A)$ is the node belonging to each of the separators, while the largest minimal transversal consists of one distinct node from each of the two element

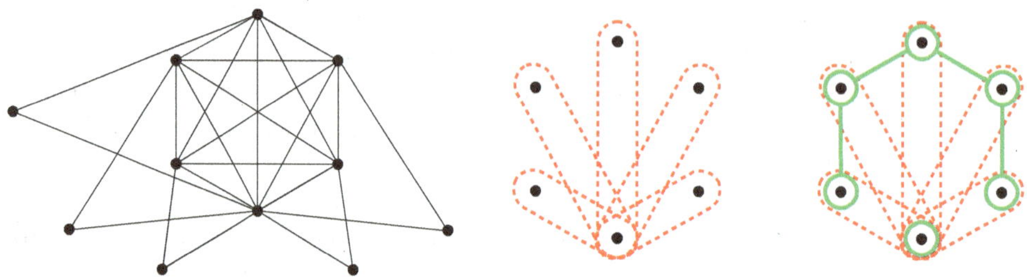

**Figure 7.10**
A network with essential separators of size 2 (in red) having two minimal transversals: one of size 1 and one of size 5 (in green).

separators. The price of anarchy (POA) will be proportional to the ratio of extra nodes that protect, and this is of order $(n-1)/2$. In other words, the POA is unbounded.

To summarize, our study of decentralized defense shows that the equilibrium choices of nodes and the Adversary can be usefully studied in terms of transversals and separators of the underlying network. Moreover, we have shown that the strategic structure of the problem is very rich, admitting features of both strategic substitutes and complements (for definitions of these concepts, refer to chapter 4 on network structure and human behavior). The welfare gap between decentralized equilibrium and first best outcomes is unbounded: interestingly, individual choice may lead to too little or too much protection relative to the choice of a single, centralized Defender.

### 7.3.2 Design and Defense

In the previous section, we studied the problem of defending a given network. While a network may be fixed in the short or medium run, it is reasonable to suppose that in the long run it is possible to alter it through appropriate link investments—lack of investment can erode an existing link while significant investments can give rise to new links. With this idea in mind, we now move on to the longer term and consider the question of design and defense of a network that faces threats. We use a model taken from Dziubiński and Goyal (2013).

#### 7.3.2.1 A model

In this model, there are two stages and two players (a Designer and an Adversary). In the first stage, the Designer chooses a network and a subset of nodes to defend. In the second stage, the Adversary observes the network and defense and then chooses a subset of nodes to attack.

As before, let the set of nodes be given by $N = \{1, \ldots, n\}$, where $n \geq 3$. The Designer chooses links between pairs of nodes to create network $g$, and chooses to protect a subset of nodes $\mathcal{D}$. Thus he chooses $(g, \mathcal{D})$. In the second stage, the Adversary assigns their attack budget $k > 0$ to a subset of nodes $X \subseteq N$, with $|X| \leq k$. This attack strategy is called a *cut*. Recall that given network $g$, the removal of $X$ nodes creates a *residual network*, $g - X$.

As in the previous section, in order to focus on network issues, we consider a simple model of conflict. Defense is perfect: a protected node cannot be removed by an attack. On the other hand, an unprotected node is removed with certainty if it is attacked. Given defense $\mathcal{D}$ and cut $X$, set $Y = X \setminus \mathcal{D}$ is removed from the network.

Both links and defense resources are costly: a link costs $c_L > 0$, and the protection of a node costs $c_D > 0$. The cost of a defended network $(g, \mathcal{D})$ is

$$c_L|g| + c_D|\mathcal{D}|. \tag{7.11}$$

The payoff to the Designer from choosing $(g, \mathcal{D})$ when the Adversary chooses cut $X$ is

$$\Pi^D(\mathcal{D}, X; g) = \Phi(g - (X \setminus \mathcal{D})) - c_L|g| - c_D|\mathcal{D}|. \tag{7.12}$$

The payoff to the Adversary is

$$\Pi^A(\mathcal{D}, X; g) = -\Phi(g - (X \setminus \mathcal{D})). \tag{7.13}$$

The objective of the Designer is to maximize the payoff, while the goal of the Adversary is to minimize the value of the residual network. We shall refer to this as the *Design and Defense Game*.

We study the subgame perfect equilibrium of this game. The Designer seeks the defended network that copes best with the worst attack the Adversary can launch. This is a setting in which the Designer and the Adversary have diametrically opposed interests.

Facing a defended network $(g, \mathcal{D})$, the Adversary will choose a set of nodes to eliminate, $X$, such that

$$\Phi(g - (X \setminus \mathcal{D})) = \min_{\substack{Y \subseteq N \\ |Y| \leq k.}} \Phi(g - (Y \setminus \mathcal{D})) \tag{7.14}$$

Therefore, the Designer chooses $(g, \mathcal{D})$ such that for all cuts $X$ with $|X| \leq k$,

$$\Pi^D(\mathcal{D}, X; g) \geq \max_{\substack{g' \subseteq g^N \\ \mathcal{D}' \subseteq N}} \left( \left( \min_{Y \subseteq N, |Y| \leq k} \Phi(g' - (Y \setminus \mathcal{D}')) \right) - (|\mathcal{D}'|c_D + |g'|c_L) \right). \tag{7.15}$$

#### 7.3.2.2 The pure connectivity problem

To develop a feel for the economic forces at work, we start with the simple case in which a network is valuable if and only if it is connected.

Formally, suppose that the value function $\Phi$ of residual network is

$$\Phi(g) = \begin{cases} 1, & \text{if the network is connected,} \\ 0, & \text{otherwise.} \end{cases} \tag{7.16}$$

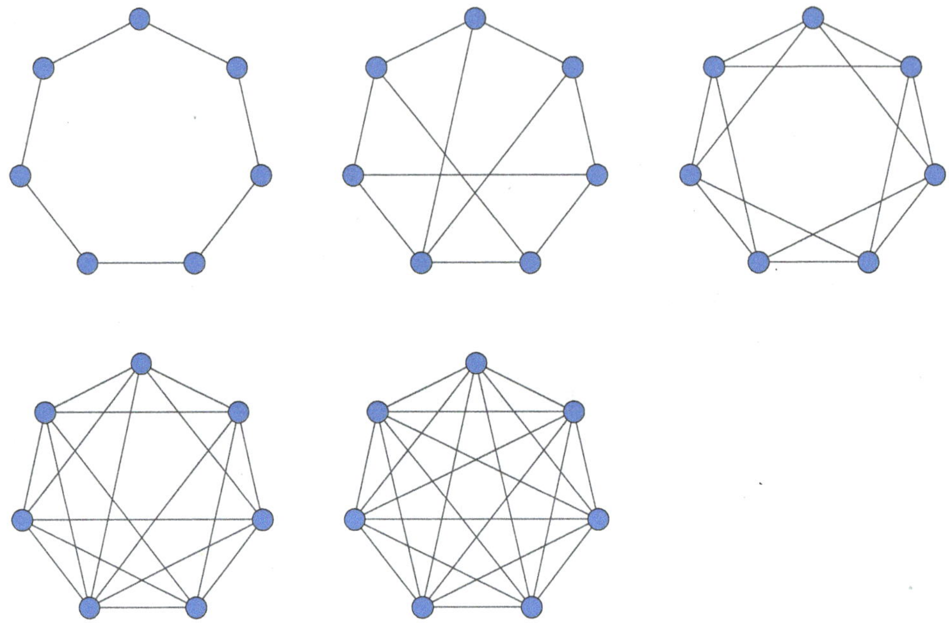

**Figure 7.11**
Harary networks: $n = 7$, connectivity $k = 2, \ldots, 6$.

Therefore, the Designer either chooses the empty network with no defense or selects a lowest-cost network-defense strategy $(g, \mathcal{D})$ such that for all $X \subseteq N$ with $|X| \leq k$, $g - (X \setminus \mathcal{D})$ is connected.

Given $k \geq 2$, network $g$ is *k-connected* if either $|N| = k + 1$, or $|N| \geq k + 2$ and there is a separator $X \subseteq N$ if and only if $|X| \geq k$. A $k$-connected network with the minimum number of links is called *minimal k-connected*. The set of minimal $k$-connected networks is denoted by $\mathcal{M}(k, n)$.

It is easy to see that every node of a $k$-connected network has a degree at least $k$, as otherwise it could be separated from the rest of the network by removing fewer than $k$ nodes. Thus the minimal number of links in such a network is $\lceil nk/2 \rceil$. Harary (1962) showed that this number of links is also sufficient. We provide some examples of Harary graphs in figure 7.11. The following result reveals that the equilibrium of the Design and Defense Game has a very simple structure.

**Proposition 7.3** *Consider the Design and Defense Game and suppose that $k \leq n - 2$. In equilibrium,*

1. *The Designer chooses the protected network $(g, \mathcal{D})$, which is as follows:*
   - *If $c_L < 1/\left\lceil \frac{n(k+1)}{2} \right\rceil$ and $c_D > c_L \left( \left\lceil \frac{n(k-1)}{2} \right\rceil + 1 \right)$, then $g \in \mathcal{M}(k, n)$ and $\mathcal{D} = \varnothing$.*

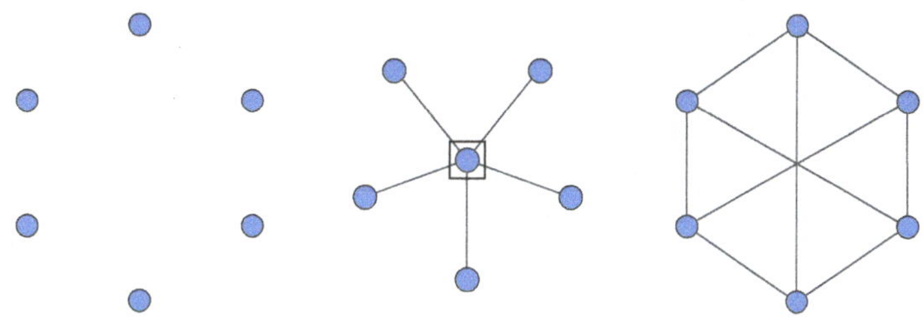

**Figure 7.12**
Equilibrium networks: $n=6$, $k=2$.

- *If* $c_L(n-1)+c_D<1$ *and* $c_D<c_L\left(\left\lceil\frac{n(k-1)}{2}\right\rceil+1\right)$, *then g is a star and the central node is protected.*
- *Otherwise, g is empty and* $\mathcal{D}=\varnothing$.

2. *The Adversary chooses a separating cut for* $(g,\mathcal{D})$ *if it exists, and if it does not exist, then all cuts yield the same payoff.*

In other words, faced with an Adversary who can eliminate $k$ nodes, the Designer chooses one of three possible networks: a $k$-connected network (connectivity is maintained even after $k$ nodes are eliminated), a center-protected star network (connectivity is maintained through a protected hub after the spokes are eliminated), or an empty network. The formal statement delineates the costs of linking and protection under which each of these three networks are optimal. We now spell out the details of these computations.

The payoffs to the Designer from the $(k+1)$–connected network, the center-protected star network, and the empty network are $1-\lceil n(k+1)/2\rceil c_L$, $1-c_D-(n-1)c_L$, 0, respectively. The payoff to the Adversary is $-1$ when faced with a $(k+1)$–connected network or the center-protected star, and it is 0 when faced with the empty network. Figure 7.12 illustrates three equilibrium outcomes—empty network, center-protected star, and 3-connected network.

The arguments underlying the result are as follows. In the first step, we clarify the nature of networks under zero or positive defense. In the case of no defense, the network is either empty or connected. If it is connected, then the residual network must be connected as well, regardless of any cuts. Thus, in the case of no defense, the Designer must choose either an empty or a minimal $(k+1)$–connected network. In the case of positive defense, the residual network must again be connected. So the initial network set up by the Designer must be connected. Observe that connectedness of the residual network can be guaranteed by a star network with 1 unit of defense assigned to the center. This protected network has a minimal number of links across all connected networks and minimal defense across all networks with positive defense. Any other network with the same number of links must be a tree, and any tree requires protecting all internal nodes (i.e., nonleaves) to stay connected after an attack

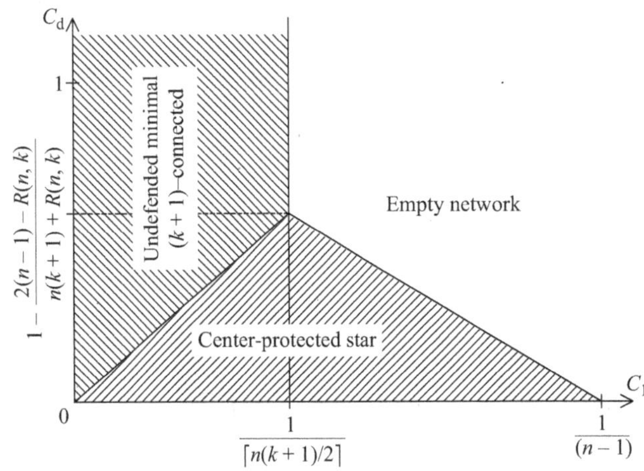


**Figure 7.13**
Equilibrium outcomes and costs of linking and defense.

of the Adversary. Thus the center-protected star is the only candidate for the Designer who is optimizing.

The payoff to the Designer from the empty network is 0. Observe that in a $(k+1)$–connected network, every node must have a degree at least $k+1$; otherwise, it can be isolated by the deletion of its neighbors. Harary (1962) proved that the degree $k+1$ for every node (except possibly for one node, which has degree $k+2$)—so $\lceil n(k+1)/2 \rceil$ links in all—is also sufficient for $k+1$ connectedness. Applying this theorem, we can write the payoff from the minimal $(k+1)$-connected network as

$$1 - c_L \left\lceil \frac{n(k+1)}{2} \right\rceil. \tag{7.17}$$

Finally, the payoff from the center-protected star is

$$1 - c_L(n-1) - c_D. \tag{7.18}$$

A comparison of the payoffs from the empty network, a minimal $(k+1)$–connected network, and a center-protected star yields the desired parameter restrictions. ■

Figure 7.13 presents the optimal defended networks, as we vary the costs of defense and linking. We say that $R(n,k) = n(k+1) \bmod 2$, so $R(n,k) = 1$ if $n$ is odd and $k$ is even, and $R(n,k) = 0$ otherwise. We can see that if the cost of linking, $c_L$, is higher than $1/\lceil n(k+1)/2 \rceil$, then only a center-protected star network or empty network can be optimal. Raising the cost of defense makes the empty network more attractive. Similarly, if the cost of defense, $c_D$, is higher than

$$1-\frac{2(n-1)-R(n,k)}{n(k+1)-R(n,k)}, \tag{7.19}$$

then only a minimal $(k+1)$–connected network or an empty network can be optimal (and raising the cost of linking makes the latter more attractive). On the other hand, if the costs are sufficiently low, $c_L < 1/\lceil n(k+1)/2\rceil$ and

$$c_D < 1-\frac{2(n-1)-R(n,k)}{n(k+1)+R(n,k)}, \tag{7.20}$$

then either a minimal $(k+1)$–connected network or a center-protected star is optimal, depending on the relation between the costs, $c_D/c_L$. If $c_D/c_L$ is sufficiently low, that is, lower than $\lceil n(k-1)/2\rceil+1)$, then the center-protected star is optimal, and if it is higher, then the minimal $(k+1)$–connected network is optimal.

#### 7.3.2.3 Remarks on model

This description of optimal defended networks is obtained under the assumption of a perfectly reliable defense. Our model can also be used to study the case of an imperfect defense. Suppose that there is a given probability of successful defense that is less than 1. The Designer will be averse to creating a protected hub network if the protection level is low, which may lead them to create a network with multiple protected hubs. A question at the end of this chapter explores equilibrium networks with imperfect defense.

Next consider the issue of Adversary's budget. In the model we assumed a fixed budget. Suppose instead, in line with the previous section, that attacking each node has a cost $c_A > 0$. Given the Designer's objective of keeping the network connected, the Adversary will choose a maximum of $k$ units of attack where $k \times c_A \leq 1$. So the Designer will play as in the game studied previously, with $k = 1/c_A$ units of attack. This implies that as $c_A$ increases, the maximum number of units of attack falls, and this makes the center-protected star less attractive relative to the $(k+1)$–connected network. An increase in the cost of linking, $c_L$, makes the center-protected star more attractive, while increases in the cost of defense, $c_D$, result in a decrease in the attractiveness of the center-protected star.

Finally, we note that the analysis so far is restricted to the connectivity network value function. The arguments that we have developed can be used to study more general network value functions that satisfy assumption (7.1). The following result covers the general network value setting.

**Proposition 7.4** *Consider the Design and Defense Game. Suppose that $1 \leq k \leq n$ and assumption 7.1 holds. In equilibrium,*

1. *The Designer chooses defense $|\mathcal{D}| = 0$, 1, or $n$. If $|\mathcal{D}| = 0$, a variety of networks—including the empty network and a $(k+1)$–connected network—can arise. If $|\mathcal{D}| = 1$, the network is a star with a protected center. If $|\mathcal{D}| = n$, the network is either empty or minimally connected (a tree).*

2. *The Adversary chooses a separating cut if* $(g, \mathcal{D})$ *permits such a cut. When* $(g, \mathcal{D})$ *permits no separating cuts, every cut yields the same payoff to the Adversary and is optimal.*

*Proof.* Suppose that $(g, \mathcal{D})$ is an equilibrium strategy of the Designer and $|\mathcal{D}| = d > 0$. We will show that either $d = 1$ and $g$ is a star with a protected center, or $d = n$ and the network is either empty or a tree. The proof is constructive.

Let $C_1, \ldots, C_m$ be the components of $g$, and $g_1, \ldots, g_m$ be the subnetworks of $g$ over these components. Without loss of generality, suppose that component $C_1$ contains a protected node (at least one such component must exist since $d > 0$). Component $C_i$ contains at least $|C_i| - 1$ links. Starting from $g$ and keeping $d$ constant, we construct a network $g'$ with defense $\mathcal{D}'$ as follows:

- Convert $g_1$ to a star network $g'_1$ with a protected node at the center.
- From each of the components $C_2, \ldots, C_m$, remove all but one node and connect each the removed nodes to the center of $g'_1$.
- If feasible, move defense from protected nodes in one-node components to unprotected nodes in the newly created star $g'_1$, thus obtaining a new defense, $\mathcal{D}'$.

Observe that $g'$ has $m$ components, as does $g$, and component $C'_1$ contains $n - (m - 1)$ nodes, while all the components $C'_2, \ldots, C'_m$ contain exactly one node. The number of links in $g'$ is weakly smaller than the number of links in $g$ (with equality only if all components of $g$ were minimally connected—that is, trees). The value of network $g'$ is larger than the value of network $g$ as $f(.)$ is increasing and convex and $f(0) = 0$. Finally, any $k$-cut $X$ applied to $g'$ causes weakly less damage than the cut on network $g$, as it does not disconnect any paths between nonattacked nodes. Thus the pair $(g', \mathcal{D}')$ yields a weakly higher payoff than $(g, \mathcal{D})$.

There are two cases to consider, corresponding to $d = 1$ and $d > 1$, which follow next.

*Case* $d = 1$*:* In this case, only the "center" of component $C'_1$ is protected. As $f$ is convex, it is optimal for the Adversary to attack component $C'_1$ first. So $(g', \mathcal{D}')$ dominates $(g', \varnothing)$ only if $|C'_1| > k + 1$. As this is an optimal outcome, it follows that the marginal value of the last periphery node, $n - (m - 1)$, is greater than the cost of link $c_{\mathrm{L}}$. It now follows from the convexity of $f(.)$ that linking an additional single node to the center of $g'_1$ is strictly profitable. Iterating, we conclude that if $d = 1$, then the optimal network is a center-protected star.

*Case* $d > 1$*:* The convexity of $f$ implies that all the nodes must be defended and the network must be connected. First, as $f(.)$ is increasing and convex, the Adversary will start by attacking unprotected periphery nodes (if any) in component $C'_1$. Again, due to the convexity of $f$, it is better to protect a periphery node in component $C'_1$ rather than a node in some other component. The convexity of $f$ implies that marginal returns from protecting additional periphery nodes are increasing, while the cost of protection is linear. Thus payoff to the Designer is strictly increased by protecting all periphery nodes in $C'_1$. Arguments analogous to those used in the case of $d = 1$ imply that if there are singleton nodes with protection, then attaching them to the center of $g'_1$ will strictly increase the payoff to the Designer as well.

Finally, consider the situation in which all nodes from $g'_1$ are protected and all singleton isolated nodes are not protected. If this is optimal, then the cost of linking and protection, $c_L + c_D$, is smaller than the marginal value of doing so—$f(|C'_1|) - f(|C'_1| - 1)$. The convexity of $f$ implies that the marginal value of adding an extra periphery node and protecting it is strictly larger, while the cost is still $c_L + c_D$. It follows that the star network with all protected nodes would yield a higher utility to the Designer than configuration $(g', \mathcal{D}')$. Observe, finally, that the payoff in any tree with all nodes protected is equal. This completes the argument.

We now discuss the architecture of equilibrium networks when defense size $|\mathcal{D}| = 0$. When $k = 1$, the equilibrium network is either empty or a cycle containing all nodes. It is not profitable to have more than $n$ links since a cycle guarantees the maximal payoff $f(n-1)$ in the face of attack $k = 1$. A network with positive number of links less than $n$ is not optimal due to the convexity of $f$. When the budget of the Adversary is $k = n - 2$, the equilibrium network is either an empty or a complete network: a nonempty incomplete network can be disconnected by the Adversary with budget $k = n - 2$, so depending on the costs of linking $c_L$ the Designer will choose either an empty or a complete network. This completes the proof of the result. ■

Let us summarize what we have learned about optimal defense and the design of infrastructure networks. If defense is relatively cheap, it is best to protect a single node and create a hub-spoke network. By contrast, if defense is relatively costly, then it is best to economize on defense and instead to create a dense network, thereby minimizing the disruption caused by the elimination of some nodes of the network by the adversary. Chapter 6, on infrastructure, shows that airlines, railways, and roads exhibit hub-spoke like structures. Our theoretical results point to the robustness of such networks from a security perspective.

## 7.4 Protecting Networks against Contagious Threats

> Our daily life, economic vitality, and national security depend on a stable, safe, and resilient cyberspace. We rely on this vast array of networks to communicate and travel, power our homes, run our economy, and provide government services.
> US Department of Homeland Security (DHS)

Connections among individuals, cities, countries, and computers facilitate the exchange of goods, resources, and information and generate value. However, these connections may serve as a conduit for the spread of damaging attacks. The Internet reflects this tension clearly. Connectivity facilitates communication but is also used by hackers, hostile governments and firms, and botnet herders to spread viruses and worms that compromise user privacy and jeopardize the functioning of the entire system. In this section, we will study the design and defense of networks in the face of threats that are contagious and spread through the connections of a network. We start with a brief discussion of cyberattacks.

Perhaps the first known instance of a worm that exploits programming weakness and the interconnections of the Internet is the *Morris Worm*. The Morris Worm was launched in 1988 by Robert Morris, a graduate student at Cornell University, and appeared to have infected around 10 percent of the then-existing Internet (which had roughly sixty thousand computers). We next present other examples of cyberattacks that exploit weaknesses in computer programming and connections across the Internet to compromise the functioning of physical infrastructure:

- Ransomware is a type of malicious software that infects a computer and restricts users' access to it until a ransom is paid to unlock it. We present one example of ransomware to illustrate how it works. The Colonial Pipeline transports gasoline, diesel, jet fuel, and other refined products from the Gulf Coast to Linden, New Jersey, and provides roughly 45 percent of the fuel used in the US East Coast. On the morning of May 7, 2021, an employee found a ransom note from hackers on a control-room computer, informing them that the computer access had been blocked and that they would have pay a ransom to gain access. By that night, the company's chief executive officer had paid the ransom (USD 4.4 million). In return, the company received a decryption tool to unlock the systems that the hackers had penetrated. But even that payment could not prevent a shutdown of the pipeline for six days. The stoppage led to a run on gasoline along parts of the East Coast, which pushed prices to the highest levels in more than six years and left thousands of gas stations without fuel. Eventually, the US Department of Justice recovered part of the ransom–USD 2.3 million—from the hackers. (Wall Street Journal, 2021).
- On December 23, 2015, hackers successfully gained access and control of the supervisory control and data acquisition (SCADA) systems of three energy distribution companies in Ukraine and temporarily disrupted the electricity supply to consumers. This attack led to roughly 230,000 people being without electricity for a period lasting from one to six hours at the peak of winter.
- Stuxnet is a malicious computer worm first uncovered in 2010 and thought to have been in development since 2005. It targets SCADA systems, as in the Ukraine attack, and it caused lasting damage to the nuclear program of Iran. Although there is no official acknowledgment, it is widely believed that the Stuxnet attack on Iran arose out of a collaboration between Israel and the US.

Identity theft is widely prevalent. Let us consider some numbers to develop a feel for the scale of the problem. In 2009, it was estimated that roughly 10 million computers were infected with malware designed to steal online credentials. The annual damages caused by malware is of the order of \$11 billion in Europe, while in the US, the annual costs of identity theft are estimated at \$2.8 billion (Moore, Clayton, and Anderson, 2009). One indicator of the economic magnitude of the problem is the valuation of security firms: Intel bought

McAfee in 2010 for $7.68 billion. Finally, we mention intellectual property theft. This theft could be from research laboratories, private firms, and universities, and it can involve corporate firms, independent operators, as well as national governments. Due to its nature, the theft is hard to measure, and estimates of its value vary greatly.

Using data from actual attacks, in their influential paper on computer security, Staniford, Paxson, and Weaver (2002) identify stealth worms and viruses as the main threats to security in computer networks. They argue that adversaries scan a network to explore its topology and the vulnerabilities of nodes prior to an attack. In the first instance, the objective is to deploy a worm on selected nodes in the network. The deployed worms then exploit communication between nodes to progressively take control of neighboring nodes in the network. The likelihood of the capture of a node and the spread of the worm in a network depends on the strength of the worm, the topology of connections, and the vulnerabilities of individual nodes.

The likelihood of the successful infection of a host is higher the more sophisticated the malware and the greater attention devoted by the Adversary to a node. On the other hand, it is lower with greater investment in security software and more specialized personnel assigned to it. These features of the conflict between security and attacks call for a model of contest on the node.

Deployed worms propagate through the network by progressively taking control of neighboring hosts. The worm replicates and then attaches itself to packages of data sent between connected hosts. The probability that the worm succeeds in infecting neighboring hosts varies with the level of security installations on them and the quality of malware being used. This transmission of a worm via communication links, the relative immobility of security installations, and the subsequent conflict between a virus and the security installed on neighboring hosts are the basis of contagion dynamics. In the next section, we will study the design and defense of networks that are subject to attack and contagion dynamics.

### 7.4.1 A Model of Attack, Defense, and Network Design

The theoretical model is taken from Goyal and Vigier (2014). In this model, there are two players—the Designer and the Adversary—and two stages. In the first stage, the Designer chooses a network and a profile of defense across the nodes. The Adversary observes these choices of the Designer and decides on how to allocate their resources to attack particular nodes and also on how to route these resources to attack other nodes in case of successful attacks.

There is a collection of nodes $N=\{1,\ldots,n\}$, with $n\geq 2$. The Designer chooses links between the nodes and allocates $d\in\mathbb{N}$ resource units across the nodes. Let $\underline{d}=(d_1,d_2,\ldots,d_n)$ denote the vector of allocated resources, where $d_i\in\mathbb{N}$ and $\sum_{i\in N} d_i\leq d$. The network-defense pair $(g,\underline{d})$ defines a strategy for the Designer. The strategy that $g$ is a star network and all defense resources are allocated to the central node (a center-protected star) plays a prominent role. We will refer to this strategy as a *CP-star* and denote it as $(g^s,\underline{d}^s)$.

The model supposes that there is a Designer that can choose links and protection to maximize some collective utility. Clearly, in practice, independent individuals will have varying degrees of freedom to choose links and protection. The analysis will therefore identify first best networks that should be seen as a benchmark against which more decentralized outcomes can be measured.

The value of a network is given by assumption 7.1. Given a defended network $(g, \underline{d})$, let $\mathcal{P}$ denote the subset of protected nodes and $\mathcal{U}$ the subset of unprotected nodes. Further, for $i \in N$, let $\mathcal{U}_i \subsetneq \mathcal{U}$ denote the subset of unprotected nodes that can be reached from $i$ through a path such that each node on that path lies in $\mathcal{U}$. Similarly, let $\mathcal{P}_i \subset \mathcal{P}$ denote the subset of protected nodes that can be reached from $i$ through a path such that each node on that path lies in $\mathcal{U}$.

The Designer moves first and chooses a strategy $(g, \underline{d})$. This is observed by the Adversary, who then chooses a strategy $(\underline{a}, \mathcal{R})$. The Adversary first allocates $a \in \mathbb{N}$ units across the nodes, $\underline{a} = (a_1, a_2, \ldots, a_n)$, where $a_i \in \mathbb{N}$ and $\sum_{i \in N} a_i \leq a$. The matrix $\mathcal{R} = \left(r_{ij}\right)_{i,j \in N}$ describes subsequent routing of successful attack resources. Row $i$ in matrix $\mathcal{R}$ specifies a pecking order on $\mathcal{P}_i$: resources on node $i$ relocate to node $j_1 \in \mathcal{P}_i$, with $r_{ij_1} = 1$. If $j_1$ has already been captured, resources are relocated to node $j_2 \in \mathcal{P}_i$, with $r_{ij_2} = 2$, and so forth (in other words, we are taking the view that the Adversary has limited resources and cannot costlessly replicate the worm that has captured a node). The details of the dynamics of attack are described next after a description of the contest on a node.

Attack resources $a_i$ and defense resources $d_i$ located on node $i$ engage in a *contest* for control of the node. If $a_i + d_i > 0$, then, following Tullock (1980), we set the following:

$$\text{probability of successful attack} = \frac{a_i^\gamma}{a_i^\gamma + d_i^\gamma}, \tag{7.21}$$

where $\gamma > 0$. If $a_i$ is 0, then the probability of successful attack is 0, regardless of the value of $d_i$: a node is safe if it is not under attack. An important property of the contest success function is that it is homogenous of degree 0 in resources, so scaling up the resources has no proportional impact on the probability of winning. We assume that all contests are statistically independent (i.e., the probability of winning on a node $i$ depends only on the resources allocated to it, $a_i$ and $d_i$).

The discrete-time dynamics of attack then proceed as follows:

- At time $\mathbf{t = 0}$: The attack begins with unprotected nodes. For all $i \in \mathcal{U}$ such that $a_i > 0$, the Adversary (1) captures $i$, (2) captures $\mathcal{U}_i$ and (3) relocates the $a_i$ attack resources to node $j = \arg\min_{k \in \mathcal{P}_i} \{r_{ik}\}$. In particular, if there is only one element in $P_i$, then the Adversary allocates $a_i$ resources to that node.
- At time $\mathbf{t = 1}$: Let $N^1$ denote the set of uncaptured nodes at the beginning of period $t = 1$ and $\underline{a}^1$ the allocation of attack resources at that point in time (all attack resources now target protected nodes). A contest takes place at all $i$ such that $a_i^1 > 0$, following the rules defined in equation (7.21).

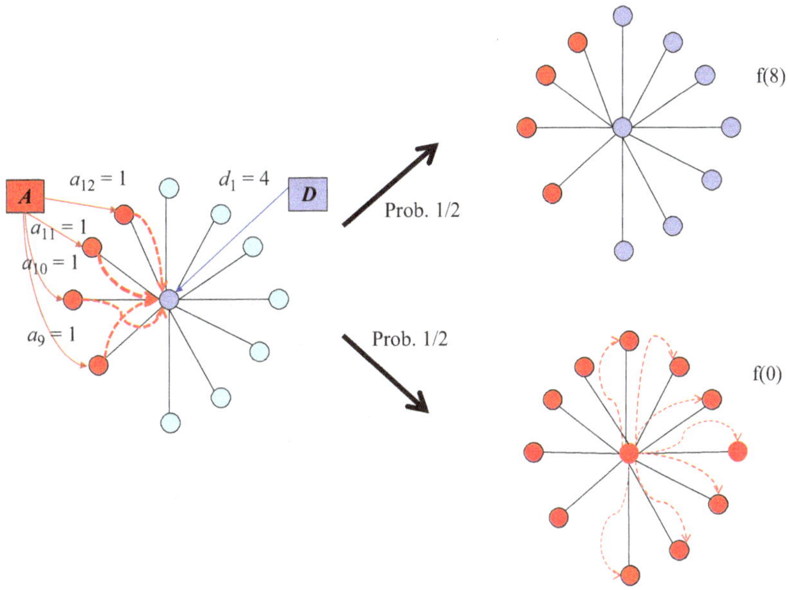


**Figure 7.14**
Dynamics of attack in a CP-star: $n = 12$, $a = d = 4$.

1. If *attack succeeds at i*, then the Adversary (a) eliminates all $d_i$ defense resources located there, (b) captures node $i$, (c) captures any remaining node in $\mathcal{U}_i$ and (d) relocates the $a_i^1$ attack resources to node $j = \arg\min_{k \in \mathcal{P}_i \bigcap N^2}\{r_{ik}\}$. If $\mathcal{P}_i \bigcap N^2 = \emptyset$, then the $a_i^1$ attack resources are eliminated.
2. If *defense succeeds at i*, then the Designer eliminates all $a_i^1$ attack resources located there.

- At time $\mathbf{t = 2}$: Let $\underline{a}^2$ denote the allocation of attack resources at the beginning of period $t = 2$ and $N^2$ the set of uncaptured nodes. If $\underline{a}^2 = \underline{0}$, then the process terminates. Otherwise, it follows the rules laid out as in period $t = 1$, and this continues until no nodes remain.

To develop an appreciation of the dynamics of conflict, it is helpful to locate them in a specific network with resource configurations. Figure 7.14 considers the dynamics in a star network. The number of nodes is 12, and the resources of Adversary and Designer are both equal to 4. The Designer allocates all 4 units to the central node, while the Adversary allocates 1 unit each to 4 unprotected peripheral nodes. These attack units capture the 4 peripheral nodes and then simultaneously attack the central node. Given the Tullock contest, the Designer and Adversary have an equal probability of winning. If the Designer wins the contest, the attack resources are eliminated. There are 8 surviving connected nodes. If the Adversary wins, the central node is captured and the defense resources are eliminated.

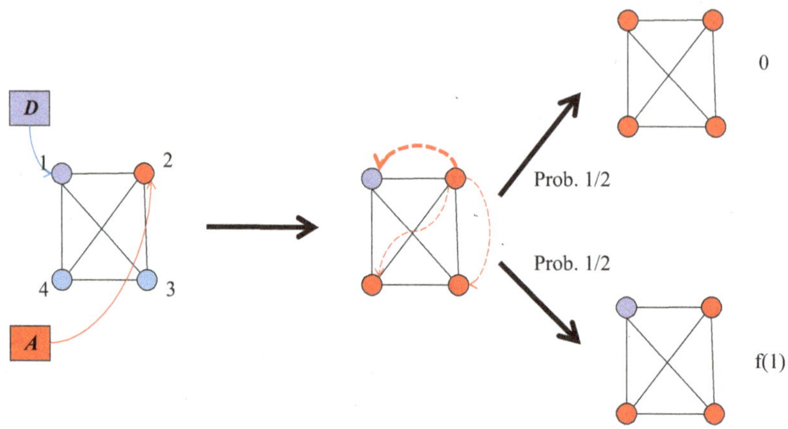


**Figure 7.15**
Dynamics of attack in a complete network: $n=4$, $a=d=1$.

The attack resources then capture the remaining 7 undefended peripheral nodes. The expected payoff of the Designer is

$$\frac{1}{2}f(8)+\frac{1}{2}f(0)=\frac{1}{2}f(8). \tag{7.22}$$

Figure 7.15 illustrates the dynamics of conflict in the complete network, with $n=4$ and $a=d=1$. The Designer allocates their resources to node 1, while the Adversary allocates theirs to node 2. Since node 2 is undefended, it is captured at time $t=0$, followed by the undefended nodes 3 and 4, which are linked to it. At time $t=1$, the attacking unit then spreads to node 1. Given the Tullock contest function, the Designer and Adversary win with equal probability. The expected payoff of the Designer is $f(1)/2$.

Let us now define the resulting networks once conflict has played out. Note that by construction, in every round with both attack and defense resources, one of the two must decline strictly (by at least 1 unit). Thus the dynamics can last at most $a+d$ rounds. Given a defended network $(g,\underline{d})$ and attack strategy $(\underline{a},\mathcal{R})$, the dynamics of conflict described here yield a probability distribution on $\mathcal{G}(g)$. Let $\mathbb{P}(g'|g,\underline{d},\underline{a},\mathcal{R})$ denote the probability that the subnetwork $g'$ is the residual network of surviving nodes after all conflicts have ended. Define $\Pi^e(g,\underline{d},\underline{a},\mathcal{R})$ to be the expected payoff of the Designer, given the defended network $(g,\underline{d})$ and attack strategy $(\underline{a},\mathcal{R})$. Then

$$\Pi^e(g,\underline{d},\underline{a},\mathcal{R})=\sum_{g'\in\mathcal{G}(g)}\mathbb{P}(g'|g,\underline{d},\underline{a},\mathcal{R})\Pi(g'). \tag{7.23}$$

Let $\overline{\Pi}^e(g,\underline{d})$ denote the minimum expected payoff of the Designer playing strategy $(g,\underline{d})$:

$$\overline{\Pi}^e(g,\underline{d})=\min_{\underline{a},\mathcal{R}}\Pi^e(g,\underline{d},\underline{a},\mathcal{R}). \tag{7.24}$$

With these pieces of terminology in place, we are now ready to define optimal networks for the Designer.

**Definition 7.1** *A defended network* $(g, \underline{d})$ *is optimal if* $\overline{\Pi}^e(g, \underline{d}) \geq \overline{\Pi}^e(g', \underline{d}')$ *for all defended networks* $(g', \underline{d}')$.

We start with the optimal architecture and defense at the level of a single component. Then we consider the pure problem of number of components in the absence of any defense resources. We take up the general problem of optimal defended networks when defense allocation, the architecture of individual components, and the number of components are all decision variables for the Designer in a problem at the end of the chapter. Discrete optimization problems are marked by divisibility issues. For simplicity, let us start with the case where the ratio of attack-to-defense resources is an integer, $a/d \in \mathbb{N}$. The case of $a < d$ is taken up later in this chapter.

### 7.4.2 Connected Networks

Consider the set of connected networks. A defended core network consists of (1) a protected set $x \in \{1, \ldots d\}$ of nodes that constitute a connected subgraph and (2) the $n - x$ unprotected nodes (if any exist), each of which has a single link to a protected node. We will show that such *a defended core network is optimal in the class of connected networks.*

The first step is to show that it is optimal for protected nodes to constitute a connected subgraph. Suppose that there is a pair of protected nodes that is connected only via a path of unprotected nodes. Then, given our assumptions on conflict and contagion, the Designer can add a link between this pair of protected nodes without risking loss. Thus we can limit our attention to defended networks in which the set of protected nodes constitutes a connected subgraph.

Next, we rule out a path of unprotected nodes between any two protected nodes. Observe that, as per the previous step, these unprotected nodes play no role in connecting $i$ and $j$ (or any other pair of protected nodes). So the alternative network, in which these unprotected nodes on the path between $i$ and $j$ have a single link to node $i$, causes no loss for the Designer. Indeed, in the new network, these unprotected nodes' survival is contingent only on node $i$'s survival, whereas in the old network, it was contingent on the survival of both node $i$ and node $j$. So any outcome in which node $j$ is captured but node $i$ is not brings about a strict gain for the Designer.

Finally, we show that a link between two unprotected nodes is never optimal. Suppose that $i$ and $j$ are unprotected and have a link between them. As per the previous step, these unprotected nodes must be linked to the same protected node (such as $k$). Let $I$ denote the set of unprotected nodes connected to $k$ through a path of unprotected nodes. Given the dynamics of conflict spelled out earlier, it is then immediate that the alternative network, in which all nodes in $I$ have a single link to node $k$, yields a weakly higher payoff to the Designer compared to the original network (because connecting them can only result in

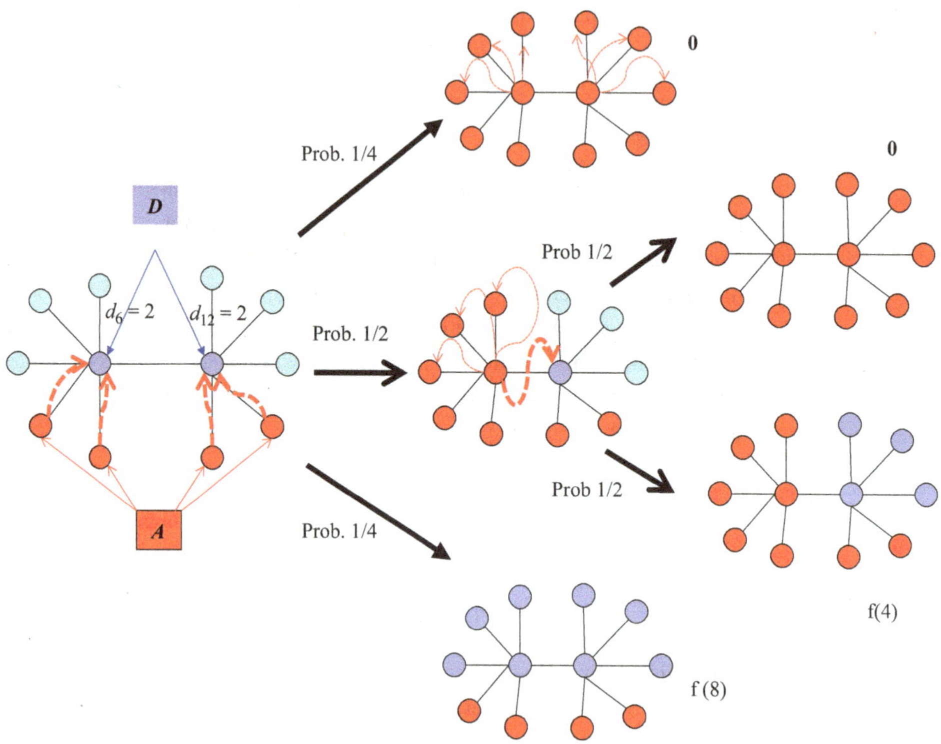


**Figure 7.16**
Attack and defense on a two-hub network: $n = 12$, $a = d = 4$.

some being infected at $t = 0$ that would otherwise only be infected at $t = 1$ if the protected node was infected).

The CP-star is an example of a defended core network. Faced with the CP-star, the Adversary's best response is to allocate 1 resource unit to exactly $a$ periphery nodes. The $a$ periphery nodes are captured and the attack resources then mount a concerted attack on the central node. If the attack on the central node succeeds, all remaining periphery nodes are subsequently captured. If the attack fails, the Designer is left with $n - a$ connected nodes. The expected payoff of the Designer in a CP-star is

$$\overline{\Pi}^e(g^s, \underline{d}^s) = \frac{d^\gamma}{d^\gamma + a^\gamma} f(n - a). \tag{7.25}$$

To develop an intuition for the nature of optimal networks, next consider a defended network with two hubs, as depicted in figure 7.16. There are 12 nodes in all, and $a = d = 4$. This is a core-periphery network with two hubs: the Designer allocates 2 units of defense to each hub. In the mimic strategy, the Adversary allocates 2 resource units to peripheral nodes connected to one hub and 2 resource units to peripheral nodes connected to the other hub. In the first instance, the Adversary captures these 4 peripheral nodes. The resources then target their respective hub nodes.

There are four possible outcomes of this attack strategy: both hubs survive, both hubs are captured, or one hub survives and the other is captured. Given the equal resources engaged in contests, it follows that the first two outcomes each arise with probability $1/4$. The two outcomes define terminal states of the dynamics, represented at the top and bottom of figure 7.16. There is a probability of $1/2$ that one of the hubs survives and the other is captured (in the initial period). This is represented in the middle of the figure. The capture of a hub triggers the capture of its respective peripheral nodes. All attack resources then target the surviving hub, inducing a second round of contests. There is a probability of $1/2$ that the hub survives the attack, and a probability of $1/2$ that it is captured. If the hub is captured, that triggers the capture of the remaining peripheral nodes.

To summarize, in the two-hub protected network, the probability $P$ on surviving nodes is as follows:

There is a probability of $1/2$ that all nodes are captured,
a probability of $1/4$ that 4 nodes survive,
and a probability of $1/4$ that 8 nodes survive.

Consider the outcomes under the CP-star network: the Adversary optimally chooses to first capture 4 peripheral nodes and then mount an attack on the hub. Thus either all nodes are captured or none are captured. The probability of outcomes $P''$ is as follows:

There is a probability of $1/2$ that all nodes are captured,
and a probability of $1/2$ that 8 nodes survive.

Let us compute the expected payoffs to the Designer for a specific network value function: $f(n) = n^2$. The expected payoff to the Designer from the two-hub network is

$$\frac{1}{2}0 + \frac{1}{4}16 + \frac{1}{4}64 = 20. \tag{7.26}$$

The expected payoff to the Designer from the CP-star network is

$$\frac{1}{2}0 + \frac{1}{2}64 = 32. \tag{7.27}$$

Thus we have shown that the minimum payoff to the Designer from a CP-star payoff is larger than the payoff from two-hub protected network for the Designer.

The computations for the example with the CP-star and two-hub network rely on a particular structure of an attack strategy: the Adversary first captures $a$ unprotected nodes and then launches concerted attacks on respective protected hub nodes. This construction underlies the notion of a *mimic* attack strategy.

Let $a = xd$, where $x \in \mathbb{N}$ and is an integer, and consider a defended network $(g, \underline{d})$. Label nodes in $\mathcal{P}$ by $i_1, i_2, \ldots, i_k$. For each node in $\mathcal{P}$, the Adversary allocates 1 resource unit to exactly $x$ times $d_i$ nodes in $\mathcal{U}_i$ (the unprotected neighbourhood of $i$) thereafter relocating each of these resource units to node $i$. This attack strategy is referred to as a "mimic strategy," as it amounts to attacking every protected node with attack resources that mimic the overall ration $a/d$.

We make the notion of a mimic strategy more formal as follows: Given the defended network $(g, \underline{d})$, say that $(\underline{a}, \mathcal{R})$ mimics defense if and only if there is a set of $a$ distinct nodes, $\{j_1, \ldots, j_a\}$, such that

1. $\{j_1, \ldots, j_{\frac{a}{d}d_{i_1}}\} \in \mathcal{U}_{i_1}$;
   $\{j_{\frac{a}{d}d_{i_1}+1}, \ldots, j_{\frac{a}{d}d_{i_1}+\frac{a}{d}d_{i_2}}\} \in \mathcal{U}_{i_2}; \cdots;$
   $\{j_{\frac{a}{d}d_{i_{k-1}}+1}, \ldots, j_{\frac{a}{d}d_{i_{k-1}}+\frac{a}{d}d_{i_k}}\} \in \mathcal{U}_{i_k}$.
2. $r_{j_s i_1} = 1, \forall s$ s.t. $s \le \frac{a}{d}d_1$;
   $r_{j_s i_2} = 1, \forall s$ s.t. $\frac{a}{d}d_1 + 1 \le s \le \frac{a}{d}d_1 + \frac{a}{d}d_2; \cdots;$
   $r_{j_s i_k} = 1, \forall s$ s.t. $\frac{a}{d}d_{k-1} + 1 \le s \le \frac{a}{d}d_{k-1} + \frac{a}{d}d_k$.

Part (1) refers to the initial allocation of attack resources and part (2) pertains to the moves from the initial success to subsequent protected nodes. Roughly speaking, successful attacks combine at the same protected node to maximize the prospects of a successful attack. Figures 7.14 and 7.16, with attack and defense resources both equal to 4, both offer instances of a mimic attack strategy.

Mimic strategies do not always exist. To see this, consider a defended core-periphery network with 12 nodes, $n = 12$, and attack and defense resources equal to 4, $a = d = 4$: the network has two hubs, with the first hub being linked to 9 peripheral nodes and the second hub being linked to 1 peripheral node. If the Designer allocates 2 units to each hub, then no attack strategy can mimic a defense on this defended network.

**Remark** *Given defended network $(g, \underline{d})$, a mimic attack strategy exists if and only if the following condition holds:*

$$\left| \bigcup_{s=1}^{k'} \mathcal{U}_{i_s} \right| \ge \frac{a}{d} \sum_{s=1}^{k'} d_{i_s} \quad \forall \{i_1, i_2, \ldots, i_{k'}\} \subset \mathcal{P}. \tag{7.28}$$

We are now ready to state the following result.

**Proposition 7.5** *Consider the game with contagious attacks. Assume that network value is given by assumption 7.1, $a/d \in N$, $n > a + 1$, and consider the class of connected networks. Then the optimal network is either a CP-star or a network that precludes a mimic strategy.*

*Sketch of Proof*: Consider a defended network $(g, \underline{d})$ other than a CP-star, which admits a mimic strategy. We show that there is an attack strategy $(\underline{a}, \mathcal{R})$ that keeps the payoff of the Designer strictly below the payoff that is guaranteed from the CP-star. Suppose the defended network $(g, \underline{d})$ contains $\mathcal{P} = \{i_1, \ldots, i_k\}$ protected nodes. Clearly, if $k = 1$, then there must be two nodes in $\mathcal{U}$ with a link between them. Allocating 1 resource unit to each of these unprotected nodes guarantees the elimination of $a+1$ nodes. As there is only 1 defended node and the networks are connected, under our attack dynamics, the probability of a successful attack on the defended node is equal in the two defended networks (the given network and the CP-star). This means that the expected payoff to Designer is

$$\Pi^e(g,\underline{d},\underline{a},\mathcal{R}) \leq \frac{d^\gamma}{d^\gamma+a^\gamma} f(n-a-1) < \frac{d^\gamma}{d^\gamma+a^\gamma} f(n-a) = \overline{\Pi}(g^s,\underline{d}^s). \tag{7.29}$$

Next, consider the case of $k \geq 2$ defended nodes. Construct the sequence of sets $(N_{i_s})_{1\leq s\leq k}$ recursively as follows:

$$N_{i_1} = \mathcal{U}_{i_1}\,;\; N_{i_2} = \mathcal{U}_{i_2} - N_{i_1}\,;\; \cdots\,;\; N_{i_k} = \mathcal{U}_{i_k} - \bigcup_{s=1}^{k-1} N_{i_s}. \tag{7.30}$$

Let $n_{i_s} = |N_{i_s}|$, $s = 1, \ldots, k$. Note that by the connectedness of $g$, $\bigcup_{s=1}^{k} N_{i_s} = \mathcal{U}$.

Suppose first that $n_{i_s} \geq \frac{a}{d} d_{i_s}$, $\forall s$, and attack mimics defense in such a way that 1 resource unit is allocated to exactly $\frac{a}{d} d_{i_s}$ nodes in $N_{i_s}$, with each of these resource units thereafter relocating to node $i_s$.

Observe that since $N_{i_s} \subset \mathcal{U}_{i_s}$, a necessary condition for nodes in $N_{i_s}$ to survive the attack is that $i_s$ itself survives the attack. Also, a protected node $i_s$ may be attacked through the attack resources allotted to nodes within $\mathcal{U}_{i_s}$ or by resources originally allocated to an attack using resources that come via a successful attack on some other protected node $i'_s$. It therefore follows that the distribution of the total number of surviving nodes is first-order stochastically dominated by the distribution of

$$(n_{i_1}+1-a_{i_1})I_1 + \cdots + (n_{i_k}+1-a_{i_k})I_k, \tag{7.31}$$

where $\{I_1, \ldots, I_k\}$ denotes a set of independent Bernoulli random variables with $\text{Prob}(I_s = 1) = \frac{d^\gamma}{d^\gamma+a^\gamma}$, $\forall s \in \{1, \ldots, k\}$. This dominance relation holds because in the latter expression, we are ignoring indirect attacks launched from protected nodes that have been successfully attacked on other protected nodes. By way of illustration, note that in the previous example with two-hubs (see figure 7.16), the probability distribution of surviving nodes after a direct attack, $P'$ (directly eliminated nodes plus those unprotected nodes that are neighbors of the attacked nodes), is as follows: there is a probability of 1/4 that all nodes are captured, a probability of 1/2 that 4 nodes survive, and a probability of 1/4 that 8 nodes survive. This distribution first-order stochastically dominates the distribution of actual surviving nodes in the two-hub network, which is given by $P$.

Since the network value function $f$ is increasing, we have

$$\Pi^e \leq \mathbb{E}\left[f\left(\sum_{s=1}^{k}(n_{i_s}+1-a_{i_s})I_t\right)\right]. \tag{7.32}$$

The final step is to note that

$$\mathbb{E}\left[f\left(\sum_{s=1}^{k}(n_{i_s}+1-a_{i_s})I_s\right)\right]<\mathbb{E}\left[f\left(\left(\sum_{s=1}^{k}n_{i_s}+1-a_{i_s}\right)I_1\right)\right]=\mathbb{E}\left[f\left((n-a)I_1\right)\right]. \tag{7.33}$$

Let us discuss the derivation of this equation. First, note that the probability distribution of eventually surviving nodes under the CP-star is a mean-preserving spread of the distribution of surviving nodes under $(n_{i_1}+1-a_{i_1})I_1+\cdots+(n_{i_k}+1-a_{i_k})I_k$. By way of illustration, note that in the CP-star example, the probability distribution of surviving nodes is as follows: there is a probability of $1/2$ that all nodes are captured and a probability of $1/2$ that 8 nodes survive. This distribution is a mean preserving spread of the distribution of surviving nodes $P'$. This observation, combined with the assumption that the network value function $f(.)$ is increasing and convex, yields strict inequality. ■

Proposition 7.5 suggests that defended networks violating equation (7.28) may be attractive for the Designer since they preclude the use of mimic strategies by the Adversary. Observe, for instance, that in a setting where $n=3$, $f(n)=n^2$, and $a=d=2$, a CP-star yields an expected payoff of $1/2$ for the Designer. On the other hand, the complete network with two protected nodes, which violates equation (7.28), yields at least 1. This shows that in some circumstances, defended networks that violate equation (7.28) may dominate a CP-star. It is possible to show that the attractiveness of networks that do not admit a mimic strategy depends on the number of nodes, $n$. Indeed, as $n$ grows, we can generalize the arguments presented in proposition 7.5 to show that CP-protected networks are approximately optimal across all possible defended networks. This point is further developed in a question at the end of the chapter.

Observe that we are assuming that the resources of the Adversary are larger than the resources of the Defender, $a \geq d$. When $a<d$, the Designer may find it attractive to create a spread-out network and to allocate their resources across more nodes. This is perhaps most easily seen in an example. Suppose that $a=1$, $f(n)=n^2$. The coefficient of conflict $\gamma$ is very small, so the probability of successful attack is close to $1/2$ regardless of the resources allocated to a node. Suppose next that the Adversary has only one unit ($a=1$), while the Designer has two ($d=2$). In a CP-star, the best the Adversary can do is to use the mimic strategy and target a periphery node, which means that the expected payoff of the Designer is roughly $f(n-1)/2$. In a two-hub network with both hubs protected, the best the Adversary can do is to target a periphery node. The probability of eliminating a single hub is 1/2, and the probability of eliminating both hubs is 1/4, so the expected payoff to the Designer is roughly $f(n-1)/2+f(n-2)/4$. It is clear that the two-hub network dominates the CP-star.

### 7.4.3 Optimal Number of Components

So far, we have restricted our attention to connected networks. Recall that the pressure toward connectivity comes from the convexity of the network. This convexity is also central to an understanding of the desirable number of components. To see this, it is helpful to start

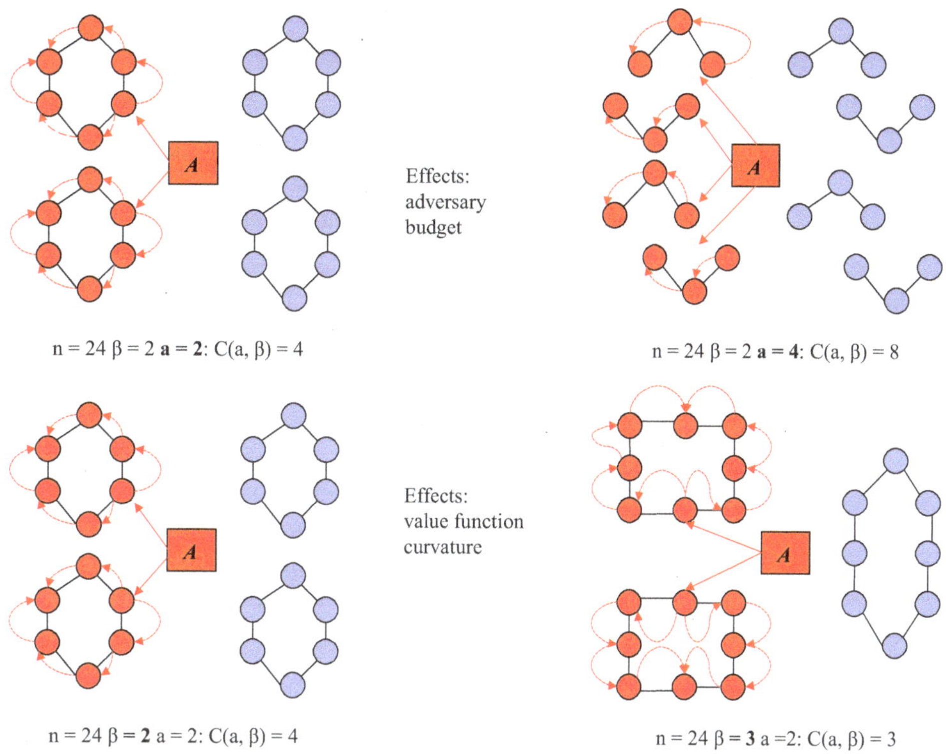


**Figure 7.17**
Optimal number of components: $f(m) = (m)^{\beta}$, $n = 24$.

with the case where $d = 0$ and to consider network value functions $f(n) = n^{\beta}$, with $\beta > 1$. We interpret $\beta$ as a measure of the convexity of the network value function. As unequal components will lead the Adversary to target the larger ones, it is better for the Designer to choose equal-sized components. A question at the end of the chapter works through this intuition. The exact number of components depends on $\beta$ and the magnitude of the Adversary's resources. So you may get a sense of these effects, figure 7.17 illustrates the optimal number of components as we vary the attack resources and the degree of convexity. Consider the effects of attack resources. Given $\beta = 2$, the optimal number of components increases from 4 to 8 as we increase the attack resources from 2 to 4. Next, consider the effects of convexity. Given attack resources $a = 4$, the optimal number of components falls from 4 to 3 as we raise the curvature by moving from $\beta = 2$ to $\beta = 3$.

Now let us summarize what we have learned about optimal defense and design of networks in the context of attacks that can spread through connections in the network. We have shown that so long as attack resources exceed defense resources, a highly centralized network with the protected center is optimal. This observation is consistent with the practice of traffic monitoring at key nodes by security personnel (Anderson [2020]). The optimality of a single protected node rests on the relative value of attack and defense resources and the convexity of the network value function. If the network value function is not always convex or the Defender has more resources than the Adversary, then multiple hub-nodes or components can be optimal. These theoretical insights draw our attention to the economic considerations that determine whether robust networks will be connected or disconnected and whether they will have highly concentrated protection or if they will exhibit dispersed protection.

## 7.5 Reading Notes

The problem of network defense has traditionally been studied in operations research, electrical engineering and computer science; for introduction and overviews of this research, see, for example, Alpcan and Başar (2011); Aspnes, Chang, and Yampolskiy (2006); Smith (2008); and Grötschel, Monma, and Stoer (1995).

The network interdiction problem involves an Adversary intervening to damage links or nodes in order to compromise the flow in a network. Early studies by Wollmer (1964) and Cunningham (1985) study the problem of network design and defense in which the conflict is on links. For instance, a link is eliminated if the Adversary assigns more resources than the Designer (thus conflict is modeled as an all-pay auction). The models presented in this chapter build on this formulation through a consideration of contests on nodes (the all-pay auction is a special case and corresponds to the situation when the coefficient of the contest function becomes very large). Network interdiction remains a very active field of study. Gueye, Walrand, and Anantharam (2010) and Laszka, Szeszlér, and Buttyán (2012) look at a model in which the network operator chooses a spanning tree of a given network to route messages, and the Attacker simultaneously chooses an edge to be removed. Aspnes, Chang, and Yampolskiy (2006) (and the literature that comes afterward) study protection choices by nodes faced with a viral infection; upon infecting a node, the virus travels through the network. This is related to the study of contagious threats presented in section 7.4. Network interdiction also remains a field of active research in economics; for recent work, see Bloch, Chatterjee, and Dutta (2021).

The subject of network robustness has also received attention in the statistical physics and network science literature. In an influential article, Albert, Jeong, and Barabási (2000) argue that highly unequal networks with hubs are vulnerable to strategic attacks since potential adversaries can significantly reduce their functionality by removing only a few hub nodes. By contrast, the theoretical models presented in this chapter bring out the attractiveness of these networks from the perspective of threats and security. How can we reconcile these perspectives? The contrasting results offer complementary perspectives and highlight the importance of defense resources and the convexity of the network value function.

In these papers, connectivity of the network is the goal. The network value function introduced in section 7.2 assumes that the value of a network is the sum of the value of its components, and the value of a component is increasing and convex in size. This formulation generalizes the idea of connectivity. The component additive and convex and increasing function builds on ideas in the research on communication networks such as Metcalfe's and Reed's laws.

Sections 7.3.1 and 7.3.2 study the two-player problem of optimal design and defense. For news coverage of the effects of natural disasters and human attacks on infrastructure networks, see Eun (2010), Kliesen (1995), India Today (2011) and Luft (2005). Early theoretical work in this field includes Bier, Oliveros, and Samuelson (2006); Clark and Konrad (2007); and Kovenock and Roberson (2012). This two-stage model with observability of first-stage actions is consistent with the approach in the large body of engineering literature on security and networks, such as Tambe (2011) and Alpcan and Başar (2011). The theoretical models in this chapter are taken from Dziubiński and Goyal (2013, 2017). The discussion on cybersecurity draws on Goyal and Vigier (2014) and Perlroth (2021). Also, see Schneider (2022) and Gordon and Rosenbach (2022) for discussions of cybersecurity as it relates to international relations.

The results on protected central nodes are related to the well-known and widely studied "key player" problem: what nodes should be targeted to attain a goal? For an introduction to key player problems, see Borgatti (2003, 2005). For an early contribution to the study of key problems in economics, see Ballester, Calvó-Armengol, and Zenou (2006). Chapters 4, 14, and 16 in the book take up the general problem of targeting. The discussion in this chapter suggests that for the problem of attack and defense, the key players are nodes that lie in separators and transversals. These nodes are typically distinct from nodes that maximize familiar notions of centrality. For a detailed discussion of differences, see Dziubiński and Goyal (2017).

There is also a strand of work that studies decentralized defense and linking by individual nodes. In section 7.3.1.2, we study an example of decentralized defense, which provides a first impression of the challenges of decentralization in security problems. We have not discussed decentralized choice of links (with or without contagion) due to space considerations. The interested reader is referred to Acemoglu, Malekian, and Ozdaglar (2016); Goyal et al. (2016); and Cerdeiro, Dziubiński, and Goyal (2017).

## 7.6 Questions

1. Consider the Network Defense Game studied in section 7.3.1. Suppose that the network value function is $f(n) = n^2$. The Designer chooses which nodes to protect, and observing these choices, the Adversary decides on which nodes to attack. The cost of defending a node is $c_D$, while the cost of attacking a node is $c_A$. A defended node cannot be damaged by an attack, while an undefended node, if attacked, is eliminated along

with its links. Write the payoffs of the Defender and the Adversary. Suppose that the Designer seeks to maximize the value of the residual network net the cost of defense, while the Adversary seeks to minimize the value of the residual network less the cost of attack. Verify the threshold values for the costs of defense and attack of the star network with four nodes (as in figure 7.3).

2. (Dziubiński and Goyal [2013]). Consider the problem of defense and design with imperfect defense. Suppose that there is a probability $\pi \in [0, 1]$ that a defended node can be eliminated by attack. Fix $n = 6$ and $k = 2$. Show that the equilibrium networks in this case depend on value of $p$ and are either the empty network, a center-protected star, a complete bipartite network with one part of size 2 fully protected, a fully protected 2-connected network with minimal number of links (a cycle), or a 3-connected network with minimal number of links and no defense.

3. Consider the Network Defense Game. Suppose that $n$ is large and the cost of attack satisfies

$$f(n-2) - f(n-3) < c_A < f(n-1) - f(n-2).$$

   (a) Show that with this cost of attack, the Adversary removes 2 nodes from the complete network over $n$ nodes, 1 node from the complete network containing $n-1$ nodes, and 0 nodes from the complete network containing $n-2$ or fewer nodes.

   (b) Suppose that the cost of defense satisfies

$$(f(n) - f(n-2) - f(1))/n < c_D < (f(n) - f(n-2))/n.$$

   With this cost of defense, show that the Defender protects all the nodes in a complete network with $n$ nodes because $f(n) - nc_D > f(n-2)$ (and we know that in a complete network, the Defender either protects all or no nodes in equilibrium).

   (c) Now consider a network with $n-1$ nodes in a clique with one node linked to a single element of the core (let's call it $i$). Show that if such a network is not protected, the Adversary will remove node $i$ only, disconnecting the network into a clique of size $n-2$ and a single isolated node. Then show that with this cost of defense, the Defender is inactive.

   (d) Complete the argument by showing that the payoff to the Defender is larger in the core-periphery network than in the complete network.

4. Consider the Design and Defense game presented in section 7.3.2. Suppose that units of attack $1 \le k \le n-2$, and suppose that the network value is component additive and the value of a component is increasing and convex in size. The Designer moves first and chooses the network and the defense of nodes. The Adversary observes the choice of Designer and then chooses to attack $k$ nodes. The payoff to the Designer from choosing $(g, \mathcal{D})$ when the Adversary chooses a cut $X$ is

$$\Pi^D(\mathcal{D}, X; g) = \Phi(g - (X \setminus \mathcal{D})) - c_L|g| - c_D|\mathcal{D}|, \tag{7.34}$$

where $c_L$ is the cost of links and $c_D$ is the cost of perfectly protecting a node. The payoff to the Adversary is

$$\Pi^A(\mathcal{D}, X; g) = -\Phi(g - (X \setminus \mathcal{D})). \tag{7.35}$$

The objective of the Designer is to maximize the payoff, while the goal of the Adversary is to minimize the value of the residual network. Show that in a subgame perfect equilibrium of this game,

- The Designer chooses defense $|\mathcal{D}| = 0$, 1, or $n$. If $|\mathcal{D}| = 0$, a variety of networks—including the empty network and a $(k+1)$–connected network—can arise. If $|\mathcal{D}| = 1$, the network is a star with a protected center. If $|\mathcal{D}| = n$, the network is either empty or minimally connected (i.e., a tree).
- The Adversary chooses a separating cut if $(g, \mathcal{D})$ permits such a cut. When $(g, \mathcal{D})$ permits no separating cuts, every cut yields the same payoff to the Adversary and is optimal.

5. This is a question on the design and defense of networks with contagious attacks as discussed in section 7.4. Define $C(a, \beta) = \frac{\beta a}{\beta - 1}$. Observe that $C(a, \beta)$ is increasing in the quantity of attack resources, $a$, and falling in the parameter of convexity, $\beta$. Assume that (*A.1*) holds, $d = 0$, and suppose that $f(n) = n^\beta$, where $\beta > 1$. Show that if $C(a, \beta) \in \{a+1, \ldots, n\}$ and divides by $n$, then the unique equilibrium network consists of $C(a, \beta)$ equal-sized components.

6. Consider the network design and defense game with contagion attacks as discussed in section 7.4. Suppose that $n = 12$, $a = d = 2$, and the network value function is as follows:

$$f(n) = \begin{cases} n^2 & \text{for } 0 < n \leq 6 \\ 36 + 0.2(n-6) & \text{for } 6 < n \leq 12. \end{cases} \tag{7.36}$$

Show that a network with two protected hubs yields a lower expected payoff to the Designer than a center-protected star.

7. (Goyal and Vigier [2014]). Consider the model of the design and defense of networks that face contagious attacks. Suppose payoffs satisfy assumption 7.1, $a < d$, $d \geq 2$, $n > a + d$. Show that
   (a) If $\gamma$ is large, a CP-star is optimal.
   (b) If $\gamma$ is small, the optimal defended network is either a CP-star or has $d$ nodes in the core. In particular, if $a = 1$ then a core with $d > 1$ nodes strictly dominates the CP-star.

8. (Goyal and Vigier [2014]). Consider the model of the design and defense of networks that face contagious attacks. Suppose payoffs satisfy assumption 7.1, $a/d$ is an integer, $n > a + 1$. Show that the center-protected star is (close to) optimal in the class of connected networks.

9. Define $\ell = \lim_{n\to\infty} f(n-1)/f(n)$. As $f$ is an increasing function, $\ell$ is either equal to 1 or less than 1. Suppose that network payoffs satisfy assumption 7.1. Let $a/d \in \mathbb{N}$, $n > a+1$, and let $\epsilon > 0$.
   (a) If $\ell < 1$ then CP-star is $\epsilon$-optimal for large $n$ among all defended networks.
   (b) If $\ell = 1$ then optimal defended network may contain multiple components.
10. Albert, Jeong, and Barabási (2000) consider the resilience of connectivity of a network to the removal of nodes. They show that networks with power law degree distributions are robust against random deletion of a fraction of nodes, but are vulnerable to the targeted elimination of a small fraction of most connected nodes. How can we reconcile this result with the result presented in this chapter on the optimality of center-protected star networks?

# 8 Intermediaries and Platforms

## 8.1 Introduction

In many markets, the benefit that consumers get is a function of their ability to communicate with other users on the network. In these markets, network effects are *direct*: the more agents on a network, the larger the communication opportunities. Examples of products with direct effects include telephone, fax, email, and online networks such as Facebook and Twitter. In many other markets, it is helpful to think of products as consisting of components and the value of a product as increasing the number of suppliers of products that are used in combination with the product. In such a market, the network effect is said to be *indirect*. Examples of markets with indirect network effects include computer operating systems (Microsoft Windows or the Apple Macintosh), smart phones, credit card systems (such as Visa and Mastercard), trading intermediaries (such as Amazon and eBay), and video-game consoles (PlayStation and Nintendo). This chapter studies the functioning of markets with network effects.

We will start with a consideration of direct network effects. As the utility of a product increases in the number of its users, as a product gains market share, it becomes more and more attractive relative to other competitors. This creates a tendency for such markets to be dominated by a single product. Consumer preference for different products may offset this pressure and we explore the circumstances under which markets are covered by multiple and individual firms, respectively. We then take up the issue of technological change in such markets. If a product or a technology is dominant, switching to a new product may entail a switch to a product with a very small user base. This may discourage technological change. We examine the circumstances under which technological change is excessive or too slow, and we also study the price and nonprice strategies of firms in such markets.

We then turn to markets with indirect effects. Consider a computer operating system: software developers want to create products for Windows (or for iPhone or Android) because of the potential consumer base. Consumers in turn are attracted to an operating system if it offers a wider range of applications. Similarly, people want to use Visa cards because they are widely accepted, and merchants want to accept them because most people carry them.

Traders want to trade in markets where they can easily find counterparties and the markets are liquid. Another example is online social networks (Facebook, LinkedIn, and Twitter) that bring together individual users and software developers and firms that wish to advertise their products. A third example is a market creator that brings together buyers and sellers, such as New York Stock Exchange/Nasdaq exchanges for public equities, eBay and Amazon's e-commerce platforms, Apple's App Store for developers and consumers, and Google's ad platform for websites and advertisers. These examples suggest that markets with two-sided or multisided network effects are quite common.

This chapter will focus on two aspects of a firm's strategy in such markets—pricing and openness. Pricing presents some novel features: for instance, the value to a user on one side of the market will depend on the number of users of the other side of the market. It is not uncommon that consumers are paid to carry a credit card, while merchants pay the credit card for each transaction. This motivates a study of the economic considerations that determine optimal prices on different sides of a market.

We next take up the notion of openness: a firm decides on how many sides of a market it wants to be active. For instance, Apple markets both its hardware and its operating system, while Microsoft is focused on producing its operating system and allows independent producers to supply the hardware (this contrast has slightly changed with the launch of the Surface range of products). In this sense, Microsoft may be seen to be more open than Apple. We discuss the considerations that are involved in the choice of the number of sides that a firm is active. Another aspect of openness relates to competing platforms: should a firm seek to be compatible or incompatible with other firms (or, alternatively, partially compatible)?

An important and recurring theme throughout this chapter is the dynamics of competition among intermediaries. The text closes with an experimental examination of this competition. We present models in which traders need connections to trade. Connections are costly, which leads traders to economize on links. This in turn gives rise to intermediaries. The interest is in understanding the dynamics of competition among potential intermediaries and the circumstances under which we see a dominant intermediary.

## 8.2 Network Externalities

A key feature of many economic contexts is that the value of choosing a platform is increasing in the number of others who are already part of the network. A first observation is that network effects naturally give rise to multiple equilibria. To see this in the simplest setting, consider the following example.

Suppose that there are $n$ individuals, each of whom has a choice between two computer software programs A and B. We shall suppose that individuals have the same preferences over the different computer programs. Let individual returns from a choice $x \in \{A, B\}$, when $k$ persons are adopting the same program, be given by

$$u_x(k), \quad x \in \{A, B\}, \quad k \in \{1, \ldots, n\}. \tag{8.1}$$

The idea of positive network effects is reflected in the following assumption:

$$u_x(k+1) > u(x,k), \forall x,\ k \in \{1, \ldots, n-1\}. \tag{8.2}$$

To simplify the exposition, let us also suppose that network effects are significant. Thus for every individual $i$,

$$u_A(n) > u_B(1); u_B(n) > u_A(1). \tag{8.3}$$

When individual utility satisfies this assumption, it is easy to see that there are two natural Nash equilibria: everyone chooses A or everyone chooses B.

As there are multiple equilibria, the outcome is sensitive to the expectations that persons have about each other. So a program may be chosen because everyone expects it to be: this may be, for instance, because it happened to be popular in the recent past. Thus recent trends may be reinforced. Moreover, this suggests that once a software is widely used, it may be difficult for users to change, even when a new superior program becomes available. This raises the possibility of inefficient lock-ins. We take up these issues in the next section. In the discussion so far, we have assumed that all individuals have the same preferences over the programs. Differences in preferences are important, and we will come back to this point later in the chapter.

### 8.2.1 Installed Base, Dynamic Choice, and Lock-Ins

One of the implications of this analysis is that if everyone has coordinated around action A, then this action will remain optimal and the outcome will persist even if, due to technological change, a new product $B$ becomes available that is superior (i.e., $u_B(k) > u_A(k)$), for all $k$). This suggests that in settings with network effects, there can be a lock-in into old, established ways of doing things. We explore the scope of this argument with the help of a simple model. We consider a model that is a simplified version of one given by Farrell and Saloner (1986).

At the start, there is a group of consumers $n_0$, who have adopted product $A$, also referred to as the "old technology." In period 1, a group of consumers $n_1$, can choose to either buy product $A$ or refrain from buying. In between periods 1 and 2, product $B$, also referred to as the "new technology" becomes available in the market. In period 2, consumers $n_2$ choose between buying $A$ or $B$ or abstaining from buying altogether. We now specify the payoffs from the different actions. The payoff from the old technology (per period, for periods 1 and 2) is given by

$$\begin{aligned} &u_A(k), && \text{where } k \text{ is the network size.} \\ &u_A(0) \geq 0, && u_A(k+1) > u_A(k), k \in \{1, \ldots, n-1\}. \end{aligned} \tag{8.4}$$

An example satisfying this requirement is $u_A(k) = a + bk,\ \ a, b > 0$.

The payoff from the new technology per period is

$$\begin{aligned} &u_B(k), && \text{where } k \text{ is the network size.} \\ &u_B(0) \geq 0, && u_B(k+1) > u_B(k), k \in \{1, \ldots, n-1\}. \end{aligned} \tag{8.5}$$

The first point to note is that period 1 consumers only know about the old technology. Hence they choose action $A$ since it is better than the outside option. In period 2, technologies $A$ and $B$ are both available, and consumers choose action $B$ if

$$u_B(n_2) > u_A(n_0 + n_1 + n_2). \tag{8.6}$$

Thus consumers in period 2 may choose action $A$ even if $u_B(k) > u_A(k)$ for all $k$. For concreteness, suppose that the old technology has the payoff $a + bk$, while the new technology has the payoff $c + dk$. This inequality tells us that it is possible for consumers to persist with the old technology even if $c > a$ and $d > b$ (so long as $a + b(n_0 + n_1 + n_2) > c + dn_2$).

This is the simplest expression of the traditional argument of how lock-in into old, established ways of doing things may arise. While the possibility of such lock-in seems quite robust, it is not clear whether such an outcome is good or bad or needs to be remedied. This leads us to examine the conditions under which technological change is optimal.

Aggregate social welfare under each choice is as follows:

$$\begin{aligned} W(old) = {} & n_0[u_A(n_0 + n_1) + u_A(n_0 + n_1 + n_2)] \\ & + n_1[u_A(n_0 + n_1) + u_A(n_0 + n_1 + n_2)] \\ & + n_2[u_A(n_0 + n_1 + n_2)] \end{aligned} \tag{8.7}$$

$$\begin{aligned} W(new) = {} & n_0[u_A(n_0 + n_1) + u_A(n_0 + n_1)] \\ & + n_1[u_A(n_0 + n_1) + u_A(n_0 + n_1)] \\ & + n_2[u_B(n_2)]. \end{aligned} \tag{8.8}$$

We will say that technological change is optimal if it maximizes the total consumer surplus across the generations. Therefore, comparing the two expressions, adopting a new technology is optimal if and only if

$$\begin{aligned} W(new) > W(old) \iff & n_2[u_B(n_2) - u_A(n_0 + n_1 + n_2)] \\ & > (n_0 + n_1)[u_A(n_0 + n_1 + n_2) - u_A(n_0 + n_1)]. \end{aligned} \tag{8.9}$$

These computations allow us to move on to the question of whether there is too little or too much technological change in markets with network effects. A comparison of equations (8.6 and 8.9) yields the following observation: *private incentives for switching to a new technology are greater than what is socially desirable.* The reason for too much technological change is that active period 2 consumers only compare their own payoffs from making a decision on technology. However, choosing the new technology generates a *negative externality* on the payoffs of earlier-generation consumers in terms of the lack of growth of the network of the old technology, which is ignored by period 2 consumers. They therefore overestimate the benefits of the new technology and have excessive incentives to adopt the new technology from a social point of view.

The possibility of too much technological change naturally raises the issue: are there circumstances under which there could be too *little* change? We need to extend the simple model described here to address this question.

Consider a situation where both period 1 and period 2 consumers can choose between new and old technology and payoffs are such that period 2 consumers find it optimal to buy any good that period 1 consumers bought. First, note that consumers in period 1 choose the old technology if

$$\begin{aligned} & u_A(n_0+n_1)+u_A(n_0+n_1+n_2)>u_B(n_1)+u_B(n_1+n_2) \\ & \Longleftrightarrow u_A(n_0+n_1)-u_B(n_1)>u_B(n_1+n_2)-u_A(n_0+n_1+n_2). \end{aligned} \tag{8.10}$$

On the other hand, social welfare under the new and old technology is, respectively,

$$\begin{aligned} W(old)= & n_0[u_A(n_0+n_1)+u_A(n_0+n_1+n_2)] \\ & +n_1[u_A(n_0+n_1)+u_A(n_0+n_1+n_2)] \\ & +n_2[u_A(n_0+n_1+n_2)] \end{aligned} \tag{8.11}$$

$$\begin{aligned} W(new)= & n_0[u_A(n_0)+u_A(n_0)] \\ & +n_1[u_B(n_1)+u_B(n_1+n_2)] \\ & +n_2[u_B(n_1+n_2)]. \end{aligned} \tag{8.12}$$

If $u(n_0)\approx u(n_0+n_1)\approx u(n_0+n_1+n_2)$, then

$$\begin{aligned} W(new)>W(old) \Longleftrightarrow & (n_1+n_2)[u_B(n_1+n_2)-u_A(n_0+n_1+n_2)] \\ & >n_1[u_A(n_0+n_1)-u_B(n_1)]. \end{aligned} \tag{8.13}$$

A comparison of equations (8.10 and 8.13) reveals that *consumers may persist with the old technology, even if the new technology is socially desirable, because they do not take into account the effects of their actions on future consumers.*

Thus individual incentives may generate too little or too much technological change relative to what is socially desirable. Our discussion helps identify the nature of externalities that generate these outcomes. Too much technological change or *excessive momentum* comes about when current consumers ignore the interests of the installed base (i.e., the users of the existing technology). This may be termed *backward externality.* By contrast, too little change, or *excessive inertia*, arises because current consumers ignore the interests of future consumers who could benefit from a growing network of new-technology users. This may be termed *forward externality*. Both forward and negative externality are present in markets with network effects, and such markets are therefore likely to generate technological change that can be too slow or too fast relative to what is socially desirable. Our analysis also raises the question: which type of externality is more likely to arise, and in which markets? An understanding of this issue requires at the very least a model in which both the supply and demand sides of the market are active.

So far, we have only looked at the demand side of the market. In the next section, we take a first look at the supply side as we consider some strategies that firms can use in such markets.

### 8.2.2 The Strategies of Firms

Firms use a variety of strategies to promote their products and introduce new technologies; some of these strategies, such as introductory pricing and product preannouncements, are common in markets with no network effects as well, but they take on particular significance when network effects are important.

*Preannouncements:* Recall that in the basic model, only period 2 consumers can choose between old and new technology. Moreover, period 1 consumers had no choice but to decide buy in period 1. To see the role of product preannouncements, it is useful to modify the model slightly. Suppose, first, that the firm introducing the new technology in period 2 can preannounce the launch. Second, suppose that consumers in period 1 can postpone their decision and buy in period 2. We examine the incentives of the firm to preannounce and the implication of such an action.

Suppose there is a preannouncement. Consumers in period 1 can either buy the old technology or wait until period 2 and buy the new technology or buy nothing. In making their decision, they compare

$$u_A(n_0+n_1)+u_A(n_0+n_1+x)x \in \{0, n_2\} \tag{8.14}$$

with

$$u_B(n_1+n_2), \tag{8.15}$$

where we have assumed that period 2 consumers always buy good $B$. Period 1 consumers choose the new technology if

$$u_B(n_1+n_2) > u_A(n_0+n_1)+u_A(n_0+n_1+x). \tag{8.16}$$

It is worth noting that if

$$u_B(n_1+n_2) > u_A(n_0+n_1+n_2), \tag{8.17}$$

but

$$u_B(n_2) < u_A(n_0+n_1+n_2), \tag{8.18}$$

then in the absence of preannouncements, the new technology would not be adopted, while with a preannouncement, the new technology in principle can be adopted. Thus *preannouncements play a crucial role in shaping technological evolution in network markets.*

*Introductory Pricing:* In the previous discussions, we have highlighted the role of the installed base; the larger the size of $n_0$, the more difficult it is to get consumers to switch to a new technology. This suggests that firms have an incentive to build a network rapidly. This raises the question: can firms induce faster growth of the network through pricing? The essential idea is the following: the firm starts by selling cheap to attract consumers, and once the network is established, it charges high prices to subsequent consumers and recovers any initial losses it may suffer.

To see the role of this strategy, we return to the model where period 1 and period 2 consumers can choose between new and old technologies. We focus on the case (the set of parameters) in which period 1 consumers stick with the old technology. This is the case covered in the previous analysis. Recall that this happens if

$$u_A(n_0+n_1)+u_A(n_0+n_1+n_2) > u_B(n_1)+u_B(n_1+n_2). \tag{8.19}$$

It is worth noting that this inequality can hold even if

$$W(new) > W(old). \tag{8.20}$$

This happens due to the loss in payoff in the transition period:

$$u_B(n_1) \ll u_A(n_0+n_1). \tag{8.21}$$

Now we examine the role of an introductory price strategy in this setting. Can the firm set prices in such a way as to induce period 1 consumers to choose the new technology, and is this in the interest of this firm?

Suppose that in period 1, the firm sets the prices as follows:

$$p_1 = [u_B(n_1)+u_B(n_1+n_2)] - [u_A(n_0+n_1)+u_A(n_0+n_1+n_2)]. \tag{8.22}$$

This is the maximum price that the firm can set that will make consumers in period 1 still buy the new technology. It is worth noting that this price is negative. Such a strategy makes sense only if these losses in period 1 are somehow recouped (and then some) by larger profits earned in period 2.

We next examine the maximum prices that the firm can charge in period 2. Note that in period 2, consumers compare $u_A(n_0+n_2)$ and $u_B(n_1+n_2)$. Thus the firm can set a price such that these two payoffs are equal. In other words, the sets are as follows:

$$p_2 = u_B(n_1+n_2) - u_A(n_0+n_2). \tag{8.23}$$

Finally, we check if this strategy is attractive for the firm. Note that the previous strategy is the best of the class of strategies that induce consumers to switch to the new technology, while the strategy with no switching generates a payoff of 0. Thus the firm finds it attractive to use this introductory pricing strategy if the combined profits from the two periods is positive. The combined profits are given by

$$\begin{aligned} &n_1[u_B(n_1)+u_B(n_1+n_2) - \{u_A(n_0+n_1)+u_A(n_0+n_1+n_2)\}] \\ &+ n_2[u_B(n_1+n_2) - u_A(n_0+n_2)]. \end{aligned} \tag{8.24}$$

What are the circumstances under which this expression is positive? From the previous discussion, recall that adopting the new technology is socially optimal if and only if

$$W(new) > W(old) \Longleftrightarrow (n_1+n_2)[u_B(n_1+n_2) - u_A(n_0+n_1+n_2)]$$
$$> n_1[u_A(n_0+n_1) - u_B(n_1)]. \quad (8.25)$$

We have thus shown that *introductory pricing strategy is attractive for a firm if and only if it is socially optimal.*

So far, we have considered a setting in which consumers have same preferences with regard to the products on offer. An important feature of markets with network effects is that the products are not identical and consumers have different valuation of the products. The next section studies the effect of such differences for competition among platforms.

### 8.2.3 Competition among Networks

We consider a simple model with two platforms, A and B, located at points 0 and 1 of the unit interval. Let $F(x)$ be the fraction of consumers with $b < x$; in our setting, for simplicity, $F(x) = x$; that is, consumers are located uniformly on the unit interval. The consumer located at point $b$ has an intrinsic benefit b from platform B, and intrinsic benefit $1 - b$ from platform A.

There is an advantage to joining a larger network: the benefit of joining a network with $d$ consumers is $kd$. We assume that consumers can choose no more than one of the platforms. The prices of the two platforms are given by $(p_A, p_B)$.

Let us solve for the equilibrium prices and network sizes. To begin, suppose that the networks are of size $x_A$ and $x_B$, with $x_A + x_B = 1$. This assumes that the market is fully covered; full market coverage can be ensured by a suitably high stand-alone value of the platform.

Consider the optimal choice of a consumer: the net utility of choosing platform A is

$$1 - b + kx_A - p_A. \quad (8.26)$$

The net utility from platform B is

$$b + kx_B - p_B. \quad (8.27)$$

It is optimal to choose A if $1 - b + kx_A - p_A \geq b + kx_B - p_B$. In other words, a consumer will choose platform A if

$$b \leq \frac{1}{2}(1 + k(2x_A - 1) + p_B - p_A), \quad (8.28)$$

where we have set $x_B = 1 - x_A$.

In an interior equilibrium, the marginal consumer must be indifferent between the two products and the expected network size must correspond to the actual networks. Thus, in the uniform distribution case, in equilibrium it must be true that the marginal consumer, $x_A$, must be equal to the size of network $A$ and this must correspond to the expected network; that is,

$$x_A = \frac{1}{2}(1 + k(2x_A - 1) + p_B - p_A). \tag{8.29}$$

We shall say that network effects are weak (strong) if the marginal returns from an increase in network size are less (greater) than 1.

To develop a feel for how the magnitude of network effects matters, let us consider some examples. First, suppose that network effects are weak, so $k < 1/2$. We can solve for the network size as a function of prices to obtain:

$$x_A = \frac{1}{2} + \frac{1}{2(1-k)}(p_B - p_A). \tag{8.30}$$

The profit of platform A may be written as

$$\Pi_A(p_A, p_B) = \frac{p_A}{2}\left[1 + \frac{1}{1-k}(p_B - p_A)\right]. \tag{8.31}$$

The first-order conditions of the optimal price for platform A yields the following condition:

$$1 + \frac{1}{1-k}(p_B - 2p_A) = 0. \tag{8.32}$$

It is natural to focus on symmetric equilibrium, as the platforms are symmetric in this model. The equilibrium price is given by

$$p_A = p_B = 1 - k. \tag{8.33}$$

We see that prices are falling in the magnitude of network effects. In particular, for $k = 0$, with zero network effects, we get a price of 1, which corresponds to the equilibrium price for the baseline Hotelling model. Thus, with small network effects, both networks are active and of equal size. This is illustrated in figure 8.1.

Next, let us consider the case of strong network effects. Suppose that $k = 1$. For simplicity, suppose that prices are equal ($p_A = p_B$). The demand for platform A is then given by $y_A = F(-1/2 + 2x_A)$, as shown in figure 8.2. Notice that there are now three equilibria: one in which all consumers go to platform A, a second one in which all consumers go to platform B, and a third one that is interior. However, the interior equilibrium is unstable, as a slight change in network size leads through the strong network effect away from the interior equilibrium and toward one of the single-platform outcomes. Equilibrium ($x_A = 1, x_B = 0$) is supported by prices ($p_A = 1, p_B = 0$), while equilibrium ($x_A = 0, x_B = 1$) is supported by prices ($p_A = 0, p_B = 1$). Thus strong network effects push toward a single dominant platform.

These computations suggest that if network effects are modest relative to the diversity of consumer tastes, that can account for the coexistence of multiple platforms/standards. A prominent example is operating systems: Apple and Microsoft operating systems have

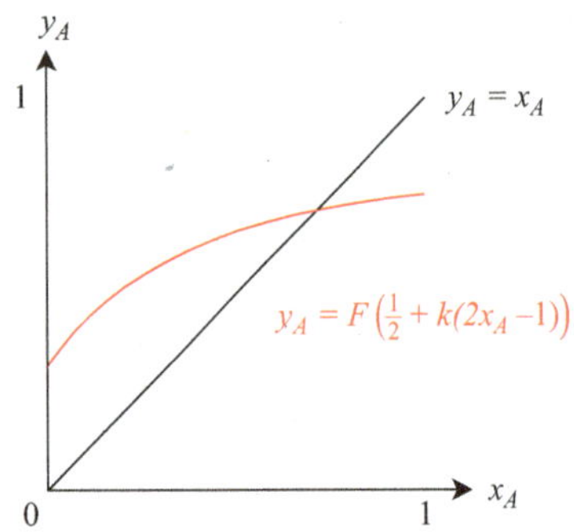


**Figure 8.1**
Weak network effects.

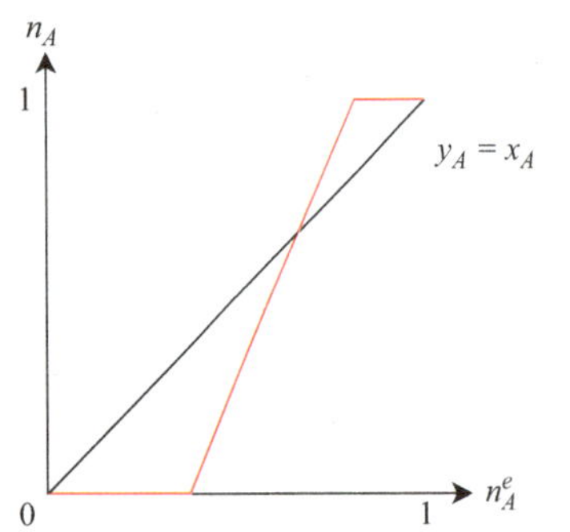


**Figure 8.2**
Strong network effects.

thrived by focusing on different segments of the market: business for Microsoft and graphics and education for Apple. Another example of a market with multiple platforms is gaming: PlayStation and Nintendo cater to different markets. PlayStation focuses on hardware, third-party games, and traditional gamers, while Nintendo is more focused on its own games and a wider population of casual gamers.

Ride hailing is another example, in which multiple online platforms compete with the traditional taxi model. Uber was the first mover in 2009; in the years following that launch, a number of competitors have emerged, particularly Lyft, Grab, Ola, and Didi Chuxing. The first operates solely in the US market (and a small part of Canada), Ola is strong in India, and the latter two operate in the lucrative Southeast Asian and Chinese markets, respectively. Uber and Lyft control 65 percent and 30 percent of the ride-hailing market in the US, respectively. Ola and Uber control 50 percent and 35 percent of the market in India, respectively, and Didi Chuxing controls 90 percent of the market in China.

By contrast, in the market for Internet search, Google is overwhelmingly dominant in many of the large economies, such as the US (88 percent), India (95 percent), the UK (85 percent), France (91 percent), Japan (74 percent), Brazil (96 percent), Nigeria (98 percent), and Germany (97 percent). Google shares the market equally with Yandex RU in Russia, and it is not allowed to operate at all in China. The choice of a search engine is driven mainly by a desire for accurate and relevant results. There is little difference in consumer preference in this dimension. A search engine delivers more useful results if it has access to more past searches. Therefore a larger market share in the past generates more data, which can give rise to tipping in favor of a dominant platform in the future.

Let us summarize what we have learned in this section. An important aspect of many economic activities is that the returns from choosing an action are increasing with the number of others who adopt the same action. A variety of product markets also share this characteristic.

We have argued that markets with strong network effects exhibit multiple equilibria, which are typically extremal, with one product/technology usually taking over the market. The nature of the eventual winner in the market depends on the expectations that consumers have regarding the behaviors of other consumers.

We have examined in some detail the effects of historical factors in shaping the evolution of such markets. Once an economy is in one equilibrium—choosing a certain network technology—it may be difficult to transit to a new superior technology due to the disadvantage that the new technology has a small network. This is known as the "installed base effect." Several authors have argued that the installed base effect typically inhibits technological change. Our analysis explored this contention and identified the different types of externalities inherent in such markets and how they drive technological change. Our analysis of the demand side of the market suggests that this is not necessarily true, and individual incentives for adopting new products can be greater as well as less than what is socially optimal. This motivated an examination of the role of the supply side of the market.

We examined two strategies that firms frequently use in such markets—product preannouncements and introductory pricing. We argued that these strategies facilitate a switch to new technology.

Finally, we examined a context in which consumers have different preferences for platforms. The pressure toward a dominant platform depends on the relative size of the network effect. When the network effect is modest, preferences for different platforms lead to coexistence of platforms. By contrast, when these networks are large, one platform takes over the entire market.

## 8.3 Compatibility

The term "compatibility" refers to the ability of a consumer to use one platform to reach a seller that uses another one. A well-known example of compatibility concerns banks and automated teller machine (ATM) networks. A depositor with one bank can use that bank's

ATM network, but can also use the networks of other banks depending on the agreements between them. The networks are more or less compatible depending on the charges that apply to outside ATM networks. The example of ATM networks offers an instance of compatibility arising from interconnection. But compatibility may have a more technological aspect: for instance, two products are compatible if they can operate together to generate value. A common example is Blu-ray discs and DVDs. A DVD can be played on a Blu-ray player, but a Blu-ray disc cannot be played on a standard DVD player. Thus compatibility may sometimes be one-sided. We study incentive of firms to make their products compatible using a model taken from Katz and Shapiro (1985).

There are $n$ firms that choose quantities, and there are consumers who choose whether to buy or not. Moreover, they care about the size of the network of firms they are dealing with. They are willing to pay more for large networks. Expectations play a major role, as in the earlier model of network externalities.

Let $y_i^e$ be the size of firm $i$'s network *as expected* by consumers. We will assume that consumers have the same expectations. Then a consumer $r$'s valuation is given by

$$\begin{gathered} r+v(y_i^e) \\ v(0)=0, v'(\cdot)>0 v''(\cdot)<0 \\ \lim_{y\to\infty} v'(y)=0. \end{gathered} \tag{8.34}$$

Now let's take a moment to consider the assumptions about $v$. As we are studying the role of network effects, it is natural to assume that the returns from a network are increasing in size. A decreasing rate of increase helps ensure that multiple firms are active in the market. Assume that $r$ is uniformly distributed on $[-\infty, A]$, where $A>0$.

In making a choice between two products (networks) $i$ and $j$, a consumer compares the net payoffs from them,

$$r+v(y_i^e)-p_i, \tag{8.35}$$

as against

$$r+v(y_j^e)-p_j. \tag{8.36}$$

All consumers are identical with regard to their preferences across the two products, so it follows that if one consumer favors $i$ over $j$, then so will all consumers. For two distinct networks $i$ and $j$ to be active, they must be equally attractive to everyone:

$$r+v(y_i^e)-p_i=r+v(y_j^e)-p_j \Longleftrightarrow p_i-v(y_i^e)=p_j-v(y_j^e). \tag{8.37}$$

Let us define $p_i-v(y_i^e)=\phi$ as the hedonic price of a product. The condition in equation (8.37) says that for two firms to be active, their hedonic prices should be the same. We can use this to compute the aggregate demand. All consumers with high enough $r$ will buy as follows:

$$r \geq p_i - v(y_i^e) = \phi$$

$$\text{Demand} = A - \phi = A - [p_i - v(y_i^e)]. \tag{8.38}$$

In equilibrium, the quantity sold by firm $i$ is equal to this number as well. Let $x_i$ be the sales of firm $i$, and let $z = \sum_i x_i$ be the aggregate sales:

$$z = A - [p_i - v(y_i^e)] \Longleftrightarrow p_i = A + v(y_i^e) - z \tag{8.39}$$

Thus higher $y_i^e$ leads to higher $p_i$, and lower $z$ leads to higher $p_i$. Observe that if there were no network effects, $v(y_i^e) = 0$ and $p_i = A - z$, as in the standard Cournot model.

To keep the computations simple, we assume that firms have zero production costs. We next turn to compatibility. Two products are said to be compatible if consumers buying one of the products can enjoy the benefits of the networks of either of them. This compatibility may require technical modifications or add-on features, so we assume that it is costly to make products compatible. In particular, firm $i$ incurs a cost of $F_i > 0$ when making its product compatible with that of firm $j$. Given these assumptions, the payoffs to firm $i$ are as follows:

- Pay-off under *full compatibility:* $\pi_i = x_i(A - z + v(z)) - F_i$
- Pay-off under *incompatibility:* $\pi_i = x_i(A - z + v(y_i^e))$

Notice that taking expectations and outputs of other firms as given, we can work out an equilibrium as in the standard Cournot model. Thus, given expectations $y$ about network sizes of various firms, there is a unique equilibrium, in the market. In this equilibrium, the quantities are given by

$$x_i^* = \frac{A + nv(y_i^e) - \sum_{j \neq i} v(y_j^e)}{n+1}. \tag{8.40}$$

Thus expectations of consumers concerning network size translate into cost advantages or disadvantages for the firms sponsoring the various networks. To see this, note that if $v(y_i^e) = 0, \forall i$ we get $x_i^* = \frac{A}{n+1}$, which is the standard Cournot equilibrium output. Moreover, for every set of expectations, there is a corresponding equilibrium. We will focus on the fulfilled expectations equilibrium next.

**Fulfilled expectations equilibrium** In such an equilibrium, the expected network size is equal to the actual network size. Thus, $y_i^e = x_i, \ \forall i$.

Standard computations allow us to say that the equilibrium profits are given by $x_i^2$, while the consumers, surplus is given by $z^2/2$. This suggests that firms extract the entire surplus generated by network effects. Let us briefly explain this outcome next. Note that $r = A - z$. Hence,

$$CS = \int_{A-z}^{A} (\rho + z - A)\, d\rho. \tag{8.41}$$

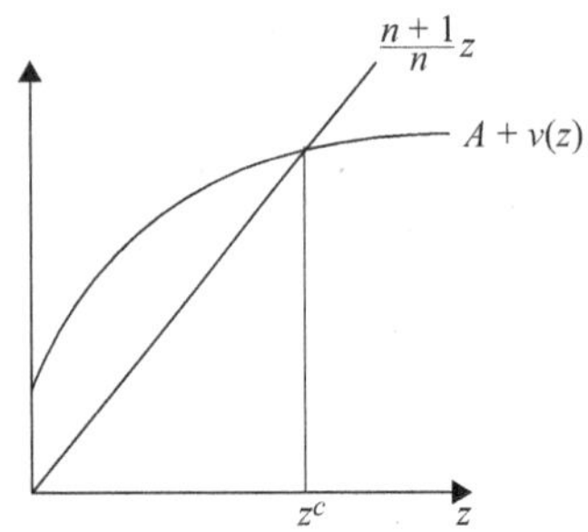


**Figure 8.3**
Equilibrium in the full compatibility case.

Consumer $r$ expects

$$r+v(y_i^e)-p_i=r+v(y_i^e)-A-v(y_i^e)+z=r-A+z. \tag{8.42}$$

We are now ready to study the equilibrium outcomes under different levels of compatibility in the market.

### 8.3.1 Compatibility and Equilibrium

*Full Compatibility Case:* This is a situation in which all firms are compatible with each other. Letting $z^e=\sum_{i=1}^{n} x_i$ and $y_i^e=z^e$, the equilibrium quantity of firm $i$ is given by

$$x_i^*=\frac{[A+v(z^e)]}{n+1}, \forall i=1,\ldots,n. \tag{8.43}$$

Following from figure 8.3, the aggregate output is implicitly defined as follows:

$$z^c=\frac{n}{n+1}(A+v(z^c)). \tag{8.44}$$

Given our assumptions on the function $v(.)$, it is possible to check that the equilibrium is unique.

*Complete Incompatibility Case:* In this case, different types of equilibria are possible:

- Symmetric outcomes: $x_i=x$, $\forall i=1\ldots n$
- Natural oligopoly: $x_i=x$, $\forall i=1\ldots k$, $x_i=0$, $i=k+1\ldots n$.
- Asymmetric outcomes: Different outputs for active firms

For simplicity, we will only take up the symmetric outcomes case. The profits are given by $x_i(A+v(y_i^e-x_i-\sum_{j\neq i}x_j))$. Taking derivatives, the first-order conditions are

$$x_i=A+v(y_i^e)-\sum_{j=1}^{n}x_j. \tag{8.45}$$

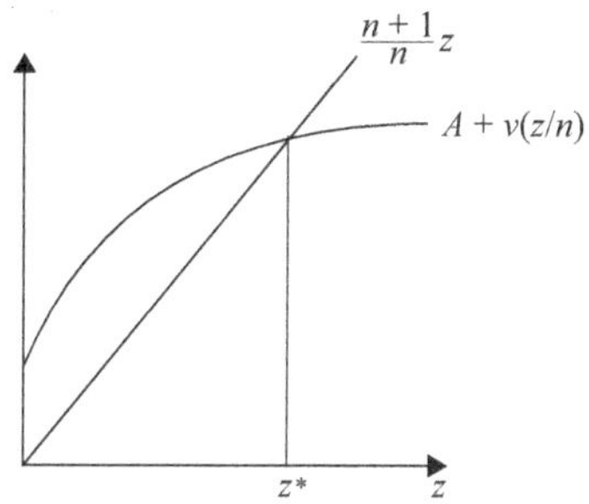


**Figure 8.4**
Equilibrium in the complete incompatibility case.

Rewriting and simplifying equation (8.45) we obtain:

$$2x_i = A + v(y_i^e) - \sum_{j \neq i} x_j. \tag{8.46}$$

The aggregate output in a symmetric equilibrium is implicitly defined as

$$z\frac{n+1}{n} = A + v\left(\frac{z}{n}\right). \tag{8.47}$$

Putting together the cases with full compatibility and incompatibility yields us the following result.

**Proposition 8.1** *Under full compatibility, there is a unique symmetric equilibrium in which $x_i^* = z^c/n$ and aggregate output/sales $z^c$ are implicitly defined by*

$$z^c = \frac{n}{n+1}(A + v(z^*/n)). \tag{8.48}$$

*Under incompatibility, there is a unique symmetric equilibrium in which $x_i = z^*/n$ and aggregate output/sales $z^*$ are implicitly defined by*

$$\frac{n+1}{n}z^* = A + v(z^*/n). \tag{8.49}$$

Figures 8.3 and 8.4 illustrate the equilibrium in the incompatibility and compatibility cases. We now take up the effects of compatibility on total output. Recall that the first-order conditions for individual firms are as follows:

$$x_i = A + v(y_i^e) - z. \tag{8.50}$$

Adding up for all firms and rearranging gives

$$(n+1)z = nA + \sum_{i=1}^{n} v(y_i^e). \tag{8.51}$$

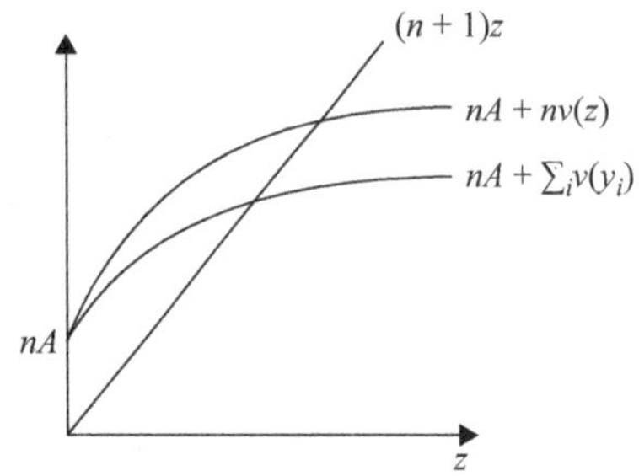


**Figure 8.5**
Total output under compatibility (top) and incompatibility (below).

If there is complete compatibility, then $y_i^e = z\ \forall i \in N$. If there is incomplete compatibility, then $y_i^e < z$ for some i as illustrated in figure 8.5. This tells us that aggregate output is higher under full compatibility as compared to incompatibility.

We next turn to the effects of compatibility on individual firms' output. Here, matters are considerably more complicated. We will establish the following result.

**Proposition 8.2** *Suppose two groups of firms make their products mutually compatible. If, in the precompatibility phase, total output is less than A, then in any postcompatibility equilibrium, (1) the average output of firms in the compatibility group will increase, (2) the output of any firm not in the merging coalitions will fall, and (3) total industry output will rise.*

Let us sketch the arguments underlying this result. Suppose there are $J$ groups of firms, each of which is compatible within itself but incompatible with every other group. In the precompatibility phase, first-order conditions for individual firms (assuming that all firms behave symmetrically within a group) satisfy

$$x^j = A - z + v(m^j x^j), \tag{8.52}$$

where $m^j$ is the number of firms in group $j = 1, 2 \ldots J$. Let $\tilde{x}^j$ and $\tilde{z}$ be the individual firm output and total output after compatibility for groups 1 and 2, respectively.

We now construct an argument by contradiction. Suppose that aggregate output $\tilde{z} < z$. Then for groups $j \geq 3$, the output satisfies $\tilde{x}^j = A - \tilde{z} + v(m^j \tilde{x}^j)$. However, $A - \tilde{z} + v(m^j x^j)$ lies above $A - z + v(m^j x^j)$, so the equilibrium output $\tilde{x}^j > x^j$. Similarly, we may argue that $\tilde{x}^j < x^j$ if $\tilde{z} > z$ and $\tilde{x}^j = x^j$ if $\tilde{z} = z$.

Next, consider the two groups $j = 1, 2$, which make compatible products compatible. For these firms in $j = 1, 2$,

$$A - z + v(m^1 \tilde{x}^1 + m^2 \tilde{x}^2) > A - z + v(m^j x^j). \tag{8.53}$$

Thus if $\tilde{z} < z$, then $\tilde{x}^j > x^j$, $\forall j = 1, 2$. But this means that if $\tilde{z} < z$, then all firms produce more in the postcompatibility world. This is a contradiction. Thus $\tilde{z} > z$. Next, from these arguments, the claims about the output of the firms in groups $j \geq 3$ and firms in groups 1 and 2 follow. ■

It is important to be clear about the content of this result. The result shows that aggregate output by firms in these two groups must increase: $m^1\tilde{x}^1 + m^2\tilde{x}^2 > m^1x^1 + m^2x^2$. This does not imply that every firm in the combining groups increases output! It may well be that one group loses output while another group gains output. This will be important next, when we examine the incentives to achieve compatibility.

### 8.3.2 Incentives for Compatibility

There are different ways in which products can be made compatible. We will start with the case of mutual compatibility. In this case, all the firms involved must agree to make their products compatible.

We consider a two-firm setting to illustrate some of the issues.

- The equilibrium under incompatible products is given by

$$x^1 = A - z + v(x^1) \tag{8.54}$$

$$x^2 = A - z + v(x^2). \tag{8.55}$$

- A symmetric equilibrium under compatibility is given by

$$\tilde{x}_1 = \tilde{x}_2 = x^c = A - \tilde{z} + v(\tilde{z}) \Longleftrightarrow \frac{3}{2}z^c = A + v(z^c). \tag{8.56}$$

Let us start with the case where the firms are in a symmetric situation in a pre-compatibility setting:

$$\frac{3}{2}z^I = A + v\left(\frac{z^I}{2}\right). \tag{8.57}$$

Clearly, $z^I < \tilde{z}^c$ and profits $\pi^I = (x^I)^2 < (x^c)^2 = \pi^c$.

This suggests that the profits of both firms increase after moving to compatibility and the increase in profits is equal. So if one firm wants compatibility, so does the other firm. If $F_i = F$ is the cost of compatibility, then firms choose compatibility if $F \leq \pi^c - \pi^I$.

The social welfare is given by $W = \sum \pi + CS$. Typically, $CS$ is an increasing function of aggregate output, so firms will underestimate the value of moving to compatible products.

There is another issue: if the costs of compatibility are different, $F_i \neq F_j$, then the incentives for compatibility are different and transfers may be needed to facilitate compatibility. We then have to check the condition

$$\sum_i F_i \leq \sum_i (\pi_i^c - \pi_i^I). \tag{8.58}$$

Let us now take up the case in which the firms are in an asymmetric equilibrium in the pre-compatibility setting. Suppose $x_1^I > x_2^I$ in the initial equilibrium. Then note that the change in profits due to compatibility will be quite different for the two firms. Recall that under incompatibility, the profits are given by

$$\pi_1^I = (x_1^I)^2 \tag{8.59}$$

$$\pi_2^I = (x_2^I)^2. \tag{8.60}$$

Meanwhile, the profits under compatibility are given by $\pi_1^c = \pi_2^c = (z^c)^2/4$. Thus it follows that $(\pi_1^c - \pi_1^I) < (\pi_2^c - \pi_2^I)$, which implies that the larger firm under incompatibility will have less incentive to switch to compatibility. This is consistent with the following empirical observation: dominant firms are generally averse to compatibility.

In this model, we have assumed that compatibility between different products is attainable, and at some cost. This is a good starting point, but there are sometimes technological constraints on how well products can be made to work together. For instance, consider the case of digital and analog technology. More generally, there may be a trade-off between performance and compatibility.

One consideration suggested by the computations given here is that low cost of compatibility will facilitate the emergence of a common standard. In the context of multisided platforms, this suggests the following general point: if a side of the market can join many platforms at little cost, then that would make multiple standards attractive. It has been suggested that the modest costs of providing video games for multiple standards have led to increased distribution of games across multiple game systems (such as PlayStation, Nintendo, and Xbox) and a less-concentrated game system market (Corts and Lederman (2009).

In this model, we have assumed that competition between the firms is considered in terms of quantity of choice. This moderates the effect of competition, and firms can earn positive profits even when they choose a compatible product. If firms compete in price, then there would be a greater need to differentiate themselves from each other. The ability of firms to differentiate themselves on some dimension is important in the choice of compatibility. Movie producers provide a highly differentiated good. Consequently, they were quick to settle on the VHS standard. More recently, this was also a factor in the emergence of Blu-ray as a single standard. By contrast, if content providers cannot differentiate themselves, then they must do so by choosing separate standards, which leads to the adoption of multiple standards (Ellison and Fudenberg [2003]).

Let us now summarize what we have learned in this section. Network effects depend on the compatibility of products. If two software programs are distinct but files in one program can be read and understood equally well in the other, then the two software programs can be said to be perfectly compatible, essentially constituting a single network. However, if files in one program cannot be read at all in the other, then the two programs are incompatible. We examined the effects of compatibility on market outcome—outputs, consumer surplus, and profits—and then examined the incentives of firms to make their products compatible.

Our analysis suggests that compatibility usually increases value, and thus the size of any surplus. Compatibility usually also increases the aggregate output of firms. However, the impact on the profits of firms is unclear. It may be that some firms lose out, while others gain. In general, larger firms are less interested in choosing compatibility than small firms are. Finally, the firm's incentive for making products compatible is less than what is socially desirable.

## 8.4 Standards

We now examine the choices that firms have with regard to compatibility more systematically. For expositional simplicity, we will focus on the case in which two firms are compatible if and only if they have the same standard and make the same product. We first introduce a typology of compatibility choices, and then we connect the incentives to the discussion of the Katz-Shapiro model in section 8.3. This section draws heavily on Belleflamme and Peitz (2015).

Suppose there are two firms, denoted by 1 and 2. They choose between two possible versions of their products, A and B. The two versions are incompatible, so the firms can be compatible only if they choose the same version. For easy reference, we present the payoffs in matrix 8.1:

| 1 \ 2 | $A$ | $B$ |
|---|---|---|
| $A$ | $\pi_1^{A,A}, \pi_2^{A,A}$ | $\pi_1^{A,B}, \pi_2^{A,B}$ |
| $B$ | $\pi_1^{B,A}, \pi_2^{B,A}$ | $\pi_1^{B,B}, \pi_2^{B,B}$ |

The form of competition will depend on the compatibility choices. Matrix 8.1 tells us that there are four cases to consider.

- **Firms choose the same product version.** Let us refer to this as "straightforward standardization." There is straightforward standardization on version A if there is a unique Nash equilibrium in which both firms choose A. This occurs when $\pi_1^{A,A} > \pi_1^{B,A}$ and $\pi_2^{A,A} > \pi_2^{A,B}$ and either $\pi_1^{A,B} > \pi_1^{B,B}$ or $\pi_2^{B,A} > \pi_2^{B,B}$.
- **Firms agree that standardization is best, but they disagree about whether version A or B is better.** This is the situation referred to as "the Battle of the Sexes." Now both $(A, A)$ and $(B, B)$ are Nash equilibria: $\pi_1^{A,A} > \pi_1^{B,A}$ and $\pi_2^{A,A} > \pi_2^{A,B}$ and $\pi_1^{B,B} > \pi_1^{B,A}$ and $\pi_2^{B,B} > \pi_2^{A,B}$. But firms rank the equilibria differently: $\pi_1^{A,A} > \pi_1^{B,B}$ and $\pi_2^{B,B} > \pi_2^{A,A}$.
- **The firms strictly prefer to compete to become the de facto standard in the market: this leads to a standards war.** For instance, if firm 1 wants version A while firm 2 wants

version B, then $(A, B)$ is the only Nash equilibrium in the game, with $\pi_1^{A,B} > \pi_1^{B,B}$ and $\pi_2^{A,B} > \pi_2^{A,A}$ and either $\pi_1^{A,A} > \pi_1^{B,A}$ or $\pi_2^{B,B} > \pi_2^{B,A}$.

- **Firms have contrasting strategies: firm 2 prefers incompatibility, while firm 1 prefers to be compatible.** In this setting, there is no Nash equilibrium in pure strategies because $\pi_1^{A,A} > \pi_1^{B,A}$ and $\pi_1^{B,B} > \pi_1^{A,B}$ and $\pi_2^{A,B} > \pi_2^{A,A}$ and $\pi_2^{B,A} > \pi_2^{B,B}$.

It is helpful at this point to briefly discuss a well-known instance of a standards war that took place at the start of the twenty-first century. This was about the new generation of DVD: Blu-ray and HD DVD. Both technologies used blue-light lasers that increased disc capacity. The two formats were incompatible. Each standard was backed by a powerful collection of hardware firms: Blu-ray was backed by Sony, Panasonic, Philips, Pioneer, Dell, and Apple, while HD DVD was backed by Toshiba, NEC, Microsoft, and Intel. The main content providers were movie producers, and even here, some of them were producing exclusively in Blu-ray, while one of them was producing exclusively in HD DVD. It seemed as though each standard had a good chance to prevail. However, in early February 2008, Toshiba announced that it would stop the production of HD DVD players and recorders. This brought the standards war to an end. The tipping point apparently came when Warner Brothers, following the lead of a number of other movie producers, decided that it would produce exclusively on Blu-ray.

We will now explore more systematically the economic circumstances under which these different outcomes arise. The discussion will focus on two variables—the size of the installed bases of the firms and the relative advantage/disadvantage of the firms vis-a-vis the different technologies. We extend the Katz-Shapiro model of compatibility to incorporate these two variables. Each firm has an installed base of users, $\beta_i$, with $i = 1, 2$. The firms compete for new consumers; let $q_i^e$ denote the number of expected new consumers for firm $i$. Thus the expected size of the network of firm $i$ will be $n_i^e = q_i^e + \beta_i$. Suppose that $\gamma \in \{0, 1\}$ is the level of compatibility. The expected network benefit to adopting product $i$ is then given by

$$g_i = v[(\beta_i + q_i^e) + \gamma(\beta_j + q_j^e)]. \tag{8.61}$$

### 8.4.1 Fulfilled Expectations Equilibrium

As in the previous analysis in this chapter, we will study the equilibrium in which consumer expectations are fulfilled. Building on the methods of analysis in section 8.3 above, and assuming that there is a unit measure of consumers with initial valuations between 0 and 1, we can then write the inverse demand for product $i$ as

$$p_i = 1 + v(\beta_i + \gamma\beta_j) - (1 - v)q_i - (1 - \gamma v)q_j. \tag{8.62}$$

The firms seek to maximize their profits $\pi_i = (p_i - c_i)q_i$., where $c_i \geq 0$ is the per-unit cost of production. It is straightforward to check that the fulfilled expectations equilibrium quantities and profits are

$$q_i^* = \frac{2(1-v)[1-c_i+v(\beta_i+\gamma\beta_j)]-(1-\gamma v)[1-c_j+v(\beta_j+\gamma\beta_i)]}{4(1-v)^2-(1-\gamma v)^2} \tag{8.63}$$

$$\pi_i^* = (1-v)(q_i^*)^2. \tag{8.64}$$

These expressions bring out interesting implications of compatibility: (1) setting $\gamma = 1$ raises the equilibrium quantities, and (2) setting $\gamma = 0$ mitigates the installed base advantages and cost advantages. To develop these implications more fully, we further simplify the model: suppose that costs take on two values, $c > 0$ and $c = 0$. Firm 1 has an advantage in product A, and hence its cost is 0 for product A and $c$ for product B. Firm B has an advantage in product B, hence its cost is 0 for product B and $c$ for product A. Also, for simplicity, set $v = 1/4$. Finally, suppose that firm 1 has the installed base $\beta_1 = \beta > 0$, while firm 2 has no installed base ($\beta_2 = 0$). Going forward with these assumptions, we now write the payoffs of the firm under standardization. As the products are compatible, they have the same network benefit, given by $\frac{1}{4}[\beta + q_1 + q_2]$. The inverse demand function is given by

$$p_1 = p_2 = \frac{1}{4}(4+\beta-3(q_1+q_2)). \tag{8.65}$$

The payoffs of the firms will be different due to differences in the cost of production. Let us consider standardization on product A. In that case, the payoffs of firms 1 and 2 are as follows:

$$\pi_1 = \frac{1}{4}[4+\beta-3(q_1+q_2)]q_1; \ \pi_2 = \frac{1}{4}[4+\beta-3(q_1+q_2)]q_2 - cq_2. \tag{8.66}$$

Taking first-order conditions and solving for equilibrium, we get

$$q_1^* = \frac{1}{9}[4+\beta+4c] \ \ q_2^* = \frac{1}{9}[4+\beta-8c] \tag{8.67}$$

$$\pi_1^* = \frac{1}{108}[4+\beta+4c]^2 = \pi_1^{AA} \ \ \pi_2^* = \frac{1}{108}[4+\beta-8c]^2 = \pi_2^{AA} \tag{8.68}$$

Similar computations yield the following equilibrium quantities and profits for the equilibrium with standardization on product B:

$$q_1^* = \frac{1}{9}[4+\beta-8c] \ \ q_2^* = \frac{1}{9}[4+\beta+4c] \tag{8.69}$$

$$\pi_1^* = \frac{1}{108}[4+\beta-8c]^2 = \pi_1^{BB} \ \ \pi_2^* = \frac{1}{108}[4+\beta+4c]^2 = \pi_2^{BB} \tag{8.70}$$

Consider next the incompatibility situations. We start with the case where each firm picks its less preferred product, thereby incurring cost $c$. Recall that firm 2 suffers from a smaller user base. Firm 1 has user base $\beta + q_1$, while firm 2 has user base $q_2$. Firm 1 and firm 2 payoffs can then be written as

$$\pi_1 = \frac{1}{4}[4+\beta-3q_1-4q_2)]q_1 - cq_1;\ \pi_2 = \frac{1}{4}[4-3q_2-4q_1)]q_2 - cq_2. \tag{8.71}$$

Taking first-order conditions and solving for equilibrium, we get

$$q_1^* = \frac{1}{10}[4(1-c)+3\beta] = q_1^{BA}\ \ q_2^* = \frac{1}{10}[4(1-c)-2\beta] = q_2^{BA} \tag{8.72}$$

$$\pi_1^* = \frac{3}{400}[4(1-c)+3\beta]^2 = \pi_1^{BA}\ \ \pi_2^* = \frac{3}{400}[4(1-c)-2\beta]^2 = \pi_2^{BA}. \tag{8.73}$$

Finally, we can compute the equilibrium for case AB by noting that all costs are 0. This yields

$$q_1^* = \frac{1}{10}[4+3\beta] = q_1^{AB}\ \ q_2^* = \frac{1}{10}[4-2\beta] = q_2^{AB} \tag{8.74}$$

$$\pi_1^* = \frac{3}{400}[4+3\beta]^2 = \pi_1^{AB}\ \ \pi_2^* = \frac{3}{400}[4-2\beta]^2 = \pi_2^{AB}. \tag{8.75}$$

Matrix 8.2 summarizes our computations.

| 1 \ 2 | A | B |
|---|---|---|
| A | $\frac{[4+\beta+4c]^2}{108}, \frac{[4+\beta-8c]^2}{108}$ | $\frac{3[4+3\beta]^2}{400}, \frac{3[4-2\beta]^2}{400}$ |
| B | $\frac{3[4(1-c)+3\beta]^2}{400}, \frac{3[4(1-c)-2\beta]^2}{400}$ | $\frac{[4+\beta-8c]^2}{108}, \frac{[4+\beta+4c]^2}{108}$ |

### 8.4.2 Describing Equilibrium Outcomes

Let us now explain the different equilibria that can arise as a function of the two key parameters, $c$ and $\beta$. Both firms choosing product A is an equilibrium if $\pi_1^{AA} \geq \pi_1^{BA}$ and $\pi_2^{AA} \geq \pi_2^{AB}$. Substituting these payoffs from matrix 8.2, we get

$$(1)\ \pi_1^{AA} \geq \pi_1^{BA} \leftrightarrow \beta \leq \frac{4}{17} + \frac{76}{17}c. \tag{8.76}$$

$$(2)\ \pi_2^{AA} \geq \pi_2^{AB} \leftrightarrow \beta \geq -\frac{1}{7} + \frac{20}{7}c. \tag{8.77}$$

Similarly, both firms choosing product B is an equilibrium if $\pi_1^{BB} \geq \pi_1^{AB}$ and $\pi_2^{BB} \geq \pi_2^{BA}$. Substituting these payoffs from matrix 8.2, we get

$$(3)\ \pi_1^{BB} \geq \pi_1^{AB} \leftrightarrow \beta \leq \frac{4}{17} - \frac{80}{17}c. \tag{8.78}$$

$$(4)\ \pi_2^{BB} \geq \pi_2^{BA} \leftrightarrow \beta \geq -\frac{1}{7} - \frac{19}{7}c. \tag{8.79}$$

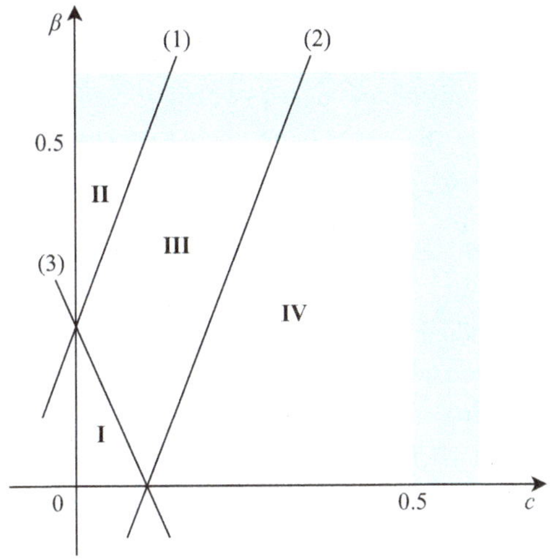


**Figure 8.6**
Installed base size and technology costs.

Similarly, for AB to be an equilibrium, $\pi_2^{AB} \geq \pi_2^{AA}$ and $\pi_1^{AB} \geq \pi_1^{BB}$: this means $\beta \leq -\frac{1}{7} + \frac{20}{7}c$ and/or $\beta \geq \frac{4}{17} - \frac{80}{17}c$.

Finally, for BA to be an equilibrium, it must be the case that $\pi_1^{BA} \geq \pi_1^{AA}$ and $\pi_2^{BA} \geq \pi_2^{BB}$. However, observe that $\pi_2^{BA} \geq \pi_2^{BB}$ is always violated, as $\beta \geq 0$. So BA can never be an equilibrium. This is intuitive, as firm 2 prefers to choose its technology (B) and this incentive is reinforced if doing so also gives firm 2 access to the installed base of firm 1.

To get an overall picture, we plot the three inequalities given in equations (8.76–8.78) as shown in figure 8.6.

In area I, the standardization outcomes AA and BB are both equilibria. This happens because the costs are very modest, so both firms are open to moving to the other technology, and the installed base is sufficiently small that firm 1 is not entirely averse to having firm 2 choose a compatible product (in return for sharing a network of new users).

In area II, the benefits from the installed base are large and the costs of choosing product A are not, so firm 1 has a strong incentive to choose product A. However, firm 1 does not wish to share its network with firm 2, so there is no pure strategy equilibrium.

In area III, straightforward standardization on product AA is the unique outcome. The costs of product A are modest, so firm 2 is eager to adopt product A. Firm 1 finds the costs of switching to product B greater than the potential costs of sharing its installed base with firm 2.

In area IV, the costs of switching products are large, so each firm sticks to its preferred product. This leads to a standards war, outcome AB.

Let us now summarize what we have learned in this section. Premarket standardization is more likely to emerge if the installed base effects and costs of different technologies are both small or the installed base advantage makes switching technologies worthwhile for new entrants. By contrast, a standards war is more likely to occur when the installed base effects are modest relative to the cost differences across technologies for the firms involved.

## 8.5 Multisided Platforms

So far in this chapter, we have studied a very simple setting, in which there is one group and the returns from choosing an action depend on how many others from that group choose the same action. We now turn to richer settings, with multiple groups. Consider the Windows operating system: having more users makes it more attractive for software developers, and more software programs make the operating system more attractive for users. In this example, there are positive effects for the two groups of users and software developers. On the other hand, in a newspaper, an increase in the number of readers makes it more attractive to advertisers, but more advertising probably makes the newspaper less attractive to readers. This draws attention to the richness of effects across groups: sometimes effects are positive on both sides (as in the Windows example), while in other cases the effects can go in opposite directions (as in the newspaper example).

The issues that we studied in the simple setting with one group—the emergence of a dominant platform and the risks of lock-in into an inefficient platform—remain pertinent. But the setting with multiple groups also raises new questions, such as how a platform should price access to its services. We now study this pricing problem.

Let us start with one platform serving two sides of the market, $A$ and $B$. Demand on one side $D_i$, is increasing with the size of the other side $j$.

$$D_A(p_A, E(D_B)) = V + \beta_{AB}E[D_B] - p_A$$
$$D_B(p_B, E(D_A)) = V + \beta_{BA}E[D_A] - p_B, \tag{8.80}$$

where $\beta_{AB}$ and $\beta_{AB}$ reflect the magnitude of the cross-side demand effects and $E(D_B)$ and $E(D_A)$ reflect the expected demands on the other side.

The profits of the platform can be written as the sum of the profits from the two sides of the market:

$$\Pi(p_A, p_B) = D_A(p_A, E(D_B))p_A + D_B(p_B, E(D_A))p_B. \tag{8.81}$$

To make progress, we again consider fulfilled expectations equilibrium. In other words, the expected demand is equal to the true demand:

$$E[D_A(p_A, E(D_B))] = V + \beta_{AB}E[D_B] - p_A$$
$$E[D_B(p_B, E(D_A))] = V + \beta_{BA}E[D_A] - p_B. \tag{8.82}$$

Given the prices, $p_A$ and $p_B$, we therefore have a demand system of two equations in two unknowns, $D_A$ and $D_B$.

We can solve these two equations and obtain consistent demands:

$$D_A(p_A,p_B)=\frac{V(1+\beta_{AB})-\beta_{AB}p_B-p_A}{1-\beta_{AB}\beta_{BA}}$$

$$D_B(p_A,p_B)=\frac{V(1+\beta_{BA})-\beta_{BA}p_A-p_B}{1-\beta_{AB}\beta_{BA}}. \tag{8.83}$$

Observe that an increase in $p_A$ lowers the demand of side A and, due to cross-side positive externalities, also lowers the demand for side B.

If we substitute these demands from equation (8.83) in the profit expression equation (8.81), we obtain

$$\Pi(p_A,p_B)=p_A\frac{V(1+\beta_{AB})-\beta_{AB}p_B-p_A}{1-\beta_{AB}\beta_{BA}}+p_B\frac{V(1+\beta_{BA})-\beta_{BA}p_A-p_B}{1-\beta_{AB}\beta_{BA}}. \tag{8.84}$$

Equipped with equation (8.46), we can compute optimal prices. To develop a feel for the problem, it is helpful to start with the benchmark case, $\beta_{AB}=\beta_{BA}=0$. It is easy to see that the optimal price will be $V/2$, as in the monopoly pricing of independent markets. Next, let us consider the case of cross-group externalities.

Solving for optimal prices, we arrive at

$$p_A=\frac{V(-1+\beta_{BA})}{-2+\beta_{AB}+\beta_{BA}}$$

$$p_B=\frac{V(-1+\beta_{AB})}{-2+\beta_{AB}+\beta_{BA}}. \tag{8.85}$$

To develop an appreciation of the cross-effects, suppose that $\beta_{AB},\beta_{BA}>0$ and $\beta_{AB}+\beta_{BA}=1$. Applying this assumption and substituting these prices from (8.85) in equation (8.84) yields:

$$p_A=\frac{V}{2}+V\left(\frac{1}{2}-\beta_{BA}\right)$$

$$p_B=V(1-\beta_{AB}). \tag{8.86}$$

Let us examine the effects of the cross-group externality term. Suppose that $\beta_{AB}>1/2$, so $\beta_{BA}=1-\beta_{AB}<1/2$. Consumers on side A gain more from side B than vice versa. It then follows that the optimal price is higher for side A than for side B. This is intuitive: an increase in the demand of group B raises the demand of group A more than the converse, so the firm sets a higher price for group A and a lower price for group B. This intuition is also reflected in the price elasticity for the two groups. The price elasticity expressions for

**Table 8.1**
Platform pricing: premium prices in red, subsidy prices in blue.

| Industry | Platforms | Premium/Subsidy |
|---|---|---|
| Employment | Naukri, Zhaopin, LinkedIn | Employers/Workers |
| Retail | Amazon, Alibaba | Sellers/Buyers |
| Lodging | Tujia, Airbnb | Sellers/Consumers |
| Ride-hail | Uber, Lyft | Drivers/Passengers |
| Payments | Visa, MasterCard | Sellers/Consumers |
| Operating systems | Windows, Mac | Programmers/Users |
| Newspapers | *Guardian, New York Times* | Advertisers/Readers |

the two groups may be written as follows:

$$\epsilon_{D_A,p_B} = \frac{\beta_{AB}}{1-\beta_{AB}\beta_{BA}} \frac{p_B}{D_A} \tag{8.87}$$

$$\epsilon_{D_B,p_A} = \frac{\beta_{BA}}{1-\beta_{AB}\beta_{BA}} \frac{p_A}{D_B}. \tag{8.88}$$

We see that if $\beta_{AB} > 1/2$, then the cross-price elasticity for side A (with respect to price B) is higher. This means that the platform can set fairly asymmetric prices to exploit cross-side network effects. A question at the end of the chapter examines this point.

Table 8.1 presents examples of well-known platforms and their pricing strategies—the side they charge high price, and the side they charge a low price. Our analysis suggests that if other aspects of the market are broadly similar then the side that creates larger positive cross-effects is offered a relatively lower price to access the platform.

Let us summarize what we have learned so far in this section. We have studied the optimal pricing by a platform that serves multiple consumer segments. The key insight was that over and above the standard considerations, as reflected in the price elasticity of demand, cross-effects on demand give rise to discrimination in pricing across different sides of the market: in particular, the side of the market that exerts a larger positive effect on the demand of the other side faces a relative lower price to access the platform.

### 8.5.1 Openness

Openness pertains to how many sides of a market a firm should pursue. A prominent example is the different choices of Apple and Microsoft. Apple produces both its computer hardware and its operating system, whereas Microsoft controls only the operating system and counts on independent manufacturers to supply most of the hardware. In this market, Microsoft manages a three-sided market among consumers, software providers, and hardware providers, whereas Apple manages a three-sided market, between consumers and software providers. So we may say that Microsoft is more open, as it manages a three sided market while Apple manages a two-sided market.

A firm may change its strategy on openness as its market evolves. This is because an entrant firm faces a chicken-and-egg problem: to establish a large demand on one side of the market, a firm should establish itself on the other side of the market, and that can in principle be addressed by providing one side of the market itself. An example of this sequence of strategies is Amazon, which first established itself as an online book retailer before introducing its Amazon Marketplace, where sellers set prices on all kinds of products and interact with consumers. Thus there is a sense in which it may be better to think of two-sided strategies rather than two-sided markets because the number of sides is to some extent endogenous.

## 8.6 Chains of Intermediation

Intermediaries are a defining feature of banking, retail, and information services, and are a prominent feature of the modern economy more generally. A central theme in this chapter has been competition between different intermediaries and platforms. This section presents an experimental examination of this competition. In particular, inspired by examples like Amazon, we study a scenario where traders need connections to be able to trade. Intermediaries lower the costs of exchange or reduce friction between buyers and sellers. In line with the earlier discussions on network effects, intermediation has a reinforcing aspect: the more actors use an intermediary, the more attractive it becomes for other actors to use. The earlier sections have highlighted how these network pressures may give rise to highly visible, globally dominant intermediaries. This section explores the dynamics of competition among the intermediaries from an experimental perspective. The goal is to better understand the mechanisms underlying the emergence of such dominant intermediaries. The experiment is taken from Choi, Goyal, and Moisan (2020).

We consider a setting in which trades between two actors can be realized if they have a direct link or are indirectly linked through a chain of intermediaries. These links are costly to maintain. For concreteness, consider a network with $n$ actors in which all pairs are linked (i.e., the complete network). In this setting, every bilateral exchange involves direct trading: there is no intermediation. However, $n(n-1)/2$ links are formed. By contrast, consider the hub-spoke network, in which all the exchanges involving pairs of spokes—that is, $(n-1)(n-2)/2$ pairs—entail intermediation (and possibly large rents for the hub). The complete network contains $n(n-1)/2$ links, while the hub-spoke network contains $n-1$ links: thus, there is a large saving in linking costs in the hub-spoke network. A network may be sparse and connected without a concentration of intermediation power. An instance of such a network is a cycle containing all actors: in this setting, there are only $n$ links, and because everyone is symmetrically located, every actor earns an equal payoff. So the cycle reconciles efficiency and equity. The experiment helps us understand the economic mechanisms that give rise to cycle and the hub-spoke networks respectively.

We will consider a network formation model that builds on the work of Goyal and Vega-Redondo (2007), Kleinberg, Suri, Tardos, and Wexler (2008) and Galeotti and Goyal (2014). Individuals choose to form links with each other and then use the network thus constructed to engage in exchanges. If an actor maintains links with many others, they incur large linking costs but in return avoid paying rents to intermediaries. If, on the other hand, they maintain few links, then their linking costs will be modest, but they will either not undertake many exchanges (as they have no path connecting them to several traders) or conduct their exchanges with the help of intermediaries to whom they may have to pay rents. In this environment, there is also an incentive to form links in order to become an intermediary and to extract rents.

We start by presenting a theoretical model and then we discuss an experiment.

### 8.6.1 Model

We study a network formation game. The set of players is denoted by $N = \{1, \ldots, n\}$, where $n \geq 3$. Players propose links with others: a link is realized only if it is reciprocated. Formally, the strategy of a player $i$ is a vector of link proposals $s_i = [s_{ij}]_{j \in N \setminus \{i\}}$, with $s_{ij} \in \{0, 1\}$ for any $j \in N \setminus \{i\}$. The strategy set of player $i$ is denoted by $S_i$. A link between agents $i$ and $j$ is formed if both propose a link to each other (i.e., $g_{ij} = s_{ij}s_{ji}$). A strategy profile $s = (s_1, s_2, \ldots, s_n)$ induces an undirected network $g(s)$. For ease of exposition, we will drop dependence of $g$ on $s$, and simply write network as $g$, in this section. There is a path between $i$ and $j$ in network $g$ if either $g_{ij} = 1$ or if there is a distinct set of players $i_1, \ldots, i_n$, such that $g_{ii_1} = g_{i_1 i_2} = g_{i_2 i_3} = \ldots = g_{i_n j} = 1$. The component of player $i$ in a network $g$ is denoted by $C_i(g)$.

Suppose that players are traders who can exchange goods and that this exchange creates a surplus of $V$. This exchange can be carried out only if these traders have a link or there is a path between them. There is a fixed cost of $k > 0$ per individual for every link that is established. On the other hand, any proposal that is not reciprocated carries no cost. If two traders have a link, it would be natural that they split the surplus equally, each earning $V/2$. If they are linked indirectly, then the allocation of the surplus depends on the nature of competition between the intermediary agents. One idea is to view these paths as perfect substitutes. Another possibility is that the paths offer differentiated trading possibilities.

**Criticality pricing** Suppose that paths between traders are perfect substitutes. If two paths connecting a pair of traders are perfect substitutes then their lengths do not matter. This suggests that if intermediaries on two paths were competing to gain business, they would be unable to extract any surplus from the traders. If this is true, then the only way an intermediary can hope to earn profits is if it is somehow indispensable, that is, it lies on all paths between two traders. We shall say that a trader is *critical* for a pair of players A and B if it lies on all paths between them (for a model of pricing in networks that develops the notion of critical traders, see chapter 16).

Denote by $T(j,k;g)$ the set of players who are critical for $j$ and $k$ in network $g$, and let $t(j,k;g)=|T(j,k;g)|$. Following Goyal and Vega-Redondo (2007), for every strategy profile $s=(s_1,s_2,\ldots,s_n)$, the net payoffs to player $i$ are given by

$$\Pi_i^{crit}(s)=\underbrace{\sum_{j\in C_i(g)}\frac{V}{t(i,j;g)+2}}_{\text{access benefits}}+\underbrace{\sum_{j,k\in N\setminus\{i\}}V\frac{I_{i\in T(j,k;g)}}{t(j,k;g)+2}}_{\text{brokerage rents}}-\eta_i(g)k, \tag{8.89}$$

where $I_{i\in T(j,k)}\in\{0,1\}$ stands for the indicator function specifying whether $i$ is critical for $j$ and $k$.

The following result provides a description of pairwise stable networks for a game with payoffs given by equation (8.89). (see chapter 3 for a definition of pairwise stable networks).

**Proposition 8.3** *Suppose payoffs are given by equation (8.89). There exists a pairwise stable network. Pairwise stable networks include the star network if* $V/6<k<\frac{Vn}{3}-\frac{V}{6}$*, the cycle network if* $k<\sum_{i=1}^{n-2}\frac{Vi}{2(2+i)}$*, and the empty network if* $k>\frac{V}{2}$*. The complete network is not pairwise stable for* $n\geq 4$.

A general observation is that pairwise stable networks cover a wide range of structures that include the star and the cycle. So incentives in this model sustain networks with very small diameter as well as very large diameter. As the cycle is pairwise stable this suggests that incentives are compatible with equality.

Let us briefly examine the inequalities in proposition 8.3. The conditions on the pairwise stability of the star network arise from two incentive constraints: spokes must not wish to form a link (this yields the constraint $V/6<c$) and the central hub must wish to form a link with a spoke (this yields the constraint $c<Vn/3-V/6$). The inequality in the pairwise stability of the empty network arises because two isolated individuals earn $V/2$ on forming a link. In the cycle network, there are no gains to forming any new links because that does not enhance access or give rise to brokerage rent. Deleting a link gives rise to a line network with the player at one end of it: comparing the payoffs from a cycle with a line give rise to the inequality in the proposition. Finally, we note that with more than 4 players, a complete network is not pairwise stable as a player can delete a link without incurring any brokerage rents or losing access to any other player.

**Betweenness pricing** We next turn to betweenness pricing, taken from Kleinberg, Suri, Tardos, and Wexler (2008). Let $n_{jk}=(d(j,k;g)-1)$ denote the number of intermediaries on a shortest path between $j$ and $k$ in network $g$. Trade surplus between $j$ and $k$ is equally distributed between the source and destination ($j$ and $k$, respectively), and among the intermediaries on the shortest path. If there are multiple shortest paths, one of them is randomly chosen. Therefore, the ex-ante expected return for any trader $i$ is in proportion to the shortest paths between $j$ and $k$ that $i$ lies on. We write $b^i_{jk}(g) \in [0, 1]$ to denote the *betweenness* of player $i$ between $j$ and $k$. Formally,

$$b^i_{jk}(g) = \frac{\#\text{ of shortest paths between } j \text{ and } k \text{ on which i lies}}{\#\text{ of shortest paths between } j \text{ and } k}.$$

Given a strategy profile $s = (s_1, s_2, \ldots, s_n)$, the net payoffs to player $i$ are given by

$$\Pi_i^{btwn}(s) = \underbrace{\sum_{j \in C_i(g)} \frac{V}{n_{ij}+2}}_{\text{access benefits}} + \underbrace{\sum_{j,k \in N \setminus \{i\}} V \frac{b^i_{jk}}{n_{jk}+2}}_{\text{brokerage rents}} - \eta_i(g)k \tag{8.90}$$

We next state the result on pairwise stable networks with betweenness-based pricing.

**Proposition 8.4** *Suppose that payoffs are given by equation (8.90). There exists a pairwise stable network. Pairwise stable networks include the complete network if $k < V/6$, the star network if $V/6 < k < Vn/3 - V/3$, and the empty network if $k > V/2$. Given any $k$ and $V$, the cycle is not pairwise stable for large enough $n$.*

The arguments for pairwise stability of the empty network and the star are the same as under criticality pricing. A first difference emerges when we consider the complete network: we note there are always returns from forming an additional link as that shortens the path length. Hence the complete network is pairwise stable if $k < V/6$. In the cycle network, the gain in benefits (access benefits and brokerage rents) for adding a link between two players sitting at opposite points of the cycle increases with $n$. As a result, if $n$ is sufficiently large, a cycle is not pairwise stable. Finally, observe that for any values of $k > 0$, and $n \geq 3$, at least one of complete, star, or empty network is pairwise stable.

Turning to efficiency, observe that the intermediation rents cancel out when we sum across individuals. A network is said to be efficient if it maximizes the sum of the trade surpluses realized minus the costs of any links. Goyal and Vega-Redondo (2007) prove that an efficient network is either an empty network or a minimally connected network. The total payoffs in the latter case are $\frac{Vn(n-1)}{2} - 2(n-1)k$, and they equal 0 in the case of an empty network. So it follows that an efficient network is minimally connected if $k < \frac{Vn}{4}$, and empty otherwise. A prominent example of a minimally connected network is a star network.

Finally, payoff inequality varies significantly across stable network structures. The outcome is equal in an empty network and a cycle network. By contrast, in the star network (under both criticality and betweenness), the hub and spoke earn, respectively,

$$V(n-1)\left[\frac{1}{2} + \frac{n-2}{6}\right] - (n-1)k \qquad V\left[\frac{1}{2} + \frac{n-2}{3}\right] - k. \tag{8.91}$$

The ratio of the two payoffs grows without bound, in $n$, highlighting large inequalities in large groups.

As is common in network formation games, there are multiple stable networks with very different properties. For instance, there are $n$ star networks, each corresponding to a different player as the hub. In addition, under criticality pricing, the cycle network is also stable. Finally, the empty network is stable alongside the star network for a wide set of parameters. Thus, while the forces of efficiency and equity point to the cycle and the star, individuals face multiple challenges to getting on such networks, and it is far from clear what networks will arise. Next, we present an experiment with human subjects to delineate the scope of the theory, particularly the ways in which pricing rules shape incentives to form links and thereby determine the architecture of the intermediation network.

### 8.6.2 Experiment

We will set the value of trade between any two traders to be $V = 10$. The cost of a link is $k = 80$. With these parameters, the star network is efficient. It is, however, very unequal: in the star network, the hub and spokes earn 8,745 and 252, respectively. On the other hand, in the cycle network, every player earns 335. The ratio of maximum to median payoffs in the star network is 35; the cycle network, by contrast, is approximately efficient (as it is only one link more than in a star) and as every node is symmetrically located the payoffs are equal. This tension between inequality and efficiency is a key element in this experiment.

The analysis of pairwise stable networks, efficiency, and inequality suggests the following hypothesis.

**Hypothesis** *Under both pricing treatments, subjects create networks that are efficient. Under criticality pricing, networks are equal and spread out with significant average distances. Under betweenness pricing, networks are unequal, with small average distance.*

**Design of experiment** We will consider four groups of 100 subjects per pricing rule. Each group of 100 subjects play the network formation game six times. Each play is referred to as a round; a round lasts six minutes. The first round is a trial round with no payoffs paid out. The first minute of every round is a trial round. We pick an instant from the last 5 minutes to pay out payoffs. In a round, at any instant, the subject is shown the entire network of reciprocated links. In addition, every subject is shown all outstanding link proposals—made and received—that involve them. Every subject is also provided full information on the payoffs of everyone (this is done by mentioning the numeric value of the payoffs for every subject next to their player ID. However, subjects are not shown unreciprocated links among other pairs. This was done to keep the information options available to a subject manageable.

At any instant a subject can make or remove a proposal to another subject by simply double-clicking on the corresponding node in the computer screen. Any reciprocated proposal leads to the formation of a link. Every subject is also shown the magnitude of access benefits, brokerage rents, overall cost of linking, and net payoffs. Finally, subjects are also provided with information about the net payoffs of every other player (given within the corresponding node of the network). A session with 6 rounds lasted 90 minutes on average. Subjects earned on average 16.4 euros, including a 5 euros show-up fee. The experiments were carried out at the University of Valencia in Spain.

### Findings

We begin by presenting snapshots of the typical dynamics under the two pricing rules. Figures 8.7(a) and 8.7(b) show the snapshots of the criticality treatment at minute 3 and minute 6, respectively. Network structures are sparse and connected and fairly dispersed. There is no single player who occupies a dominant network position and extracts large brokerage rents. Figures 8.7(c) and 8.7(d) show that the dynamics in the betweenness treatment are quite different. At minute 3, one subject (represented in red) starts to emerge as a hub and becomes a dominant hub at the end of the game.

These snapshots bring out three points. First, under both pricing protocols, subjects create sparse and connected networks. Second, the pricing protocol leads to the emergence of equal and dispersed networks under criticality and to unequal and small distance networks in betweenness pricing. Third, there is little inequality in the criticality treatment while the hub in the betweenness treatment earns large brokerage rents, and, as a result, there is great payoff inequality in the betweenness treatment. Let us examine the data more systematically.

First, consider efficiency. We define efficiency by the ratio of the aggregate payoffs as a function of aggregate payoffs obtained in a star network (that is, an efficient network). Figure 8.8 plots the time series for efficiency levels. We note that under criticality pricing, subjects create networks that attain high levels of efficiency in excess of 0.7. The situation is quite different under betweenness pricing: here efficiency starts at a very low level and increases rapidly to reach close to 0.5. Thus, there is a large difference in the efficiency of the network created under the two pricing protocols.

The level of efficiency depends on the connectivity of subjects (the realization of trade between subjects) and on the number of links created by subjects. It turns out that the connectivity of subjects is very high and that it is similar across pricing rules—it is on average 98.7 percent under criticality pricing and 98.1 percent under betweenness pricing. As connectivity is high and comparable, the differences in efficiency across treatments must be due to variations in the number of links. We turn to this issue next.

Figures 8.9(a) and 8.9(b) show that there is a large difference in the number of links. Under criticality pricing, the average degree lies between 2 and 3; by contrast, under betweenness pricing, the average degree is higher, between 4 and 5. Thus, there is a significant difference in the number of links created by subjects in the two pricing treatments.

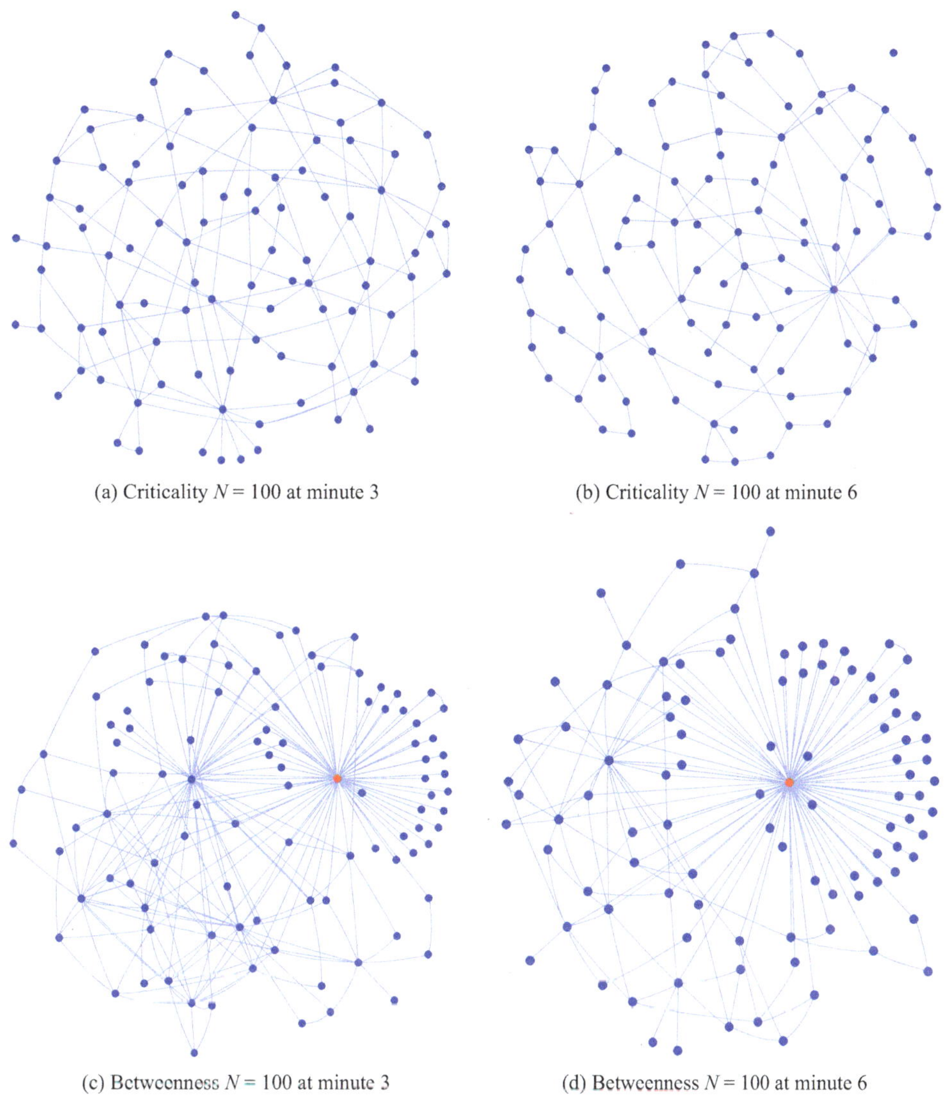

Figure 8.7
Snapshots of the dynamics. *Source*: Choi, Goyal, and Moisan (2022).

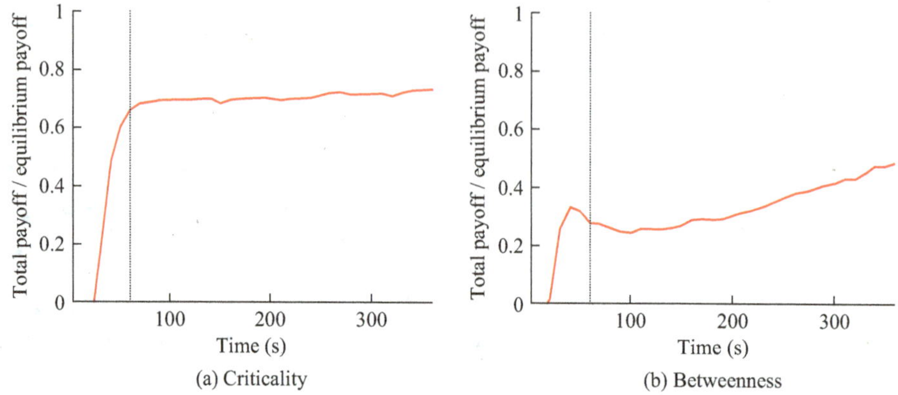


**Figure 8.8**
Efficiency. *Source*: Choi, Goyal, and Moisan (2022).

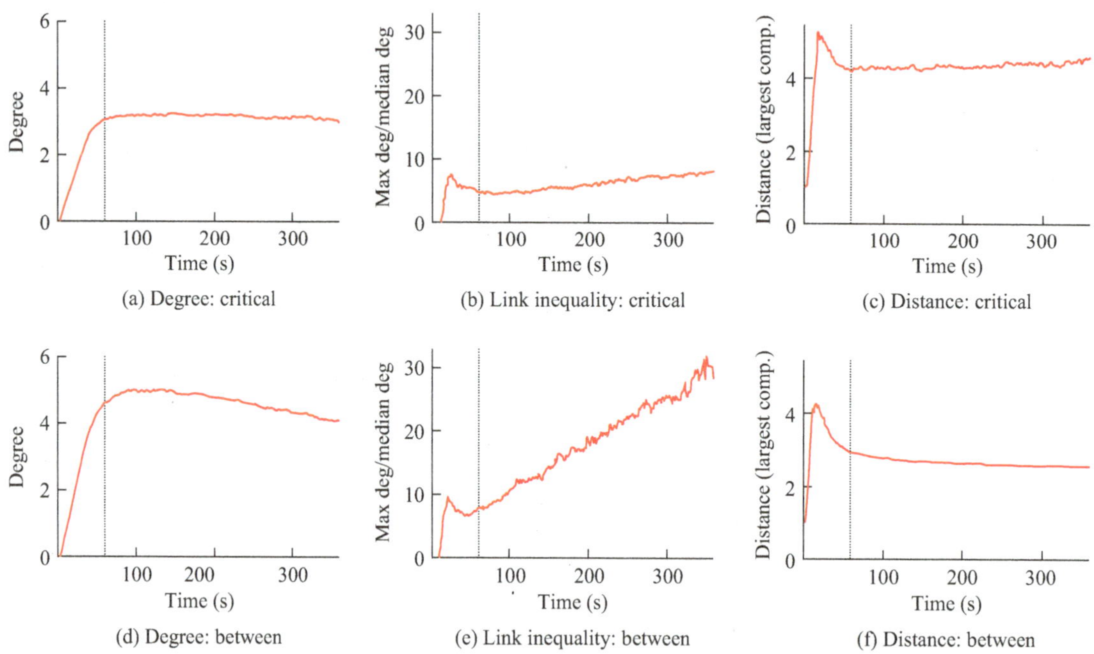


**Figure 8.9**
Network structure. *Source*: Choi, Goyal, and Moisan (2022).

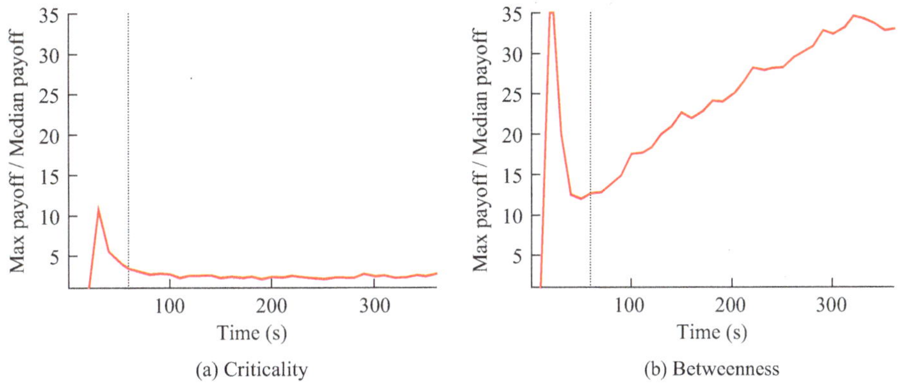


**Figure 8.10**
Payoff inequality. *Source*: Choi, Goyal, and Moisan (2022).

We next turn to the distribution of degrees in the networks. Figures 8.9b and 8.9e show that link inequality is modest and remains stable under criticality pricing. We see that the ratio of maximum degree to median degree remains below 10 throughout the experiment. By contrast, this ratio is much larger and it is increasing under betweenness pricing—it is in excess of 30 by the end of the game. This difference in degree inequality is first order and is closely related to our next network measure, average distance.

Figures 8.9c and 8.9f show that average distance is above 4 in the criticality treatment and close to 2 in the betweenness treatment. To put these numbers in perspective, note that in a cycle in the average distance is of order n/3 = 33, while in the star network the average distance is (roughly) equal to 2. Thus the average distances under criticality pricing are lower than the predicted average distance in a cycle (this should not come as a surprise; following the logic of the Watts and Strogatz [1998] model, recall that the average distances in a cycle would fall off sharply with a few additional links placed randomly in a circle). However, the average distance under betweenness is close to that predicted in a star network.

Finally, consider the payoff distribution. Figure 8.10 presents time series of the ratio of maximum payoff divided by the median payoff. We see that payoff inequality is very modest under criticality pricing—the ratio lies between 2 and 3. But payoff inequality is very large under betweenness pricing—the ratio is over 34! This large difference in payoff inequality mirrors the difference in degree inequality that we noted above and points to the key role of brokerage rents.

To summarize: subjects create sparse networks. The efficiency of the network is high under criticality pricing and moderate under betweenness pricing. Pricing has powerful effects—on the number of links, on average distances and on degree and payoff inequality. We next examine the incentives that give rise to these differences.

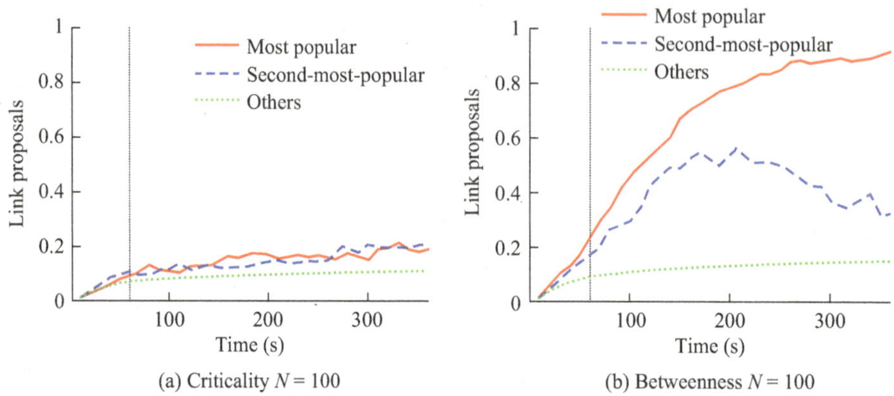


**Figure 8.11**
Link proposals. *Source*: Choi, Goyal, and Moisan (2022).

### Pricing rules and linking incentives

We start by examining the number of link proposals made by the different types of subjects (measured in terms of how many link proposals they have received): the most popular individual, the second-most-popular individual, and the other individuals. Figure 8.11 plots the time series of the average ratio of the number of link proposals made by each type to the total number of link proposals. We see that there are major differences in the link proposals made by the two most popular individuals. Under criticality pricing, most subjects form two links and no one forms a very large number of links, which keeps the average degree close to 2. By contrast, under betweenness pricing, a number of individuals compete for the hub position by making a large number of link proposals. Notably, the number of link proposals by the most popular individual is growing over time. In addition, the second-most-popular subject proposes a large number of links. These proposals are reciprocated, and as a result, there is a high fraction of subjects with three or more links. This pushes up the average degree.

The different link proposals under the two pricing rules arise out of the possibility of generating intermediation rents—under criticality pricing, there is very little incentive to propose once individuals are in a cycle, as there are no brokerage rents to be earned. By contrast, under betweenness, additional links create shorter paths and generate brokerage rents. Other individuals respond positively to the proposals, as this enables them to access traders at shorter lengths. However, as the network evolves and the average distance goes down, the returns to links with multiple hubs declines. Table 8.2 presents the relationship between the number of links and payoffs and places that in the context of equilibrium outcomes.

It shows that under criticality pricing, subjects with 2 links earn more than those with either 1 link or 3 links. In contrast, subjects with 1 link earn the most under betweenness pricing. Moreover, the difference in payoffs grows over time as the network evolves and

**Table 8.2**
Payoffs associated with forming 1, 2, or 3 links: Last 2.5 minutes

| | Criticality | Betweenness |
|---|---|---|
| | $N = 100$ | $N = 100$ |
| 1 link | 235 | 202 |
| 2 links | 311 | 131 |
| 3 links | 231 | 70 |
| Equilibrium | 335 | 252 |

*Source*: Choi, Goyal, and Moisan (2022).
*Note*: Equilibrium payoffs are based on the cycle network under criticality, and the star network (spokes' payoffs) under betweenness.

average distances gradually come down. The rate at which links come down is slow, however, which accounts for the relatively low level of efficiency even at the end of 6 minutes.

Let us summarize what we have learned in this section. We have examined the effects of pricing rules on the formation of intermediation networks. The theory is permissive: a wide range of networks are pairwise stable. The experiments yield a number of striking results. In particular, we find that under criticality pricing, subjects create efficient and sparse networks with relatively large average distances. These networks lead to fairly egalitarian payoffs. By contrast, under betweenness pricing, subjects create sparse networks with lower efficiency. These networks have very unequal degrees and support extreme payoff inequality. Pricing rules create different incentives for linking and this helps account for the different networks we observe in the laboratory.

## 8.7 Reading Notes

The literature on markets with network goods goes back a long way. For a seminal discussion of pricing and multiple equilibrium in such markets, see Rohlfs (1974). The analysis of inertia, excess momentum, and lock-ins originated with Farrell and Saloner (1985) and Arthur (1989). David (1985) offers an influential discussion of lock-ins using the example of the QWERTY keyboard. More generally, the issue of technological change has been extensively studied in the context of network externalities; see, for example, de Bijl and Goyal (1995). The analysis of the compatibility problem draws on the seminal work of Farrell and Saloner (1986) and Katz and Shapiro (1985, 1986). For surveys of the early literature on markets with network effects, see Besen and Farrell (1994) and Katz and Shapiro (1994) and for a nontechnical introduction to firm strategies in markets with network effects, see Shapiro and Varian (1995).

The literature on indirect network effects can be traced back to the early work of Chou and Shy (1990) and Church and Gandal (1992, 1993). Within this body of literature, two issues have received a great deal of attention: optimal pricing strategies and emergence of a dominant platforms. For optimal pricing, see Armstrong (2006), Caillaud and Jullien (2003), and Rochet and Tirole (2003, 2006). For research on dominant platforms, see Rochet and Tirole (2002) and Ellison and Fudenberg (2003). For an early empirical analysis of network effects, see Rysman (2004, 2007). Rysman (2009) provides a survey of the literature on two-sided markets. For a textbook treatment of platforms, see Belleflame and Peitz (2022).

The experiment on trading and network formation is part of a large body of literature on intermediation. Influential early work examines pricing by intermediaries and their ability to reduce friction, and thereby extract surpluses; see Rubinstein and Wolinsky (1987); Choi, Galeotti, and Goyal (2017); and Manea (2018). Condorelli and Galeotti (2016) provide a survey of this work. For experiments on trading in networks and on intermediation, see Gale and Kariv (2009); Charness, Corominas-Bosch, and Frechette (2007); and Choi, Galeotti, and Goyal (2017). The theory is based on the theoretical models presented in Goyal and Vega-Redondo (2007) and Kleinberg, Suri, Tardos, and Wexler (2008). The criticality-based pricing rule is taken from Goyal and Vega-Redondo (2007), while the betweenness-based pricing rule is taken from Kleinberg, Suri, Tardos, and Wexler (2008). The exposition here draws on the recent experimental paper of Choi, Goyal, and Moisan (2020).

In addition to these papers, in writing this chapter, I have drawn on the industrial organization textbook of Belleflamme and Peitz (2015) and the lecture notes of Jonathan Levin at Stanford and Andrea Galeotti at the London Business School (LBS).

## 8.8 Questions

1. Markets with positive adoption externalities are prone to dominance by single firms. Discuss.
2. Markets with demand-side externalities may exhibit too little or too much technological change. Discuss.
3. (Belleflamme and Peitz [2015]). Consider the Hotelling model with linear transport costs, where two firms, 1 and 2, are located at the ends of the unit interval. Assume that the unit mass of consumers is uniformly distributed on this unit interval. Suppose that the products offered exhibit network effects. Let the choice of consumer $x \in [0, 1]$ be given by $a_x \in \{1, 2\}$. A consumer located at point $x \in [0, 1]$ has utility

$$r - tx - p_1 + vn_1^e, \text{ if } a_x = 1 \tag{8.92}$$

$$r - t(1-x) - p_2 + vn_2^e, \text{ if } a_x = 2, \tag{8.93}$$

where $n_i^e$ is the expected number of consumers buying product $i \in \{1, 2\}$. Let us assume that $r$ is sufficiently large that the market is covered (i.e., $n_1^e = 1 - n_2^e$). Both firms produce at zero marginal costs.

We consider a two-stage game: in stage 1, both firms simultaneously announce prices, and in stage 2, observing these prices, consumers choose whether to buy product 1 or 2.

We will consider the subgame perfect equilibrium of the two-stage game. In particular, we will study the fulfilled expectations equilibrium in stage 2 and then, given that stage 2 equilibrium, we will work backward and solve for equilibrium in firm prices (in stage 1).

(a) Show that if $t > v$, then there is a unique fulfilled expectations equilibrium in stage 2 for any pair of prices. Assuming that $t > v$, solve for the equilibrium in the first-stage game of pricing. Discuss the network effects, $v$, on this equilibrium.

(b) Show that if $t < v$, then there could be multiple fulfilled expectations equilibria in stage 2 for some pairs of prices.

4. (Belleflamme and Peitz [2015]). Consider a monopoly platform that serves two groups of users. Each group $i = a, b$ comprises a unit mass of users. The platform charges membership fees of $M_a$ and $M_b$ for two types of users. The marginal costs of serving users are set equal to zero. A user of group $i$ enjoys utility

$$U_i = \alpha_i + \gamma_i n_j - M_i, \tag{8.94}$$

where $\alpha_i$ is the stand-alone or intrinsic value of being on the platform, $\gamma_i$ is the marginal benefit of an additional user on the other side of the market, and $n_j$ is the number of users on side $j$. We shall assume that $\alpha_i$ is drawn from a uniform distribution on interval $[0, v]$ and $\gamma_a, \gamma_b > 0$.

(a) Derive the demand on a side of the market as a function of firm prices and the number of users on the other side.

(b) Solve for the system of demand equations derived in the previous part to express the number of users as a function of the prices $M_a, M_b$.

(c) Now consider an asymmetric externality setting: set $\gamma_a = \gamma$ (with $0 < \gamma < 1$) and $\gamma_b = 0$; and to simplify matters, also assume that $v_a = v_b = 1$. Solve for the optimal prices of the monopolist.

5. Consider an $n$-player network formation game. Link formation is two-sided. Every pair of players that has a path between the players creates a total surplus of 1. Suppose that the surplus is shared equally with the critical traders necessary for trade to occur between a pair of traders.

(a) Consider a game with five players and write all the critical players in a cycle network and star network.

(b) Suppose the payoffs are as given in equation (8.89). Discuss the different incentives to create links.

(c) Suppose $n = 5$. Derive the conditions of costs of links under which a star and a cycle network are pairwise stable.

6. Carry out the computations and establish the following result from section 8.6, about criticality based pricing: pairwise-stable networks include an empty network if $k > \frac{V}{2}$, a

star network if $\frac{V}{6} < k < \frac{Vn}{3} - \frac{V}{6}$, and a cycle network if $k < \sum_{i=1}^{n-2} \frac{Vi}{2(2+i)}$. The complete network is not stable for $n \geq 4$.

7. Consider an $n$-player network formation game. Link formation is two-sided. Every pair of players that has a path between them creates a total surplus of 1. Suppose that the surplus is independent of the length of the path. The payoffs are shared with players who lie on the shortest paths between the two traders in the exchange.
   (a) Consider a game with 6 players, numbered 1 to 6, who are located on a cycle network. Write the payoffs of a player under betweenness pricing, using the payoffs expression as in equation (8.90).
   (b) Consider a game with 5 players, numbered 1 to 6, who are located on a star network (with player 1 as the hub). Write the payoffs of the players under betweenness pricing.
   (c) Show that a star is pairwise stable and also efficient (under suitable costs of linking).
   (d) Show that, for fixed costs of linking, as the number of players gets large, the cycle is not pairwise stable.
8. The star is pairwise stable and efficient under both criticality pricing and betweenness pricing. However, in the experiments on brokerage discussed in the chapter, subjects only create the star under betweenness pricing.
   (a) Discuss the circumstances under which criticality-based pricing and betweenness-based pricing are respectively reasonable.
   (b) Discuss the economic forces leading to the high diameter network under criticality pricing and to the small diameter and unequal network under betweenness pricing.

# 9 Financial Contagion

## 9.1 Introduction

The financial crisis of 2007–2008 drew attention to the great interconnectedness of the global financial system. The collapse of a large American financial services firm, Lehman Brothers, set off a financial contagion that spread across the US and in due course had profound effects on financial markets across the world. This contagion poses a number of questions: What is the nature of interconnectedness among financial institutions? How do these interconnections transmit shocks? Do more connections amplify or dampen shocks to individual institutions? Does the structure of the network matter? If so, what are the structural features of networks that are relevant for setting policy? The aim of this chapter is to develop a theoretical framework that can help us reason about these issues.

Section 9.2 sets the stage by describing some empirical features of the financial sector, which consists of banks and institutions spanning a wide range of activities: mortgages, insurance, supply credit, and short-term bank liquidity. The diversity of activities makes the network of financial linkages potentially very complex.

Section 9.3 begins the theoretical study by introducing the basic interlinkage of obligations among financial institutions and their ties with outsiders. We argue that the valuation/net worth of a bank depends on the valuations of other banks, which in turn depend on the valuation of the original bank. This circularity in valuation is a fundamental feature of financial networks. Thus the health of a financial system depends on the fundamentals and the network structure, but beliefs/expectations about valuations also play an important role.

Section 9.4 presents a simple model of liquidity shocks that is used to motivate the formation of interbank linkages. The analysis of this model highlights a fundamental trade-off in financial networks: linkages reduce the exposure of individual banks to idiosyncratic shocks, at the same time, by exposing a bank to the risks of other banks, they open a path for the spread of defaults across institutions.

Section 9.5 presents a general setting with an arbitrary number of financial institutions and a rich class of linkages that include cross-ownerships as well as borrowing and lending relations. The study of this model shows that both the nature of the link and the architecture of the network play a role in shaping financial contagion. A key insight concerns the relation between the size of shocks and the nature of optimal networks. Linkages provide protection against individual shocks, and thereby make the system more resilient, but large shocks create the possibility of systemic failure. Thus interlinkages are a double edged sword.

Section 9.6 takes up the issue of network complexity and opacity. The spread of a shock of a bank onto other banks depends on the connections which that bank has and the structure of the network. However, this structure is often very poorly understood by the participants in the network and outsiders such as policy makers and regulators. We present a model to examine the implications of network opacity on the behavior of banks.

Section 9.7 studies the forces that lead to the formation of core-periphery networks. The conventional view is that institutions establish links with one another as a way of diversifying different types of risk and facilitating intermediation. This model focuses on the intermediation element; banks choose borrowing and lending links strategically in a way that tilts the division of surplus along an intermediation chain in their favor. This strategic behavior pushes investment banks toward forming many links with each other and occupying a core position in the network. The resulting network exhibits higher systemic risk than for a network that maximizes the aggregate surplus.

## 9.2 The Financial Sector: Some Background

This section lays out the broad features of interdependence among financial institutions. We discuss five topics: (1) the globalization in the trade of goods and movement of capital; (2) the growth of market concentration in the financial sector; (3) correlations in portfolios held by leading financial institutions; (4) the core-periphery network connecting financial institutions; and (5) the large costs of default and bankruptcy. Finally, we discuss a number of case studies of financial contagion. The exposition here draws on Jackson (2019), Jackson and Pernoud (2021), and Glasserman and Young (2016).

*Globalization:* World trade grew from just under 20 percent of world gross domestic product (GDP) at the end of World War II to over 60 percent by 2015. This growth in trade was supported and mirrored by a growth in financial interconnectedness. To get a sense of the changes in financial interconnectedness during this time, let us consider a much more recent period. In 2000, 17 percent of equities and 18 percent of bonds around the world were held by foreigners; by 2016, the corresponding numbers were 27 percent for equities and 31 percent for bonds. Similarly, in 2016, more than \$132 trillion out of a total world investment of just over \$300 trillion came from foreigners. This international connectedness is accompanied by a great measure of linkage within the financial sector. Take, for example, the US: Duarte and Eisenbach (2018) estimate that 23 percent of the assets of bank holding companies and 48 percent of their liabilities come from within the US financial system.

*Consolidation:* The financial sector has grown enormously, but market concentration has grown too. To get an impression of these trends, consider the situation in the US: In 1980, there were 14,000 commercial banks, with total assets of $2 trillion. In 2018, there were only 4,700 banks, but they held total assets of $16.5 trillion. We see that the number of banks has dropped to a third of what it was, while the assets have increased by a factor of 8. Thus, in 1990, the five largest banks in the US held 10 percent of total assets; in 2007, they held 35 percent; and in 2015, they held 45 percent of all financial assets. The concentration can be seen as the global level: in 2016, the 10 largest banks in the world held assets worth $26 trillion. To put that in perspective, the combined GDP of the US and China in that year was $29 trillion, and the world GDP was $75 trillion.

*Complexity:* An important feature of the financial sector over time is a great expansion in the range of instruments available. Consider the case of mortgages. A hundred years ago, a mortgage was typically issued by a bank, and often that was the sole intermediary between that borrower and the bank's depositors. The bank performed a number of functions: it took in deposits, it assessed the worthiness of loans, and it monitored the loans and the payments of the borrowers.

Over time, the number of parties involved in mortgages has grown: a mortgage may now be issued through a broker, who provides sales and marketing expertise. The brokers work with a large number of firms that do the actual issuing of the mortgages. They specialize in documenting the circumstances of the borrowers and the properties involved, and then they often resell the mortgages. Mortgages are typically purchased and held en masse by entities that collect payments and then resell these payments in various tranches (packages of mortgages grouped by risks and maturities) in the form of mortgage-backed securities. The securities are in turn bought by banks (and other investment companies), which then package them together in portfolios, either to pay interest to their depositors or offer them as investment funds to private investors. Along the way, various parties insure and hedge their risks via a variety of derivatives and insurance contracts that are sold by entirely different firms.

*Core-Periphery Structures:* The interbank lending networks have a core-periphery structure: a core of very large national/international banks and a periphery of smaller (but often still large) regional banks. The core banks are highly interconnected, whereas the rest of the network is usually very sparse (a regional bank interacts with a few of the core banks). These empirical studies motivate the study of the economic forces that give rise to core-periphery networks.

*Correlations:* In the financial crisis of 2008, many financial institutions were heavily exposed to the same mortgage and subprime mortgage markets and had extensive exposure to each other at the same time. Since then, several studies have examined this sort of correlation explicitly. For instance, German banks are more likely to lend to banks with portfolios similar to their own: going from the 25th to 75th percentile of similarity in portfolios between two banks increases their lending to each other by 31 percent. There is also a similar pattern when we look at the extensive margin in terms of the probability that two banks lend to each other (for a discussion of these and other relationships among financial institutions, see Elliott, Georg, and Hazell [2020]).

*Bankruptcy Costs:* The costs of default or bankruptcy are very large (see James, 1991). Consider the Lehman Brothers default. There were initially $1.2 trillion of claims made by creditors. The courts ultimately allowed only $362 billion of that amount to be recognized. These creditors received 28 percent of their claims. This is probably an extreme example, but it does help to bring out the fact that bankruptcy costs can be very large. More generally, bankruptcy recovery rates are on average under 60 percent, suggesting that over 40 percent of the value of a company is lost in the process. These bankruptcy costs are due to legal fees and the drop in asset value. The magnitude of these bankruptcy costs is therefore a first-order factor in understanding the economic costs of contagion.

### 9.2.1 The Anatomy of a Crisis

Here, we discuss the collapse of Lehman Brothers, drawing on Wiggins, Piontek, and Metrick (2019) and Wiggins and Metrick (2019). At the time of its collapse on September 15, 2008, Lehman was the fourth-largest financial institution in the US. It sought chapter 11 protection, initiating the largest bankruptcy in American history. At the point of its bankruptcy, Lehman had $639 billion in assets and $613 billion in liabilities. Lehman's collapse turned out to be a seminal event in the financial crisis of 2008, that began in the American subprime mortgage industry in 2007, spread to the credit markets, and then burned through the world's financial markets. Estimates of the cost to the American economy based on lost output range from a few trillion dollars to over $10 trillion. The global costs were even greater. These large losses arose despite the unprecedented efforts of several major American institutions (like the Federal Reserve, the US Treasury, the Federal Deposit Insurance Corporation), as well as the central banks of many of the world's largest economies. What were the pathways that led from the collapse of one institution to a global economic crisis whose consequences are still being felt more than a decade later?

Let us begin with the immediate cause of Lehman's demise: exposure to the subprime mortgage and real estate markets in the US. When these markets began to slow in 2007, they sparked a retraction in the shadow banking system for short-term loans as concerns about unknown exposure to securitized subprime mortgages spread to other types of assets. Lehman, like many of the largest investment banks, relied on these short-term markets to raise billions of dollars each day. In 2008, it had assets of $680 billion, supported by a mere $22.5 billion of equity. Thus a 5 percent fall in real estate value could wipe out all of its capital. When the other institutions refused to roll over its loans, Lehman was doomed.

Turning now to the spread of the default, it is important to set out the broader economic context. Through the late 1990s and in 2000–2005, there were two large-scale forces at work: on the one hand, there was a funding glut due to large surpluses from oil-rich countries; and on the other hand, the US government had a policy encouraging home ownership. This was accompanied by generous funding through two federal government agencies, Fannie Mae and Freddie Mac, which supported mortgages worth $5 trillion. Housing and mortgages were felt to constitute a very safe market. Private banks borrowed and lent heavily in the housing market. By 2005, loans were increasingly being made to individuals and households with little creditworthiness. Lehman had underwritten very large mortgage loans and borrowed vast amounts of money to fund these loans. Many other major institutions had invested large amounts in Lehman as well.

By 2005–2006, as borrowers defaulted on their housing loans, there were foreclosures, which in turn led to housing sales and lower housing prices. By early 2007, several home mortgage lenders filed for bankruptcy protection, and on July 31, 2007, Bear Stearns halted all redemptions and liquidated two of its mortgage funds. By August 2007, lenders were becoming increasingly reluctant to lend, fearing that borrowers were holding subprime mortgages that could become illiquid and be marked down to market:

> Although subprime mortgages constituted only a small fraction of the portfolios of most structured credit vehicles, cautious lenders pulled back from even those that likely had no exposure to subprime mortgages. The resulting pressure in turn transmitted to major banks that had sponsored or provided funding guarantees to vehicles. (Bernanke, 2010, p. 3).

Beginning in early 2008, Lehman faced increasing questions about the value of its real estate assets and increased difficulty in trying to sell those assets. Lehman was increasingly forced to deliver nonreal-estate assets to secure funding. By March 2008, after the near-collapse of Bear Stearns, there was a fear that Lehman would fall. This is indeed what happened: it filed for bankruptcy on September 15, 2008.

In the next few months, 22 Lehman affiliates around the world were taken into bankruptcy and had their accounts frozen. The fire sales of assets and the unwinding of Lehman's large stock of derivatives quickly escalated. As Lehman's counterparts began to take account of their exposures, they recorded very large potential losses. In September 2008 alone, a number of major international banks and institutions had to be saved by their respective governments: Bradford and Bingley in the UK, Fortis in the Netherlands, Glitnir in Iceland, and the entire financial sector in Ireland. Although Lehman was the only major international financial institution to actually collapse, 15 to 18 other major institutions worldwide were saved from that fate through very large government support.

Another important aspect of the Lehman Brothers collapse relates to the role of regulatory agencies:

> So the agencies were concerned. They gathered information. They monitored. But no agency regulated . . .
>
> The SEC knew that Lehman was reporting sums in its reported liquidity pool that the SEC did not believe were in fact liquid; the SEC knew that Lehman was exceeding its risk control limits; and the

SEC should have known that Lehman was manipulating its balance sheet to make its leverage appear better than it was. Yet even in the face of actual knowledge of critical shortcomings, and after Bear Stearns' near collapse in March 2008 following a liquidity crisis, the SEC did not take decisive action.

Statement by Anton R. Valukas, examiner, Lehman Brothers bankruptcy, before the Committee on Financial Services of the US House of Representatives regarding "Public Policy Issues Raised by the Report of the Lehman Bankruptcy Examiner." (April 20, 2010)

The Lehman collapse and its aftermath illustrate the many ways in which financial contagion can occur. These include a direct loss imposed on the Federal Reserve Primary Fund, fears about the quality of all money funds (a form of information contagion), a run on funding as creditors pulled back lending, and potential fire sales. Network opacity heightened these pressures: a major concern throughout the evolving crisis was that "there was no way to know who would be owed how much and when payments would have to be made — information that would be critically important to analyze the possible impact of a Lehman bankruptcy on derivatives counter-parties and the financial markets" (Government, 2011, p. 329).

Let us now summarize a few key points from the discussion of this case. Financial networks contain very large banks and financial institutions throughout the world. The linkages among these institutions spread across a wide range of entities: mortgages, insurance, supply credit, and short-term bank liquidity. The wide range of these items makes the network of financial linkages as a whole potentially very complex. Moreover, the linkages between banks are not public knowledge; they are only known to these institutions. This makes the network very opaque, and it is often very difficult to work through the implications of any shock.

## 9.3 Building Blocks of Financial Networks

A financial network consists of nodes that are financial institutions and links that represent various types of obligations between them. We start by describing these two elements of such a network. The exposition draws on Glasserman and Young (2016).

It is helpful to start with the financial institutions; for simplicity, they will be referred to as "banks" in what follows. Figure 9.1 presents a stylized balance sheet of a bank. Let a bank be denoted by $i$. The bank has two types of assets—outside and in-network. Outside assets are claims on nonfinancial entities, such as mortgages and commercial loans. In-network assets are claims on other banks; they include interbank loans and exposures through derivatives. We denote by $\bar{p}_{ki}$ the obligation of bank $k$ to bank $i$. The bank's liabilities include obligations to nonfinancial institutions such as depositors and obligations $\bar{p}_{ij}$ to other banks, $j$. The difference between the bank's assets and liabilities yields its net worth, $e_i$.

A key function of the bank is to facilitate payments among sellers, buyers, and other banks. These payments are central to the large value payment systems, such as CHAPS in the UK, FEDWIRE in the US and TARGET2 in Europe. Another key function is the allocation of capital by intermediating between lenders and borrowers/investors. This function calls

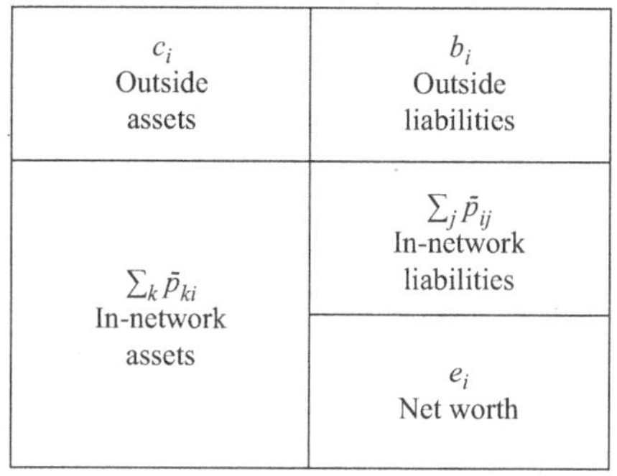


**Figure 9.1**
Balance sheet of a bank.

for a sequence of relationships between depositors and borrowers/investors. In carrying out this function, the bank invests the outside liabilities $b_i$ in outside assets $c_i$. This gives rise to liquidity exposures for the bank: to mediate between lenders that prefer short maturities and borrowers that prefer longer maturities, the bank is led to engage in interbank borrowing and lending. This motivation for interbank links will be central to our study of financial contagion in section 9.4.

A third important function is to mediate among parties that have different appetites for risk-taking: the bank provides risk transfer from agents seeking to reduce risk to others willing to bear greater risk. Banks also help corporations manage their exposure to exchange rates, interest rates, and commodity prices through derivatives and other contracts; the banks hedge this risk by trading with other banks.

Let us now discuss briefly how a network can act as a mechanism for the transmission of shocks from one bank to another. Suppose that the outside assets of bank $i$ fall (say, due to a fall in the value of real estate). A drop in $c_i$ is initially absorbed by the bank's net worth, $e_i$. But if the shock is sufficiently large, the net worth is wiped out, the bank is unable to fully repay its liabilities, and it defaults. Its actual payment, $p_{ij}$, to bank $j$ will be less than its promised payment, $\bar{p}_{ij}$ . If the payment shortfall is sufficiently large, the assets of bank $j$ may not cover its liabilities, and it may also default. This in turn could lead to defaults by creditors of bank $j$. In this way, an asset shock to bank $i$ can spread through linkages from one bank to another.

Figure 9.1 also suggests another important route through which bank balance sheets may interact: common exposure to outside assets. If a bank declares a fall in its mortgage assets, this reveals information to other banks that hold similar assets. This could give rise to information contagion. This form of contagion is amplified if the banks in question also have debt linkages.

So far, we have considered the downward flow of a shock from an originating bank to its creditors. However, financial linkages often feed back: bank $i$ may borrow from bank

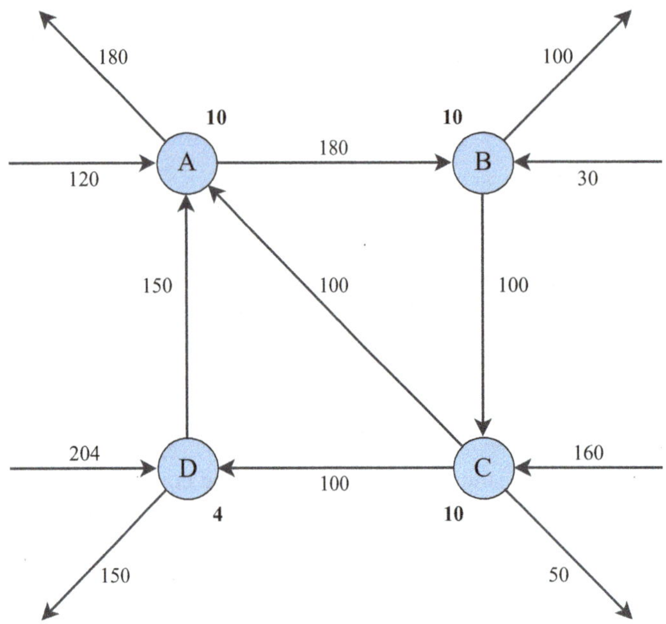


**Figure 9.2**
Financial network showing payments.

*j*, which may in turn borrow from bank *i*. Thus a shock on bank *i* may rebound on itself via a cycle of linkages. Let us consider a numerical example to appreciate the role of such financial cycles.

This example is based on the network presented in figure 9.2. The number on each directed edge represents a payment obligation, and each node's net worth is shown in bold. So bank C is owed 160 by mortgage holders, and it owes 50 to a set of depositors. In addition, C is owed 100 by bank B, and it owes 100 apiece to banks A and D. The difference between bank C's assets $(160 + 100)$ and its liabilities $(50 + 100 + 100)$ leave it with a net worth of 10.

Suppose that the economy is hit by a shock that causes some households to default on their payments to bank C: instead of the promised 160, they pay only 40. Then C defaults because its assets total $100 + 40 = 140$, whereas it owes 50 to the outside sector and 200 to other banks. Suppose that C's remaining assets are paid pro rata to C's creditors. Let us consider the spillover effects of this default.

To begin, suppose that the value of C's assets is 140. Then the pro rata rule implies that C pays $(140/250) \times 100 = 56$ to D, 56 to A, and 28 to the outside depositors. Now D has assets worth $204 + 56 = 260$ and debts totaling 300, so D is in default. The pro rata rule implies that D pays 130 to A and 130 to its outside depositors. At this stage, A's assets have an interim value of $120 + 130 + 56 = 306$, whereas its nominal obligations come to 360.

Thus, A defaults, and the pro rata rule implies that it pays half of its assets (namely 153) to B and an equal amount to outside depositors.

At this juncture, B's assets are worth $153 + 30 = 183$, whereas its obligations total 200. Therefore, B defaults, and the pro rata rule implies that it pays 91.5 to C and 91.5 to outside depositors. Therefore the value of 140 assigned to C's assets was incorrect.

That value reflected the initial outside shock of 40, but it assumed a full repayment of 100 from bank B. In fact, B is able to pay at most 91.5, so C's assets are worth at most 131.5, and the cycle must be repeated.

### 9.3.1 Keeping Accounts

We now present a general approach to computing the correct profile of payments between banks. This approach is taken from Eisenberg and Noe (2001), and it starts with a network of obligations. The goal is to study how shocks to particular institutions or assets propagate through a network.

Following the previous discussion, the model has four key ingredients: (1) a set of $n$ nodes $N = \{1, 2, \ldots, n\}$ representing various financial entities, such as banks, broker-dealers, and insurance companies; (2) an $n \times n$ liabilities matrix $\bar{P} = [\bar{p}_{ij}]$, where $\bar{p}_{ij} \geq 0$, represents the payment due from node i to node j at the end of the current period and $p_{ii} = 0$ for every $i$; (3) vector $c = (c_1, c_2, \ldots, c_n)$, where $c_i \geq 0$, represents the total payments due from nonfinancial entities to node i; and (4) vector $b = (b_1, b_2, \ldots, b_n)$, where $b_i \geq 0$ represents the total payments due from node $i$ to nonfinancial entities. The numbers $c_i$ and $b_i$ will be called $i$'s outside assets and outside liabilities, respectively.

The asset side of node $i$'s balance sheet is given by $c_i + \sum_{j \neq i} \bar{p}_{ji}$, while the liability side is given by $\bar{p}_i = b_i + \sum_{j \neq i} \bar{p}_{ij}$. The node's net worth is

$$e_i = c_i + \sum_{j \neq i} \bar{p}_{ji} - \bar{p}_i \tag{9.1}$$

Let us assume that initially, the net worth of every node is strictly positive.

Consider a shock given by an $n$-vector $x = (x_1, x_2, \ldots x_n)$, where $0 \leq x_i \leq c_i$ for $1 \leq i \leq n$. The direct effect of the shock $x$ is to reduce the net worth of each node $i$ to the value:

$$e_i(x) = c_i - x_i + \sum_{j \neq i} \bar{p}_{ji} - \bar{p}_i. \tag{9.2}$$

If the net worth $e_i(x)$ is negative, node $i$ defaults. We shall assume that all debt obligations have equal priority and in case of default, the assets are distributed to the creditors in proportion to the nominal amounts they are owed. (The equity holders are wiped out, since their claim is on the firm's net worth, provided that the latter is positive, which it obviously is not.) The problem is to determine a consistent set of payments conditional on the initial shock. Recall that we encountered this problem in our illustration of a default cascade based on figure 9.3.

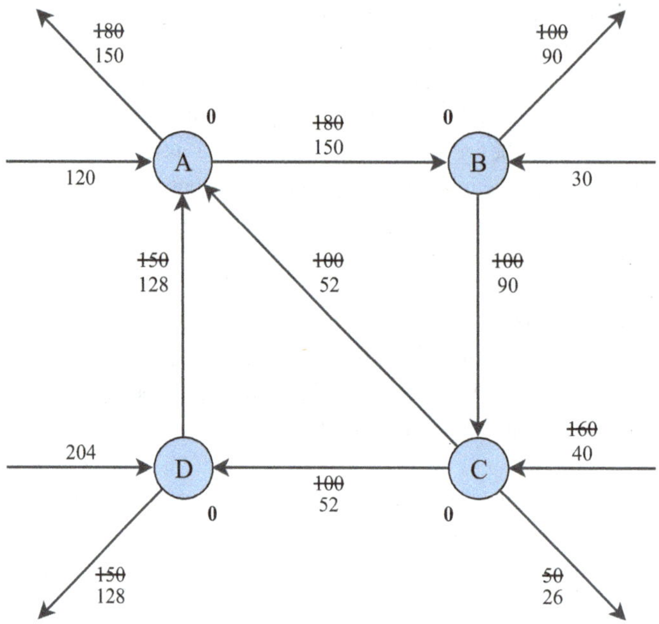


**Figure 9.3**
Eisenberg-Noe method.

To this end, let us define the relative liabilities matrix $A = (a_{ij})$ to be the $n \times n$ matrix, with the following entries:

$$a_{ij} = \bar{p}_{ij}/\bar{p}_i \text{ if } \bar{p}_i > 0 \tag{9.3}$$

$$a_{ij} = 0 \text{ if } \bar{p}_i = 0. \tag{9.4}$$

The term $a_{ij}$ represents the proportion that $i$'s obligations to node $j$ represent of its total liabilities to all other nodes and to the external sector. Suppose that the outside assets suffer a shock, $x$. We shall say that node $i$ suffers a direct default if $x_i > e_i = c_i + \sum_{j \neq i} \bar{p}_{ji} - \bar{p}_i$. The pro rata allocation rule implies that $i$'s payments are proportional to the various claims against $i$'s assets. The complication is that the value of $i$'s assets depends on the payments made by others to $i$. Thus $i$'s payment to $j$ (conditional on $x$) satisfies

$$p_{ij}(x) \leq a_{ij} \left( c_i - x_i + \sum_{k \neq i} p_{ki}(x) \right), \tag{9.5}$$

where $\sum_{k \neq i} p_{ki}(x)$ is the sum of the payments to $i$ from the other nodes in the system. In particular, payment $p_{ki}(x)$ will be less than $\bar{p}_{ki}$ if node $k$ is also in default. We shall say that payments $p_{ij}(x)$ are consistent if, for all $i$ and $j$,

$$p_{ij}(x) = \bar{p}_{ij} \wedge a_{ij}\left(c_i - x_i + \sum_{k \neq i} p_{ki}(x)\right). \tag{9.6}$$

We note here that the symbol $a \wedge b$ indicates the largest number smaller than $a$ and $b$.

This condition can be expressed in a more compact form as follows. Let $p_i(x)$ denote the total payment from $i$ to all other nodes in the financial system plus its payments to the outside sector. Let $p(x) = (p_1(x), p_2(x), \ldots p_n(x))$ be the corresponding payments vector. These payments are consistent if they are feasible. In other words, for every $i$,

$$p_i(x) = \bar{p}_i \wedge \left(c_i - x_i + \sum_j a_{ji} p_j(x)\right). \tag{9.7}$$

Any vector $p(x) \in R^n_+$ satisfying equation (9.7) is called a "clearing vector." We will show next that there is a clearing vector for any shock realization $x$.

For a given shock realization $x$, let $p = p(x)$ and define the mapping $\phi : R^n_+ \to R^n_+$ as follows:

$$\forall i, \phi_i(p) = \bar{p}_i \wedge \left(c_i - x_i + \sum_j p_j a_{ji}\right). \tag{9.8}$$

Starting with $p_0 = \bar{p}$, let

$$p_1 = \phi(p_0), p_2 = \phi(p_1), \ldots \tag{9.9}$$

Observe that this algorithm yields a monotone decreasing sequence $p_0 \geq p_1 \geq p_2 \ldots$ Since the sequence is bounded below by the zero vector, it must converge. Let limit $p' = p'(x)$. Since $\phi$ is continuous, $p'$ satisfies equation (9.7); hence, it is a clearing vector.

We will now show that the net equity of the clearing vector is unique. This step of the argument requires some additional mathematical notation.

We start with a partially ordered set, $\{\mathcal{L}, \geq\}$.

For $S \subseteq \mathcal{L}$, let $\wedge S$ denote the greatest lower bound; that is, $\hat{s} \in \mathcal{L}$, such that (i) $\hat{s} \leq s$ for all $s \in S$ and (ii) $\hat{s} \geq s'$ for all other lower bounds $s' \in \mathcal{L}$. Similarly, let $\vee S$ denote the least upper bound; that is, $\tilde{s} \in \mathcal{L}$, such that (i) $\tilde{s} \geq s$ for all $s \in S$ and (ii) $\tilde{s} \leq s'$ for all other upper bounds $s' \in \mathcal{L}$. $(\mathcal{L}, \geq)$ is a complete lattice if and only if for every $S \subseteq \mathcal{L}$, (i) $\wedge S \in \mathcal{L}$ and (ii) $\vee S \in \mathcal{L}$.

In this setting, note that $\mathcal{L} := \prod_i [0, \bar{p}_i]$ and (ii) a partial order $\geq$ is given by

$$p \geq p' \text{ if and only if } p_i \geq p'_i \text{ for all } i. \tag{9.10}$$

Thus, for $S \subseteq \prod_i [0, \bar{p}_i]$,

$$(\wedge S)_i = \min_{s_i : s \in S} s_i \tag{9.11}$$

$$(\vee S)_i = \max_{s_i : s \in S} s_i. \tag{9.12}$$

It is straightforward to check that for any $S \subseteq \mathcal{L}$, (i) $\wedge S \in \mathcal{L}$ and (ii) $\vee S \in \mathcal{L}$. Thus $(\mathcal{L}, \geq)$ is a complete lattice. Moreover, the mapping $\Phi(p): \mathcal{L} \to \mathcal{L}$ is order preserving: if $p \geq p'$, then $\Phi(p) \geq \Phi(p')$ because all organizations are repaid more given $p$. Functions $\Phi$ with this property are called "isotone."

The Tarski fixed-point theorem (Tarski [1955]) tells us that if a partially ordered set $(\mathcal{L}, \geq)$ is a complete lattice and $\Phi: \mathcal{L} \to \mathcal{L}$ is isotone, then letting $\mathcal{P}$ be the set of fixed points of $\Phi$, $\mathcal{P}$ is nonempty and $(\mathcal{P}, \geq)$ is a lattice.

Equipped with this result, we can show that the net equity is unique. Suppose that there are two clearing vectors, $p$ and $p'$. These two vectors constitute fixed points of $\Phi$. As the set of fixed points is a lattice, it follows that (i) $\hat{p} := p \wedge p'$ is a fixed point and (ii) $\tilde{p} := p \vee p'$ is a fixed point as well.

Moreover, note that $\tilde{p}_i \geq \hat{p}_i$ for all $i$, and $\tilde{p}_i > \hat{p}_i$ for some $i$. Thus more banks fail and all banks have weakly lower equity value under $\hat{p}_i$, which means that total equity must be strictly smaller. The total equity under $\hat{p}$ is given by

$$\sum_i \sum_j [\Pi_{ij}\hat{p}_j + e_i - \hat{p}_i] = \sum_i e_i. \tag{9.13}$$

It is easy to see that the sum of net equity under $\tilde{p}$ is also equal to $\sum_i e_i$. This is a contradiction that completes the argument for the uniqueness of net equity. ■

Let us now the summarize what we have learned in this section. We have described the basic features of interlinkages of obligations between banks and the relations to outside players. The valuation/net worth of a bank depends on the valuations of other banks, which in turn depend on the valuation of the original bank. This circularity in valuations is a fundamental feature of financial networks and shows that the health of a financial system depends on the fundamentals, but beliefs/expectations also play an important role.

## 9.4 Liquidity Shocks and Financial Contagion

The discussions in section 9.2 have drawn attention to the role that interconnections among banks played in spreading the collapse of Lehman Brothers. This section presents a simple model of liquidity shocks and how financial linkages can help overcome them. But we will also see how these linkages create a pathway through which shocks on a single bank or financial institution can spread to other banks. Our discussion will draw attention to the role of the network structure in shaping this trade-off. The model discussed here is taken from Allen and Gale (2000).

Depositors have different timings for liquidity. Longer-term investments yield larger returns. The uncertainty in liquidity timing and the differential returns between short- and long-term investments create the potential for a mismatch between liquidity demand and investment returns. If liquidity shocks are negatively correlated then banks can make deposits in each other to tide over them. These linkages give rise to networks that have different levels of robustness to shocks.

This is a three-period model, where the time periods are denoted by $t = 0, 1, 2$. There is a single consumption good, which can be invested for future use. The consumer is either type 1 or type 2. Type 1 values only period 1 consumption, while type 2 values only period 2 consumption. The type is revealed at period $t = 1$. All consumers are ex ante identical, so there is a probability of $\omega$ that consumers need liquidity in period $t = 1$ and a probability of $1 - \omega$ that they need liquidity in period $t = 2$. There are two assets: short asset, which invested for one period yields 1; and long asset, which yields $r < 1$ after one period and $R > 1$ after two periods. There are four regions A, B, C, and D. In each region, there is a continuum of consumers. Regions are identical in their compositions of different types of consumers.

Let $c_1$ be the consumption for a period 1 consumer and $c_2$ the consumption of period 2 consumer. The utility of consumers depends on consumption in periods 1 and 2 and is given by $U(c_1, c_2) = u(c_1)$ if type 1 and $U(c_1, c_2) = u(c_2)$ if type 2. The utility function $u(.)$ is increasing and strictly concave (risk aversion). There are two states of nature: $S_1$ and $S_2$. In state $S_1$, regions A and C have a large fraction of period 1 consumers, $\omega_H$, and regions B and D have a low fraction of type 1, $\omega_L$. The opposite is true in state $S_2$. The two states are equally likely. Thus aggregate demand for liquidity is constant across states and is given by $2\omega_H + 2\omega_L$.

We now turn to the optimal consumption paths for consumers. First, note that all consumers in all regions are identical. As consumer preferences are concave, a utilitarian planner that seeks to maximize the sum of the utilities must assign the same ex ante utility to all individuals in all regions. As all banks are identical, they too must make the same investments. Let a bank allocate (per capita) $x$ to the long asset and (per capita) $y$ to the short asset. The planner chooses $x$ and $y$ such as $x + y \leq 1$, with a view to maximizing the expected utility of consumers. As the planner's choice can be implemented in a competitive equilibrium among the banks, we shall assume that the banks do likewise.

We note here an important implication of the structure of uncertainty: in both states 1 and 2, total consumption must be equal. In other words, there is no aggregate uncertainty. So the optimal plan is to allocate returns of $x$ to cover type 2 consumers and allocate returns of $y$ to cover type 1 consumers. Define this idea as follows:

$$\gamma = (\omega_H + \omega_L)/2, \quad \gamma c_1 = y, \quad (1 - \gamma)c_2 = Rx. \tag{9.14}$$

The planner maximizes $\gamma u(c_1) + (1 - \gamma)u(c_2)$. Let us substitute for $c_1$ and $c_2$ from equation (9.14). It follows that in the social optimum, the marginal utilities must be equal:

$$u'(c_1) = Ru'(c_2). \tag{9.15}$$

Since $R > 1$, $c_1 < c_2$. Type 2 consumers therefore have no incentive to pretend to be type 1 consumers and withdraw their deposits in period 1.

Observe that this optimal investment strategy provides a rationale for interbank deposits. A bank in region A cannot implement this strategy on its own (i.e., in isolation), as it will not be able to meet the liquidity demands of its depositors in state 1. On the other hand, a bank in region A and another in region B can exchange deposits and, depending on the state, can then liquidate their deposits and thereby meet the high liquidity needs. We now describe three interbank deposit networks, each of which allows the optimal allocation to be feasible: complete, cycle, and two disconnected pairs.

### 9.4.1 The Role of Networks

A *complete* network is one in which each region holds deposits in all other regions. The size of the deposit is $z=(\omega_H-\gamma)/2$ (see figure 9.4). A representative bank in a region will invest $(x,y)$, as in the social optimum (note that deposits cancel each other out, so the allocation remains feasible at time $t=0$). In period $t=1$, with probability 1/2, we are in state $S_1$: region A has a high demand for liquidity and liquidates all its deposits in other regions. Region C does likewise. Regions B and D, however, will retain their deposits. So the net inflow of liquidity into region A is given by $(\omega_H-\gamma)c_1$, and this is exactly what is required to cover the liquidity demand in state $S_1$:

$$(\omega_H-\gamma)c_1+\gamma c_1=\omega_H c_1. \tag{9.16}$$

Simplifying, we get $\gamma c_1=y$, the first best allocation requirement. So deposits of regions B and D remain in place, and in period $t=2$, they are liquidated to pay $1-\omega_L$ period 2 consumers the promised $c_2$.

A *cycle network* is one in which each region holds deposits in only one other region. The size of the deposit is given by $z=(\omega_H-\gamma)$ (see figure 9.4). The representative bank in a region will invest $(x,y)$, as in the social optimum. In period $t=1$, with probability 1/2, we are in state $S_1$: region A has a high demand for liquidity and liquidates all its deposits in region B. Region C does likewise in region D. Regions B and D retain their deposits. The net inflow of liquidity into region A is given by $(\omega_H-\gamma)c_1$: this is exactly what is required to cover the liquidity demand in state $S_1$:

$$\omega_H c_1=\gamma c_1+(\omega_H-\gamma)c_1. \tag{9.17}$$

The situation is similar for region C. Deposits of regions B and D remain in place, and in period $t=2$, they will be liquidated to pay $1-\omega_L$ period 2 consumers the promised $c_2$. The liquidity balance for region A in period $t=2$ is $[(1-\omega_H)+(\omega_H-\gamma)]c_2=Rx$, and this simplifies to $(1-\gamma)c_2=Rx$, which is prescribed by the social optimum.

A *disconnected network* is one in which pairs of regions hold deposits in each other. The size of the deposit is $z=(\omega_H-\gamma)$ (see figure 9.4). The representative bank in a region will invest $(x,y)$, as in the social optimum. In period $t=1$, with probability 1/2, we are in state $S_1$: region A has a high demand for liquidity and liquidates all its deposits in region B. Region B retains deposits in region A. Region C liquidates its deposits in region D, while

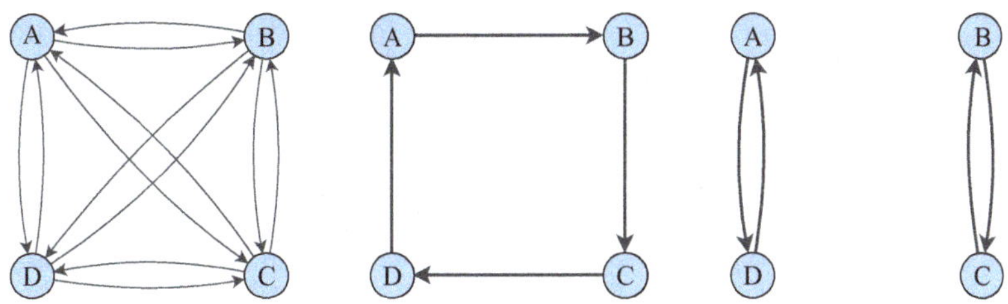


**Figure 9.4**
Interbank networks: (a) complete; (b) cycle; (c) disconnected pairs.

region D retains them in region C. So the net inflow of liquidity into region A is given by $(\omega_H - \gamma)c_1$, and this is exactly what is required to cover the liquidity demand in state $S_1$:

$$\gamma c_1 + (\omega_H - \gamma)c_1 = \omega_H c_1. \tag{9.18}$$

Simplifying equation (9.18), we get $\gamma c_1 = y$, the first best allocation requirement. The situation is similar for region C. So deposits of regions B and D remain in place, and in period $t = 2$, they will be liquidated to pay $\omega_H$ period 2 consumers the promised $c_2$.

We have shown how interbank deposits help the system attain the first best allocation (something that is unattainable under autarchy). Now we show how these linkages can act as a conduit for the spread of shocks and lead to the breakdown of the system as a whole. To study financial contagion in its simplest form, let us suppose that there is an *unanticipated* shock to the system that leads to excess aggregate liquidity. We will show how the shock can spread across from one region and lead to a systems breakdown.

### 9.4.2 Shocks and Robustness

Let there be a new state $S$ in addition to states $S_1$ and $S_2$. This state has $\gamma + \epsilon$ type 1 individuals for region A (with $\epsilon > 0$) and $\gamma$ type 1 consumers in all regions. In other words, there is excess aggregate liquidity demand in state $S$.

Suppose that we arrive at state $S$: The bank in region A cannot pay off its type 1 consumers by using its own deposits, $y$: this is because from the first best allocation, $\gamma c_1 = y$. What can such a bank do? It can liquidate its deposits in other regions and/or it can liquidate its long assets. What is the optimal order in which to liquidate assets?

Observe that the cost of liquidating its own short assets is 1: they yield 1 now, and upon reinvestment, they will also yield 1 in the next period. Liquidation of deposits in another bank leads to a current payoff of $c_1$ and a loss of $c_2$ in the next period. Finally, if it liquidates its own long asset, then it gives up R in return for $r$. To study the spread of shocks, we will suppose that

$$\frac{R}{r} > \frac{c_2}{c_1}. \tag{9.19}$$

This condition implies a pecking order for liquidation, starting with own short assets, then deposits in other banks, and finally own long assets. We now study how the liquidation of the bank in region A plays out in the various networks.

Let us start with the cycle. Recall that each bank holds an $(x, y)$ initial allocation and promises to pay $c_1$ to type 1 consumers and $c_2$ to type 2 consumers. To make this feasible, a bank in each region holds $[\omega_H - \gamma]$ deposits in one other region (so banks in region A hold deposits in region B, B in region C, C in D and D in A, and so forth). Next, consider the effects of state $S$ as mediated through the network. As D holds deposits in region A, the focus is on the effects on D and via D on other regions.

At date 1, a bank is said to be *solvent* if it can meet demands from consumers and other banks from its short assets and deposits on other banks, *insolvent* if it needs to liquidate some of its long-term assets, and *bankrupt* if even the long-term assets do not suffice to cover all the demands in period 1.

The value of a deposit in the bank in region A, at date 1, is $c_1$ if the bank is not bankrupt, and it is $q^A$ if it is bankrupt. Define $q^A$ as the value under bankruptcy. This liquidation value equates the value of assets, $y + rx + zq^B$, and liabilities, $(1+z)q^A$, and is given by

$$q^A = \frac{y + rx + zq^B}{1+z}. \tag{9.20}$$

If the bank in region B is not bankrupt, then $q^B = c_1$ and we can compute $q^A$ directly; if it is, then we must work out $q^B$, which may depend on the value of $q^C$ and so forth. If a bank cannot cover its liquidity needs from its short assets and deposits, it liquidates some of its long assets. This is possible without a *run*, so long as type 2 consumers are assured of a return of $c_1$. In other words, a bank must keep at least $[1 - \omega_H]c_1/R$ units in long-term assets. This yields a *buffer* that is given by

$$b(\omega) = r\left[x - \frac{(1-\omega_H)c_1}{R}\right]. \tag{9.21}$$

Bankruptcy occurs when extra liquidity required by region A exceeds the buffer:

$$\epsilon c_1 > b(\omega). \tag{9.22}$$

Bankruptcy in region A in turn means that the assets of the bank in region A are worth $q^A < c_1$ at date 1. Deposits of region D in region A now entail a loss of $(c_1 - q^A)z$. This creates a liquidity shortage in region D. What is the magnitude of the shortage and its systemic implications? Observe that $q^A$ is increasing with the value of deposits of banks in region $B$. So the maximum value of assets of bank in region A is given by

$$\bar{q}^A = \frac{y + rx + zc_1}{1+z}. \tag{9.23}$$

This in turn means that the minimum loss to the bank in region D is $z(c_1 - \bar{q}^A)$. The bank in region D will be bankrupt if this loss exceeds the buffer $b(\gamma)$:

$$z[c_1 - q^A] > b(\gamma). \tag{9.24}$$

The following result summarizes this discussion.

**Proposition 9.1** *Suppose that equations (9.19), (9.22), and (9.24) hold. Then state S leads to bankruptcy in region A, which spreads through the network and leads to bankruptcy in all regions.*

We have developed all the arguments underlying proposition 9.1 except for the observation that bankruptcy in region D implies an even greater loss in region C deposits. This is because $q^D < q^A$: $q^A$ is computed under the assumption that $q^B = c_1$, while $q^D$ is computed under the assumption that $q^A < c_1$. So if region D bankrupts, then the losses are even greater for region C, which will lead to bankruptcy in that region and subsequently in region B as well.

The network structure can determine the possibility of financial contagion. To illustrate this point, let us now take up the complete network. Recall that the deposits are $[\omega_H - \gamma]/2$ in each region. In state $S$, the bank in region A faces a liquidity demand of $[\gamma + \epsilon]c_1$ and short-term assets yield $y$, so there is a deficit of liquidity. Under equation (9.22), this leads to bankruptcy in region A. The value of the deposit in region A is

$$\tilde{q}^A = \frac{y + rx + \frac{3}{2}zc_1}{1 + \frac{3}{2}z}. \tag{9.25}$$

By definition, $\tilde{q}^A < c_1$, so there is a loss in each of the other regions. The size of this loss is

$$\frac{z}{2}\left[c_1 - \tilde{q}^A\right]. \tag{9.26}$$

This loss may be smaller than the loss in the cycle network since the size of each link is smaller ($z/2 < z$). Thus moving from a cycle network to the denser complete network can avert financial contagion. This suggests that adding linkages reduces contagion.

We now turn to the disconnected network to illustrate that the effects of additional links on financial contagion are nonmonotonic. Recall that in the disconnected network, banks A and D and B and C separately hold deposits in each other. The deposit size is $z = [\omega_H - \gamma]$. Bankruptcy in region A now leads to bankruptcy in region B, but there is no contagion, as there are no links across to banks C and D. The connectivity of the network offers some risk insurance and liquidity smoothing, but also contains the contagion.

Let us now summarize what we have learned with this model. Resilience issues arise out of a tension between the benefits of links and the potential spillovers. The push toward efficient risk sharing necessitates connections between banks, which creates the potential for systemic contagion and widespread collapse. We have examined a very specific type of linkage and looked at very simple networks with four banks/regions. In the next section, we will take up more general networks and other types of connections to further elaborate on the role of financial linkages in shaping contagion.

## 9.5 Financial Shocks and Optimal Networks

The discussion in section 9.2 suggests that the linkages between banks can have bases ranging from debt to equity to common exposure to the same assets. In section 9.4, we studied a setting with four sets of banks with deposit-based links. In this section, building on the Eisenberg-Noe model, we propose a general theoretical framework that accommodates an arbitrary number of financial institutions and allows for ownership links in addition to deposits. The analysis will reveal that it is both the content of the relationship, as well as the topology of the network that will matter for financial contagion. The framework presented here builds on the work of Cabrales, Gottardi, and Vega-Redondo (2017); Elliott, Golub, and Jackson (2014); Glasserman and Young (2015); Acemoglu, Ozdaglar, and Tahbaz-Salehi (2015b), and Acemoglu, Ozdaglar, and Tahbaz-Salehi (2015a). The exposition draws on Cabrales, Gale, and Gottardi (2016).

Let there be $N$ banks. Each bank has liabilities and assets. The liabilities are to external investors and are given by $\ell$. The assets are claims to returns on $N$ projects. The return on a project $i$ is given by $R - s_i$, with $s_i \in [0, R)$. The banks have financial linkages to each other. It is important to observe that the value of the assets of bank $i$, $v_i$, is contingent on the value of bank $v_j$, as they both depend on vector $r$, which describes the realizations of the returns of the $N$ projects (so for each bank $i$, let $r_i = R - s_i$ if a shock hits the return of project $i$, and $R$ otherwise). We will write this relationship as follows (keeping in mind that $v_i$ is contingent on the value of $v_j$):

$$v = f(A; r), \tag{9.27}$$

where $f : R_+^{N\times N} \times R_+^N \to R^N$ and $A$ is an $N \times N$ nonnegative matrix with entry $a_{ij}$. Matrix $A$ describes the pattern of the linkages among the banks. Function $f(.,.)$, captures the effect of linkages on a bank's value. If the value $v_i$ of the assets of firm $i$ is less than the value $\ell$ of its liabilities, the firm defaults. The default of a bank lowers the value of other banks and may trigger further defaults. Thus linkages bring out correlations between the status of banks.

We now turn to interpretations of the nature of linkages.

**Links as equity exchange** There are various types of links that banks maintain with each other. Cabrales, Gottardi, and Vega-Redondo (2017) propose the following interpretation. Bank $i$ initially controls its own project, $i$. The bank exchanges claims to the returns to projects with other banks that constitute its immediate neighbors. The pattern of exchanges at each round is described by matrix $B$, where the elements of row $i$ describe bank $i$'s trades with its immediate neighbors. After $K$ rounds of exchange, we arrive at the linkage matrix $A = B^K$, and $f(A; r) = Ar$. This means that at the end of the exchanges, bank $i$ has access to returns given by $\sum_j a_{ij} r_j$.

In a similar spirit, Elliott, Golub, and Jackson (2014) propose that banks start with full ownership of returns to a project and then exchange equity with each other. Letting $c_{ji}$ denote the fraction of the outstanding equity of firm $i$ sold to firm $j$, and $c_{ii}$ the fraction of returns owned by external investors, we get $c_{ii} = 1 - \sum_{j \neq i} c_{ji}$. This leads a bank to own direct and indirect shares in the returns to various projects that are given by a linear combination of the returns of the underlying projects, with weights given by the matrix

$$A = \hat{C}(1 - C)^{-1}, \tag{9.28}$$

where $\hat{C}$ is the diagonal matrix with entry $\hat{c}_{ii}$, and $C$ is the matrix with entry $c_{ij}$ (and all diagonal terms set equal to 0). Mutual ownership here reflects equity. This means that a bank that has a share in another firm also must bear any losses due to insolvency of that bank. Letting $\beta$ be the loss due to insolvency, we arrive at the following formulation of a bank's valuation:

$$v = f(A; r) = A(r - \beta 1_{v_i < l}), \tag{9.29}$$

where $1_{v_i<\ell}$ denotes the vector of indicator functions taking value 1 if $v_i < \ell$, and 0 otherwise, for $i = 1, \ldots, N$. Observe that $v$ is determined as a fixed point of the function defined in equation (9.29). This is because the level of $v$ determines whether a bank is solvent: if a bank is insolvent, then it has to pay the additional default cost, which affects its valuation. We illustrate this fixed-point feature of valuations as follows: Suppose that $N = 2$, and let the matrix of cross-ownerships be given by

$$A = \begin{bmatrix} 0.7 & 0.3 \\ 0.3 & 0.7 \end{bmatrix}. \tag{9.30}$$

In this example, let $R = 1$ and suppose that $s_i$ takes on value 0 or 0.5; let $\ell = 0.8$ and $\beta = 0.5$. First, consider the case when project 1 yields 1 and project 2 yields 0.5. Then firm 2 defaults, but firm 1 does as well, due to the fraction of default costs it must bear. By contrast, if both projects yield 1, then there are two possible valuations: both firms are solvent or both firms default. In other words, the belief that a firm may default suffices to generate losses in banks' valuation, which triggers a default even when the returns on the underlying projects are adequate to cover liabilities.

This example is extremely simple, but it helps to bring out the self-fulfilling nature of default cascades. Moreover, they are generated by network interdependencies interacting with beliefs. When there are costs associated with bankruptcy, these cascades are not just transfers that fail; the failures trigger real economic costs, and therefore the multiplicity can have large economic consequences. This multiplicity is a fundamental feature of this environment and is a consequence of the default cost: note that if there are no default costs, then we are back in the scenario described in section 9.3: the valuations are unique.

**Links as borrowing and lending relations** Financial linkages between banks often represent borrowing and lending; Glasserman and Young (2015) and Acemoglu, Ozdaglar, and Tahbaz-Salehi (2015b) study debt linkages. Under the debt interpretation, $a_{ij}$ denotes the payments from bank $i$ to bank $j$. The total liabilities of bank $i$ are then given by $\ell_i + \sum_j a_{ij}$. As in the other interpretations, firm $i$ has access to the returns from project $i$, and thus the book value of its assets is $r_i + \sum_{j \neq i} a_{ji}$. The firm remains solvent if the actual value of the assets can cover the liabilities. In other words, the actual payments made by firm $i$ to firm $j$ will thus depend on the value of the assets of its debtors. Therefore, the obligations $A$ create interdependence between the valuations of the banks. The actual valuation $v_i$ of bank $i$ will thus depend on the realizations of projects $r = (r_1, \ldots, r_N)$ and the rules on how the banks settle claims in case of inadequate returns.

Suppose that all claims have equal seniority. Then we can use the methods developed in section 9.3 to solve for clearing vectors and bank valuations. For any vector of realized returns $r$, the final repayment from a bank $i$ is obtained as a solution to the following system:

$$p_i(r)\left(\sum_{j \neq i} a_{ij} + \ell\right) = \left(\sum_{j \neq i} a_{ij} + \ell\right)\left(\sum_{j \neq i} p_j(r) a_{ji} + r_i\right). \tag{9.31}$$

The actual payments made by firm $i$ to firm $j$ are then

$$p_{ij}(r) = p_i(r) a_{ij}, \tag{9.32}$$

where $p_i(r) \in [0, 1]$ and $p_i(r) = 1$ if firm $i$ does not default. Firm $i$ defaults if the actual value of its assets is less than the value of its liabilities:

$$\sum_{j \neq i} p_j(r) + r_i < \sum_{j \neq i} a_{ij} + \ell_i. \tag{9.33}$$

In this setting, we know that there is a unique solution of payments, $p(r)$ (generically). The value of the firms' assets net of their internal liabilities, therefore, is given by

$$v = f(A; r) = r + (A^T - A)p(r). \tag{9.34}$$

### 9.5.1 The Spread of Defaults

We are now ready to consider the issue of financial contagion—the process whereby shocks affecting one bank are transmitted by financial linkages and lead to defaults by other banks. The interest will be on the role of the network of financial linkages in transmitting the initial shock. To develop some basic intuitions, it is convenient to restrict our attention to regular networks where each bank is equally exposed and the pattern of exposure is also the same (i.e., the matrix $A$ is symmetric). We will consider the impact of a shock on bank 1.

We will study the minimum shock on bank 1 needed to ensure that a certain number of banks default. In particular, we will derive this minimal shock $s(k)$ for $k$ defaults as a function of the architecture of the network. Let $r_j$ be the vector with elements $(R - s(k), R, \ldots, R)$, such that $f(A; r_k)$ has $k$ components less than or equal to $\ell$ (at least one of them being equal) and the other $N - k$ strictly greater than $\ell$. In other words, a shock of size $s(k)+\epsilon$ where $\epsilon$ is a small positive number, will lead to the default of $k$ banks. We will study how the values of $s(1),\ldots,s(N)$ vary with the network of linkages as reflected in matrix $A$. It is instructive to focus our attention on two very stylized networks: the complete network, where every bank is equally linked to all other banks; and the one-directional ring network, where every bank is linked to one other bank.

*Cross-ownership Linkages:* Consider the interpretation that financial linkages involve cross-ownerships and sharing the returns of the projects. Under this interpretation, let us define a complete network as one in which every bank owns share $c/N-1$ of every other bank. The residual $1-c$ of a bank is owned by outside investors. Applying the formula $A=\hat{C}(I-C)^{-1}$ yields

$$A^C=\begin{bmatrix} \alpha & \frac{1-\alpha}{N-1} & \cdots & \frac{1-\alpha}{N-1} \\ \frac{1-\alpha}{N-1} & \alpha & \cdots & \frac{1-\alpha}{N-1} \\ \cdots & \cdots & \cdots & \cdots \\ \frac{1-\alpha}{N-1} & \frac{1-\alpha}{N-1} & \cdots & \alpha \end{bmatrix}. \tag{9.35}$$

The complete network reflects common exposure of a set of banks to the same set of assets. Let us define a ring network as one in which every bank $i\geq 2$ owns share $c$ of bank $i-1$ and bank $n$ owns share $c$ of bank 1. We represent this as

$$A^R=\begin{bmatrix} \alpha & \frac{(1-\alpha)^2}{1-\alpha^{N-1}} & \cdots & \frac{(1-\alpha)^2}{1-\alpha^{N-1}}\alpha^{N-2} \\ \frac{(1-\alpha)^2}{1-\alpha^{N-1}}\alpha^{N-2} & \alpha & \cdots & \frac{(1-\alpha)^2}{1-\alpha^{N-1}}\alpha^{N-3} \\ \cdots & \cdots & \cdots & \\ \frac{(1-\alpha)^2}{1-\alpha^{N-1}} & \frac{(1-\alpha)^2}{1-\alpha^{N-1}}\alpha & \cdots & \alpha \end{bmatrix}. \tag{9.36}$$

In the ring network, the distance reflects the difference in exposure to a set of assets.

Figure 9.5 presents a complete network and a ring network. We will assume that every bank $i$ is more exposed to the returns of its own project $i$ than to the returns of each of the other projects. It can be verified that condition $\alpha>(1-\alpha)^2/(1-\alpha^{N-1})$ ensures this property for both the complete and the ring networks.

Let $s^C(1)$ and $s^R(1)$ denote the minimal size of the shock leading to the default of one bank under the complete network and the ring network, respectively. This minimum shock is the same for both networks and is given by the following equation:

$$\alpha(R-s(1))+(1-\alpha)R=\ell. \tag{9.37}$$

This yields the insight that $s^C(1)=s^R(1)>(R-\ell)/\alpha$: thus, linkages to other banks allow a bank to remain solvent for larger shocks than an isolated bank can do. Turning to a larger number of defaults, consider the complete network. Observe that every bank (other than 1) faces an identical asset and liability situation. Hence either there is zero defaults, one default, or all the banks default. In other words, the minimum shock needed for two or more defaults

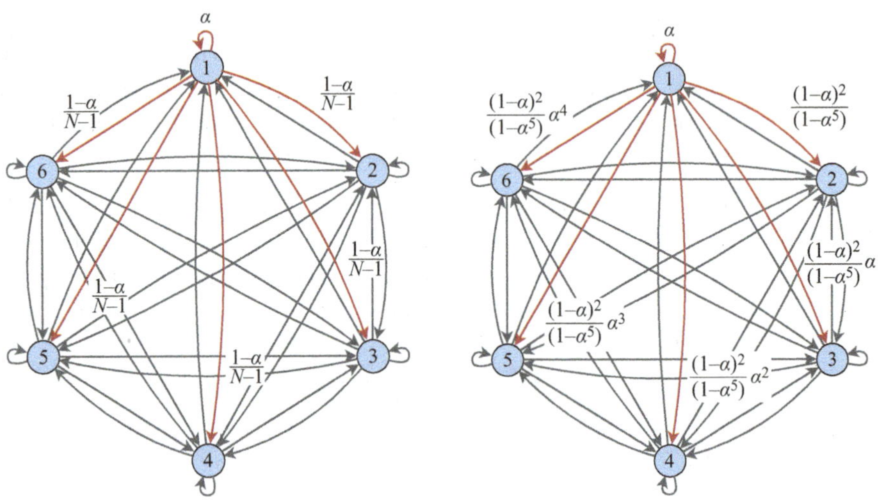


(a) Complete (b) Ring

**Figure 9.5**
Networks with cross-ownership (shares between node 1 and other nodes).

is the same, $s^C(2) = \ldots = s^C(N)$. This shock is given as a solution to the following equation:

$$\frac{1-\alpha}{N-1}\left[(R-\beta-s^C(N)\right]+\left[1-\frac{1-\alpha}{N-1}\right]R=\ell. \tag{9.38}$$

This suggests that the shock must be large enough to cause the second (and thus $N$th) bank to fail to recapture enough shares to cover its liabilities after the insolvency caused by the first shock. This equation considers the threshold from the point of view of bank $i \neq 1$. Suppose that only bank 1 has gone bankrupt and all others are solvent. What is the largest shock that could be sustained such that this bank can cover its liabilities? Any shock greater than this would lead to the bank (and hence all other banks) going bankrupt.

Observe that in the ring network, the off-diagonal terms in $A^R$ decrease with distance from the diagonal. This naturally suggests a higher threshold of the number of defaults. The exact thresholds for different $k$ values may be obtained as solutions to the following equation:

$$\left[\sum_{i=0}^{j-3}\right]\frac{(1-\alpha)^2}{1-\alpha^{N-1}}(R-\beta)+\frac{(1-\alpha)^2}{1-\alpha^{N-1}}\alpha^{j-2}(R-s^R(j)-\beta)$$

$$+\left[\sum_{i=j-1}^{N-2}\right]\frac{(1-\alpha)^2}{1-\alpha^{N-1}}R+\alpha R=\ell. \tag{9.39}$$

As the off-diagonal elements are falling in number $N$, one immediate implication is that the threshold values on minimal shocks are all increasing with the number of banks/projects. In other words, other things being the same, a larger system permits greater diffusion of exposure, which makes it more difficult for a shock on one firm to lead to contagion.

Let us next compare the thresholds in the complete and the ring networks. It is simpler to take up the case for large and small default costs separately. First, consider small $\beta$. An inspection of matrices $A^C$ and $A^R$ reveals that the largest (smallest) off-diagonal term in the ring network is larger (smaller) than the common off-diagonal term in the complete network. This suggests that generalized default of all banks will be more difficult in the ring network than in the complete network, but localized defaults by a small set of banks will be easier in the ring network than in the complete network.

Let us turn next to large costs of default. When default costs are large, a default of a single bank leads to default by all banks. The key to understanding this result is to note that when $\beta$ is small, the size of the shock that needs to be absorbed is roughly equal to the size of the shock hitting firm 1, $s_1$. By contrast, when $\beta > 0$ is large, the size of the shock is larger and grows on average as more banks default. There is an amplification created by the default costs. This yields the desired conclusion: the default of a single bank leads to the default of all banks. Indeed it is possible to show that when default costs are large, generalized default of all banks is easier in a ring network than in the complete network. This last step is the subject of a question at the end of the chapter.

The following result summarizes out discussion.

**Proposition 9.2** *Shock thresholds for the default are rising in the number of banks/projects, N. If default costs, $\beta$, are small, then $s^R(2) < s^C(N) < s^R(N)$. If default costs are large, then either all or none of the firms default, $s^m(N) \leq s^m(1)$ for $m \in \{C, R\}$. The threshold for all firms defaulting is lower in the ring network, $s^R(N) < s^C(N)$.*

This result sets the stage for the derivation of optimal networks in a given environment. Given that there is a uniform cost for bank defaults, the welfare loss due to contagion is proportional to the number of banks that default.

An inspection of proposition 9.2 gives an insight into how levels of shock can translate into relative effectiveness of different networks in containing contagion. We will say that a network $g$ dominates another network $g'$ if the more banks default under $g'$ than under $g$. With this definition in hand, we can state the following result on the ranking of networks in terms of their potential for contagion.

**Proposition 9.3** *(i) If shock $s \leq s^R(2)$ or $s > s^R(N)$, then the ring and the complete networks are equivalent. (ii) If $s^R(2) < s \leq s^C(N)$, then the complete network dominates the ring network. (iii) If $s^C(N) < s \leq s^R(N)$, then the ring network dominates the complete network.*

So far, we have focused only on the density of connections in the network. But other aspects of the network can in principle play an important role. To see this, let us take up the possibility of segmenting the system of $N$ firms into disjoint components. Fragmentation of the network into separate components can be an effective instrument for limiting contagion and dominate complete and ring networks. For concreteness, consider situations like (iii) in proposition 9.3. In this situation, the network that consists of disjointed and complete components typically dominates a single ring structure.

In the discussion so far, we have focused on the role of the network topology and the nature of the linkage (equity versus debt). In practice, the details of the network connections are often not easily available. It is therefore worth noting that a higher-level statistic is important: the level of integration of a bank with other banks. In the equity model, this is captured by $1-\alpha$, while in the debt context, this is captured by the value of $a$. An inspection of equations (9.37–9.39) reveals that the threshold for one default is increasing in $1-\alpha$, while the threshold for $j>1$, $s(j)$ decreases with $1-\alpha$. This contrasting effect on a single and multiple default nicely brings out the trade-off involved in financial linkages.

*Debt Linkages:* We now study the role of financial networks when the linkages represent debt relations. Let us start by noting that complete and ring networks can be constructed in a straightforward way: in the complete network, set $a_{ij}=a_{ji}=a/(N-1)$, where $a>0$, for all $i,j$. In the ring network, set $a_{i,i+1}=a$ for all $i$, and $a_{ij}=0$ otherwise. We will also set $\beta=0$. Let us start by noting that the effect of the size of the system, $N$, remains unchanged: The minimal size of the shock needed for all defaults of all banks grows with $N$. This is true because as $N$ grows, the magnitude of a shock on directly linked banks becomes smaller, which makes them less likely to default. However, for a given $N$, the effects of networks are quite different when links denote debt.

Observe that when linkages represent debt, changes in the number of linked banks have no effect on the individual threshold for default, so long as aggregate liabilities remain unchanged. This is because an individual bank retains full right to the returns to its project, and thus the threshold. Hence when linkages represent debt, their presence does not provide any insurance to a bank against idiosyncratic shocks. A second major difference pertains to the relative attractiveness of the complete and ring networks. When debt to external creditors (i.e., outside the network) is senior to debt within the network, the threshold shock needed to get all banks to default is the same in the complete and ring structures. However, for the ring network, we have $s^R(1)<s^R(j)<s^R(N)$ for $1<j<N$ for shocks of intermediate size between $s^R(1)=R-\ell$ and $s^R(N)$. In this range of shock values, therefore, there are multiple failures in the ring structure and only a single failure in the complete structure. Thus, when linkages represent debt, the complete network always dominates the ring network.

Let us summarize what we have learned in this section. We have developed a model of financial linkages among banks; the linkages may reflect cross-ownerships or debt contracts. To bring out the main points in a transparent way, we have focused on two simple networks that are symmetric—the complete network and the ring network. We find that: (1) the ways in which defaults or financial distress spreads from one bank to another depend both on the nature of the bilateral ties and the topology of the network. (2) the architecture of the optimal networks depend on the nature of the risks faced by individual banks: when shocks are small, greater linkages between institutions may be best, but when the shocks are large, it may be better to fragment the network into separate components.

## 9.6 Incomplete Network Information and Fire Sales

Our discussion in section 9.2 points to two features of financial linkages: the first relates to the content of the link, which can be very varied, reflecting the diversity of financial instruments; the second is that actors in the market have very limited knowledge of the network. The complexity of the network reflects both these aspects. This complexity comes together with limited information about the network. These factors are important in the decision making of managers, as they can potentially magnify the uncertainty in the market. Federal Reserve chair Ben Bernanke captures this concern as follows:

> Our financial system is extremely complex and interconnected, and Bear Stearns participated extensively in a range of critical markets. The sudden failure of Bear Stearns likely would have led to a chaotic unwinding of positions in those markets and could have severely shaken confidence. The company's failure could also have cast doubt on the financial positions of some of Bear Stearns' thousands of counterparties and perhaps of companies with similar businesses .... Moreover, the adverse impact of a default would not have been confined to the financial system but would have been felt broadly in the real economy through its effects on asset values and credit availability. (Testimony to the Senate on April 3, 2008, following the Fed's Bear Stearns intervention)

The role of domino effects in elevating complexity and uncertainty was also highlighted by Andrew Haldane, the chief economist at the Bank of England, when he wrote that at times of stress, "knowing your ultimate counterparty's risk becomes like solving a high-dimension Sudoku puzzle" (Haldane 2013, p. 15).

In section 9.4, we presented a model that illustrated amplification mechanisms created by connections that could lead to contagion and systemic collapse. One assumption in that model was that the network of exposures is fully known and understood by the banks. This section presents a model of financial crises that builds upon the idea that complexity, a dormant factor during normal times, becomes acutely relevant and self-reinforcing during crises. The model is taken from Caballero and Simsek (2013).

When banks face liquidity shocks, they adjust to them by maintaining linkages with other banks. The new element is complexity: this is reflected in the incomplete knowledge of how far a bank is from the center of the shock. The model has three periods, labeled $t=0, 1, 2$. To avoid strategic considerations, we will assume that there is a continuum of banks—specifically, there are $n$ distinct continuums of banks, denoted by $\{b_j\}_{j=0}^{n-1}$. Each of these continuums consists of identical banks. We shall refer to a continuum $b_j$ as bank $b_j$. Banks start with a given balance sheet at date 0 (which will be described shortly), but they only consume at date 2. Banks can transfer their date 0 dollars to date 2 by investing in one of two ways. First, banks can keep their dollars in cash, which yields 1 dollar at the next date per dollar invested. Second, banks can invest in a long-term asset. Each unit of the long-term asset yields $R > 1$ at date 2 (and no dollars at date 1). The asset is supplied at date 0 at a normalized price of 1 dollar. The return structure captures the standard liquidity and return trade-off, which is prevalent in financial markets.

Each bank initially has $y$ dollars and $1 - y$ units of legacy assets. At date 0, the only decision point, banks can trade legacy assets in a secondary market at an endogenous price of $p$. This price cannot exceed 1 because legacy assets and new assets are identical (and the price of the latter is 1). A key assumption is that the only buyers of legacy assets are the other banks. In the absence of adequate demand, this legacy asset sells at an outside valuation of $p_{scrap} < 1$. Selling at $p_{scrap}$ will be referred to as a *fire sale*.

Every bank $b^i$ has a deposit at bank $b^{i-1}$, which yields $z$ in period 1; bank 1 has a deposit at bank n. These are unsecured deposits that reflect large interbank exposures. So bank $i$ is owed $z$ by bank $i - 1$ and owes $z$ in turn to bank $i + 1$, at time 1. This creates a cycle of exposures (as in equation 9.6).

Banks' exposures form a financial network. For simplicity, assume that the network is a cycle (see figure 9.6). The notation $b_{j+1} \to b_j$ means that $b_{j+1}$ has claims on bank $b_j$. As banks are ordered around a cycle, bank $b_0$ has claims on bank $b_{n-1}$. The key idea that financial networks are complex is captured as follows: Bank A may know whom it is lending to or borrowing from, but it does not know where its creditor got its money from and to whom its debtor bank lends. In particular, it will be assumed that banks have only local knowledge: $i$ knows who bank $i - 1$ is but does not know whom bank $i - 1$ lends to; in other words, it does not know the identity of bank $i - 2$.

Let us define permutations of n banks on a cycle using the mapping $\sigma : \{0, 1, \ldots, n-1\} \to \{0, 1, \ldots, n-1\}$. This permutation assigns bank $j$ to slot $i = \sigma(j)$. Let $N^i(\sigma)$ be the set of potential permutations for bank $i$. Banks do not know the realization, $\sigma$. In particular, let $N_j(\sigma) \subset N$ denote the set of financial networks that bank $b_j$ deems possible, given the actual realization. We refer to the collection $\{N_j(\sigma)\}_{j,\sigma}$ as an uncertainty model for banks.

At date 0, banks hear that bank $b_i$ has had an unexpected shock in period 1. Let $\theta > 0$ be the size of the shock, which is known to all banks. This shock is senior to the short-term claims of its creditor bank.

At this point, banks choose to buy or sell liquidity. The bank's goal is to maximize its equity value at date 2, subject to meeting the liquidity needs at date 1. Suppose, for simplicity, that a bank can either use all cash to buy assets $B$ or sell all assets to keep cash $S$. If a bank buys assets, then a bank facing a shock will get $z$ and owe $z$, which cancel each other out. So it has a liquidity net need of $\theta$, and it cannot cover these needs. So the bank sells its legacy assets and keeps cash.

Selling legacy assets is a precautionary move to avert a potential liquidity crisis: but the bank may not be able to cover liquidity in spite of that, as $\theta$ may be too large. In that case,

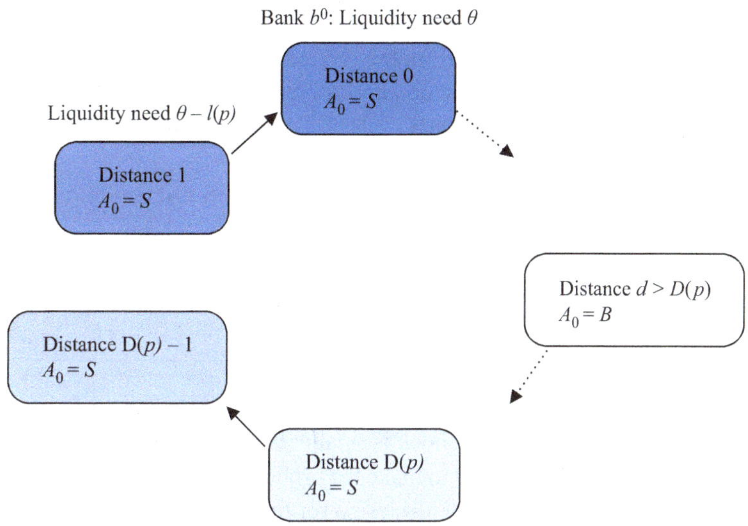


**Figure 9.6**
Outcomes with complete network information.

it is insolvent and pays $q_1 \leq z$ to the creditor bank, and its date 2 value is $q_2 = 0$. If, on the other hand, it is able to cover the liquidity needs, it pays $q_1 = z$ to the depositor bank and its date 2 equity value is $q_2 \geq 0$.

The bank makes a choice at date 0: it considers the range of possible financial networks, $N_j(\sigma)$, and chooses an action that is robust to this uncertainty. We assume that the bank chooses an action that maximizes the minimum payoff that it can get across all possible network location permutations. Let $N^i(\sigma)$ be the set of possible permutations for bank $i$ given its knowledge of the network. Each bank chooses to buy or sell assets to solve:

$$\max_{B,S} \min_{\tilde{\sigma} \in N^i(\sigma)} q_2^i(\tilde{\sigma}). \tag{9.40}$$

Legacy assets are traded at date 0 in a centralized market. The net supply of the legacy asset is

$$NS = (1-y)\sum_j \mathbf{1}_{\{A^j=S\}} - \frac{y}{p}\sum_j \mathbf{1}_{\{A^j=B\}}, \tag{9.41}$$

where $p = 1$ if $NS \leq 0$, $p \in (p_{scrap}, 1)$ if $NS = 0$, and $p = p_{scrap}$ if $NS \geq 0$. $p_{scrap}$ is the minimum price for the legacy asset.

An equilibrium consists of bank actions, debt payments, and equity values $\{A_0^j(\sigma), q_1^j(\sigma), q_2^j(\sigma)\}$ and a price level $p \in [p_{scrap}, 1]$ for legacy assets such that markets clear and banks solve their optimization problems.

Consider bank actions and payoffs $\{A_0^j(\sigma), q_1^j(\sigma), q_2^j(\sigma)\}$. To study this model, it is useful to define the bank's distance from the original distressed bank. The distressed bank $b_0$ has distance $d=0$ from itself. The neighbor of the original distressed bank has distance $d=1$. We will say that there is a *domino effect* of size $D$ if banks within distance $d \leq D-1$ are insolvent and all banks $d \geq D$ are solvent.

There is a *flight-to-quality* of size $F$ if banks with distance $d \leq F-1$ choose $S$ and all banks $d \geq F$ choose $B$.

To provide a baseline, we start with the analysis of the perfect information case: all banks know the true network permutation $\sigma$. To develop the equilibrium for this setting, it is convenient to make the following assumption:

**Assumption (A)** *$ny > \lceil\theta\rceil$, and $z+y+(1-y)p_{scrap} \geq \theta$.*

The first part says that the shock is smaller than the aggregate cash holdings of all banks. This assumption is necessary to make the problem worth studying. Clearly, if this condition is violated, then all banks will always go for fire sales after a shock. The second part of the assumption is for notational simplicity only.

### 9.6.1 Complete Network Information

The analysis proceeds in three steps: first, we solve for optimal bank choice given the price and choice of others; second, we solve for equilibrium among banks taking the price as given; and finally, we solve for the price.

Let us start with a bank at distance $d$ from the distressed bank: the net liquidity need for bank at distance $d$ from distressed bank 1 is $z - q_1(d-1) + \theta \mathbf{1}_{d=0}$. The potential liquidity supply upon liquidation of legacy assets, then, is $l(p) = p(1-y)+y$. If the liquidity need is 0, then the bank chooses $B$. If the liquidity need lies in $(0, l(p))$, then it can pay off its needs by selling, so optimal action is to sell its legacy assets, $S$. Finally, if the need is larger than $l(p)$, then the bank is insolvent regardless of what it does, and its equity value is 0. However, its value to debt holders is larger if it sells its assets, so it chooses $S$. Observe that the original distressed bank 1 receives its deposit returns from bank $n$. Hence the liquidity need is $\theta > 0$ and the bank chooses $S$. If $l(p) \geq \theta$, then the original bank avoids insolvency and the domino effect $D(p)=0$.

If $l(p) < \theta$, bank 1 cannot address its liquidity needs. It therefore only transfers $q_1(0) = z + l(p) - \theta < z$ to bank 2. Now, note that due to assumption (A), $z' \geq 0$. As there is a shortfall in its payments, bank 2 too has a positive liquidity need, given by $z - q_1(0) = \theta - l(p) > 0$. So this bank also chooses $S$. Observe that if $2l(p) \geq \theta$, then bank 2's available liquidity exceeds the need; therefore domino stops at bank 1. If not, then bank 2 is also insolvent and passes on $q_1(1) = l(p) + q_1(0)$, and so forth. Eventually, we get the pattern that payment by a distance-$k$ insolvent bank is given by $q_1(k) = l(p)[k-1] + q_1(0)$. The definition of $D(p)$ says that it is the first integer where $\theta \leq l(p)[D(p)+1]$. Assumption (A) implies that both the domino effect and the flight-to-quality are contained (i.e., $D(p) < n$ and $F < n$).

We are now ready to describe the equilibrium in the full information setting.

**Proposition 9.4** *Suppose assumption (A) holds and there is full information on the network structure. Then:*

*(i) the unique equilibrium price is $p = 1$ (no fire sales).*

*(ii) the domino effect of size $\lceil \theta \rceil - 1$ and a flight to quality of size $\lceil \theta \rceil$.*

*(iii) the aggregate amount of new asset purchase is $Y = ny - \lceil \theta \rceil$.*

The main step in the argument is to show that the price of legacy asset is 1—the rest follows from that fact. Observe that the net demand for an asset at price $p$ is

$$\frac{y(n - D(p) - 1)}{p} - (1 - y)(D(p) + 1). \tag{9.42}$$

By definition, $D(p) + 1 = \left\lceil \frac{\theta}{l(p)} \right\rceil$, and substituting and simplifying and using assumption (A) yields the property that net demand is positive, and this implies that the price of asset is 1.

Figure 9.6 illustrates this result. The basic idea is very simple. Banks closest to the distressed bank 0 use their liquidity $l(p)$ to cover the losses of bank 0. As the shock passes from one bank to the next, the liquidity need decreases by $l(p)$. From the definition of $D(p)$, it then follows that banks with distance $d \leq D(p)$ choose to sell. All but the last of them is insolvent. The last bank with distance $d = D(p)$ avoids insolvency because it is able to meet its liquidity needs and pay its immediate neighbor in full. It then follows that all the banks at distance $d > D(p)$ have zero liquidity need and optimally choose to buy long-term assets. There is, therefore, a domino effect of size $D(p)$ and a flight to quality of size $D(p) + 1$.

### 9.6.2 Incomplete Network Information

We now study bank choices under incomplete network knowledge and the max-min decision rule. Recall that the local knowledge assumption says that the bank knows the identity of the bank that owes it money, but only that bank. There are two scenarios for a nondistressed bank $i$: (1) the distressed bank is the borrower $i - 1$; and (2) the distressed bank is not the borrower bank. In the latter case, the worst case scenario is that the distressed bank is bank $i - 2$. The optimal choice of bank $i$ depends on the size of the shock $\theta$. If $\theta \leq 2l(p)$, then $D(p) \leq 1$ and the flight-to-quality size is $F = D(p) + 1$. Observe that if $\theta < 2l(p)$, then it is common knowledge that the distressed bank and its immediate depositor can take care of liquidity needs. If bank $i$ is a distressed bank or its depositor, then it will know the true state of the world. The distressed bank always chooses $S$ and the depositor chooses $S$ or $B$, depending on whether $\theta$ is smaller than $l(p)$ or not. All other banks will choose B. On the other hand, if $\theta > 2l(p)$, then $D(p) \geq 2$ and the flight-to-quality size is $F = n$. If $\theta > 2l$, all banks sell assets.

Equipped with this simple rule of behavior for banks, the following result describes the equilibrium in the incomplete network knowledge setting.

**Proposition 9.5** *Suppose assumption (A) holds and there is incomplete network knowledge.*

(i) *If* $\theta < 2l(p_{scrap})$*, then there is a unique equilibrium with* $p = 1$*,* $D(p) = \lceil\theta\rceil - 1$*, and the flight-to-quality size of* $F = \lceil\theta\rceil$*. The aggregate amount of new asset purchase is* $Y = ny - \lceil\theta\rceil$*.*

(ii) *If* $\theta > 2$*, then there is a unique equilibrium with price* $p = p_{scrap}$*,* $D(p) = \lceil\theta\rceil$*, and flight-to-quality size of* $F = n$*, and the aggregate amount of new asset purchases is 0.*

(iii) *If* $\theta \in (2l(p_{scrap}), 2)$*, then there are two equilibria, one corresponding to the fair value* $p = 1$ *case and the other to the* $p = p_{scrap}$ *case.*

The main point to note here is the flight-to-quality phenomenon: all banks sell their assets, so price collapses to scrap value as soon as $\theta > 2$.

Figure 9.7 illustrates this result. It plots the equilibrium actions corresponding to low and high $\theta$. In the low $\theta$ case, the shock is smaller than the available liquidity of original distressed bank and its immediate neighbor. The top part of figure 9.7 shows that the equilibrium outcome is the same as in the full information case. Note that banks at distance $d \geq 2$ act as if they are at distance 2. With this small shock, the bank at distance 2 does not suffer any losses from cross-exposures and chooses action $B$, as do all banks at distance $d \geq 2$.

The lower panel of figure 9.7 covers the case of shock $\theta$, which is larger than the liquidity of two banks. Thus the bank at distance 2 chooses action $S$, and so do all banks. This leads to a flight-to-quality size $n$.

Let us now summarize what we have learned in this section. The effects of a shock on a bank on other banks depend on the connections of the originator bank and the structure of the network. However, this structure is often very poorly understood by the participants in the network and by outsiders such as policy makers and regulators. The study of behavior with incomplete network knowledge is at a very early stage. The model presented in this section is very stylized, but it helps bring out in a stark manner how complexity and risk aversion can give rise to very large fire sales in response to a shock on a single bank.

## 9.7 The Formation of Financial Networks

In section 9.2, we presented evidence that interbank markets exhibit a core periphery structure. This section presents a model taken from Farboodi (2021) to understand the forces that lead to such networks.

There are three periods, $t = 0, 1, 2$, and one good, funding. There are two types of agents: banks and households. There are $K$ banks in all: banks are of two types, $I$ and $NI$, and banks in group $I$ have access to investment opportunities and banks in group $NI$ don't. There are $K_I$ and $K_{NI}$ banks of the two types; assume $K_{NI} \geq K_I$.

The investment opportunity is a risky asset that is linearly scalable. Every bank $i \in I$ receives the opportunity to invest in the risky asset with probability $q$. The probability is identical and independent across banks.

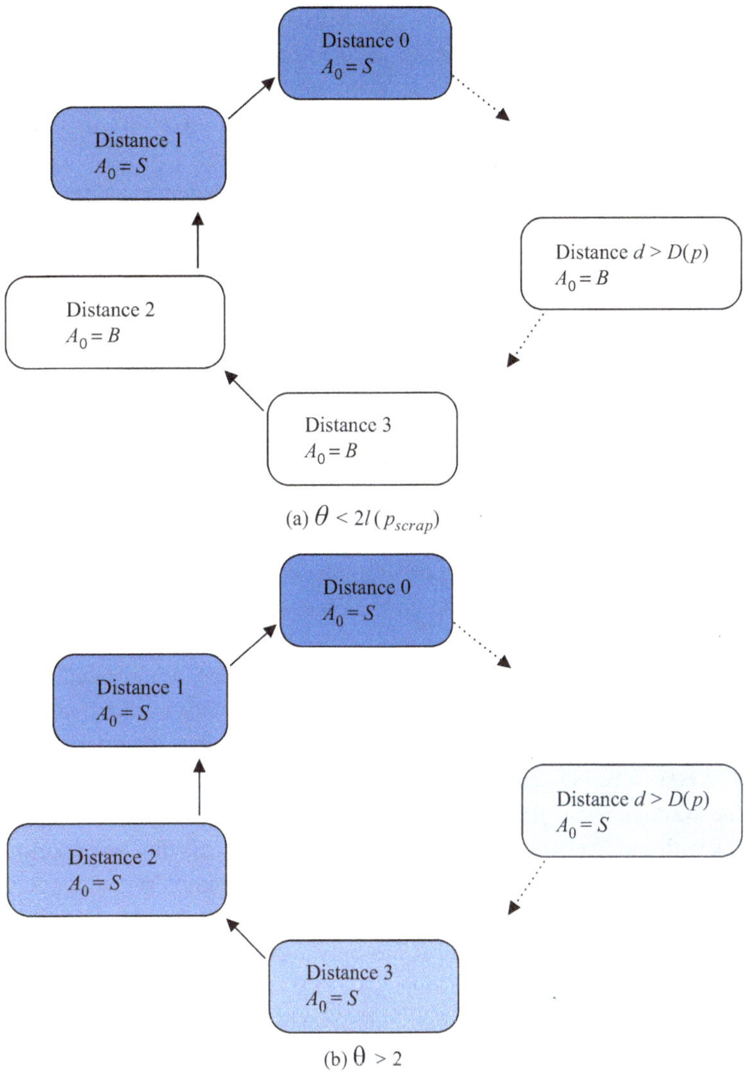


**Figure 9.7**
Outcomes with incomplete network information.

At $t = 0$, banks raise funding from households and create lending and borrowing relationships. A link $g_{ij}$ means bank $i$ is committed to lending to bank $j$. At $t = 1$, investment opportunities are realized and borrowing takes place along a subset of borrowing links created at $t = 0$. At $t = 2$, the returns from investment are realized. The returns are random: there is a probability $p$ that investment yields $R$ and a probability $1 - p$ that investment yields 0. The probability of return is identical and independent across banks. Over and above this investment, every bank has a value $V_i$, which reflects the value of the other businesses, assets, and services that the bank provides. If the bank fails, this value is lost. For simplicity, suppose that $V_i = V_I$ for all $i \in I$ and $V_j = V_{NI}$ for all $j \in NI$.

A bank can raise funding from two sources. At $t = 0$, a bank $j \in NI$ raises resources from a continuum of households $hh_j$ of measure 1. A household is endowed with 1 unit of funding. Households lend to banks so long as they break even. In addition to households, in period $t = 1$, after observing the investment opportunities, a bank can borrow from other banks that created borrowing links with them in period $t = 0$.

The financial network is a directed graph, with $K$ nodes representing the banks and a directed link from $i$ to $j$ representing a lending commitment. A bank chooses its links over which it can borrow or lend in order to maximize its expected profit net of failure cost. For concreteness, we will focus on an example with four banks: two banks of type $I$ and two banks of type $NI$.

To borrow on the interbank market at date $t = 1$, banks need to enter potential agreements at $t = 0$. Potential agreements are similar to credit lines except that they have no limit. An agreement established at $t = 0$ is a promise by the lender to deliver at least 1 unit to the borrower if the borrower receives an investment opportunity or if the borrower has a credit line to another bank that has received an investment opportunity. A bank can create a lending link with another bank only if it can deliver on it: there is thus an opportunity cost to creating a link with a potential borrower. To see this in the simplest setting, consider figure 9.8(b). Observe that the network on the left in panel (a) is not feasible: the $NI$ bank has committed to lending to two $I$ banks, but it has only 1 unit of household funds. The network on the right is feasible.

We will assume that there is an exogenously given division of surplus between the investing bank and the banks that directly or indirectly lend to it. In particular, we will assume that when bank $i$ raises funding from households and lends directly to bank $j$, which makes the investment, then $i$ and $j$ receive a share $\alpha$ and $1 - \alpha$ of the surplus. If, on the other hand, $i$ raises the funding and lends to $j$, which in turn lends to $K$, which invests, then $i$, $j$, and $k$ receive $\alpha^2$, $\alpha(1 - \alpha)$, and $1 - \alpha$, respectively.

The final return of the project at $t = 2$ is not contractible. Contracts are bilateral and take the form of contingent debt. The face value of the debt is such that given the network and the realization of investment opportunities, each bank along the intermediation chain receives its appropriate share, as described previously.

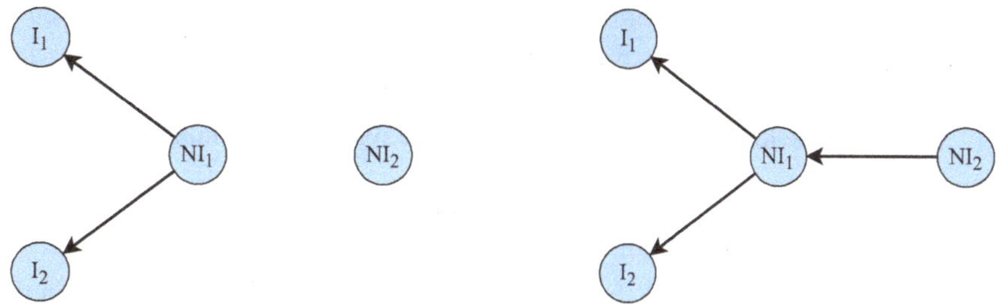


**Figure 9.8**
Examples of networks.

A network structure $G$ is blocked by a coalition $B$ of banks if there is another (feasible, individually rational) network structure $G'$ and a coalition $B$, such that (1) $G'$ can be reached from $G$ by a set of bilateral deviations by banks $b, b' \in B$ and unilateral deviations by $b \in B$; and (2) every bank $b \in B$ is strictly better off in $G'$ than in $G$. A network is said to be *stable* if it is not blocked by any coalition of banks.

We now develop a description of various networks that are stable and compare them to efficient networks.

### 9.7.1 Stable and Efficient Networks

Let us begin by noting the incentives of an NI lender and an I borrower, respectively:

$$(1-\alpha)(pR-1) > (1-p)V_I; \;\; \alpha(pR-1) > (1-p)V_{NI}. \tag{9.43}$$

This relationship is in their joint interest if the expected returns of project $pR-1$ are greater than the expected cost of default $(1-p)(V_I + V_{NI})$; that is, $pR-1 > (1-p)(V_I + V_{NI})$. Observe that if the lender and borrower find it attractive to create the link, then it is also in their collective interest. In other words, individual incentives to create a link are lower than desirable. For the study of networks to be interesting, indirect lending must be profitable. This motivates the restriction on parameter values: $\alpha^2(pR-1) > (1-p)V_{NI}$.

A key concept in the analysis of stable networks is intermediation spread. Consider the arrangement where bank $i$ lends 1 unit at face value $D$ to $j$, which invests the unit. Consider next the indirect arrangement, in which $i$ lends 1 unit to $kj$ at face value $D_1$, which lends the unit at face value D2 to $j$, and $k$ makes the investment. The face value of the debt is set in such a manner so as to ensure that in expectation, each party (including the intermediator) receives its share of expected net surplus. Formally,

$$D_1 = \frac{(\alpha^2(pR-1)+1}{p} < D_2 = D = \frac{\alpha(pR-1)+1}{p}. \tag{9.44}$$

$D_2 - D_1$ represents the intermediation spread. The intermediation spread provides a measure of the incentive for a bank to move from being an indirect to a direct lender.

In particular, recall that in deciding whether to form a link, a bank compares the returns from the link against the risks of failure. With this in mind, let us define

$$\kappa = \frac{\alpha(1-\alpha)X}{(1-p)V_I}, \tag{9.45}$$

where $X = pR - 1$ is the net expected return of a 1-unit investment in the project: $\kappa$ is the ratio of the intermediation spread per unit divided by the expected cost of default for an I bank. We can define a similar ratio for an NI bank. It is helpful to define the following pieces of additional notation:

$$\tilde{\kappa} = \max\{\alpha, (1-\alpha)\frac{V_{NI}}{V_I}\}\ \bar{\kappa} = 1 + \frac{q}{2(1-q)}. \tag{9.46}$$

In what follows, we will assume that a pair of NI and I banks always have an incentive for form a link—that is, conditions are met ($\kappa \geq \tilde{\kappa}$). Let us start by delineating the set of networks that can be stable. Observe that if $k \geq \tilde{k}$ then every NI bank must be creating a link in any stable network. So the only candidates for a stable network are as in figure 9.10. Within this set, networks (d), (g), and (h) can be eliminated using straightforward arguments. Network (d) cannot be stable because bank $NI_1$ has 2 units of loans available, so it can increase its profits by forming a link with bank $I_2$. Bank $I_2$ clearly has an incentive to form this link, given $\kappa \geq \tilde{\kappa}$. Next, consider network (g): Observe that bank $NI_2$ has an incentive to connect with $I_1$ so as to access its investment opportunity (this is strictly profitable in the state when bank $I_2$ does not have an opportunity). Bank $I_1$ can hope to raise its intermediation rents by forming this link, as it can act as an intermediator for bank $I_2$. Finally, consider network (h). Clearly, banks $NI_1$ and $I_2$ have an incentive to carry out the deviation because by doing so, they sidestep bank $I_1$ and thereby lower their intermediation payments to $I1$. Putting points together, we are left with networks (a)–(c) and (e).

The next proposition provides a characterization of equilibria in the economy with four banks. Networks (a), (b), (c), (d), and (e) are as in figure 9.10.

**Proposition 9.6** *Suppose that $\kappa \geq \tilde{\kappa}$. Then network (a) is stable if $\kappa \leq \bar{\kappa}$; networks (b) and (c) are stable if $\kappa \leq 1/2$; network (d) is stable if $\kappa \geq 1$; and network (e) is stable if $\kappa \geq 1/2$.*

The proof of the proposition involves checking the incentives of banks. A question at the end of the chapter asks for these details to be worked out. Here, we will focus on the incentives for the formation of a core-periphery network (d), in which the I banks constitute the core.

Consider the two networks (a) and (e). Observe, that in network (a), an I bank is involved in a default only if it made an investment. By contrast, in network (d), all banks are involved, so long as one of the I banks is active. Thus there is higher systemic risk in network (d). We will now show that there are circumstances under which the two I banks and bank $N_2$ have an

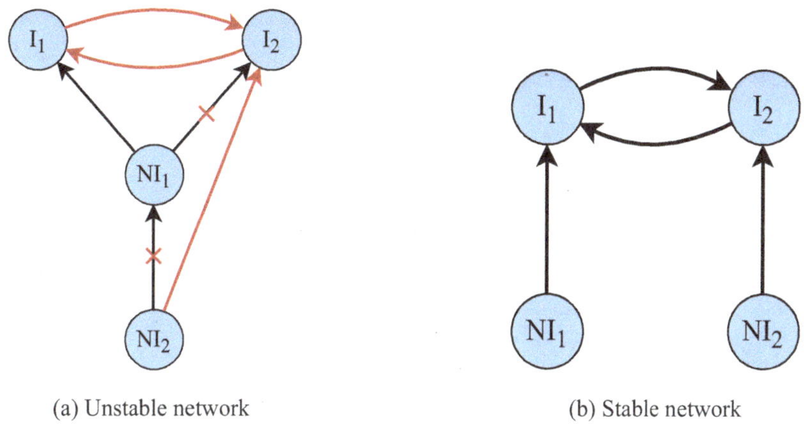


**Figure 9.9**
Deviations by banks.

incentive to deviate from network (a) and create network (d). This deviation is illustrated in figure 9.9. Consider the different investment opportunities that may arise. If only $I_2$ receives the investment opportunity, then $I_1$ serves as the intermediator for $NI_1$ and captures some intermediation rents. The cost is the potential for default that is triggered if investment in $I_2$ fails. So banks $I_1$ and $I_2$ will undertake this deviation if the intermediation spread $(D_2 - D_1)$ is sufficiently high relative to the cost of the default. This yields the condition $\kappa \geq 1$. Note that $NI_2$ must benefit from joining the coalition.

We next discuss efficient networks, that is, the network that maximizes the total surplus subject to feasibility and individual rationality. Given condition $\kappa \geq \tilde{\kappa}$, it follows that every $NI$ bank must have a link. Moreover, it is strictly better to have both $NI$ banks feeding into both $I$ banks, in the event that only one $I$ bank receives the investment opportunity. Given this maximum investment size, the goal is to minimize the expected loss of default due to the failure of project(s). This yields the star network in figure 9.10(a), with an $NI$ bank at the center.

Figure 9.11 summarizes our study of stable and efficient networks. It shows how stable networks may be underconnected or overconnected relative to efficient networks. The underconnectedness arises due to the familiar problem of positive externalities in linking (and incomplete appropriation of surplus), while the overconnectedness arises because banks have incentives to create links to divert surpluses for themselves.

These arguments have been developed in the context of a four-bank example. Figure 9.12 illustrates the pattern of core-periphery networks that arises when we consider many $I$ and $NI$ banks.

Let us now summarize what we have learned from this model of intermediation. Financial institutions have incentives to capture intermediation rents through borrowing and lending decisions. By doing so, they tilt the division of surplus along an intermediation chain in

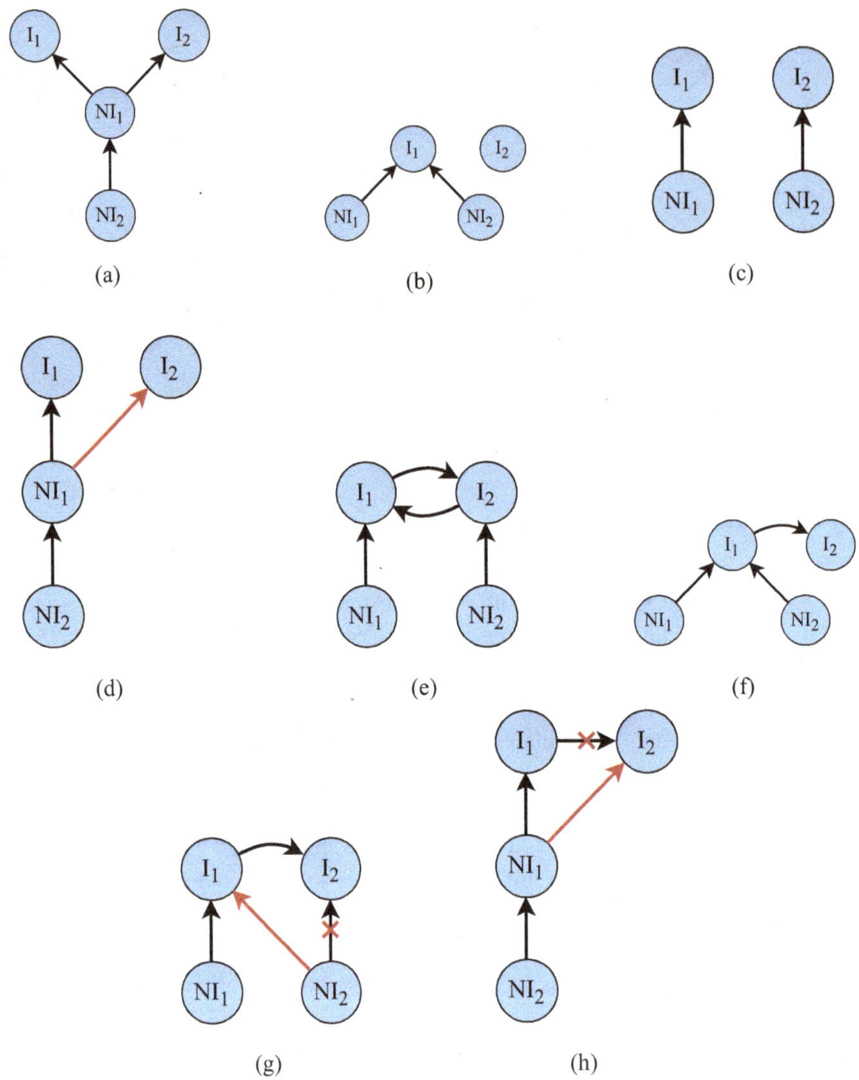


**Figure 9.10**
Candidates for stable networks.

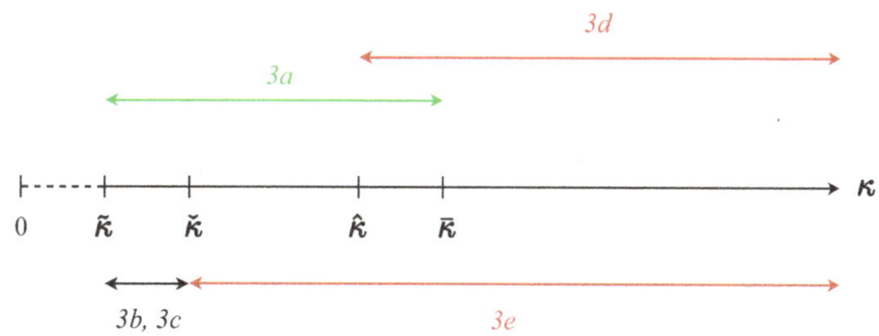


**Figure 9.11**
Stable and efficient networks: summary.

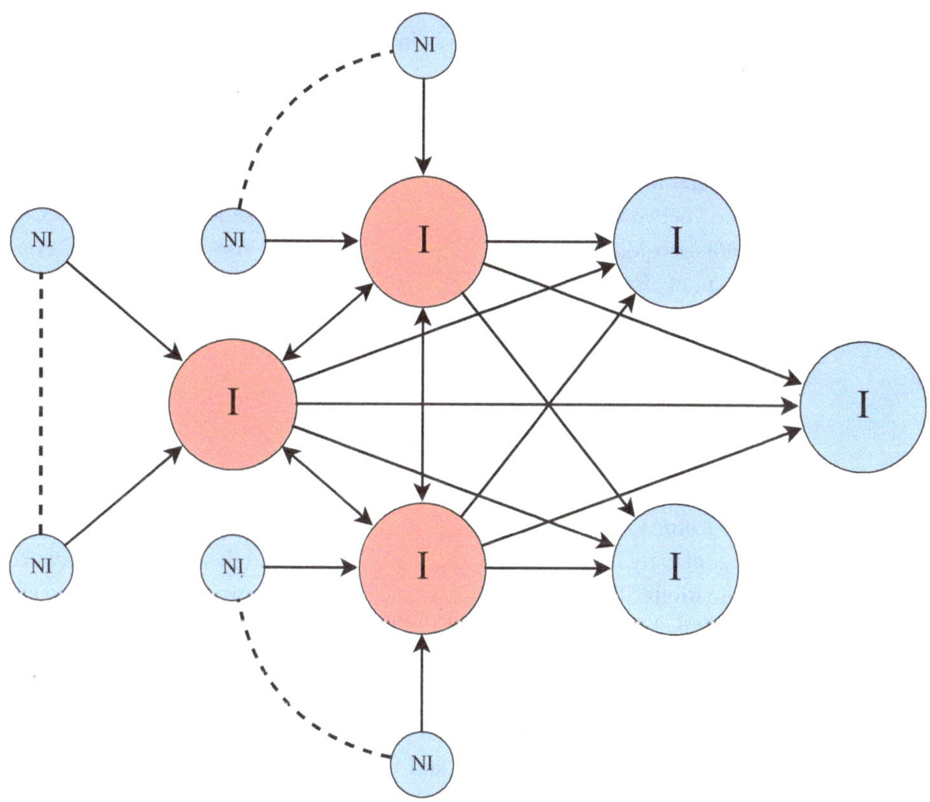


**Figure 9.12**
Core-periphery with many banks.

their favor. The key finding is that these strategic incentives create pressure for the creation of a core-periphery network. This network exhibits excessive exposure to counter-party risk relative to the efficient network.

## 9.8 Reading Notes

Financial contagion is an old idea: financial booms and busts may be seen as instances of this phenomenon, and they go back a long way; classic historical studies include Kindleberger (2001) and Mackay (2018). This chapter focuses on the narrower question of how measurable connections between institutions reflected in their borrowing/lending and equity relations can create a pathway for the spread of shocks, and how various structures of connections can give rise to the amplification of original shocks. The study of networks and their impact on financial contagion is important, as it provides a basis for the design of appropriate targeted interventions.

The literature on financial networks has grown especially rapidly since the financial crisis of 2008. The empirical research describes the rich variety of connections between financial institutions. It has also plotted a wide range of network relations. Empirical studies of networks include Martinez-Jaramillo, Alexandrova-Kabadjova, Bravo-Benitez, and Solórzano-Margain (2014); Anand, Craig, and von Peter (2014); Anand, van Lelyveld, Banai, et al. (2018); and Bech and Atalay (2010) for the US; and Upper and Worms (2004) and Craig and Von Peter (2014) for Germany; and Blasques, Bräuning, and Van Lelyveld (2018) for the Netherlands.

A number of papers have empirically studied the process of financial contagion, see, for example, Wiggins, Piontek, and Metrick (2019); Wiggins and Metrick (2019); and Khandani and Lo (2007). For overviews of this work, see Glasserman and Young (2016), Jackson (2019), and Jackson and Pernoud (2021).

Turning to theoretical studies of financial contagion, Eisenberg and Noe (2001) present an elegant early model of bank networks that clarifies the deeply interconnected nature of bank obligations. This model takes as given the linkages between financial institutions. Allen and Gale (2000) provide a foundation for linkages between banks based on a combination of negatively correlated timings of liquidity shocks. These two early papers, along with Rochet and Tirole (1996), form the basis of most of the subsequent literature on financial contagion. The more recent body of literature has taken a more sophisticated approach to the modeling of networks and bankruptcy costs play a more prominent role; see, for example, Rogers and Veraart (2013); Cabrales, Gottardi, and Vega-Redondo (2017); Elliott, Golub, and Jackson (2014); Galeotti and Ghiglino (2021); Gai and Kapadia (2010); Gai, Haldane, and Kapadia (2011); Glasserman and Young (2015); Gofman (2017); Acemoglu, Ozdaglar, and Tahbaz-Salehi (2015b); and Acemoglu, Ozdaglar, and Tahbaz-Salehi (2015a). There are a number of excellent surveys of this work, see for example, Cabrales, Gale, and Gottardi (2016); Glasserman and Young (2016); and Jackson and Pernoud (2021).

There is a growing body of literature on the formation of financial networks. The conventional view is that institutions establish links with one another as a way of diversifying risk and facilitating intermediation. At a general level, the process of liquidity intermediation and the incentives of various actors to create rents are central to these models. In this perspective, the early theoretical models of network formation, as in Goyal and Vega-Redondo (2007), provide a general approach to brokerage and intermediation and the architecture of networks. A number of papers place this general approach within a finance context with the appropriate instruments and institutional constraints, including Acemoglu, Ozdaglar, and Tahbaz-Salehi (2015a); Erol and Vohra (2018); Babus and Hu (2017); Gofman (2017); Wang (2016); Cabrales, Gottardi, and Vega-Redondo (2017); In't Veld and Hommes (2020); Castiglionesi and Navarro (2007); and Georg (2013). We presented a model taken from Farboodi (2021), as it helps us understand some of the economic forces that give rise to a core-periphery financial network.

## 9.9 Questions

1. In the network given in figure 9.13,
   (a) Consider a shock that lowers the inflow to bank A from 210 to 140. Compute the net equity of the banks after this shock.
   (b) Consider a shock that lowers the inflow to bank A from 210 drops to 20. Compute the net equity of the banks after this shock.

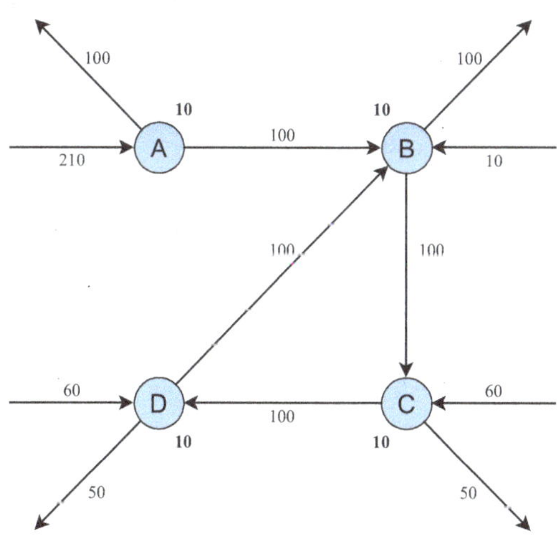


**Figure 9.13**
Original network.

2. Consider the four-region economy model discussed in section 9.4. The liquidity demands in state $S_i$, $i=1,2$ as specified in the table here. Each state takes place with equal probability.

Regional liquidity demand

| State | Region A | B | C | D |
|---|---|---|---|---|
| $S_1$ | 0.75 | 0.25 | 0.75 | 0.25 |
| $S_2$ | 0.25 | 0.75 | 0.25 | 0.75 |

There is a liquid asset that represents a storage technology. Investment in a long-term asset is available at $t=0$. Per unit invested in the long-term asset, the yield is of $r=0.4$ at $t=1$ (premature liquidation), and of $R>1$ at $t=2$. Assume that the period utility function is of the form $u(c_t)=\ln(c_t)$.

(a) Denote as $y$ and $x$ the per capita amounts that the social planner invests in the short- and long-term assets, respectively. The feasibility constraint is thus $y+x\leq 1$. Given that at $t=0$, the probability of being an early or a late consumer equals 0.5, derive the first best allocation. Verify that this allocation is incentive compatible.

(b) Consider decentralization. Describe the combination of investment decisions and interbank deposits that achieve the first best allocation when (i) the representative bank of a region holds deposits in the representative banks of all other regions (a complete structure); and (ii) the representative bank of region A deposits in the representative bank of region B, and the latter deposits in the representative bank of region C, and so on (an incomplete structure). For each case, explain the sequence of withdrawals if state $S_1$ takes place.

(c) Now suppose that a state $\bar{S}$, which was assigned zero probability at $t=0$, takes place. In this state, regions B, C, and D have a liquidity demand of 0.5, but region A faces a demand of $0.5+\varepsilon$.

(i) Consider the incomplete structure and set $\varepsilon=0.1$ and $R=1.5$. Show that there is no contagion. Would your results change if $\varepsilon$ were larger?

(ii) Suppose now that $\varepsilon=0.1$ and $R=1.2$. Show that there is contagion when the structure is incomplete, but not when it is complete.

3. Consider the model described in section 9.5. Show that when default costs are large, generalized default of all banks is easier in a ring network than in the complete network.

4. This question is inspired by the idea of the robust yet fragile networks (see, e.g., Cabrales, Gottardi, and Vega-Redondo [2017] and Acemoglu, Ozdaglar, and Tahbaz-Salehi [2015a]). Consider a model where banks face shocks of size $z$ with distribution

$F$. Consider the class of networks in which nodes are partitioned into equal-sized distinct cliques (the empty and complete networks are extreme examples of this class). Suppose that every bank has assets worth 1. A bank fails if the total assets in its clique is smaller than the shock $z$. There is a positive cost of a bank failure.

(a) Develop a model to examine the trade-offs between small and large cliques.

(b) How does the nature of $F$ relate to the optimal size of cliques?

(c) Chapter 8 studied the design and defense of networks that face contagious shocks. There we showed that multiple components may be optimal depending on the nature of the conflict technology and the relative size of the Defender and Adversary resources. Discuss the similarities and differences between the models and the results.

5. Consider the model of network formation presented in section 9.7. Suppose that $\kappa \geq \tilde{\kappa}$, with $\kappa$ and $\tilde{\kappa}$ being as defined in that section. Show that network (a) is stable if $\kappa \leq \bar{\kappa}$; networks (b) and (c) are stable if $\kappa \leq 1/2$; network (d) is stable if $\kappa \geq 1$; and network (e) is stable if $\kappa \geq 1/2$.

# 10 Wars

## 10.1 Introduction

War and violent conflict are recurring themes and continue to be important in the twenty-first century. Historically, war occurred between neighboring kingdoms, and a war between two rulers would in turn affect their neighbors. Larger wars have generally brought multiple opponents into play, and alliances play a central role in such wars. In different ways, then, inter-linkages across parties are an important feature of conflict. We would like to understand how the patterns of physical contiguity shape wars, how alliances affect the belligerence of different parties, and what the incentives to create alliances are. This chapter develops theoretical models in which interlinkages are represented as networks. This leads us to approach these questions by formulating games of conflict on networks and by setting up models of network formation.

We take the view that relations between actors—whether of enmity or friendship—can be modeled as signed links of a network, with positive links signifying amity and negative links indicating enmity. The first object of study is how a given pattern of links affects the incentives and the intensity of war. The theoretical framework combines networks with contest success functions (CSFs) and gives rise to a game on a network. The analysis draws attention to the role of connections—the sum of friendly and unfriendly links—in shaping behaviors. We apply this insight to understand the fighting intensities of different groups in the Great War of Congo. This framework permits a consideration of policy questions such as the effects of the withdrawal of particular foreign powers and of an arms embargo on the intensity of a conflict. In the discussion on contests in networks, the network is taken as a given. This is a reasonable starting point as most groups stuck to their alliances during the Great War of Congo, but if we take a longer time perspective then it is clear that alliances evolve—with old alliances lapsing and new alliances being formed. There arises the question of what alliance structures are stable more generally. This is the subject to which we turn next.

Here, we present a theoretical model for the study of stable alliances. In this model, countries can attack each other, form alliances, and trade with each other. The study of this model helps us understand the forces that shape incentives to form alliances and wage war. In particular, we show that in the absence of large trade flows, attempts to form alliances and attack opponents lead to shifting and unstable alliances: this instability makes peace hard to sustain. But if there are large gains from trade between countries, then alliances will be formed, and these alliances in turn will deter war. We apply these theoretical insights to understand the frequency of wars in the years prior to World War II and the long period of peace after that.

Finally, we use networks as a representation of contiguity and access and study the dynamics of war and conquest. Kingdoms are nodes, and the links represent contiguity. The resource base of kingdoms and the technology of war affect their chances at winning a war. Victory in a war brings rewards in the form of new territories (which come with their own resources). Winning rulers therefore expand their kingdoms and can wage war against new opponents. The theoretical analysis uncovers the role of the resources, the technology, and the network in shaping the incentives of individual rulers to wage war. The attack strategies of rulers determine the dynamics of conflict and the paths of conquest. We apply the theoretical insights of the model to reflect upon the processes that gave rise to the First Chinese Empire, the Roman Empire, and the Spanish Empire in the Americas.

## 10.2 Netwars

Individual actors and organisms seek to acquire more resources and expand their influence. One possible avenue through which to obtain resources is to appropriate them through conflict. However, agents may face constraints on whom they can target for conflict. The extensive literature on wars shows that a significant majority of them take place among physically proximate entities. Caselli, Morelli, and Rohner (2014) offer interesting empirical evidence on the role of physical contiguity in wars. Traditional models of conflict have focused on bilateral conflicts. As bilateral conflicts create spillovers on other conflicts, and as the spillovers are mediated by the pattern of neighborhood relations, it is important to understand the principles of interconnected conflict. We start with an early model of conflict on networks taken from Franke and Öztürk (2009).

There is a set of individuals $N=\{1,\ldots,n\}$, with $n\geq 3$, located on nodes of an (undirected) network $g$. The links between individuals reflect enmity: so, for instance, links can be thought of as a shared border between two regions/countries. The set of rivals of individual $i$ is given by $N_i(g)$. Individual $i$ is engaged in $n_i(g)=|N_i(g)|$ conflicts. Individual $i$ chooses strategy $e_i(g)=(\{e_{ij}\}_{j\in N_i(g)})$, which specifies a level of effort $e_{ij}$, for every $j\in N_i(g)$. The outcome of each bilateral conflict is probabilistic and depends on the investment in conflict by $i$ and $j$. For concreteness, we will suppose that with investments $e_{ij}$ and $e_{ji}$, the probability of winning for $i$ is given by

$$p_{ij}(e_{ij},e_{ji})=\frac{e_{ij}}{e_{ij}+e_{ji}} \tag{10.1}$$

so long as $e_{ij}+e_{ji}>0$. If $e_{ij}+e_{ji}=0$, the probability of either player winning is $1/2$. The cost of investment is given by the function

$$c(e_i)=\left(\sum_{j\in N_i} e_{ij}\right)^2. \tag{10.2}$$

Assume that the prize from winning a conflict is $Z$, while the cost of losing is $-Z$. The payoffs of individual $i$ under effort profile $e=(e_1,\ldots,e_n)$, are given by

$$\Pi_i(e)=Z\sum_{j\in N_i}[p_{ij}(e_{ij},e_{ji})-p_{ji}(e_{ij},e_{ji})]-c(e_i). \tag{10.3}$$

Let $e^*(g)=(e_1^*,\ldots,e_n^*)$ be a Nash equilibrium. We will suppose that there is a unique equilibrium and all links are actively contested. Define $E_i^*(g)=\sum_{j\in N_i(g)} e_{ij}^*$ as the aggregate fighting effort of player $i$ in network $g$. Equilibrium investments satisfy, for every individual $i\in N$ and for every link $g_{ij}$,

$$\frac{Ze_{ki}^*}{[e_{ik}^*+e_{ki}^*]^2}=E_i^*(g), \forall k\in N_i. \tag{10.4}$$

Define $E^*(g)=\sum_{i\in N} E_i^*(g)$ as the aggregate intensity of conflict. The following result describes equilibrium outcomes in two well-known networks.

**Proposition 10.1** *A conflict equilibrium exhibits the following properties:*

- *Regular networks: Conflict intensity is increasing in degree and in the number of individuals. Individual investment and expected payoff is decreasing in degree. Expected payoff is negative for all individuals.*
- *Star network: Conflict intensity is increasing in the number of peripheral individuals. For the central individual, link-specific (aggregate) investment is decreasing (increasing), and the expected payoff is decreasing in the number of peripheral individuals. For the peripheral player, conflict investment is declining and payoffs are increasing in the number of peripheral individuals.*

The result is fairly intuitive: involvement in a greater number of conflicts leads to a worse expected outcome for an individual as the convex costs of conflict come into play. In the star network, a greater number of peripheral players benefits the peripheral players at the expense of the hub.

While the result is obtained for specific networks only, it offers a first impression of how the interconnections in conflict shapes individuals' fighting efforts. In a regular network, increasing density of the network raises the overall level of conflict and lowers payoffs. The central individual facing more peripheral opponents is obliged to make larger investments but earns a lower payoff. The peripheral players gain as their number grows because the central opponent player is more overstretched, and hence less effective.

In the present model, the links represent enmity and the conflict investments are link specific. In the next section, we take up the more general setting with ties of both enmity as well as amity (as reflected in alliances). In order to make analytical progress, we will simplify the effort formulation and assume that there is a single effort for every individual and a single prize at stake.

## 10.3 Alliances and Conflict

Large-scale wars like the two world wars, the Korean War, and the Vietnam War involve alliances among many nation-states. Indeed, alliances have been a central feature of wars and violent conflicts throughout history. In this section, we study wars between parties who are members of alliances.

When players A and B form an alliance, they hope to support each other—possibly by sharing resources and information. Thus an alliance may strengthen the position of both A and B vis-á-vis other opponents. This benefit comes with a potential downside: the effort of A benefits A, but it also benefits B. This spillover makes A's effort a public good and can lower the incentives of A to exert effort. An alliance between A and B will have effects on other opponents: they may be obliged to raise their efforts in the face of such an alliance. Moreover, in large-scale conflicts, it may be the case that A and B are in an alliance, while B is in an alliance with other players, X and Y. With these preliminary observations in place, let us consider the following model of fighting in a network of alliances taken from König, Rohner, Thoenig, and Zilibotti (2017).

The set of players is $N=\{1,\ldots,n\}$, where $n\geq 3$. Players have relations that are positive (allies) and negative (enemies). There is a prize of value $V$, which may reflect the value of land and natural resources. The relations among the players are captured in a network of links, $g$. A pair of players can be *allies*, *enemies*, or *neutral*. Thus, for any pair of players $i,j$, a link is as follows:

$$g_{ij}=\begin{cases}1, & \text{if } i \text{ and } j \text{ are allies,}\\ -1, & \text{if } i \text{ and } j \text{ are enemies,}\\ 0, & \text{if } i \text{ and } j \text{ are in a neutral relationship.}\end{cases} \tag{10.5}$$

The players simultaneously choose fighting efforts, so player $i\in N$ chooses effort $x_i\in\mathbb{R}$. The role of the network is modeled in a specific manner: a player's effort is reinforced by the efforts of its friends and weakened by the efforts of its enemies. This idea is captured in the idea of effective effort, $\varphi_i$ as follows:

$$\varphi_i(g,\mathbf{x})=x_i+\beta\sum_{j=1}^{n}g_{ij}^{+}x_j-\gamma\sum_{j=1}^{n}g_{ij}^{-}x_j, \tag{10.6}$$

where $g_{ij}^{+}$ refers to links between allies, $g_{ij}^{-}$ refers to links between enemies, and $\beta,\gamma\in[0,1]$ are spillovers from allies and enemies, respectively.

It is worth noting some special cases of this formulation: when there are no friends or enemies, the model yields a standard contest between $n$ opponents. Observe that the notion of allies is subtle: consider an example with two allies. They contest for a prize, but each one's efforts are boosted by the efforts of their ally. On the other hand, when the two opponents are enemies, their efforts are dampened by each other's efforts.

Given network $g$ and effort profile $x = (x_1, \ldots, x_n)$, the payoff to player $i$ is determined by a Tullock contest function:

$$\Pi_i(g, \mathbf{x}) = V \times \frac{\varphi_i(g, \mathbf{x})}{\sum_{j=1}^{n} \varphi_j(g, \mathbf{x})} - x_i. \tag{10.7}$$

Here, our interest is in interior solutions, outcomes in which all players are active, and we will assume that such outcomes exist and are unique. From chapter 4 we know that in games on networks, Nash equilibrium efforts are interior and unique when spillovers across group effects are suitably small.

### 10.3.1 Equilibrium Conflict

In such an active outcome, every player will set its efforts at a level where the marginal costs are equal to the marginal returns. Differentiating individual payoffs with respect to efforts, we arrive at the following first-order condition for the optimal individual efforts:

$$\frac{\partial \pi_i}{\partial x_i} = V \frac{\sum_{j=1}^{n} \varphi_j - \varphi_i(1 + \beta d_i^+ - \gamma d_i^-)}{\left(\sum_{j=1}^{n} \varphi_j\right)^2} - 1 = 0, \tag{10.8}$$

where we have dropped the dependence of $\varphi$ on the network and the efforts, set $d_i^+$ to be the number of allies, and set $d_i^-$ as the number of enemies of player $i$. Observe that a player's efforts augment the efforts of its friends (enemies), thus making them more (less) competitive in the contest.

We would like to express the equilibrium effort of a player explicitly in terms of the network. To do so, it is helpful to proceed via a derivation of equilibrium-effective effort. The first step is to rewrite the first order condition to obtain the following expression for effective effort:

$$\varphi_i = \frac{1}{1 + \beta d_i^+ - \gamma d_i^-} \left(1 - \sum_{j=1}^{n} \varphi_j\right) \sum_{j=1}^{n} \varphi_j. \tag{10.9}$$

Summing over all players yields

$$\sum_{i=1}^{n} \varphi_i = \left(1 - \frac{1}{\sum_{i=1}^{n} \frac{1}{1+\beta d_i^+ - \gamma d_i^-}}\right). \tag{10.10}$$

The following pieces of new notation help us in simplifying the expressions:

$$\Gamma_i^{\beta,\gamma}(g) = \frac{1}{1+\beta d_i^+ - \gamma d_i^-}, \text{ and } \Lambda^{\beta,\gamma}(g) = 1 - \frac{1}{\sum_{i=1}^n \Gamma_i^{\beta,\gamma}(g)}. \tag{10.11}$$

We may refer to $\Gamma_i$ as the local hostility level, as it is increasing in the number of enemies of $i$ and decreasing in the number of allies of $i$. Using the new notation, equilibrium aggregate effective effort is given by

$$\sum_{i=1}^n \varphi_i = \Lambda^{\beta,\gamma}(g). \tag{10.12}$$

This in turn allows us to write the individual effective effort as

$$\varphi_i(g, \mathbf{x}) = \Lambda^{\beta,\gamma}(g)(1 - \Lambda^{\beta,\gamma}(g))\Gamma_i^{\beta,\gamma}(g). \tag{10.13}$$

Define $\Gamma^{\beta,\gamma}(g) \equiv (\Gamma_1^{\beta,\gamma}(G), \ldots, \Gamma_n^{\beta,\gamma}(G))^\top$. Equilibrium effort may be expressed in matrix form as follows:

$$(\mathbf{I}_n + \beta\mathbf{G}^+ - \gamma\mathbf{G}^-)\mathbf{x} = \Lambda^{\beta,\gamma}(G)(1 - \Lambda^{\beta,\gamma}(G))\Gamma^{\beta,\gamma}(G). \tag{10.14}$$

When the matrix $\mathbf{I}_n + \beta\mathbf{G}^+ - \gamma\mathbf{G}^-$ is invertible,

$$\mathbf{x} = (\mathbf{I}_n + \beta\mathbf{G}^+ - \gamma\mathbf{G}^-)^{-1}\left(V\Lambda^{\beta,\gamma}(G)(1 - \Lambda^{\beta,\gamma}(G))\Gamma^{\beta,\gamma}(G)\right). \tag{10.15}$$

It is useful to briefly reflect on the strategic effects in this environment. First, consider the direct effects of a player's enemies. As an enemy raises their efforts, it follows from equation (10.6) that an individual's effective efforts go down. This raises the marginal returns from own efforts. Thus the efforts of enemies are strategic complements. Similarly, we can reason that the efforts of friends are strategic substitutes. Turning to indirect effects, consider the enemies of my enemies. As they raise efforts, an individual's enemies raise efforts, which induces the individual in question to raise their efforts. On the other hand, as the friends of an individual's friend raise efforts, the friends lower efforts, which induces the individual in question to raise their efforts. This brief discussion helps us see the complex interplay of positive and negative strategic effects through the paths of the network.

The principal result of the analysis provides a relation between the Katz-Bonacich centrality of a player and their war effort. To develop a sense for how allies and enemies shape network centrality and efforts, we present an example of a line network in figure 10.1. In this network, there are five nodes, and we set $\gamma = 0.1, \beta = 0.1$. In the case where all links represent enemies, the Katz-Bonacich centrality related to the network of hostilities measures the local hostility levels along all walks reaching $i$ using only hostility connections, where walks of length $k$ are weighted by the geometrically decaying hostility externality $\gamma^k$. As the discounted number of walks emanating from a node in a line network is higher, the

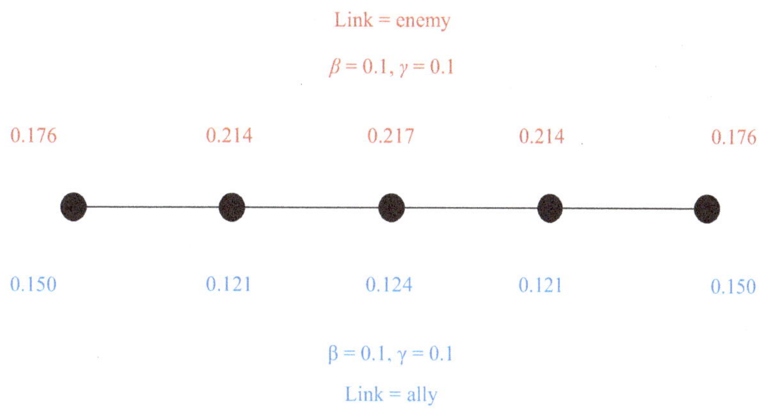


**Figure 10.1**
Line network: enemies in red; allies in blue.

more central an agent is, the player in the middle of the line has the highest centrality and centralities decrease moving away from the middle of the path.

Next, consider the situation where the links reflect friendships. The centrality is determined by $b_{\cdot,i}\left(-\beta, G^{+}\right)$. Thus a player's neighbor gets negative weight, and their neighbor's neighbor gets positive weight. This means that centrality is falling as we move from the edge of the line to the next player, and then rising again as we arrive at the center of the line. Let us now develop the relation between networks and the fighting effort for networks that combine both friendship and enmity links.

Define $c_i^{\beta,\gamma}(G)$ as player $i$'s centrality in network $G$. The vector of Katz-Bonacich centralities are given by:

$$\mathbf{c}^{\beta,\gamma}(G) \equiv \left(\mathbf{I}_n + \beta \mathbf{G}^{+} - \gamma \mathbf{G}^{-}\right)^{-1} \Gamma^{\beta,\gamma}(G). \tag{10.16}$$

Equipped with this definition of centrality, equilibrium effort levels can be expressed as

$$x_i(G) = \Lambda^{\beta,\gamma}(G)\left(1 - \Lambda^{\beta,\gamma}(G)\right) c_i^{\beta,\gamma}(G). \tag{10.17}$$

Equilibrium payoffs are given by

$$\pi_i(G) = \left(1 - \Lambda^{\beta,\gamma}(G)\right)\left(\Gamma_i^{\beta,\gamma}(G) - \Lambda^{\beta,\gamma}(G)\, c_i^{\beta,\gamma}(G)\right). \tag{10.18}$$

For sufficiently small cross-player effects (i.e., when $\beta$ and $\gamma$ are close to 0), the centrality measure defined in equation (10.16) may be expressed as a sum of centrality in the friends network, centrality in the enemies network, and a term that captures higher-order cross-relation effects; that is,

$$\mathbf{c}^{\beta,\gamma}(G) = \mathbf{b}(\gamma, g^{-}) + \mathbf{b}(-\beta, g^{+}) - \mathbf{\Gamma}^{\beta,\gamma}(g) + O(\beta\gamma), \tag{10.19}$$

where

$$\mathbf{b}(\gamma, g) = (\mathbf{I}_n - \alpha \mathbf{g})^{-1} \boldsymbol{\Gamma}^{\beta,\gamma}(g) \tag{10.20}$$

is the Katz-Bonacich centrality (this is similar for $\mathbf{b}(-\beta, g^+)$), while $O(\beta\gamma)$ involves second- and higher-order terms.

One interesting implication of these derivations is that the ratio of the efforts of two players is equal to the ratio of their centralities:

$$\frac{x_i(G)}{x_j(G)} = \frac{c_i^{\beta,\gamma}(G)}{c_j^{\beta,\gamma}(G)}. \tag{10.21}$$

When higher-order terms are ignored, the centrality measure is increasing in $\gamma$ and in the number of first-degree enemies, whereas it is decreasing in $\beta$ and in the number of first-degree alliances. We use this simple prediction of the theory next, in our study of the Great War of Congo.

### 10.3.2 Case Study: The Great War of Congo

The Democratic Republic of Congo (in what follows, Congo), with a population of over 86 million, is one of the largest countries in Africa. This population belongs to over 200 ethnic groups. Congo gained independence from Belgium in 1960 but has experienced instability and wars for extended periods. As a result of this political instability, it is one of the poorest countries in the world, in spite of having very large deposits of a number of valuable minerals such as copper, gold, diamonds, cobalt, uranium, coltan, and oil. Income level in 2020 was at 40 percent of the 1960 level; the per capita income was \$400, which is less than 1 percent of what it is in the US. The quality of life is very low: life expectancy in Congo is 20 years lower than in the US. A major reason for this dire situation is violent conflict. The conflicts in Congo involve many interconnected domestic and foreign actors. Our discussion of the Great War of Congo draws on König, Rohner, Thoenig, and Zilibotti (2017) and the *Encyclopedia Britannica*.

The first point to note is that the war in Congo is closely connected with ethnic conflicts in neighboring countries such as Rwanda and Uganda. In 1994, Hutu radicals took control of the Rwandan government and allowed ethnic militias to carry out the killing of nearly a million Tutsis and moderate Hutus. After they lost power in Rwanda, over a million Hutus fled Rwanda and sought refuge in the Congo (which was then ruled by Mobutu Sese Seko). These Hutu militias ran into conflict with local Tutsi groups. As ethnic tensions mounted, a large coalition of African countries, which included Uganda and Rwanda, supported an anti-Mobutu rebellion led by Laurent-Desire Kabila. The First Congo War (1996–1997) ended with Kabila's victory.

However, Kabila's relationship with Uganda and Rwanda soon turned sour, and he ordered all Rwandan and Ugandan troops to leave the country. As a result, new ethnic clashes erupted in eastern Congo, and the crisis escalated into a larger war. This led to the Second Congo War.

**Table 10.1**
Main groups: Allies, enemies, and fights

| Name | Allies | Enemies | Total Links | Fights |
|---|---|---|---|---|
| FARD-JK | 16 | 26 | 42 | 88 |
| FARD-LK | 21 | 16 | 37 | 49 |
| Uganda | 9 | 13 | 22 | 21 |
| RCD-G | 4 | 14 | 18 | 41 |
| RCD-K | 5 | 13 | 18 | 28 |
| RWA94 | 7 | 10 | 17 | 8 |
| RWA00 | 4 | 11 | 15 | 17 |
| RCD | 11 | 4 | 15 | 8 |

*Source*: www.acleddata.com.

The Second Congo War lasted from 1998 until 2003 is regarded as the deadliest war of the twenty-first century. The eastern part of the Congo became a bloody battlefield that was as bitterly contested as the Western Front in World War I. The armies of nine countries and a number of militias were involved. Angola, Namibia, Chad, Sudan, and Zimbabwe backed Kabila's Congolese government forces, while troops from Burundi, Rwanda, and Uganda supported anti-Kabila rebels. Mass rapes were reported in areas of conflict, and large sections of the Congo were stripped of resources as organized combat between professional armies gave way to brigandage and plunder. It is estimated that over three million people (mostly civilians) were killed in the fighting or died of disease or malnutrition during the war. A peace agreement was signed in 2002 and the war officially ended in 2003, but fighting has continued in different parts of Congo even after that.

After a major reshuffling at the end of the First Congo War, the web of alliances and enmities between the main armies and rebel groups has remained largely stable in the period 1998–2010. There are 80 groups in all; for a complete list, see König, Rohner, Thoenig, and Zilibotti (2017). There were 4 Congolese state army groups, 47 domestic Congolese nonstate militias, 11 foreign government armies, and 18 foreign nonstate militias.

We will think of a group as a player and represent it as a node in the network. The average degree of a node is 5.35 (here, degree refers to both friends and enemies; this is therefore a sparse network), the average distance in the network is 2.35 (groups are close to each other), and the network is unequal, as the most connected groups have a very large number of links. Table 10.1 presents an overview of the eight most connected groups: the Conglolese Army under Joseph Kabila (FARD-JK), the Conglolese Army under Laurent Kabila (FARD-LK), Uganda, Rally for Congolese Democracy, Goma (RCD-G), Rally for Congolese Democracy, Kisangani (RCD-K), Military Forces of Rwanda 1994–1999 (RWA94), Military Forces of Rwanda 2000– (RWA00), and Rally for Congolese Democracy (RCD). Figure 10.2 summarizes the relations between the 80 groups that were active during

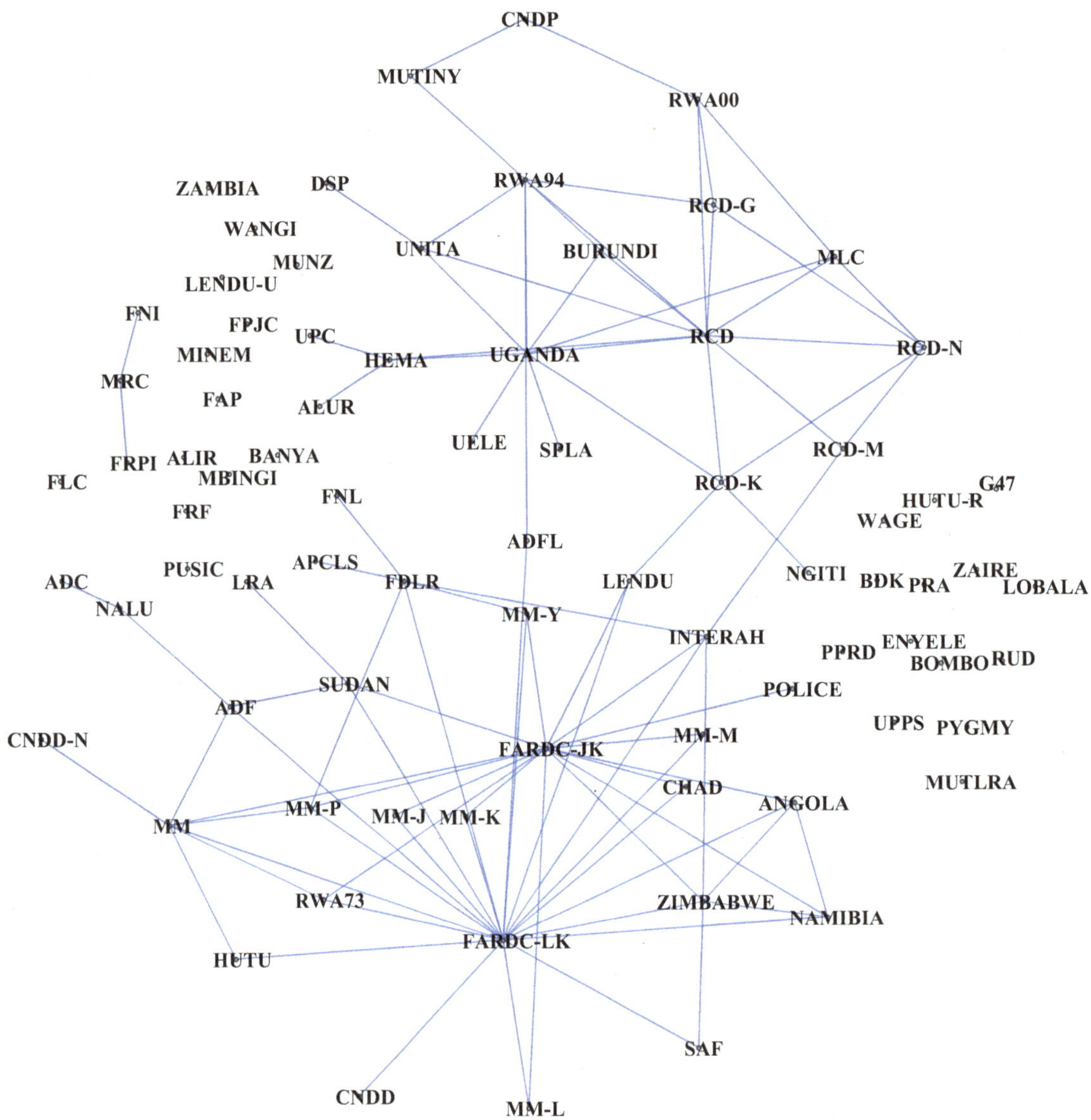


**Figure 10.2**
The Great War in Congo: friends. *Source*: www.acleddata.com.

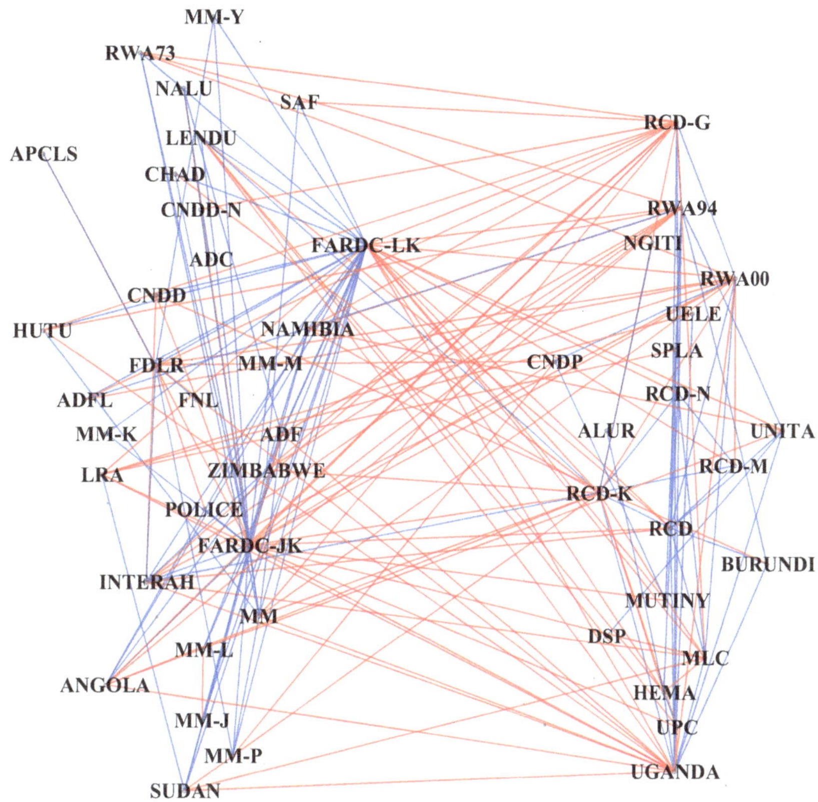


**Figure 10.3**
The Great War in Congo: friendship in blue, enmity in red. *Source*: www.acleddata.com.

the Second Congo War: friends are portrayed in blue, enemies in red, and absent ties in neutral.

Table 10.1 highlights the great inequality in the number of links, which helps us see the effects of the number of allies and enemies on fighting effort. We see that even among groups with the same number of links, the relative number of allies and friends matters—more enemies lead to higher levels of fighting. Let us now describe the network of friends and enemies.

An initial thought would be that friends and enemies would be neatly separated: this would suggest that an enemy of A would be an enemy of all friends of A and a friend of A would be friends of all friends of A. The actual pattern of relations in Congo is richer and more complicated. To see this, we proceeded as follows. We first plotted the friendship ties only, as shown in figure 10.2. Then we removed all nodes that have no friends and added the enmity links among the remaining groups. This yields the network given in figure 10.3.

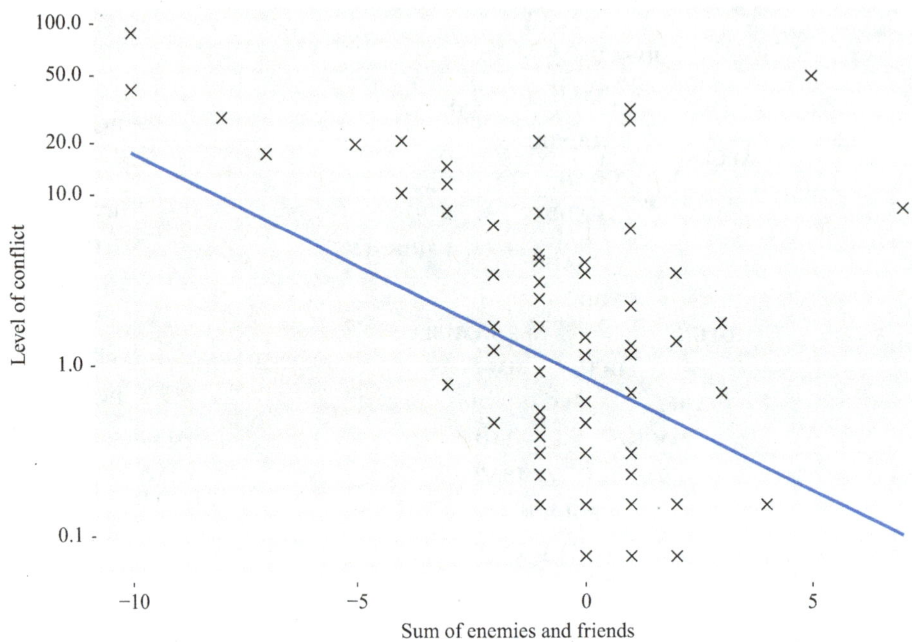


**Figure 10.4**
Friends and enemies and level of fighting. *Source*: www.acleddata.com.

We see that there is a dense web of friendship ties within two large clusters, but we also see that there are enmity ties within these clusters and some friendship ties across the clusters. These figures suggest why it might be helpful to go beyond a cluster-level analysis and consider the details of the pairwise links.

The data source for the fighting effort is the Armed Conflict Location & Event Data (ACLED) Project (www.acleddata.com). This data set contains 4,676 geolocalized violent events in the Congo involving 80 groups. The theory predicts that friends depress and enemies raise the fighting effort of a group. Figure 10.4 plots this relationship in the Great Congo War. On the $x$-axis, we plot the (log of) the sum of numbers of friends (positive) and enemies (negative), and on the $y$-axis, we present the number of fights. The patterns of fighting are broadly consistent with the predictions of the theory.

The network approach to the study of the war can help us uncover the potential effects of various changes in the environment. For instance, we can ask how the withdrawal of foreign players like Uganda and Rwanda would affect the fighting. This question can be addressed by comparing the fighting level observed with the fighting level in a network in which these two groups, Uganda and Rwanda, are taken out of the network. Given their centrality in the alliance network, their withdrawal could sharply reduce the level of fighting. By contrast, the removal of peripheral players like Zaire or Zambia would have relatively minor effects on the level of conflict.

Similarly, we can examine the implications of arms embargoes on certain groups. Such an embargo would raise the costs of fighting for these groups. An increase in the costs of fighting for a group will lower the fighting by that group, which will lower the fighting of its enemies and raise the fighting of its allies. These effects will percolate through the network of alliances. Imposing an embargo on a central group can therefore significantly lower the overall level of fighting.

Let us now summarize what we have learned about large-scale wars from this model. The model helps us appreciate how the network of relations shapes the fighting efforts of opponents and the aggregate level of fighting. A key prediction of the model is that individual fighting effort is increasing in the number of enemies and falling in the number of friends. This prediction is consistent with the empirical evidence from the Great War of Congo. In this model, the focus is on war and there is no other economic activity. In the next section, we expand the scope of the inquiry along two dimensions—one, we allow for trade and two, we study the incentives to form alliances.

## 10.4 Alliances, Trade, and War

The frequency of wars between countries has declined significantly over the past 200 years. In particular, wars were more common from 1800 until World War II than in the period since then. One way of developing a better feel for the great change in frequency of wars is to consider the number of wars in a year in relation to the number of distinct pairs of countries in that year. Between 1820 and 1959, we find that there were 0.00056 wars per year per pair of countries. By contrast, from 1960 to 2000, the average was only 0.00005 wars per year. Thus wars were a tenth as likely in the period after 1960 as before. Figure 10.4 provides an overview of this trend. This section examines the factors that can account for this change in frequency of war. Let us begin by noting that two other variables have registered significant changes over the same period the density and stability of alliances and the size of international trade.

Our data is taken from the Directed Dyadic Interstate War Data Set (Maoz et al. [2019]). The nature of military alliances changed dramatically over this period. Between 1816 and 1950, a country had 2.5 alliances on average (and if we exclude the 1940s, this number drops even further, to 1.7). By contrast, between 1951 and 2003, the number of alliances per country grows by a factor of more than 4, reaching over 10.5. Thus, there were significantly more alliances after World War II than before it. This change in the number of alliances was accompanied by a great change in their persistence or stability. To see this, we ask what fraction of alliances at year $t$ are also present at year $t+5$. For the period from 1816 to 1950, we find this number of to be 0.695. By contrast, the number of the period from 1950 to 2003 is 0.949! In other words, there is a 30 percent chance that a given alliance disappears in the

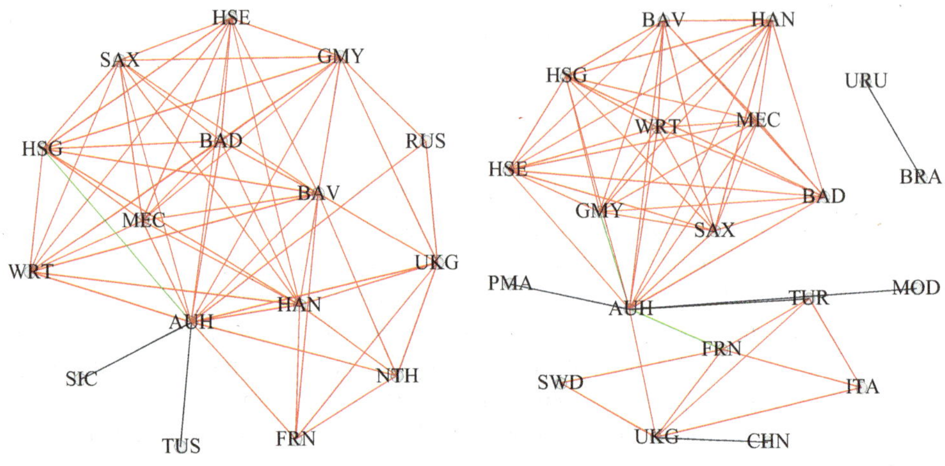


**Figure 10.5**
Alliances: multilateral in red, bilateral in gray, and both in green. *Source*: Maoz, Johnson, Kaplan, et al. (2019).

next five years in the period prior to the World War II, while there is only a 5 percent chance that this happens in the period after it.

Figures 10.5–10.7 present alliance networks from the nineteenth and twentieth centuries to illustrate these trends. In the early nineteenth century, the networks were sparse and rapidly evolving. This is brought out by figure 10.5. The labels for the entities in figure 10.5 are as follows: AUH—Austria-Hungary; BAD—Baden; BAV—Bavaria; BRA—Brazil; CHN—China; FRN—France; GMY—Germany; HAN—Hanover; HSE—Hesse Electoral; HSG—Hesse Grand Ducal; ITA—Italy; MEC—Mecklenburg-Schwerin; MOD—Modena; NTH—Netherlands; PMA—Parma; RUS—Russia; SAX—Saxony; SIC—Two Sicilies; SWD—Sweden; TUR—Turkey; TUS—Tuscany; UKG—United Kingdom; URU—Uruguay; WRT—Wuerttemburg. We also see that the alliance network is sparse and evolving.

Figures 10.6 and 10.7 illustrate the situation after World War II. This period witnessed increasingly dense networks with largely stable alliances separated by continent and ideology: the networks contain densely connected subsets of states, which are bridged by a few larger countries.

Turning to international trade, we note that there are two major periods of growth. The first period covered the latter half of the nineteenth century and lasted until World War 1. The second period began after World War II and lasted roughly until 2010. Table 10.2 provides an overview of this trend. We see that trade increased dramatically after World War II, growing by almost a factor of 4.

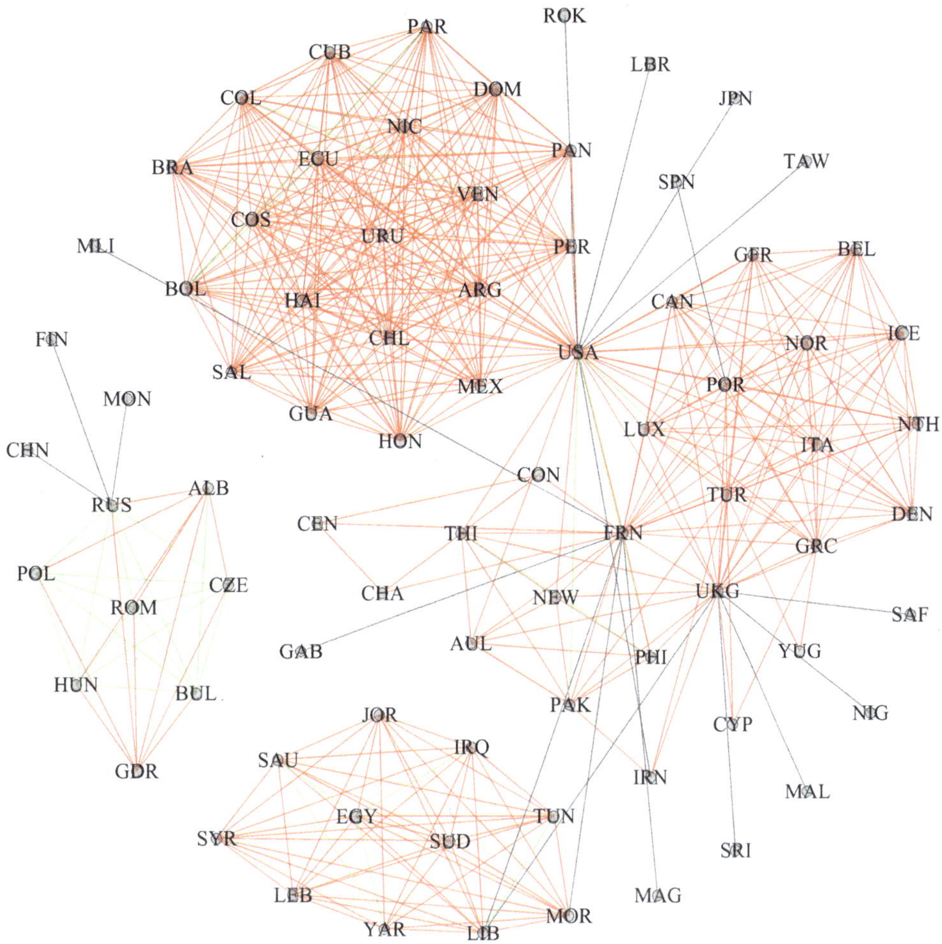


**Figure 10.6**
Alliances: 1960 (multilateral in red, bilateral in gray, and both in green). *Source:* Maoz, Johnson, Kaplan, et al. (2019).

### 10.4.1 A Model of Alliances

Given this empirical background, we now turn to a theoretical model taken from Jackson and Nei (2015) that helps us understand the co-movements in the frequency of war, the changes in trade, and the nature of alliances. There are $N = \{1, \ldots, n\}$, $n \geq 3$, countries. Individual countries can attack each other, form alliances, and trade with each other. A link between two countries signifies an alliance. The collection of alliances is denoted by network $g$. Let $g - i$ denote the network obtained by deleting all alliances that involve country $i$. Each country $i \in N$ is endowed with military strength $M_i \in \mathbb{R}_+$. For any subset of countries $C \subseteq N$,

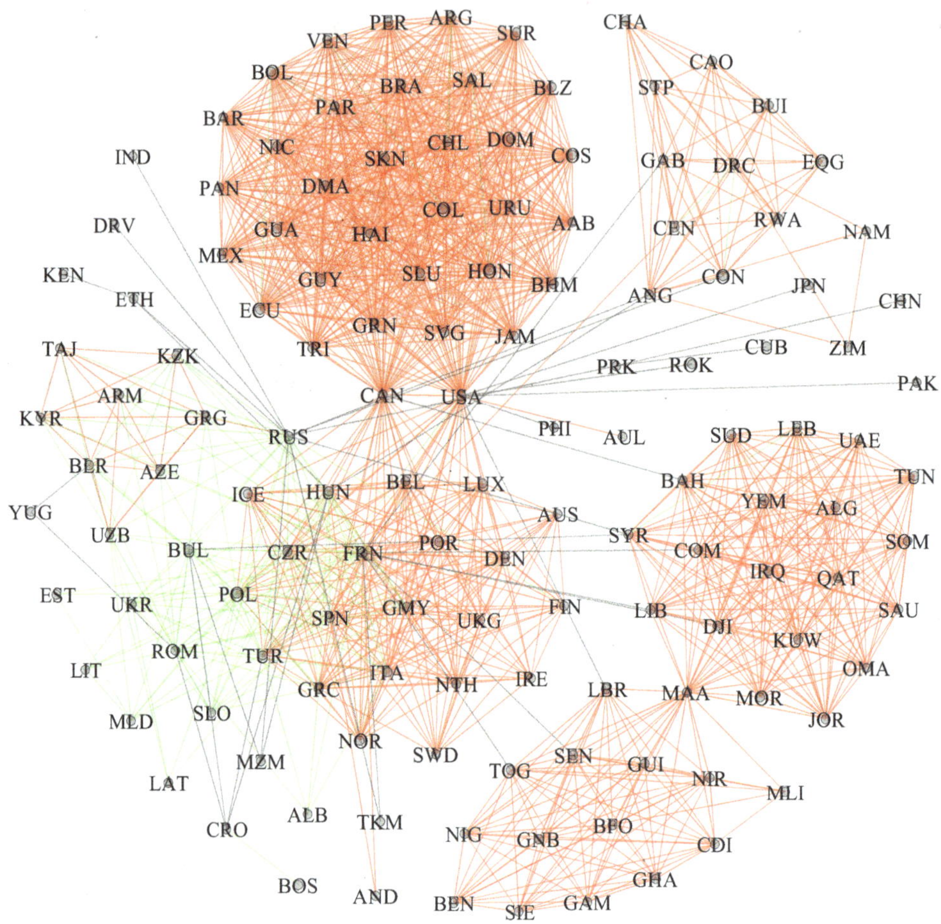


**Figure 10.7**
Alliances: 2000 (multilateral in red, bilateral in gray, and both in green). *Source*: Maoz, Johnson, Kaplan, et al. (2019).

let $M(C) = \sum_{i \in C} M_i$ be their collective military strength. If there is a war between $C_1$ and $C_2$, with $C_1$ being the aggressor, then $C_1$ wins if $M(C_1) > \rho M(C_2)$. The parameter $\rho > 1$ reflects the relative advantage of being the defender, and $\rho < 1$ reflects the relative advantage of being the aggressor.

The notion of vulnerability plays a key role in the analysis. Country $i$ is vulnerable at network $g$ if there is a country $j$ and a coalition $C \subseteq N_j(g) \cup \{j\}$ such that $j \in C$, $i \notin C$, and

$$M(C) > \rho M(i \cup (N_i(g) \cap C^c)), \tag{10.22}$$

**Table 10.2**
World merchandise exports as percentage of gross domestic product (GDP)

| Year | 1850 | 1880 | 1913 | 1950 | 1973 | 1985 | 1993 | 2012 |
|---|---|---|---|---|---|---|---|---|
| Percent | 5.1 | 9.8 | 11.9 | 7.1 | 11.7 | 14.5 | 17.1 | 25.3 |

*Source*: Jackson and Nei (2015), Krugman (1995).

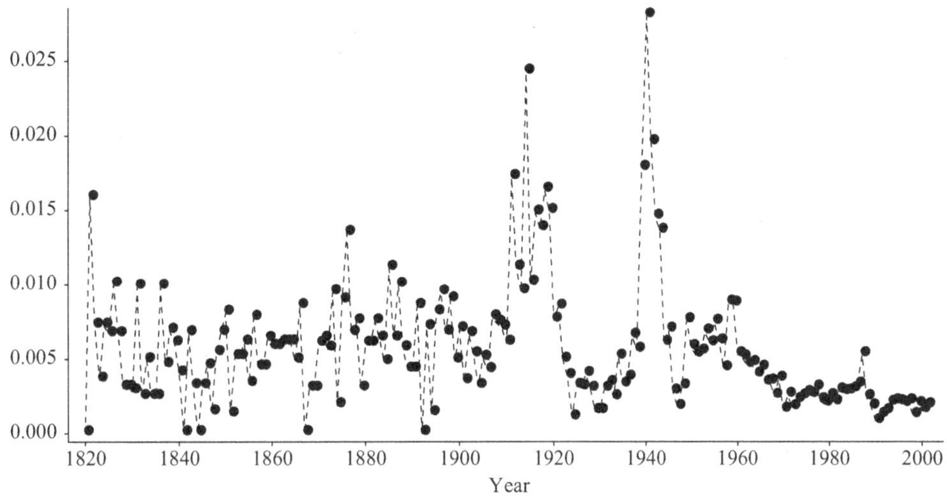


**Figure 10.8**
Probability of war between country pairs: 1820–2000. *Source*: Jackson and Nei (2015).

where $C^c$ is the complement of $C$. In this instance, country $j$ is said to be a potential aggressor. This is saying that there is a coalition of $j$ and some of their neighbors such that the combined might of the coalition is greater than the defensive might of $i$ and its neighbors (those that are not in the coalition). This definition thus brings out the role of alliance ties: an alliance creates the potential for asking for support when faced with a threat (however, as ties are not exclusive, it is possible that an ally may also switch sides and become part of a rival group). This definition of feasible attacking and defending coalitions may be interpreted as another assumption about the technology of war (in the same spirit as the CSF).

This idea is illustrated in figure 10.9. Country 2 and its allies (3 and 4) attack country 1 (which is defended by 5). Country 1 is vulnerable if $M(\{2,3,4\}) > \rho M(\{1,5\}$. Without getting into further detail, we may assume that winning is desirable and losing a war is undesirable.

We are interested in understanding alliance networks that are stable in the sense that no country is vulnerable, no one wishes to delete an alliance, and no pair of countries wishes to

**Figure 10.9**
(left) Vulnerable country; (right) ring network.

add an alliance link. Suppose that there is a cost $c_{ij} > 0$ to keeping a link between a pair of countries $i, j$. These costs will be taken to be small relative to the spoils of a successful war.

With this notation in place, a network $g$ is war-stable if all of the following occurs:

- No country is vulnerable at $g$ (or else that country will be invaded and conquered).
- $\forall g_{j,k} \notin g$, no country is vulnerable at $g + g_{jk}$ (which discourages new links).
- $\forall g_{jk} \in g$, both $j$ and $k$ are vulnerable at $g - g_{jk}$ (which discourages the deletion of existing links).

The notion of war-stability (and the other stability definition war-and-trade stable discussed next) has the same essential structure as the usual pairwise stability notion introduced in chapter 3. In all cases, the considerations are very similar: links have to benefit both parties, and all beneficial links are added. The definitions of stability in this section place these considerations in the context of war and peace and alliances.

Taken one at a time, the requirements for stability are reasonable, but they are difficult to satisfy jointly. To see this tension between the three requirements, let us consider the complete network. For this network to be war-stable, no country must be vulnerable. But this means that for every country, $\rho M(i) \geq M(N \setminus \{i\})$. This, however, implies that country $i$ is not vulnerable in network $g - g_{ik}$ for any $j \neq i$, thereby showing that the complete network is not war-stable.

Consider next a regular network, as depicted in figure 10.9. There are five countries in this network. Let us first ensure that no country wishes to form a link. Consider link $g_{53}$. In order for country 1 not to be vulnerable to the addition of this link, it must be that $\rho M(1) \geq M(\{2, 3, 4, 5\})$ (as it must not be vulnerable to 3 and its allies 2, 4, and 5). But note that this implies that 1 is not vulnerable (with respect to any coalition of rivals) in the original ring, even if it deletes a link. This contradicts the war-stability of the ring network.

On the other hand, the empty network is war-stable if no country is vulnerable and no two countries can gang up to successfully attack a third country. Suppose that the resources of countries are ordered as follows: $M_1 \geq M_2 \geq \ldots \geq M_n$. Then a sufficient condition for the empty network to be war-stable is that $\rho M(\{n\}) \geq M(\{1,2\})$.

These considerations are general and form the basis for the following result.

**Proposition 10.2** *If $n \geq 3$, then there are no nonempty, war-stable networks.*

In other words, there is no network with alliances that is war-stable. The argument shows that there is a very fine line between profitable alliances and vulnerability: if an alliance between $i$ and $x$ is necessary for sustaining $i$, then $x$ could form an alliance with another country $z$ that would render $i$ vulnerable. This suggests that there may be rapidly shifting alliances as countries try to take advantage and navigate this delicate balance. This is reminiscent of the empirical patterns from the nineteenth century that we mentioned previously: during the nineteenth century and the first half of the twentieth century, roughly one-third of the alliances present at any time were dissolved within a five-year period. The dynamics of shifting alliances went hand in hand with the frequency of wars in this period.

Here is a sketch of the proof for this result. Consider a nonempty, war-stable network, $g$. There must be a country $i$ that has an alliance with country $k$. In order for this link to be incentive compatible (i.e., there must be no incentive to delete a link), $i$ must be vulnerable in $g - g_{ik}$. Thus, there is some $j$ and $C \subset N_j(g - g_{ik}) \cup \{j\}$ with $i \notin C$ and $M(C) \geq \rho M(C')$, for every $C' \subset \{i\} \cup N_i(g - g_{ik}) \cap C^c$, where $C^c$ is the complement of set $C$.

As $g$ is war-stable, $i$ is not vulnerable at $g$: it must be that $k \notin C$, and in particular that $g_{jk} \notin g$. However, if link $g_{jk}$ is added to create network $g + g_{jk}$, then $C \cup \{k\}$ can defeat $i$ because $M(C \cup \{k\}) \geq M(C)$, and therefore $M(C \cup \{k\}) \geq \rho M(C')$ for any feasible $C'$ that can defend $i$; that is,

$$M(C \cup \{k\}) \geq M(C) > \rho M(C') \tag{10.23}$$

for any feasible $C'$ that can defend $i$ in $g + g_{jk}$. This means that $j$ and $k$ can form a link that makes $i$ vulnerable, contradicting the hypothesis that $g$ is war-stable. As $g$ was an arbitrary nonempty network, this also completes the proof. ■

Turning to the period after World War II, a major change was the introduction of nuclear weapons. It has been widely argued that this profoundly altered the incentives to wage large-scale wars. One way to interpret this within the model is to say that with the widespread availability of nuclear weapons, countries were no longer vulnerable to attacks. The only war-stable network is the empty network. However, the empirical evidence presented here shows that alliances became more popular and their stability increased greatly. Moreover, this trend was accompanied with an increase in international trade. To reconcile these trends, we introduce international trade into the theoretical model.

### 10.4.2 A Model of Alliances and Trade

Suppose that a country earns payoff $u_i(g)$ from network $g$. The utility reflects gains from trade. Let us adapt the notion of vulnerability as follows: Denote by $E_{ik}(g, C)$ the net gains to country $k$ if country $i$ is conquered by coalition $C$ (of which $k$ is a member). Given network

$g$, country $i$ is said to be *vulnerable despite trade* if there exists a country $j$ and a coalition $C \subseteq N_j(g) \cup \{j\}$ such that $j \in C$, $i \notin C$, and

- $M(C) > \rho M(i \cup (N_i(g) \cap C^c))$ and
- $u_k(g-i) + E_{ik}(g, C) \geq u_k(g)$, with a strict inequality for some $k$.

The utility $u_k(g-i)$ brings out the potential implications of an elimination of $i$, as it may enhance or lower the payoffs of country $k$. We will say that a link $g_{jk}$ is war-beneficial if it lets $j$ and $k$ attack a third country, $i$, and the net gains to conquering $i$ outweigh any losses to adding the link for both $j$ and $k$ (i.e., the definition of vulnerable despite trade from before, but with the left side being $u_k(g+g_{jk}-i) + E_{ik}(g, C)$ and the inequality being strict for at least one of $j$ or $k$). Let us define network g to be *war-and-trade stable* if the following are true:

- No country is vulnerable despite trade at g,
- $\forall g_{jk}=0$, if $u_j(g+g_{jk}) > u_j(g)$ then $u_k(g+g_{jk}) < u_k(g)$, and $g_{jk}$ is not war-beneficial, and
- $\forall g_{jk}=1$, either $u_j(g-g_{jk}) \leq u_j(g)$ or $j$ is vulnerable despite trade at $g-g_{jk}$, and similarly for k.

In other words, a network of alliances is war and trade stable if no country is vulnerable despite trade, if no two countries can add an alliance that is mutually profitable (through economics or war), and either economic or conquest considerations prevent every country from severing any of its links.

For simplicity, we will consider a symmetric setting in what follows. Suppose that utility from a network depends only on the degree and the number of alliances. Thus

$$u_i(g) = f(d_i(g)) - cd_i(g), \tag{10.24}$$

where $d_i(g)$ is the degree of $i$. Let the function $f$ be concave and nondecreasing, and suppose that there is a $d \leq n-1$ such that $f(d) < cd$. Finally, let $d^*$ maximize $f(d) - cd$. This is a simple model of gains from trade and costs of having trading relationships that abstracts from heterogeneity in goods and trading partners, and from interdependencies in trading relationships beyond diminishing returns.

The reward from conquest is important in what follows. We will set $E_{ij}(g; C)$ as the reward to country $i$ from conquering country $j$. We set $E_{ij}(g; C) = E(d_i(g))/|C|$, so the rewards from conquest depend on the degree of the conquered country and are divided equally among the members of the winning coalition. Let us refer to the game with these assumptions as the symmetric payoffs game.

**Proposition 10.3** *Consider the symmetric payoffs game with $d^* \geq 2$. If $E(d^*) \leq 2[f(d^*) - f(d^*-1) - c]$, then a $d^*$-regular network is war and trade stable if*

$$\rho \geq \frac{d^*+1}{d^*-1}.$$

Recall that a network is pairwise stable if no two countries weakly benefit from adding a link (at least one strictly), and no single country benefits from deleting a link. Note that any network that is $d^*$ regular is pairwise stable. Suppose that $g$ is pairwise stable with respect to $u$. Then it follows that if no country is vulnerable despite trade at $g$ or $g + g_{jk}$, then $g$ must be war and trade stable. So, to prove the result, we need to show that this is true under the given assumption on $E(.)$, for any $d^*$- regular network.

First, note that no country $i$ is vulnerable to any coalition $C$ that does not include any of its neighbors (even if this comes from the addition of a link that does not involve any neighbors) because $\rho \geq (d^* + 1)/d^* - 1)$. Thus, we need only verify vulnerability to a coalition that involves at least one neighbor (and possibly involves the addition of a link).

Next, observe that a neighbor that has $d^*$ links will not want to attack $i$. This is because any coalition that succeeds must involve at least two countries, and if all neighbors have $d^*$ links, then under the condition $E(d^*)/2 \leq (f(d^*) - f(d^* - 1) - c)$, being part of such a coalition is not profitable. Finally, consider the case where all $i$'s neighbors in the attacking coalition have $d^* + 1$ links. This means that the coalition involves at most two of $i$'s neighbors, as at most one new link can be formed. However, $\rho \geq (d^* + 1)/(d^* - 1) \geq (d^* + 2)/(d^*)$, so the attacking coalition cannot defeat $i$ and its remaining neighbors, regardless of whether it contains one or two of $i$'s neighbors. ■

Observe that the regular networks identified as war and trade stable are not war-stable. Thus we have shown one route through which economic forces—working through gains from trade—support stable networks, and thereby place limits on the extent of conflict. The condition shows that with sufficient gains from trade—reflected in the condition $E(d^*) \leq 2 \leq [f(d^*) - f(d^* - 1) - c]$—the potential spoils of a war against a trading partner are outweighed by the loss in trade value, so countries are never attacked by one of their own allies.

Let us now summarize what we have learned about alliances, trade, and war. We considered a model of network formation that yields two interesting insights. The first is that in a pure conflict setting, individual attempts to form alliances and attack opponents lead to shifting and unstable alliances. This instability is consistent with the constantly shifting structures and recurring wars that occurred throughout the nineteenth and early twentieth centuries. The second insight is that the presence of large gains from trade can sustain stable alliance structures where no country is vulnerable to attack by a coalition of enemies. This too is consistent with the empirical trends. In the period since 1950, wars have greatly subsided in parallel with the huge increase of trade.

So far in this chapter, we have studied static models of war. However, in history, important wars have altered the power and prosperity of the parties involved and have reconfigured the subsequent relations between them. Indeed, the fear of such a long-term change in the relative power of Sparta and Athens was the primary cause of the Peloponnesian War according to the great Greek historian Thucydides. In the next section, we study the dynamics of war and conquest.

## 10.5 Conquest and Empire

*The history of the world .... is an imperial history, the history of empires. Empires were systems of influence or rule where ethnic, cultural or ecological boundaries were overlapped or ignored. Their ubiquitous presence arose from the fact that .... the endowments needed to build strong states were very unequally distributed. Against the cultural attraction, or physical force, of an imperial state, resistance was hard, unless reinforced by geographical remoteness or unusual cohesion.*
(Darwin 2007, p. 491)

A recurring theme in history is the that the presence of small kingdoms is accompanied by bloody conflicts; rulers fight each other incessantly, small parcels of land are exchanged, treasures are plundered, and the capture of human beings is common. However, once a ruler acquires a large advantage relative to his neighbors, he then quickly goes on to take them over, one after the other, and create an empire. Classical studies on the formation of empire include Polybius (2010), Tacitus (2009), and Khaldun (1989). We begin by discussing three major historical empires to bring out general features of the formation of empires.

### 10.5.1 Historical Background

#### The first Chinese Empire

We start with an examination of one of the turning points in world history: the emergence of the first empire in China in 221 BC. Our discussion draws on Lewis (2010) and Overy (2010). In China, the years between 475 BC and 221 BC are referred to as the Warring States Period: this period was characterized by almost uninterrupted warfare between seven major states. The seven major kingdoms were Qin (located in the far west); the three Jins (located in the center on the Shanxi plateau–Han south along the Yellow River, Wei located in the middle, Zhao the most northernmost of the three); Qi (centered on the Shandong Peninsula); Chu (with its core territory around the valleys of the Han River); and Yan (centered on modern-day Beijing). Initially, wars led to changes in the power of the dynasties, but all the kingdoms survived. However, from 320 BC to 221 BC, there was a major consolidation, and by 221 BC, the Qin defeated all the other kingdoms and unified the entire area under one ruler, Qin Shi Huang. Figure 10.10 illustrates these dynamics.

The Qin empire was bounded by forests in the south, deserts and the Tibetan Plateau on the west, wasteland in the north, and the Pacific Ocean in the east. These geographic features, especially in the south, west, and east, presented a physical constraint on further expansion.

#### The Roman Empire

The Roman Empire has had a profound impact on the history of the Mediterranean area (and more broadly across Europe) over the past 2,500 years. Our discussion draws on

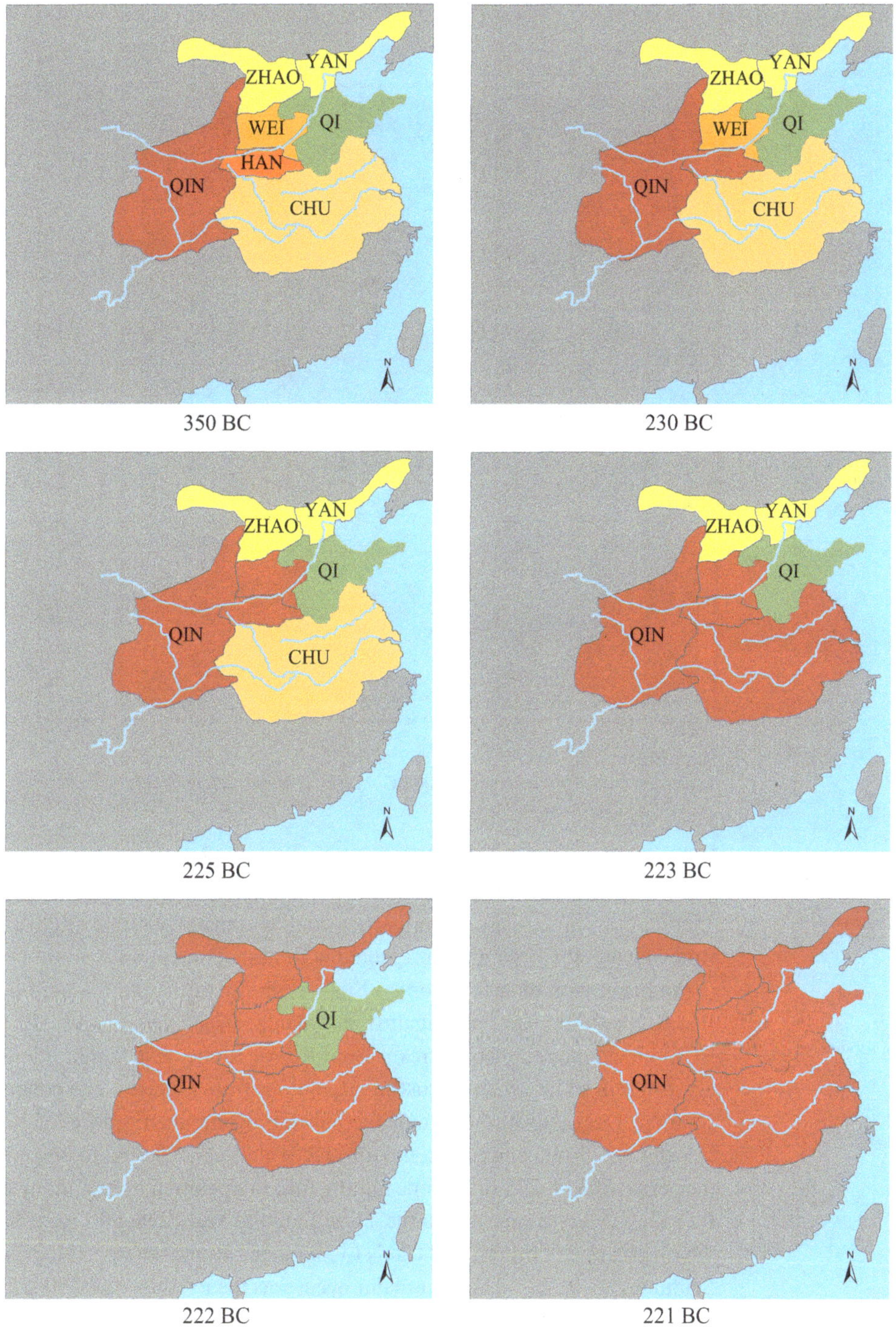


**Figure 10.10**
The first Chinese Empire: dynamics. *Source*: Overy (2010).

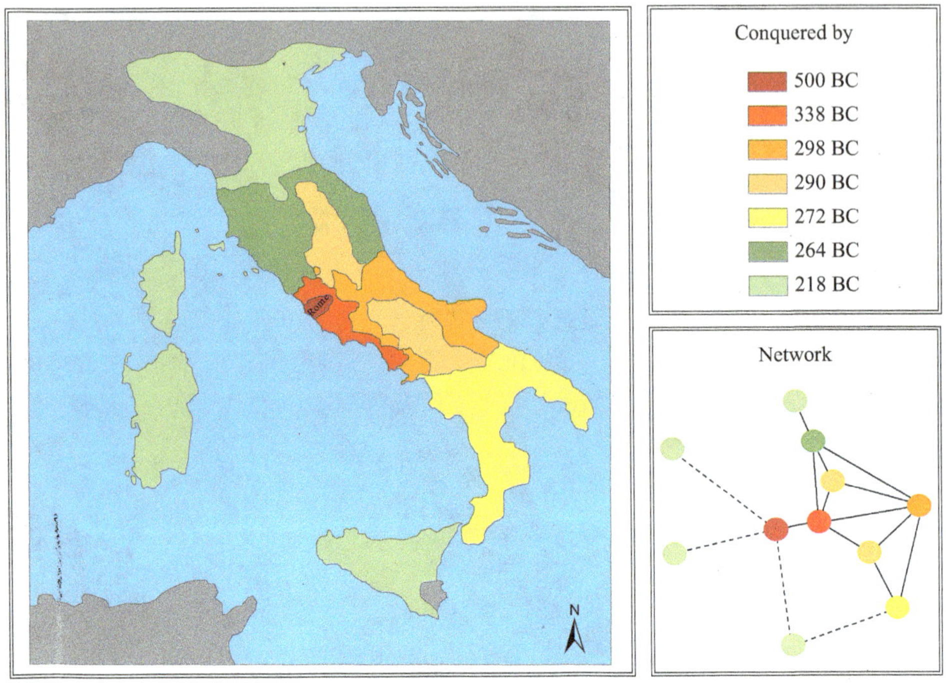


**Figure 10.11**
Expansion of the Roman republic, 500 BC–218 BC. *Source*: Scarre (1995).

Kelly (2006) and Polybius (2010). Figures 10.11 and 10.12 summarize the expansion of Roman empire over the period 500 BC—30 BC. In these figures, we distinguish physical contiguity from sea-based contiguity, which was made possible after the development of a Roman navy; the latter are represented with dashed lines.

We begin with the early Roman Empire and first describe the period of 500 BC to 272 BC. Rome's first major war against an organized state was fought with Fidenae (437–426 BC), a town located just upstream from Rome. Rome next fought a long and difficult war against Veii, an important Etruscan city not far from Fidenae. The conquest of Veii opened southern Etruria to further Roman expansion. Rome then proceeded to found colonies at Nepet and Sutrium and forced the towns of Falerii and Capena to become its allies. During the period of 348–295 BC, Rome rapidly rose to a position of hegemony in Italy south of the Po valley. A key moment was the Third Samnite War (298–290 BC): Samnites persuaded the Etruscans, Umbrians, and Gauls to join them. Rome emerged victorious in the Battle of Sentinum in 295 BC. The next major event was the Pyrrhic War, 280–275 BC. The conflict between Rome and Pyrrhus lasted five years, ending in a final Roman victory in 275 BC at Beneventum.

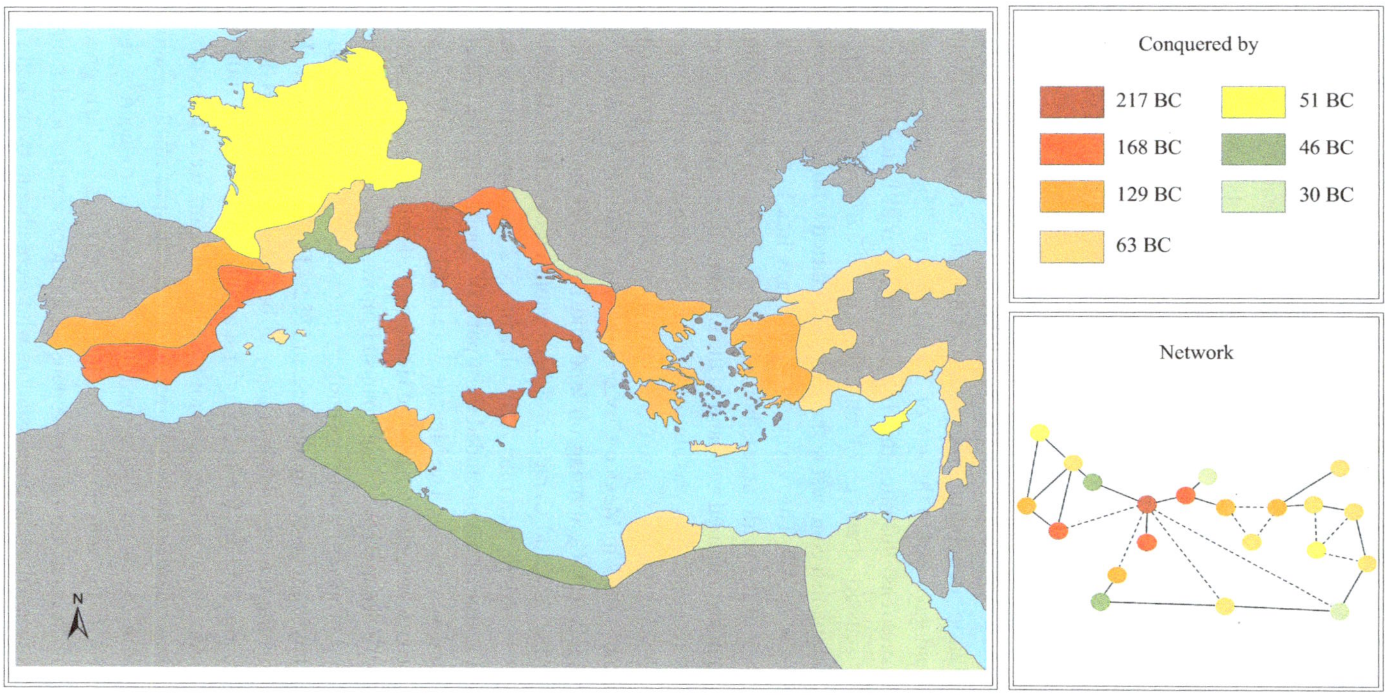


**Figure 10.12**
Expansion of the Roman republic, 217 BC–30 BC. *Source*: Wittke, Olshausen, Szydlak et al. (2010).

The period from 272 BC to 30 BC witnessed a massive expansion of the Roman Empire across the Mediterranean Sea and most of modern western Europe. Rome first began to make war outside the Italian peninsula during the Punic Wars against Carthage (in North Africa) around 264 AD. By 146 AD, Rome had defeated Carthage and taken over direct control over large parts of North Africa, and through its conflict with Carthage, it also expanded its influence in Iberia. The wars with Macedonia led to control over Greece by 148 BC, and the defeat of the Selucid emperor in 188 BC led to control over Asia Minor. Further conquests over the next hundred years would result in Rome's conquest of large parts of modern Spain and most of modern France (Kelly [2006], Polybius [2010]). Figure 10.12 illustrates this growing hegemony.

### The Spanish Empire in the New World

European imperial expansion starting from around 1500 AD reshaped the medieval world and gave rise to the age of global empires. The expansion of the Spanish domains in the Americas illustrates this instance of imperial history in a especially dramatic form. Our discussion draws on Elliott (2006), and the *Encyclopedia Britannica*.

Spanish conquest in the Americas started with the first voyage of Christopher Columbus in 1492 AD. This voyage created a new link in the contiguity network, as it made a new part of the world accessible. Equipped with superior technology from Europe, the Spanish quickly captured an island in the Caribbean (subsequently named Hispaniola). The Indigenous population was almost entirely annihilated, and the island became part of the Spanish domain. Moving on to Central America, the Spanish conquistador Hernán Cortés defeated the Aztecs in Mexico City by 1521 AD, and the Aztec Empire was largely conquered by 1532 AD. Continuing on land and by sea, Spanish conquest had reached Cartagena by 1532 AD, and Caracas had been captured by 1567 AD. Farther south, Francisco Pizzaro defeated the Inca ruler Atahualpa in 1532, and Spain set up the viceroyalty of Peru in 1542, a vast area that included most parts of South America (other than the Portuguese Empire and Venezuela). The Mayans were finally defeated in 1697, and the area of southern Mexico, Belize, Guatemala, and Honduras fell into Spanish hands. In the same year, El Salvador also became part of the Spanish Empire. Figure 10.13 illustrates this process.

European military technology played a central role in the dramatic speed and scale of these conquests. For instance, in 1532 AD, Pizarro captured the Inca emperor with 167 men fighting an imperial Inca army of between 5,000 and 10,000 men. In 1536, 190 conquistadors held out for a year against an Inca army of over 100,000 men (Hoffman [2015]). In addition to military superiority, the Europeans were helped by the vulnerability of Indigenous populations in America to diseases such as smallpox and measles. Almost 95 percent of the Aztec population died due to diseases introduced by the Spanish during this period. The Indigenous population under the Incas was similarly greatly reduced due to epidemics of diseases. So the Indigenous populations and its leadership could not present any real resistance to the conquistadors who were able to overwhelm opponents with significantly larger armies.

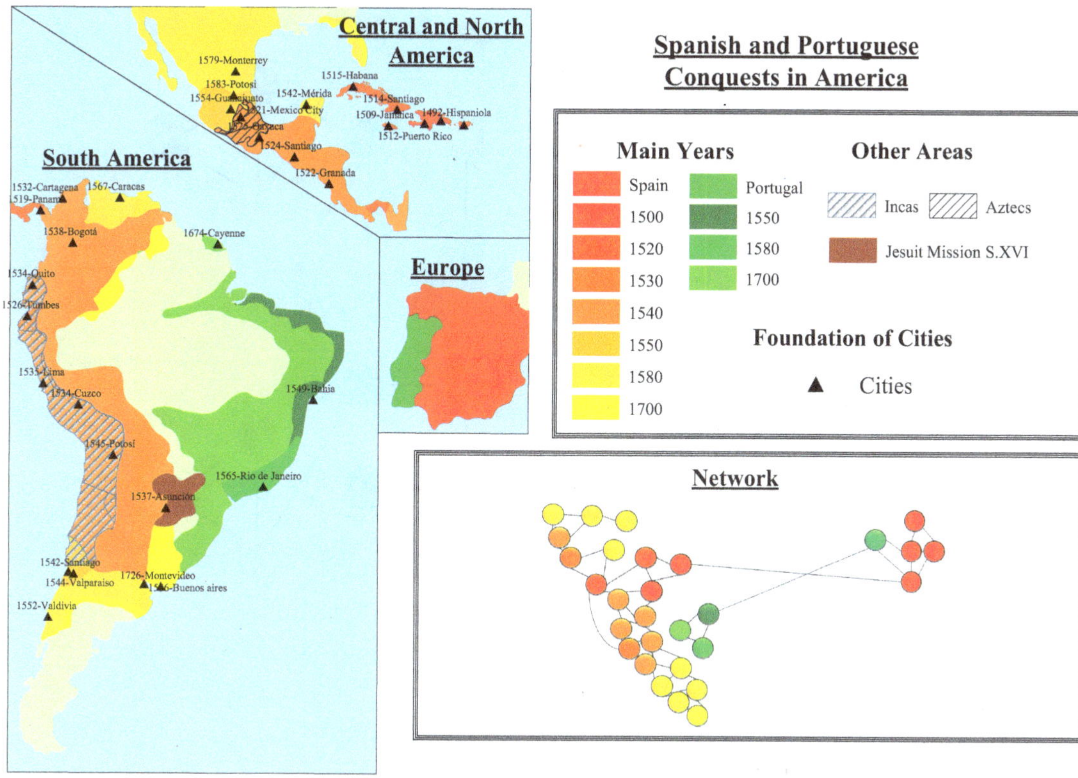


**Figure 10.13**
Spanish and Portuguese conquests in America. *Source*: O'Brien (2005).

This record of war and conquest in China, Rome, and America motivates the study of the following questions: what are the circumstances under which rulers will choose to fight? What is the optimal timing of attack, now or later? When will the resource advantage of ruled translate into domination over their neighbors? What are the limits to the size of an empire? The next section proposes a theoretical framework to explore these questions.

### 10.5.2 A Dynamic Model of Wars and Conquest

We study a dynamic game in which rulers seek to maximize the resources they control by waging war and capturing new territories. There are three building blocks in our model: the interconnected kingdoms, the resource endowment for every kingdom, and the CSF. This model is taken from Dziubinski, Goyal, and Minarsch (2017).

Let $V = \{1, 2, \ldots, n\}$, where $n \geq 2$ is the set of vertices. A node $i \in V$ is endowed with resources, $r_i \in \mathbb{R}_{++}$. The nodes are connected in a network, represented by an undirected graph $g$. A link between two nodes signifies access. Access may reflect physical contiguity,

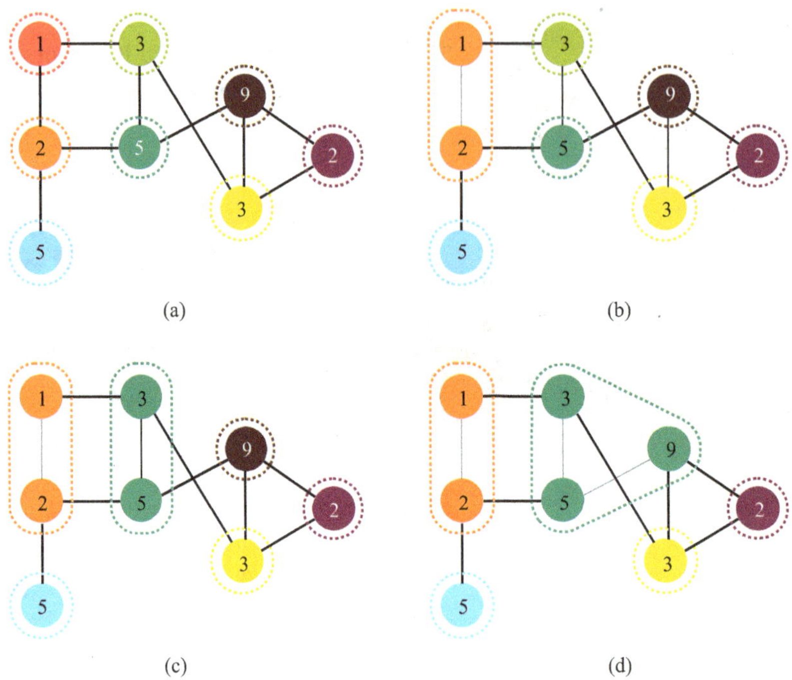


**Figure 10.14**
Neighboring rulers.

but in principle, it goes beyond geography: we do not restrict our attention to planar graphs. So our model allows virtual links (i.e., links made possible by advances in military and transport technology).

Every node $i \in V$ is controlled/owned by one ruler. At the beginning, there are $\mathbb{N} = \{1, 2, \ldots, n\}$ rulers. Let $\mathbb{O} : V \to \mathbb{R}$ denote the ownership function. The resources of ruler $i \in \mathbb{N}$ under $\mathbb{O}$, are given by

$$R_i(\mathbb{O}) = \sum_{v \in \mathbb{O}^{-1}(i)} r_v. \tag{10.25}$$

The network, together with the ownership configuration, induces a neighbor relation between the rulers: two rulers $i, j \in N$ are *neighbors* in network $g$ if there exists $u \in V$, owned by $i$, and $v \in V$, owned by $j$, such that $g_{uv} \in g$. Figure 10.14 illustrates nodes, resource endowments, and connections; nodes controlled by the same ruler share a common color. The light line between nodes represents the interconnections, the dotted lines encircling nodes owned by the same ruler indicate the ownership configuration, and the thick lines between nodes reflect the induced neighborhood relation between rulers.

When two rulers fight, the probability of winning is specified by a CSF. Here, we consider symmetric CSFs with no ties. Given two rulers, $A$ and $B$, with resources $x_A \in \mathbb{R}_{++}$ and

$x_B \in \mathbb{R}_{++}$, respectively, $p(x_A, x_B)$ is the probability that $A$ wins the conflict and $p(x_B, x_A)$ is the probability that $B$ wins the conflict. We shall use the Tullock contest function in our analysis of conflict:

$$p(x,y) = \frac{x^\gamma}{x^\gamma + y^\gamma}, \tag{10.26}$$

where $\gamma > 0$. Larger resources enhance the prospects of success. In this discussion, for expositional simplicity, we will focus on the case where $\gamma > 1$. Here, the probability of success rises more than proportionately with respect to the ratio of resources.

The game takes place in discrete time: rounds are numbered $t = 1, 2, 3 \ldots$. At the start of a round, one of the rulers is picked with equal probability from the set of remaining rulers. The chosen ruler, such as $i$, chooses either to be peaceful or to attack one of their neighbors. If a ruler attacks a rival, they do so with all their current resources. If they choose peace, one of the remaining rulers is asked to choose between war and peace, and so forth. If no ruler chooses war, the game ends. If the attacker loses, the round ends. Otherwise, the attacker is allowed to attack neighbors until they lose, choose to stop, or there are no neighbors left to attack. When two rulers $i$ and $j$ fight, the winner takes over the entire kingdom of the loser (and also inherits the boundaries, and hence the connections). For simplicity, we assume that there are no losses or costs of war; our arguments also hold so long as the losses are relatively small.

This dynamic is illustrated in figure 10.14: the orange kingdom wins the war with the red kingdom and expands. This expansion brings it in contact with new neighbors, the light- and dark-green kingdoms. The game ends when all rulers choose to be peaceful (the case of a single surviving ruler is a special case, as there is no opponent left to attack). Observe that, given these rules, the game ends after at most $n-1$ rounds. It may end earlier, of course: this happens if all the rulers choose peace in a round.

A *state* is a pair $(\mathbb{o}, P)$, where $P \subseteq N$, is the set of rulers who were picked prior to i and chose peace at $\mathbb{o}$. Ruler $i$, picked at state $(\mathbb{o}, P) \in \mathbb{O} \times 2^{N\setminus\{i\}}$, chooses a sequence of rulers to attack. A sequence $\sigma$ is *feasible* at $\mathbb{o}$ in graph $G$ if either $\sigma$ is empty or if $\sigma = j_1, \ldots, j_k$ for all $1 \le l < k$, $j_l \notin \{i, j_1, \ldots, j_{l-1}\}$, and $j_l$ is a neighbor of one of the rulers from $\{i, j_1, \ldots, j_{l-1}\}$ under $\mathbb{o}$ in $G$. A sequence $\sigma$ is *attacking* if it is nonempty. Let $N^*$ denote the set of all finite sequences over $N$ (including the empty sequence). A *strategy* of ruler $i$ is function $s_i$ : $\mathbb{O} \times 2^{N\setminus\{i\}} \to N^*$ such that for every ownership configuration, $\mathbb{o} \in \mathbb{O}$, and every set of rulers, $P \subseteq N \setminus \{i\}$, $s_i(\mathbb{o}, P)$ is feasible at $\mathbb{o}$ in $G$. Observe that the only feasible sequence for rulers who do not own any nodes, and for the ruler who owns all nodes, is the empty sequence. Given ruler $i \in N$ and graph $G$, the set of strategies of $i$ is denoted by $S_i$; $\mathbf{S} = \prod_{i \in N} S_i$ denotes the set of strategy profiles.

The probability that ruler 1 with resources $R_1$ wins a sequence of conflicts with rulers with resources $R_2, \ldots, R_m$, accumulating the resources of the losing opponents at each step of the sequence is

$$p_{\text{seq}}(R_1,\ldots,R_m)=\prod_{k=2}^{m}p\left(\sum_{j=1}^{k-1}R_j,R_k\right). \tag{10.27}$$

Given $\mathbb{O}$, a set of rulers, $P$, and a strategy profile $\boldsymbol{s}=(s_1,s_2,\ldots,s_n)\in\boldsymbol{S}$, the probability that the game ends at $\mathbb{O}'$ is given by $F(\mathbb{O}'\mid\boldsymbol{s},\mathbb{O},P)$. We shall refer to a final ownership configuration as an *outcome*. The expected payoff to ruler $i$ from strategy profile $\boldsymbol{s}\in\boldsymbol{S}$ at state $(\mathbb{O},P)$ is

$$\Pi_i(\boldsymbol{s}\mid\mathbb{O},P)=\sum_{\mathbb{O}'\in\mathbb{O}}F(\mathbb{O}'\mid\boldsymbol{s},\mathbb{O},P)R_i(\mathbb{O}'). \tag{10.28}$$

Every ruler seeks to maximize their expected payoff; in other words, the capture of resources occupies center stage in this model.

The goals of rulers and the motivations for war have been extensively studied. In the history of the Peloponnesian War by Thucydides, we already find a discussion of this subject. Thucydides (1989) says that there are three motives for war: greed, fear, and honor. Hobbes (1886) elaborates on these motivations as follows.

> So that in the nature of man, we find three principal causes of quarrel. First, competition; secondly, diffidence; thirdly, glory. The first maketh men invade for gain; the second, for safety; and the third, for reputation. The first use violence, to make themselves masters of other mens persons, wives, children, and cattle; the second, to defend them; the third, for trifles. (p. 64)

These observations are consistent with historical evidence. The Roman Empire was founded on a series of hard-fought campaigns. During the second and first centuries BC, Roman generals waged ever more extensive wars and campaigns. Victory yielded land for the expanding Roman population, large numbers of slaves, and huge quantities of booty: in the 50 years from 200–150 BC, the equivalent of 30 metric tonnes of gold was seized. In 62 BC, the victorious Pompey returned from the east with booty worth nearly 70 metric tonnes of gold (Kelly [2006]). Equally important was the high esteem in which successful generals were held. The highest honour for a general in Rome was a Triumph: a march of the general with his army through the city.

The second example concerns European global empires:

> The arch-characteristic of European imperialism was expropriation. Land was expropriated to meet the needs of plantations and mines engaged in long-distance commerce. Slave labor was acquired and carried thousands of miles to serve the same purpose. Native peoples were displaced, and their rights nullified, on the grounds that they had failed to make proper use of their land. Both native peoples and slaves (by different forms of displacement) suffered the effective expropriation of their cultures and identities. (Darwin 2007, p. 24)

Control over resources remains a major motivation for wars in the contemporary world. For instance, the presence of large oil reserves has been suggested as a potential explanation for conflict in the Middle East. The historical and political science literature has suggested a potential role for natural resources in many wars. Motivated by this descriptive literature and the relatively large number of changes in boundaries between countries in the twentieth century, Caselli, Morelli, and Rohner (2015) present evidence that the location of oil resources has significant and quantitatively important effects on interstate conflicts in the period after World War II.

Returning to the formal model, we say that strategy profile $\boldsymbol{s} \in \boldsymbol{S}$ is a Markov perfect *equilibrium* of the game if and only if, for every ruler $i \in N$, every strategy $s_i' \in S_i$, and every state $(\mathbb{o}, P) \in \mathbb{O} \times 2^{N \setminus \{i\}}$, it holds that $\Pi_i(\boldsymbol{s} \mid \mathbb{o}, P) \geq \Pi_i([s_i', \boldsymbol{s}_{-i}] \mid \mathbb{o}, P)$. Standard arguments can be employed to establish that for a connected network $G$, for any symmetric CSF $p$, and any resource endowment $\boldsymbol{r} \in \mathbb{R}^V_{++}$, there is an equilibrium and all equilibria are payoff equivalent.

### 10.5.3 The Incentives to Wage War

The first step is to understand the basic incentives to wage war. In our model, a ruler picked to fight needs to decide whether to fight or to remain peaceful, and if fighting is desirable, then to decide whom to attack. The answer to these questions turns on coefficient $\gamma$ in the contest function. When $\gamma > 1$, $x^\gamma$ has increasing returns to scale, and when $\gamma < 1$, it has diminishing returns to scale. This is critical in shaping the expected returns to waging war. In particular, suppose that $x > y$. It is then easy to check the following:

1. If $\gamma > 1$, then $(x+y)p(x,y) > x$ (*rich rewarding*).
2. If $\gamma < 1$, then $(x+y)p(x,y) < x$ (*poor rewarding*).

Under a rich rewarding CSF, the expected resources of the richer player are higher than their current resources and the expected resources of the weaker player are lower. The opposite is true in the case of a weak rewarding CSF. This means that if rulers have unequal resources and are myopic, no peace is possible (so long as $\gamma \neq 1$). In our game, rulers are farsighted and care only about the long-run outcome. In this setting, a ruler may decide not to fight a neighbor, as that would bring them in contact with a more powerful ruler.

To develop a feel for some of the forces at work in this setting, we present two examples next. The first concerns the role of the contest success function.

**Example 10.1** *The role of technology*

Suppose that three rulers, located in a complete network, have equal resources given by $x$. Let $\gamma = 0$. If two rulers have fought, then the state must contain one ruler with resources $2x$ and the other ruler with resources $x$. It follows that the poorer ruler has a strict incentive to wage a war. Anticipating this, consider the incentives of rulers at the initial state with three active rulers. As rulers have equal resources and the network is complete, all three rulers have the same incentives. As the probability of surviving two wars is $1/4$, the expected payoff from waging a war is $3x/4$. This tells us that there are no wars in equilibrium. By contrast, consider very large $\gamma$. When there are two rulers, one of them must have $2x$ resources and the other $x$. The ruler with more resources wins a war with probability close to 1, and therefore they expect to increase payoffs. Anticipating this order of moves in the two-ruler state, at the initial state, all three rulers have a strict incentive to wage war. This is because at the initial state, the expected payoff on waging a war is $3x/2$, which is larger than the expected payoff from no one fighting. We see that with large $\gamma$, rulers will wage war, leading to a hegemony. This example brings out the role of the technology of war in shaping the dynamics of conquest. △

**Example 10.2** *The role of resources*

As before, for simplicity, consider three rulers linked to each other. Suppose that resources are very unequal: for example, rulers 1 and 2 have equal resources, $x$, and ruler 3 has resources $3x$. When $\gamma = 0$, the two poorer rulers now wish to fight, while the rich ruler does not. The outcome is war and hegemony. As $\gamma = 0$, the probability of becoming a hegemon is equal for the three rulers. Thus conflict and conquest are equalizing. Next, consider the case where $\gamma$ is very large. Now ruler 3 will win any war they fight, so they have a strict incentive to fight two wars. The outcome will be the hegemony of ruler 3. In this setting, war reinforces initial inequality. △

We now turn to a more general study of the dynamics of conquest. Consider three rulers with resources $x$, $y$, and $z$. The expected payoffs to waging two wars are

$$p(x,y)p(x+y,z)(x+y+z), \tag{10.29}$$

while the expected payoff to waiting is

$$p(x,y+z)(x+y+z). \tag{10.30}$$

It is possible to show that a ruler prefers to wage two wars if $\gamma > 1$ and prefers to wait if $\gamma < 1$. Thus, if $\gamma > 1$, there is a no-waiting property, while if $\gamma < 1$, then opponents prefer to wait. This is because if $\gamma > 1$, then $x^\gamma$ is supermodular, and because of that, $p$ has the no-waiting property; and if $\gamma < 1$, then $x^\gamma$ is submodular, and because of that, $p$ has the waiting property. Thus we note that rich rewarding $p$ is necessarily no-waiting (because increasing returns to scale imply supermodularity) and poor rewarding $p$ is necessarily waiting (because diminishing returns to scale imply submodularity). A question at the end of the chapter further explores this relationship between $\gamma$ and the incentives to wage war.

### 10.5.4 Equilibrium Analysis: Strong Rulers and Hegemony

We build on this incentive to develop the equilibrium analysis of the game of conquest. Given ownership configuration $\mathbb{o}$, the set of *active* rulers at $\mathbb{o}$ is

$$\text{Act}(\mathbb{o}) = \{i \in \mathbb{R} : \varnothing \subsetneq \mathbb{o}^{-1}(i) \subsetneq V\}. \tag{10.31}$$

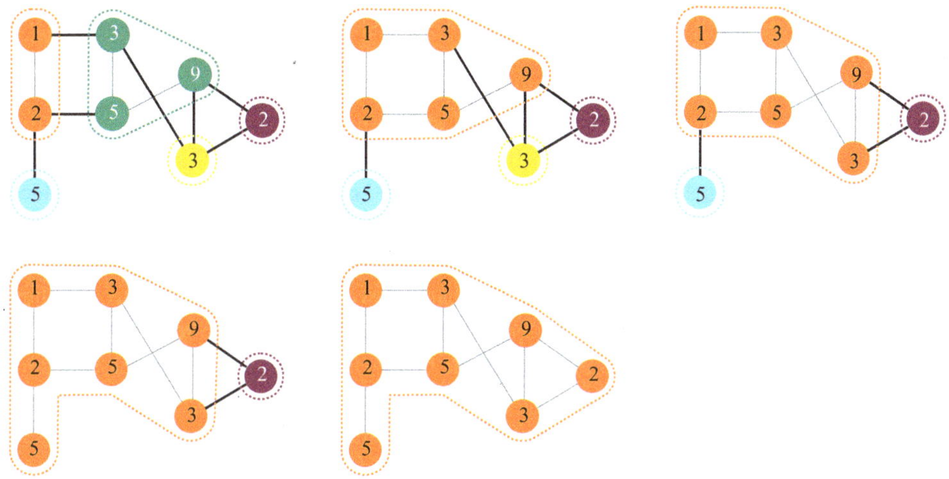

**Figure 10.15**
Full attacking sequence (f.a.s.).

In other words, an active ruler is someone who controls at least one vertex but does not control all vertices. An ordering of the elements of the set $\mathrm{Act}(\mathbb{o}) \setminus \{i\}$, $\sigma$, such that the sequence $\sigma$ is feasible for $i$ in $G$ under $\mathbb{o}$, is called a *full attacking sequence (f.a.s.)*. Figure 10.15 illustrates the execution of such a sequence (for the orange kingdom).

Our main result on war and conquest and the extent of empire concerns the rich rewarding case.

**Proposition 10.4** *Consider a rich rewarding contest success function that satisfies equation (10.26). Suppose g is a connected network, and let* $\mathbf{r} \in \mathbb{R}^V_{++}$ *be a generic resource profile. In equilibrium, every active ruler chooses to attack a neighbor if* $|A(\mathbb{o})| \geq 3$*, and at least one of the active rulers attacks their opponent if* $|A(\mathbb{o})| = 2$*. The outcome is hegemony, and the probability of becoming a hegemon is unique for every ruler.*

The result predicts incessant fighting, preemptive attacks, and long attacking sequences for all rich rewarding contest functions, any connected network, and generic resources.

The argument builds on the notion of a strong ruler. A ruler is said to be *strong* if they have an attacking sequence $\sigma = i_1, \ldots, i_k$, where for all $l \in \{1, \ldots, k\}$,

$$\sum_{j=0}^{l-1} R_{i_j}(\mathbb{o}) > R_{i_l}(\mathbb{o}). \tag{10.32}$$

In other words, at every step in the attacking sequence, the ruler has more resources than the next opponent. The set of strong rulers at ownership configuration $\mathbb{o}$ is

$$\mathrm{S}(\mathbb{o}) = \{i \in \mathrm{Act}(\mathbb{o}) : i \text{ has a strong f.a.s. } \sigma \text{ at } \mathbb{o}\}. \tag{10.33}$$

A ruler who is not *strong* is said to be *weak*. It is worth noting that in any state, the ruler with the most resources is strong, while the ruler with the least resources is weak. Thus both sets are nonempty in every network and for generic resource profiles.

The first step in the proof shows that, assuming that all other rulers choose peace in all states, it is optimal for a strong ruler to choose a full attacking sequence. This is true because the CSF is rich rewarding, so a strong ruler has a full attacking sequence that increases their resources in expectation, at every step along the sequence. The second step extends the argument to cover opponents that choose war. If opponents are active, then the no-waiting property tells us that it is even more attractive not to give them an opportunity to move. For a strong ruler, it is therefore a dominant strategy to use an optimal full attacking sequence. The final step in the proof covers nonstrong or weak rulers to establish that with three or more active rulers, it is optimal for *every* ruler to choose a full attacking sequence. Observe that we have already shown that every nonstrong ruler knows that they will be facing an attack sooner or later. This means that waiting can only mean that the opposition will become larger and richer. The no-waiting property then tells us that every ruler must attack as soon as possible. If there are only two active rulers, then the richer ruler has a strict incentive to attack the poorer one (this follows from the definition of the rich rewarding contest function). ■

We now study the role of the network in shaping conquest dynamics. A preliminary remark is that for fixed resources and sufficiently large $\gamma$, it is never optimal to attack a richer ruler if other options are available. The optimal strategy for a strong ruler must involve attacking a poorer ruler at every stage in the attack sequence. Such a sequence is clearly not available for a weak ruler: the probability of a weak ruler becoming a hegemon converges to zero as $\gamma$ grows. Whether a ruler is strong or weak depends on both the distribution of resources and the position of the ruler in the contiguity network. Figure 10.16 helps bring out this point: relatively rich kingdoms, such as those with resources 16 and 17, are weak, while less rich kingdoms, such as those with resources 8 and 9, are strong.

It is helpful to define the boundary of a set of vertices $U \subseteq V$ in $G$ as

$$B_G(U) = \{v \in V \setminus U : \text{ there exists } u \in U \text{ s.t. } uv \in E\}. \tag{10.34}$$

A set of vertices, $U$, is *weak* if $G[U]$ is connected, $B_G(U) \neq \varnothing$, and for all $v \in B_G(U)$, $r_v > \sum_{u \in U} r_u$. A weak set of vertices is surrounded by a boundary consisting of vertices, each of which is endowed with more resources than the sum of the resources of the vertices within the set. It is easy to see that for any initial state $\mathbb{O}$, a ruler is weak if their vertex belongs to a weak set; otherwise, the ruler is strong.

### 10.5.5 Relating Theory and Historical Experience

It is illuminating to view the rise of the three historical empires we discussed earlier in this chapter through the lens of the model presented in section 10.5.1.

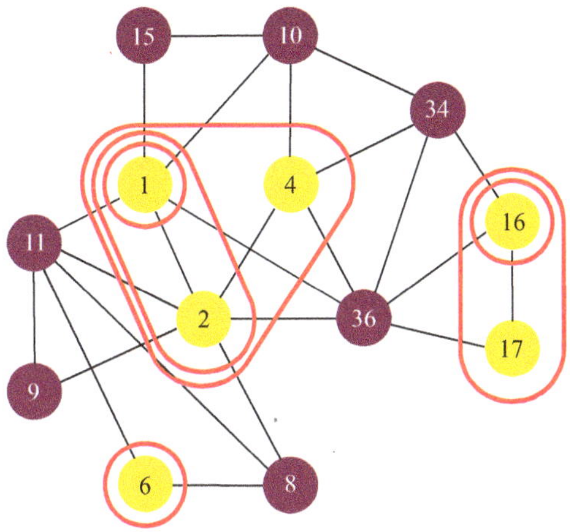


**Figure 10.16**
Weak rulers (surrounded by thick red lines) and strong rulers.

**Chinese Empire** In line with the theoretical prediction, over a period stretching several hundred years, there was incessant warfare. To appreciate the time-line of gradual and then very rapid expansion of empire, consider a slight variation on the contest function, in which a tie arises with a probability related to the size of the armies of the opponents. In the period prior to 360 BC, the armies were small and the battles indecisive for the fate of a ruler. The period after 360 BC witnessed major reforms by the Qin minister, Shang Yang. After these reforms and the accompanying technological developments, the scale and violence in a war changed dramatically: now elimination of the losing ruler and conquest of his kingdom became much more likely, especially in a war between the Qin and one of the other warring states:

> [T]he rise of Qin to dominance and its ultimate success in creating a unified empire depended on two major developments. First, under Shang Yang it achieved the most systematic version of the reforms that characterized the Warring States. These reforms entailed the registration and mobilization of all adult males for military service and the payment of taxes. While all Warring States were organized for war, Qin was unique in its extension of this pattern to every level of society, and in the manner in which every aspect of administration was devoted to mobilizing and provisioning its forces for conquest. (Lewis 2010, pp. 38–39).

These reforms meant that the ruler had the resources—in terms of both army size and tax revenue—to wage large-scale wars. Equipped with such a large army, the Qin ruler was able to implement a long attacking sequence: in 230 BC, Qin conquered Han, the weakest of the Seven Warring States. In 225 BC, Qin conquered Wei, followed in 223 BC by Chu. The size of the army was crucial in this contest: the first Qin invasion failed, when 200,000 Qin troops were defeated by a much larger Chu army with around 500,000 troops. The

**Table 10.3**
Chinese kingdoms: Army size and end year

| Kingdom | Size of Army | End Year |
|---|---|---|
| Qin | 800,000 | – |
| Chu | 800,000 | BC 223 |
| Qi | 600,000 | BC 221 |
| Zhao | 500,000 | BC 222 |
| Wei | 400,000 | BC 225 |
| Han | 300,000 | BC 230 |
| Yan | 300,000 | BC 222 |

*Source*: Zhao and Xie (1988, p. 18–19).

following year, Qin mounted a second invasion, with 600,000 men, defeating the Chu state. At their peak, the combined armies of Chu and Qin are estimated to have had in excess of a million soldiers. Qin conquered Zhao and Yan in 222 BC. Finally, in 221 BC, Qin turned its attention to the last surviving Warring State opponent: the Qi. In the face of this great threat, Qi surrendered.

In line with the theory, there was a tendency to attack the weaker states before the stronger ones. Han, the weakest of the seven, was the first to fall. Qin's policy of attacking the nearby states and befriending the faraway states was determined partly by proximity and partly by the fact that Han and Wei were relatively weak, while Qi and Chu had the most resources. Yan was also a weak state and was the object of attack by Zhao and Qi. Table 10.3 lists the size of the armies during the late Warring States period.

Our final observation concerns the frontiers of the empire. Recall that the Qin empire was bounded by forests in the south, deserts and the Tibetan Plateau in the west, wasteland in the north, and the Pacific Ocean in the east. These physical features, especially in the south, west, and east, presented a physical constraint on further expansion. We may therefore interpret China as a distinct component of the world network, somewhat isolated from other parts of the world. The first Chinese Empire was a hegemon that was limited by the connectivity of the physical contiguity network.

**Roman Empire** Turning next to the Roman Empire, our theoretical analysis draws attention to four features in this process. Again, in line with the theoretical prediction, Rome was at war for much of this period: its vast territory had been acquired through a long series of hard-fought campaigns during a period of over 500 years. The second point pertains to the pace of expansion: over the period 500 BC–272 BC, the expansion was slow and limited to the Italian peninsula. This relatively slow pace of expansion would be consistent with outcomes in a slighted extension of our model, in which the probability of ties is proportional to the size of the armies employed. However, once Rome had taken over the Italian

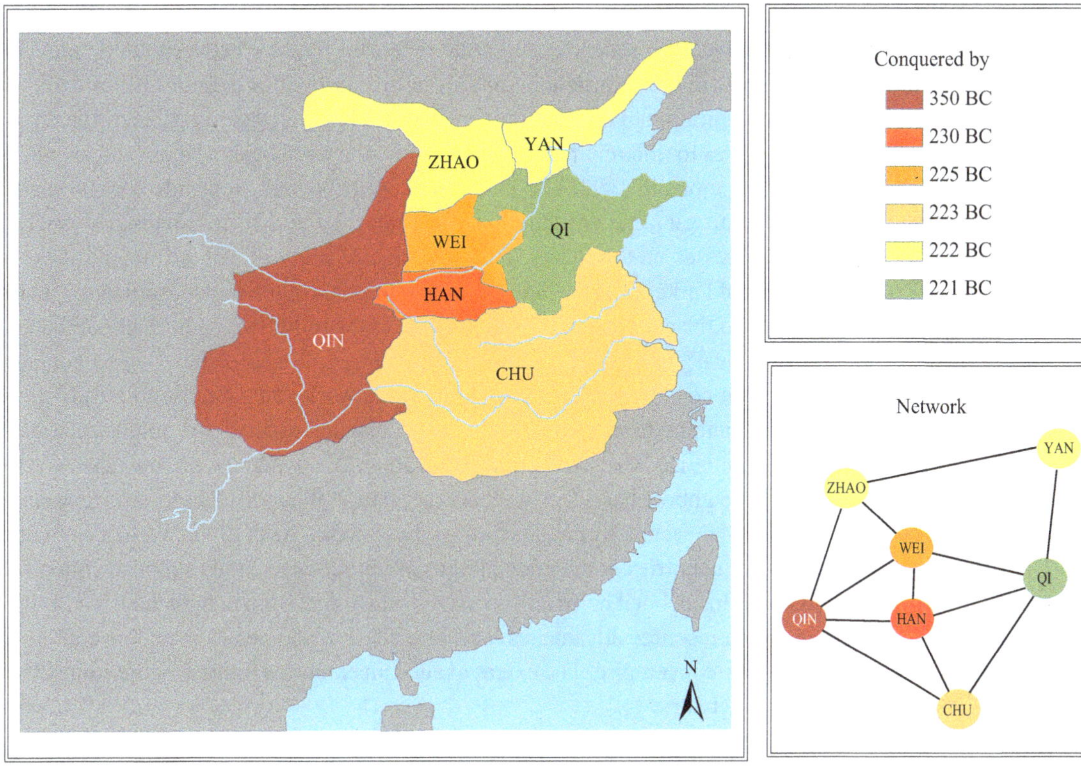


**Figure 10.17**
The first Chinese Empire: Summary. *Source*: Overy (2010).

peninsula, further expansion was rapid. Polybius (2010) presents a detailed discussion of the expansion during the period from 220 BC to 167 BC, a period that saw Rome take over parts of North Africa, Greece, and Asia Minor. Later, during the period until 30 BC, saw a further massive expansion of Roman rule to almost the entire coast around the Mediterranean Sea and much of modern western Europe. The final observation concerns the limits of the empire: the boundaries came to be defined by the Atlantic Ocean in the west, the Rhine and the Danube River in the north, the Sahara Desert in the south, and the Euphrates River in the east. Over the subsequent four hundred years, these boundaries would be contested, but they would describe the limits of the empire broadly: they are consistent with the theoretical prediction that the size of the empire is limited by the connectivity of the contiguity network.

**Spanish Empire** Our theoretical analysis draws attention to three aspects of this development. The first is the developments in Europe involving the successes of the Castilian kingdom through the fifteenth century. These successes set the stage for even further expansion across the world. The second point is the incessant fighting between the Spanish and the native kingdoms in both North and South America during this period. The third and key point is the reconfiguration of the contiguity network. This was made possible by the discovery of new sea routes to different parts of the world—the Caribbean islands (and eventually Americas) by Columbus in 1492 AD. This discovery happened alongside a major change in the technology of war—the advancement of gunpowder and corresponding advances in the design of fortresses and the navy; for a systematic study of military revolutions, see Rogers (1995a) and Parker (1988). Taken together, these developments significantly altered the configuration of the contiguity network, as well as the military resources of combatants: previously "unknown" parts of the world now became accessible and open to conquest. Imperial expansion now proceeded along this new network and gave rise to a truly global Spanish empire spanning three continents: Europe, North America, and South America.

Let us now summarize what we have learned about the dynamics of conquest. Wars of conquest among neighbors have been a recurring feature of history. These wars give rise to dominant rulers, who eventually create empires. Even today, most of the world's population lives in a few large countries or integrated large communities like the European Union. The model is highly stylized, but it helps us understand why rulers want to fight, how institutional reforms can create resource advantages, and how these resources can support contiguous expansion, leading to an empire. The extent of such an empire is limited by the connectivity of the contiguity network.

## 10.6 Reading Notes

This chapter provides an introduction to the study of wars and networks. For a popular overview of some issues in network-based conflict, see Arquilla and Ronfeldt (2001) and Zhu and Levinson (2011). The formal literature brings together contest success functions and networks within a unified framework. For an introduction to contest functions, see Konrad (2009), for an overview of economics literature on conflict, see Garfinkel and Skaperdas (2012). For a survey of the literature on on conflict in networks, see Dziubinski, Goyal, and Vigier (2016).

Section 10.3 covered static models of conflict on networks and drew heavily on the work of Franke and Öztürk (2015) and König, Rohner, Thoenig, and Zilibotti (2017). The model of Franke and Öztürk (2015) builds on a large literature of contests and conflict; for example, see Hillman and Riley (1989) and Appelbaum and Katz (1986). The model in König, Rohner, Thoenig, and Zilibotti (2017) builds further on this strand of work and the theory of games on networks, especially in the use of centrality measures discussed by Freeman (1979) and introduced into economics by Ballester, Calvó-Armengol, and Zenou [2006]).

In the discussion on the Great War of Congo, the network is taken as a given. This is a reasonable starting point, and it is plausible as well, as most groups stuck to their alliances during the Second Congolese War. But it is clear that large-scale interventions will alter the environment, which will give rise to new incentives for forming and dissolving alliances. These considerations led us to examine stable alliance structures and their effects on the frequency of wars. We presented a model taken from Jackson and Nei (2015); for related work in a similar vein see Huremovic (2014) and Hiller (2017). We note that an important concern in the study of alliances is free riding among the parties; for an elegant summary of the literature on this topic, see Bloch (2012). The study of alliances where efforts is endogenous remains an open problem.

The final part of this chapter moved from static models of conflict to the dynamics of conquest and appropriation. Classical studies on the formation of empire include Polybius (2010), Tacitus (2009), and Khaldun (1989). Starting with Gibbon (1776), there is a long tradition of modern work on empires; well-known examples are Braudel (1995), Darwin (2007), Elliott (2006), Lewis (2010), Morris and Scheidel (2009), and Thapar (1997, 2002). Section 10.5 located contests in a dynamic context and built on the work of Hirshleifer (1995) and Krainin and Wiseman (2016) and the large body of historical work on the motivations underlying war and conquest (Thucydides (1989), Hobbes (1886), and Darwin (2007). The presentation in section 10.5 is based on Dziubiński and Goyal (2017). For related models of predation and violence, see Piccione and Rubinstein (2007), Jordan (2006), Krainin and Wiseman (2016), Levine and Modica (2013), and Turchin (2007). The distinctive feature of the model is the central role of networks in shaping conflict.

I thank Sebastian Cortes Corrales for preparing the figures on imperial expansion presented in section 10.5.

## 10.7 Questions

1. Consider the model of contests on networks from section 10.2.

   (a) Assume that there is a unique and interior equilibrium effort in a regular network. Show that equilibrium effort for every link and every player in a regular network of degree $d$ is given by

   $$e^* = \frac{1}{2}\sqrt{\frac{Z}{d}}. \tag{10.35}$$

   Show that the equilibrium payoff for every player is $-(dZ)/4$.

   (b) Assume that there is a unique and interior equilibrium effort in a star network. Let $e_c$ denote the equilibrium effort of the central agent (in every link) and $e_p$ the equilibrium effort of every peripheral agent.

(i) Show that equilibrium efforts are as follows:

$$e_i = p_i \sqrt{\frac{Z}{\sqrt{n-1}}}, \forall i \in \{c, p\}, \tag{10.36}$$

where $p_c = 1/(1+\sqrt{n-1})$ and $p_p = 1 - p_c$. Thus the central agent's link-specific effort and the peripheral agent's effort are both decreasing in $n$. Show that the aggregate effort of the central agent is increasing in $n$.

(ii) Show that equilibrium payoff of central agent is

$$-\frac{(n-1)(\sqrt{n-1}+n-2)}{(1+\sqrt{n-1})^2}Z, \tag{10.37}$$

while the equilibrium payoff of the peripheral agent is

$$\frac{n-2-\sqrt{n-1}}{(1+\sqrt{n-1})}Z. \tag{10.38}$$

(iii) Show that the equilibrium payoff of the central agent is decreasing, while the equilibrium payoff of the peripheral player is increasing in $n$.

2. This question considers fighting in a model of alliances presented in section 10.3. Groups simultaneously choose a single fighting effort, $x_i \in \mathbb{R}$. The efforts of a group are reinforced by the efforts of its allies and weakened by the efforts of its enemies. Effective effort, $\varphi_i$ is defined as

$$\varphi_i(g, \mathbf{x}) = x_i + \beta \sum_{j=1}^{n} g_{ij}^{+} x_j - \gamma \sum_{j=1}^{n} g_{ij}^{-} x_j, \tag{10.39}$$

where $g_{ij}^{+}$ refers to links between allies, $g_{ij}^{-}$ refers to links between enemies, and $\beta, \gamma \in [0,1]$ are spillovers from allies and enemies, respectively. Given network $g$ and effort profile $x = (x_1, \ldots, x_n)$, the payoff to group $i$ is determined by the following Tullock contest function:

$$\Pi_i(g, \mathbf{x}) = V \times \frac{\varphi_i(g, \mathbf{x})}{\sum_{j=1}^{n} \varphi_j(g, \mathbf{x})} - x_i. \tag{10.40}$$

In a regular network, $G_{k^+,k^-}$, every group $i$ has $d_i^+ = k^+$ alliances and $d_i^- = k^-$ enmities. Given the symmetric structure, there is a symmetric Nash equilibrium. Show that this equilibrium effort and payoff vectors are given by

$$x\left(k^+, k^-\right) \equiv x_i\left(G_{k^+,k^-}\right) = \left(\frac{1}{1+\beta k^+ - \gamma k^-} - \frac{1}{n}\right) \times \frac{1}{n}, \tag{10.41}$$

$$\pi\left(k^+, k^-\right) \equiv \pi_i\left(G_{k^+,k^-}\right) = \frac{1+(1+n)(\beta k^+ - \gamma k^-)}{n(1+\beta k^+ - \gamma k^-)} \times \frac{1}{n}. \tag{10.42}$$

Show that the fighting effort of every group $x$ is decreasing in $k^+$ and increasing in $k^-$, while $\pi$ is increasing in $k^+$ and decreasing in $k^-$.

3. Consider the symmetric setting of proposition 10.3 with a concrete functional form $f(d) = \sqrt{d}$ and six agents, $N = \{1, 2, 3, 4, 5, 6\}$.
   (a) Let $c = 0.4$. Find $d^*$.
   (b) Consider the network $g = \{g_{12}, g_{23}, g_{34}, g_{45}, g_{56}, g_{61}\}$ (a cycle). For what values of $E(d^*)$ and $\rho$ is this network war and trade stable?
   (c) Consider the network $g = \{g_{12}, g_{23}, g_{31}, g_{45}, g_{56}, g_{64}\}$ (two disconnected triangles). For what values of $E(d^*)$ and $\rho$ is this network war and trade stable?
   (d) Suppose $d^* = 1$ (a case that is not covered by proposition 10.3). Describe 1-regular networks. What conditions on $E(d^*)$ and/or $\rho$ make such a network war and trade stable?
   (e) Prove the lack of existence of war-stable networks in one of the other coalition formation rules (e.g., attacking countries all in the same component, an attacked country being defended by its neighbors).
   (f) Work through the existence in the one case where that is so (attacking and defending coalitions both have to be cliques, $\rho \in (1, 4/3)$).
4. Consider the conquest game from section 10.5. Suppose that three rulers are connected to each other. A ruler can fight the two rulers one after the other or wait and just fight the victor of the fight between the other two. Assume that the probability of winning is given by the Tullock contest function with parameter $\gamma \geq 0$. Show that fighting two battles is better if $\gamma > 1$, while waiting and fighting a single battle with the winner of the battle between the other two rulers is better if $\gamma < 1$.
5. Consider the conquest game from section 10.5. Suppose three rulers are connected to each other. A ruler can fight the rich neighbor followed by the poor neighbor or the other way around. Assume that the probability of winning is given by the Tullock contest function with parameter $\gamma \geq 0$. Show that the sequence with the poor neighbor followed by the rich neighbor is optimal if $\gamma > 1$; the converse holds true if $\gamma < 1$.
6. Consider the role of defensive alliances in the conquest game from section 10.5. Suppose that in a round, once a ruler has been picked, all the other active rulers have an opportunity to create alliances. An alliance brings together the resources of all its members to defend a member of the alliance against an attack.
   (a) Suppose that the contest function is Tullock and $\gamma$ is large. Assume first that a ruler who is threatened can form an alliance with anyone in the network. In this case, hegemony will obtain only if there is a ruler who controls more than one-half of the aggregate resources.

(b) Next, suppose that an alliance can only consist of path-connected rulers in the residual contiguity network involving all rulers other than the ruler currently picked. Consider a line network with an odd number of rulers. The central vertex has $(n+1)/2$ resources, and each of the other $n-1$ rulers controls exactly 1 unit of resources. Show that it is optimal for the central vertex to launch a full attacking sequence, and if $\gamma$ is large, then the probability of the central ruler becoming the hegemon is close to 1.

# III SOCIAL NETWORKS

# 11 The Law of the Few

## 11.1 Introduction

Massive online networks are a defining feature of life in the early twenty-first century. These networks perform a variety of functions and differ in their structures. However, many of them exhibit a great inequality in the level of activity and number of connections across nodes. These properties were first identified in the context of offline social networks by Katz and Lazersfeld (1966) and Lazarsfeld, Berelson, and Gaudet (1948) but they are greatly amplified in large scale online networks like Twitter and the World Wide Web. For instance, on Twitter, the top 10 percent of the tweeters make over 80 percent of all tweets; the vast majority of users had hardly any followers but there exists a club of users who each have over 25 million followers! The *Law of the Few* says that in social groups, individuals get most of their information from a very small subset of the group. This chapter uses the economic theory of network formation to explore the origins of such great inequality.

We are constantly looking for information so as to make better decisions. We experiment with different alternatives, we read surveys, and we connect with others, hoping to learn from their experiences, and also to learn from what they may have learned from their friends and colleagues. There are rewards to making more informed decisions, but acquiring information is costly. Experiments take time and involve resources; similarly, reading takes time and effort, and talking with others takes time and also has other associated costs. The rewards of connecting and spending time with someone will depend on how well informed they are and how much new information they have for us. In turn, the novelty of information they provide depends partly on how well connected they are to people whom we don't already know. Moreover, the quality of the information accessed from contacts—its timeliness and accuracy—is higher if the information has to travel less far in the social network.

We combine these ideas on information with the theory of strategic network formation introduced in chapter 3, to propose the following model of information sharing: there is a group of individuals each of whom has some information that is of value to everyone. An individual can access the information from another person by forming a link with them. However, the links are costly. The theory illustrates how a comparison of the costs and rewards of linking leads individuals to join a network, and as they join up, the network becomes larger, which makes it more attractive for others to join. This reinforcing aspect of joining a network pushes toward growth and connectivity. Turning to the architecture of networks, as the quality of information accessed is higher if someone is closer to one in the network, which leads individuals to form links with highly connected and central individuals. The resulting network has a hub, which means that it has a small diameter.

Turning to the performance of networks, a network is said to be *efficient* if it maximizes the sum total of individual rewards minus the sum total of linking costs. This formulation has the virtue of defining performance in terms of the concerns of the users of the network. What are efficient networks, and how do they relate to networks that individuals created by individuals? We build on the above reasoning, with regard to network value growing in its size, to establish that an efficient network is either connected or empty. We then note that the star network economizes on the number of links *and* also minimizes on distances between nodes. It is thus efficient across a large range of parameters.

While the reasoning underlying the process of network formation appears to be simple, the informational demands on an individual who is comparing the costs and benefits of forming a link are very great: they need to understand the benefits of connecting to different combinations of individuals. So they need to figure out the shortest paths to different members of the network. Moreover, as they contemplates their options, other individuals are active and the network is evolving. So it is far from clear if the theory is meaningful as a guide to network formation in practice.

To develop an appreciation of the scope of an economic approach to reasoning about networks, we present an experiment on this model that is conducted with human subjects. To make the setting realistic, we consider a group of 100 subjects. Individuals can form and delete links with each other over a period of six minutes. The experiment in this chapter reveals that individuals successfully navigate a very complex environment to create networks in line with the theory.

A key element of the law of the few is specialization in information gathering from external sources: only a small subset of the group invests in personally acquiring information, while the vast majority connect with this minority to learn about the world. In the theory described above, everyone has an equal amount of information at the outset. We next turn to a study of the distribution of information that individuals will personally acquire.

We extend the theory to allow individuals to choose how much information they acquire themselves. This richer model creates an additional trade-off: individuals compare the costs of personally acquiring information against the costs of linking with others in order to access the information they have acquired. The key observation is that if an individual acquires a great deal of information, then it becomes attractive for others not to acquire information on their own, but rather to link with this information-rich individual. The substitutability between information acquisition by others and by oneself sets up a potential route to specialization: the main result is that in large populations, the fraction of individuals who personally acquire information is negligible. The small active subset constitutes a clique, and everyone forms a link with every member of the clique (creating a core-periphery network).

While the theory yields a sharp result, the computational challenges facing an individual are formidable. Now, in addition to the network structure, individuals have to keep track of the effort invested by others in acquiring information. We present an experiment with human subjects in a laboratory to explore the scope of the theory. We consider a group with 100 subjects that chooses information purchase and linking over a period of six minutes. The experiment reveals that subjects specialize in information purchase and linking very much in line with the theoretical prediction.

## 11.2 Empirical Background

Throughout history, information has been passed on mostly via interpersonal communication. But in the first part of the twentieth century, with the coming of age of radio, television, and newspapers, there was a expectation that this would change. Mass media would be central to communication and largely shape individual opinions and decisions.

However, in a series of path-breaking surveys, Lazarsfeld, Berelson, and Gaudet (1948) and Katz and Lazarsfeld (1966) showed that while mass media was important, the majority of individuals (as both consumers and voters) made their decisions based on information and advice garnered through social interactions. Their empirical studies led them to propose a *two-step model* of information. The mass media puts out information that is directly accessed by a small fraction of people, and the rest of the population relies on social contacts with this select few. These studies showed that information gathered through social connections played a crucial role in shaping attitudes and decisions pertaining to fashion, moviegoing, purchasing goods, voting, and public affairs.

In particular, in their book *People's Choice* Lazarsfeld, Berelson, and Gaudet (1948) studied the determinants of voting behavior in the presidential election of 1940 in the small Midwest town of Erie, Ohio. The study involved repeated interviews of a sample of 2,400 voters from May to October 1940 and showed that personal interactions played a key role in shaping voting decisions. In their book *Personal Influence*, Katz and Lazarsfeld (1966) conducted a survey of 800 female residents of Decatur, Illinois, and identified 40 percent of the sample as potential leaders in either marketing, fashion, or public affairs.

In subsequent years, the role of social influence has been widely documented. For instance, Feick and Price (1987) found that 25 percent of their sample of 1,531 individuals acquired a great deal of information about food, household goods, nonprescription drugs, and beauty products, and those people were widely accessed by the rest of the group.

Research on virtual social communities reveals a similar pattern of communication. Zhang, Ackerman, and Adamic (2007) studied the Java Forum, an online community of users who ask and respond to queries concerning Java. They identified 14,000 users and found that 55 percent of these users only asked questions, 12 percent both asked and answered questions, and about 13 percent only provided answers.

In chapter 1, we presented a case study of two information networks—Twitter and the World Wide Web. The introduction to this chapter recalled some aspects of Twitter network that are especially striking.

## 11.3 A Simple Theory of Linking

This section presents a model of the formation of information networks, that is taken from Goyal (1993) and Bala and Goyal (2000a). There is a large group of individuals $N=\{1,\ldots,n\}$, each of whom has been given a distinct piece of information with value 1. Person $i$ can access person $j$ by forming a link with them. A strategy of player $i \in N$ is a (row) vector $g_i=(g_{i1},\ldots,g_{ii-1},g_{ii+1},\ldots,g_{in})$, where $g_{ij}\in\{0,1\}$ for each $j\in N\backslash\{i\}$. Player $i$ has a link with $j$ if $g_{ij}=1$. The set of pure strategies of player $i$ is denoted by $\mathcal{G}_i$. A strategy profile is denoted by $g=\{g_1,\ldots,g_n\}$. There is an equivalence between the set of strategy profiles $\mathcal{S}$, and the set of all directed networks on $n$ nodes. In what follows, we will use network notation. Links are *one-sided* in the sense that they can be formed on an individual initiative and the individual forming the link incurs the costs of doing so. The cost of a link is $k>0$.

While the decision to link is taken unilaterally, a link is undirected for the purposes of communication. A link created by A to B allows both A and B to access each other's information: this is the original information (worth 1) that they started with and any information that they have acquired by forming links with others. With this in mind, to describe the flow of information, define $\hat{g}_{ij}=\max\{g_{ij},g_{ji}\}$ and define network $\hat{g}$ correspondingly.

The quality of information decays as it passes along the network: this may be due to the time it takes or the noise that gets added to it. To make this idea precise, let us define $\delta\in(0,1)$ as a measure of decay. So if person A is one link away from an isolated person B, then A has access to $\delta\times 1=\delta$ information from B. If, on the other hand, A is two links away from B, then A has access to $\delta^2\times 1=\delta^2$ information from B. Consider the network depicted in figure 11.1(a). In this network, A is distance 1 away from B and C, distance 2 from D, and distance 3 from E. Individual A has access information $\delta$ each from B and C, information $\delta^2$ from $D$, and $\delta^3$ from E. Building on this example, we shall say that the information accessed by individual $i$ in network $g$ is

$$1+\sum_{j\in N}\delta^{d(i,j;\hat{g})}. \tag{11.1}$$

The first term, 1, here refers to own information. The term $d(i,j;\hat{g})$ counts the distance between individual $i$ and node $j$ in network $g$. The summation across individuals reflects the idea that every person has a distinct piece of information.

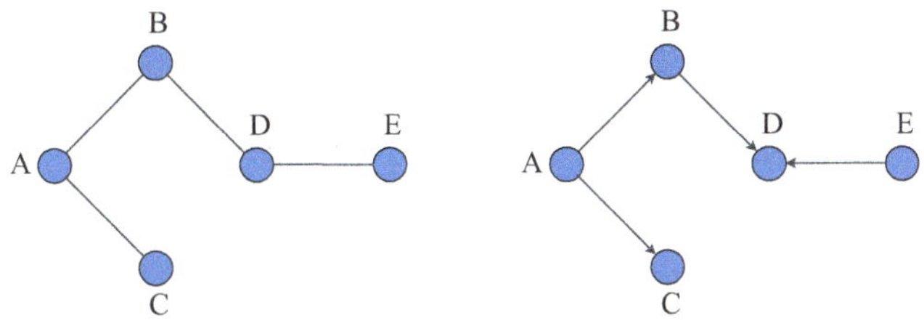

(a) Direct and indirect access (b) Linking patterns

**Figure 11.1**
Access and decay.

For expositional purposes, we are taking a very simple and stylized model of information in this section. These payoffs are generalized in section 11.4, and a question at the end of the chapter further explores a game of linking with general payoffs.

The linking decisions of individuals give rise to a directed network. An example of such a network is illustrated in figure 11.1(b). The arrow in the line from A to B indicates that A has formed a link with B. In this network, A has formed two links, while B and E have formed one link each.

Figure 11.1 illustrates the flow of information. Let us define $d_i(g)$ as the number of links created by person $i$ in network $g$. The net payoff of individual 1 in the network in figure 11.1 is given by $1 + 2\delta + \delta^2 + \delta^3 - 2c$. More generally, the payoff to an individual $i$ in network $g$ is given by

$$\Pi_i(g) = 1 + \sum_{j \in N} \delta^{d(i,j;\hat{g})} - d_i(g)k. \tag{11.2}$$

A Nash equilibrium of this network formation game is a strategy profile $g^*$ such that every player is choosing an optimal strategy given the choices of others; that is,

$$\Pi_i(g_i^*, g_{-i}^*) \geq \Pi_i(g_i', g_{-i}^*), \forall g_i' \in \mathcal{G}_i. \tag{11.3}$$

We next study the Nash equilibrium of the network formation game described above.

### 11.3.1 Equilibrium Networks

First, we note than an equilibrium network must be connected or have no links at all. We will establish this claim by contradiction. Suppose that $g$ is an equilibrium network and there were two distinct groups of connected nodes (i.e., two components X and Y), in it. One of them must be weakly larger than the other. Suppose that X contains (weakly) more nodes than Y. As the network is not empty, in component X, there must be an individual A who has created a link with someone else, such as B. We will argue that individual C, who is in component Y, will find it strictly profitable to form a link with B. Such a link will give C access to everyone that A accessed through their link with B, and in addition, it will give her access to A (via B). So if A finds is profitable to form the link with B, then C must find it even more profitable. This shows that the network with two distinct components X and Y cannot be an equilibrium. The argument we propose is general and can be applied to rule out any network with links and multiple components. This is a contradiction that completes the proof.

This line of reasoning also brings out a general feature of the economics of linking: when an individual forms links with another person, other individuals will have even greater incentives to follow suit. This is a valuable insight and rules out networks with multiple components.

Recall the examples in chapter 1—regular networks as well as different types of core-periphery networks are all connected. Connectedness is thus a fairly permissive requirement. Does economic behavior by individuals imply any further restrictions on network architecture?

We consider the role of the two economic variables, the costs of linking $k$, and the level of decay $\delta$ in shaping incentives for linking. If costs are very small, $k < \delta - \delta^2$, then it is attractive to directly link with everyone, which gives rise to a complete network. The maximum return to a single link is a return to a single neighbor and $n-2$ indirect neighbors, $\delta + (n-2)\delta^2$. If the cost of a link is more than this return, then no one will form any links and the equilibrium network will be empty. For costs between these two thresholds, a wide range of networks may arise in equilibrium.

To illustrate some of the possibilities here, let us start with the case of $k > \delta$. In this case, the empty network is an equilibrium. In addition, if $k < \delta + (n-2)\delta^2$, then the star is also an equilibrium. This brings out the challenge of coordination problems in the linking game. An individual's incentive to form or delete links, therefore, depends on the linking behavior of others. If no one forms links the returns to linking are too small and the best response is to also form no links. This suggests that links are strategic complements. On the other hand, if everyone forms links with everyone, then the best response is to again form no links: here links are strategic substitutes. This possibility suggests that linking games have a rich strategic structure. Finally, observe that if $\delta - \delta^2 < k$, then no two spokes will wish to form a link, and since $k < \delta + (n-2)\delta^2$, it is optimal to form a single link with the hub. Thus the star is an equilibrium if $\delta - \delta^2 < k < \delta + (n-2)\delta^2$. These observations are summarized in the following result.

**Proposition 11.1** *Consider the game of linking with payoffs given by equation (11.2). An equilibrium network is either empty or connected. The complete network is a unique equilibrium if $k < \delta - \delta^2$. The star is an equilibrium if $\delta - \delta^2 < k < \delta + (n-2)\delta^2$. The empty network is an equilibrium for $k > \delta$ and the unique equilibrium if $k > \delta + (n-2)\delta^2$.*

To appreciate the arguments at a more general level, it is helpful to consider the situation where $k > 1$ and $\delta$ is close to 1. As decay is small, there cannot be a cycle in an equilibrium network. Let us consider a network without a cycle that is not a star. In such a network, there will be at least one pair of individuals who are at distance 3 or greater apart. Denote the agents farthest apart as $i$ and $j$. They must each have 1 link (as there are no cycles in the

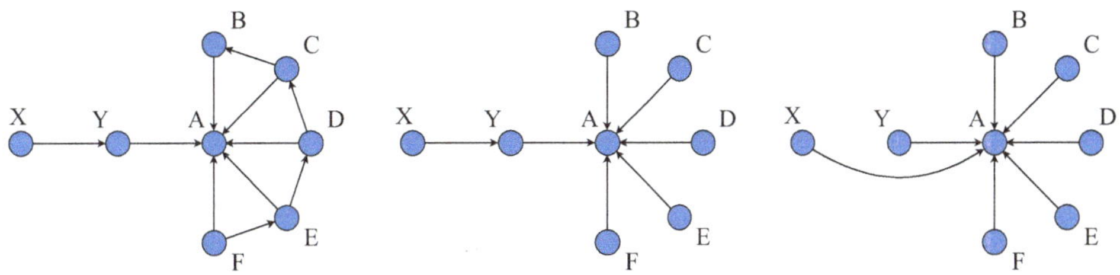


**Figure 11.2**
Salience of the hub-spoke architecture.

network). Since $k > 1$, it follows that each of them must be paying for their link. Suppose that individual $j$ earns a weakly higher payoff than player $i$. Let $j$ have a link with player $l$ on the unique path between $i$ and $j$. Since the distance between $i$ and $j$ is greater than 2, it must be true that individual $i$ has no link with $l$. Individual $i$ can earn a strictly higher payoff if they delete their current link and instead form a link with individual $l$. This is because they will be at the same distance from all players as player $j$ in the original network, and, in addition, they will be closer to $j$ in the new network than in $g$. Hence the distance between any two individuals in an equilibrium network cannot be greater than 2. The final step in the argument is to note that the star is the only acyclic network in which every pair of players is at a distance of 2 or less.

Figure 11.2 walks through the logic of this argument with the help of pictures. Start with the network in figure 11.2(a). In this network, individual F has no incentive to have a direct link with E: they can access E via A, and the loss in benefits $\delta - \delta^2$ is smaller than the saving in cost $k$. It is similar for individuals B–E. If we were to delete links, we arrive at the network in figure 11.2(b). Notice next that X has a strict incentive to delete their link with Y and instead form a link with A. This allows X to shorten the distance to B, C, D, E, and F. The distance to Y goes from 1 to 2, but the distance to A correspondingly declines from 2 to 1. This link switch by X yields the star in figure 11.2(c). This helps us appreciate how individual incentives push toward sparse and unequal networks with a small diameter.

### 11.3.2 Efficient Networks

Recall that the social welfare from a network $g$, $W(g)$, is the sum of individual utilities:

$$W(g) = \sum_{i \in N} \Pi_i(g). \tag{11.4}$$

Network $g$ is said to be efficient if $W(g) \geq W(g')$ for all $g' \in \mathcal{G}$.

If the costs of linking are very small, $k < 2(\delta - \delta^2)$, it is easy to see that it is socially desirable to form a direct link between every pair of individuals. On the other hand, if the costs of links are very large, then at an intuitive level, it is clear that no links would be justifiable. We also note that while there is a very rich range of possible networks, the star network is attractive because it economizes on the number of links and at the same time keeps the average distance between individuals very low (there are $n-1$ links in a star—the minimum number of links it takes to connect $n$ nodes—and the average distance is less than 2). The following result summarizes these observations.

**Proposition 11.2** *Suppose that payoffs are given by equation (11.2). The unique efficient network is (i) the complete network if* $0 < k < 2[\delta - \delta^2]$*, (ii) the star network if* $2[\delta - \delta^2] < k < 2\delta + (n-2)\delta^2$*, or (iii) the empty network if* $2\delta + (n-2)\delta^2 < k$*.*

We provide a proof of this result here, as the arguments are of general interest (the reader will notice that the proof follows the same lines as the proof of efficiency in the connections model in chapter 3).

The joint marginal gains to players $i$ and $j$ from forming a link are bounded from below by $2[\delta - \delta^2]$. If $k < 2[\delta - \delta^2]$, then it follows that forming a link increases social welfare. This means that any incomplete network is welfare dominated by the complete network: in this parameter range, the complete network is uniquely efficient.

Next, fix component $C_1$ in $g$, with $|C_1| = m$. Suppose that $m \geq 3$. Let $l \geq m-1$ be the number of links in the component. Then the welfare in $C_1$ is bounded from above by

$$m + l(2\delta - k) + [m(m-1) - 2l]\delta^2. \tag{11.5}$$

This is because a link ensures direct benefits of $2\delta$ to each of the connected pairs, the cost of a link is $k$, and the closest all other pairs of individuals could be is distance 2. If the component is a star, then social welfare is

$$m + (m-1)[2\delta - k] + (m-1)(m-2)\delta^2, \tag{11.6}$$

where the first term, $m$, reflects stand-alone benefits, the second term collects the direct benefits minus the costs of links, and the third term reflects the benefits of all pairs who are distance 2 apart.

Under the hypothesis that $2(\delta - \delta^2) < k$, equation (11.5) can never exceed equation (11.6) and the two are exactly equal for $l = m-1$. It can be determined that the star is the only network with $m$ players and $m-1$ links in which every pair of players is at a distance of 2 or less. Hence any other network with $m-1$ links must have at least one pair of players who are at a distance of 3 or more. This implies that social welfare in any other network with $l = m-1$ links is strictly less than social welfare in the star network. Thus, in an efficient network, a component must be a star.

Consider next an efficient network with multiple stars, with $m$ and $m'$ individuals, respectively. As the network is efficient, the component must have nonnegative welfare. It can be shown by direct computation that a single component with $m + m'$ players has higher social welfare than two components with the star structure. Thus a single star maximizes social welfare in the class of all nonempty networks. Social welfare in a star is given by equation (11.6), where we replace $m$ with $n$. It can be checked that the start welfare exceeds welfare in the empty network if $2\delta + (n-2)\delta^2 > k$. This completes the argument. ■

### 11.3.3 Relation between Equilibrium and Efficient Networks

An important feature of an economic approach is the systematic exploration of the relation between what individuals wish to do and their collective interest. Let us examine this relation in our model. When individual A forms a link with B, A gains access to B, but B also gains access to A. The latter benefit is not taken into account by A if they care only about their own payoffs: as a result, in our model, networks created by individuals are typically underconnected relative to the networks that they would collectively prefer. This point is clearly brought out both when the costs of linking are small and when they are large. If $\delta - \delta^2 < k < 2[\delta - \delta^2]$, then the complete network is efficient but not an equilibrium (as the returns from firsthand links to an individual are less than the cost of the links). Similarly, if $\delta + (n-2)\delta^2 < k < 2\delta + (n-2)\delta^2$, then the star network is efficient, but no individual has an incentive to form any links: as a result, the unique equilibrium is the empty network.

In this model, linking is driven by the individual desire to access others at a short distance and minimal cost. The theory yields three insights: (1) there are economic pressures for individuals to create sparse and unequal networks that have a short diameter; (2) there are powerful strategic interaction effects that give rise to the possibility of multiple equilibria and create serious coordination difficulties for individuals (e.g., the empty and the star networks are both equilibria for a wide range of parameters); and (3) individual incentives to form links are generally lower than social benefits, so networks created by individuals will generally be sparser than what they would collectively like.

We next comment on how the economic approach relates to the Erdős-Rényi model of random graphs (presented in chapter 2). Recall that in this model, there are two parameters: the probability of linking and the number of nodes. An important result of that model is that the probability of linking must remain at a level above a threshold to ensure that the network remains connected. In a certain sense, the cost of linking performs a similar role in the economic model of linking presented in this section. As the number of nodes grows, the connected network is sustainable for larger and larger costs of link $k$ (recall that the star network is stable so long as $k < \delta + (n-2)\delta^2$). On the other hand, the arguments in the individual linking model reveal a robust multiplicity of outcomes as pointed out earlier. Coordination issues are central to an economic approach. On the other hand, as the number of nodes grows, the Erdős-Rényi model yields graphs with certain properties that arise with a probability close to 1. This suggests an important distinction between the economic approach and the statistical approach of the Erdős-Rényi model. Finally, the economic approach offers a definition of the performance of networks founded on individual objectives and helps us appreciate the tension between individual incentives and collective returns. This goes beyond the Erdős-Rényi model, and it opens up the space for thinking about interventions that can improve the network.

While the ingredients of the theory are few—the costs of linking and the benefits of linking—and the arguments are simple, it is also clear that in practice, an individual who is comparing the costs and benefits of forming a link faces a very complex decision: this person needs to understand the rewards from linking with different individuals (and also subsets of individuals). To do so, they must be able to compute the shortest paths to various individuals in a large and evolving network. Moreover, even in simple cases, there are multiple stable networks (e.g., the empty network and the star network in the previous discussion), so it is far from clear what networks will actually emerge if individuals were given the payoffs as in the model. To address this concern, we now turn to an experiment with human subjects who play this linking game.

### 11.3.4 Experiment

We report the findings of an experiment on link formation taken from Choi, Goyal, and Moisan (2020). The payoff function is as in equation (11.2). The value of benefits is $V = 10$ and the decay parameter is $\delta = 0.9$. The costs of linking are $k = 200$. In order to better mimic the environment of very large networks the experiment is run with a group of 100 subjects.

Given these parameter values, proposition 11.1 tells us that the empty and star networks are both equilibria. In the star network, the hub and spokes earn 901 and 613, respectively. Thus the star network exhibits significant inequality—the hub earns roughly 50 percent more than the spokes. Individual payoffs in the empty network equal 10. Finally, proposition 11.2 tells us that the star network is the unique efficient network.

Looking ahead, to study the data arising from these large groups, it is more reasonable to consider the statistical properties of networks. With this in mind, we study general aspects of a star network such as density of links, degree inequality, and average distances and state the hypothesis to be tested as follows.

**Hypothesis 11.1** *Subjects create a network that is efficient: it is sparse, unequal, and exhibits small average distances.*

The experiment consists of a continuous-time game that is played over 6 minutes. There are six rounds in all. At any point, an individual can choose to form and delete links with anyone else. The first minute is a trial period, and the subsequent 5 minutes are the game, with payment consequences. At the end of each round, every subject is informed, of a time moment randomly chosen for payment. The subjects are provided detailed information on everyone's behavior at the chosen moment, through the corresponding network structure. The first round is a trial round with no payoff relevance, and the only the last five rounds were relevant for subjects' earnings. In analyzing the data, we will focus on the subjects' behavior and group outcomes from these last five rounds.

During a round, at every moment, each subject is informed about the links in their own component and about their own payoff (but not the payoff of any other subject). Figure 11.3 presents the screen observed by a subject. At any instant in the six-minute game, a subject can form or delete a link with any other subject by simply double-clicking on the corresponding node in the computer screen. If the subject forms a link with another subject on the right side of the screen (i.e., someone who is not in the same component), that subject (along with the entire component to which they belong) would be transferred to the left side

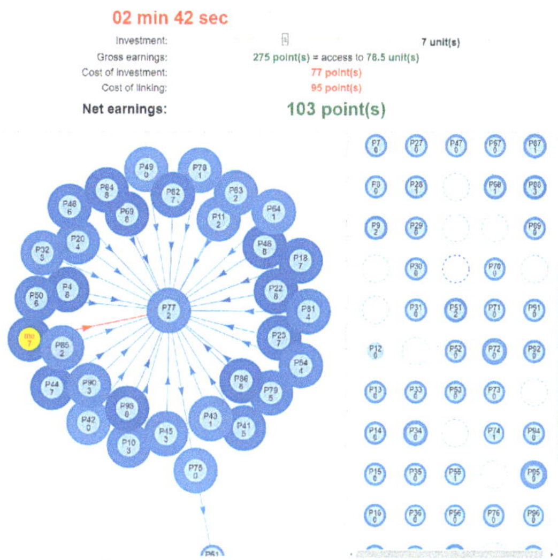


**Figure 11.3**
Decision screen: linking experiment.

of the computer screen. In a case in which the subject removes a link to another subject, that subject would be transferred to the right side of the computer screen if they are no longer part of the same component and remain on the left side of the screen otherwise.

On average, a session lasted 90 minutes and subjects earned 15.3 euros (this includes a 5-euro show-up fee). The experiments were conducted in the Laboratory for Research in Experimental and Behavioral Economics (LINEEX) at the University of Valencia and the Laboratory for Experimental Economics (LEE) at the Jaume I University of Castellon.

To get a first impression of the outcome of the experiment, we present snapshots of the network at four points in figure 11.4. These plots suggest that subjects create sparse networks with a few highly connected individuals. Over time, one dominant hub emerges. This means that all the individuals are close to each other. As the number of links and small distances are key to efficiency, these snapshots suggest that individual linking gives rise to networks that attain high levels of efficiency.

There were four groups and each group took part in five payoff relevant rounds, so we have data from twenty rounds in all. We summarize the data from these rounds in figure 11.5 with the help of average time series on four measures—the total number of links, degree inequality, average distance, and efficiency. The data used from every round of the game consists of 360 observations (snapshots of every subject's choices) selected at intervals of 1 second. The time series is constructed as follows: for a fixed second $t$ and for a round $r$, consider the number of links created, $l_{tr}$. Sum $l_{tr}$ across the twenty rounds and then divide by 20 to obtain an average. This number shows up as the total number of links for second $t$ in the plot.

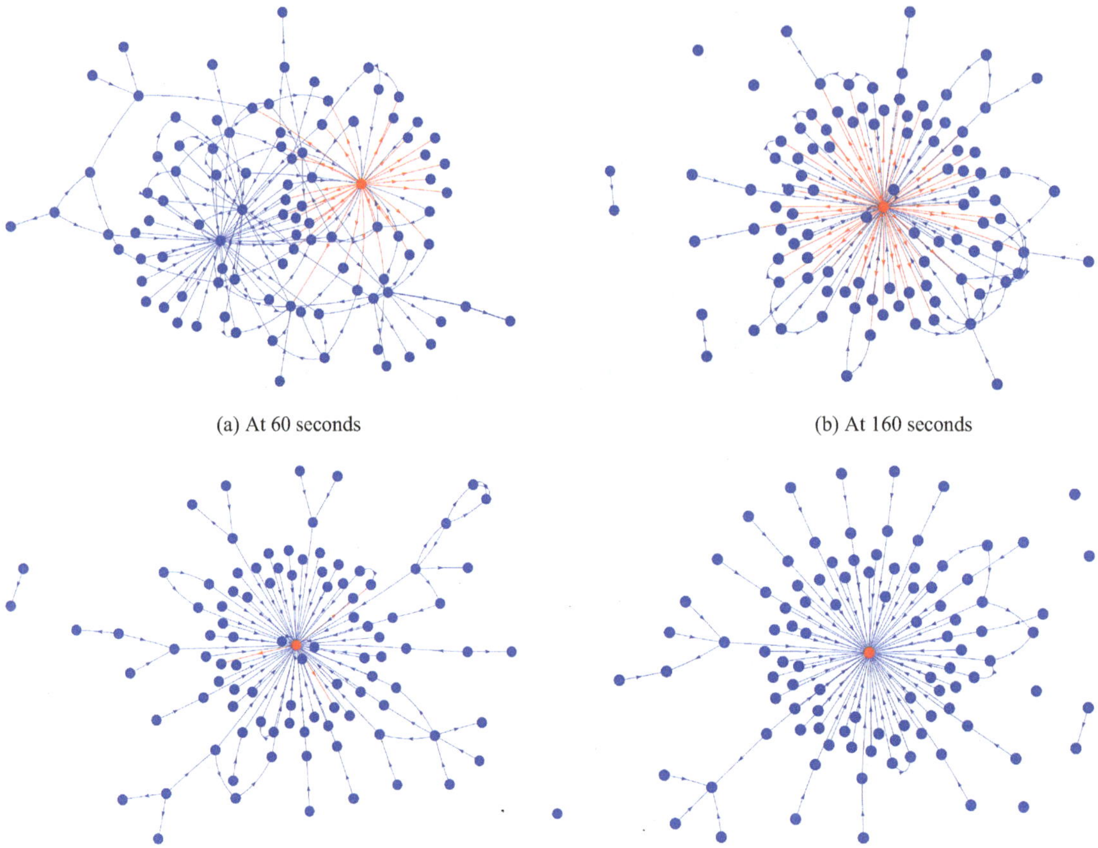

(a) At 60 seconds (b) At 160 seconds

(c) At 260 seconds (d) At 360 seconds

**Figure 11.4**
Evolution of an information network. *Source*: Choi, Goyal, and Moisan (2020).

By way of background, we note that in these experiments, subjects rapidly coordinate their linking activity and create connected networks: the average size of the largest component was 96.3. So almost everyone belonged to the same component. The statistics on distance that follow pertain to this component.

Figure 11.5(a) plots the total number of links. The number of links grew at first, reaching a level of 250, and then declined steadily until it was a little over 100 by the end of the experiment. Recall that in a group of 100, the minimal number of links needed for connectedness is 99. Thus subjects were successful in keeping the links close to a minimum.

Next, we consider degree inequality: Figure 11.5(b) presents the ratio of the highest degree to median degrees. At the start of the experiment, this ratio is close to 1, but then it

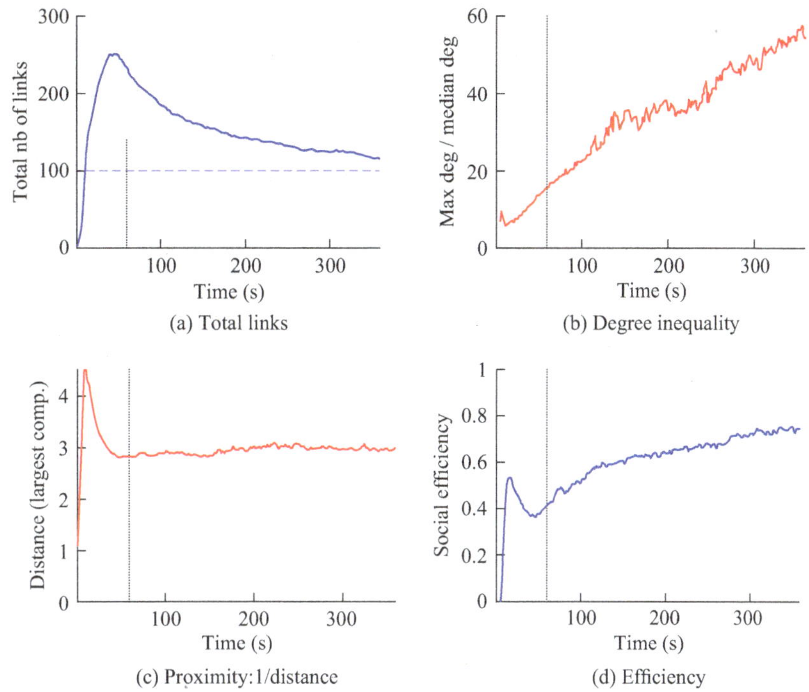


**Figure 11.5**
Findings: Network structure and efficiency. *Source*: Choi, Goyal, and Moisan (2020)

grows steadily, and by the end, it reaches over 50. In other words, the most connected node had a degree that is over 50 times more than the median degree.

Figure 11.5(c) presents the evolution of average distance. We see that fairly early in the experiment, the distance was under 3 and remains so until the end of the experiment. In view of the group size of 100 and the small number of links, this is a very low average distance (which is close to the average distance of a star network).

Finally, we take up relative efficiency: Figure 11.5(d) presents total payoffs attained as a fraction of the maximum possible total earnings. Starting at 50 percent, subjects were able to steadily increase the efficiency, and by the end of the experiment, they were attaining close to 80 percent relative efficiency.

We conclude here with some remarks on the behavior of the highly connected individuals. Figure 11.6 shows that there is intense competition among a couple of individuals to become the hub: this competition takes the form of forming many links. We interpret these links as investments: by forming these links, an individual gets close to others. This makes them attractive as a connector. Once an individual has induced others to link with them, they start deleting links, which induces the newly isolated individuals to respond by forming a

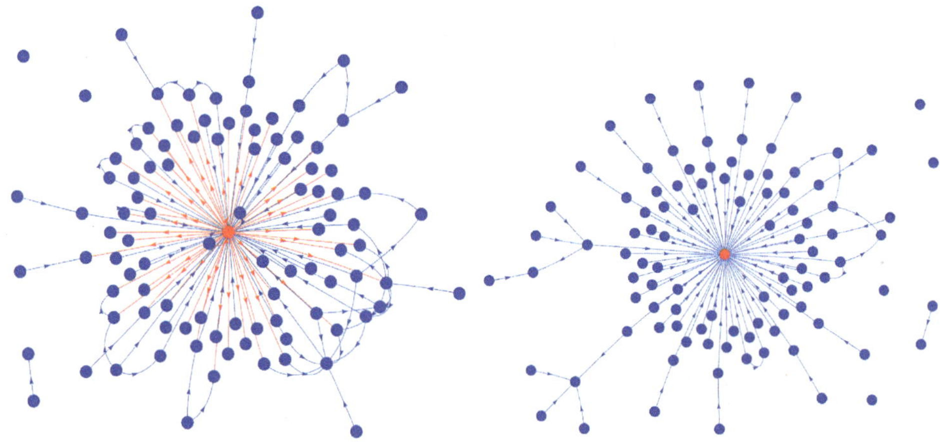

(a) Minute 3 (b) Minute 6

**Figure 11.6**
Competition to become a hub (red links are formed by the red player). *Source*: Choi, Goyal, and Moisan (2020).

link. This process ends with the hub forming almost no links, and everyone connecting with them.

To summarize: The long-run outcome of a sparse network with a hub is consistent with the theory developed in the previous section. However, the experiment reveals an interesting dynamic of large investments and intense competition that underlies the formation of the network. This dynamic goes beyond the theoretical arguments previously developed for the star network being an equilibrium in the static model.

## 11.4 Who Buys Information?

A key element in the law of the few is specialization in information acquisition: only a small subset of society actually invests in acquiring information, while most of the others simply connect with them to learn about the world. In the theory presented in section 11.3, at the outset, everyone has an equal amount of information. To understand the determinants of specialization in the purchase of information, we supplement the choices available to individuals. In this richer model, therefore, there are three ingredients: linking, a decay factor, and efforts in the purchase of information. The discussion in this section is based on Galeotti and Goyal (2010).

There is a set of individuals $N = \{1, \ldots, n\}$, where $n \geq 2$. Every individual chooses an effort level, $x_i$, and a set of links with others, $g_i$. A link formed by $i$ with $j$ allows $i$ to access information that $j$ personally bought, as well as the information that $j$ accesses from those they connect to. Let $s_i = (x_i, g_i)$ be the strategy of individual $i$, and let $s = (s_1, \ldots, s_n)$

denote the strategy profile of the individuals. The payoff of an individual $i$ given a strategy profile $s$ is

$$\Pi_i(s) = f\left(x_i + \sum_{l=1}^{l=n-1} a_l \sum_{j\in N_i^l(\hat{g})} x_j\right) - cx_i - d_i(g)k, \tag{11.7}$$

where $a_l \geq 0$ and $a_{l+1} \leq a_l$ for all $l \geq 1$ ($N_i^l(\hat{g})$ refers to individuals that are distance $l$ from individual $i$ in graph $\hat{g}$), $c > 0$, $k > 0$, and $d_i(g)$ is the number of links created and paid for by individual $i$. In the previous scenario, everyone started with 1 unit of information, and for simplicity, we assumed that the value of information increases linearly in the number of people accessed. In the present context, if we were to use a similar linear formulation and the marginal value of information was constant at, say, $r$, then individuals would demand either zero or an infinite amount of information, depending on whether $r$ was smaller or larger than $c$. Therefore, to make the problem of information demand interesting (and have an interior optimum), we will assume that the marginal value of information declines as an individual has more of it.

**Assumption 11.1** *$f(0) = 0$, $f(.)$ is strictly increasing and concave. There exists a number $z$ such that $f'(z) = c$, i.e., the marginal benefit is exactly equal to the marginal cost at $z$.*

Diminishing marginal returns is a reasonable assumption in an information-sharing setting: for instance, we may think of action $x$ as draws from a distribution (e.g., the price distribution for a product). If the different draws are independent across individuals and players are interested in the lowest price, then the value of an additional draw, which is the change in the average value of the lowest-order statistic, is positive, but the number of draws is declining. Another possible interpretation is in terms of individuals choosing an action whose payoffs are unknown. Every individual has access to a costly sample of observations, which may reflect personal experience with a product or a technology. A link with another player then allows access to their personal experience. The returns from accessing more samples of information—own and others—are increasing but concave.

Next, we study the Nash equilibrium of this game of information purchasing and linking. For concreteness, and to develop intuitions, following Goyal, Rosenkranz, Weitzel, and Buskens (2017), we will provide a specific functional form for the value of information:

$$f(y) = \begin{cases} y(29 - y) & \text{if } y \leq 14 \\ 196 + y & \text{else.} \end{cases} \tag{11.8}$$

Let us discuss the diminishing returns property with the help of this functional form. Suppose that an individual has 5 units of information. How much is 1 more unit of information worth? To figure this out, we need to work out the difference $f(6) - f(5)$. In this example, this number is $138 - 120 = 18$. Similarly, one can check that if one already has 8 units of information, the next unit is worth $180 - 168 = 12$. So we see that the value of additional units of information declines as one has more information. In particular, if the cost $c = 11$, then this example the value of $z$ is given by 9. This number will play an important role in the discussion that follows.

We next discuss the individual incentives for the acquisition of information and the formation of links. The problem at hand is complicated, so we will proceed in steps. First, we will consider the situation where $a_1 = 1$ and $a_l = 0$ for all $l \geq 2$. This corresponds to a situation of high information decay: an individual gains utility from the information they get from their neighbors, but does not get any utility from the neighbors of neighbors.

Consider an individual in isolation, who will choose information up to the point that the incremental value of an additional unit is less than or equal to the cost of information. Then the individual who is on their own will choose exactly 9 units. To see this, observe that the value of the 10th unit is $190 - 180 = 10 < 11$. Suppose that A has chosen 9. What would be the response of the other individuals?

For concreteness, label an individual B. How much information should this person buy, and should B link with A? B accesses 9 units if they link with A. The cost of this information is $11 \times 9 = 99$, and it costs $k$ to access A. So it is in B's interest to link with A if $k < 99$. Observe that once an individual has linked with A, they have access to 9 units of information, so the incremental value of additional information is smaller than the cost of information; thus they will choose to acquire 0 units of information personally. The same reasoning applies to all individuals other than A. Therefore, once A chooses 9, if $k < 99$, then every other individual can do no better than forming a link with A and choosing 0 purchases of information. Thus the star network with A choosing purchase level 9 and all other individuals choosing purchase level 0 and forming a link with A constitutes an equilibrium.

### 11.4.1 Direct Information Access

To develop this theme further, suppose that $a_2 = 0$, so information decays rapidly and only direct neighbors are useful. Consider a situation where three individuals A, B, and C all choose 3. It follows that individual D will link with A only if the cost of the link is smaller than the cost of the information that D accesses from A. This cost of information is $11 \times 3 = 27$. So if $k < 33$, then D will find it profitable to form a link with A, and it is similar for B and C. So it follows that the network in which A, B, and C (with each choosing 3 units of purchase) constitute a core and everyone links to them constitutes an equilibrium.

In particular, for B to link with A, the link must be cheaper than the cost of the information that A acquires. Suppose that A acquires $z$. For B to link to A, it must be the case that $k < cz$; otherwise, B would be better off purchasing $z$ on their own and not forming the link with A.

To develop an complete understanding of equilibrium outcomes, a key issue concerns the sum total of purchases undertaken by individuals. In the previous discussion, we have considered outcomes in which the total purchases of all individuals $z = 9$. In principle, it is possible that the total purchases exceed $z$. The simplest situation arises when $k > cz$: there is a unique equilibrium in which everyone chooses $z$ and no links are formed. However, the interesting case is when $k < cz$: even in this case, the total purchases of all individuals may exceed $z$.

To see this, consider a game with four individuals. The following is an equilibrium outcome: there are two components of two individuals each, and everyone chooses $z = 4.5$, while one individual chooses a link with the other individual in each component. However, note that in this equilibrium, the individual who is choosing a link is indifferent between linking with their current match and an individual in the other component. This suggests that the linking is not a strict best response. Bearing this in mind, we can now state a result that describes all strict equilibrium of the game of activity and linking. Define $I(s) = \{i \in N | x_i > 0\}$ as the set of individuals who chose the positive purchase $x_i > 0$ under strategy profile $s$. The proportion of active players in a strategy profile $s$ is given by $|I(s)|/n$.

**Proposition 11.3** *Consider the game of information purchase and linking with payoffs given by (11.7). Suppose that $a_1 = 1$ and $a_l = 0$ for all $l \geq 2$. Suppose that assumption 11.1 holds and $k < cz$. In a strict Nash equilibrium, $s^*$, the sum of information purchases of all individuals is equal to $z$. In a large society, in such equilibria, the fraction of active individuals who choose a positive purchase is negligible. This active subset constitutes a clique, while the rest of the individuals form a link with every individual in the clique.*

Now let us sketch out the arguments underlying the proof of this result. Fix a strategy profile $s$. The total information accessed by individual $i$ under strategy profile $s$, $y_i$, is the sum of their own purchase and the purchase of their neighbors:

$$y_i = x_i + \sum_{j \in N_i(\hat{g})} x_j. \tag{11.9}$$

We start by noting an important implication of the assumptions on payoffs. In equilibrium, it must be true that for every individual, $y_i \geq z$. If $y_i < z$, then $i$ can profitably raise their effort, as the marginal benefit of the effort at $y_i$, $f'(y_i)$, is greater than the marginal cost of effort, $c$ (this follows from the concavity of $f$ and the definition of $z$). This implies that for any active individual $i$ with $x_i > 0$, it must be the case that $y_i = z$. We have already shown that $y_i \geq z$. Suppose that $y_i > z$, then $i$ can profitably lower their effort, as the marginal benefit of the effort, $f'(y_i)$, is less than the marginal cost of effort.

We next sketch the argument for why the sum total of purchases in a strict equilibrium must equal $z$. If the total purchases exceed $z$, then we know from the previous step that there must be active individuals who are accessed by some individuals, but not others. It is possible to show that only two configurations of purchases are possible: one where all positive purchase individuals choose the same activity level, and a second one, in which they choose two different positive levels (this is an exercise at the end of the chapter). In both cases, it is possible to show that equilibrium implies that the cost of linking must exactly equal the cost of a purchase undertaken by such an individual. But then players are indifferent between forming a link and making the corresponding purchase themselves.

In other words, the strategies of the players are not a strict best response to the strategies of others.

As the total purchase equals $z$ and everyone must access at least $z$, it follows that in equilibrium, every individual must access every active individual. This in turn implies that the active individuals must constitute a clique and inactive players must form a link with every member of this clique.

Finally, consider the specialization in information purchases. Recall that we are considering an equilibrium in which the total purchase is $z$. We have noted already that for every $i$, $x_i + \sum_{j \in N_i(\hat{g})} x_j \geq z$. This means that every player who acquires information personally is accessed by every player in equilibrium. There is therefore at most one player $i \in I(s)$ with no incoming links (i.e., $g_{ji} = 0$, for all $j \in N$). For all other players $l \in I(s)$, there must be at least one player $j \in I(s)$ such that $g_{jl} = 1$; but this implies that $x_l > k/c$. So the number of "incoming links" players who acquire information personally, $I(s) - 1$, is bounded from above by $(zc)/k$. It follows that $I(s)/n \leq ([zc/k] + 1)/n$. The right side can be made arbitrarily small by raising $n$. This completes the argument underlying the proof. ■

Figure 11.7 illustrates core-periphery networks in which the core is of size 1, 2, 3, and 4.

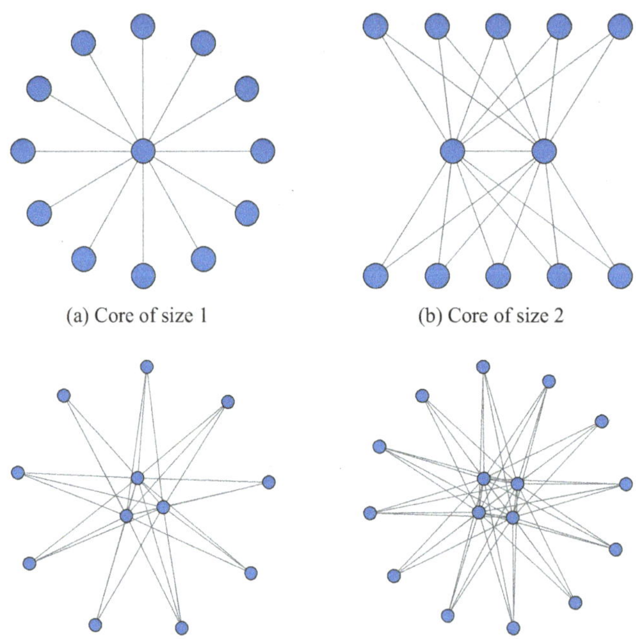

(a) Core of size 1 (b) Core of size 2

(c) Core of size 3 (d) Core of size 4

**Figure 11.7**
Core-periphery networks.

What does the law of the few imply for individual and collective welfare? A first point to note is that as the cost of purchase is linear and total effort is the same across these networks, the total cost of effort is equal across the different sizes of cores. Moreover, in these core periphery networks, all individuals also access exactly $z$ units of information. As links are costly, it then follows that the equilibrium with a single core element is most economical and hence maximizes aggregate utility across all core-periphery networks.

Next, consider the appropriate level of information purchase. Observe that the purchase level $z$ equates the return to a single individual with the cost of purchase. However, the social return to an incremental unit of purchase $z+1$ is really $n$ times the private return. Thus the hub individual will choose a level of purchase that is lower than what is collectively desirable. Moreover, the gap between the individually optimal and the socially desirable levels of purchase grows with the number of individuals. In large societies characterized by a law of the few network, very little information is actually collected relative to what would be desirable.

Proposition 11.3 says that the number of players personally acquiring information is small relative to the number of players in large societies. But the result is permissive with regard to the identity of the hub player. A recurring theme in the empirical literature is that even though hubs seem to have similar demographic characteristics as the others, they have distinctive attitudes that include greater attention to general market information and greater enjoyment in collecting this information. One way to incorporate this empirical observation in the model is to suppose that some players have slightly lower costs of acquiring information (or slightly larger benefits from information) than others. It turns out that this modification has powerful and clear-cut effects on who becomes a hub of the network.

To see these effects in the simplest way, let us suppose that one individual, such as Mr. A has slightly lower costs of purchasing information than others. For this low-cost player, the optimal information level, $z_A$, is greater than the optimal information level for other players $z$. From the arguments developed in proposition 11.4, we know that aggregate information purchase by the rest of the population is at most $z$. This means that A must personally purchase some information (i.e., $x_A > 0$). If $x_A = z_A > z$, then the best response of everyone else is clearly to purchase no information and to form a link with A.

Next, consider the case of $x_A < z_A$: we know, from our discussions earlier in this chapter that the optimality of A's choice implies that $x_A + y_A = z_A$, so there is a player $i \neq A$ with $x_i > 0$ and $x_i + y_i = z$. A key observation is that if someone wants to link with $i$, then it must be profitable for everyone else to do likewise. But then $i$ accesses all information, $z_A > z$, and this contradicts the optimality of $i$'s choices. Thus *no* player can have a link with player $i \neq A$ in equilibrium. Hence, $i$ must form a link with player A and, from the optimality of linking, so must every other player. Thus, in any equilibrium, the low-cost player is the unique hub. Finally, since every player is choosing positive effort, the equilibrium values of $x_A$ and $x_i$ are given by the two equations $x_A + (n-1)x_i = z_A$ and $x_A + x_i = z$. A question at the end of the chapter works through the details of this argument.

### 11.4.2 Indirect Information Access

In the discussion so far, we have assumed that information flows across direct links only. And we have shown that core-periphery networks in which core nodes are active (and constitute a clique) and periphery nodes choose zero purchases but form links with the core members constitute the unique outcome. We now take up the more natural case of indirect information transmission. To develop a feel for the rich range of possibilities that arise, we assume that payoffs are given by equation (11.8) and that neighbors are worth 1, two-removed neighbors are worth 1/2, and all other farther away neighbors are worth 0, that is, $a_1 = 1$, $a_2 = 1/2$, and $a_l = 0$, for all $l \geq 3$. For concreteness, we will also assume that $c = 11$ and $k = 90$.

We start by noting that with $c = 11$ and a reward function $f$ as given by equation (11.8), the optimal purchase level is given by $z = 9$. The star network with an active hub is an equilibrium in this setting, as in the earlier model with no indirect flow of benefits. We refer to this as the "pure influencer" outcome. The left side of figure 11.8 illustrates this outcome. But now a qualitatively very different configuration of purchases can arise in equilibrium. Let us develop this equilibrium next.

In this equilibrium, the network is a star: the hub invests 0 and the spokes each invest $18/n$. Thus each spoke has access to exactly $z = 9$ units of information. The hub is content as they are accessing $18(n-1)/n$ units of information and not incurring any costs. The spokes are content because the link with the hub yields $9(n-2)/n$ units of information and their $18/n$ purchase supplements this so that they access 9 units in all (this equates the marginal cost with the marginal rewards). Observe that the cost of effort accessed via the central node—which is $11 \times 9(n-2)/n$—is larger than the cost of the link—which is given by 85 (for a sufficiently large number of peripheral nodes). We refer to this is as the "pure connector" outcome, as the hub does not personally purchase any information but is a connector among active spokes. The right side of figure 11.8 illustrates this outcome.

Let us briefly relate the equilibrium outcomes with the empirical research on personal influence. Katz and Lazarsfeld (1966) emphasize that social influencers typically have more social ties and also acquire more information (via radio, newspapers, and television). We interpret this as a situation in which influencers acquire information. This is the case depicted in figure 11.8(a). In other instances, hubs acquire some—possibly a small amount of—information personally, but their numerous contacts provide much new information, which they then communicate to their neighbors and friends. Here, the highly connected individual functions primarily as a connector. This is the case depicted in figure 11.8(b). The interested reader is referred to Gladwell (2006) for an engaging discussion of connectors.

The theory is still relatively simple. It has four ingredients—the costs of information, the costs of linking, and the benefits of direct and indirect linking—but the individual who is contemplating how much information to purchase and with whom to link faces a very complex set of computations. Such a person needs to keep an eye on the purchase of individuals and the different paths that connect them to each other. This problem is greatly compounded when the networks are evolving. Also, we must note that there is a great multiplicity of

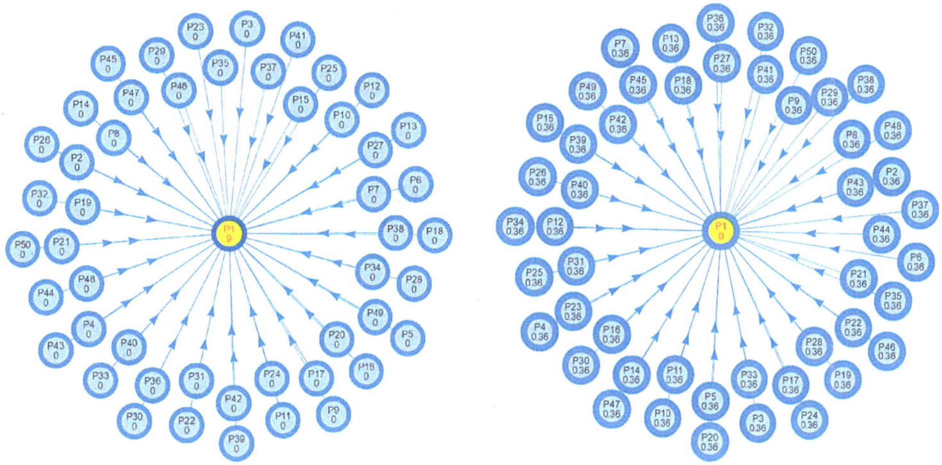

(a) The hub as pure influencer (b) The hub as pure connector

**Figure 11.8**
Examples of equilibria.

equilibrium networks—there are core-periphery networks with cores of different sizes and the identities of the individuals who constitute the core are not pinned down. To develop a better understanding of the scope of the theory in proving an account for the law of the few, we therefore take this game to the laboratory.

#### 11.4.2.1 Experiment

This section reports the findings of an experiment that is taken from Choi, Goyal, and Moisan (2019). Human subjects make choices concerning purchases and linking over a six-minute interval. The reward function is as given in equations (11.7) and (11.8). The first minute of the experiment is for subjects to get used to the game and is purely for practice; it does not count for payoffs. Once the six minutes end, an instant is picked at random from the last five minutes. The earnings of the subjects are computed for this instant, and they are paid these earnings.

For simplicity, the purchases are assumed to take on integer values only, and there is an upper bound, $\overline{x} = 20$. The cost of a unit of information is $c = 11$ and the cost of a link is $k = 95$; finally, $a_1 = 1$, $a_2 = 1/2$, and $a_l = 0$, for all $l \geq 3$. Given these parameters, the stand-alone optimum effort $z$ is equal to 9. We will assume that the group consists of 100 individuals.

Given these parameter values, proposition 11.3 tells us that there is a pure influencer equilibrium in which a single individual chooses 9 and all other individuals choose 0 and form a link with this positive-purchase player. Our discussion in the previous section also reveals that there is a pure connector outcome, with 18 peripheral individuals choosing 1 while the rest of the subjects choose 0. This outcome constitutes an approximate pure connector equilibrium (this is an "approximate" equilibrium because the periphery player who chooses purchase level 1 and forms a link with the hub earns 79.25, whereas they could earn 81 by deleting the link and instead choosing purchase level 9).

In the pure influencer equilibrium, the hub chooses an information purchase of 9, while the spokes choose 0. The hub earns 81 while the spokes each earn 85. In the pure connector equilibrium, the hub chooses purchase level 0, 18 spokes choose 1 each, and the other spokes choose 0. The hub earns 198, the active spokes 74, and the inactive spokes 85. Hence, there is little earnings inequality in the pure influencer equilibrium, but there is significant inequality in the pure connector equilibrium.

We have noted in our discussion on efficiency that for any given level of information purchase, the hub-spoke network maximizes the aggregate player welfare. Putting together our characterization of equilibrium with our observations on efficiency and equity suggests the following hypothesis.

**Hypothesis 11.2** *Subjects create a network that is efficient: it is sparse, exhibits an unequal number of connections, and has small average distances. The most connected subject makes large information purchases and the other subject makes small purchases.*

There were three groups of 100 subjects. Each group played a six minute continuous time game a total of six times. The first round was a trial round, and only the last five rounds were relevant for payoffs.

In each round, the first minute was a pure trial period and did not matter for payoffs. An instant was chosen at random from the last 5 minutes to determine the payoff for that round. Therefore in our analysis we will restrict pay attention to the last five rounds for each of the groups, that is, on a total of fifteen rounds. Thus a total of 300 subjects participated in the experiment. At the beginning, each subject was endowed with an initial balance of 500 points and added positive earnings to or subtracted negative earnings from that initial balance. Subjects' total earnings in the experiment were the sum of earnings across the last five rounds and the initial endowment. Each session lasted on average 90 minutes and subjects earned roughly 18 euros (including a 5-euro show-up fee). The experiments were conducted in LINEEX at the University of Valencia and the LEE at the Jaume I University of Castellon.

Figures 11.9 and 11.10 present snapshots of the experiment at four points in time. Initially, at minute 1, subject P26 emerges as a hub with the maximum information purchase 20. There are other subjects who make maximal purchases (such as P97). At minute 3, P26 continues to be a hub but has substantially lowered their purchase. Due to this shading of purchase, they start to lose some of their links to subject P97 (who has kept their purchase at 20). The transition becomes clearer at the 5-minute mark, when the initial hub subject P26 has lost most of their links to the emerging hub P97. Figure 11.10(b) confirms that this transition to node P97 as the hub is stable until the end of the game.

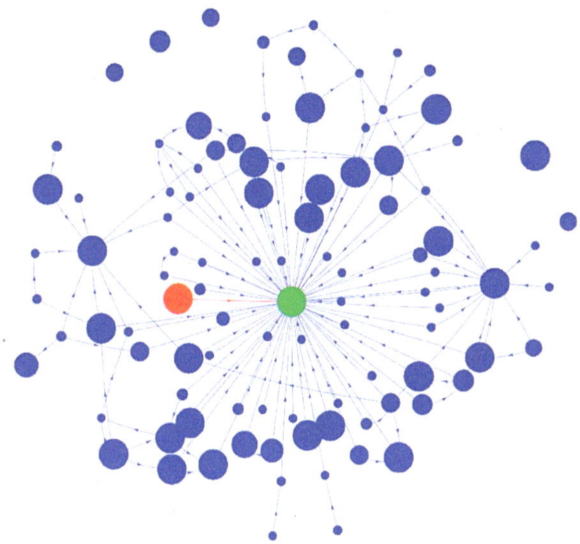

(a) At minute 1

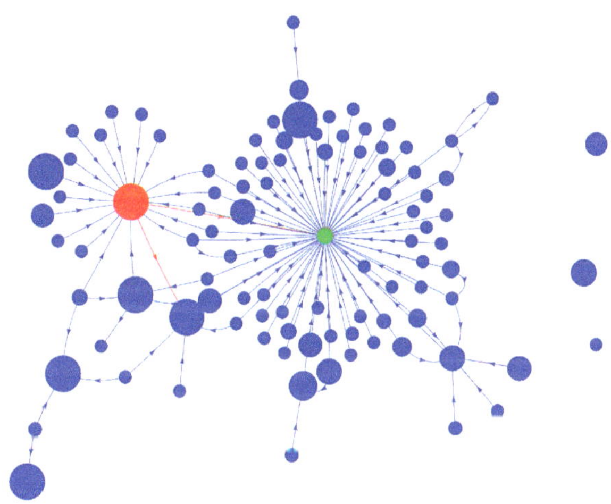

(b) At minute 3

**Figure 11.9**
Competition in efforts to become a hub. *Source*: Choi, Goyal, and Moisan (2019).

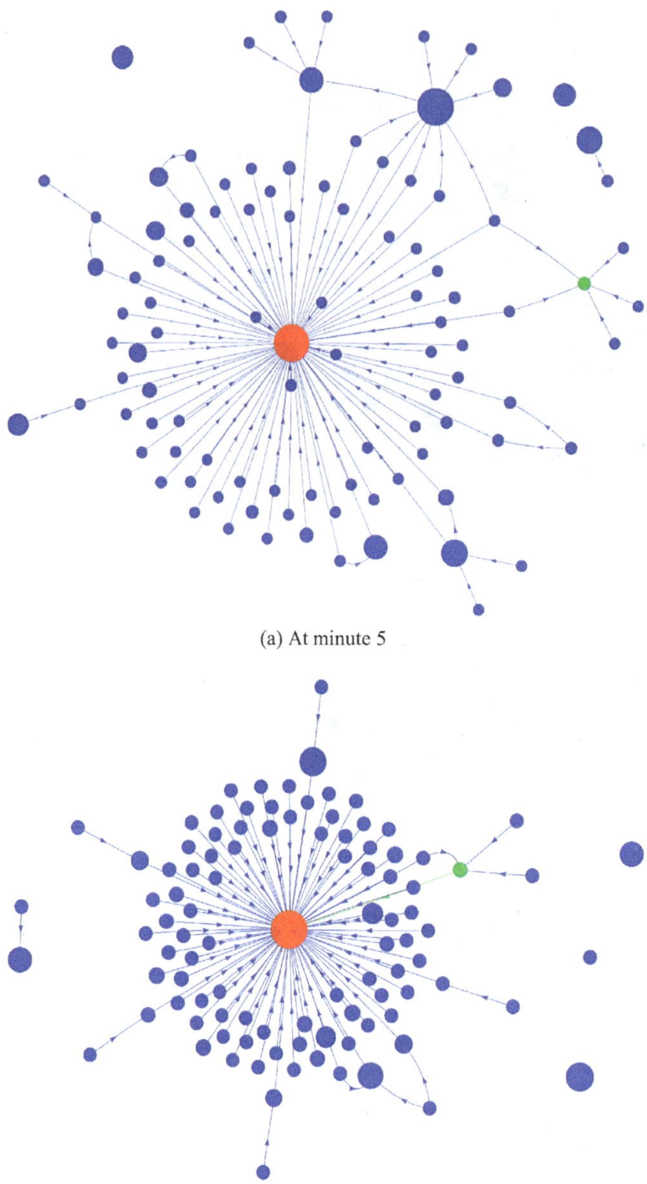

(a) At minute 5

(b) At minute 6

**Figure 11.10**
Emergence of a pure influencer. *Source*: Choi, Goyal, and Moisan (2019).

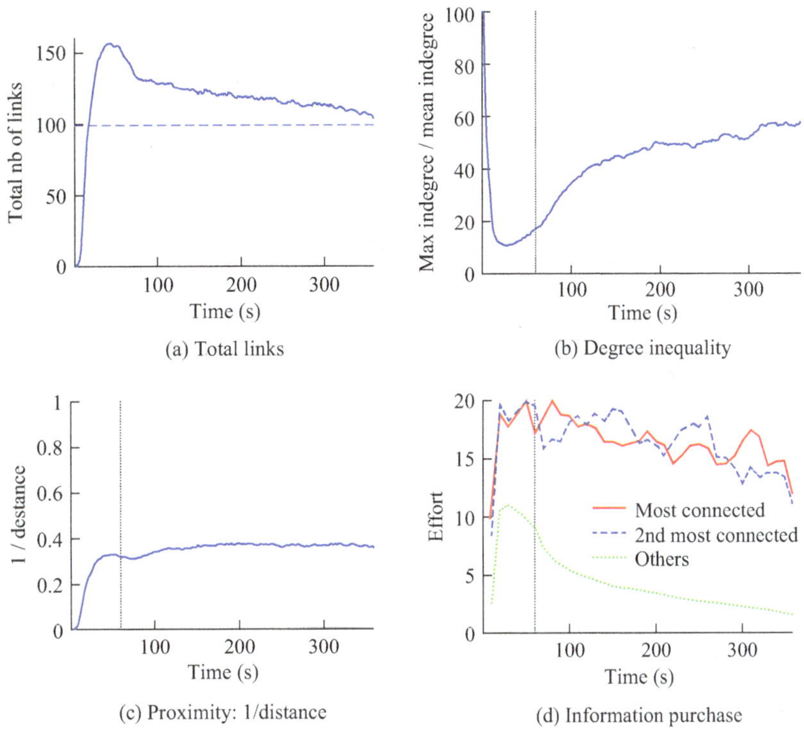


**Figure 11.11**
Findings: network structure and information purchase. *Source*: Choi, Goyal, and Moisan (2019).

Figure 11.11 summarizes the data on purchases and networks gathered from these sessions. Let us start with a preliminary remark about the connectivity of the network. The average size of the largest component was 94.8 across the rounds and the groups. So practically everyone belonged to the same component and the network may be viewed as being connected.

Figure 11.11(a) presents the evolution of number of total links across the experiment: at the start groups formed 150 links on average, but the number cames down steadily as the game proceeded and eventually it was close to 100. In a group of 100, this is basically the minimum number of links needed to ensure connectivity of the network.

Figure 11.11(b) presents the evolution of the ratio of the maximum in-degree to the mean indegree. At the start, this ratio is very high, and it comes down by the end of the first minute. After that instant, it rises consistently, and throughout the payoff-relevant period of the experiment, from second 60 until second 360, the ratio grows steadily and eventually reaches 60. Thus subjects create a network with very unequal degrees.

Figure 11.11(c) presents the evolution of average distance (in the main component). The proximity between two nodes is the inverse of the distance. The figure shows that proximity reaches 0.4 by second 60 and then stays at this level for the rest of the experiment. In other words, the average distance in the network was under 2.5 practically throughout the experiment (a number that is only slightly larger than proximity 2, which would occur in a star network).

Finally, figure 11.11(d) presents the time series of purchases of three types of individuals: the most connected individuals and everyone else. The plot shows that the top two connected individuals at any point make much larger purchases, and all the other individuals make small purchases that are tailing off and becoming negligible.

These large purchases of information by competing hubs has the effect of lowering their payoffs. Indeed, the two most connected individuals earn less than the individuals who make low purchases. In a pure connector equilibrium, the hub player earns large rents, so there is an incentive to make large information purchases to become a hub. The puzzling aspect is that these competing hubs purchase too much information for too long, and as a result, there is not enough time left to recover their investments. It is possible that they fail to anticipate that the benefits they can reap as a hub later do not sufficiently compensate for the early costs of competing. This could be due to computational complexity: it is indeed difficult to compute expected payoffs from being a hub, and the only way for subjects to find that out may be to actually reach that position, when it is too late to realize that the significant costs they already paid are not worth the benefits. In the treatment discussed so far, subjects were shown their own payoffs, but not the payoffs of others. We now consider a treatment in which subjects are shown the payoffs of everyone.

Sharing everyone's payoff can potentially help because this information can reduce computational complexity: subjects do not need to compute expected payoffs for being a hub or wait until they reach that position to find out; they can simply observe how much others earn by reaching such a position. If they see that payoffs are not large, then they may compete less aggressively. This treatment also tests the alternative hypothesis on status or efficiency because seeing others' payoffs should not have any effect on their behavior in that case.

As in the baseline treatment, this experiment also considers three groups, and for each group, there are five payoff-relevant rounds, so there were fifteen rounds in all. The experiment reveals that showing information on everyone's payoffs to subjects has a powerful effect: the hub chooses low effort in the majority of the rounds. Indeed, in 40 percent of the twenty rounds, the hub chooses to make 0 information purchases, giving rise to the pure connector outcome. This is in sharp contrast to the pure influencer outcome observed in all the rounds in the baseline information treatment discussed previously. Complexity of the environment may be an explanation for the excessive information purchases by the hub in the baseline treatment. Figures 11.12 and 11.13 present a representative instance of the dynamic that leads to the pure connector outcome.

To summarize, we find that subjects make choices that lead to extreme specialization in the purchasing of information and in linking. This is very much in line with the law of the few. However, this experiment draws attention to the dynamics of competition and the role

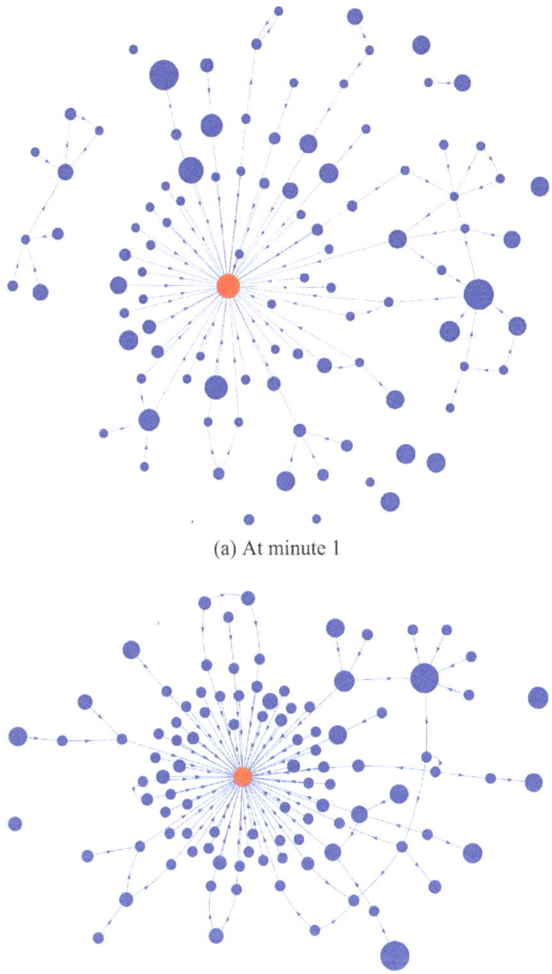

(a) At minute 1

(b) At minute 3

**Figure 11.12**
Snapshots with payoff information: Competition to become a hub. *Source*: Choi, Goyal, and Moisan (2019).

of informational complexity in shaping behavior; these factors go beyond the arguments we have used to prove the equilibrium properties in the static model.

## 11.5 Monetizing Network Status

In our examination of social networks so far, we have taken the view that individuals form links and exert effort (to purchase information or to tweet) solely for the purpose of acquiring information. In real-world networks like Twitter or Facebook, links and followers may be

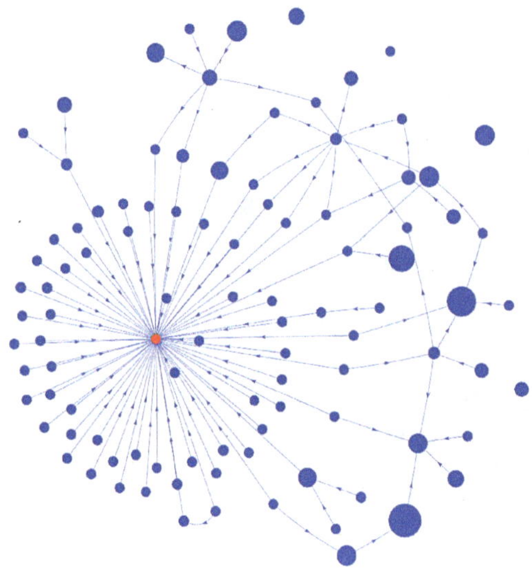

(a) At minute 5

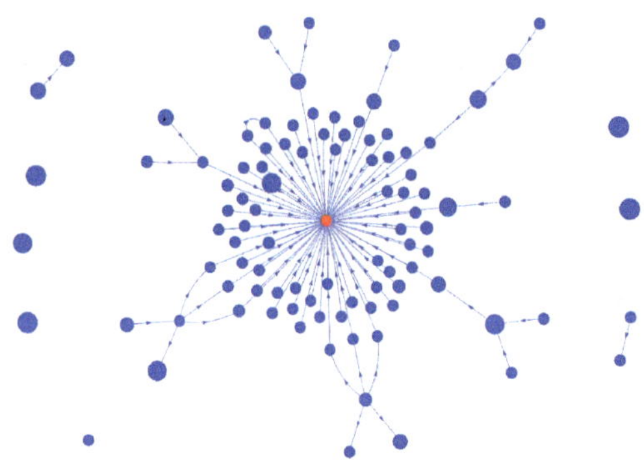

(b) At minute 6

**Figure 11.13**
Emergence of a pure connector. *Source*: Choi, Goyal, and Moisan (2019).

used to generate monetary returns. This section explores the implications of such returns for the structure and functioning of communication networks. The discussion is based on Galeotti and Goyal (2010) and van Leeuwen, Offerman, and Schram (2020).

In the model of information purchase and linking presented in section 11.4, we may interpret the cost incurred in the formation of a link as a payment that the player forming the link makes to the person receiving the link. In this case, $k$ becomes a transfer and the payoffs to player $i$ in a strategy profile $s = (x, g)$ are given by

$$\Pi_i(s) = f\left(x_i + \sum_{j \in N_i(\hat{g})} x_j\right) - cx_i - d_i(g)k + \sum_{j \in N} g_{ji}k. \tag{11.10}$$

Observe that the last term involving transfers is independent of the strategy of $i$. It then follows that for all $s_{-i} \in S_{-i}$ and $s_i, s_i' \in S_i$, $\hat{\Pi}_i(s_i, s_{-i}) \geq \hat{\Pi}_i(s_i', s_{-i})$ if and only if $\Pi_i(s_i, s_{-i}) \geq \Pi_i(s_i', s_{-i})$. Therefore our methods of analysis and our findings from section 11.4 carry over to the alternative model, where link formation costs are transfers from one individual to another. Note that the payoff in equation (11.7) corresponds to the case with no indirect information communication. This means that the equilibrium outcomes will be as described in proposition 11.3.

While the profile of information purchases and the network remain unchanged, there is a profound difference in the distribution of payoffs. The active individuals in the core will earn link-based transfers that will increase linearly with the size of the population. In large populations, therefore, there will arise a great gap in payoffs between the core and the periphery (which is quite different from the payoff distribution in the baseline model with no monetary transfers). Our discussion in the previous paragraph suggests that the Nash equilibrium of the static game is unaffected by this possibility. However, in a dynamic setting where individuals make efforts and form links over time, the potential for such large earnings can make a profound difference to behavior and to the nature of the network that arises. We have seen this dynamic in one form already in the experiments presented on the pure linking game in section 11.3 and on information purchase and linking in section 11.4. In both these experiments, we see intense competition to become a hub so as to earn slightly larger returns than the periphery. We expect these pressures to be amplified when the payoffs are substantially larger for the hub.

A recent experiment by van Leeuwen, Offerman, and Schram (2020) shows that this is indeed the case. They consider a repeated game setting in which, at each stage, the players play the static game of information purchase and linking. They have a $2 \times 2$ design: two group sizes (four and eight members) and two payoff models (one without link-based payment transfers and one with such transfers). Their main results are as follows: In the baseline model without link-based payments, there is little specialization in information purchases or linking in both group sizes. Link-based transfers have a dramatic impact, and these effects interact with size. Subjects specialize in efforts, and a star network emerges. Moreover, the efforts of the hub are much larger in the larger group than in the smaller group. This is in line with the intuitions we spelled out before: a larger group means a larger payoff for the individual who becomes the hub. This leads individuals to compete more vigorously to become the hub, which is reflected in larger information purchases by them. Indeed, the hub subjects choose efforts that are close to the first-best level of effort (and thus are significantly greater than the equilibrium level). In this experiment, the efforts of the hubs are so great that the net earnings of the hub are not very different from those of the peripheral individuals. This similarity in payoffs between peripheral individuals and hubs lends stability to the outcome: there is no great incentive for the various individuals to switch places.

Putting together the models and experiments reported in this chapter, we are led to the view that individual attempts to economize on the costs of linking and information purchases and to effectively access information from others lead to a law of the few. The theory also points to an important welfare problem in these networks: individual efforts possess public good features, so equilibrium efforts will be less than what is in their collective interest. In small societies, monetizing network connections can circumvent this public good problem by inducing hubs to exert large effort. However, as the group scales up in size, the theory suggests that there may exist a pure connector outcome in which the hub earns large rents, without making an effort. The experiments offer support in favor such a pure connector outcome.

## 11.6 Reading Notes

The interest in influencers and the importance of social communication dates from the early work of Katz and Lazarsfeld (1966) and Lazarsfeld, Berelson, and Gaudet (1948). For more recent research on the role of influencers in social communication, see Feick and Price (1987) and Beck, Dalton, Greene, and Huckfeldt (2002) and Zhang, Ackerman, and Adamic (2007). For a engaging popular introduction to the subject of personal influence in social networks, see Gladwell (2006).

For case studies on Twitter and the World Wide Web, see chapter 1. For an overview of online communities, see Goyal (2012), and for a firms' perspective on online networks and platforms, see Belleflamme and Peitz (2022). Online social and information networks perform a variety of functions and differ on many dimensions. In this chapter, the emphasis is on inequality in the level of activity and connectivity across nodes. These properties were first identified in the context of offline social networks by Katz and Lazersfeld (1966) and Lazarsfeld, Berelson, and Gaudet (1948) but research shows that they are greatly amplified in large-scale online networks like Twitter and the World Wide Web. This chapter uses the economic theory of network formation to explore the origins of these properties of networks. For a general introduction to the economic theory of network formation, see chapter 3 of this book.

Building on the models presented in chapter 3, in this chapter we present a model of network formation in which individuals can unilaterally decide to form links. Unilateral link formation has the advantage that it allows us to use the tools of noncooperative game theory to analyze the games of linking. This facilitates a study of a number of questions using familiar methods. We start with an exposition of the two-way flow model in Bala and Goyal (2000a), which yields simple and intuitive results on network structure and on the relation between equilibrium and efficient networks. It also shows that there typically are multiple equilibria in this model that reflect the complementarity of links. The two-way flow model has been developed along various dimensions over the years. Researchers have examined richer models of benefits, link formation protocols, bounded rationality of individuals, and heterogeneity across individuals in costs and benefits (see, e.g., Galeotti, Goyal, and Kamphorst [2006]; Ferri [2007]; and Hojman and Szeidl [2008]); for surveys of the research in this line of work, see Goyal (2007), Jackson (2008), and Mauleon and Vannetelbosch (2016).

The chapter then turns to an experimental test of this theory. There is by now a large body of experimental work on networks; for surveys, see Choi, Gallo, and Kariv (2016) and Breza (2016). In particular, the pure linking game has been the subject of extensive experimental work: Callander and Plott (2005), Falk and Kosfeld (2012), and Goeree, Riedl, and Ule (2009) present experiments on the same model with small groups (four and six subjects and simultaneous moves in discrete time). Network formation with asynchronous choice and continuous time was studied in an early paper by Berninghaus, Ehrhart, and Ott (2006), and more recently by Goyal, Rosenkranz, Weitzel, and Buskens (2017). The use of continuous time in repeated game experiments has been explored in a number of recent papers, such as Friedman and Oprea (2012) and Calford and Oprea (2017). The chapter presents a large scale experiment on network formation taking place in continuous time. This experiment is taken from Choi, Goyal, and Moisan (2020).

With a view to studying specialization in effort levels and linking, the chapter then considers a richer theoretical model that adds effort-level choice to the linking choice. The presentation is based on a model from Galeotti and Goyal (2010). A number of subsequent papers have explored this framework, including Kinateder and Merlino (2017), Baetz (2015), Perego and Yuksel (2016), Sethi and Yildiz (2016), and Herskovic and Ramos (2020). These models may be seen as combining the two-way linking model of Bala and Goyal (2000a) with the public goods model in the network model of Bramoullé and Kranton (2007).

We note that in the model of linking and efforts/information purchase studied in this chapter, the benefits function $f(.)$, is increasing and concave. This means that marginal return to increasing personal effort is falling in response to the total effort of the neighbors. In other words, the efforts of neighbors are strategic substitutes. Several steps in the analysis exploit this feature of the reward function. In follow-up work, Baetz (2015) and Hiller (2017) study a model in which efforts of neighbors are strategic complements. Complementarity can give rise to a multilayered network in which more highly linked subsets of individuals exert greater effort than less well connected individuals. For a survey of games of linking ands assorted activities, the interested reader is urged to consult Vega-Redondo (2016).

We have presented a large-scale experiment of this richer model on information purchasing and linking. The presentation of the experiment is taken from Choi, Goyal, and Moisan (2019). This experiment offers strong support for specialization in purchasing and linking, in line with the law of the few. However, the experiment also reveals dynamics that go well beyond the arguments invoked in the static model. We then present a related experimental paper by van Leeuwen, Offerman, and Schram (2020), which considers a finitely repeated version of Galeotti and Goyal (2010) in which they include monetary transfers based on incoming links.

The models in this chapter focus on individuals in social networks and do not consider the role of profit-making firms. In practice, large social networks are run by firms that seek to maximize profits. See chapters 8, 15, and 16 for discussions on how firms (and platforms) interact with information networks.

## 11.7 Questions

1. Consider a model in which link creation in unilateral, while benefits flow both ways (as in this chapter). In particular, if A forms a link with B, then both A and B can access each other. Suppose that there is no decay. Define $\hat{g}_{ij} = \max\{g_{ij}, g_{ji}\}$. Let $N_i(\hat{g})$ be the set of individuals that $i$ can access in network $g$. The payoff to individual $i$ in network $g$ is

$$\Pi_i(g) = 1 + n_i(\hat{g}) - d_i(g)c, \tag{11.11}$$

where $n_i(\hat{g}) = N_i(\hat{g})$ is the number of individuals accessed by $i$ in network $\hat{g}$, and $c$ is the cost of a link.

   (a) Show that an equilibrium network is either connected or empty.

   (b) Show that the connected equilibrium network is a tree.

   (c) Describe the efficient networks as a function of $c$ and $n$.

   (d) Show that a strict Nash equilibrium is a hub-spoke network (in which the hub forms all the links) for $c < 1$ and the empty network for $c > 1$.

2. (Hojman and Szeidl [2008]). Suppose that the payoffs to individual $i$ in network $g$ are given by

$$\Pi_i(g) = f(a_1 n_i^1(g) + \cdots + a_{n-1} n_i^{n-1}(g)) - d_i)c, \tag{11.12}$$

where $N_i^k(\hat{g})$ is the number of individuals who are at geodesic distance $k$ from individual $i$ in the undirected network associated with network $g$, $a_1 \geq a_2 \geq a_3 \geq \ldots \geq a_d$, and $c > 0$. Assume that $f(\cdot)$ is an increasing and concave function; communication takes place only within a certain distance (there is $D < n$ such that $a_{d'} = 0$ for all $d' \geq D$); and that there are eventually strongly diminishing returns to communication (there is $M$ such that for $m \geq M, f(m) - f(m/2) \leq c$). Show that if the number of players is large enough, relative to $M$ and $D$, and if $a_2 > a_3$, then the star network in which peripheral players form links with the hub is a unique equilibrium network.

3. Consider a game of efforts and linking. Every individual chooses an action $\{0, 1\}$ and chooses unilaterally to connect to a subset of other players. The cost of action 0 is zero, and the costs of action 1 is $c$. The cost of a link is $k$, where $k \in (0, c)$. Let $s_i = (a_i, g_i)$ be the strategy of player $i$ and $s = (s_1, \ldots, s_n)$ be the strategy profile of all players. Given a directed network $g$, define $\hat{g}_{ij} = \max\{g_{ij}, g_{ji}\}$ and the corresponding network $\hat{g}$. Let

$N_i(\hat{g}) = \{j|\hat{g}_{ij} = 1\}$, and let $y_i = a_i + \sum_{j \in N_i(\hat{g})} a_j$ denote the sum of efforts of player $i$ and their neighbors in network $g$. Suppose that $f(y_i) = 1$ if $y_i \geq 1$, and 0 otherwise. The payoff to a player from a strategy profile $s$ is given by

$$\Pi_i(s) = f(y_i) - a_i.c - d_i.k, \tag{11.13}$$

where $d_i$ is the number of links formed by $i$ under strategy profile $s$. Describe the equilibrium when $k < c$ and the equilibrium when $k > c$.

4. Consider a game of efforts and linking as in question 3. Suppose, however, that the efforts of neighbors are strategic complements (instead of strategic substitutes). Define $b_i = \sum_{j \in N_i(\hat{g})} a_j$. Let the payoff to a player from strategy profile $s$ be given by

$$\Pi_i(s) = x_i \times b_i - a_i.c - d_i.k, \tag{11.14}$$

where $d_i$ is the number of links formed by $i$ under strategy profile $s$. Describe the equilibrium of this game, and discuss how moving from substitutes to complements alters the equilibrium.

5. Consider the game of information purchasing and linking as described in section 11.4. Suppose that the assumptions of proposition 11.3 hold. Let $\mathbf{s}^* = (\mathbf{x}^*, \mathbf{g}^*)$ be a Nash equilibrium of the game. Show that:
   (a) If $\sum_{i \in N} x_i^* = z$, then $\mathbf{g}^*$ is a core-periphery network, hubs purchase information personally and spokes purchase no information personally.
   (b) If $\sum_{i \in N} x_i^* > z$, then the following is true:
      (i) Every player $i \in I(\mathbf{s}^*)$ chooses $x_i^* = \frac{z}{\Delta+1} = \frac{k}{c}$ and has $\Delta \in \{1, \ldots, n-2\}$ links within $I(\mathbf{s}^*)$, while every player $j \notin I(\mathbf{s}^*)$ forms $\Delta + 1$ links with players in $I(\mathbf{s}^*)$.
      (ii) High-information-level players choose $\bar{x}^* = \frac{k}{c}$, low-information-level players have $\eta$ links with high-information-level players, and they are not neighbors of each other and choose information $\underline{x}^* = \hat{y} - \eta\frac{k}{c}$, where $\frac{\hat{y}c}{k} - 1 < \eta < \frac{\hat{y}c}{k}$.

6. Consider the game of information purchasing and linking as described in section 11.4. Suppose that the cost of purchasing information is $c_i = c$ for all $i \neq 1$, but $c_1 = c - \epsilon > 0$, where $\epsilon > 0$ is a small number. Let $z_1 = \arg\max_y f(y) - c_1 y$. Clearly, so long as $\epsilon > 0$, $z_1 > z$, and $z_1 \to z$ as $\epsilon \to 0$. Suppose that $k < f(z_1) - f(z) + cz$. Show that in a strict Nash equilibrium $\mathbf{s}^* = (\mathbf{x}^*, \mathbf{g}^*)$, the following is true:
   (a) $\sum_{i \in N} x_i^* = z_1$.
   (b) The network is a star and player 1 is the hub.
   (c) Either $x_1^* = z_1$ and spokes choose $x^* = 0$, OR $x_1^* = [(n-1)z - z_1]/[n-2]$ and $x^* = [z_1 - z]/[n-2]$.

7. Consider the game of information purchasing and linking as described in section 11.4. Let $s = (e_i, g_i)$ be the strategy of individual $i$, and let $s = (s_1, \ldots, s_n)$ denote the strategy

profile of the individuals. The payoff of an individual $i$ given a strategy profile $s$ is

$$\Pi_i(s) = f\left(x_i + \sum_{l}^{n-1} a_l \sum_{j \in N_i^1(\hat{g})} x_j\right) - cx_i - d_i(g)k, \tag{11.15}$$

where $a_l = 1$ for all $l \geq 1$, $c > 0$ and $k > 0$, and $d_i$ is the number of links created and paid for by individual $i$. Define $z$ as $f'(z) = c$.

(a) Show that the star network with the hub choosing $z$ and all other individuals choosing effort 0 and forming a link with the hub is an equilibrium, so long as $k < cz$.

(b) What are the conditions under which a pure connector outcome is an equilibrium?

# 12 Social Coordination

## 12.1 Introduction

We can view any form of communication as a form of coordination, one in which the speaker and the listener agree on a set of meanings for the words that are being spoken. Indeed, almost all human activity involves coordination, ranging from our use of time, when and how we eat, what we wear, and the languages and technologies, such as fax machines or telephones, we use. As coordination is so central to human life, it is important for societies to have norms or standards. And once a norm becomes established, any single person would be reluctant to change actions, as miscoordination is costly. For change to come about, therefore, there must be coordination, and this is one reason why social and cultural change is often so difficult. At the heart of coordination is the fact that it arises out of interaction among people. In this chapter, we will explore how the patterns of interaction matter as societies work their way toward norms, how they respond to new circumstances and arrive at new norms, and how they navigate the tension between differing personal tastes and the benefits of coordination on common norms.

In the next section, we start by laying out the logic of the coordination problem in a setting with two individuals. We clarify the advantages of coordination and the possibility of more and less risky courses of action. We then locate individuals in their neighborhoods, which are embedded in a social network. We study the relation between the structure of a network and the prospects of common and diverse social norms. The simple logic of the coordination problem helps us develop a powerful intuition on this issue: a person will choose A if a large enough faction of her neighbors also choose A. Building on this idea, we say that a subgroup of individuals is *p-cohesive* if everyone in the group has at least fraction $p$ of their links within the group. Societies have diverse social norms if they contain multiple cohesive subgroups.

We turn next to the issue of changing norms. Suppose that a society has an established norm and a new superior action becomes available. What are the networks in which the new action will be adopted, and where will adoption fail? The answer lies in the cohesiveness of societies. Adoption will spread, and the new norm will take over the entire network only if there is no suitably cohesive subgroup in the society. How can established norms be changed in cohesive societies? One possibility is to create special insulated conclaves in which new norms can be experimentally tried, and as they succeed, the conclaves can be appropriately integrated with the main network. We discuss Special Economic Zones (SEZs) set up in China (and in other countries) as an instance of a policy in which the network itself is reconfigured.

The possibility that the network changes leads us to develop a framework in which individuals choose links with others and also choose an action in the coordination game. We study the dynamics of evolving networks and how they interact with choices in the coordination game. Our analysis reveals that the possibility of choosing links has powerful effects on social coordination.

The first part of the chapter studies a setting in which all individuals earn the same payoffs from different outcomes. We then turn our attention to the setting where everyone prefers to coordinate, but individuals differ on how they view the coordinated outcomes. One motivation for the study of heterogeneous preferences comes from contemporary discussions on cultural integration. An important feature of modern societies is that there exist large migrant communities often with their own distinct cultural background that differs from the majority on grounds of religion, cuisine, and language. For instance, while individuals would like to successfully coordinate on a common language, communities would prefer to coordinate on their own language. Similar considerations arise when we consider dress codes or norms relating to religion, giving rise to a tension between diverse preferences and a desire for a common coordination norm. We study how patterns of interaction shape social norms when such communities interact.

We develop a framework to study the process of formation of neighborhoods in a setting where coordination is important, but individuals coming from different communities have differing preferences over norms. This allows us to define the tension between diverse norms and social efficiency (which arises when everyone conforms to the same norm). The theoretical analysis shows that a variety of network structures, ranging from full integration and conformism to segregation and diversity, are theoretically possible. We test this model in the laboratory and find that when subjects are obliged to interact with everyone, they choose to conform to the action preferred by the majority. But if they are allowed to choose their own connections, then they create segregated neighborhoods and settle on diverse norms (even though this is socially suboptimal).

Elements of the coordination problem appear in a wide variety of concrete and practical settings. To appreciate the fundamental issues, it is sometimes easier to work with simple and stylized models. This is the reason why the discussion in this chapter is carried out on an abstract level. For a discussion of issues of coordination that arise in markets, the reader is urged to consult chapter 8, on platforms and intermediation.

**Table 12.1**
Coordination game

| 1 \ 2 | $A$ | $B$ |
|---|---|---|
| $A$ | $a, a$ | $d, e$ |
| $B$ | $e, d$ | $b, b$ |

## 12.2 Coordination in a Network

The problem of coordination arises in its simplest form when the optimal course of action is to conform to what others are doing. A well-known example is the choice of what software to use to draft documents. As we work with colleagues, we prefer to use the software that they are using. To bring out the basic elements of the coordination problem, we start with the case of two individuals, 1 and 2, choosing between two actions, A and B. The rewards to a player depend on their own action and the action of the other player. Table 12.1 shows how payoffs are determined as a function of the choices of individuals.

Choosing the same action is better than choosing different actions: the payoff from coordinating on either $a$ or $b$ is thus larger than miscoordinating, $d$ and $e$. It is possible that coordinating on one action is better than coordinating on the other action, so generally $a$ and $b$ will not be equal. This difference is going to be important later in this chapter when we discuss efficient and inefficient norms (and also when we talk about the introduction of a new superior technology).

A key element in the coordination problem is that individuals make decisions without knowing each other's choices. This uncertainty suggests a natural thought experiment: which action would be best if the other individual is equally likely to choose the other action? The answer to this question would depend on the relative value of $a+d$ versus $b+e$. These considerations are summarized in the following restrictions on the values of the payoffs:

$$a > d,\ \ b > d,\ \ d > e,\ \ a + d > b + e. \tag{12.1}$$

Choosing A is optimal when the other individual chooses A, and the same applies for B. In other words, the action combinations $(A, A)$ and $(B, B)$ are both Nash equilibria. The assumption that $a + d > b + e$ means that if a player places equal probability on the opponent playing the two actions, then it is strictly better to choose $A$. Following Harsanyi and Selten (1988), we will say that A is the *risk-dominant* action if $a + d > b + e$. Observe that A may be risk-dominant even if $a$ is smaller than $b$; in other words, the efficient and the risk-dominant actions may not be the same.

As our interest is in social coordination, we now extend this game to allow for several individuals. There are $N = \{1, \ldots, n\}$, with $n \geq 3$, individuals located on the nodes of network

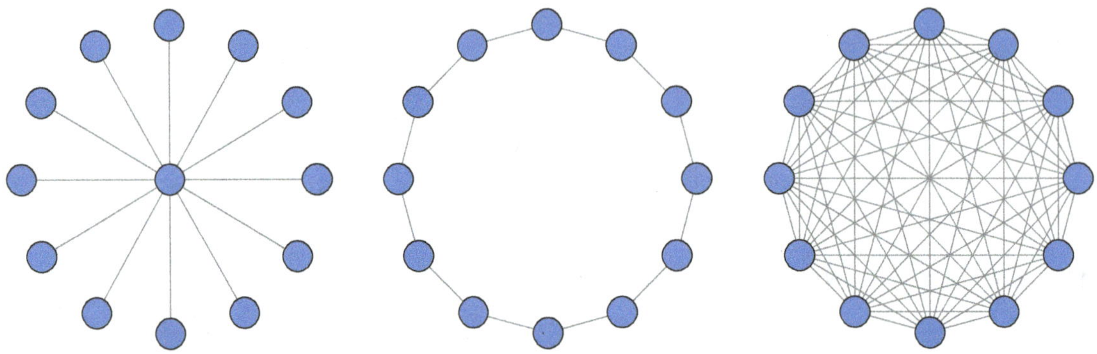

(a) Star network (b) Circle network (c) Complete network

**Figure 12.1**
Simple networks.

$g \in \mathcal{G}$. We assume that player $i$ plays the coordination game with each of their neighbors, $N_i(g) = \{j \in N | g_{ij} = 1\}$. For concreteness, figures 12.1 presents three simple networks—the complete network, the star network, and local interaction around a circle network. In the star network, every individual is in the neighborhood for the hub, while only the hub is in the neighborhood of each of the spokes. In the complete network, the neighborhood of every individual includes every other person. In the circle network, the neighborhood of any person consists of the individuals on either side.

Individual $i$ chooses an action, $s_i$, from set $\{A, B\}$. Let $s = (s_1, \ldots, s_n)$ be the profile of actions chosen by individuals and $S = \{A, B\}^n$ be the set of all possible strategy profiles. In a two-player game, let $\pi(x, y)$ denote the payoff to player $i$ when this player chooses action $x$ while her opponent chooses action $y$. The payoff to an individual in a network is the sum of the payoffs that they earn from each of the bilateral interactions in the neighborhood. Assuming that individuals choose the same action on all interactions, given network $g$, the payoff to individual $i$ from a strategy profile $s$ is

$$\Pi_i(s|g) = \sum_{j \in N_i(g)} \pi(s_i, s_j). \tag{12.2}$$

To develop an understanding of coordination in networks, it is useful to start with the three networks in figure 12.1. A preliminary observation is that in all three networks, everyone choosing the same action—whether A or B—is an equilibrium. This is a direct implication of the payoff that we have assumed: it is optimal to choose the action that everyone in your neighborhood chooses. This suggests that global conformism is always an outcome.

We turn next to a study of the circumstances under which different parts of a network adopt different actions. In the networks given in figure 12.1, global conformism is the *only* possible equilibrium. This is easiest to see in the star network: clearly, every spoke will choose the action chosen by the hub. Next, consider the complete network: no two individuals can choose different actions. Label the individuals 1 to $n$. Suppose that 1 chooses A and $n$ chooses B. The payoff of 1 is given by $[n(A)-1]a+n(B)d$, where $n(A)$ is the number of individuals choosing action A and $n(B)$ is the number of individuals choosing B. Similarly, the payoff to individual $n$ is $[n(B)-1]b+n(A)e$. As inidividual 1 is happy with their action, choosing A must be better than choosing B: $[n(A)-1]a+n(B)d$ must be at least as large as $n(B)b+[n(A)-1]e$. Similarly, for individual $n$ to be happy with their choice, the payoff from choosing A, $n(A)a+(n(B)-1)d$, must be less than what they earn with action B, $[n(B)-1]b+n(A)e$. Putting together these implications, we get the following requirement:

$$[n(A)-1]a+n(B)d \geq n(B)b+[n(A)-1]e > [n(B)-1]b+n(A)e \geq n(A)a+[n(B)-1]d. \tag{12.3}$$

The strict inequality occurs because we have assumed that equation (12.1) holds, so $b>e$. Comparing the first and the last expressions in equation (12.3) yields an impossibility, as $a>d$ by assumption.

The argument for global conformity on the circle network relies on a similar construction: for diversity to exist, there must be a boundary between an A and a B region: on one side of the boundary, an individual chooses A, while on the other, an individual chooses B. As the individuals at the boundary choosing A and B have one A and one B neighbor each, they must earn $a+d$ and $b+e$, respectively. But given our assumption about the payoffs given by equation 12.1, choosing A is strictly better than choosing B, so diversity is not sustainable.

This raises the following question: what are the networks for which diversity is possible? To develop a first impression of how networks sustain diversity, following Goyal (2007), we consider a class of societies in which there are multiple communities and intracommunity interaction is stronger than intercommunity interaction. Figure 12.2 presents network structures with two communities that reflect this idea. The number of cross-community links reflect the level of integration in this society.

To develop an understanding of the relation between integration and diversity, consider some payoff parametric values. Suppose that $d=e=0$. Next, fix $a=4$ and $b=2$. It can be verified that the community of individuals 1–4 choosing A and the community of individuals 5–8 choosing B constitute an equilibrium in network I, but not in networks II or III. Next, suppose that $a=4$ and $b=3$: as we have raised the value of coordinating on action B, diversity is now an equilibrium in both networks I and II (but not in III).

For two actions to emerge as social norms in different neighborhoods of a social network, it suffices that every individual in each neighborhood is content with their choice. This would hold if, for everyone in a community, a sufficient fraction of connections were within the community choosing the same action. To make this concrete, fix network $g$ and parameters $a$ and $b$ and set $d=e=0$. Diversity of social norms will occur if there are two distinct subsets of connected individuals $C_A$ and $C_B$ with the following property: for each $i \in C_A$, the

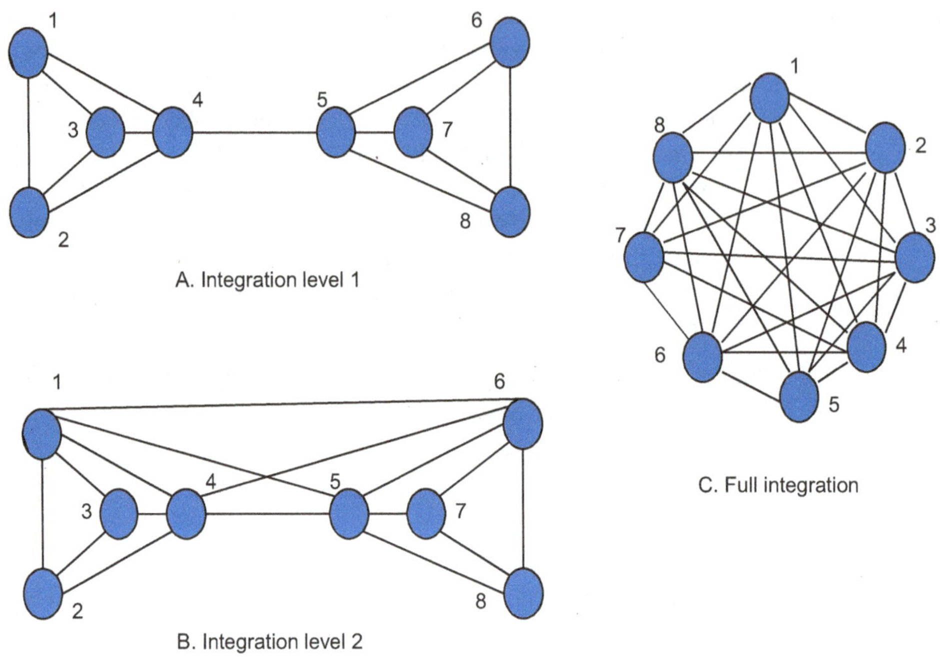


**Figure 12.2**
Networks with varying levels of integration.

fraction of contacts within the community $p_i \geq b/(a+b)$; and for every $i \in C_B$, the fraction of contacts within that community $p_i$ is greater than $a/(a+b)$. Returning to the previous example with $a=4$ and $b=2$, for the two norms to coexist, we require that $p_i \geq 1/3$ for individuals in the A community and $p_i \geq 2/3$ for all individuals in the B community.

Fix the community $C_k$, $k=A, B$, and consider the person $i$ with the lowest fraction $p_i$. The possibility of sustaining action A in community $C_A$ depends on whether $p_i \geq b/a+b$ (in what follows, we will define $q=b/(a+b)$). And the same goes, for community B. The subset of connected individuals $C_k$ in a network is *p-cohesive* if $p_i \geq p$ for every individual in $i \in C_k$.

Equipped with the concept of cohesiveness, we can summarize our discussion on conformity and diversity as follows.

**Proposition 12.1** *Suppose that $d=e=0$, and let $q=b/(a+b)$. Everyone choosing the same action—conformism—is a Nash equilibrium in every network. Diversity is an outcome if and only if there are distinct subsets of nodes $C_A$ and $C_B$, with $C_A$ being q-cohesive and $C_B$ being $1-q$-cohesive.*

This result sets the stage for an examination of the process of change from one social norm to another.

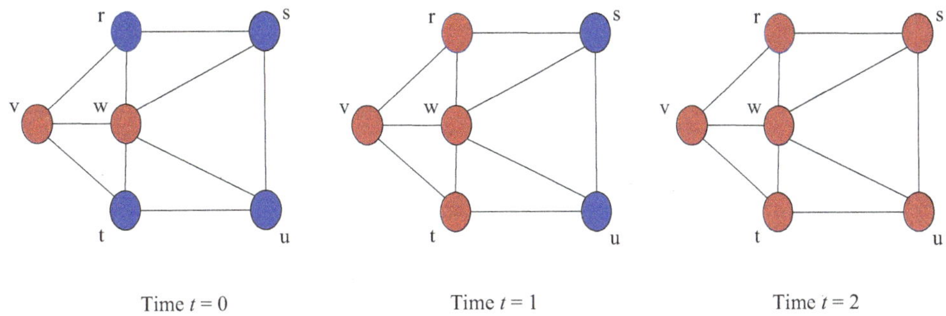


**Figure 12.3**
Coordination dynamics on a simple network.

## 12.3 A Change in a Convention

We will suppose that a society has a well-established social norm: everyone chooses B. At some point, a new and superior action, A, becomes available. The action may involve a new technology, such as the fax machine or telephone or a new software program. It may refer to a norm concerning being on time (punctuality) or a norm on which side of the road to drive. We study how the network structure determines whether this new norm will be adopted by the society. Our discussion draws on Goyal (1996) and Morris (2000); the exposition is based on Easley and Kleinberg (2010).

To focus on the issue of change, we will set $d = e = 0$ and suppose that $a > b$ in equation (12.1). Further, suppose that the dynamics of adoption take place over time, which is numbered $t = 0$, moving to 1 to 2 and so forth. The process starts at $t = 0$; a subset of the society adopts action A. These are the individuals who have been offered a new and advanced technology for free. Everyone else is choosing B. At every point from $t = 1$ onward, an individual who was with action B at time $t - 1$ chooses between A and B. The choice maximizes their payoff, taking as given the profile of actions of others (i.e, it is a best response to last-period actions by others). Observe that the process of choice will continue either until everyone has adopted A or there is a moment in time when no new person switches from B to A. Recall the threshold: $q = b/(a + b)$: this is the minimum fraction of neighbors choosing A needed for someone to switch from B to A. If an individual has a fraction of neighbors below $q$ choosing A, then they will persist with B.

To develop a feel for the dynamics of adoption, consider the network figure 12.3. Suppose $a = 3$ and $b = 2$, so the threshold is $q = 2/5$. Suppose that at $t = 0$, we start with $v$ and $w$ as the two nodes that switch to A. At $t = 1$, nodes $r$ and $t$ switch as the fraction of As in their neighborhood, 2/3, is greater than the threshold $q = 2/5$. But $s$ and $u$ persist with B, as the fraction of A choosing neighbors, 1/3, is less than the threshold $q = 2/5$. At $t =$ 2, $s$ and $u$ also switch to A, as the fraction of their A neighbors 2/3 is now greater than

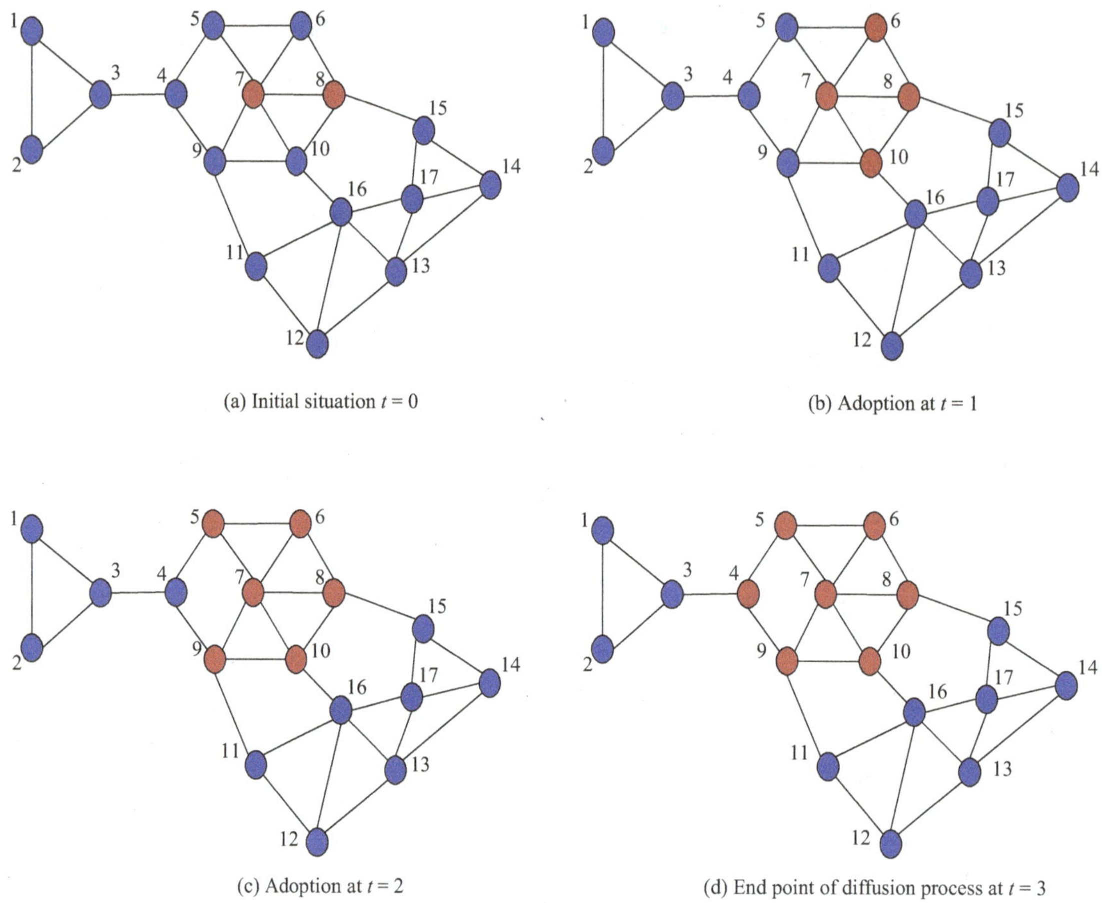


**Figure 12.4**
Cohesive groups blocking contagion.

the threshold $q = 2/5$. So at $t = 2$, everyone adopts A. A *complete cascade* happens when everyone switches to action A.

We next examine potential barriers in the form of network structure to a complete cascade. The discussion in the previous section has already given us some idea of when a cascade will be blocked; this could happen if there is a sufficiently cohesive community of individuals who choose B. To develop this point a little further, consider the network figure 12.4. The process starts with nodes 7 and 8 choosing A. In this network, there are two subsets of nodes in the residual network that are tightly knit: nodes 1–3 and nodes 11–17. In particular, each of them are $2/3$ cohesive. So the maximum exposure to A would be $1/3$, which is smaller than the threshold $2/5$. This means that every individual in either of these groups will find it optimal to persist with $B$. This simple example paves the way for a general result on adoption dynamics in networks.

**Proposition 12.2** *Consider a set of initial adopters of behavior A. Let the threshold be q for nodes in the remaining network. Then the following applies:*

- *If the remaining network contains a group of nodes with greater than $1-q$ cohesiveness, then a complete cascade does not occur.*
- *Moreover, whenever a set of initial adopters does not cause a complete cascade, the remaining network must contain a group with cohesiveness greater than $1-q$.*

Consider part 1: Suppose the remaining network contains a group that is greater than $1-q$ cohesive, $X$. If a complete cascade occurs, then there must be a time at which the first node in group X switches from B to A. We know that this node has greater than a $1-q$ fraction of neighbors within $X$ who all choose B. But then it would be optimal for the node to choose B. This is a contradiction. So it cannot be the case that a complete cascade occurs.

Next, consider part 2: Suppose the cascade stops before complete adoption. Let the set of action B choosers at the end point of the process be given by $Y$. Consider node $y \in Y$. Since $y$ does not adopt A, it must be the case that their fraction of neighbors within $Y$ must exceed $1-q$. Indeed, this must be true for all nodes in $Y$. So $Y$ has cohesiveness greater than $1-q$. ■

So a new norm will permeate a society if and only if it contains no suitably cohesive subgroups. This discussion naturally suggests the following question: what is the maximal receptiveness of a society? More precisely, we can ask: given a network, what is the largest threshold $q$ that will support a complete cascade?

To study this problem, it is helpful to consider large societies, networks with an infinite set of nodes. At the start, everyone chooses B. A finite set of nodes change to A. The *cascade capacity* of a network is the largest value of threshold $q$ for which there is a complete cascade.

We discuss some examples here to explore the issues. Consider a cycle network in which everyone has degree 2. Working through the computations, as in the earlier examples, it is easy to verify that there is a complete cascade for any $q < 1/2$. Moreover, there is no switching to A, and hence no cascade at all for $q > 1/2$. So the cascade capacity of a cycle is $q = 1/2$. Next, consider a grid with degree 8: everyone is connected to all neighbors to the top, bottom, left, and right, and on each diagonal. Suppose there is a square of 9 nodes that adopt A. Consider the neighbors of this square. The most receptive person would be someone who has the (maximal) 3 neighbors in the square. So it follows that an action A with $q > 3/8$ will not spread. Arguing analogously, it can be seen that any $q < 3/8$ will lead to a complete cascade. So the cascade capacity of the grid is $3/8$. Observe that for $q \in (3/8, 1/2)$, action A fails to spread. In other words, an action that yields superior payoffs may fail to spread due to the cohesiveness of the existing network.

Equipped with these observations, we are ready to state the following result.

**Proposition 12.3** *There is no network for which cascade capacity exceeds* $1/2$.

The argument underlying this proposition goes as follows: Take a new action with $q > 1/2$. At any point $t$, some individuals are choosing A and others are choosing B. Label an edge in the network as AA if it connects two nodes that are choosing A, AB if the edge connects two nodes that choose A and B, and BB if the edge connected two nodes that both choose B. Observe that expansion of the set of A adopters happens only along edges of type AB. At the start ($t = 0$), there is a finite set of adopters of A. Let $I_0$ be the number of AB edges that connect these A adopters to nonadopters. We will show that at every point from $t = 1$ onward, the number of AB edges *falls strictly*. So there are at most $I_0$ active periods in the dynamics. This means that the cascade is incomplete.

Consider node $x$, which switched at time $t$. As $q > 1/2$, the number of AB edges for this node must be strictly greater than the number of BB edges. So it follows, after the switch by $x$, that the number of AB edges for $x$ falls strictly. This is true for every node that switches at time $t$. Hence the number of AB edges falls strictly at time $t$ compared to at time $t - 1$. This completes the argument. ■

This result has a reassuring implication: a new action A, which is less efficient than the existing action B, can have some success, but it can never completely take over any entire network.

The discussion also draws attention to the difficulties in introducing large-scale change to cohesive societies. One way to overcome the resistance to change is to initiate movement from one community to a new location, which helps to erode the cohesiveness of a community. One strand of research explores this route from a theoretical perspective. Let us discuss this approach briefly next.

Building on Ely (2002), Mailath, Samuelson, and Shaked (1994), Bhaskar and Vega-Redondo (2004), and Oechssler (1997), let us consider a world with many islands. Individuals care about the average payoffs from interactions, and they earn payoffs from interactions with everyone on an island. Moving from one island to another leads to the severing of all ties with the former island, and instead the playing of the game with all players on the new island. In a sense, then the neighborhood becomes a matter of choice–the choice of an island.

Now imagine that everyone is on one island and playing the inefficient action. Then the possibly experimental move of a few individuals to a new island can lead to the emergence of a location with an efficient convention. Individuals left behind on the old island can now migrate to this newly inhabited island with an efficient convention, which can lead to a transition from a situation where everyone is choosing the inefficient action to one in which everyone is on a new island and choosing the efficient action. Observe that it takes only a few initial experimental individuals to move to the new island for this transition to take place. Thus the possibility of moving to a new, as-yet-unoccupied location creates a pathway from inefficient to efficient outcomes (so long as individuals care only about average payoffs). The basic insight flowing from this work is that if individuals can easily separate/insulate themselves from those who are playing an inefficient action, then efficient enclaves will be formed and eventually attract the migration of others who will adopt the efficient action eventually.

At an abstract level, this is a compelling account of the change of coordination norms. To make it a little concrete, we discuss one example of a large-scale transformation of social norms where immigration has been central: the creation of Special Economic Zones in China and in other countries.

### 12.3.1 An Application: Special Economic Zones in China

In 1979, the Chinese leadership introduced four Special Economic Zones in the neighborhood of Hong Kong as part of a larger reform of its economic system. These Special Economic Zones included the cities of Shenzhen, Zhuhai, and Shantou in Guangdong province and the city of Xiamen in Fujian province. In these zones, private ownership of capital and market-oriented labor laws were put in place. These laws were very different from the institutional arrangements in China at that point. Individuals from the rest of the country could come in to these special zones with their skills and their savings. By 1984, the Chinese leadership expanded the scope of these zones by opening 14 other coastal cities—Dalian, Qinhuangdao, Tianjin, Yantai, Qingdao, Lianyungang, Nantong, Shanghai, Ningbo, Wenzhou, Fuzhou, Guangzhou, Zhanjiang, and Beihai. Over the past four decades, these special zones have witnessed extraordinary growth. Some of them now have a population over 10 million.

Reasoning in terms of our theoretical framework, the special economic zones and the coastal cities offer individuals an opportunity to move out of their traditional network and create new, relatively insulated conclaves. Once these individuals are in these conclaves, their interactions are governed by new norms and a new and large collection of networks emerges. At the same time, outmigration has the potential to mitigate the constraints of the old social network. The combination of new networks in the conclaves and the erosion of the old network may create the circumstances for large-scale adoption of new social norms across the entire network.

## 12.4 Co-Evolution: Conventions and Networks

This section studies the evolution of conventions in an environment where the network itself changes with time. To appreciate the impact of evolving networks, we begin with a discussion of evolving conventions in a given network and then introduce changing networks. The exposition here draws on Young (1998) and Goyal (2007, 2012).

### 12.4.1 Exogenous Networks

We first study the setting where the network is fixed and exogenously given. The dynamics take place over discrete points in time numbered as $t = 1, 2 \ldots$. At each point, with probability $p \in (0, 1)$, a player gets an opportunity to revise their strategy. Faced with this opportunity, a player chooses an action that maximizes the payoff, under the assumption that the strategy profile of neighbors remains the same as in the previous period. If more than one action is optimal, then the player sticks with the current action. Let the action of $i$ at period $t$ be $s_i^t$, where $s_t^i \in S$. The profile of actions at time $t$ is given by $s_t$. Therefore, the strategy for player $i$ at time $t$ maps the action profile at time $t-1$ into an action at time $t$: $s_t^i : S^N \to S$. If player $i$ is not active in period $t$, then set $s_i^t = s_i^{t-1}$. This simple best-response strategy revision rule generates, for every network $g$, a transition probability function $P_g(ss') : S \times S \to [0, 1]$, which governs the evolution of the state of the system $s^t$. A strategy profile (or state $s$) is said to be absorbing if the dynamic process cannot escape the state once it reaches it (i.e., $P_g(ss) = 1$). Here, we will study the relation between absorbing states and the structures of local interaction. The dynamics of choice in networks are summarized in the following result.

**Proposition 12.4** *Given network g, and starting from any initial strategy profile $s^0$, the dynamic process $s^t$ converges to an absorbing strategy profile in finite time, with a probability of 1. Moreover, there is a equivalence between the set of absorbing strategy profiles and the set of Nash equilibria of the static social game.*

The arguments underlying this result are as follows: Let us start at state $s_0$. Consider the set of players who are not playing a best response. If this set is empty, then the process is at a Nash equilibrium profile; and this is an absorbing state of the process, as no player has an incentive to revise strategy. Suppose, therefore, that there are some players who are currently choosing action A but would prefer B. Allow them to choose B, and let $s_1$ be the new state of the system (this transition occurs with positive probability, given the decision rules used by individuals). Now inspect the players doing A in state $s_1$ who would like to switch actions. If there are such players, then have them switch to B and define the new state as $s_2$. Clearly, this process of having the A players switch will end in a finite time (since there are a finite number of players in the society). Let the state with this property be $\hat{s}$. Either there will be no players left choosing A or there will be some players choosing A in $\hat{s}$. In the former case, the process is at a Nash equilibrium.

Next consider the latter situation, in which some players choose A while others choose B. Check if there are any players choosing B in state $\hat{s}$ who would like to switch actions. If there are none, then the process is at an absorbing state. If there are A players who would like to switch, then follow the process as outlined previously to reach a state in which there is no player who wishes to switch from B to A. Let this state be denoted by $\bar{s}$. Next, observe that no player who was choosing A (and did not want to switch actions) in $\hat{s}$ would be interested in switching to B. This is true because the game is a coordination game and the set of players choosing A has weakly increased in the transition from $\hat{s}$ to $\bar{s}$. Hence the process has arrived (with positive probability) at a state in which no player has any incentive to switch actions. This is an absorbing state of the dynamics; since the initial state was arbitrary and the transition occurs with positive probability, the theory of Markov chains says that the transition to an absorbing state will occur in a finite time, with a probability of 1. ■

We conclude this discussion by noting that for a profile $s$ to be an absorbing state, it must be the case that from some point in time $t$, no individual has an incentive to switch actions. But if this is so, then everyone must be playing a best response to the choices of everyone else. But this means that such a strategy profile must be a Nash equilibrium. Similarly, it is easy to see that every Nash equilibrium profile offers no incentive for anyone to switch actions; therefore it constitutes an absorbing state of the dynamics.

Thus every Nash equilibria can be supported via a natural dynamic process. To select across different equilibria in networks, we need to go beyond these dynamics. We will explore the scope of the following general idea in the next discussion. Suppose that $s$ and $s'$ are the two absorbing states of the best-response dynamics described earlier. Given that $s$ is an absorbing state, a movement from $s$ to $s'$ requires an error or an experiment on the part of one or more of the players. Similarly, a movement from $s'$ to $s$ requires errors on the part of some subset of players. State $s$ is said to be *stochastically stable* if it requires relatively more errors/experiments to move from $s$ to $s'$ than the other way around. If it takes the same number of mutations to move between the two states, then they are both stochastically stable.

To develop the analysis of stochastically stable states, let us spell out some details of this experiment process. Assume that, conditional on receiving a revision opportunity at any point in time $t$, a player chooses a strategy at random with some small probability $\epsilon > 0$. Given a network $g$, and for any $\epsilon > 0$, it follows that in this experimental dynamic process, there is a positive probability of transitioning from any state $s$ to any other state $s'$. In other words, the experimental dynamic process defines a Markov chain that is aperiodic and irreducible: from standard results, it follows that the process has a unique invariant probability distribution on states (Kemeny and Snell [1983] and Seneta [2006]). Denote this distribution by $\mu_g^\epsilon$. The analysis will study the support of $\mu_g^\epsilon$ as the probability of experiments becomes very small (i.e., as $\epsilon$ converges to 0). Define $\lim_{\epsilon \to 0} \mu_g^\epsilon = \hat{\mu}_g$. State $s$ is said to be *stochastically stable* if $\hat{\mu}_g(s) > 0$.

We now present some examples that help us appreciate the effects of the network of interaction, $g$, on the set of stochastically stable states.

**Example 12.1** *The complete network*

This example considers a complete network in which every player is a neighbor of every other player. Suppose that player 1 is deciding on whether to choose $A$ or $B$. It is easy to verify that at least $k = (n-1)(b-d)/[(a-e)+(b-d)]$ players need to choose $A$ in order for $A$ to be optimal for player 1. Similarly, the minimum number of players needed to induce player 1 to choose $B$ is $l = (n-1)(a-e)/[(a-e)+(b-d)]$. Given the assumption that $a+d > b+e$, it follows that $k < n/2 < l$. If everyone is choosing $A$, then it takes $l$ experiments to transit to a state where everyone is choosing $B$; likewise, if everyone is choosing $B$, then it takes $k$ mutations to transit to a state where everyone is choosing $A$. It follows, therefore, that the risk-dominant action B is the unique stochastically stable outcome. ■

**Example 12.2** *Local interaction around a circle*

Following Ellison (1993), we consider local interactions with immediate neighbors around a circle. Suppose that at time $t-1$, every player is choosing $B$. Now suppose that two adjacent players, $i$ and $i+1$, choose action $A$ at time $t$ due to an experiment with the process. It is now easy to verify that in the next period, $t+1$, the immediate neighbors of $i$ and $i+1$, players $i-1$ and $i+2$, will find it optimal to switch to action $A$ (due to the assumption that $A$ is risk-dominant and $a+d>b+e$). Moreover, in period $t+2$, the immediate neighbors of $i-1$ and $i+2$ have a similar incentive, so there is a process under way that leads to everyone choosing action $A$ within a finite time. On the other hand, if everyone is choosing $A$, then $n-1$ players must switch to $B$ to induce a player to switch to action $B$. This is true because so long as at least one of the neighbors is choosing $A$, the optimal action is to choose $A$. Thus the risk-dominant action $A$ is the unique stochastically stable state. ■

The simplicity of these arguments suggests the following conjecture: the risk-dominant outcome occurs in all networks. This conjecture is false, as example 12.3 illustrates.

**Example 12.3** *The star network*

Following Jackson and Watts (2002b), we consider a star network and suppose that player 1 is the central player. The first point to note about a star network is that there are only two possible equilibrium configurations, both involving social conformism. A study of stochastically stable actions, therefore, involves a study of the relative stability of these configurations. However, it is easily verified that in a star network, a perturbation that switches the action of player 1 is sufficient to get a switch of all the other players. As this is also the minimum possible number of mutations, it follows that both states are stochastically stable. ■

These examples suggest that network structure matters for the stability of outcomes; however, the partition of networks where the various equilibria are stochastically stable appears to be an open problem. We have so far assumed that the network is fixed. In many situations of interest, individuals faced with a coordination problem can orient their network. This is especially true over time. Pupils may pick new friends as they choose new languages or sports activities; similarly, businesses may pick new partners as they change their standards or technologies. We now turn to a study of the coevolution of networks and actions in the coordination game.

### 12.4.2 Endogenous Networks

Following Goyal and Vega-Redondo (2005), we consider a model of links and actions. There is a set of players $N \in \{1, 2, \ldots, n\}$, where $n \geq 3$. A player chooses a link-action pair, $(g_i, a_i)$, where $g_i$ refers to the links that are formed and $a_i \in \{A, B\}$ refers to the action in the accompanying coordination game. Let $g = \{g_1, \ldots, g_n\}$ be a profile of links chosen by the players. A profile of link decisions defines a directed network. Given network $g$, let us say that $i$ and

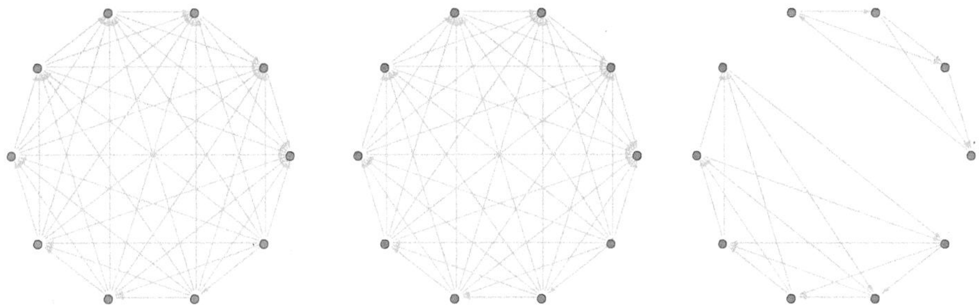


**Figure 12.5**
Equilibria with endogenous networks.

$j$ are directly linked if at least one of them has established a link with the other (i.e., a link between $i$ and $j$ exists if $\max\{g_{ij}, g_{ji}\} = 1$). Every player who establishes a link with some other player incurs a cost of $c > 0$. To understand payoffs, we therefore need to keep track of who forms a link and who receives a link: if $g_{ij} = 1$ and $g_{ji} = 0$, then we shall say that $g_{ij}$ has an active link for player $i$ and a passive link for player $j$. Given a strategy profile $s = (s_1, \ldots, s_n)$, the payoffs of player $i$ are

$$\Pi_i(s) = \sum_{j \in N_i(g)} \pi(a_i, a_j) - \eta_i(g)c, \tag{12.4}$$

where $\pi(a_i, a_j)$ are the payoffs in the bilateral game between two connected players $i$ and $j$, and $\eta_i(g)$ is the number of links formed by player $i$ in strategy profile $g$. The payoffs $\pi(a_i, a_j)$ are taken from the matrix 12.1. We start with a brief discussion of the equilibrium of the linking and coordination game.

In what follows, to focus on the more interesting case, we will suppose that $b > a$, so there is a tension between risk dominance and efficiency in the coordination game: action $A$ corresponds to the risk-dominant action, but action $B$ corresponds to the efficient action. Observe that if the costs of linking are greater than the efficient payoffs, $c > b$, then no links will be worthwhile: the network must be empty. So in what follows, we restrict our attention to the case of $c < b$. Our next observation is that if $c > a$, then two players will be linked in an equilibrium only if they are both playing the efficient action. A final comment pertains to the small costs of linking: if $c < a$, then complete networks with everyone choosing A or everyone choosing B are both equilibria. Interestingly, when $c > e$, then there also are equilibria with two component networks where players choose a different action across the components. Figure 12.5 presents some equilibria of this game of linking and actions.

Moving to the dynamics, we start by noting an immediate counterpart of proposition 12.4: there is an equivalence between the set of Nash equilibria of the static game of linking and actions and the best-response dynamics. We examine the role of experiments in selecting across these equilibria. As in the dynamic model with experiments considered previously, we suppose that at regular intervals, individuals choose links and actions to maximize (myopically) their respective payoffs. Occasionally, they may also experiment. Our interest is in the nature of long-run networks and actions, when the probability of these experiments is small. The perturbed dynamics of actions and endogenous networks lead to very sharp predictions.

**Proposition 12.5** *Consider the dynamic model of linking and actions with experiments. Define a number $\bar{c}$, where $e < \bar{c} < a$. Suppose that the probability of experiments is small. If $0 < c < \bar{c}$, in the long run, the network is complete and all players choose the risk-dominant action A. If $\bar{c} < c < b$, then the long-run network is complete and choose efficient action B. Finally, if $c > b$, then the long-run network is empty and actions are undetermined.*

A proof of the result will take us too far afield, but let us try and spell out the main ideas informally. So long as costs of linking are below $b$, in the long run, the network is complete. This means that partially connected networks are ephemeral: to see why this is the case, suppose for simplicity that $b > c > e$: so players will only maintain links with each other if they are playing the same action. Then note that starting from two components with distinct actions, a single experiment will take an individual from one action such as A to the other action $B$ and with links to the corresponding component. The players in the erstwhile $A$ component will now best respond by disconnecting their links with this experimenting individual. We can iterate this process one experiment at a time, and at each point, the outcome may be a Nash equilibrium. The process converges with everyone in a complete component choosing $B$. This suggests that the two-component configurations with distinct action configurations are fragile. It is easy to check that the complete network with conformism is not fragile in this way. As a small exercise, the interested reader may wish to check that a variant of this argument would work for small costs of links as well.

Next, note that in the complete network, players always coordinate on the same action (i.e., social conformism obtains). We can adopt the arguments we discussed in section 12.2 to show this. Moreover, recall from section 12.1 that if the complete network were fixed, then the risk-dominant action would be uniquely stochastically stable. Thus the dynamics of linking must account for the sharp transition from all A to all B as we move $c$ from under $\bar{c}$ to above $\bar{c}$.

We observe that threshold $\bar{c}$ is strictly below $a$; that is, there is some interval of values $c \in (\bar{c}, a)$ where the complete network with risk-dominant action is a Nash equilibrium, and yet it is not stochastically stable. Rather, the efficient action is uniquely stochastically stable. This interval shows that the study of the dynamics allows us to go beyond what we could infer simply by examining the Nash equilibrium of the static game.

We now discuss the role of trembles/experiments in shaping the co-evolution of networks and coordination game equilibrium. Starting from a complete network and everyone choosing A, suppose that some players were to experiment with action $B$. If the costs of linking are very small, everyone will maintain the links as they are. In essence, a player must make fresh choices as if they were in a complete network. In this case, from our arguments in example 12.1, the risk-dominant (and inefficient) convention prevails since, under complete connectivity, this convention is harder to destabilize than the efficient but risk-dominated one.

Next, suppose that the costs of links are higher and lie in the range $c > \bar{c}$. Now it is no longer profitable for the nonexperimenting players to maintain any links with the experimenters. They will delete their links and the network is no longer complete. If enough links are deleted in this manner, the experimenters are adrift in a new complete component that is playing the efficient action. So long as there are enough experimenters, those left behind will have an incentive to switch actions and form links with the experimenters. Let the minimum number of experimenters be $M_{AB}$. We could similarly contemplate a transition from a complete network with everyone choosing $B$ to a complete network where everyone chooses $A$, and compute the minimum number of experimenters needed for this transition; let us denote it as $M_{BA}$. Recalling our discussion of stochastic stability, we note that the key comparison is between $M_{AB}$ and $M_{BA}$. It turns out $M_{AB} > M_{BA}$ for $c < \bar{c}$ and $M_{AB} < M_{BA}$ for $c > \bar{c}$. The details of the computations are fairly involved, so we omit them here; see Goyal and Vega-Redondo (2005) for a complete proof. ■

#### 12.4.2.1 Fixed locations versus evolving networks

We briefly discuss the relationship between migrating between locations (as discussed in the previous section) and evolving networks (as discussed in this section).

The basic insight flowing from the changing location approach is that if individuals can easily separate/insulate themselves from those who are playing an inefficient action, then efficient enclaves will be formed and eventually attract the migration of others who will adopt the efficient action. One may be tempted to associate easy mobility with low costs of forming links. However, the considerations involved in the two approaches turn out to be somewhat different. Let us elaborate on this point briefly.

Recall from our discussion of the coordination dynamics in the endogenous networks case that, in the network formation approach, the risk-dominant outcome prevails if the costs of forming links are small. There are two main reasons for this contrast. First, in the network formation approach, players do not indirectly choose their patterns of interaction with others by moving across a prespecified network of locations (as in the case of player mobility). Rather, they directly construct their interaction network (with no exogenous restrictions) by choosing those agents with whom they want to play the game. Second, the cost of link formation is paid per link formed and thus becomes truly effective only if it is high enough. Thus it is precisely the restricted mobility of high costs that helps insulate (and thus protect) the individuals who are choosing the efficient action. If the costs of link formation are low, then the extensive interaction that this facilitates may have the unfortunate consequence of rendering risk-dominance considerations decisive.

#### 12.4.2.2 Minimal effort games

In the problems we have studied so far, individuals choose between two actions, $A$ and $B$. It is easy to extend the problem to have $k \geq 2$ actions. A variant of this game is the *weakest-link* or the *minimum effort* game. We follow Riedl, Rohde, and Strobel (2016) in describing the game. Let $N = \{1, \ldots, n\}$ be a group of players and $S = \{1, \ldots, k\}$ be the set of effort levels available to every player. Players simultaneously choose an effort level $s_i \in S$. Let $s = (s_1, \ldots, s_n)$ be the strategy profile of players, $b$ the marginal cost of effort, and $a$ the marginal return from the effort in the group, with $a > b > 0$. The payoff of player $i$ facing strategy profile $s$ is

$$\Pi_i(s) = a \min_{j \in N}\{s_j\} - bs_i + c, \tag{12.5}$$

where $c > 0$ ensures nonnegative payoffs for all strategy profiles. The restriction $a > b > 0$ implies that every player has a monetary incentive to align their effort level with the minimum level chosen by the other players. Therefore, any strategy profile in which all players choose the same effort level constitutes a Nash equilibria. These equilibria are Pareto-ranked, from the highest- to the lowest-effort equilibrium. Also, observe that the strategy profile in which everyone chooses the lowest effort pairwise risk-dominates every other equilibrium.

In this game, individuals choose from among a finite set of actions $\{1, \ldots, k\}$, where $k \geq 2$. The gross payoffs to an individual from an action profile are given by the minimum action chosen among all players while a higher action is costlier. The structure is such that the rewards of higher actions more than compensate for this cost. Thus there are $k$ coordination game equilibria, each corresponding to a different action chosen by everyone (for a binary version of this game, see chapter 4, on network structure and human behavior). Therefore, there are $k$ Nash equilibria and they are Pareto-ranked, with a higher matched action profile payoff dominating a lower action profile.

There is a large body of experimental literature on this game: a robust finding is that subjects generally choose the lowest action as the group of players grows (i.e., they chose the worst equilibrium of the game). For weakest-link games played in fixed groups, the seminal papers by Harrison and Hirshleifer (1989) and Van Huyck, Battalio, and Beil (1990) indicated that when played in pairs, substantial coordination on the Pareto-dominant equilibrium occurs, whereas efficient coordination breaks down completely when groups grow large (typically beyond size 8). This result has been replicated by a number of experimental studies over the years; for an overview of the literature, see Riedl, Rohde, and Strobel (2016).

Our interest is in understanding how the possibility of partner choice will shape the nature of social coordination. Here are some examples of this interaction of actions and partners. For instance, in the global public good of preventing the outbreak and spread of infectious diseases, the country with the poorest preventive measures determines the likelihood of an outbreak. Governments with higher standards can respond not only by lowering their own costly preventive measures, but also by restricting trade or traveling to and from countries with low standards. Here is a second example: in groups of coauthors of a paper, the slowest/lowest-effort member determines the speed of progress. In response to poor effort by a researcher, their coauthors may reduce their own efforts or terminate the collaboration altogether.

With these examples in mind, let us consider a variant of this game, in which players choose links with each other and play the weakest-link game. Observe that as in our earlier discussion of the baseline coordination game, there are equilibria with a complete network and with everyone playing any one of the actions. Next, we discuss experimental evidence on this game that is taken from a recent paper by Riedl, Rohde, and Strobel (2016), which examines the behavior of subjects in versions of the repeated weakest-link games, with and without link choice. The researchers consider two group sizes: 8 and 24 members. In their Baseline Treatment (BT), 8 players are located in a complete network and simultaneously choose an integer (which they interpret as effort) from the set $\{1, \ldots, 8\}$. Everyone choosing 1 is the least efficient Nash equilibrium and everyone choosing 7 is the most efficient. They have a Neighborhood Treatment (NT) that adds a link decision to the BT treatment: interaction between any two players is endogenous and requires mutual consent. Recall that a player's payoff is determined by the minimum effort in her neighborhood. Further, in line with our field examples, which exhibit returns from increasing interaction neighborhood size, we provide incentives to endogenously form larger neighborhoods. The treatments are designed in such as way that when each player chooses to connect with everyone else (i.e., create a complete network), the incentives on actions in the weakest-link game under NT coincide with those of BT.

The main results are as follows: In the first round, there is little difference between treatments. The average effort level is 5.66 in BT and 5.99 in NT. However, the subsequent evolution of efforts is very different across the rounds. In the BT treatment, the frequency of the lowest effort (11 percent in round 1) increases strongly, and this effort level is the main choice from round 19 onward. The frequency of the highest effort level deteriorates over time from 64 percent to about 30 percent in the last few rounds. By contrast, in the NT treatment, the frequency of the lowest effort is never above 4 percent, and the frequency of the highest effort (7) increases strongly from about 60 percent in the first round to above 94 percent (where it mostly remains) after round 4.

More generally, efficient coordination is rarely observed in groups of size 8 and never in groups of size 24. This echoes the classical findings of Van Huyck, Battalio, and Beil (1990) and Harrison and Hirshleifer (1989). Matters are very different with endogenous links: under NT, subjects quickly coordinate on the fully efficient equilibrium and virtually all subjects form links with everyone else (thereby creating a complete network).

Riedl, Rohde, and Strobel (2016) suggest the following mechanism as an explanation for this result: subjects who face link deletion from individuals who put in high effort respond by raising their own effort. Over time, this leads almost all individuals to choose high effort, which encourages all individuals to form links with each other, resulting in a complete network with almost universal high effort. We see that the link dynamics play a central role in the emergence of the high-effort outcome.

## 12.5 Social Coordination with Heterogeneous Preferences

So far, we have assumed that all individuals have the same preferences about the outcomes, as reflected in equal payoffs of the row and column players in the outcomes $(A, A)$ and $(B, B)$. It is easy to see, however, that sometimes players may wish to coordinate with each other but one of them prefers the A outcome while the other player prefers the B outcome. Let us take up some examples of this.

In 2017, in a widely publicized incident in the Netherlands, the public transportation company Qbuzz refused to interview an immigrant who had applied for a job because he refused to shake hand with female clients (on account of his religious beliefs). The company felt that the behavior of the applicant went against social norms in the Netherlands (and would probably put off potential customers). This is an instance of norms on greeting: physical contact between a man and woman is accepted in some communities, while it is entirely prohibited in other communities. So individuals may have very different rankings concerning norms.

Language is another context in which a similar tension arises: members of different communities prefer their own mother tongue to be the common language of communication. In modern societies the language of official communication is of central importance and so it is perhaps only natural that this tension appears in many countries. These differences in preferences create the following tension: individuals would like to coordinate on the same action, but their utility from the outcomes differs.

### 12.5.1 Exogenous Networks

Consider the following simple modification of the model discussed in section 12.4.

There is a group of individuals who each choose between two actions, A and B. Everyone prefers to coordinate on one action, but some individuals prefer action A while others prefer action B. To develop an understanding for how this difference can have a large impact on individual decisions, consider the simple setting of a complete network. Recall that in section 3, we showed that in a setting where individuals interact with everyone, conformism must occur. Now consider the modified situation in which some individuals prefer action A over B, while others prefer B over A.

Suppose there are 15 individuals in all, and 8 prefer A while 7 prefer B. This preference is reflected in the payoffs: in the two-person game, individuals of type A earn 4 from coordinating on action A and 2 from coordinating on action B. The payoffs of type B go the other way: B types earn 4 from coordinating on B and earn only 2 from coordinating on A. Now it is easy to see that with these preferences, conformism on either action remains an outcome. But there is also an outcome in which the A types choose action A, while the B types choose action B, that is, a Nash equilibrium. The wedge in the payoffs between actions across types of agents thus gives rise to the possibility of diverse norms, even in a complete network.

Observe, however, that for diversity to be an equilibrium, the minority must not be too small. So, for example, if there were 3 type B individuals in a society with 15 members, then it is no longer possible to sustain an outcome in which the type B members choose B and the type A members choose action A. Type B individuals earn $2 \times 4 = 8$ in such an outcome and could earn $12 \times 2 = 24$ if they were to switch to action A. The prospects of diversity will depend on the values of payoffs and the relative size of the minority.

An important point to note is that these prospects are considerably brighter if we move away from the complete network. For instance, take the society with 15 members where 12 are of type A and 3 are of type B, but partition them into two distinct cliques corresponding to the type of individual. Now it is easy to see that diversity is a Nash equilibrium: the clique with type A individuals chooses A, while the clique with type B individuals chooses B. This simple example brings out the role of interaction structure in shaping the prospects of diversity and motivates the study of coordination problems in which individuals have heterogenous preferences. The discussion in this section will draw on a literature in economics and sociology and in game theory (e.g, Schelling [2006]; Kearns, Judd, Tan, and Wortman [2009]; and Goyal et al. [2021]).

To develop the arguments formally, we extend the coordination game presented in section 12.2 by assigning different payoffs to players upon successful coordination. This leads us to the Battle of the Sexes game. For ease of exposition, let us write the payoffs in the Battle of the Sexes game as played on a network. There are two actions in the game: A and B. Every individual $i$ has type $\theta_i \in \{A, B\}$. Individuals are located on network $g$. Individual $i$ chooses action $s_i \in \{A, B\}$. Recall the payoffs of coordination game in equation (12.1): for simplicity, set $d = e = 0$. The payoff to individual $i$ from strategy profile $\mathbf{s}$ is

$$u_i(\theta_i, s, g) = \lambda_{s_i}^{\theta_i} \left(1 + \sum_{j \in N_i(g)} I_{s_i = s_j}\right), \tag{12.6}$$

where $I_{s_j = s_i}$ is the indicator function for $i$'s neighbor $j$, who chooses the same action as $i$. We set $\lambda_{s_i}^{\theta_i} = \alpha$ if $s_i = \theta_i$ and $\lambda_{s_i}^{\theta_i} = \beta$ if $s_i \neq \theta_i$. Let $\alpha > \beta > 0$.

We note that conformism on either action A or B remains an equilibrium for all networks, as in the baseline coordination game with aligned preferences. Moreover, diversity in actions also can arise, and we expect that it should be easier to sustain in the Battle of the Sexes game than in the baseline coordination game. Thus we will face the problem of multiple equilibria, as in the basic coordination problem. But differences in preferences now raise a new issue: how does the location in networks of individuals with particular preferences shape coordination in the group? We present an experiment taken from Kearns, Judd, Tan, and Wortman (2009) to develop a feel for how networks matter.

#### 12.5.1.1 Experimental evidence: Heterogeneity, networks, and coordination

The setting of the experiment is as follows: there are 36 individuals located on a network. Every individual inhabits a node in the network and can choose one of two colors, red or blue; moreover, the colours can be asynchronously updated as often as desired during a 1-minute interval. Subjects are able to view the current color choices of their immediate neighbors in the network at all times, but otherwise, they have no information on the current choices of the others in the network. No other communication between subjects is permitted.

The experiment offers payoffs to individuals only if all 36 subjects arrive at the same colour choice before the end of the 1 minute (in this sense, the pressure to coordinate is even greater than in the Battle of the Sexes game, where payoffs depend only on the extent of local coordination). For concreteness, we will suppose that there are two types of players: Blue players, who are paid \$1.25 for Blue consensus and \$0.75 for Red consensus; and Red players, who are paid \$1.25 for Red consensus and \$0.75 for Blue consensus. To reiterate, payments are made only if global unanimity is reached, whether on red or blue. This requirement of unanimity is extreme, but it helps us to develop the main points in a simple way.

There are three design variables underlying the experiment: the number of individuals with different preferences, their placement in the network, and the structure of the network. There are two broad categories of experiments: the Cohesion experiments and the Minority Power experiments. The networks used have roughly the same number of edges (roughly 100), but we consider two networks: an Erdős-Rényi network and a preferential-attachment network.

In the Cohesion experiments, vertices were divided into two equal groups corresponding to their colour preferences. One goal of the experiment was to examine how variations in the network structure—from Erdős-Rényi to Preferential Attachment—could alter social coordination choices. Figure 12.6 presents examples of networks with these features.

In the Minority Power experiments, all networks were generated via preferential attachment. A minority of the vertices with the highest degrees (i.e., number of neighbors) were then assigned incentives preferring red to blue (the size of the minority varied between 6, 9, and 14), the remaining majority of subjects were Blue types. One objective of the Minority experiment was to examine the influence of a small but well-connected group of individuals on collective behavior. Figure 12.7 presents networks and locates players with colour preferences in the networks.

The authors ran experiments with a variety of payoff configurations, but here we will restrict ourselves to discussing the symmetric case: the Blue subjects and the Red subjects exhibited the same payoff differences (\$1.25 versus \$0.75).

At any instant in time, a subject sees the current color choices of neighbors. The subject's payoffs for the experiment are shown; there is a bar that displays the time that has elapsed in the experiment and a "game progress" indicator that measures the fraction of edges in the network that choose the same color on each end.

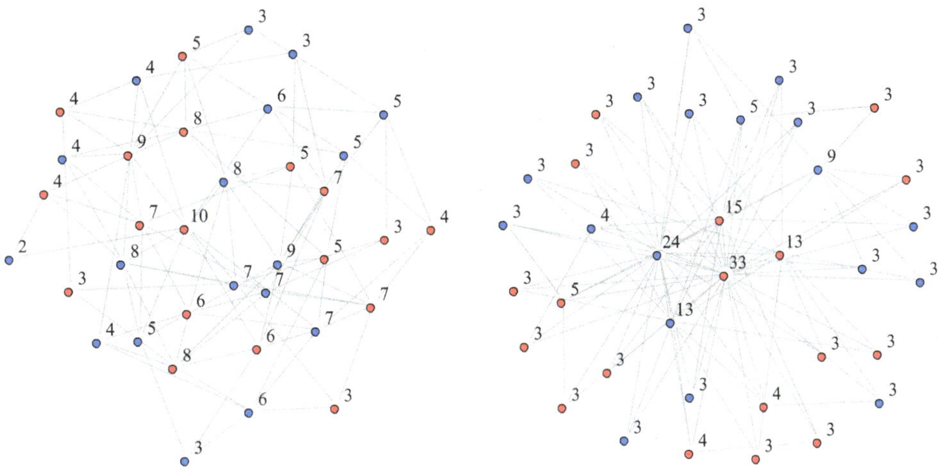

(a) Erdős-Rényi network (b) Preferential attachment network

**Figure 12.6**
Cohesion experiment configurations: two equal groups of 18.

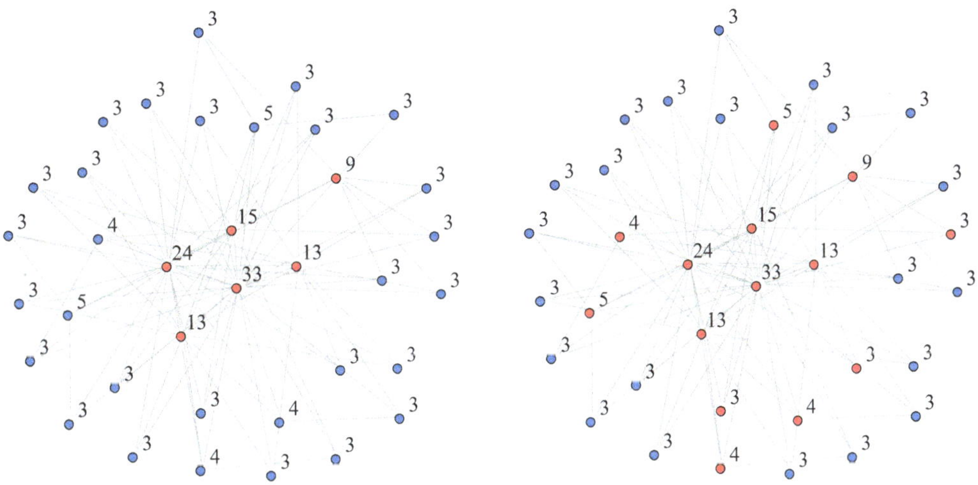

(a) Minority of 6 (b) Minority of 14

**Figure 12.7**
Minority power configurations: preferential attachment networks.

Let us summarize the main findings here. On the issue of whether groups arrived at consensus, there was a significant difference in the success rate between the Cohesion experiments and the Minority Power experiments: subjects found it significantly easier to reach consensus in the Minority Power experiments. A second observation is that in all the cases where the group was successful in the Minority Power experiment, the global consensus was reached on the colour preferred by the well-connected minority. Together, these results suggest that not only can an influentially positioned minority group reliably override the majority preference, but such a group can in fact facilitate global unity.

Our next observation is that within the Cohesion experiments, unanimity was much more likely in the preferential-attachment network as compared to the Erdős-Rényi network. When we combine this with the high success rate of the preferential-attachment Minority Power experiments, we are led to the view that for this class of consensus problems, preferential-attachment networks are easier for subjects as compared to the Erdős-Rényi networks.

### 12.5.2 Endogenous Networks

Modern societies experience large-scale migrations of people from rural to urban areas and from one country to another. Diversity of preferences on issues of shared interest arise naturally, and as examples in the previous section illustrate, this can give rise to a tension between the preference for diversity and the need for common standards or norms. This tension raises the following possibility: a community may sustain its preferred way of doing things—on dress or diet or religion— through social segregation, and this would come at the cost of social coordination. The discussion here is based on Advani and Reich (2015) and Goyal, Hernández, Martínez-Cánovas, et al. (2021).

#### 12.5.2.1 A model with linking and coordination

There is $N = \{1, 2, \ldots, n\}$, with $n \geq 3$ individuals. There are two actions in the coordination game: A and B. Every individual $i$ has a type, $\theta_i \in \{A, B\}$. Individuals first choose links with others, and then they choose between actions A and B. Links are binary, $g_{ij} \in \{0, 1\}$: a link is formed between $i$ and $j$ if both wish to form it. After the network is created, individual $i$ chooses action $x_i : g \to \{A, B\}$. In equation (12.1), we will suppose that $d = e = 0$. The payoff to individual $i$ from strategy profile $s = (x, g) = (x_1, \ldots, x_n, g_1, \ldots, g_n)$ is

$$u_i(\theta_i, x, g) = \lambda^{\theta_i}_{x_i(g)} \left( 1 + \sum_{j \in N_i(g)} I_{\{x_i(g) = x_j(g)\}} \right) - |N_i(g)|k. \tag{12.7}$$

$I_{x_j = x_i}$ is the indicator function for $i$'s neighbor $j$ who chooses the same action as $i$. We will denote $\overline{g}_{ij}$ as reflecting the situation where $i$ and $j$ have proposed having a link to each other, and therefore the link has actually been formed. We set $\lambda^{\theta_i}_{x_i(\overline{g})} = \alpha$ if $x_i(\overline{g}) = \theta_i$ and $\lambda^{\theta_i}_{x_i(\overline{g})} = \beta$ if $x_i(\overline{g}) \neq \theta_i$. To focus our attention on the interesting case, we will assume $\beta > k$.

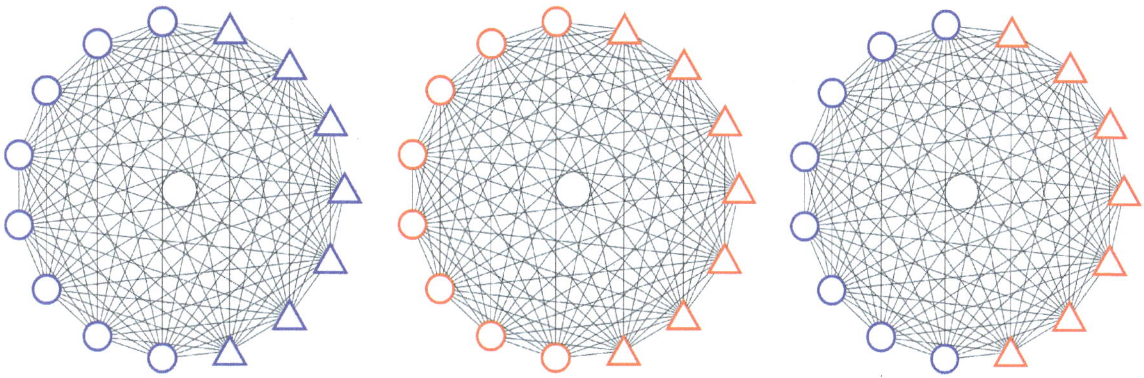

(a) Integration and conformity to blue

(b) Integration and conformity to red

(c) Integration and diversity

**Figure 12.8**
Pairwise-stable outcomes for $k = 0$.

To understand strategic behavior in our setting, we adapt the pairwise stability notion from Jackson and Wolinsky (1996) (as presented in chapter 3) to our setting. In the spirit of their definition, we say that a network and corresponding equilibrium action profile is stable if no individual can profitably deviate either unilaterally or with one other individual. Given a network action pair $(\overline{g}, x(\overline{g})), x_{-ij}(\overline{g})$ refers to the choices of all players except for players $i$ and $j$. Equipped with this terminology, we can define pairwise network action profile as follows.

**Definition 12.1** *A network-action pair $(\overline{g}, x(\overline{g}))$ is pairwise stable if the following is true:*

1. *$x(\overline{g})$ is an equilibrium action profile given network $\overline{g}$.*
2. *For every $\overline{g}_{ij} = 1$, $u_i(x, \overline{g}) \geq u_i(x', \overline{g} - \overline{g}_{ij})$ and $u_j(x, \overline{g}) \geq u_j(x'', \overline{g} - \overline{g}_{ij})$, where $x'(\overline{g} - \overline{g}_{ij})$ and $x''(\overline{g} - \overline{g}_{ij})$ are some equilibrium action profiles given network $\overline{g} - \overline{g}_{ij}$.*
3. *For every $\overline{g}_{ij} = 0$, $u_i(x, g) \geq u_i(x', g + g_{ij})$ or $u_j(x, g) \geq u_j(x', \overline{g} + \overline{g}_{ij})$, where $x'(\overline{g} + \overline{g}_{ij})$ is some equilibrium action profile given network $\overline{g} + \overline{g}_{ij}$.*

Figures 12.8 and 12.9 illustrate the pairwise stable network and action profiles. A *circle* node represents a player in the majority and a *triangle* a player in the minority. Majority players prefer action A, represented by blue, while minority players prefer action B, represented by red. The border color of a node displays its chosen action.

Individual decisions on linking create the possibility of fruitful interaction and the choices in the coordination game determine the actual payoffs. It is possible, then, to study how well individuals do and the group does as a result of the choices that individuals make. We will say that an outcome is efficient if it maximizes the sum of the payoffs of all individuals.

An interesting general property is the following: individuals creating the complete network and everyone choosing the majority's preferred action maximizes the sum of the

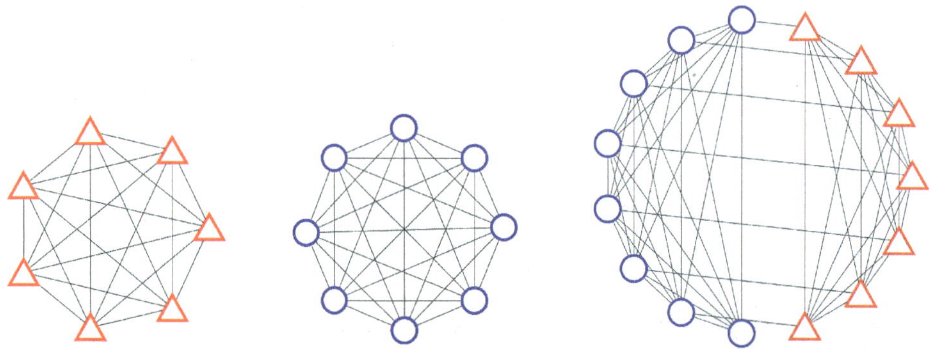

(a) Segregation and diversity (b) Partial integration and diversity

**Figure 12.9**
Pairwise-stable outcomes for $k = 0$.

individual utilities. To develop some intuition for the property, let us consider the complete network. Fixing the behavior of one group, observe that the total aggregate payoffs can only decrease when the other group mixes actions. We therefore only need to compare the two outcomes: (1) where everyone conforms to action *up*, and (2) where everyone conforms to action *down*. The concluding step shows that conformity on *up* is better if and only if the group that prefers *up* constitutes a majority. Observe that this argument holds for arbitrary values of $\alpha$ and $\beta$. Thus conformity is preferred, even if $\alpha$ is much larger than $\beta$: this is because the minority collectively gains less than what the majority loses when the minority switches from conformism to diversity. We note that the socially efficient outcome is invariant with respect to the value of the linking cost $k$ (so long as it is less than $\beta$). A question at the end of the chapter works through the details of this argument.

As the theory is permissive—allowing both connected and partially connected networks and both conformism and diversity—we turn to an experiment to help us develop a better understanding of the problem. The focus of the experiment is on the effects of endogenous linking: we first consider a treatment in which the complete network is given and subjects choose an action, and then take up a treatment in which individuals choose links as well as actions.

#### 12.5.2.2 Experimental evidence: Linking, conformism, and diversity

We consider groups of 15 subjects with a majority of 8 (that prefer *up*) and a minority of 7 (that prefer *down*). There are three groups in a session and two sessions per treatment (i.e., six groups per treatment). Every group plays the game 25 times. The first 5 (rounds) are just a trial, and subjects are paid based on their actions in the last twenty rounds.

The parameters of the payoffs are as follows: coordinating on preferred action brings 4, and coordinating on the less preferred action brings 2. The cost of the link, $k$, is set equal

**Table 12.2**
Equilibrium payoffs

| Player type | Equilibrium payoffs | | | |
|---|---|---|---|---|
| | Endogenous | | Exogenous | |
| | 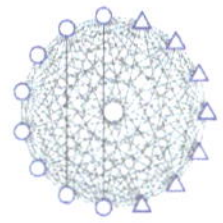 |   | 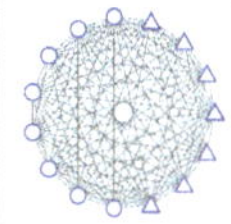 | 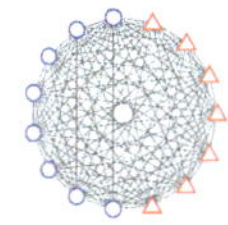 |
| Minority (Δ) | 30 | 28 | 30 | 28 |
| Majority (O) | 60 | 32 | 60 | 32 |

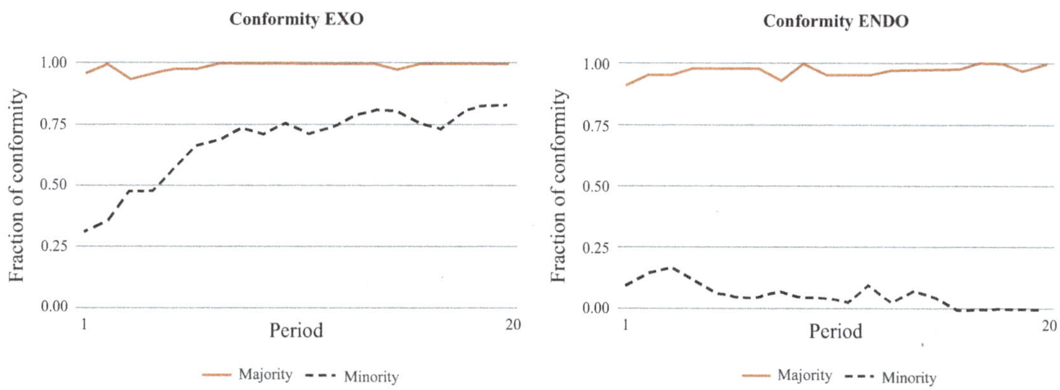


(a) Exogenous network (b) Endogenous network

**Figure 12.10**
Coordination game choices.

to 0 in order to facilitate comparison across the exogenous and endogenous link treatments. The theoretical predictions are set out in table 12.2.

Turning to the experimental findings, we start by describing the linking patterns. Subjects create roughly 94.5 links (out of a maximum possible 105), and the individual average degree is 12.59 (out of a maximum possible 14). There are no differences in connectivity between majority and minority players. The interesting point is that practically all subjects are fully connected to everyone of their own type: almost all the missing links are those between subjects who prefer different actions.

Next, we turn to the choice of actions in the two treatments with exogenous and endogenous links. Figure 12.10 shows that the average numbers of subjects choosing the majority's action in the two networks are 12.68 and 8.18, respectively. This difference is entirely due to the choices of the minority.

One reason for why this outcome is surprising is that the minority could be earning more by conforming with the majority's preferred action. With this payoff loss in mind, let us compare the payoffs of the minority subjects in the two treatments. It turns out that the average minority payoffs under the exogenous complete network are *not* significantly different from the average payoffs obtained with the diversity outcome under the endogenous treatment. This is due to the slower rate of convergence under exogenous networks.

This leads to the following tentative explanation: Due to the large number of individuals and the different preferences, subjects face a very complex coordination problem. They use cues from the environment and any instruments that they have available to simplify this problem. In the experiment, relatively greater linking with own types correlates strongly with rapid convergence to choosing preferred actions (i.e., to diversity actions).

## 12.6 Appendix: Advanced Material

### 12.6.1 Potential Functions and Stochastic Stability

In the discussion in section 12.4, we started with a myopic best-response decision rule and supplemented it with small but persistent mutations and looked at what happens as the probability of mutations becomes small. The key assumption was that errors take place independent of the payoffs. We now explore the issue of payoff-sensitive experiments. Following the work of Blume (1993) and Young (1998), one strand of the literature has studied the log-linear best response. We will present the dynamics under this rule and develop the formal arguments in detail as they involve the use of potential functions, a concept that is general interest for the study of games on networks (a point also made in chapter 4).

Let us suppose that in any period $t$, an individual $i$ located in network $g$ is drawn at random and chooses $\alpha$ according to a probability distribution, $p_i^{\gamma}(\alpha|s^t, g)$, where $\gamma > 0$ and $s^t$ is the strategy profile at time $t$:

$$p_i^{\gamma}(\alpha|s^t, g) = \frac{e^{\gamma \Pi_i(\alpha, s^t_{-i}|g)}}{e^{\gamma \Pi_i(\alpha, s^t_{-i}|g)} + e^{\gamma \Pi_i(\beta, s^t_{-i}|g)}}. \tag{12.8}$$

For large values of $\gamma$, the probability distribution will place most of the probability mass on the best-response action. Define $\Delta_i(s|g) = \Pi_i(\beta, s_{-i}|g) - \Pi_i(\alpha, s_{-i}|g)$. Then for large $\gamma$, the probability of action $\alpha$ is

$$p_i^{\gamma}(\alpha|s^t, g) = \frac{e^{-\gamma \Delta_i(s^t|g)}}{1 + e^{-\gamma \Delta_i(s^t|g)}} \cong e^{-\gamma \Delta_i(s^t|g)}. \tag{12.9}$$

The probability of not choosing the best response is exponentially declining in the payoff loss from the deviation. It turns out that dynamics of the log-linear decision rule are extremely well behaved. To develop some intuition for the dynamics, let us return to the star network example. In that network, the simplest way to implement a transition is via a switch in the action of the central player. In the standard model, with payoff-insensitive mutations, the probability of the central player switching from $A$ to $B$ is the same as the other way around. Matters are very different under the log-linear response rule. If there are many peripheral players, then there is a significant difference in the payoff losses involved and the probability of switching from $A$ to $B$ is significantly smaller than the probability of switching from $B$ to $A$.

Our main result with the log-linear decision rule says that in the long run, behavior is network invariant: in all networks, the risk-dominant outcome prevails. As the proof builds on the ideas of potential functions, a concept that is of general interest for the study of games on networks more generally, we present it completely here.

A game has a *potential* if there is a real-valued function $F(x,y)$ and a rescaling of the utility functions such that whenever a player deviates unilaterally, the change in payoff equals the change in the potential. For a symmetric two-player game, this means that there is a symmetric function $F(x,y)=F(y,x)$, such that for some rescaling of utilities, $\pi_i$, and for all $x,x',y\in S_i$,

$$\pi_i(x,y)-\pi_i(x',y)=F(x,y)-F(x',y). \tag{12.10}$$

Next, note that if a symmetric two-player game admits a potential, then so does the corresponding social game on network $g$. To see this, let $x$ be a profile of actions in the social game, and suppose that player $i$ deviates by choosing $x_i'$. Let $x'=(x_i',x_{-i})$. Then

$$\begin{aligned}\Pi_i(x|g)-\Pi_i(x'|g) &= \sum_{j\in N_i(g)}[\pi_i(x_i,x_j)-\pi_i(x_i',x_j)]\\ &= \sum_{j\in N_i(g)}[F(x_i,x_j)-F(x_i',x_j)]\\ &= \sum_{g_{h,k}=1}F(x_h,x_k)-\sum_{g_{h,k}=1}F(x_h',x_k'),\end{aligned} \tag{12.11}$$

where $g_{h,k}=1$ refers to all links that are present in network $g$. It follows that a potential for the social game is

$$F^*(x|g)=\sum_{g_{h,k}=1}F(x_h,x_k). \tag{12.12}$$

Given network $g$, let $P_g^\gamma$ be the probability transition matrix corresponding to the dynamic process and the log-linear decision rule with $\gamma>0$. We are now ready to state and prove the following result that is taken from Young (1998).

**Proposition 12.6** *Consider a symmetric two-person game with potential function $F$. Let $g$ be an undirected graph. For every $\gamma>0$, the adaptive process $P_g^\gamma$ has the following unique stationary distribution:*

$$\mu_g^\gamma=\frac{e^{\gamma F^*(x|g)}}{\sum_{z\in S}e^{\gamma F^*(z|g)}} \tag{12.13}$$

*and the stochastically stable states of the social game are those that maximize $F^*(x)$.*

The proof of this result is as follows: For simplicity, write $\mu$ instead of $\mu_g^\gamma$ and $P$ instead of $P_g^\gamma$. The detailed balanced condition states

$$\mu(x)P(xy) = \mu(y)P(yx) \text{ for all } x, y \in S. \tag{12.14}$$

Let us begin by showing that $\mu$ satisfies this detailed balance condition. First, observe that $P(xy) > 0$ only if either $x = y$ or $x$ and $y$ differ for exactly one player. Note that any player is chosen with a probability of $1/n$. This means that

$$\mu(x)P(xy) = \frac{1}{n}\left[\frac{\exp(\gamma F^*(x))}{\sum_{z\in S}\exp(\gamma F^*(z))}\right] \times \left[\frac{\exp(\gamma \sum_{j\in N_i}\pi_i(y_i, x_j))}{\sum_{z_i\in S_i}\exp(\gamma \sum_{j\in N_i}\pi_i(z_i, x_j))}\right]. \tag{12.15}$$

Define

$$\lambda = \frac{1}{n}\left[\frac{1}{\sum_{z\in S}\exp(\gamma F^*(z))}\right]\left[\frac{1}{\sum_{z_i\in S_i}\exp(\gamma \sum_{j\in N_i}\pi_i(z_i, x_j))}\right]. \tag{12.16}$$

This allows us to rewrite equation (12.15) as

$$\begin{aligned}
\mu(x)P(xy) &= \lambda \exp\left[\gamma[\sum_{g_{h,k}=1} F(x_h, x_k) + \sum_{j\in N_i(g)} \pi_i(y_i, x_j)]\right] \\
&= \lambda \exp\left[\gamma[\sum_{g_{h,k}=1} F(x_h, x_k) + \sum_{j\in N_i(g)} [\pi_i(x_i, x_j) - F(x_i, x_j) + F(y_i, x_j)]]\right] \\
&= \lambda \exp\left[\gamma[\sum_{g_{h,k}=1} F(y_h, y_k) + \sum_{j\in N_i(g)} \pi_i(x_i, x_j)]\right] \\
&= \mu(y)P(yx).
\end{aligned} \tag{12.17}$$

This proves that $\mu(.)$ satisfies the detailed balanced condition. Given that the detailed balance condition holds, it follows that

$$\sum_{x\in S}\mu(x)P(xy) = \sum_{x\in S}\mu(y)P(yx) = \mu(y)\sum_{x\in S}P(yx) = \mu(y). \tag{12.18}$$

Thus $\mu$ is an invariant distribution, and since the process is irreducible, it is the unique invariant distribution. The claim on stochastically stable states now follows from the behavior of $\mu$ as $\gamma \to \infty$.

Note that there is a potential function in the coordination game: $F(\alpha, \alpha) = a - e$, $F(\alpha, \beta) = F(\beta, \alpha) = 0$, and $F(\beta, \beta) = b - d$. Next, define $w_\alpha(x)$ ($w_\beta(x)$) as the total number of player-pairs who choose $\alpha$ ($\beta$) in profile $x$. Then it follows that the probability of profile $x$

in the invariant distribution $\mu(x)$ is proportional to $e^{(a-e)w_\alpha+(b-d)w_\beta}$. If $\alpha$ is risk dominant, then $a-e>b-d$, and it follows that $\mu(.)$ places all probability mass on the state in which everyone chooses the risk-dominant action. ■

Potential functions can be used to study games on networks more generally; the interested reader is referred to Bramoullé, Kranton, and D'Amours (2014) and Bramoullé and Kranton (2016).

### 12.6.2 Thresholds, Networks, and Common Knowledge

In the models so far, we have been concerned with coordination problems played on networks and in which individuals earn payoffs out of interactions that occur locally on links in a network. In this section, we very briefly touch upon a rather different class of situations: let us suppose that people are aware that a demonstration against the government is being planned for tomorrow. If a large number of people show up, then the protest will be successful (e.g., the government may be forced to change its stance) and everyone in society—including the demonstrators—will benefit. But if only a few people show up, then the demonstrators may be dispersed or arrested, and it would have been better not to turn up for the protest. This is an example of a situation in which benefits from an action are contingent on how many others do likewise. It is therefore reminiscent of the examples considered in chapter 8. However, there is an added layer of difficulty: there may not be enough time to collect information on how many people are planning to turn up, so individuals may have to make decisions based on knowledge gathered over time from their existing social networks. Alternatively, the collective action may be an uprising against a repressive regime, so individuals can only trust their immediate neighbors with any information.

We would like to understand what features of a network facilitate the organization of such collective actions. Our discussion outlines a model of collective action of thresholds in networks that draws on the work of Chwe (2000) and Granovetter (1978). The exposition in this section draws on Easley and Kleinberg (2010).

Suppose that everyone knows about an upcoming protest against the government. Individuals differ in their willingness to take a risk that is captured by a threshold: a threshold of 4, for instance, means that this person will show up if for the protest if they are sure that at least 4 people (including this person) will show up. These individuals are located in a network. A link in this network indicates that the two connected individuals know each other's threshold. Therefore, every person knows the thresholds of all their neighbors in the network. Who will turn up for the Protest, and who will stay at home? Will a protest take place if there are enough people with thresholds that support it?

Next, we will discuss some examples of small networks to address these points. Let us assume that everyone knows the social network. Consider the network given in figure 12.11(a). Suppose that $w$ would join the protest only if at least 4 people (in all) do. Since there are only 3 people in total, this means $w$ will never turn up for the protest. Node $v$ has a threshold of 3. They know that $w$'s threshold is 4, so they know that $w$ will not turn up. Since $v$ requires 3 people in order to be willing to join, $v$ knows that there will not be enough

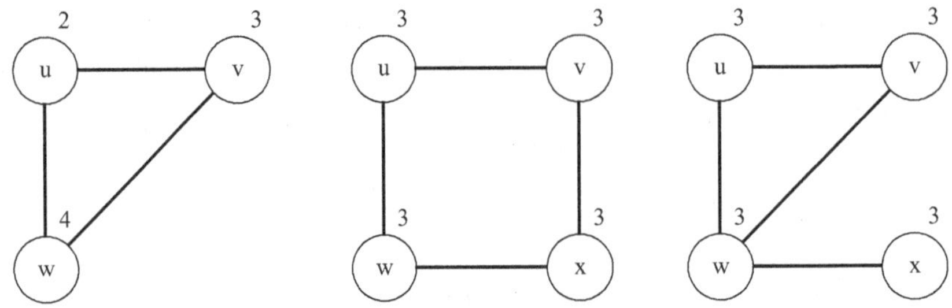


(a) Three-player network (b) Circle (c) Network with clique

**Figure 12.11**
Thresholds, networks, and protest. *Source*: Easley and Kleinberg (2010).

people joining the protest, and so $v$ will not turn up either. Finally, $u$ only requires 2 people to participate, but they know the thresholds of both $w$ and $v$ and know that no one else will join. Hence, $u$ also will not join.

We next take up a slightly more interesting network, as in figure 12.11(b). Let us consider the situation from $u$'s perspective; suppose that $u$'s threshold is $x$. They know that $v$ and $w$ each have a threshold of 3, and that $u$, $v$, and $w$ will individually feel safe taking part in a protest that contained all three of them. However, as they know the network, they can infer that $v$ and $w$ do not know each other's thresholds. This means that they are not sure that enough people are going to turn up for the protest, so they will not choose to protest either. How about $u$? Observe that in this network, $u$ does not know $x$'s threshold: it could be very high, like 5. In that case, node $v$, seeing neighbors with 3 and a high threshold like 5, would not join the protest. The case is similar for $w$. So if $u$ joined the protest, they would be the only one. Therefore, it is not safe for $u$ to join. As $u$'s situation is the same as for all four nodes, it follows that no protest will happen. Observe that in this example, every node knows that there are three nodes with thresholds of 3, and this number is enough for a protest to form. But each of the nodes holds back from joining the protest because it cannot be sure that the other nodes know this fact.

Things would turn out very differently if the link from $v$ to $x$ were moved and connected $v$ and $w$ instead. This yields the network shown in figure 12.11(c). In this new network, observe that each of $u$, $v$, and $w$ knows that there are three nodes with threshold 3, and each of them also knows that each of the others knows this fact, and so forth. In other words, this fact is common knowledge among the three of them. This suffices for them to have the confidence to choose the protest action.

This simple example points to a general insight: for a given set of individuals with protest thresholds that are compatible for a protest to actually go on, the network that connects them must have the ability to generate common knowledge about this fact. In the example we have explored here, we have shown that the clique structure among individuals with appropriate thresholds is useful in generating common knowledge. This logic can be extended to the case

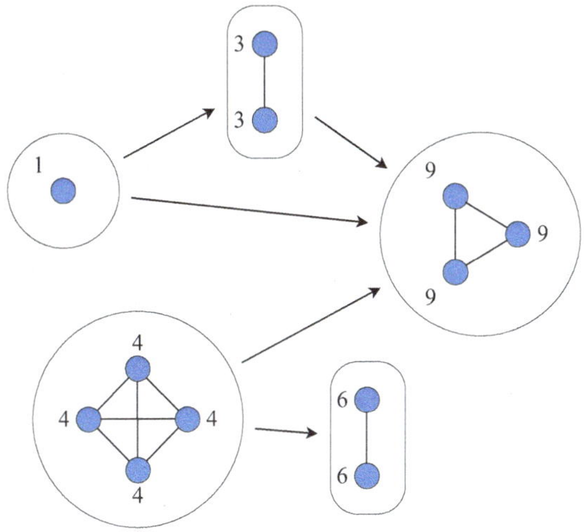


**Figure 12.12**
Hierarchy of cliques. *Source*: Chwe (2000).

of individuals with different thresholds: these groups of individuals with different thresholds can be located in a hierarchy of cliques where the smallest thresholds are at the top of the hierarchy.

Figure 12.12 presents an example of such a network. In this network, there are individuals with thresholds 1, 3, 4, 6, and 9. The two individuals with a threshold, 3 are connected to each other and commonly observe an individual with a threshold, thereby establishing common knowledge of 3 individuals with 3 or fewer thresholds. The 4 individuals with threshold 4 constitute a clique among themselves; similarly, the two individuals with threshold 6 observe each other and commonly observe all the individuals with threshold 4, thereby ensuring common knowledge that 6 individuals have the appropriate threshold. Finally, the three individuals with threshold 9 are connected to each other, and in addition, they commonly observe all individuals with thresholds 1, 3, and 4, thereby establishing common knowledge that at least 9 individuals have a threshold of 9 or lower.

The reader may recall that overlapping neighborhoods were also a factor in coordination on the risky action in the study of games in networks in chapter 4. For further elaborations on this connection between networks, common knowledge, and real-world illustrations, see Chwe (2000).

## 12.7 Reading Notes

The literature on coordination problems goes back a long way. One may reason from introspection and seek to arrive at a solution. In this spirit, Thomas Schelling offers an excellent introduction to the notion of focal points as a solution to the coordination problem in his book *The Strategy of Conflict* (Schelling [1960]). The idea of a risk-dominant action comes from Harsanyi and Selten (1988). For recent work in this tradition, see Bacharach (1999) and Sugden (2004). David Lewis offers a philosopher's perspective on how conventions help resolve problems of social coordination in his book *Convention: A Philosophical Study* (Lewis [1969]). The dynamics of choice offer an alternative perspective in which societies solve coordination problems through the gradual accumulation of precedent. In his book *The Civilizing Process*, Norbert Elias (1978) offers an early historical and conceptual contribution on this subject. For a more recent theoretical perspective on the evolution of conventions, see the book *Individual Strategy and Social Structure* (Young [1998]). The study of coordination equilibrium in networks remains an active field of study in economics. For a survey, see Vega-Redondo (2016). For recent research, see Jackson and Storms (2019), Galeotti, Golub, Goyal et al. (2021), and Leister, Zenou, and Zhou (2022).

The study of coordination games on networks has been an active field of study for close to three decades. Blume (1993) and Ellison (1993) introduced the study of binary-action coordination problems among players located on simple networks (like the cycle and lattices). The exposition in sections 12.2 and 12.3 draws on Goyal (2007). The section focuses on the static problem of coordination. A number of authors have explored dynamics of learning and coordination, and some of this work studies the role of network structure.

Blume (1993) studied coordination games on lattices and showed convergence of behavior to the risk-dominant action. An early result on the convergence of dynamics to a Nash equilibrium in regular networks (where every player has the same number of neighbors) is presented in Anderlini and Ianni (1996). Ellison (1993) showed that local interaction has implications for the speed of convergence—specifically, that local interaction among neighbors on a cycle facilitates faster convergence than for random (or global) interactions. Cassar (2007) provides evidence for faster convergence under local interactions. On the issue of equilibrium selection (Pareto-dominant versus risk-dominant equilibrium), Blume (1993) and Ellison (1993) show that learning dynamics under local interaction lead to the risk-dominant outcome. In a slightly different vein, Berninghaus, Ehrhart, and Keser (2002) and Cassar (2007) present experimental evidence that local interaction with high clustering—as in the small-world network of Watts and Strogatz (1998)—leads to the Pareto-dominant outcome.

The material on the introduction of a new norm in a society with existing norms in section 4 is taken from Goyal (1996) and Morris (2000); our exposition draws on exposition on Easley and Kleinberg (2010). The introduction and diffusion of new conventions and social norms is a central feature of the process of economic development. Chapter 17 further examines the issue of how network structure affects the adoption of new activities. In that chapter we also comment on the changes in the social network as part of the process of economic development.

The existence of multiple strict Nash equilibria in simple games of coordination has motivated a very large body of literature that explores equilibrium selection/refinement criteria.

One strand of this work that has been very fruitful examines the role of perturbations (trials or experiments). A number of models of experiments have been proposed. In this chapter, we discussed stochastic stability at some length. The notion of stochastic stability was introduced by Foster and Young (1990), Kandori, Mailath, and Rob (1993), and Young (1993). The basic model of stochastic stability says that experiments are made independent of the costs. This assumption has been explored by a number of authors.

Following Blume (1993) and Young (1998), we present one possible elaboration on this formulation—the log-linear best response—in which the probability of experiments declines exponentially in the payoff losses. We show that the log-linear best-response rule has a powerful implication: players select the risk-dominant equilibrium in all networks. As the proof uses the notion of potential functions, a concept of wider interest in the study of games on networks, we present the formal definitions and the details of the proof. The material is more advanced and it is presented in the appendix.

We mention one other rule here to further draw out the importance of decision rules for the dynamics and the selection of equilibrium. This is the imitate the best payoff action. Robson and Vega-Redondo (1996) study this rule in the context of social coordination games and show that, taken with random matching, it leads to the efficient action being the unique, stochastically stable action. The study of imitation dynamics in a model with local interaction and suitable informational constraints appears to be an open problem.

The discussion of coordination games in networks suggests that the interaction structure has important effects on social coordination. These networks of interaction evolve over time as individuals reconfigure their network. We present a theoretical model in which individuals choose links and an action in the coordination game. This framework draws on the work of Goyal and Vega-Redondo (2005), Jackson and Watts (2002b), and Gilles and Johnson (2000). The minimum effort game (also referred to as the "weakest-link game") allows a more general treatment of risk versus efficiency, and it has been the subject of extensive study; important contributions include Van Huyck, Battalio, and Beil (1990); Crawford (1995); and Weber (2006); for an overview of the literature, see Riedl, Rohde, and Strobel (2016). Experiments on the weakest-link game show that as group size grows subjects tend toward the minimum effort equilibrium. We discuss the recent work of Riedl, Rohde, and Strobel (2016) that shows how endogenous linking can dramatically alter subject behavior leading them to select the efficient equilibrium.

The final part of the chapter takes up the study of coordination problems in a setting where individuals differ in their preferred equilibrium. The study of identity, tastes, and its impact on coordination is spread across several disciplines. The dynamics of how preferences on neighborhoods can give rise to sharp patterns of segregation were highlighted by Thomas Schelling in his influential work *Micromotives and Macrobehavior* (Schelling 2006). For a general introduction to contemporary debates surrounding identity, see Fukuyama (2018). For an introduction to the study of identity in economics, see Akerlof and Kranton (2000).

Game theory offers us a natural formulation of coordination games with conflicting preferences: the Battle of the Sexes game. The chapter presents this game and discusses how network structure can affect social coordination. Section 12.6 draws on the work of Advani and Reich (2015); Kearns, Judd, Tan, and Wortman (2009); and Goyal, Hernández, Martínez-Cánovas, et al. (2021). In a closely related paper, Kearns, Judd, and Vorobeychik (2012) study endogenous linking in a game of voting with biased voters. In this game, players must coordinate on the *same* vote to earn a payoff. They find that with endogenous linking, subjects form rich networks but fail to reach coordination. This finding is consistent with those of the experiment in Goyal et al. (2021) that are presented in section 12.5.1 There is a strand of research that studies coordination in a network when individuals have heterogeneous preferences, see e.g., Calvo-Armengol, de Marti, and Prat (2011), Galeotti, Golub, Goyal et al. (2021), and Genicot (2022).

The study of thresholds in social action has a distinguished history, for early contributions see Granovetter (1978) and Schelling (2006). We presented a model taken from Chwe (2000), in which social structure serves to locally communicate the thresholds of individuals. The role of communication networks in facilitating protest movements has been highlighted in the context of the Arab Spring movement; see, for example, the discussion in Acemoglu, Hassan, and Tahoun (2018).

## 12.8 Questions

1. Discuss the relation between the $q-core$ of a network (discussed in chapter 4) and a *p-cohesive* set of nodes in a network (as discussed in this chapter).
2. Consider the stochastic block model of random graphs discussed in chapter 2. Suppose there are $n$ individuals and $m$ groups, with $n \geq m$. The probability of a link between nodes of the same group is $p_s$ and the probability of a link across groups is $p_d$, with $p_s > p_d$. Relate the parameters of linking $p_s$ and $p_d$ to the concept of cohesiveness in networks.
3. Consider the model of myopic best-response dynamics studied in this chapter. Suppose that the network is as in figure 12.13. At the start, everyone is choosing action $B$. Suppose that every node has threshold $q=2/5$ for switching to action $A$. Now, let $e$ and $f$ and $k$ form a three-node set $S$ that initially chooses action $A$.
   (a) Which other nodes will eventually switch to A?
   (b) Find a subset of nodes outside $S$ that blocks behavior A from spreading to all nodes.
   (c) Suppose that we can add one node to the set $S$ of initial adopters. Is it possible to do it in a such a way that the new four-node set causes a cascade at threshold $q=2/5$?
4. (From Goyal and Janssen [1997]). In some contexts, we can choose a flexible option in addition to the two actions, A and B. We can learn two languages or carry two credit cards. Someone who is flexible can effectively engage with individuals who choose either

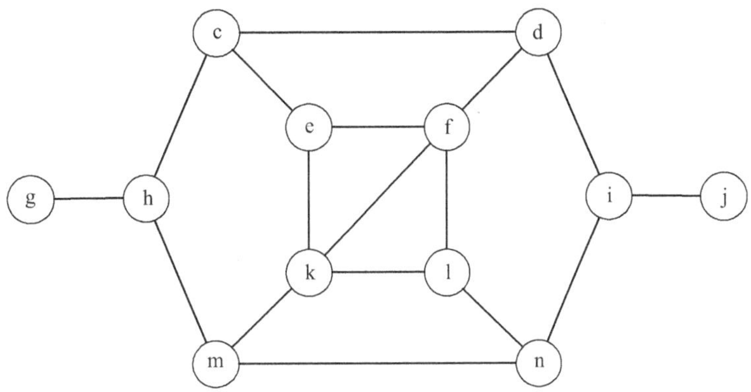


**Figure 12.13**
Network example.

**Table 12.3**
Coordination game with flexible action

| 1 \ 2 | $A$ | $B$ | $B$ |
|---|---|---|---|
| $A$ | $a, a$ | $d, e$ | $a, a-c$ |
| $B$ | $e, d$ | $b, b$ | $b, b-c$ |
| $(A, B)$ | $a-c, a$ | $b-c, b$ | $a-c, a-c$ |

of the two actions. Suppose that the cost of choosing the flexible action is $c > 0$. Then the matrix of payoffs with actions $A$, $B$ and $(A, B)$ can be written as in table 12.3: where $a > d$; $b > d$; $d > e$; $a + d > b + e$; $a < b$; $a > c > 0$.

(a) Compute the Nash equilibrium of this two-person game.

(b) Suppose that there are $n$ players located around a circle. Every player interacts with one neighbor on either side. Payoffs of a player are the sum of earnings from the games with the two neighbors. Describe some of the Nash equilibria of this local interaction game.

(c) Suppose for simplicity that there is a continuum of agents that are located around a cycle network. Players interact with neighbors the size of which is a variable of interest. Suppose that at the start there is an interval of players who choose $A$ and rest of the players choose $B$. What are the conditions under which the dynamics will lead to efficient action and inefficient action taking over the entire population?

(d) Develop examples of networks in which the flexible action is played in equilibrium.

(e) Use the theoretical analysis in this section to comment on the sustainability of bilingual states.

5. Consider the static game of linking and coordination games, studied in section 12.4.2. Assume that $a > b; b > d; a + d < b + e$. Show that the following hold.
   (a) If $c < min\{e, b\}$, then an equilibrium network is complete.
   (b) If $e < c < b$, then an equilibrium network is either complete or can be partitioned into two complete components.
   (c) If $b < c < a$, then an equilibrium network is either empty or complete.
   (d) If $c > a$, then the unique equilibrium network is empty.

   Describe the action profiles that correspond to these networks.
6. Consider the two-stage game of linking and actions in the coordination game studied in section 12.5.2. Show that if $k < \beta$, then a complete network with everyone coordinating on the majority's preferred action maximizes the sum of individual utilities.
7. Consider the two-stage game of linking and actions in the coordination game studied in section 12.5.2. Suppose there are 15 players and 8 players prefer "up," while 7 players prefer "down." Assume that coordinating on preferred action brings 6, coordinating on the less preferred action brings 4. Mis-coordination payoff is set equal to 0. The cost of link, $k$, is set equal to 2. Describe the pairwise stable outcomes of this game.

# 13 Communication and Social Learning

## 13.1 Introduction

> In these democratic days, any investigation into the trustworthiness and peculiarities of popular judgements is of interest. The material about to be discussed refers to a small matter, but it is much to the point.
> —Galton (1907, pp. 450–451).

In his piece *Voice of the People*, Francis Galton (1907) discusses the merits of estimating the weight of an ox by asking individuals. Eight hundred persons submitted a guess, and the guesses ranged from 1,074 (5th percentile) to a bit over 1,293 pounds (95th percentile). The median guess was 1,207, while the correct weight was 1,198 pounds. The median weight was thus less than 1 percent off the correct weight, and Galton also found that more than 50 percent of the guesses lay within roughly 3 percent of the true weight. This competition gives us a first feel for the so-called wisdom of the crowd: individuals typically hold a variety of views that reflect their experiences and expertise. However, if we were to take an average of their opinions—by identifying the median or the mean—then we could arrive at something close to the truth.

A century or so later, democratic politics has become more common across the world, and as the scale of social media has grown, our opinions and beliefs matter for an ever-widening range of subjects. For instance, we decide on whom to hire, where to work, which computer or car to buy, what to eat to remain healthy, which fruits or vegetables to plant, what combination of inputs to use to grow a crop, where to go for a vacation, how real global warming is, and if it is real, what should be done about it. New goods, services, and new ideas are regularly being added to existing options. In this world of change and expanding choices, we try to inform ourselves of the available alternatives and then make decisions. As there are often many aspects of these decisions and it is costly to invest time and effort into making them, we necessarily seek the opinions and thoughts of others. The sharing of information via mass media and personal interaction is therefore a central feature of day-to-day life. This chapter studies the role of patterns of communication in shaping individual opinions and behaviors.

To set the stage, we begin by presenting a number of case studies on opinions and choices and the role of social interaction. These case studies cover empirical contexts ranging across medicine, agriculture, climate change, fishing, and domestic and international politics. Taken along with our discussions of social networks and communication in chapters 1 and 11, they motivate an inquiry into general principles that govern social influence in networks of communication.

Here, we lay out a theoretical framework in which individuals carry out activities that generate information, and then they share this information with others. The information sharing shapes opinions, and these opinions then lead to new actions that generate new information, and so forth. Our goal is to understand how the information-sharing connections among individuals affect the generation and flow of information. This allows us to understand the circumstances under which information is adequately generated and successfully aggregated and the determinants of the rate at which this aggregation takes place. Motivated by the case study of Twitter in chapter 1 and the case studies in this chapter, we devote special attention in our theoretical studies to networks with unequal connections and to the role of homophily.

We explore models with fully rational individuals as well as bounded rational individuals. It turns out that on some of the fundamental questions (such as whether opinions converge and whether they are correct), the theoretical predictions of a fully rational and a bounded rational model are similar. But there are questions on which a bounded rational approach—as epitomized in the DeGroot model—allows us to obtain more complete answers. For instance, take the question of the wisdom of crowds: when is a large group going to have correct beliefs and choose the right actions? The (fully rational) Bayesian model helps us develop the intuition that influential individuals may interfere with information aggregation and social learning and offers sufficient conditions on networks to obtain a correct consensus. The DeGroot model yields a complete answer to this question: a large group of individuals learns the truth if and only if there are no overly influential individuals in it. In other words, the absence of influential individuals is both necessary and sufficient for the wisdom of crowds to manifest. Similarly, concerning the role of homophily, the Bayesian model provides examples with a diversity of beliefs and choices, while the DeGroot model shows that homophily slows learning, which sustains the diversity of opinions for much longer. Section 13.5 presents experimental evidence that offers support for these theoretical predictions on the role of network inequality and homophily.

In the models in sections 13.3–13.5, individuals embedded in social networks learn by observing their neighbors: in these models, the neighbors themselves do not make choices about whether to share information. The spread of misinformation on social media draws attention to the motivations and the choices of individuals with regard to verification and the sharing of information in social networks. Section 13.6 studies the incentives of individuals to verify information before sharing it in social networks. A supplementary materials section at the end of the chapter presents the sequential choice model of learning and also presents an experiment on the effects of networks on learning.

## 13.2 Evidence about Social Influence

This section starts with a discussion of the classical early studies on social influence carried out by sociologists in the period between 1940 and 1965. It then presents studies on innovation in agriculture, followed by a discussion of the role of social influence in shaping views and behaviors concerning climate change and the environment.

### 13.2.1 Early Studies

In the early twentieth century, with the coming of radio, television, and newspapers, it was believed that the views and decisions of individuals would be largely shaped by mass media. In *People's Choice*, Lazarsfeld, Berelson, and Gaudet (1948) studied the determinants of voting behavior in the American presidential election of 1940 in the small Midwest town of Erie, Ohio. The study involved repeated interviews of a sample of 2,400 voters from May to October 1940. It showed that individual voters identified personal interactions and specific individuals as critical to a change in how they voted.

Building on this study, in a subsequent book called *Personal Influence*, Katz and Lazarsfeld (1966) studied marketing, fashion, film viewing, and public affairs. They conducted a survey of 800 female residents of Decatur, Illinois, in 1945–1946. In this survey, they identified a fraction of their sample as potential "opinion leaders"—these individuals were instrumental in the respondents changing their opinions and their choices. This work also highlighted another feature of the nature of social influence—the opinion leaders are "not a group apart"; opinion leadership is not a trait possessed by some and not by others. Rather, opinion leaders are scattered across the various strata of society—and the leadership arises from day-to-day personal relationships.

The spread of modern medicines is a major factor in explaining the remarkable improvements in the longevity and quality of human life over the past hundred years. There is considerable uncertainty on the effectiveness of a drug or a new treatment when it is first introduced. Thus information about the efficacy of the treatment is vital to facilitating its adoption. An early study on medical innovation pertains to the adoption of the antibiotic tetracycline in four Midwestern towns of the US in the 1950s. Coleman, Katz, and Menzel (1966) examine the timing of the first prescription of the drug by a physician. The timing ranged widely—some doctors adopted within the first four months, while many others had not adopted the drug even after a year.

In this study, physicians were asked to complete a survey with questions concerning their personal characteristics and social contacts. A total of 125 general practitioners, internists, and pediatricians were studied—they constituted 85 percent of the doctors in these fields practising in the four towns. The doctors were asked three questions: To whom did they most often turn for advice and information? With whom did they most often discuss their cases in the course of an ordinary week? Who were the friends, among their colleagues, whom they saw most often socially? Physicians could nominate up to 3 doctors in response to each of these questions.

The main finding was that there is a positive correlation between the number of social connections and the speed of adoption. Consider the 36 doctors who were mentioned as friends by no one: at the 6-month point, only 30 percent of them had prescribed the drug; and at the 8-month point, only 42 percent of these doctors had prescribed the drug. By contrast, consider the 33 doctors who were mentioned as friends by 3 or more other doctors: at the 6-month point, 70 percent of them had prescribed the drug, and by the 8-month point, over 91 percent of these doctors had prescribed the drug.

### 13.2.2 Innovation in Agriculture

The adoption of new technologies is central to change in agriculture and the process of economic development. For a new technology to be adopted by a farmer, its fit with the local circumstances must be understood. This usually calls for experimentation with various input combinations. As neighboring farmers face similar circumstances, it is natural that they should learn from each other's experiences. Next, we present two studies that document the importance of this type of social learning.

*High-Yielding Variety (HYV) Seeds in India, 1960s:* Foster and Rosenzweig (1995) collect data on 4,118 households for the crop years 1968–1969, 1969–1970, and 1970–1971. This data covered information on areas planted with new, high-yielding seed varieties (of wheat and rice). Farmers' adoption of HYVs occurred at an accelerated rate over this 3-year period: consider villages where there was some adoption of HYV seeds by 1970: in this set of villages, only 19 percent were using HYV seeds by 1968, 29 percent by 1969, and 42 percent by 1970. Moreover, among farmers using HYV seeds in the 1970–1971 crop year, acreage under HYV seeds grew from only 4 percent of cultivated land in the 1968–1969 crop year to over 20 percent in 1970–1971.

The main finding was that imperfect information about the appropriate input combination was a key obstacle to the adoption of HYV seeds. In particular, they found that farmers with experienced neighbors were significantly more profitable and devoted more of their land to new technologies than those with inexperienced neighbors.

*Pineapple in Ghana in the 1990s:* In this period, an established system of maize and cassava intercropping was transformed into intensive production of pineapple for export to European markets. The interest here is in how farmers learned their appropriate level of input use.

Conley and Udry (2010) collect data in three villages of southern Ghana for the 1996–1998 period. In the sample villages, pineapple was grown by less than 10 percent of farmers in 1990 and by over 46 percent of farmers in 1997. In all, 180 households were drawn from a population of 550 households. The focus was on 132 farmers who cultivated pineapple on a total of 406 plots. Of these plots, 288 were planted during the survey period, and the study focuses on the determinants of 113 observed changes in fertilizer use.

The information network of every farmer was plotted; spatial proximity was a contributing factor to information links, but farmers often held ties with farmers farther away too. A farmer used their own experience with inputs and profits and combined it with the experience of their information neighbors to decide on input use in subsequent periods.

The main finding was that changes in fertilizer use by a farmer were affected by the experience of their information neighbors—if the experience of neighbors using the same fertilizer mix was negative, that led to a change in the farmer's behavior. Moreover, the responsiveness to news in the information neighborhood was inversely related to the level of their own experience: veteran pineapple farmers responded less to news from their neighbors than novice farmers.

### 13.2.3 Climate Change and Environment

We now present studies on the role of social networks in shaping beliefs about climate change and fishing behaviors.

*Opinions on Climate Change:* There is robust evidence that temperature has increased over the past hundred years, and there is wide agreement among scientists that human activity has played an important role in bringing about this increase. Yet there are significant differences in popular opinion on both issues. In a 2019 Pew survey of Americans, one-half of those surveyed believed that human activity contributes a great deal to climate change, 30 percent felt that it plays some role in climate change, and 20 percent believed that it plays no role at all in climate change (Funk and Hefferon [2019]). These differences were strongly correlated with the political positions of the respondents. For instance, among liberal Democrats, 84 percent felt that human activity contributes a great deal to climate change, while among conservative Republicans, only 14 percent felt that way.

*Fishing and Sharks:* Hawaii's longline fishery is a limited-entry industry supplying domestic and international markets with fresh tuna and swordfish. It is the largest commercial fishing sector in the Hawaiian islands. From 2008 to 2012, there were 122–129 active vessels that completed between 1,205 and 1,381 annual fishing trips. They generated revenues of $65 to $94 million per year. A major concern for these fisheries is that they encounter sharks while fishing for tuna and swordfish. This can lead to the capture of a species of sharks that is under threat.

Barnes, Lynham, Kalberg, and Leung (2016) collect data on the social network among fishers and how that related to the number of sharks captured. The fisher group is composed of three distinct ethnic groups: Vietnamese Americans (VA), European Americans (EA), and Korean Americans (KA). The social network of fishers (i.e., who shares information

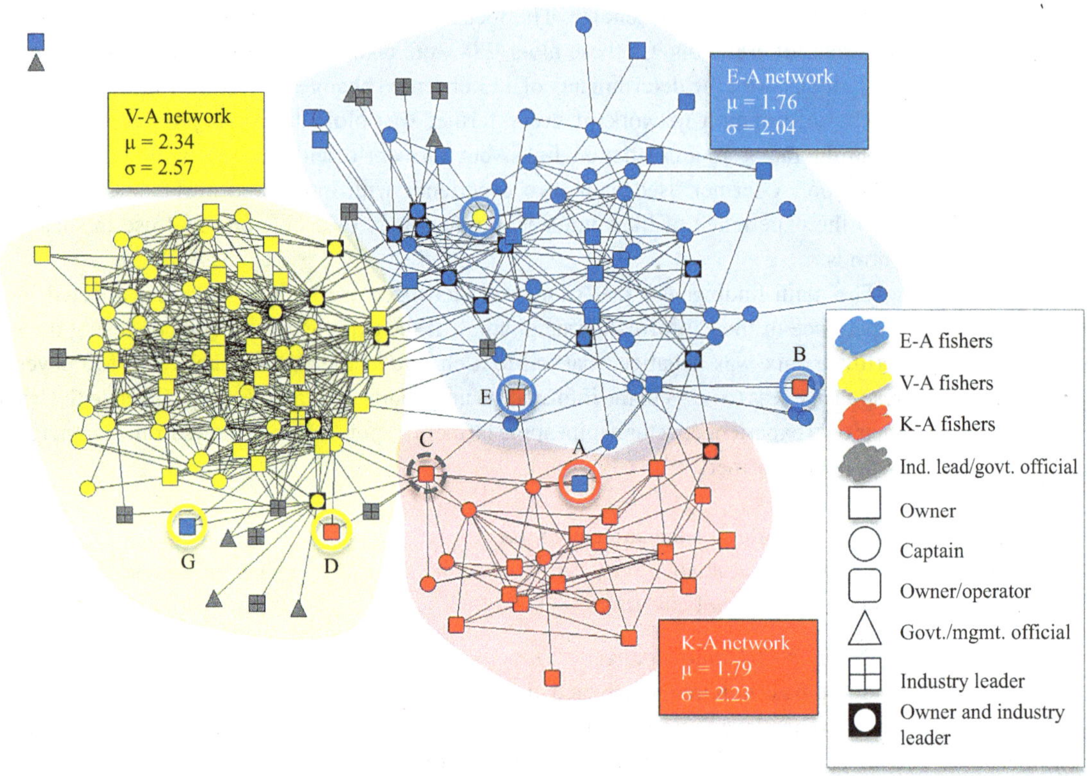


**Figure 13.1**
Social networks and sharks bycatch. Each node corresponds to an individual fisher color, coded by ethnicity or an actor deemed important for information sharing by respondents (i.e., industry leader, government, or management official). Information-sharing groups are delimited by color. Two isolates not connected to anyone are located in the upper-left corner. Circled nodes denote outliers. Those with solid lines represent fishers who have a majority of ties outside their ethnic group, with the color of the circle corresponding to the group with which they have a majority of ties. Those with gray dashed lines denote nodes with an equal proportion of ties both within and outside their ethnic group. Courtesy of Michele L. Barnes.

with whom) exhibits strong homophily: fishers organize themselves into three distinct communities, which overlap strongly with ethnicity. Out of 159 fishers, only 6 have a majority of ties outside their ethnic group, while 1 has an equal proportion of intraethnic and interethnic group ties. We will refer to these 6 as outliers. The network is shown in figure 13.1, which reports mean ($\mu$) and standard deviations ($\sigma$) in shark bycatch (per 1,000 hooks) in Hawaii's tuna fishery for 2008–2012: there is a big difference across the three communities.

To examine the role of networks, the authors focus on the behaviors of the outliers whose connections span groups with very different rates of shark bycatch. They find that the behaviors of these outliers are closer to the behaviors of their respective information neighborhoods than with their own ethnic group. The effect of information networks can be very large: if, for instance, the three ethnic communities were to catch sharks at the same rate as the EA ethnic group, then roughly 46,339 sharks might have been avoided (leading to a 12 percent reduction in overall shark bycatch for Hawaii).

### 13.2.4 Domestic and International Politics

*Weapons of Mass Destruction (WMD) in Iraq:* The case for the invasion of Iraq in 2003 centered on the argument that Saddam Hussein's regime had WMD and that this posed a threat to regional stability and international peace. In a poll conducted in October 2004, Americans held very different views on this issue: 47 percent of Republican respondents believed that Iraq had WMD, while only 9 percent of Democrats thought so. Over a year later, a poll conducted in March 2006 found that, in spite of new information and the passage of time, the percentages had barely changed: the numbers stood at 41 percent for Republicans and 7 percent for Democrats (see Golub and Jackson [2012] and "Iraq: The Separate Realities of Republicans and Democrats," available from the World Public Opinion webpage, www.worldpublicopinion.org).

*2020 US Presidential Election:* The US President is elected based on votes of an electoral college. The electoral college brings together individual states. The winner of a state gets all the electoral votes of that state. A candidate may win a state with a small margin (less than 10,000) votes. Thus the number of electoral votes a candidate secures could in principle be at variance with the size of the popular vote that they get. The 2020 election was between Joseph Biden, the Democratic candidate, and Donald Trump, the incumbent Republican president. Biden won the election by a margin of over 7 million votes. US federal and state officials have repeatedly said that they have no evidence that votes were compromised during this election. In the period since the election, a number of legal challenges were filed against the result, all of which were rejected by the courts. Next, we discuss the popular opinion on two issues: (1) whether the election was fair, and (2) whether Biden was the legitimate winner. We draw on two polls conducted by Reuter/Ipsos in November 2020 and in May 2021 (https://www.ipsos.com/).

The poll conducted in November 2020 surveyed a nationally representative sample of 1,346 American adults (including 598 Democrats, 496 Republicans, and 149 independents). The poll found that 28 percent of Americans in total and 59 percent of Republicans believed that Donald Trump had won the election. More than six months after the election and after the many court decisions had been handed down, little had changed. In a poll conducted in May 2021 with a sample of 2,007 adults (909 Democrats, 754 Republicans, and 196 independents), 25 percent of all Americans believed that Donald Trump was the winner. Furthermore, there was a big divide on this question across party lines: 53 percent of Republicans and only 3 percent Democrats held this view.

These two studies suggest that differences on factual matters can persist in spite of communication and the accumulation of evidence over time. These differences appear to be highly correlated with the political positions of those surveyed.

The case study on Twitter in chapter 1 drew attention to the extraordinary size of the network and the great inequality in connections across individuals (recall figure 0.5 from the introduction chapter.). The case studies in this section draw attention to the role of social interactions in shaping opinions and behaviors. In the next two sections, we develop theoretical models to explore the role of social communication in shaping social learning and human behavior.

## 13.3 Learning a New Technology

A common theme in these case studies is that individuals have incomplete information on the various available alternatives. A second feature of some of the case studies—such as innovation in agriculture—is that individuals may be able to learn from experience (their own as well as that of their neighbors). This learning has the capacity to shape future actions. These considerations motivate the following model, taken from Bala and Goyal (1998, 2001). The exposition draws on Goyal (2011) and Golub and Sadler (2016).

There is a set of individuals $N = \{1, \ldots, n\}$, with $n \geq 2$, who choose between two actions, $a_0$ and $a_1$. Action $a_0$ may be thought of as a known technology—it yields 1 and 0 with equal probability. Action $a_1$ is the unknown technology—it may be high quality or low quality. If it is high quality, it yields 1 and 0 with probabilities $\pi$ and $1 - \pi$, where $\pi \in (1/2, 1)$. If it is low quality, then it yields 1 or 0, with a probability of $(1 - \pi)$ and $\pi$, respectively. Individuals have a prior belief $\mu_i \in (0, 1)$ that the quality of technology $a_1$ is high.

The expected utility from action $a_0$ is

$$U(a_0, \mu_i) = \frac{1}{2} \cdot 1 + \frac{1}{2} \cdot 0 = \frac{1}{2}. \quad (13.1)$$

For an individual with belief $\mu_i$, the expected utility from action $a_1$ is

$$U(a_1, \mu_i) = \mu_i[\pi 1 + (1 - \pi)0] + (1 - \mu_i)[(1 - \pi)1 + \pi 0] = 2\pi\mu_i - \mu_i - \pi + 1. \quad (13.2)$$

An individual who seeks to maximize utility will choose the new technology, $a_1$ if $\mu_i > 1/2$ and action $a_0$ if $\mu_i < 1/2$.

We now consider the individual learning problem. Suppose that an individual chooses actions repeatedly. Trials with the known technology $a_0$ do not reveal any new information on its quality or the quality of $a_1$. However, when the individual tries the unknown technology $a_1$, the outcomes yield information about its quality. If the action yields outcome 1, then the individual will update their belief about the quality of the action upward, while if the outcome is 0, than they will lower their belief about the quality of the action. Formally, new information is incorporated through an application of the Bayes theorem. Starting with a belief $\mu_i > 1/2$, suppose that the individual tries action $a_1$ and the outcome is 1. Then the posterior belief that $a_1$ is of high quality is

$$\mu_i'(1) = \frac{\mu_i \pi}{\mu_i \pi + (1-\mu_i)(1-\pi)}. \tag{13.3}$$

On the other hand, if the outcome is 0, the posterior belief is

$$\mu_i'(0) = \frac{\mu_i(1-\pi)}{(\mu_i(1-\pi) + (1-\mu_i)\pi)}. \tag{13.4}$$

As $\pi > 1/2$, $\mu_i'(1) > \mu_i$ and $\mu_i'(0) < \mu_i$: this is the sense in which the experience with action $a_1$ yields information and shapes the evolution of beliefs over time.

We can now consider the learning dynamics if an individual chooses actions repeatedly. Let time be indexed as $t = 1, 2, \ldots$. In period 1, an individual chooses an action that maximizes their payoff for that period, in other words, they choose $a_1$ if $\mu_{i,1} > 1/2$ and $a_0$ if $\mu_{i,1} < 1/2$. More generally, they choose optimal action with respect to the beliefs $\mu_{i,t}$ for $t = 1, 2, \ldots$ At the end of the period, they observe the outcome of their own actions. At the start of the next period, they update the prior $\mu_{i,1}$, and arrive at the belief $\mu_{i,2}$. They then make a decision in period 2, and so forth.

Let us briefly comment on the long-run outcomes of learning. Suppose that an individual starts with an optimistic prior concerning action $a_1$ (i.e., $\mu_{i,1} > 1/2$). A simple computation on equation (13.4) tells us that there is a sequence of 0s that would lead the person to a posterior below the threshold of 1/2. The probability of such a sequence is positive, regardless of whether the action is high or low quality. Hence, the individual will stop trying action $a_1$ with positive probability. Once they stop, they will persist with action $a_o$ forever, as there is no further information revealed by trials with that action. Thus their beliefs dictate choosing $a_o$, and an individual can fail to learn that action $a_1$ is optimal with positive probability.

We now locate this individual in a directed social network in which they can also observe the trials of their neighbors. What are the prospects of learning in a network?

Consider a directed network $g$: a link $g_{ij} \in \{0, 1\}$ represents information access: if $g_{ij} = 1$, then individual $i$ observes the actions and outcomes of the actions of individual $j$. The set of neighbors of individual $i$ is given by $N_i(g) = \{k \in N | g_{ik} = 1\}$; let $\eta_i(g) \equiv |N_i(g)|$ be the *out-degree* of individual $i$. Define $N_{-i}(g) = \{k \in N | g_{ki} = 1\}$ as the individuals who observe $i$; set $\eta_{-i}(g) \equiv |N_{-i}(g)|$ as the *in-degree* of individual $i$.

Figure 13.2 presents examples of information networks (which build on the discussion in chapter 1). In the circle network, every person has a local neighborhood consisting of four individuals. Prominent social networks like Twitter combine two key elements: local neighborhoods (which reflect homophily) and extreme inequality in degree. We accommodate them by moving from a circle network to a network with a *royal family*. This is accomplished as follows: we create a directed link from everyone to six selected individuals. This

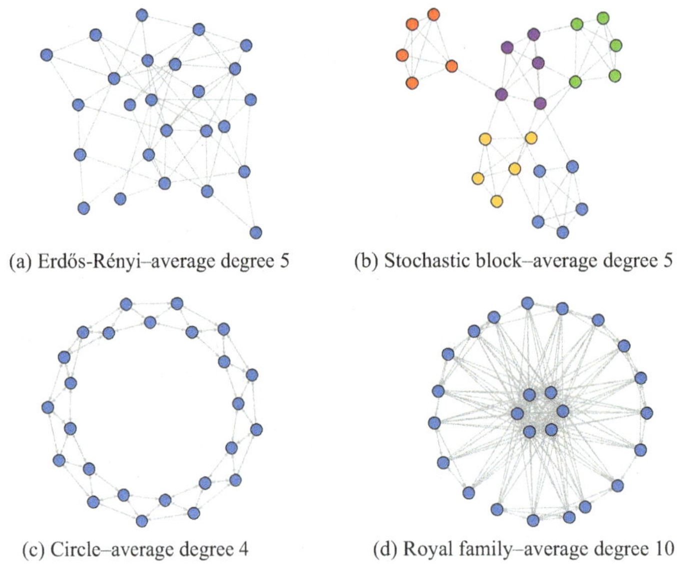


**Figure 13.2**
Simple networks: $n = 25$.

gives rise to a network with essentially two types of individuals: the royal family, each of whose members has $n - 1$ links, and those outside the royal family (with 10 links).

Recall that there is a directed path from $j$ to $i$ in $g$ if $g_{ij} = 1$ or there are distinct players $j_1, \ldots, j_m$ that are different from $i$ and $j$ such that $g_{i,j_1} = g_{j_1,j_2} = \ldots. = g_{j_m,j} = 1$. Network $g$ is said to be *strongly connected* if there is a path between any pair of players $i$ and $j$. All four networks in figure 13.2 are strongly connected.

So an individual $i$ located in network $g$ observes their own actions and their outcomes and the actions and outcomes of their neighbors $N_i(g)$. They use these with the actions to update their beliefs over time.

We note that in principle, the choice of a neighbor reveals something about their priors, and that over time, it may also reveal something about the actions and experiences of the neighbors of their neighbor. So, for instance, if a neighbor, having chosen action $a_0$ for several periods, switches to action $a_1$, this probably means that they have learned something about action $a_1$ by observing their neighbors. For simplicity, we will first assume that an individual makes no inferences from the choice of actions of the neighbors. We then return to the issue of indirect inferences about neighbors of neighbors.

All the ingredients of the learning from the neighbors model are now in place. Next, we will explore the influence of network $g$ on the evolution of individual actions, beliefs, and utilities, $(a_{i,t}, \mu_{i,t}, U_{i,t})_{i \in N}$, over time, $t = 1, 2 \ldots$

### 13.3.1 Information Aggregation

Individual actions are an optimal response to beliefs, which in turn evolve in response to the information generated by actions. Thus the dynamics of actions and beliefs feed back on to each other. Over time, as an individual observes the outcomes of their own actions and the actions and outcomes of neighbors, their beliefs will evolve depending on the particularities of their experience. However, it seems intuitive that as time goes by and their experience grows, additional information should have a smaller and smaller effect on their beliefs about action $a_1$. As actions respond to beliefs, we would expect that as beliefs settle down, so should actions and utilities. Moreover, as an individual observes their neighbors period after period, we would expect that they should be able to do as well as them. Iterating on this improvement principle, we note that individual A should do as well as their neighbors, who do as well as their neighbors. Putting together these points yields the following result on learning and information aggregation.

**Proposition 13.1** *The beliefs, actions, and utilities of individuals converge in the long run. If the society is strongly connected, then every individual chooses the same action and earns the same utility.*

We discuss the arguments underlying this result in general terms now. First, observe that if an individual with belief $\mu_i$ tries action $a_1$, then their expected belief after the action is

$$(\mu_i\pi + (1-\mu_i)(1-\pi))\mu_i'(1) + (\mu_i(1-\pi) + (1-\mu_i)\pi)\mu_i'(0) = \mu_i. \tag{13.5}$$

Equation (13.5) says that the expected posterior belief is equal to the current belief: the beliefs are a martingale. Standard arguments from the theory of martingales tell us that beliefs converge to a limit belief; for an introduction to the study of martingales, see Williams (1991).

Second, consider actions and utilities: an individual's action is optimal with respect to their beliefs. Thus the long-run actions of any individual must be optimal with respect to their long-run beliefs. Someone who observes this individual can in principle imitate this action and therefore earn the same payoff. While this observation is intuitively plausible, we need to be careful in the reasoning: the principal complication is that individual $i$ observes the actions and corresponding outcomes of a neighbor $j$ but does not observe the actions and outcomes of the neighbors of $j$. The claim that $i$ does as well as $j$ if they observe $j$, then, rests on the idea that all payoff-relevant information that $j$ has gathered is implicitly reflected in the choices that they make over time. In particular, if $j$ chooses a certain action in the long run, then this action must be the best action for them, conditional on all their information. However, individual $i$ observes these actions and the corresponding outcomes and therefore can do as well as $j$ simply by imitating $j$.

This improvement via imitation logic extends along paths: in a strongly connected society, every individual has a directed path to every other individual, so it follows that everyone must do as well as everyone else. Thus, all players converge on the same action and earn the same utility. This discussion provides an outline of the arguments underlying the result; a question at the end of the chapter works through the formal details.

### 13.3.2 Learning Optimal Actions

We started our examination of learning in networks with the issue of whether an individual located in a social network will eventually learn the optimal action to take. This section shows that the answer to this question depends on the structure of the network.

To see the role of the network in the simplest setting, suppose that action $a_1$ has a high quality and all individuals start with the prior beliefs $\mu_{i,0} > 1/2$. We will also assume that

$$\min_{i \in N} \mu_{i,1} > \frac{1}{2} \quad \max_{i \in N} \mu_{i,1} < \frac{1}{1+x}, \tag{13.6}$$

where $x = (1-\pi)/\pi \in (0, 1)$. In period 1, everyone tries action $a_1$. Suppose that individuals are located in a Royal Family network, as shown in figure 13.2(d). In this example, every person observes their four local neighbors and the six members of the royal family.

Suppose that every individual in the royal family is unlucky in the first period and gets an outcome of 0. Any individual in the circle can hope to get at most five positive signals from their local neighborhood. Thus any person in this society will have a minimum residual of one negative signal. Given the assumptions about priors, it is easily verified that this negative information is sufficient to push the posteriors below the critical cutoff level of $1/2$. Thus every individual will switch to action $a_0$ in period 2.

Observe that action $a_0$ yields no new information in period 2. So beliefs in period 3 will remain as in period 2. Everyone will choose action $a_0$ in period 3, and this will remain the case for all subsequent periods. Thus the society is locked into the suboptimal action $a_0$ forever. Finally, observe that this argument holds regardless of the size of the society. This example provides one illustration of the breakdown of the wisdom of crowds.

The royal family plays a crucial role in this breakdown of learning. To see this, consider the circle network, in which everyone observes their four immediate neighbors, as in figure 13.2(c). As action $a_1$ is of high quality, from elementary considerations, it follows that if an individual tries this action forever, then there is a set of sample paths with positive probability on which the number of 1s always remains greater than the number of 0s. Similar sequences of actions can be constructed for each of the four neighbors of player $i$. Exploiting the independence of actions across players, it follows that the probability of the five players $\{i-2, i-1, i, i+1, i+2\}$ receiving positive information on average is strictly positive. Let this probability be $q > 0$. Recalling our assumption of the absence of indirect inference from the neighbors of neighbors, we conclude that the experience of individuals outside their neighborhood cannot lower the beliefs of individual $i$ (when the outcomes of the neighbors are uniformly positive). Thus the probability of individual $i$ choosing the suboptimal action $a_0$, in the long run, is bounded from above by $1-q$.

We can construct a similar set of outcomes for individual $i+5$, whose information neighborhood is $\{i+3, i+4, i+5, i+6, i+7\}$. From the independent and identical nature of trials by different individuals, the probability of this sample of paths is also $q > 0$. As individuals $i$ and $i+5$ do not share any neighbors, the two events,

$$\{i \text{ doesn't try optimal action}\}$$

and

$$\{i+5 \text{ doesn't try optimal action}\},$$

are independent. The probability of the joint event

$$\{\text{ neither i nor i} + 5 \text{ try the optimal action}\}$$

is bounded from above by $(1-q)^2$. In a society where the neighborhood is given by $N_i = \{i-2, i-1, i+1, i+2\}$, the probability of learning can be made arbitrarily close to 1 by raising the number of such individuals. In other words, the wisdom of crowds appears in a sufficiently large circle network.

More generally, we can say that two individuals A and B are *locally independent* if their neighborhoods are disjoint (i.e., they share no neighbors in common). Locally independent individuals who start with action $a_1$ all have a positive probability—which is independent—of persisting with that action forever. This argument shows us that in a *large* society, if enough people start by trying action $a_1$, then some of these players will obtain positive results and continue using the optimal action forever. They will thereby gather sufficient information and learn the true quality of this action. Then, from strong connectedness, it follows that they will also ensure that everyone chooses the optimal action in the long run. Our discussion is summarized in the following result.

**Proposition 13.2** *Consider a strongly connected society. The probability that everyone chooses an optimal action in the long run can be made arbitrarily close to 1 by suitably increasing the number of locally independent optimistic players.*

Our discussion provides us an outline of the arguments underlying this result; the details of the proof of the result are developed in a question at the end of the chapter.

### 13.3.3 Homophily

Proposition 13.1 says that in a strongly connected society, all individuals will obtain the same utility. In our baseline model with two actions, there is a unique optimal action in either state of the world. To see the role of homophily in the simplest way, imagine that in addition to $a_o$ and $a_1$, there is an action $a_2$ that can be of a high or low type (with probabilities for outcome 1 given by $\pi$ or $1-\pi$, as for action $a_1$). There are four states of the world corresponding to both $a_1$ and $a_2$ being of high or low quality, and two states corresponding to the case where one is of high quality and the other of low quality. Now we can apply the arguments of proposition 13.1 to infer that in a strongly connected society, all individuals must

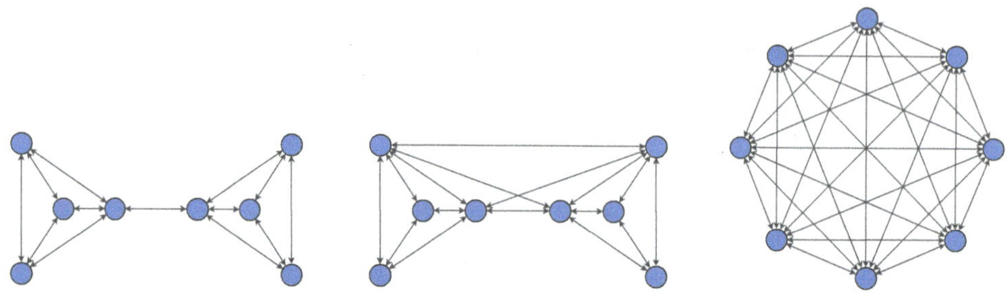

(a) Minimal (b) Intermediate (c) Full

**Figure 13.3**
Levels of integration: $n = 8$.

earn the same utility in the long run. However, in the state where both $a_1$ and $a_2$ are high quality, proposition 13.1 leaves open the possibility that some individuals choose action $a_1$, while others choose action $a_2$. We now examine the role of homophily in this specific situation.

Suppose that all individuals start with the same priors on the true state. Let us consider a society with two communities and vary the level of integration of the communities. Figure 13.3 presents three networks with varying levels of integration: the networks in panels (a) and (b) exhibit imperfect integration (with most individuals linked more within their own group as compared to outside the group), and the network in panel (c) is complete and exhibits full integration. Building in the arguments in the previous section, we can say that it is possible that the 4 individuals on the left start with action $a_1$ and persist with that action forever, while 4 individuals on the right start with action $a_2$, receive positive signals on that action, and persist with that action forever. Crucially, the bridge agents that connect the two communities are more exposed to their own groups and therefore persist with the group's action. Thus it is the selective exposure of individuals to information that sustains diversity of actions in the long run. In the complete network, everyone receives the same information and therefore must choose the same action (here, we are abstracting from the case of indifference). The formal details of the proof of this result are outside the scope of this chapter; the interested reader is urged to consult Bala and Goyal (2001).

### 13.3.4 Variations on the Model

In the model described previously, we assumed that individuals do not make inferences from the choice of actions of their neighbors about the information that the neighbors are accessing from their own neighbors. This places a restriction on the rationality of individuals. It is possible to relax this assumption. A rich strand of recent research explores the implications of networks when individuals are fully rational. We consider a model originally proposed by Gale and Kariv (2003) and that has been subsequently studied by a number of authors, including Mossel, Sly, and Tamuz (2014, 2015) and Chandrasekhar, Larreguy, and Xandri (2020).

In this model, individuals receive a single informative signal at the beginning of the game. In each period, each player makes a guess about the true state. For simplicity, and to avoid strategic interaction issues, suppose that individuals choose an action that maximizes single-period utility. Given this behavior, however, belief updating based on observed neighbors' choices is fully rational: in other words, indirect inferences about the signals of the neighbors of neighbors are allowed. In this context, the improvement-through-imitation principle holds: individuals can ensure themselves the same expected utility as a neighbor through imitation, and they may improve based on their other information.

Building on this principle, it is possible to show that the insights of propositions 13.1 and 13.2 can be generalized and shown to hold when individuals make indirect inferences about neighbors of neighbors through changes in the guesses and actions of their neighbors. In particular, strong connectedness ensures that everyone chooses an action that yields the same expected utility. This action is optimal in undirected networks but may fail to be optimal in networks that contain a royal family.

At different points in this section, we have commented on the complexity of making inferences about information that others hold, especially about the information of the neighbors of neighbors. These types of inferences appear to be implausible, and especially so when we consider networks with hundreds or even thousands of individuals. With these concerns in mind, we now turn to a study of information aggregation and opinion formation when individuals follow bounded rational rules.

## 13.4 A Model of Communication and Social Influence

Galton's study of weights (discussed in the introduction to this chapter) draws attention to two central ideas: (1) information is diverse and dispersed among different individuals in the community; and (2) this information, when put together, provides an accurate estimate of the truth of the matter at hand. In Galton's (1907) orginal study, individuals were asked to submit their guesses, but in many contexts, individuals talk and share ideas. This section presents a model that examines this process of communication: does social communication allow individuals to gain access to all useful information available, and how quickly is this accomplished? The material in this section is taken from DeMarzo, Vayanos, and Zwiebel (2003), and Golub and Jackson (2010, 2012). Our exposition draws on Goyal (2011), Jackson (2008), and Golub and Sadler (2016).

There is a set $N = \{1, 2, \ldots, n\}$ with $n \geq 2$ individuals, each of whom starts with a belief at date 0, a number given by $p_i(0) \in [0, 1]$. Individuals are located in a network that reflects the weight that individual $i$ assigns to the opinions of others: the weight that $i$ assigns to the opinion of $j$ is given by $w_{ij}$, where $w_{ij} \geq 0$. For simplicity, it will be assumed that for every $i$, the sum of weights equals 1 (i.e., $\sum_{j \in N} w_{ij} = 1$). Let the $n \times n$ matrix of weights be given by $W$.

In period $t \geq 1$, an individual $i$ updates their belief by taking an average of their own belief $p_i(0)$ and the opinions of others. Thus, in period $t = 1$,

$$p_i(1) = \sum_{j \in N} w_{ij} p_j(0). \tag{13.7}$$

The belief at time period $t \geq 1$ is similarly obtained by combining the opinions at time $p(t-1)$ with weights $w$:

$$p_i(t) = \sum_{j \in N} w_{ij} p_j(t-1). \tag{13.8}$$

Define for any $t \geq 0$ the vector of beliefs at the start of that period:

$$p(t) = (p_1(t), p_2(t), p_3(t), \ldots, p_n(t)). \tag{13.9}$$

Now we discuss how the dynamics of opinions $p(t)$ are shaped by the initial opinions and the network of interaction, especially the following questions:

- What are the circumstances under which individual opinions settle down?
- When does consensus (i.e., all individuals settle on the same opinion) occur?
- When does the updating of opinions lead to efficient aggregation of information?
- What are the effects of homophily on opinion dynamics?

It is helpful to begin with some simple examples to appreciate the dynamics of opinion formation. Consider a society with three individuals in which the weights are as follows:

$$W = \begin{bmatrix} 1/3 & 1/3 & 1/3 \\ 1/2 & 1/2 & 0 \\ 0 & 1/4 & 3/4 \end{bmatrix}. \tag{13.10}$$

Figure 13.4 illustrates this matrix in network form. Suppose that we start with initial opinions $p(0) = (1, 0, 0)$. Consider the opinions in periods 1 and 2, respectively:

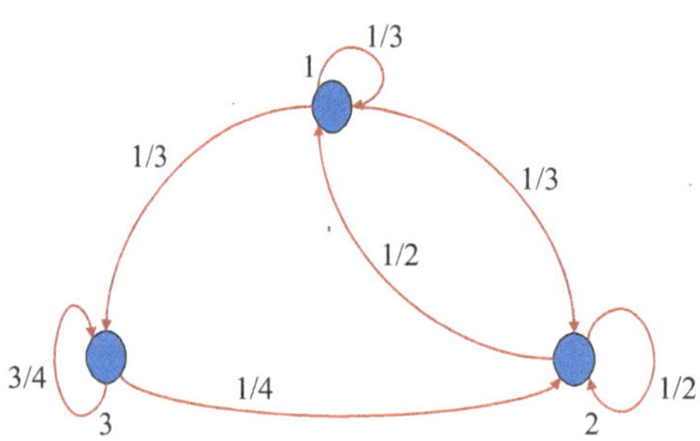


**Figure 13.4**
Simple weighted network.

$$p(1) = Wp(0) = \begin{bmatrix} 1/3 & 1/3 & 1/3 \\ 1/2 & 1/2 & 0 \\ 0 & 1/4 & 3/4 \end{bmatrix} \times \begin{bmatrix} 1 \\ 0 \\ 0 \end{bmatrix} = \begin{bmatrix} 1/3 \\ 1/2 \\ 0 \end{bmatrix}. \tag{13.11}$$

$$p(2) = Wp(1) = \begin{bmatrix} 1/3 & 1/3 & 1/3 \\ 1/2 & 1/2 & 0 \\ 0 & 1/4 & 3/4 \end{bmatrix} \times \begin{bmatrix} 1/3 \\ 1/2 \\ 0 \end{bmatrix} = \begin{bmatrix} 5/18 \\ 5/12 \\ 1/8 \end{bmatrix}. \tag{13.12}$$

As individuals communicate and update their opinions, we see that their opinions become more similar: at the start, individual 1's opinion was 1, while individuals 2 and 3 held the opinion 0. By period 2, individual 1 has moved to 5/18, individual 2 has moved to 5/12, and individual 3 has moved to 1/8. So individual 1's opinion moves down while the opinions of 2 and 3 move up.

The rate of change of opinion depends on the weights that individuals put on their own opinions and the opinions of others. Observe that individual 1 places equal weight on all three, while individual 3 places weight only on individuals 2 and 3. Nevertheless, as individual 2 places weight on 1, the opinion of 1 has an influence on 3 over time. Indeed, as these individuals communicate further, their opinions will continue to evolve. As weights remain unchanged over time, this evolution is captured in the simple formula

$$p(t) = Wp(t-1) = W^t p(0). \tag{13.13}$$

To understand the evolution of beliefs, it is therefore sufficient to keep track of the matrix $W^t$ and the initial opinions $p(0)$. In particular, $W^t$ "converges" to a matrix $W^*$:

$$\begin{bmatrix} x & y & z \\ x & y & z \\ x & y & z \end{bmatrix}, \tag{13.14}$$

where the row vector $(x, y, z)$ corresponds to the stationary distribution of $W$ if we view $W$ as a Markov matrix.

In our $3 \times 3$ example, $W^*$ is given by

$$\begin{bmatrix} 3/11 & 4/11 & 4/11 \\ 3/11 & 4/11 & 4/11 \\ 3/11 & 4/11 & 4/11 \end{bmatrix}. \tag{13.15}$$

In the long run, an individual influences everyone in equal measure. The existence of $W^*$ in turn means that the long-run opinion $p(\infty)$ is

$$p(\infty) = W^* p(0) = \begin{bmatrix} 3/11 \\ 3/11 \\ 3/11 \end{bmatrix}. \tag{13.16}$$

Thus, repeated communication and updating lead to the convergence of all individuals to the same opinion. We next examine the conditions for convergence and consensus more systematically.

### 13.4.1 Convergence and Consensus

It is useful to start with a two-person example. Suppose that the initial opinion is $p(0) = (1, 0)$ and the weighted matrix is

$$W = \begin{bmatrix} 0 & 1 \\ 1 & 0 \end{bmatrix}. \tag{13.17}$$

It is then easy to see that in period 1, $p(1) = Wp(0) = (0, 1)$, and in period 2, $p(2) = W^2 p(0) = (1, 0)$. Indeed, the opinions cycle indefinitely, taking on the values $(1, 0)$ in odd periods and $(0, 1)$ in even periods. In this example, the cycling of beliefs arises because the matrix $W^t$ alternates every two periods. Observe that the society is *strongly connected* because individuals place all their weight on each other. A simple way to avoid a cycle in opinions is to suppose that an individual places at least some weight on their own opinion, that is, $w_{ii} > 0$, for $i \in N$. To see this, suppose the weighted matrix is given by

$$W = \begin{bmatrix} 0.1 & 0.9 \\ 1 & 0 \end{bmatrix}. \tag{13.18}$$

It is easy to verify that opinions in periods 1 and 2 are, respectively,

$$p(1) = \begin{bmatrix} 0.1 & 0.9 \\ 1 & 0 \end{bmatrix} \begin{bmatrix} 1 \\ 0 \end{bmatrix} = \begin{bmatrix} .1 \\ 1 \end{bmatrix} \quad p(2) = \begin{bmatrix} 0.1 & 0.9 \\ 1 & 0 \end{bmatrix} \begin{bmatrix} .1 \\ 1 \end{bmatrix} = \begin{bmatrix} .91 \\ .1 \end{bmatrix}. \tag{13.19}$$

Indeed, opinions evolve smoothly. In the long run,

$$p(\infty) = \begin{bmatrix} .53 \\ .47 \end{bmatrix}. \tag{13.20}$$

The other issue pertains to the similarity of opinions of individuals: at an intuitive level, opinions become similar if two individuals are neighbors of each other (i.e., they place positive weight on each other). In a network, the opinions of 1 will become similar to the opinion of 2 if there is a path from 1 to 2. However, it is possible that there is a path from 1 to 2 but no path from 2 to 1. In that case, 1 is influenced by 2, but 2 is immune to the opinion of 1. A simple example of such a society is described in the following weighted matrix:

$$W = \begin{bmatrix} 1 & 0 & 0 & 0 & 0 \\ 1/5 & 1/5 & 1/5 & 1/5 & 1/5 \\ 1/5 & 1/5 & 1/5 & 1/5 & 1/5 \\ 1/5 & 1/5 & 1/5 & 1/5 & 1/5 \\ 0 & 0 & 0 & 0 & 1 \end{bmatrix}. \tag{13.21}$$

Suppose that $p(0) = (1, 0, 0, 0, 0)$. Individual 1 will then not change their views over time, as they place no weight on anyone else; similarly, individual 5 will not change their views over time. However, individuals 2–4 will update their views, and indeed, as they assign equal weight to individuals 1 and 5, their long-run opinion will be the average of the opinions of 1 and 5 (i.e., 1/2). Observe that the weights that 2–4 place on each other eventually disappear: as a result, in the long run, the opinions will converge to $p^* = (1, 1/2, 1/2, 1/2, 0)$. This example brings out the possibility of convergence without consensus. It also highlights the role of stubborn individuals, who are not receptive to the opinions of others (but others are open to them).

Let us develop sufficient conditions on the weighted network matrix for convergence and consensus. Formally, we require that there is $f \geq 1$ such that all entries of the iterated matrix $W^f$ are positive (i.e., $w_{ij}^f > 0$). An adjacency matrix that satisfies this property is called *primitive*. To see why primitive matrices will exhibit convergence, observe that if $w_{ij}^f \geq \underline{w}$ for some $\underline{w}$, then the range of opinions must shrink over time. Setting $w_{max}(t)$ and $w_{min}(t)$ as maximum and minimum beliefs at the point of time $t$, we can infer that

$$w_{\max}(t+f) - w_{\min}(t+f) \leq (1-\underline{w})[w_{\max}(t) - w_{\min}(t)] < w_{\max}(t) - w_{\min}(t). \quad (13.22)$$

Therefore, in a society with a primitive matrix $W$, opinions will converge to a common consensus belief. We now turn to the issue of social influence: how much influence does an individual have on the consensus belief of their society?

### 13.4.2 Social Influence

Let us examine how the influence of an individual 1 on individual 2 evolves in a social network over time. At time 1, this influence is captured by the number $w_{21}$, as this is the weight placed by 2 on 1. At time 2, the influence of 1 on 2 is captured by paths of length 2 that start from 2 and end at 1: this situation is captured by the term $w_{21}^2$. More generally, at time $t$, the influence of $i$ on any individual $j$ is given by $w_{ji}^t$. Therefore, to understand the influence of $i$ on $j$ in the long run, we need to examine $w_{ji}^*$.

As $W^t$ converges to $W^*$, $w_{ji}^*$ is well defined for every pair $i$ and $j$. To get a feel for evolving social influence, consider an example with three individuals that satisfies the properties of positive own-weights (1 and 3) and strong connectedness:

$$W = \begin{bmatrix} 1/2 & 1/2 & 0 \\ 0 & 0 & 1 \\ 1/4 & 0 & 3/4 \end{bmatrix}. \quad (13.23)$$

Figure 13.5 presents the network corresponding to the weighted matrix. The limit influence $W^*$ is given by

$$W^* = \begin{bmatrix} 2/7 & 1/7 & 4/7 \\ 2/7 & 1/7 & 4/7 \\ 2/7 & 1/7 & 4/7 \end{bmatrix}. \quad (13.24)$$

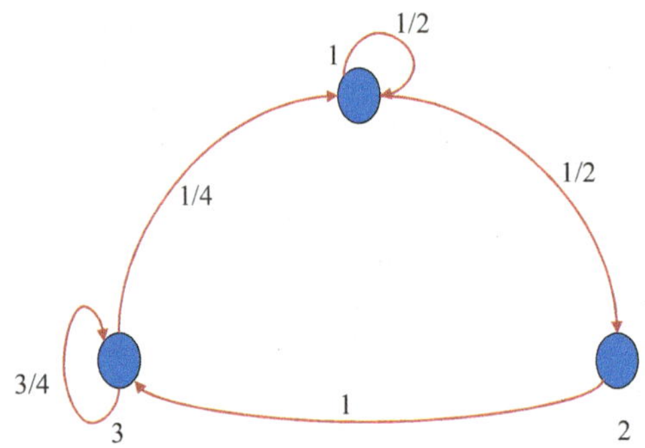


**Figure 13.5**
Weighted network 2.

We note that in a strongly connected society, the influence of $i$ on every individual is the same; we will refer to this as the *social influence* of $i$ on the society and denote it by the number $s_i$. The social influence vector is denoted by $s=(s_1,\ldots,s_n)$.

As $W$ is strongly connected, it is easy to see that every individual must have a positive social influence. The social influence of an individual may be expressed as a weighted sum of the influence of their neighbors as follows:

$$s_i = \sum_{j\in N} W_{ji} s_j. \tag{13.25}$$

Recalling the recursive nature of centrality as discussed in chapter 1, we will say that the social influence of a node is proportional to its left eigenvector centrality. As $W$ is strongly connected and primitive and the rows sum to 1, it follows from standard results in the theory of Markov chains that $W^*$ always exists and that there is a unique left-side unit eigenvector (with the eigenvector corresponding to eigenvalue 1); for an overview of the theory of Markov chains and matrix algebra, see Kemeny and Snell (1983) and Seneta (2006). Our discussion is summarized in the following result.

**Proposition 13.3** *Suppose that the matrix $W$ is primitive. Then the following is true:*

1. *The influence of individual $j$ on individual $i$ converges:*

$$\lim_{t\to\infty} w^t_{ij} = s_j. \tag{13.26}$$

2. *The opinions $p(t)$ converge to $p(\infty)$. The limit opinion $p(\infty)=sp(0)$.*
3. *The social influence vector $s$ is defined as the (unique) solution to*

$$s\cdot W = s. \tag{13.27}$$

If individual $i$ receives more weight than individual $j$ (i.e., $W_{ki}\geq W_{kj}$ for every $k$), then $i$ is more influential than $j$. This follows from equation (13.25), which also implies that

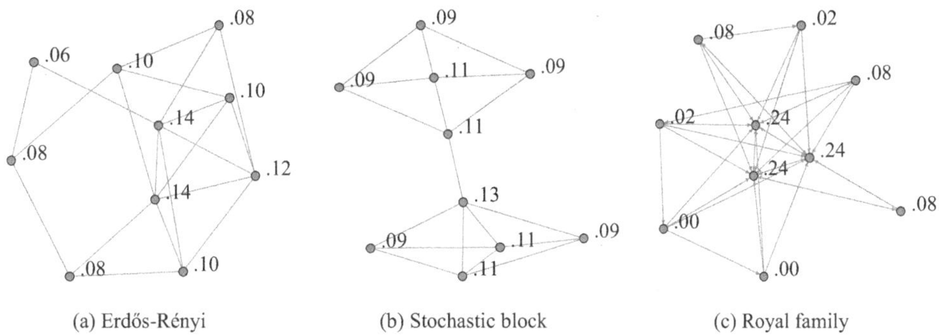


**Figure 13.6**
Social influence in networks: $n = 10$, average degree $= 4$.

if $i$ receives the same weight as $j$ but $i$ receives weight from those who have more social influence, then $i$ in turn will have more influence. Next, note that if all links are symmetric ($w_{ij} = w_{ji}$ for all pairs $i,j$), then every individual will have the same social influence. A question at the end of the chapter works through the details of this feature of social networks.

To illustrate this result, we next consider long-run opinions in some well-known networks. First, consider a set of graphs in which links are binary and undirected, so $g_{ij} = g_{ji}$ and $g_{ij} \in \{0, 1\}$. For every person, set $g_{ii} = 1$, to ensure that the weights matrix is primitive. Then normalize the weights by setting $w_{ij} = g_{ij}/d_i$, for every $i \in N$. Figure 13.6 presents three networks of a society with 10 individuals—an Erdős-Rényi graph, a Stochastic Block random graph, and a Royal Family graph. In all cases, the true state is 0.5. Every individual draws signals that have equal probability on $\{0.2, 0.5, 0.8\}$. These signals are drawn independently. So in period 0, $p_i(0) \in \{0.2, 0.5, 0.8\}$. Individuals then update their opinions using the weighted matrix defined by the graphs. The numbers next to the nodes present the social influence of individuals in each of the networks. Observe that the range of social influence is modest in the Erdős-Rényi and Stochastic Block networks, while it is large in the case of the Royal Family network. The ratios of maximum social influence to minimum social influence are 2.33, 1.45, and 12 in the Erdős-Rényi, Stochastic Block, and Royal Family network, respectively.

### 13.4.3 Complete Learning

We turn to an issue that lies at the heart of contemporary discussions: could individuals in a large society hold opinions that are contrary to evidence over extended periods of time? One way to think about this is to suppose that there is a true state and individuals acquire impressions about it through personal inquiry or efforts. As individuals come to this issue with their own personal experiences, they may arrive at slightly different beliefs about the true state. A famous story along these lines is the Galton problem that was discussed in the introduction to this chapter. The conditions under which individual idiosyncracies cancel out and the average of these views corresponds to the truth have been studied in the theory of probability. A well-known theorem in probability theory, the strong law of large numbers, tells us that if individual impressions are independent and unbiased, then the average opinion would become a better and better measure for the actual facts as the number of individuals grows. In other words, a large crowd will be "wise." This section examines how this central intuition is affected by the presence of network connections that route social communication.

To fix ideas, it is helpful to suppose that there is a true state, given by $\theta \in \mathbb{R}$. Individual $i$'s belief about this true state at period 0 is given by $p_i(0)$, where $p_i(0) = \theta + \rho_i$ and $\rho_i$ reflects some idiosyncratic term. For concreteness, suppose that every person draws this $\rho_i$ from the same distribution and the draw is independent. Suppose that $\rho_i \sim \mathcal{N}(0, \sigma^2)$. In period 0, individual $i$'s opinion or belief about the state of the world is simply $p_i(0)$. In period 1, individual $i$ updates their view of the world upon the observation of others' signals. Bayes's rule then yields

$$p_i(1) = \sum_{j \in N} w_{ij} p_j(0), \tag{13.28}$$

where $w_{ij}$ is a measure of the precision of $j$'s signal.

We start with a consideration of some simple examples. First, consider the simple case where everyone communicates their signal to everyone else: in other words, suppose that the social network is complete and every individual places weight $1/n$ on everyone. In this case, in period 1, everyone will have the same opinion, given by

$$p_i(1) = \frac{1}{n} \sum_{i \in N} p_i(0) = \theta + \frac{1}{n} \sum_{i \in N} \rho_i, \forall i \in N. \tag{13.29}$$

where the first equality holds because everyone places the same weight on everyone and the second equality holds due to the definition of individual signals. In principle, the sum of the values of $\rho_i$ is uncertain, as they are drawn from distribution $F$. However, a classical result in probability theory—namely, the strong law of large numbers—tells us that the variance of this term becomes negligible as the number of individuals grows (for a classical exposition of this theorem, see Billingsley [2008]). In other words, the belief in the completely connected egalitarian network will approximate the true value of $\theta$ in large groups from period 1 onward.

We now turn to opinion formation in networks more generally. The principal complication is that repeated updating privileges more connected individuals over less connected individuals. This in turn means that the former come to acquire a disproportionate social influence, which can bias the opinion of society at large. Let us develop this idea with the help of an example of hub-spoke networks, given by the following matrix:

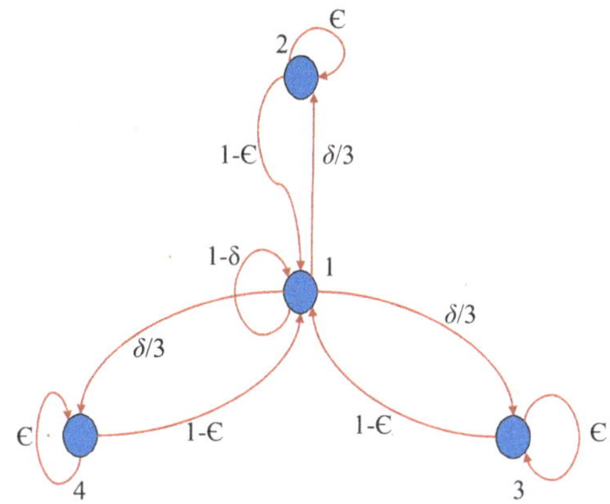


**Figure 13.7**
Weighted hub-spoke network.

| | 1 | 2 | 3 | 4 |
|---|---|---|---|---|
| 1 | $1-\delta$ | $\delta/3$ | $\delta/3$ | $\delta/3$ |
| 2 | $1-\epsilon$ | $\epsilon$ | 0 | 0 |
| 3 | $1-\epsilon$ | 0 | $\epsilon$ | 0 |
| 4 | $1-\epsilon$ | 0 | 0 | $\epsilon$ |

Figure 13.7 illustrates the network corresponding to this matrix. It is easy to verify that for general $n$, with individual 1 at the center, the social influence vector is

$$s_1 = \frac{1-\epsilon}{1-\epsilon+\delta}; \; s_j = \frac{\delta}{(n-1)(1-\epsilon+\delta)}, \; j \neq 1. \tag{13.30}$$

This means that the long-run belief is

$$p^* = \theta + s_1\rho_1 + \frac{\delta}{(n-1)(1-\epsilon+\delta)} \sum_{j=2}^{n} \rho_j. \tag{13.31}$$

We can see that $p^*$ will not be equal to $\theta$, even when $n$ gets large, because it will always assign positive weight to the signal of the hub, and this signal will generally not equal 0. In other words, a large society organized in a hub-spoke structure will *not* arrive at the truth through communication. Importantly, observe that in a large society, we know from the strong law of large numbers that sufficient information will be available to reach the truth. So we can conclude that the network structure prevents information aggregation.

The example also gives us the reason for the breakdown in communication: the hub individual comes to acquire disproportionate social influence compared to everyone else.

Observe that the influence of all other individuals becomes negligible as the size of society $n$ grows, while the social influence of 1 remains unchanged. This means that it is the signal of individual $i$—$\rho_1$—that biases public opinion.

We have seen that influential individuals are sufficient to block correct opinions. It turns out that they are also necessary: in other words, any society where no single individual possesses significant social influence will eventually converge to the correct view (this is a more or less a direct consequence of the strong law of large numbers). We summarize our discussion in the following result.

**Proposition 13.4** *Fix some initial beliefs $p^n(0)$, and let $W_n$ be a sequence of primitive matrices. Let $s^n$ be the social influence and $p^n$ be the limit belief in a network with n individuals. The limit beliefs converge (in probability) to the truth, $\theta$, if and only if individual social influence disappears as the society grows large; that is,*

$$\lim_{n\to\infty} \max_i s_i^n \to 0. \tag{13.32}$$

Our example of the hub-spoke network illustrates the basic intuition underlying this result; a question at the end of the chapter works through the argument for general networks.

Proposition 13.4 is illustrated with the help of figure 13.8. Here, we consider two networks with 50 individuals apiece—the Erdős-Rényi and the Royal Family networks. The average degree is the same in the two networks: 3. The left side of the graphics illustrates the networks. We generate beliefs at random and then run the opinion dynamics process. The right side presents the limit belief. The true state is $\theta = 1/2$. We see that in the Erdős-Rényi network, the limit belief is very close to the true state, at 0.48. On the other hand, the limit belief in the Royal Family—0.40—is a fair distance from the truth. The reason for this breakdown of aggregation is the large social influence of the royal family (which drew a signal lower than the true state).

Our previous discussion of the persistence of diverse opinions in the case studies on climate change and fishery and on WMD and presidential elections motivates the following question: what features of the social interaction lead to a persistence of diverse opinions and slow the convergence of opinions? This is the subject of the next section.

### 13.4.4 Homophily

Let us start with a simple example to develop some intuition. To begin, consider an Erdős-Rényi graph with $n$ individuals and a probability of linking given by $p$. Next, consider a variant of the Erdős-Rényi graph in which the individuals are divided into distinct groups and the probability of linking within a group is higher than the probability of linking across groups. Suppose that there are $m$ equal groups, and, for simplicity, suppose that the probabilities are perfectly symmetric: $p_s$ is the probability of a link between two individuals within a group, and $p_d$ is the probability of a link between two individuals who belong to different groups; we assume that $p_s > p_d$. This $p_s, p_d$ model is a special case of the Stochastic

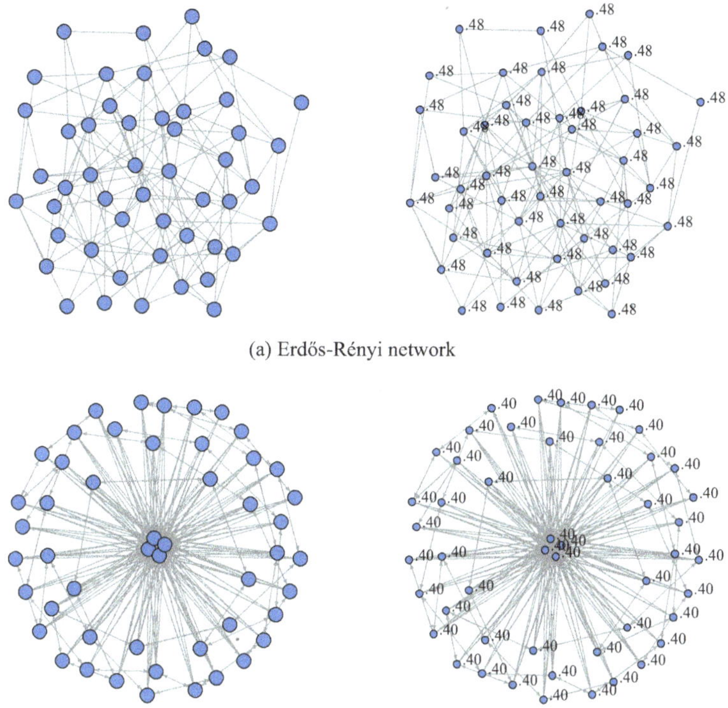

(a) Erdős-Rényi network

(b) Prominent groups: Royal family.

**Figure 13.8**
Network structure and wisdom of crowds.

Block model, in which probabilities of pairwise meetings within same group are equal and given by $p_s$. Similarly, the probability of a pair from two different groups meeting, $p_d$, is also equal for all such pairs. We will refer to this model as the "Islands Model" in the rest of this section. Figure 13.9 illustrates networks generated using the Islands Model.

Let us draw out a relation between homophily and the Islands Model. In this model, the average probability of linking is given by

$$p = \frac{p_s + (m-1)p_d}{m}. \tag{13.33}$$

Recall from chapter 1 that the extent of homophily can be defined as the difference between the same and different linking probabilities, with a normalization for dividing by the number of islands, $m$:

$$IH = \frac{p_s - p_d}{mp} = \frac{\frac{p_s}{mp} - \frac{1}{m}}{1 - \frac{1}{m}}. \tag{13.34}$$

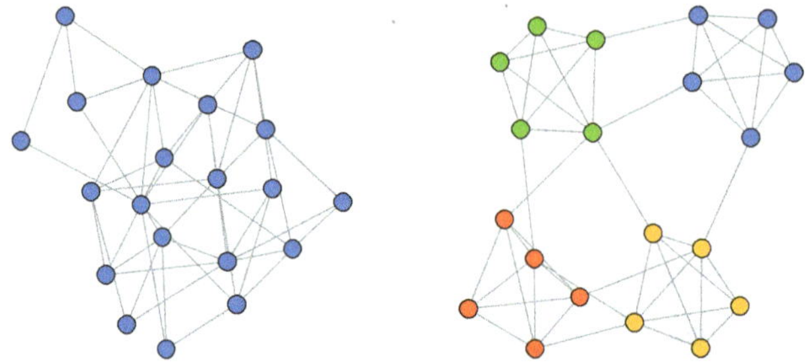

(a) Erdős-Rényi network: $p = 0.25$

(b) Islands network: $vm = 4, p_s = 1, p_d = 0.05$

**Figure 13.9**
Homophily and networks: $n = 20$.

The final formula, on the right side, is known as Coleman's Homophily Index (after the sociologist James Coleman): it provides a measure of how much a group's fraction of own-type links ($p_s/mp$) exceeds its population share ($1/m$) as a ratio of how big this difference could be $\left(1 - \frac{1}{m}\right)$. Positive $IH$ indicates homophily, while negative $IH$ indicates heterophily. Observe that this ratio varies between 0 (when $p_s = p_d$) and 1 (when $p_s > 0$ and $p_d = 0$). We see that it is increasing in the ratio $p_s/p_d$. And it can be verified that it equals 0 for the Erdős-Rényi network and it equals 0.826 for the Islands Model with $p_s = 1$ and $p_d = 0.05$.

Consider the dynamics of opinion in the Erdős-Rényi network and the Islands Model. Both networks are strongly connected and egalitarian. As before, the true state is 0.5 and the long-run belief in both networks is a good approximation. However, the structure of the network has a profound impact on the speed of convergence. In the Erdős-Rényi network, opinions of all individuals are close to 0.5 by period 5. On the other hand, in the Islands Model, there is considerable dispersion of opinions in period 5. In particular, in period 5, the opinions range from 0.41 to 0.6. Indeed, even at time $t = 15$, when Erdős-Rényi beliefs have converged to 0.51, there remains a considerable dispersion of opinion in the Islands Model: the opinions of three communities are 0.47, 0.47, and 0.48, while members of one community hold the opinion 0.50. Figures 13.10 and 13.11 illustrate the impact of homophily on the pace of social learning and the persistence of diverse beliefs.

These examples provide a first impression of how the rate of convergence of beliefs may be shaped by homophily. We now develop this idea more systematically.

For expositional simplicity, let us consider binary links, $g_{ij} \in \{0, 1\}$ and define weights of the matrix $W$ as $w_{ij} = g_{ij}/d_i$. We may then diagonalize the matrix $W$ as follows:

$$W = S \begin{bmatrix} 1 & 0 & 0 & 0 \\ 0 & \lambda_2 & 0 & 0 \\ 0 & 0 & \lambda_3 & 0 \\ .. & .. & .. & .. \\ 0 & .. & .. & \lambda_n \end{bmatrix} S^{-1}, \tag{13.35}$$

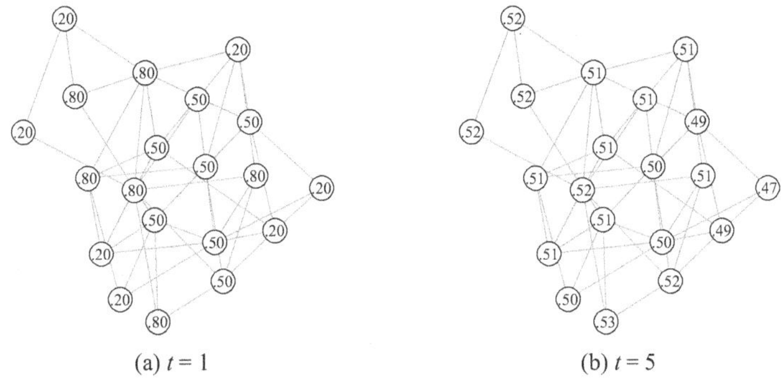


**Figure 13.10**
Opinion dynamics in Erdős-Rényi networks.

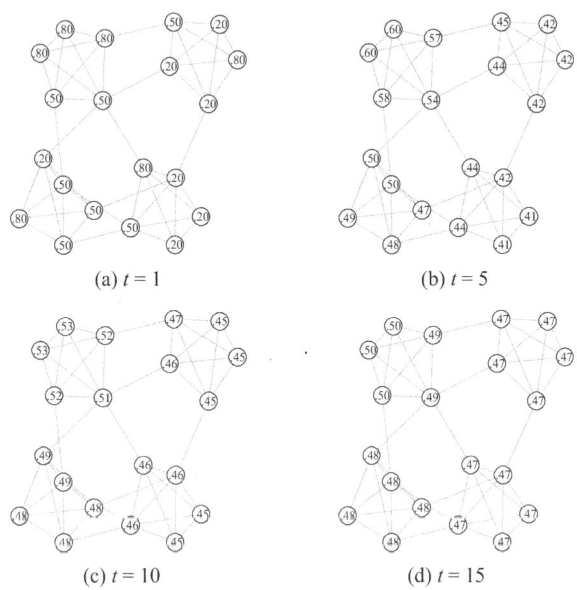


**Figure 13.11**
Opinion dynamics in Islands Model.

where the columns in $S$ are the right eigenvectors and the rows in $S^{-1}$ are the left eigenvectors of $W$. The eignevalues are presented in descending order, $\lambda_1, \lambda_2, \ldots, \lambda_n$; note that as all rows sum to 1 for this matrix, the largest eigenvalue $\lambda_1 = 1$ (for a discussion of such properties of stochastic matrices, see Seneta [2006]).

We have shown that in any society, if $W$ is primitive, then opinions converge to a consensus $p(\infty)$. It is possible to show that the distance between the period $t$ belief and the long-run belief is an increasing function of the second eigenvalue of matrix $W$. This second

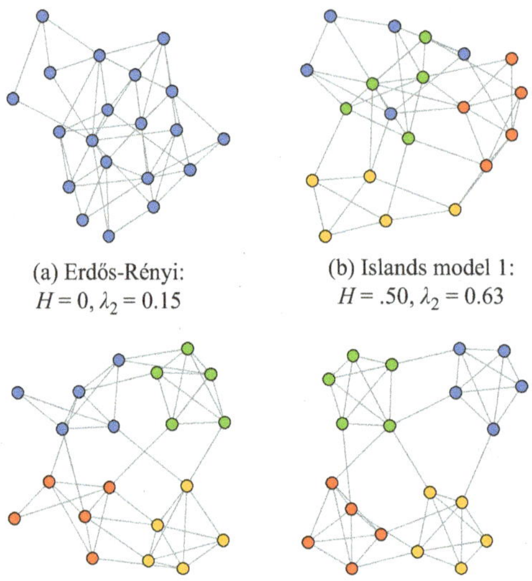

(a) Erdős-Rényi: $H = 0, \lambda_2 = 0.15$

(b) Islands model 1: $H = .50, \lambda_2 = 0.63$

(c) Islands model 2: $H = 0.70, \lambda_2 = 0.81$

(d) Islands model 3: $H = .83, \lambda_2 = .87$

**Figure 13.12**
Homophily and second eigenvalues.

eigenvalue of the weighted matrix, $W$, is closely related to the level of homophily in the society. To see this in the simplest way, let us construct the Islands Model with progressively higher levels of homophily (by varying $p_s$ and $p_d$) and present their second eigenvalues. In all cases, the number of nodes $n = 20$, and the average degree is 5. These networks are presented in figure 13.12. Our discussion leads to the following result.

**Proposition 13.5** *Consider an Islands Model with a primitive $W$: the rate of convergence of opinions to consensus is negatively related to the level of homophily.*

A proof of this result goes beyond the scope of this chapter; the interested reader is urged to consult Golub and Jackson (2012) for more detail.

To summarize, we have studied a model of communication in which individuals repeatedly update their opinions by averaging across the opinions of their neighbors. This analysis yields a number of powerful conclusions. The first is that if a society is strongly connected, then everyone will hold the same opinions (i.e., consensus occurs). The second is that the influence of a person on this consensus opinion is given by their eigenvector centrality. The third is that the consensus belief in a large society reflects all available information if and only if no one possesses significant social influence. Finally, the rate at which a society aggregates the information to arrive at a consensus depends on the extent of homophily: greater homophily leads to longer persistence of disagreement.

## 13.5 Experimental Evidence on Social Learning

Our discussion in section 13.2 reveals that in a variety of important contexts, we rely on information gathered from others to make decisions, these others in turn get their information from their social contacts.

Our discussions in the introduction chapter, and chapters 1 and 11, suggest that real world social networks are often very large and that they exhibit two key features: deep inequalities (the average connection is small but the variance is very large) and homopohily (tendency of people with similar traits to form links with each other). The theory of opinion formation and learning we have presented in sections 13.3 and 13.4 tells us that these network features have a powerful impact on opinions and behavior. In this section, we present experimental evidence on the role of networks in shaping opinions and behavior. The discussion here is based on Choi, Goyal, Moisan, and To (2022).

The theoretical model is a simplified version of the models studied in the previous two sections. There is a set of individuals $N = \{1, \ldots, n\}$, with $n \geq 2$, who choose between two actions, Green and Red. There are two states, Green and Red. Action Green yields a payoff of 1 if the true state is Green, and zero otherwise. Likewise, action Red yields a payoff of 1 if the true state is Red, and zero otherwise.

Time is discrete and proceeds as $t = 1, 2 \ldots$. At the start, individuals believe that the two states are equally likely. They observe a noisy but informative signal on the true state: individual $i$ receives a binary signal $s_i \in \{Green, Red\}$. The probability of receiving the Green (Red) signal that is conditional on the true state being Green (Red) is $p \in (1/2, 1)$. Thus, upon receiving a Green signal, the expected payoff to an individual from action Green is $p$, and the payoff is $1 - p$ from action Red. In period $t$, an individual chooses action $a_{i,t} \in \{Green, Red\}$.

Individuals are located in an information network, $g$. At time $t$, individual $i$ observes the actions of their neighbors $N_i(g)$ from period 1 until period $t - 1$. The signal at the start and the observations on neighbors' guesses in subsequent periods are inputs into choices at time $t$.

In the first period, individuals choose an action that mimics the signal $s_i$. In periods $t \geq 2$, they choose an action $a_{i,t}$ that corresponds to the majority action in their neighborhood in the previous period. Let us also suppose that individuals randomize (with equal probability) between the two actions if there is no clear majority.

We consider three archetypal networks: the Erdős-Rényi (ER) network, the Stochastic Block (SB) network, and the Royal Family (RF) network. Figure 13.13 (a) presents examples of these networks. To develop a hypothesis, we run simulations under the behavioral rule described previously. The signals are randomly drawn independently and with the same distribution for 40 subjects with signal quality $p = 0.7$. The group-level variable $c_t$ measures the extent to which group actions at time $t$ move toward either a correct or an incorrect

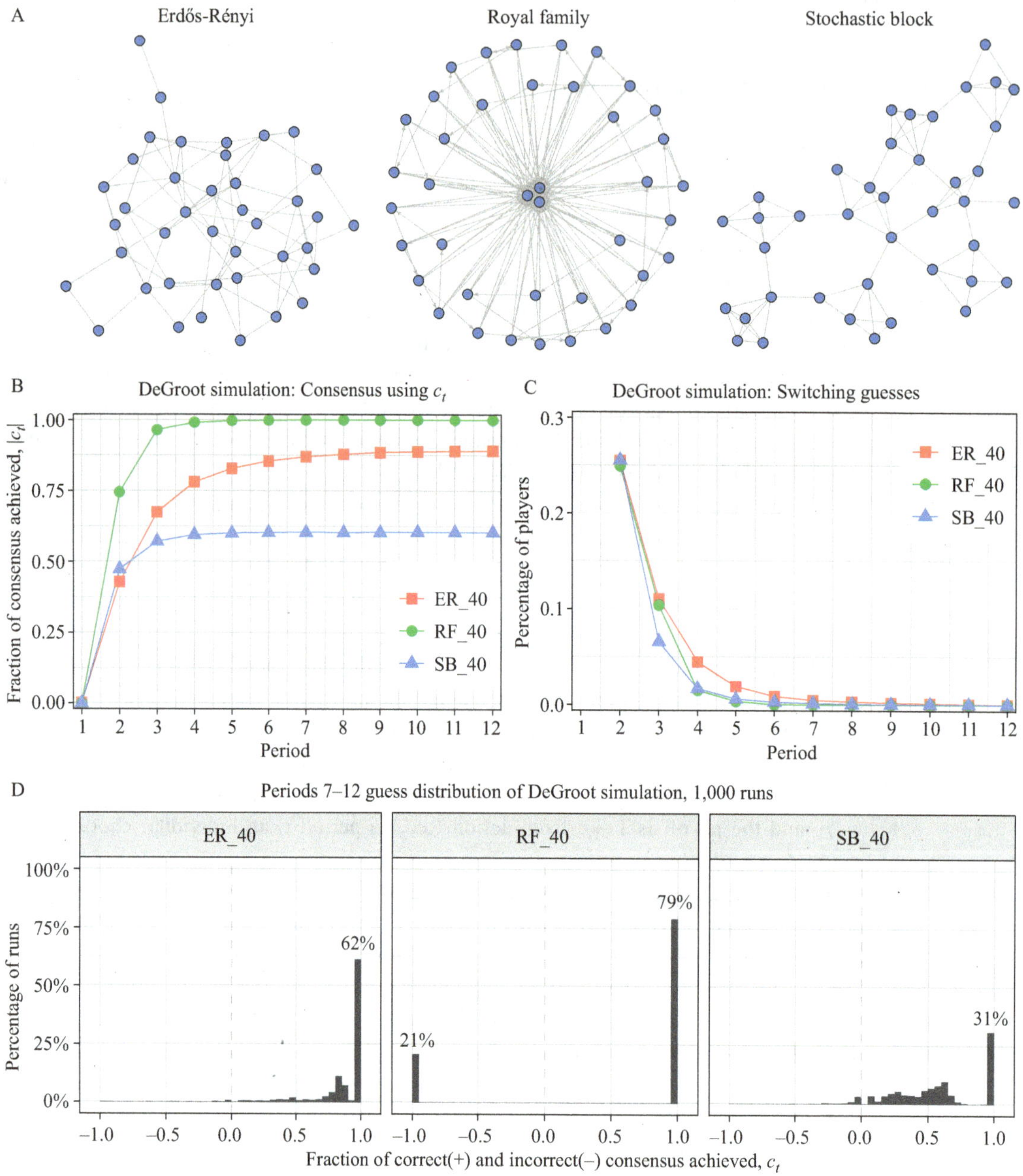


**Figure 13.13**

Canonical networks and DeGroot simulations of 1,000 runs. (A) Average degree is approximately equal to 4; diameters in ER, RF, and SB are equal to 5, 38, and 9, respectively. (B) By period 4, the RF network (green) achieves complete consensus in almost all cases. The SB network (blue) realizes 60 percent of possible consensus, and the ER network (red) achieves 87 percent of the maximum possible consensus. (C) By period 7, switching frequency is negligible. (D) In periods 7–12, 62 percent of cases in the ER network reach correct consensus, whereas it is 31 percent in the SB network and 79 percent in the RF network. Almost all the remaining cases yield a breakdown of correct consensus (38 percent in ER, 66 percent in SB) or incorrect consensus (21 percent in RF). *Source*: Choi, Goyal, Moisan, and To (2022).

consensus relative to the initial assignment of signals:

$$c_t = \begin{cases} (n_t - n_0)/(n - n_0) & \text{if } n_t \geq n_0, \\ (n_t - n_0)/n_0 & \text{if } n_t < n_0, \end{cases} \tag{13.36}$$

where $n_0$ denotes the number of correct signals received by individuals at time 0 and $n_t$ denotes the number of correct actions made at time $t$. This variable ranges between $-1$ (incorrect consensus) and 1 (correct consensus). If the number of individuals choosing a correct action is the same as that of correct signals, $c_t = 0$.

Using 1,000 runs of the DeGroot simulations, figure 13.13(b) shows the evolution of consensus, measured by the absolute value of $c_t$; and figure 13.13(c) shows the fraction of players switching actions between periods $t$ and $t-1$. We note that learning occurs rapidly: most of the consensus achieved in the simulation happens at the first few periods. Network structure has a significant impact on consensus dynamics: the RF network achieves consensus by period 4 in almost all cases; the SB network realizes only about 60 percent of the possible consensus by period 4 and remains at that level afterward. Learning in ER continues a bit longer and achieves about 87 percent of the possible consensus by period 7. Figure 13.13(d) presents the distribution of $c_t$ at periods 7–12. It shows that in the ER network, correct consensus obtains in 62 percent of the cases; in the SB network, correct consensus is obtained in 31 percent of cases. In the RF network, consensus occurs in nearly all cases: correct consensus in 79 percent of cases and incorrect consensus in 21 percent of cases.

These simulations lead to three hypotheses:

1. Individual choices converge to a limit action.
2. Breakdown of consensus is higher in SB than in ER and RF.
3. Incorrect consensus is higher in RF than in ER and SB.

Let us now describe the experiment. Each experimental session consisted of a group of 40 subjects who played six rounds of the learning game. Groups of subjects were assigned to one of three experimental conditions, each associated with a distinct network structure: ER, SB, or RF. Four independent groups participated in each experimental condition, and no subject participated in more than one experimental session.

At the start of each round, subjects were informed about a bag containing 10 balls. The color composition of the bag was unknown to the subjects. They were told that the bag contains either 7 red and 3 green balls (the RED bag) or 7 green and 3 red balls (the GREEN bag). Each subject drew a ball from the bag and saw its color. There was a probability of 0.7 of getting the correct signal. For 12 periods, subjects were asked to make a guess on whether the bag is RED or GREEN. At the end of the round, one period (from 1 to 12) was picked at random to determine actual payoffs in the round: subjects earned 3 euros if their guess matched the color of the bag (GREEN or RED), and 0 euros otherwise. The total earnings for

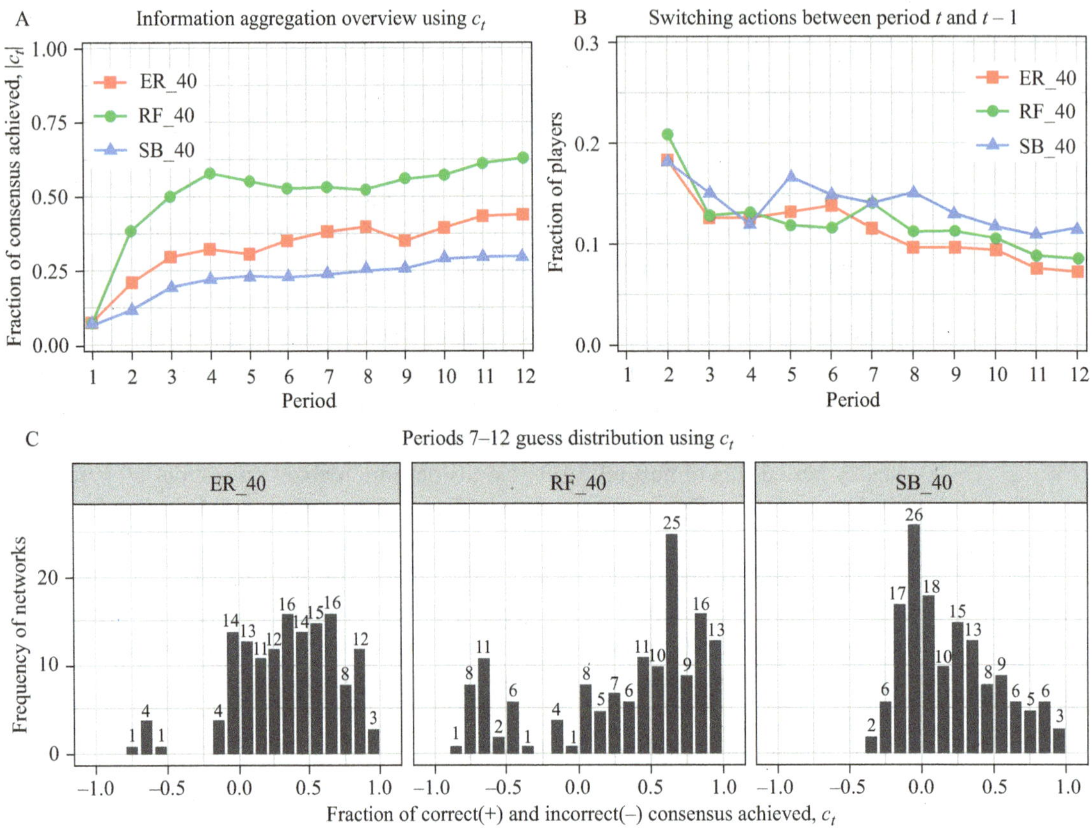


**Figure 13.14**

Learning and consensus. (A) By period 12, RF, ER, and SB reach 63 percent, 44 percent, and 30 percent of the possible consensus, respectively. (B) Switching frequency falls below 10 percent by period 12. (C) Distribution of $c_t$ is uniform between 0 and 1 for ER, bimodal around 1 and −1 for RF, and modal around 0 for SB. *Source*: Choi, Goyal, Moisan, and To (2022).

a subject corresponded to the sum of earnings in each round and a 5-euro show-up fee. The experiment lasted approximately 1.5 hours. The average payment per subject was 19.3 euros.

Figure 13.14 summarizes our experimental findings on network effects. Figure 13.14(a) shows the evolution of consensus across rounds and groups. Figure 13.14(b) presents the switching frequency from period $t-1$ to period $t$. Figure 13.14(c) presents the distribution of $c_t$ in the last six periods (i.e., between period 7 and period 12) in each network.

We begin by discussing the dynamics of learning in figures 13.14(a) and 13.14(b). Most of the learning occurs in the early periods; by period 4, the RF network reaches 58 percent of the maximum margin of consensus and the SB network reaches 22 percent, while the ER network achieves 35 percent by period 6. The quick learning is consistent with the simulations. There remains a small amount of switching near the end; the frequency of switching falls to 10 percent eventually.

Figure 13.14(c) shows the distribution of $c_t$ across the three networks in the periods 7–12. The distribution of the RF network is bimodal near the two types of consensus, as $c_t = 1$ and $c_t = -1$, the SB network has a mode around the value of $c_t = 0$, indicating a high likelihood of no learning and the persistence of diverse opinions, and the ER network generates a distribution somewhat uniformly spread between 0 and 1.

To consolidate these findings, let us define binary variables of correct consensus (if $c_t > k$), incorrect consensus (if $c_t < -k$), and breakdown of consensus (if $-k \leq c_t \leq k$) based on the value of $c_t$. Let us fix $k$ to be 0.3. Then, consistent with the second hypothesis, the fraction of breakdown of consensus is highest in the SB network: it is 40 percent in the ER network, 19 percent in the RF network, and 65 percent in the SB network. Finally, consistent with the third hypothesis, the fraction of incorrect consensus is highest in the RF network: it is 4 percent in the ER network, 20 percent in the RF network, and 1 percent in the SB network.

We study the impact of network structure on social learning using a laboratory experiment. At the start, subjects observe a private signal and then make a guess. In subsequent periods, subjects observe their neighbors' previous guesses before guessing again. We locate these individuals in three social networks—Erdős-Rényi (reflecting a baseline setting with homogeneous decentralized contacts), Stochastic Block (reflecting homophily), and Royal Family (reflecting "influencers" and local interaction). In line with theoretical predictions, we find that networks have powerful effects on social learning: a society with hubs and influencers is more likely to arrive at incorrect consensus, a society with homophily is more likely to persist with diverse beliefs. The behavior of individuals closely matches the predictions of DeGroot updating rule.

In section 13.3–13.5, individuals learn by observing their neighbors but in these models, the neighbors themselves do not makes choices about whether to verify or to share information.

In actual practice, individuals often verify a piece of information before passing it on to their friends and acquaintances. In the next section, we study the incentives to verify and share information and how it is affected by the network structure.

## 13.6 Verifying and Sharing Information

Our discussion of early evidence in section 11.2 suggest that social connections have been essential for information dissemination historically. In recent decades, the role of social exchange of information has gained momentum with the use of massive online networks. In 2016, 14 percent of Americans said they use social media as their primary sources of news with over 70 percent of Americans getting at least some of their news from social media. This development has taken place in parallel with the concern about the spread of false information concerning a number of issues—such as politicians, health remedies, vaccines and firm values (Allcott and Gentzkow 2017, Levy 2021). These discussions have drawn attention to the importance of individual decisions on verifying and on sharing information.

Verification of content is central to preventing misinformation in traditional news media. However, with consumers shifting toward social media for news and information, centralized fact-checking (third-party identification of inaccuracies before or after content dissemination) faces the challenge of scalability due to the growing volume of online contents posted every day. Moreover, a perceived lack of trust in centralized fact-checking compromises its scope (for instance, 70 percent of Republicans and 48 percent of Americans believe that fact-checkers are biased [Walker and Gottfried 2019]). This highlights the importance of verification of information by online media users. This section sketches a model taken from Goyal, Safranov, and To (2022) and uses it to think of the ways in which platforms and social networks shape incentives of individuals to verify information before passing it on to their neighbors and how that shapes the quality of information that circulates in the network.

The setting of the model is as follows: there is a set of $N = \{1, \ldots, n\}$, individuals who are located at nodes of a large (undirected) network. A piece of information arrives to a seed individual in the network. The news has some exogenous probability of being true. The seed decides whether to verify the news (at a cost) and then whether to share the news. Similarly, a nonseed individual in the network who receives a piece of information faces a choice about verifying and sharing. Individuals derive benefits from sharing news, these benefits are proportional to the number of direct neighbors. They incur a reputation damage from sharing news that is false.

We assume that verification reveals the veracity of news perfectly; this means that an individual who verifies news will only share it if it is true. Thus an individual can (1) share without verification, (2), not share and not verify, and (3), verify information and only share true news. As the interest is in large networks, it is reasonable to assume that an individual's degree is known only to herself, and moreover, that the identity of the sender is unknown (whether they are a seed or not). Thus the strategy of an individual is a function from their degree to one of the three actions described above. The model is solved using the concept of Bayesian Nash equilibrium. Our discussion will focus on two aggregate outcomes: one, how much does a piece of news travel, and two, what is the quality of the news that spreads in the network.

A preliminary remark is that the game of verification exhibits a strategic substitutes property: when other agents verify more, indirect news is more likely to be true, which lowers incentives to personally verify the news. We restrict attention to equilibrium that is symmetric in the sense that every seed and nonseed with the same degree chooses the same action, respectively. It turns out that in this model, there exists a unique equilibrium. In this equilibrium, the seed of any degree verifies with a (weakly) higher probability as compared to a nonseed with the same degree and the probability of verification is (weakly) increasing in the degree of an individual.

We next examine the role of two key aspects of the environment—the ex-ante quality of the information and the structure of the network.

Consider the perceived accuracy of information: this is the probability that the news is correct at the point that it arrives at the seed of the network. When accuracy is very low, either the seed kills it or if their costs of verification are low then they verify and share if the news is correct. The nonseed anticipates this and therefore never verifies any news they receive in this low accuracy scenario. On the other hand, when accuracy is very high, the seed and the nonseed share it without verification. In the intermediate information accuracy range, sharing both with and without verification are possible depending on the costs of verification for an individual. This reasoning suggests one that more news is shared as ex-ante accuracy grows and two, that there may be a nonmonotonicity in the quality of news (prevalent in a network) as a function of the ex-ante accuracy of the news.

Consider next the role of the network. When information accuracy is below a threshold, the degree and the network do not matter; the seed verifies, and if true, then shares information (if their costs of verification are small) or does not verify and does not share. Above the threshold accuracy level, network structure becomes relevant for the nonseeds. As seed verification is increasing in degree, a denser network implies more connected seed and hence a higher likelihood of verification and therefore a higher quality of received news—from strategic substitutes property, this then means that the nonseed with any degree verifies with lower probability.

Equipped with these results on equilibrium, we can examine the incentives of a platform to invest in information quality. We are interested in questions such as: how does network structure shape quality of information chosen by a platform and how does that shape the spread and quality of information in a network? Consider the model with a social media platform that invests in information accuracy with a goal to maximize the spread of information in the network. As we have noted above, the spread of news—as measured by the probability of news reaching a nonseed node—is increasing in the accuracy of information chosen by the platform. We also noted that there is a threshold accuracy level above which a seed (and also a nonseed) always shares news, either with or without verification. The general problem is quite complicated, but under suitable assumptions on the costs of verification and the network degree distributions it is possible to derive closed-form solutions on optimal accuracy: it is falling in the platform's costs of acquiring accuracy and beyond a certain cost the platform chooses zero level of accuracy. The network structure affects the rate at which the accuracy falls with costs and also the threshold cost at which it declines to zero.

## 13.7 Appendix

### 13.7.1 Sequential Models of Learning

For completeness, we present a canonical model of social learning in this appendix: there is a single sequence of privately informed individuals who take one action each. Before making their choice, an individual gets to observe the actions of all the people who have made a choice earlier. The actions of the predecessors potentially reveal their private information. An individual can therefore use the information revealed via the actions of others (together with their own private information) to make decisions. This model was introduced in Banerjee (1992) and Bikhchandani, Hirshleifer, and Welch (1992); for a general treatment of this model, see Smith and Sørensen (2000). An extensive body of literature has grown around this basic model. See Smith and Sørensen (2000) for an elaboration of the general model, and Golub and Sadler (2016) and Chamley (2004) for comprehensive surveys. The principal question is: do individuals eventually learn and choose the optimal action?

A basic insight is that learning can lead to herding, where everyone may choose the wrong action. Consider a setting in which private signals are equally accurate and individuals assign equal weight to their own signals and the signal of others. To fix ideas, suppose that there are two actions and two states. For simplicity, suppose that in state 1, action 1 is optimal, while in state 0, action 0 is optimal. Suppose that agents initially believe that the states are equally likely. At the point of entry, the agent in period $t$ observes a private signal: the probability of signal $x$ when the true state is $x$ is $q$, where $q > 1/2$. The probability that the signal is $x$ when the true state is $y \neq x$ is $1 - q < 1/2$. Assume that signals are drawn independently, conditional on the true state in every period. Now suppose that the first two individuals observe a signal in favor of state (and hence action) 1. They will both choose action 1. Consider agent 3, who observes this sequence of 1s. Given that the information from others is as accurate as their own, two signals in favor of state 1 will overrule their own signal in favor of action 0. So agent 3 will also choose action 1, regardless of their own signal. In that case, the action does not convey any information about agent 3's signal. In particular, agents 4 and above are in the same situation as agent 3, so they too will ignore their own private information and choose action 1. Thus the sequence of individuals may herd on action 1.

Observe that this argument applies whether or not 1 is in fact an optimal action. So we have shown that there is a strictly positive probability that society may herd on the wrong action. Finally, observe that private signals arrive independently (and exogenously) over time, so eventually, there will always be enough information to infer the optimal action. This illustrates how observational learning may fail to aggregate private information.

One way to avoid inefficient herding is that agents draw signals with different levels of accuracy. This will induce private beliefs that vary across agents. In particular, if some agents receive very strong signals—signals that make one state much more likely than the other state—then they may choose to ignore past observations and choose an action that reflects their private signal. Suppose that the private belief about state 0, given by $\mu_t^0$, ranges between $\underline{\beta}$ and $\overline{\beta}$. Let us say that the beliefs are bounded if $\underline{\beta} > 0$ and $\overline{\beta} < 1$, and unbounded if $\underline{\beta} = 1 - \overline{\beta} = 0$. It is fairly straightforward to verify that if agents have bounded beliefs, then inefficient herding may occur, while if beliefs are unbounded, then observational learning will lead to an efficient choice of actions eventually.

In this model, the social network is elementary: a person at time $t$ gets to observe everyone who came before them. Let us briefly consider a variation with a richer network structure. Following Acemoglu, Dahleh, Lobel, and Ozdaglar (2011), we may introduce social networks in this model of sequential learning as follows: suppose that the agent at time $t$ can draw a sample from the past, $N_t \subset \{1, 2, \ldots, t-1\}$. Let this sample be drawn with some probability distribution $\mathcal{L}_t$. Some examples of such distributions are the following:

- $\mathcal{L}_t(\{1, 2, \ldots t-1\}) = 1$: This corresponds to the standard model, in which every agent observes the entire past history of actions.
- $\mathcal{L}_t(t-1) = 1$: Every agent observes only the immediately preceding agent.
- $\mathcal{L}_t$: This assigns equal probability to picking every subset of the past sequence of agents.

We can study the impact of social networks by varying the nature of the distribution $\mathcal{L}_t$.

For expositional simplicity, let us assume that beliefs are unbounded. Recall that if the observation window is the entire past history, then the arguments given here ensure that actions converge in probability to optimal actions. We examine the network needed to ensure learning.

A simple example illustrates the key idea: suppose that there is a positive probability such that for all $t \geq 2$, $\mathcal{L}_t(1) = p > 0$. Suppose that Mr. 1 chooses action 1. Under the assumption of unbounded beliefs, we know that at any point, there is a possibility of an agent with extremal signals (and the corresponding private beliefs) that sharply favor one state over the other. But under our hypothesis, there is a strictly positive probability that such an agent observes a single agent, Mr. 1, who has chosen action 1. It is then easy to see that this agent will choose an action that depends solely on their private signal. As beliefs arise independently over time and observation neighborhoods are independent across agents, it follows that there is a strictly positive probability that agents will choose an action in line with their private beliefs. This prevents asymptotic learning.

To avoid this problem, Acemoglu, Dahleh, Lobel, and Ozdaglar (2011) develop the property of expanding observations in social networks. A social network is said to satisfy expanding observations if, for all $k \in N$,

$$\lim_{t \to \infty} \mathcal{L}_t \left( \max_{n \in N_t} < k \right) = 1. \tag{13.37}$$

If the network does not satisfy this property, then it is has nonexpanding observations. Expanding observations rules out the example discussed previously, in which every agent samples agent 1 with strictly positive probability. It is possible to show that *if beliefs satisfy the unbounded beliefs assumption and networks satisfy the expanding observations assumption, then actions converge to the optimal action eventually.*

Let us sketch the main ideas underlying this result. First, we establish a generalized "improvement principal." Suppose that every agent $t$ gets to observe one person from the past; then there is a strict increase in the probability of Mr. t making the correct choice compared to the person they observe. This argument builds on the earlier discussion of the improvement upon "imitation" principle across neighbors in section 13.3. The second step is to show that this improvement principle can be extended to allow multiple observations. The third step exploits expanding observations to infer that later agents will have access to new information, so the expected utilities must converge to the maximum possible value (i.e., actions must converge to the optimal one).

We conclude here with a comment on the relation between the expanding assumptions property and RF network. Note that the key obstacle to complete learning in the repeated action setting is asymmetry in observation: there is a small group of agents who observe few others but are observed by everyone. In the sequential learning model, the expanding observations property of social networks ensures that agents eventually assign zero probability to any fixed set of early agents. This ensures that new information arrives in the system and ensures long-run learning.

### 13.7.2 An Experiment on Social Learning

We describe an experiment on wisdom of crowds that examines the effect of networks on information aggregation. The experiment is taken from Becker, Brackbill, and Centola (2017).

Individuals are engaged in an estimation task. Individuals guess once and they can revise their guesses two more times. In the control treatment, individuals are simply asked if they wish to revise their guess. In the social network treatment, after the first guess, they are shown the average of the guesses in their network neighborhood and asked to guess a second time. At the start of the third round, they get to see the guesses in the second round. Then they make a third guess. Participants are rewarded a monetary prize the value of which depended on the accuracy of their final estimate.

Subjects were allotted either to one of the two social networks or to a control condition (with no information sharing). In the decentralized network treatment, participants were placed in a regular network with degree 4, while in the centralized network treatment a single person was connected to everyone else (as in a star network). Subjects were not provided any information about their social networks—this was to ensure that subject experience was similar across the two network conditions. Subjects in the control condition were not placed into social networks, but were instead given the opportunity to answer the same questions without being exposed to social influence.

There were 40 subjects in the three treatments. In total, there were 13 experimental trials in each of the two networks (thus 1040 network subjects in all) plus 8 trials with the control group (comprising 320 subjects). The subjects were recruited using Mechanical Turk.

The principal findings are as follows: in the control treatment, there was a negligible decrease in dispersion of estimates and a small increase in accuracy of average estimate from round 1 to round 3. By contrast, the dispersion of opinions declined by over 40 percent in the two network treatments. In the decentralized network, the accuracy of estimate increased by over 20 percent. In the centralized network, the effects on accuracy of estimate depended on the "quality" of central agent's signal (relative to others). If the signal neutralized the bias of the signals of the other 39 individuals then social interaction led to much more accurate estimates by everyone. If the signal reinforced the bias then social interaction led to poorer estimates. For instance, if the true value is 100 and the group mean is 90, a central node with an estimate of either 105 (more accurate) or 120 (less accurate) will pull the group toward the truth. On the other hand, if the central node's initial estimate is 70, that would pull the group away from the truth.

## 13.8 Reading Notes

The study of social communication and influence has a long and distinguished history. Pioneering work was carried out by a group of sociologists around the mid-twentieth century. Lazarsfeld, Berelson, and Gaudet (1948) present an early empirical study of social influence on voting behavior. Katz and Lazarsfeld (1966) expand the scope of this early study to examine the role of social influence in marketing, fashion, film viewing, and public affairs. Coleman, Katz, and Menzel (1966) report on the adoption of a medical drug, tetracycline, among a group of physicians in the early 1950s. Rogers (1995b) provides an overview of the early work on communication and innovation.

Economists studying technological change in agriculture have focused on social learning in shaping the adoption of new input combinations for a variety of crops. An early contribution is Foster and Rosenzweig (1995), which explored HYV seeds in India. More recent work includes Bandiera and Rasul (2006), Munshi (2004), and Duflo, Kremer, and Robinson (2006). Most of this research presents evidence on social informational spillovers (without paying attention to the details of the network structure). Conley and Udry (2010) take a step forward in this area by collecting data on the information networks of farmers and presenting evidence on the role of such information neighborhoods in shaping the adoption of fertilizers in the cultivation of pineapple.

The case study on fishery in Hawaii is taken from Barnes, Lynham, Kalberg, and Leung (2016). The case study on climate change is taken from Funk and Hefferon (2019).

Establishing causality in network effects poses a number of challenges, which are greatly exacerbated when the network is endogenous. There is a body of sophisticated literature on these issues; see Manski (1995); Brock and Durlauf (2001); and Bramoullé, Djebbari, and Fortin (2009). Partly in response to these difficulties, recent research has used experiments to uncover network effects on opinion formation and behavior. We present in this chapter a case study on the wisdom of crowds taken from Becker, Brackbill, and Centola (2017). Christakis and Fowler (2007, 2013) study various aspects of learning and behavior in networks using both observational and experimental data.

The theoretical literature on information sharing and learning in networks may be seen as broadly following two approaches. One studies choices that generate information and social interactions that spread this information. As information spreads, it alters beliefs and thereby shapes the choice of subsequent actions. In this way, current choice and the network shape the generation of new information. This approach builds on the insights of the statistical literature on bandit-arms (Berry and Fristedt [1985]) and is very close in spirit to the economic development work on the adoption of new crops (as in Conley and Udry 2010). The model of learning in (directed) networks presented in section 13.3 was introduced in Bala and Goyal (1998), which established that connectedness was sufficient to ensure convergence of actions and utilities. This paper also identified the role of influential individuals in inhibiting learning and showed that egalitarian networks guarantee complete learning. Bala and Goyal (2001) studied the role of homophily and network integration in sustaining the diversity of beliefs and actions. In closely related work, Ellison and Fudenberg (1993, 1995) study social learning and the prospects of long-run diversity (they are less concerned with the network architecture dimensions of the learning process). These models involve collective experimentation, but, in the interests of tractability, they abstract from strategic considerations relating to the choice of actions; for an early study of strategic forces in collective experimentation, see Bolton and Harris (1999).

A second and more widely studied approach endows individuals with signals and examines the aggregation of this information via social interaction. The simplest model is one in which a sequence of individuals learn from the actions of previous individuals; influential early work in this tradition includes Banerjee (1992) and Bikhchandani, Hirshleifer, and Welch (1992). This model was elaborated upon by Smith and Sørensen (2000). For a model of sequential learning in which individuals learn from observing past actions and outcomes of the action, see Bala and Goyal (1995). Chamley (2004) presents an overview of the first generation of social learning models. This line of work was brought into a network setting by Gale and Kariv (2003), which proposes a model of guesses: individuals guess on the true state of the world and then update their guesses after observing the guesses of their neighbors. An interesting and technically sophisticated line of research explores observational learning in networks; for instance, see Rosenberg, Solan, and Vieille (2009); Acemoglu, Dahleh, Lobel, and Ozdaglar (2011); Mossel, Sly, and Tamuz (2015); and Mueller-Frank (2013). Mueller-Frank (2013) studies a general setting that goes beyond the case of decision rules that maximize expected utility, and allows arbitrary choice correspondences; he also permits the decision rules not to be common knowledge. Chen, Mueller-Frank, and Pai (2021) examine general conditions under which an outside principal can learn the true state without knowing the details of the information structure of individuals.

Within the information aggregation literature, there is also an alternative (a bounded rational) approach to information sharing and opinion formation. This approach is called

"DeGroot updating," as it builds on a model proposed by DeGroot (1974). Section 13.4 presented a model of DeGroot learning. Early antecedents of this approach to updating and consensus-reaching include French (1956) and Harary (1959). DeMarzo, Vayanos, and Zwiebel (2003) introduce the DeGroot model to economics and obtain a number of key early results on connectedness, social influence, and the rate of convergence to consensus. In more recent work, Golub and Jackson (2010, 2012) studied correct and incorrect consensus and the effects of homophily on the rate of convergence to consensus.

The binary state/action model was introduced by Gale and Kariv (2003) and has become a workhorse model for the study of observational learning and information aggregation in networks; for recent theoretical studies of this model, see Mossel, Sly, and Tamuz (2014, 2015). For more recent surveys of research on social learning in networks, see Goyal (2011) and Golub and Sadler (2016).

The dynamics of opinion formation and behavior have been extensively studied from an experimental perspective. Early contributions in the field of economics include Choi, Gale, and Kariv (2005) and Mobius, Phan, and Szeidl (2015). For a survey of research in economics, see Choi, Gallo, and Kariv (2016) and Breza (2016); and for recent research that tests the binary state, binary action model, see Grimm and Mengel (2020); Chandrasekhar, Larreguy, and Xandri (2020); and Choi, Goyal, Moisan, and To (2022). For experiments on learning in sociology and communications, see Centola (2011) and Centola and Baronchelli (2015).

We note that most of this research literature assumes that individuals can observe the choices and experience of their neighbors. There is a also a small but interesting strand of research that examines how networks affect the incentives of individuals to share their information. This work places the classical work of Crawford and Sobel (1982) within a network setting. Early contributions in this field include Galeotti, Ghiglino, and Squintani (2013) and Hagenbach and Koessler (2010). For a recent contribution that combines these two papers with network formation, see Goyal, Safranov, and To (2022).

There is a large literature on issues relating to verification and sharing of news in networks, recent papers include Kranton and McAdams (2022); Charlson (2022); Mostagir, Ozdaglar, and Siderius (2022); Candogan and Drakopoulos (2020); Chen and Papanastasiou (2021); Keppo, Kim, and Zhang (2022); Tornberg (2018); Nguyen, Yan, Thai et al. (2012); Hsu, Ajorlou, and Jadbabaie (2020); Acemoglu, Ozdaglar, and Siderius (2021). In addition to the questions relating to the amount and the accuracy of information that circulates in social networks, this literature also studies a number of questions relating to the role of the platform in shaping opinion formation in networks. It is impossible to do justice to this very exciting and currently very active field of work in this book. In section 13.6 our goal was to provide a very brief introduction to some of the issues that are being studied with the help of a parsimonious model. The model we presented was taken from Goyal and To (2022).

A slight different strand of the literature on news markets studies how the revenue generating process of media producers could bias content. Gentzkow and Shapiro (2006) find that news producers who benefit from having a reputation for accuracy slant their news toward consumers' initial beliefs. Besley and Prat (2006) and Gentzkow et al. (2006) find that producers who earn revenue from advertising reduces bias; In contrast, Ellman and Germano (2009) show that newspapers bias their news toward their advertisers.

## 13.9 Questions

1. The first three questions help the reader work through the mathematical details of propositions 13.1 and 13.2. To be able to make the arguments precise, let us describe the probability space in which all actions and realizations take place. This probability space is denoted by $(\Omega, \mathcal{F}, P^\theta)$, where $\Omega$ is the space of all outcomes, $\mathcal{F}$ is the $\sigma$ field, and $P^\theta$ is the probability measure induced over sample paths in $\Omega$ by the state $\theta \in \Theta$. In the two-action example discussed in the chapter, there are two states: $\theta_1$, in which action $a_1$ is optimal; and state $\theta_0$, where action $a_0$ is optimal.

   Let $\Theta$ be endowed with the discrete topology, and suppose that $\mathcal{B}$ is the Borel $\sigma$-field on this space. For rectangles of the form $\mathcal{T} \times H$, where $\mathcal{T} \subset \Theta$ and $H$ is a measurable subset of $\Omega$, let $P_i(\mathcal{T} \times H)$ be given by

$$P_i(\mathcal{T} \times H) = \sum_{\theta \in \mathcal{T}} \mu_{i,1}(\theta) P^\theta(H) \tag{13.38}$$

   for each individual $i \in N$. Each $P_i$ extends uniquely to all $\mathcal{B} \times \mathcal{F}$. We will assume that every individual's prior belief lies in the interior of $\mathcal{P}(\Theta)$ (i.e., individuals assume every state is possible). The stochastic processes are defined on the measurable space $(\Theta \times \Omega, \mathcal{B} \times \mathcal{F})$.

   A typical sample path takes the form $\omega = (\theta, \omega')$, where $\theta$ is the state of nature and $\omega'$ is an infinite sequence of sample outcomes:

$$\omega' = ((y^a_{i,1})_{a \in A, i \in N}, (y^a_{i,2})_{a \in A, i \in N}, \ldots), \tag{13.39}$$

   with $y^a_{i,t} \in Y^a_{i,t} \equiv Y$. Let $C_{i,t} = b_i(\mu_{i,t})$ denote the action of individual $i$ in period $t$, $Z_{i,t}$ the outcome of this action, and let $U_{i,t} = u(C_{i,t}, \mu_{i,t})$ be the expected utility of $i$ with respect to their own action at time $t$. Given this notation, the posterior beliefs of individual $i$ in period $t+1$ are

$$\mu_{i,t+1}(\theta|g) = \frac{\prod_{j \in N_i^d(g) \cup \{i\}} \phi(Z_{j,t}; C_{j,t}; \theta) \mu_{i,t}(\theta)}{\sum_{\theta' \in \Theta} \prod_{j \in N_i^d(g) \cup \{i\}} \phi(Z_{j,t}; C_{j,t}; \theta) \mu_{i,t}(\theta)}. \tag{13.40}$$

   In what follows, we will take $\theta_1$ to be the true state of nature. Note that

$$Q^{\theta_1} = \{\omega = (\theta, \omega') | \theta = \theta_1\} \tag{13.41}$$

   has $P^{\theta_1}$ probability 1. It will be assumed that the strong law of large numbers holds on $Q^{\theta_1}$. All statements of the form with probability 1 are with respect to measure $P^{\theta_1}$.

- Show that the following statement is true:

  The utilities of individuals converge: $\lim_{t\to\infty} U_{i,t}(\omega) = U_{i,\infty}(\omega)$, for every $i \in N$ with probability 1. If the society is strongly connected, then every individual gets the same long-run utility: $U_{i,\infty}(\omega) = U_{j,\infty}(\omega)$ for every pair of individuals $i, j \in N$ with probability 1.

2. Turning to the result on long-run optimal actions, recall that if $\mu_{i,0} \geq 1/2$, then the optimal action is $a_1$.

   - Show that the following property holds:

     Let $B(\delta_{\theta_1})$ be the set of beliefs on which optimal action corresponds to optimal action in state $\theta_1$. Fix an individual $i \in N$ with $|N_i(g)| + 1 \leq K$. For any $\lambda \in (0, 1)$, there is a set of sample paths $W_i$ satisfying $P^{\theta_1}(W_i) \geq \lambda$ and $d(\lambda) \in (0, 1)$ such that if $\mu_{i,1}(\theta_1) \geq d(\lambda)$, then

$$\omega \in W_i \Rightarrow A_i(\omega) \subset B(\delta_{\theta_1}). \tag{13.42}$$

     That is, if the path of outcomes lies in $W_i$, then the path of actions taken must converge to $a_1$.

3. We now explore the role of network structure in shaping social learning. For an individual whose prior $\mu_{i,1}(\theta_1) \geq d(\lambda)$, there is a set of sample paths $W_i$ with probability $\lambda$, such that $i$ will choose an optimal action forever on sample paths $\omega \in W_i$. Recall that two individuals $i$ and $j$ are said to be *locally independent* if they share no neighbors (i.e., $N_i(g) \cup \{i\} \cap N_j(g) \cup \{j\} = \emptyset$). A pairwise, locally independent group of individuals is a subset of $N$, such that any two persons $i, j$ in the set are mutually locally independent. Fix two numbers $K > 0$ (which sets an upper bound to the size of the neighborhood) and a $\bar{\lambda} > 0$ (which relates to the likelihood of positive information on action $a_1$). Let $\bar{d} = d(\bar{\lambda})$ be the corresponding value, whose existence is guaranteed by the previous step. Consider the collection of individuals $i \in N$ such that $|N_i| \leq K$ and $\mu_{i,1}(\theta_1) \geq \bar{d}$ are satisfied. Let $N_{K,\bar{d}}$ be a maximal group of pairwise, locally independent individuals chosen from this collection.

   - Show that the following statement is true:

     Assume a strongly connected society. Then

$$P^{\theta_1}(\cup_{i \in N}\{A_i(\omega) \not\subset B(\delta_{\theta_1})\}) \leq (1 - \bar{\lambda})^{N_{K,\bar{d}}}. \tag{13.43}$$

     In particular, if, for some $\bar{\lambda} > 0$ and $\bar{d} = d(\lambda)$, $|N_{K,\bar{d}}| \to \infty$, then the probability of everyone choosing the optimal action goes to 1.

4. Consider the model of Bayesian learning in a network. The network is as follows: individuals observe their neighbors and a set of common individuals (i.e., $N_i = \{i-1, i+1\} \cup \{7, 8, 9, 10, 11\}$ for all $i \in N$). Suppose that everyone is optimistic and that beliefs satisfy the following condition:

$$\inf_{i \in N} \mu_{i,1} > \frac{1}{2}; \; \sup_{i \in N} \mu_{i,1} < \frac{1}{1+x^2}, \tag{13.44}$$

where $x = (1-\pi)/\pi \in (0,1)$. Provide the reasoning to establish that there is a strictly positive probability for everyone to choose action $a_0$ from period 2 onward.

5. Show that one or more agents having positive self-weight and strong connectedness of the network are sufficient for the corresponding weighted matrix to be primitive.
6. (From Jackson [2008]). Consider the model with DeGroot updating. This question presents a slightly more general version of the convergence result in proposition 13.3. In network $g$, define a closed set of agents as $C \subset N$, such that there is no directed link from an agent in $C$ to an agent $j \notin C$, and there is no pair $i \in C$ and $j \notin C$, such that $W_{ij} > 0$. Show that every network contains at least one closed and strongly connected set of agents. Next, show that every network can be partitioned into a collection of strongly connected and closed groups and remaining agents who each have at least one directed path to an agent in a strongly connected and closed group.
7. Matrix $W$ is periodic if all cycles in the matrix are of equal length. Show that opinions converge for $W$ if and only if every set of nodes that is strongly connected and closed is aperiodic. Show that opinions converge to consensus in a strongly connected network that has an aperiodic $W$.
8. (From Jackson [2008]). Consider the network given in figure 13.15; the link pointing from $i$ to $j$ indicates the weight that $i$ places on $j$. Observe that this network is not strongly connected such that agent 1 will retain his original opinion through time. However, the other individuals in this society are influenced by each other. Compute the social influence vector and the limit beliefs in this society.

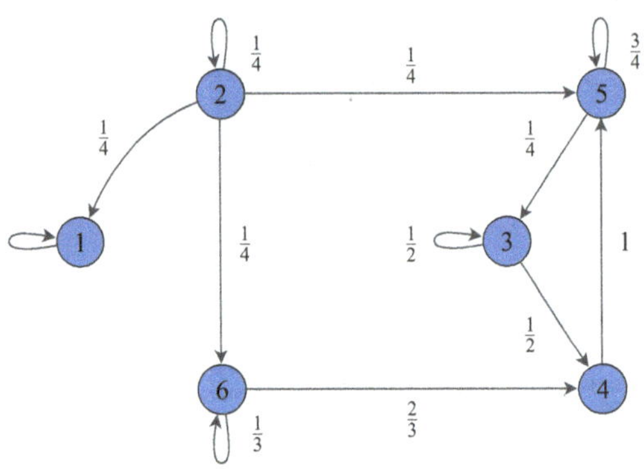


**Figure 13.15**
A network with multiple closed groups.

9. (From Jackson [2008]). Suppose the network is strongly connected and aperiodic. Show that if $W_{ij} = W_{ji}$, for every pair $i,j$ of individuals, then $s_i = 1/n$ for every $i \in N$. (Hint: Use proposition 13.3.)

# 14 Epidemics and Diffusion

## 14.1 Introduction

Large-scale diseases have had a profound impact on human history; influenza, measles, tuberculosis, and sexually transmitted diseases continue to infect millions of people every year. In extreme instances, such as the spread of smallpox, measles, and tuberculosis in Central and South America—epidemics can lead to the collapse of entire civilizations. The spread of a disease is determined by the properties of the pathogen in question (its contagiousness, the length of its infectious period, and its severity) and on how infected individuals interact with others. This chapter studies the relation between the networks of interaction and the dynamics of epidemics. It concludes with an application to the diffusion of human behaviors in networks.

We start in section 14.2 with a brief overview of the empirical evidence on major disease epidemics. The discussion covers important episodes of epidemics in history and then turns to contemporary epidemic diseases. We note that some diseases can be had only once, while others can be contracted multiple times; some need only casual contact, while others need close or intimate contact to spread. We also note that some diseases exhibit explosive growth, while others persist at low levels. How can we explain the extinction of some diseases and the persistence of others? What is the role of contact networks in shaping the persistence of epidemics? What sort of policies can help in alleviating these epidemics? This chapter will develop theoretical models in order to understand these questions.

The pathogen and the network are closely intertwined: even within the same population, the contact networks for two diseases can have very different structures, depending on the diseases' respective modes of transmission. For a highly contagious disease, involving air-borne transmission based on coughs and sneezes, the contact network will include a huge number of links, including any two people who sat together on a bus or an airplane. For a disease requiring close contact, such as a sexually transmitted disease, the contact network will be much sparser, with fewer pairs of people being connected.

At an intuitive level, the spread of a disease from one person to others should depend on its infectiousness and on how many contacts this person has had. Our first step is to formalize this idea in the context of a model where, starting with a single infected person, every person meets $k$ distinct and new individuals. We study the conditions under which the disease will spread and when it will die out. The analysis clarifies the key role of the *reproductive number*, which is the product of the infectiousness and the number of contacts. We show that in this simple network, a disease will spread if and only if the reproductive number is larger than 1. We then turn to the spread of diseases in more general networks.

We introduce the Susceptible-Infected-Recovered (SIR) model of disease dynamics: a node either is susceptible to a disease (S), is infected by the disease (I), or has recovered from the disease (R). The aim is to understand how infectiousness and network structure determine the size of the epidemic. A key observation is that we can study the dynamics of the disease in terms of an equivalent static model—we refer to this static formulation as a *percolation*. From this perspective, we show how methods from random graph theory can be employed to understand how far a disease spreads in Erdős-Rényi random graphs. We then study disease spread in general random graphs (building on the discussion of configuration model in chapter 2). We show that the disease is more likely to spread the greater the dispersion in degree relative to the mean degree in the network. This ratio of variance to mean degree may be interpreted as a measure of the relative influence of a node: greater variance indicates the presence of individuals whose degree is much higher than the average. Recall from our discussions in chapters 1, 2, and 5 that this ratio can grow without bound in scale-free/power law networks: this means that diseases with arbitrarily small infectiousness can spread to a large population in such networks.

We then turn to diseases that an individual can suffer from multiple times. This calls for a modification of the basic SIR model, and leads us to the Susceptible-Infected-Susceptible (SIS) model. Individuals can be in one of two states: they are susceptible (S) or infected (I); once they recover from a disease, they become susceptible (S) again. A prominent example of such a disease is the flu. We locate this SIS process on a network and study the size of infection. The analysis yields an insight that is similar to what we found for the SIR model: diseases with arbitrarily small infectiousness can be sustained by scale-free networks.

Our theoretical results on the permeability of networks are empirically relevant. In chapter 1, we presented a study of romantic and sexual relationships in an American high school and showed that there is a giant component in that network: this suggests that once a sexually transmitted disease takes hold, it can infect a very large number of people. Our results on scale-free networks draw attention to the role of a superspreader event, an event that brings together large numbers of people from different parts of a country can facilitate the explosive spread of a disease. We present a case study of major religious festivals in India in this context. Similarly, in chapter 1, we showed that computer and information networks (like Twitter and the World Wide Web) have a very unequal degree distribution. Our theoretical results suggest that these networks may be vulnerable to the diffusion of worms and viruses.

We then turn to the diffusion of behaviors and optimal targeting of interventions. We show that random vaccinations may be helpful to contain diseases in homogenous random graphs like the Erdős-Rényi network, but that they are very ineffective in scale-free networks. However, targeting highest-degree nodes for vaccination can be very effective in scale-free networks.

Finally, we present a case study of the adoption of microfinance in South Indian villages. This study draws attention to the advantages of seeding more central nodes in facilitating the diffusion of new products. Identifying more central individuals requires investments in network information that may be very large and motivates an enquiry into the value added of optimal versus random seeding. We conclude with a discussion of the circumstances in which random seeding may be attractive.

This chapter ends with a section that contains supplementary material on the Bass model of diffusion.

## 14.2 Empirical Background

In this section, we provide a very brief description of a few diseases—plague, smallpox, tuberculosis, influenza, and acquired immunodeficiency syndrome (AIDS)—that have had large-scale impacts on society.

### 14.2.1 Plague

Plague, caused by a bacterium called, *Yersinia pestis*, has been the cause of some of the most devastating epidemics in history—the Black Death in the fourteenth century and a pandemic in Asia in the late nineteenth and early twentieth centuries. *Yersinia* causes three types of plague in humans: bubonic, pneumonic, and septicemic. Plague is transmitted between animals and humans by the bite of infected fleas, direct contact with infected tissues, and inhalation of infected respiratory droplets. Plague can be a very severe disease, with a case-fatality ratio of 30 percent to 60 percent for the bubonic type; pneumonic plague is almost always fatal when left untreated. We focus on the time line and impact of the Black Death in this discussion. We draw on documents provided by the Centers for Disease Control and Prevention (CDC) (https://www.cdc.gov/plague) and the *Encyclopedia Britannica* (https://www.britannica.com/event/Black-Death).

The plague that caused the Black Death probably originated in China in the early- to mid-1300s. In 1347, the plague decimated the army of the Khan Janibeg while he was besieging the Genoese trading port of Kaffa (now Feodosiya) in Crimea. Janibeg catapulted plague-infested corpses into the town in an effort to infect his enemies. From Kaffa, Genoese ships carried the epidemic west to Mediterranean ports, affecting Sicily (1347), North Africa, mainland Italy, Spain, and France (1348), and Austria, Hungary, Switzerland, Germany, and the Low Countries (1349). A ship from Calais carried the plague to Dorset, England, in 1348. The plague reached the extreme north of England, Scotland, Scandinavia, and the Baltic countries in 1350.

Roughly one-third of the European population—around 25 million people—is estimated to have died from the plague between 1347 and 1351. The population of western Europe did not again reach its pre-1348 level until the beginning of the sixteenth century (150 years later).

The Black Death had profound and wide-ranging effects on society. Trade suffered, and wars were temporarily abandoned. There were more long-lasting effects as well, as a large number of workers died and the balance of power between landlords and tenants altered. This led to landowners paying wages and money rents. Wages for artisans and other workers increased. Commentators view the Black Death as a turning point, bringing large-scale changes in the feudal structures of society that ultimately led to the Renaissance in Europe.

Plagues are no longer a major source of concern today—the total number of cases at a global level rarely exceeds a few thousand. This is because we understand how plagues spread and because there are drugs that can effectively treat those who become infected.

### 14.2.2 Spanish Flu

The 1918 influenza pandemic was perhaps the biggest pandemic of the twentieth century. A virus called influenza type A, subtype H1N1, was the cause of this pandemic. Influenza is transmitted from person to person through airborne respiratory secretions. Our discussion draws on the *Encyclopedia Britannica* (https://www.britannica.com/event/influenza-pandemic-of-1918-1919) and the website of the CDC (https://www.cdc.gov/flu/pandemic-resources/).

The origins of the flu are unclear, but it was first widely discussed by the press in Spain and this gave the pandemic its name. As World War I was drawing to an end, the movement of troops was probably a key mechanism for the spread of this virus. By the summer of 1918, the virus had reached parts of Russia, Africa, Asia, and New Zealand. This first wave was comparatively mild. But a second, more lethal wave began in August/September 1918. During this wave, pneumonia developed quickly, with patients often dying only two days after experiencing the first symptoms. As social distancing measures were enforced, the second wave began to die down toward the end of November. However, once those measures were relaxed, a third wave began in the winter and early spring of 1919. Although not as deadly as the second wave, the third wave still claimed a large number of lives. By that summer, the virus had run its course in many parts of the world. Some historians suggest that there was a fourth wave in winter 1920, although it was far less virulent.

It is estimated that about 500 million people—roughly one-third of the world's population—were infected with this virus. The number of deaths is estimated to be at least 25 million, though some scholars claim that it was more than 50 million.

As no vaccine was available and there were no antibiotics to treat secondary bacterial infections that can be associated with influenza, health policy measures were limited to nonpharmaceutical interventions. These included limits on contact and interactions (e.g., isolation, quarantine, and restrictions on public meetings) and improvements in personal hygiene (e.g., use of disinfectants). While the Spanish flu has become part of history, influenza remains a health problem of major concern even today: there are three to five million cases of acute influenza and between 250,000 and 500,000 deaths annually.

### 14.2.3 AIDS

AIDS is a transmissible disease of the immune system caused by the human immunodeficiency virus (HIV). HIV is a lentivirus (the term literally means "slow virus," and it is a member of the retrovirus family) that slowly attacks and destroys the immune system, the body's defense against infection, leaving an individual vulnerable to a variety of other infections (and malignancies) that eventually cause death. This virus is transmitted by the direct transfer of bodily fluids—such as blood and blood products, semen and other genital secretions, or breast milk—from an infected person to an uninfected person. AIDS is the final stage of HIV infection, during which time fatal infections and cancers frequently arise. Our discussion draws on documents from the CDC website (https://www.cdc.gov/hiv/).

The origins of HIV remain unclear. A virus that is genetically similar to HIV has been found in chimpanzees and gorillas in western equatorial Africa. That virus is known as simian immunodeficiency virus (SIV). It was originally thought to be harmless in chimpanzees, but in 2009 a team of researchers investigating chimpanzee populations in Africa found that SIV causes AIDS-like illness in the animals. SIV may have migrated to humans through the consumption of the flesh of infected chimpanzees.

The first cases of AIDS may be traced to CDC reports published in 1981. These reports drew attention to pneumonia in five homosexual men in Los Angeles that was likely acquired through sexual contact. The reports also described an outbreak of a rare cancer called Kaposi sarcoma in homosexual men in New York City and San Francisco. Researchers subsequently established that the infections and cancers were manifestations of an acquired immunodeficiency syndrome, which became known as AIDS.

According to the World Health Organization (WHO), about 36.7 million people were living with HIV, approximately 1.8 million people were newly infected with HIV, and about 1 million people died of HIV-related causes in 2016. In the period 1981–2016, about 35 million people died of HIV infection. From wreaking havoc on certain populations (such as the gay community in San Francisco in the 1980s) to infecting more than one-third of adults in sub-Saharan African countries such as Botswana, Swaziland, and Zimbabwe at the turn of the twenty-first century, AIDS continues to have a devastating social impact. AIDS appears to have been brought under control in rich countries but much less so in poor countries.

### 14.2.4 Tuberculosis

Tuberculosis is an infectious disease that is caused by a tubercle bacillus called *Mycobacterium tuberculosis*. The tubercle bacillus is a small, rod-shaped bacterium that is extremely hardy; it can survive for months in a state of dryness and can also resist the action of mild disinfectants. Infection spreads primarily through the respiratory route directly from an infected person who discharges live bacilli into the air. Minute droplets ejected by sneezing, coughing, and even talking can contain hundreds of tubercle bacilli that may be inhaled by a healthy person. Our discussion here draws on the *Encyclopedia Britannica* (https://www.britannica.com/science/tuberculosis).

During the eighteenth and nineteenth centuries, tuberculosis reached near-epidemic proportions in the rapidly urbanizing and industrializing societies of Europe and North America. Indeed, consumption (as it was then known) was the leading cause of death for all age groups in the Western world from that period until the early twentieth century. Since the 1940s, though, antibiotic drugs have reduced the length of treatment to months instead of years, and drug therapy has done away with the old tuberculosis sanatoriums where patients were nursed for years and frequently died.

Due to a combination of more hygienic living conditions and antibiotic drugs, the rate of deaths from tuberculosis in developed countries declined sharply over the first half of the twentieth century. In England and Wales, the death rate dropped from 190 per 100,000 population in 1900 to 7 per 100,000 in the early 1960s. In the US, during the same time period, it dropped from 194 per 100,000 to approximately 6 per 100,000. In the early twenty-first century, tuberculosis is mainly a disease of the developing world, especially in regions of Africa, South and Southeast Asia, and the eastern Mediterranean. There are 8–10 million new cases of tuberculosis each year, and between 1.6 million and 2 million die.

### 14.2.5 Smallpox

Smallpox is caused by the *Variola* virus (major or minor). The disease begins with a high fever, headache, and back pain, and then proceeds to an eruption on the skin that leaves the face and limbs covered with pockmarks (or pox). Smallpox spreads from one person to another through close contact, usually by inhalation of the virus that had been expelled in the breath or saliva droplets of an infected person. Despite the hardiness of the *Variola* virus, smallpox is not highly infectious; infected persons usually did not infect more than two to five of their closest contacts. Our discussion draws on the *Encyclopedia Britannica* (https://www.britannica.com/science/smallpox) and the CDC website (https://www.cdc.gov/smallpox/).

There is evidence of the prevalence of smallpox going back 3,000 years to the time of the pharaohs in Egypt. For centuries, it was one of the world's most-dreaded plagues, killing as many as 30 percent of its victims, most of them children. Those who survived were permanently immune to a second infection, but they faced a lifetime of disfigurement, and in some cases blindness.

There are systematic records of smallpox epidemics starting in the seventeenth century: a huge pandemic spread from Europe to the Middle East in 1614, and epidemics occurred regularly in Europe throughout the seventeenth and eighteenth centuries. In the eighteenth century, an estimated 400,000 people died annually of smallpox. Introduced to the Americas by European conquerors and settlers, smallpox decimated Indigenous groups in North America, including the Aztecs of Mexico, the Incas of South America, and the Araucanians of Chile. The Australian Aboriginal populations also suffered large losses from the disease in the nineteenth century. It is estimated that over 300 million people have died due to smallpox in the twentieth century. But this was also one of the first diseases to be controlled by a vaccine, following the experiments of the English physician Edward Jenner in 1796. The WHO began an intensive global eradication program against smallpox in 1967, and in 1980, the disease was officially declared eradicated.

### 14.2.6 COVID-19

COVID-19 is an acute disease that is caused by a coronovirus. The main symptoms are a high temperature, a continuous cough, and a loss of the sense of smell and taste. Over time, a variety of other complications may arise, such as acute pneumonia. The first cases of COVID-19 were identified in the Chinese city of Wuhan in December 2019. It spreads through contact with infected individuals. As of August 2021, it is estimated that over 200 million people have been infected and over 4 million people have died due to COVID. It is the most devastating epidemic of the twenty-first century. Our discussion draws attention to the role of contact networks in the explosive spread of COVID in India in 2021. The data is taken from www.coronavirus.jhu.edu.

The first cases in India were detected in January 2020, but throughout the rest of the year, rates of infection remained below 50,000 per day. Similarly, death rates remained below 500 per day through most of 2020. In the first quarter of 2021 (January until mid-March), the rates of infection and mortality were very low. However, by the end of March, the rate of infection started climbing. Over the period of mid-April to mid-May, over 250,000 new cases were recorded daily. As a result, from the end of April to mid-June, over 3,000 deaths were recorded daily. We elaborate next on one of the events believed to have led to a massive increase in infections in April and May 2021.

As COVID spreads through human-to-human contact, an event that brings very large numbers of individuals together can dramatically increase the rate of infection. We illustrate this point through a discussion of the Kumbh Mela in India in April 2021. Our discussion draws on an article in the *Guardian* from May 30, 2021: https://www.theguardian.com/world/2021/may/30/

On April 12, India registered 169,000 new COVID-19 cases. However, in the same week, millions of people were gathering on the banks of the Ganges River in the holy city of Haridwar to celebrate the Kumbh Mela, one the holiest festivals in the Hindu calendar. By the time the festival ended, on April 28, more than 9 million people had attended. By April 15, more than 2,000 festivalgoers had already tested positive for COVID-19. We now briefly describe how the Kumbh Mela acted as a key spreader of COVID-19 infection by tracing the routes taken by two pilgrims from different parts of the country. Figure 14.1 presents a snapshot of the spread of the disease across space.

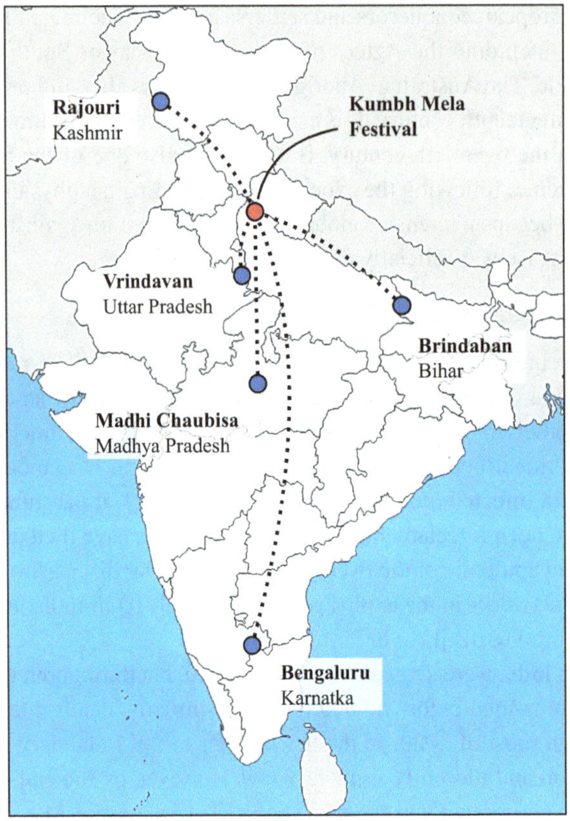


**Figure 14.1**
Superspreader event: Kumbh Mela. *Source*: May 30, 2021. *The Guardian*.

We start with the case of Thakur Puran Singh, 79, from Rajouri in Kashmir. Singh and his extended family drove to Haridwar on April 9. For the next five days, the family took multiple swims in the Ganges. On April 16, the day after returning home, Singh began to experience COVID symptoms, and by April 21, his condition had deteriorated, and he died shortly afterward. Eight days later, his elder brother, Balwant Singh, also died. A test-and-trace official said that more than two dozen people contracted the virus after contact with Singh's family members. We turn next to the case of a 67-year-old woman from Nandini Layout, a suburb of Bengaluru, who tested positive for COVID days after returning from the Kumbh Mela. She lived with her daughter-in-law, who worked in a hospital: tests soon confirmed she too had COVID. Testing teams at the hospital found that 12 patients and 3 staffers had contacted the diease. In addition, 18 other close contacts of the woman were eventually diagnosed with COVID, but the true spread of the virus was probably even higher.

### 14.2.7 Computer Viruses

The discussion so far has focused on biological diseases that infect human beings. Over the past three decades, with the growth of the Internet, the spread of computer viruses and worms has become important. In 2009, roughly 10 million computers were infected with malware designed to steal online credentials. It is estimated that in Europe, annual damage caused by malware is around 9.3 billion euros, while in the US, the annual costs of identity theft are estimated at \$2.8 billion. For a general overview of computer security issues, see Anderson (2020).

We present here a short discussion of one computer epidemic called ILoveYou, caused by a worm that originated in Philippines on May 5, 2000. It spread westward across the world: Hong Kong, Europe, and then to the US. Within 10 days, over 50 million infections had been recorded. Once the worm infected a computer, it would overwrite files and spread itself through email messages sent to contacts of the captured computer. It is estimated that this worm caused \$5.5 to \$8.7 billion in damages and it cost around \$15 billion to remove it (https://en.wikipedia.org/wiki/ILOVEYOU). For a discussion on other computer viruses see chapter 7.

Let us summarize a few points arising from these case studies. Large-scale disease epidemics are a major occurrence in human history and account for several million deaths every year, even with the modern medicine of today. The scale and persistence of COVID reaffirm the seriousness of the threat posed by such diseases. Many of these diseases originated in animals, while some of them have human origin. The mode of contagion of these diseases varies greatly: in some cases, it requires frequent and intimate contact among humans (such as with AIDS), while in others, infection can spread via casual contact (such as with flu), and in still others, infection occurs via third-party agents (such as plague) that carry disease from an infected person to an uninfected one. Some diseases (like smallpox) can infect a person only once, while others (like flu and COVID) can infect the same person multiple times. Finally, human responses to diseases range from the development of vaccines, to limitations on contact, to changes in standards of hygiene. In all these cases, patterns of human interaction play a central role in the spread of diseases.

## 14.3 A Simple Threshold for Epidemics

In this section, we consider a model in which there is an initial infected individual who remains infected for some time, and during this period, they can transmit the disease to those they come in contact with. Each of these contacts in turn also have a set of distinct contacts, who have their contacts, and so forth. The infectiousness of the disease is captured in a number $p \in (0, 1)$ that may be interpreted as the probability that a contact is infected. Suppose for simplicity that everyone has $k$ contacts. Our goal is to understand how $p$ and $k$ determine the size of the epidemic. The exposition here draws heavily on Easley and Kleinberg (2010).

The contact network is illustrated in figure 14.2; in this network, the number of contacts is $k = 4$, and we present the first three layers of the network. This network is a tree with

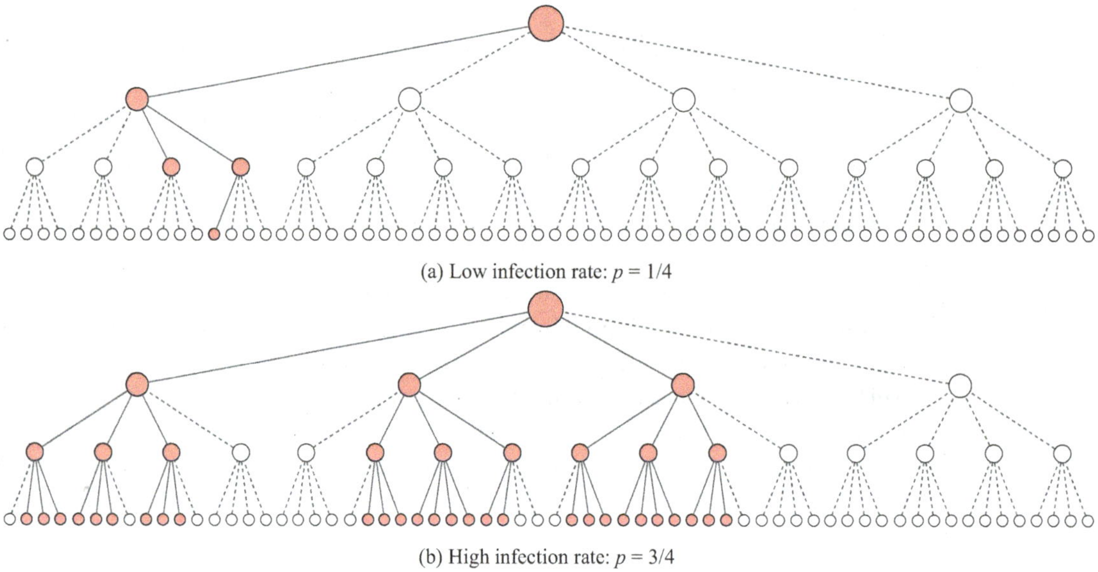


**Figure 14.2**
Spread of disease: varying infectiousness.

a single root—the initially infected individual. Every node is connected to $k$ nodes in the level below it, and every node (other than the root) is connected to a single node in the level above it. As we wish to understand whether a disease will persist indefinitely, we will find it convenient to work with a tree that is infinite.

To appreciate the basic forces at work, it is helpful to plot a few examples of disease spread through the network. Figure 14.2 illustrates the evolution of an epidemic that infects 1 person in the first level, 2 in the second level, and 1 again in the third level (and possibly none in subsequent layers). It also shows a more virulent epidemic, with 3 people infected in the first level, 9 infected in the second level and 28 at level three (and possibly even more in the subsequent levels). As a result, the disease spreads explosively. We may interpret the difference between figures 14.2(a) and 14.2(b) as arising from differences in the infectiousness of the disease: the value of $p$ is much higher in the latter case.

Figure 14.3 brings out the role of connectivity of the network: there is relatively little infection in the network in figure 14.3(a), while there is persistent and continuing infection in figure 14.3(b). These diagrams suggest that if the disease ever fails to infect at a certain level, then it will die out. In other words, there are two possibilities—either the disease dies out after a finite number of steps or it continues to infect people in every wave, proceeding infinitely through the contact network. Figures 14.2 and 14.3 suggest that higher $p$ and $k$ make a long-lasting epidemic more likely. To make this idea more precise, we will define a fundamental notion in epidemics: the *reproductive number*.

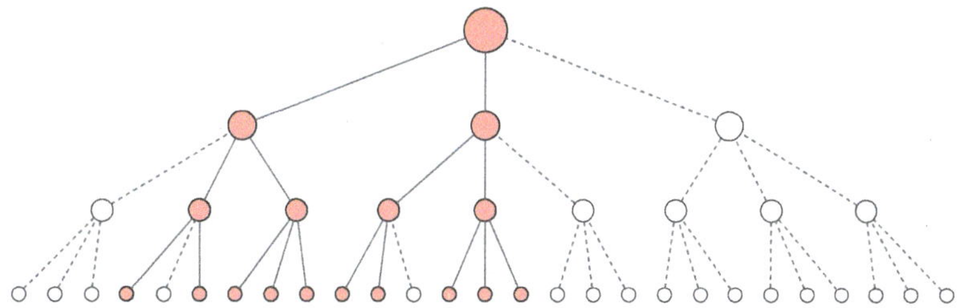

(a) Low connectivity, $k = 3$

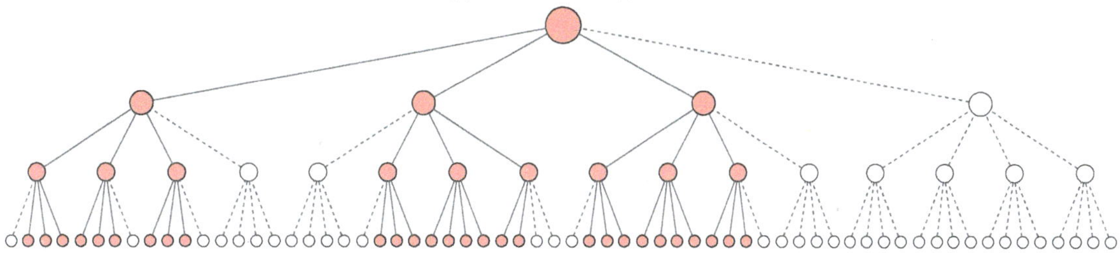

(b) High connectivity, $k = 4$

**Figure 14.3**
Spread of disease: varying $k$.

The reproductive number, denoted as $R_0$, is the expected number of new cases of the disease caused by a single individual. In our model, everyone meets $k$ new people and infects each of them with probability $p$. The reproductive number here is given by $R_0 = pk$. We will show that the outcome of the disease is determined by whether $R_0$ is smaller or larger than 1.

Let $q_n$ denote the probability that the epidemic survives for at least $n$ levels—in other words, that some individual in the $n$th level of the tree becomes infected. Let $q^*$ be the limit of $q_n$ as $n$ goes to infinity; we can think of $q^*$ as the probability that the disease persists indefinitely. We will establish the following result.

**Proposition 14.1** *Consider a tree network with a single root, and suppose that infection spreads from the root downward. If $R_0 < 1$, then $q^* = 0$, and if $R_0 > 1$, then $q^* > 0$.*

It is instructive to work through the argument step by step. Note that the number of individuals at any given level exceeds the number at the previous level by a factor of $k$, so the number at level $n$ is $k^n$. Let us examine the expected number of infected individuals at different levels. For level $n$, this will be a random number ranging from 0 to $k^n$.

Define $X_d$ to be a random variable equal to the number of infected individuals at level $d$. For every person $j$ at level $n$, let $Y_{nj}$ be a random variable equal to 1 if $j$ is infected, and equal to 0 otherwise. Then

$$X_n = Y_{n1} + Y_{n2} + \cdots + Y_{nm}, \tag{14.1}$$

where $m = k^n$. Using the result that the expectation of the sum of random variables is equal to the sum of their expectations, we may rewrite equation (14.1) as

$$E[X_n] = E[Y_{n1} + Y_{n2} + \cdots + Y_{nm}] = E[Y_{n1}] + E[Y_{n2}] + \cdots + E[Y_{nm}]. \tag{14.2}$$

Note that $E[Y_{nj}] = 1 \times Pr[Y_{nj} = 1] + 0 \times Pr[Y_{nj} = 0] = Pr[Y_{nj} = 1]$, so the expectation of any $Y_{nj}$ is just the probability that $j$ gets infected. But what is the probability that $j$ at level $n$ gets infected? This happens when each of the $n$ contacts leading from the root to $j$ successfully transmits the disease. The probability of this event is $p^n$: $E[Y_{nj}] = p^n$. Equipped with this formula, the expected number of infections at level $n$ is given by:

$$E[X_n] = p^n k^n = (pk)^n = R_0^n. \tag{14.3}$$

Equipped with this formula, let us return to the original object of interest, $q^*$. We note that

$$E[X_n] = 1Pr[X_n = 1] + 2Pr[X_n = 2] + 3Pr[X_n = 3] + \cdots \tag{14.4}$$

An equivalent way to write the expected value is

$$E[X_n] = Pr[X_n \geq 1] + Pr[X_n \geq 2] + Pr[X_n \geq 3] + \cdots \tag{14.5}$$

It follows, then, that the expected value $E[X_n] \geq Pr[X_n \geq 1]$. However, $Pr[X_n \geq 1]$ is the definition of $q_n$; thus $E[X_n] \geq q_n$. But if $R_0 < 1$, then $R_0^n \to 0$ as $n$ grows; hence $q_n$ must also converge to 0. This shows that $q^* = 0$ when $R_0 < 1$.

Let us take up the case of $R_0 > 1$ next. It is easy to see that $E[X_n]$ grows and is unbounded in $n$. However, this is not generally sufficient to ensure that the disease persists. A question at the end of the chapter examines this issue. So we need to dig a little deeper into the structure of the model. Our method is to compute $q_n$ in terms of $q_{n-1}$, and we will use equation (14.5) to work out the value of $q^*$.

Consider the following event: *The disease spreads through the root node's first contact j and then continues to persist down to n levels in the part of the tree reachable through j.* For this event to obtain, we need $j$ to catch the disease directly from the root, which happens with probability $p$. At this point, $j$ becomes completely analogous to the root node of its own branching process, consisting of all nodes reachable from it downward in the tree. So, for the event to occur, after $j$ is infected, the disease must persist for the remaining $n - 1$ levels: by definition, this occurs with probability $q_{n-1}$. As $j$ is infected by the root with probability $p$, it follows that the probability of the event is $pq_{n-1}$. This event fails to hold with a probability of $1 - pq_{n-1}$. There is an identical copy of the event for each of the direct contacts of the root node, and each fails to hold with probability $1 - pq_{n-1}$. As each of them starts with a different root and we are considering a tree network, the events are independent, so the probability that they all fail to hold is $(1 - pq_{n-1})^k$.

But by definition of $q_n$, we know that the probability that the event fails to occur is $1 - q_n$. Hence,

$$1 - q_n = (1 - pq_{n-1})^k. \tag{14.6}$$

Simplifying, we get

$$q_n = 1 - (1 - pq_{n-1})^k. \tag{14.7}$$

We are interested in values of $q_n$ as $n$ gets large. Let us define function $f(x) = 1 - (1 - px)^k$, then we can write equation (14.7) as $q_n = f(q_{n-1})$. Now our goal is to study the limit of the sequence $1, f(1), f(f(1)), f(f(f(1))), \ldots$, which is obtained by applying $f$ repeatedly. Function $f$ satisfies the following properties:

1. $f(0) = 0 \quad \text{and} \quad f(1) = 1 - (1 - p)^k < 1.$ (14.8)
2. $f'(x) = pk(1 - px)^{k-1}$ is positive but monotonically decreasing.
3. $f'(x)$ at $x = 0$ is equal to $f'(0) = pk = R_0$. (14.9)

In the case $R_0 > 1, f(x)$ therefore lies above $x$ for small values of $x$. Putting together these observations, and noting that $f$ is a continuous function on the range $x \in [0, 1]$, we conclude that there is a unique value $x^* > 0$ such that $x^* = f(x^*)$. This concludes the proof. ■

The threshold property developed in proposition 14.1 highlights a sharp transition at the threshold point. Suppose $R_0$ is just slightly below 1 and we increase probability $p$ by a little. This could result in a positive probability of a large outbreak. Similarly, if $R_0$ is just slightly above 1, then slightly reducing $p$ to push $R_0$ below 1 would eliminate the risk of a large epidemic outbreak. For example, if $k = 3$ and $p = 0.4$, then $q^* = .44$. Reducing $p$ to 0.35 reduces $q^*$ to .14; reducing $p$ further, to below 1/3, reduces $q^*$ to 0. As $R_0$ is the product of $p$ and $k$, we can think of two basic types of public-health policies to lower $R_0$: quarantining people (which lowers $k$), and encouraging changes in behavior such as wearing masks or being more hygienic (which lowers $p$).

In the model of this section, the disease can only move from higher to lower levels and there is only one route to the spread of the disease from an upstream to a downstream node (as the network is a tree). As we turn to more general networks, we will need to think about both these assumptions. We first take up the case of a disease that a person can get only once (such as smallpox), and then we study a disease that a person can get multiple times (such as flu).

## 14.4 The Susceptible-Infected-Recovered (SIR) Model

Here, we consider a model of a disease that an individual can suffer from only once. There are therefore three states for an individual: they may be susceptible, infected, or recovered. This is the Susceptible-Infectious-Recovered (SIR) model. Our discussion will focus on the relation between network structure and the spread of a disease; we will draw on the exposition of the basic theory in Easley and Kleinberg (2010) and Jackson (2008).

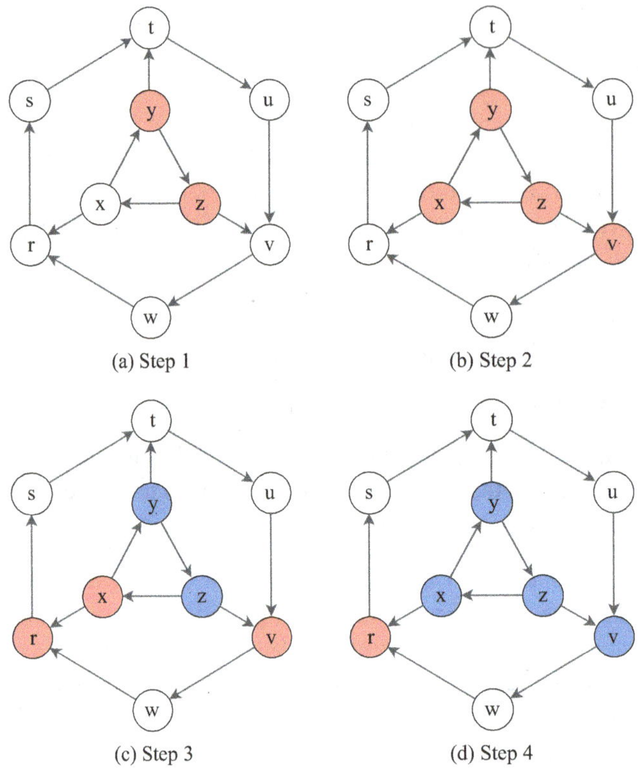


**Figure 14.4**
The SIR process.

The dynamics of infection are determined by the contact network, the probability of contagion $p$, and the length of infection time $t_I$. At the start of the process, some nodes are in state $I$ and all other nodes are in state $S$. A node $v$ that enters state $I$ remains infectious for $t_I$ steps. During each of these $t_I$ steps, $v$ has a probability $p$ of passing the disease to each of its susceptible neighbors. After $t_I$ steps, node $v$ is no longer infectious or susceptible to further bouts of the disease and is referred to as "recovered" or "removed."

Figure 14.4 presents an example of the SIR model unfolding on a contact network. At each step, blank nodes are in a susceptible state, the shaded nodes in red are in the $I$ state, and the shaded nodes in blue are in the $R$ state. Notice that the basic model in section 14.3 is a special case of the SIR model: it corresponds to the case $t_I = 1$ and a contact network that is an infinite tree, with each node connected to a fixed number of neighbors in the level below it.

We now explain how a network structure can alter the dynamics as compared to the basic tree structure described in the previous section. The simplest way to see this is to reconsider

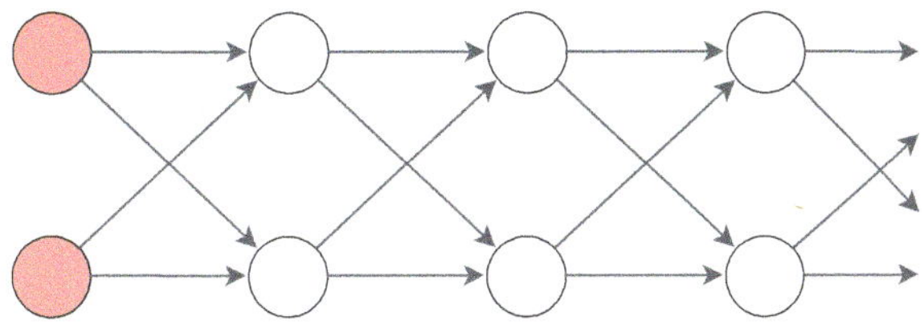

**Figure 14.5**
Tunneling in networks. *Source*: Easley and Kleinberg (2010).

the threshold result given in proposition 14.1. Recall that in the tree network, the disease dies out if and only if the reproductive number $R_0 < 1$. We will show that this result is no longer true when we consider more general networks.

Consider the network illustrated in figure 14.5, and suppose that these levels of two nodes continue indefinitely to the right. To fix ideas, let us consider an SIR epidemic in which $t_I = 1$, the infection probability p is 2/3, and the two nodes at the far left are the only nodes that are infected at the start.

In this simple network, each infected node has edges to two nodes in the next layer: as every link comes alive with probability $2/3$, the expected number of new cases is $2 \times 2/3 = 4/3 > 1$. Hence in this example, $R_0 > 1$. In the original model with the tree network from the previous section, we know that this means that there is a strictly positive probability that the disease will persist indefinitely.

However, in the network in figure 14.5, the disease will die out almost certainly after reaching only a finite number of steps. To see this, note that in each layer, there are four edges leading to the next layer. As each can fail with probability $1/3$, there is a probability $(1/3)^4 = 1/81$ that all four edges will fail to transmit the disease. It follows that there is a probability of at least $1/81$ that each layer will be its last. Therefore, from standard reasoning, the disease will cease to spread after a finite number of layers, with probability 1.

This is a very simple example, but it helps us understand that network structure can be more or less conducive to the spread of a disease. This happens because the network forces the disease to pass through a narrow tunnel, in which a small breakdown in contagion can wipe it out.

### 14.4.1 Percolation

We have presented the SIR model as a dynamic process, in which the state of the nodes evolves over time, one step at a time. This is illuminating because it captures the temporal patterns of the disease as it spreads through a network. In this section, we will explore an alternative perspective on the spread of a disease that is static and at the same time equivalent in a suitable sense. The static formulation is very helpful, as we can use models of random graphs to understand disease progression.

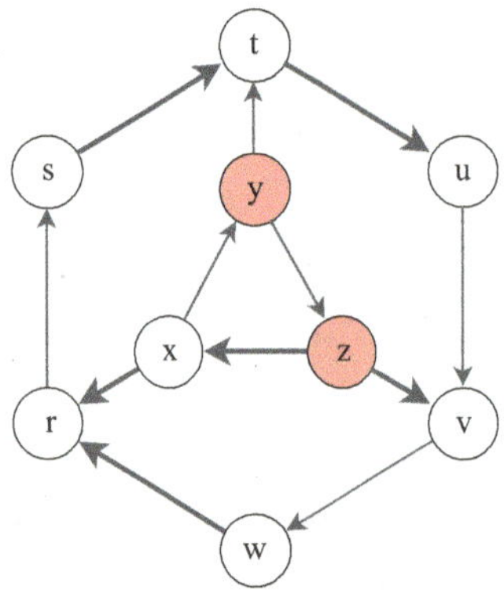


**Figure 14.6**
From SIR to percolation: open edges are shown in thick links.

Let us consider the basic SIR model, in which $t_I = 1$. Consider a point in an SIR epidemic when a node $v$ has just become infectious, and it has a susceptible neighbor $w$. Node $v$ has one period—and therefore one chance—to infect $w$, and it succeeds with probability $p$. The outcome of this random event can be thought of as the outcome of a coin flip that has probability $p$ of coming up heads. To understanding how far a disease travels, it is important to examine whether the disease will proceed from $v$ to $w$, but it is not important when the coin was flipped. Keeping in mind this atemporal interpretation, we can now take one link in a network at a time and ask whether it comes up heads, and we can assume that the coin toss is independent across links. Once we have stored the results of all the coin tosses, we can proceed to examine the extent of spread of the disease as follows.

The links in the contact network for which the coin flip was heads (i.e., successful) are declared open; the remaining edges are interpreted as blocked. This thought process is represented in figure 14.6, which shows a sample result of coin flips that is consistent with the pattern of infections in the example from figure 14.4. And we can now see how to use the open and blocked edges to understand the course of the disease in this network. Let us start with some initially infected nodes, and then node $v$ will become infected if and only if there is a path consisting only of open edges from one of these infected nodes to $v$. Figure 14.6 is a concise way to summarize the course of such a disease. This static view of the progression of a disease is referred to as *percolation*, and this concept has been extensively studied by physicists and mathematicians. We now use the percolation perspective to understand the SIR process in a network.

Starting from an initially infected node, a disease will spread to another node so long as there is a path from the initially infected node to the node in the subgraph of open edges in the original network. In other words, to understand the extent of spread of the disease, we need to know the distribution of the component sizes of the open subgraph. This leads us to an exposition of one of the most celebrated results in graph theory: the distribution of component sizes in the Erdős-Rényi model of random graphs. Our discussion here will be informal; for more a formal treatment of the material, the interested reader should consult Bollobas (1998 and 2004).

Consider the Erdős-Rényi model (as in chapter 2) on $n-1$ nodes with a probability of any given link being $p > 1/n$ (in principle, $p$ is a decreasing function of $n$ increases), but we are suppressing this dependence for simplicity. Add a new node, numbered $n$. Connect this last node with the existing $n-1$ nodes, where the probability of each link is independent and given by $p$. Let $q$ be the fraction of nodes in the largest component of the original network. For large $n$, the number $q$ will also be a fairly good approximation of the share of nodes in the largest component in the network with $n$ nodes. The only case where this may not be true is when the new node successfully connects two hitherto-unconnected large components. However, the likelihood of this happening becomes negligible under the assumption $p(n-1) > 1$ (the details are provided in the proof of connectedness of Erdős-Rényi graphs given in chapter 2). The new node is not in the largest component if none of its neighbors are in the giant component; if the new node has degree $d$, then for large $n$, this probability is roughly equal to $(1-q)^d$.

Generalizing this reasoning, the probability that a node with degree $d$ is not a member of the largest component is $(1-q)^d$. This leads us to the identity: the fraction of nodes outside the largest component, $1-q$, is equal to the expected probability of a node lying outside the largest component; that is,

$$1-q=\sum_d (1-q)^d P(d). \tag{14.10}$$

Recall the Poisson degree distribution:

$$P(d)=\frac{e^{-(n-1)p}((n-1)p)^d}{d!}. \tag{14.11}$$

Substituting for $P(d)$ in equation (14.10), we get

$$1-q=\sum_d \frac{e^{-(n-1)p}((n-1)p)^d}{d!}(1-q)^d. \tag{14.12}$$

Recalling the definition

$$\sum_d \frac{((n-1)p)^d(1-q)^d}{d!}=e^{(n-1)p(1-q)}, \tag{14.13}$$

we arrive at the following approximation for $q$:

$$q=1-e^{-q(n-1)p}. \tag{14.14}$$

A first point to note is that $q = 0$ is always a solution to this equation. Whether there is a positive solution depends on the value of $p$. Intuitively, if $p$ is very small, then the network will be fragmented. To derive the threshold probability, define $f(q) = 1 - e^{-q(n-1)p}$. Observe that $f(0) = 0$. Consider the first derivative,

$$f'(q) = (n-1)pe^{-q(n-1)p}, \tag{14.15}$$

and the second derivative,

$$f''(q) = -((n-1)p)^2 e^{-q(n-1)p}. \tag{14.16}$$

Function $f(.)$ is concave as the second derivative is negative. Next, observe that $f(1) = 1 - e^{-(n-1)p} < 1$, so long as $p(n-1)$ is bounded. So $f(q) = q$ at some $q > 0$ if and only if $f'(0) = (n-1)p > 1$. We summarize our discussion as follows.

**Proposition 14.2** *In the Erdős-Rényi graph, the size of the giant component becomes negligible and the network is fragmented in case $p(n-1) < 1$; the giant component is nonvanishing in a large network only if $p(n-1) > 1$.*

We note that the threshold for Erdős-Rényi graphs is very much in the spirit of the reproductive number result obtained for trees in the previous section (see proposition 14.1).

What can we say about general random graphs? Recall that in chapter 3, we introduced the configuration model as a way to think of general degree distributions. We now study giant components in networks that have been generated using the configuration model.

Let $P^n(d)$ describe the degree distribution for a network with $n$ nodes. As we are interested in properties of networks for large $n$, for reasons of tractability, we place some restrictions on $P^n(d)$ as $n$ grows. We place the following restrictions:

1. $P^n(d)$ converges uniformly to a degree distribution $P$ with a finite mean.
2. There exists an $\epsilon$ such that $P^n(d) = 0$ for $d > n^{\frac{1}{4}-\epsilon}$.
3. $(d^2 - 2d)P^n(d)$ converges uniformly to $(d^2 - 2d)P(d)$.
4. $E_{P^n}[d^2 - 2d]$ converges uniformly to its limit (which may be infinite).

The high-level idea is the following: starting at a random node, we should be able to trace larger and larger neighborhoods as the distance increases. The first step in the argument is to note that below the threshold, as we move outward from a node, we do not encounter an already visited node (in other words, the network is a tree). Consider a link in a network generated using a configuration model that satisfies the four conditions listed here. The probability that a link connected two nodes that already have a path between them in a component with $s$ nodes is the probability that both nodes of the link lie in the component: this is proportional to $(s/n)^2$. Thus the fraction of links that end up in cycles is of the order

$$\sum_i \left[\frac{s_i}{n}\right]^2, \tag{14.17}$$

where $s_i$ is the size of component $i$ in the network. Let $S$ be the size of the largest component. Then it follows that, since $\sum_i s_i = n$, this sum is smaller than $S/n$. If we are below the threshold at which the giant component emerges, then, by definition, $S/n$ is converging to 0 for large $n$. This completes a sketch of the argument that the network is a collection of trees below the threshold. For a more precise statement and the details of the proof, see Molloy and Reed (1995).

Let us now turn to the size of the giant component above the threshold. Define $\phi$ as the number of nodes that can be found on average by tracing the paths outward from an end node taken from a link picked at random in the network (as it gets large). As there are no cycles, the number of nodes reached starting from a link is 1 plus the number of nodes reached starting from each of the neighbors of the node. Define $\langle d \rangle = E[d] = \sum_d P(d)d$ and $\tilde{P}(d) = \frac{P(d)d}{\langle d \rangle}$. Then

$$\phi = 1 + \sum_{d=1}^{\infty} \frac{P(d)d}{\langle d \rangle}(d-1)\phi. \tag{14.18}$$

Simplifying, we obtain

$$\phi = 1 + \frac{(\langle d^2 \rangle) - \langle d \rangle}{\langle d \rangle}\phi. \tag{14.19}$$

This yields

$$\phi = \frac{1}{2 - \frac{\langle d^2 \rangle}{\langle d \rangle}}. \tag{14.20}$$

Equipped with equation (14.18), we can now compute the threshold for the emergence of the giant component. Observe that $\phi$ is finite if $2\langle d \rangle - \langle d^2 \rangle > 0$. Thus there is a giant component if

$$2\langle d \rangle - \langle d^2 \rangle > 0. \tag{14.21}$$

This in turn yields the threshold $2\langle d \rangle = \langle d^2 \rangle$. To appreciate the implications of this result, let us apply it to some well-known degree distributions.

First, consider the Erdős-Rényi random graph: recall that when $n$ is large, this graph has a Poisson degree distribution so that $\langle d^2 \rangle = \langle d \rangle + \langle d \rangle^2$. Our threshold result then tells us that the giant component emerges if $\langle d \rangle > 1$. Turning next to a regular network with degree $k$, $\langle d \rangle^2 = 2\langle d \rangle$ implies that $k = 2$. Finally, for a scale-free degree distribution $P^n(d) = cd^{-\gamma}$, the term $\langle d^2 \rangle$ diverges when $\gamma < 3$. This means that there is a giant component for all degree distributions that satisfy the finite mean condition mentioned previously.

We next turn to the size of the giant component. Recall that equation (14.10) does not assume a specific degree distribution, so the same formula applies for the configuration model:

$$1 - q = \sum_d (1-q)^d P(d). \tag{14.22}$$

A first-order stochastic shift in degree distribution means that the right side of equation (14.22) is smaller for every finite $q$, which in turn means that the $1-q$ that solves the equation must be smaller (i.e., the giant component must be larger). This is intuitive, as we are implicitly raising the probability of linking. A question at the end of the chapter explores the implications of varying degrees distributions for the size of the giant component.

We now apply the result to the study of vaccination policies.

### 14.4.2 Random Vaccination

Suppose that some fraction $\pi$ of nodes have been vaccinated against a disease like COVID and are therefore immune. How does that affect the size of the epidemic? The initially infected person interacts with their neighbors, of whom $\pi$ are immune.

To address this question, it is helpful to lay out the sequence of events: first, a network is formed. Second, a fraction of nodes $n\pi$ is deleted at random, leaving a residual network in place. Finally, we identify the component of a randomly chosen initial infection in the residual network.

We first take up the Erdős-Rényi random graph. As node vaccination is random, we may study the extent of spread of the disease by considering an alternative network with $n(1-\pi)$ individuals in which all links are created with probability $p$. Recall from our earlier computations that the threshold for the emergence of a giant component is given by $pn(1-\pi)=1$: thus the disease is contained within a small/finite component if $pn(1-\pi)<1$, and it spreads over a unbounded component if $pn(1-\pi)>1$. Moreover, the fraction of nodes that will be infected is given by the number $q$, where $q$ solves

$$q = 1 - e^{-q(1-\pi)np}. \tag{14.23}$$

Taking logs, we can use the following equation to write $q$ in a more useful form:

$$-(1-\pi)np = \frac{log(1-q)}{q}. \tag{14.24}$$

We can infer that an increase in $p(1-\pi)n$ leads to a corresponding increase in the size of the giant component, and hence in the size of the infected fraction of the population.

Let us now turn to disease spread in a network with a general degree distribution. We start with a study of the configuration model. For the network obtained after the deletion of $\pi$ nodes, we get the following threshold property for the emergence of a giant component:

$$2\langle d\rangle_{\pi} = \langle d^2\rangle_{\pi}. \tag{14.25}$$

To apply this formula, we need to have an expression for the degree distribution of the network, $P_{\pi}$, after the immune nodes have been deleted. Let us start with a node in the original network $P$. The probability that a node starting with degree $d'$ has a degree $d \leq d'$ is given by

$$\binom{d'}{d}(1-\pi)^d \pi^{d'-d}. \tag{14.26}$$

The degree distribution in the modified network after eliminating immune nodes is

$$P_\pi(d) = \sum_{d' \geq d} P(d') \binom{d'}{d} (1-\pi)^d \pi^{d'-d}. \tag{14.27}$$

Next, note that

$$E_\pi[d] = \sum_d \sum_{d' \geq d} dP(d') \binom{d'}{d} (1-\pi)^d \pi^{d'-d}. \tag{14.28}$$

This expectation may be rewritten as

$$E_\pi[d] = \sum_{d'} P(d') \sum_{d' \geq d} d \binom{d'}{d} (1-\pi)^d \pi^{d'-d}. \tag{14.29}$$

It can be expressed more compactly as $\sum_{d'} P(d') M_\pi(\hat{d}; d')$, where $M_\pi(\hat{d}; d')$ is the expectation of $\hat{d}$ from a binomial distribution with parameter $(1-\pi)$ and a maximum of $d'$ draws. It then follows that $M_\pi(d; d') = d'(1-\pi)$ and $M_\pi(d^2; d') = \langle d \rangle^2 + d'\pi(1-\pi)$. Using these facts, we may write

$$\langle d \rangle_\pi = \langle d \rangle (1-\pi) \tag{14.30}$$

$$\langle d^2 \rangle_\pi = \langle d^2 \rangle (1-\pi)^2 + \langle d \rangle \pi (1-\pi). \tag{14.31}$$

Using equation (14.25), the threshold for a giant component of susceptible nodes is given by a $\pi$ that solves

$$\langle d^2 \rangle (1-\pi) = \langle d \rangle (2-\pi). \tag{14.32}$$

Solving for $\pi$, we get

$$\pi = \frac{\langle d^2 \rangle - 2\langle d \rangle}{\langle d^2 \rangle - \langle d \rangle}. \tag{14.33}$$

Let us consider a few examples of networks in order to develop an appreciation for the threshold in equation 14.33. In the regular network, every node has degree $k$. The threshold is then given by $\pi = (k-2)/(k-1)$. So if $k = 2$, then the threshold is $\pi = 0$; in other words, immunization of any positive fraction of nodes eliminates the spread of the disease. On the other hand, if $k = 3$, then $\pi = 0.5$, meaning that we would need to vaccinate at least one-half of the nodes to prevent a serious epidemic. We recall from the earlier discussion that in the Erdős-Rényi network (with a Poisson degree distribution), $\langle d^2 \rangle = \langle d \rangle^2 + \langle d \rangle$ and $\langle d \rangle = (n-1)p$. This implies that the threshold is given by $\pi = 1 - \frac{1}{(n-1)p}$, or equivalently by $pn(1-\pi) = 1$. This threshold is reminiscent of the basic threshold with regard to the reproductive number obtained in proposition 14.1.

Finally, consider the scale-free network with the degree distribution $P(d)$ proportional to $d^{-\gamma}$. Recall that $\langle d^2 \rangle$ is diverging for $\gamma < 3$. This immediately implies that the threshold value for $\pi$ is 1. In other words, the disease spreads to a giant component even when virtually all nodes are immune. This means that nodes with very high degrees play a central role in the spread of disease.

Thus whether a network successfully diffuses a disease or not depends on the relationship between the variance and the mean. When the variance is sufficiently large relative to the mean, the network will diffuse the disease even when large parts of the population are immune. This motivates the study of targeted vaccination policies, which follows.

### 14.4.3 Targeted Vaccination

Suppose that the policy maker knows the degrees of everyone and can target individuals based on those degrees. Let us consider the policy of immunizing a fraction $\pi$ of the highest-degree individuals. To assess the impact of this policy, we start with a network formed with the original degree distribution $P(d)$. Suppose that a share $H$ of the highest-degree individuals are deleted. For simplicity, suppose that all nodes with degrees higher than $\bar{d}(\pi)$ are immunized and deleted. This in turn means that all links emanating from these immunized nodes are also deleted, which lowers the degree of the remaining nodes. In other words, if we are immunizing a fraction $\pi$, then

$$\sum_{d=1}^{\bar{d}(\pi)} P(d) = 1 - \pi. \tag{14.34}$$

Observe that we have removed share $\pi$ of nodes, but as these are the highest-degree nodes, we have removed a higher fraction of links, given by

$$f(\pi) = \frac{\sum_{d=\bar{d}(\pi)+1}^{\infty} P(d)d}{\langle d \rangle}. \tag{14.35}$$

Thus a node in the residual network loses each of its links with a probability of $f(\pi)$. The new degree distribution is given by

$$P_{\pi,H}(d) = \sum_{d=1}^{\bar{d}(\pi)} \frac{P(d')}{1-\pi} \binom{d'}{d} (1-f(\pi))^d f(\pi)^{d'-d}. \tag{14.36}$$

Building on the thresholds obtained in equation 14.32, and using equation 14.36, we arrive at

$$\langle d^2 | d \le \bar{d}(\pi) \rangle (1 - f(\pi)) = \langle d | d \le \bar{d}(\pi) \rangle (2 - f(\pi)), \tag{14.37}$$

where $\langle . | d \le \bar{d}(\pi) \rangle$ is the expectation with respect to the original distribution (which is truncated at $\bar{d}(\pi)$).

We use this threshold to clarify the effects of immunizing the high-degree nodes in scale-free networks. It is convenient to work with a continuous approximation of the degree distribution. Let the density be given by $(\gamma - 1)d^{-\gamma}$. Observe that

$$\int_1^x (\gamma - 1)d^{-\gamma} dd = 1 - x^{-\gamma+1}. \tag{14.38}$$

Next, we note that

$$\int_1^{\bar{d}(\pi)} P(d)dd = 1 - \pi. \tag{14.39}$$

Substituting for the density, we get

$$\int_1^{\bar{d}(\pi)} (\gamma - 1)d^{-\gamma} dd = 1 - \pi. \tag{14.40}$$

Hence $1 - \bar{d}(\pi)^{1-\gamma} = 1 - \pi$, implying $\pi = \bar{d}(\pi)^{1-\gamma}$, and so $\bar{d}(\pi) = \pi^{1/(1-\gamma)}$. We can obtain an explicit formula for $f(\pi)$ using the density $P(d)$ as follows:

$$f(\pi) = \frac{\sum_{d=\bar{d}+1}^{\infty} P(d)d}{\langle d \rangle} \tag{14.41}$$

$$= \frac{\lim_{t\to\infty} \int_{\bar{d}(\pi)}^{t} (\gamma - 1)d^{-\gamma+1}dd}{\lim_{t\to\infty} \int_1^t (\gamma - 1)d^{-\gamma+1}dd}. \tag{14.42}$$

$$= \frac{\frac{1}{-\gamma+2} \lim_{t\to\infty} [d^{-\gamma+2}]_{\bar{d}\pi}^{t}}{\frac{1}{-\gamma+2} \lim_{t\to\infty} [d^{-\gamma+2}]_1^t} \tag{14.43}$$

Taking limits with respect to $t$ and substituting for $\bar{d}(\pi)$, we obtain $f(\pi) = \pi^{(\gamma-2)/(\gamma-1)}$. Let us next obtain an explicit expression for $\langle d^x | d \leq \bar{d}(\pi) \rangle$:

$$\langle d^x | d \leq \bar{d}(\pi) \rangle = \int_1^{\bar{d}(\pi)} d^x (\gamma - 1)d^{-\gamma} dd \frac{1}{1-\pi} \tag{14.44}$$

$$= (\gamma - 1)[d^{x-\gamma+1}]_1^{\bar{d}(\pi)} \frac{1}{x - \gamma + 1} \frac{1}{1-\pi}. \tag{14.45}$$

$$= \frac{\gamma - 1}{\gamma - 1 - x} \frac{1}{1-\pi} [1 - \bar{d}(\pi)^{-\gamma+1+x}] \tag{14.46}$$

Note that the term, $1/1 - \pi$, is a rescaling due to truncated distribution. Substituting for $x = 1$ and $x = 2$ in equation (14.46), we obtain

$$\langle d | d \leq \bar{d}(\pi) \rangle = \frac{(\gamma - 1)(1 - \bar{d}(\pi))^{-\gamma+2}}{(\gamma - 2)(1 - \pi)} \tag{14.47}$$

$$\langle d^2 | d \leq \bar{d}(\pi) \rangle = \frac{(\gamma - 1)(1 - \bar{d}(\pi))^{-\gamma+3}}{(\gamma - 3)(1 - \pi)}. \tag{14.48}$$

Substituting for $f(\pi)$ and for $\langle d | d \leq \bar{d}(\pi) \rangle$ and $\langle d^2 | d \leq \bar{d}(\pi) \rangle$ in equation 14.37, the threshold may be expressed as

$$(\gamma - 2)[1 - \pi^{(\gamma-3)/(\gamma-1)}] = (\gamma - 3)[2 - \pi^{(\gamma-2)/(\gamma-1)}]. \tag{14.49}$$

To get a sense of the large effects of targeted immunization, let us consider a few examples: If we set $\gamma = 2.5$, then the threshold equation (14.49) above is simplified and yields $\pi^{1/3} + \pi^{-1/3} = 3$, which means that $\pi = 0.06$. Thus immunizing only 6 percent of the (highest-degree) nodes is sufficient to eliminate the large-scale spread of the disease. By contrast, the immunization of a positive fraction of nodes at random cannot eliminate the risk of large-scale spread. If we raise the coefficient and set $\gamma = 2.9$, then the corresponding threshold is 0.030, thus suggesting that as coefficient $\gamma$ grows, the fraction of high-connected nodes that is needed shrinks.

This section has presented the SIR model. We first showed through an example how the threshold level of the reproduction number depends on the network structure. This set the stage for a more systematic study of threshold levels and how they depend on networks. We showed that this issue can be usefully reformulated as a question on the circumstances under which a giant component emerges in a large graph. We first established a threshold result for the infection rate in the Erdős-Rényi graph. As empirical networks exhibit very unequal degrees, we then examined general degree distributions and obtained the key result that a giant component emerges for arbitrarily low rates of infectiousness if the variance in degrees is large enough relative to the mean degree. Finally, we applied the threshold results to understand the attractiveness of various types of vaccination policies.

## 14.5 The Susceptible-Infected-Susceptible (SIS) Model

We now take up diseases that people can suffer from multiple times. The mechanics of the disease spread are as follows: initially, some nodes are in an infectious state, $I$, while all others are in a susceptible state, $S$. A node $v$ that enters state $I$ remains in it for a fixed number of steps $t_I$. During each of these $t_I$ steps, $v$ has probability $p$ of passing the disease to each of its susceptible neighbors. After $t_I$ steps, the node is no longer infectious, so it returns to state $S$. This gives rise to the SIS model. This model has been studied in a number of research papers, such as Pastor-Satorras and Vespignani (2001a, 2001b) and López-Pintado (2008). Our discussion draws on Jackson (2008) and López-Pintado (2008). As in section 14.4, the interest here will be on the relation between the structure of networks and the spread of disease.

We will study the dynamics of disease using an SIS model in a network. The networks will be described by degree distribution $P(d)$. An individual of degree $d_i$ will have $d_i$ interactions with other individuals during a given period. The probability that individual $i$ meets with an individual who has degree $d$ is

$$\frac{P(d)d}{\langle d\rangle}, \tag{14.50}$$

where $\langle d\rangle = E(d)$ is the expected degree in distribution $P$. Thus individuals are more likely to meet individuals who have higher degrees. Define $\rho(d)$ as the fraction of $d$-degree nodes who are infected. The average proportion of infected individuals is given by $\sum_d \rho(d)P(d)$.

Using this notation and the degree distribution of contacts, we may write the expected probability of meeting an infected person as

$$\theta = \sum_d \frac{P(d)d\rho(d)}{\langle d \rangle}. \tag{14.51}$$

Observe that $\theta$ is different from the average rate of infection in the population:

$$\rho = \sum_d P(d)\rho(d). \tag{14.52}$$

We next turn to the important question of how an infection arises out of interactions. In principle, this can take different forms. It may be that $i$ gets infected if they meet a single infected individual. An alternative is that they get infected only if the fraction of infected individuals in the neighborhood is above a certain threshold. We will suppose that there is a linear rate $v$ at which an infected person passes on infection. For simplicity, suppose that the probability that a degree $d$ individual becomes infected is given by $v\theta d$, where $v \in (0, 1)$. If we assume that $vd \leq 1$ for the highest degree in the network, this allows us to interpret this term as a probability. This expression is a good approximation of the probability of infection when $v$ is small.

In the SIS model, an infected individual recovers and becomes susceptible again. Let the recovery rate—from infection to susceptible—in any period be given by $\delta > 0$. We note that while this formulation makes the model tractable, it implicitly assumes that the duration of infection has no bearing on the probability of recovery.

We start with a comment on the finite model: as in our earlier discussions, if the network is finite and the recovery rate $\delta$ is independent across persons, then everyone will eventually be in a susceptible state: the long-run outcome is an infection rate of zero. In what follows, we will impose limits on the size of the network and assume an infinite population.

We will study the steady state of the process of disease spread. Our interest will be in the conditions on the probability of infection $v$, the rates of recovery $\delta$, and the network $P$ under which infection rates are positive.

In a steady state, the rate of new infections must equal the rate at which infected individuals move to a susceptible state. In other words, for every degree $d$,

$$(1-\rho(d))vd\theta = \rho(d)\delta. \tag{14.53}$$

Defining $\lambda = v/\delta$, we can write the steady-state infection rate for degree $d$ as

$$\rho(d) = \frac{\lambda\theta d}{\lambda\theta d + 1}. \tag{14.54}$$

Recall that

$$\theta = \sum_d \frac{P(d)\rho(d)d}{\langle d \rangle}. \tag{14.55}$$

Substituting for the steady state $\rho(d)$, we obtain

$$\theta = \sum_d \frac{P(d)\lambda\theta d^2}{(\lambda\theta d + 1)\langle d\rangle}. \tag{14.56}$$

A first point to note is that $\theta = 0$ is always a steady state of this process. Let us examine the conditions under which there also exists a nonzero steady state.

It is helpful to begin with the simple case in which all individuals have the same degree (i.e., the network is regular). We can rewrite the formula for steady state infection rates as

$$\theta = \frac{\lambda\theta d}{(\lambda\theta d + 1)}. \tag{14.57}$$

In the positive solution for this equation,

$$\theta = 1 - \frac{1}{\lambda d}. \tag{14.58}$$

Positive infection obtains if $d\lambda > 1$ (this threshold is reminiscent of our results in the SIR model, as well as the threshold obtained in proposition 14.1). Given a net rate of infection $\lambda$, we require the degree to be large. On the other hand, for a given degree, we require the net rate of infection to be large.

To see the role of networks, let us next consider a scale-free distribution: $P(d) = 2d^{-3}$. Substitute this distribution in the expression for the steady-state infection rate and we get

$$\theta = \sum_d \frac{2d^{-3}\lambda\theta d^2}{(\lambda\theta d + 1)\langle d\rangle}. \tag{14.59}$$

Let us solve for a nonzero $\theta$. First, note that we can rewrite the right side of this equation as

$$\frac{2\lambda\theta}{\langle d\rangle} \sum_d \frac{\frac{1}{\lambda\theta}}{d(d + \frac{1}{\lambda\theta})}. \tag{14.60}$$

Set $x = 1/\lambda\theta$. Taking a continuous approximation, we get

$$\frac{2\lambda\theta}{\langle d\rangle} \int_1^\infty \frac{x}{d(d+x)} dd. \tag{14.61}$$

Rearranging, we get

$$\frac{2\lambda\theta}{\langle d\rangle} \int_1^\infty \left[\frac{1}{d} - \frac{1}{d+x}\right] dd. \tag{14.62}$$

Integrating and simplifying, we get

$$\frac{2\lambda\theta}{\langle d\rangle} log\left(1 - \frac{1}{\lambda\theta}\right). \tag{14.63}$$

Simplifying and rearranging, we obtain

$$\theta = \frac{1}{\lambda(e^{\frac{1}{\lambda}} - 1)}. \tag{14.64}$$

Observe that this expression is always positive, regardless of the value of $\lambda$: in other words, infection rate is positive in the steady state, no matter how low the infectiousness of the disease is. A comparison of this result with the positive threshold in the regular graph gives a first intuition for how degree inequality may facilitate the spread of a disease.

To develop a more general understanding for the prospects of infection in networks, we examine the following question: Suppose that a small fraction of the population is infected. Would the dynamics take us toward a zero infection steady state or a significant positive infection rate? Next, we follow López-Pintado (2008) in addressing this question.

We start by defining the function

$$H(\theta) = \sum_d \frac{P(d)d}{\langle d \rangle} \left( \frac{\lambda d\theta}{\lambda d\theta + 1} \right). \tag{14.65}$$

Function $H(.)$ keeps track of the number of people who become infected starting from $\theta$. If $H(\theta) > \theta$, then the new infection rate will be larger than the initial rate, while if $H(\theta) < \theta$, then the new rate will be less than the initial rate. Therefore, fixed points of the function $H(\theta) - \theta$ correspond to the steady states of the dynamic process. First, note that $H(0) = 0$, so zero infection is always a steady state.

It is easily verified that $H(\theta)$ is increasing and strictly concave in $\theta$. Also, observe that $H(1) < 1$. So there is a positive infection steady state if and only if $H'(0) > 1$. Moreover, if it exists, such a positive steady state will be unique (due to the strict concavity of $H$).

When $H'(0) > 1$, at low values of $\theta$, function $H$ pushes the infection rate away from 0, so the zero infection rate steady state is unstable. On the other hand, if $H'(0) < 0$, then there is only one steady state, and at low values of $\theta$, function $H$ pushes back toward this unique zero-rate steady state. Let us now examine the conditions under which $H'(0) > 1$.

Differentiating $H(.)$ with respect to $\theta$ yields

$$H'(\theta) = \sum_d \frac{P(d)d}{\langle d \rangle} \frac{\lambda d}{(\lambda d\theta + 1)^2}. \tag{14.66}$$

We can rewrite this to obtain

$$H'(0) = \lambda \langle d^2 \rangle / \langle d \rangle. \tag{14.67}$$

The right side of the equation is greater than 1 if and only if

$$\lambda > \frac{\langle d \rangle}{\langle d^2 \rangle}. \tag{14.68}$$

In a regular graph, $\langle d \rangle = d$ and $\langle d^2 \rangle = [\langle d \rangle]^2$. Equation (14.68) is equivalent to $\lambda > 1/d$, which is the condition we obtained in equation (14.58). If, on the other hand, $P(d)$ is scale free, then we know that $\langle d^2 \rangle$ grows without bound as $n$ grows, so the inequality is satisfied for all $\lambda > 0$.

Finally, consider the Poisson degree distribution, in which $\langle d^2 \rangle = (\langle d \rangle)^2 + \langle d \rangle$. So we can rewrite the inequality in equation (14.68) as

$$\lambda > \frac{1}{\langle d \rangle + 1}. \tag{14.69}$$

The threshold for the Poisson degree distribution lies between the thresholds for the regular and scale-free degree distribution cases.

The intuition for this result is as follows: high-degree individuals serve as conduits for the disease to spread. This means that even very low rates of net infection (i.e., low $\lambda$) leave open the possibility for the hubs to be infected because they have a very large number of contacts. Moreover, once the hub is infected, it can in turn infect many other nodes due to its high degree. The contrast with regular networks is clear: everyone has the same degree. If the degree is high enough, infection persists, otherwise not. In a Poisson distribution with the same average degree, there are individuals with higher as well as lower degrees. The existence of the higher degrees helps lower the threshold needed for the positive infection steady state. Moving from Poisson to scale-free networks further increases the variance in degrees, giving rise to even higher-degree nodes. This further lowers the threshold needed for a positive infection rate steady state.

This section introduced the SIS model. The principal insight was that the level of spread of a disease depends on the relative magnitude of the variance in degrees as opposed to the mean degree. This yields a positive threshold for infectiousness in Erdős-Rényi graphs. However, in scale-free graphs, the variance in degrees grows without bound, so diseases with arbitrarily small levels of infectiousness can persist in the population.

## 14.6 Diffusion of Behaviors

Information on new products or behaviors spreads through personal contact in a population. So we would like to understand how best to implant the information at a few select points so that it benefits the largest number of individuals. In this section, we will present a case study of the diffusion of microfinance in Indian villages that will draw attention to the role of centrally seeded nodes. We will then examine circumstances when random seeding can perform close-to-optimal seeding.

We discuss the diffusion of micro-finance in south Indian villages of Karnataka. This study is taken from Banerjee, Chandrasekhar, Duflo, and Jackson (2013). For a general introduction to microfinance, the reader is referred to chapter 17, on economic growth. There is a sample of 75 villages where the microfinance institution, Bharatha Swamukti Samsthe (BSS), was planning to start operating. These villages are spread across five districts in Karnataka, India (we discussed these villages in chapter 1 and will also take them up in chapter 17). In 2006, six months before BSS's entry into any village, a baseline survey was conducted in all 75 villages, which had very limited access to any type of formal credit prior to this move of BSS.

In 2007, after this data collection was completed, BSS began operations in some of these villages. The study covers a period from 2006 until 2011. Over this period, BSS had entered 43 of the villages. There were large differences in the adoption rate of microfinance across the villages. We examine the role of the seeding points in explaining these differences.

We start by noting that, with a view to maximizing adoption, BSS sought out a number of village leaders, including teachers, leaders of self-help groups, and shopkeepers—individuals whom BSS expected to be well connected and credible. BSS held a private meeting with a subset of these leaders who were amenable. In this meeting, credit officers explained the program and asked the leaders to help organize a meeting to present information about microfinance to other villagers. These people, therefore, were the seeding points into a village.

A first thought is that villages in which the seeds had a greater degree would perform better. Figure 14.7 provides a first impression of the correlation between the network location of leaders and the eventual adoption of microfinance. Figure 14.7(a) shows that degree centrality is not strongly correlated with the diffusion of microfinance. This leads us to dig deeper into the location of seeds in the local village network.

Next, we will explore the idea that diffusion of microfinance is a dynamic process and direct as well as indirect connections of seeds will play a role. Let us consider the following process: First, the initial households have one opportunity to choose whether to take up microfinance. Second, the seeds have one opportunity to talk with their network neighbors: this happens with probability $q_p$ if they adopt, and probability $q_n$ if they do not. In subsequent periods, households that have been informed choose to adopt or not, they also pass information to their neighbors, and so forth. Let us say that the process stops after $T$ periods; observe that if $q_n = 0$ and $T$ grows without bound, then the process is a variant of the SIR model (susceptible before exposure to microfinance, infected if adopting, and removed after the period of communication is over). The finite number of periods is reasonable, as we will be studying relatively small networks. There are therefore two parameters in this diffusion process: $q_p$ and $q_n$.

In the data from these 75 villages, the values of the parameters were estimated as follows: $q_p = 0.35$, $q_n = 0.07$. Thus nonadopters are much less likely to share information, but they matter for diffusion because a large share of villagers are nonadopters.

With these parameters in hand, we can compute the centrality measures for different nodes in a network. Let us define the communication centrality of a leader as the estimated number of adopters, under the assumption there is only one seed and the diffusion is as it is in the model with the parameters. Figure 14.7(b) shows a positive correlation between communication centrality and adoption rates. This supports the idea that good injection points can make a large difference in diffusion.

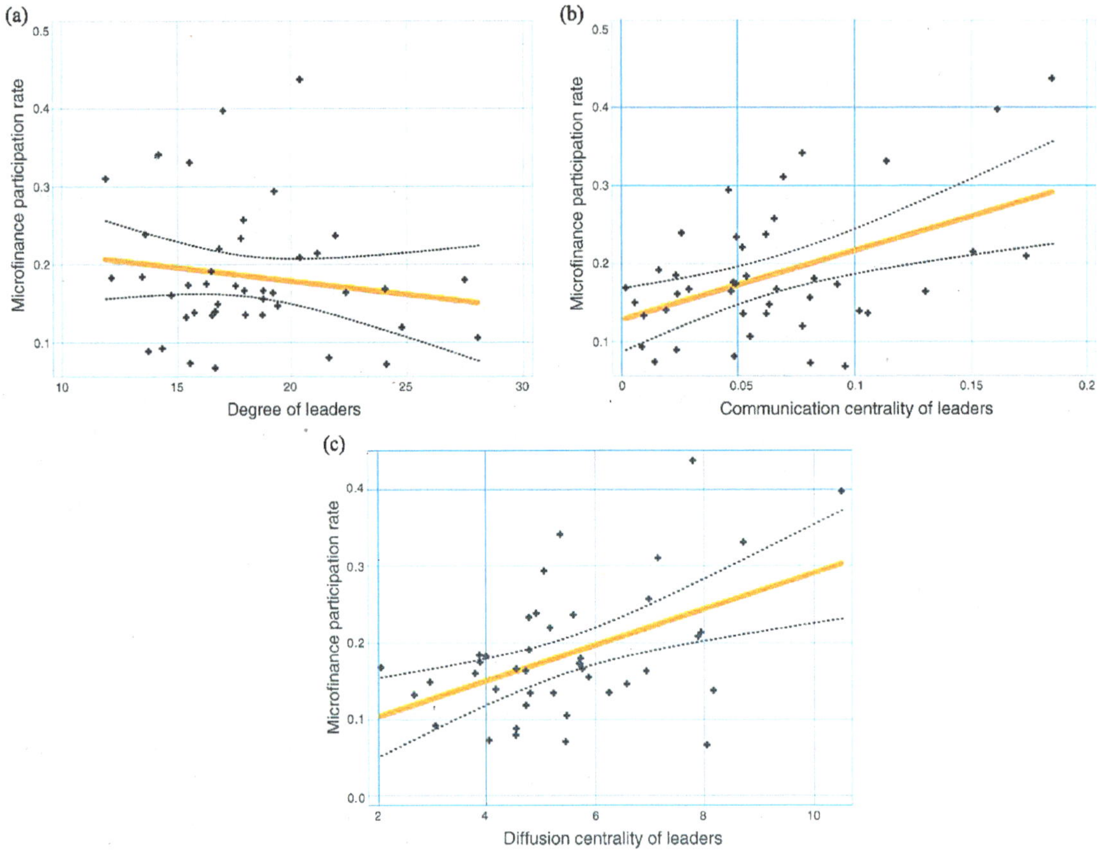


**Figure 14.7**
Injection points. *Source*: Figure 2 in Banerjee, Chandrasekhar, Duflo, and Jackson (2013).

Indeed, we can simplify the model further and compute a measure of diffusion centrality as follows: set $q_n = q_p = q$. Define the diffusion centrality of node $i$, in network $g$, as the vector:

$$C_D(g, q, T) = \left[ \sum_{t=1}^{T} (qg)^t \right] \cdot 1. \tag{14.70}$$

This is a measure of the expected number of times that all individuals, taken together, hear from individual $i$. When $T = 1$, diffusion centrality is proportional to degree centrality. If $T \to \infty$, diffusion centrality is proportional to Katz-Bonacich centrality or eigenvector centrality, depending on whether $q$ is smaller than the first eigenvalue of the adjacency matrix or smaller than its inverse (for a discussion on the measures of centrality, see chapter 1). In the intermediate region of $T$, diffusion centrality differs from these standard centrality measures. Figure 14.7(c) shows that the average diffusion centrality of leaders is positively correlated with adoption rates for microfinance. Here, the $q$ value is set equal to the inverse of the first eigenvalue of the adjacency matrix of the village social network. The value of $T$ is taken from the number of trimesters that a village was exposed to the microfinance, and it was set equal to 6.6.

### 14.6.1 On the Value of Targeting in Diffusion Problems

This microfinance case study draws attention to the role of identifying seed nodes. However, collecting detailed information on networks is costly, and even if we did collect all the available information, there are computational limitations on working out the optimal seeds. It is therefore important to understand how much benefit there is from optimal seeding strategies, and when it justifies the expense. Our discussion in this section draws on Akbarpour, Malladi, and Saberi (2020).

Consider a population of $n$ individuals who are connected to each other through a social network. At time $t=0$, a small collection of individuals—the seeds—are informed, and everyone else is uninformed. An individual has one chance to speak to each of their uninformed neighbors. This information sharing is successful with probability $c \in (0, 1)$, independently for each neighbor. If the information sharing is successful, then the neighbor becomes informed at the next period. This informed neighbor now speaks to each of their neighbors at time $t+1$, and so forth. The process continues until there is no individuals left with an opportunity to be informed. This is therefore a variant of the SIR model considered in section 14.4.

To quantify the value of network information, we contemplate two scenarios. In scenario 1, suppose that there is access to full network data, and, in addition, we know the communication links that come alive (as in the percolation model studies discussed earlier in this chapter). Moreover, suppose that we can compute the optimal $s$ seeds. In scenario 2, we ignore the network and simply pick $s+x$ initial seeds uniformly at random. We are interested in understanding the value of $x$ for which diffusion in scenario 2 will exceed that in scenario 1. Observe that comparing this omniscient seeding with random seeding provides a generous upper bound for the value of network information; this is because, for all realizations of the random communication graph, the omniscient strategy will perform at least as well as the optimum.

The main insight is as follows: the difference in the expected fraction of informed individuals between the random seeding strategy, with $s+x$ seeds, and the omniscient strategy, with $s$ seeds, disappears as we increase $x$. The intuition underlying this result can be appreciated through a consideration of some well-known networks.

First, consider networks that are homogenous (where nodes are similar). In such networks, it would not matter how we seed them. Thus optimal seeding should be similar to random seeding in Erdős-Rényi networks. Next, consider unequal networks, such as networks with a hub. Observe that targeting seeds at random will involve nodes that are connected to the hubs. Thus random seeds are very likely to get information across to the hubs, who will in turn spread it to everyone else. Optimal seeding will directly target the hubs. Thus random seeding is likely to reach hubs with a one-period lag as compared to optimal seeding. This suggests that so long as timing is not critical, random seeding will do almost as well as optimal seeding.

To develop a better feeling for the relative reach of random versus optimal seeding, let us consider the reach of various targeting strategies in the Indian villages considered in Banerjee, Chandrasekhar, Duflo, and Jackson (2013). Figure 14.8 compares the average performance of random, degree-central, diffusion-central, eigenvector-central, and omniscient seeding strategies (for a definition of centrality measures, see chapter 1).

Figure 14.8 presents diffusion for different values of the communication probability $p$. We see that under both values of costs $c = 0.1$ and $c = 0.2$, random seeding with a few extra seeds compares well with network-guided seeding heuristics. For instance, when $c = 0.1$, random, with 5 seeds, performs as well as degree- and diffusion-central seeding, with 2 seeds, and better than omniscient, with 1 seed. When $c = 0.2$, random, with 5 seeds, performs better than all heuristics with an equal number of seeds, and better than omniscient, with 1 seed.

We turn finally to a comparison to optimal seeding and omniscient seeding (this is the case where the external observer knows the links that actually get activated). Let us denote the average degree in the underlying social network by $d$. Simulations show that when the average number of activated links is $d = 1.5$, random with 3 extra seeds beats both optimal and omniscient seeding. Similarly, when $d = 2$, random with 2 and 3 extra seeds beat both optimal and omniscient seeding.

We conclude with two comments on the scope of this reasoning. The first point pertains to timing, and we have already alluded to it. It is clear that in hub-spoke or scale-free networks, optimal seeding will be faster than random seeding because random seeding will get to hubs only indirectly, while optimal seeding will directly target the hubs. A second point pertains to the mechanics of the diffusion process: if information and behavior are related to thresholds of the neighbors affected, then random seeding may yield poorer outcomes than optimal seeding. To see this, let us consider the example of the hub-spoke network again. Suppose a person believes that a piece of information or adopts an action only if a high enough fraction of their neighbors adopt it. Random seeding will then fail to persuade the hub—with many connections—and that would lead to a failure of diffusion. Optimal seeding will take this into account and target a collection of hub-nodes that will ensure widespread diffusion.

## 14.7 Supplementary Material

By way of background to the study of diffusion, we present the Bass model (Bass, [1969]). In this model, there are two motivations for adopting an opinion or product: (1) a spontaneous desire, and (2) social influence. Social influence is assumed to operate at the global level

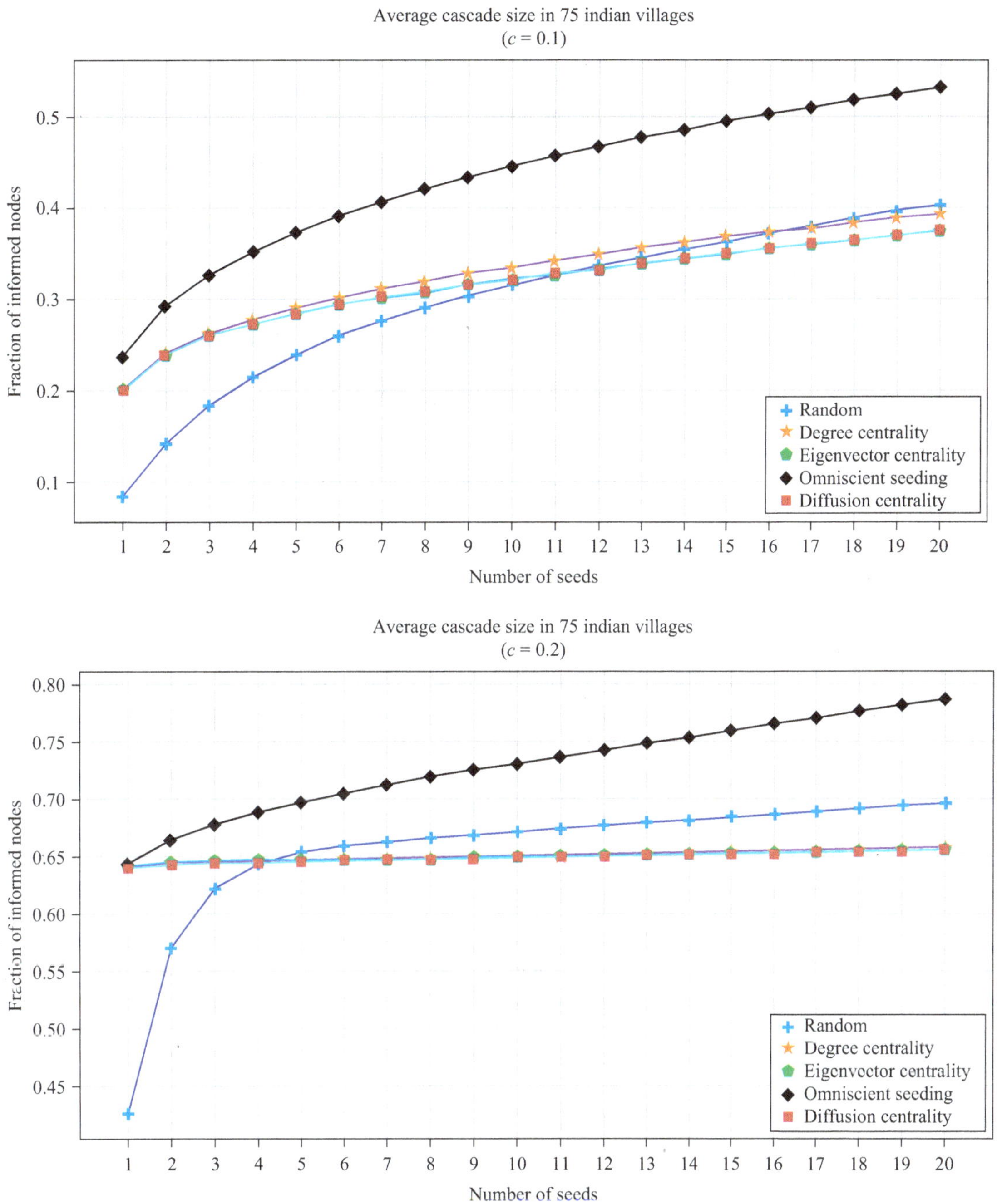


**Figure 14.8**
A comparison of average diffusion for various seeding strategies (omniscient, random, degree-, diffusion-, and eigenvector-central seeding) across Indian village network data. Two levels of communication probabilities are shown. *Source*: Akbarpour, Malladi, and Saberi (2020).

and depends on the aggregate measure of adopters in a society. By contrast, the focus in this chapter was on models in which the details of the social interaction were spelled out.

Suppose time is discrete $t = 1, 2, \ldots$. Let $F(t)$ be the fraction of the population that has adopted a product at time $t$, expressed as follows:

$$F(t) = F(t-1) + p(1 - F(t-1)) + q(1 - F(t-1))F(t-1), \tag{14.71}$$

where $p$ captures the rate of spontaneous adoption and $q$ reflects the magnitude of social influence. Observe that $(1 - F(t-1))$ is the share of the population that has not adopted the product. The last term in equation (14.71) says that the social influence acts on the fraction of the population that has not adopted $(1 - F(t-1))$ and the size of the effect is $F(t-1)$. We may express the rate of adoption in continuous time as follows:

$$\frac{dF(t)}{dt} = (p + qF(t))(1 - F(t)). \tag{14.72}$$

If we set the initial condition $F(0) = 0$ and assume that $p > 0$, then we get the following solution to the differential equation:

$$F(t) = \frac{1 - e^{-(p+q)t}}{1 + \frac{q}{p} e^{-(p+q)t}}. \tag{14.73}$$

As we vary the two parameters $p$ and $q$, we trace a range of adoption curves. The Bass curve can be enriched by introducing pricing and advertising effects, among others.

An important feature of the Bass diffusion curve that has been widely studied is that it gives rise to an $S$-shaped adoption curve—the rate of adoption is small initially, speeds up, and then tapers off over time. The intuition for this is that when adoption is close to zero, there is little social influence, so the rate is given by $p$. As adoption progresses, the social influence kicks in and adoption enters a reinforcement phase, with rapid adoption. However, as the fraction of adopters expands, while the scope of social influence expands, there is a smaller and smaller fraction of nonadopters left, leading to an eventual fall in the rate of adoption. The $S$-shaped adoption curve has been widely studied in empirical research (see, e.g., Ryan and Gross [1943], Griliches [1957], and Coleman, Katz, and Menzel [1966]).

## 14.8 Reading Notes

Infectious diseases have had profound effects on human history. A number of diseases continue to be widespread, causing large-scale mortality. The experience of COVID-19 in 2020–2021 shows that diseases can still cause global upheaval. The spread of disease depends on its inherent infectiousness and the ways in which it spreads. Diseases differ greatly in these two dimensions. There is a vast body of literature spanning many disciplines on the nature of infectious diseases. It is impossible to cover all the different strands of work. The focus in this chapter is on theoretical models that bring out the role of networks in the spread of diseases and in the design of policies to limit their spread. Two well-known, book-length overviews of infectious disease research are Anderson and May (1992) and Bailey (1975).

We have concentrated on infectious biological diseases in this chapter, but it is clear that diffusion of information and computer viruses may be amenable to similar methods of analysis. Indeed, some of the mathematical results we have discussed were first developed in the context of nonbiological infections. For expositional simplicity, we have limited ourselves to biological diseases. The final section, on the diffusion of microfinance, serves to illustrate the general applicability of these methods.

The SIR and SIS models were originally studied in the context of large, compartmentalized populations with individuals belonging to different groups and interacting with uniform probability. Early work goes back to Ross (1916) and Ross and Hudson (1917a, 1917b). An early SIR model was presented in Kermack and McKendrick (1927). These models were gradually elaborated to include richer interaction structures; for instance, see Anderson and May (1992). Explicit models of networks were introduced in Kretzschmar and Morris (1996) and Pastor-Satorras and Vespignani (2001a). The literature on diseases and epidemic dynamics on networks has grown a great deal over the past two decades. For a panoramic overview of the theoretical research on epidemics in complex networks, see Pastor-Satorras, Castellano, Van Mieghem, and Vespignani (2015).

Some of the key results on the role of network structure in shaping the spread of disease have been inspired by the spread of computer viruses; see in particular Pastor-Satorras and Vespignani (2001a); Cohen, Erez, Ben-Avraham, and Havlin (2001); and Cohen, Erez, and Havlin (2000).

Finally, we draw on research on dynamic processes and percolation on random graphs. Special mention must be made of Molloy and Reed (1995) and Chung and Lu (2002b) in this connection. For an overview of this line of work, the reader is referred to the excellent collection of articles in Newman, Barabasi, and Watts (2006).

There is a vast literature spanning various disciplines on the diffusion of information and behavior; Rogers (1995b) presents an important overview of the early literature. As we discuss in chapter 13, on communication and social learning, an early study of diffusion in social networks is Coleman, Katz, and Menzel (1966); other early studies on diffusion include Ryan and Gross (1943) and Griliches (1957). More recently, easy availability of data on large-scale networks has led to a revival of interest in the problem of optimal targeting. Domingos and Richardson (2001) provide a formal statement of the problem of optimal seeding, and Kempe, Kleinberg, and Tardos (2003) develop a model of optimal seeding. They explore the computational challenges involved in optimal seeding and propose appropriate algorithms that are computationally efficient. The problem of optimal influence strategies remains an active field of research; for example, for recent theoretical contributions, see Galeotti and Goyal (2009) and Goyal, Heidari, and Kearns (2019). Our case study of microfinance is based on Banerjee, Chandrasekhar, Duflo, and Jackson (2013);

for other closely related recent empirical studies on diffusion in social networks, see Beaman, BenYishay, Magruder, and Mobarak (2021); Kim, Hwong, Stafford, et al. (2015); and Cai, De Janvry, and Sadoulet (2015).

## 14.9 Questions

1. In the basic tree network example with a single original infected node, show that $E[X_n] = R_n$ going to infinity is consistent with $P(q_n \geq 0) \to 0$ as $n$ grows.
2. This question explores an aspect of the proof of proposition 14.1. In the basic tree network with a single original infected node, use the construction of $f$ to demonstrate that $q^* = 0$ when $R_0 < 1$.
3. (From Easley and Kleinberg [2010]). Imagine that you're advising a group of agricultural officials who are investigating measures to control the outbreak of an epidemic in its early stages within a livestock population. On short notice, they are able to try to control the extent to which the animals come in contact with each other, and they are also able to introduce higher levels of sanitization to reduce the probability that one animal passes the disease to another. Both of these measures cost money, however, and the estimates of the costs are as follows: If the officials spend $x$ dollars controlling the extent to which animals come into contact with each other, then they expect each animal to come into contact with

$$40 - \frac{x}{200{,}000} \tag{14.74}$$

others. If the officials spend $y$ dollars introducing sanitization measures to reduce the probability of transmission, then they expect the probability that an infected animal passes it to another animal to be

$$0.04 - \frac{y}{100{,}000{,}000}. \tag{14.75}$$

The officials have \$2 million budgeted for this activity. Their current plan is to spend \$1 million on each of the two measures. Using what you know about epidemics, would you advise them that this is a good use of the available money? If so, why? If not, can you suggest a better way to allocate the money?
4. Consider diffusion with immune nodes, as discussed in section 14.4. Fix a degree distribution $P(d)$ and suppose that the threshold $\pi$ for the emergence of a giant component of susceptible nodes lies between 0 and 1. Consider a first-order stochastic shift in the degree distribution to $P'(d)$: how does the threshold change? Similarly, consider a mean-preserving spread of the degree distribution $P''(d)$ and study how the threshold changes (for definitions of first-order stochastic dominance and mean preserving spread, refer to chapter 1).

5. (From Jackson [2008]). This question provides a foundation for the linear infection model studied in section 14.5. Suppose that the probability of becoming infected in any given meeting with an infected individual is $v$. Then the probability of becoming infected in $d$ random meetings with individuals who are independently infected with probability $\theta$ is

$$\sum_{x=1}^{d}(1-(1-v)^{x})\binom{d}{x}\theta^{x}(1-\theta)^{d-x}. \tag{14.76}$$

Equation (14.76) sums across the number of infected neighbors, $x$, that an individual with $d$ neighbors is likely to have, where $\binom{d}{x}\theta^{x}(1-\theta)^{d-x}$ is the probability of having $x$ infected meetings. The term $(1-(1-v)^{x})$, then, is the probability of not becoming infected in any of the meetings with infected individuals. Show that if $v$ is small relative to $d$ (so that $(1-v)^{x}$ is approximately equal to $1-vx$, for any $x \leq d$), then equation (14.76) reduces to $v^{d}\theta$.

6. (From López-Pintado [2008]). Consider the SIS model. Suppose that the probability of infection depends not on the absolute number of neighbors, but on the average rate of infection in the neighborhood. This suggests that the probability of getting infected with degree $d$ is $v\theta$, where $\theta$ is the neighbor infection rate. Show that $\rho(d)$ is independent of $d$: $\rho = \theta = \frac{\lambda-1}{\lambda}$ if $\lambda > 1$, and 0 otherwise.

# 15 Social Ties and Markets

## 15.1 Introduction

Traditional models in economics assume that individuals are anonymous and act in isolation. Over the past two decades, economists have developed models that include social networks alongside the familiar notions of strategy, information, prices, and competition. This chapter studies the role of social networks in product markets, in labor markets, and in financial markets.

In our discussion on product markets, we will study how firms can use knowledge of social networks to better design advertising, product placement, and pricing strategies. In our study of advertising and placement, we will explore ways in which a firm can use information on the social network to improve its performance. Building on our study of games on networks in chapter 4, we will show that optimal firm strategies will depend both on the level as well as the content of the network interaction. In some situations, an increase in network connectivity calls for an increased engagement from the firm, while in other instances, the converse may hold. In a similar vein, we show that in some settings, it is optimal for a firm to target the most connected individuals, while in others, it is better to target poorly connected ones.

We then study how firms can use information about networks to price discriminate across consumers. The general finding is that firms will find it attractive to tailor prices to the network location of consumers, offering discounts to consumers who are highly influential and charging markups to consumers who are more susceptible to influence.

We next take up the role of social ties in labor markets. We start with an overview of the wide-ranging empirical evidence on this subject. This discussion brings out the extensive use of social ties in job search and recruitment by both workers and firms. We then present theoretical models to understand how the use of social ties affects wages, employment, and inequality in labor markets.

We present a very brief discussion of the role of social networks in financial markets in the material on reading notes in section 15.4.

## 15.2 Product Markets

In the theory of industrial organization, a firm traditionally chooses prices, advertising strategy, and product quality against a background assumption that individuals are anonymous and act in isolation from each other (for a classical exposition of this theory, see Tirole [1988]). However, a number of studies have brought out the important role of friends, neighbors, and colleagues in shaping consumer choice. Social influence is channeled through two primary routes—information sharing and a desire to be compatible. For a discussion on the many motivations for information sharing, see chapter 13 and for a discussion on pressures to choose compatible products, see chapter 8. In the past, the practical use of such social influences for advertising and pricing was limited due to the absence of good data on social networks. The recent trends in the availability of large amounts of data on social networks, along with advances in information technology, now make it possible for firms to harness the power of social networks to further their goals.

In particular, the massive quantities of data available on social network sites such as chat rooms, social networking websites, and newsgroups, has given rise to measures of the *network value of a customer*: the expected increase in sales that results from marketing to that customer. For instance, social networking sites like Facebook and Twitter help firms target consumers by sharing their demographic characteristics and information on their social interactions, and new firms have emerged that use these data to create a profile of consumers' online behavior and their influence score. For instance, take the website and social media app Klout, which created a Klout influence score that firms paid for the privilege of using.

At the outset, it is useful to distinguish between the level and the content of a social interaction. There are a number of different aspects to the level of interaction. A natural statistic is the number of people someone talks to or the number of friends they have, which is the degree. In many of the models in this chapter, we will use degree as a measure of social networks. Empirical work suggests that degree distributions vary across product categories and are correlated with individual demographic characteristics. In some cases, further details on the social network may be available. This will lead us to also study models in which the firm has complete information on the network.

The content of interactions refers to how an individual's action affects the returns to others (for an extended discussion on content of interaction, refer to chapter 4). For instance, an interaction may involve word-of-mouth communication about product quality and prices. In this case, the presence of a single informed neighbor leads to product awareness, and possibly purchases. Alternatively, an interaction may involve working together on a project: in this, an individual may choose a word processing software. A sufficient proportion of neighbors need to choose an action before an individual will switch to this action.

### 15.2.1 Advertising and Seeding

We now study the problem of a firm that chooses advertising intensity in order to maximize profits. The behavior of these individuals is influenced by their interactions. Our discussion will draw attention to the content and the level of interaction in shaping optimal firm strategy. In this setting, content refers to the sharing of information about new products and the sharing of computer files in collaborative work. The level of interaction will be modeled in terms of the network degree distribution. The discussion is based on Galeotti and Goyal (2009).

There is a unit measure of individuals $N=[0,1]$ who are located in a social network. For individual $i\in N$, the level of social interaction is parameterized by degree $k$. Suppose that every individual draws $k$ others with probability $P(k)\geq 0$, $k\in\mathcal{K}$, where $\mathcal{K}=\{0,1,\ldots,\bar{k}\}$; $\sum_{k\in\mathcal{K}}P(k)=1$. Conditional on degree $k$, they make $k$ draws from the population, using a uniform distribution on the unit interval. As there is a continuum of individuals, the probability of drawing the same person two or more times is zero. We say that there is a fraction $P(k)$ of individuals who choose a $k$-sized sample. In what follows, we will refer to $P$ as the "out-degree distribution." It will be convenient to define $\hat{k}=\sum_{k\in\mathcal{K}}P(k)k$ as the mean out-degree. As we wish to focus on out-degrees here, we assume that everyone has the same in-degree (and that it is equal to the mean out-degree, $\hat{k}$).

The firm seeks to maximize its profits by selling its product to population $N$. The firm knows the degree distribution $P(\cdot)$ and chooses an action $x\in[0,1]$. We will say that the profits from an individual influenced by $k$ others are given by $\phi_k(x)$, where $\phi_k(\cdot):[0,1]\to\mathbb{R}$. For ease of exposition, we will assume that $\phi_k(\cdot)$ is twice continuously differentiable. The expected profits of the firm from strategy $x$ are

$$\Pi(x|P)=\sum_{k\in O}P(k)\phi_k(x)-C(\alpha,x), \tag{15.1}$$

where $C(\alpha,\cdot):[0,1]\to\mathcal{R}$ is the cost of effort and parameter $\alpha\geq 0$ indicates the efficiency in generating efforts.

Here, we develop two examples to clarify how the content of interaction among consumers shapes the returns function $\phi_k(\cdot)$.

**Example 15.1** *Word-of-mouth communication*

Consider a firm advertising to a group of consumers who share product information among themselves. The price of the product is 1, while the cost of producing the good is zero. Every buyer has inelastic demand and the reservation value is 1. These buyers are unaware of the product; the firm uses advertising to inform them of it.

The firm chooses the fraction of individuals who will receive advertisements $x\in[0,1]$. Let the cost of effort $x$ be $\alpha x^2/2$, where $\alpha>0$. A consumer buys either if they receive the advertisement from the firm or receive information via word-of-mouth communication from her neighbors. Thus the expected profits from a degree $k$ buyer are

$$\phi_k(x) = 1 - (1-x)^{k+1}. \tag{15.2}$$

Note that $\phi_k(x)$ is increasing and concave in $x$ and $k$. Given the degree distribution, $P$, the expected profits are

$$\Pi(x|P) = \sum_{k \in O} P(k)[1 - (1-x)^{k+1}] - \frac{\alpha}{2}x^2. \tag{15.3}$$

Note that we have assumed that information travels only one link; a question at the end of the chapter explores the case of indirect information transmission. ■

**Example 15.2** *Adoption externalities*

Suppose that a firm is introducing a new product into the market. This product exhibits positive externalities: individual returns from a product depend on how many neighbors buy it. Examples of such products include fax machines, telephones, video-conference technologies, online games, online social networks, and file-sharing tools. There are two periods, 1 and 2. In period 1, the firm seeds the network by distributing free samples of the product. Let $x \in [0, 1]$ be the fraction of individuals who are sent free samples, and let the price of the product equal 1. A consumer with degree $k$, of whom $s$ are using the product, buys the product with probability $\psi(k, s)$. Suppose that a consumer earns $v = 1$ if all neighbors adopt, and 0 otherwise. Then returns from a $k$-degree individual are

$$\phi_k(x) = (1-x)x^k. \tag{15.4}$$

On the right-hand-side, the first term is the probability of not receiving a free sample, and the second term is the probability that all neighbors receive a seed. This function is increasing and convex for low $x$, and decreasing and concave for large $x$, and it is decreasing and convex in $k$. The expected profits under $x$ are

$$\Pi(x|P) = \sum_{k \in O} P(k)(1-x)x^k. \tag{15.5}$$

Expected profits are zero at $x = 0$ and $x = 1$ and positive for all $x \in (0, 1)$. The cost of production and dissemination of samples is zero, but a free sample has an implicit cost for the firm since a consumer who gets a free product does not buy at a positive price later. ■

Here we will focus on the effects of networks in the word-of-mouth. Questions at the end of the chapter explore the example with adoption externalities.

#### 15.2.1.1 Network effects with word-of-mouth communication

First, consider the effects of networks on profits. Suppose for simplicity that in equation (15.3), $\alpha = 1$. Then the optimal strategy of a firm that ignores word-of-mouth advertising is to set $x = 1$ and earn profits as $\Pi(1) = 1/2$. Suppose next that everyone has degree $k$. The

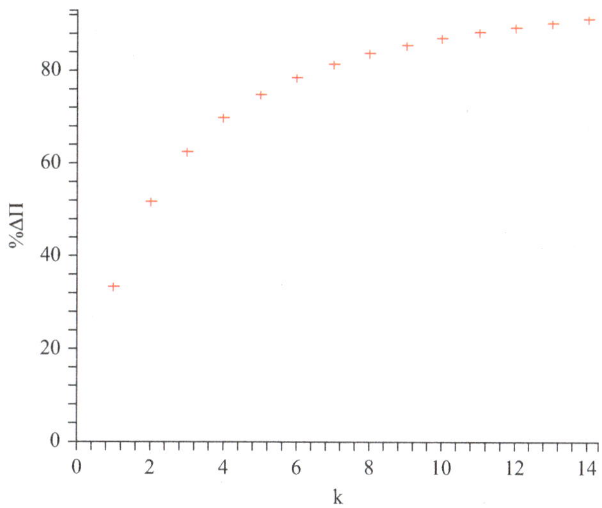


**Figure 15.1**
Incorporating word of mouth. Percent profit difference, $P(k) = 1, k = 1, 2, \ldots,$ and $\alpha = 1$.

optimal strategy of a firm that incorporates word-of-mouth communication is given by $x_k^*$, where $x_k^*$ solves as follows:

$$(k+1)(1-x_k^*)^k - x_k^* = 0. \tag{15.6}$$

Let $\Pi(x_k^*)$ be the profits from optimal advertising, and let us define the advantages of using social networks using the difference in profit, $[\Pi(x_k^*) - \Pi(1)]/\Pi(1)$. These advantages are plotted in figure 15.1: we note that if $k \geq 10$, then the optimal use of word of mouth can raise profits by more than 80 percent.

Denote the optimal strategy under a degree distribution $P$ by $x_P^*$. The interior optimal strategy $x_P^*$ solves as follows:

$$\sum_{k=1}^{\bar{k}} P(k)(k+1)(1-x_P^*)^k - \alpha x_P^* = 0. \tag{15.7}$$

Observe that optimal $x_P^*$ is falling in $\alpha$. Turning to the effects of networks, consider a first-order stochastic shift from $P$ to $P'$ (refer to chapter 1 for definitions of changes in degree distribution). An informed individual will inform more of their cohort, but an uninformed individual is more likely to hear from others. The first pressure increases incentives for advertisements, while the second pressure lowers them. The derivative of the marginal returns with respect to degree $k$ at $x_P^*$ is

$$\frac{\partial^2 \phi_k(x_P^*)}{\partial x \partial k} = (1-x_P^*)^k \left[1 + (k+1)\ln(1-x_P^*)\right]. \tag{15.8}$$

For low $x_P^*$, the marginal returns are increasing, while for high $x_P^*$, the marginal returns are falling. This suggests that if the costs of advertising are large (small), then optimal advertising increases (decreases) with word of mouth. The intuition is as follows: If $\alpha$ is large, $x_P^*$ is small; at this stage, word of mouth and advertising are complements. If, on the other hand, $\alpha$ is low, then $x_P^*$ is high and the relation is one of substitutes.

Turning to profits, observe that the term $[1-(1-x)^{k+1}]$ is increasing in $k$, so profits under $P'$ are larger, keeping strategy fixed at $x_P^*$. It follows, then, that profits increase with an increase in word of mouth.

Let us next examine the effects of greater dispersion in social connections. Consider a mean-preserving spread change from $P$ to $P'$. The effects depend on the curvature of marginal returns with respect to $k$:

$$\frac{\partial^3 \phi_k(x_P^*)}{\partial x \partial k^2} = (1-x_P^*)^k \ln(1-x_P^*) \left[2+(k+1)\ln(1-x_P^*)\right]. \tag{15.9}$$

For small $x_P^*$, this effect is negative, while for large $x_P^*$, it is positive. Hence marginal returns are concave in $k$ for large costs of ads and convex in $k$ for small costs of ads. This suggests that if the costs of advertising are large (small), then advertising falls (rises) under a mean-preserving spread of word-of-mouth communication. Turning to profits, recall that $[1-(1-x)^{k+1}]$ is concave in $k$. This means that profits fall under a mean-preserving spread of word-of-mouth communication. These observations are summarized in the following result.

**Proposition 15.1** *Suppose that a firm's expected payoffs are given by equation (15.1).*

- *If the costs of advertising are large (small), then optimal advertising increases (falls) with word of mouth; profits always increase in word of mouth.*
- *If the costs of advertising are large (small), then optimal advertising falls (rises) with greater dispersion in word of mouth; profits fall with greater dispersion in word of mouth.*

**Role of network information** A recurring idea in marketing and public health is that organizations can target key individuals in networks to amplify the power of their messages or their strategies. To consider optimal targeting in this setting, suppose that the firm knows the distribution of degrees $P$ and is able to partition set $N$ into $\bar{k}$ groups. $P(k)$ into the fraction of individuals in group $k$, and individuals in group $k$ have degree $k$. The strategy is vector $\mathbf{x} = (x_1, \ldots, x_{\bar{k}})$, where $x_k \in [0, 1]$ indicates the effort that the firm targets to the group $k \in \mathcal{K}$. It follows that $\mathbf{x} \in [0, 1]^{\bar{k}}$. Strategy $\mathbf{x}$ leads to total effort $\theta(\mathbf{x}) = \sum_{k \in O} P(k) x_k$. Let the expected profits from a degree $k$ individual be given by $\phi_k(x_k, \theta(\mathbf{x}))$. The expected returns from a degree $k$ consumer are

$$\phi_k(x_k, \theta(\mathbf{x})) = 1-(1-x_k)(1-\theta(\mathbf{x}))^k. \tag{15.10}$$

This is the probability that an individual with degree $k$ will be informed either from direct advertisements or word of mouth. Observe that $\phi_k(x_k, \theta(\mathbf{x}))$ is concave in the first argument (i.e., the marginal returns are decreasing in degree). The expected profits of the monopolist are

$$\Pi(\mathbf{x}|P) = \sum_{k\in\mathcal{K}} P(k)[1-(1-x_k)(1-\theta(\mathbf{x}))^k] - \frac{\alpha}{2}(\theta(\mathbf{x}))^2.$$

A threshold strategy $\mathbf{x}$ has $\tilde{k}\in\mathcal{K}$ such that $x_k = 1$ if $k < \tilde{k}$, $x_{\tilde{k}} \in [0,1]$, and $x_k = 0$ if $k > \tilde{k}$. The marginal returns from a degree $s$ individual are

$$P(s)\left[(1-\theta(\mathbf{x}))^s + \sum_{k\in O} P(k)k(1-x_k)(1-\theta(\mathbf{x}))^{k-1} - \alpha\theta(\mathbf{x})\right]. \tag{15.11}$$

If $x_s^* > 0$ for $s\in O$, then $\frac{d\Pi(\mathbf{x}^*|P)}{dx_s^*} \geq 0$. For all $s \in O$, the latter two terms are equal, the first term is strictly declining in $s$, and so is the optimal strategy. Now suppose $1 > x_{s'}^* \geq x_s^* > 0$ for some $s' < s$. Since $x_s^* > 0$, it follows that $\frac{d\Pi(\mathbf{x}^*|P)}{dx_s} \geq 0$. However, $(1-\theta(\mathbf{x}^*))$ only depends on $\theta(\mathbf{x}^*)$, so $\frac{d\Pi(\mathbf{x}^*|P)}{dx_{s'}} > 0$. Thus the optimal strategy $\mathbf{x}^*$ targets low-degree individuals and ignores high-degree consumers. The intuition for this is simple: consumers who are poorly connected are less likely to hear about product from word of mouth.

**Incoming and outgoing links** In the discussion so far, we have assumed that all nodes have the same number of incoming links, that is every node has the same influence. To explore the role of influencers, let us instead suppose that every individual draws a sample of the same size, but some individuals are drawn more than others. If an individual is sampled by $l$ other individuals, this means that there are $l$ links pointing to individual $i$. We will refer to this as the "in-degree." We can apply the methods of analysis described in this chapter to study optimal advertising and targeting in this setting. In line with intuition, optimal advertising will target individuals with higher in-degrees. A question at the end of the chapter explores this model.

To summarize, we have studied the effects of networks on optimal advertising and product placement in the word-of-mouth example; in this study, we exploited properties of the content function as reflected by $\phi_k$. We have seen that the example with adaption externalities leads to payoff function with different properties. Questions at the end of the chapter explore the role of social networks in that context.

### 15.2.2 Pricing Network Effects

We study price discrimination based on network information. Consider a product whose value is increasing in the consumption of other consumers. Suppose that consumer A interacts with a large number of other individuals, who only interact with them. The firm would find it easier to get these consumers to buy its product if A buys it. There is therefore an priori case for subsidizing consumer A and possibly selling the product with a markup to these other consumers. This section explores the scope of this argument; the discussion is based on Fainmesser and Galeotti (2016).

#### 15.2.2.1 A model with degree distributions

There are $N = \{1, \ldots, n\}$, $n \geq 2$ individuals located in a network. A tie between two individuals $i$ and $j$, $g_{ij}, \in \{0, 1\}$. Link $g_{ij}$ reflects the influence of $j$ on $i$. We will allow influence to be asymmetric: so $g_{ij}$ may be different from $g_{ji}$.

Suppose that the firm faces constant marginal cost, normalized to zero, and that consumer $i$'s demand, $x_i$, is decreasing in the price faced and is increasing in the consumption of their peers:

$$x_i = 1 - p_i + \gamma \sum_j g_{ij} x_j, \tag{15.12}$$

where $\gamma \geq 0$, captures social influence. This formulation allows both divisible and indivisible products. In the latter case, we interpret $x_i$ as the probability that individual $i$ will buy the product.

The out-degree of individual $i$ is $k_i = \sum_j g_{ij}$ and the in-degree, $l_i = \sum_j g_{ji}$. Letting $P(k)$ be the fraction of consumers with out-degree $k$ and $H(l)$ be the fraction of consumers with in-degree $l$, it follows that the average in-degree is equal to the average out-degree; that is,

$$\hat{l} = \sum_l l H(l) = \sum_k P(k) k = \hat{k}. \tag{15.13}$$

Let $\sigma_k^2$ denote the variance in out-degrees and $\sigma_l^2$ the variance in in-degrees.

To begin, let us assume that the firm knows the distributions $P(k)$ and $H(k)$, as well as the in-degree and the out-degree of every consumer. We will think of the out-degree, $k$, as a measure of susceptibility and the in-degree, $l$, as a measure of influence. We will set $x(k; l)$ as the demand of a consumer with susceptibility $k$ and influence $l$. The firm sets prices $(p(k, l))_{k,l}$ for various segments. Faced with these prices, consumers make purchase decisions $x = (x_i)_{i \in N}$.

As the costs of production are equal to 0, the profit from consumers of type $(k, l)$ is

$$\pi(k, l) = x(k, l) p(k, l). \tag{15.14}$$

The profit from price strategy $\mathbf{p}$ is

$$\Pi(\mathbf{p}) = \sum_k P(k) \sum_l H(l) x(k, l) p(k, l). \tag{15.15}$$

Facing price profile $\mathbf{p}$, the utility of a consumer from different purchase choices will depend on the choices of their neighbors (due to the peer effects term in the demand). To ensure that the demands do not explode, we assume that $\gamma \times k^{max} < 1$. Under this condition, for any $\mathbf{p}$, there is a unique demand equilibrium given by

$$x(k, l) = 1 - p(k, l) + \gamma \frac{1 - \bar{p}}{1 - \gamma \bar{k}} k, \tag{15.16}$$

where $\bar{p}$ is the average price paid by a neighbor of $i$ and is given by

$$\bar{p} = \sum_l \frac{H(l)l}{\hat{l}} \sum_k P(k)p(k,l). \tag{15.17}$$

In the demand equation (equation 15.16), the first term reflects individual differences in stand-alone valuation of the good, so the demand is decreasing in the price offered, $p(k;l)$. The second term captures the peer effects. In particular, note that an additional out-degree shifts demand upward by

$$\gamma \frac{1-\bar{p}}{1-\gamma\bar{k}}. \tag{15.18}$$

This term is a product of the peer effect parameter, $\gamma$, and the average consumption of a neighboring node. The average consumption is increasing in the average connectivity of the network and decreasing in the average price paid by neighboring nodes.

**Effects of networks on pricing** We first compute the demands and profits when the firm sets a uniform price (that ignores peer effects). The optimal price is 1/2. Faced with this price, the demand will depend only on susceptibility level and is given by

$$x(k) = \frac{1}{2}\left[1 + \frac{\gamma}{1-\gamma\bar{k}}k\right]. \tag{15.19}$$

The total profits are then given by

$$\frac{1}{4}\left[\frac{1}{1-\gamma\bar{k}}\right]. \tag{15.20}$$

When we turn to optimal pricing with peer effects, we again need to be aware of the potential of peer effects leading to the possibility of having multiple sets of optimal prices. To rule that out, we require that peer effects be sufficiently low.

Observe that when a firm increases the price, $p(k;l)$, there are two standard effects: a larger margin on sales and a lowering of demand. But there is also a third effect, which is due to peer effects: the increase in price lowers the demand of segment $(k,l)$ and indirectly reduces the average consumption that all consumers expect from their neighbors.

**Proposition 15.2** *Suppose that peer effects $\gamma k^{max} < 1/2$. The optimal pricing policy $\mathbf{p}$ is*

$$p(k,l) = \frac{1}{2} + \frac{\gamma\hat{k}}{2C\hat{k}^2}\left[(\gamma\sigma_l^2 + 2\hat{k})k - (\gamma\sigma_k^2 + 2\hat{k})l\right], \tag{15.21}$$

*where $C = 4 - 4\hat{k}\gamma - \gamma^2(\sigma_k^2 + \sigma_l^2) - \gamma^2\sigma_k^2\sigma_l^2$. The consumption levels $\mathbf{x}$ are given by*

$$x(k,l) = \frac{1}{2}\left[1 + \frac{(\gamma\sigma_l^2 + 2\hat{l})k - (\gamma\sigma_k^2 + 2\hat{k})l}{\hat{k}^2 C}\hat{k}\gamma\right]. \tag{15.22}$$

The optimal pricing strategy thus has a simple structure: there is a baseline price, $1/2$; and there is a markup that is increasing in the susceptibility, $k$, and falling in the influence, $l$. It is instructive to work through the algebra step by step. Recall that firm profits are given by

$$\Pi(\mathbf{p})=\sum_l\sum_k kH(l)P(k)p(k,l)x(k,l). \tag{15.23}$$

Taking the derivative with respect to the price, we obtain

$$\frac{\partial\Pi(.)}{\partial p(k,l)}=0\Longleftrightarrow p^*(k,l)=\frac{1}{2}\left[1+\frac{\gamma}{1-\gamma\hat{k}}((1-\bar{p})k-\phi l)\right]. \tag{15.24}$$

where $\phi=\frac{1}{\hat{k}}\sum_l\sum_k H(l)P(k)kp^*(k,l)$. Using $p^*(k,l)$ and the definition of $\bar{p}$, we obtain

$$\bar{p}^*=\frac{1}{2}\left[1+\frac{\gamma}{1-\gamma\hat{k}}((1-\bar{p}^*)\hat{k}-\phi\frac{\sigma_l^2+\sigma_{\hat{k}^2}}{\hat{k}})\right]. \tag{15.25}$$

Similarly, we substitute for $p^*(k,l)$ in the definition of $\phi$ to obtain

$$\phi=\frac{1}{2}\left[1+\frac{\gamma}{1-\gamma\hat{k}}((1-\bar{p}^*)\frac{\sigma_k^2+\hat{k}^2}{\hat{k}}-\phi\hat{k})\right]. \tag{15.26}$$

We therefore have a system of two equations, (15.25) and (15.26), in two unknowns, $\bar{p}^*$ and $\phi$. We can solve the two equations to obtain

$$\bar{p}=\frac{\hat{k}(\gamma\hat{k}-1)(2\hat{k}+\gamma\sigma_k^2)}{-4\hat{k}^2+4\hat{k}^3\gamma+\hat{k}^2\gamma^2\sigma_k^2+\hat{k}^2\gamma^2\sigma_l^2+\gamma^2\sigma_k^2\sigma_l^2}$$

$$\phi=\frac{2\hat{k}^2+2\hat{k}^3\gamma+\hat{k}^2\gamma^2\sigma_k^2+\hat{k}\gamma\sigma_l^2-\gamma^2\sigma_k^2\sigma_l^2}{-4\hat{k}^2+4\hat{k}^3\gamma+\hat{k}^2\gamma^2\sigma_k^2+\hat{k}^2\gamma^2\sigma_l^2+\gamma^2\sigma_k^2\sigma_l^2}. \tag{15.27}$$

Substituting these values of $\bar{p}$ and $\phi$ into equation (15.24), we obtain the optimal prices:

$$p^*(k,l)=\frac{1}{2}+\frac{\gamma\hat{k}}{2}\left[\frac{(\gamma\sigma_l^2+2\hat{k})k-(\gamma\sigma_k^2+2\hat{k})l}{\hat{k}^2(4-4\hat{k}\gamma-\gamma^2(\sigma_k^2+\sigma_l^2)-\gamma^2\sigma_k^2\sigma_l^2)}\right]. \tag{15.28}$$

When we substitute these optimal prices into equation (15.16), we obtain the required equilibrium demand expression. ■

We now compute numerical examples to illustrate the effects of networks on pricing and consumption.

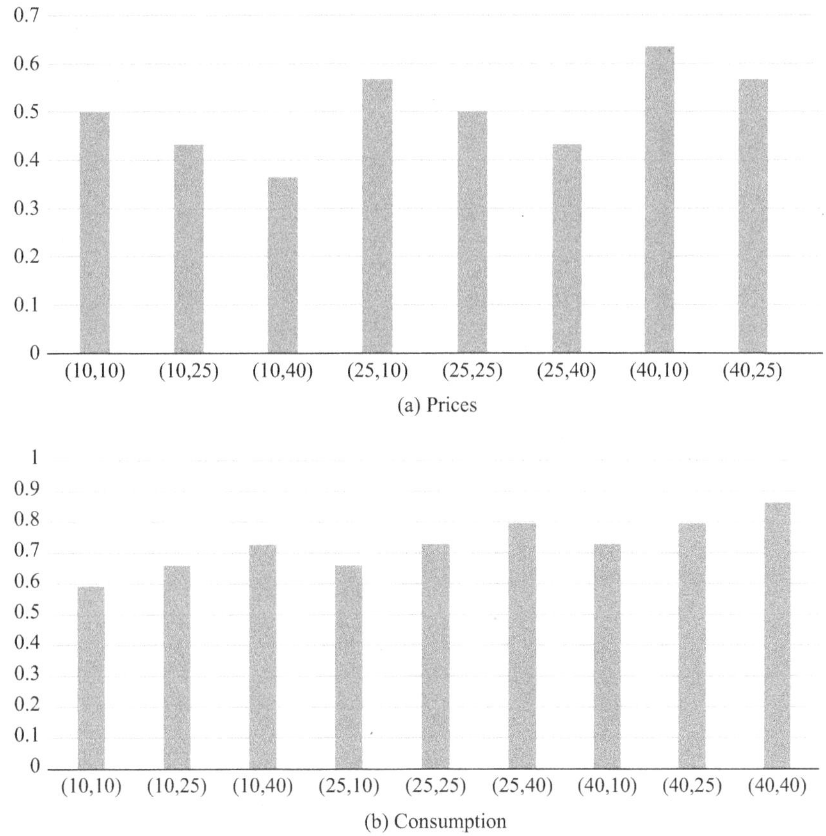


**Figure 15.2**
Optimal prices and equilibrium consumption in networks.

**Example 15.3** *The effects of networks on pricing*

Suppose that $\gamma = 0.012$. The distribution $F(\cdot)$ is as follows. one-third of the population has susceptibility 10, one-third has susceptibility 25 and one-third has susceptibility 40. The distribution of influence is identical. The optimal prices are presented in figure 15.2(a). In this graph, under each bar, reflecting the level of the price, the first number is the out-degree and the second number is the in-degree. We note that the prices are increasing in susceptibility and falling in influence. The consumption of different types is plotted in figure 15.2(b): it is increasing in both influence (due to lower prices) and susceptibility (due to larger peer effects). The profits of the firm are 0.362.

Proposition 15.2 tells us that optimal prices depends on the mean-linking $\hat{k}$ and the variance in links. Let us illustrate the effects of changes in mean and variance. Consider the network with the following susceptibility distribution, $F''(.)$: 20 percent of the population

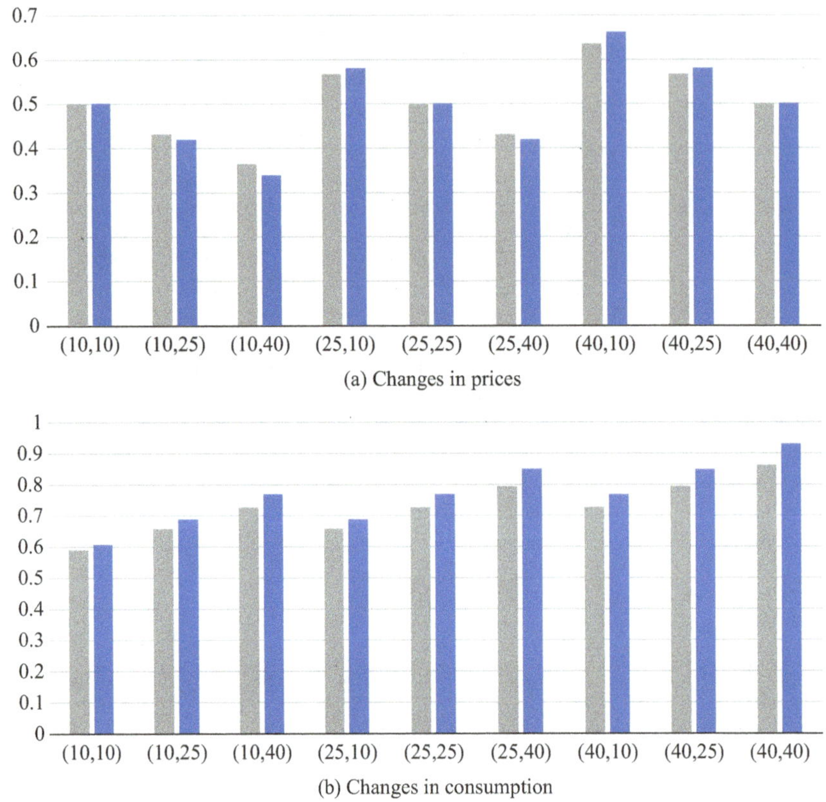


**Figure 15.3**
Effects of changes in network: $F$ in gray, $F''$ in blue.

has susceptibility 10, 30 percent has susceptibility 25, and 50 percent has susceptibility 40. The distribution of influence is $H''(.) = F''(.)$. It can be verified that $F''$ first-order stochastically dominates $F$ (and hence has a higher mean). Optimal prices and equilibrium consumption are presented in figure 15.3. An increase in susceptibility means that all consumers have access to higher positive peer effects, which pushes up the prices. The rise in prices is modest, but figure 15.3(b) also shows that the effects on consumption are more significant. As a consequence, profits of the firm go up from 0.36 to 0.44. ■

#### 15.2.2.2 A model of pricing with complete network knowledge

So far, we have studied the effects of networks in terms of degree distribution. In some cases, a firm may have more complete knowledge of the network. To see how additional information can be used by a firm, we will consider the case where a firm has complete information about the network. We will see that the optimal pricing strategy has a similar structure to the one described previously: consumers are offered a baseline price, a markup that depends on how much the consumer is susceptible to influence, and a price discount that depends on the amount of influence that the consumer exercises on others. Our discussion is based on Bloch and Quérou (2013) and Candogan, Bimpikis, and Ozdaglar (2012).

Suppose that the firm sets prices targeted at specific individuals $\mathbf{p} = (p_1, \ldots, p_n)$. Let $\mathbf{q} = (q_1, \ldots, q_n)$ denote the consumption profile. Given network $g$ (with a corresponding adjacency matrix $G$), prices $\mathbf{p}$, and consumption $\mathbf{q}$, individual $i$'s utility is given by

$$u_i = \underbrace{\alpha x_i - \frac{\beta}{2} x_i^2}_{\text{A: Utility from own usage}} + \underbrace{x_i \sum_j g_{ij} x_j}_{\text{B: Utility from friends' usage}} - \underbrace{p_i x_i}_{\text{C: Cost of usage}} . \tag{15.29}$$

Observe that marginal utility to own consumption is increasing in the consumption of neighbors (i.e., consumption choices of neighbors are strategic complements). We suppose that $\alpha > 0$ and $\beta > 0$ and assume that $\beta$ is sufficiently large that the negative quadratic term eventually dominates. Define the average influence between $i$ and $j$ in a network $g$ by

$$\bar{g}_{ij} = \frac{g_{ij} + g_{ji}}{2}. \tag{15.30}$$

The profit of the firm is

$$\sum_{i=1}^{n} (p_i - c) x_i, \tag{15.31}$$

where $c > 0$ is the cost of production for the firm. As in the incomplete information setting, we will consider a two-stage game. In the first stage, the firm sets prices, and in the second stage, the consumers play an equilibrium in consumption choices:

$$\begin{array}{lll} \max_{\mathbf{p} \in \mathcal{P}} & \sum_{i=1}^{n} (p_i - c) x_i & \\ \text{s.t.} & x_i \in \arg\max u_i(x_i, \mathbf{x_{-i}}), & \text{for all } i. \end{array} \tag{15.32}$$

Fix some prices $\mathbf{p}$. The first-order condition for consumer $i$ is

$$\alpha - \beta x_i + \sum_{j=1}^{n} x_j g_{ij} - p_i = 0. \tag{15.33}$$

Define $S = \{i : x_i > 0\}$. The first-order condition for individual $i \in S$ is

$$\alpha - \beta x_i + \sum_{j \in S} x_j g_{ij} - p_i = 0. \tag{15.34}$$

The best response for consumer $i$ may be written as

$$x_i = \frac{1}{\beta} \max \left\{ \alpha - p_i + \sum_{j=1}^{n} g_{ij} x_i, 0 \right\}. \tag{15.35}$$

This can be written in matrix form as

$$\beta x_S = \alpha \mathbf{1}_S - p_S + G_S x_S. \tag{15.36}$$

Rearranging terms in equation (15.36), the equilibrium consumption for an active consumer is

$$x_S = \frac{1}{\beta}\left[I - \frac{1}{\beta}G_S\right]^{-1}(\alpha \mathbf{1}_S - p_S). \tag{15.37}$$

Equipped with this expression for equilibrium demand, we now solve for optimal prices. We will assume that $\alpha > c$. This ensures that marginal utility at $x_i = 0$ is greater than the cost of production, thereby creating space for profitable exchange between the firm and consumers. It is possible to show that in a subgame perfect equilibrium, consumption is positive for every consumer (a question at the end of the chapter works through this property). Given the positive consumption property, the firm faces the following problem:

$$\max_p \quad (p - c\mathbf{1})^T x$$

$$\text{s.t.} \quad x = \frac{1}{\beta}\left(I - \frac{1}{\beta}G\right)^{-1}(\alpha \mathbf{1} - p).$$

This may be rewritten as

$$\max_p \quad (p - c\mathbf{1})^T \left(I - \frac{1}{\beta}G\right)^{-1}(\alpha \mathbf{1} - p). \tag{15.38}$$

The first-order condition for the firm's problem is

$$\left(I - \frac{1}{\beta}G\right)^{-1}(\alpha \mathbf{1} - p) - \left(I - \frac{1}{\beta}G^T\right)^{-1}(p - c\mathbf{1}) = 0. \tag{15.39}$$

Setting $M = I - \frac{1}{\beta}G$, we can rewrite the first-order condition as

$$M^{-1}(\alpha \mathbf{1} - p) - M^{-T}(p - c\mathbf{1}) = 0, \tag{15.40}$$

and after rearranging terms, we get

$$p = \left(\frac{\alpha + c}{2}\right)\mathbf{1} - \frac{M - M^T}{2}\left(\frac{M + M^T}{2}\right)^{-1}\left(\frac{\alpha - c}{2}\right)\mathbf{1}. \tag{15.41}$$

Let us define Bonacich centrality in graph $G$:

$$C(G, \hat{\alpha}) = (I - \hat{\alpha}G)^{-1}\mathbf{1}. \tag{15.42}$$

Since $M = I - \frac{1}{\beta}G$, it follows that

$$\left(\frac{M+M^T}{2}\right)^{-1}\mathbf{1}=\left(I-\left(\frac{G+G^T}{2\beta}\right)\right)^{-1}\mathbf{1}=C\left(\frac{G+G^T}{2},\frac{1}{\beta}\right). \tag{15.43}$$

We are now in a position to state the following result.

**Proposition 15.3** *Consider a monopoly firm choosing optimal prices with complete information on a network with adjacency matrix G. Optimal pricing is given by*

$$\mathbf{p}=\underbrace{\frac{\alpha+c}{2}\mathbf{1}}_{\text{Nominal price}}+\underbrace{\frac{\alpha-c}{4\beta}GC\left(\frac{G+G^T}{2},\frac{1}{\beta}\right)}_{\text{Markup—influenced by others}}-\underbrace{\frac{\alpha-c}{4\beta}G^TC\left(\frac{G+G^T}{2},\frac{1}{\beta}\right)}_{\text{Discount—influence on others}}. \tag{15.44}$$

The intuition underlying this result is as follows: if an agent influences others, then giving them a discount raises the consumption of their peers and raises profits, while if they are influenced by others, then their marginal utility is higher and they can pay more for the product. In this respect, the intuition is very much like in the earlier model of pricing conditional on the degrees of individuals. What is new here is that the influence is measured in terms of degree *and* the centrality of neighbors.

It is instructive to consider the case when influence and susceptibility are symmetric (i.e., $g_{ij}=g_{ji}$). This means that $G=G^T$. Proposition 15.3 tells us that the optimal price is uniform. There are two forces at work: on the one hand, greater connectivity means greater utility, which pushes toward higher prices. On the other hand, greater connectivity also means greater externalities, which push toward lower prices (as that boosts direct demand, and hence the demand of neighbors). In the linear model under study, these two effects cancel out exactly. Observe that with uniform prices, individual consumption will be proportional to Bonacich centrality.

To summarize: in this section, we studied price discrimination with incomplete as well as complete network information. Our analysis shows that firms will tailor prices to the network location of consumers, offering subsidies and discounts to consumers who are highly influential and charging markups to consumers who are more susceptible to influence.

## 15.3 Labor Markets

Workers like jobs that fit their skills and location preferences, and firms are looking to hire workers with the right skills for the jobs they need to fill. But both workers and firms face information constraints: workers do not know which firms have vacancies, and firms have imperfect information on the ability of workers who apply for jobs. It is natural, therefore, for workers to tap into their social connections to find out more about available jobs, and for firms to ask their current employees for information on applicants. This section explores the implications of the use of social connections on the functioning of labor markets. Our exposition here draws on Goyal (2007; 2017) and Topa (2019).

In the context of labor markets, social interactions range widely, from the simple transmission of information about job openings at a particular firm (letting a social contact know that a position is available at firm X) to the provision of a referral (recommending a social contact to a potential employer for a given position). Referrals can occur informally, but they can also be institutionalized as a recruiting tool by firms: firms set up formal referral systems for their employees, giving them the opportunity to refer potential candidates for a given position and rewarding them for a successful hire.

We start with a presentation of empirical evidence on the use of social ties. There is extensive evidence for the use of social ties in locating jobs. On the other side of the market, we present evidence for the use of referrals by firms. Finally, we present some evidence about the correlation between social networks and employment and wage levels.

This discussion sets the stage for a study of theoretical models on the use of social ties in labor markets. We first take up a model of referrals by firms to hire workers whose quality is unknown. This model highlights the role of social structure in shaping the functioning of the market, and thereby determining wage levels and inequality.

### 15.3.1 Empirical Background

> Despite modernization, technology, and the dizzying pace of social change, one constant in the world is that where and how we spend our working hours, the largest slice of life for most adults, depends very much on how we are embedded in networks of social contacts—the relatives, friends, and acquaintances that are not banished by the never-ending proposals to pair people to jobs by some automatic technical procedures such as national computerized matching.
> —Granovetter (1995, p. 141).

Empirical studies on the uses of social ties have looked at the use of contacts by both employees and employers. With regard to the use of personal contacts by workers, we take up three questions: (1) To what extent do workers rely on personal sources of information in obtaining jobs? (2) How does the use of personal contacts vary with the nature of the job and across countries? (3) How productive is this reliance upon contacts in terms of wages of the jobs obtained? Our discussion draws on survey papers by Ioannides and Datcher Loury [2004], Beaman [2016], and Topa [2019].

Early work by Rees (1966), Myers and Shultz (1951), and Granovetter (1973) demonstrate the extensive use of social connections in obtaining information about jobs. Myers and Shultz (1951) study textile workers and find that almost 62 percent of those surveyed obtained their first job via personal contacts, in contrast to only 15 percent who obtained their job from agencies and advertisements. Similarly, Granovetter (1973) showed that almost one-half of the people surveyed received information about their current job from a personal acquaintance. Table 15.1 presents a high-level summary of some of the early empirical work on the use of social contacts in labor markets.

These findings have inspired an extensive body of empirical research. While most of the literature has focused on referral usage by unemployed job seekers, recent work has

**Table 15.1**
Information on jobs.

| Source | Contacts | Application | Emp. Agency | Ads | Other | Sample Size |
|---|---|---|---|---|---|---|
| 1. Rees and Schultz (1970) | | | | | | |
| Typist | 37.3 | 5.5 | 34.7 | 16.4 | 6.1 | 343 |
| Keypunch operator | 35.3 | 10.7 | 13.2 | 21.4 | 19.4 | 280 |
| Accountant | 23.5 | 6.4 | 25.9 | 26.4 | 17.8 | 170 |
| Janitor | 65.5 | 13.1 | 7.3 | 4.8 | 9.3 | 246 |
| Janitress | 63.6 | 7.5 | 5.2 | 11.2 | 12.5 | 80 |
| Truck driver | 56.8 | 14.9 | 1.5 | 1.5 | 25.3 | 67 |
| Tool and die maker | 53.6 | 18.2 | 1.5 | 17.3 | 9.4 | 127 |
| 2. Granovetter (1974) | | | | | | |
| Professional | 56.1 | 18.2 | 15.9 | –[a] | 9.8 | 132 |
| Technical | 43.5 | 24.6 | 30.4 | – | 1.4 | 69 |
| Managerial | 65.4 | 14.8 | 13.6 | – | 6.2 | 81 |
| 3. Corcoran et. al. (1980) | | | | | | |
| White males | 52.0 | –[b] | 5.8 | 9.4 | 33.8 | 1499 |
| White females | 47.1 | – | 5.8 | 14.2 | 33.1 | 988 |
| Black males | 58.5 | – | 7.0 | 6.9 | 37.6 | 667 |
| Black females | 43.0 | – | 15.2 | 11.0 | 30.8 | 605 |

*Notes*: [a]Agencies and advertisements are collected together and reported under employment agencies.
[b]Gate applications are included under "other."
*Source*: Goyal (2007).

highlighted that social networks and referrals are widely used during on-the-job searches by employed workers as well. Indeed, for employed workers, many job offers come about without the workers actively looking for a job but as the result of informal networking activities.

Turning to variations in the use of social ties across different types of jobs, a broad finding is that there is a negative correlation between age, education, and occupational status and the likelihood of finding a job through personal contacts. This is observed in the 1978 Panel Study on Income Dynamics (Corcoran, Datcher, and Duncan [1980]), a study of an Indianapolis labor market (Marsden and Campbell [1990]), and a 1970 Detroit-area study (Marsden and Hurlbert [1988]). A similar negative correlation is also observed across European countries (Pellizzari [2010]).

A number of the studies find that personal contacts are an efficient way of finding jobs: a higher proportion of jobs found via contacts are likely to be accepted (Blau and Robins [1990]; Holzer [1988]). Turning to the relation between wages of jobs found via personal contacts, the evidence is mixed. Early work by Ullman (1966) suggests that there is a positive relation between wages and hiring via contacts. In more recent work, Pellizzari (2010) finds that in some countries (i.e., Austria, Belgium, and Netherlands), there is a wage premium for jobs found via personal contacts while in other countries (i.e., Greece, Italy, Portugal, and the UK), there is a wage penalty for jobs obtained via contacts. For a theoretical study of these empirical patterns, see Granovetter (1994).

While most of the literature has focused on the use of social networks and referrals from the perspective of the job seeker, a growing body of research has also looked at the employer's use of formal or informal referrals. In an early study, Holzer (1987) find that over 35 percent of the firms interviewed filled their last vacancy via referral. Similarly, Marsden and Campbell (1990), in their study of 53 Indiana establishments, find that roughly 51 percent of the jobs had been filled through referrals.

More generally, looking at the process—from initial contact to job application to interview to hire—referrals seem to be associated with a higher probability of being hired relative to other job search or recruiting methods. Referred workers typically receive higher starting wages (relative to nonreferred), but the wage gap tends to shrink with tenure at the firm. Referred workers are also less likely to separate from their employers—a possible sign of better match quality (see Dustmann, Glitz, and Schönberg (2009) and Brown, Setren, and Topa [2016]). Finally, the literature suggests that the joint distribution of the referrer and the referred characteristics matter for referral outcomes: for instance, referrals from employees who are older or at a higher staff level are associated with salary advantages that are stronger and persist longer.

Granovetter (1973) studied the use of contacts in labor markets in the US state of Massachusetts. He defined the strength of a tie as follows: a tie was said to be strong if two people had interacted twice a week, medium for interactions less than twice a week but more than once a year; weak if the pair had interacted less than once a year. A key finding pertained to the wide use of social contacts: over one-half of the workers who found jobs did so via social contacts. A second key finding pertained to the nature of social ties that were used by workers: of the 54 workers who had found their last job through a social contact, 16.7 percent found the job via a strong tie, 55.7 percent through a medium tie, and 27.6 percent through a weak tie. Thus the vast majority of those who used social contacts relied on nonstrong ties. This led him to coin the phrase *the strength of weak ties*.

A major concern of research has been to find a clear line of causality from social connections to job market outcomes. A difficulty here is to find detailed data on social networks and at the same time also have data on employment status. Another difficulty is that there may be reverse causation: employment status may shape social connections. Recent research has made progress in untangling these chains of effects and we discuss some of this work now.

We start with some evidence on correlations between social networks and employment. Conley and Topa (2002) study the spatial patterns of unemployment in Chicago over two decades, 1980 and 1990. Their focus is on the investigation of unemployment clustering with respect to distance metrics that reflect the structure of agents' social networks. With this in mind, these metrics are measures of physical distance, travel time, and the difference in ethnic and occupation distributions. Their empirical analysis reveals that there is a strong positive and statistically significant spatial dependence in the distribution of raw unemployment rates, at distances close to zero, for all these metrics. This correlation decays roughly monotonically with distance.

They also conduct a study of two-metric correlations. When the physical, travel time, or occupation metric is coupled with the ethnic metric, the latter drives most of the variation in spatial clustering: once we condition on ethnic distance, physical distance, and other indicators have relatively little impact on the correlations. On the other hand, when physical or travel time metrics are combined with distance in occupations, the correlations decline in both distances. Finally, they find that the variations in raw unemployment rates are well explained by tract-level variables. This study suggests that social interaction effects at the tract level may be modest.

A large body of continuing research studies interaction effects. One way to approximate the social interaction is to examine households at a finer level of granularity. This is the route taken in Bayer, Ross, and Topa (2008), who study block-level outcomes for the city of Boston. They find evidence that households with similar characteristics located in the same block have more similar employment outcomes than households located in different blocks. Their work also examines and rules out the reverse causation possibility—individuals are in the same block because they have similar employment outcomes.

Another route taken to study the effects of social networks is to connect variations in group size to outcome variables of interest. This strand of work has found strong social interaction effects on employment and wage outcomes. For instance, Munshi (2003) studies Mexican migration to the US. He uses variations in rainfall in Mexico as an exogenous shock: this rainfall affects incentives to move, and hence the rate of migration out of regions in Mexico for reasons that are unrelated to market conditions in the US. He finds that having a higher number of migrants who arrived more than three years ago has a positive effect on migrants' employment rate. In a similar vein, Beaman (2013) studies the employment rates and wages of refugees in the US and finds that the larger the number of political refugees from a foreign country allocated to a given area at least two years prior, the higher the current employment rate and wages of the refugees.

### 15.3.2 Theoretical Models

On the one hand, referrals can potentially reduce the asymmetric information between firms and workers and lead to a better match between workers and firms. On the other hand, if workers of one type are better connected than other types, this could also give them an advantage in the market, which could in turn give rise to wage inequality. Here, we present a theoretical model on the use of referrals to examine these issues. The model is taken from Montgomery (1991). Our exposition is based on Goyal (2007).

#### 15.3.2.1 A model of referrals

There are two periods, 1 and 2. There are a large number of firms and workers. In each period, a firm hires one worker. The output of a firm is equal to the ability of the worker who works for the firm. Workers know their ability, while firms do not. In period 1, all firms therefore have an expectation on the average quality of worker and pay wages corresponding to this average. During period 1, a firm learns the ability of its worker. At the start of period 2, it has a choice between asking the period 1 worker for the name of a potential worker and offering a referral wage, or simply posting a wage in the market, which can be taken by any of the large number of workers. There are a large number of firms competing for workers, so wages are set to equate expected ability to wages and ex-ante (at the start of period 1) expected profits of firms are equal and zero.

We now describe the model more formally.

*Workers:* There are a large number of workers who all live for one period. The number of workers is equal in each period. There are two types of workers: High and Low, and let us say that there is an equal number of each type. The productivity of a High type is 1, while the productivity of Low type is 0. Workers know their own ability, but firms do not.

*Firms:* There are a large number of firms; every firm employs one worker in each period. The profit of a firm is equal to the productivity of worker minus the wage that is paid to the worker. Wages are set at the start of each period and cannot be made contingent on the output. A simple way to model this is to suppose that wages are set prior to learning the productivity of workers.

*Social structure:* Each period 1 worker knows at most one period 2 worker, and the probability of knowing someone is $r \in [0, 1]$. Conditional upon holding a tie, period 1 worker knows a period 2 worker of their own type with probability $\alpha > 1/2$. The assumption that $\alpha > 1/2$ captures the idea that it is more likely that a worker knows someone with the same ability as themselves. The social structure is thus defined by two parameters: $r$, reflecting the density of links; and $\alpha$, reflecting the inbreeding bias in the links. Since links are randomly assigned, it is possible that some period 2 workers have many connections, while others have none.

*Timing of offers:* At the start of period 1, firms hire workers through the market: the market clears at wages given by $w_{M1}$. After this recruitment, production occurs in period 1. Every firm learns the ability of its worker. At the start of period 2, a firm decides on whether to hire through the market or via referral. If a firm decides to offer a referral wage, this is denoted by $w_{R_i}$. These wages are communicated via social contacts to workers in period 2. The workers in period 2 compare wage offers and decide whether to accept one of them. If a worker rejects all offers, then they go to the market. Similarly, if a firm's referral offer is rejected, then it goes to the market. The market in period 2 clears at wage $w_{M2}$.

**Equilibrium analysis** We first discuss the baseline case with no social ties. In the absence of social ties, the two periods are completely independent. The probability that a firm hires a High-type worker is equal to $1/2$ in both periods; hence the market wage is 1/2 in both periods. Every worker earns $1/2$, and all firms make zero ex-ante profits.

Let us now take up the case with assortative social ties: $r > 0$ and $\alpha > 1/2$. In this world, learning about the period 1 worker gives the firm some information on the ability of a contact of its own period 1 worker. If the period 1 worker has High ability, then the firm expects that a worker contacted via a referral is more likely to be a High type. The converse is true if the period 1 worker has Low ability. A firm will want to hire via referral only if its period 1 worker has High ability.

There cannot be a single referral wage for all firms: if there is such a single referral wage $x$, then a firm can deviate and set a slightly higher wage $x+\epsilon$ for some small $\epsilon$. All workers will prefer this slightly raised wage offer. Thus the deviating firm can strictly raise its probability of acceptance by paying a slightly higher wage. Firms will offer prices drawn from a distribution that has support on an interval $[w_{M2}, \bar{w}_R]$, where $\bar{w}_R$ refers to the maximal referral wage offered by any firm. We next note that the probability density is positive for all wages in the interval. To see why this is the case, suppose that there is an interval of wage levels $[\underline{w}, \bar{w}] \subset [w_{M2}, \bar{w}_R]$, for which the probability is zero. Observe that the firm offering a referral wage $\bar{w}$ can lower the wage slightly. This will have no effect on the probability of acceptance but will strictly increase the surplus of the firm (upon acceptance of the offer). In other words, a wage offer of $\bar{w}$ cannot be optimal.

In period 2, a majority of the workers receiving (and accepting) the referral wages will be the High-type workers. This implies that those who go on to the decentralized market will on average be lower quality than 1/2: in other words, there is a *lemon effect* created by the use of social connections for referral wages.

With these observations in mind, let us comment on the profits of firms. A firm that has a High-type worker in period 1 can hope to make positive profits in period 2. This is because it will use referral wages and there is imperfect competition between firms who use referrals. Expected profits are positive (and constant) across the wages in support of the distribution $[w_{M1}, \bar{w}_R]$. As there is free entry in the market for firms, the expected profits in the two periods must be zero. In period 2, firms with High-type workers will earn positive profits, but not the others. To compensate for this possibility of positive profits, firms have to set the wage at $w_{M1}$, which is higher than the expected quality of workers in period 1, $w_{M1} > 1/2$. These points are summarized in the following result.

**Proposition 15.4** *Consider the model of referrals. In an equilibrium, the following properties hold:*

1. *A firm makes a referral offer in period 2 if and only if it employs a high-ability worker in period 1.*
2. *Referral wage offers are dispersed over the interval $[w_{M2}, \bar{w}_R]$, and the density of the referral wage is positive over the interval.*
3. *Period 2 wages are characterized by a lemon effect: $w_{M2} < 1/2$.*
4. *An increase in the density of links, $r$, or in the in-breeding bias, $\alpha$, leads to a fall in $w_{M2}$, as well as an increase in the maximal referral wage, $\bar{w}_R$.*

We now present the proof for this result. As is standard, we start from the last period, starting from period 2 market wages, $w_{M2}$, the profits of firms offering referral wages, and then work backward to period 1 market wages, $w_{M1}$, and finally the distribution of referral offers.

To compute the market wages, we need to understand the referral wages. Consider the decision problem of a High-type worker, $H$, faced with a referral wage, $w_{R_i}$. The probability that they accept a referral wage is

$$\begin{aligned}\text{Prob}(H \text{ accepts } w_{R_i}) &= \text{Prob}(H \text{ receives no higher offer } w_{R_j}\ \forall j \neq i)\\ &= \prod_{j\neq i} \text{Prob}(H \text{ receives no higher offer } w_{R_j})\\ &= \prod_{j\neq i} (1 - \text{Prob}(H \text{ receives } w_{R_j} > w_{R_i})) \qquad (15.45)\end{aligned}$$

where

$$\text{Prob}(H \text{ receives } w_{R_j} > w_{R_i}) = \text{Prob}(\text{firm } j \text{ makes an offer})\text{Prob}(\text{offer } w_{R_j} > w_{R_i}). \qquad (15.46)$$

Suppose that $F(\cdot)$ is the distribution of referral wages. Then this last expression is equal to

$$\left(\frac{\alpha r}{N}\right)(1 - F(w_{R_i})), \qquad (15.47)$$

noting that there are $N$ High-type workers and $\alpha$ and $r$ have the specified meaning.

Substituting from (15.47) in equation (15.45) yields us

$$\text{Prob}(H \text{ accepts } w_{R_i}) = \left(1 - \left(\frac{\alpha r}{N}\right)(1 - F(w_{R_i}))\right)^{N-1}. \qquad (15.48)$$

From standard considerations, it follows that

$$\lim_{N\to\infty} \text{Prob}(H \text{ accepts } w_{R_i}) = e^{-\alpha r(1-F(w_{R_i}))}. \qquad (15.49)$$

Similarly, for large values of $N$

$$\text{Prob}(L \text{ accepts } w_{R_i}) = e^{-(1-\alpha) r(1-F(w_{R_i}))}. \qquad (15.50)$$

Note that

$$\text{Prob}(H \text{ accepts } w_{R_i}) < \text{Prob}(L \text{ accepts } w_{R_i}), \qquad (15.51)$$

because a High-type worker is more likely to receive more offers since $\alpha > 1/2$.

Note next that

$$\text{Prob}(\text{market}|H) = \text{Prob}(H \text{ accepts } w_{M_2}) = e^{-\alpha r} \qquad (15.52)$$

$$\text{Prob}(\text{market}|L) = \text{Prob}(L \text{ accepts } w_{M_2}) = e^{-(1-\alpha) r}. \qquad (15.53)$$

The assumption that there is a continuum of workers allows us to derive the expected productivity of workers in the period 2 market:

$$\text{Prob}(H|\text{market}) = \frac{\text{Prob}(\text{market}|H)\text{Prob}(H)}{\text{Prob}(\text{market}|H)\text{Prob}(H) + \text{Prob}(\text{market}|L)\text{Prob}(L)}$$

$$= \frac{e^{-\alpha r}}{e^{-\alpha r} + e^{-(1-\alpha)r}} \tag{15.54}$$

In this derivation, we have used the assumption that Prob$(H) =$ Prob$(L) = 1/2)$.

Note that we use underlying $\alpha$ and $r$, not realized values. This is not a problem since we are assuming a continuum of workers. With finite $N$, the precise number of $H$ types will vary depending on realization. Next, observe that the expected productivity is $w_{M2}$, given that the market is competitive. Hence

$$w_{M2} = \frac{e^{-\alpha r}}{e^{-\alpha r} + e^{-(1-\alpha)r}}. \tag{15.55}$$

Notice that $w_{M2} < 1/2$, which means that the market wage is less than the average period 2 productivity!

The profit earned by a firm that has a period 1 High-ability worker and chooses to offer a referral wage:

$$\begin{aligned} E(\Pi|w_R) = {} & \text{Prob}(H \text{ hired}|w_R)(1 - w_R) \\ & + \text{Prob}(L \text{ hired}|w_R)(-w_R) \end{aligned} \tag{15.56}$$

We then apply Bayes's rule:

$$\begin{aligned} & \text{Prob}(H \text{ hired}|w_R) \\ & = \text{Prob}(\text{offer made } H)\text{Prob}(H \text{ accepts } w_R) \\ & = \alpha r e^{-\alpha r(1-F(w_R))}. \end{aligned} \tag{15.57}$$

Similarly,

$$\text{Prob}(L \text{ hired}|w_R) = (1-\alpha) r e^{-(1-\alpha)r(1-F(w_R))}. \tag{15.58}$$

Thus,

$$E(\Pi_H|w_R) = \alpha r e^{-\alpha r(1-F(w_R))}(1 - w_R) + (1-\alpha) r e^{-(1-\alpha)r(1-F(w_R))}(-w_R). \tag{15.59}$$

For $w_R \in [w_{M2}, \bar{w}_R]$ to be offered, firms must earn the same profit at all these wages:

$$\alpha r e^{-\alpha r(1-F(w_R))}(1 - w_R) + (1-\alpha) r e^{-(1-\alpha)r(1-F(w_R))}(-w_R) = c \ \forall \ w_R. \tag{15.60}$$

Recalling that $w_R = w_{M2} = \frac{e^{-\alpha r}}{e^{-\alpha r} + e^{-(1-\alpha)r}}$, and we get

$$c(\alpha, r) = \frac{(2\alpha - 1)r}{e^{\alpha r} + e^{(1-\alpha)r}}. \tag{15.61}$$

Note that $c(\alpha, r) > 0$ since $\alpha > 1/2$. Thus such a firm will always offer referral wages. It may be checked that $c(\cdot)$ is increasing in both $\alpha$ and $r$.

We next derive $\bar{w}_R$. By definition, $F(\bar{w}_R) = 1$:

$$\begin{aligned} \alpha r(1-\bar{w}_R) + (1-\alpha)r(-\bar{w}_R) &= \tfrac{(2\alpha-1)r}{e^{\alpha r}+e^{(1-\alpha)r}} \\ \Longrightarrow \qquad \alpha r - r(\bar{w}_R) &= \tfrac{(2\alpha-1)r}{e^{\alpha r}+e^{(1-\alpha)r}} \\ \Longrightarrow \qquad r(\alpha - \bar{w}_R) &= \tfrac{(2\alpha-1)r}{e^{\alpha r}+e^{(1-\alpha)r}} \\ &= c(\alpha, r) \end{aligned} \tag{15.62}$$

Hence

$$\bar{w}_R = \alpha - c/r. \tag{15.63}$$

We now show that firms hiring a low-type worker in period 1 will not make a referral offer in period 2:

$$E(\Pi_L|w_R) = (1-\alpha)re^{-\alpha r(1-F(w_R))}(1-w_R) + \alpha re^{-(1-\alpha)r(1-F(w_R))}(-w_R) \tag{15.64}$$

$$\begin{aligned} \tfrac{\partial E(\Pi_L|w_R)}{\partial w_R} = &(1-\alpha)re^{-\alpha r(1-F(w_R))}(1-w_R)\alpha r(F'(w_R)) \\ &+ (1-\alpha)re^{-\alpha r(1-F(w_R))}(-1) \\ &+ \alpha re^{-(1-\alpha)r(1-F(w_R))}(-w_R)\alpha r(-F'(w_R)) \\ &+ \alpha re^{-(1-\alpha)r(1-F(w_R))}(-1) \end{aligned} \tag{15.65}$$

$$\begin{aligned} \frac{\partial E(\Pi_H|w_R)}{\partial w_R} = &\alpha re^{-\alpha r(1-F(w_R))}(1-w_R)\alpha r(F'(w_R)) \\ &+ \alpha re^{-\alpha r(1-F(w_R))}(-1) \\ &+ (1-\alpha)re^{-(1-\alpha)r(1-F(w_R))}(-w_R)\alpha r(-F'(w_R)) \\ &+ (1-\alpha)re^{-(1-\alpha)r(1-F(w_R))}(-1). \end{aligned} \tag{15.66}$$

It is intuitive that

$$\frac{\partial E(\Pi_L|w_R)}{\partial w_R} < \frac{\partial E(\Pi_H|w_R)}{\partial w_R}. \tag{15.67}$$

The latter is zero for all $w \in (w_{M2}, \bar{w}_R)$. Hence $\Pi_L(w_R)$ is maximized at $w_{M2}$.

It can be checked that

$$E(\Pi_L|w_{M2}) = \frac{(1-2\alpha)e^{-r}}{e^{-\alpha r} + e^{-(1-\alpha)r}} < 0 \tag{15.68}$$

since $\alpha > 1/2$. By going to the market, it can ensure that $E\Pi_L = 0$. Hence a firm with an low-type worker in period 1 will *not make a referral offer*.

Given free entry in period 1, firms set wages to equate expected profits:

$$w_{M1}(\alpha, r) = \frac{1}{2} + \frac{1}{2}c(\alpha, r) = \frac{1}{2}(1 + c(\alpha, r)). \tag{15.69}$$

■

The intuition for the effects of changes in density of connections $r$ and inbreeding bias $\alpha$ is as follows. An increase in $r$ and $\alpha$ both strengthen the lemon effect: a greater proportion of High-type workers are employed via referrals. This lowers the average quality of workers who enter the market, which lowers $w_{M2}$. Turning next to the maximal referral wage, note that an increase in $r$ increases the number of offers that a period 2 worker receives, which increases competition and pushes up wages. Similarly, an increase in $\alpha$ increases the average type of a worker via referrals, which also pushes up the maximal referral wage. Thus an increase in either $r$ or $\alpha$ leads to a greater wage dispersion.

As was noted earlier in the chapter, the presence of social connections implies that market wages in period 1 exceed the average quality of workers (i.e., $w_{M1} > 1/2$). An increase in $r$ or $\alpha$ drives up the profits of firms that make a hire through referrals. The zero-profit market equilibrium condition implies that wages in period 1 must adjust to account for this. In other words, an increase in $r$ or $\alpha$ pushes up the first-period market wage $w_{M1}$. Since expected profits are zero in equilibrium, this implies a redistribution from period 2 referred workers to period 1 workers.

The social structure of contacts has powerful implications for wage inequality. A period 2 worker's wage is determined by the number and quality of ties that they hold. A Low-quality period 2 worker is likely to have ties mostly with Low-type period 1 workers; by contrast a High-type period 2 worker is more likely to have ties with a High-type worker. This suggests that a High-type period 2 worker is more likely to receive referral wage offers and will be at an advantage compared to a situation in which the social structure was absent. Moreover, even among High-type workers, those who have more links with High-type period 1 workers will receive more offers and therefore will earn higher wages.

Let us now summarize what we have learned in this section. Labor economists have long recognized that many workers find jobs through friends and relatives. We have presented a stylized economic model that combined elements of market competition, asymmetric information, and social structure within a common framework. This allows us to study the relationship between social structure and wages. The analysis reveals that social connections can generate inequality and how the use of referrals by firms can lead to higher profits for them. Moreover, an increase in the density of social ties or homophily (by ability) will create greater wage dispersion.

#### 15.3.2.2 Sharing information about jobs

In section 15.3.1, we discussed the role of strong and weak ties in shaping the flow of information on jobs. We also presented evidence on spatial correlation of employment status. In this section, we begin with a model of network formation to explain when individuals will form weak and strong links and how that will shape overall employment outcomes. We then present a model of the dynamics of information flow in a social network to develop a deeper understanding of spatial and intertemporal correlations in employment status.

Boorman (1975) offers a seminal contribution on the uses of strong and weak ties in labor markets. There are many individuals, each of whom decides how to allocate their time between strong and weak links. Strong links take more time to form than weak links. So an individual faces a trade-off between having many ties that are weak or a few ties that are strong. If an individual has $S$ strong ties and $W$ weak ties, then they face the following budget constraint with respect to time:

$$W + \lambda S = T, \tag{15.70}$$

where $\lambda > 1$ is a factor indicating the extra time needed for a strong tie and $T$ is the overall time available.

In the model, with probability $\mu$ an individual needs a job. Every person gets news about a job with some exogenous probability $p$. If they do not need the job, then they can pass the information of the vacancy to a neighbor/contact. The individual first picks someone with whom they have a strong tie. If there is no one in this set, they pick someone with whom they have a weak tie. They send the information to one of the unemployed weak contacts. If there is no such person, then the job information is left unused. Suppose for simplicity that the network is a tree, so there are no cycles and common neighbors. Let $q_w$ and $q_s$ be the probability of not hearing about a job from a weak and a strong tie, respectively. The probability of hearing about a job is

$$p + (1-p)(1 - q_s^S q_w^W). \tag{15.71}$$

Starting with an allocation of strong and weak links, we can derive the values of $q_s$ and $q_w$. Equipped with these probabilities, we can then ask what the optimal allocation across strong and weak ties. This will define an equilibrium allocation between strong and weak ties. The model allows for multiple equilibria. Boorman uses simulations to develop intuitions about the structure of networks and the implications for the functioning of the labor market. An increase in $\lambda$ raises the relative cost of strong ties: this will mean fewer strong ties. A decrease in $\mu$ means that individuals are less likely to need a job, and this means that a weak link may suffice. This in turn pushes up the allocation toward a weak links. High $\mu$ leads to greater number of strong ties (and hence fewer ties in all).

The paper by Boorman draws attention to an interesting externality in networking: as the number of strong ties goes up, the total number of ties falls; as a result, job information may be wasted. The model also brings out the difficulties of analytically solving models with networks and markets. To make progress, we therefore turn to a simpler model of information sharing in a given network. The model is taken from Calvó-Armengol and Jackson (2004); our exposition follows Goyal (2007).

**15.3.2.2.1 A dynamic model of information sharing in networks** Consider a set of $N = \{1, \ldots, n\}$, $n \geq 2$ individuals/workers who all have the same skills. Time evolves in discrete periods $t = 1, 2, \ldots$. At the end of time $t$, a worker is either employed ($s_{i,t} = 1$) or unemployed

($s_{i,t}=0$). The vector $s_t=\{s_{1t},\ldots,s_{nt}\}$ describes the employment status of everyone at the end of time $t$. By convention, the employment status at the start of time $t+1$ is set to be equal to the employment status at the end of time $t$.

Period $t$ starts with the arrival of new information on jobs. Every worker hears about new jobs with probability $a \in (0,1)$. Suppose that this probability is identical and independent across workers. If the worker is unemployed, they take the job; if they are employed, then they pass the information to one of their unemployed contacts. If workers know no one who is unemployed and is employed themselves, then the information is wasted. The pattern of contacts is captured by the undirected network $g$. The probability that worker $j$ gets a job that worker $i$ originally heard about is

$$p_{i,j}(s)=\begin{cases} a & \text{if } s_i=0 \text{ and } i=j \\ \frac{a}{\sum_{k:s_k=0} g_{i,k}} & \text{if } s_i=1, s_j=0, \text{ and } g_{i,j}=1 \\ 0 & \text{otherwise.} \end{cases} \tag{15.72}$$

There is a competitive aspect to connections: if worker $i$ knows other workers who are unemployed, then this lowers the probability of worker $j$ getting the information. There is a second, more subtle effect that goes in the opposite direction. The existence of other workers linked to worker $i$ also means that it is more likely that $i$ will get information from them about jobs, which in turn means that it is more likely that they will pass on information about jobs that they receive to worker $j$. To study the effect of indirect connections, it is helpful to recall that a pair of workers, $i$ and $j$, are said to be path-connected in network $g$ if there is a path between them.

Finally, a worker loses his job with probability $b \in (0,1)$, with this probability being identical and independent across individual workers.

The model has been deliberately kept very simple to bring out the essential implications of the network transmission of information. It is possible to generalize the model to allow for heterogeneity in skills and indirect transmission of information, as well as to make the transmission of information sensitive to the wages that various workers are earning. For the analysis of such a general model, see Calvó-Armengol and Jackson (2004).

To summarize, at the start of period $t$, the employment status of workers is given by vector $s_{t-1}$. Workers receive information on new jobs, which is shared via the social network. Some workers may lose jobs, and these factors together define a new employment status, $s_t$, at the end of the period. Next, we will examine how network $g$ shapes the employment status of workers

**Networks and employment** We first take up the relationship between the employment statuses of workers in the same network. Two workers, $i$ and $k$, who are linked to the same worker $j$, compete for the information of worker $j$, and this may induce a negative correlation between the employment statuses of $i$ and $k$. On the other hand, worker $k$ receives information on jobs as well, and this information may be used by worker $j$ to get a job.

This in turn may allow worker $j$ to pass information on jobs to worker $i$, which may lead a positive correlation between the employment statuses of $i$ and $k$. We will show that the second effect prevails: the employment status of path-connected workers is therefore positively correlated.

Let us define a few pieces of notation so we can spell this out more precisely. Observe that starting at an employment state, $s_t$, the arrival probability $a \in (0, 1)$, the job loss probability $b \in (0, 1)$, and a network of information communication together define the employment status at time $t+1$. In other words, the probability of transition between employment statuses can be described by a finite-state (reflecting the set of possible employment statuses of all individuals) Markov chain. Moreover, as $a$ and $b$ are both positive, there is a positive probability of transitioning from any state to any other state. From standard results in the theory of Markov chains, we conclude that there is a unique invariant distribution $\mu$ on the set of employment states (Seneta [2006], Billingsley [2008]). The first observation about this invariant distribution is that *the employment statuses of path-connected workers are positively correlated.* The intuition underlying this result is simple: if a group of workers are all employed, then it is more likely that they will share information on new jobs, which in turn makes it more likely that their friends and neighbors will be employed too. Next, we present an example to illustrate this positive correlation.

**Example 15.4** *Positive correlation of employment status*

Suppose that $n = 4$, $a = .100$, and $b = .015$. Consider four networks—an empty network ($g^e$), a network with one link ($g^1$), a cycle network with four links ($g^w$), and a complete network with six links ($g^c$). These networks are presented in figure 15.4. Table 15.2, taken

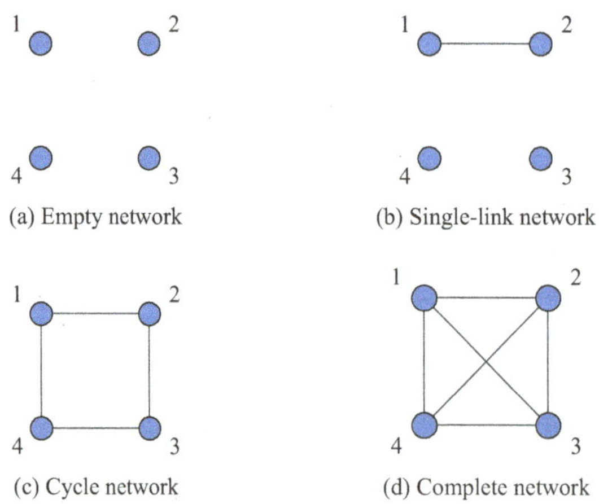


**Figure 15.4**
Examples of networks, $n = 4$.

**Table 15.2**
Employment in networks

| g | Prob($s_1 = 0$) | Corr($s_1$,$s_2$) | Corr($s_1$,$s_3$) |
|---|---|---|---|
| $g^e$ | .132 | — | — |
| $g^1$ | .083 | .041 | — |
| $g^{cycle}$ | .063 | .025 | .019 |
| $g^c$ | .050 | .025 | .025 |

*Source*: Calvó-Armengol and Jackson (2004).

from Calvó-Armengol and Jackson (2004), presents the probability of being employed and the correlations in employment status across workers in a network. Observe that workers 1 and 2 are directly connected in networks $g^1$, $g^w$, and $g^c$, while workers 1 and 3 are indirectly connected in network $g^w$ and directly connected in $g^c$.

In the empty network, there is no information sharing on jobs: every worker has the same probability of unemployment, given by 0.132. As links are added in the social network and more information about jobs among the workers is shared, less information about jobs is wasted. The result is that the probability of being unemployed falls: it is 0.083 in the single-link network, 0.063 in the cycle network, and 0.050 in the complete network. This suggests that a worker in a denser network faces better employment prospects. The next observation is about the correlation between the employment prospects of different workers. This correlation is positive across all workers, and it is higher for directly linked workers 1 and 2 than for the indirectly linked workers 1 and 3 in the cycle network. ■

We now turn to the question of how the duration of unemployment affects future employment prospects. The model delivers a crisp result for this question: *the conditional probability that a worker will be employed in a given period is decreasing with the length of their observed unemployment spell*. In other words, there is a positive duration dependence. The intuition goes as follows: the longer the duration of unemployment of an individual, the more likely it is that their neighbors, and the neighbors of their neighbors, are also unemployed. In other words, a longer duration of unemployment reveals that a worker's environment is poor, which in turn leads to low forecasts for future employment of the worker. To develop a better feel for this result, we present example 15.5.

**Example 15.5** *Positive duration dependence*

Let us again consider the four-worker economy discussed in example 15.4. Table 15.3, also taken from Calvó-Armengol and Jackson (2004), presents the probability of being employed, conditional on 1, 2, and 10 periods of unemployment.

In the empty network, the probability of getting employed depends solely on getting information about a new job, and then on not losing the job. These events do not depend on the duration of unemployment, and this explains the unchanging number in the first row

**Table 15.3**
Duration dependence in networks

| g | 1 Period | 2 Periods | 10 Periods | Limit |
|---|---|---|---|---|
| $g^e$ | .099 | .099 | .099 | .099 |
| $g^1$ | .176 | .175 | .170 | .099 |
| $g^c$ | .305 | .300 | .278 | .099 |

*Source*: Calvó-Armengol and Jackson (2004).

of the table. However, as the network gets denser, a longer duration of unemployment tells us more about the status of the other workers (in particular, that the other workers are not employed). This negative information in turn means that the other workers are less likely to share any information they will get, and this implies that a longer duration of unemployment lowers the probability of getting a job in the near future. ■

In the model discussed here, the structure of links is kept very simple. It is reasonable to expect that the links will vary with employment status because it may be easier for two employed people to maintain a tie than for an employed and an unemployed person. Similarly, it may be easier for two workers of the same ethnicity to maintain a link. These ideas broadly suggest a type of *in-breeding bias* in links. Bramoullé and Saint-Paul (2010) show that if linking is more likely between persons with the same employment status, then duration dependence arises in a strong form. A longer duration of unemployment leads to fewer employed contacts, which lowers access to job information, which in turn prolongs unemployment. More recent research uses the models we have presented in this section to further explore role of homophily in networks in shaping employment and inequality.

Let us briefly summarize what we have learnt on the role of social networks in labor market.

Employees and employers use social ties extensively to secure a better match. Social ties are used for referrals and to access information on job vacancies. The use of social ties yields better matches between employers and employees. However, individuals who are socially connected will also exhibit positive correlation in their employment status. The use of social connections by firms tends to favor those who are well connected and therefore inequality in connections is mirrored in wage and unemployment differentials.

## 15.4 Reading Notes

The industrial organization literature on consumption externalities starts with Rohlfs (1974). In the two decades after this paper, most of the research focused on the role of group size. We presented an overview of this research in chapter 8, on platforms and intermediation. In the 1990s, as economists began to examine networks more systematically, interest progressed beyond the size of the group and onto a systematic exploration of the effects of network structure.

There is a longstanding interest in using network knowledge in better targeting behavioral changes. The growth in our knowledge of empirical networks has further spurred the development of formal models. The literature on targeting in networks spans several disciplines. Domingos and Richardson (2001) is probably the first paper to study algorithms that maximize sales in a social network. They consider a model where consumers can be of two types, 0 and 1, reflecting whether they buy the product or not. Consumers' probability of buying a product depends on two factors: marketing expenditures and the probability that their direct neighbors have bought the product. The paper compares the performance of three algorithms: a single-pass algorithm that only looks at one iteration, a greedy algorithm that increases marketing expenditures wherever they increase payoffs and a hill-climbing algorithm that increases expenditures where it matters most. Using data on an experimental program of movie recommendations, EachMovie (from the years 1996–1997), they compute the multiplier effect of marketing expenditures. A key finding is that the distribution of multipliers is very skewed, such that targeted marketing strategies can be very profitable.

In an influential contribution, Kempe, Kleinberg, and Tardos (2003) study the optimal targeting problem within the framework of standard diffusion processes. The objective of the firm is to select an initial set of nodes in the social network in order to maximize the total number of informed nodes. They show that the optimal strategy is computationally hard and then establish bounds on the efficiency of the hill-climbing algorithm; these bounds draw attention to the specifics of the dynamic processes. The role of the dynamics process (in other words, the content of interaction) is also illustrated in a model of competitive contagion in networks by Goyal, Heidari, and Kearns [2019]).

The chapter mostly restricts itself to the economics research on this subject. But it is worth noting there was a precursor to Klout-like scores in the 1950s literature in sociology and communication on the two-step flow of communication, which argues that the mass media did not directly influence consumption, but it was opinion leaders who were influenced by the mass media, and they in turn influenced members of their community (Katz 1957). Also, see the discussions of the role of social networks in chapter 11, on the law of the few, and chapter 13, on learning and communication.

Economists have focused on the structure of optimal or equilibrium outcomes and the effects of different network statistics in shaping these optimal strategies. The model that we used was taken from Galeotti and Goyal (2009). It combines the formulation of advertising from Butters (1977) with the word-of-mouth communication model of Ellison and Fudenberg (1995). Building on our discussions in chapter 4, we draw attention to the content and the level of interaction in shaping optimal firm policies.

A major issue in the design of peer-leader network intervention policies is to identify the influencers. A general practice is to submit questionnaires to members of the targeted group.

Subjects are asked, among other things, to answer questions about their social network, such as to nominate their best friends, to nominate other individuals with whom they talk about specific issues, and other topics. Individuals who receive more nominations from others are identified as network leaders. In turn, network leaders are asked to attend a training session and then to communicate what they have learned to their acquaintances. For a detailed discussion on the implementation of these policies, see Valente, Hoffman, Ritt-Olson, et al. (2003). The model from Galeotti and Goyal (2009) is used to explore optimal targeting in networks and to explore the ways in which the content of interaction shapes the optimal target.

Pricing in markets with network effects has been discussed at length in chapter 8. In that chapter, the focus was on size of the networks, while here, we discussed richer statistics of the network, such as degrees and centrality. The material on optimal pricing in networks draws on Fainmesser and Galeotti (2016); the model with complete network knowledge is taken from Bloch and Quérou (2013) and Candogan, Bimpikis, and Ozdaglar (2012). For a survey of this literature, see Goyal (2017) and Bloch (2016). The literature on pricing remains active; for a recent contribution to competitive pricing in networks, see Fainmesser and Galeotti (2020).

It is clear that consumer search and their word-of-mouth communication interacts with firm advertising; for an early attempt at integrating social networks with search and pricing in product markets, see Galeotti (2004). We draw attention to an interesting paper by Campbell (2013) that combines pricing with advertising in the presence of word of mouth communication. In this model, consumers learn about a product via communication from their contacts. Information travels through paths in a random graph.

The word of mouth creates a positive externality of consumption: a lower price increases direct demand and, through word of mouth, has a further indirect demand enhancement effect. This suggests that optimal prices will be lower in the presence of word-in-mouth communication. While this intuition is true in some simple settings, Campbell (2013) shows that it is not true in general. In particular, in empirically interesting cases with correlations in valuations across connected consumers, this result no longer obtains. The paper then turns to the effects of networks on optimal pricing—in particular, first-order and second-order stochastic shifts in degree distribution and the effects of clustering. Finally, the paper examines the nature of optimal advertising: an interesting finding is that optimal targets for advertising may sometimes be less connected individuals (as they may not have heard about the product from contacts). This is consistent with the result on targeting consumers with low degrees in the word-of-mouth model presented in section 15.2.1.

The study of social networks in shaping labor markets has a long and distinguished history. The aim of our discussion was to draw attention to some of the main themes in this work. A large body of literature has documented the widespread use of referrals and social connections across both developed and developing countries. In addition to the information in the chapter, we note here a few other studies. Burks, Cowgill, Hoffman, and Housman

(2015) use personnel data from nine large firms in three industries to document the use of referrals and their impact on outcomes. Similarly, Gavazza, Mongey, and Violante (2018) use a novel survey of recruitment costs and practices for a sample of about 400 US firms. It contains information on the amount of resources spent by employers on employee referrals (among many other recruiting channels). Ioannides and Datcher Loury (2004), (Topa 2011, 2019), Beaman (2016), Granovetter (1995), and Pellizzari (2010) provide excellent overviews of the literature. Then there is research on the effects of the use of social ties on the efficiency and the inequality in the labor market; see Conley and Topa (2002) and Bayer, Ross, and Topa (2008).

The theoretical models help us develop a better understanding of how social networks interact with the asymmetric/inperfect information and market competition. The model of referral by firms is taken from Montgomery (1991). For recent elaborations of this model that further develop the role of homophily in creating inequality, see Bolte, Immorlica, and Jackson (2020). Turning to the social sharing of job information, we start with the early model of Boorman (1975) and then turn to the more recent work of Calvó-Armengol and Jackson (2004). For a more recent elaboration on the theme of correlations in employment status across connected workers, see Bramoullé and Saint-Paul (2010).

In the referral model, a High-type worker has no way of signaling their ability. In labor markets, workers often can use mechanisms such as certificates and educational degrees to communicate their ability and skills. This leads naturally to the study of the role of social connections when workers also have access to such signaling mechanisms. Casella and Hanaki (2008) study this question using an extension of Montgomery (1991). The model contrasts signals and networks in the following plausible way: a signal can be bought at a cost, and it offers a proof of ability that is valid across all potential employers, while a personal contact allows access to a single employer and communicates a candidate's ability via the assortative tie hypothesis (as in the referral model discussed previously). This model yields a simple insight: in a context where certificates are imperfect signals of ability, for signals to work well, they must be costly to acquire. However, if they are costly to acquire, then social ties (which are cheap) become attractive, and signals are not used. These contradictory pressures on signals imply that social networks are quite resilient even in the presence of anonymous mechanisms such as educational certificates.

We conclude with a very brief discussion of the literature on the role of social networks in financial markets. Financial markets are one setting where the standard market model of anonymous traders and common prices that reveal information of traders has been especially dominant. A recent body of literature examines the role of social networks in shaping the functioning of financial markets. We have not covered this literature, though, as it is mainly empirical, and the focus of this chapter was on theoretical models. We conclude with a few pointers to interesting lines of enquiry. In a fascinating paper, Cohen, Frazzini, and Malloy (2008) study the role of school ties in facilitating the flow of financially valuable information on firms. School ties typically had been formed years earlier, and their formation is frequently independent of the information to be transferred. Social connections provide a useful tie because one side has private information and the other side has an incentive to access this private information. The value of the social tie can be computed relatively objectively in terms of returns to investments. Cohen, Frazzini, and Malloy (2008) find that portfolio managers place larger bets on a firm if they went to school with its senior managers (or board members) and their investment on these firms outperforms other investments.

Turning to more general social interaction effects, Hong, Kubik, and Stein (2005) find that US fund managers located in the same city commit to correlated investment decisions. Such correlated choices may be due to peer-to-peer communications or because fund managers in a given area condition their decisions upon common sources of information. In a similar spirit, Kuchler et al. (2022) show that institutional investors are more likely to invest in firms located in regions to which they have stronger social ties. Interestingly, however, these investments do not earn a differential return. Firms located in regions that have stronger social ties with institutional investors have higher valuations and liquidity.

There is also a small strand of research on theoretical models of social networks in financial markets; for instance, see Ozsoylev, Walden, Yavuz, and Bildik (2014); Walden (2019); and Colla and Mele (2010). These papers study asset pricing in markets where traders are located in information networks and obtain results on the relation between social network topology and equilibrium prices and trading. For a survey of social networks in finance, see Allen and Babus (2009) and Hirshleifer (2020).

There is a small but interesting body of empirical research on how social ties—based on the flow of immigrants between two countries—can lead to positive effects on international trade. For an introduction to and overview of this literature, see Rauch (2001).

## 15.5 Questions

1. Consider the word-of-mouth example in section 15.2.1. This question explores the value of network information. Show that the value of network information is increasing with a mean-preserving spread in degree distribution. Hint: Compare the profits of targeted versus untargeted firm strategies, and show that this difference in increasing in a mean-preserving spread of degree distribution.
2. Consider the model of optimal pricing with complete network information discussed in section 15.2.2.2.
   (a) Show that in a subgame perfect equilibrium every consumer must choose a positive quantity.
   (b) Suppose $n = 6$. Consider the star network. Suppose all spokes assign weight 0.5 to the centre and the centre assigns weight 1 to the link with each spoke. Compute optimal prices to different customers in this network.

(c) Suppose $n=6$. Consider the star network. Suppose all spokes assign weight 1 to the centre and the centre assigns weight 0.5 to the link with each spoke. Compute optimal prices to different customers in this network.

(d) Suppose $n=6$. Consider networks with binary links that take values 0 or 1. Suppose that links are symmetric. Compute the optimal price in the empty, complete, and the star network.

3. An important element in viral marketing is the idea that information can be passed from person to person via social connections. Let us extend the model in section 15.2.1 to allow for this possibility as follows. Suppose that every buyer has the same degree, such as $k$, and suppose that information flows $r$ steps; $r \geq 1$ is an integer that indicates the radius of information diffusion. Assume that there is no overlap in neighborhoods.

(a) Given information radius $r$ and strategy $x$, show that the probability that a consumer with $k$ friends becomes aware of the product is

$$\phi_k(x|r) = 1 - (1-x)^{\sum_{s=0}^{r} k^s}. \tag{15.73}$$

(b) Next, show that the expected profits to firm $\mathcal{M}$ are

$$\Pi(x|k,r) = 1 - (1-x)^{\sum_{s=0}^{r} k^s} - \frac{\alpha}{2}x^2. \tag{15.74}$$

(c) Verify that (I) $\phi_k(x|r)$ is increasing and concave in $x$, $k$, and $r$; (II) the function $\phi_k(\cdot)$ exhibits increasing marginal returns from degree for low values of $x$, and otherwise, it exhibits decreasing marginal returns from degrees; and (III) $\frac{\partial^2 \phi_k(x,r)}{\partial x \partial r}$ is positive for low values of $x$, and negative otherwise.

(d) Using properties I–III, show that the effects of an increase in the level of word-of-mouth communication on optimal advertising strategy and profits presented in the chapter extend to richer patterns of information diffusion (i.e., $r \geq 1$). Then, show that an increase in the radius of information flow is analogous to an increase in the level of word-of-mouth communication.

4. Consider the model in section 15.2.1 and let us apply it to the choice of product quality. There is asymmetric information between firms and consumers about quality, and consumers share their experience about product quality via word-of-mouth communication. Suppose that there is one firm that is selling to a set of consumers. The set of buyers is $\mathcal{N} = [0, 1]$; each buyer has inelastic demand, and their reservation value for the object is $v = 1$ if the quality is HIGH, but the reservation utility $v = 0$ if the quality is LOW. At the start, all consumers are pessimistic about the product's quality so that no one is willing to pay a positive price. Hence, the only way that the firm can generate sales is to give away free samples of the product and hope that the consumers will pass on good information about it. Consider a two-period model, where in period 1, the firm chooses the number of samples to give away for free ($x \in [0, 1]$), and in period 2, it chooses the price

to charge ($p \geq 0$). Moreover, to simplify matters, suppose that there are no direct costs of producing the good, which implies that the only cost is an indirect one, via the loss of potential sales. Given that consumers only buy if they are informed that the product quality is HIGH, it is optimal for the firm to set price $p = 1$ in the second period.

(a) Show that the payoffs to a firm from a consumer with degree $k$ are then given by

$$\phi_k(x) = (1 - x)[1 - (1 - x)^k]. \tag{15.75}$$

$(1 - x)$ refers to the probability that a consumer has not been given the product for free in period 1.

(b) Verify that $\phi_k(x)$ is concave in $x$ and is increasing and concave in $k$.

(c) For a given distribution, $P$, show that the expected profits under strategy $x$ is:

$$\Pi(x|P) = (1 - x) \sum_{k \in O} P(k)[1 - (1 - x)^k]. \tag{15.76}$$

(d) The monopolist chooses $x$ to maximize profits. Show that the effects of changes in $P$ on the optimal strategy depend on how marginal returns change with respect to $k$, as in the model in this chapter.

5. (Galeotti and Goyal [2009]). Consider a variant of the model in section 15.2.1 that allows us to consider adoption externalities. Suppose that $\psi(k, s) = s/\bar{k}$ for all $s, k \in O$: here, the probability that a consumer buys a product is increasing with the number of neighbors who have already bought the product, but it is independent of the consumer's neighborhood size.

(a) Under this assumption, show that the expected profits to the firm from a degree $k$ buyer are

$$\phi_k(x) = (1 - x)x\frac{k}{\bar{k}}. \tag{15.77}$$

(b) Verify that $\phi_k(x)$ is increasing and linear in degree and exhibits increasing (decreasing) marginal returns in degree for low (high) $x$.

6. (Galeotti and Goyal [2009]). This question considers a variant of the model discussed in section 15.2.1. Suppose that all consumers have the same out-degree but have different in-degrees. Let $I = \{1, \ldots, \bar{l}\}$, and let $H : O \rightarrow [0, 1]$ be a probability distribution, where $H(l)$ indicates the fraction of individuals in $\mathcal{N}$ that are sampled by $l$ others. The mean of $H$ $\hat{l} = \sum_{l \in I} H(l)l$. If an individual is sampled by $l$ other individuals, there are $l$ links pointing to individual $i$. Note that $P$ and $H$ satisfy the condition $\hat{l} = \hat{k}$. For simplicity, we focus on the case where $P(\hat{k}) = 1$; in other words, everyone draws a sample of the same size (and so the out-degree distribution is degenerate).

(a) For a given strategy $x \in [0, 1]$, show that the expected net profits are

$$\Pi(x|P) = [1 - (1-x)^{\hat{k}+1}] - \frac{\alpha}{2}x^2. \tag{15.78}$$

(b) Suppose that $H'$ first-order stochastically dominates $H$. Show that profits under $H'$ are higher than profits under $H$.

(c) Consider targeted strategies. Suppose that the firm knows the in-degree of individuals. Let a targeted strategy be denoted by $\mathbf{x} = \{x_1, x_2, \ldots, x_{\bar{l}}\}$, where $x_l$ is the effort that firm spends on targeting consumers with in-degree $l$. Let us denote by $\tilde{H}(l)$, the probability that consumer $i$ samples a consumer who has in-degree $l$. Using Bayes's rule, we can express $\tilde{H}(l)$ as follows:

$$\tilde{H}(l) = \frac{H(l)l}{\hat{l}}. \tag{15.79}$$

Given a targeted strategy $\mathbf{x}$, let $\omega(\mathbf{x}) = \sum_{l \in I} \tilde{H}(l)x_l$. Show that expected profits from strategy $\mathbf{x}$ are

$$\Pi(\mathbf{x}|H) = 1 - \sum_{l \in I} H(l)(1-x_l)(1-\omega(\mathbf{x}))^{\hat{l}} - \frac{\alpha}{2}(\theta(\mathbf{x}))^2, \tag{15.80}$$

and for any $s \in I$, we have that

$$\frac{d\Pi(\mathbf{x}|H)}{dx_s} = H(s)\left[(1-\omega(\mathbf{x}))^{\hat{l}} + s\sum_{l \in I} H(l)(1-x_l)(1-\omega(\mathbf{x}))^{\hat{l}-1} - \alpha\theta(\mathbf{x})\right]. \tag{15.81}$$

(d) Show that it is optimal to use an increasing cutoff strategy.

7. This question studies the role of social networks in labor markets and is based on the model presented in section 15.3. Consider a two-period model with the following features. Workers know their ability while firms do not know it. In each period a firm hires one worker. The output of a firm is equal to the ability of the worker who works for the firm. In period 1, all firms have same average quality of worker, and pay wages corresponding to this average. During period 1, a firm learns the ability of its worker. At the start of period 2, it has a choice between asking the period 1 worker for the name of contact and offering a referral wage, *or* simply posting a wage in the market. Competition between firms means that wages equal expected ability of workers. And that profits of firms are equal to zero over two periods. Each period 1 worker knows at most one period 2 worker, possessing a social tie with probability $r \in [0, 1]$. Conditional upon holding a tie, period 1 worker knows a period 2 worker of his own type with probability $\alpha > 1/2$. The social structure is thus defined by, $r$ and $\alpha$.

(a) Explain why a firm will offer a referral wages in period 2 only if its current worker is of high ability. Then show that the optimal referral wage offer must involve randomization.

(b) Show that period 2 wages are characterized by a lemons effect: the market wage is below one half.

(c) Social connections create inequality in the labor market. Comment.

# IV BROADER THEMES

# 16 Networked Markets

## 16.1 Introduction

In the theory of general equilibrium and oligopoly, the background assumption is that firms and consumers interact anonymously and globally (anyone can buy and sell from anyone else) at a common price. In practice, bounds of trust and cooperation lead to personalized relations, and geographical distance and national boundaries place restrictions on who can undertake exchange with whom. These restrictions may be modeled in terms of ties that are either present or absent in a network. This chapter presents models of networked markets that help us understand the ways in which prices and quantities are determined in such settings.

We start with a study of a group of sellers, each of whom wishes to sell an indivisible good to a group of buyers. In a world where valuations of all sellers are 0 and the valuations of all buyers are 1, the standard model says that a law of one price obtains, with the price being equal to 1 if there are more buyers than sellers and 0 if there are more sellers than buyers. We examine how this prediction is affected if there are restrictions on who can trade with whom. We locate the buyers and sellers in a bipartite graph. The complete bipartite graph corresponds to the case where all buyers and sellers can trade with each other. Our analysis shows that the law of one price obtains only under very special circumstances: when the local environment facing sets of buyers and sellers corresponds to the global ratio: in other words, a price of 1 obtains only if all buyers find themselves in a situation where they are connected to sellers with an excess number of buyers to sell to. Similarly, a uniform price of 0 obtains only if all buyers find themselves in a situation where they are connected to sellers with too few buyers to sell to.

We then take up pricing in chains of intermediaries between an initial seller and an eventual buyer. Examples of this model are supply chains and financial markets. We study price formation via three protocols: posted prices, bargaining, and auctions. The discussion draws attention to the complexity of the problem and reveals aspects of networks that will be important in shaping pricing and the distribution of surplus. We find that the notion of critical nodes is helpful in organizing arguments. Roughly speaking, a node is critical in a network if it lies on all paths between the original seller and the eventual buyer. Critical traders earn larger payoffs than noncritical nodes.

The last part of the chapter takes up research collaboration ties among oligopolistic firms. Research alliances among firms are common and have been widely studied. Networks of research collaboration exhibit a number of distinctive features: the average degree is relatively small but unequal, and the network has a core-periphery architecture (implying that the average distance between firms in the network is relatively small). We build on classical models of price (Bertrand) and quantity (Cournot) competition to propose a model of network formation that sheds light on the economic forces that can help explain the emergence of these network properties. The analysis reveals that research collaboration among firms has powerful effects on the competitive position of firms. These effects are reinforced if firms are allowed to make transfers to other firms to form collaboration ties, as would be involved in technology exchange agreements between a large firm and a start-up. This reinforcement of advantages can give rise to highly unequal networks.

## 16.2 Bilateral Exchange

In a textbook model of buyers and sellers, the price is determined by the intersection of the demand and supply curves. This classical formulation assumes that all buyers and sellers can trade with each other. In practice, participation in trading may be restricted, and some buyers may be able to trade with only a subset of sellers, and vice versa. This could be due to transport costs or restrictions imposed by national boundaries, or due to high contracting costs. When trading options are limited, sellers may be able to charge more because many buyers are dependent solely on them, even if the aggregate picture is one in which sellers are on the long side and buyers are on the short side. This section studies the formation of prices and the allocation of trading surpluses in such settings. We start with a model of bargaining and then take up auctions in networks.

### 16.2.1 Bargaining in Networks

We will consider a model consisting of buyers and sellers, with trading restrictions between them. The model is taken from Corominas-Bosch (2004).

We will consider a market comprising of B buyers and S sellers. Each seller has a single indivisible good, which they value at 0; every buyer has a known valuation for the good equal to 1. The trading relationships are represented by a bipartite network (see figure 16.1): in such a network, a buyer and a seller have a link if and only if they can trade. The simplest cases of such networks involve a buyer and a seller, or two sellers and a single buyer (and vice versa). Note that the complete bipartite network in which all sellers can trade with all buyers is an example of a special interest, as it corresponds to the classical market with no trading restrictions/frictions.

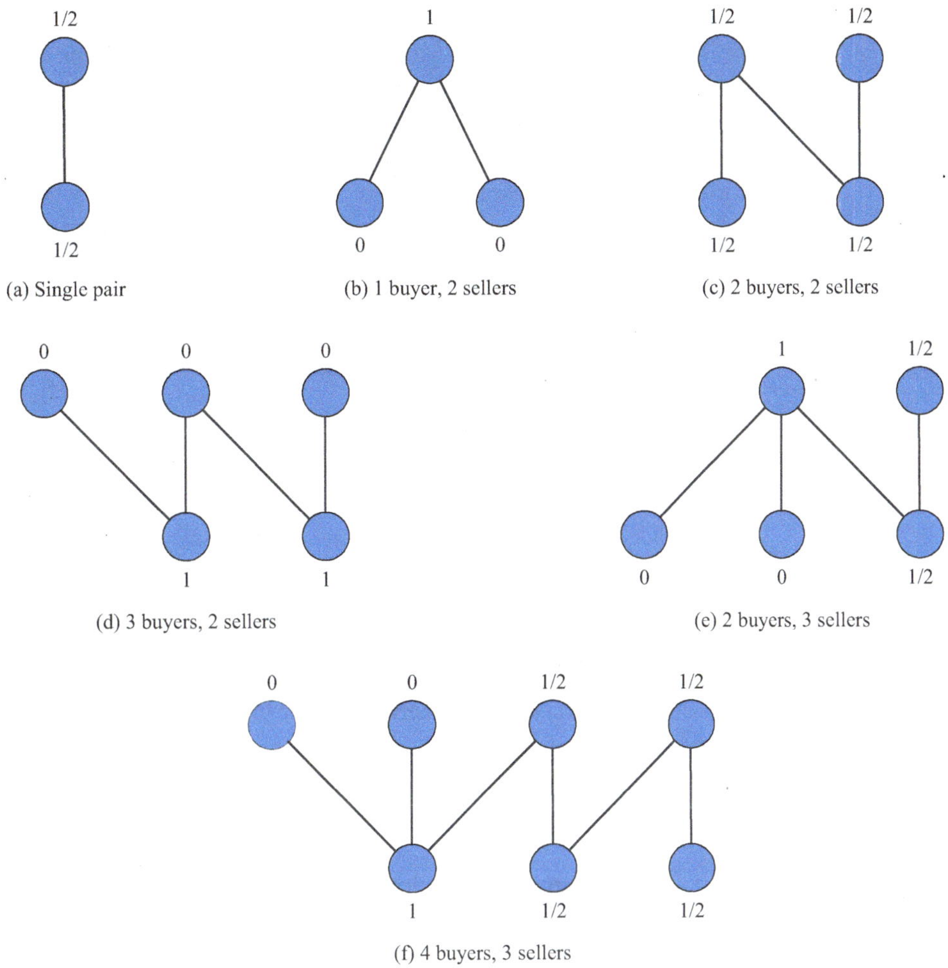


**Figure 16.1**
Examples of bipartite networks. *Source*: Jackson (2008).

Let us start by recalling how prices will be determined in an introductory economics textbook model: we can derive the demand and supply curves by aggregating the individual schedules. Note that price $p$ means that the buyer's payoff is $1-p$, while the seller's payoff is $p$. As every buyer can trade with every seller, there must be a single price for all transactions. We will refer to this outcome as the competitive benchmark. In this outcome, the equilibrium price is determined by the relative sizes of $B$ and $S$. If $B > S$, then the demand and supply curves will support the price of 1, while if $B < S$, then the only price that can equate demand with supply is 0.

Let us next consider settings with trade restrictions. To facilitate an easy comparison with the Walrasian model, we consider a simple and relatively synchronized bargaining process. Time proceeds in discrete steps ($t = 1, 2, \ldots$). In period 1 and all subsequent odd-numbered periods, every remaining seller makes an offer, which is observed by the remaining connected buyers. Buyers who wish to trade accept one of the prices that they see, while those who do not wish to trade reject all prices that they observe. Those who have an agreed trade make the transaction at the agreed price and leave the market (in case of a tie with two traders buying from one seller, we randomly pick one trade). In round 2 and all subsequent even-numbered rounds, buyers make offers and connected sellers respond. To focus on the network structure, let us suppose that all traders discount the future at the rate $\delta \in (0, 1)$. If a buyer (seller) trades at time $t$, they earn $\delta^t(1-p)$ ($\delta^t p$). We study the relation between network structure and prices.

Consider the simplest network with a pair of traders or three traders. If two buyers are linked to a single seller, then $p = 1$; if two sellers are linked to a single buyer, then $p = 0$. In the case of disjoint pairs of traders, $p = 1/(1+\delta)$ (this comes from the well-known Rubinstein-Stahl model of alternating offers).

Turning to richer and larger networks, there are indirect chains of links that are important in bargaining. For instance, a seller realizes that the response of their connected buyer depends on how many sellers they are connected to, and then on how many buyers they in turn are connected to (and so forth). The first step in the study of this problem is the following observation: every bipartite network can be broken into subnetworks in which either the buyers are in the majority, the sellers are in the majority, or the two sides are in balance. This decomposition is helpful because prices in these subnetworks are either 1, 0, or (roughly) 1/2, respectively.

### 16.2.2 Network Structure and Prices

A seller-surplus local network, $g^s$, is one in which sellers are on the long side and every subset of sellers can be matched with buyers with a cardinality at most as great as the seller. We refer to the buyer-surplus local network as $g^b$ and the balanced subnetwork as $g^e$. Let $N_g(V_0)$ be the set of vertices linked to a set of vertices $V_0$. We are now ready to define the concept of a nondeficient set.

**Definition 16.1** *A set of nodes $V$ with $V \subseteq S$ or $V \subseteq B$ is nondeficient in network $g$ if $|N_g(V_0)| \geq V_0$ for every $V_0 \leq V$.*

Every bipartite network $g$ can be decomposed into a number of subgraphs: $g_1^s, g_2^s, \ldots, g_{n_s}^s$ (of the seller surplus type), $g_1^b, g_2^b, \ldots, g_{n_b}^b$ (of the buyer surplus type), and a third category $g_1^e, g_2^e, \ldots, g_{n_e}^e$ (of the balanced type). Moreover, a seller in $g_i^s$ is linked only to buyers in some $g_j^S$, and a buyer in $g_l^b$ is linked only to sellers in some $g_x^b$. Finally, a given node always belongs to the same type of subgraph across all possible decompositions.

This decomposition can be implemented as follows:

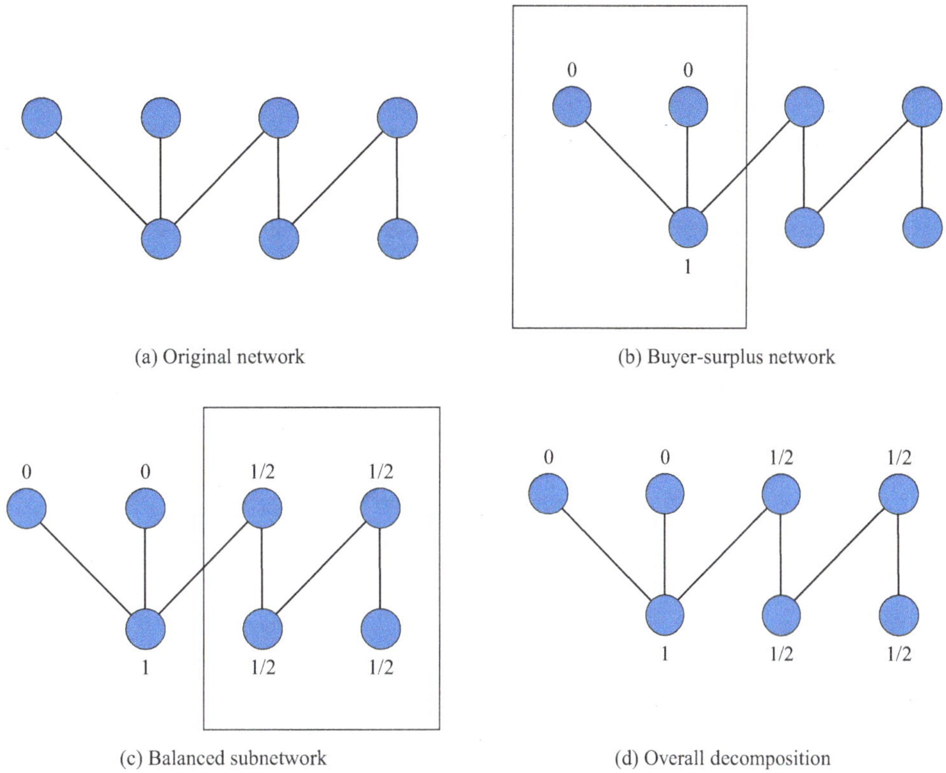


**Figure 16.2**
Implementing the algorithm (the numbers indicate payoffs when $\delta \to 1$). *Source*: Jackson (2008).

1. Start with two or more sellers who are linked *only* to the same buyer. Ignore the other links of this buyer. The buyer gets 1 and the sellers get 0. Take these traders out of the network.
2. Consider the residual network and repeat step 1, but with the role of the traders reversed.
3. Proceed inductively in the number of traders: identify $k$ sellers who have links with at most $k-1$ buyers. Alternatively, identify $k$ buyers who have links with at most $k-1$ sellers. Assign the payoffs correspondingly.
4. We are left with balanced sets of traders, with $k$ buyers linked to $k$ sellers.

We illustrate how this algorithm works by applying it to the last network in figure 16.1. This yields figure 16.2: we identify a buyer surplus subgraph and then identify a balanced subnetwork. This yields us a decomposition of the network and a corresponding allocation of surplus.

This decomposition allows us to develop the following description of prices in the various types of subnetworks. There is a subgame perfect equilibrium of the bargaining game in which the price is 0 in subgraphs $g^s$, the price in subgraphs $g^b$ is 1, and the price in subgraphs $g^e$ is $1/(1+\delta)$.

Let us sketch the argument underlying this pricing outcome. Consider the profile in which all sellers in a $g^b$ subgraph propose 1 and all buyers accept it. Suppose that a buyer rejects this proposal. Then in equilibrium, the trade will take place among the remaining buyers and sellers in the subgraph. So the buyer will be disconnected from all the sellers in the original subgraph $g^b$. So their only hope is a positive payoff from their links in other subgraphs. But the decomposition we obtained tells us that this buyer is linked only to sellers in other $g^b$ subgraphs. In such a subgraph, sellers propose 1 and the buyers linked to them agree to the proposal. The buyer will see all their links to sellers deleted at the end of the round. The buyer will therefore be isolated and earn 0 from the deviation. Thus accepting a price of 1 is optimal for this buyer.

We summarize our analysis in the following result.

**Proposition 16.1** *Consider a network with S sellers and B buyers and a decomposition as computed as described previously.*
*If $S > B$, then g will support the competitive outcome if and only if every subgraph is of type $g^s$.*
*If $S < B$, then g will support the competitive outcome if and only if every subgraph is of type $g^b$.*
*If $B = S$, then g will support the competitive outcome if and only if every subgraph is of type $g^e$.*

These arguments are intuitive, but the decomposition underlying the proof involves careful consideration of the direct and indirect connections in the buyer-seller network. It is therefore very unclear if actual behavior in such settings will conform to the theoretical predictions. With this observation in mind, we report the findings of an experiment with a small buyer-seller network (with seven traders). The experiment is taken from Charness, Corominas-Bosch, and Frechette (2007).

Let us consider the following network: there are four sellers and three buyers. Sellers 1 and 2 linked only to buyer 1, seller 3 has links with buyers 1 and 2, while seller 4 has links with buyers 2 and 3. Sellers 1 and 2 and buyer 1 are in one subgraph, and sellers 3 and 4 and buyers 2 and 3 are in the other subgraph. The theoretical prediction is that sellers 1 and 2 make 0, while buyer 1 makes 1, and sellers 3 and 4 and buyers 2 and 3 make 1/2 each. The network and the theoretical predictions are presented in figure 16.3(a).

The principal experimental finding concerns the average payoffs, to wit: seller 1 (0.07), seller 2 (0.08), seller 3 (0.53), seller 4 (0.51), buyer 1 (0.85), buyer 2 (0.47), and buyer 3 (0.49). These are presented in figure 16.3(b). We conclude that the experimental outcome corresponds closely to the theoretical predictions of the model.

The Corominas-Bosch (2004) paper provides an elegant microfoundation for the Walrasian benchmark: it tells us that the law of one price obtains only when all local markets reflect the global balance of buyers versus sellers. So, in a market with surplus sellers,

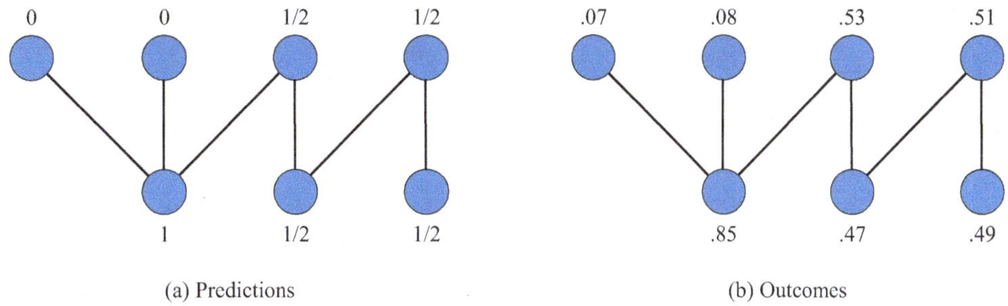


**Figure 16.3**
Experiments on buyer-seller bargaining. *Source*: Charness, Corominas-Bosch, and Frechette (2007).

the outcome may entail some sellers who make large profits because they are locally in a buyer-surplus market.

We have taken the network as given so far, but given the trading outcome on any network, we can now take a step back and ask what sort of networks would form if buyers and sellers can build links with each other. A question at the end of the chapter works through the incentives to create networks in this setting.

We have examined price determination in a network via a process of bargaining: in our model, everyone knows the network and also knows that all buyers value the good at 1, while all sellers value the good at 0. In practice, it is more natural to suppose that there will be limited information about valuations and the connections of others. The theory of bargaining in networks—with incomplete information about either of these dimensions—is very much a field of ongoing research. The interested reader is referred to the excellent survey by Manea (2016). Prices may be determined by agents posting a price (as firms often do) and through an auction among connected buyers. A problem at the end of the chapter explores posted prices in networks. We conclude this section with a brief discussion of auctions in networks that also allow for link formation.

### 16.2.3 Auctions in Networks

We consider a model of auctions in networks that is based on Kranton and Minehart (2001). In stage 1, players choose to form links that determine potential trade patterns. In stage 2, buyers simultaneously make bids to the seller. The winner is determined using a second-price auction. Assume that the valuations of the buyers are uniformly distributed on the unit interval.

To fix ideas, suppose that there are two buyers and one seller. In the single-link network, a buyer bids 0. In the two-link network, the buyers submit valuations equal to their valuation, so the expected price is the expected value of the second-highest valuation. It maybe verified that the expected valuation of the winner is 2/3 (which is also the total value of the surplus generated), while the expected price is equal to $1/3$. Each buyer expects to earn $1/6$, together they expect to earn $1/3$, and the seller expects to earn $1/3$.

What are the incentives of the traders to form a network? Let us first characterize the efficient networks: observe that the expected social value of one buyer is $1/2$, while the expected social value of selling to two buyers is $2/3$. This implies that the empty network is efficient if $c > 1/2$, the single-link network is efficient if $1/6 < c < 1/2$, and the two-link network is efficient if $c < 1/6$.

Next, consider stage 1 with unilateral links formed by buyers. Observe that the empty network is an equilibrium if no buyer has an incentive to form a link: simple computations reveal that if the cost of a link is $c > 1/2$, then the empty network is an equilibrium. Now consider the single-link network. A buyer is willing to form a link so long as $c < 1/2$, and the second buyer has no incentive to form a link if $c > 1/6$.

We have thus shown that a single-link network is an equilibrium if $1/6 < c < 1/2$, and the two-link network is an equilibrium if $c < 1/6$. ■

In this example, the efficient and equilibrium networks coincide. A question at the end of the chapter explores the role of linking protocol—one-sided versus two-sided—in this result.

## 16.3 Intermediaries

Section 16.2 considered direct ties between initial sellers and final buyers. However, as the examples in earlier chapters indicate, supply chains are a defining feature of the modern economy. They are prominent in agriculture, manufacturing, transport and communication, international trade, and finance. The routing of economic activity, the allocation of surplus and the efficiency of the system depend on the prices set by the various intermediaries. This section studies the formation of prices in a network of intermediaries. We start with models of posted prices and then take up models of bargaining and auctions. The exposition in this section draws on Condorelli and Galeotti (2016).

Motivated by the example of supply chains, let us consider a simple model, in which intermediaries set a bid price to buy upstream and an ask price to sell downstream (as in Blume, Easley, Kleinberg, and Tardos [2009]). The intermediary has no consumption value for the object and is connected to subsets of buyers and sellers. This may be seen as a natural next step from the bipartite networks considered in the previous section. In this model, a seller has 1 unit of an indivisible good, and every buyer demands 1 unit of the same good. The consumption value of buyers and sellers may differ, but it is commonly known.

The trading proceeds in two stages. In the first stage, an intermediary offers a bid price to each seller to whom they are connected, and an ask price to each buyer to whom they are connected. In the second stage, sellers and buyers choose the best offer from the offers of intermediaries open to them (it is possible that they then choose not to buy or sell). A large penalty is imposed on intermediaries that sell more units than they have acquired. This assumption ensures that in equilibrium, intermediaries will not default on their price commitment to

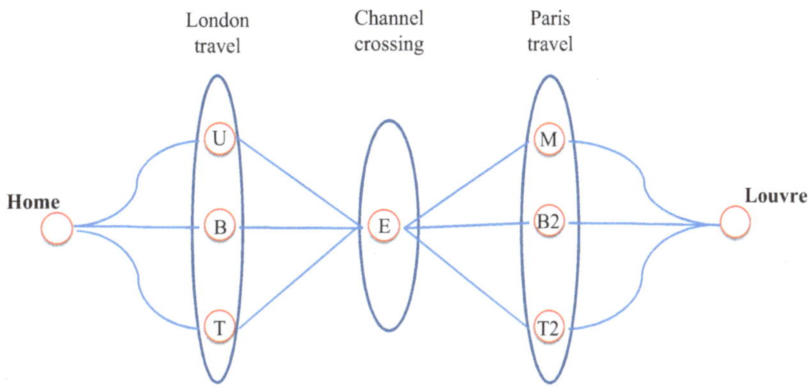


**Figure 16.4**
Traveling from home in London to the Louvre in Paris.

buyers. It is possible to show that every Nash equilibrium of this game results in an efficient outcome (i.e., every possible beneficial trade is realized). An intermediary makes a positive profit if and only if they are *essential*, that is, if attainable social surplus would fall in the absence of this intermediary. In the special case with only one buyer and one seller, an intermediary is essential if they lie on the unique path between them. A question at the end of the chapter works through an equilibrium in specific networks based on this model.

In this model, there is only one layer of intermediation between initial sellers and eventual buyers. Let us move beyond this two-step network to more complete multipartite networks with longer paths in which all traders post bid and ask prices simultaneously. In this case, the object flows from the initial seller to the highest bidder in tier 1, from the buyer in tier 1 to the highest bidder in tier 2, and so forth. The object stops moving either when it is acquired by intermediary $i$ and $i$'s ask is strictly higher than the best bid of any of their downstream buyers, or if it has reached an eventual buyer. This formulation with bid and ask prices is explored in Gale and Kariv (2009). We would like to study a richer set of networks, and this leads us to simplify the pricing process slightly. Our discussion will focus on a model of posted prices taken from Choi, Galeotti, and Goyal (2017).

### 16.3.1 A Model of Posted Prices

By way of motivation for this model, let us consider a tourist who wishes to travel by train from London to see the Louvre in Paris. The first leg of the journey is from her home to the St. Pancras Station in London. She can use the London Underground, a bus or a taxi to get from home to St Pancras. Once at the station, the only service provider to Gare du Nord station in Paris is Eurostar. Upon arriving at Paris Nord Station, she again has a number of alternatives (e.g., Metro, bus, or taxi) to get to the Louvre. We can represent the possibilities with the help of a network similar to what is shown in figure 16.4: this network consists of alternative paths, each constituting local transport alternatives in London and in Paris and

Eurostar. Each of these service providers sets a price with a view to maximizing its profits. The traveler picks the cheapest path. How does the network shape prices, and which route will the tourist eventually choose?

This example suggests the following model: there is a source node, $\mathcal{S}$, and a destination node, $\mathcal{D}$. A path between the two is formed by a sequence of interconnected nodes, each occupied by an intermediary. The source node and the destination node and all the paths between them together define a network. The passage of goods (or people) from source to destination generates a surplus. Let us suppose that the value is known, and for simplicity, set it equal to 1. Intermediaries (who all have zero cost) simultaneously post a price; the prices determine a total cost for every path between $\mathcal{S}$ and $\mathcal{D}$. The tourist moves along a least-cost path; so intermediaries earn payoffs only if they are located on it.

Every node $i$ is called an *intermediary*; let $N=\{1,2,3,\ldots,n\}$, $n\geq 1$ denote the set of intermediaries. A path $q$ between $\mathcal{S}$ and $\mathcal{D}$ is formed by a sequence of distinct nodes $\{i_1,\ldots,i_l\}$, such that $g_{\mathcal{S}i_1}=g_{i_1i_2}=\cdots=g_{i_l\mathcal{D}}=1$. The nodes $N\cup\{\mathcal{S},\mathcal{D}\}$ and the paths $\mathcal{Q}$ define network $g$. Every intermediary $i$ simultaneously posts price $p_i\geq 0$. Let $p=\{p_1,p_2,\ldots,p_n\}$ denote the price profile. Throughout this discussion, we will restrict attention to pure pricing strategies. Network $g$ and price profile $p$ define a cost for every path $q$ between $\mathcal{S}$ and $\mathcal{D}$:

$$c(q,p)=\sum_{i\in q} p_i. \tag{16.1}$$

A *least-cost* path $q'$ is one such that $c(q',p)=\min_{q\in\mathcal{Q}} c(q,p)$. Payoffs arise from active intermediation: intermediary $i$ obtains $p_i$ only if they lie on a feasible least-cost path. Define $c(p)=\min_{q\in\mathcal{Q}} c(q,p)$. Path $q$ is feasible if $c(q,p)\leq 1$, where 1 is the value of an economic good generated by the path. All paths generate the same value, 1. If there are multiple least-cost paths, one of them is chosen randomly to be the active path. Given $g$ and $p$, we denote by $\mathcal{Q}=\{q\in\mathcal{Q}: c(q,p)=c(p), c(p)\leq 1\}$ the set of feasible least-cost paths. Given price profile $p$, intermediary $i$'s payoff is

$$\pi_i(p)=\begin{cases} 0 & \text{if } i\notin q,\ \forall\, q\in\mathcal{Q} \\ \frac{\eta_i}{|\mathcal{Q}|}p_i & \text{if } i\in q,\ q\in\mathcal{Q}, \end{cases} \tag{16.2}$$

where $\eta_i$ is the number of paths in $\mathcal{Q}$ that contain intermediary $i$.

We study a pure-strategy Nash equilibrium of the posted price game. Price profile $p^*$ is a Nash equilibrium if, for all $i\in\mathcal{N}$, $\Pi_i(p^*)\geq\Pi_i(p_i,p^*_{-i})$ for all $p_i\geq 0$. An equilibrium is efficient (inefficient) if trade occurs (does not occur). Equilibrium $p^*$ is said to be efficient if $c(p^*)\leq 1$; otherwise, equilibrium $p^*$ is inefficient.

To build some intuition for how network structure affects pricing, let us consider two simple networks. The first has two paths between $\mathcal{S}$ and $\mathcal{D}$, each with a distinct node. These two intermediaries compete in price: this is very much like price competition between firms selling a homogenous product. Standard arguments tell us that the firms will set a price equal to 0. The second contains a single line with two nodes between $\mathcal{S}$ and $\mathcal{D}$. The outcome is a pair of prices that sums to 1; this is as in the Nash model of two players bargaining over a cake of size 1. Observe that in the first network, the prices of the two competing firms are strategic complements, while in the latter network (when the two prices add up to 1), they are strategic substitutes. These examples illustrate how classical models of price formation constitute special cases of our framework and how networks and the strategic structure are intimately related.

Let us build on these examples to make some observations on pricing in general networks. If there are multiple routes between source and destination, then the players located on these nodes become competitors who are supplying a route, which is a homogenous product. If the routes are distinct—they have no common intermediary—then we should expect that the outcome would be like the Bertrand outcome: all intermediaries set a price of 0. It is possible to verify that this price profile constitutes a Nash equilibrium. However, it is not the unique equilibrium: to see why, consider a simple network with two paths, with two intermediaries on each path. There is an equilibrium in which intermediaries on one path miscoordinate and each sets a price of 1, while each of the intermediaries on the other path sets a price of 1/2.

Turning next to the case where some intermediaries are common to the paths, consider the special case where an intermediary lies on all paths. In this situation, we claim that the traveler must earn zero surplus. Suppose that they earn a positive surplus in equilibrium. This means that the cheapest path adds up to less than 1. But then the intermediary who lies on all paths can raise their price so that the prices add up to 1. This is a strictly profitable deviation for the intermediary and contradicts the claim that we were in equilibrium.

Building on chapter 1, let us define the *betweenness centrality* of intermediary $i$ as $BC_i = \eta_i/|\mathcal{Q}|$, where $BC_i \in [0, 1]$. Intermediary $i$ is said to be *critical* if $BC_i = 1$.

**Proposition 16.2** *In every network, there is an efficient equilibrium. Any equilibrium $p^*$ is either inefficient ($c(p^*) > 1$), allows intermediaries to extract all surplus ($c(p^*) = 1$), or gives no surplus to intermediaries ($c(p^*) = 0$). In a network with critical traders, an efficient equilibrium results in full extraction by intermediaries.*

Let us sketch the proof for this result. When equilibria are efficient, only two outcomes are possible with regard to surplus extraction—either all of a surplus accrues to intermediaries or none of it does. To see why this is true, note that if there is a critical trader, then trade cannot occur at a price less than full surplus because the critical trader can simply increase their price and thereby strictly increase their profits. If there is no critical trader, then the argument is a little more complicated. If the feasible least-cost path is unique, then intermediaries in that path exercise market power, and if intermediation costs are below the full surplus, then an intermediary on that path could slightly increase their intermediation price while guaranteeing that exchange takes place through them. In contrast, when there are multiple feasible least-cost paths, then there is price competition among intermediaries

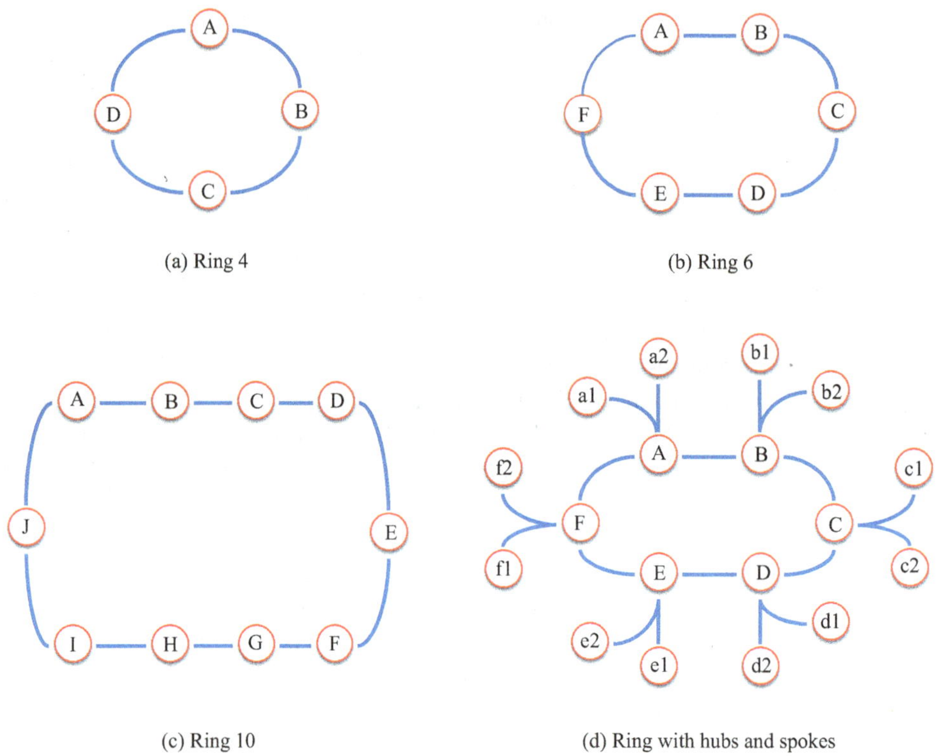


**Figure 16.5**
Examples of networks. *Source*: Choi, Galeotti, and Goyal (2017).

on these paths. In that case, whenever intermediation costs are larger than zero, an intermediary demanding a positive price gains by undercutting their price. Price competition drives intermediation costs down to zero.

Criticality dictates that all surpluses must accrue to intermediaries, but the theory is permissive about how they are distributed among them. To see this point, consider the Ring with Hubs and Spokes network presented in figure 16.5, and suppose that $\mathcal{S}$ and $\mathcal{D}$ are located on $(a_1, d_1)$. Then, there is an equilibrium in which all surplus accrues to the critical intermediaries (e.g., $A$ and $D$ charge $1/2$ and all other intermediaries charge 0). However, there is also an equilibrium in which the entire surplus is earned by noncritical intermediaries (e.g., $A$ and $D$ charge 0, $B$ and $C$ charge $1/2$, and $F$ and $E$ charge 1).

The theoretical analysis suggests some broad patterns for how networks affect pricing, but open questions remain due to the multiplicity of equilibria: we know, for instance, that miscoordination can lead to the breakdown of trade, and even when trade occurs, surplus may flow to noncritical traders. Now we conduct an experiment with the networks in figure 16.5 that allows us to examine the roles of coordination, competition, and market power.

**Table 16.1**
Frequency of trading

| Network | Minimum Distance of Buyer-Sell Pair | | | | |
|---|---|---|---|---|---|
| | All (≥ 2) | 2 | 3 | 4 | 5 |
| Ring 4 | 1.00 | 1.00 | – | – | – |
| | (480) | (480) | | | |
| Ring 6 | 1.00 | 1.00 | 1.00 | – | – |
| | (420) | (289) | (131) | | |
| Ring 10 | 1.00 | 1.00 | 1.00 | 1.00 | 1.00 |
| | (240) | (49) | (87) | (69) | (35) |
| Ring with Hubs | 0.95 | 1.00 | 0.94 | 0.90 | 0.90 |
| and Spokes | (420) | (126) | (155) | (109) | (30) |

*Note*: The number of group observations is reported in parentheses.
*Source*: Choi, Galeotti, and Goyal (2017).

The ring networks with 4, 6, and 10 traders allow us to focus on coordination and competition. For every choice of $\mathcal{S}$ and $\mathcal{D}$, there are always two competing paths of intermediaries. In ring 4, for any nonadjacent pair, there are two paths with a single intermediary each. Rings 6 and 10 allow situations with a higher (and possibly unequal) number of intermediaries on either path.

The Ring with Hubs and Spokes network allows us to study of the impact of market power: for instance, if $\mathcal{S}$ is located at $a_1$ and $\mathcal{D}$ is located at $a_2$, intermediary $A$ is a pure monopoly, while if $\mathcal{D}$ is $b_1$, then the intermediaries $A$ and $B$ play a symmetric Nash demand game. This network also creates the space for both market power and competition to come into play. For instance, if $\mathcal{S}$ is located at $a_1$ and $\mathcal{D}$ is located at $e_1$, then there are two competing paths: a shorter path (through $A$, $F$, and $E$) and a longer path (through $A$, $B$, $C$, $D$, and $E$). Traders $A$ and $E$ are the only critical intermediaries.

The first finding is that the level of efficiency is remarkably high in all networks. Trading in rings with 4, 6, and 10 intermediaries occurs with probability 1. In the Ring with Hubs and Spokes, trading occurs with probability around 0.95. Table 16.1 summarizes the data.

We next turn to the issue of surplus extraction by intermediaries. Figure 16.6 presents a summary of the findings. As we move along the $x$-axis, we cover the various networks. On the $y$-axis, we have the share of surplus accruing to intermediaries. In the Ring with Hubs and Spokes, when $\mathcal{S}$ and $\mathcal{D}$ are served by a sole critical intermediary, surplus extraction is in the region of 99 percent. When $\mathcal{S}$ and $\mathcal{D}$ are connecting via one single path with two intermediaries, the game played by the two intermediaries is analogous to a symmetric Nash demand game. The intermediaries extract, in total, around 96 percent of the surplus, and they share it roughly equally. Finally, when there are two competing paths and critical traders, the intermediation cost ranges between 62 percent and 83 percent. In the case without critical intermediaries, this cost falls sharply to around 28 percent, which is comparable to the low-cost outcome found in the rings.

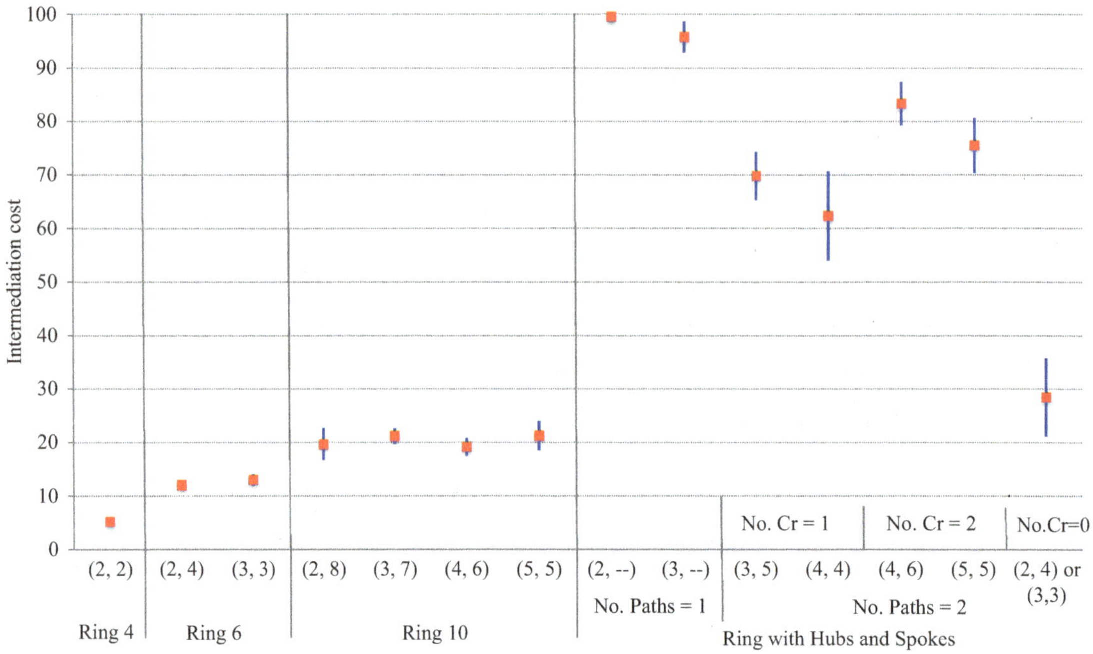


**Figure 16.6**
Costs of intermediation (numbers on $x$-axis indicate short and long paths between source and destination; No. Cr refers to number of critical nodes). *Source*: Choi, Galeotti, and Goyal (2017).

The final issue pertains to the sharing of surpluses between critical and noncritical traders. Figure 16.7 summarizes the data. We cover the possible distances and critical-noncritical configurations as we move along the $x$-axis. The $y$-axis presents the prices. The graph reveals that in the Ring with Hubs and Spokes, critical intermediaries set higher prices and earn a much higher share of surplus than noncritical intermediaries.

To summarize: trading in a network is generally efficient, and critical intermediaries capture practically all the surplus.

In this model, there is full information on the size of the surplus. In practice, traders will normally not know the value of the surplus. Let us briefly discuss the implications of this imperfect information. Suppose that to fix ideas, that value is uniformly distributed on the unit interval. This defines a new game on a network: the strategies remain as before, but the profits of intermediaries are altered due to the incomplete information on valuations.

To develop an idea of how incomplete information matters, we discuss the two simple network examples as discussed previously. In the two-path case, nothing essential changes: prices are still set at 0. But in the line network with two nodes, there is an outcome where both intermediaries set a price equal to $1/3$, so there is no trade with probability $2/3$. It is

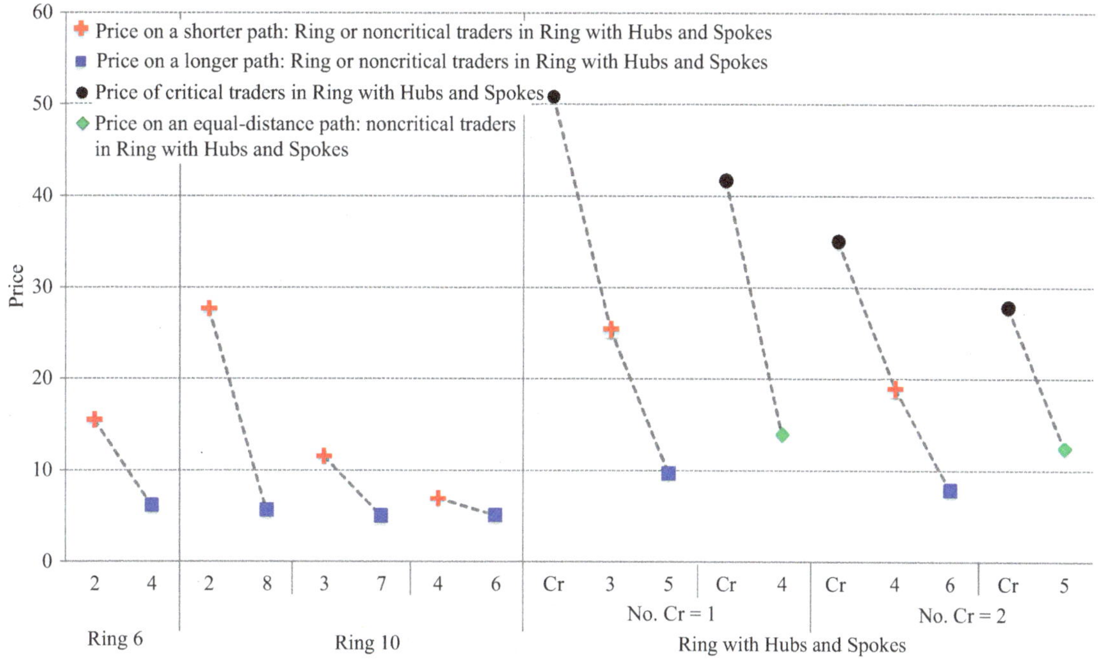


**Figure 16.7**
Competition among intermediaries. *Source*: Choi, Galeotti, and Goyal (2017).

easy to see that with three intermediaries, the price will be 1/4, so the probability of no trade is 3/4. Thus individual prices are falling, aggregate price is rising, and the probability of trade is falling in the number of critical traders. These points can be shown to hold in more general networks, a point that is developed in a question at the end of the chapter.

The discussion on post prices reveals that critical nodes play an important determinant of prices and trading patterns. This suggests that traders have an incentive to form links in order to become critical nodes in the trading network. For a model of network formation with intermediation rents, see section 8.6 in chapter 8.

As in the previous section on bipartite networks, to deepen our understanding of pricing in networks, we will next explore price formation via bargaining.

### 16.3.2 A Model of Bargaining

We next consider a model of bargaining among intermediaries that is based on Manea (2018). In this model, there is a single seller who a single unit of an indivisible good, which can be resold through a chain of intermediaries until it reaches a final buyer. The details of timing and moves are as follows:

- At every stage, the current owner of the good selects a bargaining partner among their downstream neighbors in the network.
- The two traders negotiate the price of the good. With probability $p$, the current owner makes an offer and the partner either accepts or rejects it. With probability $1-p$, the downstream trader makes an offer. Regardless of who makes the offer, once an offer is rejected, bargaining in that stage ends. The current owner has an opportunity to select a new trader in the next stage (they may select the same partner again).
- On the other hand, if an offer is accepted, then the two traders exchange the good at the agreed price. If the new owner is an intermediary, they have an opportunity to resell the good to downstream neighbors following the same protocol. The final buyer consumes the good upon purchase.

Traders have a common discount factor $\delta \in (0, 1)$. At any point in the game, the strategy of an active trader is conditioned on current ownership: the strategy consists of an offer of a price to sell or an offer to buy at a price. The strategy of the respondent is to accept or reject the offer. As past actions do not matter, we will study the Markov perfect equilibrium of the bargaining game. In other words, the traders condition their offers and responses only on current ownership status and potential buyers downstream.

To draw out the role of the network architecture, let us assume that all traders have zero costs and all buyers have a common value $v > 0$. A preliminary observation is the following: any seller/intermediary linked to two or more buyers will extract the full surplus of $v$, as traders become patient (this is reminiscent of our model of bargaining in bipartite networks). In the rest of this section, the discussion will proceed under the assumption that players are very patient (i.e., $\delta \to 1$).

With these points in mind, let us consider the class of connected networks that are acyclic—these are networks in which there is a path leading from the original seller to every final buyer and a well-defined progression from the original owner downstream. Building on the previous discussion, we will want to identify the sellers who act as a gateway to competing buyers without having to compete themselves to buy the good from the upstream seller. We do this as follows. Start with the final buyers: add all intermediaries who are linked to at least two buyers, then add all intermediaries linked to at least two traders already present, and so on until no more traders have two or more links to traders already present in layer 0. This defines layer 0 in the induced network. Consider all the traders who do not belong to layer 0. Start with traders who have only one link with a trader in layer 0, then add all intermediaries who have at least two links with intermediaries currently in layer 1, and repeat until there is no one with two or more links with traders in the emerging layer 1. This completes the construction of layer 1. Proceed recursively until all agents have been assigned to layers 0,1, 2....

To develop a feel for the economic pressures at work in this environment, let us restrict attention to a special class of networks (inspired by the previous example of travel from

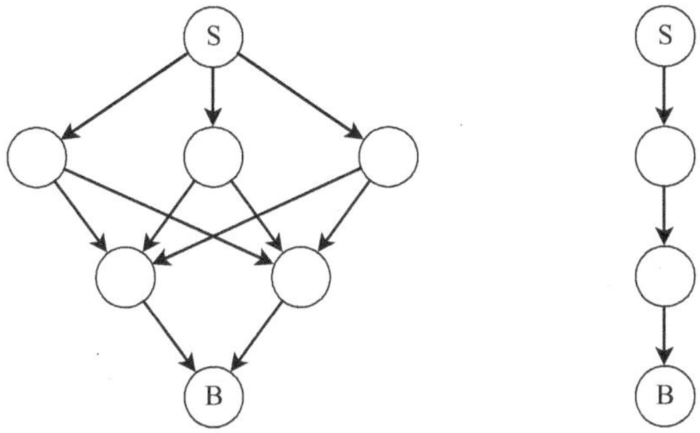


(a) Competitive network (b) Line network

**Figure 16.8**
Complete multipartite networks. *Source*: Condorelli and Galeotti (2016).

London to Paris). We will consider a complete multipartite network, a network with a single initial seller and a single final buyer and $L \geq 1$ intermediating tiers. Every node in a level is linked to every node in the adjacent levels above and below it. A node is critical if it is the unique member of a tier. Given the layer $x$, let $k_x \in \{0, \ldots, L-x\}$ be the number of downstream tiers that have critical traders. Let $k$ be the number of tiers with critical traders in them. Figure 16.8 presents examples of such networks. Note that in the competitive network, there are multiple intermediaries at every tier of the network. By contrast, in the line network, there is a unique—critical—intermediary at both tiers 1 and 2.

The study of bargaining in these networks yields a clear set of predictions as summarized in proposition 16.3. Recall that $p$ is the probability that the current owner makes an offer to a partner.

**Proposition 16.3** *Fix a complete multipartite network and let $\delta \to 1$. In equilibrium, (i) the reservation value of intermediary i at level x converges to $p^{k_x+1}v$; (ii) the payoff of the initial seller converges to $p^{k+1}v$ and payoff of the buyer converges to $(1-p)v$; and (iii) the payoff of noncritical intermediaries converges to 0, while the payoff of critical trader at level x converges to $(1-p)p^{k_x+1}v$.*

We start with part (i) of proposition 1. The proof relies on a backward induction argument. When the object reaches an intermediary in the last tier, we have a standard two person bargaining game with a random proposer. In this game, when $\delta \to 1$, the intermediary obtains payoff $pv$ and the buyer obtains $(1-p)v$. The resale value of an intermediary in tier $L$ is then $pv$. Suppose next that the object has reached intermediary $i$ in tier $L-1$. If tier $L$ contains a critical trader $j$, then there is a standard bargaining game between intermediaries $i$ and $j$: the total size of the cake is $j$'s resale value $pv$. In this game, intermediary $i$ obtains an expected payoff of $p^2v$, which is their resale value. When tier $L$ has more than one intermediary, the current owner, $i$, has multiple potential buyers in tier $L$, each with a resale of $pv$. We invoke the observation given earlier to infer that competition among intermediaries will lead $i$ to extract all surplus (i.e., his resale value is $pv$). Part (i) of the proposition now follows, by iterating backward. Given part (i), it is straightforward to verify the other two parts.

We return to the networks in figure 16.8 to appreciate the role of networks. Let us start with the line network. In this case, the resale value of intermediaries is as follows: $p^3v$ for the initial seller, $p^2v$ for the first intermediary, and $pv$ for the last intermediary. This suggests that the resale value is falling along with the distance from the final customer. As the equilibrium payoff of an intermediary $i$ is $(1-p)$ times their resale value, the ranking of equilibrium payoffs is the same as the ranking of their resale values. The payoff of the initial seller is decreasing in the number of intermediaries, while the payoff of the final buyer is $v(1-p)$.

In this model, $p$ is naturally interpreted as a measure of the bargaining power of upstream traders. An increase in $p$ leads to an increase in payoffs of the initial seller and a decrease in the payoff of the final buyer. Interestingly, the payoff of an intermediary changes nonmonotonically with $p$: at first, it increases and then it eventually decreases (due to the presence of multiple layers in the network).

Turning to the competitive network in figure 16.8, we see that the number of critical traders is $k=0$. Proposition 16.3 tells us that intermediaries have the same resale value, equal to 0, regardless of their location. The initial seller and the final buyer obtain $vp$ and $v(1-p)$ because the intermediary layers earn zero payoff. This suggests that horizontal mergers—which lead the competing traders in a tier to collude—are very profitable. For instance, if all intermediaries in one tier decide to merge, their total payoff would increase from 0 to $pv(1-p)$; the seller's payoff decreases from $pv$ to $p^2v$.

Finally, we take up price formation through auctions in intermediation networks. Following Kotowski and Leister (2019), let us suppose that there is a single source and possibly multiple eventual buyers (each of whom values the good at $v>0$). There are tiers of intermediaries between the original owner and buyers. In each tier, traders compete to provide intermediation services. The current owner conducts a second-price auction among the traders in the immediate downstream layer to sell their good. The new owner does likewise until the good arrives at a buyer. The network is common knowledge, but intermediaries have private information about their own costs. If the cost of trading is High, then the intermediary drops out of the network.

In this setting, trader behavior is determined by two network characteristics—the number of layers and the number of intermediaries in each layer—and the probability of High- versus Low-cost intermediaries. If there are two or more Low-cost intermediaries in each layer, the original owner will extract a full surplus. Therefore, an intermediary earns rents only if it is the sole Low-cost player in its layer (i.e., it is critical). With a greater probability of High cost, intermediate layers can in principle earn rents in the event that their competitors in the same layer have turned out to be High cost. However, this possibility has correspondingly negative effects on the resale value for upstream traders. The authors show that the resale value is increasing in the probability of being Low cost and in the number of traders in each layer.

The models discussed in this section show how standard pricing protocols—posted prices, bargaining, and auctions—can be used to study price formation and intermediation in networks. In all cases, critical traders appear to be central to shaping market power. Our discussion shows that the location within a network and the structure of the network have powerful effects on patterns of trade and on earnings. In particular, we found that critical intermediaries earn larger payoffs than noncritical traders. So it pays to occupy a critical spot in a network. This suggests that traders have an incentive to create links that would become critical. Similarly, other traders have an incentive to circumvent such critical traders by creating new ties. Chapter 8, on platforms and intermediaries, studies this process and presents experimental evidence on the role of pricing protocols in shaping network formation.

## 16.4 Research Alliances in Oligopoly

Research alliances among firms are common: firms collaborate with both firms in their own industry and those outside it, and these alliances are nonexclusive, so a firm often takes part in multiple projects with different partners. Empirical research reveals the following stylized facts about research and development (R&D) networks: the average degree is relatively small, the degrees are unequal, there is a core-periphery architecture, and the average distance between firms in the network is small (König, Liu, and Hsieh 2021). This section studies the origins and implications of these network patterns. We present a model taken from Goyal and Joshi (2003), Goyal and Moraga-González (2001), and König, Tessone, and Zenou (2014). Our exposition draws on Goyal (2007, 2017).

Firms produce services and products that involve the use of different bodies of knowledge. The complexity of technology means that an individual firm is at the frontier of some of, but not all the aspects of business. Research collaboration can be seen as a mechanism for firms to pool their distinct technological advantages. For firms producing goods that involve many different technologies, such as automobiles, there are many areas in which they can form potentially profitable collaboration partnerships.

Prior to competing in a market, firms can choose to collaborate on research. Collaboration lowers the costs of partner firms. Lower costs are advantageous as they lead to larger market share and profits. On the other hand, collaboration with other firms involves resources and is therefore costly. So a firm compares the costs and returns from collaboration when deciding on how many links to form. At the heart of the analysis is the issue of how a collaboration link between two firms alters the incentives of other firms to form collaboration links (throughout this discussion, we will assume that there is no collusion in the market stage among research collaborators).

There are two stages. In stage 1, $n$ firms play a game of two-sided link formation. Every firm announces a set of firms, $s_i = \{s_{i1}, s_{i2}, \dots, s_{in}\}$, with whom it wishes to form links. A link is formed between two firms if both announce an intention to form a link with each other. The collection of links formed defines an undirected network $g(s)$. Let $N_i(g)$ be the collaboration partners of firm $i$ in network $g$, and define $\eta_i(g) = |N_i(g)|$. There are $K > n$ components in the item that firms produce, and we will assume that all firms use the same $K$ components. Let the cost for firm $i$ of component $k$ be given by $c_{i,k}$. The marginal cost of production for firm $i$ is given by $c_i = \sum_{k=1}^{K} c_{i,k}$. The component-wise cost $c_{i,l}$ takes on a value of $c^H$ or $c^L$, with $c^H > c^L$. Assume that for each firm $i$, there is one and only one $\hat{k}$ such that $c_{i,\hat{k}} = c^L$. Moreover, suppose that $c_{j,\hat{k}} = c^H$ for all other firms, $j \neq i$. Then it follows that if two firms form a collaboration link, then both can reduce their costs by $c^H - c^L$. Define $\gamma = c^H - c^L$.

It follows, then, that the marginal cost of firm $i$ is given by

$$c_i(g) = \gamma_0 - \gamma\eta_i(g), \quad i \in N, \tag{16.3}$$

where $\gamma_0 > 0$ is a positive parameter representing a firm's marginal cost when it has no links and $\gamma > 0$ is the cost reduction from a link. The cost is a linear and declining function of the number of collaboration links with other firms. Given network $g$, the profile of costs is $c(g) = \{c_1(g), c_2(g), \ldots, c_n(g)\}$. In this formulation, the cost reduction in each link is exogenously fixed.

In stage 2, firms compete in the market by choosing quantities or setting prices. Suppose that firms face an inverse linear demand given by $P = 1 - Q$, where $P$ is the price and $Q = \sum_{i=1}^{n} q_i$ is the total output produced by the firms. Define $L(g_{-i}) = \sum_{j \in N} \eta_j(g) - 2\eta_i(g)$ as the total number of links of all firms in network $g$, *except* for the links that involve firm $i$. For network $g$, using the standard formulas for Cournot models with heterogenous costs (see, e.g., Vives [1999]), the equilibrium quantity of firm $i$ can be written as

$$q_i(g) = \frac{(1-\gamma_0) + (n-1)\gamma\eta_i(g) - \gamma L(g_{-i})}{(n+1)}, \quad i \in N. \tag{16.4}$$

To ensure that each firm produces a strictly positive quantity, we assume that $(1 - \gamma_0) - (n-1)(n-2)\gamma > 0$. It is easy to verify that the Cournot profits for firm $i$ in network $g$ are given by $q_i^2(g)$.

To complete the model, assume that every link involves a fixed cost, $c > 0$. The net payoffs of firm $i$ in network $g$ are given as follows:

$$\Pi_i(g) = \left[\frac{(1-\gamma_0) + (n-1)\gamma\eta_i(g) - \gamma L(g_{-i})}{(n+1)}\right]^2 - \eta_i(g)c. \tag{16.5}$$

In the case of price competition, we will assume that all demand accrues to the lowest-price firm; if there are multiple lowest-cost firms, then the demand is equally shared among them. We study the architecture of pairwise equilibrium networks and payoff distributions (see chapter 3, for the definition of a pairwise equilibrium).

In a market with a homogeneous product, a firm will attract demand only if it is a lowest-price firm and if there are many such firms, then they will share the demand equally. Anticipating this, in stage 1, a firm will invest in costly links only if it hopes to become a lowest-cost firm. Either there is only one lowest-cost firm or there are multiple lowest-cost firms. In either event, if there are costs to forming links, however small, then in both cases, there will be firms that have formed links and will make zero profits in the market: in other words, they will have negative earnings. Hence the empty network is a unique pairwise equilibrium.

By contrast, if firms compete in quantities, then an inspection of the equilibrium quantity in equation (16.4) reveals that profits are increasing in own links $\eta_i(g)$. This means that a firm has an incentive to form a link with every other firm, so long as the cost of links is sufficiently small. We conclude that the complete network is a unique pairwise equilibrium. Thus the nature of market competition—price versus quantity—has a decisive impact on the nature of collaboration networks.

As networks shape the costs and quantities produced, they will determine the utility of consumers. Recall that social welfare in this market is the sum of firm profits and consumer surpluses. Let us now derive the efficient networks in the two markets. We first consider the nature of efficient networks under quantity competition. Let $c(k)$ denote the marginal cost of a firm with $k$ links. Social welfare is defined as

$$W(g) = \frac{1}{2}Q^2(g) + \sum_{i \in N} \pi_i(g). \tag{16.6}$$

It is possible to show that the complete network is a unique network that maximizes social welfare. When two firms form a link, that lowers their costs and increases their market shares and profits. However, other firms lose out in market share. The computations show that aggregate quantity sold is increasing in links. The final step is to show that the gains of the firm with the additional links, along with the increase in consumer surpluses due to the larger aggregate quantity sold, are greater than the loss of the other firms.

Turning to the case of price competition, let $\underline{c}$ be the minimum cost attainable by a firm in any network; this is achieved when a firm has $(n-1)$ links. It is possible to show that a network maximizes social welfare if and only if two firms attain the minimum cost, $\underline{c}$. The argument is straightforward: with two maximally connected firms, costs attain their minimum value and price competition therefore pushes both firms to charge the minimal price. This maximizes consumption (and consumer surplus). It turns out that it also maximizes the total surplus. A question at the end of the chapter works through these computations.

To summarize, we have embedded a standard oligopolistic competition within a network formation game and shown that market competition and networks interact in interesting ways: market competition shapes incentives to form links and create networks. These networks then shape the nature of the competition. The interaction between competition and networks, therefore, can have large effects on social welfare.

### 16.4.1 Large Costs of Linking

We next turn to study the case of network formation when the costs of linking are large. Larger costs will reinforce the lack of incentives to form links in the pricing competition case. We therefore focus on quantity competition in the rest of this section.

As a firm will compare the marginal cost of a link with the marginal returns from a link, we need to understand the curvature of the returns as a function of the links in the network. We note from equation (16.5) that a firm's quantity (and therefore its profits) are declining in the links of other firms. Given network $g$, the marginal gross returns from an additional link, $g_{i,j}$, are given by

$$\Pi_i(g+g_{i,j}) - \Pi_i(g) = \frac{(n-1)\gamma}{(n+1)^2}\left[\lambda(n) + 2(n-1)\gamma\eta_i(g) - 2\gamma L(g_{-i})\right], \tag{16.7}$$

where $\lambda(n) = 2(1-\gamma_0) + (n-1)\gamma$. Thus the marginal gross returns from an additional link are increasing in the number of own links $\eta_i(g)$ and decreasing in the number of links of other firms $L(g_{-i})$. The total cost of links is linearly increasing in the number of links. So any two firms that have a link must be linked with each other. This observation has an important implication: any pair of firms that has at least one link in the network must also have a link with each other. Let us define a network with a dominant group as follows: there is a set of firms $1 < k < n$, which constitutes a clique, and all firms outside the group are singletons. Equipped with these observations we are ready to state our next result on pairwise equilibrium networks.

**Proposition 16.4** *Suppose that payoffs are given by equation (16.5). A pairwise equilibrium network either is empty, contains a dominant group, or is complete.*

The key to the proof is a simple observation: the marginal returns in own links are increasing and convex, and marginal costs of links are constant, so if two firms have one or more links, then in a pairwise equilibrium network, they must also be linked to each other. As every pair of firms that has any connections must in turn be linked with each other, the only possibility is that there is a clique of connected firms and a few isolated firms. Figure 16.9 illustrates network architectures that can arise in pairwise equilibrium.

Let $g^k$ refer to a dominant group network in which the dominant group has $k$ firms. A firm in the dominant group should not have any incentive to delete any subset of its links. Given that payoffs are increasing and convex in own links, it is sufficient to check if a firm has an incentive to delete all its links. Let $Y(k)$ denote the difference in the payoff of a firm in the dominant group of size $k$ minus the payoff when the firm becomes isolated. Using equation (16.5), the incentive constraint may be written as follows:

$$Y(k) \equiv \frac{(n-1)\gamma}{(n+1)^2}\left[2(1-\gamma_0) + (k-1)(n+3-2k)\gamma\right] \geq c. \tag{16.8}$$

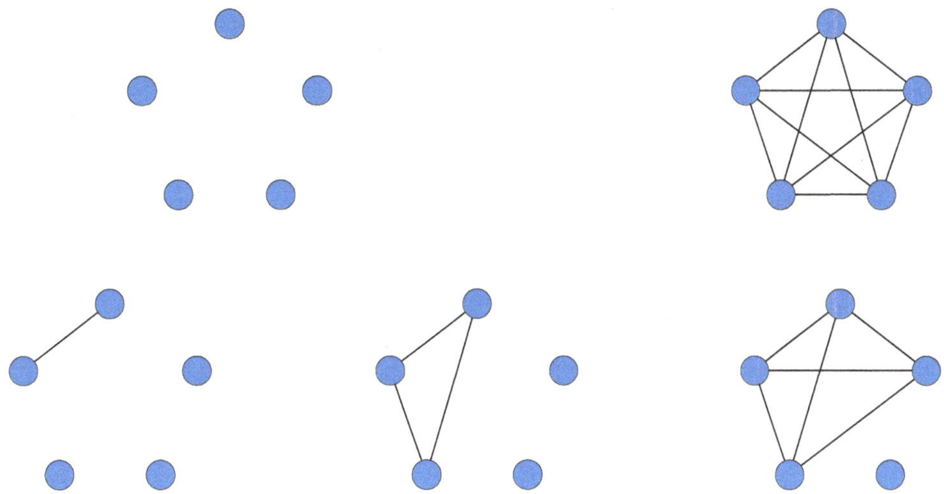

**Figure 16.9**
Pairwise equilibrium networks, $n = 6$.

The left side of equation (16.8) reveals an interesting property of payoffs: the average returns from links are nonmonotonic with respect to the size of the dominant group. They are initially increasing until a critical size $k^*$, and declining thereafter. Due to the increasing returns property, a firm in the dominant group would like to link with any isolated firms. So for the dominant group to be an equilibrium, the isolated firm must find the link unprofitable. Let us define $X(k)$ as the difference in payoff with and without a link. This yields the following incentive constraint for isolated firms:

$$X(k) \equiv \frac{(n-1)\gamma}{(n+1)^2}\,[2(1-\gamma_0)+(n-1)\gamma-2k(k-1)\gamma] < c. \tag{16.9}$$

We see that the marginal returns to the isolated firm are declining with the size of the dominant group. An increase in the costs of forming links will make a smaller dominant groups sufficient to deter the isolated firms from forming a link. Figure 16.10(a) illustrates the incentives of firms in the dominant group and the isolated firms as a function of the size of the dominant group.

In figure 16.10, the terms $F0$, $F1$, $F2$, and $F3$ are defined as follows:

$$F0 = \frac{(n-1)\gamma}{(n+1)^2}\,[2(1-\gamma_0)+(n-1)(3-2n)\gamma]$$

$$F1 = \frac{(n-1)\gamma}{(n+1)^2}\,[2(1-\gamma_0)+(n-1)(3-n)\gamma]$$

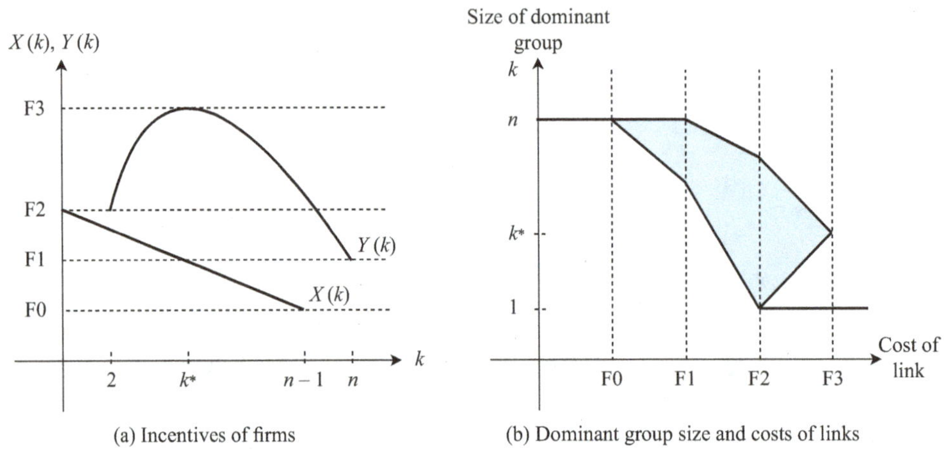


**Figure 16.10**
Dominant group and costs of links. *Source*: Goyal and Joshi (2003).

$$F2 = \frac{(n-1)\gamma}{(n+1)^2}\,[2(1-\gamma_0)+(n-1)\gamma]$$

$$F3 = Y(k^*).$$

We see that with the low costs of forming links, the incentive constraint of an isolated firm is binding. As the costs of links increase, smaller dominant groups are sufficient to discourage an isolated firm from forming a link. This suggests that larger costs of links will sustain a wider range of dominant group sizes. However, there is a complication: once we move beyond a certain cost level, the incentive constraint for a firm in the dominant group comes to bind. This implies that at high cost levels, small and large dominant groups are not sustainable; only medium-sized groups are sustainable. Figure 16.10(b) summarizes these findings.

Our discussion draws attention to a number of points. We see that for a wide range of costs of linking, equilibrium networks will contain a moderate-sized dominant group. Networking opportunities give rise to asymmetries. These asymmetries are economically significant: firms in the dominant group have more links and lower costs than firms outside it. In a model of quantity competition, this means that they have a larger market share. We can go further and show that firms in the dominant group will also earn more profits. A question at the end of the chapter asks you to work through the computations.

The results in this section show how firms can use collaboration links as a strategy to create market dominance and increase profits. But the architecture of these networks differs from the empirically observed networks in one critical aspect: empirical networks have a core set of firms that have links with a large number of firms who are relatively poorly linked. Let us reexamine this model to understand the forces that may push one toward this architecture.

### 16.4.2 Transfers and Market Power

In our model, the marginal returns to a firm from an additional link are increasing in own links and declining in the links of others. When a high-degree firm forms a link with a low-degree firm, it earns a higher marginal payoff compared to the low-degree firm. Thus a high-degree firm may have an incentive to offer transfers to a low-degree firm to encourage link formation.

Let $t^i = \{t^i_{i1}, \ldots, t^i_{in}\} \in \mathbb{R}^n$, with $t^i_{ij}$ being the transfer from firm $i$ to firm $j$ on link $g_{ij}$. We will assume that $t^i_{ij} \geq 0$ for all $i, j \in N$, and $t^i_i = 0$ for all $i \in N$. Once transfers are allowed, a link is attractive for firms $i$ and $j$ so long as the joint marginal returns exceed the total costs of the link. Let us define a notion of stable networks that builds on the idea of pairwise equilibrium and incorporates this idea.

**Definition 16.2** *Network g is stable against transfers if the following is true:*

1. *For all* $g_{i,j} = 1$, $[\Pi_i(g) - \Pi_i(g - g_{ij})] + [\Pi_j(g) - \Pi_j(g - g_{i,j})] > 2c.$
2. *For all* $g_{i,j} = 0$, $[\Pi_i(g + g_{i,j}) - \Pi_i(g)] + [\Pi_j(g + g_{i,j}) - \Pi_j(g)] < 2c.$
3. *There are transfers* $t^i \in R^n$, $i = 1, 2, \ldots, n$ *such that*

$$\Pi_i(g) - \eta_i(g)c - \sum_{j \in N_i(g)} (t^i_{ij} - t^j_{ji}) \geq \Pi_i(g_{-i}), \tag{16.10}$$

where $\Pi_i(g_{-i})$ refers to the profit of firm $i$ after it deletes all its links.

As payoffs remain as before, it follows that there can be at most one nonsingleton component in a stable network. Note that the dominant group was sustained by the resistance of the isolated firm to forming a link. However, now a firm in the dominant group can offer a transfer to induce an isolated firm to form links. Moreover, once it forms a link with one isolated firm, the increase in total number of links among other firms lowers the marginal payoffs of any other isolated firm. However, the marginal returns to the dominant group go up, as it now has one more link. It turns out that the positive effect on the dominant firm dominates the negative effect on the isolated firm. As a result, once a dominant firm forms a link with one isolated firm, it will go all the way and form a link with all isolated firms (by suitably raising the transfers). We state this next, as a property that we will invoke to establish results about networks that are stable against transfers.

**Property** *Suppose that g is stable against transfers. If* $g_{i,j} = 1$ *for distinct* $i, j \in N$, *then* $g_{i,k} = 1$ *for all* $k \in N$, *such that* $\eta_k(g - g_{i,k}) \geq \eta_j(g - g_{i,j})$.

This property helps us establish that the star network is stable against transfers.

**Proposition 16.5** *Let $n \geq 4$. Suppose that payoffs are given by equation (16.5). Then there exist numbers $F_H$ and $F_L$, where $0 < F_L < F_H$, such that the star network is stable against transfers if and only if $c \in (F_L, F_H)$.*

Let us now work through the details of these computations to appreciate the role of transfers in generating market power and augmenting the profits of well-connected firms.

Suppose that $g^s$ is a star network; denote the central firm by $n$ and typical firms at the spokes by $i$ and $j$. If firm $n$ deletes all its links, then the resulting network is empty, $g^e$. If firm $i$ or firm $n$ deletes a link, then we get the network $g^s - g_{n,i}$. They will wish to maintain their link if

$$[\pi_n(g^s) - \pi_n(g^s - g_{n,i})] + [\pi_i(g^s) - \pi_j(g^s - g_{n,i})] > 2c. \tag{16.11}$$

The requirement that firms $i$ and $j$ have no incentive to form a link may be written as follows:

$$[\pi_i(g^s + g_{i,j}) - \pi_i(g^s)] + [\pi_j(g^s + g_{i,j}) - \pi_j(g^s)] < 2c. \tag{16.12}$$

We wish to define transfers such that firms have no incentive to isolate themselves by deleting all their links. There are transfers $t_i$, for $i = 1, 2, \ldots, n$, such that

$$\pi_n(g^s) - (n-1)c + \sum_{j \in N_n(g)} (t_j^n - t_n^j) \geq \pi_n(g^e)$$

$$\pi_i(g^s) - c + (t_n^i - t_i^n) \geq \pi_i(g^s - g_{n,i}), \forall i \in N \backslash \{n\}. \tag{16.13}$$

The gross profits for firms under different networks are

$$\pi_n(g^s) = \frac{[1 - \gamma_0 + (n-1)^2\gamma]^2}{(n+1)^2}, \quad \pi_n(g^e) = \frac{[1-\gamma_0]^2}{(n+1)^2},$$

$$\pi_n(g^s - g_{n,i}) = \frac{[1 - \gamma_0 + (n-2)(n-1)\gamma]^2}{(n+1)^2},$$

$$\pi_i(g^s) = \frac{[1 - \gamma_0 + (3-n)\gamma]^2}{(n+1)^2}, \quad \pi_i(g^s - g_{n,i}) = \frac{[1 - \gamma_0 - 2(n-2)\gamma]^2}{(n+1)^2},$$

$$\pi_i(g^s + g_{i,j}) = \frac{[1 - \gamma_0 + 2\gamma]^2}{(n+1)^2}. \tag{16.14}$$

After substituting for profits from equation (16.14) we can rewrite equation (16.11) as follows:

$$\frac{\gamma(n-1)[4(1-\gamma_0) + (n-1)\gamma(2n-3) - \gamma(3n-7)]}{(n+1)^2} > 2c.$$

Similarly, equation (16.12) can be rewritten as follows:

$$\frac{2\gamma(n-1)[2(1-\gamma_0) + \gamma(2-n+3)]}{(n+1)^2} < 2c. \tag{16.15}$$

Let us define $F'$ and $F_L$ as follows:

$$F' = \frac{\gamma(n-1)[4(1-\gamma_0)+(n-1)\gamma(2n-3)-\gamma(3n-7)]}{2(n+1)^2},$$

$$F_L = \frac{2\gamma(n-1)[2(1-\gamma_0)+\gamma(2-n+3)]}{2(n+1)^2}. \tag{16.16}$$

Equations (16.11) and (16.12) are satisfied if and only if the fixed costs are such that $F_L < f < F'$. It is easily verified that $F_L < F'$ if $n > 3$.

Finally, let us construct the transfers. For the star to be stable, it must be the case that the spokes have no incentive to form a link with each other. Given the symmetry in their situation, it follows that their marginal payoffs from the additional link are the same. This requirement, along with increasing returns, imply that if the star is to be stable, then it must be the case that each of the spoke firms also do not have any incentive to form a link with the central firm. Thus transfers have to be made by the central firm to each of the spokes. The minimum value of this transfer is given by

$$t_n^i = \pi_i(g^s - g_{n,i}) - \pi_i(g^s) + c. \tag{16.17}$$

Substituting the profit expressions from equation (16.14) in equation (16.17) yield us the following minimum value of transfer:

$$t_n^i = c - \frac{(n-1)\gamma[2(1-\gamma_0)-\gamma(3n-7)]}{(n+1)^2}. \tag{16.18}$$

We wish to show that the central firm has an incentive to make such transfers to each of the spoke firms rather than delete all links. This incentive is satisfied if and only if

$$\pi_n(g^s) - (n-1)(c+t_n^i) \geq \pi_n(g^e). \tag{16.19}$$

After some rearrangement, this requirement can be expressed as

$$\frac{(n-1)\gamma[4(1-\gamma_0)+(n-1)^2\gamma-\gamma(3n-7)]}{(n+1)^2} \geq 2c. \tag{16.20}$$

Define $F''$ as follows:

$$F'' = \frac{(n-1)\gamma[4(1-\gamma_0)+(n-1)^2\gamma-\gamma(3n-7)]}{2(n+1)^2}. \tag{16.21}$$

It can be verified that $F'' > F_L$, for all $n > 3$. Finally define $F_H = \min\{F', F''\}$. ■

Transfers are critical to the emergence of a star network. If the marginal returns of a peripheral firm from the link with the central firm are positive, then it follows, from the property of increasing returns in own links, that the peripheral firm would also want to form links with all the other peripheral firms. Thus a star is stable only in a situation where the links in the star are not individually profitable for the peripheral firms. In other words, all the links between the central firm and the peripheral firm are sustained by transfers from the central firm! The network is sustained by transfers from the central firm. It is possible to show that in spite of these transfers, the central firm earns a larger payoff than do the peripheral firms. A question at the end of the chapter works through these computations.

These arguments can be used to build a general description of networks that are stable against transfers. Consider a partition of firms (based on degree) $\{h_1(g), \ldots, h_m(g)\}$ with $h_l(g) \cap h_k(g) = \emptyset$ for $l \neq k$, and $\cup_{l=1}^{m} h_l(g) = N$. Following Mahadev and Peled (1995), we define a nested split graph.

**Definition 16.3** *A network g is said to have a nested split structure if*

1. *For $i \in h_1(g)$, $g_{i,j} = 1$ if and only if $j \in h_m(g)$.*
2. *If $g_{i,j} = 1$ for $i \in h_l(g)$ and $j \in h_{l'}(g)$, then $g_{i,k} = 1$ for any $k \in h_{l''}(g)$, where $l'' \geq l'$.*
3. *Suppose $i \in h_{m-l}(g)$. Then $g_{i,j} = 1$ if and only if $j \in h_k(g)$ for $k > l$.*

We note that as we move up the partition, the neighborhood of a firm in layer $l$ is nested within the neighborhood of firms in layer $l + 1$. Equipped with this definition, we establish the following result.

**Proposition 16.6** *Let $n \geq 4$ and $g \neq g^c$ be a connected network. If g is stable against transfers, then it has a nested, split-graph structure.*

Figure 16.11 presents nested split networks that are stable against transfers for $n = 6$. The reasoning underlying the nested split structure is as follows: Consider a connected network $g$ that is stable against transfers. Suppose that there is a firm $i \in h_{x_1}$. Since the network is connected, $\eta_i(g) \geq 1$. It is possible to show that firm $i$ does not form a link with any $j \notin h_{x_m}$. If $i$ did form a link, then from property (ii) in definition 16.2, it follows that firm $j$ would have a link with all firms (i.e., $j \in h_{x_m}$, a contradiction). Since $\eta_i(g) \geq 1$, it must form a link with $k \in h_{x_m}$, but then from property (ii) in definition 16.2 (on stable network against transfers), it follows that $\eta_k(g) = n - 1$, and so $x_m = n - 1$. A question at the end of the chapter works through the arguments that show how stability against transfers satisfies the properties of a nested split graph.

The discussion in this section has been carried out in a model where all firms compete in quantities and are present in a single market. It is possible to generalize the model to allow for firms to be active in multiple markets and for demand across markets to be interrelated. In such a setting, the incentives of a firm to conduct research would depend on the markets that it is active in, the presence of other in different markets, and in the interrelations across the markets. Building on our discussion in chapter 4, this economic setting may be represented as a game on a network. Galeotti, Goyal, and Kalbfuss (2022) show that firm research strategies, when firms compete in overlapping markets with interrelated demands, can be understood in terms of the principal components on the matrix that describes the

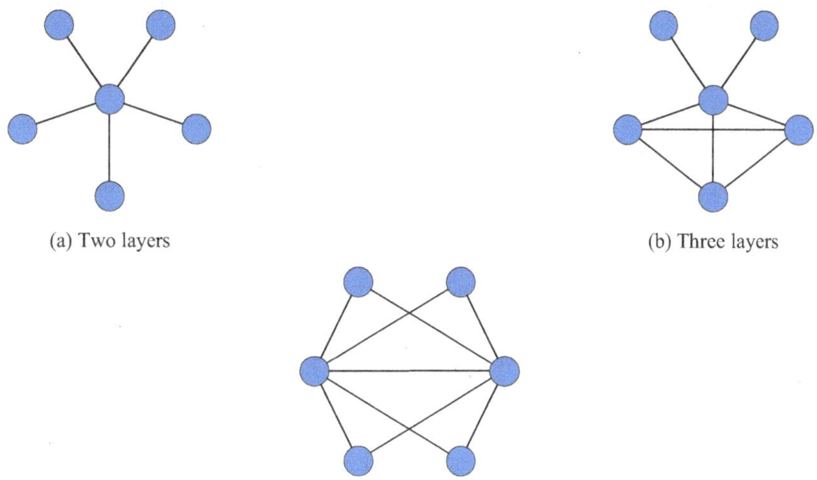

(a) Two layers

(b) Three layers

(c) Two layers

**Figure 16.11**
Nested-split graphs, $n = 6$.

interrelations of demands across markets. The study of which firms participate in which markets remains an open problem.

Now let us summarize what we have learned in this section. Research collaboration among firms has powerful effects on the competitive position of firms. These effects can be further reinforced if firms are allowed to make side payments and transfers—as would be involved, for instance, in technology exchange agreements between a large firm and a start-up. The reinforcement of advantages can give rise to nested-split graph structures. In these networks, firms earn very unequal profits.

## 16.5 Reading Notes

The study of exchange and power in social networks has a long tradition in sociology; for early contributions, see Homans (1961), Blau (2017), and Emerson (1976). It was recognized early on by these authors that a network creates possibilities for trade and bargaining power and gives rise to considerations of equity. Cook and Emerson (1978) present an early experiment on how network location shapes the division of surplus among the actors that prefigure some of the main themes of research, and Cook and Emerson (1987) provide a good summary of the early work in this field. For an overview of some of the sociology research on economic exchange and price formation, see Granovetter (2005).

The issues of bargaining power were central to early work on networks in economics (see, e.g., Myerson [1977b]). The role of networks was also highlighted in early work by

Kirman (1997); Weisbuch, Kirman, and Herreiner (2000); and Tesfatsion (1997). Starting with Corominas-Bosch (2004) and Polanski (2007), a number of papers in the economics literature have explored the issue of bargaining power in networks. In the model of Corominas-Bosch (2004), the bargaining process is centralized: a single price is announced to all linked traders at the same time. In recent work, Abreu and Manea (2012) study a model with decentralized matching: in every period, a single pair of linked traders is picked to bargain. They show that this change from centralization to decentralized trading can have large effects: bargaining may end in disagreement; a pair of traders may refuse to trade at one stage but agree to trade at a subsequent point. See Manea (2016) for an excellent overview of the research on bargaining in networks.

Price formation may be based on posted prices and auctions. We presented, very briefly, a discussion of auctions in networks. For an early and influential contribution to this subject, see Kranton and Minehart (2001). Our discussion, both in the bargaining problem and in the auction case, draws attention to the role of link formation in shaping the architecture of networks and the efficiency of the trading system. For a systematic exploration of inefficiencies in bilateral trading networks, see Elliott (2015) and Elliott and Nava (2019). Finally, it is worth noting that all the work we have discussed in this chapter assumes that traders know the network. The issue of price formation with imperfect information on valuations and networks remains an active field of research.

There is a large body of research on intermediaries, and it is clearly not possible to provide a good coverage of the main ideas within the space of a book chapter. In our choice of material, we have focused on research where networks play a central role. Condorelli and Galeotti (2016) provide a comprehensive overview of the theoretical literature. One way of organizing this large body of literature is to consider the price formation protocol used—auctions, bargaining, or posted prices. We have presented models with posted prices and bargaining and briefly discussed auctions. In addition to the papers mentioned in the chapter, we would like to mention the following other contributions. On posted prices, see Acemoglu and Ozdaglar (2007); on bargaining, see Gofman (2011) and Siedlarek (2015). We have restricted our attention to models where traders choose prices; for models where traders choose quantities, see Babus and Kondor (2018), Malamud and Rostek (2017), and Nava (2015).

In the model of bargaining presented in this chapter, it was assumed that every seller knows the value of the good to the buyers. In many settings, the value of the good is known to some traders, but not to other. Condorelli, Galeotti, and Renou (2017) study a situation where the good either has Low or High value to a trader. This valuation is independent of others' valuations and is private information. Trading proceeds as follows: the current owner makes a take-it-or-leave-it offer to a neighbor. If the neighbor accepts, then trade takes place; if not, then he makes an offer to other neighbors. The process of bargaining can reveal the private information of traders. The authors show that in equilibrium, High-valuation traders always consume the product they own, while Low-valuation traders seek out potential trading partners. The novelty relative to the earlier bilateral bargaining literature is that the search for a High-valuation trader will involve possibly many other traders in the network. A trader that lies on all paths between trader $i$ and the original seller is termed a critical node: such nodes earn higher payoffs. For a general discount factor $\delta \in (0, 1)$, the analysis is intricate, and trading exhibits complicated behavior: prices may be nonmonotonic and trading inefficient. However, in the limit, as $\delta \to 1$, trading is efficient: the traders will locate a High-valuation trader (if one exists).

Research collaboration among firms is widespread, with potentially important implications for the performance of firms and the functioning of the economy at large. The traditional approach to collaboration is to consider coalitions of firms; notable early contributions include Bloch (1995) and d'Aspremont and Jacquemin (1988). Following Goyal and Moraga-González (2001) and Goyal and Joshi (2003), there is now also a large body of literature on R&D networks. For a study of efficient R&D networks, see Westbrock (2010); for a systematic study of nested-split graphs, see König, Tessone, and Zenou (2014); and for a detailed study of empirical patterns on R&D networks, see König, Liu, and Hsieh (2021). For a mathematical treatment of nested-split graphs, the interested reader is referred to Mahadev and Peled (1995). We discussed a simple model based on oligopoly competition to bring out the economic aspects of collaboration. Research collaboration among firms has also been extensively studied in sociology, organization theory, and business strategy. We mention three themes in this work that bear upon R&D networks.

In the model of R&D alliances we presented, the implicit assumption is that there is no informational asymmetry between firms about skills and expertise or about the level of research effort. In practice, there will be significant informational asymmetries that will give rise to a variety of incentive problems (and large transaction costs). To mitigate these pressures, a firm may prefer repeated collaboration with existing partners or to collaborate with firms about whom they can get reliable information via existing and past common partners. These considerations inform the social embeddedness perspective in economic sociology; for instance, see Granovetter (1985); Powell Walter (1990); Gulati (2007); Raub and Weesie (1990); Shan, Walker, and Kogut (1994); and Podolny and Page (1998). Networks also shape the nature of contracts and governance structures on collaboration links among firms. Collaboration agreements become less formal if partners are embedded in social networks of previous collaboration links; for an overview of this research, see Gulati (2007).

A second comment pertains to the theoretical modeling. We assumed that firms could join any number of alliances, but these alliances were restricted to being bilateral. In actual practice, firms join multiple alliances, and the alliances typically have more than two partners. This suggests that a more natural model would involve firms that join multiple alliances, each of which may be of arbitrary size. See Ding, Dziubinski, and Goyal (2021) for a study of stable R&D alliance profiles in such a model.

Collaboration among scientists and academics raises somewhat related considerations, and there is a parallel strand of work that explores the role of networks in that sphere; for instance, see Goyal, van der Leij, and Moraga-González (2006); Fafchamps, Van der Leij, and Goyal (2010); and Ductor, Fafchamps, Goyal, and Van der Leij (2014). Fafchamps,

Van der Leij, and Goyal (2010) examine the formation of coauthor relations among economists over the period 1970–1999. They find that a new coauthor collaboration emerges faster between two researchers if they are closer in the preexisting coauthor network among economists. This proximity effect on collaboration is strong: being at a distance of 2 instead of 3 raises the probability of initiating a collaboration by 27 percent.

## 16.6 Questions

1. (From Jackson [2008]). Suppose that the assumptions of the Corominas-Bosch model hold. Apply the decomposition discussed in this chapter to compute the bargaining payoffs in the networks given in figure 16.12.

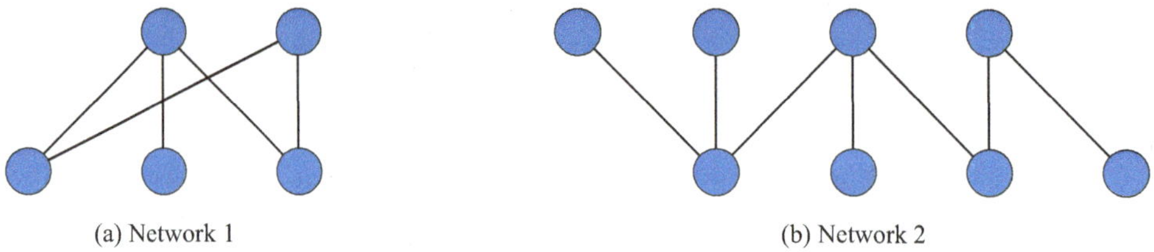


**Figure 16.12**
Buyer-seller networks.

2. Consider the Corominas-Bosch model and suppose that a link is two-sided and entails a cost of $c > 0$ for each trader. Show that if $c < 1/2$, then the efficient network will entail a maximal set of disjoint pairs. Show next that if $c < 1/2$ and the discount factor is close to 1, then pairwise-stable networks (as defined in chapter 3, on the costs and benefits of links) coincide with efficient networks.
3. Let us consider a market with price-setting firms. The sellers and buyers are located in a bipartite network. Every firm has a unit good to sell with reservation value 0. Consumers' utility from the good is 1 and is known to firms. Every firm sets a single price, and the network is commonly known.
   (a) Show that if two sellers are linked only to a single consumer, then they cannot set a price 1 in equilibrium.
   (b) If there is a consumer who is linked to only one seller, then the seller who is linked to this captive consumer can always make a profit of 1.
   (c) Consider a network with three sellers and three consumers. Seller 1 is linked to consumers 1 and 2, seller 2 is linked only to consumer 2, and seller 3 is linked to consumers 2 and 3.
      (i) Compute the pricing equilibrium in this network.

(ii) Compute the outcome of the Corominas-Bosch bargaining game in this network.

(iii) How would you explain the differences in prices and allocations of surplus in these two games?

4. Consider the model of auctions in networks considered in section 16.2.2. Suppose that stage 2 is as presented there but that in stage 1, linking is two-sided. Suppose that a seller and a buyer both have to pay cost $c$ for a link to be created. Examine the incentives to create links and compare efficient and pairwise-stable networks in that example.

5. (From Easley and Kleinberg [2010]). Consider the trading model with a single layer of intermediaries, as in section 16.3. Suppose there are two buyers (B1 and B2), two sellers (S1 and S2), and two intermediary traders (T1 and T2). The sellers each have one unit of the object and value it at 0. The buyers each demand one unit and value it at 1. The network is as follows: seller S1 and Buyer B1 can trade only with intermediary T1, seller S2 and Buyer B2 can trade with both intermediaries T1 and T2. The pricing protocol is as explained in section 16.3.

   (a) Check if these prices and this flow of goods constitutes an equilibrium of the trading game.

      (i) T1's bid price to Seller S1 is 0, his bid price to Seller S2 is 1/2, his ask price to Buyer B1 is 1, and his ask price to Buyer B2 is 1/2. T2's bid price to Seller S2 is 1/2 and his ask price to Buyer B2 is 1/2.

      (ii) One unit of the good flows from Seller S1 to Buyer B1 through Trader T1; and, one unit of the good flows from Seller S2 to Buyer B2 through trader T2.

   (b) Suppose now that we add a third trader (T3) who can trade with Seller S1 and Buyer B1. This trader cannot trade with the other seller or buyer, and the rest of the trading network remains unchanged. Check if these prices and this flow of goods constitutes an equilibrium of the trading game.

      (i) The prices on the old edges are unchanged from those in the part above.

      (ii) The prices on the new edges are: a bid of 1/2 to Seller S1 by Trader T3 and an ask of 1/2 to Buyer B1 by Trader T3.

      (iii) The flow of goods is the same as in the part above.

6. Consider the trading model with a single layer of intermediaries, as in section 16.3. Suppose there are S sellers, B buyers, and T intermediary traders. Show that (i) every Nash equilibrium of this game results in an efficient outcome (every possible beneficial trade is realized). (ii) an intermediary trader earns profits in equilibrium only if it is essential.

7. Consider the model of posted-pricing by intermediaries as in section 16.3.1. There is a single SOURCE and a single DESTINATION and a collection of $n$ intermediary traders

located on nodes of an undirected connected network in between the source and destination. The value of exchange is 1. The network of traders and the valuations are common knowledge. Traders post prices simultaneously; they have zero costs. Source and destination compare the costs of different paths and choose the lowest cost path if it is less than 1 (randomizing across paths if there are multiple lowest cost paths). Source and destination divide the residual surplus equally, after paying the cost of the path.

(a) Suppose $n = 8$. Consider a line network with source at one end and destination at other end. Describe an equilibrium price profile with trade and another equilibrium price profile with no trade.

(b) Suppose $n = 8$. Consider a circle network with source and destination that are maximal distance apart. Describe an equilibrium price profile with trade and another equilibrium price profile with no trade.

(c) An equilibrium outcome is said to be efficient if trade takes place with certainty. Show that for any network there exists an efficient pure strategy Nash equilibrium.

8. Consider the model of posted-pricing by intermediaries as in section 16.3.1. There is a single SOURCE and a single DESTINATION and a collection of $n$ intermediary traders located on nodes of an undirected connected network in between the source and destination. The value of exchange is unknown and has a uniform distribution on unit interval. The network of traders is common knowledge. Traders have zero costs and post prices simultaneously. Source and destination compare the costs of different paths and choose the lowest cost path if it is less than the valuation (randomizing across paths if there are multiple lowest cost paths). Source and destination divide the residual surplus equally, after paying the cost of the path.

   (a) Consider a line network with source at one end and destination at other end. Describe an equilibrium price profile for $n = 3$ and $n = 4$. Compute the corresponding probability of trade

   (b) Next consider a line with $n$ intermediary traders: compute a symmetric equilibrium price and the corresponding probability of trade as a function of number of traders $n$.

9. Consider the model of bargaining among intermediaries in section 16.3.2. Suppose that final buyer has a valuation, suppose that the final buyer has a valuation of 1 and each trader has a small but positive transaction cost, $c$. Consider the network in figure 16.13. Using the ideas of critical traders and bargaining power, show that in equilibrium, the object will move via intermediary 1 or 2 and it reaches the final buyer via at least three intermediaries.

10. (From Goyal and Joshi [2003]). Consider the two-stage model of network formation and price or quantity competition (as discussed in section 16.4). Show that with small costs of linking, the complete network maximizes social surplus with quantity competition,

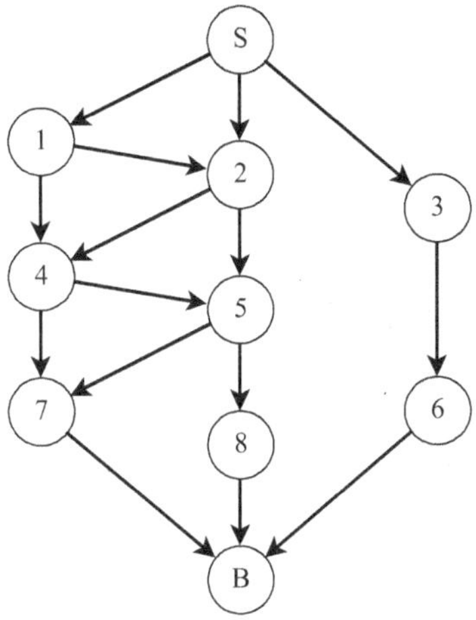


**Figure 16.13**
Short and long paths.

while a network with two maximally connected firms maximizes social welfare under price competition.

11. Consider the model of network formation and quantity competition as presented in section 16.4. Show that in a pairwise equilibrium network, firms in the dominant group earn higher profits as compared to isolate firms.

12. Consider the model of network formation and quantity competition with transfers as presented in section 16.4.2. Show that in the star network, the central firms earns higher profits than do the peripheral firms.

13. Consider the model of network formation and quantity competition with transfers presented in section 16.4.2. This question works through different properties of networks that are stable against transfers.

    (a) Suppose that $g$ is connected and not complete. Show that it must contain firms with different degrees. Use property (ii) in definition 16.2 on stable against transfers to establish that there must be a difference of at least two degrees between any two firms who have different degrees.

    (b) Note that if $i, j \in h_1(g)$ and $g$ is connected, then $\eta_i \geq 1$. Next, show that $i$ cannot be connected to a firm outside $h_m(g)$. So it must be connected to a firm in $h_m(g)$. Then apply property (ii) in definition 16.2 on stable against transfers to show that a firm with the highest degree must have degree $n - 1$.

    (c) Apply Property (ii) in definition 16.2 on stable against transfers to establish part (ii) in the definition 16.3 of nested split networks.

(d) Property (iii) in definition 16.3 of nested split graphs is proved using an argument by induction. Start with $l = 1$ and show that if $i \in h_{m-1}(g)$, then $g_{i,j} = 0$ for $j \in h_1(g)$. Next, suppose that the hypothesis is true for $\hat{l} \geq 1$, and show that it also holds for $\hat{l} + 1$.

14. Consider the model of network formation and quantity competition as presented in section 16.4. Suppose that the firms initially have different costs of production. Discuss how this might alter incentives for linking and might shape networks.

15. Consider the model of network formation and quantity competition as presented in section 16.4. Next, suppose a setting in which firms have different costs of linking. A natural way to model such differences is to suppose that firms can be divided into groups based on cultural, legal, market, or geographical proximity. The costs are low within a group but high across the groups. Reason about how such differences in costs of links can shape networks.

# 17 Communities and Economic Growth

## 17.1 Introduction

> Modern economic growth of nations has two distinctive features: in *all* cases it involves a sustained and substantial rise in product per capita, and in *almost all cases* it involves a sustained and substantial rise in population. . . . implying even higher rates of growth of total product.
> —(Kuznets 1961, p. 14)

> It has long been the majority view among sociologists, anthropologists, political scientists, and historians that . . . (economic) behavior was heavily embedded in social relations in premarket societies but became much more autonomous with modernization. This view sees the economy as an increasingly separate, differentiated sphere in modern society, with economic transactions defined no longer by the social or kinship obligations of those transacting but by rational calculations of individual gain.
> —(Granovetter 1985, p. 482).

This chapter studies the role of communities in the process of economic growth and development. Sustained economic growth can have very large effects on income over time—a rate of increase of 20 percent per decade means a rise of 6.7 times the initial value over a century; over two centuries, this growth rate will lead to an income level over 38 times the initial level. These rates appear to be high but were realized by a number of countries, including Sweden, the US, and France, during the period 1850–1900. During 1950–1990, a number of other countries—such as South Korea and Japan—registered still higher rates. Finally, in the years since 1980, China (and, in later years, India) have recorded even higher growth rates. As economic growth is closely associated with changes in a number of quality-of-life indicators, its impact on human well-being over a period of time can be enormous.

However, one of the enduring facts about economic growth is that it remains very uneven. A number of countries have achieved sustained growth over the past 200 years, but there still are a fairly large number of countries where growth has been slow and a few where growth has barely occurred. This unevenness leads to an examination of the sources of economic growth:

> . . . a rise in per capita product usually means an even larger rise in product per unit of labor input—since some of the extra product is ordinarily exchanged for more leisure, a concomitant of a higher standard of living. However, marked rises in product per labor unit, when population and therefore labor force are increasing, are usually possible only through major innovations, i.e., applications of new bodies of tested knowledge to the processes of economic production. . . . But this also means structural change as new industries appear and old industries recede in importance—which, in turn, calls for the capacity of society to absorb such changes: society must be able to accommodate itself to and adopt the successive innovations that raise per capita productivity.
> —(Kuznets 1961, p. 14).

If development is about creating new knowledge and investing in its uses to create new products and services, differences in growth must lie in the various responses to new innovations.

We start by briefly recalling the common features of economic development across time and space. The discussion then discusses specific cases relating to migration, education, and investments in trade and industry, where we can see varying responses by societies to similar opportunities. We examine the role of communities in explaining these differences.

Communities, and more generally social networks, perform a number of functions in developing countries. An important role is to support business activity: a small number of communities dominate the trade and manufacturing sectors in many developing countries—for instance, expatriate Indian communities dominated East African business during and even after British colonial rule until the 1970s, and ethnic Chinese have controlled business in South East Asia, and this dominance may have grown with trade liberalization. In India, a small number of Hindu castes and non-Hindu communities continue to dominate business activity. A second role for community connections is to find jobs for their members. Friends and members of the origin community in Europe helped secure jobs for migrants to the American Midwest during the nineteenth and early twentieth centuries. A caste-based working class formed in the Indian cities that grew under British colonial rule and remain prominent to this day. A third role for community-based networks is to provide insurance for their members. Private-sector and state provision of insurance is limited—agrarian economies face weather-related uncertainties that generate fluctuations in income. Social arrangements provide wide-ranging help to households in the face of such shocks in smoothing their consumption.

These functions of community-based networks interact powerfully with the opportunities that the development process opens up for individuals: in this chapter, we present three empirical case studies—on migration, patterns of education choice, and the transition from agriculture to manufacturing—to illustrate this point. These case studies motivate an inquiry into the role of social structure in shaping individual responses.

It is helpful to place the discussion of change and the take up of new opportunities in a broader context. The issue of social coordination and change was taken up in a number of earlier chapters: we studied the weakest-link games in chapter 4 and the issue of technological change in markets with network externalities in chapter 8. Chapter 12 discussed the issue of social coordination and we studied the responsiveness to different social structures to new, possibly welfare enhancing, social norms.

In this chapter, we build on these discussions in earlier chapters to propose a new model that locates individuals in a social network and considers their level of engagement in a network activity and their take-up of a market opportunity. Network activity involves personalized interactions and reciprocal exchanges—the returns to an individual from taking part in it are thus increasing in the number of their neighbors who are also active in networks. The market opportunity is anonymous, and agents are price-takers. The key issue is the relation between network activity and market opportunity: we say that they are substitutes if greater network activity lowers the returns from market opportunity and complements if greater network activity enhances the returns from market opportunity.

As returns from network activity are increasing in the number of neighbors who take it up, we can use the analysis of games of complements from chapter 4, on network structure and human behavior. There, we drew attention to the role of a *q-core* of the network as the maximal group of active individuals. Building on that analysis, we show that when networks and markets are substitutes, individuals within the q-core stay out of the market opportunity, while those outside it take it up. By contrast, when the two activities are complements, individuals within the relevant q-core take up both the network and market activity, while those outside the q-core remain inactive on both dimensions. Denser networks lead to larger q-cores: in the case of substitutes, this will mean a lower take-up of market opportunity and in the case of complements, it will mean a higher level of take-up.

New market opportunities can in principle benefit or harm a society. Our analysis reveals that when network activity and market opportunity are substitutes, the appearance of markets can leave everyone worse off due to negative externalities of people moving out of social networks. On the other hand, in the complements case, taking up market opportunity raises participation in the network and therefore creates positive spillovers for everyone, thereby necessarily raising social welfare. Our model also sheds light on the question of whether new market opportunities raise or lower inequality. In the substitutes case, inequality in the traditional society is necessarily lowered; in the complements case, the converse holds.

We next turn to the effects of economic change on social structure. A key feature of the process of economic growth is the movement of labor from agriculture to manufacturing and the service industry. This is accompanied with a corresponding movement of people from the rural countryside to the cities. The salience of this large-scale process has led many scholars to take the position that, while economic life historically was bound up with social relations (involving family and close friends), modern economic life is largely divorced from such ties. We present a number of empirical studies concerning the expansion of market activity to illustrate the capacity of social ties to metamorphose and reconfigure in response.

In some cases, social ties weaken, while in other cases they strengthen. These case studies thus pose a challenge to the traditional perspective on the role of social ties in economic activity. We conclude by arguing that the economic principle of whether markets and social ties are complements or substitutes is also helpful in understanding these empirical patterns on the evolution of social networks over time.

## 17.2 The Patterns of Economic Growth

We start by presenting basic statistics on per capita income for a group of countries in table 17.1. The obvious point to note is that even in 2018, after almost a century of political movements and research on the determinants of economic growth, the differences in per capita income across countries remain very great. There are countries like Australia, the US, and Germany with per capita incomes in excess of $55,000, and at the same time, we have several large countries, such as Bangladesh, Congo, and Kenya, with per capita incomes below $2,000.

**Table 17.1**
Per capita incomes

| Countries | US Dollars | PPP |
|---|---|---|
| Australia | 57,396 | 51,036 |
| Bangladesh | 1698 | 4550 |
| Belgium | 47,472 | 52,254 |
| Brazil | 9001 | 14,952 |
| Canada | 46,234 | 49,994 |
| China | 9771 | 15,376 |
| Congo | 561 | 1111 |
| Egypt | 2549 | 11,643 |
| France | 41,470 | 46,447 |
| Germany | 47,615 | 54,456 |
| Ghana | 2202 | 5302 |
| India | 2010 | 6,697 |
| Indonesia | 3893 | 11,646 |
| Kenya | 1710 | 4294 |
| Japan | 39,289 | 41,473 |
| Mexico | 9,673 | 20,396 |
| Nigeria | 2028 | 5281 |
| Pakistan | 1,482 | 4,855 |
| South Korea | 31,380 | 39,661 |
| Russia | 11,288 | 28,556 |
| South Africa | 6,374 | 12,938 |
| Turkey | 9370 | 28,139 |
| UK | 42,962 | 46,868 |
| US | 62,887 | 62,887 |

*Source*: World Bank 2018.

These numbers give a first impression of the range of income levels; this variation remains very great even after adjustments are made for price and commodity bundle differences across countries. For instance, even at purchasing power parity (PPP), a number of large countries have per capita income in 2018 that is less than one-tenth of the per capita income of the US.

We noted in the introduction to this chapter how even small rates of per capita growth can lead to a massive aggregate change if they are sustained over 50 or 100 years. The other side to this observation is that starting from a certain income today and moving back in time, a relatively short stretch of time will bring us to a point where income is very low. Indeed, it would be difficult to sustain life if income were any lower. In other words, *sustained economic growth is very much a modern phenomenon.* It is this realization that inspires the hope that differences in per capita income can be bridged relatively quickly, if only there were a good understanding of the process of economic growth.

Table 17.2 presents the growth rates of select countries over the past 50 and 100 years. There are enormous variations in growth rates—as noted in the introduction, some countries, like Japan and South Korea, have sustained rates of growth of income of over 50 percent for every decade over that 50-year period. Even more impressively, China's per capita income has grown 65 percent every decade. On the other hand, a number of large countries have hardly registered any growth—for instance, Congo actually registered a decline in per capita income, Ghana grew by 8.5 percent, and Argentina grew at the modest rate of 13 percent per decade over the past 50 years.

It is important to bear in mind the difference in the environment for the first countries that created sustained economic growth—such as England and France—compared to the situation faced by poor countries in the contemporary world. This point is brought out by the next set of data on the income of these countries over the past 25 years. Table 17.3 presents per capita income (in terms of PPP) on the same set of countries, but now expressed as a ratio of the US per capita. We see that while some countries like China have registered large gains, but that other countries have registered little movement, and several countries (e.g., Pakistan, Congo, and South Africa) have actually fallen further behind.

The income levels may be seen as creating different levels of opportunity for the populations of these countries. But it is possible to go beyond opportunity and to look directly at measures of human well-being. Figure 17.1 suggests that literacy can range from 40 percent to 100 percent and life expectancy can range from 55 to 85 years. These are an extraordinarily wide ranges. In addition, it is interesting to observe that the two quality-of-life indicators are highly correlated with per capita income, up to the point where a country attains a per capita income of around \$20,000. Robert Lucas sums up the power of these data as follows:

> Rates of growth of real per-capita income are ... diverse, even over sustained periods ... Indian incomes will double every 50 years; Korean every 10. An Indian will, on average, be twice as well off as his grandfather; a Korean 32 times .... We do not see how one can look at figures like these without seeing them as representing possibilities. Is there some action a government of India could take that would lead the Indian economy to grow like Indonesia's or Egypt's? If so, what, exactly?

**Table 17.2**
Percent change per decade—past 50 and 100 years

| Countries | PC Income 50 Yrs | Pop. 50 Yrs | PC Income 100 Yrs | Pop. 100 Yrs |
|---|---|---|---|---|
| Argentina | 13.86 | 16.83 | 11.66 | 23.05 |
| Australia | 26.07 | 18.17 | 19.16 | 17.68 |
| Bangladesh | 17.98 | 24.53 | N/A | N/A |
| Belgium | 30.56 | 3.51 | 19.75 | 4.33 |
| Brazil | 27.97 | 26.96 | 24.61 | 25.64 |
| Canada | 24.95 | 17.29 | 21.59 | 19.01 |
| China | 65.82 | 18.22 | 29.72 | 12.18 |
| Colombia | 24.28 | 27.99 | 25.78 | 25.84 |
| Congo | −18.62 | 33.59 | N/A | 18.56 |
| Egypt | 35.15 | 26.42 | N/A | 21.36 |
| France | 28.25 | 7.53 | 22.10 | 4.18 |
| Germany | 29.00 | 3.75 | 20.70 | 4.22 |
| Ghana | 8.61 | 30.36 | N/A | 21.57 |
| India | 36.09 | 22.84 | 17.19 | 13.44 |
| Indonesia | N/A | N/A | N/A | N/A |
| Iran | 29.02 | 31.07 | N/A | 20.26 |
| Japan | 50.29 | 8.53 | 33.17 | 11.08 |
| Kenya | 9.67 | 38.08 | N/A | 22.13 |
| Mexico | 22.94 | 28.53 | 17.43 | 22.07 |
| Nigeria | 16.91 | 29.39 | N/A | 21.60 |
| Pakistan | 31.28 | 29.99 | N/A | N/A |
| South Korea | 80.76 | 17.58 | N/A | 16.82 |
| Russia | N/A | 7.55 | N/A | N/A |
| South Africa | 12.36 | 29.42 | 13.29 | 24.66 |
| Turkey | 31.27 | 26.09 | N/A | N/A |
| UK | 25.46 | 3.50 | 18.14 | 3.76 |
| US | 23.52 | 13.13 | 20.69 | 13.96 |

*Source*: World Bank (2018).

If not, what is it about the "nature of India" that makes it so? The consequences for human welfare involved in questions like these are simply staggering: once one begins to think about them, it is hard to think about anything else.
Lucas (1988, pp. 4–5)

### 17.2.1 Growth, Structural Transformation, and Technology

One way to describe economic growth is to say that it involves a change in the types of economic activity that are undertaken by a society. This can be seen in changes in the allocation of labor force and aggregate output across broad sectors of the economy. It is customary to separate economic activity in three sectors—agriculture and related industries, such as forestry and fishing; mining, manufacturing, and construction; and all other activities. Perhaps the most striking change in the process of economic growth is in the share of agriculture. Figure 17.2 presents the relation between the share of agriculture in labor force and the share of agriculture in national income, in relation to per capita income.

**Table 17.3**
Per capita incomes relative to US

| Countries | 1990 | 2000 | 2015 |
|---|---|---|---|
| Argentina | 30.12 | 31.98 | 35.23 |
| Australia | 72.55 | 72.43 | 81.44 |
| Bangladesh | 3.56 | 3.66 | 6.26 |
| Belgium | 78.09 | 76.50 | 81.33 |
| Brazil | 28.05 | 24.94 | 25.95 |
| Canada | 84.35 | 80.54 | 78.43 |
| China | 4.11 | 8.04 | 22.75 |
| Colombia | 20.88 | 18.33 | 24.46 |
| Congo | 3.70 | 1.23 | 1.59 |
| Egypt | 15.55 | 15.95 | 19.98 |
| France | 73.76 | 71.83 | 71.91 |
| Germany | 81.33 | 74.88 | 83.92 |
| Ghana | 5.18 | 4.88 | 9.01 |
| India | 5.03 | 5.77 | 9.62 |
| Indonesia | 12.90 | 13.06 | 18.03 |
| Iran | 30.21 | 28.37 | 23.35 |
| Japan | 81.89 | 73.86 | 71.09 |
| Kenya | 6.18 | 4.45 | 5.92 |
| Mexico | 33.83 | 30.52 | 32.18 |
| Nigeria | 8.62 | 6.35 | 9.55 |
| Pakistan | 8.10 | 7.26 | 7.70 |
| South Korea | 34.63 | 49.77 | 62.93 |
| Russia | 33.53 | 18.78 | 42.39 |
| South Africa | 26.88 | 21.23 | 22.09 |
| Turkey | 35.66 | 26.38 | 45.10 |
| UK | 70.41 | 72.69 | 74.83 |
| US | 100.00 | 100.00 | 100.00 |

*Source*: World Bank (2018).

We see that the share of agriculture in labor force moves from 80 percent to 1 percent, and the share of agriculture in national income similarly moves from 50 percent to 1 percent, as we go from the very poor to the richest countries. This is a very robust feature of economic growth—an increase in per capita income is accompanied by a significant fall in the importance of agriculture as a share of the national economy.

The rural-urban relation is central to the process of economic growth. There are two flows in this relation—that of labor from farms to factories and that of food from agriculture to cities to feed workers who have left the farms. Figure 17.3 presents the relation between per capita income and share of rural population. We see that the share of rural population falls progressively as we move up the income levels—all the way from 80 percent to less than 20 percent.

In the first half of the twentieth century, theories of growth and development were deeply concerned about the relationship between agriculture and the rest of the economy. There was an early realization that agriculture must be able to spare labor, and productivity must grow

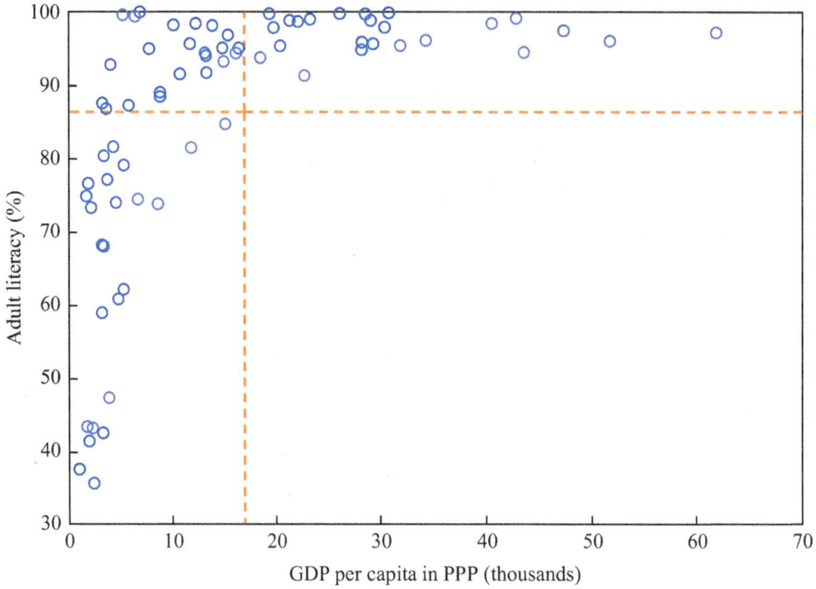


(a) Literacy

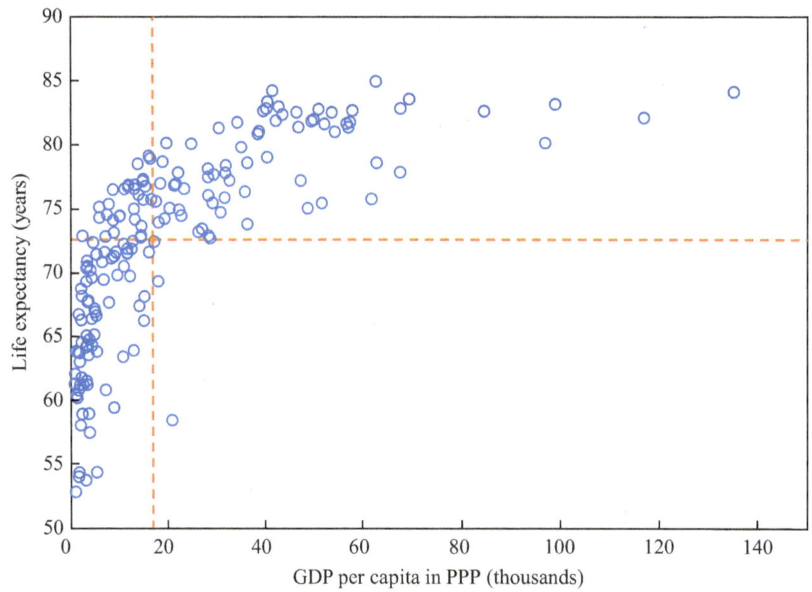


(b) Life expectancy

**Figure 17.1**
Quality of life and per capita income. *Source*: World Bank (2018).

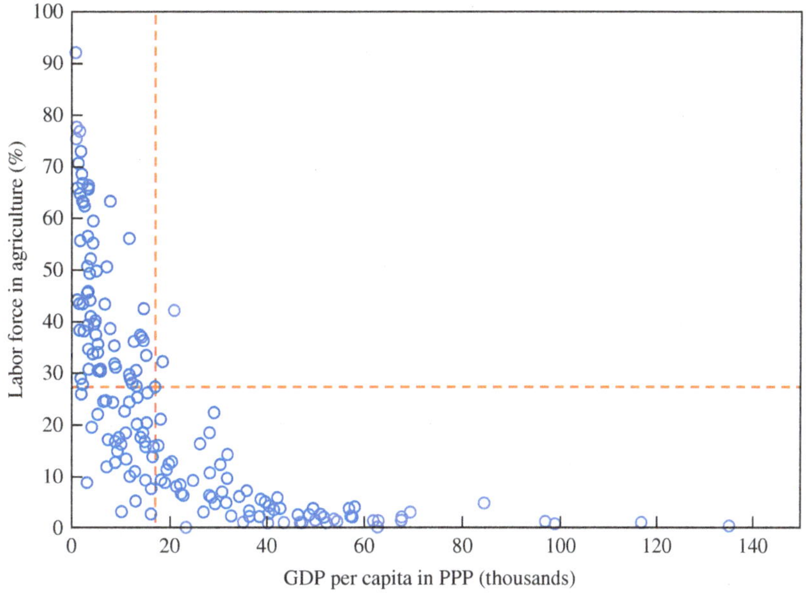


(a) Share in labor force

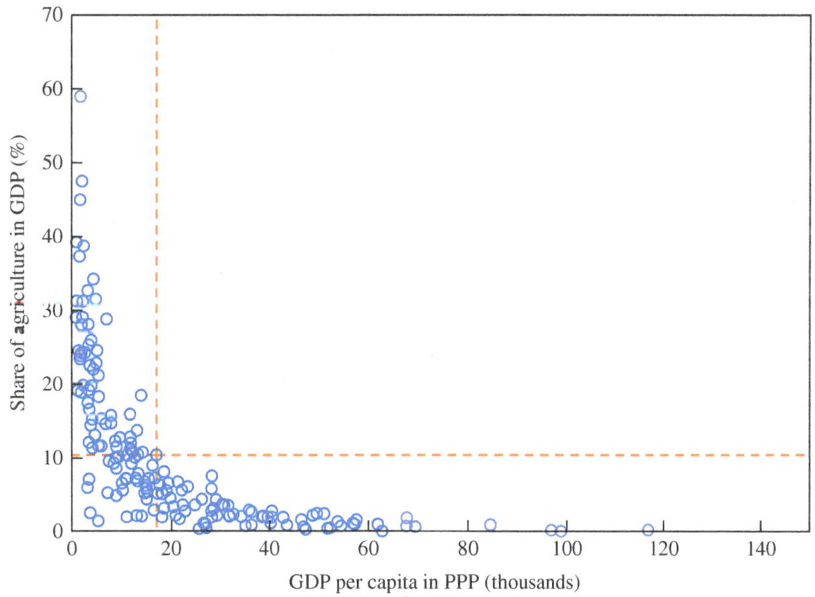


(b) Share in national income

**Figure 17.2**
Agriculture in economy. *Source*: World Bank 2018.

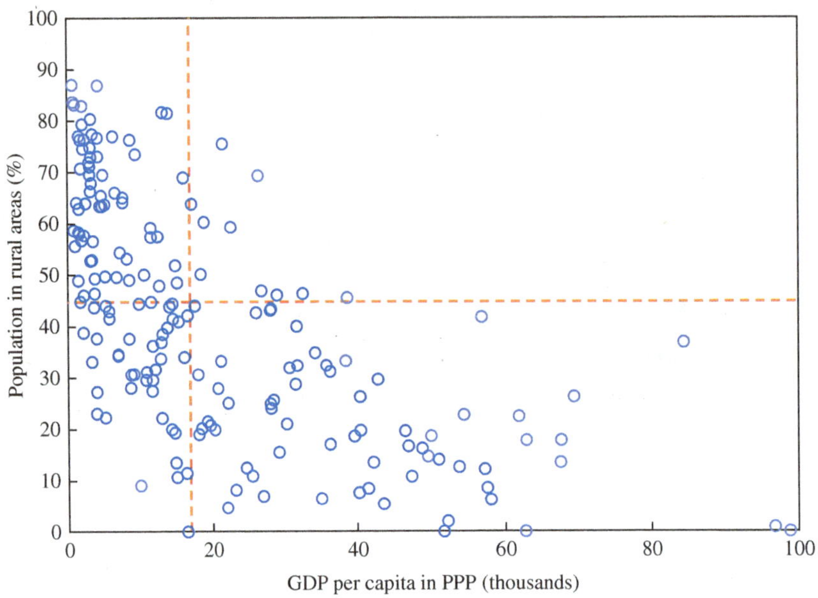


**Figure 17.3**
Share of rural population. *Source*: World Bank 2018.

in agriculture so that it could feed the laborers who were moving to industry. Fundamental to this process of growth, therefore, was the relocation of labor away from villages and countryside to cities—in other words, large-scale migration.

However, this raises the question: once labor has moved to manufacturing, what are the possibilities for further growth? Our discussion in the introduction suggests that ever-widening circles of scientific discovery and continuous technological change are central to sustained economic growth.

Ever-widening circles of scientific discovery and continuous technological change are central to sustained economic growth:

> Continuous technological progress and, underlying it, a series of new scientific discoveries are a necessary condition for the high rate of modern growth in per capita income combined with a substantial rate of growth in population. As evidence, we need only note the industries that loom large in an advanced economy: many of the electrical, internal combustion, and chemical fields were entirely unknown a hundred years ago, and even the older industries are permeated by processes whose origin lies in relatively recent scientific discoveries.
> Kuznets (1961, pp. 29–30).

This suggests that one way to understand the uneven rates of growth in different countries is to examine the ways that communities and social structure shape the take up of new opportunities.

## 17.3 Traditional Society and New Opportunities

In this section we discuss the historical experience of societies to new economic opportunities in relation to migration, to education, and investments in trade and manufacturing.

**Example 17.1** *Economic growth in China*

China has witnessed the same degree of industrialization in three decades as Europe had over the course of two centuries; for a discussion on this growth, see Greif and Tabellini (2017). This economic transformation began in the early 1980s with the establishment of township-village enterprises and accelerated with the entry of private firms in the 1990s. Starting with almost no private firms in 1990, there were 15 million registered private firms in 2014 (they accounted for over 90 percent of all registered firms in the country). Alongside this growth in numbers, the share of registered capital held by private firms has grown sharply: by 2014, private firms held 60 percent of all registered capital in the economy. China's growth has had profound effects on the flow of goods and services and capital and on the balance of political influence across the world.

Governments at the local (county), provincial, and central levels played an important role in China's economic transformation. There still remains the question of how this growth in private firms occurred without effective legal systems and well-functioning financial institutions (i.e., without the preconditions generally believed to be necessary for market-based development). How did millions of individuals born in rural areas transition into the role of entrepreneurs, setting up and successfully running such a vast array of extraordinarily successful companies? ■

**Example 17.2** *Rural-urban migration differences*

We have seen that a central element in the process of economic development is the transformation of the economy from one in which most people work in agriculture and live in villages to an economy in which most people work in manufacturing or services and live in cities. The pace of rural to urban migration is thus a key factor in economic development, and there are big differences in this rate. Our discussion here draws on Munshi and Rosenzweig (2016).

In India, the rural-urban wage gap (after correcting for cost-of-living differences) was 25 percent in 2000—this gap is large, and it has remained so for decades. This gap is also significantly larger than the wage gap in other large, developing countries such as China and Indonesia—one estimate puts the difference as large as 16 percent higher in India. This large wage gap is accompanied by relatively low levels of rural-urban migration in India. For instance, the rate of rural-urban migration as a fraction of rural population was around 5.34 percent for India in 2005, while it was close to 14 percent for Brazil for 1997.

The low migration mobility in India is reflected in its urbanization rates. For the period 1975–2000, consider the relative rates across four large, developing countries: Indonesia,

China, India, and Nigeria. Urbanization in all four countries was low in 1975—around 15–20 percent of the population lived in cities. However, India fell far behind the rest by 2000—the fraction of urbanized population is almost 15 percent less than in the other three countries. What are the reasons for these differences in migration rates across these countries? ■

**Example 17.3** *Education*

One of the commonly observed features of economic growth is that literacy becomes universal and large sections of the population go in for secondary and postsecondary school education. There are major differences in the rate at which education is adopted by different countries and by different communities within a country. We briefly explore the take-up of English-language education in Mumbai for the purpose of bringing out the role of social networks in shaping take-up rates. The discussion here draws on Munshi and Rosenzweig (2006).

Mumbai was a leading manufacturing center in India throughout the twentieth century. In the last decade of the century, larger-scale liberalization of the Indian economy led to a shift in the city's economy toward the corporate and financial sectors. Jobs in these sectors required a knowledge of English, unlike most jobs in the manufacturing sector. As these sectors expanded, the returns to learning English grew substantially. Over the period 1980–2000, the returns to years of schooling increased only slightly for both men and women. On the other hand, the English premium increased sharply, rising from 15 percent in 1980 to 24 percent in 2000 for men, and from negligible in 1980 to 27 percent in 2000 for women.

This rise in returns to learning English elicited a strong response from families with children of school age children: enrollment rates in English-medium schools grew significantly for both boys and girls, and for all castes. At the start, in 1980, there were large differences across castes in the take-up of English-language schooling for both boys and girls. The fraction of high-caste boys and other (medium and low) castes going to English-language schools was 45 percent and 10 percent, respectively, while the fraction of high-caste girls and other castes going to English-language schools was 35 percent and 15 percent, respectively. Over the period 1980–2000, the differences across castes persist for boys but narrow significantly for girls: the fraction of high-caste boys and other castes going to English-language schools was 60 percent and 35 percent, respectively, while the fraction of high-caste girls and other castes going to English-language schools was 45 percent and 35 percent, respectively. Why did lower-caste boys fail to take advantage of this new economic opportunity as well as the lower-caste girls? ■

We now present a theoretical model to help us uncover a number of general principles that can help us understand the relation between social networks and market opportunities.

## 17.4 A Theoretical Model

We present a model taken from Gagnon and Goyal (2017). There is a community with $n$ individuals. The social relations between these individuals are reflected in a social network, $g$. Ties are binary and undirected: $g_{ij} \in \{0, 1\}$ for any pair of individuals $i$ and $j$. Individuals can take part in network activity $x$ (this could be sharing labor services or sharing income) and a market opportunity $y$ (such as learning a language, migrating, or investing in a new enterprise). Suppose for simplicity that both $x$ and $y$ are binary—$x_i \in \{0, 1\}$ and $y_i \in \{0, 1\}$. Let $a_i$ denote the action choice of person $i$ and let $\mathbf{a}$ denote the profile of actions chosen. A key variable is the number of neighbors who choose the network opportunity. Let

$$\chi_i(\mathbf{a}) = \sum_{j \in N_i(\mathbf{g})} x_j \tag{17.1}$$

be the number of neighbors who choose the network action, and let $\Phi_i(\mathbf{a} \mid \mathbf{g})$ denote individual $i$'s payoffs under action profile $\mathbf{a}$ in network $\mathbf{g}$. If an individual abstains from network exchange, then the network does not affect their payoffs: choosing $x_i = 0$ may be thus interpreted as "leaving the network." If an individual chooses inactivity, $a_i = (0, 0)$, then they earn 0. The payoffs to the market action by itself (i.e., $a_i = (0, 1)$), are given by $\pi_y \in \mathbb{R}$. If individual $i$ chooses $a_i = (1, 0)$, her payoffs are given by $\phi_0(\chi_i(\mathbf{a}))$, and if the individual chooses $a_i = (1, 1)$, they are given by $\phi_1(\chi_i(\mathbf{a}))$. To summarize,

$$\Phi_i(\mathbf{a} \mid \mathbf{g}) = \begin{cases} 0, & \text{if } a_i = (0,0) \\ \pi_y, & \text{if } a_i = (0,1) \\ \phi_0(\chi_i(\mathbf{a})), & \text{if } a_i = (1,0) \\ \phi_1(\chi_i(\mathbf{a})), & \text{if } a_i = (1,1). \end{cases} \tag{17.2}$$

We note that the payoff function $\phi_i(.)$ is the same across individuals. This is a useful starting point, as it allows us to focus on network-based differences between individuals. Toward the end of this section, we will discuss how heterogeneity across individuals along other dimensions, such as talent or wealth, interact with network differences.

Network-based activity involves individuals carrying out favors or barter exchanges. It is therefore reasonable to suppose that payoffs from network action $x$ display local complementarity. These ideas are reflected in the following assumption.

**Assumption 17.1** *Both $\phi_0(\cdot)$ and $\phi_1(\cdot)$ are strictly increasing in $\chi_i(\mathbf{a})$.*

Turning to the relation between the network and market opportunities, the key idea is that the market action affects the marginal returns from network action. Define the function:

$$\xi(\chi_i(\mathbf{a})) = \phi_1(\chi_i(\mathbf{a})) - \phi_0(\chi_i(\mathbf{a})) - \pi_y. \tag{17.3}$$

Observe that $\xi(\cdot)$ is the difference between the marginal returns to $x$ when $y_i = 1$, $\phi_1(\cdot) - \pi_y$, and the marginal returns to $x$ when $y_i = 0$, $\phi_0(\cdot) - 0$.

Network and market actions are said to be *substitutes* if $\xi(\cdot)$ is negative and weakly decreasing in $\chi_i(\mathbf{a})$. They are said to be *complements* if $\xi(\cdot)$ is positive and weakly increasing in $\chi_i(\mathbf{a})$. Thus, our notion of substitutes combines a substitutes relation between an individual's network action and market action and a strategic substitutes relation between the network action of their neighbors and their own market action. The relation between social networks in traditional occupations with semiskilled labor and markets for white-collar jobs may be seen as an example of substitutes. In a similar spirit, our definition of complements subsumes a complements relation between an individual's network and market action and a strategic complements relation between the network action of their neighbors and their own market action. Trust in traditional community ties may be seen as a complement to trading in products with high but uncertain valuation, like diamonds. These ideas are reflected in our next definition.

**Assumption 17.2** $\xi(0) = 0$. *Network and market actions are either substitutes or complements.*

We suppose that $\xi(0) = 0$, which is a simplifying normalization: if no one in the neighborhood adopts action $x$, then the network is not functioning, and so action $y$ does not affect the marginal payoffs from action $x$. To develop intuitions underlying the arguments, it is helpful to consider the following example of a payoff function:

$$\Phi_i(\mathbf{a} \mid \mathbf{g}) = (1 + \theta y_i) x_i \chi_i(\mathbf{a}) + y_i - p_x x_i - p_y y_i, \tag{17.4}$$

where $p_x \geq 0$ and $p_y \geq 0$, are the prices of actions $x$ and $y$, respectively. Observe that $x$ and $y$ are substitutes for $\theta \in [-1, 0]$ and complements for any $\theta \geq 0$. We now study the nature of equilibria and how they depend on the primitives of the model—network $g$ and the relation between the market and network opportunities $\theta$.

### 17.4.1 Communities and Markets: Trade-Offs

To develop a feel for the economic trade-offs involved and how they shape individual choices, let us work through an example with the linear payoffs example, as in equation (17.4). Let us set $\theta = -0.9$, $p_x = 4.1$ and $p_y = 0.5$. This is the case for substitutes. Observe that $\pi_y = 1 - 0.5 > 0$: market activity on its own is profitable, and therefore, inactivity, $a_i = (0, 0)$, is never optimal. Next, observe that $a_i = (1, 1)$ is never optimal: the payoff from $a_i = (1, 1)$, $-p_x + 1 - p_y$ is always smaller than the payoff from action $a_i = (0, 1)$, $1 - p_y$. To compute the optimal action, therefore, we need to compare pure network activity with pure market activity. It is easily verified that pure network activity is more profitable if and only if $\chi_i \geq 5$ (as this is the lowest integer that is greater than 4.1). So, for an individual to choose network activity, they must have at least five neighbors also choose it. It now follows, from reasoning as given in chapter 4 on network games, that the maximal group of individuals who will choose network activity corresponds to a 4-core of the network.

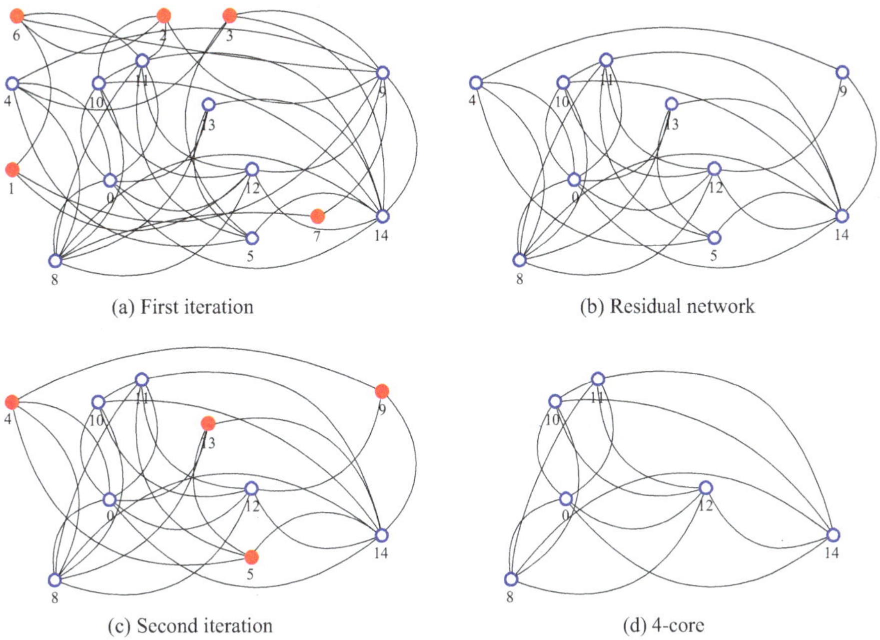


**Figure 17.4**
Algorithm to obtain a $q$-core. *Source*: Gagnon and Goyal (2017).

Figure 17.4 illustrates the derivation of a 4-core. All individuals outside the 4-core will take up the market action.

Next, consider the setting with complements: set $\theta = 1.1$ and make $p_x = 7.5$ and $p_y = 2$. Market action is not profitable on its own, as $\pi_y = 1 - 2 < 0$. Next, observe that $a_i = (1, 0)$ is never optimal: for it to be optimal, $\chi_i - p_x \geq 0$, which means that $\chi_i > 0$. However, the payoff from $a_i = (1, 1)$, $(1 + 1.1)\chi_i - p_x + 1 - p_y$ is always larger than $\chi_i - p_x$ because $\theta = 1.1 > p_y - 1$. To compute the optimal action, therefore we need to compare action $a_i = (1, 1)$ with the payoff from inactivity. Simple computations reveal that joint network activity and market action are optimal if and only if $\chi_i \geq 5$. So, for an individual to choose network activity, they must have at least five neighbors choose the network activity. It now follows, from reasoning as in chapter 4 on network games, that the maximal group of individuals who will choose network activity corresponds to the 4-core of the network. All individuals outside the 4-core will take up inactivity.

These computations serve as a basis for more general arguments concerning individual choices across a wide range of payoff functions. First, we observe that as in the weakest-link game, the local complementarity in the network action, $x$, creates the potential for coordination failure and the possibility of zero-activity outcomes. As the interest is on the interaction between the network and market action, it is simplest to abstract from the coordination problem in the network activity. In what follows, therefore, we will focus on the maximal equilibrium—equilibrium $\mathbf{a}^*$ is said to be *maximal* if there is no other equilibrium that Pareto-dominates it. Restricting our attention to a maximal equilibrium is helpful as, for a given payoff function and a given network, there is a unique maximal equilibrium. With these observations in mind, we are ready to state our first result.

**Proposition 17.1** · *Suppose that assumptions 17.1 and 17.2 hold. For a given network* $\mathbf{g}$*, a maximal equilibrium exists and is generically unique.*

We begin with existence in the complements case: start from a profile where everyone chooses $a_i = (0, 0)$. Iterate through best responses: noting that actions are complements, any increase in action $x$ by one individual provokes a further increase (weakly) in others' actions. As the action set is binary, the process must converge and the limit is an equilibrium. In the substitutes case, the argument is a little more involved and exploits the payoff structure more directly to construct different types of equilibrium in the cases where the market action alone is attractive and where it isn't. The existence of a maximal equilibrium follows from noting that the set of strategies (and hence the set of equilibria) is finite.

Next, consider the case of substitutes: it is helpful to separate the analysis into two parts:

1. $\pi_y \leq 0$: If $\phi_0(0) > 0$, then $a_i^* = (1, 0)$ for all $i \in N$ is an equilibrium. If $\phi_0(0) \leq 0$, then $a_i^* = (0, 0)$ for all $i \in N$ is an equilibrium.
2. $\pi_y > 0$: If $\phi_1(0) \leq \pi_y$, then $a_i^* = (0, 1)$ for all $i \in N$ is an equilibrium. Finally, if $\phi_1(0) > \pi_y$, then $a_i^* = (1, 1)$ for all $i \in N$ is an equilibrium (due to complementarity in returns from action $x$ across individuals).

Turning to uniqueness, suppose that there are two distinct profiles $\mathbf{a}$ and $\mathbf{a}'$ that are both maximal equilibria. This means that there are individuals $i$ and $j$ such that $i$ does strictly better under $\mathbf{a}$, while $j$ fares strictly better under $\mathbf{a}'$.

Consider first the case of complements. Define a new profile $\hat{\mathbf{a}}$, with $\hat{x}_i = \max\{x_i, x_i'\}$ and $\hat{y}_i = \max\{y_i, y_i'\}$ for all $i$. If $\hat{\mathbf{a}}$ constitutes an equilibrium, then it follows that $\hat{\mathbf{a}}$ Pareto-dominates $\mathbf{a}$ and $\mathbf{a}'$, as there is a strict inequality for at least a pair of agents. This contradicts the hypothesis that $\mathbf{a}$ and $\mathbf{a}'$ are maximal equilibria. If $\hat{\mathbf{a}}$ does not constitute an equilibrium, then iterate using best responses starting from $\hat{\mathbf{a}}$. Observe that all actions are complements, so best responses can only lead to an increasing number of individuals choosing $x = 1$ and/or $y = 1$. As in the existence proof, this process converges and the limit is an equilibrium. Note that at every iteration stage, the payoffs of every individual are weakly rising relative to $\hat{\mathbf{a}}$, which again contradicts the hypothesis that $\mathbf{a}$ and $\mathbf{a}'$ are maximal.

Finally, consider uniqueness for the substitutes case. Construct profile $\hat{\mathbf{a}}$, where $\hat{x}_i = \max\{x_i, x_i'\}$ and $\hat{y}_i = \min\{y_i, y_i'\}$ for all $i$. Suppose that $\hat{\mathbf{a}}$ constitutes an equilibrium. Clearly, the payoffs of all individuals choosing $x = 1$ under either $\mathbf{a}$ or $\mathbf{a}'$ must be weakly larger in $\hat{\mathbf{a}}$ (due to local complementarity in $x$). Also, note that individual $k$ switches from $y_k = 1$

(or $y'_k = 1$) to $\hat{y}_k = 0$ only if $\min\{y_k, y'_k\} = 0$. As the payoffs from $y$ are independent of others' choices, this must entail a weak increase in individual $k$'s payoffs. Hence, $\hat{\mathbf{a}}$ Pareto-dominates $\mathbf{a}$ and $\mathbf{a}'$, which contradicts the hypothesis that $\mathbf{a}$ and $\mathbf{a}'$ are maximal equilibria. The case where $\hat{\mathbf{a}}$ does not constitute an equilibrium can be studied by iteration as in the complements case described previously; details are omitted here. ■

### 17.4.2 Networks and Market Participation

We now turn to understanding the relation between networks and equilibrium behavior. An individual chooses among four possible opportunities: namely, (0, 0), (1, 0), (0, 1), and (1, 1). Recall that both $\phi_0(\cdot)$ and $\phi_1(\cdot)$ are strictly increasing in the level of network activity. Assuming that these payoffs increase sufficiently, there are $q_1 \geq 0$ and $q_2 \geq 0$ such that

$$\phi_0(\chi_i) > \max\{0, \pi_y\} \text{ if and only if } \chi_i > q_1 \tag{17.5}$$

$$\phi_1(\chi_i) > \max\{0, \pi_y\} \text{ if and only if } \chi_i > q_2. \tag{17.6}$$

Next, recall from the definition of substitutes, in equation (17.3), that $\phi_0(\cdot)$ increases "faster" than $\phi_1(\cdot)$ with respect to $\chi_i \in \mathbb{N}_+$. This means that there is $q_3 \geq 0$ such that

$$\phi_0(\chi_i) > \phi_1(\chi_i) \text{ if and only if } \chi_i \geq q_3. \tag{17.7}$$

Similarly, in the case of complements, there is $q_4 \geq 0$ such that

$$\phi_1(\chi_i) > \phi_0(\chi_i) \text{ if and only if } \chi_i \geq q_4. \tag{17.8}$$

The network and market opportunities are strong substitutes if $q_3 < q_1$. They are strong complements if they are complements and $q_4 < q_2$. Observe that strong substitutes rule out cases where $a_i = (1, 1)$ is optimal for any $\chi_i \in \mathbb{N}_+$. Following similar logic, we note that the property of strong complements rules out action $a_i = (1, 0)$ being optimal for any $\chi_i \in \mathbb{N}_+$. It can be verified that in the payoff function example (equation [17.4]) and the network activity, $x$, and the market action, $y$, are strong substitutes if $\theta \in (-1, 0)$ and $\theta(n-1) < p_y - 1$, and they are strong complements if $\theta > 0$ and $\theta > p_y - 1$.

In the case of strong substitutes, only individuals in the $q_1$-core will choose $a_i = (1, 0)$, while those outside it will either choose $a_i = (0, 1)$ if $\pi_y > 0$, or $a_i = (0, 0)$ if $\pi_y \leq 0$. To develop some intuition about what individuals in the $q_1$-core will choose, consider the case where $\pi_y \leq 0$. Individuals choose between $a_i = (1, 0)$ and $a_i = (0, 0)$. They prefer the network action if they have at least $q_1$ neighbors who choose $x = 1$. Observe that if all individuals in the $q_1$-core choose $x = 1$, then it follows that equation (17.5) is satisfied for all of them. Hence, players in the $q_1$-core all obtain larger payoffs by playing (1, 0) than by remaining inactive, and the converse is true for players outside the $q_1$-core.

In the case of strong complements, only individuals in the $q_2$-core choose $a_i = (1, 1)$, while individuals outside the $q_2$-core choose either $a_i = (0, 1)$ (if $\pi_y > 0$), or $a_i = (0, 0)$ (if

$\pi_y \leq 0$). Consider the case where $\pi_y > 0$. Individuals choose between $a_i = (1, 1)$ and $a_i = (0, 1)$ and prefer the former if and only if equation (17.6) is satisfied. If all individuals in the $q_2$-core choose $x = 1$, then equation (17.6) is satisfied for individuals in the $q_2$-core, so all individuals in the $q_2$-core (and those individuals only) must strictly prefer $a_i = (1, 1)$ to $a_i = (0, 1)$.

We summarize the discussion as follows.

**Proposition 17.2** *Suppose that assumptions 17.1 and 17.2 hold. Let* $\mathbf{a}^*$ *be the maximal equilibrium.*

1. ***Strong substitutes:*** $a_i^* = (1, 0)$ *if and only if* $i \in \mathbf{g}^{q_1}$. *If* $i \notin \mathbf{g}^{q_1}$, *then* $a_i^* = (0, 0)$ *if* $\pi_y \leq 0$, *and* $a_i^* = (0, 1)$ *if* $\pi_y > 0$.
2. ***Strong complements:*** $a_i^* = (1, 1)$ *if and only if* $i \in \mathbf{g}^{q_2}$. *If* $i \notin \mathbf{g}^{q_2}$, *then* $a_i^* = (0, 0)$ *if* $\pi_y \leq 0$, *and* $a_i^* = (0, 1)$ *if* $\pi_y > 0$.

In other words, if networks and markets are strong substitutes, then all individuals in $\mathbf{g}^{q_1}$ choose network activity only. Individuals outside $\mathbf{g}^{q_1}$ choose the market action only if $\pi_y > 0$, and choose inactivity if $\pi_y \leq 0$. If networks and markets are strong complements: all individuals in $\mathbf{g}^{q_2}$ choose both network and market activity. Individuals outside $\mathbf{g}^{q_2}$, choose the market action only if $\pi_y > 0$, and choose inactivity if $\pi_y \leq 0$.

To develop a better understanding of the uses of proposition 17.2, we present equilibrium outcomes in two familiar networks on figure 17.6: the regular network, with degree 3, and a core-periphery network, with an equal number of nodes and links. In the case of strong substitutes (figure 17.6[a]), peripheral individuals, who benefit the least from network exchange, choose the market action, while all other individuals choose the network action. Everyone chooses the network action in the regular network. In the case of complements, the opposite holds: for the given prices, only the best-connected individuals (in the core of the core-periphery network) can afford to choose the market (and the network) action; all other individuals choose inaction. In the regular network, no one has sufficient connections: inactivity is pervasive.

Figures 17.5 and 17.6 help us appreciate the role of the topology of networks and the strategic relation between market and network activity in shaping behavior. In the case of substitutes, the first thought would be that highly connected nodes should adopt the network action, while less connected nodes adopt the market action. The analysis of the model goes beyond this intuition. Consider the network in figure 17.5: node 9 has a higher degree than node 10, and yet it chooses the market action, while the latter chooses the network action. This is because node 10 forms part of the 4-core while node 9 does not. Turning next to the impact of the strategic relation between network and market opportunities, let us compare behavior in the panel (a-substitutes) and the panel (b-complements) of figure 17.6. In the substitutes case, the nodes lying *outside* the relevant $q$-core choose market action, while in the complements case, the nodes *within* the relevant $q$-core do so.

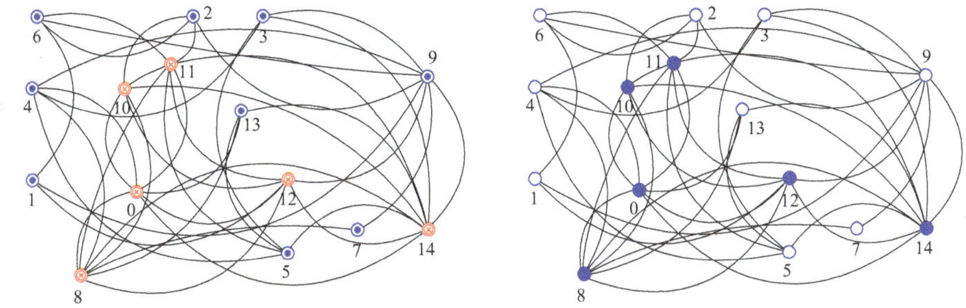

(a) Substitutes ($\theta = -1, p_x = 4.1, p_y = 0.5$) (b) Complements ($\theta = 1.1, p_x = 7.5, p_y = 2$)

○ x = y = 0 ⊗ x = 1, y = 0 ⊙ x = 0, y = 1 ● x = y = 1

**Figure 17.5**
Adoption patterns. *Source*: Gagnon and Goyal (2017).

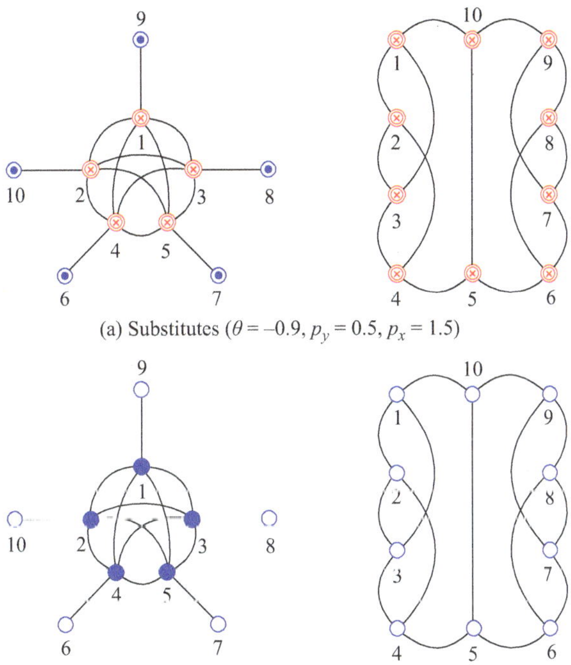

(a) Substitutes ($\theta = -0.9, p_y = 0.5, p_x = 1.5$)

(b) Complements ($\theta = 1, p_y = 1.5, p_x = 6.5$)

○ x = y = 0 ⊗ x = 1, y = 0 ⊙ x = 0, y = 1 ● x = y = 1

**Figure 17.6**
Core-periphery and regular networks. *Source*: Gagnon and Goyal (2017).

We say that one network $\mathbf{g}'$ is denser than another network $\mathbf{g}$ if $g_{ij} \leq g'_{ij}$ for any pair $i, j \in N$, and the inequality is strict for at least one such pair. We say that an individual is well connected if they lie in the appropriate $q$-core (e.g., the $q_1$-core in the case of strong substitutes and the $q_2$-core for strong complements).

Proposition 17.2 says that the key to market participation is the size of $\mathbf{g}^q$ and the value of $\pi_y$. For instance, in the case of strong substitutes, if $\pi_y > 0$, then the set of market participants is simply the complement of set $\mathbf{g}^{q_1}$. Similarly, in the case of strong complements, if $\pi_y < 0$, then every individual in $\mathbf{g}^{q_2}$ adopts the market action. This suggests that, loosely speaking, market participation is falling in the size of the core set in the case of substitutes, while the converse is true in the case of complements. This implies that market participation is weakly lower in denser networks when $x$ and $y$ are substitutes, and weakly larger when they are complements. Moreover, market action $y$ is adopted by less-connected individuals in the case of substitutes, and by well-connected ones in the case of complements.

### 17.4.3 Impact of Markets on Welfare

Our theoretical framework allows an examination of the circumstances under which the introduction of markets is welfare enhancing. To do so, we compare welfare in a society before and after the arrival of market action $y$. Given network $\mathbf{g}$ and action profile $\mathbf{a}$, aggregate welfare is given by

$$W(\mathbf{a} \mid \mathbf{g}) = \sum_{i \in N} \Phi_i(a_i, \mathbf{a_{-i}} \mid \mathbf{g}). \tag{17.9}$$

In the case of complements, the introduction of $y$ weakly facilitates the adoption of network action $x$. The introduction of $y$ thus implies weakly larger individual payoffs for everyone, and hence a larger aggregate welfare. However, if $x$ and $y$ are substitutes, the effects of the introduction of the market are less clear. A switch away from the network activity to the market action by some individuals leads to a drop in the payoffs of the individuals who remain with the network action. This negative effect can dominate any gains enjoyed by the market participants. Example 17.4 illustrates this point.

**Example 17.4** *When markets lower social welfare*

Consider the core-periphery network in figure 17.6, and suppose that the payoff function is as in equation (17.4), which we present here for easy reference:

$$\Phi_i(\mathbf{a} \mid \mathbf{g}) = (1 + \theta y_i) x_i \chi_i(\mathbf{a}) + y_i - p_x x_i - p_y y_i. \tag{17.10}$$

In this payoff function, fix $\theta = -0.9$ and $p_x < 1$. Prior to the introduction of $y$, all individuals choose $x = 1$. Suppose now that market action $y$ becomes available. If $0 < 0.1 < p_y \leq p_x < 1$, then all periphery individuals choose $y = 1$, while core individuals stick to $x = 1$. Periphery individuals increase their payoffs by $0 < p_x - p_y < 1$ following their switch. On the other hand, a periphery individual's switch entails a decrease of exactly 1 in the benefits of the core individual to which they are connected. The net effect of the introduction of the market action is thus strictly negative.

### 17.4.4 Markets and Inequality

We now turn to the impact of markets on inequality. To appreciate the issues in the simplest way, we examine the ratio of the highest payoffs to the lowest payoffs. Given network **g**, this ratio is denoted by $\mathcal{R}(\mathbf{g})$:

$$\mathcal{R}(\mathbf{g}) \equiv \frac{1+\max\{\Phi_i(a_i^*, \mathbf{a}_{-\mathbf{i}}^* \mid \mathbf{g})\}_{i\in N}}{1+\min\{\Phi_i(a_i^*, \mathbf{a}_{-\mathbf{i}}^* \mid \mathbf{g})\}_{i\in N}}, \tag{17.11}$$

where $a^*$ is the maximal equilibrium in network $g$.

$\mathcal{R}(\mathbf{g})$ is close in spirit to other traditional metrics of inequality, including the *range*, the *20:20 ratio*, and the *Palma ratio*. The range is the difference between the payoffs of the wealthiest and poorest individuals of a population. The 20:20 ratio and the Palma ratio reflect the payoff ratios of the wealthiest 20 percent to the poorest 20 percent, and the wealthiest 10 percent to the poorest 40 percent, respectively. While $\mathcal{R}(\mathbf{g})$ has the same structure as these two measures, it requires less information about the payoff distribution, and thus about the network structure.

Let $\mathcal{R}_0(\mathbf{g})$ denote the inequality prior to the introduction of a market and $\mathcal{R}_1(\mathbf{g})$ its level after the introduction of market action. Note that rising $\mathcal{R}(\mathbf{g})$ implies increasing inequality.

In the case of strong substitutes, it is easiest to see the argument when we start from a premarket situation where well-connected individuals choose $x$. The introduction of the market clearly offers the less connected individuals a potentially better option. Their switch to the market action can only lower the payoffs of the best connected who remain with the network action. Hence the minimum payoffs must weakly rise and the maximum payoffs must (weakly) fall, with the introduction of the market. Thus markets unambiguously lower inequality.

When $x$ and $y$ are strong complements, we can focus on two action profiles, $(0, 0)$ and $(1, 1)$. Individuals who benefit the most from network exchange will also benefit the most from markets. When market take-up is partial, markets will thus unambiguously raise inequality. Let us define market participation in a network $g$, $\mathcal{M}(\mathbf{g})$, as the number of individuals who choose $y = 1$ in the unique maximal equilibrium in that network. When market participation is complete ($\mathcal{M}(\mathbf{g}) = 1$), the worst-off individuals may benefit relatively more or less than the best-off individuals from the newly available market $y$, depending on the social structure and the payoffs to the two opportunities. Example 17.5 elaborates on this point.

**Example 17.5** *Networks and inequality*

Consider the network in figure 17.7 and the payoff function in equation (17.4). Fix $p_x = 4.1$. In such a case, the best-off individuals before the introduction of $y$ are individuals

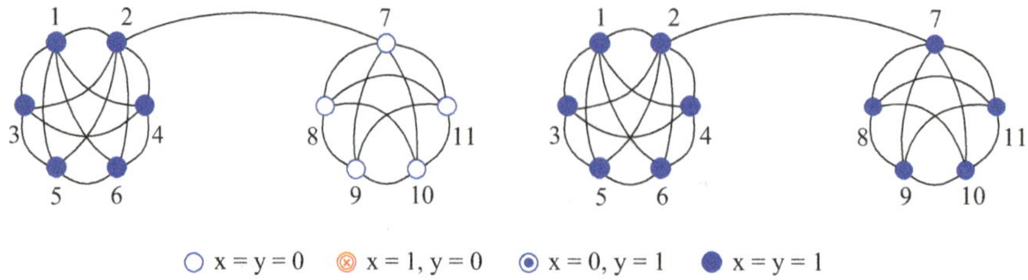


**Figure 17.7**
Prior to market: $p_x = 4.1$. Postmarket: $p_x = 4.1$; $p_y = 1.05$ or $p_y = 2$. *Source*: Gagnon and Goyal (2017).

1 to 6, with payoffs of 0.9, while all other individuals have payoffs of 0. This means that inequality is given by $\mathcal{R}_0(\mathbf{g}) = 1.9$. Now suppose that $y$ is introduced at a price $p_y = 1.05$. Then the earnings of individuals 1, 7, and 3–6 are 5.85, while those of individuals 2 and 8–11 are 7.85 and 3.85, respectively. Consequently, $\mathcal{R}_1(\mathbf{g}) = 1.825$, which indicates falling inequality.

Next, suppose that $p_y = 2$. Then the payoffs to individuals 1, 7, and 3–6 is 4.9, while those of individuals 2 and 8–11 amount to 6.9 and 2.9, respectively. Consequently, inequality is given by $\mathcal{R}_1(\mathbf{g}) = 2.026$; there is thus an increase in inequality with the arrival of a market.

We summarize the effects of social structure on social efficiency and inequality as follows.

**Proposition 17.3** *Consider the interaction between networks and markets:*

- *In the case of strong substitutes, a new market opportunity may lower aggregate payoffs but it weakly decreases inequality.*
- *In the case of strong complements, a new market opportunity will raise aggregate efficiency. It will also raise inequality so long as take-up is partial ($\mathcal{M}(\mathbf{g}) \in (0,1)$). If take-up is complete ($\mathcal{M}(\mathbf{g}) = 1$), then the effects on inequality are ambiguous.*

In the discussion so far, we have assumed that individuals differ only with regard to network location. Individuals may be heterogeneous in other dimensions that affect the extent to which they can benefit from markets (e.g., human capital and initial wealth).

### 17.4.5 Individual Heterogeneity and Responses to Markets

Suppose that the benefits from the market action, $\pi_y$, are different across individuals. We assume that this heterogeneity does not affect the other determinants of the payoff function (i.e., returns to $x$ and degree of complementarity between $x$ and $y$). To bring out the interaction between types of heterogeneities, consider the following variation of the linear payoffs case:

$$\Phi_i(a_i, \mathbf{a}_{-\mathbf{i}}|\mathbf{g}) = (1 + \theta y_i)\, x_i \chi_i(\mathbf{a}) - p_x x_i + \pi_y^i \tag{17.12}$$

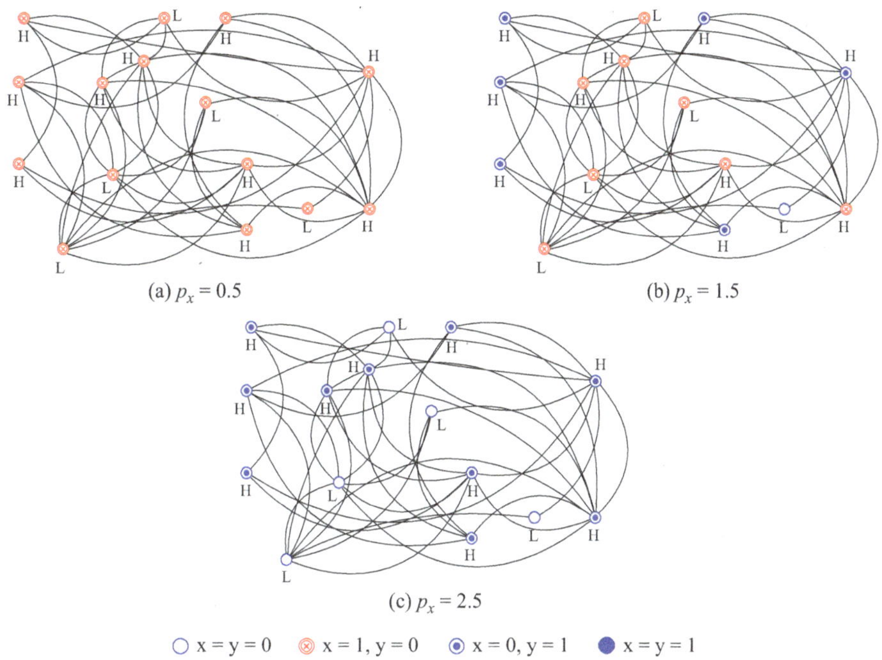


**Figure 17.8**
Implications of heterogeneity on market action: $q_H = 2$ and $q_L = 5$. *Source*: Gagnon and Goyal (2017).

with $\theta = -0.9$. Suppose that individuals have either high or low returns from $y$ with $\pi_y^H = 3$ and $\pi_y^L = -1$. The first thing to note is that high-market-value individuals require larger returns from network action $x$ to remain in the network. Figure 17.8 illustrates the equilibrium adoptions of $x$ and $y$ for different values of $p_x$.

We see that as we move to higher prices for network action, it is the higher-value, not the lowest-connected individuals who switch to market action (as in figure 17.8[b]). Further, it is possible for the market action to be adopted as stand-alone by certain individuals, while others opt for $a^* = (0, 0)$ (as in figure 17.8[c]).

Building on these observations, we can develop a general analysis of equilibrium actions with network and market value heterogeneity. A question at the end of the chapter explores this point.

Our results on inequality in proposition 17.3 may change considerably. One example is if returns to market activity, $\pi_y^i$, are negatively correlated with membership in the $q$-core. To see this, recall that in our benchmark model, only poorly connected individuals (i.e., those out of the $q_1$-core), opt for the market action. These individuals are also the worst off in the premarket situation, which explains why inequality always goes down with the introduction of markets in the case of substitutes. But if these poorly connected individuals have high returns to $y$ while others have no returns at all, then the introduction of markets may make the poorly connected individuals the best-off—indeed, they are better off than the erstwhile rich individuals, and thereby inequality is exacerbated.

Let us now summarize what we have learned from the theoretical model. We develop a model where individuals located in a social network choose a network action and a market action. The key to our results, as well as to understanding the empirical patterns, is the relation between the two activities (i.e., whether they are strategic complements or substitutes). We show that equilibrium individual behaviors can be described in terms of the *q-core* of the social network. We show that in the case of substitutes, it is the individuals who benefit the least from network exchange (i.e., individuals outside the q-core) who adopt markets. Conversely, in the case of complements, well-connected individuals find markets more attractive. Markets always raise aggregate welfare if the two activities are complements, but they may lower welfare when the two activities are substitutes. Inequality in social networks is reinforced by markets in the case of complements but lowered in the case of substitutes. We now relate these empirical findings on the rise of manufacturing and services, migration, and take-up of modern education.

### 17.4.6 Using the Model to Understand Empirical Patterns

In this section, we use the model as a lens through which to better understand the case studies presented in section 17.3.

*Trading and Manufacturing in China:* In the absence of well-functioning markets and legal institutions, how did large-scale industrialization and urbanization of China take place? A number of authors have drawn attention to the role of communities in the Chinese growth process (i.e., Allen, Qian, and Qian [2005]; Dai, Mookherjee, Munshi, and Zhang [2020]; Song, Storesletten, and Zilibotti [2011]; Fleisher, Hud, McGuiree, and Zhang [2010]; Nee and Opper [2012]; Peng [2004]; and Greif and Tabellini [2017]).

We start by noting the importance of the production clusters in the Chinese growth process (for a discussion of these clusters, also see chapter 12, on social coordination). Thousands of firms, large and small, with many specializing in a strictly defined production process, are agglomerated in a densely populated region, where a specific manufactured consumer good is churned out in very large quantities: these regions are sometimes referred to as the world's "socks city," "sweater city," "kids' clothing city," and "footwear capital." Members from clans and lineages migrate to production clusters in groups. It has been argued that informal mechanisms based on reputation and trust have been at work to allow millions of entrepreneurs, most of whom were born in rural areas, to establish and grow private companies.

Let us briefly discuss lineages in China. Patrilineal lineages—also referred to as clans—have long been associated with Chinese society. Almost 100 years ago, Max Weber (1951) observed that clan organization was well preserved in China. A clan rests on blood ties, confers cultural identity, and has clearly nominated leaders. Clans are characterized by rules and obligations that have high ethical standing. Upon taking power in 1949, the Communist Party took a number of steps to suppress lineage organizations: it confiscated clan communal land and properties, deprived clan elders of their power, repealed clan codes, and injected the ideology of class consciousness and class struggle to diffuse clan identity. In spite of an official policy against clans during the Communist period, there is evidence to show that clans persisted, albeit in a dormant form, through the Communist period, and they revived greatly after the market reforms of 1979. There is strong empirical support for the role of lineages and clans in furthering private enterprise and economic activity in production clusters.

Seen through the lens of our model, in the setting of China with its limited legal and market institutions, activity in social ties may be seen as complementary to entrepreneurial market activity. In line with our theoretical work, lineages or clans that have dense networks are able to better leverage social connections to grow private enterprises.

*Migration:* Why are levels of rural-urban migration in India much lower than other comparable developing economies? Migration could be low because formal insurance in cities is very weak and/or informal insurance works particularly well in villages. There is little evidence to suggest that formal insurance is significantly better in other developing countries compared to India. In addition, research has documented evidence for very high levels of informal risk-sharing throughout the developing world, not just in India.

It would appear that the key is the size of networks that engage in informal insurance: if the group or network is small, then consumption will still fluctuate appreciably as the group is too small to smoothen all shocks. On the other hand, if the group is very large, then the smoothing would be much more effective. It would seem that what is exceptional about India is the size, spatial spread, and scale of caste-based insurance networks: as the network is very large and spread out and comprehensive in its coverage, it has the ability to smoothen individual-level and even village-level shocks a great deal more effectively than in other countries. To put it in the language of our model, in India, villagers are members of networks with larger q-cores compared to villagers in other developing countries. Proposition 17.2 suggests that villagers in India are less likely to take up the market opportunity of migration. This is consistent with the empirical record.

*English-Language Education:* Turning next to education, the developments can be understood in terms of the theoretical framework as follows: a significant fraction—68 percent—of men in blue-collar jobs found their current job through a relative or a member of their subcaste. Thus network connections appear to be important for blue-collar jobs in manufacturing. On the other hand, the prospects of getting a white-collar job appear to depend on number of years of schooling and proficiency in English. Thus networks are relatively unimportant for white-collar jobs. Parents choose the language of instruction: a Marathi-language school may be interpreted as action $x$ in the model, and an English-language school as market action $y$. These choices are mutually exclusive: in other words, we are in a setting with perfect substitutes (viz., $\theta$ is close to $-1$ in example 17.4).

In lower-ranking subcastes, as girls are not part of the network, they do not expect to secure blue-collar jobs through their network. The situation is very different for boys, as they are part of well-functioning networks. Proposition 17.2 suggests that this difference in access to networks will lead girls to take English-language education more than boys. This difference is consistent with the empirical record. This differential take-up of English-language education has implications for overall social well being and inequality. Proposition 17.3 suggests that girls move into white-collar jobs, their families will withdraw from lower-caste networks, which would erode these networks over time. This is costly for those who remain in the network and may lower the welfare of these subcastes. On the other hand, greater take-up of white collar jobs will raise incomes for girls relative to boys, which will help reduce gender inequality.

## 17.5 *La Longue Duree*

In the introduction of this chapter and in section 17.2, we discussed large-scale patterns of economic change in historical context. A key feature of the process of economic growth is the movement of labor from agriculture to manufacturing and services. This is accompanied by a corresponding movement of people from the rural countryside to urban cities. Traditionally, the salience of this large-scale process has led many scholars to take the position that, while historically economic life was bound up with social relations (involving family and close relations), modern economic life is largely divorced from such social ties. The three empirical cases in section 17.3 point to the resilience and the persistent presence of social networks and a reassessment of this perspective.

In the context of migration, social networks can shape the overall rate of movement of people from villages to cities. However, over the past several decades, millions of people have moved from villages to cities. A number of studies in India and other parts of the world demonstrate the emergence and great resilience of community-based networks in shaping the functioning of labor markets in manufacturing and services in cities. Indeed, these community-based networks were a major consideration in the case study concerning the adoption of English-language education: it was the presence of strong working class networks that discouraged the take-up of English-language education among lower-caste men in Mumbai. This case study reveals that, almost a century after the setting up of large mills and factories in Mumbai, community-based networks are highly effective, as they continue to exercise a decisive influence on the occupational choices of individuals. The transition from an agricultural rural economy to an urban manufacturing economy leads to an evolution of ties that can take very different forms, depending on the context: in some cases, ties are eroded (as when families leave the working class networks and move into white-collar jobs), while in other cases, the relations are reconfigured and possibly strengthened (as when a community moves collectively into the trade and manufacturing sectors).

There is therefore a two-way flow of influence between community-based networks and market activity: networks shape participation in markets, and markets in turn shape the structure of social networks. This co-evolution of markets and social networks is a central aspect of the economic growth process, and it takes place over long periods of time. We discussed the impact of social networks on participation in markets in section 17.3; here, we discuss the flow from markets to networks.

In recent years, a number of researchers have dug deeper into the details of how social ties–and indeed, the topology of the network—is affected when traditional communities come in contact with new opportunities in a changing economy. Next, we discuss case studies taken from this line of work to bring out the rich range of spillovers and interdependencies between formal institutions and market opportunities and traditional social ties.

**Example 17.6** *Expansion in commercial banking and social lending*

Consider the effects of new bank accounts on the social network of informal ties of borrowing and lending. Our discussion is taken from Comola and Prina (2021).

In 2010, these accounts were offered randomly to women in 19 villages located in the vicinity of the town of Pokhara in Nepal. The bank did not charge any opening, maintenance, or withdrawal fees and paid interest comparable to the alternatives available in the Nepalese market. Customers could make transactions at the local bank's branch offices in the villages, which were open twice a week for approximately three hours, or at the bank's main office, located in downtown Pokhara, during regular business hours. The take-up and usage rate of the savings accounts offered to the treatment group were very high—84 percent of the households that were offered the account opened it and used it actively, depositing an average of 8 percent of their baseline weekly household income almost once a week for the first year after getting the account. How did these bank accounts affect informal ties between the villagers?

The study of village networks is based on a starting survey in 2009 (prior to when the bank accounts were offered) and an ending survey in 2011 (conducted after they were offered). In all, the sample included 915 households. In the survey, the female head of household was asked to provide a list of people (inside or outside the village) whom the household could rely on most (and/or who could rely on them most) for help, in cash or in kind, and with whom they regularly exchanged gifts and/or loans. Respondents could list as many names as they wished.

At the start, households reported having 1.42 partners on average, of whom 0.64 lived in the village. The network was therefore very sparse—network density was low (only 2 percent of the potential within-village links were present) and it was also very fragmented, with 312 households (34 percent of the sample) being isolated. The introduction of bank accounts leaves the number of binary links virtually unchanged: 656 links at the start versus 658 at the end. However, there was an important reshuffling in the distribution of links—the probability of a tie between new bank account holders increased, and that of ties between nonaccount holders declined. ■

**Example 17.7** *Community-driven development projects and economic networks*

International donors, multilateral organizations, and national governments increasingly use bottom-up approaches, such as community-driven development (CDD) programs, which involve local communities in project design and implementation. The scale of these programs is extensive—they represent between 5 percent and 10 percent of the overall World Bank lending portfolio; roughly $85 billion was allocated to supporting close to 400 programs in 94 countries during the decade 2000–2010. We next discuss the impact of CDD on informal social ties. Our presentation draws on Hess, Jaimovich, and Schündeln (2020) and Jaimovich (2015).

The Gambian CDD program allocated funds for village-level development projects to about a third of all rural villages in the country. The program was implemented between 2008 and 2009 in close to 500 poor villages that were chosen randomly from a set of 900 candidates. The resource allocation was equivalent to one-half of the households' annual income. A major goal of CDDs is to encourage and facilitate community-level interactions. To accomplish this, villagers were deeply involved at all stages, ranging from identification of the potential projects to their maintenance. A total of 38 meetings were mandated—20 of which intended to involve the whole village, while the other 18 involved meetings of community-based organizations. The most common subprojects were farm implements and inputs, milling machines, water pumps, seed stores and cereal banking, and draft animals.

Data was collected in 2014 from 56 villages, half of whom had been exposed to CDD. Ties were measured on six economic domains (land, labor, inputs, food, gifts, and credit) and two social domains (friendship and kinship). The effect of the CDD is estimated by comparing the probability of a link between any two individuals between villages that were and were not exposed to the program.

It is helpful to trace, at a high level, a few channels through which CDD participation can shape informal social ties. One argument is that by bringing together villagers in a sustained interaction, the program would also increase informal ties. A second argument is that CDD exposes a village to markets and uniform prices, which may lead to a shift away from informal ties and toward market relations. A third argument pertains to the possibility of elite capture and very unequal benefits accruing from the program, which could create disputes and disrupt social ties.

The empirical study reveals that the CDD program led to a more formal economy—it eroded informal economic ties, eliminating roughly one of six transactions between households, and raised the number of transactions with individuals outside the village. The loss of ties was higher in villages where the projects performed poorly, as well as villages where the gains were shared unequally. ■

**Example 17.8** *Entry into diamond markets and social ties*

Investments in manufacturing or trading require financial and social capital that are often beyond the capacity of a single individual. Individuals may have to turn to their communities to put together these forms of capital. We discuss here how a historically disadvantaged subcaste moved from agriculture into the international diamond business using its community network, and how its entry led in turn to changes in the network. The discussion is based on Munshi (2011).

Diamonds constitute one of the principal exports for India. But India does not produce rough diamonds. These diamonds are imported, cut, and polished in domestic factories and then exported. The diamond mines of Argyle, Australia, were discovered in 1979. At that time, two traditional Indian communities, the Palanpuris and the Marwaris, controlled the business end of the diamond industry, while the cutting and polishing was done by a lower caste of agricultural labor contractors, the Kathiawaris. After the supply shock, some of the Palanpuri businessmen, who had branches in Antwerp, Belgium, helped their Kathiawari contacts enter the business by supplying rough diamonds to them. This initial group of Kathiawari firms encouraged more of their community members to follow their lead: by 2005, there were hundreds of Kathiawari-owned firms in the Indian diamond industry.

The first entry of Kathiawars into the market was made possible through connections with well-established Palanpuri diamond merchants based in Antwerp. This is the first point where network connections come into play. The second entry occurred after the initial Kathiawari enterprises had established themselves: using a strong, caste-based community, successive members entered the diamond market, and as they did so, the base of the Kathiawari community grew further. An examination of the patterns of transition reveal that at the start in 1975, almost 70 percent of the new Kathiawaris who joined the diamond market had parental connections. However, over the next two decades, this fraction declined sharply: by 2004, only 20 percent of the newly joining Kathiawaris had paternal connections in the diamond industry: rather, they were entering on the strength of their ties with the Kathiawari community.

So far, we have discussed the consequences of social networks for behavior and market entry, but the transition of a community from one activity to another also has consequences for the social network itself. An examination of the patterns of marriage relations within the communities reveals an interesting change: the frequency of intra-industry (and intra-caste) marriages increases significantly for the Kathiawaris. Practically none of the early Kathiawari entrants in the diamond market (i.e., those who entered prior to 1975) married within the industry. By 2004, almost 50 percent of the entrants were marrying within the industry. Their (intra-industry) marriage rate was higher than the corresponding marriage rates for the Palanpuris and Marwaris (which remained largely unchanged over this period). ■

### 17.5.1 Microfinance and Social and Economic Networks

**Example 17.9** *Expansion of microfinance and social lending*

Muhammad Yunus founded the Grameen Bank in Bangladesh in 1983. By 2007, Grameen had made loans of more than $6 billion to microentrepreneurs in developing countries. A distinctive feature of the scheme is that it targeted borrowers with no credit history (i.e., those who had limited access to traditional banking). Yunus would go on to win the Nobel Peace Prize in 2006 for his work. Since 1986, microfinance (MF) institutions have grown rapidly: according to the Microcredit Summit Campaign 2012, the number of very poor families with a microloan has grown more than 18-fold, from 7.6 million in 1997 to 137.5 million in 2010. We study the impact of the introduction of MF on social networks. Our presentation is based on Banerjee, Breza, Chandrasekhar, et al. (2021).

MF brings people together in its application process and the repayment phrase. On the other hand, by providing loans, it lowers the need for local loans within the village. It is therefore a priori whether the introduction of MF will erode or strengthen informal sharing and related social networks within the village.

The study covers 75 villages in Karnataka, a state in southern India. We discussed properties of these networks in chapter 1. Bharatha Swamukti Samsthe (BSS) offered a conventional group-based microcredit program: borrowers (who were only women) were formed into groups of five and are jointly liable for their loans. The starting loan is approximately 10,000 rupees (a little over $200) and is repaid in 50 weekly installments. Between 2007 and 2010, BSS entered 43 of these 75 villages. We call these the "MF villages," and the remaining villages as the "nonMF villages." The social network is studied at two points in time: 2006 (prior to the introduction of MF) and 2012 (after the introduction).

The first finding is that the introduction of MF is associated with a 11 percent decline in the probability of a link between any two households in an MF village compared to a nonMF village. Turning to the composition of these link deletions, let us classify households in terms of those that adopted MF and those that did not. The second finding is that links between two nonMF-type households fell by more than the links between two MF households. This is somewhat surprising as it would seem that the value of the link between two nonMF households has not changed. A third finding is that it is not just the financial ties of borrowing and lending that have eroded, but other social ties that involve advice and support have dissolved as well. ■

Putting these studies—on bank accounts, development projects, entry in diamond markets, and MF—together with the earlier studies in section 17.3, shows that market opportunities can both substitute for social ties and complement social relations. In the diamond industry, market opportunities spurred on and strengthened social ties. Similarly, in the bank accounts case, access to formal financial institutions appears to reinforce social ties. However, in the development project and MF cases, opportunities arising out of formal institutions and greater market opportunities eroded informal economic ties based on borrowing and lending, and to the extent that other social relations are complementary to these ties, they also have a negative effect on the broader social network.

The theoretical model proposed in section 17.3 can be elaborated to make these ideas a little more precise. Suppose that, in addition to the choices of the network activity, $x$, and the market action, $y$, individuals can choose links. These links are costly. To pursue this reasoning, it is helpful to incorporate these costs of links within the linear example presented in equation (17.4). The augmented payoffs may be written as

$$\Phi_i(\mathbf{a} \mid \mathbf{g}) = (1+\theta y_i)x_i\chi_i(\mathbf{a}) + y_i - p_x x_i - p_y y_i - c(\eta_i), \tag{17.13}$$

where $\eta_i$ is the number of links formed by $i$ and $c(\eta_i)$ is the total cost of the links. It will be convenient to assume that $c(0) = 0$ and these costs are strictly increasing and are a convex function of the number of links. An individual contemplating an additional link will earn extra payoffs only if they are choosing the network activity. In the event that they are choosing only the network activity, the return from an additional neighbor who also chooses the network activity is 1, while in the event that they choose both the network and the market action, the additional reward is $1+\theta$. It follows that an individual will forms links until the point that the marginal reward and the marginal cost are equal. Recall that $\theta < 0$ in the case of substitutes and $\theta > 0$ in the case of complements. This means that the additional reward, $1+\theta$, is larger than 1 if network and market are complements and less than 1 if they are substitutes. As cost $c(.)$ is increasing and convex in the number of links, it then follows that an individual will form more links in the case where these activities are complements. The number of links defines the density of the network—thus networks will grow stronger when individuals in a traditional community face new opportunities that complement the network activity, while they will weaken when they are substitutes.

## 17.6 Reading Notes

At the midpoint of the twentieth century, with the decolonization process in full swing, the sources of economic growth and the reasons for its uneven spread across countries emerged as a major field of study. The work of Simon Kuznets provided an empirical foundation for this literature. We draw upon the discussion in the beautifully self-contained "Six Lectures on Economic Growth" (Kuznets [1961]). The fundamental role of sectoral transformation away from agriculture and toward manufacturing and services was the motivation for the theoretical models of economic growth inaugurated by the work of Lewis (1954) and the models of migration initiated by Harris and Todaro (1970). The exposition in section 17.2 draws on Ray (1998). We also touch upon themes from other older texts on economic development, such as Myrdal (1972), Nurkse (1966), and Hirschman (1958). For overviews of the modern theory of economic growth, see the excellent books by Acemoglu (2009) and Aghion and Howitt (1998).

Section 17.2 discusses how social structure can help us understand individual and social responses to new opportunities. The discussion draws on the wide-ranging research of Marcel Fafchamps, Kaivan Munshi, Chang-Tai Tsieh, Guido Tabellini, and Avner Grief and their collaborators. In particular, the case studies in this section draw on Munshi and Rosenzweig (2006); Munshi and Rosenzweig (2016); Dai, Mookherjee, Munshi, and Zhang (2020); Bai, Hsieh, Song, and Wang (2020); Bai, Hsieh, Song, and Wang (2020); and Greif and Tabellini (2017).

The theoretical model is taken from Gagnon and Goyal (2017)—this model combines the traditional idea that markets and networks are substitutes (as in the early work of Kranton [1996]) with the possibility that they can be complements. Building on the research on network games and social coordination, these ideas are located within a social network. They suggest the concept of the q-core as an organizing principle. The exposition on the relation between social ties and market opportunities draws on the elegant essay on the relation between markets and social ties by Hirschman (1997), the popular book by Sandel (2000), and the survey paper by Goyal (2017).

The traditional perspective on social structure and economic growth sees the process as one in which the role of social ties in economic life is gradually eroded. Karl Polanyi's *The Great Transformation* is a well-known early work on this subject (Polanyi 1944). Section 17.5 discusses the enduring role of social networks in the process of change. It starts with a number of case studies on how new opportunities—such as markets and the arrival of other formal institutions—lead to changes in the social network. An important sphere in which social networks are especially important is informal risk sharing. There is a large body of research on the limits of such insurance: Our discussion on social ties draws on the extensive work of Marcel Fafchamps and his collaborators (Fafchamps and Lund [2003]; Fafchamps and Gubert [2007]; and Fafchamps [2011]); Christopher Udry (Conley and Udry [2010]; and Udry [1994]); and Ray Fisman (2003) on informal insurance and social networks in developing countries. For recent work that takes on an explicit network perspective, see Ambrus, Mobius, and Szeidl (2014); Ambrus and Elliott (2021); Bloch, Genicot, and Ray (2008); Bramoullé and Kranton (2007); and Munshi and Rosenzweig (2016). Until recently, however, relatively little attention had been given to the interaction between formal insurance markets and informal risk sharing in networks. A notable early exception is Arnott and Stiglitz (1991), who show that due to moral hazard problems, a developed informal insurance system can hamper the development of formal insurance markets. For a recent study of formal and informal insurance in agriculture, see Mobarak and Rosenzweig (2013).

The case studies in section 17.5 are taken from recent papers on the relations between formal institutions and social networks—the study on microfinance (MF) by Banerjee, Breza, Chandrasekhar, et al. (2021); the study on bank accounts by Comola and Prina (2021); the study of the diamond market by Munshi (2011); and the study on CDD projects by Heß, Jaimovich, and Schündeln (2020) and Jaimovich (2015).

Economic growth interacts with the environment and the base of natural resources. In many parts of the developing world, the lives of communities depend intimately on the quality of the local natural resources (examples of which include waterways, fisheries, pastures, and forests) that they can access. We do not cover these important interactions in this book. For an introduction to the subject, see Dasgupta (1993), and for a study of rules that communities use to manage natural resources, see Ostrom (1990).

## 17.7 Questions

1. Consider the model of network and market activity described in section 17.4. Players simultaneously choose network action $x_i \in \{0, 1\}$ and market action $y_i \in \{0, 1\}$. Define $a_i = (x_i, y_i)$. Suppose that in network $g$ faced with the action profile $a = (a_1, a_2, \ldots, a_n)$, the payoff function for player $i$ is given by

$$\Phi_i(a|g) = (1+\theta y_i)x_i\chi_i(a|g) + y_i - x_ip_x - y_ip_y, \tag{17.14}$$

where $\chi_i(a|g)$ is the number of neighbors in network $g$ who choose the network action, and $p_x \geq 0$ and $p_y \geq 0$ are the prices of actions $x$ and $y$, respectively. We say that actions $x$ and $y$ are substitutes if $\theta \in [-1, 0]$ and complements if $\theta \geq 0$. A Nash equilibrium is said to be maximal if there is not no other equilibrium that Pareto-dominates it.

   (a) Suppose that $\theta = -1$, $p_x = 4$, and $p_y = 0.5$. Describe how the network shapes behavior in the maximal equilibrium.

   (b) Suppose that $\theta = 1$, $p_x = 7$, and $p_y = 2$. Describe how the network shapes behavior in the maximal equilibrium.

   (c) Assess the impact of markets on aggregate welfare (measured as the sum of individual payoffs) and inequality (measured as a ratio of highest versus lowest income) in these two settings.

2. Consider the model of network and market activity described in section 17.4. Players simultaneously choose a network action $x_i \in \{0, 1\}$ and a market action $y_i \in \{0, 1\}$. Define $a_i = (x_i, y_i)$. Suppose that in a network $g$ faced with a action profile $a = (a_1, a_2, \ldots, a_n)$, the payoff function for player $i$ is given by

$$\Phi_i(a|g) = (1+\theta y_i)x_i\chi_i(a|g) + y_i - x_ip_x - y_ip_y \tag{17.15}$$

where $\chi_i(a|g)$ is the number of neighbors in network $g$ who choose the network action, and $p_x \geq 0$ and $p_y \geq 0$, respectively, are the prices of actions $x$ and $y$. We say that the actions $x$ and $y$ are substitutes if $\theta \in [-1, 0]$ and complements if $\theta \geq 0$. A Nash equilibrium is said to be maximal if there does not exist another equilibrium that Pareto dominates it.

(a) Suppose that $p_x = 6$ and $p_y = 0.5$. What is the range of parameter values of $\theta$ for which network and market activity are strong substitutes?

(b) Do there exist values of $\theta < 0$ and $p_x$ and $p_y$ for which it is optimal to choose actions $(x_i, y_i) = (1, 1)$?

(c) Suppose that $p_x = 9$ and $p_y = 4$. What are the range of parameter values of $\theta$ for which network and market activity are strong complements?

(d) Do there exist values of $\theta > 0$ and $p_x$ and $p_y$ for which it is optimal to choose actions $(x_i, y_i) = (1, 0)$?

3. In chapter 12, we studied coordination games on networks and drew attention to the role of network cohesiveness as a determinant of behavior. In the model in section 17.4, our analysis draws attention to the role of the $q$-core in understanding behavior. Discuss the relationship between cohesiveness and the $q$-core of a network.

4. Consider the model of network and market activity described in section 17.4. Suppose that individuals are heterogenous with respect to the returns from market activity and that returns to market activity are negatively related to membership of the q-core. Reason how the arrival of markets may well increase inequality even if networks and markets are substitutes.

5. Consider the case study of the impact of MF on social networks as discussed in section 17.5.4.

(a) We found that ties between non-MF household fell by more than ties between MF households, and finally that ties of advice also fell. How can we account for this change in social networks?

(b) We found that informal ties of advice also declined. Use ideas from the theory of network formation—that links of various individuals may be strategic complements or substitutes—to reason about this change in social networks.

6. When social networks and markets are substitutes, there may arise the possibility of multiple equilibria: one with large social networks and small markets, and another with small social networks and well-developed markets. Moreover, once large social networks are in place, it may be difficult for markets to develop. Discuss (and, if possible, provide examples of) such outcomes.

7. Social ties become less important with modernization because well-functioning markets provide services traditionally provided by social relations in traditional societies. Discuss.

# 18 Trust

## 18.1 Introduction

> Virtually every commercial transaction has within itself an element of trust, certainly any transaction conducted over a period of time. It can be plausibly argued that much of the economic backwardness in the world can be explained by the lack of mutual confidence.
> —Arrow (1972, p. 357).

> "individuals will rationally place trust if the ratio of the probability that the trustee will keep the trust to the probability that he will not is greater than the ratio of the potential loss to the potential gain . . ."
> —Coleman (1990, p. 104).

Transactions in which trust is important include those in which goods and services are provided in exchange for future payment; employment contracts in which managers rely on employees to accomplish tasks that are difficult to monitor; and investments and savings decisions that rely on assurances by governments/banks that they will not expropriate these assets. In some situations, it is possible that the parties to a transaction will get to know one another and may carry out transactions with each other in the future. However, in other situations, it is more natural to imagine that the parties are strangers and unlikely to meet ever again. Imagine, for example, a passenger arriving at an international airport and taking a taxi ride. The passenger and driver are unlikely to meet after the taxi drops off the passenger in town.

In this chapter, we will study both types of situations. In the former situation, we will think of trust as being local to a small group of individuals (as in the quote from Coleman above), while in the latter, we will consider trust among strangers—generalized trust.

We start with an exploration of local trust. From this perspective, trust is viewed as a solution to a social dilemma—it is in the collective interest of individuals to cooperate and choose a certain course of action, but each individual has an interest in deviating from this course of action for their own advantage. Good behavior today is sustained by the anticipation of receiving rewards tomorrow. The magnitude of rewards and the possibility of punishments implemented by connected members lead us to a study of social relations, in particular the role of common neighbors in a network. These considerations lead us to the concept of *network closure*. To formally examine how direct and indirect connections come into play, we develop a model of links as *social collateral*. A relationship offers a stream of possible benefits in the future. Individuals can carry out transactions and trust each other to behave well because if they did not do so, then they would forsake these future benefits. An investor may borrow money using the link as collateral. This approach yields a key insight: the amount a person can borrow depends on the level of trust that exists, and this trust is defined as the *minimum cut* of the network. We present evidence from urban Peru and rural India to illustrate the role of network closure.

We turn next to generalized trust; here, we start with a presentation of data on measures of generalized trust in different countries and show how that is correlated to economic performance. This sets the stage for a study of the determinants of generalized trust. As a first step, we think of trust as arising out of beliefs and expectations about behavior. We conceive of culture as describing these beliefs and expectations and present evidence of how two central cultural elements—religion and ethnicity—shape trust.

In the final section of the chapter, we take up the relation between local and generalized trust. A recurring theme is the tension between the group-based cooperation that underlines local trust (and excludes nonmembers) and the demands of generalized trust. We present a simple model of favoritism to bring out the origins of group-based cooperation and its broader negative consequences. This is followed by a discussion of the role that formal institutions and social structure play in helping to bridge the gap between local and generalized trust.

## 18.2 Local Trust

We start with a famous description of local trust:

> Wholesale diamond markets exhibit a property that to an outsider is remarkable. In the process of negotiating a sale, a merchant will hand over to another merchant a bag of stones for the latter to examine in private at his leisure, with no formal insurance that the latter will not substitute one or more inferior stones or a paste replica. The merchandise may be worth thousands, or hundreds of thousands, of dollars. Such free exchange of stones for inspection is important to the functioning of this market. In its absence, the market would operate in a much more cumbersome, much less efficient fashion.
>
> Inspection shows certain attributes of the social structure. A given merchant community is ordinarily very close, both in the frequency of interaction and in ethnic and family ties. The wholesale diamond market in New York City, for example, is Jewish, with a high degree of intermarriage, living in the same community in Brooklyn, and going to the same synagogues. It is essentially a closed community.
>
> Observation of the wholesale diamond market indicates that these close ties, through family, community, and religious affiliation, provide the insurance that is necessary to facilitate the transactions in the market. If any member of this community defected through substituting other stones or through stealing stones in his temporary possession, he would lose family, religious, and community ties. The strength of these ties makes possible transactions in which trustworthiness is taken for granted and

> trade can occur with ease. In the absence of these ties, elaborate and expensive bonding and insurance devices would be necessary- or else the transactions could not take place.
> Coleman (1988, p. S98–99).

It is clear that a high degree of trust in others saves us from having to incur large costs by drawing up contracts with them and having to monitor their activities. Coleman's description presents us with a context in which the overlapping social connections, reflected in trading links, of intermarriage, common religious affiliation, and physical proximity help in creating and sustaining trust and facilitating the functioning of a very high-value market.

We now turn to the sources of local trust:

> If A does something for B and trusts B to reciprocate in the future, this establishes an expectation in A and an obligation on the part of B. This obligation can be conceived as a credit slip held by A for performance by B. If A holds a large number of these credit slips, for a number of persons with whom A has relations, then the analogy to financial capital is direct. These credit slips constitute a large body of credit that A can call in if necessary—unless, of course, the placement of trust has been unwise, and these are bad debts that will not be repaid. In some social structures, it is said that "people are always doing things for each other." There are a large number of these credit slips outstanding, often on both sides of a relation (for these credit slips appear often not to be completely fungible across areas of activity, so that credit slips of B held by A and those of A held by B are not fully used to cancel each other out). . . . This form of social capital depends on two elements: trustworthiness of the social environment, which means that obligations will be repaid, and the actual extent of obligations held. Social structures differ in both these dimensions, and actors within the same structure differ in the second.
> Coleman (1988, p. S102).

We now move forward from bilateral relations and locate individuals in a network. A central idea in the literature pertains to the notion of *network closure*. Network closure was first introduced in the context of dropout rates in high schools in the US (Coleman 1981). Figure 18.1 illustrates the idea of network closure: in the network on panel (a), individuals 1, 2, and 3 are linked, but 2 and 3 do not close the circle of connections. In the network on panel (b), there is a link between 2 and 3 that does close the circle. Let us discuss the dropout study and place network closure in that context.

The High School and Beyond (HS&B) is a national longitudinal study originally funded by the US Department of Education's National Center for Education Statistics (NCES). The HS&B is part of the National Education Longitudinal Studies program, which seeks to document the educational and personal development of young people, following them over time as they begin to take on adult roles and responsibilities.

Our discussion draws heavily on Coleman (1981). The study uses the HS&B data from 893 public schools, 84 Catholic schools, and 27 other private schools. Most of the other private schools were independent schools with no religious affiliation. The focus is on the dropout rates of pupils as they approach their last year of high school. The dropout rates between sophomore and senior years are 14.4 percent in public schools, 3.4 percent in Catholic schools, and 11.9 percent in other private schools. The dropout rate at Catholic

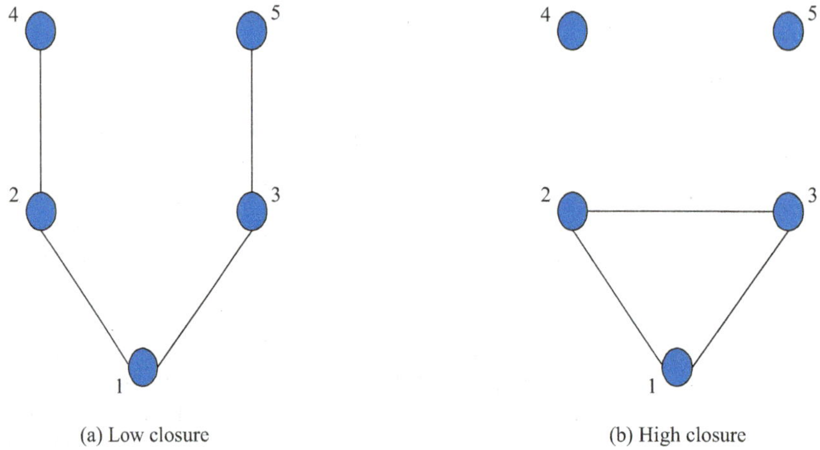


**Figure 18.1**
Network closure.

schools is one-quarter of the rate at public schools and about a third of the rate at other private schools. These large differences persist after we adjust for differences in economic and demographic differences between the families sending their children to these schools. Interestingly, for public schools, the dropout rates of pupils from Catholic families are only slightly lower than those of nonCatholics. What are the reasons for this large difference?

The low dropout rates of the Catholic schools, the absence of low dropout rates in the other private schools, and the independent effect of frequency of religious affiliation point to the importance of the social network in the adult community surrounding the schools. The difference in this structure of this community can be understood with the help of figure 18.2. The vertical lines represent relations across generations (between parent and child), while the horizontal lines represent relations within a generation. In both figure 18.2(a) and figure 18.2(b), the point labeled P1 represents the parent of child C1, and the point labeled P2 represents the parent of child C2. The lines between C1 and C2 represent the relations among pupils in the school. There is a rich set of connections between the pupils as they see each other at school, and this develops a set of expectations and norms about each other's behavior. The two communities differ, however, in the presence or absence of links among the parents of children in the school. The network of parents in school II has intergenerational closure—the parents' friends are the parents of their children's friends. The social network of parents in school I, on the other hand, exhibits no closure. Thus, in school II, P1 and P2 can discuss their children's activities and come to some consensus about standards and sanctions. This is not possible in the network of school I. Network closure helps the community of parents to develop shared norms and more effectively impose sanctions in response to deviations from those norms. P1 is reinforced by P2 in sanctioning their child's

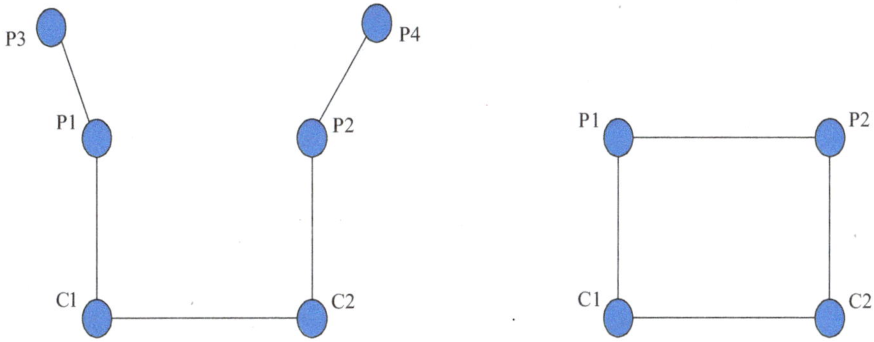


(a) School I: Low closure (b) School II: High closure

**Figure 18.2**
Intergenerational closure.

actions; beyond that, P2 constitutes a monitor not only for their own child, C2, but also for the other child, C1. Parents and their children in Catholic schools were embedded in a network with intergenerational closure, as in school II, while their public-school counterparts were located in a network like school I.

Next, we present two other examples of the use of social ties that serve to further bring out the role of network closure in supporting economic transactions. These examples are taken from Karlan, Mobius, Rosenblat, and Szeidl (2009).

The first example pertains to a Norwegian shipowner who was in need of a ship that had undergone repairs in an Amsterdam shipyard. The shipyard would not release the ship unless a cash payment was made of 200,000 pounds. The ship would remain tied up for the weekend, and the shipowner would lose at least 20,000 pounds. But he did not have the 200,000 pounds, so he reached out to a London banker in Hambros, hoping that he would have contacts in Amsterdam. After hearing the situation, the Hambros man looked at the clock and said, "It's getting late, but I'll see whether we can catch anyone at the bank in Amsterdam . . . stay at the phone." Over a second phone, he dictated to a secretary in the bank a telex message to the Amsterdam bank: "Please pay 200,000 pounds telephonically to (name of shipyard) on understanding that (name of ship) will be released at once."

In this example, the shipowner borrowed 200,000 pounds from an Amsterdam bank with which he had no direct connection. He accomplished this by combining two relations: his connection with the London banker and the connection between the London and Amsterdam banks. The London banker acted as a trust intermediary: he provided access and created the necessary trust for the transaction.

The second example of how networks generate trust is the guanxi system in China. The term "guanxi" refers to a trusted relationship that can be used to obtain services, either directly or indirectly, from that person's social network. Consider the example of a buyer and a seller who share guanxi with a common acquaintance. This third person can act as a trust source—*zhongjian ren*—by introducing the buyer to the supplier. The intermediary vouches for the buyer by assuring the supplier that should the buyer exploit the supplier, the intermediary will compensate for any loss.

These examples illustrate ways in which activity between one pair of individuals can be supported by links to other individuals whom the pair knows in common. The intuitive appeal of the idea of network closure motivates a more general study that takes account of the overall structure of the network of connections. However, before exploring this issue, we briefly comment on other approaches to local trust not based on self-interest.

One route to trust proceeds as follows: an individual may act in a trustworthy way because this course of action is prescribed by their sense of identity. A core element in the theory of identity concerns the idea that our notion of the self arises out of interactions with others. Our views of who we are and how we should act hinge on what we learn from others with whom we interact. Thus interactions with others may shape our notion of goals and aspirations and the appropriate way of behaving. To act in a certain way that is consistent with one's sense of identity is to act based on a different understanding than that which is based on a computation of material costs and benefits. At a more general level, as we move away from instrumental to intrinsic motivations, identity may be seen as being related to social norms. We will discuss the role of social norms at length in section 18.4, but at this point, it is probably worth noting that social interactions may play a role of sustaining norms. We will return to this theme in section 18.6.

## 18.3 Social Collateral

In this section, we consider a situation where a borrower needs the assets of a lender to produce a social surplus. In the absence of legal contract enforcement, borrowing must be secured by an informal arrangement supported by the social network: connections in the network have associated consumption value, which serves as social collateral to enable borrowing. The discussion here and the theoretical model are taken from Karlan, Mobius, Rosenblat, and Szeidl (2009).

We start with three numerical examples to illustrate the basic logic of using relationships as collateral. In figure 18.3, individual $s$ would like to borrow an asset, like a car, from agent $t$. In figure 18.3(a), the network consists of just the two individuals $s$ and $t$; the value of their relationship is given by 2. This summarizes the total benefits, which may include the social benefits from friendship or the discounted present value of future transactions. We take the view that these benefits may be used as collateral by $s$ to borrow from $t$, so $t$ will lend the asset only if its value does not exceed the relationship value of 2.

Let us enrich the situation slightly now and consider the network as shown in figure 18.3(b), where $s$ and $t$ have a common friend, $u$. The value of the relationship between $s$ and $u$ is 3, and that between $u$ and $t$ is 4. Here, the common friend increases the borrowing

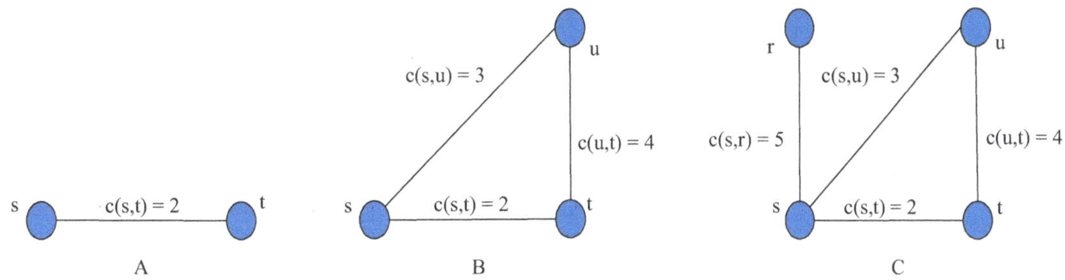


**Figure 18.3**
Social collateral. *Source*: Mobius and Rosenblat (2016).

limit by $\min\{3, 4\} = 3$, the weakest link on the path connecting the borrower and the lender through $u$. This common friendship raises the amount that can be borrowed by $s$ from $t$ to 5. The logic is that the intermediate agent $u$ vouches for the borrower and acts as a guarantor of the loan transaction. If $s$ chooses not to return the car, for example, they are breaking their promise of repayment to $u$ and therefore lose $u$'s friendship. Since the value of this friendship is 3, it can be used as collateral for a payment of up to 3. For the lender $t$ to receive this amount, $u$ must prefer transmitting the payment to losing the friendship with them. This logic also explains why we need to consider the weakest link.

Finally, figure 18.3(c) considers a coalitional deviation. Assume that the borrower also has a cousin $r$, with whom they have a relationship valued at 5. In principle, $r$ can act as a guarantor for $s$, raising the borrowing limit by an additional 5, to a total of 10. However, $r$'s threat to break off their relationship with the borrower is not credible: for any loan amount exceeding 5, the borrower could propose a side deal to intermediary $u$ and the cousin such that $u$ can reimburse the lender for the guaranteed amount (which is at most 3) while transferring 0 to $r$ in case of a default. Observe that as there is no onward link from $r$ to any other individual, $r$ incurs no loss as a result of $s$ reneging on their promise, Thus the intermediary $u$ and $r$ are not worse off as a result of this side deal. The borrower will use their friendship and therefore incur a combined loss of at most 5 (a loss of 3 to $u$ and a loss of 2 to $t$). However, as they borrowed an amount exceeding 5, she is strictly better off under such a side deal. Hence, a punishment of the borrower that involves individuals like $r$, who are unconnected to the lender, is not credible.

### 18.3.1 A Model

We now develop this idea and apply it in a general network, $G$, with nodes $N = \{1, \ldots, n\}$. For every pair $i$ and $j$ in $N$, there is a capacity given by $c_{ij}$. This capacity is zero if no link is present and positive if there is a link. For simplicity, suppose that capacity is symmetric (i.e., $c(u, v) = c(v, u)$). A special case that is interesting arises when all positive links have the same capacity $c > 0$, such that $\forall\, i, j \in N$, $c_{ij} \in \{0, c\}$.

To understand the relation between networks and the limits of borrowing, it is helpful to explicitly define a sequence of actions that involve the borrower, the lender, and the other individuals in the network:

- STAGE 1: Realization of needs. Two agents $s$ and $t$ are randomly selected from the social network. Agent $t$, the lender, has an asset that agent $s$, the borrower, desires. The lender values the asset at $V$, and it is assumed that V is drawn from some distribution F over $[0; 1)$. The identity of the borrower and the lender, as well as the value of V, are publicly observed by all players.
- STAGE 2: Borrowing arrangement. The borrower publicly proposes a transfer arrangement to all agents in the social network. The role of this arrangement is to punish the borrower and compensate the lender in the event of a default. A transfer arrangement consists of a set of transfer payments $h(u; v)$ for all $u$ and $v$ agents involved in the arrangement. Here, $h(u; v)$ is the amount $u$ promises to pay $v$ if the borrower fails to return the asset to the lender. Once the borrower has announced the arrangement, all agents involved have the opportunity to accept or decline. If all involved agents accept, then the asset is borrowed and the borrower earns income $\omega(V)$, where $\omega$ is a nondecreasing function with $\omega(0) = 0$. If some agents decline, then the asset is not lent, and the game moves directly to stage 5.
- STAGE 3: Repayment. Once the borrower has used the asset, they can either return it to the lender or steal it and sell it for a price of $V$. If the borrower returns the asset, then the game moves to stage 5.
- STAGE 4: Transfer payments. All agents observe whether the asset was returned in stage 3. If the borrower did not return the asset, then the transfer arrangement is activated. Each agent makes the promised payment $h(u; v)$ in full or pays nothing. If some agent $u$ fails to make a prescribed transfer $h(u; v)$ to $v$, then they lose their friendship with agent $v$ (i.e., the $(u; v)$ link goes bad). If $(u; v)$ link is lost, then the associated capacity is set to zero for the remainder of the game. We let $\tilde{c}(u; v)$ denote the new link capacities after these changes.
- STAGE 5: Friendship utility. At this stage, agents derive utility from their remaining friends. The total utility enjoyed by agent $u$ from their remaining friends is simply the sum of the values of all remaining relationships (i.e., $\sum_{v \in N} \tilde{c}(u; v)$).

Now, we study the pure-strategy subgame perfect equilibrium of the game. In particular, we would like to understand the limits placed by network $G$ on the amount that $s$ can borrow from lender $t$.

### 18.3.2 Analysis of Equilibrium

In any equilibrium where promises are kept, transfers have to satisfy the capacity constraint

$$h(u; v) \leq c(u; v). \tag{18.1}$$

This inequality reflects the incentives facing an individual. If the borrower fails to return the asset, individual $u$ has to decide whether to make their promised transfer payment $h(u; v)$ to $v$. The cost of making the payment is $h(u; v)$, while the cost of not making the payment is the value of the relationship that is foregone. In any equilibrium where promises are kept, $u$ must prefer the friendship over the monetary value of the transfer, leading to equation (18.1).

Consider the two-agent network, consisting of $s$ and $t$. We argue that the extent of borrowing $V \leq h(s; t)$. To see why, suppose that borrower $s$ defaults. Then the lender receives the transfer payment $h(s; t)$, but they must break even, which requires that $V \leq h(s; t)$. On the other hand, for the borrower to prefer to return the asset, they must prefer not to default, which again requires $V \leq h(s; t)$. Combining this inequality with the capacity constraint (1) yields

$$V \leq c(s; t), \tag{18.2}$$

showing that borrowing is limited by the total social assets available to $s$ in this simple network. The value of the total social assets is referred to as the "maximum flow" in the network. It is also easy to see that when equation (18.2) is satisfied, there is an equilibrium that implements borrowing: just set $h(s; t) = V$. Intuitively, the collateral value of friendship can be used to elicit payment, and thus solve the agency problem.

The maximum flow is easy to infer in this two-agent network, but it is a much more complicated object in a general network with several individuals and with links having different capacities. As a next step, let us consider a three-agent network, with $s$ and $t$ and an intermediary, $u$. A natural transfer arrangement that implements borrowing in this network is one in which agent $u$ acts as an intermediary who elicits and transits payments from $s$ to $t$ in the case of no compliance and gets zero net profits. To formalize this arrangement, simply set $h(s; u) = h(u; t) = V$. For this arrangement to be in the interest of the individuals, the capacity constraint (1) must be satisfied for both links involved: $V \leq c(s; u)$ must hold such that $s$ delivers the transfer to $u$, and $V \leq c(u; t)$ is needed to ensure that $u$ passes the transfer to $t$. Combining these yields the weakest-link inequality

$$V \leq min[c(s; u); c(u; t)] \tag{18.3}$$

Here, the maximum flow is defined, taking into account the links that $s$ and $t$ have with the intermediary.

However, networks with more than two agents generally admit other subgame perfect equilibria that can implement borrowing even if (18.3) fails. To do this in the simplest way, let us return to a network like the one depicted in figure 18.3 and consider the network with four individuals. Assume that borrower $s$ has a strong link to their cousin $v$, with a capacity value of $c(s; v) = V + 1$. The borrower might then propose an informal arrangement in which they promise to pay their cousin a transfer of $h(s; v) = V + 1$ if they fail to return the asset. This arrangement provides the right incentives to the borrower and is a subgame perfect equilibrium, even though (18.3) fails.

However, there is a potential problem with this arrangement: the borrower could circumvent it by entering a side deal with $v$, in which they steal the asset and share the proceeds with the cousin (who in equilibrium would otherwise receive nothing). The lender, conscious of these side deals, will not lend to $s$ if the loan is supported by transfer arrangements that are vulnerable to such deals. To address this issue, we define a subgame perfect equilibrium that is side-deal proof.

Consider the subgame starting in stage 2, after the identities of the borrower and the lender and the value of the asset are realized, and for any pure strategy $\sigma$, let $U_u(\sigma)$ denote the total utility of agent $u$ in this subgame. We formalize the idea of a side deal as an alternative transfer arrangement $\tilde{h}(u; v)$ that s proposes to a subset of agents $S \subset W$ after the original arrangement is accepted. If this side deal is accepted, agents in $S$ are expected to make transfer payments according to eh, while agents outside $S$ continue to make payments described by $h$. In order for the side deal to be credible to all participating agents, it must be accompanied by a proposed path of play that these agents find optimal to follow.

Thus, a *side deal* with respect to a strategy profile $\sigma$ is a set of agents $S$, a transfer arrangement $\tilde{h}(u, v)$ for all $u, v \in S$, and a set of continuation strategies $\{\tilde{\sigma}_u | u \in S\}$, proposed by $s$ to agents in $S$ at the end of stage 2, such that

1. $U_u(\tilde{\sigma}_u, \tilde{\sigma}_{S\backslash u}, \sigma_{-S}) \geq U_u(\sigma'_u, \tilde{\sigma}_{S\backslash u}, \sigma_{-S}), \forall \sigma'_u, \forall u \in S$.
2. $U_u(\tilde{\sigma}_S, \sigma_{-S}) \geq U_u(\sigma_S, \sigma_{-S}), \forall u \in S$.
3. $U_s(\tilde{\sigma}_S, \sigma_{-S}) > U_s(\sigma_S . \sigma_{-S})$.

In other words, condition (1) says that all agents $u$ involved in the side deal are best-responding on the new path of play (i.e., that the proposed path of play is an equilibrium for all agents in $S$, conditional on others playing their original strategies). Condition (2) says that if any agent $u \in S$ refuses to participate in the side deal, then play reverts to the original path given by $\sigma$. Finally, condition (3) ensures that borrower $s$ strictly benefits from the side deal.

A pure strategy profile is a side-deal proof equilibrium if it is a subgame perfect equilibrium that allows no side deals.

We now introduce a few more pieces of notation that are helpful. An $s \rightarrow t$ flow with respect to capacity $c$ is a function $f : G \times G \rightarrow \mathcal{R}$ that satisfies the following:

1. Skew symmetry: $f(u, v) = -f(v, u)$.
2. Capacity constraints: $f(u, v) \leq c(u, v)$.
3. Flow conservation: $\sum_w f(u, w) = 0$, except if $u = s$ or $t$.

The value of the flows is the amount that leaves the borrower: $|f| = \sum_w f(s, w)$. Let $T^{st}(c)$ denote the maximum flow among all $s \rightarrow t$ flows.

There is a side-deal proof equilibrium that implements borrowing between $s$ and $t$ if and only if the asset value $V$ satisfies $V \leq T^{st}(c)$. Thus the maximum flow sets a limit to borrowing between $s$ and $t$. Let us go through the argument underlying this result. A well-known result on flows in graphs tells us that the maximum flow between $s$ and $t$ is equal to the minimum cut between them. So what is a minimum cut? A *cut* is a partition of nodes into two sets $S$ and $T$, with $s \in S$ and $t \in T$, and the value of the cut is given by the sum of all links between nodes in the sets $S$ and $T$. A *minimum cut* is a partition that minimizes the value of the cut across all partitions.

To develop a feel for the idea of a minimum cut, let us consider a few examples. Consider the three networks in figure 18.3. In a network with two individuals $s$ and $t$, there is only one link, and so there is a unique cut. The maximum flow is simply the capacity of the link. In a network with three individuals, the minimum cut corresponds to the the partition with 1 in one set and 2 and 3 in the other set. The minimum cut is given by 5. Finally, consider the network with four individuals. It is easy to see that the existence of individual leaves the minimum cut unaltered relative to the network with three individuals, so it is also given by 5.

Equipped with this result on the maximum flow and minimum cut, we can state a simple but powerful theoretical result: the size of the loan for $s$, $V$ is limited by the maximum flow in the network. First, observe that any amount $V \leq T^{st}(c)$ can be borrowed. Simply use the flows that define $T^{st}$ to construct the transfers in stage 2. By hypothesis, $V \leq T^{st}(c)$, so such a flow is incentive feasible. Also, note that each intermediary node acts as a pure conveyor in such a flow. The intermediary node merely passes the transfers onward from borrower to lender. Next, we argue that no loan larger than the maximum flow is feasible. Consider a loan that is larger than the maximum flow. This means that it also exceeds the minimum cut in the network. In other words, there is a cut in the network $S$ and $T$, such that the value of the cut is smaller than $V$. But then there is a side deal with the members of set $S$, in which $V$ is shared between the members of $S$. The side deal is attractive to members of $S$, as they get to keep $V$ and it exceeds the sum total of anticipated rewards that they forgo from members of $T$.

Let us say that trust is equal to the size of the loan that can be taken out. We can summarize our discussion so far as follows.

**Proposition 18.1** *The maximum flow is given by the minimum cut of the network. The level of trust in the network is defined by its maximum flow.*

The maximum flow therefore defines payoffs in a network. The payoffs to $s$ in network $G$ with capacities $c$ are

$$\Pi^{st}(c) = \Pi^{st}(T^{st}(c)), \tag{18.4}$$

where $\Pi(z) = \int_0^z \omega(v) f(v) dv$ (recalling that $\omega(v)$ is the value to the borrower and $f$ is the distribution of $v$). This value is computed conditional on the pair $(s, t)$ being picked.

We now examine how network structure shapes borrowing possibilities. One remark is that an increase in capacities raises the maximum flow and therefore raises the borrowing potential in the network. Let us next look at the deeper structure of the network (while bearing in mind the idea of network closure).

### 18.3.3 The Role of Network Closure

At an intuitive level, networks have high closure if the neighborhoods of connected agents have large overlap (as in figure 18.1). However, there are also considerations that suggest that a network with low closure may be more advantageous. The idea here is that closure involves linking individuals who already have paths between them. Thus links are in some sense redundant. To the extent that links are costly and therefore scarce, closure is wasteful (Granovetter [1973]; Burt [1994]). Thus networks with low closure lead to higher performance as they allow agents to reach many others through the network.

At an intuitive level, high network closure is associated with having multiple paths to a smaller set of agents. Using the concept of network flows, let us count the total number of paths of an agent. Suppose that all existing links have the unit value 1. Then network flow $T^{st}(c)$ is effectively the number of disjoint paths between $s$ and $t$, $T^s(c) = \sum_{t \in N} T^{st}(c)$.

We use figure 18.4 (which is a relabeling of figure 18.1) to elaborate on the role of network closure. In the diagrams, $s$ has a total of four paths in both networks (where the background assumption is that each of the links has capacity 1). In figure 18.4(a), there are four paths that reach four different people, while in figure 18.4(b) they reach only two people, but there are two paths connecting $s$ with either of them. More generally, define $P^s(n)$ as the share of paths $s$ has with individuals to whom they have at least $n$ paths. In the networks in figure 18.4, $P^s(2) = 0$ in figure 18.4(a) and $P^s(2) = 1$ in figure 18.4(b). Clearly, $P^s(0) = 1$ always, and $P^s(n)$ is weakly falling in $n$.

The important point to note is that higher closure increases trust but reduces access. For example, in figure 18.2(b) two people trust $s$ with assets of value $V = 2$; access is low as only two people are available for a loan, but loans of value 2 can be taken in this closed network. In contrast, in figure 18.2(a), $s$ can borrow from four people, but the asset value can be no more than 1: access has increased, but at the cost of a reduction in the size of the loan that can be taken out.

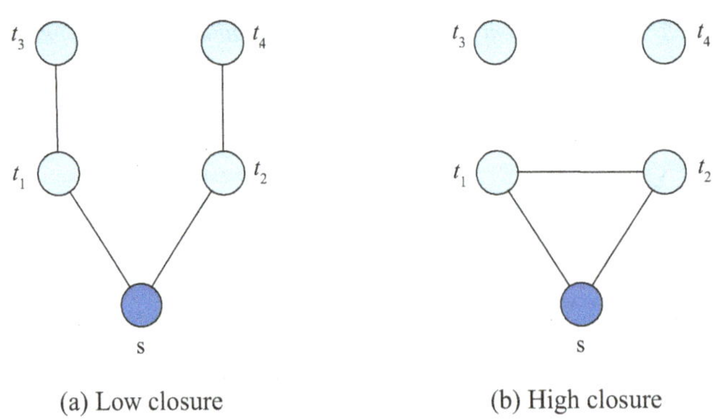


**Figure 18.4**
Closure versus access. *Source*: Karlan, Mobius, Rosenblat, and Szeidl (2009).

The attractiveness of closure depends on the relative value of high- versus low-value loans. To formalize this trade-off between access and pairwise trust, define $\tilde{\omega}(V) = f(V)\omega(V)$ as the frequency-weighted profits from the ability to borrow $V$. Observe that $\tilde{\omega}(V)$ depends on both the probability that an asset of value $V$ is needed ($f(V)$) and on the profits that this asset generates ($\omega(V)$). An economy is a high-value environment if $\tilde{\omega}(V)$ is increasing, and it is a low-value exchange environment if $\tilde{\omega}(V)$ is decreasing.

We will say that the network neighborhood of $s$ has a higher closure than the neighborhood of $s'$ if both of the following are true:

1. $T^s(c) = T^{s'}(c)$ so that $s$ and $s'$ have the same total number of paths.
2. For each $n$, $P^s(n) \geq P^{s'}(n)$, so that a greater share of paths connect $s$ to people with whom $n$ has many paths.

Thus if the neighborhood of $s$ has higher closure, then $s$ is connected to fewer people through many paths. To facilitate a comparison of networks, it is helpful to define payoffs of individuals as a function of the network.

Define $q_s(j)$ as the proportion of paths of $s$ with agents to whom they have exactly $j$ paths. Note that

$$P^s(n) = 1 - \sum_{j=1}^{j=n-1} q^s(j). \tag{18.5}$$

Thus an increase in closure may be interpreted as a first-order stochastic shift in density $q_s(j)$. Recall that there are $N$ individuals in all, so $s$ can have 1 out of $N-1$ individuals as a potential lender (so $N=4$ in both panels of figure 18.2). Let $M$ be the total number of paths, observe that in both networks in figure 18.2, we have $M=4$. Now $q_s(j)$ is the share of total paths that connect to agents with exactly $j$ paths. So the number of paths that satisfies this criterion for $j$ paths is $Mq_s(j)$. Next, observe that the number of potential lenders who have $j$ paths is given by $Mq_s(j)/j$ (as there are $j$ paths for each such individual). The probability of requesting a favor from any of them equals

$$\frac{1}{N-1}\frac{Mq_s(j)}{j}. \tag{18.6}$$

The payoff on meeting such an individual is $\Pi(j)$, and therefore the expected payoff to $s$ in network is

$$\frac{1}{N-1}\sum_j \frac{Mq_s(j)}{j}\Pi(j), \tag{18.7}$$

where we have assumed that all links have capacity 1. This in turn can be rewritten as

$$\frac{1}{N-1}\sum_j Mq_s(j)\frac{\Pi(j)}{j}. \tag{18.8}$$

This expression is simply the expected value of $\Pi(j)/j$ under density $q_s(j)$. In a high-value environment, $\Pi(V)$ is convex because the first derivative, $\Pi(V)' = \tilde{w}(V)$, is increasing. Since $\Pi(0) = 0$, it follows that $\Pi(V)/V$ is nondecreasing in $V$. In this case, a first-order stochastic dominance shift in density $q_s(j)$ increases the expected payoff. The converse holds in low-value exchange environments.

These considerations allow us to state our main result on network closure.

**Proposition 18.2** *In a high-value exchange environment, a neighborhood with higher closure leads to a higher expected payoff to s. Conversely, in a low-value exchange environment, a neighborhood with higher closure leads to a lower expected payoff to s.*

This result speaks to a classical question on the relative attractiveness of high- and low-closure networks. In a low-value exchange environment, the access provided by low closure is more attractive because knowing more people (directly or indirectly) increases the likelihood that $s$ can obtain a low-value asset. This is consistent with theories put forward by Granovetter (1973) and Burt (1994) concerning the strength of weak ties and the benefits of a dispersed social network in providing access to assets such as small favors, information, or advice. In contrast, in a high-value exchange environment, network closure is better. Here, a reduction in access is more than compensated for by the fact that, through their dense connections, $s$ will be able to borrow even high-value assets. This would be critical for parents bringing up children (where norms need to be established, monitoring needs to be carried out, and sanctions need to be applied) or for diamond merchants in New York (where the exchange of valuable stones requires high trust between dealers).

### 18.3.4 Empirical Evidence on Networks and Social Collateral

Here, we present two case studies for the uses of social collateral that draw attention to the role of network closure. The discussion here is based on Karlan, Mobius, Rosenblat, and Szeidl (2009); Mobius and Rosenblat (2016); and Jackson, Rodriguez-Barraquer, and Tan (2012).

*1. Informal Loans in Peruvian Towns*

The first case study pertains to two Peruvian shantytowns in the Northern Cone of Lima. The data is from the year 2005. There are 299 households in all. The network describes, for each pair of households, how much time is spent with the friend or acquaintance per week and whether there were any loans made over the past year. Households have, on average, 8.6 links, and the average geographic distance between connected agents (i.e., agents who have spent time together) is 42 and 39 meters in the two communities; this is considerably less than the geographic distance between two randomly selected addresses, which is 132 and 107 meters, respectively. There were 254 informal loans; 167 borrowers in 138 households reported to have borrowed on average about \$23 from 173 lenders during the past 12 months. Thus, informal borrowing is very common in these communities: 46 percent of all households have at least one household member who borrowed money in this manner.

**Table 18.1**
Social relations and propensity to borrow

| Direct Time \ Indirect Time | Below average | Above average |
|---|---|---|
| Above average | 21 | 42 |
| Below average | 14.5 | 22.5 |

*Source*: Mobius and Rosenblat (2016).

The amount of time spent together provides a proxy for the strength of a relationship. This can be used to construct capacity of ties. Suppose that capacity of a link $(u, v)$ is given by $c(u, v) = c\tau(s, t)$, where $\tau(s, t)$ is the time spent together by $s$ and $t$. For concreteness, let us consider only direct and indirect ties with one common intermediary. This allows a simple decomposition of the trust flow between $s$ and $t$ as follows:

$$T^{st}(c) = c\tau(s;t) + c \sum_{v \in N_s \cap N_t} \min(\tau(s;v); \tau(v;t)), \tag{18.9}$$

where the first term represents the direct flow and the second is the indirect flow. Here, $N_s$ is the set of direct friends of agent $s$.

Table 18.1 groups all social links of each borrower into four categories depending on whether the direct flow between borrower and lender is below or above the average direct flow, and whether the indirect flow between borrower and friend is below or above the average indirect flow. Table 18.1 suggests that direct and indirect ties are strongly correlated with the frequency of informal loans. When we move from below-average direct and indirect ties to above-average direct and indirect ties, the frequency of loans grows almost three times—from 14.5 percent to 42 percent. Moreover, considering only strong direct ties, there is close to a doubling of frequency from 22.5 percent to 42 percent when we move from weak to strong indirect ties. Indirect flows thus play an important role in creating social collateral for borrowing.

*2. Favor Exchange in South India*
The second case study is about favor exchange among households in rural southern India The study covers 75 villages in the southern Indian state of Karnataka. These are the same villages that were included in the rural networks discussion in chapter 1. The average number of households sampled in a village is 193.5. The average number of links per household is 2.89. Table 18.2 summarizes the relation between having common friends and favor exchange.

To get a first impression of the level of social collateral, we present the distribution of pairs with respect to the number of common friends in figure 18.5.

We consider the following types of favors:

- Borrow kerosene and rice: If you needed to borrow kerosene or rice, to whom would you go?

**Table 18.2**
Common friends and favors

| | Percentages |
|---|---|
| Favor exchange with common friends | 59 |
| Favor exchange without common friends | 41 |
| Favor exchange within a subcaste | 68 |
| Favor exchange outside a subcaste | 32 |
| Money or kerorice favors with common friends | 61 |
| Money or kerorice favors without common friends | 39 |

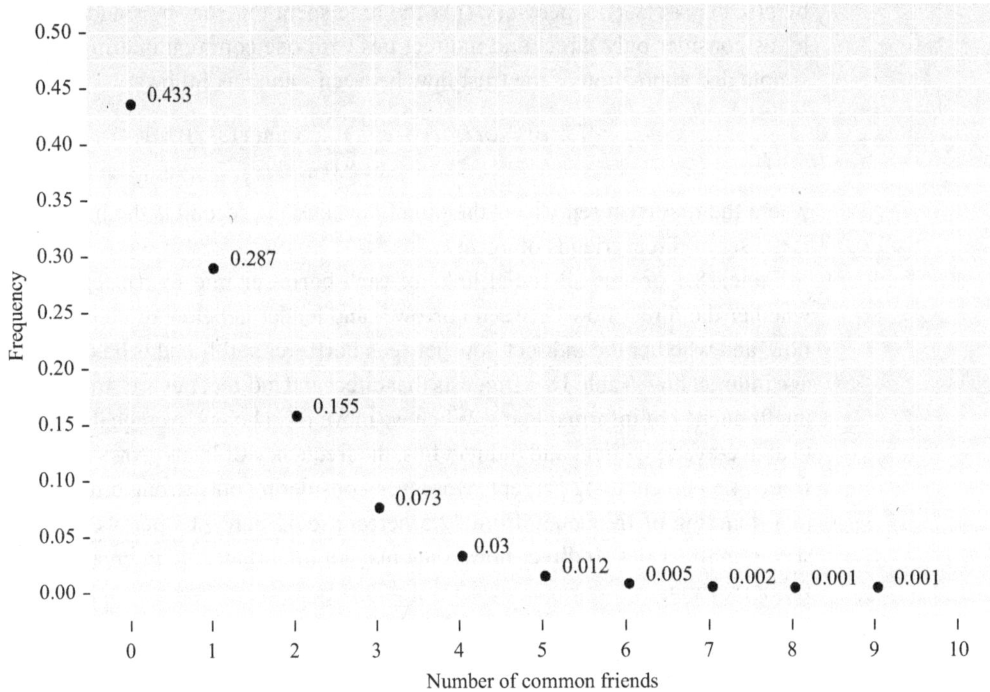


**Figure 18.5**
Distribution of common friends. *Source*: Jackson, Rodriguez-Barraquer, and Tan (2012).

**Figure 18.6**
Common friends and favors. *Source*: Jackson, Rodriguez-Barraquer, and Tan (2012).

- Lend kerosene and rice: Who would come to you if they needed to borrow kerosene or rice?
- Borrow money: If you suddenly needed to borrow 50 INR for a day, whom would you ask?
- Lend money: Who do you trust enough that if they needed to borrow 50 INR for a day, you would lend it to them?
- Advice come: Who comes to you for advice?
- Advice go: If you had to make a difficult personal decision, whom would you ask for advice?
- Medical help: If you had a medical emergency and were alone at home, whom would you ask for help in getting to a hospital?

First, we consider the relation between common friends and any of these seven favors. Figure 18.6 presents the relation between the number of common friends and the probability of favor exchange. This graph shows that there is a positive relation: the greater the number of common friends, the higher the fraction of favor exchange (except in the case of nine common friends, which is probably due to the very small number of such links). If we interpret the number of common friends as higher social collateral, then this positive correlation

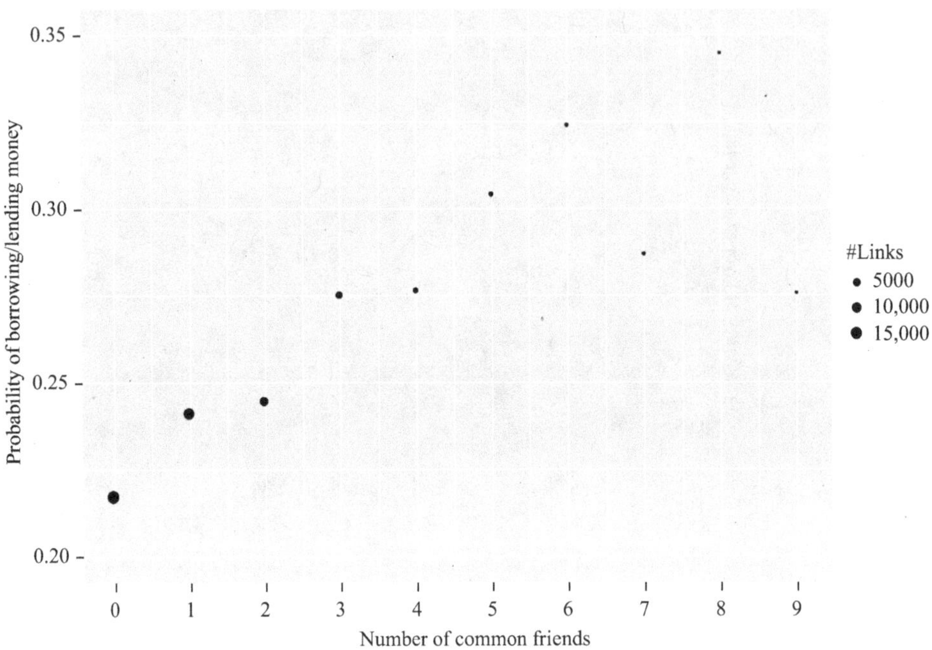


**Figure 18.7**
Common friends and large favors. *Source*: Jackson, Rodriguez-Barraquer, and Tan (2012).

is consistent with the theory: a greater number of common friends can support a wider range of favors, which raises the probability of a favor.

The size of social collateral would probably matter for large favors more than for small favors. With this idea in mind, we look at potentially higher-value favors—loans of money and loans of kerosene and rice. Figure 18.7 presents the fraction of large-favor exchange pairs as a function of the number of common friends. It reveals that the fraction of pairs undertaking large favors increases with the number of common friends.

### 18.3.5 Repeated Interactions and Common Friends

Section 18.3.1 presented a model of social collateral in which a link reflected anticipated future rewards. In this section, we briefly elaborate on the repeated interactions implicit in these rewards. The discussion draws on a theoretical model due to Jackson, Rodriguez-Barraquer, and Tan (2012).

Consider a group of individuals, $N = \{1, \ldots, n\}$, with $n \geq 2$ that are connected in an undirected network. The neighbors of $i$ in network $g$ are denoted as $N_i(g) = \{j | g_{ij} = 1\}$. The degree of i is the number of neighbors, and is denoted by $d_i(g) = |N_i(g)|$.

Time proceeds in discrete periods, $t = 0, 1, \ldots$. In any period, there is a chance that an individual needs a favor from a friend or will be called upon to do a favor for a friend. To be precise, there is probability $p$ that individual $i$ will be called upon to do a favor for any of his neighbors. It is assumed that at most, one favor will be needed across all agents in any period (i.e., $n(n-1)p \leq 1$).

Doing a favor costs $c > 0$, and the value of the favor is $v$. We will focus on the case where $v > c$. Thus the value of a favor to the receiving agent exceeds the cost to the providing agent, so favor exchange is good for overall welfare. Individuals discount future payoffs using a factor of $0 < \delta < 1$.

To develop a feel for the trade-offs involved, observe that in the situation with two individuals who do favors for each other, each would expect a discounted payoff of

$$\frac{p(v-c)}{1-\delta}. \tag{18.10}$$

So an individual called upon to do a favor compared the cost $c$ with the stream of benefits given in equation (18.10). Suppose that costs exceed these benefits—then two individuals cannot sustain favor exchange in isolation. How can a network help in this situation?

Consider individual $i$ who is located in network $g$. Suppose they refuse an offer to a friend, $j$. Building on the idea of social punishments in the social collateral model, a possibility is that $j$ informs their common acquaintances, and these acquaintances all decide not to offer any favors to $i$ in the future. Let $N_{ij}(g) = N_i(g) \cup N_j(g)$ be the set of common acquaintances of $i$ and $j$ in network $g$. Now, individual $i$, located in network $g$, compares the cost of doing the favor today, $c$, with the loss in stream of benefits from the common acquaintances and person $j$; that is,

$$\frac{(N_{ij}(g)+1)p(v-c)}{1-\delta}. \tag{18.11}$$

This simple computation provides a simple rule of thumb: the size of favors that can be sustained in the network will grow with the number of common acquaintances between $i$ and $j$; this observation is consistent with the evidence presented in section 18.3.

The discussion in this section focuses on the ways in which the structure of relations provides a form of collateral that allows cooperative relations to exist. The social collateral argument rests on detailed information about transfers and the strength of ties being available to potential partners. In the introduction to this chapter, we mentioned the role of trust in a one-off interaction among strangers. The next section takes up that topic.

## 18.4 Generalized Trust

In this section, we start by presenting evidence on measures of generalized trust and then examine its sources. We will use the following generalized trust question:

- Generally speaking, would you say that most people can be trusted, or that you can't be too careful when dealing with others? The two possible answers are
  1. Most people can be trusted.
  2. Need to be very careful.

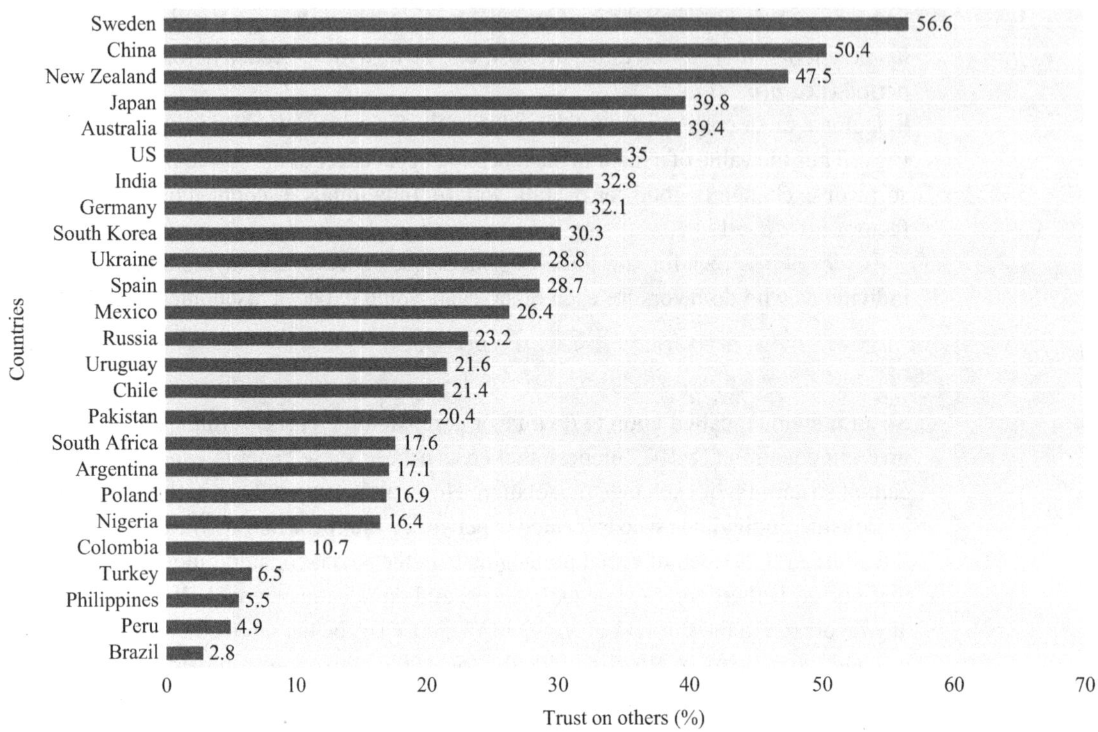


**Figure 18.8**
Trust levels in 1995. *Source*: World Value Survey Wave 3.

We will measure trust in terms of the fraction of respondents who answered 1. The same question has been used by a variety of other questionnaires, such as the European Social Survey, the General Social Survey, the World Values Survey, Latinobarometro, and the Australian Community Survey.

Figures 18.8 and 18.9 summarize the data for a set of countries for the years 1995 and 2017. They report the fraction of respondents who responded with "Most people can be trusted." There are very great variations in level of trust across countries, and these differences are fairly stable. In Sweden, for instance, the trust level is 56 percent and 60 percent, while in Brazil, the level of trust is 2.8 percent and 5.5 percent, respectively in the two years.

We next discuss the relation between this measure of trust and broad economic indicators. Figures 18.10 and 18.11 present a simple scatterplot on the relation between trust and per capita income for the years 1995 and 2017. We plot trust on the $x$-axis and the level of per capita income on the $y$-axis. We see that there is a clear positive correlation between trust and income levels for both years. These correlations motivate an examination of the sources of large differences in trust across countries.

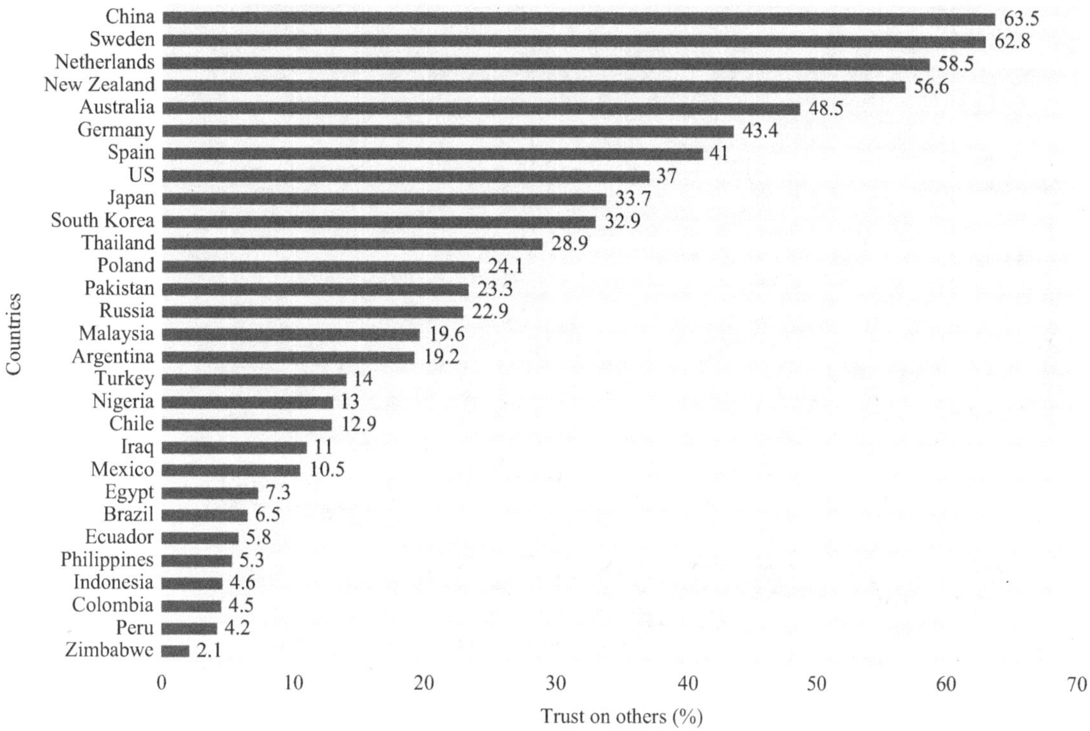


**Figure 18.9**
Trust levels in 2017. *Source*: World Value Survey Wave 7.

We will trace differences in trust to culture. To appreciate the pathways through which culture may influence trust, we start our discussion with the trust game. There are two players, a trustor and a trustee. The trustor has a sum of money, $M$. In the first stage of the game, they can choose to pass a part of this money, $m$, where $m \in [0, M]$ to the trustee. Any amount passed to the trustee gains in value, so the trustor receives $3m$. In the second stage of the game, the trustee can decide how much of this $3m$ to return to the trustor. It is clear that if the trustor prefers more money to less money, then they should retain all of $3m$. Anticipating this, the trustor will choose to transfer 0 in stage 1. Thus the money available to the trustor and trustee will be $M$ and 0, respectively. However, both players are better off if the trustor and trustee can agree to each transfer money to each other. For instance, if the trustor transfers all of $M$ and the trustee transfers half of what they receive, then both players will earn $1.5M$, and they will both be better off than in the no-transfer outcome.

One resolution to this dilemma sees individual action as arising out of social obligations, expectations, and norms. This perspective emphasizes the role of the social context—how social relations and the broader culture give meaning to individual choice and thereby shape

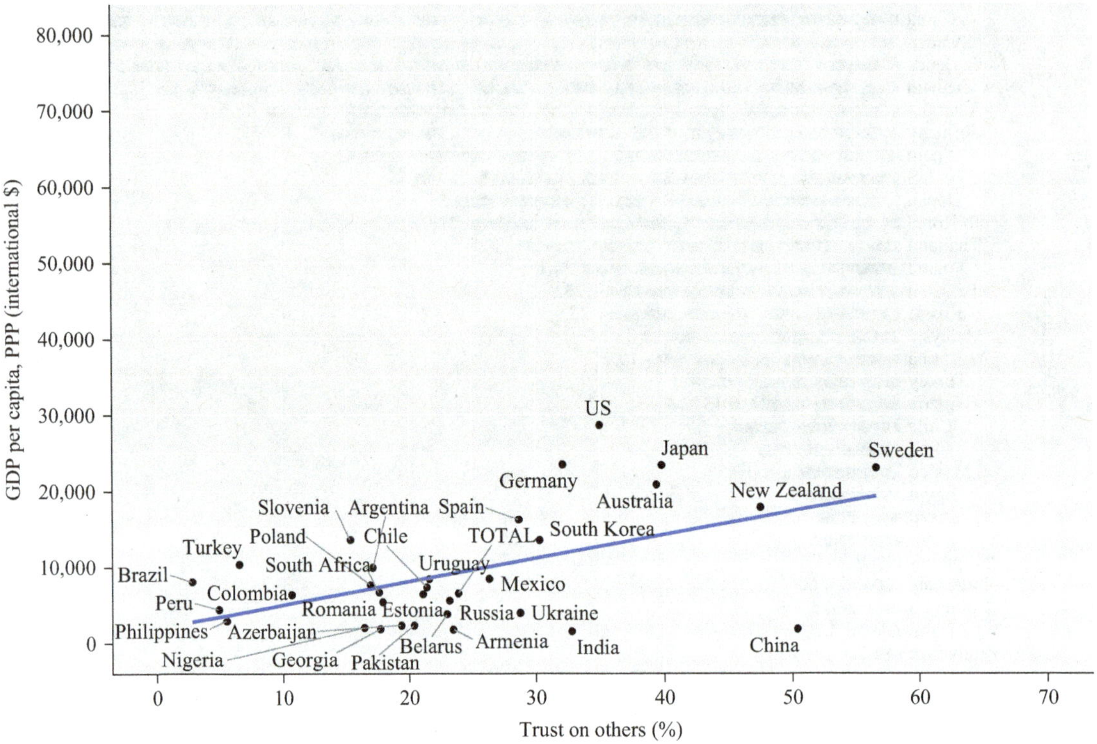


**Figure 18.10**
Trust and Income (1995). *Source*: World Value Survey Wave 3.

action. In this line of thought, players solve this dilemma through trust. Trust can be thought of as the subjective probability with which an individual believes that another individual or group of individuals will perform a particular action (see e.g., Gambetta [1988]).

Individual A may trust B because they know that B adheres to certain norms, and these norms prescribe certain behaviors. These norms may entail trustworthy behavior toward own group members or more generally toward everyone, even strangers:

> A prescriptive norm within a collectivity that constitutes an especially important form of social capital is the norm that one should forgo self-interest and act in the interests of the collectivity. A norm of this sort, reinforced by social support, status, honor, and other rewards, is the social capital that builds young nations (and then dissipates as they grow older), strengthens families by leading family members to act selflessly in "the family's" interest, facilitates the development of nascent social movements through a small group of dedicated, inward-looking, and mutually rewarding members, and in general leads persons to work for the public good. In some of these cases, the norms are internalized; in others, they are largely supported through external rewards for selfless actions and disapproval for selfish

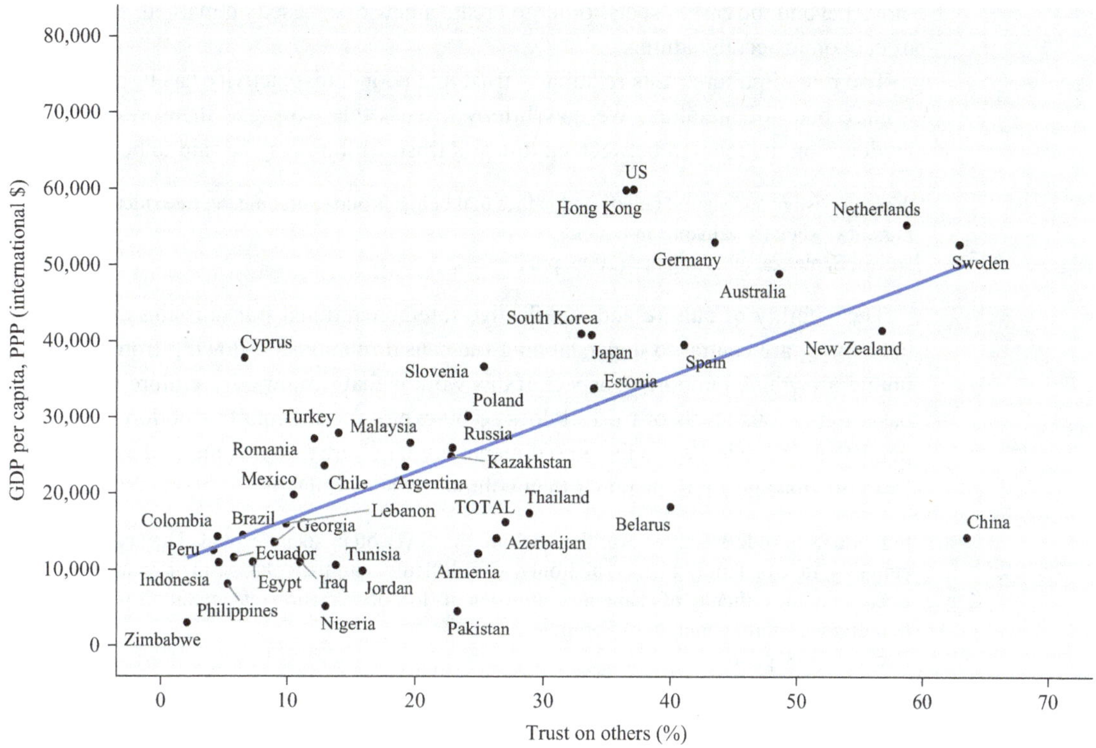


**Figure 18.11**
Trust and Income (2017). *Source*: World Value Survey Wave 7.

> actions. But, whether supported by internal or external sanctions, norms of this sort are important in overcoming the public goods problem that exists in collectivities.
> Coleman (1988, pp. S104–S105).

Thus a certain norm may be sustained through a combination of mechanisms (which involve the internalization of prescriptions that may form part of someone's identity, as well as a range of social pressures). In the previous section, we discussed the role of self-interest and ongoing social relations in supporting cooperative behavior in small groups. We now turn to the role of higher-level social norms in shaping trust in large, anonymous groups.

An important line of thought going back at least to Max Weber (2002), argues for a central role for culture in shaping economic activity. Any new economic order, argued Weber, faces initial resistance. Economic incentives are not sufficient to motivate entrepreneurs to break apart from the preexisting order. Weber argued that the Protestant Reformation came with the message that the pursuit of wealth should be regarded not merely as an advantage, but as a duty. This powerful injunction opened the way for individuals (and communities) to move beyond the earlier social order to create a new one, based on markets and the pursuit of economic accumulation.

The role of culture in its relation to trust and cooperative activity has been explored by a large body of literature. We now briefly discuss this work and then present empirical evidence on the relation between culture and trust. Culture may be said to be

> those persistent and shared beliefs and values that help a group overcome the free rider problem in the pursuit of socially valuable activities.
> Guiso, Sapienza, and Zingales (2006, pp. 23–24).

The stability of culture and its effective intergenerational transmission through family upbringing are central to understanding the causal relationship flowing from trust to economic growth. An important aspect of this work is that it shows that culture may provide a basis for various levels of trust. It does so by exploiting the intuitive notion that culture is persistent, which leads to a focus on dimensions of culture that are inherited by an individual from previous generations rather than voluntarily accumulated:

> Individuals have less control over their culture than over other social capital. They cannot alter their ethnicity, race or family history, and only with difficulty can they change their country or religion. Because of the difficulty of changing culture and its low depreciation rate, culture is largely a "given" to individuals throughout their lifetimes.
> Becker (1998, p. 16).

In this spirit, let us restrict our attention to cultural aspects like religion and ethnic background, which can more reasonably be treated as invariant over an individual's lifetime.

Guiso, Sapienza, and Zingales (2003) present the effect of religion on trust using the World Values Survey. The dependent variable is a dummy equal to 1 if an individual replies "Most people can be trusted" to the question "Generally speaking, would you say that most people can be trusted or that you have to be very careful in dealing with people?" The coefficients of interest pertain to the religions shown in figure 18.12 (where the omitted category is "No religious affiliation"). The graph suggests that being raised in a religious family raises the level of trust by 20 percent (this effect differs across denominations).

Similarly, ethnic origin has large effects on trust. To see this, let us replicate the same regression exercise within the US, based on data from the General Social Survey, which measures the ethnic origin of the respondent's ancestors and allows us to study whether the culture transmitted by those ancestors who migrated from different countries plays a role in the beliefs of people living in the US. Figure 18.13 indicates a strong effect of ethnic origin: note that these effects are computed relative to Americans with British descendants. This suggests that the level of trust that an American has toward others depends in part upon where their ancestors came from.

We conclude this discussion by showing that cultural traits are persistent. Figure 18.14 plots the impact of having ancestors from different parts of the world, compared to having

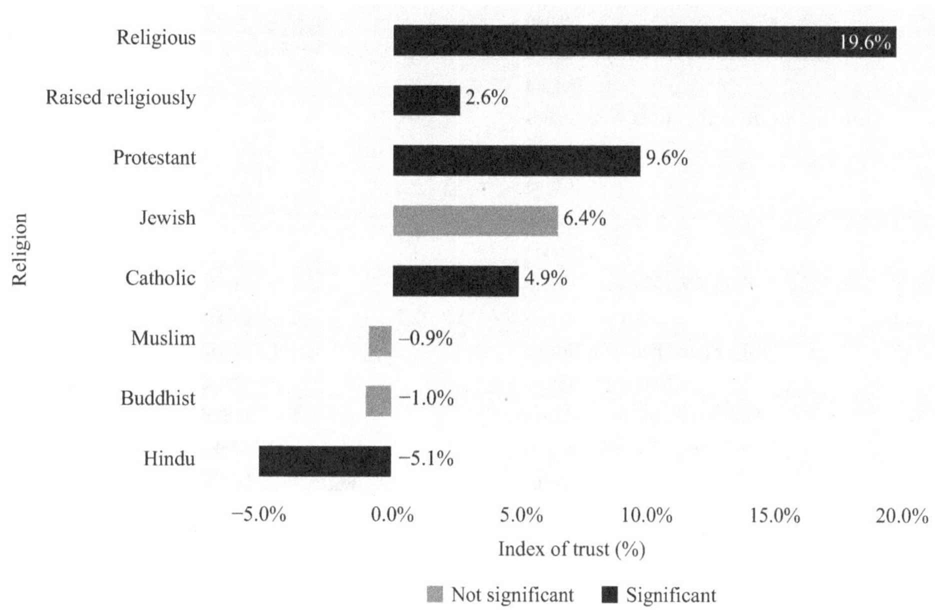


**Figure 18.12**
Religion and trust. *Source*: Guiso, Sapienza, and Zingales (2006).

British ancestors, and this finding is compared to the difference between the current level of trust in these parts of the world minus the trust in Great Britain from the World Values Survey. This graph reveals a strong persistence in the differences in trust levels (the correlation is 0.6). This finding is consistent with the idea that beliefs about trust have a cultural component that is transported to the New World and continues to shape individual beliefs even in the new environment (several generations later).

## 18.5 Local and Generalized Trust

In our previous discussion of the diamond market, high trust within the small Jewish community, which helps sustain economic activity, also makes it difficult for individuals who do not belong to the community to participate in that market. This draws attention to a widely noted feature of network-based trust—namely, that it may inhibit wider exchange with outsiders, and therefore it will be harmful to overall economic performance. In a wide-ranging study on trust, Fukuyama (1995) draws attention to a tension between different types of trust. He argues that prosperous countries tend to be those where loyalty to the extended family is not a dominant feature of social ties. Overweening family ties create rigidities and constrain the circle of trust. In particular, he argues that in countries like France and Italy (and

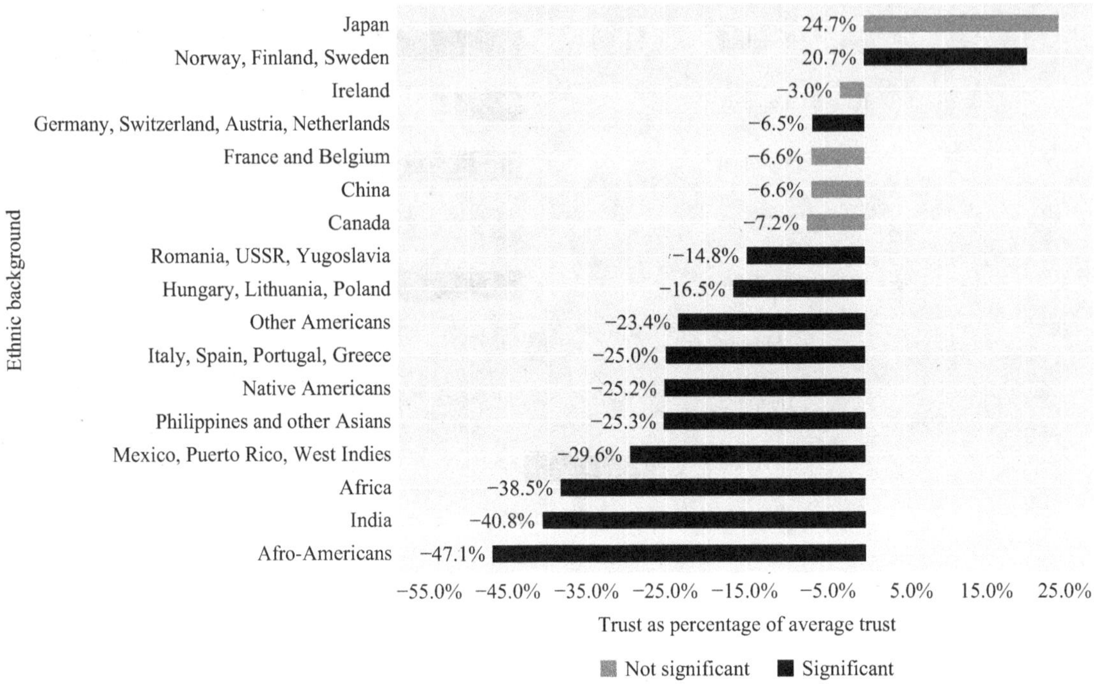


**Figure 18.13**
Ethnicity and trust. *Source*: Guiso, Sapienza, and Zingales (2006).

South Korea), social bonds are subordinated to family ties and other dysfunctional loyalties, creating rigidities, provoking state intervention, and dampening economic growth. By contrast, in Germany, Japan, and the US, family ties are not dominant and business relations between people can be conducted informally and flexibly on the basis of generalized trust.

We next discuss group based favoritism. Favoritism refers to the act of offering jobs, contracts, and resources to members of one's own social group in preference to others outside the group. Over the years, a large body of literature has documented the prominent role of groups in the practice of favoritism in developing countries. For instance, in Tunisia, members of the extended family of President Ben Ali and his wife routinely appropriated economic opportunities and granted each other special privileges; popular resentment against such favoritism played an important role in the Arab Spring in 2011. Appropriation of resources and contracts by dominant tribal groups in the African countries (such as the Democratic Republic of Congo and Nigeria), by caste groups in India, by dominant ethnic minorities in many countries has been extensively documented. The aim of this section is

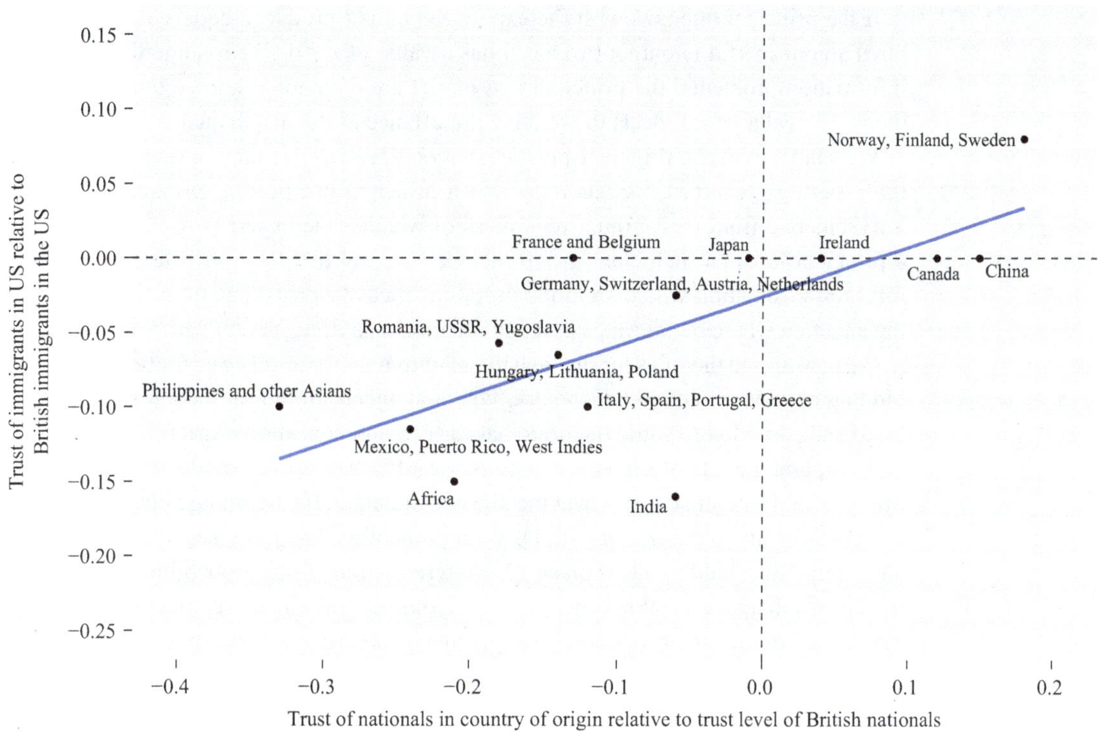


**Figure 18.14**
Persistence of culture. *Source*: Guiso, Sapienza, and Zingales (2006).

examine the economic circumstances that give rise to favoritism and then to study its consequences for the welfare of society as a whole. We present a theoretical model taken from Bramoullé and Goyal (2016).

### 18.5.1 A Model

We consider a society with $n$ individuals, who are partitioned into two groups, $\mathcal{A}$ and $\mathcal{B}$, of sizes $g_A$ and $g_B$ with $g_A + g_B = n$, respectively; we will assume throughout that $n \geq 3$.

One individual is picked uniformly at random and gets an economic opportunity. Call that person the "principal." To realize this opportunity, this principal needs to transact with an agent. One other individual is picked uniformly at random among the remaining individuals in the group to be the expert. Thus the probability that a pair of individuals $i$ and $j$ are principal and expert, respectively, is given by $p$ and defined as

$$p = \frac{1}{n}\frac{1}{n-1}. \tag{18.12}$$

If the principal interacts with the expert, the output produced equals 1. If the principal hires a nonexpert, the output produced has a value of $L \leq 1$. We assume that there are no information problems: the principal and expert are commonly known once nature draws them. The value of $L$ reflects the relative importance of the match quality.

We shall say that a principal practices *market behavior* if they always offer the job to the expert. By contrast, we shall say that a principal practices *favoritism* if they always hire someone from their group, regardless of whether the expert is in their group. When a principal hires an inefficient group member, we say that they provide a *favor*. We will refer to the situation where a unique group practices favoritism as *limited favoritism*, and the situation where both groups practice favoritism as *widespread favoritism*.

We now turn to the rules for the division of output. In the absence of frictions, competitive bidding provides a natural benchmark. Potential agents all bid for a contract; the expert is hired and earns $1 - L$, while the principal earns $L$ and nonexperts earn 0.

To capture the role of frictions and rents, we adopt a two-stage model. In the first stage, a principal and an agent bargain over the division of output. If bargaining fails, the opportunity disappears with probability $q \in [0, 1]$. With probability $1 - q$, the second stage is reached and competitive bidding takes place. One interpretation of this probability is that it reflects the fact that bargaining takes time, and during this time, alternative competing opportunities may arise. Another interpretation is simply that it takes time to locate potential partners, and during this period, the exchange or economic opportunity may be superseded by alternatives. Payoffs in the first stage are determined via Nash bargaining. We now work out the payoff outcomes in this bargaining model.

Consider an interaction between the principal and the expert. Their reservation utilities are $(1 - q)L$ and $(1 - q)(1 - L)$, respectively. It then follows that their Nash bargaining payoffs are then equal to

$$L - q\left(L - \frac{1}{2}\right) \text{ and } 1 - L + q\left(L - \frac{1}{2}\right), \text{ respectively.} \tag{18.13}$$

Next, consider bargaining between the principal and a nonexpert. The reservation utilities are $(1 - q)L$ and 0. So their first-period payoffs are given by $L - \frac{1}{2}qL$ and $\frac{1}{2}qL$, respectively. As $q$ increases, frictions worsen and payoffs get increasingly further from the competitive benchmark.

This model provides a parsimonious representation of transaction costs and rents. We note that if $L > \frac{1}{2}$ and $q > 0$, then experts earn more than under frictionless competition, and their rents are equal to $q\left(L - \frac{1}{2}\right)$. These rents are increasing in the level of friction, $q$, and falling in the unimportance of match quality, $L$.

We denote by $\pi_j(F, M)$ the expected payoff of an individual in group $j \in \{\mathcal{A}, \mathcal{B}\}$ when their group practices favoritism while the other group practices market behavior; analogous notation is used for the other combinations. We will sometimes write $\pi_j(F)$ when the behavior of outsiders is irrelevant.

### 18.5.2 Group Incentives

The analysis starts with group incentives for the practice of favoritism. Suppose that group members can commit, ex ante, to a common norm of behavior. What are the circumstances under which they would choose to engage in favoritism?

When the expert is in the same group as the principal, in-group bias and efficiency are aligned. In this case, favoritism does not affect payoffs. Favoritism comes into play when the expert is an outsider to the group. A favor then costs $\frac{1}{2}q(1-L)$ to the principal, relative to market behavior, and yields $\frac{1}{2}qL$ to the favored group member. The group gains $q\left(L-\frac{1}{2}\right)$, while the other group loses $1-L+q\left(L-\frac{1}{2}\right)$ and society loses $1-L$. This happens every time the principal is in the group while the expert is an outsider, hence there is a probability of $pg_Ag_B$. Therefore, the expected net group gain from favoritism is equal to $pqg_Ag_B\left(L-\frac{1}{2}\right)$, while the other group loses $pg_Ag_B\left(1-L+q\left(L-\frac{1}{2}\right)\right)$ and society loses $pg_Ag_B(1-L)$. The per capita gain from a collective switch to favoritism is thus:

$$\pi_A(F)-\pi_A(M)=pqg_B\left(L-\frac{1}{2}\right). \qquad (18.14)$$

Observe that this equality holds no matter what the other group does. These points are summarized in the following statement.

**Proposition 18.3** *A group gains from favoritism if and only if $q>0$ and $L>\frac{1}{2}$. The rewards to favoritism for a group are increasing in both $q$ and $L$.*

An important message is that if $L>1/2$, then *frictions* are both necessary and sufficient for a group to desire favoritism. If the total payoff from an inefficient *within-group* match is higher than the fraction of an efficient match's payoff that stays in the group, then the group gains from favoritism. Therefore, groups may choose to practice favoritism even in the absence of informational frictions, social preferences, or social dilemmas. When $q>0$ and $L>\frac{1}{2}$, experts earn rents in their economic transactions. Group gains from favoritism are precisely proportional to these rents and are increasing in the extent of frictions $q$ and $L$. As market frictions are greater and match quality is less important (and hence $L$ is larger) in developing countries, this result also suggests that favoritism is more attractive in poor countries.

In addition, if a group faces discrimination or if there are other significant contracting costs with outsiders, principals in the group may not be able to get a fair reward for economic opportunities in dealings with outsiders. Terms of trade would then be group-specific, and our analysis easily extends to such situations. A group would then gain from favoritism when expert outsiders earn rents, no matter what happens for expert insiders. We finally observe that, under competitive bidding, $q=0$ and the principal's group is indifferent between favoritism and the market rule.

When $L>\frac{1}{2}$ and $q>0$, the game played by the two groups has the structure of a prisoner's dilemma. Playing favoritism is a dominant strategy for each group.

### 18.5.3 The Consequences of Favoritism

Let us consider the economic consequences of the practice of favoritism. Suppose, to begin with, that everyone abides by the market rule: principals hire experts. An individual is a principal with probability $\frac{1}{n}$ and earns $L-q\left(L-\frac{1}{2}\right)$. Similarly, they are an expert with probability $\frac{1}{n}$ and then they earn $1-L+q\left(L-\frac{1}{2}\right)$. Therefore their expected payoff is

$$\pi_A(M,M)=\pi_B(M,M)=\frac{1}{n}. \tag{18.15}$$

As expected, the market generates equal payoffs across individuals. Moreover, total welfare is simply the sum of the individuals' utilities and is equal to 1.

Next, suppose that group $\mathcal{A}$ practices favoritism while group $\mathcal{B}$ abides by the market rule. Consider an individual $i$ in $\mathcal{A}$. There are three possibilities:

1 With probability $\frac{1}{n}$, individual $i$ is the principal. Then the expert is a group member with probability $\frac{g_A-1}{n-1}$, in which case $i$ earns $L-q\left(L-\frac{1}{2}\right)$. Or, with the remaining probability $\frac{g_B}{n-1}$, the expert is an outsider and $i$ provides a favor and earns $L-\frac{1}{2}qL$.

2 With probability $\frac{1}{n}$, individual $i$ is the expert. Since the other group does not practice favoritism, $i$ is always hired and earns $1-L+q\left(L-\frac{1}{2}\right)$.

3 Individual $i$ obtains a favor when the principal is another group $\mathcal{A}$ member while the expert is an outsider. In addition, the opportunity to receive a favor is shared with all group members. So with probability $\frac{(g_A-1)g_B}{n(n-1)}\frac{1}{g_A-1}$, the favored individual $i$ earns $\frac{1}{2}qL$. Formally,

$$\pi_A(F,M)=\frac{1}{n}\left(\frac{g_A-1}{n-1}\left(L-q\left(L-\frac{1}{2}\right)\right)+\frac{g_B}{n-1}\left(L-\frac{1}{2}qL\right)\right)$$
$$+\frac{1}{n}\left(1-L+q\left(L-\frac{1}{2}\right)\right)+\frac{(g_A-1)g_B}{n(n-1)}\frac{1}{g_A-1}\left(\frac{1}{2}qL\right). \tag{18.16}$$

Regrouping and simplifying give us the expected payoff to individual $i$ in group $\mathcal{A}$, which practices favoritism, while group $\mathcal{B}$ does not:

$$\pi_A(F,M)=p\left[n-1+qg_B\left(L-\frac{1}{2}\right)\right]. \tag{18.17}$$

In contrast, group $\mathcal{B}$ loses $1-L+q\left(L-\frac{1}{2}\right)$ per favor provided. So the individual's expected payoff is

$$\pi_B(M,F)=p\left[n-1-g_A\left(1-L+q\left(L-\frac{1}{2}\right)\right)\right]. \tag{18.18}$$

We see that $\pi_A(F,M)>\pi(M,M)>\pi_B(M,F)$. Starting from a market, a switch to favoritism by one group increases the payoffs of the group members at the expense of the payoffs of the outsiders. Interestingly, holding $n$ constant, payoffs in the favoritism group are *decreasing* in its size. Benefits from exclusive favors are lower when they have to be shared with more individuals. Payoffs in group $\mathcal{B}$ also decrease as group $\mathcal{A}$ grows. Moreover, members in group $\mathcal{B}$ lose more than what insiders gain, and the payoff advantage to group $\mathcal{A}$,

$$\pi_A(F,M) - \pi_B(M,F) = p\left[qn\left(L - \frac{1}{2}\right) + g_A(1-L)\right], \tag{18.19}$$

is positive and increasing with the size of group $\mathcal{A}$.

Now consider a society with *widespread favoritism*. An expert in group $\mathcal{A}$ is hired only when the principal is also a group member. Therefore,

$$\pi_A(F,F) = p[n-1-g_B(1-L)], \tag{18.20}$$

and by symmetry, $\pi_B(F,F) = p[n-1-g_A(1-L)]$. Recall that $\pi_A(M,M) = \pi_B(M,M) = p(n-1)$, so individuals in *both* groups lose relative to the market!

Inequality is now a consequence of differences in group size. Since

$$\pi_A(F,F) - \pi_B(F,F) = p(g_A - g_B)(1-L), \tag{18.21}$$

individuals in the larger group earn more than individuals in the smaller group. As both groups are practicing favoritism, a larger group means more access to opportunities. Holding $n$ constant, increasing the size of the larger group magnifies this effect: it raises payoffs in the larger group and lowers them in the other group.

Finally, consider aggregate social welfare. Recall that welfare drops by $1-L$ every time a favor is given. Total welfare loss is then equal to $pg_Ag_B(1-L)$ under limited favoritism and $2pg_Ag_B(1-L)$ under widespread favoritism. In either case, welfare loss is maximized in a society with two groups of equal size.

We summarize these arguments as follows.

**Proposition 18.4** *The welfare effects of favoritism are as follows:*

- *Limited favoritism: Individuals in the favoritism group earn more than in the market, while individuals in the other group earn less than in the market. The payoff to the favoritism group is declining in group size. However, payoff difference between the two groups is increasing with the size of the favoritism group.*
- *Widespread favoritism: All individuals earn lower payoffs compared to the market. The individuals in the larger group earn more than those in the smaller group; this difference is increasing in the size of the larger group.*
- *Social welfare is lower under favoritism and is minimized in a society with two equal-size groups.*

Thus, group-based favoritism *always* reduces aggregate social welfare. We have provided a simple theoretical model of group-based favor exchange that leads to lower economic performance. What can the groups and the society as a whole do to overcome these inefficiencies?

### 18.5.4 Institutions to Reduce Favoritism

One way to overcome inefficiencies from favoritism is to create formal legal and executive institutions that create and implement fair practice. These institutions involve innovations in institutional design and will entail costs. A simple way to think about the problem would be to say that there is a fixed cost, $F > 0$, to establish such institutions. The society as a whole would find it worthwhile to install such institutions if the returns were greater than the costs. Recall that the institution will help rectify principal and expert matching in situations where the principal and the expert are in different groups. The likelihood of this happening increases with an increase in the size of the smaller group and is maximized when the two groups are of equal size. Thus a society is more likely to install formal monitoring institutions when the two groups are of relatively similar size, or equivalently, the greater the similarity in the size of the groups, the higher the costs the society is willing to incur to prevent favoritism.

In this simple story, the assumption is that, once established, the formal institution can successfully prevent favoritism. But installing institutions is generally not enough: they have to be monitored for successful performance. The monitoring of institutions calls for effort and initiative from individuals. Therefore, the extent to which formal institutions are able to address the problem of favoritism may depend on the associations and the broader culture of public spiritedness that exist in a society. The relation between formal institutions and social structure is studied in the next chapter.

## 18.6 Scaling up Trust: The Role of Social Networks

> . . . we need to understand the relationship between trust relations among individuals and in small communities and those in large networks of interaction. This question has received little attention.
> Granovetter (2017, p. 85).

In our discussion of network closure and social collateral, a recurrent theme is that particular forms of social networks can help sustain cooperation and local trust. In our discussion on generalized trust in the previous section, we mostly concentrated on the role of culture—interpreted in terms of expectations and beliefs concerning individual behaviors in matters regarding public goods—in sustaining trust. In this section, we explore the role of social interactions and structures in sustaining such beliefs. In particular, we will examine ways in which the structure of the social network can help sustain social norms by providing a pathway from the small scale and local to the large scale and societal.

Let us begin with a few empirical observations. Ermisch and Gambetta (2008), using trust games with a representative sample of the British population, find that people with strong family ties have a lower level of trust in strangers than people with weak family ties. They argue that this is because of the level of outward exposure: factors that limit exposure limit subjects' experience, which also impairs their motivation to deal with strangers. Greif and Tabellini (2017) provide a historical analysis of this opposition by comparing the bifurcation of societal organization between premodern China and medieval Europe. Premodern China sustained cooperation within the clan (e.g., a kinship-based hierarchical organization in which strong moral ties and reputation among clan members played the key role). By contrast, in medieval Europe, the main example of a cooperative organization is the city, where cooperation is across kinship circles, and external enforcement played a bigger role. There is also empirical evidence on a negative relation between strong family-based ties and political and social engagement; for instance, see Alesina and Giuliano (2010, 2011).

Studies in this spirit lend support to a widely held and influential view that local group–based favor exchange is incompatible with generalized trust. A number of prominent authors have written about this tension. As we noted in the previous section, Fukuyama (1995) argues that strong favor exchange within kin-based groups undermines generalized trust. Similarly, Henrich (2020), in his study of WEIRD (an acronym for "Western, Educated, Industrialized, Rich, and Developed") societies argues for the distinctiveness of societies in which individuals hold on to abstract principles of fairness and are able to successfully undertake anonymous impersonal exchange, in contrast to the majority of societies in the world where kin-based norms are dominant (and rely on favor exchange within groups). The model presented in the previous section offered a formulation of this tension: favor exchange within a group came at a the expense of losses at the aggregate level.

On the other hand, some authors have written about the possibilities of scaling up personalized trust through an appropriate network structure. To see how this may be accomplished, consider the case of South Korea, a country that on the one hand conforms to a Confucian family system and on the other hand has an economy dominated by large, professionally managed, and highly successful companies (such as LG, Samsung, and Hyundai). Another prominent example of a large, professionally managed conglomerate controlled by a community is the Tata Group in India. One possibility that could explain these examples is that a kinship group can scale up its operations substantially by locating close members of the family in strategic positions of a large network. This is accompanied by cross-ownership among the relevant firms to ensure overlapping financial control:

> The typical evolution was that an original family firm expanded not by getting larger but by setting up branches as independent companies or by buying already-established businesses. Authority, however, remained highly centralised across the component companies. Reputation and personal trustworthiness are crucial, contracts unimportant.... These business groups can be very large and diversified, but control is maintained through pyramids—family firms that control other firms that control still other firms, etc—and dense interlocking directorates.
>
> Thus family members who have strong trust relations with the central family group are strategically sprinkled through the many holdings in such a way as to knit the entire structure together. Employees who are not in direct touch with the core family members may nevertheless trust the motives of that group through their direct ties to the local family representatives and work harder and more effectively than if they had no commitment to the central group.
>
> Granovetter (2017, pp. 87–88).

In this example, it is possible that key members of the family were deliberately located at certain positions in the network to monitor and collect information and to enforce norms.

To see how such a social structure can come about without deliberate intervention, we turn next to discussing a large community of researchers. Here, we present data on research economists. Let us recall from chapter 1 the broad facts about this community: over the period 2000–2009, there were over $151,000$ authors who published papers. The average number of coauthors, 1.95, was very small, but the most connected 100 authors had 25 coauthors on average. Somewhat remarkably, in spite of the very low average degree, the largest component contained over 67,000 nodes (this constitutes over 44 percent of all nodes), with an average distance of only 9.80. The key to understanding the average small distance is highly connected authors: the deletion of the 5 percent most connected authors completely fragmented it. Thus the most connected authors spanned the research profession and held it together.

Van der Leij and Goyal (2011) study the location of the topology of the network with an interest in the role of strong ties in sustaining it. They measure the strength of a tie by the number of papers written together by the coauthors. They find that there is a positive correlation between the degree of authors and the strength of their tie. They also find that these strong ties are critical to holding the network together: in particular, the deletion of strong ties fragments the network at a much faster rate than the deletion of weak ties among authors.

We illustrate these points with the help of local network plots of leading economists. Figures 18.15 and 18.16 present the network of weighted links in the coauthor network around two leading economists over the period 1990–2009, Jean Tirole and Esther Duflo. These economists are connected with strong ties to key economists, who in turn also have many links. The strong ties and the close access that a large set of economists have to Tirole and Duflo (and therefore also to each other) facilitate the process of creating a tightly knit global community with shared norms on important research questions and the appropriate methods to address them.

We bring these observations together by presenting a stylized network that illustrates these structural possibilities—such as highly connected nodes, strong ties between high-degree nodes, and small average distances—as in figure 18.17.

The network of economics co-authors is therefore a small world—in the sense that the average distances are small—and perhaps equally importantly the small world is held together by individuals who have high degree and have strong ties with other highly connected nodes. In a general sense, we expect strong ties to facilitate cooperative norms and the central location of these highly connected nodes to facilitate easy diffusion of ideas and of social norms. Thus, these empirical features of the network offer us a pathway for the building up of possibly general trust based on patterns of local interaction. The structure we have uncovered here also has clear points of contact with the discussions on models of network formation that were discussed in chapters 2 and 3.

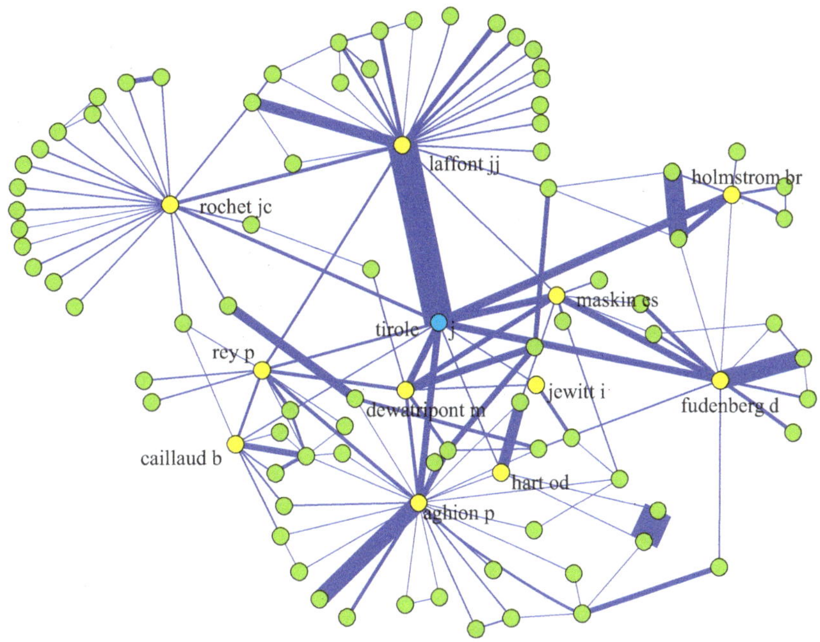


**Figure 18.15**
Local network of collaboration of Jean Tirole in the 1990s. *Note*: This diagram shows all authors within distance 2 of Tirole, as well as the links between them. The width denotes the strength of a tie. Some economists might appear twice or are missing due to the use of different initials or misspellings in EconLit. The image was created by the software program Pajek. *Source*: van der Leij and Goyal (2011).

## 18.7 Supplementary Material: Names of Journals

The network of boards of editors of economics journals includes 28 journals: *Journal of Health Economics* (JHE), *Review of Economics and Statistics* (REStat), *Review of Economic Studies* (REStud), *Econometric Theory* (ET), *Journal of Monetary Economics* (JME), *Quarterly Journal of Economics* (QJE), *Journal of Economic Literature* (JEL), *Journal of Business and Economic Statistics* (JBES), *Econometrica* (ECMA), *Review of Financial Studies* (RFS), *RAND Journal of Economics* (RAND), *Economic Journal* (EJ), *Journal of Environmental Economics and Management* (JEEM), *Journal of Finance* (JoF), *Journal of Econometrics* (JoE), *Journal of International Economics* (JIE), *European Economic Review* (EER), *World Bank Economic Review* (WBER), *International Economic Review* (IER), *American Economic Review* (AER), *Journal of Human Resources* (JHR), *Journal of Labor Economics* (JLE), *Journal of Political Economy* (JPolE), *Journal of Public Economics* (JPubE), *Games and Economic Behavior* (GEB), *Journal of Economic Theory* (JET), *Journal of Economic Perspectives* (JEP), and *Journal of Financial Economics* (JFE).

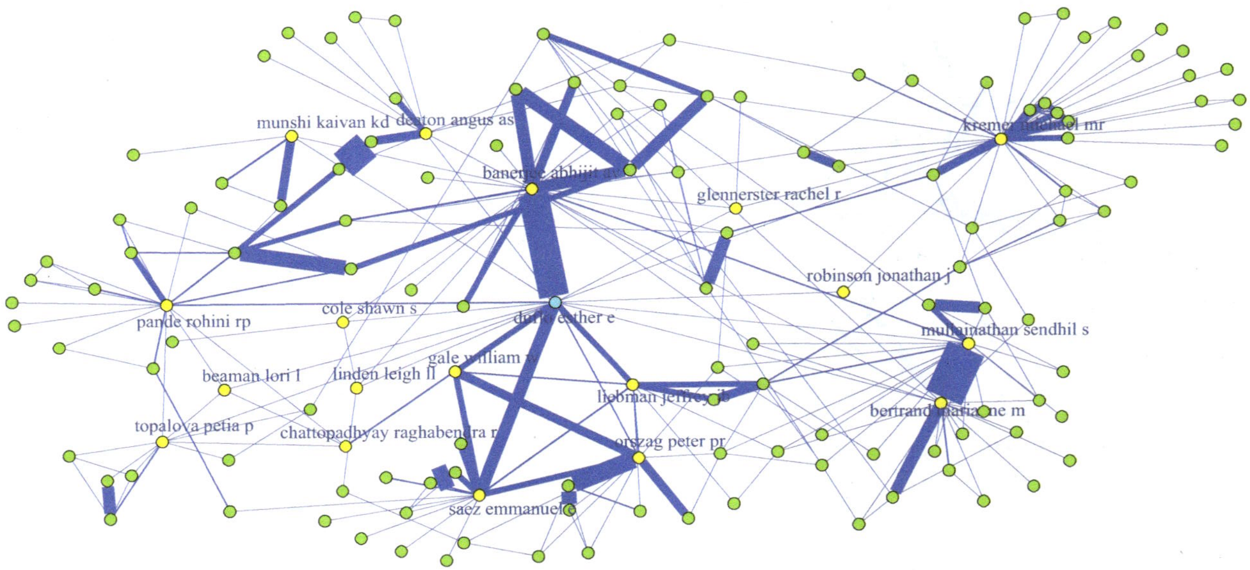


**Figure 18.16**
Local network of collaboration of Esther Duflo, 2000–2009. *Note*: The diagram shows all authors within distance 2 of Duflo, as well as the links between them. Some economists might appear twice or are missing due to the use of different initials or misspellings in EconLit. The width denotes the strength of a tie. The image was created by the software program Pajek.

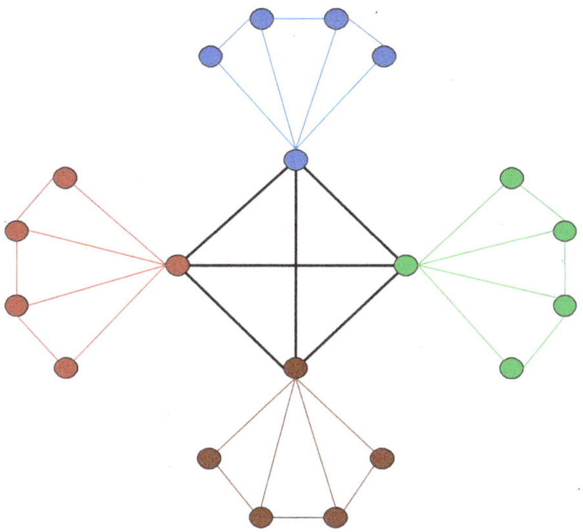

**Figure 18.17**
Key individuals and strong ties.

## 18.8 Reading Notes

The study of trust spans many disciplines. It is closely connected to the ideas of social capital in sociology and political science and of reputations and repeated interactions in game theory. More recently, a large strand of research in economics studies the role of culture in shaping trust.

For an early and classical discussion of the role of trust in reducing transaction costs, see Arrow (1972, 1974). The origins of the ideas on social capital may be found in Bourdieu (1977, 1984), Jacobs (2016), and Loury (1976). Coleman (1988, 1994) provided a broad conceptual foundation for social capital and also drew attention to the importance of network closure for norms of monitoring and cooperation. Gambetta (1988) provides an introduction to different perspectives on the subject of trust, and Dasgupta and Serageldin (2001) and Portes (1998) give an excellent overview of the literature on social capital. Mention must also be made of the Russell Sage series on Trust (especially Cook, Levi, and Hardin (2009) and Wellman and Wortley (1990).

The impetus provided by the work in the 1980s, and especially Coleman's work, led to two distinct strands—a microeconomic approach more focused on local trust and a line of macroeconomics concerned with the role of culture in understanding generalized trust. We briefly discuss the evidence on trust in section 18.2. The material there draws on the Global Values Surveys, Coleman (1988, 1994) and the empirical work of Knack and Keefer (1997).

Economists have traditionally studied questions of cooperation and social norms using models of repeated games. For a survey of this literature, see Mailath and Samuelson (2006).

A general message from this work is that cooperation is difficult to sustain in large communities with anonymous interactions. In section 18.3, we focus on small communities and examine the role of networks closure in sustaining cooperation. For a survey of the work on networks and repeated games, see Nava (2016). To bring out the role of networks in the simplest way, we focus in section 18.3 on a model of social collateral taken from Karlan, Mobius, Rosenblat, and Szeidl (2009). The empirical study of Peruvian towns comes from the same paper. The case study of favor exchange in rural India is taken from Jackson, Rodriguez-Barraquer, and Tan (2012), which also provides a general theory of favor exchange in networks that we draw on to elaborate the role of common neighbors.

We do not discuss this point in the chapter, but it should be clear that shared norms based on altruism and identity are not incompatible with the role of self-interest in sustaining cooperation even in small groups. Networks evolve in response to changes in the larger environment; for a study of networks that support cooperation in a changing environment, see Vega-Redondo (2006). For an early study of repeated games and network structure, see Haag and Lagunoff (2006).

There is a large body of literature on the relations between culture, trust, and economic performance in political science and sociology. Max Weber's work on the Protestant ethic remains a powerful influence in this field. Similarly, Edward Banfield's early study of amoral familism in southern Italy casts a long shadow on our understanding of the importance of culture (Banfield [1958]). He attributes underdevelopment to the excessive pursuit of narrow self-interest by its inhabitants, a condition that he labels "amoral familism." More recently, Fukuyama (1995), argues for a key role for culture and the fabric of society in our understanding of economic success and failure. Similarly, (Putnam, Leonardi, and Nanetti [1993]), in their study of the differences between North and South Italy, argue for the positive effects of civic culture on the quality of political institutions.

Trust can be measured using surveys and laboratory experiments. Empirical research investigating the link between economic performance and trust usually draws on answers from survey questions. The reason for this is the availability of surveys that have covered a large number of countries since the beginning of the 1980s. Nevertheless, these surveys raise difficulties in interpretation. It is not clear how respondents interpret some questions: for instance, whom do they have in mind when they think of trustworthiness? Some of these points are taken up in the next chapter.

This work in political science and the positive empirical correlations between generalized trust and a number of economic performance indicators was demonstrated by Knack and Keefer (1997) and Zak and Knack (2001) drew the attention of economists to the study of trust.

A large body of subsequent work studies the role of culture in shaping trust and economic performance. Influential contributions in this field include Algan and Cahuc (2010); Bisin and Verdier (2000); Guiso et al. (2003, 2006); and Glaeser, Laibson, Scheinkman, and Soutter (2000). For a survey of this work, see Algan and Cahuc (2014) and Guiso, Sapienza, and Zingales (2011). The issue of trust and distrust in large-scale settings is examined in Aghion, Algan, Cahuc, and Shleifer (2010); Nunn and Wantchekon (2011); and La Porta, Lopez-de Silanes, Shleifer, and Vishny (1997). Section 18.4 presents the game of trust and provides a brief summary of the relation between culture and trust.

The game of trust was introduced in Berg, Dickhaut, and McCabe (1995); for a related game of trust, see Dasgupta (1988). This game has been used to systematically investigate the elements of trust—in terms of own behavior, expectations of other's behavior, and so forth (Glaeser, Laibson, Scheinkman, and Soutter (2000); Glaeser, Laibson, and Sacerdote [2002]). There is also a strand of literature that examines the relation between survey-based trust measures and actual behavior in trust games; for instance, see Glaeser, Laibson, Scheinkman, and Soutter (2000).

Section 18.6 takes up the relation between local and generalized trust. Bourdieu (1984), Banfield (1958), and Fukuyama (1995) draw attention to the tension between local trust and generalized trust. We present a simple model of within-group favor exchange to examine this tension. This model of group-based favor exchange is taken from Bramoullé and Goyal (2016). We briefly comment on the role of formal institutions in overcoming the negative consequences of group-based favor exchange. The discussion on local trust draws attention to the relation between social networks and individual level incentives for cooperative behavior and favor exchange. The discussion on generalized trust on the other hand focuses on beliefs abut others' behavior and the role of culture in shaping these beliefs. There appears to be a missing link between the two narratives. Following Wrong (1961), we may see local trust may be an instance of under-socialized behavior while generalized trust with its emphasis on culture and values may be seen as an instance of an oversocialized model, in which individuals choose actions because they are expected to do so by society.

This leads us in the last section of the chapter to an examination of social networks as a mediating construction that can help provide a bridge between the local and generalized trust. We draw on Granovetter (2017) and Van der Leij and Goyal (2011) to discuss the aspects of social structure that can facilitate scaling up of social norms and trust from the local setting to larger collectivities.

This discussion forms a bridge to the next chapter, where we study the role of formal institutions and social structure in scaling up trust in a society.

## 18.9 Questions

1. Consider the model of social collateral considered in section 18.3.
   (a) Compute the maximum loan that individual $S$ can take from individual $T$ in network given in figure 18.18(a). Suppose there is the possibility to allocate an additional unit of obligation to a link. Identify a link whose strengthening would raise loan capacity of S and a link whose strengthening would have no impact on loan capacity.

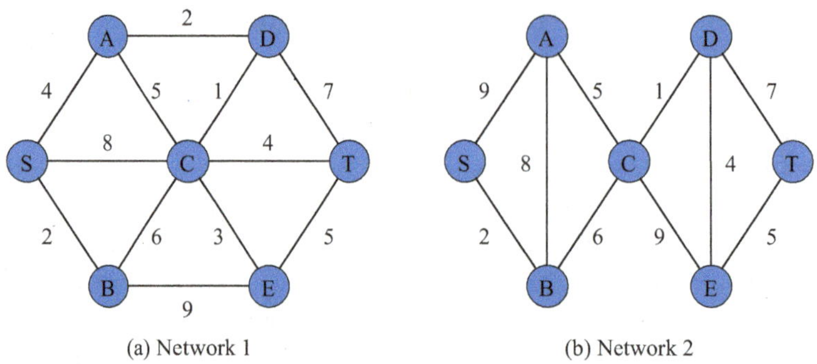


**Figure 18.18**
Social collateral in networks.

(b) Compute the maximum loan that individual $S$ can take from individual $T$ in network given in figure 18.18(b). Suppose there is the possibility to allocate an additional unit of obligation to a link. Identify a link whose strengthening would raise loan capacity of S and a link whose strengthening would have no impact on loan capacity.

2. (Jackson, Rodriguez-Barraquer, and Tan 2012) Consider the model of favor exchange discussed in section 18.3.5. Define the *support* of a link $g_{ij}$ in network $g$ as the number of common neighbors that $i$ and $j$ have in the network $g$. The model shows that higher support would facilitate greater favor exchange. How does the support compare with clustering in the network (as defined in chapter 1)?

3. (Bramoullé and Goyal [2017]). Consider the model of group favoritism discussed in section 18.5.1. We showed there that a group has a collective interest in practicing favoritism. Now imagine that individuals are concerned about their own private payoffs only.

   (a) What are the circumstances under which a principal will offer an opportunity to someone from their own group rather than an expert who lies outside the group?

   (b) Are there circumstances under which a group benefits from favor exchange but individuals within the group would prefer to offer the opportunity to an expert outside the group?

4. This question explores variations on the model of group-based favoritism presented in section 18.5.1.

   (a) For historical and institutional reasons, it is often the case that one group of individuals—for instance, a tribe, linguistic group, or ethnic group in power—is more likely to hear about economic opportunities than other groups. Similarly, for historical reasons, some groups may have greater expertise than other groups. Using the

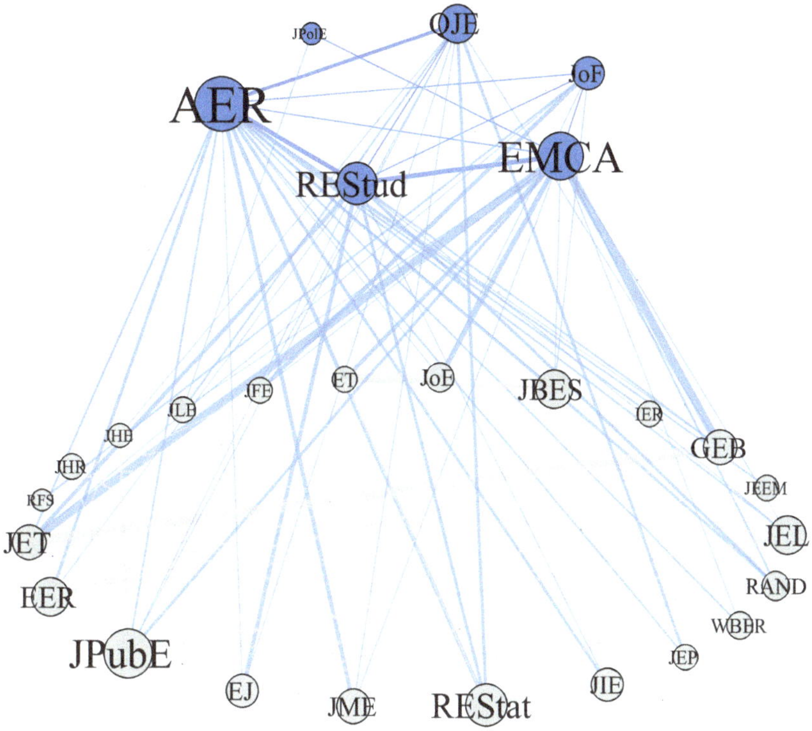


**Figure 18.19**
The editorial boards of economic journals in 2010. The node size reflects the number of editors; the link thickness indicates the number of common editors. Courtesy of Lorenzo Ductor and Bauke Visser.

model, show that heterogeneity in opportunities across groups makes favoritism easier to sustain, while heterogeneity within a group makes favoritism less sustainable.

(b) We assumed that individuals have linear preferences. Show that risk aversion will reinforce the pressure toward favoritism in groups.

5. The problem of trust arises only in large, anonymous groups. Discuss.

6. Cultural beliefs form a natural foundation for trust among strangers. Discuss the role of social structure in sustaining such cultural beliefs.

7. Figure 18.19 presents a network of ties between the boards of leading economic journals in 2010. The list of these journals is provided in section 18.7 (containing Supplementary Material). We see that the network is connected and most of the links are relatively weak. Interestingly, the network is held together through a hierarchical structure—the general-interest journals share common editors with the field journals, and there are relatively few ties among general-interest journals and field journals, respectively. Use this network

in combination with the discussion in section 18.6 to discuss the social-structure basis of shared norms in economics.

8. In the theory of small worlds as described in chapter 2, starting from a ring network, as we rewire links with small probability, the average distance falls very sharply. This fall is central to the small world phenomenon. One possible interpretation of these rewired links is to think of them as weak ties and to think of the original (unrewired) as strong ties. However, the empirical evidence on co-authorship discussed in section 18.6 suggests that it is the strong ties that connect hubs and therefore play a more important role in reducing distances. Discuss the role of the strength of ties and the topology of the network in the process of socialization and in shaping the level of trust in a society.

# 19 Groups, Impersonal Exchange, and State Capacity

Americans of all ages, all conditions, all minds constantly unite. Not only do they have commercial and industrial associations in which all take part, but they also have a thousand other kinds: religious, moral, grave, futile, very general and very particular, immense and very small: Americans use associations to give fetes, to found seminaries, to build inns, to raise churches, to distribute books, to send missionaries to the antipodes; in this manner they create hospitals, prisons, schools. Finally, if it is a question of bringing to light a truth or developing a sentiment with the support of a great example, they associate. Everywhere that, at the head of a new undertaking you a see the government in France and a great lord in England, count on it that you will perceive an association in the United States.
—Tocqueville (2004, p. 489).

When historians record the history of our time, 300 years from now, the end of the Cold War will be at most a third story in that history. Events in the Middle East will be the second story. When the history of our times is written, the events in Asia, the changes in the lives of so many people so quickly, and its ramifications for the global system will be the most important story.
—Summers (2007, p. 4).

## 19.1 Introduction

The role of kin-based groups in its relation to economic performance remains highly contested. The dominance of kin-based groups—where we interpret kin broadly to refer to family, tribes, caste, lineage—is an impediment to the evolution of broader circles of trust; as generalized trust is important for impersonal exchange and impersonal exchange is central to efficient economic activity, strong, group-based ties inhibit economic performance. On the one hand, there are well-known examples of societies centered on nuclear families and weak kinship groups that are economic and social failures. On the other hand, there are prominent instances of societies with strong family and kin-based groups that have enjoyed rapid economic growth. This suggests that kin-based groups have a rich and varied relationship with economic performance. The goal of this chapter is to develop a theoretical framework that helps us identify principles to understand this relationship.

In section 19.2, we begin by showing a negative correlation between the strength of kin-based institutions and generalized trust. This is the point of departure for a number of case studies of how various societies organize economic and political activity—those with small kin-based groups, as well as those with large and powerful kin-based groups. Of particular interest is the relation between kin-based groups, the nature of impersonal exchange, and the role of the state.

Section 19.3 draws on anthropology, sociology, political science, and economics to discuss, in very broad terms, a number of concepts that we use to locate the experience of different countries within a common framework.

Section 19.4 presents a theoretical model, the ingredients of which are social structure (kin-based groups and horizontal social linkages across groups), economic exchange (within and across groups), and the formal institutions of the state. Kin-based exchange is frictionless, but it is constrained by the size of the group; exchange outside the group has the potential to be more valuable, but it entails transaction costs. The magnitude of these costs depends on the effectiveness of the state and formal institutions, as well as on generalized trust. Generalized trust in turn is correlated with the quality of civic community and is measured by the strength of ties across kin-based groups in a society. A larger state and greater civic community both reduce friction.

The model proceeds as follows: given a social structure, individuals choose their level of civic engagement. These choices determine the civic capital in a society. Given the civic capital, individuals decide on the tax rate through majority voting. The tax revenue shapes the size of the state. Given civic capital and state capacity, individuals finally choose whether to limit themselves to kinship-based exchange or to engage in impersonal exchange.

Our analysis draws attention to the role of the social structure in defining the level of civic engagement and the size of the state, how these outcomes determine the relative magnitude of group-based and impersonal exchange, and how that in turn shapes economic performance.

## 19.2 Empirical Background

We begin with a brief recapitulation of our discussion on trust in chapter 18. On the World Values Survey, the key question on generalized trust is:

> Generally speaking, would you say that most people can be trusted, or that you can't be too careful when dealing with others?

The two possible responses are "Most people can be trusted" and "Need to be very careful." The fraction of population giving the first answer is interpreted as a measure of trust. The survey shows that there are very great variations in the level of trust across countries, and these differences are stable over time. For instance, in Sweden, the trust level is 56 percent and 60 percent, while in Brazil, the level of trust is 2.8 percent and 5.5 percent in

1995 and 2017, respectively. In that chapter, we showed that generalized trust is positively correlated with income. The wide variations in generalized trust and the positive correlation warrant a closer examination of the sources of trust. We discussed the contrast between local and generalized trust, introduced the role of culture, and examined the relation between stable indicators of culture, such as religious affiliation and ethnicity, and generalized trust. We now take that discussion further. We introduce the notion of universalism and then study how these two variables, generalized trust and universalism, are related to the strength of kin-based groups in a society.

Universalism is defined in terms of responses to a hypothetical scenario, the *passenger's dilemma*:

> You are riding in a car driven by your friend. He hits a pedestrian. You know that he was going at least 35 miles per hour in an area of the city where the maximum allowed speed is 20 miles per hour. There are no witnesses, except for you. His lawyer says that if you testify under oath that he was driving only 20 miles per hour, it may save him from serious legal consequences.
>
> Do you think:
>
> 1. that your friend has a definite right to expect you to testify (as his close friend), and that you would testify that he was getting 20 miles per hour, or
> 2. that your friend has little or no right to expect you to testify and that you would not falsely testify that he was only going 20 miles per hour?

Surveys have been conducted with managers and businesspeople in countries across the world. The first response is interpreted as *particularistic* or *relational*, while the second response is interpreted as *universalistic* or *nonrelational*. In a number of countries such as South Korea, Venezuela, and Nepal, the vast majority of responses were (1). By contrast, in a number of other countries like the US, Canada, and Switzerland, over 90 percent of respondents answered (2).

The studies on generalized trust and universalism are striking in a number of ways. There is wide variation in outcomes with regard to both variables. Further, countries that score high on one measure do not always score high on the other. For instance, some Asian countries like South Korea and Japan score highly on generalized trust but poorly on universalism. Finally, there are some outlier countries—such as the US, Germany, Switzerland, and Sweden—that score very highly on both measures. Following the terminology coined by Joseph Henrich and his collaborators, we will refer to these countries as WEIRD (meaning "Western, Educated, Industrialized, Rich, Developed"). Let us next examine the relation between the strength of kin-based groups and universalism and generalized trust.

### 19.2.1 Kinship and Weirdness

In our discussions on local trust in chapter 18, we elaborated on the idea of how favor exchange can arise through personal connections. This was a very concrete and specific instance of how kinship-based networks can support trust. More generally, there are many features of kin-based institutions that promote a sense of trust and depend on interconnectedness with those within the group. At the same time, and also as noted in our discussions in chapter 18, kin-based norms may breed a sharper recognition of those within and those outside the group, and this appreciation can undermine generalized trust. Building on this observation, we examined how strong, kin-based institutions affect generalized trust, but now we take care to pose the question on generalized trust in a manner that distinguishes between (within-kinship-group) insiders and (nonkin) outsiders. Our discussion draws on Henrich (2020) and Enke (2019).

The questions on trust distinguish between different sets of people. They ask how much individuals trust (1) their own families, (2) their neighbors, (3) people they know, (4) people they don't know, (5) people they have met for the first time, (6) foreigners, and (7) adherents to religions other than their own. We construct an in-group trust measure by averaging people's responses to the first three categories about family, neighbors, and people they know. Similarly, we can construct a measure of out-group trust by averaging responses to responses to the latter four categories. When we take the difference between the two averages, we arrive at the Out-In-Group Trust. Figure 19.1 summarizes the data on this measure (the data is from 75 countries; however, it must be noted that it does not cover large parts of Africa and the Middle East).

The first point to note is that, as with generalized trust, there is also great variation in Out-In-Group Trust across countries. We next note an interesting and more subtle issue: there are countries—such as China—where individuals responded very positively to the original generalized trust question in the World Values Survey, but where the Out-In-Group Trust measure is low. One way to interpret this discrepancy between the generalized trust measure and the Out-In-Group Trust measure is as follows: when facing the generalized trust question, individuals may think that it is about people they meet on a day-to day basis. If they mostly meet own kin-based members then their response would be to say that such individuals can be trusted. However, when asked specifically about different types of individuals in the seven categories mentioned previously, individuals may be more precise about their trust attitudes. Equipped with this more sophisticated notion of generalized trust, let us now turn to the relation between kin-based institutions and Out-In-Group Trust and universalism.

Kin-based institutions possess a wide range of features and they differ in many ways from each other. A natural place to start is rules and practices concerning marriage: some societies allow men to have multiple wives, while others allow only one (this variable is termed "polygamy versus monogamy"). A related feature pertains to which partners are allowed and which are disallowed: in some societies, marriages between uncles and nieces or between first or second cousins are allowed, whereas in others, even marriages between fifth cousins is disallowed (this variable is termed "cousin marriage").

A second dimension pertains to habitation: in some societies, the expectation is for multiple generations such as parents, their sons, and the families of the sons to live together; in other societies, the norm is that children live with their parents until adulthood and they then

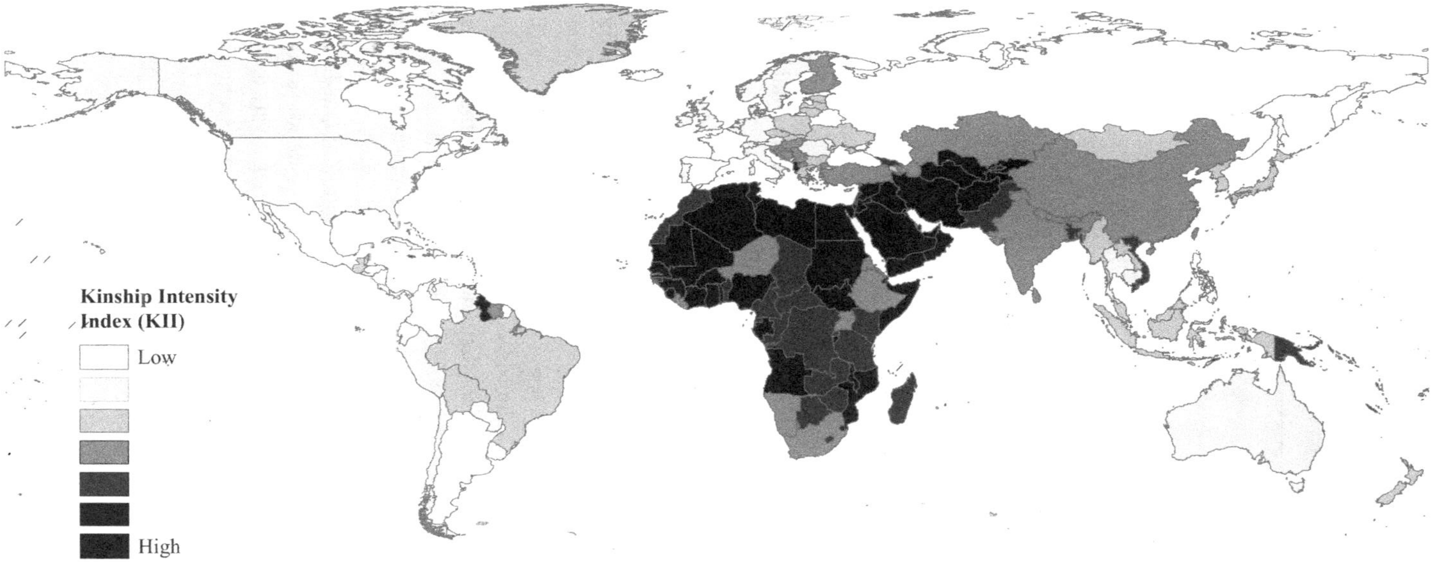


**Figure 19.1**
World map of kinship patterns. *Source*: Figure 6.1 in Henrich (2020).

**Table 19.1**
Distribution of kinship traits

| Traits | % of Preindustrial Societies |
|---|---|
| Bilateral descent | 28 |
| Cousin marriage | 25 |
| Monogamy | 15 |
| Nuclear family | 8 |
| Neolocal residence | 5 |

*Source*: Table 5.1 in Henrich (2020).

move to set up their own households (this variable is termed "joint versus nuclear family"). Finally, there is the issue of descent: in some societies, descent is traced solely through the male side (father and son), while in others, decent is traced through both the paternal and the maternal sides (this variable is termed "paternal versus bilateral descent").

Building on these considerations, we will study the following attributes of kinship institutions: (1) bilateral descent, (2) second or closer cousin marriage, (3) monogamy, (4) nuclear family, and (5) separate/neolocal residence. Anthropologists have collected data on these traits from over 1,200 preindustrial societies (available in the Database of Places, Language, Culture, and Environment at D-PLACE.org). The frequencies of these traits vary from 28 percent for bilateral descent to 5 percent for neolocal residence. Table 19.1, taken from Henrich (2020), summarizes this data.

Table 19.1 is based on data from the late nineteenth and early twentieth centuries. Moving forward in time to the twenty-first century, let us briefly consider the empirical patterns on marriage among individuals related through the extended family. For concreteness, let us consider marriages between relations that are second or closer cousins. At one end of the spectrum, in the Middle East and Africa, more than a quarter of all marriages fall in this category. At the other end of the spectrum, in countries like the US, Britain, and the Netherlands, only about 0.2 percent of marriages fall in this class. Large countries like China and India fall in the middle, with intermediate levels of cousin marriage (around 1 in 10 marriages is a cousin marriage).

Figure 19.2 plots the global distribution of Out-In-Group Trust. When we place the evidence on kinship groups alongside the evidence on generalized trust and universalism, we find that stronger kinship relations are negatively associated with Out-In-Group Trust and universalism. Figures 19.3 and 19.4 present scatter plots of these relations and the best linear fit.

These statistical correlations are striking. As we are interested in understanding the relation between kinship institutions and economic performance, let us now put together what we have learned on kinship-based institutions and generalized trust and universalism, together with some data on economic performance for a few specific countries.

The set of WEIRD countries includes the US, the UK, Canada, North Western Europe, and Australia and New Zealand. These countries are characterized by low strength of

**Figure 19.2**
World map of Out-In-Group Trust. *Source*: Figure 6.5 in Henrich (2020).

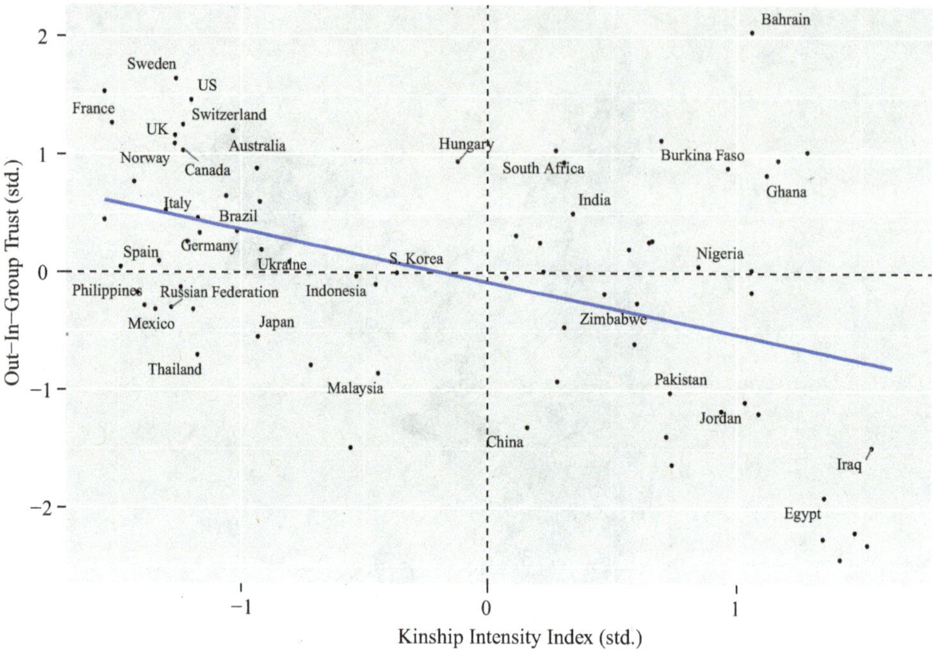


(a) Kin-based groups and Out-In-Group Trust

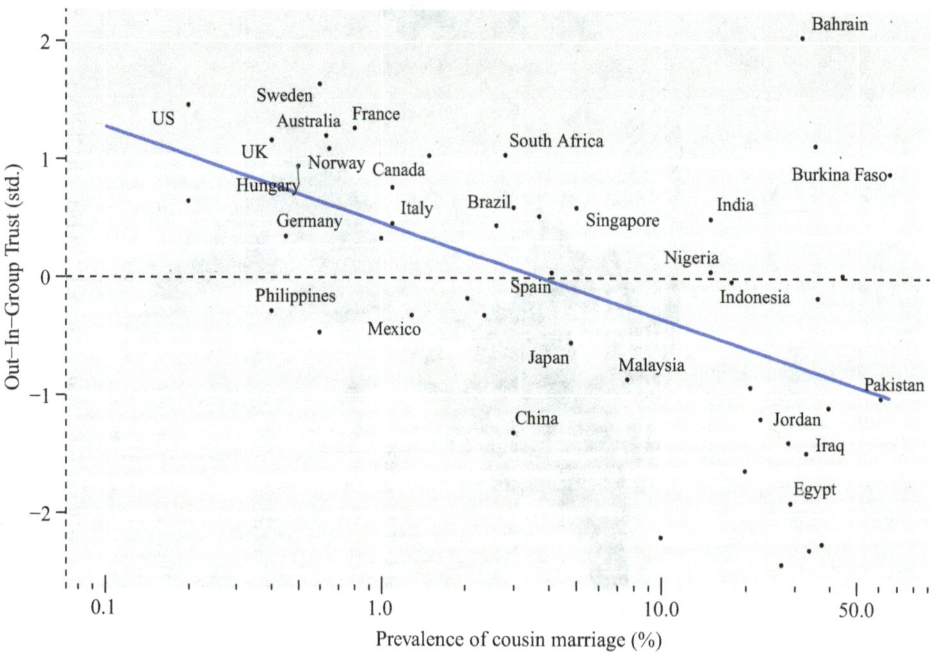


(b) Cousin marriage and Out-In-Group Trust

**Figure 19.3**
Society and Out-In-Group Trust. *Source*: Figure 6.6 in Henrich (2020).

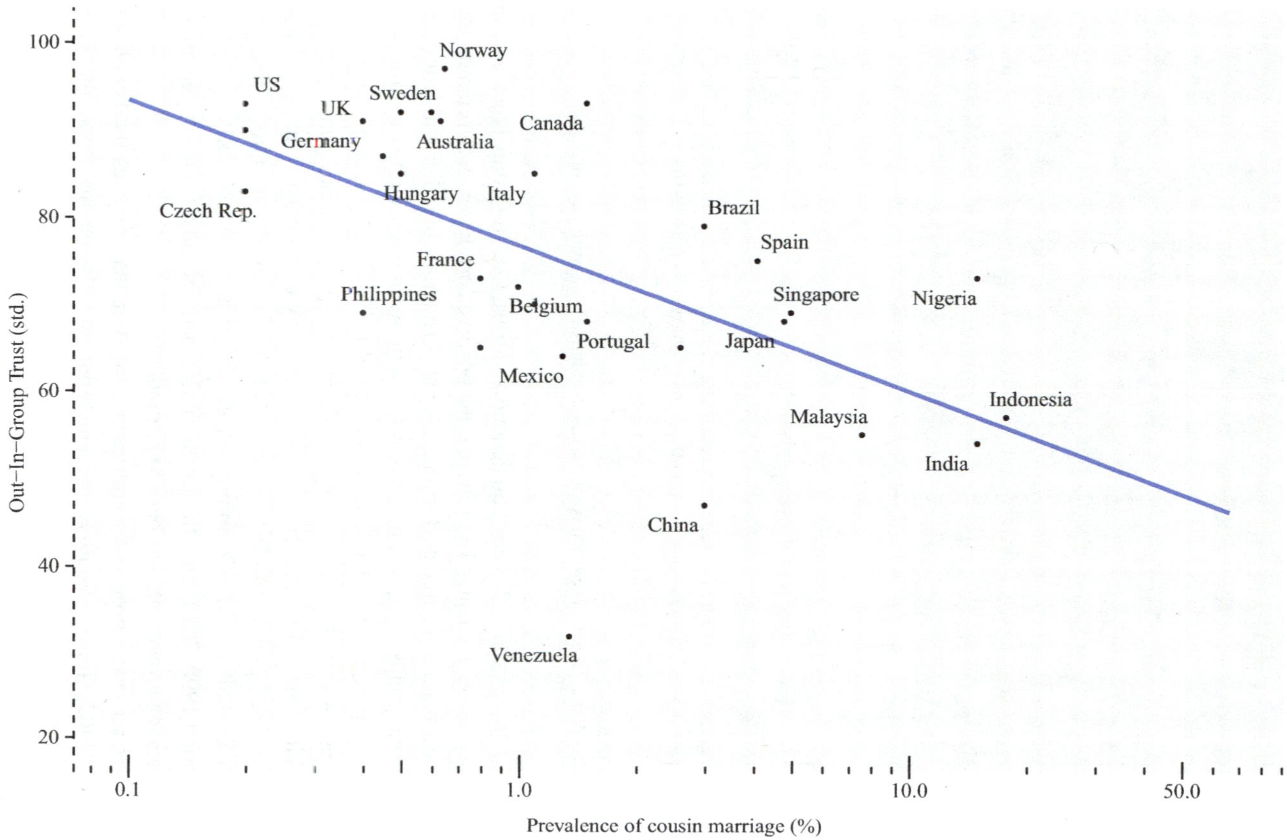


**Figure 19.4**
Cousin marriage and universalism. *Source*: Figure 6.7 in Henrich (2020).

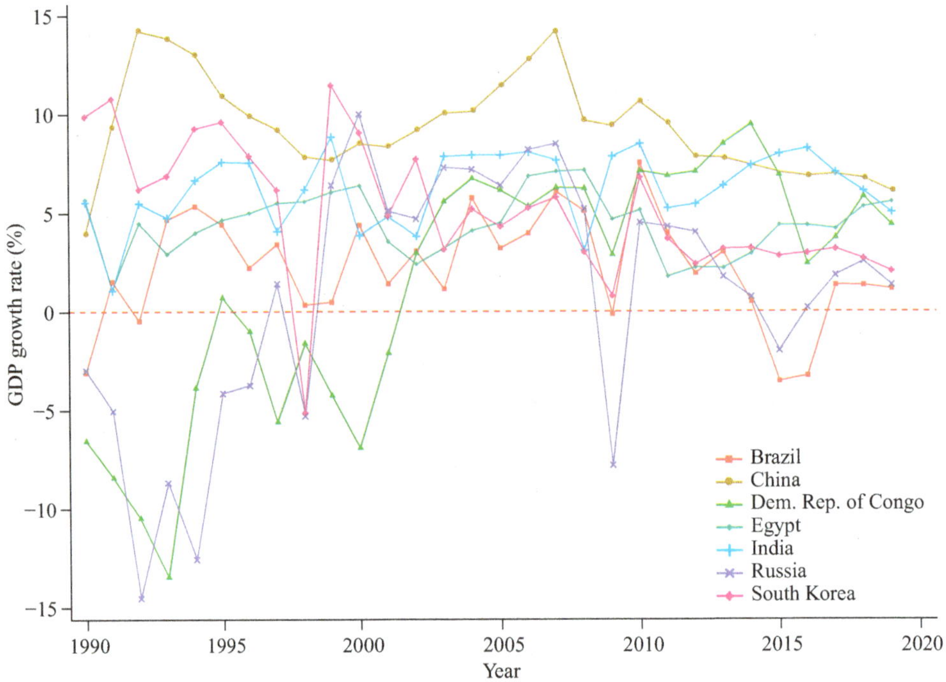


**Figure 19.5**
Rate of economic growth in selected countries. *Source*: https://data.worldbank.org/.

kinship groups and high scores on generalized trust, Out-In-Group Trust, and universalism. Our discussion in chapter 18 brought out a positive correlation between measures of generalized trust and economic performance. That correlation, together with our observations on kin-based groups, suggest a negative relation between the strength of kin-based groups and economic performance. Once we move out of the WEIRD group of countries, the picture becomes considerably richer. The growth rates are presented in figures 19.5 and 19.6.

Moving east in Europe, let us consider formerly communist countries. Russia has weak kinship-based groups, modest generalized trust, modest Out-In-Group Trust, and low universalism. After the fall of communism, economic performance has been very uneven. Over the period 1990–2020, growth rates have fluctuated widely, from −5 percent to 5 percent. The average growth rate has been very modest.

Consider next a group of countries in East Asia that includes the People's Republic of China (PRC), Taiwan, South Korea, and Singapore. Within this group, there are significant variations that we will discuss in the second case study in this chapter. Here, we comment on the experience of the PRC. In the PRC, kinship groups are strong, as is generalized trust. But a closer examination of the sources of trust revealed that Out-In-Group Trust is low to modest. In addition, the PRC scores low on universalism. These patterns must be set alongside the extraordinary economic success of the PRC. For example, the Chinese economy has grown at a rate averaging around 8 percent over the period 1990–2020 (see figure 19.5). These very high growth rates raise questions about the compatibility of strong, kin-based institutions and economic performance that will be taken up in a case study later.

Moving south in Asia, let us next consider India: kinship-based groups are strong, as is generalized trust. But a closer examination of the evidence suggests that Out-In-Group Trust is modest. Moreover, India also has a low score on universalism. These institutional and cultural arrangements are accompanied by impressive economic performance growth rates over the 1990–2020 period, with rates of growth ranging between 4 percent and 8 percent (see figure 19.5). We will examine kinship-based institutions in India in a case study later.

Turning to Latin America and South America, consider Brazil: kinship-based groups are weak and the generalized trust score is very low. In addition, Out-In-Group Trust and universalism scores are modest. Economic performance over the period 1990–2020 has been very uneven, with rates of growth ranging between 0 percent and 6 percent. Figure 19.5 presents the data.

Finally, we take up two countries in Africa: the Democratic Republic of the Congo and Egypt. We will discuss the case of the Democratic Republic of Congo is some detail later. Here, we note that the population of the Congo consists of a very large number of ethnic groups with limited experience of cohabiting the same country. We note that the rate of economic growth was very low for a long period of time until 2003, when the Great War of Congo ended. The rate of growth has improved significantly after that time. In Egypt, the strength of kinship groups is high (as reflected in high rates of cousin marriage), generalized trust is low, and Out-In-Group Trust is very low. Economic performance over the past two decades has been uneven, with rates of growth ranging from 2 percent to 6 percent (see figure 19.5).

We summarize the growth rates in income for these countries in figures 19.5 and 19.6. For ease of comparison, we place these countries in two separate plots. One plot contains Brazil, China, Egypt, India, Democratic Republic of Congo, South Korea, and Russia, and the second plot contains a set of the WEIRD countries (Australia, Canada, France, Germany, Netherlands, the UK, and the US).

Our discussion on kinship institutions and "weirdness" suggests a few high-level observations. The strength of kinship-based groups has a negative relationship with Out-In-Group Trust and with universalism. Also, the relationship between the strength of kinship-based groups and economic performance is less clear: on the one hand, some societies with weak kinship-based ties (the WEIRD societies) have performed well for extended periods of time and continue to do so, but there are countries (like Brazil) that have performed much less well. On the other hand, there are societies with strong, kinship-based ties (such as South Korea, China, and India) that have registered very high rates of growth, and there are others (such as the Congo) that have performed less well. We now turn to a closer study of a few

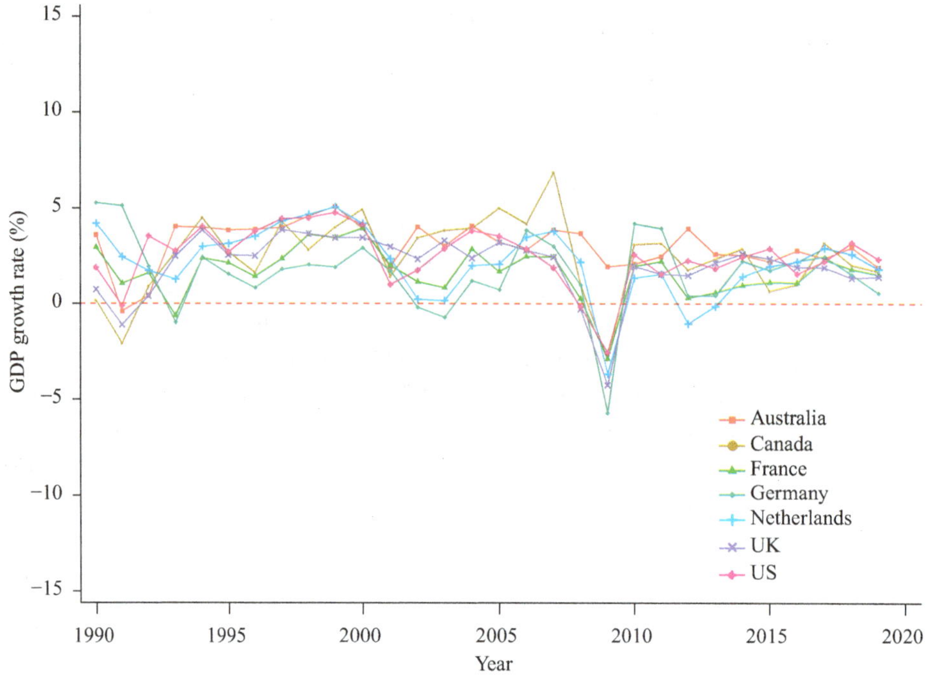


**Figure 19.6**
Rate of economic growth in selected WEIRD countries. *Source*: https://data.worldbank.org/.

countries, which draws attention to the relation between kinship groups, trust, and the nature of the state.

### 19.2.2 Lineages and Clans

*China*: The Chinese constitute the world's largest racial, linguistic, and cultural group. They are spread across a vast geographic area and live in wide variety of states, from the communist PRC, to overseas Chinese settlements in South East Asia (Taiwan, Hong Kong, Singapore, and Malaysia), to industrial democracies like the UK, the US, and Canada. We now discuss the role of lineage and extended families in Chinese communities. Our discussion draws on a wide range of sources that include Allen, Qian, and Qian (2005); Dai, Mookherjee, Munshi, and Zhang (2020); Song, Storesletten, and Zilibotti (2011); Fleisher, Hud, McGuiree, and Zhang (2010); Nee and Opper (2012); Peng (2004); Greif and Tabellini (2017); and especially on Fukuyama (1995).

Let us briefly recapitulate some of the main points of our discussion in chapter 17, on economic growth and communities. We start by noting that China has witnessed the same degree of industrialization in three decades as Europe did over the course of two centuries (Summers [2007]). This economic transformation began in the early 1980s with the establishment of township-village enterprises (TVEs) and accelerated with the entry of private firms in the economy in the 1990s. Starting with almost no private firms in 1990, there were 15 million registered private firms by 2014 (accounting for over 90 percent of all registered firms). Alongside this growth in numbers, the share of registered capital held by private firms has grown sharply: by 2014, private firms held 60 percent of all registered capital in the economy. Depending on how the accounting is done, China is now the world's largest or second-largest economy. Its growth has had profound effects on the flow of goods and services and capital and on the balance of political influence across the world.

The dynamism of the Chinese economy is reflected along different dimensions. Take, for instance, in the list of the world's largest firms by revenue by *Fortune* magazine. In 1990, there were no Chinese firms on the list; by 2020, China and Hong Kong accounted for most of the firms on it. Indeed, there are more Fortune Global 500 companies based in mainland China and Hong Kong than in the US—124 versus 121. In 2020, China had more firms on the list than France, Germany, and Britain combined! A second feature of this economic growth that is worth noting is that in spite of the very high growth rates of private-sector firms, many of the largest firms in China are state-owned. Again, let us look at the largest firms by revenue: in 2020, 84 (i.e., 68 percent) of the Chinese firms in the largest Fortune 500 firms worldwide are state owned.

We next turn to the role of kin-based groups and the state in Chinese economic growth. Governments at the local (county), provincial, and central levels played an important role in China's economic transformation. Local governments provide the infrastructure to support production clusters, which are a distinctive feature of the Chinese economy (for a discussion of production clusters, see chapter 12 on coordination problems.) Provincial governments and the central government supported firms by giving them subsidized credit and aggressively promoting exports. In addition, large parts of the economy are still dominated by state firms (as noted here). But there remains the question of how this growth in private firms occurred without effective legal systems and well-functioning financial institutions (i.e., those that function without the preconditions generally believed to be necessary for market-based development). Specifically, how did millions of individuals who were born in rural areas transition into the role of entrepreneurs, setting up and successfully running such a vast array of extraordinarily successful companies?

Patrilineal lineages—also referred to as "clans"—have long been associated with Chinese society; see, for instance, Weber (1951). A clan rests on blood ties, confers cultural identity, and has clearly nominated leaders. Clans are characterized by rules about obligations that have high standing. The Communist Party took a number of steps to suppress lineage organizations, but recent research shows that clans persisted through the communist period and they have reconstituted themselves and been revived after the market reforms of 1979. In chapter 17, we provided an account of the role of lineages and clans in shaping economic growth. (See chapter 17 for a brief discussion of the role of lineages and clans in shaping economic growth in China.)

*South Korea:* We next turn to South Korea, as another instance of a society based on strong family ties, to illustrate a possible configuration of society, state, and markets. First, we note the extraordinary economic growth that started in 1960 and that has made South Korea one of the technologically most advanced countries in the world today. Second, we note the state support and the dominance of internationally powerful, large, private-sector firms. A third point is that in 2020, there were 14 Korean firms on *Fortune* magazine's list of the 500 largest firms in the world by revenue, and most of those were controlled by a few large conglomerates (the chaebols), of which only a few are state-owned.

We will discuss the story of Samsung next, as it serves to bring out the broader contours of the growth process in South Korea. The information is taken from Wikipedia (https://en.wikipedia.org/wiki/Samsung), and the broader argument concerning Korea draws on Fukuyama (1995) and Granovetter (2017).

Samsung is one of the world's largest producers of electronic devices today, including a wide variety of consumer and industry electronics, such as appliances, digital media devices, semiconductors, memory chips, and integrated systems. It produces about a fifth of South Korea's total exports. Samsung was founded as a grocery trading store on March 1, 1938, by Lee Byung-Chull. He started his business in Taegu, Sourth Korea, trading noodles and other goods produced in and around the city and exporting them to China and its provinces. After the Korean War, Lee expanded his business into textiles. During that period, his business benefited from policies adopted by the Korean government that helped large domestic firms by shielding them from competition and providing them with easy financing. During the 1970s, the company expanded its textile-manufacturing processes and entered other new industries through the launching of new subsidiaries such as Samsung Heavy Industries, Samsung Techwin, and Samsung Shipbuilding.

Samsung first entered the electronics industry in 1969. In the 1970s, it acquired a 50 percent stake in Korea Semiconductor. The late 1970s and early 1980s witnessed the rapid expansion of Samsung's technology businesses. Separate semiconductor and electronics branches were established. Samsung Data Systems (now Samsung SDS) was established in 1985 to serve the growing need for systems development. In the 1990s, Samsung continued its expansion into global electronics markets with a number of its technology products, ranging from semiconductors to computer monitors and liquid crystal display (LCD) screens. The 2000's saw the birth of Samsung's Galaxy, one of the top-selling smart phones in the world. Since 2006, the company has also been the top-selling global manufacturer of televisions. As of 2020, it includes over 60 firms ranging across most sectors of the Korean economy and constituting over 20 percent of its total exports. Notable affiliates include Samsung Electronics, Samsung Heavy Industries, Samsung Engineering, and Samsung C&T.

In this highly diversified conglomerate, the convention is that the top management positions are typically held by male members of the family of the founder, Lee Byung-Chull. By way of illustration, consider Samsung Electronics: the chairman, Lee-Kun Hee, is the son of the founder, while the vice-chairman (and chairman designate), Lee Jae-yong, is the son of Lee-Kun Hee. The firms in the Samsung group are closely interconnected through a network of cross-ownership. For instance, Samsung Electronics is a dominant shareholder in Samsung Heavy Industries.

The Samsung story shows how strong family ties combined with deep and sustained state support can give rise to world-leading firms.

### 19.2.3 The Caste-Based Society

Hindu society is centered on castes. Formally, there are four castes, but a large part of the population lies outside these four castes (and is referred to as 'Dalits'). The central rule in Hindu society involves marriage within a caste (known as "endogamy"). This rule has been followed over the past 2,000 years, and even today, 9 out of 10 marriages respect this rule. There are roughly 3,000–4,000 subcastes, each of which has on average approximately 250,000 members. Within a village, there is spatial clustering based on caste, but caste members are usually spread across many villages, as well as in urban centers. Thus caste networks have an interesting structure: local spatial clustering within a village alongside a wide spatial spread. The local clustering is accompanied by rules on social interaction both horizontally as well as vertically across a caste. Caste has been a major factor shaping social relations and continues to be a powerful presence in contemporary Indian society, economy, and democracy. The discussion here draws on Srinivas (1987), Beteille (1965), Mayer (1960), Munshi ((2019), and Munshi and Rosenzweig (2015). We recall that the role of caste in shaping informal exchange was discussed in chapter 1, and its role in shaping gender differences in education choice was discussed in chapter 17.

Historically, caste networks helped smooth the consumption of their members in the face of income fluctuations. More recently, since the middle of the nineteenth century, they have expanded into the urban labor market and into business when new opportunities became available. As a result, in contemporary India, caste networks shape participation in labor markets, allocation of capital, and entry into new markets. Indeed, a distinctive feature of the Indian economy is that the large and dynamic private sector is dominated by large conglomerates centered on extended family and subcaste networks.

One reason for the prominence of caste is that it has a important relation to trust. Munshi and Rosenzweig (2015) present cross-country results from wave 5 of the World Values Survey (conducted between 2005–2009) on questions relating to trust and tolerance of outsiders. Restricting the sample to countries with a population in excess of 20 million that are classified by the World Bank as low, lower-middle, or upper-middle income, India ranks close to the top of the list with regard to trust in neighbors. On the face of it, this appears to be strong evidence for generalized trust. However, on measures of tolerance of neighbors following a different religion or speaking a different language, India ranks at the bottom. This suggests that an alternative interpretation may be more accurate: Indian respondents are essentially reporting that they have a high degree of trust in their fellow caste members living nearby.

Caste is the basis for one of the most extensive and aggressive affirmative action programs in the world: in many parts of the country, over half of all public-sector jobs are reserved for members of historically disadvantaged castes. At different levels of the political system, positions may be reserved for particular communities.

At a more general level, since India's independence from British rule in 1947, caste has also become a central pillar of representative democracy. Parties come to power on the basis of alliances across caste groups. The ability of a party to win elections, therefore, depends on how successful it is in forming partnerships with the different caste groups. Politicians make decisions that favor a group, the group rewards the politicians by voting—at a group level—for them. Caste has become the natural social unit around which "vote banks" are organized. It can be said that the democratic process has reinforced caste identity and strengthened kinship-based groups.

We conclude this discussion with a brief comment on some aspects of Indian economic growth since independence from Britain in 1947. Since the early years after independence, the Indian government has played a prominent role in shaping the pace and the direction of economic change. However, economic growth was modest until the early 1990s. It has picked up over the past 25 years, partly due to the liberalization of the market and the opening of the economy to foreign firms and capital. Figure 19.5 presents an overview of the economic growth rate over the period 1990–2020. The dynamism in the economy is also reflected in the list of the world's largest firms. In 1990, there were no Indian firms on the Fortune 100 list, but there were 10 Indian firms there in 2010 and 7 by 2020. In spite of the dynamism of the private sector, we note that some of the largest firms in India are still state owned: for example, in the list of 7 largest firms, 4 were state owned. Another feature of the Indian economy is that family-based conglomerates control the largest private firms.

### 19.2.4 Civic Community and Democracy in Italy

In their landmark study, Putnam, Leonardi, and Nanetti (1993) argue for a central role for civic community in the effective functioning of representative democratic institutions. They study the impact of a political reform in Italy that shifted budgetary authority from the national government to the regions (in several key areas such as education and health care). The result is that starting at 10 percent in the prereform period, the control of regions over the national budget increased to over 25 percent by 1977. How did this shift in resources and authority affect the performance of government in the 20 regions of Italy?

The first finding is that there were large differences in the performance of the regional governments across the regions based on independent measures of policy process, pronouncements, and implementation. These differences were consistent with citizens' assessments of regional governments. Figure 19.7 provides a mapping of the levels of performance.

The second finding is that these differences in the performance of regional governments were closely related to the civic culture. Civic culture was seen as a combination of civil associations, voter turnout at referenda, lack of clientelism, and local newspaper circulation.

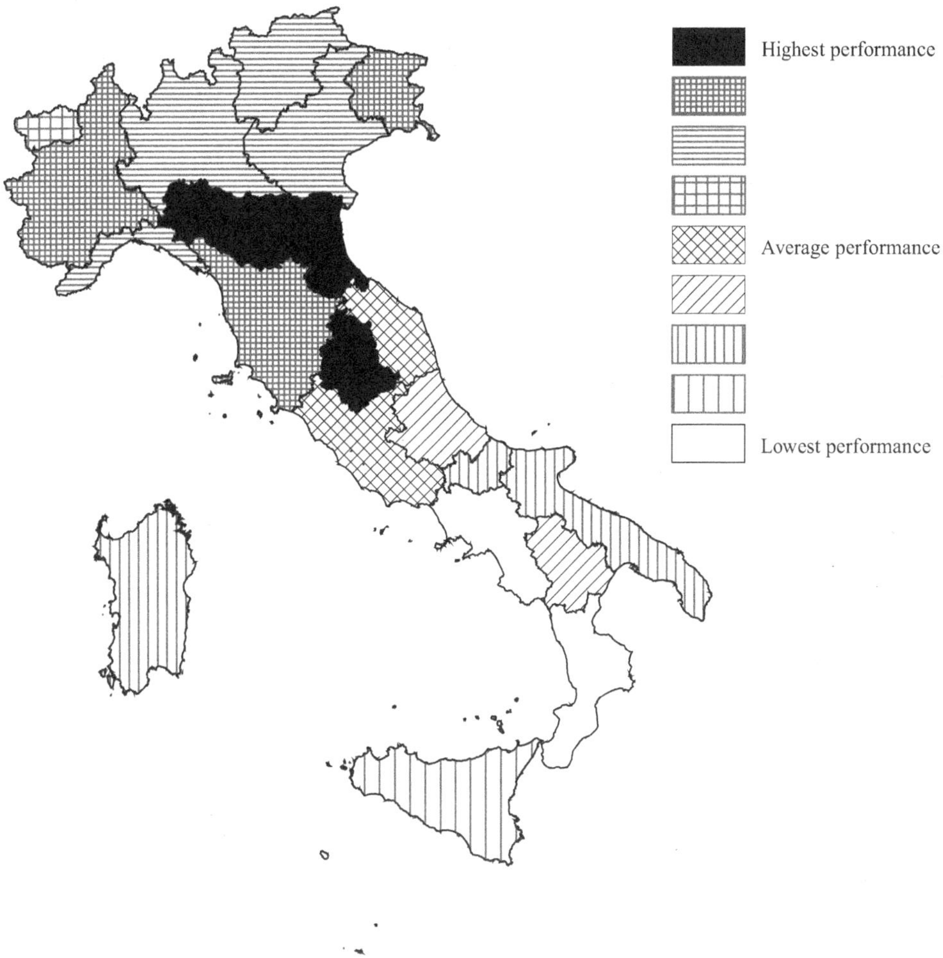


**Figure 19.7**
Performance of regional governments. *Source*: Figure 4.1 in Putnam, Leonardi, and Nanetti (1993).

Civil associations include sports societies, leisure clubs, music and theater, and health and social services. Figure 19.8 charts the levels of civic community in Italy's 20 regions according to these factors. A comparison of figures 19.7 and 19.8 reveals a very strong correlation between civic culture and institutional performance: northern regions were characterized by high levels of civic engagement, and the southern regions by hierarchically organized public life and far less engagement.

The third finding is that the origins of differences in civic culture in late-twentieth-century participation may be traced to differences in the modes of governance in the early medieval period. The republicanism of Italian regions at the beginning of the fourteenth century

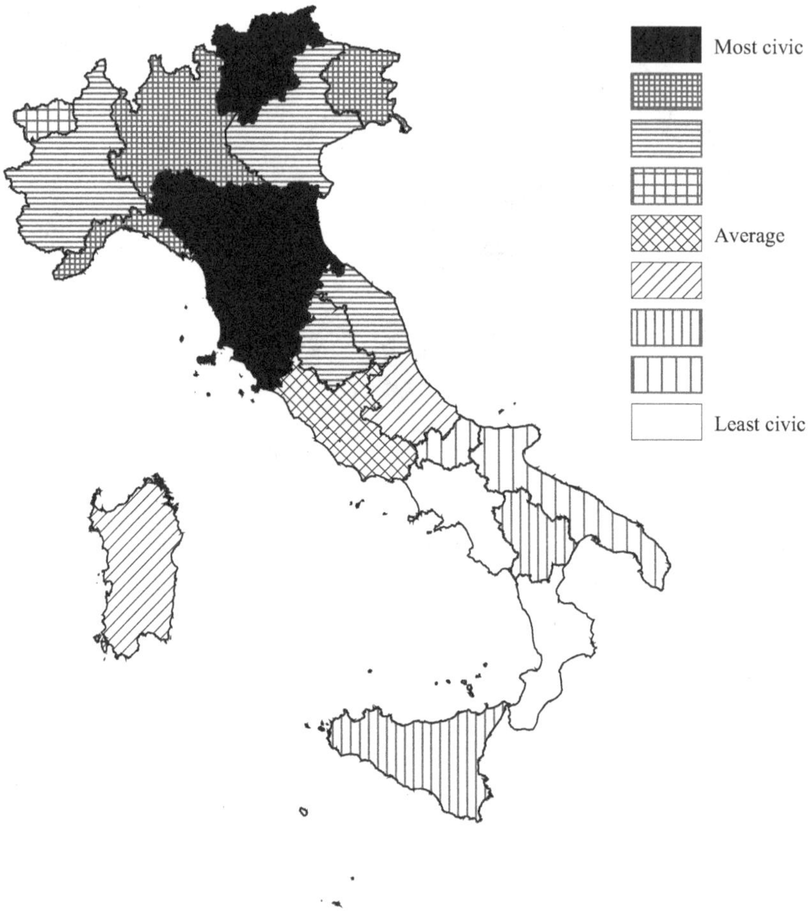


**Figure 19.8**
Civic capital in regions. *Source*: Figure 4.4 in Putnam, Leonardi, and Nanetti (1993).

corresponds closely to the strength of the civic tradition in the twentieth century. The parallel between this pattern and the distribution of civic norms and networks in the 1970s, as displayed in figure 19.8, is remarkable. The southern territories once ruled by the Norman kings constitute the seven least civic regions in the 1970s. Almost as precisely, the papal states (minus the communal republics that lay in the northern section of the pope's domains) correspond to the next three or four regions up the civic ladder in the 1970s. At the other end of the scale, the heartland of republicanism in 1300 corresponds uncannily to the most civic regions of today, followed closely by the areas still farther north, in which medieval republican traditions had proved somewhat weaker. The persistence of the high and low civic community cultures in North and South Italy over several hundred years suggests that, once attained, these widely differing social configurations are very stable.

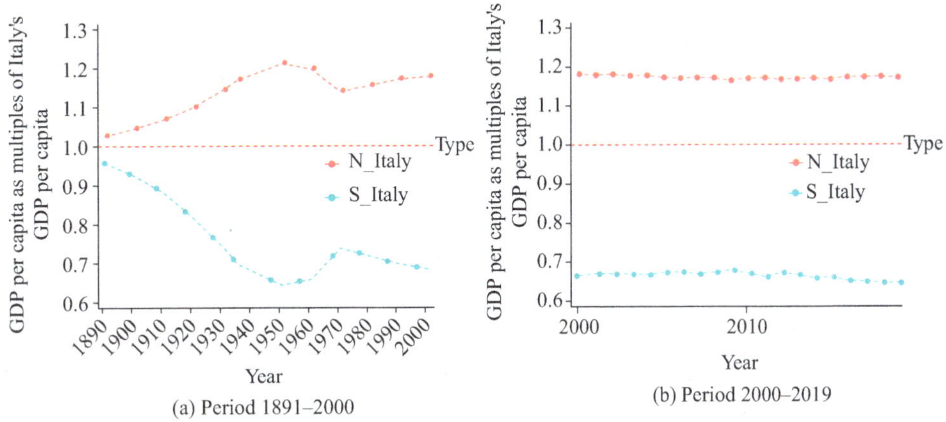


**Figure 19.9**
Economic differences between North and South Italy. *Source*: Daniele and Malanima (2014) and https://ec.europa.eu/eurostat/.

The differences in civic culture and quality of governance are reflected in large and persistent income differences. Figure 19.9 presents trends on these income differences over the last 120 years.

### 19.2.5 Ethnic Fragmentation

The Democratic Republic of the Congo (in what follows, simply Congo) has a population of 68 million and is the largest subSaharan African country. Congo gained independence from Belgium in 1960. For a discussion on ethnic fragmentation and wars in Congo, see chapter 10. Here we discuss the patterns of economic growth and then turn to aspects of society and the state.

Figure 19.5 presents the growth rate in gross national product (GNP) over the period 1990–2020. It shows that growth rates have fluctuated widely and the average has been low over this period. In 2020, the per capita income was around $580, a figure that is less than 1 percent of Switzerland's per capita income. This low income is reflected in a life expectancy that is 20 years less than Switzerland's. As indicated in figure 19.6, economic growth was very poor for an extended period lasting until 2003, but it has picked up since then. This record of economic performance must be viewed against the background of Congo's extraordinary wealth of natural resources: it has some of the world's largest reserves of copper, diamonds, cobalt, and coltan (a mineral that is used primarily in the production of tantalum capacitors used in many electronic devices, including mobile phones).

An important feature of Congo is that the population belongs to over 200 ethnic groups. There are close affinities between several of these ethnic groups and groups in adjoining countries: as a result, developments in Congo are closely connected to developments in neighboring countries such as Rwanda and Uganda. These kinship ties are an important aspect of the Great War of Congo (1996–1997, 1998–2003). The state in Congo has failed to provide one of the essential services expected of a government—that of providing secure borders. It has also been unable to offer personal and economic security within its borders. The result is that the citizens have not been able to take advantage of the vast mineral resources in the country, leaving Congo one of the poorest and most insecure countries in the world.

Let us now summarize what we have learned in this section. First, we found that there are very great variations in the strength of kin-based institutions across the world. Second, the relation between kinship groups and economic performance is complicated. WEIRD societies like the US, North Western European countries, New Zealand, and Australia suggest a positive correlation between weak kinship ties and economic performance. There are countries like Brazil that have weak kinship groups and low generalized trust and have a record or uneven economic performance. On the other hand, there are countries like South Korea, China, and India that have strong kinship groups but a good-to-strong record of economic growth. Finally, there are countries with strong kinship groups, such as Congo and Egypt, with poor-to-uneven economic performance. A recurring theme in these case studies is the important role of the state. We next develop a theoretical framework to better understand these empirical patterns.

## 19.3 Conceptual Considerations

In this section, we consider a theoretical framework with a focus on economic activity and social welfare. The discussion introduces a number of concepts and explains their background.

First, we consider individuals in their relation to kinship-based groups. Ties between individuals belonging to the same group are close and reliable. The size of the groups is a key variable, and it is one indication of the strength of kinship-based relations in a society (Fukuyama [1995] and Henrich [2020]). Ties between individuals belonging to different groups is another important element: the ties may be civic and relate to common memberships of a variety of associations, as in Putnam, Leonardi, and Nanetti (1993)'s study of democracy in Italy, or integrated business organizations and professional associations as in Varshney (2001)'s study of Hindu-Muslim communal violence (where associations involving members of different religious communities are seen as embodying bridging capital) in the terminology of Putnam, Leonardi, and Nanetti (1993).

Second, we suppose that individuals earn utility from economic activity and engagement in civic activities. Economic activity can be carried out within a group or with other individuals outside the group. Economic activity takes place in the presence of asymmetric information, search and matching frictions, and commitment problems. Kin-based interaction helps to overcome some of these frictions, but at the cost of restrictions on who can work with whom. Economic exchange across kinship groups thus entails transaction costs: the magnitude of these costs will depend on the effectiveness of formal institutions and the level of generalized trust in a society. We borrow these ideas from North and Thomas (1973), North (1990), and Williamson (1985) and the recent literature on kin-based exchange and Fukuyama (1995) and Henrich (2020), and they underly the following observations from Fukuyama (1995):

> By contrast, people who do not trust one another will end up cooperating only under a system of formal rules and regulations, which have to be negotiated, agreed to, litigated, and enforced, sometimes by coercive means. This legal apparatus, serving as a substitute for trust, entails what economists call "transaction costs." Widespread distrust in a society, in other words, imposes a kind of tax on all forms of economic activity, a tax that high-trust societies do not have to pay.
> (pp. 27–28).

Third, we consider the state, which carries out redistribution and provides a range of public goods such as education, health, and infrastructure. The state may run large-scale, public-sector firms that produce key inputs for other sectors, such as iron, steel, coal, and oil; and it also may run banks that provide credit to private and public firms. The state is supported by tax revenue and also contains formal institutions that help enforce contracts and lower transaction costs of impersonal economic exchange. It is therefore important to understand who makes decisions on tax rates and what their incentives are. Our approach to the political economy of taxation draws on a long tradition in political economy and state capacity, as summarized in Besley and Persson (2013).

Fourth, we specify the relation between the state and civic community and how this bears on impersonal market exchange (here we draw, among others, on Huntingdon [1968]). The state and civic community may be complementary: this is the idea developed in the influential work of Putnam, Leonardi, and Nanetti (1993), and it is a key theme in Acemoglu and Robinson (2019)—the effectiveness of the state is only as good as the strength of the social institutions.

> . . . the failure of democracy to consolidate itself in many parts of the world may be due less to the appeal of the idea itself than to the absence of those material and social conditions that make it possible for accountable government to emerge in the first place. That is, successful liberal democracy requires both a state that is strong, unified, and able to enforce laws on its own territory, and a society that is strong and cohesive and able to impose accountability on the state. It is the balance between a strong state and a strong society that makes democracy work, not just in seventeenth-century England but in contemporary developed democracies as well.
> Fukuyama (2011, pp. 479–480).

While complementarity between civic society and state is widely noted, there is also an influential strand of thinking that argues for their substitutability. This idea is implicit in Polanyi (1944), which says that the growth of national markets for labor was accompanied by a growing role for the government and the weakening of local social ties. This idea is consistent with the line of work that stresses the importance of greater involvement of the state in countries that have joined the development process at a later point in time (see e.g., Gerschenkron [1962]). It is also consistent with the idea of Fukuyama (1995) and others who have argued that strong, kinship-based groups and weak civic institutions may be supported by a powerful and an active state. The example of an activist state in France is mentioned in this context. More generally, it is possible to see some aspects of civic engagement as being complementary to the activities of the state, while others are substitutes.

Fifth, we use a notion of civic capital as a composite that combines beliefs and expectations and social structure. In this, we draw upon Fukuyama (1995) and Geertz (1973).

> Cultural anthropologists and sociologists distinguish between culture and what they term social structure. Culture in this sense is restricted to meanings, symbols, values and ideas and encompasses phenomena like religion and ideology. Geertz' own definition of culture is "an historical transmitted pattern of meanings embodied in symbols, a system of inherited conceptions expressed in symbolic forms by means of which they communicate, perpetuate, and develop their knowledge about and attitudes toward life." Social structure, by contrast, concerns concrete social organizations such as the family, clan, legal system, or nation. In this sense, Confucian doctrines about the relationship between fathers and sons belong to culture; the actual Chinese family is social structure.
>
> ... I will not make use of this distinction between culture and social structure because it is often difficult to distinguish between the two: values and ideas shape concrete social relationships, and vice versa. The Chinese family has a patrilineal structure in large measure *because* Confucian ideology gives preference to males and teaches children to honor their fathers. Conversely, Confucian ideology seems reasonable to those who have been brought up in Chinese families.
>
> Fukuyama (1995, p. 34).

In the next section, we will present a model of civic capital that arises out of social structure and expectations about behavior. In this model, expectations and beliefs, as well as the autonomy of individuals in shaping them, will play a major role. See Swidler (1986) for a discussion on different ways of accommodating individual agency within notions of culture.

## 19.4 A Model of State Capacity

This section presents a theoretical framework within which we can locate different types of societies and assess their economic performance. The framework is taken from Bramoullé, Goyal, and Morelli (2022). It builds on the model of network and market activity in chapter 17 (taken from Gagnon and Goyal [2017]) and the model of group favoritism in chapter 18 (taken from Bramoullé and Goyal [2016]), and we also incorporate the concepts of group fractionalization (taken from Alesina, Devleeschauwer, Easterly, et al. 2003), and state capacity (taken from Besley and Persson [2013]).

We now consider a society composed of individuals who belong to kinship groups. Denote by $N = 1, \ldots, n$ the set of individuals and by $M = 1, \ldots, m$ the set of groups, with $m \geq 2$. The size of group $j$ is $s_j$ and $\sum_{j \in M} s_j = N$. Nuclear families give rise to small groups; castes, tribes, extended families, lineages, or clans give rise to larger groups. For simplicity, we will suppose that individuals within a group are fully connected to each other. In addition, there may be links between individuals across groups. We denote this network of cross-group links by $g_o$.

There are three stages in the model. In stage 1, individuals decide on the level of civic activity (which defines civic capital in the society). In stage 2, the tax rate is determined and tax revenue is used to build state capacity. In stage 3, individuals decide on whether they will conduct exchange within their kinship group or in impersonal markets.

Individuals earn utility through economic exchange. Exchange could take place either between individuals within the same group or between individuals in different groups. The return from an exchange depends on the quality of the match between the individuals and the costs of transaction between them. The ideal match yields a value of 1, while a nonideal match yields $r \in [0, 1]$. We assume that every individual is equally likely to be an ideal match. The ideal match is then an individual in one's own group with a probability proportional to the size of one's group minus 1 ($s_i - 1$), and someone from another group with probability proportional to $n - s_i$.

Economic exchange within a group has lower transaction costs: this may be due to advantages of repeated interaction and cooperative norms within a group, or it may reflect group-level altruism. For simplicity, let us say that the within-groups transaction costs are zero. An ideal match with a group yields the full value, 1, while a nonideal match yields $r < 1$. The return from exchange between members belonging to different groups depends on the formal institutions and on civic culture. This return is denoted by $F(T, K) \leq 1$, where $T$ is the amount of government funds invested in the functioning of impersonal markets and $K$ is the level of civic culture.

A larger revenue can support a more extensive set of executive and legal institutions that would enhance the quality of contract enforcement. Similarly, high civic capital would support higher levels of generalized trust, which in turn would mitigate the transaction costs among members of different groups. This leads us to suppose that function $F$ is increasing with respect to both $T$ and $K$. We will explore both the situation in which state and civic capital complement each other and the situation in which weaknesses in one can be offset by expansion in the other. We introduce the concepts of strategic complements and substitutes to model these relations.

**Assumption 19.1** *$F(0, 0) = 0$, $F \leq 1$, and $F$ is weakly increasing and concave in both arguments. We shall say that civic capital and government are complements if $F$ displays increasing differences for $T' \geq T$ and $K' \geq K$:*

$$F(T', K') - F(T, K') \geq F(T', K) - F(T, K).$$

*Civic capital and government are substitutes if $F$ displays decreasing differences:*

$$F(T', K') - F(T, K') \leq F(T', K) - F(T, K).$$

By way of illustration, consider a specific functional form: $F(T, K) = \phi T^{\alpha} K^{\alpha}$. If we assume that $\alpha \in (0, 1)$, then the function satisfies assumption 19.1 and displays complements. By contrast, $F(T, K) = \phi(T + K)^{\alpha}$, with $\alpha \in (0, 1)$ satisfies assumption 19.1 and displays substitutes (note that with both these functional forms, $F \leq 1$, when $T$ and $K$ are small and $\phi$ is also small enough).

The government is funded by taxes on individual citizens. Let $t \in [0, 1]$ be the tax rate. Suppose that individual $i \in N$ starts with initial income $y_i$. Set $Y = \sum_i y_i$. Government's resources are equal to tax earnings, $tY$. We study a utilitarian social planner and compare that with the choices of a majority-based democratic government.

Finally, in stage 3, given a level of tax revenue, individuals choose whether to take part in impersonal exchange. Let $x_i \in \{0, 1\}$ denote the two options on within group and outside group; it takes a value of 1 if an individual engages in outside exchange and a value of 0 otherwise. When $x_i = 1$, individual $i$ matches an ideal partner, while when $x_i = 0$, $i$ matches someone in their own group. For simplicity, assume that an individual gets to keep the entire value of the exchange that they initiate. The ideal partner is an outsider with probability $\frac{n-s_i}{n-1}$. An individual's payoff from tax rate $t$, action $x_i$ and group size $s_i$ is thus equal to

$$u_i = (1-t)y_i + x_i \left[ F(T,K)\frac{n-s_i}{n-1} + \frac{s_i-1}{n-1} \right] + (1-x_i) \left[ r\frac{n-s_i}{n-1} + \frac{s_i-1}{n-1} \right], \tag{19.1}$$

and we see that the individual strictly prefers to engage in outside exchange, $x_i = 1$, if and only if $F(T,K) > r$. It is worth noting that the decision on whether to participate in within-group or outside exchange does not depend on income or group size. In other words, either all individuals engage in outside exchange or none do, and individual utility can be rewritten as

$$u_i = (1-t)y_i + max(F(T,K), r)\frac{n-s_i}{n-1} + \frac{s_i-1}{n-1}. \tag{19.2}$$

### 19.4.1 Utilitarian Outcome

We consider a utilitarian planner who seeks to maximize the sum of utilities. This provides a benchmark normative analysis and will serve as a basis to assess performance of a democratic government later. As is standard, we start at the second stage of the model and take the level of civic culture, $K$, as given.

We note that, in this setting, the only use of tax revenue is to improve state capacity. This improvement mitigates the transaction costs of impersonal exchange. Transaction costs arise when ideal matches lie across groups. Therefore the social return to improving state capacity is intimately related to the proportion of exchanges that will involve individuals of different groups.

Given a group structure, the fraction of ideal exchanges that will be across groups is given by

$$f = 1 - \sum_{j \in M} \left(\frac{s_j}{n}\right)^2. \tag{19.3}$$

Following Alesina, Devleeschauwer, Easterly, et al. (2003), we will refer to $f$ as a measure of *fractionalization*.

The fractionalization index takes the value of 0 if all individuals belong to a single group, and it is maximized if all individuals belong to different groups. Thus $0 \leq f \leq 1 - \frac{1}{n}$. When the number of groups is fixed, fractionalization decreases following a mean-preserving spread in size. Moreover, if all groups have the same size, fractionalization increases with the number of groups.

Our first result characterizes optimal taxation and brings out the relation between state capacity, the fractionalization index, and civic capital.

**Proposition 19.1** *Suppose that F satisfies assumption 19.1 and that $\frac{\partial F}{\partial T}(0,K) > \frac{1}{2}$ and $\frac{\partial F}{\partial T}(Y,K) < \frac{1}{n}$. Let $t_u^*$ be the tax rate chosen by an utilitarian planner. Then, equation (19.4) has a solution $t_u \in [0,1]$*

$$\frac{\partial F}{\partial T}(t_u Y, K) = \frac{n-1}{n^2}\frac{1}{f} \tag{19.4}$$

*If $F(t_u Y, K) < r$, then $t_u^* = 0$ and $\forall i, x_i = 0$. If $F(t_u Y, K) > r$, $t_u^* = t_u$ and $\forall i, x_i = 1$.*

*Proof.* Define $W = \sum_i u_i$, with

$$W = (1-t)Y + max(F(T,K), r)\sum_i \frac{n-s_i}{n-1} + \sum_i \frac{s_i - 1}{n-1}. \tag{19.5}$$

Using the definition of fractionalization, we may write aggregate out-group exchange as follows:

$$\sum_i \frac{n-s_i}{n-1} = \frac{n^2 - \sum_{j\in M} s_j^2}{n-1} = \frac{n^2}{n-1} f. \tag{19.6}$$

Consider a situation where $\forall i, x_i = 1$. Then,

$$\frac{\partial W}{\partial t} = -Y + Y\frac{\partial F}{\partial T}(tY,K)\frac{n^2}{n-1}f, \tag{19.7}$$

and since $F$ is concave in $T$,

$$\frac{\partial^2 W}{\partial t^2} = Y^2 \frac{\partial^2 F}{\partial T^2}\frac{n^2}{n-1} f \leq 0. \tag{19.8}$$

Moreover, since there are at least two groups, $f \geq \frac{2(n-1)}{n^2}$. Therefore,

$$\frac{\partial W}{\partial t}(0,K) = Y\left(-1 + \frac{\partial F}{\partial T}(0,K)\frac{n^2}{n-1}f\right) \geq Y\left(-1 + \frac{\partial F}{\partial T}(0,K)2\right).. \tag{19.9}$$

This means that

$$\frac{\partial W}{\partial t}(0,K) > 0 \text{ if } \frac{\partial F}{\partial T}(0,K) > \frac{1}{2}. \tag{19.10}$$

Since $f \leq 1 - \frac{1}{n}$,

$$\frac{\partial W}{\partial t}(1,K) = Y\left(-1 + \frac{\partial F}{\partial T}(Y,K)\frac{n^2}{n-1}f\right) \leq Y\left(-1 + \frac{\partial F}{\partial T}(Y,K)\right)n. \tag{19.11}$$

This means that

$$\frac{\partial W}{\partial t}(1,K) < 0 \text{ if } \frac{\partial F}{\partial T}(Y,K) < \frac{1}{n}. \tag{19.12}$$

Therefore, the first-order condition $\frac{\partial W}{\partial t} = 0$ has an interior solution, $0 < t_U < 1$, under the stated conditions.

Finally, observe that this is the solution of the planner's program only if $F(t_u Y, K) > r$. If $F(t_u Y, K) < r$, agents choose not to engage in impersonal markets even when the planner sets the best possible tax rate. Therefore, investing in impersonal markets is socially not worthwhile, and $t_u^* = 0$. ■

Proposition 19.1 shows that the optimal tax rate is a weakly increasing function of fractionalization. Impersonal exchange may bring higher benefits than exchange within groups only when the ideal match is an outsider. Our measure of fractionalization provides a measure of out-group exchange. As we have noted, fractionalization is high when there are many groups and when group sizes are the same. Thus societies with high fractionalization are precisely those where impersonal markets generate high social benefits, and therefore they are also societies in which a large state would be especially valuable.

We now examine the relation between optimal tax and civic capital.

**Corollary 19.1** *Suppose that the conditions for proposition 19.1 hold and civic capital and governments are complements. Then there is a threshold value of civic capital $\overline{K}_u$ such that $t_u^* = 0$ if $K < \overline{K}_u$ and $t_u^* = t_u > 0$, and it is increasing in $K$ if $K > \overline{K}_u$.*

*Proof.* First, note that the tax rate is positive ($t_u^* > 0$) only if $F(t_u^* Y, K) > r$. Next, implicitly differentiate the optimal tax rate with respect to $K$:

$$Y\frac{\partial t_u}{\partial K}\frac{\partial^2 F}{\partial T^2} + \frac{\partial^2 F}{\partial T \partial K} = 0 \tag{19.13}$$

Since $\frac{\partial^2 F}{\partial T^2} < 0$, $t_u$ is weakly increasing with respect to $K$ under complements (i.e., when $\frac{\partial^2 F}{\partial T \partial K} \geq 0$). We may therefore define the threshold $\bar{K}_u$ as the solution to $F(t_u Y, \bar{K}_u) = r$. Under assumption 19.1, $F(0,K) = 0$: it then follows that the optimal tax is a discontinuous function of civic capital $K$: optimal tax $t_u^* = 0$ for $K \leq \bar{K}_u$ and then is strictly positive and increasing in $K$ for $K > \overline{K}_u$. ■

As the optimal tax rate is a discontinuous and weakly increasing function of civic capital $K$, civic capital must reach a specific threshold for public investment in impersonal exchange to be socially worthwhile.

To bring out the different aspects of the utilitarian optimization problem, we present example 19.1 with an explicit functional form.

**Example 19.1** *Optimal tax rates*

Suppose that $F(T,K)=\phi T^{\alpha}K^{\alpha}$ with $0<\alpha<1$. In this case,

$$\frac{\partial F}{\partial T}(0,K)=\infty, \tag{19.14}$$

while

$$\frac{\partial F}{\partial T}(Y,K)=\phi\alpha\frac{K^{\alpha}}{Y^{1-\alpha}}. \tag{19.15}$$

Therefore

$$\frac{\partial F}{\partial T}(Y,K)<\frac{1}{n} \tag{19.16}$$

if $Y$ is large enough. This means that the conditions of proposition 19.1 are satisfied and $t_u$ solves

$$\phi\alpha t_u^{\alpha-1}Y^{\alpha-1}K^{\alpha}=\frac{n-1}{n^2}\frac{1}{f}, \tag{19.17}$$

leading to

$$t_u=\left(\frac{n^2}{n-1}\alpha\phi f\right)^{\frac{1}{1-\alpha}}Y^{-1}K^{\frac{\alpha}{1-\alpha}}. \tag{19.18}$$

We see that $t_u$ is increasing in civic capital $K$, and this function is concave if $\alpha\leq\frac{1}{2}$ and convex if $\alpha\geq\frac{1}{2}$. Then,

$$F(t_uY,K)=\left(\frac{n^2}{n-1}\alpha f\right)^{\frac{\alpha}{1-\alpha}}\phi^{\frac{1}{1-\alpha}}K^{\frac{\alpha}{1-\alpha}}. \tag{19.19}$$

This means that $t_u^*=0$ if $K<\overline{K}_u$ and $t_u^*=t_u$ if $K>\overline{K}_u$, where the threshold $\bar{K}_u$ is given by

$$\overline{K}_u=\frac{n-1}{n^2}\frac{1}{\alpha f}\phi^{\ \frac{1}{\alpha}}r^{\frac{\alpha}{1-\alpha}}. \tag{19.20}$$

■

We note that corollary 19.1 relies on the complements property. Under substitutes, $t_u$ is weakly decreasing in $K$ because $\frac{\partial^2 F}{\partial T\partial K}<0$. But the optimal tax rate $t_u^*=t_u$ if and only if $F(t_uY,K)>r$. There is a positive direct effect of increasing $K$, but there is also an indirect negative effect via $t_u^*$. The two effects go in opposite directions, so the effects of $K$ on optimal tax rate $t_u^*$ may be nonmonotonic ($t_u^*$ may initially decline in $K$, then be equal to zero for a range of $K$ values, and then become positive and decline again in $K$).

### 19.4.2 Democratic State

We next study optimal taxes in a democratic society. Building on the theory of the median voter, we say that a profile of tax $t$ and exchange choice $(x_1, \ldots, x_n)$ is majority stable if (1) given $t$, $x_i$ is optimal for every $i$; and (2) given $(x_1, \ldots, x_n)$, $t$ equals the median of the distribution of individual-specific tax rates.

When $\forall i, x_i = 0$, a positive tax rate brings no benefit, and all agents prefer zero tax. Conversely, if $t = 0$, $x_i = 0$ is optimal when $F(0, K) < r$. By contrast, when $x_i = 1$ for all $i \in N$, the preferred tax rate of agent $i$, $t_i$, solves

$$\max_{0 \le t \le 1} (1-t)y_i + F(tY, K)\frac{n-s_i}{n-1} + \frac{s_i - 1}{n-1}. \tag{19.21}$$

Since $1 \le s_i \le n-1$, an interior solution is guaranteed if

$$\frac{\partial F}{\partial T}(0, K) > \frac{n-1}{n-s_i}\frac{y_i}{Y} \tag{19.22}$$

and

$$\frac{\partial F}{\partial T}(Y, K) < \frac{n-1}{n-s_i}\frac{y_i}{Y}. \tag{19.23}$$

The interior tax rate is given as a solution to

$$\frac{\partial F}{\partial T}(t_i Y, K) = \frac{n-1}{n-s_i}\frac{y_i}{Y}. \tag{19.24}$$

Since $F$ is concave in $T$, preferred tax rates in the population increase with $\frac{n-s_i}{y_i}$. Therefore, the median of the distribution of preferred individual tax rates is the tax rate of the individual with a median value of $\frac{n-s_i}{y_i}$. This observation yields the following result on optimal taxes in a democratic society.

**Proposition 19.2** *Let $d$ be an individual with the median value of $\frac{n-s_i}{y_i}$. Suppose that $F$ satisfies assumption 19.1 and $\frac{\partial F}{\partial T}(0, K) > \frac{n-1}{n-s_d}\frac{y_d}{Y}$ and $\frac{\partial F}{\partial T}(Y, K) < \frac{n-1}{n-s_d}\frac{y_d}{Y}$. The following equation has a solution $t_d \in [0, 1]$*

$$\frac{\partial F}{\partial T}(t_d Y, K) = \frac{n-1}{n-s_d}\frac{y_d}{Y}. \tag{19.25}$$

*An outcome $(t_d^*, x^*)$ is either (1) $t_d^* = 0$ and $\forall i, x_i = 0$ if $F(0, K) \le r$; or (2) $t_d^* = t_d$ and $\forall i, x_i = 1$ if $F(t_d Y, K) \ge r$. When civic capital and governments are complements, there is a threshold value of civic capital $\overline{K}_d$ such that $t_d^* = 0$ if $K < \overline{K}_d$ and $t_d^* = t_d$ if $K > \overline{K}_d$, and $t_d^* = t_d > 0$ is increasing in $K$ if $K > \overline{K}_d$.*

If $F(t_d Y, K) > r$, then there is a majority-stable profile $(t, x)$, in which the optimal tax rate $t_d^* > 0$, and everyone engages in impersonal exchange, $x_i = 1$ for all $i \in N$. However, the profile of zero tax and no impersonal exchange is always stable so long as markets cannot function without formal institutions (i.e., if $F(0, K) = 0$).

### 19.4.3 Utilitarian versus Democratic Outcomes

A preliminary observation is that with democratic governance, there is a potential coordination problem: an active state and impersonal market bring higher welfare, but society can be stuck in the equilibrium with no tax and no market. Moving beyond the coordination problem, we note that even the active government outcome will generally be different from the utilitarian optimum.

To see why, let us examine the optimal tax rates and the democratic tax rates in greater detail. Define $\bar{y} = Y/n$ as the average income and $\bar{s} = \sum_i s_i/n$ as the average size of the group across individuals. Note that these are population averages and $\bar{s}$ usually differs from the average size when we average across groups, $\sum_j s_j/m$. Equipped with this notation, we can state the following implication of proposition 19.2.

**Corollary 19.2** *The tax rate chosen by a democratic government is weakly lower than the socially optimal tax rate if* $\frac{n-s_d}{y_d} \leq \frac{n-\bar{s}}{\bar{y}}$. *It is weakly higher than the socially optimal tax rate if* $\frac{n-s_d}{y_d} \geq \frac{n-\bar{s}}{\bar{y}}$.

*Proof.* Since $\frac{\partial F}{\partial T}(T, K)$ is weakly decreasing in $T$, comparing equations (19.4) and (19.25) shows that $t_d < t_u$ if and only if

$$\frac{n-1}{n^2}\frac{1}{f} < \frac{n-1}{n-s_d}\frac{y_d}{Y}. \tag{19.26}$$

We can simplify this condition and rewrite it as $\frac{n-s_d}{y_d} < \frac{nf}{\bar{y}}$. If $F(t_u Y, K) > r$, then $t_u^* = t_u > t_d^*$ because $t_d^* = t_d$ or 0. If $F(t_u Y, K) < r$, then $F(t_d Y, K) < r$ and $t_u^* = t_d^* = 0$. Similar arguments can be made for the case where the democratic society has a higher tax rate. ■

There is therefore tension between the utilitarian optimum and the median voter's preferred tax rate. This is because the marginal benefits from impersonal markets depend on $n - s_i$, the size of the group of outsiders, while marginal costs depend on income $y_i$ through taxation. In a democracy, the tax rate is controlled by the median ratio $\frac{n-s_d}{y_d}$. By contrast, a utilitarian planner considers aggregate benefits and aggregate costs, and state size is then controlled by the ratio of averages, $\frac{n-\bar{s}}{\bar{y}}$. Corollary 19.2 draws attention to these two ratios.

To further understand the impact of the kinship groups, let us assume that everyone has the same income. In that case, from equations (19.4) and (19.25), it follows that the tax rate is lower in a democracy where median group size is greater than average group size (i.e., $s_d \geq \bar{s}$). Applying the formula of fractionalization, this happens equivalently when

$$f \geq 1 - \frac{s_d}{n}. \tag{19.27}$$

Therefore, holding the median group size fixed, *the tax rate is likely to be lower, and hence the state size smaller, in a democracy when fractionalization is higher*.

Let us elaborate further on its implications for the relation between the democratic outcomes and the utilitarian optimum. We note that this inequality holds, for instance, in the presence of one large group containing a majority of people. In that case, the median voter belongs to this large group, and their expected benefits from impersonal markets are relatively small, leading to a small state in a democracy and potentially large welfare losses (compared to the utilitarian outcome).

Next, consider the converse problem: when the state is too large relative to the social optimum. Start from a situation with $m$ groups of equal size $s$. Here, $\bar{s}=s_d=s$ and democratic outcomes are efficient. Consider a small change in the group structure, with small gains in size for some groups and correspondingly small losses in size for other groups. The median group size remains unchanged, but the fractionalization is lower: this means that a positive tax rate in a democratic society is too high compared to the first-best rate.

The fact that individual preferred policies depend on group sizes can give rise to interesting regime shifts. To illustrate this point, consider a society composed of one large group of size $s$ and many small groups of size 2. The median voter is in one of the small groups if $s<\frac{n}{2}$ and in the large group if $s>\frac{n}{2}$. The average group size $\bar{s}$ lies strictly between 2 and $s$. Therefore, a small change in $s$ from slightly above $n/2$ to slightly below $n/2$ leads to a drastic expansion in the size of the state from inefficiently small to inefficiently high.

We close this section by drawing out an implication of the discontinuous shifts in optimal tax rates at the thresholds $\bar{K}_u$ and $\bar{K}_d$.

**Corollary 19.3** *Suppose that the conditions for proposition 19.1 and 19.2 hold and civic capital and governments are complements. The threshold value for civic capital under democratic regime is higher than under the social optimum,* $\overline{K}_d \geq \overline{K}_u$, *when* $\frac{n-s_d}{y_d} \leq \frac{n-\bar{s}}{\bar{y}}$; *the opposite is true otherwise:* $\overline{K}_d \leq \overline{K}_u$ *when* $\frac{n-s_d}{y_d} \leq \frac{n-\bar{s}}{\bar{y}}$.

*Proof.* From the arguments in corollary 19.2, we know that the utilitarian optimum tax rate is weakly lower than the democratic tax rate if

$$\frac{n-s_d}{y_d} \leq \frac{n-\bar{s}}{\bar{y}}. \tag{19.28}$$

Recall that $\bar{K}_u$ and $\bar{K}_d$ are defined by the following equations:

$$F(t_u Y, \bar{K}_u)=r \tag{19.29}$$

$$F(t_d Y, \bar{K}_d)=r. \tag{19.30}$$

As $t_d \leq t_u$, it then follows that $\bar{K}_d > \bar{K}_u$.

A similar argument may be used to prove the second part of the corollary that covers the case $n-s_d d/y_d \leq n-s/\hat{y}$. ■

To appreciate how fractionalization and civic capital shape tax rates and the size of the state, we work through example 19.2, with specific functional forms.

**Example 19.2** *State and civic culture as complements*

Suppose that $F(T,K)=fT^{\alpha}K^{\alpha}$. It may be verified that this function satisfies assumption 19.1 and state and civic culture are complements. Moreover, $\frac{\partial F}{\partial T}$ is strictly monotonic in $T$.

As $F(0,K)=0$, it follows that there exists a majority-stable outcome with zero tax and zero impersonal exchange. Turning to stable outcomes with positive tax rates, proposition 19.2 tells us that the median voter tax rate is as follows:

$$t_m=\left[\frac{\alpha fY^{\alpha}K^{\alpha}}{n-1}\frac{n-s_m}{y_m}\right]^{\frac{1}{1-\alpha}}. \tag{19.31}$$

Observe that $t_m$ is increasing in $K$ and decreasing in $s_m$ and $y_m$. Optimal taxes are increasing with the quality of civic culture because the marginal returns to bigger government are higher with better civic culture. The optimal taxation is also falling with the size of this individual's group: this is because the larger the group size, the smaller the size of the potential gains from trading with outsiders (as reflected in the term $(n-s_m)$).

An active state and impersonal exchange appear if and only if

$$\alpha^{\frac{1}{1-\alpha}}f^{\frac{2-\alpha}{1-\alpha}}(YK)^{\frac{\alpha(2-\alpha)}{1-\alpha}}\left(\frac{n-s_m}{(n-1)y_m}\right)^{\frac{\alpha}{1-\alpha}}>r. \tag{19.32}$$

Thus there is a threshold level of civic culture $K^*$ such that the tax rate is positive, and the state is active if and only if $K>K^*$.

Let us compute the aggregate welfare that obtains under the different parametric conditions. When $K<K^*$ and $t^*=0$, $x_i=0$, individual utility is

$$u_i=y_i+r\frac{n-s_i}{n-1}+\frac{s_i-1}{n-1}. \tag{19.33}$$

Aggregate utility is

$$\begin{aligned}\sum_i u_i&=Y+\frac{r}{n-1}\sum_i s_i(n-s_i)+\frac{1}{n-1}\sum_i s_i(s_i-1)\\&=Y+\frac{1}{n-1}\left(r\sum_i s_i(n-s_i)+\sum_i s_i^2-n\right).\end{aligned} \tag{19.34}$$

Since $F(0,K)=0$, everyone opts for kin-based group exchange, and therefore its share in the total exchange equals 1.

When $K>K^*$ in a stable outcome with positive tax rates $x_i=1$ for all $i\in N$, $t=t^*>0$. This in turn means that individual utility is

$$u_i=(1-t^*)y_i+F\frac{n-s_i}{n-1}+\frac{s_i-1}{n-1}. \tag{19.35}$$

Aggregate utility is

$$\sum_i u_i = (1-t^*)Y + \frac{F}{n-1}\sum_i s_i(n-s_i) + \frac{1}{n-1}\sum_i s_i(s_i-1)$$

$$= (1-t^*)Y + \frac{1}{n-1}\left(F\sum_i s_i(n-s_i) + \sum_i s_i^2 - n\right). \tag{19.36}$$

The share of kin-based exchange is

$$\frac{\sum_i s_i(s_i-1)}{\sum_i s_i(n-s_i) + \sum_i s_i(s_i-1)},$$

where

$$\sum_i s_i(n-s_i) + \sum_i s_i(s_i-1) = \sum_i s_i(n-1) = n(n-1). \tag{19.37}$$

This yields

$$\frac{\sum_i s_i(s_i-1)}{n(n-1)} = \frac{\sum_i s_i^2 - n}{n^2-n},$$

which is increasing in $\sum_i s_i^2$ (and hence it is falling in the fractionalization index). ■

Example 19.2 assumed that state capacity and civic capital are complements. A question at the end of the chapter explores the case of substitutes.

Our discussion here reveals that the relative share of kin-based and impersonal exchange, the size of the state, and economic performance are shaped by group composition and civic culture. We now take a closer look at the determinants of civic capital.

## 19.5 Sources of Civic Capital

In this section we will discuss the sources of civic capital. Building on the ideas of Tocqueville and Putnam discussed in section 19.3 , we will take the view that civic capital arises out of associational ties between individuals who may belong to distinct groups.

### 19.5.1 Horizontal Associations

Now we return to our model and recall that in stage 1, individuals choose an action $z_i \in \{0, 1\}$, where $z_i = 0$ refers to low activity and $z_i = 1$ refers to high activity. Social engagement takes time and effort, and this cost is given by $c > 0$. Let $z = (z_1, \ldots, z_n)$ denote the profile of social engagement. The civic capital in stage 2 reflects the choices in stage 1. In particular, we will suppose that $K = \sum_{i\in N} z_i$.

An individual's returns to social engagement will depend on the level of engagement of others in their neighborhood: if everyone else is narrowly focused on the short-term interests of their nuclear family, then one individual expects to earn very little from increasing their own engagement. By contrast, if an individual is surrounded by others who are highly engaged, then increasing their social commitment is more likely to be rewarding. The returns to horizontal social engagement across groups rest on the bridging ties between groups (i.e., ties between individuals that belong to different groups). Recall that $g_o$ is the network of ties outside one's own group. We will suppose that $N_i(g_o)$ is the neighborhood of individual $i$ in network $g_o$. Given the profile of actions $z$, let

$$\zeta_i = \sum_{j \in N_i(g_o)} z_i \tag{19.38}$$

be the level of engagement in the neighborhood of individual $i$.

Our analysis in section 19.4 indicates that $K$ is central to understanding the size of the government and the share of impersonal exchange. However, as a first step, to keep matters simple, we will assume that in their social engagement problem, individuals do not take into account the effects of $z_i$ choices on $K$. Recall that we are primarily concerned with the case where $n$ is large, an individual's choices on civic engagement are unlikely to have a large impact on the economywide scale of $K$, so our assumption is a reasonable approximation. With this assumption in place, given network $g_o$ and the profile of actions $z$ the utility of individual $i$ is

$$H(z_i, \zeta_i) - cz_i. \tag{19.39}$$

We will say that individual efforts and neighbors' efforts are complements if they exhibit increasing differences that is, for $\zeta_i' > \zeta_i$ and $z_i' > z_i$:

$$H(\zeta_i', z_i') - H(\zeta_i', z_i) \geq H(\zeta_i, z_i') - H(\zeta_i, z_i). \tag{19.40}$$

They are strict complements if this inequality is strict. We make the following assumptions on the function $H(.,.)$.

**Assumption 19.2** *$H(0,0) = 0$, $H(.,.)$ is weakly increasing in both arguments and exhibits complementarity.*

A simple example of such a function is $H(z_i, \zeta_i) = \zeta_i z_i$; it exhibits strict complementarity between own and neighbors' engagement.

We will assume that there is a fixed positive cost of social engagement given by $c > 0$. Observe that if everyone else chooses action $z_i = 0$, then under our assumptions on $H(.,.)$, it is a best response to choose 0 as well. Thus, regardless of the social structure, inactivity $z = (0, \ldots, 0)$ is a Nash equilibrium of the game of social engagement. Let us consider an equilibrium with positive engagement. For concreteness, let us suppose that $H(\zeta_i, z_i) = \zeta_i z_i$ In this case, the best that an individual can hope to earn from choosing $z_i = 1$ is that all their neighbors also choose 1. In other words, their payoff is bounded by the size of the neighborhood. Under the assumption that there is a fixed positive cost of social engagement

$c > 0$, it follows that an individual will choose $z_i = 1$ only if the number of neighbors is greater than or equal to $c$. The same reasoning applies to the neighbors of the individual: a neighbor will only choose action $z_i = 1$ if they have at least $c$ neighbors, and so forth.

This line of reasoning corresponds to the games we considered in chapter 4, on network structure and human behavior. We now apply the methods developed in that chapter to the problem at hand. Suppose, to fix ideas, that $c = 3.1$. An individual will choose action 1 only if the returns to choosing 1 cover the cost of 3.1. This means that at least 4 neighbors must also choose action 1. However, these neighbors will choose action 1 only if each of them has at least 3 other neighbors choosing 1 (in addition to he neighbor in question). Thus for an individual to choose 1, they must be part of a set of nodes in a network, each of which has at least 4 links with others who have 4 links, and so on. Recall that this line of reasoning led to the *3-core* of a network. For easy reference, we reproduce the definition of a q-core of a network.

**Definition 19.1** *The q-core of a network $g_o$, denoted by $g_o^q$, is the largest subgraph of $g_o$ such that all individuals in $g_o^q$ have strictly more than $q$ links to other individuals in $g_o^q$.*

Recall from our discussion in chapters 4 and 17, the procedure for obtaining the q-core of a network is as follows: Start with network $g$. In step 1, delete all the nodes (and their links) in $g$ for which degree $k \leq q$. Label the residual graph $g_1$. In step 2, delete all the nodes (and their links) in $g_1$ for which $k \leq q$. Iterate until no node with $k \leq q$ remains (i.e., when $g_t = g_{t+1}$). The residual graph in this last step is the q-core.

The equilibrium corresponding to the q-core defines the minimal and the maximal levels of social engagement in a network. The social structure thus sets an upper bound on the level of civic activity in a society. The actual outcome will depend on the beliefs that members of the community have. This suggests that in societies with large q-cores, beliefs about behavior can make a very large difference in outcomes.

A final remark concerns the utility of individuals: the payoff to an individual who chooses 0 is zero, while the payoffs of an active agent are increasing based on the number of neighbors choosing action 1. So given a positive cost $c$, it follows that payoffs are larger for nodes in the q-core compared to those outside it. Thus, for any network, total payoffs are maximized in the equilibrium corresponding to the q-core. These observations are summarized in the following result.

**Proposition 19.3** *Fix a group size profile $s = (s_1, \ldots, s_m)$ a network, $g_o$, a function $H(.,)$ satisfying assumption 19.2, and a cost $c > 0$. There exists a zero activity equilibrium and a maximal activity equilibrium that corresponds to the q-core of the network. A society with a larger q-core, therefore, has the potential to support a higher level of social engagement. Aggregate payoffs are increasing in the number of active players. Therefore, networks with larger q-cores have the potential for greater aggregate utility.*

In our model, there are two aspects of social structure: the groups and the ties across groups. We work through a simple example to appreciate the role of the social structure in shaping economic performance.

Consider a society with $n = 12$ individuals, and let $H(\zeta_i, z_i) = \zeta_i z_i$, and set ex-ante individual income $y = 1$. We consider a society with large kin-based groups and a society with small nuclear families. The former is represented as consisting of 3 groups, each of size 4, while the latter consists of 12, groups, each of size 1. To study the role of ties across groups, we consider two configurations: in one, the ties are concentrated within a few individuals, while in the other, the ties are spread out across individuals. The four configurations of group size and ties across groups are presented in figure 19.10.

Figures 19.10(a) and 19.10(b) present societies with large kin groups, while figures 19.10(c) and 19.10(d) present societies with small kin groups. Figures 19.10(a) and 19.10(c) represent societies in which the ties across kin groups are concentrated among a few individuals (i.e., they have a large 3-core) while figures 19.10(b) and 19.10(d) represent societies in which they are spread across individuals (as a consequence, they have an empty 3-core).

Suppose that the cost of social engagement is $c = 3.1$. From equation (19.3), we know that the maximal equilibrium corresponds to the 3-core of the social network. This tells us that in the societies in figures 19.10(a) and 19.10(c), individuals can support an active civic community, while in the societies in figures 19.10(b) and 19.10(d), there will be no civic engagement. To be precise, the number of active members in the maximal equilibrium is 6 in the former and 0 in the latter.

We now build on these observations to draw out the implications of civic capital for the size of the state and the magnitude of impersonal exchange. Suppose that $F(T, K) = (TK)^\alpha$, $\alpha < 1$. We note that in this case, civic capital and the size of the state are complements. As all individuals are in equal-size groups and have equal incomes, they have the same incentives. The preferred tax rate for an individual therefore corresponds to the utilitarian optimum. From proposition 19.1, it follows that in figures 19.10(b) and 19.10(d), the optimal tax rate will be zero. In the societies in figures 19.10(a) and 19.10(c), a positive tax is optimal if $F(t_U Y, K) > r$. Let us assume that $r$ is sufficiently small that this condition is satisfied in both societies. Under this assumption, differences in tax rates are mirrored in differences in impersonal exchange: in figures 19.10(a) and 19.10(c), therefore, everyone is engaged in impersonal exchange, while in figures 19.10(b) and 19.10(d), everyone is engaged in kin group exchange. This in turn has implications for utility and welfare. In figure 19.10(a), the utility for socially active and inactive individuals are, respectively,

$$(1 - t^*) + F(12t^*, 6)\frac{8}{11} + \frac{3}{11} + 0.9 \quad \text{and} \quad (1 - t^*) + F(12t^*, 6)\frac{8}{11} + \frac{3}{11}. \tag{19.41}$$

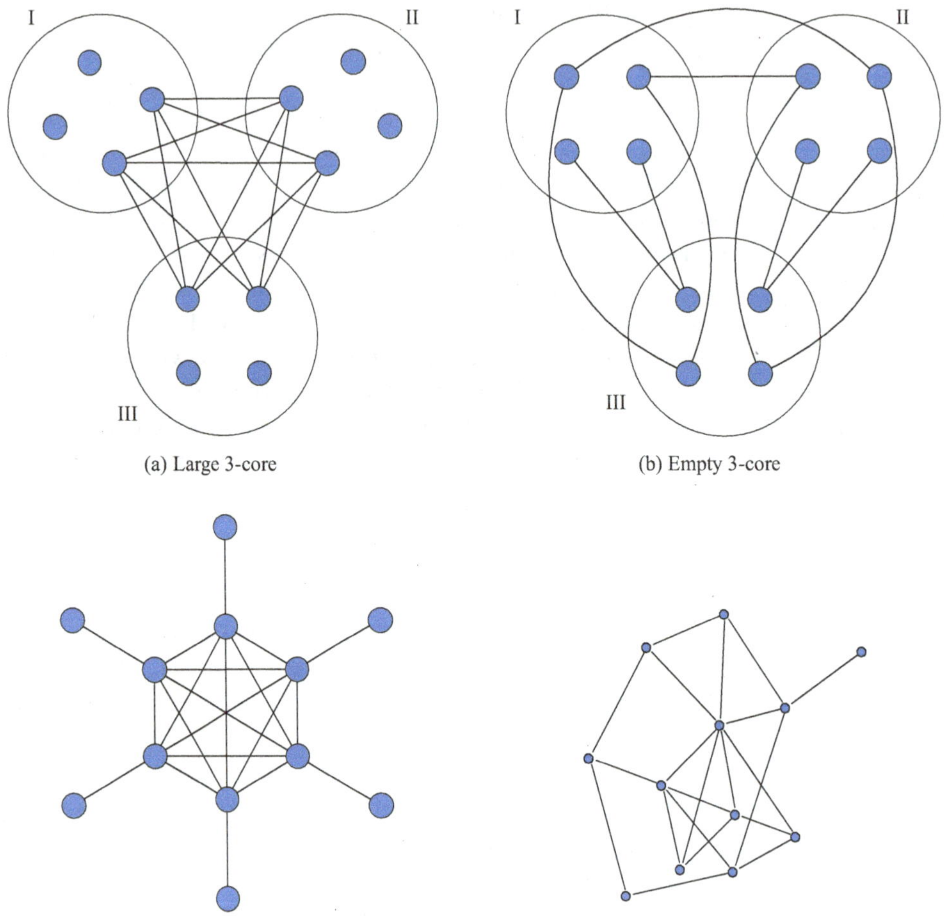


(a) Large 3-core (b) Empty 3-core

(c) Large 3-core (d) Empty 3-core

**Figure 19.10**
Examples of societies: (a) and (b) are for large groups, and (c) and (d) are for small groups.

Thus aggregate utility in figure 19.10(a) is

$$W_a^* = 12(1-t^*) + \frac{96}{11}F(12t^*, 6) + 12\frac{3}{11} + 5.4. \tag{19.42}$$

In figure 19.10(b), as there is no taxation (and therefore the state is inactive), all exchange takes place within kin-based groups. Individual utility is

$$1 + \frac{3}{11} + \frac{8}{11}r \tag{19.43}$$

**Table 19.2**
Social structure and outcomes

| Fraction \ Q-core | Large | Small |
|---|---|---|
| Small | $K^*=6, t^*>0, E^*=0.7$, high $W_a^*$ | $K^*=0, t^*=0, E^*=0$, modest $W_b^*$ |
| Large | $K^*=6, t^*>0, E^*=1$, high $W_c^*$ | $K^*=0, t^*=0, E^*=0$, low $W_d^*$ |

and aggregate utility is given by

$$W_b^* = 12[1+\frac{3}{11}+\frac{8}{11}r]. \tag{19.44}$$

It follows that the zero tax rate outcome is feasible in figure 19.10(a) and will yield the same utility but the positive tax rate is preferred. So it must yield a higher utility.
In figure 19.10(c), individual utilities are given by

$$(1-t^*)+F(12t^*,6)+1.9 \quad \text{and} \quad (1-t^*)+F(12t^*,6) \tag{19.45}$$

for the active and inactive members of the society, respectively. Thus aggregate utility in figure 19.10(c)

$$W_c^* = 12(1-t^*)+12F(12t^*,6)+6(1.9). \tag{19.46}$$

Finally, in figure 19.10(d), as there is zero taxation (and an inactive state), there is also no impersonal exchange. As group sizes equal 1, individual utility is also equal to $1+r$. Aggregate utility in figure 19.10(d) is

$$W_d^* = 12+12r. \tag{19.47}$$

The zero tax outcome is feasible in figure 19.10(c) and yields the same utility as in figure 19.10(d), but by definition, the positive tax outcome is utility maximizing. Hence figure 19.10(c) does significantly better than figure 19.10(d).
Define $E^*$ as the share of impersonal/market exchange in equilibrium. Our computations are summarized in table 19.2.

Propositions 19.1–19.3 develop relations between aspects of social structure on the one hand and the nature of formal versus informal exchange and the size of the state on the other hand. While the theory highlights the role of the q-core, we must be careful not to take this measure too literally. The q-core arises due to a specific formulation of the coordination game in civic participation; if we specify the game differently, a different but related network measure may be identified. The important point is that for civic capital to arise, we need ties that create bridges across groups in a society.

The presumption in the model that we have discussed is that ties are horizontal and range across social, political, economic, and cultural spheres (as in Putnam, Leonardi, and Nanetti (1993)'s study of North and South Italy and Varshney (2001)'s study of Indian riots). The formulation of complementarity between these ties and the state reflects a dominant strand of thought that can be traced to Tocqueville (2004).

We next turn to circumstances with limited horizontal associations and weak-bridging civic capital. There are two broad circumstances to consider that correspond to weak and strong kinship groups, respectively. When a society has both weak kinship groups and limited civic capital, there is a greater need for formal institutions but due to a complementarity between civic capital and state capacity, a democratic regime may be unable to provide adequate state capacity. These circumstances can lead to a failed state, but under some historical circumstances, such as a communist or a military takeover, it can also lead to a strong authoritarian state. We may arrive at a situation where civic capital and state capacity are substitutes.

A second situation corresponds to strong kinship groups with weak-bridging civic capital. Here, the need for the state is less pressing, as much economic exchange occurs within the group; however, due to historical circumstances such as foreign occupation or war, there may be need for public goods more broadly construed. This may give rise to mass social and political movements that can have profound implications for the nature of the state. For example, members of large and distinct kinship groups who take part in a large-scale independence movement may be led to support a large state once the foreign occupying power is expelled. These possibilities will surface next, when we map the theory onto the specific circumstances of different countries.

### 19.5.2 Mapping Theory onto the Country Case Studies

In our discussion, it will be helpful to keep in mind the $2 \times 2$ matrix table 19.2, that covers the cases of high/low fractionalization and small/large bridging capital. We will use this table as a lens through which to view the historical experience of different countries. This discussion will lead us to classify the following countries Brazil, China, Congo, Egypt, India, WEIRD countries, and South Korea in a table that is represented as table 19.3.

Let us start with the *top-left* cell in table 19.2–19.3, which depicts a society where fractionalization is low and bridging capital is high. Let us discuss the experience of India, China, and South Korea in this context.

In the case of India, the mass independent movement against British rule led by the Congress Party (and the associated social reform movements) helped build ties across the

**Table 19.3**
Countries' experience: Summary

| Bridging Capital / Fraction | Large | Small |
|---|---|---|
| Small | India, China | Egypt, Congo |
| Large | Weird Societies | Brazil, Russia |

different castes and region-based groups that dominate Indian society (for a discussion of this process, see Varshney [2001]). These ties allowed the Indian Constituent Assembly to draft a progressive constitution for independent India that created a federal country with a strong central government. Seen through the lens of our model, at this moment in time, India was a society with large groups (small fractionalization) but high bridging-capital due to the broad-based freedom movement. In the early 1950s, this bridging civic capital helped the country to create a large developmental state. In the early twenty-first century, the state continues to be heavily involved in the economy (as we noted, some of the largest firms are state controlled). The rapid economic growth over the past twenty-five years has also given rise to a large, diverse, and dynamic private sector, but private-sector firms typically form part of family-based conglomerates reflecting the larger presence of kin-based groups in Indian society. Democratic politics have matured, but voting often takes place along caste lines. Today, in the early twenty-first century, India is a country with strong kinship groups and a state that is deeply involved in its economy. The centrality of castes and region-based groups has led some observers to argue that bridging civic capital ties have eroded. Our model would predict that this erosion of bridging civic capital would lower state capacity. For a notable recent articulation of this view, see Acemoglu and Robinson (2019).

The configuration in the top-left cell of table 19.2 is also helpful to understand the experience of China. The long history of a centralized state and foreign occupation of parts of China by European powers in the nineteenth century and by Japan in the twentieth century is an important part of the historical background. The communist takeover of China in 1949 was accompanied by a mass political movement that mobilized millions of people scattered across the country who were traditionally affiliated with lineages and clans. We may interpret this mass mobilization as a form of extensive bridging ties, something that made possible the creation of the Chinese state. Indeed, throughout the 1950s and 1960s, to assert itself, the state attempted to weaken traditional lineages and clans (e.g., cousin marriage was made illegal). However, market reforms implemented after 1979 have led to a revival of traditional lineages/clans and regional networks. These networks have been an important part of the extraordinarily successful production clusters that have fueled Chinese economic growth. Moreover, close ties between the various layers of the state and lineages are an important feature of contemporary China. In the early twenty-first century, China is a country with kinship groups that are reviving and a strong state. We note that we don't have a model of decision making in a communist state so strictly speaking the experience of China lies outside our purview; the process in China can be seen as an instance of an 'authoritarian transition' in the words of Huntington (1968). For evidence on these social networks and their interactions with the state; see Allen, Qian, and Qian (2005); Dai, Mookherjee, Munshi, and Zhang (2020); and (Bai, Hsieh, and Song 2020a, 2020b).

In South Korea, kinship ties based on extended family relations are an important feature of the society, but the Japanese occupation in the early part of the twentieth century and the Korean War in the 1950s led to a strong nationalist ethos. This ethos brought together different lineage groups and that helped make possible a strong developmental state led by a sequence of generals (i.e., Park Chung-hee, Chun Doo-hwan, and Roh Tae-woo) who undertook large-scale land reforms and supported the rise of kinship-based conglomerates (this experience may be regarded as another instance of 'authoritarian transition', Huntingdon [1968]). Over time, the economy has prospered, and today, South Korea is one of the most technologically sophisticated countries in the world.

We next take up the *bottom-left* cell in table 19.2, with high fractionalization and high bridging capital. The theory predicts that these are the ideal circumstances for high taxes that support a large and effective state. These conditions describe WEIRD societies such as the US, Australia, New Zealand, and most of North Western Europe. Much has been written about these countries: the limited scope of kinship groups, the individualist psychology of their people, and the strength of out-group ties. These societies exhibit sustained economic performance, as summarized in figure 19.6.

Next, we take up the *bottom-right* cell in table 19.2, with high fractionalization and weak bridging capital. The theory predicts that a democratic state may fail to deliver on the demands made on it. However, kinship groups are small, so valuable exchange would often be with outsiders, and it is subject to high transaction costs. This failure of a democratic state to deliver creates circumstances that are ripe for alternative forms of governance. We use this cell to understand the experiences of Russia and Brazil.

In Russia (and other former communist countries in Eastern Europe), kin-based groups and bridging capital are both weak. This is partly due to its precommunist history, but over its long period of rule, from 1917 to 1990, the Communist Party actively sought to eliminate political opposition and restrict associational life (Putnam, Leonardi, and Nanetti (1993) and Fukuyama [1995]). We next draw attention to a subtle but very important relation between political and more general civic associations.

> Among all the peoples where political associations are prohibited, civil association is rare. It is hardly probable that this is an accident; and one ought rather to conclude that a natural and perhaps necessary relation exists between these two types of association. A political association draws a multitude of individuals outside themselves at the same time; however separated they are by age, mind, fortune, it brings them together and puts them in contact. They meet each other once and learn to find each other always.
>
> I do not say that there cannot be civil associations in a country where political association in prohibited; for men can never live in a society without engaging in some common undertaking. But I maintain that in a country like this, civil associations will always be very few in number, weakly conceived, unskillfully conducted, and that they will never embrace vast designs or will fail when they want to execute them
> (Tocqueville [2004], pp. 496–8).

In a society with a long history of political repression and correspondingly weak civic capital, a democratic regime will support a small state capacity. Our theory suggests that this state capacity may be much smaller than the utilitarian optimum. This difficulty was visible in the years immediately after the collapse of communism; and may help us understand why democratic politics has struggled to take root in post-communist Russia. Instead, the outcome has been de facto one-party rule. The following comment from Putnam, Leonardi and Nanetti (1993) has turned out to be prescient:

> Many of the formerly Communist societies had weak civic traditions before the advent of Communism, and totalitarian rule abused even that limited stock of social capital. Without norms of reciprocity and networks of civic engagement, the Hobbesian outcome of the Mezzogiorno—amoral familism, clientelism, lawlessness, ineffective government, and economic stagnation seems likelier than successful democratization and economic development. Palermo may represent the future of Moscow.
> Putnam, Leonardi, and Nanetti (1993, p. 183).

Turning to Brazil, at the start of the twentieth century, it was a very diverse society constituted of immigrants from different parts of Europe and Africa (and with a long history of slavery). Our discussion in section 19.2 suggests that Brazil has weak kinship groups and high fractionalization. At the same time, generalized trust is very low. These circumstances make it very difficult for society to sustain an accountable democratic state. Indeed, at the start of the twentieth century, there was a long period of very limited franchise, one-party rule, and military dictatorship. Since 1988, Brazil has had regular elections, but its economic record is uneven and its political situation remains uncertain.

Finally, we turn to the *top-right* cell in table 19.2, with high fractionalization and weak bridging capital. The theory suggests that democratic politics will struggle to support an effective state in such conditions. Depending on the specific circumstances of a country (such as conflicts with neighboring countries), this can lead to either continuing poor governance or the rise of dictatorship. Let us use the theory to understand the experiences of the Democratic Republic of Congo (hereafter Congo) and Egypt.

Consider Congo: we discuss the experience in the years after 1960 (the year that it won independence from Belgium). Independence led to a period of instability between 1960 and 1965, when Joseph-Desire Mobuto took power. Our discussion in section 19.2 drew attention to the high fractionalization and the long period of large-scale war in Congo. The Great War of Congo and the accompanying disruption of ordinary life suggest that the country has found it difficult to create an effective and accountable state. The circumstances of Congo are special in some respects—such as the very rich mineral wealth and the complicated overlaps in ethnic groups with neighboring countries—but the difficulties of creating an effective state are in line with our theory.

Turning next to Egypt, we note that it gained independence from Britain in 1922. Our discussion in section 19.2 reveals a society with high rates of cousin marriage and cousin marriage and strong kin-based groups. After a brief period of multiparty politics, from 1956 onward, Egypt has had a combination of military dictatorship and one-party rule. This has been accompanied by restrictions on political activity and limits to associations (the long-standing ban on the Muslim Brotherhood is one example). The history of Egypt through the twentieth and early twenty first century is one with a sequence of military dictatorships. These military dictatorships arose, in the first instance in the 1950s, when bridging ties were weak. But the dictatorships have discouraged political associations and have declared large civic organizations (like the Muslim Brotherhood) illegal. As they discourage political associations, they have also, following the observations of Tocqueville noted above, placed limits on the growth of civic associations.

Our theory suggests that a democratic society with low fractionalization and weak civic capital will struggle to support large state capacity. The failure of the 2011 democratic uprisings to lead to a sustainable democratic state may be seen in this perspective.

## 19.6 Reading Notes

The study of the role of culture in shaping economic change has distinguished antecedents; a prominent early study is Weber (2010). Kinship groups are an important component of culture. Indeed, Max Weber himself emphasized the importance of the role of families in his study of Chinese society (Weber [1951]). In chapter 18, on trust, we concluded by noting the tension between local (group-specific) trust and generalized trust. In that chapter, the focus was on culture and social relations. This chapter takes the discussion one step further by interpreting culture as consisting of a composite of beliefs and social structure, and by locating it within a broader conceptual framework that includes the market and the state. Here, the focus is on understanding how culture interacts with markets and the state in shaping economic performance.

We begin by providing an empirical background to the relationship between the various types of kin-based institutions and measures of trust and values (such as universalism). This is a subject that been studied in many disciplines, including anthropology, sociology, political science, and economics, as well as the theory of cultural evolution. The research draws on a wide range of intellectual traditions and theoretical and empirical methodologies. It is clearly impossible to do justice to this vast body of scholarship within a single chapter. The goal here is to provide leads into the different areas of work. For economics, see Enke (2019); Guiso, Sapienza, and Zingales (2006); Greif and Tabellini (2017); and Guiso, Sapienza, and Zingales (2016). For sociology, see Peng (2004). For political science, see Fukuyama (1995); Putnam, Leonardi, and Nanetti (1993); and Banfield (1958). Cultural evolution researchers and business scholars have explored this subject extensively; see Schulz, Bahrami-Rad, Beauchamp, and Henrich (2019) and Trompenaars and Hampden-Turner (1998). Henrich (2020) offers a comprehensive overview of the research on this subject.

In a sequence of interesting papers, Alberto Alesina and his collaborators explored the relation between the family and political and economic activity. Alesina and Giuliano (2010) construct a measure of the strength of family ties for over 70 countries. They construct this measure with the help of individual responses from the World Values Survey on the role of the family and the love and respect that children need to have for their parents. They find that when family ties are strong, there is more reliance on home production and less participation in market activities, especially for youngsters and women. Strong family ties imply a stricter division of labor, with the man working in the market and the woman working at home. In line with this practice, women's education is lower with strong family ties, and fertility levels are higher. Stronger family ties support higher levels of informal insurance, and this substitutes for insurance provided by the state. Family ties can better provide support if extended families live close to each other: this in turn leads to lower geographical mobility. Finally, and in line with the discussions in this chapter, individuals in families with strong ties trust their own family members more but nonfamily members less. In a follow-up, Alesina and Giuliano (2011) show that a larger role for the family lowers civic engagement and political participation.

We also have presented Robert Putnam's study of civic community and democracy in Italy. A large body of subsequent work has documented the robustness of the positive relation between the quality of civic community and local government and the persistence of civic traditions, using rich sets of data from different parts of Europe; for instance, see Henrich (2020) and Guiso, Sapienza, and Zingales, (2016).

We then moved beyond kinship and trust and take up the relation between kinship and economic performance. The empirical work is vast and spans many disciplines. As before, due to space considerations, the discussion in the chapter is very short and somewhat narrowly focused. in our presentation, we draw upon Allen, Qian, and Qian (2005); Dai, Mookherjee, Munshi, and Zhang (2020); Song, Storesletten, and Zilibotti (2011); Fleisher, Hud, McGuiree, and Zhang (2010); Nee and Opper (2012); Peng (2004); Greif and Tabellini (2017); and Fukuyama (1995) for work on China and other East Asian societies, upon Munshi ((2019); Beteille (1965, 1969); and Srinivas (1987) for work on caste in India; and upon Munshi (2014) for an overview of the role of communities in the development process.

Concerning the theory, our aim was to develop a framework in which economic performance occupies center stage and we can understand how culture, the state, and markets contribute to it. The model discussed here is taken from Bramoullé, Goyal, and Massimo (2022).

The modeling of the economic elements builds on the concepts of formal institutions, transaction costs, and asymmetric information. These themes lie at the heart of modern studies of economic history and of modern economic theory; for instance, see North and Thomas (1973), North (1990), and Williamson (1985). The roots of the idea that the state and market and kin-based groups may substitute for or complement each other in relation to economic activity may be traced to Polanyi (1944) and finds a more modern expression in Acemoglu and Robinson (2019) and Fukuyama (1995). That they may be substitutes is suggested by the empirical evidence from the recent development experience of a number of large countries such as China and India. Our formulation of these ideas draws on the economic theory of strategic substitutes and complements (Bulow, Geanakoplos, and Klemperer, [1985]) and on the more recent applications to formal and informal institutions; for instance, see Gagnon and Goyal (2017) and Kranton (1996). Finally, we draw upon Besley and Persson (2013) for our modeling of the politics of taxation and the role of the state, and upon Alesina, Devleeschauwer, Easterly et al. (2003) in our formulation of fractionalization.

## 19.7 Questions

Consider the model of state capacity discussed in section 19.4. Suppose that the function $f(T,K)=a(T+K)^{\alpha}$, where $\alpha \in (0,1)$.

1. Suppose that $F(T,K)=a(T+K)^{\alpha}$, where $a>0$.
   (a) Show that this function satisfies assumption 19.1.
   (b) Show that $\frac{\partial F}{\partial T}=a\alpha(T+K)^{\alpha-1}$ is monotonic in $T$.
   (c) Show that if there is a stable outcome with positive tax rates, then the median tax rate satisfies
   $$a\alpha(t_m Y+K)^{\alpha-1}=\frac{n-1}{Y}\frac{y_m}{n-s_m}. \tag{19.48}$$
   This in turn means that
   $$t_m=\left(\frac{\alpha a(n-s_m)}{y_m(n-1)}\right)^{\frac{1}{1-\alpha}} Y^{\frac{\alpha}{1-\alpha}}-\frac{K}{Y} \tag{19.49}$$
   if this value is positive.
   (d) Argue that there is a threshold $K^{**}$ such that if $K>K^{**}$, the median tax rate equals 0.
   (e) Show that the median voter's preferred tax rate, $t_m$, is decreasing in $K$ and decreasing in the size of their group, $s_m$, and their income, $y_m$.
   (f) Show that optimal taxes are decreasing in $K$ and in the size of the median individual's group size, $s_m$.
   (g) Impersonal exchange appears if $F(t_m Y,K)>r$. In other words,
   $$a\left(\frac{\alpha a Y(n-s_m)}{y_m(n-1)}\right)^{\frac{\alpha}{1-\alpha}}>r. \tag{19.50}$$
   Show that when $K>K^{**}$, $t^*=0$, $x_i=0$, individual utility is
   $$u_i=y_i+r\frac{n-s_i}{n-1}+\frac{s_i-1}{n-1}.$$
   In this case, everyone opts for kin-based group exchange, and therefore its share in total exchange equals 1.

(h) If $K < K^{**}$ and equation (19.50) is satisfied, then in a stable outcome with positive tax rates $x_i = 1$ for all $i \in N$, $t^* > 0$. Show that in this case, individual utility is

$$u_i = (1 - t^*)y_i + F\frac{n - s_i}{n - 1} + \frac{s_i - 1}{n - 1}. \tag{19.51}$$

Show that in this final case, the share of kin-based exchange is

$$\frac{\sum_i s_i^2 - n}{n^2 - n}. \tag{19.52}$$

2. Consider the model of democratic government described in section 19.4.2. This question explores the effects of group composition on democratic outcomes. Suppose that there is one large group, $S$, and several small groups of size $s$. Then the average group size lies strictly between $s$ and $S$. Discuss the conditions—on group sizes—under which the majority tax rate and the size of the state would be larger and smaller than the utilitarian optimum, respectively.
3. Consider the model of state capacity described in section 19.4.
   (a) Show that utilitarian tax rate is higher than the democratic tax rate if $s_d \geq \bar{s}$, where $s_d$ is the size of the median voter's group, and $\bar{s}$ is the average size of a group.
   (b) Construct an example for which the democratic tax rate is higher than the utilitarian optimum tax rate.
4. Corollary 19.2 develops conditions under which the threshold for the positive tax rate is higher under the democratic society than the utilitarian optimum. Discuss the ways in which an autocratic government can function and how it my be able to address the problems of underprovision of state services.
5. Difficulties in sustaining democratic governments and the persistence of authoritarian governments in many countries are due to the lack of appropriate civic capital, as embodied in horizontal associations between citizens. Discuss.
6. "Democratic politics fail to deliver on economic performance in societies with strong kinship groups." Discuss this statement with reference to the experience of South Korea, India, and China.

# References


Abreu, D., and M. Manea. 2012. Bargaining and efficiency in networks. *Journal of Economic Theory*, 147 (1): 43–70.

Acemoglu, D. 2009. *Introduction to Modern Economic Growth*. Princeton University Press.

Acemoglu, D., U. Akcigit, and W. Kerr. 2016a. Networks and the macroeconomy: An empirical exploration. In *National Bureau of Economic Research Macroeconomics Annual*, vol. 30, edited by M. Eichenbaum and J. Parker, 276–335.

Acemoglu, D., and P. Azar. 2020. Endogenous production networks. *Econometrica*, 88 (1): 33–82.

Acemoglu, D., V. Carvalho, A. Ozdaglar, and A. Tahbaz-Salehi. 2012. The network origins of aggregate fluctuations. *Econometrica*, 80 (5): 1977–2016.

Acemoglu, D., M. A. Dahleh, I. Lobel, and A. Ozdaglar. 2011. Bayesian learning in social networks. *Review of Economic Studies*, 78 (4): 1201–1236.

Acemoglu, D., T. A. Hassan, and A. Tahoun. 2018. The power of the street: Evidence from Egypt's Arab spring. *The Review of Financial Studies*, 31 (1): 1–42.

Acemoglu, D., A. Malekian, and A. Ozdaglar. 2016. Network security and contagion. *Journal of Economic Theory*, 166: 536–585.

Acemoglu, D., and A. Ozdaglar. 2007. Competition and efficiency in congested markets. *Mathematics of Operations Research*, 32 (1): 1–31.

Acemoglu, D., A. Ozdaglar, and J. Siderius. 2021. Misinformation: Strategic sharing, homophily, and endogenous echo chambers. Working paper MIT.

Acemoglu, D., A. Ozdaglar, and A. Tahbaz-Salehi. 2015a. Systemic risk and stability in financial networks. *American Economic Review*, 105 (2): 564–608.

Acemoglu, D., A. E. Ozdaglar, and A. Tahbaz-Salehi. 2015b. Systemic risk in endogenous financial networks. *Columbia Business School Research Paper*, (15–17).

Acemoglu, D., and J. A. Robinson. 2019. *The Narrow Corridor: States, Societies, and the Fate of Liberty*. Penguin Random House.

Advani, A., and B. Reich. 2015. Melting pot or salad bowl: The formation of heterogeneous communities. Technical report, IFS Working Paper W15/30.

Aghion, P., Y. Algan, P. Cahuc, and A. Shleifer. 2010. Regulation and distrust. *Quarterly Journal of Economics*, 125 (3): 1015–1049.

Aghion, P., and P. Howitt. *Endogenous Growth Theory*. MIT press, 1998.

Akbarpour, M., S. Malladi, and A. Saberi. 2020. Just a few seeds more: Value of network information for diffusion. Available at SSRN 3062830.

Akerlof, G. A., and R. E. Kranton. 2000. Economics and identity. *Quarterly Journal of Economics*, 115 (3): 715–753.

Albert, R., H. Jeong, and A.-L. Barabási. 2000. Error and attack tolerance of complex networks. *Nature*, 406 (6794): 378–382.

Albornoz, F., A. Cabrales, and E. Hauk. 2019. Occupational choice with endogenous spillovers. *The Economic Journal*, 129: 1953–1970.

Alesina, A., A. Devleeschauwer, W. Easterly, S. Kurlat, and R. Wacziarg. 2003. Fractionalization. *Journal of Economic Growth*, 8 (2): 155–194.

Alesina, A., and P. Giuliano. 2010. The power of the family. *Journal of Economic Growth*, 15: 93–125.

Alesina, A., and P. Giuliano. 2011. Family ties and political participation. *Journal of the European Economic Association*, 9 (5): 817–883.

Algan, Y., and P. Cahuc. 2010. Inherited trust and growth. *American Economic Review*, 100 (5): 2060–2092.

Algan, Y., and P. Cahuc. 2014. Trust, growth, and well-being: New evidence and policy implications. In *Handbook of Economic Growth*, vol. 2, edited by P. Aghion and S. Durlauf, 49–120. Elsevier.

Allcott, H., and M. Gentzkow. 2017. Social media and fake news in the 2016 election. *Journal of Economic Perspectives*, 31(2): 211–236.

Allen, F., and A. Babus. 2009. Networks in finance. In *Network-Based Strategies and Competencies*, edited by P. Kleindorfer and J. Wind. Wharton School Publishing.

Allen, F., and D. Gale. 2000. Financial contagion. *Journal of Political Economy*, 108 (1): 1–33.

Allen, F., J. Qian, and M. Qian. 2005. Law, finance, and economic growth in China. *Journal of Financial Economics*, 77 (1): 57–116.

Allouch, N. 2015. On the private provision of public goods on networks. *Journal of Economic Theory*, 157: 527–552.

Alpcan, T., and T. Başar. 2011. *Network Security: A Decision and Game Theoretic Approach*. Cambridge University Press.

Ambrus, A., and M. Elliott. 2021. Investments in social ties, risk sharing, and inequality. *Review of Economic Studies*, 88 (4): 1624–1664.

Ambrus, A., M. Mobius, and A. Szeidl. 2014. Consumption risk-sharing in social networks. *American Economic Review*, 104 (1): 149–82.

Anand, K., B. Craig, and G. von Peter. 2014. Filling in the blanks: Network structure and interbank contagion. *Quantitative Finance*, 15: 625–636.

Anand, K., I. van Lelyveld, Á. Banai, S. Friedrich, R. Garratt, G. Hałaj, J. Fique, et al. 2018. The missing links: A global study on uncovering financial network structures from partial data. *Journal of Financial Stability*, 35: 107–119.

Anderlini, L., and A. Ianni. 1996. Path dependence and learning from neighbors. *Games and Economic Behavior*, 13 (2): 141–177.

Anderson, R. *Security Engineering: A Guide to Building Dependable Distributed Systems*. Third Edition. Wiley.

Anderson, R. M., and R. M. May. 1992. *Infectious Diseases of Humans: Dynamics and Control*. Oxford University Press.

Antras, P., and D. Chor. 2013. Organizing the global value chain. *Econometrica*, 81 (6): 2127–2204.

Antras, P., and E. Helpman. 2004. Global sourcing. *Journal of Political Economy*, 112 (3): 552–580.

Appelbaum, E., and E. Katz. 1986. Transfer seeking and avoidance: on the full costs of rent-seeking. *Public Choice*, 48: 175–181.

Armstrong, M. 2006. Competition in two-sided markets. *RAND Journal of Economics*, 37 (3): 668–691.

Arnott, R., and J. E. Stiglitz. 1991. Moral hazard and nonmarket institutions: Dysfunctional crowding out of peer monitoring? *American Economic Review*, 81: 179–180.

Arquilla, J., and D. Ronfeldt. 2001. *Networks and Netwars: The Future of Terror, Crime, and Militancy*. Rand.

Arrow, K. J. 1972. Gifts and exchanges. *Philosophy & Public Affairs*, 1 (4): 343–362.

Arrow, K. J. 1974. *The Limits of Organization*. WW Norton & Company.

Arthur, W. B. 1989. Competing technologies, increasing returns, and lock-in by historical events. *Economic Journal*, 99 (2): 116–131.

Aspnes, J., K. Chang, and A. Yampolskiy. 2006. Inoculation strategies for victims of viruses and the sum-of-squares partition problem. *Journal of Computer and System Sciences*, 72 (6): 1077–1093.

Atalay, E., A. Hortacsu, J. Roberts, and C. Syverson. 2011. Network structure of production. *Proceedings of the National Academy of Sciences*, 108 (13): 5199–5202.

Aumann, R., and R. Myerson. 1988. Endogenous formation of links between players and coalitions: an application to the shapley value. In *The Shapley Value*, edited by A. Roth. Cambridge University Press.

Aumann, R. J. 1959. Acceptable points in general cooperative $N$-person games. In *Contribution to the Theory of Games IV, Annals of Mathematical Study*, edited by R. D. Luce and A. W. Tucker, 40, 287–324. Princeton University Press.

Babus, A., and T.-W. Hu. Endogenous intermediation in over-the-counter markets. *Journal of Financial Economics*, 125 (1): 200–215, 2017.

Babus, A., and P. Kondor. Trading and information diffusion in over-the-counter markets. *Econometrica*, 86 (5): 1727–1769, 2018.

Bacharach, M. 1999. Interactive team reasoning: A contribution to the theory of cooperation. *Research in Economics*, 23: 117–147.

Baetz, O. 2015. Social activity and network formation. *Theoretical Economics*, 10: 315–340.

Bai, C.-E., C.-T. Hsieh, and Z. Song. 2020a. Special deals with Chinese characteristics. *NBER Macroeconomics Annual*, 34 (1): 341–379.

Bai, C.-E., C.-T. Hsieh, Z. M. Song, and X. Wang. 2020b. Special deals from special investors: The rise of state-connected private owners in China. University of Chicago, Becker Friedman Institute for Economics Working Paper No. 2020-170. Available at SSRN: https://ssrn.com/abstract=3740120 or http://dx.doi.org/10.2139/ssrn.3740120.

Bailey, N. T. 1975. *The Mathematical Theory of Infectious Diseases and Its Applications*. Charles Griffin & Company Ltd.

Bala, V., and S. Goyal. 1995. A theory of learning with heterogeneous agents. *International Economic Review*, 36 (2): 303–323.

Bala, V., and S. Goyal. 1998. Learning from neighbours. *Review of Economic Studies*, 65 (3): 595–621.

Bala, V., and S. Goyal. 2000a. A noncooperative model of network formation. *Econometrica*, 68 (5): 1181–1230.

Bala, V., and S. Goyal. 2000b. A strategic analysis of network reliability. *Review of Economic Design*, 5 (3): 205–228.

Bala, V., and S. Goyal. 2001. Conformism and diversity under social learning. *Economic Theory*, 17 (1): 101–120.

Ballester, C., A. Calvó-Armengol, and Y. Zenou. 2006. Who's who in networks. Wanted: The key player. *Econometrica*, 74 (5): 1403–1417.

Bandiera, O., and I. Rasul. 2006. Social networks and technology adoption in northern Mozambique. *The Economic Journal*, 116 (514): 869–902.

Banerjee, A., E. Breza, A. G. Chandrasekhar, E. Duflo, M. O. Jackson, and C. Kinnan. 2021. Changes in social network structure in response to exposure to formal credit markets. *Review of Economic Studies*, forthcoming.

Banerjee, A., A. G. Chandrasekhar, E. Duflo, and M. O. Jackson. 2013. The diffusion of microfinance. *Science*, 341 (6144): 1236498.

Banerjee, A. V. 1992. A simple model of herd behavior. *Quarterly Journal of Economics*, 107 (3): 797–817.

Banfield, E. C. 1958. *Moral Basis of a Backward Society*. Free Press.

Baqaee, D., and E. Farhi. 2019. The macroeconomic impact of microeconomic shocks: Beyond hulten's theorem. *Econometrica*, 87 (4): 1155–1203.

Barabási, A. L. 2016. *Network Science*. Cambridge University Press.

Barabási, A. L., and R. Albert. 1999. Emergence of scaling in random networks. *Science*, 286 (5439): 509–512.

Barnes, M. L., J. Lynham, K. Kalberg, and P. Leung. 2016. Social networks and environmental outcomes. *Proceedings of the National Academy of Sciences*, 113 (23): 6466–6471.

Bass, F. M. 1969. A new product growth for model consumer durables. *Management Science*, 15 (5): 215–227.

Baumann, L. 2021. A model of weighted network formation. *Theoretical Economics*, 16: 1–23.

Bayer, P., S. L. Ross, and G. Topa. 2008. Place of work and place of residence: Informal hiring networks and labor market outcomes. *Journal of Political Economy*, 116 (6): 1150–1196.

Beaman, L. 2016. Social networks and the labor market. In *The Oxford Handbook of the Economics of Networks*, edited by Y. Bramoullé, A. Galeotti, and B. Rogers. Oxford University Press.

Beaman, L. A. 2013. Social networks and the dynamics of labour market outcomes: Evidence from refugees resettled in the U.S. *Review of Economic Studies*, 79 (1): 128–161.

Beaman, L., A. BenYishay, J. Magruder, and A. M. Mobarak. 2021. Can network theory-based targeting increase technology adoption? *American Economic Review*, 111 (6): 1918–43.

Bearman, P. S., J. Moody, and K. Stovel. 2004. Chains of affection: The structure of adolescent romantic and sexual networks. *American Journal of Sociology*, 110 (1): 44–91.

Bech, M. L., and E. Atalay. 2010. The topology of the federal funds market. *Physica A: Statistical Mechanics and its Applications*, 389 (22): 5223–5246.

Beck, P. A., R. J. Dalton, S. Greene, and R. Huckfeldt. 2002. The social calculus of voting: Interpersonal, media, and organizational influences on presidential choices. *American Political Science Review*, 96 (1): 57–73.

Becker, G. S. 1968. Crime and punishment: An economic approach. *Journal of Political Economy* 76: 169–217.

Becker, G. S. 1998. *Accounting for Tastes*. Harvard University Press.

Becker, J., D. Brackbill, and D. Centola. 2017. Network dynamics of social influence in the wisdom of crowds. *Proceedings of the National Academy of Sciences*, 114 (26): E5070–E5076.

Belleflamme, P., and F. Bloch. 2004. Market sharing agreements and collusive networks. *International Economic Review*, 45 (2): 387–411.

Belleflamme, P., and M. Peitz. 2015. *Industrial Organization: Markets and Strategies*. Cambridge University Press.

Belleflamme, P., and M. Peitz. 2022. *The Economics of Platforms*. Cambridge University Press.

Benhabib, J., A. Bisin, and M. O. Jackson. 2011. *Handbook of Social Economics: Volumes 1A-1B*. North Holland.

Berg, J., J. Dickhaut, and K. McCabe. 1995. Trust, reciprocity, and social history. *Games and Economic Behavior*, 10 (1): 122–142.

Berman, A., and R. J. Plemmons. 1979. *Nonnegative Matrices in the Mathematical Sciences*. Academic Press.

Bernanke, B. 2010. Causes of the recent financial and economic crisis. *Statment before the Financial Crisis Inquiry Commission*, Washington D.C.

Berninghaus, S. K., K.-M. Ehrhart, and C. Keser. 2002. Conventions and local interaction structures: experimental evidence. *Games and Economic Behavior*, 39 (2): 177–205.

Berninghaus, S. K., K.-M. Ehrhart, and M. Ott. 2006. A network experiment in continuous time: The influence of link costs. *Experimental Economics*, 9 (3): 237–251.

Berry, D. A., and B. Fristedt. 1985. *Bandit problems: Sequential Allocation of Experiments*. Chapman and Hall.

Besen, S. M., and J. Farrell. 1994. Choosing how to compete: Strategies and tactics in standardization. *Journal of Economic Perspectives*, 8 (2): 117–131.

Besley, T., and T. Persson. 2013. *Pillars of Prosperity: The Political Economics of Development Clusters*. Princeton University Press.

Beteille, A. 1965. *Caste, Class and Power: Changing Patterns of Stratification in a Tanjore Village*. University of California Press.

Beteille, A. 1969. *Castes: Old and New, Essays in Social Structure and Social Stratification*. Asia Publishing House.

Bharat, K., B.-W. Chang, M. Henzinger, and M. Ruhl. 2001. Who links to whom: Mining linkage between web sites. In *Proceedings 2001 IEEE International Conference on Data Mining*, 51–58. IEEE.

Bhaskar, V., and F. Vega-Redondo. 2004. Migration and the evolution of conventions. *Journal of Economic Behavior & Organization*, 55 (3): 397–418.

Bier, V. M., S. Oliveros, and L. Samuelson. 2006. Choosing what to protect: Strategic defensive allocation against an unknown attacker. *Journal of Publc Economic Theory*, 9: 1–25.

Bikhchandani, S., D. Hirshleifer, and I. Welch. 1992. A theory of fads, fashion, custom, and cultural change as informational cascades. *Journal of political Economy*, 100 (5): 992–1026.

Billingsley, P. 2008. *Probability and Measure*. John Wiley & Sons.

Bimpikis, K., O. Candogan, and S. Ehsani. 2019. Supply disruptions and optimal network structures. *Management Science*, 65 (12): 5504–5517.

Bisin, A., and T. Verdier. 2000. "Beyond the melting pot": Cultural transmission, marriage, and the evolution of ethnic and religious traits. *Quarterly Journal of Economics*, 115 (3): 955–988.

Black, F. 2009. *Business Cycles and Equilibrium*. John Wiley & Sons.

Blasques, F., F. Bräuning, and I. Van Lelyveld. A dynamic network model of the unsecured interbank lending market. *Journal of Economic Dynamics and Control*, 90: 310–342.

Blau, D. M., and P. K. Robins. 1990. Job search outcomes for the employed and unemployed. *Journal of Political Economy*, 98 (3): 637–655.

Blau, P. 2017. *Exchange and Power in Social Life*. Routledge.

Bloch, F. 1995. Endogenous structures of association in oligopolies. *RAND Journal of Economics*, 26 (3): 537–556.

Bloch, F. 2012. Endogenous formation of alliances in conflicts. In *The Oxford Handbook of the Economics of Peace and Conflict*, edited by M. Garfinkel and S. Skaperdas. Oxford University Press.

Bloch, F. 2016. Targeting and pricing in networks. In *The Oxford Handbook of the Economics of Networks*, edited by Y. Bramoullé, A. Galeotti, and B. Rogers.

Bloch, F., Chatterjee, K., and Dutta, B. 2021. Attack and interception in networks. *The Warwick Economics Research Paper Series* (TWERPS) 1338, University of Warwick, Department of Economics.

Bloch, F., and B. Dutta. 2009. Communication networks with endogenous link strength. *Games and Economic Behavior*, 66: 39–56.

Bloch, F., and B. Dutta. 2011. Strategic models of coalition and network formation. In *Handbook of Social Economics*, edited by J. Benhabib, A. Bisin, and M. O. Jackson. North Holland.

Bloch, F., G. Genicot, and D. Ray. Informal insurance in social networks. *Journal of Economic Theory*, 143 (1): 36–58, 2008.

Bloch, F., and M. O. Jackson. 2006. Definitions of equilibrium in network formation games. *International Journal of Game Theory*, 34 (3): 305–318.

Bloch, F., and M. O. Jackson. 2007. The formation of networks with transfers among players. *Journal of Economic Theory*, 133: 83–110.

Bloch, F., and N. Quérou. 2013. Pricing in social networks. *Games and Economic Behavior*, 80: 243–261.

Blöchl, F., F. J. Theis, F. Vega-Redondo, and E. O. Fisher. 2011. Vertex centralities in input-output networks reveal the structure of modern economies. *Physical Review E*, 83 (4): 046127.

Blume, L., D. Easley, J. Kleinberg, R. Kleinberg, and É. Tardos. 2013. Network formation in the presence of contagious risk. *ACM Transactions on Economics and Computation (TEAC)*, 1 (2): 1–20.

Blume, L. E. 1993. The statistical mechanics of strategic interaction. *Games and Economic Behavior*, 5 (3): 387–424.

Blume, L. E., D. Easley, J. Kleinberg, and E. Tardos. 2009. Trading networks with price-setting agents. *Games and Economic Behavior*, 67 (1): 36–50.

Bollobás, B. 1998. *Modern Graph Theory*. Spinger Verlag.

Bollobás, B. 2004. *Extremal Graph Theory*. Dover Publications.

Bolte, L., N. Immorlica, and M. O. Jackson. 2020. The role of referrals in inequality, immobility and inefficiency in labor markets. Stanford Working Paper.

Bolton, P., and C. Harris. 1999. Strategic experimentation. *Econometrica*, 67 (2): 349–374.

Bonacich, P. 1987. Power and centrality: A family of measures. *American Journal of Sociology*, 92: 1170–1182.

Boorman, S. A. 1975. A combinatiorial optimization model for transmission of job information through contact networks. *The Bell Journal of Economics*, 6(1): 216–249.

Borenstein, S. 1992. The evolution of U.S. airline competition. *Journal of Economic Perspectives*, 2 (6): 45–73.

Borgatti, S. 2005. Centrality and network flow. *Social Networks*, 27: 55–71.

Borgatti, S. P. 2003. The key player problem. In *Dynamic Social Network Modelling and Analysis: Workshop Summary and Papers*, edited by R. Breiger, K. Carley, and P. Pattison, 241–252. The National Academies Press.

Bourdieu, P. 1977. *Outline of a Theory of Practice*. Cambridge University Press.

Bourdieu, P. 1984. *Distinction: A Social Critique of the Judgement of Taste*. Harvard University Press.

Bourlès, R., Y. Bramoullé, and E. Perez-Richet. 2017. Altruism in networks. *Econometrica*, 85 (2): 675–689.

Bramoullé, Y., H. Djebbari, and B. Fortin. 2009. Identification of peer effects through social networks. *Journal of Econometrics*, 150 (1): 41–55.

Bramoullé, Y., A. Galeotti, and B. Rogers. 2016. *Oxford Handbook on the Economics of Networks*. Oxford University Press.

Bramoullé, Y., and S. Goyal. 2016. Favoritism. *Journal of Development Economics*, 122: 16–27.

Bramoullé, Y., S. Goyal, and M. Morelli. 2022. Social structure, markets, and state capacity. *Work in Progress*.

Bramoullé, Y., and R. Kranton. 2007a. Public good in neworks. *Journal of Economic Theory*, 135 (1): 478–494.

Bramoullé, Y., and R. Kranton. 2007b. Risk-sharing networks. *Journal of Economic Behavior & Organization*, 64 (3–4): 275–294.

Bramoullé, Y., and R. Kranton. 2016. Strategic interaction in networks. In *The Oxford Handbook of the Economics of Networks*, edited by Y. Bramoullé, A. Galeotti, and B. Rogers. Oxford University Press.

Bramoullé, Y., R. Kranton, and M. D'Amours. 2014. Strategic interaction and networks. *American Economic Review*, 104 (3): 898–930.

Bramoullé, Y., and G. Saint-Paul. 2010. Social networks and labor market transitions. *Labour economics*, 17 (1): 188–195.

Braudel, F. 1995. *The Mediterranean and the Mediterranean World in the Age of Philip II Volume 1*. University of California Press.

Breza, E. 2016. Field experiments, social networks and development. In *The Oxford Handbook of the Economics of Networks*, edited by Y. Bramoullé, A. Galeotti, and B. Rogers. Oxford University Press.

Britannica. 2000. *Encyclopaedia Britannica*. https://www.britannica.com/

Brock, W. A., and S. N. Durlauf. 2001. Interactions-based models. In *Handbook of Econometrics*, vol. 5, edited by J. J. Heckman and E. Leamer, 3297–3380. Elsevier.

Broder, A., R. Kumar, F. Maghoul, P. Raghavan, S. Rajagopalan, R. Stata, A. Tomkins, and J. Wienerca. 2000. Graph structure in the web. *Computer Networks*, 33: 309–320.

Brown, M., E. Setren, and G. Topa. 2016. Do informal referrals lead to better matches? Evidence from a firm's employee referral system. *Journal of Labor Economics*, 34 (1): 161–209.

Brueckner, J. K. 2006. Friendship networks. *Journal of Regional Science*, 46 (5): 847–865.

Bulow, J. I., J. D. Geanakoplos, and P. D. Klemperer. 1985. Multimarket oligopoly: Strategic substitutes and complements. *Journal of Political Economy* 93 (3): 488–511.

Burks, S. V., B. Cowgill, M. Hoffman, and M. Housman. 2015. The value of hiring through employee referrals. *Quarterly Journal of Economics*, 130 (2): 805–839.

Burt, R. S. 1994. *The Social Structure of Competition*. Harvard University Press.

Butters, G. Equilibrium distribution of prices and advertising. *Review of Economic Studies*, 44 (3): 465, 1977.

Caballero, R., and A. Simsek. 2013. Fire sales in a model of complexity. *Journal of Finance*, 68 (6): 2549–2587.

Cabrales, A., A. Calvo-Armengol, and Y. Zenou. 2011. Social interactions and spillovers. *Games and Economic Behavior*, 72: 339–360.

Cabrales, A., D. Gale, and P. Gottardi. 2016. Financial contagion in networks. In *The Oxford Handbook of the Economics of Networks*, edited by Y. Bramoullé, A. Galeotti, and B. Rogers. Oxford University Press.

Cabrales, A., P. Gottardi, and F. Vega-Redondo. 2016. Financial contagion in networks. In *The Oxford Handbook of the Economics of Networks*, edited by Y. Bramoullé, A. Galeotti, and B. Rogers, 543–568. Oxford University Press.

Cabrales, A., P. Gottardi, and F. Vega-Redondo. 2017. Risk-sharing and contagion in networks. *Review of Financial Studies*, 30 (9): 3086–3127.

Cai, J., A. De Janvry, and E. Sadoulet. 2015. Social networks and the decision to insure. *American Economic Journal: Applied Economics*, 7 (2): 81–108.

Caillaud, B., and B. Jullien. 2003. Chicken & egg: Competition among intermediation service providers. *RAND Journal of Economics*, 34 (2): 309–28.

Calford, E., and R. Oprea. 2017. Continuity, inertia, and strategic uncertainty: A test of the theory of continuous time games. *Econometrica*, 85: 915–935.

Callander, S., and C. Plott. 2005. Principles of network development and evolution: An experimental study. *Journal of Public Economics*, 89: 1469–1495.

Calvó-Armengol, A., J. de Martí, and A. Prat. 2015. Communication and influence. *Theoretical Economics*, 10 (2): 649–690.

Calvó-Armengol, A., and M. O. Jackson. 2004. The effects of social networks on employment and inequality. *American Economic Review*, 94 (3): 426–454.

Campbell, A. 2013. Word-of-mouth communication and percolation in social networks. *American Economic Review*, 103 (6): 2466–2498.

Candogan, O., K. Bimpikis, and A. Ozdaglar. 2012. Optimal pricing in networks with externalities. *Operations Research*, 60 (4): 883–905.

Candogan, O., and K. Drakopoulos. 2020. Optimal signaling of content accuracy: Engagement vs. misinformation. *Operations Research* 68(2): 497–515.

Canen, N., M. Jackson, and F. Trebbi. 2022. Social interactions and legislative activity. Available at SSRN: http://dx.doi.org/10.2139/ssrn.2823338

Carvalho, V. M. 2014. From micro to macro via production networks. *Journal of Economic Perspectives*, 28 (4): 23–48.

Carvalho, V. M., M. Nirei, Y. U. Saito, and A. Tahbaz-Salehi. 2021. Supply chain disruptions: Evidence from the great east japan earthquake. *Quarterly Journal of Economics*, 136 (2): 1255–1321.

Carvalho, V. M., and A. Tahbaz-Salehi. 2019. Production networks: A primer. *Annual Review of Economics*, 11: 635–663.

Carvalho, V. M., and N. Voigtlander. 2015. Input diffusion and the evolution of production networks. NBERWorking Paper No. 20025.

Casella, A., and N. Hanaki. 2008. Information channels in labor markets: On the resilience of referral hiring. *Journal of Economic Behavior & Organization*, 66 (3–4): 492–513.

Caselli, F., M. Morelli, and D. Rohner. 2014. The geography of inter-state resource wars. Working Paper, Columbia University.

Caselli, F., M. Morelli, and D. Rohner. 2015. The geography of inter-state resource wars. *Quarterly Journal of Economics*, 130: 267–315.

Cassar, A. 2007. Coordination and cooperation in local, random and small world networks: Experimental evidence. *Games and Economic Behavior*, 58 (2): 209–230.

Castiglionesi, F., and N. Navarro. 2007. Optimal fragile financial networks. Discussion Paper 2007-100, Tilburg University, Center for Economic Research.

Centola, D. 2011. An experimental study of homophily in the adoption of health behavior. *Science*, 334 (6060): 1269–1272.

Centola, D., and A. Baronchelli. 2015. The spontaneous emergence of conventions: An experimental study of cultural evolution. *Proceedings of the National Academy of Sciences*, 112 (7): 1989–1994.

Cerdeiro, D., M. Dziubiński, and S. Goyal. 2017. Individual security, contagion, and network design. *Journal of Economic Theory*, 170: 182–226.

Chamley, C. P. 2004. *Rational herds: Economic models of social learning*. Cambridge University Press.

Chandrasekhar, A. G., H. Larreguy, and J. P. Xandri. 2020. Testing models of social learning on networks: Evidence from two experiments. *Econometrica*, 88 (1): 1–32.

Charlson, G. 2022. In platforms we trust: Misinformation on social networks in the presence of social mistrust. Working Paper Cambridge University.

Charness, G., M. Corominas-Bosch, and G. R. Frechette. 2007. Bargaining and network structure: An experiment. *Journal of Economic Theory*, 136 (1): 28–65.

Charness, G., F. Feri, M. A. Meléndez-Jiménez, and M. Sutter. 2014. Experimental games on networks: Underpinnings of behavior and equilibrium selection. *Econometrica*, 82 (5): 1615–1670.

Chen, J., M. Elliott, and A. Koh. 2020. Capability accumulation and conglomeratization in the information age. Cambridge Working Paper in Economics 2069.

Chen, Y.-C., M. Mueller-Frank, and M. M. Pai. 2021. The wisdom of the crowd and higher-order beliefs. arXiv preprint arXiv:2102.02666.

Chen, L. and Y. Papanastasiou. 2021. Seeding the herd: Pricing and welfare effects of social learning manipulation. *Management Science*, 67(11): 6734–6750.

Choi, S., D. Gale, and S. Kariv. 2005. *Behavioral Aspects of Learning in Social Networks: An Experimental Study*. Emerald Group Publishing Limited.

Choi, S., A. Galeotti, and S. Goyal. 2017. Trading in networks: Theory and experiments. *Journal of the European Economic Association*, 15 (4): 784–817.

Choi, S., E. Gallo, and S. Kariv. 2016. Networks in the laboratory. In *The Oxford Handbook of the Economics of Networks*, edited by Y. Bramoullé, A. Galeotti, and B. Rogers. Oxford University Press.

Choi, S., S. Goyal, and F. Moisan. 2019. Connectors and influencers. C-INET Working Paper Number: 1909.

Choi, S., S. Goyal, and F. Moisan. 2020. Large scale experiments on networks: A new platform with applications. Technical Report 2063, Cambridge-INET Working Paper.

Choi, S., S. Goyal, and F. Moisan. 2022. *Brokerage: theory and experiments*. University of Cambridge.

Choi, S., S. Goyal, F. Moisan, Y. Y. T. To. 2022. Learning in canonical networks. Cambridge Working Paper in Economics WPE2235.

Chou, C.-f., and O. Shy. 1990. Network effects without network externalities. *International Journal of Industrial Organization*, 8 (2): 259–270.

Christakis, N. A., and J. H. Fowler. 2007. The spread of obesity in a large social network over 32 years. *New England Journal of Medicine*, 357 (4): 370–379.

Christakis, N. A., and J. H. Fowler. 2013. Social contagion theory: Examining dynamic social networks and human behavior. *Statistics in Medicine*, 32 (4): 556–577.

Chung, F., and L. Lu. 2002a. The average distances in random graphs with given expected degrees. *PNAS*, 99: 15879–15882.

Chung, F., and L. Lu. 2002b. Connected components in random graphs with given expected degree sequences. *Annals of Combinatorics*, 6 (2): 125–145.

Church, J., and N. Gandal. 1992. Network effects, software provision, and standardization. *Journal of Industrial Economics*, 40 (1): 85–103.

Church, J., and N. Gandal. 1993. Complementary network externalities and technological adoption. *International Journal of Industrial Organization*, 11 (2): 239–260.

Chwe, M. S.-Y. 1994. Farsighted coalitional stability. *Journal of Economic Theory*, 63 (2): 299–325.

Chwe, M. S.-Y. 2000. Communication and coordination in social networks. *Review of Economic Studies*, 67 (1): 1–16.

Clark, D., and K. A. Konrad. 2007. Asymmetric conflict: Weakest link against bestshot. *Journal of Conflict Resolution*, 51: 457–469.

Cohen, L., A. Frazzini, and C. Malloy. 2008. The small world of investing: Board connections and mutual fund returns. *Journal of Political Economy*, 116 (5): 951–979.

Cohen, R., K. Erez, and S. Havlin. 2000. Resilience of the internet to random breakdowns. *Physical Review Letters*, 85 (21): 4626–8.

Cohen, R., K. Erez, D. Ben-Avraham, and S. Havlin. 2001. Breakdown of the internet under intentional attack. *Physical Review Letters*, 86 (16): 3682.

Coleman, J. 1958. Relational analysis: The study of social organizations with survey methods. *Human Organization*, 17 (4): 28–36.

Coleman, J. S. 1981. *Public and Private Schools*, vol. 3. ERIC Document Reproduction Service.

Coleman, J. S. 1988. Social capital in the creation of human capital. *American Journal of Sociology*, 94: S95–S120.

Coleman, J. S. 1994. *Foundations of Social Theory*. Harvard University Press.

Coleman, J. S., E. Katz, and H. Menzel. 1966. *Medical Innovation: A Diffusion study*. Bobbs-Merrill Company.

Colla, P., and A. Mele. 2010. Information linkages and correlated trading. *The Review of Financial Studies*, 23 (1): 203–246.

Comola, M., and S. Prina. 2021. Treatment effect accounting for network changes. *Review of Economics and Statistics*, 103(3): 597–604.

Condorelli, D., and A. Galeotti. 2016. Intermediation in networks. In *The Oxford Handbook of the Economics of Networks*, edited by Y. Bramoullé, A. Galeotti, and B. Rogers. Oxford University Press.

Condorelli, D., A. Galeotti, and L. Renou. 2017. Bilateral trading in networks. *Review of Economic Studies*, 84 (1): 82–105.

Conley, T. G., and G. Topa. 2002. Socio-economic distance and spatial patterns in unemployment. *Journal of Applied Econometrics*, 17 (4): 303–327.

Conley, T. G., and C. R. Udry. 2010. Learning about a new technology: Pineapple in ghana. *American Economic Review*, 100 (1): 35–69.

Cook, K. S., and R. M. Emerson. 1978. Power, equity and commitment in exchange networks. *American Sociological Review*, 43: 721–739.

Cook, K. S., and R. M. Emerson. 1987. Social Exchange Theory. *Annual Review of Sociology*, 2: 335–362.

Cook, K. S., M. Levi, and R. Hardin. 2009. *Whom Can We Trust?: How Groups, Networks, and Institutions Make Trust Possible*. Russell Sage Foundation.

Corcoran, M., L. Datcher, and G. Duncan. 1980. Information and influence networks in labor markets. *Five Thousand American Families: Patterns of Economic Progress*, 8 (S 1): 37.

Corominas-Bosch, M. 2004. Bargaining in a network of buyers and sellers. *Journal of Economic Theory*, 115 (1): 35–77.

Corts, K. S., and M. Lederman. 2009. Software exclusivity and the scope of indirect network effects in the U.S. home video game market. *International Journal of Industrial Organization*, 27 (2): 121–136.

Costinot, A., J. Vogel, and S. Wang. 2013. An elementary theory of global supply chains. *Review of Economic Studies*, 80: 109–144.

Craig, B., and G. Von Peter. 2014. Interbank tiering and money center banks. *Journal of Financial Intermediation*, 23 (3): 322–347.

Crawford, V. P. 1995. Adaptive dynamics in coordination games. *Econometrica*, 63: 103–143.

Crawford, V. P., and J. Sobel. 1982. Strategic information transmission. *Econometrica*, 50 (6): 1431–1451.

Cunningham, W. 1985. Optimal attack and reinforcement of a network. *Journal of the ACM*, 32 (3): 549–561.

Currarini, S., M. O. Jackson, and P. Pin. 2009. An economic model of friendship: Homophily, minorities, and segregation. *Econometrica*, 77 (4): 1003–1045.

Dai, R., D. Mookherjee, K. Munshi, and X. Zhang. 2020. The community origins of private enterprise in China. Working Paper Cambridge and Boston University.

Daniele, V., and P. Malanima. 2014. Falling disparities and persisting dualism: Regional development and industrialisation in Italy, 1891–2001. *Economic History Research*, 10: 165–176.

Darwin, J. 2007. *After TamerLane: The Rise and Fall of Global Empires 1400–2000*. Penguin.

Dasaratha, K. 2021. Innovation and strategic network formation. *Review of Economic Studies*, forthcoming 2022. Working Paper Harvard University.

Dasgupta, P. 1988. Trust as a commodity. In *Trust: Making and Breaking Cooperative Relations*, edited by Diego Gambetta. Blackwell Press.

Dasgupta, P. 1993. *An Inquiry into Well-Being and Destitution*. Clarendon Press.

Dasgupta, P., and I. Serageldin. 2001. *Social Capital: A Multifaceted Perspective*. The World Bank.

d'Aspremont, C., and A. Jacquemin. 1988. Cooperative and noncooperative R & D in duopoly with spillovers. *American Economic Review*, 78 (5): 1133–1137.

David, P. A. 1985. Clio and the economics of qwerty. *American Economic Review*, 75 (2): 332–337.

de Bijl, P., and S. Goyal. 1995. Technological change in markets with network externalities. *International Journal of Industrial Organization*, 13 (3): 307–325.

de Sola Pool, I., and M. Kochen. 1978–79. Contacts and influence. *Social Networks*, 1: 55–51.

de Solla Price, D. 1965. Networks of scientific papers. *Science*, 149 (3683): 510–515.

de Solla Price, D. 1976. A general theory of bibliometric and other cumulative advantage processes. *Journal of the American Society for Information Science*, 27 (5): 292–306.

DeGroot, M. H. 1974. Reaching a consensus. *Journal of the American Statistical Association*, 69 (345): 118–121.

Demange, G., and M. Wooders. 2005. *Group Formation in Economics: Networks, Clubs, and Coalitions*. Cambridge University Press.

DeMarzo, P., D. Vayanos, and J. Zwiebel. 2003. Persuasion bias, social influence, and unidimensional opinions. *Quarterly Journal of Economics*, 118 (3): 909–968.

Department of Homeland Security. 2012. *Office of Infrastructure Protection Strategic Plan: 2012-2016*. Washington, DC.

Deroian, F. 2009. Endogenous link strength in directed communication networks. *Mathematical Social Sciences*, 57: 110–116.

Ding, S. 2021. A factor influencing network formation: Link investment substitutability. Working Paper Nankai University.

Ding, S., M. Dziubinski, and S. Goyal. 2021. Clubs and networks. *Cambridge Working Papers in Economics 2175*.

Dodds, P. S., R. Muhamad, and D. J. Watts. 2003. An experimental study of search in global social networks. *Science*, 301 (5634): 827–829.

Domingos, P., and M. Richardson. 2001. Mining the network value of customers. *Proceedings of the 7th Conference on Knowledge Discovery and Data Mining*, 57–66,

Donaldson, D. 2015. The gains from market integration. *Annual Review of Economics*, 7: 619–647.

Donaldson, D. 2018. Railroads of the Raj: Estimating the impact of transportation infrastructure. *American Economic Review*, 108: 899–934.

Donaldson, D., and R. Hornbeck. 2016. Railroads and American economic growth: A market access approach. *Quarterly Journal of Economics*, 131: 799–858.

Donato, D., L. Laura, S. Leonardi, and S. Millozzi. 2007. The web as a graph: How far we are. *ACM Transactions on Internet Technology (TOIT)*, 7 (1): 4–es.

Duarte, F., and T. M. Eisenbach. 2018. Fire-sale spillovers and systemic risk. *Journal of Finance*, 76 (3): 1251–1294.

Ductor, L., M. Fafchamps, S. Goyal, and M. J. Van der Leij. 2014. Social networks and research output. *Review of Economics and Statistics*, 96 (5): 936–948.

Ductor, L., S. Goyal, and A. Prummer. 2022. Gender and collaboration. *Review of Economics and Statistics*, forthcoming.

Duesenberry, J. 1949. *Income, Saving, and the Theory of Consumer Behavior*. Harvard University Press.

Duflo, E., M. Kremer, and J. Robinson. 2006. Understanding technology adoption: Fertilizer in western Kenya evidence from field experiments (preliminary and incomplete) April 14.

Durieu, J., H. Haller, and P. Sola. 2011. Nonspecific networking. *Games*, 2: 87–113

Dustmann, C., A. Glitz, and U. Schönberg. 2009. Job search networks and ethnic segregation in the workplace. University College London, Working Paper.

Dutta, B., and M. O. Jackson. 2003. On the formation of networks and groups. In *Networks and groups*, 1–15. Springer.

Dutta, B., and S. Mutuswami. 1997. Stable networks. *Journal of Economic Theory*, 76 (2): 322–344.

Dziubiński, M., and S. Goyal. 2013. Network design and defence. *Games and Economic Behavior*, 79 (1): 30–43.

Dziubiński, M., and S. Goyal. 2017. How do you defend a network? *Theoretical Economics*, 12 (1): 331–376.

Dziubinski, M., S. Goyal, and D. Minarsch. 2017. The strategy of conquest. *Journal of Economic Theory*, 191: 105161.

Dziubiński, M., S. Goyal, and A. Vigier. 2016. Conflict and networks. In *The Oxford Handbook of the Economics of Networks*, edited by Y. Bramoullé, A. Galeotti, and G. Rogers, 215–243. Oxford University Press.

Easley, D., and J. Kleinberg. 2010. *Networks, Crowds, and Markets: Reasoning about a Highly Connected World*. Cambridge University Press.

Eaton, J., and S. Kortum. 2002. Technology, geography, and trade. *Econometrica*, 70: 1741–1779.

Eisenberg, L., and T. H. Noe. 2001. Systemic risk in financial systems. *Management Science*, 47 (2): 236–249.

Elias, N. 1978. *The Civilizing Process*. Basil Blackwell.

Elliott, J. H. 2006. *Empires of the Atlantic World: Britain and Spain in America 1492–1830*. Yale University Press.

Elliott, M. 2015. Inefficiencies in networked markets. *American Economic Journal: Microeconomics*, 7 (4): 43–82.

Elliott, M., B. Golub, and M. O. Jackson. 2014. Financial networks and contagion. *American Economic Review*, 104 (10): 3115–53.

Elliott, M., C.-P. Georg, and J. Hazell. 2020. Systemic risk shifting in financial networks. *Journal of Economic Theory*, 105157.

Elliott, M., B. Golub, and M. V. Leduc. 2020. Supply network formation and fragility. Available at SSRN 3525459.

Elliott, M., and F. Nava. 2019. Decentralized bargaining in matching markets: Efficient stationary equilibria and the core. *Theoretical Economics*, 14 (1): 211–251.

Ellison, G. 1993. Learning, local interaction, and coordination. *Econometrica*, 61: 1047–1071.

Ellison, G., and D. Fudenberg. 1993. Rules of thumb for social learning. *Journal of Political Economy*, 101 (4): 612–643.

Ellison, G., and D. Fudenberg. 1995. Word-of-mouth communication and social learning. *Quarterly Journal of Economics*, 110 (1): 93–125.

Ellison, G., and D. Fudenberg. 2003. Knife-edge or plateau: When do market models tip? *Quarterly Journal of Economics*, 118 (4): 1249–78.

Ely, J. 2002. Local conventions. *The B.E. Journal of Theoretical Economics*, 2 (1): 20021002.

Emerson, R. J. 1976. Social exchange theory. *Annual Review of Sociology*, 2: 335–362.

Enke, B. 2019. Kinship, cooperation, and the evolution of moral systems. *Quarterly Journal of Economics*, 134 (2): 953–1019.

Erdős, P., and A. Rényi. 1959. On random graphs, *Publicationes Mathematicae Debrecen*, 6: 290–297.

Erdős, P., and A. Rényi. 1960. On the evolution of random graphs. *Publication of Mathematical Institute of Hungarian Academy*, 5 (1): 17–60.

Erdős, P., and A. Rényi. 1961. On the strength of connectedness of a random graph. *Acta Mathematica Scientia Hungary*, 12: 261–267.

Ermisch, J., and D. Gambetta. 2008. Do strong family ties inhibit trust? *Journal of Economic Behavior and Organization*, 75 (3): 365–376.

Erol, S., and R. Vohra. 2018. Network formation and systemic risk. Available at SSRN 2546310.

Eun, H. 2010. Impact analysis of natural disasters on critical infrastructure, associated industries, and communities. PhD thesis, Purdue University, West Lafayette, Indiana.

Fabrikant, A., A. Luthra, E. Maneva, C. Papadimitriou, and C. Shenker. 2003. On a network creation game. In *Proceedings of ACM Symposium on Principles of Distributed Systems*, pages 247–351.

Fafchamps, M. 2011. Development, social norms, and assignment to task. *Proceedings of the National Academy of Sciences*, 108 (Supplement 4): 21308–21315.

Fafchamps, M., and F. Gubert. 2007. The formation of risk sharing networks. *Journal of development Economics*, 83 (2): 326–350.

Fafchamps, M., and S. Lund. 2003. Risk-sharing networks in rural philippines. *Journal of development Economics*, 71 (2): 261–287.

Fafchamps, M., M. J. Van der Leij, and S. Goyal. 2010. Matching and network effects. *Journal of the European Economic Association*, 8 (1): 203–231.

Fainmesser, I. P., and A. Galeotti. 2016. Pricing network effects. *Review of Economic Studies*, 83 (1): 165–198.

Fainmesser, I. P., and A. Galeotti. 2020. Pricing network effects: Competition. *American Economic Journal: Microeconomics*, 12 (3): 1–32.

Fajgelbaum, P. D., and E. Schaal. 2020. Optimal transport networks in spatial equilibrium. *Econometrica*, 88: 1411–1452.

Falk, A., and M. Kosfeld. 2012. It's all about connections: Evidence on network formation. *Review of Network Economics*, 11.

Farboodi, M. 2021. Intermediation and voluntary exposure to counterparty risk. MIT working paper.

Farrell, J., and G. Saloner. 1985. Standardization, compatibility, and innovation. *RAND Journal of Economics*, 16: 70–83.

Farrell, J., and G. Saloner. 1986, December. Installed base and compatibility: Innovation, product preannouncements, and predation. *American Economic Review*, 76 (5): 940–955.

Feick, L. F., and L. L. Price. 1987. The market maven: A diffuser of marketplace information. *Journal of Marketing*, 51 (1): 83–97.

Feld, S. L. 1991. Why your friends have more friends than you do. *American Journal of Sociology*, 96 (6): 1464–1477.

Ferri, F. 2007. Stochastic stability in networks with decay. *Journal of Economic Theory*, 135: 442–457.

Fershtman, C., and D. Persitz. 2021. Social clubs and social networks. *American Economic Journal: Microeconomics*, 13 (1): 224–251.

Fishlow, A. 1965. *American Railroads and the Transformation of the Ante-bellum Economy*. Harvard University Press.

Fisman, R. 2003. Ethnic ties and the provision of credit: Relationship-level evidence from african firms. *Advances in Economic Analysis & Policy*, 3 (1): 1211.

Fleisher, B., D. Hud, W. McGuiree, and X. Zhang. 2010. The evolution of an industrial cluster in china. *China Economic Review*, 21 (3): 456–469.

Fogel, R. 1962. A quantitative approach to the study of railroads in american economic growth: A report of some preliminary findings. *The Journal of Economic History*, 22: 163–197.

Fogel, R. W. 1964. *Railroads and American Economic Growth: Essays in Econometric History*. The Johns Hopkins Press.

Foster, A. D., and M. R. Rosenzweig. 1995. Learning by doing and learning from others: Human capital and technical change in agriculture. *Journal of political Economy*, 103 (6): 1176–1209.

Foster, D., and P. Young. 1990. Stochastic evolutionary game dynamics. *Theoretical Population Biology*, 38 (2): 219–232.

Franke, J., and T. Öztürk. 2009. Conflict networks. Ruhr Economic Papers 116, University of Dortmund.

Franke, J., and T. Öztürk. 2015. Conflict networks. *Journal of Public Economics*, 126: 104–113.

Freeman, L. 1979. Centrality in social networks: Conceptual clarification. *Social Networks*, 1: 215–239.

French, J. R., Jr. 1956. A formal theory of social power. *Psychological review*, 63 (3): 181.

Friedman, D., and R. Oprea. 2012. A continuous dilemma. *American Economic Review*, 102 (1): 337–363.

Fukuyama, F. 1995. *Trust: The Social Virtues and the Creation of Prosperity*. Free Press.

Fukuyama, F. 2011. *The Origins of Political Order: From Prehuman Times to the French Revolution*. Farrar, Straus and Giroux.

Fukuyama, F. 2018. *Identity: Contemporary Identity Politics and the Struggle for Recognition*. Profile books.

Funk, C., and M. Hefferon. 2019. *US Public Views on Climate and Energy: Democrats Mostly Agree the Federal Government Should Do More on Climate, While Republicans Differ by Ideology, Age and Gender*. Pew Research Center.

Gabaix, X. 2011. The granular origins of aggregate fluctuations. *Econometrica*, 79 (3): 733–772.

Gagnon, J., and S. Goyal. 2017. Networks, markets, and inequality. *American Economic Review*, 107 (1): 1–30.

Gai, P., A. Haldane, and S. Kapadia. 2011. Complexity, concentration and contagion. *Journal of Monetary Economics*, 58 (5): 453–470.

Gai, P., and S. Kapadia. 2010. Contagion in financial networks. *Proceedings of the Royal Society A: Mathematical, Physical and Engineering Sciences*, 466 (2120): 2401–2423.

Gale, D., and S. Kariv. 2003. Bayesian learning in social networks. *Games and Economic Behavior*, 45 (2): 329–346.

Gale, D. M., and S. Kariv. 2009. Trading in networks: A normal form game experiment. *American Economic Journal: Microeconomics*, 1 (2): 114–132.

Galeotti, A. 2006. One-way flow networks: The role of heterogeneity. *Economic Theory*, 29: 163–179.

Galeotti, A. 2010. Talking, searching and pricing. *International Economic Review*, 51 (4): 1159–1174.

Galeotti, A., and C. Ghiglino. 2021. Financial linkages and portfolio choice. *Journal of Economic Theory*, forthcoming.

Galeotti, A., C. Ghiglino, and F. Squintani. 2013. Strategic information transmission networks. *Journal of Economic Theory*, 148 (5): 1751–1769.

Galeotti, A., B. Golub, and S. Goyal. 2020. Targeting interventions in networks. *Econometrica*, 88 (6): 2445–2471.

Galeotti, A., B. Golub, S. Goyal, and R. Rao. 2021. Discord and harmony in networks. doi: arXiv:2102.13309v1.

Galeotti, A., and S. Goyal. 2009. Influencing the influencers: A theory of strategic diffusion. *RAND Journal of Economics*, 40 (3): 509–532.

Galeotti, A., and S. Goyal. 2010. The law of the few. *American Economic Review*, 100 (4): 1468–1492.

Galeotti, A., and S. Goyal. 2014. Competing supply chains. Mimeo, Cambridge and Essex.

Galeotti, A., S. Goyal, and J. Kalbfuss. 2022. Spectral oligopolies. Working Paper. University of Cambridge.

Galeotti, A., S. Goyal, and R. Rao. 2021. Discord and harmony in networks. arXiv:2102.13309v1.

Galeotti, A., S. Goyal, E. Talamàs, and O. Tamuz. 2022. Taxes and market power: A principal components approach. arXiv:2112.08153v2.

Galeotti, A., S. Goyal, M. O. Jackson, F. Vega-Redondo, and L. Yariv. 2010. Network games. *Review of Economic Studies*, 77 (1): 218–244.

Galeotti, A., S. Goyal, and J. Kamphorst. 2006. Network formation with heterogeneous players. *Games and Economic Behavior*, 54: 353–372.

Galeotti, A., and F. Vega-Redondo. 2011. Complex networks and local externalities: A strategic approach. *International Journal of Economic Theory*, 7 (1): 77–92.

Galichon, A. 2016. *Optimal Transport Methods in Economics*. Princeton University Press.

Gambetta, D. 1988. *Trust. Making and Breaking Cooperative Relations*. Blackwell Press.

Garfinkel, M., and S. Skaperdas. 2012. *The Oxford Handbook of the Economics of Peace and Conflict*. Oxford University Press.

Gavazza, A., S. Mongey, and G. L. Violante. 2018. Aggregate recruiting intensity. *American Economic Review*, 108 (8): 2088–2127.

Geertz, C. 1973. *Interpretation of Cultures*. Basic Books.

Genicot, G. 2022. Tolerance and compromise in social networks. *Journal of Political Economy*, 130 (1): 94–120.

C.-P. Georg. 2013. The effect of the interbank network structure on contagion and common shocks. *Journal of Banking and Finance*, 37 (7): 2216–2228.

Gerschenkron, A. 1962. *Economic Backwardness in Historical Perspective*. Harvard University Press.

Ghiglino, C., and S. Goyal. 2010. Keeping up with the neighbors: Social interaction in a market economy. *Journal of the European Economic Association*, 8 (1): 90–119.

Gibbon, E. 1776. *The Decline and Fall of the Roman Empire*. Strahan & Cadell.

Gilles, R. P., S. Chakrabarti, and S. Sarangi. 2012. Nash equilibria of network formation games under consent. *Mathematical Social Sciences*, 64 (2): 159–165.

Gilles, R. P., and C. Johnson. 2000. Spatial social networks. *Review of Economic Design*, 5 (3): 273–299.

Gilles, R. P., and S. Sarangi. 2004. Social network formation with consent. CentER Discussion Paper No. 2004-70. Available at SSRN: http://dx.doi.org/10.2139/ssrn.603341.

Gladwell, M. 2006. *The Tipping Point: How Little Things Can Make a Big Difference*. Little, Brown.

Glaeser, E. L., D. Laibson, and B. Sacerdote. 2002. An economic approach to social capital. *The Economic Journal*, 112 (483): F437–F458.

Glaeser, E. L., D. I. Laibson, J. A. Scheinkman, and C. L. Soutter. 2000. Measuring trust. *Quarterly Journal of Economics*, 115 (3): 811–846.

Glaeser, E. L., B. Sacerdote, and J. A. Scheinkman. 1996. Crime and social interactions. *Quarterly Journal of Economics*, 111 (2): 507–548.

Glasserman, P., and H. P. Young. 2015. How likely is contagion in financial networks? *Journal of Banking & Finance*, 50: 383–399.

Glasserman, P., and H. P. Young. 2016. Contagion in financial networks. *Journal of Economic Literature*, 54 (3): 779–831.

Goeree, J. K., A. Riedl, and A. Ule. 2009. In search of stars: Network formation among heterogeneous agents. *Games and Economic Behavior*, 67 (2): 445–466.

Gofman, M. 2011. A network-based analysis of over-the-counter markets. Working Paper, Hebrew University, Jerusalem.

Gofman, M. 2017. Efficiency and stability of a financial architecture with too-interconnected-to-fail institutions. *Journal of Financial Economics*, 124 (1): 113–146.

Golub, B., and M. O. Jackson. 2010. Naive learning in social networks and the wisdom of crowds. *American Economic Journal: Microeconomics*, 2 (1): 112–149.

Golub, B., and M. O. Jackson. 2012. How homophily affects the speed of learning and best-response dynamics. *Quarterly Journal of Economics*, 127 (3): 1287–1338.

Golub, B., and Y. Livne. 2010. Strategic random networks and tipping points in network formation. Working Paper, Harvard University.

Golub, B., and E. Sadler. 2016. Learning in social networks. In *The Oxford Handbook of the Economics of Networks*, edited by Y. Bramoullé, A. Galeotti, and B. Rogers. Oxford University Press.

Gordon, S., and E. Rosenbach. 2022. America's cyber reckoning. *Foreign Affairs*, 101 (1): 10–21.

Government, U. S. 2011. Final Report of the National Commission on the Causes of the Financial and Economic Crisis in the United States. Washington D.C.

Goyal, S. 1993. Sustainable communication networks. Tinbergen Institute Discussion Paper, TI 93-250.

Goyal, S. 1996. Interaction structure and social change. *Journal of Institutional and Theoretical Economics (JITE)/Zeitschrift für die gesamte Staatswissenschaft*, 152 (3): 472–494.

Goyal, S. 2005. Strong and weak links. *Journal of the European Economic Association*, 3 (2–3): 608–616.

Goyal, S. 2007. *Connections: An Introduction to the Economics of Networks*. Princeton University Press.

Goyal, S. 2011. Learning in networks. In *Handbook of Social Economics*, vol. 1, edited by J. Benhabib, M. O. Jackson, and A. Bisin, 679–727. Elsevier.

Goyal, S. 2012. Social networks on the web. In *Handbook of the Digital Economy*, edited by M. Peitz and J. Waldfogel. Oxford University Press.

Goyal, S. 2016. Economics of networks: A perspective on the literarure. In *The Oxford Handbook of the Economics of Networks*, edited by J. Benhabib, M. O. Jackson, and A. Bisin. Oxford Univetsity Press.

Goyal, S. 2017. Networks and markets. In *Advances in Economics and Econometrics: Eleventh World Congress of the Econometric Society*, edited by M. P. Bo Honore, Ariel Pakes, and L. Samuelson. Cambridge University Press.

Goyal, S., H. Heidari, and M. Kearns. 2019. Competitive contagion in networks. *Games and Economic Behavior*, 113: 58–79.

Goyal, S., P. Hernández, G. Martínez-Cánovas, F. Moisan, M. Muñoz-Herrera, and A. Sánchez. 2021. Integration and diversity. *Experimental Economics*, 24 (2): 387–413.

Goyal, S., S. Jabbari, M. Kearns, S. Khanna, and J. Morgenstern. 2016. Strategic network formation with attack and immunization. In *Web and Internet Economics (WINE)*.

Goyal, S., and M. C. Janssen. 1997. Non-exclusive conventions and social coordination. *Journal of Economic Theory*, 77 (1): 34–57.

Goyal, S., and S. Joshi. 2003. Networks of collaboration in oligopoly. *Games and Economic Behavior*, 43 (1): 57–85.

Goyal, S., and S. Joshi. 2006a. Bilateralism and free trade. *International Economic Review*, 47 (3): 749–778.

Goyal, S., and S. Joshi. 2006b. Unequal connections. *International Journal of Game Theory*, 34 (3): 319–349.

Goyal, S., M. van der Leij, and J. L. Moraga-González. 2006. Economics: An emerging small world. *Journal of political economy*, 114 (2): 403–412.

Goyal, S., and J. L. Moraga-González. 2001. R&D networks. *RAND Journal of Economics*, 32 (4): 686–707.

Goyal, S., J. L. Moraga-González, and A. Konovalov. 2008. Hybrid R&D. *Journal of the European Economic Association*, 6 (6): 1309–1338.

Goyal, S., S. Rosenkranz, U. Weitzel, and V. Buskens. 2017. Information acquisition and exchange in social networks. *Economic Journal*, 127: 2302–2331.

Goyal, S., and E. Sadler. 2021. Strategic network formation revisited. *Mimeo University of Cambridge and Columbia University*.

Goyal, S., M. Safranov, and T. To. 2022. Verification and sharing of news in social networks. Working paper, University of Cambridge.

Goyal, S., and F. Vega-Redondo. 2005. Network formation and social coordination. *Games and Economic Behavior*, 50 (2): 178–207.

Goyal, S., and F. Vega-Redondo. 2007. Structural holes in social networks. *Journal of Economic Theory*, 137 (1): 460–492.

Goyal, S., and A. Vigier. 2014. Attack, defence, and contagion in networks. *Review of Economic Studies*, 81 (4): 1518–1542.

Granovetter, M. 1978. Threshold models of collective behavior. *American Journal of Sociology*, 83 (6): 1420–1443.

Granovetter, M. 1985. Economic action and social structure: The problem of embeddedness. *American Journal of Sociology*, 91 (3): 481–510.

Granovetter, M. 1994. *Getting a Job: A Study of Contacts and Careers*. Northwestern University Press.

Granovetter, M. 1995. *Getting a Job*. University of Chicago Press.

Granovetter, M. 2005. The impact of social structure on economic outcomes. *Journal of Economic Perspectives*, 19 (1): 33–50.

Granovetter, M. 2017. *Society and Economy: Frameworks and Principles*. Harvard University Press.

Granovetter, M. 1973. The strength of weak ties. *American Journal of Sociology*, 78 (6): 1360–1380.

Greif, A., and G. Tabellini. 2017. The clan and the corporation: Sustaining cooperation in china and europe. *Journal of Comparative Economics*, 45 (1): 1–35.

Griffith, A. 2020. A continuous model of strong and weak ties. Working Paper, Washington University.

Griliches, Z. 1957. Hybrid corn: An exploration in the economics of technological change. *Econometrica*, 25 (4): 501–522.

Grimm, V., and F. Mengel. 2020. Experiments on belief formation in networks. *Journal of the European Economic Association*, 18 (1): 49–82.

Grötschel, M., C. Monma, and M. Stoer. 1995. Design of survivable networks. In *Handbooks of Operations Research and Management Science*, edited by M. Ball, T. Magnanti, C. Monma, and G. Nemhauser. Amsterdam.

Gueye, A., J. Walrand, and V. Anantharam. 2010. Design of network topology in an adversarial environment. In *Proceedings of the 1st International Conference on Decision and Game Theory for Security*, GameSec'10, 1–20. Springer-Verlag.

Guiso, L., P. Sapienza, and L. Zingales. 2003. People's opium? religion and economic attitudes. *Journal of Monetary Economics*, 50 (1): 225–282.

Guiso, L., P. Sapienza, and L. Zingales. 2006. Does culture affect economic outcomes? *Journal of Economic Perspectives*, 20 (2): 23–48.

Guiso, L., P. Sapienza, and L. Zingales. 2011. Civic capital as the missing link. *Handbook of Social Economics*, 1: 417–480.

Guiso, L., P. Sapienza, and L. Zingales. 2016. Long-term persistence. *Journal of Eurpoean Economic Association*, 14 (6): 1401–1436.

Gulati, R. 2007. *Managing Network Resources: Alliances, Affiliations, and Other Relational Assets*. Oxford University Press.

Haag, M., and R. Lagunoff. 2006. Social norms, local interaction, and neighborhood planning. *International Economic Review*, 47 (1): 265–296.

Hagedoorn, J. 2002. Inter-firm R&D partnerships: An overview of major trends and patterns since 1960. *Research Policy*, 31 (4): 477–492.

Hagenbach, J., and F. Koessler. 2010. Strategic communication networks. *Review of Economic Studies*, 77 (3): 1072–1099.

Haldane, A. G. 2013. Rethinking the financial network. In *Fragile stabilität–stabile fragilität*, edited by Stephan A. Jansen, Eckhard Schröter, and Nico Stehr, 243–278. Springer.

Harary, F. 1959. A criterion for unanimity in French's theory of social power. In *Studies in Social Power*, edited by D. Cartwright, 168–182.

Harary, F. 1962. The maximum connectivity of a graph. *Proceedings of the National Academy of Science*, 48 (7): 1142–1146.

Harary, F. 1969. *Graph Theory*. Perseus Books.

Harris, J. R., and M. P. Todaro. 1970. Migration, unemployment and development: A two-sector analysis. *American Economic Review*, 60 (1): 126–142.

Harrison, G. W., and J. Hirshleifer. 1989. An experimental evaluation of weakest link/best shot models of public goods. *Journal of Political Economy*, 97 (1): 201–225.

Harsanyi, J. C., and R. Selten. 1988. A General Theory of Equilibrium Selection in Games. MIT Press.

Hayek, F. A. 1945. The use of knowledge in society. *American Economic Review*, 35 (4): 519–530.

Hendricks, K., M. Piccione, and G. Tan. 1995. The economics of hubs: The case of monopoly. *Review of Economic Studies*, 62: 83–99.

Hendricks, K., M. Piccione, and G. Tan. 1997. Entry and exit in hub-spoke networks. *RAND Journal of Economics*, 2 (28): 291–303.

Hendricks, K., M. Piccione, and G. Tan. 1999. Equilibria in networks. *Econometrica*, 67: 1407–1434.

Henrich. J., 2020. *The Weirdest People in the World: How the West Became Psychologically Peculiar and Particularly Prosperous*. Penguin Books.

Herings, P. J.-J., A. Mauleon, and V. Vannetelbosch. 2009. Farsightedly stable networks. *Games and Economic Behavior*, 67 (2): 526–541.

Herskovic, B., and J. Ramos. 2020. Acquiring information through peers. *American Economic Review*, 110: 2128–52.

Heß, S., D. Jaimovich, and M. Schündeln. 2020. Development projects and economic networks: Lessons from rural Gambia. *Review of Economic Studies*, 88 (3): 1347–1384.

Hiller, T. 2017. Friends and enemies: A model of signed network formation. *Theoretcial Economics*, 12 (3): 1057–1087.

Hillman, A., and J. Riley. 1989. Politically contestable rents and transfers. *Economics and Politics*, 1(1): 17–39.

Hirschman, A. O. 1958. The strategy of economic development. Technical report. Yale University Press.

Hirschman, A. O. 1997. *The Passions and the Interests: Political Arguments for Capitalism before Its Triumph*. Greenwood Publishing Group.

Hirshleifer, D. 2020. Presidential address: Social transmission bias in economics and finance. *The Journal of Finance*, 75 (4): 1779–1831.

Hirshleifer, J. 1983. From weakest-link to best-shot: The voluntary provision of public goods. *Public Choice*, 41 (3): 371–386.

Hirshleifer, J. 1995. Anarchy and its breakdown. *Journal of Political Economy*, 103: 26–52.

Hobbes, T. 1886. *Leviathan*. Ballantyne Press.

Hoffman, P. 2015. *Why did Europe Conquer the World?* Princeton University Press.

Hojman, D., and A. Szeidl. 2008. Core and periphery in networks. *Journal of Economic Theory*, 139: 295–309.

Holland, Paul W., Laskey, K. B., Leinhardt, S. 1983. Stochastic block models: First steps. *Social Networks*, 5 (2): 109–137.

Holzer, H. J. 1987. Hiring procedures in the firm: Their economic determinants and outcomes. In *Human Resources and Firm Performance*, edited by Richard Block, et. al. Industrial Relations Research Association.

Holzer, H. J. 1988. Search method use by unemployed youth. *Journal of Labor Economics*, 6 (1): 1–20,

Homans, C. C. 1961. *Social Behavior: Its Elementary Forms*. Harcourt, Brace and World.

Hong, H., J. D. Kubik, and J. C. Stein. 2005. Thy neighbor's portfolio: Word-of-mouth effects in the holdings and trades of money managers. *The Journal of Finance*, 60 (6): 2801–2824.

Hsu, C-C., A. Ajorlou, and A. Jadbabaie. 2020. News sharing, persuasion, and spread of misinformation on social networks. Available at SSRN: http://dx.doi.org/10.2139/ssrn.3391585.

Hulten, C. R. 1978. Growth accounting with intermediate inputs. *Review of Economic Studies*, 45 (3): 511–518.

Huntingdon, S. 1968. *Political Order in Changing Societies*. Yale University Press.

Huremovic, K. 2014. Rent seeking and power hierarchies: A noncooperative model of network formation with antagonistic links. Nota di Lavoro 45.2014, Fondazione Eni Enrico Mattei, Milan, Italy.

Immorlica, N., R. Kranton, M. Manea, and G. Stoddard. 2017. Social status in networks. *American Economic Journal: Microeconomics*, 9 (1): 1–30.

India Today. 2011. Political agitations affect railway service. March 26. https://www.indiatoday.in/india/north/story/political-agitations-in-the-country-affect-railway-service-131001-2011-03-26

In't Veld, Daan, M. van der Leij, and C. Hommes. 2020. The formation of a core-periphery structure in heterogeneous financial networks. *Journal of Economic Dynamics and Control*, 119.

Ioannides, Y. M., and L. Datcher Loury. 2004. Job information networks, neighborhood effects, and inequality. *Journal of economic literature*, 42 (4): 1056–1093.

Jackson, M. 2008. *Social and Economic Networks*. Princeton University Press.

Jackson, M., and S. Nei. 2015. Networks of military alliances, wars, and international trade. *Proceedings of the National Academy of Sciences of the United States of America*, 112 (50): 15277–15284.

Jackson, M., B. W. Rogers, and Y. Zenou. 2017. The economic consequences of social-network structure . *Journal of Economic Literature*, 55 (1): 49–95.

Jackson, M. O. 2019. *The Human Network: How Your Social Position Determines Your Power, Beliefs, and Behaviors*. Penguin Random House.

Jackson, M. O., and A. Pernoud. 2021. Systemic risk in financial networks: A survey. *Annual Review of Economics*, 13: 171–202. Available at SSRN 3651864.

Jackson, M. O., T. Rodriguez-Barraquer, and X. Tan. 2012. Social capital and social quilts: Network patterns of favor exchange. *American Economic Review*, 102 (5): 1857–1897.

Jackson, M. O., and B. W. Rogers. 2005. The economics of small worlds. *Journal of the European Economic Association*, 3 (2–3): 617–627.

Jackson, M. O., and B. W. Rogers. 2007. Meeting strangers and friends of friends: How random are social networks? *American Economic Review*, 97: 890–915.

Jackson, M. O. and E. Storms. 2019. Behavioral communities and the atomic structure of networks. Available at SSRN: http://dx.doi.org/10.2139/ssrn.3049748.

Jackson, M. O., and A. Van den Nouweland. 2005. Strongly stable networks. *Games and Economic Behavior*, 51 (2): 420–444.

Jackson, M. O., and A. Watts. 2001. The existence of pair-wise stable networks. *Seoul Journal of Economics*, 14: 299–321.

Jackson, M. O., and A. Watts. 2002a. The evolution of social and economic networks. *Journal of Economic Theory*, 106 (2): 265–295.

Jackson, M. O., and A. Watts. 2002b. On the formation of interaction networks in social coordination games. *Games and Economic Behavior*, 41 (2): 265–291.

Jackson, M. O., and A. Wolinsky. 1996. A strategic model of social and economic networks. *Journal of Economic Theory*, 71 (1): 44–74.

Jackson, M. O., and Y. Zenou. 2015. Games on networks. In *Handbook of Game Theory with Economic Applications*, 4: 95–163. Elsevier.

Jacobs, J. 2016. *The Death and Life of Great American Cities*. Vintage.

Jaimovich, D. 2015. Missing links, missing markets: Evidence of the transformation process in the economic networks of gambian villages. *World Development*, 66: 645–664.

James, C. 1991. The losses realized in bank failures. *The Journal of Finance*, 46: 1223–1242.

Jordan, J. 2006. Pillage and property. *Journal of Economic Theory*, 131: 26–44.

Kandori, M., G. J. Mailath, and R. Rob. 1993. Learning, mutation, and long run equilibria in games. *Econometrica*, 61 (1): 29–56.

Karinthy, F. 1929. Chain-links. *Everything Is Different*. http://vadeker.net/articles/Karinthy-Chain-Links_1929.pdf

Karlan, D., M. Mobius, T. Rosenblat, and A. Szeidl. 2009. Trust and social collateral. *Quarterly Journal of Economics*, 124 (3): 1307–1361.

Katz, E. 1957. The two-step flow of communication: An up-to-date report on an hypothesis. *Public Opinion Quarterly*, 21 (1): 61–78.

Katz, E., and P. F. Lazarsfeld. 1966. *Personal Influence, The Part Played by People in the Flow of Mass Communications*. Transaction Publishers.

Katz, L. 1953. A new status index derived from sociometric analysis. *Psychometrika*, 39–43.

Katz, M., and C. Shapiro. 1985. Network externalities, competition and compatibility. *American Economic Review*, 75 (3): 424–440.

Katz, M. L., and C. Shapiro. 1986. Technology adoption in the presence of network externalities. *Jounal of Political Economy*, 94: 822–841.

Katz, M. L., and C. Shapiro. 1994. Systems competition and network effects. *Journal of Economic Perspectives*, 8 (2): 93–116.

Kearns, M. 2007. Graphical games. *Algorithmic Game Theory*, 3: 159–180.

Kearns, M., S. Judd, J. Tan, and J. Wortman. 2009. Behavioral experiments on biased voting in networks. *Proceedings of the National Academy of Sciences*, 106 (5): 1347–1352.

Kearns, M., S. Judd, and Y. Vorobeychik. 2012. Behavioral experiments on a network formation game. In *Proceedings of the 13th ACM Conference on Electronic Commerce*, 690–704.

Kearns, M., M. Littman, and S. Singh. 2001. Graphical models for game theory. In *Proceedings of the 17th Conference Uncertainty in Artificial Intelligence*.

Kelly, C. 2006. *The Roman Empire: A Very Short Introduction*. Oxford University Press.

Kemeny, J. G., and J. L. Snell. 1983. *Finite Markov Chains: With a New Appendix "Generalization of a Fundamental Matrix"*. Springer.

Kempe, D., J. Kleinberg, and E. Tardos. 2003. Maximizing the spread of influence through a social network. *Proceedings of the 9th International Conference on Knowledge Discovery and Data Mining*, 137–146.

Keppo, J., M. J. Kim, and X. Zhang. 2022. Learning manipulation through information dissemination. *Operations Research*.

Kermack, W. O., and A. G. McKendrick. 1927. A contribution to the mathematical theory of epidemics. *Proceedings of the Royal Society of London. Series A, Containing Papers of a Mathematical and Physical Character*, 115 (772): 700–721.

Khaldun, I. 1989. *The Muqaddimah: An Introduction to History*. Bollingen Press.

Khandani, A. E., and A. W. Lo. 2007. What happened to the quants in august 2007? *Journal of Investment Management*, 5 (4): 29–78.

Kim, D. A., A. R. Hwong, D. Stafford, D. A. Hughes, A. J. O'Malley, J. H. Fowler, and N. A. Christakis. 2015. Social network targeting to maximise population behaviour change: A cluster randomised controlled trial. *The Lancet*, 386 (9989): 145–153.

Kim, Chang-Ran, and I. Reynolds. 2011. "Supply Chain Disruptions Force More Delays in Japan." Reuters, March 23. http://www.reuters.com/article/2011/03/23/us-japan-supplychain-idUSTRE72M21J20110323

Kim, Chang-Ran, and I. Reynolds. 2011. Supply chain disruptions force more delays in japan. Reuters, March 23. http://www.reuters.com/article/2011/03/23/us-japan-supplychain-idUSTRE72M21J20110323.

Kinateder, M., and L. P. Merlino. 2017. Public goods in endogenous networks. *American Economic Journal: Microeconomics*, 9: 187–212.

Kindleberger, C. 2001. *Manias, Panics and Crashes: A History of Financial Crises*. Wiley.

Kirman, A. 1997. The economy as an evolving network. *Journal of Evolutionary Economics*, 7 (4): 339–353.

Kleinberg, J., S. Suri, É. Tardos, and T. Wexler. 2008. Strategic network formation with structural holes. In *Proceedings of the 9th ACM Conference on Electronic Commerce*, 284–293.

Kleinberg, J. M. 1998. Authoritative sources in a hyperlinked environment. In *SODA*, vol. 98, 668–677. Citeseer.

Kleinberg, J. M. 2000. Navigation in a small world. *Nature*, 406: 845.

Kliesen, K. 1995. The economics of natural disasters. *The Regional Economist*, April. https://www.stlouisfed.org/publications/regional-economist/april-1994/the-economics-of-natural-disasters

Knack, S., and P. Keefer. 1997. Does social capital have an economic payoff? A cross-country investigation. *Quarterly Journal of Economics*, 112 (4): 1251–1288.

Koller, D., and B. Milch. 2003. Multi-agent influence diagrams for representing and solving games. *Games and Economic Behavior*, 45 (1): 181–221.

König, M., X. Liu, and C.-S. Hsieh. 2021. Endogenous technology spillovers in dynamic R&D networks. Working Paper.

König, M. D., X. Liu, and Y. Zenou. 2019. R&D networks: Theory, empirics, and policy implications. *Review of Economics and Statistics*, 101 (3): 476–491.

König, M., M. Rohner, D. Thoenig, and F. Zilibotti. 2017. Networks in conflict: Theory and evidence from the great war of Africa. *Econometrica*, 85 (4): 1093–1132.

König, M. D., C. J. Tessone, and Y. Zenou. 2014. Nestedness in networks: A theoretical model and some applications. *Theoretical Economics*, 9 (3): 695–752.

Konrad, K. 2009. *Strategy and Dynamic in Contests. London School of Economics Perspectives in Economic Analysis*. Oxford University Press.

Kotowski, M. H., and C. M. Leister. 2019. Trading networks and equilibrium intermediation. HKS Faculty Research Working Paper RWP18-001.

Kovenock, D., and B. Roberson. 2012. Conflicts with multiple battlefields. In *The Oxford Handbook of the Economics of Peace and Conflict*, edited by M. Garfinkel and S. Skaperdas. Oxford University Press.

Krainin, C., and T. Wiseman. 2016. War and stability in dynamic international systems. *The Journal of Politics*, 78: 1139–1152.

Kranton, R. and D. McAdams. 2022. Social connectedness and the market for information. Working Paper Duke University.

Kranton, R. E. 1996. Reciprocal exchange: A self-sustaining system. *American Economic Review*, 86 (4): 830–51.

Kranton, R. E., and D. F. Minehart. 2001. A theory of buyer-seller networks. *American Economic Review*, 91 (3): 485–508.

Kremer, M. 1993. The O-ring theory of economic development. *Quarterly Journal of Economics*, 108 (3): 551–575.

Kreps, D. 2018. *Notes on the Theory of Choice*. Routledge.

Kretzschmar, M., and M. Morris. 1996. Measures of concurrency in networks and the spread of infectious disease. *Mathematical Biosciences*, 133 (2): 165–195.

Krugman, P. 1995. Growing world trade: Causes and consequences. *Brookings Papers on Economic Activity*, 327–377.

Kuchler, T., Y. Li, L. Peng, J. Stroebel, and D. Zhou. 2022. Social proximity to capital: Implications for investors and firms. *Review of Financial Studies*, 35 (6): 2743–2789.

Kuhn, P., P. Kooreman, A. Soetevent, and A. Kapteyn. 2011. The effects of lottery prizes on winners and their neighbors: Evidence from the Dutch postcode lottery. *American Economic Review*, 101 (5): 2226–2247.

Kuznets, S. 1961. *Six Lectures on Economic Growth*. Free Press.

La Porta, R., F. Lopez-de Silanes, A. Shleifer, and R. W. Vishny. 1997. Trust in large organizations. *The American Economic Review*, Proceedings of the Hundred and Fourth Annual Meeting of the American Economic Association, 333–338.

Laszka, A., D. Szeszlér, and L. Buttyán. 2012. Game-theoretic robustness of many-to-one networks. In *Proceedings of the 3rd International ICTS Conference on Game Theory for Networks*, GameNets'12.

Layard, R. 2011. *Happiness: Lessons from a New Science*. Penguin.

Lazarsfeld, P. F., B. Berelson, and H. Gaudet. 1948. The people's choice: How the voter makes up his mind in a presidential campaign. Columbia University Press.

Lazarsfeld, P. F., and R. K. Merton. 1954. Friendship as a social process: A substantive and methodological analysis. *Freedom and Control in Modern Society*, 18 (1): 18–66.

Leider, S., M. Mobius, T. Rosenblat, and Q.-A. Do. 2009. Directed altruism and enforced reciprocity in social network. *Quarterly Journal of Economics*, 124 (1): 1815–1851.

Leister, M., Y. Zenou, and J. Zhou. 2022. Social connectedness and local contagion. *Review of Economic Studies*, 89(1): 372–410.

Leontief, W. 1941. *The Structure of the American Economy: An Empirical Application of Equilibrium Analysis*. Harvard University.

Leontief, W. W. 1951. The structure of American economy, 1919–1939: An empirical application of equilibrium analysis. Technical report.

Levine, D., and S. Modica. 2013. Conflict, evolution, hegemony and the power of the state. Working Paper 19221, NBER.

Levy, R. 2021. Social media, news consumption, and polarization: Evidence from a field experiment. *American Economic Review*, 111(3): 831–870.

Lewis, D. K. 1969. *Convention: A Philosophical Study*. Wiley-Blackwell.

Lewis, M. E. 2010. *The Early Chinese Empires*. Harvard University Press.

Lewis, W. A. 1954. Economic development with unlimited supplies of labour.

Lindquist, M. J., and Y. Zenou. 2019. Crime and networks: Ten policy lessons. *Oxford Review of Economic Policy*, 35 (4): 746–771.

Long, J. B., and C. I. Plosser. 1983. Real business cycles. *Journal of Political Economy*, 91: 39–69.

López-Pintado, D. 2008. Diffusion in complex social networks. *Games and Economic Behavior*, 62 (2): 573–590.

Loury, G. C. 1976. A dynamic theory of racial income differences. Technical report, Discussion paper,

Lucas, R. E. 1977. Understanding business cycles. *Carnegie-Rochester Conference Series on Public Policy*, 5: 7–29.

Lucas, R. 1988. On the mechanics of economic development. *Journal of Monetary Economics*. 22: 3–42.

Luft, G. 2005. Pipeline sabotage is terrorist's weapon of choice. *Energy Security*, March 28. https://www.thefreelibrary.com/Pipeline+sabotage+is+terrorist%27s+weapon+of+choice%3A+assaults+on+oil...-a0129809519

Luttmer, E. F. 2005. Neighbors as negatives: Relative earnings and well-being. *Quarterly Journal of Economics*, 120 (3): 963–1002.

Maceaes, B. 2018. *Belt and Road: A Chinese World Order*. Hurst Publishers.

Mackay, C. 2018. *Extraordinary Popular Delusions and the Madness of Crowds*. Harriman.

Mahadev, N. V., and U. N. Peled. 1995. *Threshold Graphs and Related Topics*. Elsevier.

Mailath, G. J., and L. Samuelson. 2006. *Repeated Games and Reputations: Long-Run Relationships*. Oxford University Press.

Mailath, G. J., L. Samuelson, and A. Shaked. 1994. Evolution and endogenous interactions. Working Paper, Center for Analytic Research in Economics.

Malamud, S., and M. Rostek. 2017. Decentralized exchange. *American Economic Review*, 107 (11): 3320–3362.

Mandelbrot, B. 1953. An informational theory of the statistical structure of languages. In *Communication Theory*, edited by W. Jackson, 486–502. Woburn.

Manea, M. 2016. Models of bilateral trade in networks. In *The Oxford Handbook of the Economics of Networks*, edited by Y. Bramoullé, A. Galeotti, and B. Rogers. Oxford University Press.

Manea, M. 2018. Intermediation and resale in networks. *Journal of Political Economy*, 126 (3): 1250–1301.

Manski, C. F. 1995. *Identification Problems in the Social Sciences*. Harvard University Press.

Maoz, Z., P. L. Johnson, J. Kaplan, F. Ogunkoya, and A. P. Shreve. 2019. The dyadic militarized interstate disputes (mids) dataset version 3.0: Logic, characteristics, and comparisons to alternative datasets. *Journal of Conflict Resolution*, 63 (3): 811–835.

Marsden, P. V., and K. E. Campbell. 1990. Recruitment and selection processes: The organizational side of job searches. *Social Mobility and Social Structure*, 59–79.

Marsden, P. V., and J. S. Hurlbert. 1988. Social resources and mobility outcomes: A replication and extension. *Social forces*, 66 (4): 1038–1059.

Martinez, G., M. Rostek, and J. Yoon. 2019. Games among groups. Mimeo University of Wisconsin.

Martinez-Jaramillo, S., B. Alexandrova-Kabadjova, B. Bravo-Benitez, and J. P. Solórzano-Margain. 2014. An empirical study of the mexican banking system's network and its implications for systemic risk. *Journal of Economic Dynamics and Control*, 40: 242–265.

Mas-Colell, A., M. D. Whinston, and J. R. Green. 1995. *Microeconomic Theory*. Oxford University Press.

Mauleon, A., and V. Vannetelbosch. 2016. Network formation games. In *The Oxford Handbook of the Economics of Networks*, edited by Y. Bramoullé, A. Galeotti, and B. Rogers. Oxford University Press.

Mayer, A. C. 1960. *Caste and Kinship in Central India*. University of California Press.

Merton, R. K. 1973. *The Sociology of Science: Theoretical and Empirical Investigations*. Chicago University Press.

Milgram, S. 1967. The small world problem. *Psychology Today*.

Mobarak, A. M., and M. R. Rosenzweig. 2013. Informal risk sharing, index insurance, and risk taking in developing countries. *American Economic Review*, 103 (3): 375–80.

Mobius, M., T. Phan, and A. Szeidl. 2015. Treasure hunt: Social learning in the field. Working Paper Harvard and CEU Budapest.

Mobius, M., and T. Rosenblat. 2016. Trust and social colateral. In *The Oxford Handbook of the Economics of Networks*, edited by Y. Bramoullé, A. Galeotti, and B. Rogers. Oxford University Press.

Molloy, M., and B. Reed. 1995. A critical point for random graphs with a given degree sequence. *Random Structures and Algorithms*, 6: 161–180.

Monderer, D., and L. S. Shapley. 1996. Potential games. *Games and Economic Behavior*, 14 (1): 124–143.

Montgomery, J. D. 1991. Social networks and labor-market outcomes: Toward an economic analysis. *American Economic Review*, 81 (5): 1408–1418.

Moody, J. 2001. Race, school integration, and friendship segregation in america. *American journal of Sociology*, 107 (3): 679–716.

Moore, T., R. Clayton, and R. Anderson. 2009. The economics of online crime. *Journal of Economic Perspectives*, 23 (3): 3–20.

Morris, I., and W. Scheidel. 2009. *The Dynamics of Ancient Empires: State Power from Assyria to Byzantium*. Oxford University Press.

Morris, S. 2000. Contagion. *Review of Economic Studies*, 67 (1): 57–78.

Mossel, E., A. Sly, and O. Tamuz. 2014. Asymptotic learning on bayesian social networks. *Probability Theory and Related Fields*, 158 (1–2): 127–157.

Mossel, E., A. Sly, and O. Tamuz. 2015. Strategic learning and the topology of social networks. *Econometrica*, 83 (5): 1755–1794.

Mostagir, M., A. Ozdaglar, and J. Siderius. 2022. When is society susceptible to manipulation? Management Science.

Mueller-Frank, M. 2013. A general framework for rational learning in social networks. *Theoretical Economics*, 8 (1): 1–40.

Munshi, K. 2003. Networks in the modern economy: Mexican migrants in the U.S. labor market. *Quarterly Journal of Economics*, 118 (2): 549–599.

Munshi, K. 2004. Social learning in a heterogeneous population: Technology diffusion in the indian green revolution. *Journal of Development Economics*, 73 (1): 185–213.

Munshi, K. 2011. Strength in numbers: Networks as a solution to occupational traps. *Review of Economic Studies*, 78 (3): 1069–1101.

Munshi, K. 2014. Community networks and the process of development. *Journal of Economic Perspectives*, 28 (4): 49–76.

Munshi, K. (2019). Caste and and the Indian economy. *Journal of Economic Literature*, 57 (4): 781–834.

Munshi, K., and M. Rosenzweig. 2006. Traditional institutions meet the modern world: Caste, gender, and schooling choice in a globalizing economy. *American Economic Review*, 96 (4): 1225–1252.

Munshi, K., and M. Rosenzweig. 2015. Insiders and outsiders: Local ethnic politics and public goods provision. NBER Working Paper 2172.

Munshi, K., and M. Rosenzweig. 2016. Networks and misallocation: Insurance, migration, and the rural-urban wage gap. *American Economic Review*, 106 (1): 46–98.

Myers, C. A., and G. P. Shultz. 1951. The dynamics of a labor market: A study of the impact of employment changes on labor mobility, job satisfactions, and company and union policies. Technical report.

Myerson, R. 1991. *Game Theory: Analysis of Conflict*. Harvard University Press.

Myerson, R. 1977a. Graphs and cooperation in graphs. *Mathematics of Operations Research*, 2: 225–229.

Myerson, R. B. 1977b. Graphs and cooperation in games. *Mathematics of Operations Research*, 2: 225–229.

Myrdal, G. 1972. *Asian Drama; An Inquiry into the Poverty of Nations*. Pantheon.

Nalebuff, B. J., and A. M. Brandenburger. 1997. Co-opetition: Competitive and cooperative business strategies for the digital economy. *Strategy & Leadership*, 25 (6).

Nava, F. 2015. Efficiency in decentralized oligopolistic markets. *Journal of Economic Theory*, 157: 315–348.

Nava, F. 2016. Repeated games and networks. In *The Oxford Handbook of the Economics of Networks*, edited by Y. Bramoullé, A. Galeotti, and B. Rogers. Oxford University Press.

Nee, V., and S. Opper. 2012. *Capitalism from Below: Markets and Institutional Change in China*. Harvard University Press.

Newman, M. 2018. *Networks*. Oxford University Press.

Newman, M., A.-L. Barabasi, and D. J. Watts. 2006. *The Structure and Dynamics of Networks*. Princeton University Press.

Newman, M. E., S. H. Strogatz, and D. J. Watts. 2001. Random graphs with arbitrary degree distributions and their applications. *Physical Review E*, 64 (2): 026118.

North, D. C. 1990. *Institutions, Institutional Change and Economic Performance*. Cambridge University Press.

North, D. C., and R. P. Thomas. 1973. *The Rise of the Western World: A New Economic History*. Cambridge: Cambridge University Press.

Nguyen, N. P., G. Yan, M. T. Thai, and S. Eidenbenz. 2012. Containment of misinformation spread in online social networks. In *Proceedings of the 4th Annual ACM Web Science Conference*, pp. 213–222.

Nunn, N., and L. Wantchekon. 2011. The slave trade and the origins of mistrust in africa. *American Economic Review*, 101 (7): 3221–52.

Nurkse, R. 1966. Problems of capital formation in underdeveloped countries. Basil Blackwell.

Oberfield, E. 2018. A theory of input-output architecture. *Econometrica,*, 86 (2): 559–589.

O'Brien, P. 2005. *Philip's Atlas of World History*. George Philip.

OECD. 2018. *China's Belt and Road Initiative in the Global Trade, Investment and Finance Landscape*. OECD.

Oechssler, J. 1997. Decentralization and the coordination problem. *Journal of Economic Behavior & Organization*, 32 (1): 119–135.

Olaizola, N., and F. Valenciano. 2015. A unifying model of strategic network formation. Working Paper Departamento de Fundamentos del Análisis Económico I.

Osborne, M. J., and A. Rubinstein. 1994. *A Course in Game Theory*. MIT Press.

Ostrom, E. 1990. *Governing the Commons: The Evolution of Institutions for Collective Action*. Cambridge University Press.

Overy, R. 2010. *Times Complete History of the World*. 8th edition. Times Books.

Ozsoylev, H. N., J. Walden, M. D. Yavuz, and R. Bildik. 2014. Investor networks in the stock market. *The Review of Financial Studies*, 27 (5): 1323–1366.

Page, F. H., Jr., and M. Wooders. 2010. Club networks with multiple memberships and noncooperative stability. *Games and Economic Behavior*, 70 (1): 12–20.

Papanastasiou, Y. 2020. Fake news propagation and detection: A sequential model. *Management Science*, 66(5): 1826–1846. INFORMS.

Parker, G. 1988. *The Military Revolution: Military Innovation and the Rise of the West 1500–1800*. Cambridge University Press.

Parkes, David C., and S. Seuken. 2016. *Introduction to Economics*. Cambridge University Press. Pass, R. 2019. *A Course in Networks and Markets Game-Theoretic Models and Reasoning*. MIT Press.

Pastor-Satorras, R., C. Castellano, P. Van Mieghem, and A. Vespignani. 2015. Epidemic processes in complex networks. *Reviews of Modern Physics*, 87 (3): 925.

Pastor-Satorras, R., and A. Vespignani. 2001a. Epidemic spreading in scale-free networks. *Physical Review Letters*, 86 (14): 3200.

Pastor-Satorras, R., and A. Vespignani. 2001b. Epidemic dynamics and endemic states in complex networks. *Physical Review E*, 63 (6): 066117.

Pellizzari, M. 2010. Do friends and relatives really help in getting a good job? *ILR Review*, 63 (3): 494–510.

Peng, Y. 2004. Kinship networks and entrepreneurs in china's transitional economy. *American Journal of Sociology*, 109 (5): 1045–1074.

Perego, J., and S. Yuksel. 2016. Searching for information. Working Paper Columbia University.

Perlroth, N. 2021. *This Is How They Tell Me the World Ends: The Cyberweapons Arms Race*. Bloomsbury Publishing.

Petzinger, T. 1996. *Hard Landing: The Epic Contest for Power and Profits That Plunged the Airlines into Chaos*. Three Rivers Press: Random House.

Piccione, M., and A. Rubinstein. 2007. Equilibrium in the jungle. *Economic Journal*, 117: 883–896.

Podolny, J. M., and K. L. Page. 1998. Network forms of organization. *Annual Review of Sociology*, 24 (1): 57–76.

Polanski, A. 2007. Bilateral bargaining in networks. *Journal of Economic Theory*, 134 (1): 557–565.

Polanyi, K. 1944. *The Great Transformation*. Rinehart.

Polybius. 2010. *The Histories: Volumes I-III. Loeb Classical Library*. Harvard University Press.

Portes, A. 1998. Social capital: Its origins and applications in modern sociology. *Annual Review of Sociology*, 24 (1): 1–24.

Powell Walter, W. 1990. Neither market nor hierarchy: Network forms of organization. *Research in Organizational Behavior*, 12 (2): 295–336.

Putnam, R. D., R. Leonardi, and R. Y. Nanetti. 1993. *Making Democracy Work: Civic Traditions in Modern Italy*. Princeton University Press.

Raub, W., and J. Weesie. 1990. Reputation and efficiency in social interactions: An example of network effects. *American Journal of Sociology*, 96 (3): 626–654.

Rauch, J. E. 2001. Business and social networks in international trade. *Journal of Economic Literature*, 39 (4): 1177–1203.

Ray, D. 1998. *Development Economics*. Princeton University Press.

Redding, S. J., and E. Rossi-Hansberg. 2017. Quantitative spatial economics. *Annual Review of Economics*, 9: 21–58.

Rees, A. 1966. Information networks in labor markets. *American Economic Review*, 56 (1/2): 559–566.

Riedl, A., I. M. Rohde, and M. Strobel. 2016. Efficient coordination in weakest-link games. *The Review of Economic Studies*, 83 (2): 737–767.

Robbins, L. 2007. *An Essay on the Nature and Significance of Economic Science*. Ludwig von Mises Institute.

Robson, A. J., and F. Vega-Redondo. 1996. Efficient equilibrium selection in evolutionary games with random matching. *Journal of Economic Theory*, 70 (1): 65–92.

Rochet, J.-C., and J. Tirole. 1996. Interbank lending and systemic risk. *Journal of Money, Credit and Banking*, 28: 733–762.

Rochet, J.-C., and J. Tirole. 2002. Cooperation among competitors: Some economics of payment card associations. *RAND Journal of Economics*, 33 (4): 549–70.

Rochet, J.-C., and J. Tirole. 2003. Platform competition in two-sided markets. *Journal of the European Economic Association*, 1 (4): 990–1029.

Rochet, J.-C., and J. Tirole. 2006. Two-sided markets: A progress report. *RAND Journal of Economics*, 35 (3): 645–667.

Rogers, B. W. 2006. A strategic theory of network status. *Unpublished paper, Division of Humanities and Social Sciences, California Institute of Technology*.

Rogers, C. 1995a. *The Military Revolution: Readings on the Military Transformation of Early Transformation of Early Modern Europe*. Westview Press.

Rogers, C., and L. Veraart. 2013. Failure and rescue in an interbank network. *Management Science*, 59: 882–889.

Rogers, E. M. 1995b. *Diffusion of Innovations*. Free Press.

Rohlfs, J. 1974. A theory of interdependent demand for a communications service. *Bell Journal of Economics*, 5 (1): 16–37.

Rosenberg, D., E. Solan, and N. Vieille. 2009. Informational externalities and emergence of consensus. *Games and Economic Behavior*, 66 (2): 979–994.

Ross, R. 1916. An application of the theory of probabilities to the study of a priori pathometry—part I. *Proceedings of the Royal Society of London. Series A, Containing Papers of a Mathematical and Physical Character*, 92 (638): 204–230.

Ross, R., and H. P. Hudson. 1917a. An application of the theory of probabilities to the study of a priori pathometry—part II. *Proceedings of the Royal Society of London. Series A, Containing Papers of a Mathematical and Physical Character*, 93 (650): 212–225.

Ross, R., and H. P. Hudson. 1917b. An application of the theory of probabilities to the study of a priori pathometry—part III. *Proceedings of the Royal Society of London. Series A, Containing Papers of a Mathematical and Physical Character*, 93 (650): 225–240.

Roughgarden, T. 2005. *Selfish Routing and the Price of Anarchy*. MIT Press.

Rubinstein, A., and A. Wolinsky. 1987. Middlemen. *Quarterly Journal of Economics*, 102 (3): 581–593.

Ryan, B., and N. C. Gross. 1943. The diffusion of hybrid seed corn in two Iowa communities. *Rural Sociology*, 8 (1): 15.

Rysman, M. 2004. Competition between networks: A study of the market for yellow pages. *Review of Economic Studies*, 71 (2): 483–512.

Rysman, M. 2007. An empirical analysis of payment card usage. *Journal of Industrial Economics*, 55 (1): 1–36.

Rysman, M. 2009. The economics of two-sided markets. *Journal of Economic Perspectives*, 23 (3): 125–143.

Sadler, E., and B. Golub. 2021. Games on endogenous networks. https://doi.org/10.48550/arXiv.2102.01587.

Salganik, M. J., P. S. Dodds, and D. J. Watts. 2006. Experimental study of inequality and unpredictability in an artificial cultural market. *Science*, 311 (5762): 854–856.

Salonen, H. 2015. Reciprocal equilibria in link formation games. *Czech Economic Review*, 9: 169–183.

Sandel, M. J. 2000. What money can't buy: the moral limits of markets. *Tanner Lectures on Human Values*, 21: 87–122.

Scarre, C. 1995. *The Penguin Historial Atlas of Ancient Rome*. Penguin Books.

Schelling, T. 1960. *The Strategy of Conflict*. Harvard University Press.

Schelling, T. C. 2006. *Micromotives and Macrobehavior*. WW Norton & Company.

Schneider, J. 2022. A world without trust: The insidious threat. *Foreign Affairs*, 101 (1): 22–32.

Schulz, J. F., D. Bahrami-Rad, J. P. Beauchamp, and J. Henrich. 2019. The church, intensive kinship, and global psychological variation. *Science*, 366 (November 8).

Sen, A. 1997. *On Economic Inequality*. Oxford University Press.

Seneta, E. 2006. *Non-Negative Matrices and Markov Chains*. Springer Science & Business Media.

Sethi, R., and M. Yildiz. 2016. Communication with unknown perspectives. *Econometrica*, 84 (6): 2029–2069.

Shachter, R. D. 1986. Evaluating influence diagrams. *Operations Research*, 34 (6): 871–882.

Shan, W., G. Walker, and B. Kogut. 1994. Interfirm cooperation and startup innovation in the biotechnology industry. *Strategic Management Journal*, 15 (5): 387–394.

Shapiro, C., and H. Varian. 1995. *Information Rules: A Strategic Guide to the Network Economy*. HBS Press.

Siedlarek, J. P. 2015. Intermediation in networks. Discussion Paper Series of SFB/TR 15 Governance and the Efficiency of Economic Systems 471, Free University of Berlin, Humboldt University of Berlin, University of Bonn, University of Mannheim, and University of Munich.

Simon, H. A. 1955. On a class of skew distribution functions. *Biometrika*, 42 (3/4): 425–440.

Singh, N., and X. Vives. 1984. Price and quantity competition in a differentiated duopoly. *RAND Journal of Economics*, 15 (4): 546–554.

Skyrms, B., and R. Pemantle. 2009. A dynamic model of social network formation. In *Adaptive Networks*, edited by T. Gross and H. Sayama, 231–251. Springer.

Smelser, N., and R. Swedberg. 2005. *The Handbook of Economic Sociology*. Princeton University Press.

Smith, C. 2008. Preface to special issue on *Networks: Games, Interdiction, and Human Interaction Problems on Networks*. *Networks*, 52 (3): 109–110.

Smith, L., and P. Sørensen. 2000. Pathological outcomes of observational learning. *Econometrica*, 68 (2): 371–398.

Solomonoff, R., and A. Rapoport. 1951. Connectivity of random nets. *Bulletin of Mathematical Biophysics*, 13: 107–117.

Song, Z., K. Storesletten, and F. Zilibotti. 2011. Growing like China. *American Economic Review*, 101 (1): 196–233.

Srinivas, M. N. 1987. *The Dominant Caste and Other Essays*. Oxford University Press.

Staniford, S., V. Paxson, and N. Weaver. 2002. How to own the internet in your spare time. In *Proceedings of the 11th USENIX Security Symposium*, 149–167, USENIX Association.

Stewart, G. W. 1998. *Matrix Algorithms: Basic Decompositions*. Society for Industrial and Applied Mathematics.

Sugden, R. 2004. *The Economics of Rights, Co-operation and Welfare*. Springer.

Summers, L. 2007. The rise of Asia and the global economy. *Research Monitor*, 2: 4–6.

Sundararajan, A. 2005. Local network effects and network structure. *The B.E. Journal of Theoretical Economics Contributions* 7 (1): Article 46.

Swidler, A. 1986. Culture in action: Symbols and strategies. *American Sociological Review*, 51 (2): 273–286.

Tacitus. 2009. *Annals and Histories*. Everyman's Library.

Tambe, M. 2011. *Security and Game Theory*. Cambridge University Press.

Tarski, A. 1955. A lattice-theoretical fixpoint theorem and its applications. *Pacific Journal of Mathematics*, 5 (2): 285–309.

Tesfatsion, L. 1997. A trade network game with endogenous partner selection. In *Computational Approaches to Economic Problems*, edited by H. Amman, B. Rustem, and A. Whinston, 249–269. Springer.

Thapar, R. 1997. *Asoka and the Decline of the Mauryas*. Oxford University Press.

Thapar, R. 2002. *Early India: From the Origins to 1300*. Penguin.

Thucydides. 1989. *The Peloponnesian War: The Complete Hobbes Translation*. University of Chicago Press.

Tirole, J. 1988. *The Theory of Industrial Organization*. MIT Press.

de Tocqueville, A. 2004. *Democracy in America*. Folio Society.

Topa, G. 2011. Labor markets and referrals. In *Handbook of Social Economics*, vol. 1, edited by J. Benhabib, M.O. Jackson, and A. Bisin, 1193–1221. Elsevier.

Topa, G. 2019. Social and spatial networks in labour markets. *Oxford Review of Economic Policy*, 35 (4): 722–745.

Topkis, D. M. 1998. *Supermodularity and Complementarity*. Princeton University Press: New Jersey.

Travers, J., and S. Milgram. 1969. An experimental study of the small world problem. *Sociometry*, 32 (4): 425–443. Dynamics of Networks, 130–148. Princeton University Press.

Trompenaars, A., and C. Hampden-Turner. 1998. *Riding the Waves of Culture: Understanding Cultural Diversity in Global Business*. McGraw-Hill.

Tullock, G. 1980. Efficient rent seeking. In *Toward a Theory of the Rent Seeking Society*, edited by J. Buchanan, R. Tollison, and G. Tullock, 97–112. Texas A&M University Press.

Turchin, P. 2007. *War and Peace and War: The Rise and Fall of Empires*. Penguin, New York.

Udry, C. 1994. Risk and insurance in a rural credit market: An empirical investigation in northern Nigeria. *Review of Economic Studies*, 61 (3): 495–526.

Ullman, J. C. 1966. Employee referrals-prime tool for recruiting workers. *Personnel*, 43 (3): 30–35.

Upper, C., and A. Worms. 2004. Estimating bilateral exposures in the german interbank market: Is there a danger of contagion? *European Economic Review*, 48 (4): 827–849.

US Supply Chain Policy Fact Sheet. 2012. http://www.whitehouse.gov/the-press-office/2012/01/25/fact-sheet-nation.

Valente, T., B. Hoffman, A. Ritt-Olson, K. Lichtman, and C. Johnson. 2003. Effects of a social network method for group assignment strategies in peer-led tobacco prevention programs in schools. *American Journal of Public Health*, 93: 1837–1843.

Valukas, A. 2010. *Public policy issues raised by the report of the Lehman bankruptcy examiner*. Committee on Financial Services US House of Representatives.

Van der Leij, M., and S. Goyal. 2011. Strong ties in a small world. *Review of Network Economics*, 10 (2).

Van Huyck, J. B., R. C. Battalio, and R. O. Beil. 1990. Tacit coordination games, strategic uncertainty, and coordination failure. *American Economic Review*, 80 (1): 234–248.

van Leeuwen, B., T. Offerman, and A. Schram. 2020. Competition for status creates superstars: An experiment on public good provision and network formation. *Journal of the European Economic Association*, 18: 666–707.

Varshney, A. 2001. Ethnic conflict and civil society: India and beyond. *World Politics*, 53 (3): 362–398.

Vazquez, A. 2003. Growing network with local rules: Preferential attachment, clustering hierarchy, and degree correlations. *Physical Review E*, 67: 056104.

Veblen, T. 1973. *The Theory of the Leisure Class*. Houghton Mifflin.

Vega-Redondo, F. 2006. Building up social capital in a changing world. *Journal of Economic Dynamics and Control*, 30 (11): 2305–2338.

Vega-Redondo, F. 2008. *Complex Social Networks*. Cambridge University Press.

Vega-Redondo, F. 2016. Links and actions in interplay. In *The Oxford Handbook of the Economics of Networks*, edited by Y. Bramoullé, A. Galeotti, and B. Rogers, 175–191. Oxford University Press.

Vives, X. 1999. *Oligopoly Pricing: Old Ideas and New Tools*. MIT Press.

Walden, J. 2019. Trading, profits, and volatility in a dynamic information network model. *Review of Economic Studies*, 86 (5): 2248–2283.

Walker, M. and J. Gottfried. 2019. Republicans far more likely than democrats to say fact-checkers tend to favor one side. Pew Research Center.

Wall Street Journal. 2021. Colonial pipeline CEO tells why he paid hackers a $ 4.4 million ransom. May 19. https://www.wsj.com/articles/colonial-pipeline-ceo-tells-why-he-paid-hackers-a-4-4-million-ransom-11621435636

Wang, C. 2016. Core-periphery trading networks. Available at SSRN 2747117.

Wasserman, S., and K. Faust. 1994. *Social Network Analysis: Methods and Applications*. Cambridge University Press.

Watts, A. 2001. A dynamic model of network formation. *Games and Economic Behavior*, 34 (2): 331–341.

Watts, D. 1999. *Small Worlds: The Dynamics of Networks between Order and Randomness*. Princeton University Press.

Watts, D. J. 2004. *Six Degrees: The Science of a Connected Age*. WW Norton.

Watts, D. J., P. S. Dodds, and M. E. J. Newman. 2002. Identity and search in social networks. *Science*, 296(5571): 1302–1305.

Watts, D. J., and S. H. Strogatz. 1998. Collective dynamics of "small-world" networks. *Nature*, 393 (6684): 440–442.

Weber, M. 1951. *The Religion of China*. Free Press.

Weber, M. 2002. *The Protestant Ethic and the Spirit of Capitalism and Other Writings*. Penguin.

Weber, M. 2010. *The Protestant Ethic and the Spirit of Capitalism*. Oxford University Press.

Weber, R. A. 2006. Managing growth to achieve efficient coordination in large groups. *American Economic Review*, 96 (1): 114–126.

Weisbuch, G., A. Kirman, and D. Herreiner. 2000. Market organisation and trading relationships. *The Economic Journal*, 110 (463): 411–436.

Wellman, B., and S. Wortley. 1990. Different strokes from different folks: Community ties and social support. *American Journal of Sociology*, 96 (3): 558–588.

Westbrock, B. 2010. Natural concentration in industrial research collaboration. *RAND Journal of Economics*, 41 (2): 351–371.

Wiggins, R. Z., T. Piontek, and A. Metrick. 2019. The Lehman Brothers bankruptcy A: Overview. *Journal of Financial Crises*, 1: 39–62.

Wiggins, R. Z., and A. Metrick. 2019. The Lehman Brothers bankruptcy H: The global contagion. *Journal of Financial Crises*, 1: 172–199.

Williams, D. 1991. *Probability with Martingales*. Cambridge University Press.

Williamson, D. 1985. *The Economic Institutions of Capitalism*. Free Press.

Wittke, A. M., E. Olshausen, R. Szydlak, V. Sauer, C. F. Salazar, D. Prankel, and C. Vermeulen. 2010. *Historical Atlas of the Ancient World*. Brill.

Wojcik, S., and A. Hughes. 2019. *Sizing up Twitter Users*. Pew Research Center.

Wollmer, R. 1964. Removing arcs from a network. *Operations Research*, 12 (6): 934–940.

Wrong, D. 1961. The oversocialized conception of man in modern sociology. *American Sociological Review*, 26 (2): 183–193.

Young, H. P. 1993. The evolution of conventions. *Econometrica*, 61 (1): 57–84.

Young, H. P. 1998. *Individual Strategy and Social Structure: An Evolutionary Theory of Institutions*. Princeton University Press.

Zak, P. J., and S. Knack. 2001. Trust and growth. *The Economic Journal*, 111 (470): 295–321.

Zenou, Y. 2016. Key players. In *The Oxford Handbook of the Economics of Networks*, edited by Y. Bramoullé, A. Galeotti, and B. Rogers. Oxford University Press.

Zhang, J., M. S. Ackerman, and L. Adamic. 2007. Expertise networks in online communities: Structure and algorithms. In *Proceedings of the 16th International Conference on World Wide Web*, 221–230.

Zhao, W., and S. Xie. 1988. *Zhongguo renkou shi [The Population History of China]*. Renmin Chubanshe.

Zhu, S., and D. Levinson. 2011. Disruptions to transportation networks: A review. Working Paper, University of Minnesota.

# Index

*Note:* Page numbers followed by *t* indicate tables and *f* indicate figures.